Fodor's
Southeast Asia

Fodor's Travel Publications, Inc.
New York • Toronto • London • Sydney • Auckland

Twentieth Edition

ISBN 0–679–02762–9

Fodor's Southeast Asia

Editors: Craig Seligman, Conrad Little Paulus, Melanie Roth
Contributors: Steven Amsterdam, Shann Davies, John English, Doreen Fernandez, Nigel Fisher, Luis Francia, Colleen Davis Gardephe, Echo Garrett, Robert Halliday, Eu Hooi Khaw, Dawn Lawson, Steven Levingston, John Major, Bevin McLaughlin, Linda Miller, Jack Moore, Violet Oon, Mary Ellen Schultz, Bruce Shu, Nancy van Itallie, Joan Warner
Creative Director: Fabrizio La Rocca
Cartographer: David Lindroth
Illustrator: Karl Tanner
Cover Photograph: National Geographic Traveler/Paul Chesley/ Photographers/Aspen

Design: Vignelli Associates

Special Sales

Contents

Vocabulary *541*

Index *548*

Maps

Foreword

In compiling this guide to the vast area of Southeast Asia, we have had to make some difficult choices. Rather than provide skeletal coverage of all areas of the countries included, we have selected the most popular areas and covered them in depth, although we have tried to provide at least a hint of character of some of the lesser-known but fascinating areas.

For the invaluable assistance they have provided us in putting together this guide, we would like to extend our sincere appreciation to the following: Philippine Air Lines, Philippine Department of Tourism (New York and Manila), and Philippine Convention and Visitors' Corporation (Manila).

While every care has been taken to ensure the accuracy of the information in this guide, the passage of time will always bring change, and consequently, the publisher cannot accept responsibility for errors that may occur.

All prices and opening times quoted here are based on information supplied to us at press time. Hours and admission fees may change, however, and the prudent traveler will avoid inconvenience by calling ahead.

Fodor's wants to hear about your travel experiences, both pleasant and unpleasant. When a hotel or restaurant fails to live up to its billing, let us know, and we will investigate the complaint and revise our entries where the facts warrant it.

Send your letters to the editors of Fodor's Travel Publications, 201 East 50th Street, New York, NY 10022.

Highlights
and
Fodor's Choice

Highlights

Hong Kong and Macau

The first cruise ship to take a berth in Hong Kong, *Star Pisces,* arrived in May 1994. The 40,000-ton luxury liner, with room for 1,700 passengers, sails between Taiwan and the territory, with trips that take about 22 hours each way.

The new **Museum of Coastal Defense,** scheduled to open in 1995, will be a tribute to the forces that guarded Hong Kong throughout its period as a British colony. The museum is situated at a barracks built in 1890 in Chai Wan, on the eastern side of Hong Kong island. Exhibits include historic military installations and a variety of restored 19th-century heavy weapons.

The **Peninsula Hotel** renovation should be completed by the time this book is published. Along with the new tower's 132 guest rooms and suites, business center, and banquet facilities, the hotel is opening two new restaurants—Felix, the Phillipe Starck–designed rooftop restaurant serving nouvelle Continental and Asian cuisine, and the Japanese Imasa. The lobby of the Peninsula has been spruced up and is once again is *the* place in Hong Kong to meet for tea.

The **Peak Galleria,** part of a redevelopment program by the Hongkong & Shanghai Hotels, Ltd., is now open. The complex includes a variety of shops and restaurants, including **Cafe Deco,** the trendy new restaurant where locals go to see and be seen.

The new 40,000-seat **Hong Kong Stadium,** in Wanchai, opened in March 1994 in time for the international Seven-a-Side rugby championships.

Meanwhile, the $890-million **Macau International Airport** is slated to open by the end of 1995, allowing all types of aircraft, including the Boeing 747–400, to land in Macau. The terminal will be able to handle some 4.5 million passengers daily. A **new bridge** from the airport to Zhuhai, China, is now open. It will provide a rail link to Zhuahai and Guangzhou, although work on this part of the project is not yet under way. A major reclamation of the waterfront, changing the size and appearance of Macau, is to be completed by 1999.

New hotels are on the increase in Macau, led by the Westin Resort on Coloane's Hac Sa Beach, opened in 1993. Other hotels recently opened include the 350-room, 26-story **Hotel Grandeau,** featuring a revolving restaurant, and the 451-room **Holiday Inn.** The popular **Pousada Ritz** has expanded, adding a 13-room wing.

To keep visitors apprised of the vast changes in an ever-evolving Macau, a **tourist center** was opened in 1994 adjacent to the Macau

Forum. It houses the Grand Prix Museum as well as restaurants, shops, and extensive conference facilities.

Indonesia

With the price of crude fluctuating on the world market, oil-rich Indonesia is placing more and more emphasis on its tourist industry as a source of foreign revenue. There is not a universal tourist infrastructure yet, but that's part of Indonesia's attraction: Travelers can choose between resort areas and places where tourists are still a novelty.

In the rush to attract tourists, new hotels are opening everywhere, with the emphasis on Bali, Jakarta, and Yogyakarta. In the last few years, the quiet paradise that was Bali has more than doubled the number of its hotel rooms, and even more are on the way. The congestion has driven tourists farther east to Lombok, which also is becoming cluttered with hotels and guest houses. Jakarta, once short on top-quality accommodation, now has several world-class hotels, like the Oriental, and more on the way, including the Regent—a state of affairs that, happily for the tourist, depresses room prices. In Yogyakarta, the number of hotel rooms far exceeds the number of visitors (a surfeit that should continue with a Conrad Hilton and Sheraton slated to open in the next two years), so don't be surprised at the offer of a 40% discount.

The traveler who does not want to rub shoulders with groups of camera-clicking tourists must seek other islands and settle for more modest accommodations. **Sumba,** east of Lombok, attracts travelers with its deserted shores; **North Sulawesi** and **Ambon** lie waiting to be discovered; and **Flores,** with fewer tourist amenities, offers fabulous scuba diving.

Air transportation is improving. The government has begun allowing foreign airlines access to its international airports. The national airline, **Garuda Indonesia,** has relinquished many of its domestic routes to another government airline, **Merpati,** in order to improve its international flights; and **Sempati,** a new private airline, is stimulating Merpati with some healthy competition. Domestic travel operators, such as **Satriavi,** have a network of offices with staff to meet clients at each airport and manage all travel logistics. Travel operators aside, a coterie of taxi drivers and guides are always willing to help: These local entrepreneurs know the best hotels, the best restaurants, and the best methods for sightseeing.

Malaysia

Malaysia is a far more attractive tourist destination than its government tourist office or unreliable Malaysian Airlines has managed to convey. Reservations at hotels remain easy to obtain and booking flights is no problem. Malaysia will never rival Thailand or Indonesia for diversity of appeal, but the friendliness of the people, the quality of the hotels, and the ease of travel make the country an attractive vacation destination. A further incentive is **Malaysian Airlines' "Discover Malaysia" plan,** which allows passengers to make four flights within peninsular Malaysia for M$190, and offers half-price flights to Sarawak and Sabah. Hotel prices in Malaysia are also a bargain compared with other Southeast Asian resort areas.

The newest resort is **Langkawi,** just south of the Thai border. Of this archipelago of 99 islands, only **Pulau Langkawi** has accommodations, which vary from the luxury and elegance of the **Datai** resort to chain hotels such as the **Sheraton** and small, inexpensive guest houses. The other islands, surrounded by crystal clear waters, are solely for exploring. An entirely different island is **Borneo,** which offers beach resorts in both Sarawak (the Holiday Inn Damai) and Sabah (Tanjung Aru and the new Ramada Renaissance at Sandakan). Inland, organized river trips take intrepid travelers deep into the jungle to experience the lifestyles of the Ibans and Dayaks. (Those who want their luxury can stay at the **Batang Ai Longhouse,** managed by Hilton Hotels and set deep in Sarawak's hinterland.) In stark contrast is the increasing prosperity of Malaysia's urban centers—witness the imported European cars in the streets of Kuala Lumpur and the latest fashions at such glittering new hotels as the **Kuala Lumpur Regent.**

The Philippines

The 1990 earthquake in the Philippines caused widespread damage, especially in the area around Baguio City, north of Manila. Two major hotels were demolished and some rubble remains, but otherwise the situation is back to normal. Kennon Road, one of the main routes to this resort city, is often under repair, so prospective visitors should check on alternate routes—for example, via Naguilian Road, or flying in via Philippine Air Lines.

For a while, a communist rebel group was making threats against U.S. government personnel, and several military men were killed. But with U.S. military installations phased out in 1992, such threats have all but disappeared, so there's no longer any need to worry. Still, tourists should contact the U.S. State Department, the embassy in Manila, or the consulate in Cebu before visiting remote areas.

The Philippine peso has strengthened against the dollar, but a Philippine vacation is still a bargain. At press time, the exchange rate was 28 pesos to the dollar.

Major new resorts have opened in Cebu, Davao, Marinduque, and Palawan. The premier resorts are **El Nido,** situated in a marine sanctuary off northern Palawan; **Dakak,** in northwestern Mindanao; and **Badian Beach Club** and **Shangri-La** in Cebu. Three deluxe hotels have opened in Manila, while the 2,577-room **Asiaworld Plaza Hotel** is still under construction. The Department of Tourism's **Homestay Program,** begun two years ago, continues providing foreign visitors the opportunity to stay with Filipino families in different regions, giving them a firsthand look at Philippine culture.

Singapore

The artificiality of Singapore continues to intensify. The **Hong Bao Festival,** for example, has been created during the Chinese New Year out of whole cloth. The Chinese New Year itself is a family-oriented occasion rather than a public celebration, so promoters have come up with this weeklong celebration, complete with fireworks on Marina Bay, for the benefit of the tourist trade.

Occasionally, though, less structured development is allowed. **Boat Quay** is one of the rare instances, and it has become Singapore's most popular area for strolling and dining. A clutter of restaurants have opened along this section of the Singapore River's bank, without the constraining hand of the Singapore Tourist Promotion Board, providing good food and a relaxed atmosphere for conversation and people-watching. This pleasant informality contrasts sharply with what you'll find in the newly renovated area farther upstream at **Clarke Quay.** Here warehouses have been cleaned up and developed to produce an artificial minivillage of boutiques, restaurants, and galleries. As a result, the locals shun the area; the only people you'll find here, milling about and browsing through the shops full of merchandise at inflated prices, are tourists.

Singapore **hotels,** with their attentive and highly trained staffs, used to offer some of the finest service in the world. While hotels still strive for this standard, the competition among them for staff and the finite number of Singaporeans willing to work in hotels have combined to bring about a slight faltering in hotel service. Nevertheless, Singapore's hotels still rank among the world's best, and unless there you run up against a large convention—and Singapore is increasingly a convention city—you can usually obtain special discounted rates on your rooms.

Some of the crowding from the deluge of conventioneers may be alleviated by the new convention site at Marina Square, **Suntec City,** which will include not only vast meeting halls and five towers of office buildings but also a mammoth hotel, the 1,000-room **Marina Pontiac;** the complex is scheduled for completion in 1995. Two other hotels offering what promises to be more personable service will also be making their debuts in 1995. The **Four Seasons,** opening behind the Singapore Hilton, should give that aging but efficient hotel some stiff competition. The 525-room **Traders Hotel** will be managed by the Shangri-La group, but it's designed to appeal to the traveler who wants first-class service and accommodations without the frills or the costs of a superdeluxe hotel.

At press time, Singapore's **Silk Air** was offering a new Discover Asia Airpass visitor ticket, with a $119-per-leg fixed price for flights on any Silk Air route over a 90-day period. (Some of these flights normally cost up to $400.) The Airpass must be arranged through a travel agency and purchased before leaving for Asia. Silk Air flies from Singapore to 16 mostly secondary cities, including Pattaya and Chiang Mai in Thailand, Xiamen and Hangchow in China, and Cebu in the Philippines.

The much-celebrated case of the American teen-ager convicted of vandalism in 1994 and then punished with a jail term and caning—a severe form of corporal punishment still practiced in Singapore—should serve as a lesson to all visitors. Singapore has a draconian penal code, from mandatory capital punishment for drug trafficking down to heavy fines for chewing gum in the subways. Foreigners are every bit as subject to these laws as the locals are, and if you are convicted of breaking one of them, your foreign citizenship will not win you any leniency.

Thailand

The current surfeit of **hotel rooms** in Bangkok will increase in 1995, with many now across the Chao Phraya River on the Thonburi side. It will take aggressive marketing to lure travelers over here, since they'll need a ferry to get to the Bangkok side, but the situation will further depress room prices on both sides. Even on the Bangkok side, new hotels (among them the luxury **Sheraton Towers** along Sukhumvit) are opening. As elsewhere in the region, published hotel rates have little bearing on what guests actually pay; hoteliers throughout Thailand should be offering discounts through 1996.

Bangkok **traffic** remains a nightmare. Various proposed mass transit systems keep on stalling in the bureaucratic apparatus; at press time, even the plans for the elevated train had snarled. Meanwhile, most Bangkok **taxis** have been persuaded to use meters. Use the metered cabs—you won't negotiate a better fare with a meterless one. The new **electric tuk-tuks** (open-sided three-wheel taxis) are in the testing phase; if all goes well, the streets of the capital may become quieter and less chokingly polluted.

Two vast infrastructure projects are in the works. To lessen the congestion of Bangkok, a new city, **Chachoengsao,** is being planned 100 miles to the east and will be home to many of the Thai government's bureaucracies. A second international airport is to be built southeast of Bangkok at **Nong Ngu Hao** (north of Chonburi). Both projects should be well on their way by the turn of the century.

Action is finally being taken to cure the ills in **Pattaya.** The government has allotted US$200 million for a cleanup process that should include water and sewage treatment plants. In the meantime, Pattaya is filling its hotels with package tours from eastern Europe.

Hotels and guest houses are sprouting up all over the island of **Ko Samui,** with **Chaweng** becoming the most lively beach area. The sublimely comfortable **Santiburi Resort** has been joined by **Baan Taling Ngam,** a luxury hotel managed by the Mandarin Oriental group with a spectacular cliffside location. Those seeking a beach vacation quieter than what **Phuket** and its 20,000 hotel rooms have to offer may want to cross over to the Krabi province at Ao Prang Bay. Here the beautiful **Dusit Rahwadee** has opened on a headland that can only be reached by boat.

While more frequent flights by Thai International has made getting to **Chiang Mai** easier, travelers are shortening their stays there in order to visit the **Golden Triangle** in Chiang Rai province. The region has been gaining in popularity since Myanmar relaxed its border restrictions at Mae Sai: You can now get a day visa for shopping across the border or a three-day visa for a trip inland to Kengtung. **Mae Hong Son,** too, is becoming more popular, with flights from Chiang Mai on Thai International and direct service from Bangkok on Bangkok Airways.

Until recently the airport nearest **Sukhothai** has been at Phitsanaloke. If Bangkok Airways has its way, there will be direct Bangkok–Sukhothai flights by the time you read this. In the northeast, the Friendship Bridge at **Nong Khai** opened in mid-1994, permitting vehicular traffic to cross the Mae Khong river to Laos and drive the 20 km (12.4 mi) to Vientiane. At press time, foreigners still need a Laotian visa—not obtainable at Nong Khai, and requiring about a week to process in Bangkok.

Two major events are approaching: the **total eclipse of the sun** across the country's central plain in October 1995, and the celebrations of **50th anniversary of King Bhumibol's accession to the throne** (on May 5) throughout 1996. Chiang Mai will host the **Southeast Asian Games** in December 1995 and will mark its 700th birthday the following year.

Fodor's Choice

No two people will agree on what makes a perfect vacation, but it's fun and helpful to know what others think. We hope you'll have a chance to experience some of Fodor's Choices yourself in Southeast Asia. For detailed information about each entry, refer to the appropriate chapter.

Dining

Hong Kong The Chinese Restaurant, *$$$$*

Lai Ching Heen, *$$$$*

Au Trou Normand, *$$$*

Papillon, *$$$*

A Lorcha, Macau, *$$*

Balichao, Macau, *$$*

Yung Kee, *$$*

Indonesia Kupu Kupu Barong, Bali, *$$$*

The Spice Garden, Jakarta, *$$$*

Sari Kuring, Jakarta, *$$*

Ny Suharti, Yogyakarta, *$*

Malaysia Lai Ching Yuen, Kuala Lumpur, *$$$$*

Brasserie, Penang, *$$$*

La Farfalla, Penang, *$$$*

Eden, Penang, *$$*

Yazmin, Kuala Lumpur, *$$*

Minah, Penang, *$*

Philippines Lantaw Seafoods Restaurant, Cebu City, *$$$*

Mario's, Baguio City, *$$$*

Via Mare, Manila, *$$$*

Alavar's, Zamboanga City, *$$*

Bistro Remedios, Manila, *$$*

Cafe by the Ruins, Baguio City, *$$*

Sunset Terrace, Iloilo City, *$$*

Singapore Latour, *$$$$*

Li Bai, *$$$–$$$$*

Tandoor, *$$$*

La Brasserie, *$$–$$$*

Banana Leaf Apollo, *$*

Thailand Le Normandie, Bangkok, *$$$$*

Amanpuri, Phuket, *$$$*

Royal Kitchen, Bangkok, *$$$*

Sala Rim Naam, Bangkok, *$$$*

Hong Tauw Inn, Chiang Mai, *$$*

Lodging

Brunei Sheraton Utama, *$$$*

Hong Kong Mandarin Oriental, *$$$$*

Peninsula, Kowloon, *$$$$*

The Regent, Kowloon, *$$$$*

Hotel Bela Vista, Macau, *$$$*

Hyatt Regency and Taipa Island Resort, Macau, *$$$*

Pousada de São Tiago, Macau, *$$$*

Indonesia Kupu Kupu Barong, Ubud, Bali, *$$$$*

Mandarin Oriental, Jakarta, *$$$$*

Oberoi, Legian, Bali, *$$$$*

Tanjung Sari, Sanur, Bali, *$$$*

Kul Kul Beach Resort, Kuta, Bali, *$$–$$$*

Hotel Misiliana, Rantepao, Sulawesi, *$$*

Kusuma Sahid Prince Hotel, Solo, *$$*

Malaysia Datai, Langkawi, *$$$$*

Kuching Hilton, Kuching, *$$$$*

Penang Mutiara, Penang, *$$$$*

The Regent, Kuala Lumpur, *$$$$*

Tanjung Aru Beach Hotel, Kota Kinabalu, *$$$$*

Eastern & Oriental Hotel, Penang, *$$*

Philippines Banaue Hotel, Banaue, *$$$$*

Cebu Plaza, Cebu City, *$$$$*

Manila Peninsula, Manila, *$$$$*

Philippine Plaza, Manila, *$$$$*

Casa Amapola, Baguio City, *$–$$*

Villa Angela, Vigan, *$*

Singapore Goodwood Park, *$$$$*

Sheraton Towers, $$$

The Inn of the Sixth Happiness, $

Ladyhill Hotel, $

RELC International House, $

Thailand Dusit Rahwadee, Krabi, $$$$

Dusit Thani, Bangkok, $$$$

Oriental, Bangkok, $$$$

Santiburi, Ko Samui, $$$$

Shangri-La, Bangkok, $$$$

Tara Mae Hong Son, Mae Hong Son, $$

Panviman Resort, Ko Pha Ngan, $–$$

River View Lodge, Chiang Mai, $

Museums

Hong Kong Hong Kong Museum of History

Maritime Museum, Macau

Indonesia National Museum, Jakarta

Philippines Ayala Museum, Vigan

Malacañang Palace, Manila

National Museum, Manila

University of San Carlos Museum, Cebu City

Singapore Empress Place

Pioneers of Singapore/Surrender Chambers

Thailand National Museum, Bangkok

Pim Buranaket Folklore Museum, Phitsanulok

Temples, Shrines, and Buildings

Hong Kong Temple of 10,000 Buddhas, Shatin

A-Ma Temple, Macau

Indonesia Borobudur, Yogyakarta

Prambanan, Yogyakarta

Ceremonial Houses of the Toraja, Sulawesi

Hall of Justice, Klungkung, Bali

Philippines Miagao and Molo churches, Iloilo City

Manila Cathedral, Quiapo, Binondo, and San Agustin churches, Manila

Paoay and Santa Maria churches, Ilocos Norte

Baclayon Church, Bohol

Singapore Fuk Tak Chi Temple

Sri Mariamman Temple

Thailand Suan Pakkard Palace, Bangkok

Wat Benjamabophit (Marble Temple), Bangkok

Wat Chaimongkol, Chiang Mai

Wat Phanan Choeng, Ayutthaya

Wat Phra Keo (Temple of the Emerald Buddha), Bangkok

Wat Traimitr (Temple of the Golden Buddha), Bangkok

Sights

Hong Kong The view of the coastline from the Ocean Park cable car

Crossing the harbor on the Star Ferry—second class, at water level

Tram ride from Kennedy Town to North Point

A bus ride around the island to Repulse Bay or Stanley

Malaysia Masjid Jamek Bandaraya, Kuala Lumpur

Baba Nonya Heritage, Malacca

Khoo Kongsi, Penang

Mt. Kinabalu from anywhere in Sabah

Sunset from the patio of E&O Hotel in Penang

Philippines Basilica Minore, Cebu City

Intramuros, Manila

Villa Escudero, Metro Manila

Banaue Rice Terraces, northern Luzon

Mt. Mayon, southern Luzon

Magellan's Cross, Cebu

Taluksangay, Mindanao

St. Paul Underground River National Park, Palawan

Singapore Botanic Gardens

Carved murals at the Dynasty hotel

Sultan Mosque

Zoological Gardens and Night Safari

Thailand Erawan Waterfall, Kanchanaburi

Floating Market, Damnoen Saduak

Golden Triangle, northern Thailand

    Phang Nga Bay, off Phuket

    Thai classical dancing

Beaches

Indonesia	Legian Beach, Bali
	Lombok Island
Malaysia	Batu Ferringhi, Penang
	Langkawi Pangkor Island
	Damai Beach, Sarawak
Philippines	Panglao, Bohol
	El Nido, Palawan
	Samal Island, Davao
	Boracay Island
	Santa Cruz Island, Zamboanga
Thailand	Pansea Beach, Phuket
	Nai Harn, Phuket
	Ao Phrang Bay, Krabi
	Haad Tong Nai Pan Noi, Ko Pha Ngan

Shopping

Hong Kong	Jade Market, Kansu Street, Kowloon
	Night Market at Temple Street, Kowloon
Indonesia	Antique wayang-kulit in Bali or Yogyakarta
	Batiks and leather in Yogyakarta
	Gold and silver in Bali
Malaysia	Karyaneka Handicrafts Center, Kuala Lumpur
	Batik Malaysia Berhad, Kuala Lumpur and Penang
	Selangor pewter, throughout Malaysia
	Antiques shops of Jonker Street, Malacca
Philippines	Handwoven tribal cloth, Yakan Village, Zamboanga
	Handicrafts, antiques, fresh produce, Baguio Market, Baguio City
	Madrazo tropical fruit market, Davao City
Singapore	Singapore Handicraft Centre
	P. Govindasamy Pillai for Indian silks
	China Silk House for Chinese silks

Thailand Sapphires and rubies in Bangkok

Thai silk in Chiang Mai and Bangkok

Night Bazaar in Chiang Mai

World Time Zones

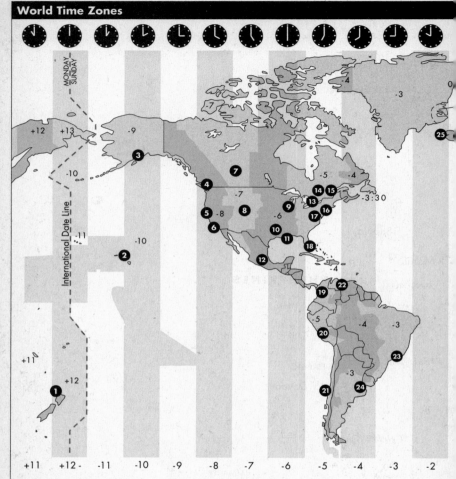

Numbers below vertical bands relate each zone to Greenwich Mean Time (0 hrs.).
Local times frequently differ from these general indications,
as indicated by light-face numbers on map.

Algiers, **29**

Anchorage, **3**

Athens, **41**

Auckland, **1**

Baghdad, **46**

Bangkok, **50**

Beijing, **54**

Berlin, **34**

Bogotá, **19**

Budapest, **37**

Buenos Aires, **24**

Caracas, **22**

Chicago, **9**

Copenhagen, **33**

Dallas, **10**

Delhi, **48**

Denver, **8**

Djakarta, **53**

Dublin, **26**

Edmonton, **7**

Hong Kong, **56**

Honolulu, **2**

Istanbul, **40**

Jerusalem, **42**

Johannesburg, **44**

Lima, **20**

Lisbon, **28**

London (Greenwich), **27**

Los Angeles, **6**

Madrid, **38**

Manila, **57**

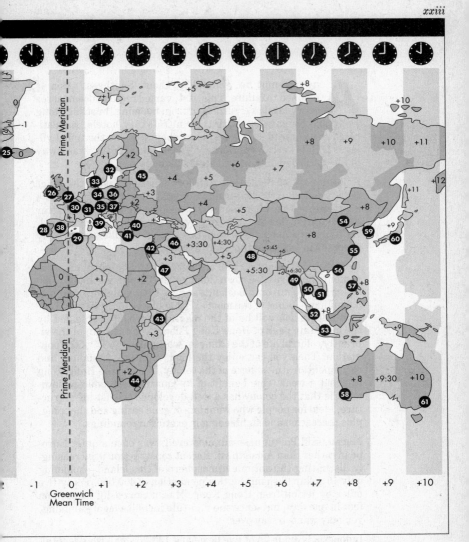

Mecca, **47**

Mexico City, **12**

Miami, **18**

Montréal, **15**

Moscow, **45**

Nairobi, **43**

New Orleans, **11**

New York City, **16**

Ottawa, **14**

Paris, **30**

Perth, **58**

Reykjavík, **25**

Rio de Janeiro, **23**

Rome, **39**

Saigon (Ho Chi Minh City), **51**

San Francisco, **5**

Santiago, **21**

Seoul, **59**

Shanghai, **55**

Singapore, **52**

Stockholm, **32**

Sydney, **61**

Tokyo, **60**

Toronto, **13**

Vancouver, **4**

Vienna, **35**

Warsaw, **36**

Washington, D.C., **17**

Yangon, **49**

Zürich, **31**

Introduction

A ny attempt to generalize about Southeast Asia is doomed to failure. This vast, varied region encompasses every level of civilization, from booming, bustling Hong Kong and Singapore—with their ultraluxury hotels, sophisticated restaurants, and world-class shopping—to the tribal villages of Sulawesi and of Borneo, where head-hunting was a way of life discarded only within recent memory.

A large part of Southeast Asia's fascination lies in the quiet beauty found in its rice-paddy landscapes—the glimpse into a simpler time that we in the West have left behind. But no matter where you go, do not expect to leave modern life entirely behind. As tourism among these societies grows, it subtly or grossly succeeds in changing them irrevocably.

Hong Kong is compact, well organized, well equipped, and convenient. The British Crown Colony—encompassing about 1,050 sq km (405 sq mi) on 235 islands and with a population of around 5.6 million—is one of the most exciting places in the world. Your first impression will be of the magnificent harbor shielded by the mountain peak of Hong Kong Island; your second, of the vibrantly colorful life of the Chinese, who make up 98% of the population. Then you can enjoy the food, nightlife, shopping, and cosmopolitan atmosphere of the colony. You can see Hong Kong in about a week. One benefit of its amazing economic achievement is that the colony has a well-developed tourist infrastructure, ideal for people who want lots of good eating and shopping, plus recreation and sightseeing in exotic surroundings.

Macau, still Portuguese-administered, was once a quiet European rather than Asian town. Recent construction is increasingly disrupting the antique atmosphere of this island—spanning only 15 sq km (6 sq mi), with a population of 400,000. Forty-five miles by jetfoil from Hong Kong, Macau can easily be seen on foot in one day, but since the nightlife includes legal gambling, you may want to stay over.

Indonesia is made up of five large and 13,600 small islands totaling more than 1,506,486 sq km (581,655 sq mi), with a population of 175 million. Its principal tourist destinations are Bali and Java. Java, the smallest of the main islands, has the capital city of Jakarta (population 7 million), which clearly reflects the successive influences on Indonesian culture: Local markets cater to its native people, the National Museum displays the heritage of former kingdoms, the cuisine is a fabulous mixture of Chinese and Dutch, and the architecture includes the pompous projects that remain from world's greatest Buddhist monument, and the palaces of the sultans in Yogyakarta and Solo.

Bali is only about 145 km (90 mi) long but has more than 3 million people and probably more than 10,000 temples. Since the destruction of Tibet, this is the last completely traditional society in which all facets of life—agriculture, economics, politics, technology, social customs, and the arts—are welded together by religion. The beaches of Bali's southern coast are highly developed to accommodate tourists, but it is in the interior that you can fully appreciate Bali's passionate and beautiful way of life. Lombok, the island to the east of Bali, is quickly becoming a resort attractive to those who find Bali too commercialized.

Sumatra to the north, with its ethnic minorities and a charming hill station at Lake Toba, has lately become a regular tourist stop, as have the Toraja highlands on the island of Sulawesi. Allow a minimum of two weeks to see Indonesia, more if you plan to go beyond Jakarta and Bali.

Malaysia's more than 329,748 sq km (127,316 sq mi) are divided into two parts, peninsular and eastern Malaysia. Its population of 16 million is made up of about 56% Malays, 34% Chinese, and 10% Indians. Peninsular Malaysia, with 83% of the population, contains the chief cities, sights, and resorts. English is common in the major cities, and the country is prosperous, although Western visitors will still find prices very low. The scenery is spectacular, with jungles and rugged hills in the interior, plantations and superb beaches in some of the coastal areas.

The capital, Kuala Lumpur (population 1.6 million), is clean and comfortable—if rather dull—with striking Victorian-Moorish architecture. The city is a 50-minute flight from Penang (the other main tourist center) and is near the Genting and Cameron highlands. The island of Langkawi is becoming a popular resort with the opening of deluxe hotels.

The states of Sarawak and Sabah in northern Borneo constitute eastern Malaysia. For tourists, this is frontier country. It has limited facilities (other than a few new luxury resorts) but offers wild jungle and mountain scenery and fascinating close-up glimpses of tribal life. Malaysia's major highlights can be seen in seven to 10 days. (Be aware that a United States travel advisory for Malaysia warns that convicted drug traffickers will receive the death penalty.)

Brunei, primarily a stopover between Sabah and Sarawak in East Malaysia, covers less than 5,760 sq km (2,226 sq mi). The tiny Malay sultanate is rich in oil revenues but still limited as to tourist facilities. Its population of 200,000 is found mostly in the sleepy tropical capital, Bandar Seri Begawan, and in longhouses on stilts along the water nearby. You can visit the country's attractions in a couple of days.

The Philippines has a population of 62 million and an area of nearly 300,000 sq km (115,831 sq mi), including seven major and 7,100 minor islands. The economic, political, and cultural center is still Manila (population 8 million), though the country's capital is Quezon City. Tourism is concentrated in Cebu and the Metro Manila area, where there are modern hotels, restaurants, and shops. Elsewhere on the main island of Luzon, hill resorts, beaches, subtropical scenery, and friendly people also draw visitors. The nation contains about 55 ethnic groups, each with distinctive languages, customs, and traditions. The five major cultures are the Ilocanos, Tagalogs, Visayans, Bicolanos, and Muslims. A couple of days will suffice to visit Manila, but if you want to see the upcountry areas and the exotic southern islands such as Cebu, plan on spending two weeks or more.

Singapore is something of an anomaly: an independent city-state, an efficient economy, a tightly run welfare system, and a remarkable multiracial social environment. With a population of 2.6 million and about 582 sq km (225 sq mi), Singapore has lost the mystery and romance of the "exotic Orient." What you will find instead is a bright, clean, modern tropical city that has neither the glamour of Hong Kong nor, mercifully, its brutal contrasts of wealth and squalor. Although the population is predominantly Chinese, Singapore's national culture is truly multiracial. A major port and shopping center, Singapore boasts excellent tourist facilities. Sightseeing takes only two or three days, but shopping often keeps visitors busy much longer.

Thailand, with a population of 54 million and an area of almost 513,998 sq km (198,455 sq mi), has become one of the world's top tourist destinations. Most of the traffic flows through the capital city of Bangkok (population 6 million), which has wonderful hotels, restaurants, nightclubs, shops, banks, and other big-city facilities. The level of development makes the city very convenient, but much of Bangkok is chaotic—like Tokyo, a monument to the problems of sudden, unplanned growth and commercialization.

Outside the capital, chief excursions are to important temples and ruins, mostly in smaller towns in the Bangkok basin—a hot, flat, wet, rice-growing plain that epitomizes subtropical Asia. The eastern and northeastern parts of the country are arid and poor; the areas' riches lie in their fantastic ruins, the spicy food, and a traditional Thai lifestyle. In the north, Chiang Mai, the rapidly developing second city, is a pleasant provincial town on a cool mountain plateau, with several good hotels and a tranquil atmosphere. A number of beach resorts are opening up for tourism. Pattaya is the leader: almost 137 km (85 mi) south of Bangkok, it is Asia's largest—and possibly tackiest—resort. Toward the Malaysian border are miles of sand beaches, fishing villages, and jungle regions. At least a week is needed to get a feel for this fascinating land.

1 Essential Information

Before You Go

Government Information Offices

Call or write to the organizations listed below for free brochures; listings of hotels, restaurants, sights, and shops; and up-todate calendars of events. The **Pacific Asia Travel Association** (1 Montgomery St., San Francisco, CA 94104, tel. 415/986–4646) can answer general questions about the area.

In the United States

Brunei Brunei has no tourist office in the United States. For information, contact the **Embassy of Brunei** (Consular Section, Watergate, Suite 300, 2600 Virginia Ave. NW, Washington, DC 20037, tel. 202/342–0159, fax 202/342–0158) or the **Brunei Permanent Mission to the United Nations** (866 UN Plaza, Room 248, New York, NY 10016, tel. 212/838–1600, fax 212/980–6478).

Hong Kong **Hong Kong Tourist Association** (590 5th Ave., New York, NY 10036, tel. 212/869–5008; 610 Enterprise Dr., Oak Brook, IL 60521, tel. 708/575–2828, fax 708/575–2829; 10940 Wilshire Blvd., Suite 1220, Los Angeles, CA 90024, tel. 310/208–4582, fax 310/208–1869).

Indonesia **Indonesia Tourist Promotion Board** (3457 Wilshire Blvd., Los Angeles, CA 90010, tel. 213/387–2078, fax 213/380–4876).

Macau **Macau Tourist Information Bureau** (70A Greenwich Ave., Box 316, New York, NY 10011, tel. 212/206–6828, fax 212/924–0882; Box 350, Kenilworth, IL 60043, tel. 708/251–6421, fax 708/256–5601; 3133 Lake Hollywood Dr., Box 1860, Los Angeles, CA 90068, tel. 213/851–3402 or 800/331–7150, fax 213/851–3684; Box 22188, Honolulu, HI 96822, tel. 808/538–7613, fax 808/536–0719).

Malaysia **Malaysia Tourist Information Center** (818 W. 7th St., Los Angeles, CA 90017, tel. 213/689–9702, fax 213/689–1530).

Philippines **Philippine Department of Tourism** (556 5th Ave., New York, NY 10036, tel. 212/575–7915, fax 212/302–6759; 447 Sutter St., 5th Floor, San Francisco, CA 94108, tel. 415/443–6666, fax 415/956–2093; 3460 Wilshire Blvd., Los Angeles, CA 90010, tel. 213/487–4525, fax 213/386–4063).

Singapore **Singapore Tourist Promotion Board** (590 5th Ave., 12th Floor, New York, NY 10036, tel. 212/302–4861, fax 212/302–4801; 333 N. Michigan Ave., Suite 818, Chicago, IL 60601, tel. 312/704–4200, fax 312/220–0020; 8484 Wilshire Blvd., Suite 510, Beverly Hills, CA 90211, tel. 213/852–1901, fax 213/852–0129).

Thailand **Tourism Authority of Thailand** (5 World Trade Center, Suite 3443, New York, NY 10048, tel. 212/432–0433, fax 212/912–0920; 3440 Wilshire Blvd., Los Angeles, CA 90010, tel. 213/382–2353, fax 213/389–7544; 303 E. Wacker Dr., Suite 400, Chicago, IL 60601, tel. 312/819–3990, fax 312/565–0359).

In Canada Indonesia and the Philippines have no tourist offices in Canada. For information, write to any U.S. office.

Brunei Brunei has no tourist office in Canada. For information, write to the **Embassy of Brunei** in Washington, DC, or the Permanent Mission to the United Nations in New York.

Hong Kong **Hong Kong Tourist Association** (347 Bay St., Suite 909, Toronto, Ontario M5H 2R7, tel. 416/366–2389, fax 416/366–1098).

Macau **Macau Tourist Information Bureau** (19 Mountalan Ave., Toronto, Ontario M4J 1H3, tel. and fax 416/466–6552; 1530 W. 8th Ave., Suite 305, Vancouver, BC V6J 1T5, tel. 604/736–1095, fax 604/736–7761).

Malaysia **Malaysia Tourist Information Center** (830 Burrard St., Vancouver, BC V6C 2K4, tel. 604/689–8899, fax 604/689–8804).

Singapore **Singapore Tourist Promotion Board** (175 Bloor St. E, Suite 1112, North Tower, Toronto, Ontario M4W 3R8, tel. 416/323–9139, fax 416/323–3514).

Thailand **Tourism Authority of Thailand** (250 St. Clair Ave. W, Suite 307, Toronto, Ontario M4V 1R6, tel. 416/925–9329, fax 416/925–2868; 10551 Shellbridge Way, Suite 157, Richmond, BC V6X 2W9, tel. 604/231–9030, fax 604/231–9031).

In the United Kingdom Contact the following offices for brochures and tourist information: **Brunei High Commission** (49 Cromwell Rd., London SW7 2ED, tel. 0171/581–0521); **Hong Kong Tourist Association** (125 Pall Mall, London SW1Y 5EA, tel. 0171/930–4775); **Indonesia Tourist Promotion Board** (3–4 Hanover St., London W1R 9HH, tel. 0171/493–0334); **Macau Tourist Information Bureau** (6 Sherlock Mews, Paddington St., London W1M 3RH, tel. 0171/224–3390); **Malaysian Tourist Development Corporation** (57 Trafalgar Sq., London WC2N 5DV, tel. 0171/930–7932); **Philippines Department of Tourism** (199 Piccadilly, London W1V 9LE, tel. 0171/439–3481); **Singapore Tourist Promotion Board** (126–130 Carrington St., London W1R 5FE, tel. 0171/437–0033); **Thailand Tourist Office** (49 Albemarle St., London W1X 3FE, tel. 0171/499–7679).

U.S. Government Travel Briefings The U.S. Department of State's **Overseas Citizens Emergency Center** (Room 4811, Washington, DC 20520; enclose S.A.S.E.) issues Consular Information Sheets, which cover crime, security, political climate, and health risks as well as embassy locations, entry requirements, currency regulations, and other routine matters. (Travel Warnings, which counsel travelers to avoid a country entirely, are issued in extreme cases.) For the latest information, stop in at any U.S. passport office, consulate, or embassy; call the interactive hotline (tel. 202/647–5225, fax 202/647-3000); or, with your PC's modem, tap into the Bureau of Consular Affairs' computer bulletin board (tel. 202/647–9225).

Tours and Packages

Package tours are a good idea if you are willing to trade independence for a guide who knows the language, a fairly solid guarantee that you will see the highlights, and some savings on airfare, hotels, and ground transportation. Listed below is a select sampling of tour operators serving the region, and of the tours they offer. Operators mix and match Southeast Asian countries in seemingly infinite varieties, so chances are that one has just the tour you have in mind. Often you can customize existing tours to suit your preferences. If you'd like to keep group travel to a minimum, look for tours with plenty of free or optional days. If your tour includes a private car with a driver, you will usually be expected to pick up the tab for the driver's lunch.

When considering a tour, be sure to find out (1) exactly what expenses are included in the price, particularly tips, taxes, side trips, meals, and entertainment; (2) ratings of all hotels on the itinerary and the facilities they offer; (3) cancellation policies for both you and the tour operator; (4) the number of travelers in your group; and (5), if you are traveling alone, the cost of the single supplement. Most tour operators request that bookings be made through a travel agent, and in most cases there is no additional charge for doing so.

Fully Escorted Tours
Multicountry

Deluxe-tour packager **Abercrombie & Kent International** (1520 Kensington Rd., Suite 212, Oak Brook, IL 60521, tel. 708/954–2944 or 800/323–7308) offers an "Oriental Capitals" tour of Singapore, Hong Kong, Tokyo, and Bangkok, plus the exotic "Borneo and Beyond" trip to Bangkok, Kuala Lumpur, Borneo, and Hong Kong. **Globus** (5301 S. Federal Circle, Littleton, CO 80123, tel. 303/797–2800 or 800/221–0090; for less extravagant touring, try its more budget-minded sister company, **Cosmos Tourama**) teams Bali, Bangkok, Singapore, and Hong Kong in a 15-day tour; and Tokyo, Hong Kong, Katmandu, Bangkok, Penang, Singapore, and Taipei in a 27-day package. "Oriental Adventure" from **Maupintour** (Box 807, Lawrence, KS 66046, tel. 913/843–1211 or 800/255–4266) includes Hong Kong, Bangkok, Bali, and Singapore. **TBI Tours** (787 7th Ave., Suite 1101, New York, NY 10019, tel. 212/489–1919 or 800/223–0266) serves up Bali, Hong Kong, Singapore, Malaysia, China, and Japan in its grand samplers. The firm also offers some of the best values through Thailand and Indochina, including a circular tour that departs from Bangkok and visits Phnom Penh, Angkor Wat, Ho Chi Minh City, Hanoi, Vientiane, and Luang Prabang. **Absolute Asia** (180 Varick St., New York, NY 10016, tel. 212/595–5782 or 800/736–8187) is a Vietnam-based company offering trips in Vietnam, China, Singapore, Myanmar (formerly called Burma), Thailand, Cambodia, and Laos. **EastQuest** (1 Union Square W, Suite 606, New York, NY 10003, tel. 212/741–1688 or 800/638–3449 outside NY) offers packages to Cambodia, Thailand, Laos, and Myanmar and, in conjunction with Bangkok Airways, organizes direct flights into Myanmar from Chiang Mai. **InterPacific Tours International** (111 E. 15th St., New York, NY 10003, tel. 212/953–6010 or 800/221–3594) has a base of operations in Hong Kong and a wide range of Orient packages (and prices) as a result. **Certified Tours** (110 S.E. 6th St., Fort Lauderdale, FL 33301, tel. 305/522–1110 or 800/233–7260) has a variety of Orient packages. **Collette Tours** (162 Middle St., Pawtucket, RI 02860, tel. 401/728–3805 or 800/832–4656) has several deluxe tours to Thailand, Singapore, China, and elsewhere in Asia. **Pacific Delight Tours** (132 Madison Ave., New York, NY 10016, tel. 212/684–7707 or 800/221–7179) offers single-country packages to Singapore, Thailand, or Hong Kong as well as mixed Orient tours. **Travel Plans International** (1200 Harger Rd., Oak Brook, IL 60521, tel. 708/573–1400 or 800/323–7600) travels out-of-the-ordinary routes in Southeast Asia. Its deluxe 18-day "Route of the Spice Traders" visits the boat-shape houses and mountain tribes of Sulawesi in Indonesia, as well as Singapore, Yogyakarta, Bali, and Hong Kong. **Cultural Tours** (9920 La Cienega Blvd., Suite 715, Englewood, CA 90301, tel. 310/216–1332, 800/282–8898, or in CA, 800/282–8899) offers a 15-day "Orient Shangri-La" tour to Hong Kong, Bangkok, Singapore, and Bali, as well as a 17-day tour of Hong Kong, Bangkok, Kuala Lumpur, Singapore, Bali, and Jakarta.

Single-Country

Several of the operators listed above also offer single-country tours. **Cultural Tours** has Hong Kong, Indonesia, and Philippines tours. **Abercrombie & Kent** runs Indonesia and Philippines tours. **Mindful Journey Tours** (1242 24th St., Santa Monica, CA 90404, tel. 310/828–5443 or 800/654–7975) offers single-country trips to Hong Kong, Singapore, and Thailand. **Natrabu** (433 California St., Suite 630, San Francisco, CA 94104, tel. 800/628–7228) runs tours throughout Indonesia and also organizes individual trips.

U.K. Operators

Bales Tours Ltd. (Bales House, Barrington Rd., Dorking, Surrey RH4 3HB, tel. 01306/76881) specializes in escorted tours, such as a 19-day tour of Indonesia, 10 days in northern Thailand, and 17 days in Bangkok and Singapore.

British Airways Holidays (Atlantic House, Hazelwick Ave., Three Bridges, Crawley, W. Sussex RH10 1NP, tel. 01293/611–611) offers numerous packages to Southeast Asia.

Kuoni Travel Ltd (Kuoni House, Dorking, Surrey RH5 4AZ, tel. 01306/740500) covers all the main Southeast Asian centers. Offerings include numerous holidays in Thailand, Singapore, Hong Kong, and Bangkok; combination tours of Indonesia, China, and Malaysia; and a 13-day "Beaches of Malaysia" package.

Tradewinds Faraway Holidays (Station House, 81–83 Fulham High St., London SW6 3JP, tel. 0171/731–8000) offers a variety of tours to Malaysia, Indonesia, Hong Kong, Thailand, and Singapore.

Special-Interest Tours

Adventure

Mountain Travel–Sobek (6420 Fairmont Ave., El Cerrito, CA 94530, tel. 800/227–2384) offers a variety of adventure outings, including sailing and hiking in Thailand and a 16-day "Thai Elephant Safari" tour, in which you visit remote hill tribes and stay in simple village houses. A tour in Indonesia's remote outpost Irian Jaya visits Melanesian tribes with roots in the Stone Age. The eight-day "Sumatran Alas River Adventure" is a rafting trip through the jungle.

Art and Archaeology

Archaeological Tours (271 Madison Ave., Suite 904, New York, NY 10016, tel. 212/986–3504) travels via Hong Kong and Jakarta en route to the temples, mountain villages, and lush tropics of Java, Sulawesi, and Bali. **InnerAsia Expeditions** (2627 Lombard St., San Francisco, CA 94123, tel. 415/922–0448 or 800/777–8183) offers an in-depth look at the cultures of Singapore, Bangkok, Hong Kong, and China. **Select Tours International** (Box 210, Redondo Beach, CA 90277, tel. 310/374–0880 or 800/356–6680) offers art and photography tours throughout Southeast Asia, including a 25-day "Art Expedition to the Indonesian Archipelago," focusing on textile arts.

Bicycling

Backroads Bicycle Touring (1516 5th St., Berkeley, CA 94710–1713, tel. 415/527–1555 or 800/462–2848) offers a 12-day "Cycle Bali" tour in spring. **Asia Pacific Adventures** (826 S. Sierra Bonita Ave., Los Angeles, CA 90036, tel. 213/935–3156 or 800/825–1680) features a 15-day cycling trip through northern Thailand.

Business

Asian Corporate Travel Service (Mindful Journeys, 1242 24th St., Santa Monica, CA 90404, tel. 310/453–1042 or 800/654–7975), in addition to air and first-class accommodations, provides such services as bilingual business cards, a letter of introduction in the language of your destination, a list of business contacts, and pretrip counseling on local business practices.

Culinary

For the serious chef, **InnerAsia** (*see* Art, *above*) opens the doors to cooking schools in Singapore and Bangkok. Led by a noted authority on Oriental cooking, the group goes behind the scenes at restaurants and into the markets. The tour is offered in conjunction with the California Culinary Academy. **Epicurean Expeditions East** (450 7th Ave., Suite 1202, New York, NY 10123, tel. 212/594–5860 or 800/732–2244) leads several plate-filling Hong Kong culinary crusades.

Music

Daily Thorpe (330 W. 58th St., Suite 610, New York, NY 10019, tel. 212/307–1555), **Great Performance Tours** (1 Lincoln Center Plaza, Suite 32V, New York, NY 10023, tel. 212/580–1400), and **Now Voyager International Tours** (Deer La., Pawlett, VT, tel. 802/325–3656) have a variety of packages throughout the year, including the world-famous Hong Kong Festival.

Natural History **Questers Worldwide Nature Tours** (257 Park Ave. S, New York, NY 10010, tel. 212/673–3120 or 800/468–8668) offers two 14-day nature and culture tours, one of Thailand and one of Malaysia (they can be taken back-to-back). The group follows wild elephant tracks looking for gibbons and tropical birds; boats down the Kok River; and takes in a wealth of temples and shrines. **Mountain Travel–Sobek** (*see* Adventure, *above*) offers a 10-day natural-history tour of Bali and Java, called "Islands of Fire." **King Bird Tours** (Box 196, Planetarium Station, New York, NY 10024, tel. 212/866–7923) arranges small group tours, focusing specifically on bird life, to most Asian countries. **Journeys** (4011 Jackson Rd., Ann Arbor, MI 48103, tel. 313/665–4407 or 800/255–8735) specializes in guided nature and culture travel, including eight-day trips for two or more people to Thailand and Vietnam. The **National Audubon Society** (700 Broadway, New York, NY 10003, tel. 212/979–3066) offers several land and cruise tours to Indonesia, China, and East Asia. **Smithsonian International Study Tours** (1100 Jefferson Dr., SW, Room 3045, tel. 202/357–4700) explore the natural and cultural riches of China, Indonesia, Singapore, Malaysia, and Thailand with land and water packages.

Photography **Craft World/Camera World Tours** (6776 Warboys Rd., Byron, NY 14422, tel. 716/548–2667) and **Voyages International** (706 Cayuga Heights Rd., Box 915, Ithaca, NY 14851, tel. 607/257–3091 or 800/633–0299) are geared to capturing perfect moments on film in Hong Kong and surrounding areas.

Scuba **Tropical Adventures Travel** (111 Second Ave. N, Seattle, WA 98109, tel. 206/441–3483 or 800/247–3483), a specialist in scuba cruises, visits some of the best dive spots in Indonesia and Thailand. Other water-sports equipment is available. **Natrabu** (*see* Single-Country Tours, *above*) offers dive packages to Indonesia.

Cruises **Abercrombie & Kent** (1520 Kensington Rd., Suite 212, Oak Brook, IL 60521, tel. 708/954–2944 or 800/323–7308) offers cruises around Indonesia, Borneo, Malaysia, Thailand, and Vietnam. The tour is noted for its high-caliber onboard lectures and programs by experts in the history, natural history, culture, and other facets of its destinations. Reserve six months to a year in advance if possible.

Cunard Cruise Lines (555 5th Ave., New York, NY 10017, tel. 800/458–9000) offers the ultimate in luxury cruises aboard the *Sea Goddess II*. Eleven-to 16-day cruises visit major and less-traveled Southeast Asian ports. The 11-day "Malaysia/Indonesia" cruise calls at eight ports.

Pearl Cruises (1510 S.E. 17th St., Fort Lauderdale, FL 33316, tel. 800/426–3588) has a variety of luxury cruises year-round, including a 23-day "Great Cities of Asia" land-sea tour. The 19-day "Spice Islands" tour calls at Singapore, Ho Chi Minh City, Nha Trang, Phuket, and seven Indonesian ports.

Independent Packages Most packages include air transportation, accommodations, and transfers to and from your hotel. Some add on meals and sightseeing and make local representatives available to answer questions and offer advice. The travel section of a local newspaper and a good travel agent are your best sources for shopping around. The airlines also provide individualized service for the independent traveler. For example, **Singapore Airlines** offers a flexible "Driveaway Holiday" fly/drive/hotel package. **Thai Airways International**'s "Royal Orchid

Holiday Discover Tours" are fly/hotel packages, which cover not only Thailand but elsewhere in Southeast Asia.

Japan & Orient Tours (3131 Camino del Rio N, Suite 1080, San Diego, CA 92108, tel. 619/282–3131 or 800/377–1080) offers flexible packages that let you design your own itinerary with options for hotels, air and ground transportation, and sightseeing. **InterPacific Tours International** (111 E. 15th St., New York, NY 10003, tel. 212/953–6010 or 800/221–3594) has four-day "TravPak Orient Vacation Stretcher" packages. **Tourcrafters** (30 S. Michigan Ave., Chicago, IL 60603, tel. 312/726–3886 or 800/621–2259) has two-day (or longer) "Short Stay" packages offering hotels in all ranges. Other good sources of independent packages are **Certified Tours** (110 S.E. 6th St., Fort Lauderdale, FL 33301, tel. 305/522–1110 or 800/233–7260), **Travel Plans International** (1200 Harger Rd., Oak Brook, IL 60521, tel. 708/573–1400 or 800/323–7600), **Delta Dream Vacations** (tel. 800/338–2010), and **United Airlines Vacations** (tel. 800/328–6877).

In the United Kingdom, **Trailfinders** (42–50 Earls Court Rd., London W8 7RG, tel. 0171/937–5400; 58 Deansgate, Manchester M3 2FF, tel. 0161/839–3636) is a leader in long-haul independent travel.

When to Go

Hong Kong and Macau Hong Kong's high tourist season, October–late December, is popular for a reason: The weather is pleasant, with sunny days and comfortable, cool nights. January, February, and sometimes early March are not only cold but also dank, with long periods of overcast skies and rain. March and April can be either cold and miserable or beautiful and sunny. By May, the cold, damp spell has broken and the temperature is warm and comfortable. The months of June through September are the typhoon season, when the weather is hot and sticky, with lots of rain.

Macau's summers are slightly cooler and wetter than Hong Kong's. In the 19th century, many Hong Kong residents summered in Macau to escape the heat.

Climate The following are average daily maximum and minimum temperatures for Hong Kong.

Jan.	64F	18C	May	82F	28C	Sept.	85F	29C
	56	13		74	23		77	25
Feb.	63F	17C	June	85F	29C	Oct.	81F	27C
	55	13		78	26		73	23
Mar.	67F	19C	July	87F	31C	Nov.	74F	23C
	60	16		78	26		65	18
Apr.	75F	24C	Aug.	87F	31C	Dec.	68F	20C
	67	19		78	26		59	15

Indonesia Indonesia's low-lying regions are uniformly hot and humid year-round. Temperatures can reach 90°F (32°C) soon after midday, and they drop no lower than 70°F (21°C) at night. The weather at higher altitudes is up to 20°F (11°C) cooler.

The best months for traveling are April–May and September–October, when you are most likely to miss the rains and the crowds. The west monsoon, from November through March, brings heavy rains: It can drizzle for several days in a row or pour half the day, with only occasional dry spells. Since most of Indonesia's attractions are under the open sky—temples and other architecture, beaches, and outdoor festivals—the monsoon can very literally dampen your enjoyment.

In the peak tourist months, June and July, popular areas (especially Torajaland) are crammed with visitors. Bali hotels also tend to be fully booked around Christmas and New Year.

Climate The following are average daily maximum and minimum temperatures for Jakarta.

Jan.	84F	29C	May	88F	31C	Sept.	88F	31C
	74	23		74	23		74	23
Feb.	84F	29C	June	88F	31C	Oct.	88F	31C
	74	23		74	23		74	23
Mar.	85F	30C	July	88F	31C	Nov.	85F	30C
	74	23		74	23		74	23
Apr.	86F	30C	Aug.	88F	31C	Dec.	85F	30C
	74	23		74	23		74	23

Malaysia and Brunei Malaysia's equatorial climate is fairly uniform throughout the year: Temperatures range from the low 90s during the day to low 70s at night. The mountains may be 10° cooler than the lowlands. Relative humidity is usually about 90%. Rain is common all year, but showers don't last long and shouldn't slow you down much. A rainy season brought on by monsoons lasts from November through February on the east coast of peninsular Malaysia, from October through April in Sarawak, and from October through February in Sabah. The heavy rains can cause delays.

During school holidays, locals tend to fill hotels, so book in advance if you plan to visit in early April, early August, or from mid-November to early January.

Climate The following are average daily maximum and minimum temperatures for Kuala Lumpur.

Jan.	89F	32C	May	91F	33C	Sept.	89F	32C
	72	22		74	23		74	23
Feb.	91F	33C	June	91F	33C	Oct.	89F	32C
	72	22		74	23		74	23
Mar.	91F	33C	July	89F	32C	Nov.	89F	32C
	74	23		72	22		74	23
Apr.	91F	33C	Aug.	89F	32C	Dec.	89F	32C
	74	23		74	23		72	22

Brunei, which lies between 4° and 6° north of the equator, is also hot and humid. (The annual mean temperature is 80°F.) Except for a narrow coastal plain, much of the country is rugged and heavily forested. Though sudden and short-lived rainstorms are prevalent throughout the year (particularly November–May), the wettest months are December and January.

Philippines The Philippines has two seasons: dry and wet. The dry season generally runs from late October through May, with temperatures ranging from cool and breezy—even chilly—in the northern highlands to scorching hot in the lowland cities. Within this seven-month span, the coolest stretch is from November through February and, since it coincides with winter months in the West, is also the peak tourist season. During this period popular spots are crowded, major hotels have high occupancy rates, and airfares are higher. Still, there are plenty of beaches and unspoiled places where crowds are either sparse or nonexistent.

If you enjoy crackling summer heat, then March through May are the best months to visit. The Catholic penitential rites of Lent are observed in late March or early April, climaxing in nationwide rituals during Holy Week, when business and government offices shut down. In contrast, May is harvest time, when fiestas are held all over the islands in a final burst of abandon before the onset of the monsoon rains.

For travelers who find themselves in the Philippines during the rainy season—June through September—it's helpful to know that most of Mindanao lies outside the typhoon belt, which cuts across Luzon and most of the Visayas. Mindanao does get rain, but not much more than during the rest of the year. Manila, on the other hand, is subject to frequent floods, while the highlands of northern Luzon become waterlogged, and mud and rock slides frequently make the roads impassable. Be sure to pack a good raincoat and waterproof boots.

Climate   The following are average daily maximum and minimum temperatures for Manila.

Jan.	86F	30C	May	93F	34C	Sept.	88F	31C
	70	21		75	24		75	24
Feb.	88F	31C	June	92F	33C	Oct.	88F	31C
	70	21		75	24		74	23
Mar.	91F	33C	July	88F	31C	Nov.	88F	31C
	72	22		75	24		72	22
Apr.	93F	34C	Aug.	88F	31C	Dec.	86F	30C
	74	23		75	24		70	21

Singapore   Singapore has neither peak nor off-peak tourist seasons. Hotel prices remain the same throughout the year, though during quiet spells many properties will discount room rates upon request (either in person or by mail). The busiest tourist months are December and July.

With the equator only 129 km (80 mi) to the south, Singapore is usually either hot or very hot. The average daily temperature is 80°F (26.6°C); it usually reaches 87°F (30.7°C) in the afternoon and drops to a cool 75°F (23.8°C) just before dawn. The months from November through January, during the northeast monsoon, are generally the coolest. The average daily relative humidity is 84.5%, though it drops to 65%–70% on dry afternoons.

Rain falls year-round, but the wettest months are November through January. February is usually the sunniest month; December, the most inclement. Though Singapore has been known to have as much as 512.2 mm (20 in) of rainfall in one 24-hour period, brief, frequent rainstorms are the norm, and the washed streets soon dry in the sun that follows.

Climate   The following are average daily maximum and minimum temperatures for Singapore.

Jan.	86F	30C	May	89F	32C	Sept.	88F	31C
	74	23		75	24		75	24
Feb.	88F	31C	June	88F	31C	Oct.	88F	31C
	74	23		75	24		74	23
Mar.	88F	31C	July	88F	31C	Nov.	88F	31C
	75	24		75	24		74	23
Apr.	88F	31C	Aug.	88F	31C	Dec.	88F	31C
	75	24		75	24		74	23

Thailand Thailand has two climates: tropical savannah in the northern regions and tropical rain forest in the south. Its three seasons run from hot (March to May) to rainy (June to September) to cool (October to February). Humidity is high all year, especially during the hot season. The cool season is pleasantly warm in the south, but in the north, especially in the hills around Chiang Mai, it can become quite chilly. The cool season is the peak season. Prices are often twice as high then as in the low seasons, yet hotels are often fully booked.

Climate The following are average daily maximum and minimum temperatures for Bangkok. The north will generally be a degree or two cooler.

Jan.	89F	32C	May	93F	34C	Sept.	89F	32C
	68	20		77	25		75	24
Feb.	91F	33C	June	91F	33C	Oct.	88F	31C
	72	22		75	24		75	24
Mar.	93F	34C	July	89F	32C	Nov.	88F	31C
	75	24		75	24		72	22
Apr.	95F	35C	Aug.	89F	32C	Dec.	88F	31C
	77	25		75	24		68	20

Information Sources For current weather conditions and forecasts for cities in the United States and abroad, plus the local time and helpful travel tips, call the **Weather Channel Connection** (tel. 900/932–8437; 95¢ per minute) from a touch-tone phone.

What to Pack

Pack light, because porters can be hard to find and baggage restrictions are tight on international flights—be sure to check on your airline's policies before you pack. And either leave room in your suitcase or bring expandable totes for all your bargains.

Clothing If you'll be traveling through several different types of climate, your wardrobe will have to reflect this. Light cotton or other natural-fiber clothing is appropriate for any Southeast Asian destination; drip-dry is an especially good idea, because the tropical sun and high humidity encourage frequent changes of clothing. Avoid exotic fabrics, because you may have difficulty getting them laundered.

Southeast Asia is generally informal: A sweater, shawl, or light-weight linen jacket will be sufficient for dining and evening wear, except for top international restaurants, where men will still be most comfortable in (and may in fact be required to wear) a jacket and tie. A sweater is also a good idea for cool evenings or overly air-conditioned restaurants.

Toiletries It might be wise to bring your favorite toilet articles (in plastic containers, to avoid breakage and reduce the weight of luggage). Make sure that bottles containing liquids are tightly capped to prevent leakage.

Footwear The paths leading to temples can be rough; in any case, a pair of sturdy and comfortable walking shoes is always appropriate when traveling. Slip-ons are preferable to lace-ups, as shoes must be removed before you enter most shrines and temples.

Miscellaneous Allow for the tropical sun by bringing along a hat and sunscreen. Mosquito repellent is a good idea, and toilet paper is not always supplied in public places. Bring an extra pair of eyeglasses or contact lenses in your carry-on luggage. If you have a health problem that requires a prescription drug, pack enough to last the duration of the trip or have your doctor write a prescription using the drug's generic name, because brand names vary from country to country (you'll need a prescription from a doctor in the country you're visiting in order to get the medication from a pharmacy there). Always carry prescription drugs in their original packaging to avoid problems with customs officials. Don't pack them in luggage that you plan to check in case your bags go astray. Pack a list of the offices that supply refunds for lost or stolen traveler's checks.

Electricity The electrical current in the countries covered in this book is 220 volts, 50 cycles alternating current (AC), except for the Phillipines, which, like the United States, runs on 110-volt, 60-cycle AC current. Unlike wall outlets in the United States, which accept plugs with two flat prongs, outlets in Southeast Asia take a variety of plug styles: Continental-type plugs, with two round prongs (Macau, some parts of the Philippines and Thailand); plugs with two round oversize prongs (some parts of Hong Kong, Malaysia, and Singapore); and plugs with three prongs (some parts of Hong Kong, Malaysia, and Singapore). Some parts of the Philippines and Thailand take plugs with two flat prongs.

Adapters, To use U.S.-made electric appliances abroad, you'll need an adapter
Converters, plug. Unless the appliance is dual-voltage and made for travel, you'll
Transformers also need a converter. Hotels sometimes have 110-volt outlets for low-wattage appliances marked "For Shavers Only" near the sink; don't use them for a high-wattage appliance like a blow-dryer. If you're traveling with an older laptop computer, carry a transformer. New laptop computers are auto-sensing, operating equally well on 110 and 220 volts, so you need only the appropriate adapter plug. For a copy of the free brochure "Foreign Electricity Is No Deep Dark Secret," send a stamped, self-addressed envelope to adapter-converter manufacturer Franzus Company (Customer Service, Dept. B50, Murtha Industrial Park, Box 142, Beacon Falls, CT 06403, tel. 203/723–6664).

Luggage Free airline baggage allowances depend on the airline, the route,
Regulations and the class of your ticket; ask in advance. In general, on domestic flights and on international flights between the United States and foreign destinations, you are entitled to check two bags—neither exceeding 62 inches, or 158 centimeters (length + width + height), or weighing more than 70 pounds (32 kilograms). A third piece may be brought aboard; its total dimensions are generally limited to less than 45 inches (114 centimeters) so that it will fit easily under the seat in front of you or in the overhead compartment. In the United States the Federal Aviation Administration gives airlines broad latitude to limit carry-on allowances and tailor them to different aircraft and operational conditions. Charges for excess, oversize, or overweight pieces vary.

If you are flying between two foreign destinations, note that baggage allowances may be determined not by piece but by weight—generally 88 pounds (40 kilograms) of luggage in first class, 66 pounds (30 kilograms) in business class, and 44 pounds (20 kilograms) in economy. If your flight between two cities abroad *connects* with your transatlantic or transpacific flight, the piece method still applies.

Safeguarding Before leaving home, itemize your bags' contents and their worth in
Your Luggage case they go astray. To minimize that risk, tag them inside and out with your name, address, and phone number. (If you use your home address, cover it so that potential thieves can't see it.) Put a copy of your itinerary inside each bag so that you can easily be tracked. At

check-in, make sure that the tag attached by baggage handlers bears the correct three-letter code for your destination. If your bags do not arrive with you, or if you detect damage, immediately file a written report with the airline before you leave the airport.

Taking Money Abroad

Traveler's Checks

Traveler's checks are preferable in metropolitan centers, although you'll need cash in rural areas and small towns. The most widely recognized are **American Express, Citicorp, Thomas Cook,** and **Visa,** which are sold by major commercial banks, usually for a fee of 1% to 3% of the checks' face value. Both American Express and Thomas Cook issue checks that can be countersigned and used by you or your traveling companion, and they both provide checks, at no extra charge, denominated in six non-U.S. currencies. (Some foreign banks charge as much as 20% for cashing traveler's checks denominated in dollars.) Buy a few checks in small denominations to cash toward the end of your trip, so you won't be left with excess foreign currency. Record the numbers of the checks, cross them off as you spend them, and keep this list separate from the checks.

Currency Exchange

Banks offer the most favorable exchange rates. If you use currency exchange booths at airports, rail and bus stations, hotels, stores, and privately run exchange firms, you'll typically get less favorable rates, but you may find the hours more convenient.

You can avoid long lines at airport currency-exchange booths by getting a *small* amount of currency before you depart at **Thomas Cook Currency Services** (630 5th Ave., New York, NY 10111, tel. 212/757–6915 or 800/223–7373 for locations in major metropolitan areas throughout the United States) or **Ruesch International** (tel. 800/424–2923 for locations). Check with your travel agent to be sure that the currency of the country you will be visiting can be imported.

Getting Money from Home

Cash Machines

Many automated-teller machines (ATMs) are tied to international networks such as **Cirrus** and **Plus.** You can use your bank card at ATMs to withdraw money from an account and get cash advances on a credit-card account if your card has been programmed with a personal identification number, or PIN. Check in advance on limits on withdrawals and cash advances within specified periods. Ask whether your bank-card or credit-card PIN will need to be reprogrammed for use in the area you'll be visiting. Four digits are commonly used overseas. Note that Discover is accepted only in the United States. On cash advances you are charged interest from the day you receive the money from ATMs as well as from tellers. Although transaction fees for ATM withdrawals abroad may be higher than fees for withdrawals at home, Cirrus and Plus exchange rates are excellent because they are based on wholesale rates offered only by major banks. They also may be referred to abroad as "a withdrawal from a credit account."

Plan ahead: Obtain ATM locations and the names of affiliated cash-machine networks before departure. For specific foreign Cirrus locations, call 800/424–7787; for foreign Plus locations, consult the Plus directory at your local bank.

Wiring Money

You don't have to be a cardholder to send or receive funds through **MoneyGram**^{SM} **from American Express.** Just go to a MoneyGram agent, located in American Express Travel Offices. Pay up to $1,000 with cash or a credit card, anything over that in cash. The money can be picked up within 10 minutes in the form of U.S. dollar traveler's checks or local currency. Call 800/926–9400 for locations and more information, or, abroad, the nearest American Express Travel Office. There's no limit, and the recipient need only present photo identification. The cost runs from 3% to 10%, depending on the amount sent, the destination, and how you pay.

You can also use **Western Union.** To wire money, take either cash or a cashier's check to the nearest agent or call 800/325–6000 and use MasterCard or Visa.

Long-Distance Calling

AT&T, MCI, and Sprint have international services that make calling home relatively affordable and convenient and let you avoid hotel surcharges. Before you go, call the company of your choice to learn the number you must dial in the country you're visiting in Southeast Asia to reach its network: **AT&T** USA Direct (tel. 800/874–4000), **MCI** Call USA (tel. 800/444–4444), or **Sprint** Express (tel. 800/793–1153). All three companies offer message delivery services to international travelers and have added debit cards so that you don't have to fiddle with change.

Passports and Visas

If your passport is lost or stolen abroad, report the loss immediately to the nearest embassy or consulate and to the local police. If you can provide the consular officer with the information contained in the passport, he or she will usually be able to issue you a new passport promptly. For this reason, keep a photocopy of the data page of your passport separate from your money and traveler's checks. Also leave a photocopy with a relative or friend at home.

All U.S., Canadian, and U.K. citizens must have a valid passport to enter any of the countries covered in this book. In addition, each country has its own visa requirements, listed below. (*Note:* Do check with your travel agent or the consulates of the countries you are planning to visit, as regulations change.)

Also, if you have visited areas infected with yellow fever, cholera, or smallpox within six to 14 days (depending on the country) of your arrival in any of the countries in the book, you will need a certificate of vaccination to be allowed in.

U.S. Citizens. You can pick up new and renewal passport application forms at any of the 13 U.S. Passport Agency offices and at some post offices and courthouses. Although passports are usually mailed within four weeks of your application's receipt, allow five weeks or more from April through summer. Call the Department of State Office of Passport Services' information line (tel. 202/647–0518) for fees, documentation requirements, and other details.

Canadian Citizens. Application forms are available at 28 regional passport offices as well as post offices and travel agencies. Whether for a first or a subsequent passport, you must apply in person. Children under 16 may be included on a parent's passport but must have their own to travel alone. Passports are valid for five years and are usually mailed within two to three weeks of an application's receipt. For fees, documentation requirements, and other information in English or French, call the passport office (tel. 819/994–3500 or 800/567–6868).

U.K. Citizens. Citizens of the United Kingdom need a valid passport to enter most Southeast Asian countries. Applications for new and renewal passports are available from main post offices as well as at the six passport offices, located in Belfast, Glasgow; Liverpool, London, Newport, and Peterborough. You may apply in person at all passport offices, or by mail to all except the London office. Children under 16 may travel on an accompanying parent's passport. All passports are valid for 10 years. Allow a month for processing.

Brunei
U.S. Citizens Visas, good for stays up to 10 days, are required to enter Brunei. To apply, contact the Embassy of Brunei (Consular Section, Watergate, Suite 300, 2600 Virginia Ave. NW, Washington, DC 20037, tel. 202/342–0159), or the Brunei Permanent Mission to the United Nations (866 UN Plaza, Room 248, New York, NY 10017, tel. 212/838–1600). Allow at least seven working days for applications to be processed.

Canadian Citizens Visas are not required for stays up to 14 days. Canadians planning longer stays in Brunei can apply for a visa at the UN Mission in New York or the embassy in Washington, DC.

U.K. Citizens Visas are not required for stays up to 30 days. For extensions, contact the Embassy of Brunei (49 Cromwell Rd., London SW7 2ED, tel. 0171/581–0521). Allow at least seven working days for processing.

Hong Kong Visas are not required for stays of up to one month for U.S. citizens, up to three months for Canadian citizens, and up to six months for U.K. citizens.

Extended-stay visas may be obtained through the nearest British embassy, consulate, or high commission, or through the Immigration Department in Hong Kong (3/F, Mirror Tower, 61 Mody Rd., E. Tsim Sha Tsui, Kowloon; tel. 3/2733–3111). Allow six weeks for processing.

Indonesia Passports must be valid for at least six months from arrival date, and all travelers must have proof of onward or return passage. Visas are not required for stays of up to 60 days for U.S., Canadian, and U.K. citizens, as long as you enter the country through one of the major gateways: Medan, Jakarta, Surabaya, Denpasar (Bali), or Biak (Irian Jaya). Other ports of entry may require a visa.

Macau Visas are not required for stays of up to 90 days for U.S., Canadian, and U.K. citizens.

Malaysia Visas are not required for stays of up to 90 days for U.S., Canadian, and U.K. citizens.

Philippines Visas are not required for stays of up to 21 days for U.S. citizens, providing travelers have a ticket for a return or onward journey. Canadian and U.K. citizens, however, do need visas; contact your nearest consulate for details.

Singapore Visas are not required for stays of up to 14 days for U.S., Canadian, and U.K. citizens.

Thailand Visas are not required for stays of up to 15 days for U.S., Canadian, and U.K. citizens, providing visitors can show proof of onward travel arrangements.

Extended-stay visas can be obtained by contacting the nearest Thai diplomatic mission or writing the Immigration Division, Soi Suan Phlu, Sathon Tai Rd., Bangkok 10120, Thailand.

Customs and Duties

On Arrival Personal effects, 8 ounces of tobacco, 2 ounces of perfume, up to 10
Brunei ounces of toilet water, and 20 ounces of liquor may be brought into
Brunei duty-free.

Hong Kong Visitors may bring 200 cigarettes, 50 cigars, or 250 grams of tobacco; 1 liter of liquor; 60 milliliters of perfume; and 250 milliliters of toilet water into Hong Kong duty-free. Firearms must be declared and handed into custody until departure.

Indonesia Two bottles of liquor and 200 cigarettes may be brought into Indonesia duty-free. Restrictions apply on the import of radios and television sets.

Macau There are no Customs restrictions for travelers entering Macau.

Malaysia Such items as cameras, watches, pens, lighters, cosmetics, perfume, portable radio cassette players, cigarettes (up to 200), and liquor (1 liter) may be brought into Malaysia duty-free. Visitors bringing in dutiable goods, such as video equipment, may have to pay a deposit (up to 50% of the item's value) for temporary importation, which is refundable when they leave. If you have to pay a tax or deposit, be sure to get an official receipt. The importation of illegal drugs into Malaysia carries the death penalty.

Philippines Personal effects (a reasonable amount of clothing and a small quantity of perfume), 400 cigarettes or two tins of smoking tobacco, and 2 liters of liquor may be brought into the Philippines duty-free.

Singapore Duty-free allowances include 1 liter each of spirits, wine, and beer; all personal effects; and less than S$50 in foods such as chocolates, biscuits, and cakes. The import of drugs, obscene articles and publications, seditious and treasonable materials, toy coins and currency notes, cigarette lighters of pistol/revolver shapes, or reproductions of copyrighted publications, videotapes, records, or cassettes is prohibited. Chewing gum in amounts deemed large enough for resale is also prohibited, as are duty-free cigarettes.

Thailand One quart of wine or liquor, 200 cigarettes or 250 grams of smoking tobacco, and all personal effects may be brought into Thailand duty-free. Visitors may bring in any amount of foreign currency; amounts taken out may not exceed those declared upon entry. Narcotic drugs, pornographic materials, and firearms are strictly prohibited.

Returning If you've been out of the country for at least 48 hours and haven't
Home already used the exemption, or any part of it, in the past 30 days, you
U.S. Customs may bring home $400 worth of foreign goods duty-free. So can each member of your family, regardless of age; and your exemptions may be pooled, so one of you can bring in more if another brings in less. A flat 10% duty applies to the next $1,000 worth of goods; above $1,400, the rate varies with the merchandise. (If the 48-hour or 30-day limits apply, your duty-free allowance drops to $25, which may not be pooled.) Please note that these are the *general* rules, applicable to most countries, including many in Southeast Asia.

Travelers 21 or older may bring back 1 liter of alcohol duty-free, provided the beverage laws of the state through which they reenter the United States allow it. In addition, 100 non-Cuban cigars and 200 cigarettes are allowed, regardless of your age. Antiques and works of art more than 100 years old are duty-free.

Canadian Once per calendar year, when you've been out of Canada for at least
Customs seven days, you may bring in C$300 worth of goods duty-free. If

you've been away less than seven days but more than 48 hours, the duty-free exemption drops to C$100 but can be claimed any number of times (as can a C$20 duty-free exemption for absences of 24 hours or more). You cannot combine the yearly and 48-hour exemptions, use the $300 exemption only partially (to save the balance for a later trip), or pool exemptions with family members. Goods claimed under the C$300 exemption may follow you by mail; those claimed under the lesser exemptions must accompany you.

Alcohol and tobacco products may be included in the yearly and 48-hour exemptions but not in the 24-hour exemption. If you meet the age requirements of the province through which you reenter Canada, you may bring in, duty-free, 1.14 liters (40 imperial ounces) of wine or liquor *or* two dozen 12-ounce cans or bottles of beer or ale. If you are 16 or older, you may bring in, duty-free, 200 cigarettes, 50 cigars or cigarillos, and 400 tobacco sticks or 400 grams of manufactured tobacco. Alcohol and tobacco must accompany you on your return.

An unlimited number of gifts valued up to C$60 each may be mailed to Canada duty-free. These do not count as part of your exemption. Label the package "Unsolicited Gift—Value under $60." Alcohol and tobacco are excluded.

For more information, including details of duties on items that exceed your duty-free limit, ask the Revenue Canada Customs, Excise and Taxation (2265 St. Laurent Blvd. S, Ottawa, Ontario, K1G 4K3, tel. 613/957–0275) for a copy of the free brochure "I Declare/Je Déclare."

U.K. Customs   From destinations outside the EU such as Southeast Asia, you may import duty-free 200 cigarettes, 100 cigarillos, 50 cigars or 250 grams of tobacco; 1 liter of spirits or 2 liters of fortified or sparkling wine; 2 liters of still table wine; 60 milliliters of perfume; 250 milliliters of toilet water; plus £136 worth of other goods, including gifts and souvenirs.

For further information or a copy of "A Guide for Travellers," which details standard customs procedures as well as what you may bring into the United Kingdom from abroad, contact HM Customs and Excise (Dorset House, Stamford St., London SE1 9PY, tel. 0171/928–3344).

Brunei   The export of certain goods, such as antiques and articles of a historical nature, is restricted. Severe penalties (including death) apply to anyone caught smuggling narcotics.

Hong Kong   Hong Kong is a free port with no duty restrictions.

Indonesia   Visitors may not export more than 50,000 rupiah per person.

Macau   Travelers may bring only 200 cigarettes, 50 cigars, or 250 grams of tobacco, plus 1 liter of spirits, duty-free into Hong Kong from Macau. Otherwise, Macau has no export duties.

Malaysia   Restrictions exist on the export of antiquities. If in doubt about any purchase, check with the director of the Museum Negara in Kuala Lumpur.

Philippines   Restrictions exist on the export of antiques, religious and historical artifacts, seashells, coral, orchids, monkeys, and birds (including endangered species such as the Philippine eagle).

Singapore   Export permits are required for arms, ammunition, explosives, animals, gold, platinum, precious stones and jewelry, poisons, and medicinal drugs. The export of narcotic drugs is punishable by death under Singapore law.

Thailand   Visitors may not export more than 500 baht per person or 1,000 baht per family passport.

Traveling with Cameras, Camcorders, and Laptops

If your camera is new or if you haven't used it for a while, shoot and develop a few test rolls of film before you leave. Store film in a cool, dry place—never in the car's glove compartment or on the shelf under the rear window. Airport security X-rays generally aren't harmful to film with ISO below 400. To protect your film, carry it with you in a clear plastic bag and ask for a hand inspection. Such requests are honored at U.S. airports, usually not abroad. Don't depend on a lead-lined bag to protect film in checked luggage—the airline may increase the radiation to see what's inside. Call the Kodak Information Center (tel. 800/242–2424) for details.

Camcorders   Before your trip, put camcorders through their paces, invest in a **and**   skylight filter to protect the lens, and check all the batteries. Most **Videotapes**   newer camcorders are equipped with batteries that can be recharged with a universal or worldwide AC adapter charger (or multivoltage converter) usable whether the voltage is 110 or 220. All that's needed is the appropriate plug. Register foreign-made camcorders with U.S. Customs before your departure when you're traveling to the Orient.

Videotape is not damaged by X-rays, but it may be harmed by the magnetic field of a walk-through metal detector, so ask for a handcheck. Airport security personnel may ask you to turn on the camcorder to prove that it's what it appears to be, so make sure the battery is charged. Note that rather than the National Television System Committee (NTSC) video standard used in the United States and Canada, the countries covered in this book use PAL technology, except for the Philippines, which uses NTSC. You will not be able to view your tapes through the local TV set or view movies bought there in your home VCR. Blank tapes bought in Southeast Asia can be used for NTSC camcorder taping, but they are pricey.

Laptops   Security X-rays do not harm hard-disk or floppy-disk storage, but you may request a hand-check, at which point you may be asked to turn on the computer to prove that it is what it appears to be. (Check your battery before departure.) Most airlines allow you to use your laptop aloft except during takeoff and landing (so as not to interfere with navigation equipment). For international travel, register your foreign-made laptop with U.S. Customs as you leave the country. If your laptop is U.S.-made, call the consulate of the country you'll be visiting to find out whether or not it should be registered with customs upon arrival. Before departure, find out about repair facilities at your destination, and don't forget any transformer or adapter plug you may need (*see* Electricity, *above*).

Staying Healthy

Shots and   Although the countries in Southeast Asia do not require or suggest **Medications**   vaccinations before traveling, the United States Centers for Disease Control offer the following recommendations:

Tetanus-diphtheria and polio vaccinations should be up-to-date—if you haven't been immunized since childhood, consider bolstering your vaccination. You should also be immunized against (or immune to) measles, mumps, and rubella. If you plan to visit rural areas, where there's questionable sanitation, you'll need an immune-serum globulin vaccination as protection against hepatitis A. If you are staying for longer than three weeks, and traveling into rural areas, antimalaria pills and a typhoid vaccination are recommended. If staying for a month or more, you should be vaccinated against rabies and Japanese encephalitis; for six months or more, against hepatitis B as well. For news on current outbreaks of infectious diseases, ask your physician and check with your state or local department of health.

A major health risk in Southeast Asia is posed by the contamination of drinking water and fresh fruit and vegetables by fecal matter, which causes the intestinal ailment known as traveler's diarrhea. It usually lasts only a day or two. Paregoric, a good antidiarrheal agent that dulls or eliminates abdominal cramps, requires a doctor's prescription in some Southeast Asian countries. Two drugs recommended by the National Institutes of Health for mild cases of diarrhea can be purchased over the counter: Pepto-Bismol and loperamide (Imodium). If you come down with the malady, rest as much as possible and drink lots of fluids (such as tea without milk—chamomile is a good folk remedy for diarrhea). In severe cases, rehydrate yourself with a salt-sugar mixture added to purified water (½ tsp. salt and 4 tbsp. sugar per quart/liter of purified water). The best defense is a careful diet. Stay away from unbottled or unboiled water, as well as ice, uncooked food, and unpasteurized milk and milk products.

According to the Centers for Disease Control (CDC), there is a limited risk of malaria and dengue in certain areas of Southeast Asia. If you plan to visit remote regions or stay for more than six weeks, check with the CDC's **International Travelers Hotline** (Center for Preventive Services, Division of Quarantine, Traveler's Health section, 1600 Clifton Rd., MSE03, Atlanta, GA 30333, tel. 404/332–4559). The hot line recommends chloroquine (Analen) as an antimalarial agent. Malaria-bearing mosquitoes bite at dusk and at night, so travelers to susceptible regions should take mosquito nets, wear clothing that covers the body, and carry repellent containing Deet and a spray against flying insects for living and sleeping areas. No vaccine exists against dengue, so if it is in the area, travelers should use aerosol insecticides indoors as well as repellents against the mosquito.

Scuba divers take note: PADI recommends that you not fly within 24 hours of scuba diving.

Finding a Doctor Many Southeast Asian hotels have physicians on call 24 hours a day. Also, the **International Association for Medical Assistance to Travelers** (IAMAT; 417 Center St., Lewiston, NY 14092, tel. 716/754–4883; 40 Regal Rd., Guelph, Ontario N1K 1B5; 57 Voirets, 1212 Grand-Lancy, Geneva, Switzerland) publishes a worldwide directory of English-speaking physicians whose qualifications meet IAMAT standards and who have agreed to treat members for a set fee. Membership is free.

Assistance Companies Pretrip medical referrals, emergency evacuation or repatriation, 24-hour telephone hot lines for medical consultation, dispatch of medical personnel, relay of medical records, cash for emergencies, and other personal and legal assistance are among the services provided by several organizations specializing in medical assistance to travelers. Among them are **International SOS Assistance** (Box 11568, Philadelphia, PA 19116, tel. 215/244–1500 or 800/523–8930;

Box 466, Pl. Bonaventure, Montréal, Québec H5A 1C1, tel. 514/874–7674 or 800/363–0263), **Medex Assistance Corporation** (Box 10623, Baltimore, MD 21285, tel. 410/296–2530 or 800/874–9125), **Near Services** (450 Prairie Ave., Suite 101, Calumet City, IL 60409, tel. 708/868–6700 or 800/654–6700), and **Travel Assistance International** (1133 15th St. NW, Suite 400, Washington, DC 20005, tel. 202/331–1609 or 800/821–2828). Because these companies will also sell you death-and-dismemberment, trip-cancellation, and other insurance coverage, there is some overlap with the travel-insurance policies discussed under Insurance, *below.*

Publications   *The Safe Travel Book* by Peter Savage ($12.95; Lexington Books, 866 3rd Ave., New York, NY 10022, tel. 212/702–4771 or 800/257–5755, fax 800/562–1272) is packed with handy lists and phone numbers to make your trip smooth. *Traveler's Medical Resource* by William W. Forgey ($19.95; ICS Books, Inc., 1 Tower Plaza, 107 E. 89th Ave., Merrillville, IN 45410, tel. 800/541–7323) is also a good, authoritative guide to care overseas.

Insurance

For U.S.   Most tour operators, travel agents, and insurance agents sell spe-
Residents   cialized health-and-accident, flight, trip-cancellation, and luggage insurance as well as comprehensive policies with some or all of these features. Before you make any purchase, review your existing health and homeowner policies to find out whether they cover expenses incurred while traveling.

Health-and-   Specific policy provisions of supplemental health-and-accident in-
Accident   surance for travelers include reimbursement for $1,000 to $150,000
Insurance   worth of medical and/or dental expenses caused by an accident or illness during a trip. The personal-accident, or death-and-dismemberment, provision pays a lump sum to your beneficiaries if you die or to you if you lose a limb or your eyesight; the lump sum awarded can range from $15,000 to $500,000. The medical-assistance provision may reimburse you for the cost of referrals, evacuation, or repatriation and other services, or it may automatically enroll you as a member of a particular medical-assistance company (*see* Assistance Companies, *above*).

Flight   Often bought as a last-minute impulse at the airport, flight insur-
Insurance   ance pays a lump sum when a plane crashes either to a beneficiary if the insured dies or sometimes to a surviving passenger who loses eyesight or a limb. Like most impulse buys, flight insurance is expensive and basically unnecessary. It supplements the airlines' coverage described in the limits-of-liability paragraphs on your ticket. Charging an airline ticket to a major credit card often automatically entitles you to coverage and may also embrace travel by bus, train, and ship.

Baggage   In the event of loss, damage, or theft on international flights, air-
Insurance   lines' liability is $20 per kilogram for checked baggage (roughly about $640 per 70-pound bag) and $400 per passenger for unchecked baggage. On domestic flights, the ceiling is $2,000 per passenger. Excess-valuation insurance can be bought directly from the airline at check-in for about $10 per $1,000 worth of coverage. However, you cannot buy it at any price for the rather extensive list of excluded items shown on your airline ticket.

Trip Insurance   **Trip-cancellation-and-interruption insurance** protects you in the event you are unable to undertake or finish your trip, especially if your airline ticket, cruise, or package tour does not allow changes or cancellations. The amount of coverage you purchase should equal the cost of your trip should you, a traveling companion, or a family member fall ill, forcing you to stay home, plus the nondiscounted one-way airline ticket you would need to buy if you had to return home early. Read the fine print carefully, especially sections defining "family member" and "preexisting medical conditions." **Default or bankruptcy insurance** protects you against a supplier's failure to deliver. Such policies often do not cover default by a travel agency, tour operator, airline, or cruise line if you bought your tour and the coverage directly from the firm in question. Tours packaged by one of the 33 members of the United States Tour Operators Association (USTOA, 211 E. 51st St., Suite 12B, New York, NY 10022; tel. 212/750–7371), which requires members to maintain $1 million each in an account to reimburse clients in case of default, are likely to present the fewest difficulties. Even better, pay for travel arrangements with a major credit card, so that you can refuse to pay the bill if services have not been rendered—and let the card company fight your battles.

Comprehensive Policies Companies supplying comprehensive policies with some or all of the above features include **Access America, Inc.** (Box 90315, Richmond, VA 23230, tel. 800/284–8300); **Carefree Travel Insurance** (Box 310, 120 Mineola Blvd., Mineola, NY 11501, tel. 516/294–0220 or 800/323–3149); **Near** (450 Prairie Ave., Suite 101, Calumet City, IL 60409, tel. 708/868–6700 or 800/654–6700; **Tele-Trip** (Mutual of Omaha Plaza, Box 31762, Omaha, NE 68131, tel. 800/228–9792); **The Travelers Companies** (1 Tower Sq., Hartford, CT 06183, tel. 203/277–0111 or 800/243–3174); **Travel Guard International** (1145 Clark St., Stevens Point, WI 54481, tel. 715/345–0505 or 800/826–1300); and **Wallach and Company, Inc.** (107 W. Federal St., Box 480, Middleburg, VA 22117, tel. 703/687–3166 or 800/237–6615).

For U.K. Residents Most tour operators, travel agents, and insurance agents sell policies covering accident, medical expenses, personal liability, trip cancellation, and loss or theft of personal property. You can also buy an annual travel-insurance policy valid for every trip (usually of less than 90 days) you make during the year in which it's purchased. Make sure you will be covered if you have a preexisting medical condition or are pregnant.

For advice by phone or a free booklet, "Holiday Insurance," that sets out what to expect from a holiday-insurance policy and gives price guidelines, contact the Association of British Insurers (51 Gresham St., London EC2V 7HQ, tel. 0171/600–3333; 30 Gordon St., Glasgow G1 3PU, tel. 0141/226–3905; Scottish Providence Bldg., Donegall Sq. W, Belfast BT1 6JE, tel. 01232/249176; call for other locations).

Student and Youth Travel

Travel Agencies **Council Travel Services (CTS),** a subsidiary of the nonprofit Council on International Educational Exchange, specializes in low-cost travel arrangements abroad for students and is the exclusive U.S. agent for several discount cards. Also newly available from CTS are domestic air passes for bargain travel within the United States. CIEE's twice-yearly *Student Travels* magazine is available at the CTS office at CIEE headquarters (205 E. 42nd St., 16th Floor, New York, NY 10017, tel. 212/661–1450) and in Boston (tel. 617/266–1926), Miami (tel. 305/670–9261), Los Angeles (tel. 310/208–3551), and at 43 branches in college towns nationwide (free in person, $1 by mail). **Campus Connections** (1100 East Marlton Pike, Cherry Hill,

NJ 08034, tel. 800/428–3235) specializes in discounted accommodations and airline fares for students. The **Educational Travel Centre** (438 N. Frances St., Madison, WI 53703, tel. 608/256–5551) offers low-cost domestic and international airline tickets, mostly for flights departing from Chicago, and rail passes. Other travel agencies catering to students include **TMI Student Travel** (1146 Pleasant St., Watertown, MA 02172, tel. 617/661–8187 or 800/245–3672) and **Travel Cuts** (187 College St., Toronto, Ontario M5T 1P7, tel. 416/979–2406).

Discount Cards For discounts on transportation and on museum and attractions admissions, buy the **International Student Identity Card** (ISIC) if you're a bona fide student or the **International Youth Card** (IYC) if you're under 26. In the United States the ISIC and IYC cards cost $16 each and include basic travel accident and illness coverage and a toll-free travel assistance hot line. Apply to **CIEE** (*see* address *above*, tel. 212/661–1414; the application is in *Student Travels*). In Canada the cards are available for $15 each from **Travel Cuts** (*see above*). In the United Kingdom they cost £5 and £4 respectively at student unions and student travel companies, including Council Travel's London office (28A Poland St., London W1V 3DB, tel. 0171/437–7767).

Hostelling A **Hostelling International** (HI) membership card is the key to more than 5,000 hostels in 70 countries; the sex-segregated, dormitory-style sleeping quarters, including some for families, go for $7 to $20 a night per person. Membership is available in the United States through **Hostelling International–American Youth Hostels** (HI-AYH, 733 15th St. NW, Suite 840, Washington, DC 20005, tel. 202/783–6161), the U.S. link in the worldwide chain, and costs $25 for adults 18 to 54, $10 for those under 18, $15 for those 55 and over, and $35 for families. Volume 2 of the *AYH Guide to Budget Accommodation* lists hostels in Asia and Australasia as well as in Canada and the United States ($13.95 including postage). HI membership is available in Canada through **Hostelling International–Canada** (205 Catherine St., Suite 400, Ottawa, Ontario K2P 1C3, tel. 613/748–5638) for $26.75, and in the United Kingdom through the **Youth Hostel Association of England and Wales** (Trevelyan House, 8 St. Stephen's Hill, St. Albans, Hertfordshire AL1 2DY, tel. 01727/855215) for £9.

The **Hong Kong Youth Hostel Association** (21A Lock Rd., Kowloon, tel. 2366–3419) provides information on inexpensive accommodations. For a list of hostels, write to the tourist authorities (*see* Government Information Offices, *above*) of Singapore (ask for the booklet *Surprising Singapore*) and Thailand.

YMCAs are located throughout Southeast Asia. For a listing of Y's worldwide, send a stamped, addressed envelope to "Y's Way," 356 W. 34th Street, New York, NY 10001, tel. 212/760–5856. They can also make reservations.

Traveling with Children

Publications
Newsletter
Family Travel Times, published 10 times a year by **Travel With Your Children** (TWYCH, 45 W. 18th St., New York, NY 10011, tel. 212/206–0688; annual subscription $55), covers destinations, types of vacations, and modes of travel.

Books
Traveling with Children—And Enjoying It, by Arlene K. Butler ($11.95 plus $3 shipping per book; Globe Pequot Press, Box 833, 6 Business Park Rd., Old Saybrook, CT 06475, tel. 800/243–0495, or

800/962–0973 in CT) helps plan your trip with children, from tod-
dlers to teens.

Tour Operators **Rascals in Paradise** (650 5th St., Suite 505, San Francisco, CA 94107,
tel. 415/978–9800 or 800/872–7225) specializes in adventurous, exot-
ic, and fun-filled vacations for families to carefully screened resorts
and hotels around the world.

Getting There
Air Fares On international flights, the fare for infants under age 2 not occupying a seat is generally either free or 10% of the accompanying adult's
fare; children ages 2 to 11 usually pay half to two-thirds of the adult
fare. On domestic flights, children under 2 not occupying a seat travel free, and older children currently travel on the "lowest applicable" adult fare.

Baggage In general, infants paying 10% of the adult fare are allowed one carry-on bag, not to exceed 70 pounds or 45 inches (length + width +
height) and a collapsible stroller; check with the airline before departure, because you may be allowed less if the flight is full. The
adult baggage allowance applies for children paying half or more of
the adult fare.

Safety Seats The FAA recommends the use of safety seats aloft and details approved models in the free leaflet **"Child/Infant Safety Seats Recommended for Use in Aircraft"** (available from the Federal Aviation
Administration, APA–200, 800 Independence Ave. SW, Washington, DC 20591, tel. 202/267–3479; Information Hotline, tel. 800/322-
7873). Airline policy varies. U.S. carriers allow FAA-approved models bearing a sticker declaring their FAA approval. Because these
seats are strapped into regular passenger seats, airlines may require that a ticket be bought for an infant who would otherwise ride
free. Foreign carriers may not allow infant seats, may charge the
child's rather than the infant's fare for their use, or may require you
to hold your baby during takeoff and landing, thus defeating the
seat's purpose.

Facilities Aloft Some airlines provide other services for children, such as children's
meals and freestanding bassinets (only to those with seats at the
bulkhead, where there's enough legroom). Make your request when
reserving. Biannually the February issue of *Family Travel Times*
details children's services on three dozen airlines ($12; *see above*).
"Kids and Teens in Flight" (free from the U.S. Department of
Transportation's Office of Consumer Affairs (R-25, Washington, DC
20590, tel. 202/366–2220) offers tips for children flying alone.

Lodging Baby-sitting services are available at almost all of the better hotels,
including Hilton, Inter-Continental, Marriott, and Ramada Inn,
and at most YMCAs in major Southeast Asian cities. At many hotels, children can stay free in their parents' room. **Club Med** (40 W.
57th St., New York, NY 10019, tel. 800/CLUB–MED) has "Mini
Clubs" for ages 4–9 and "Kids Clubs" for ages 10–11 in their Malaysian and Bali resort villages.

Hints for Travelers with Disabilities

Organizations Several organizations provide travel information for people with
disabilities, usually for a membership fee, and some publish newsletters and bulletins. Among them are the **Information Center for
Individuals with Disabilities** (Fort Point Pl., 27–43 Wormwood St.,
Boston, MA 02210, tel. 617/727–5540 or 800/462–5015 in MA between 11 AM and 4 PM, or leave message; TTY 617/345–9743); **Mobility
International USA** (Box 10767, Eugene, OR 97440, tel. and TTY 503/
343–1284; fax 503/343–6812), the U.S. branch of an international or-

ganization based in Britain (*see below*) that has affiliates in 30 countries; **MossRehab Hospital Travel Information Service** (tel. 215/456–9603, TTY 215/456–9602); the **Travel Industry and Disabled Exchange** (TIDE, 5435 Donna Ave., Tarzana, CA 91356, tel. 818/344–3640, fax 818/344–0078); and **Travelin' Talk** (Box 3534, Clarksville, TN 37043, tel. 615/552–6670, fax 615/552–1182).

In the United Kingdom   Important information sources include the **Royal Association for Disability and Rehabilitation** (RADAR, 12 City Forum, 250 City Rd., London EC1V 8AF, tel. 0171/250–3222), which publishes travel information for people with disabilities in Britain, and **Mobility International** (228 Borough High St., London SE1 1JX, tel. 0171/403–5688), an international clearinghouse of travel information for people with disabilities.

Travel Agencies and Tour Operators   **Accessible Journeys** (35 West Sellers Ave., Ridley Park, PA 19078, tel. 610/521–0339 or 800/846–4537, fax 610/521–6959) arranges escorted trips for travelers with disabilities and provides licensed caregivers to accompany those who require aid. **Flying Wheels Travel** (143 W. Bridge St., Box 382, Owatonna, MN 55060, tel. 507/451–5005 or 800/535–6790) is a travel agency specializing in domestic and worldwide cruises, tours, and independent travel itineraries for people with mobility problems.

Publications   Two free publications are available from the U.S. Consumer Information Center (Pueblo, CO 81009): "New Horizons for the Air Traveler with a Disability" (include Dept. 608Y in the address), a U.S. Department of Transportation booklet describing changes resulting from the 1986 Air Carrier Access Act and from the 1990 Americans with Disabilities Act, and the Airport Operators Council's *Access Travel: Airports* (Dept. 5804), which describes facilities and services for people with disabilities at more than 500 airports worldwide.

The 500-page *Travelin' Talk Directory* (*see* Organizations, *above;* $35 check or money order with a money-back guarantee) lists names and addresses of people and organizations who offer help for travelers with disabilities. Twin Peaks Press (Box 129, Vancouver, WA 98666, tel. 206/694–2462 or 800/637–2256) publishes the *Directory of Travel Agencies for the Disabled* ($19.95, plus $2 for shipping), listing more than 370 agencies worldwide.

The **Hong Kong Tourist Association**'s *A Guide for Physically Handicapped Visitors to Hong Kong* offers information about hotels, transportation, restaurants, services, and tourist attractions. For a free copy, contact the HKTA (*see* Government Information Offices, *above*).

Hints for Older Travelers

Organizations   The **American Association of Retired Persons** (AARP, 601 E St. NW, Washington, DC 20049, tel. 202/434–2277) provides independent travelers who are members of the AARP (open to those age 50 or older; $8 per person or couple annually) with the Purchase Privilege Program, which offers discounts on lodging, car rentals, and sightseeing, and arranges group tours, cruises, and apartment living through AARP Travel Experience from American Express (400 Pinnacle Way, Suite 450, Norcross, GA 30071, tel. 800/927–0111 or 800/745–4567).

Two other organizations offer discounts on lodgings, car rentals, and other travel products, along with such nontravel perks as magazines and newsletters: the **National Council of Senior Citizens** (1331

F St. NW, Washington, DC 20004, tel. 202/347–8800; membership $12 annually) and **Mature Outlook** (6001 N. Clark St., Chicago, IL 60660, tel. 800/336–6330; $9.95 annually).

Note: Mention your senior-citizen identification card when booking hotel reservations for reduced rates, not when checking out. At restaurants, show your card before you're seated; discounts may be limited to certain menus, days, or hours. If you are renting a car, ask about promotional rates that might improve on your senior-citizen discount.

Educational Travel The nonprofit **Elderhostel** (75 Federal St., 3rd Floor, Boston, MA 02110, tel. 617/426–7788) has offered inexpensive study programs for people 60 and older since 1975. Held at more than 1,800 educational and cultural institutions, courses cover everything from marine science to Greek myths and cowboy poetry. Participants usually attend lectures in the morning and spend the afternoon sightseeing or on field trips; they live in dormitory-type lodgings. Fees for two-to three-week international trips—including room, board, and transportation from the United States—range from $1,800 to $4,500.

Tour Operators **Saga International Holidays** (222 Berkeley St., Boston, MA 02116, tel. 800/343–0273) caters to those over age 50 who like to travel in groups.

Publications *The 50+ Traveler's Guidebook: Where to Go, Where to Stay, What to Do* by Anita Williams and Merrimac Dillon ($12.95; St. Martin's Press, 175 5th Ave., New York, NY 10010) is available in bookstores and offers many useful tips. "**The Mature Traveler**" (Box 50820, Reno, NV 89513, tel. 702/786–7419; $29.95), a monthly newsletter, contains many travel deals.

Hints for Gay and Lesbian Travelers

Organizations The **International Gay Travel Association** (Box 4974, Key West, FL 33041, tel. 800/448–8550), which has a membership of 800 travel-related businesses, will provide you with names of travel agents and tour operators who specialize in gay travel.

Tour Operators and Travel Agencies Tour operator **Olympus Vacations** (8424 Santa Monica Blvd., No. 721, West Hollywood, CA 90069; tel. 310/657–2220) offers all-gay-and-lesbian resort holidays. **Skylink Women's Travel** (746 Ashland Ave., Santa Monica, CA 90405, tel. 310/452–0506 or 800/225-5759) handles individual travel for lesbians all over the world and conducts international and domestic group trips annually.

Publications The premiere international travel magazine for gays and lesbians is *Our World* (1104 N. Nova Rd., Suite 251, Daytona Beach, FL 32117, tel. 904/441–5367; $35 for 10 issues). "**Out & About**" (tel. 203/789–8518 or 800/929–2268; $49 for 10 issues, full refund if you aren't satisfied) is a 16-page monthly newsletter with extensive information on resorts, hotels, and airlines that are gay-friendly.

Further Reading

Southeast Asia *The Travelers' Guide to Asian Customs and Manners*, by Kevin Chambers, advises on how to dine, tip, dress, make friends, do business, bargain, and do just about everything else in Asia, Australia, and New Zealand. *Shopping in Exotic Places*, by Ronald L. Krannich, Jo Reimer, and Carl Rae Krannich, discusses all major shopping districts and tells how to pick a tailor, how to bargain, and how to pack. For full reservation information with detailed descriptions of lodgings in 16 countries, read Jerome E. Klein's *Best Places to Stay in Asia*. Also, *Video Night in Kathmandu*, by Pico Iyer, is a delightful collection of essays on the *Time* correspondent's travels through Southeast Asia.

History Three highly recommended works on Southeast Asian history are *Southeast Asia*, 3rd edition, by M. Osborne; *Southeast Asia: A History* by Lea E. Williams; and *In Search of Southeast Asia: A Modern History*, edited by David J. Steinberg.

Religion Taufik Abdullah and Sharon Siddique's *Islam and Society in Southeast Asia* provides an excellent overview of the subject.

Fiction Southeast Asia has been an inspiration for much of Joseph Conrad's work, including the novels *An Outcast of the Islands*, *Lord Jim*, *The Shadow-Line*, *Victory*, *Almayer's Folly*, and *The Rescue* and the short stories "Karain," "The Lagoon," "Youth," "The End of the Tether," "Typhoon," "Flak," "The Secret Sharer," and "Freya of the Seven Isles."

Hong Kong *History of Hong Kong*, by G. B. Endicott, traces Hong Kong from its beginnings to the 1960s. Richard Hughes's *Borrowed Time, Borrowed Place* studies the colony immediately before the signing of the 1984 Sino-British agreement, and David Bonavia's *Hong Kong 1997: The Final Settlement* provides history and analysis of the agreement.

James Clavell wrote several novels with Hong Kong as a backdrop, including *Noble House; Taipan*, set in the 1840s during the Opium War; and *Hong Kong*, with a more contemporary setting. *The Honourable Schoolboy* by John LeCarré is a suspenseful spy thriller set in Hong Kong. Richard Mason's classic novel *The World of Suzie Wong* chronicles an American's adventures with a young woman in the Wanchai bar area. Also read Jan Morris's *Hong Kong*.

Indonesia *Anthology of Modern Indonesian Poetry*, edited by B. Raffle, provides insight into Indonesian society. Christopher Koch's *The Year of Living Dangerously* is a historical novel of the chaotic state of Indonesia in 1965. *The Religion of Java*, by Clifford Geertz, is a modern classic that describes the religious and social life of the Javanese.

Malaysia Denis Walls and Stella Martin's *In Malaysia* is a dramatic novel set in Malaysia. Somerset Maugham's *Ah King and Other Stories* and *The Casuarina Tree* are two volumes of short stories that capture the essence of colonial life in Malaya.

Philippines *In Our Image*, by S. Karnow, and *The Philippines*, by Onofre D. Corpuz, are good standard texts on the history of the nation. An excellent book dealing with the 1986 People Power revolution is *Endgame*, by Ninotchka Rosca, while José Ma. Sison's *The Philippine Revolution* places the People Power phenomenon in the context of earlier history. *Waltzing with a Dictator*, by R. Bonner, is an indepth study of the relationship between the United States and the Philippines. Also try Bryan Johnson's *The Four Days of Courage: The Untold Story of the People Who Brought Marcos Down*. D. Schirmer's *Philippine Reader* is a good collection of left-wing essays. *Playing with Water: Love and Passion on a Philippine Island*, by James Hamilton Patterson, is a fascinating account of a year's stay on a small island.

Singapore Maurice Collis's *Raffles* is a rich biographical account of the founder of Singapore. *Singapore Malay Society*, by T. Li, is a solid historical reference. *Saint Jack* is a novel set in Singapore by Paul Theroux.

Thailand *Monsoon Country* is a contemporary novel by Pira Sudham, who portrays life in the northeast of Thailand. For insights into Thai culture and everyday life, read Denis Segaller's *Thai Ways* and *More Thai Ways*. For a humorous account of an expatriate's life in Thailand in the 1950s, read *Mai Pen Rai* by Carol Iollinger. An excellent account of life in northern Thailand is provided by Gordon Young in *The Hill Tribes of Northern Thailand*.

Arriving and Departing

From North America by Plane

Flights are either nonstop, direct, or connecting. A **nonstop** flight requires no change of plane and makes no stops. A **direct** flight stops at least once and can involve a change of plane, although the flight number remains the same; if the first leg is late, the second waits. This is not the case with a **connecting** flight, which involves a different plane and a different flight number.

Airlines The following is a list of all major airlines that fly from the United States to Southeast Asia, and their primary transpacific hub cities and routes. To break up the lengthy flight, especially from the east coast of the United States, you may want to plan a stopover in one of these hub cities.

From the Southeast Asian hub cities listed below, the airlines branch out to myriad regional destinations. If they do not fly to your chosen destination, they often will work with other airlines that do. Generally, your carrier can reserve and ticket all your flights when you make your initial reservation.

Canadian Airlines International, tel. 800/426–7000 for your local toll-free number (Vancouver–Hong Kong).

Cathay Pacific Airways, tel. 800/233–2742 (San Francisco–Vancouver–Hong Kong).

China Airlines, tel. 800/227–5118 (Los Angeles or San Francisco–Hong Kong).

Delta Air Lines, tel. 800/241–4141 (Portland–Tokyo–Hong Kong).

Finnair, tel. 800/950–5000 (New York–Helsinki–Bangkok–Singapore).

Garuda Indonesian Airways, tel. 800/342–7832 (Los Angeles–Honolulu–Biak–Bali).

Japan Air Lines, tel. 800/525–3663 (nonstops from Los Angeles, San Francisco, Seattle, New York, Atlanta, or Chicago–Tokyo, Hong Kong, Bangkok, Singapore, or Manila).

Malaysia Airlines, tel. 800/421–8641 (Los Angeles–Tokyo–Kuala Lumpur).

Northwest Airlines, tel. 800/447–4747 (Chicago, Detroit, Los Angeles, New York, San Francisco, or Seattle–Tokyo–Hong Kong, Bangkok, Kuala Lumpur, Manila, or Singapore).

Philippine Airlines, tel. 800/435–9725 (Los Angeles or San Francisco–Honolulu–Manila).

Singapore Airlines, tel. 800/742–3333 (Los Angeles or San Francisco–Honolulu, Tokyo, or Taipei–Hong Kong–Singapore).

Thai Airways International, tel. 310/640–0097 or 800/426–5204 (Toronto–Seattle–Tokyo–Bangkok, or Los Angeles–Seoul or Tokyo–Bangkok).

United Airlines, tel. 800/538–2929 (New York or Chicago–Tokyo–Hong Kong, Bangkok, or Singapore; San Francisco–Taiwan–Bangkok, San Francisco–Seoul–Manila, and San Francisco–Hong Kong).

Flying Times Minimum flying time from west-coast United States can range from 13½ hours nonstop from San Francisco to Hong Kong to 16 hours from Seattle to Bangkok. From Chicago, it is 18 hours to Hong Kong, 20 hours to Bangkok. From New York, it is 20 hours to Hong Kong, 22 hours to Bangkok. Add more time for stopovers and connections, especially if you are using more than one carrier. Currently **Northwest Airlines,** which uses Tokyo as its Asia-Pacific hub, has the best schedule for minimizing waiting times between connecting flights. East-coast travelers departing from New York should consider using **Finnair** via Helsinki for flights to Bangkok and Singapore, where the flying time, respectively, is 17 hours and 18 hours.

Country by Nonstop and direct flights generally operate on certain days of the
Country week and differ according to time of year. If your transpacific flight is on a Southeast Asian carrier, you generally will need to fly to its west coast hub city on a U.S. domestic airline. However, this can be arranged through your Southeast Asian carrier. *All flying times reflect in-air time only.*

Hong Kong Hong Kong is served by many airlines and acts as connecting point for most Southeast Asian destinations. **United Airlines** has nonstop flights from San Francisco and Seattle; direct, one-stop flights from Los Angeles and Chicago, and a direct, two-stop flight from New York. **Cathay Pacific** offers a direct, one-stop flight from San Francisco to Hong Kong. Flying time is 15 hours nonstop from San Francisco, 18 hours from Chicago, and 20 hours from New York.

Indonesia **Garuda Indonesian Airways,** the national carrier, offers a direct, two-stop flight from Los Angeles to Jakarta or Bali. Flying time to Bali is 19 hours from Los Angeles, 23 hours from Chicago, and 25 hours from New York. Many travelers use **United Airlines** or **Northwest Airlines** for the Pacific crossing and transfer at Singapore to Garuda or Singapore Airlines for the remaining leg into Indonesia. Alternatively, flying the eastbound route on **Finnair,** the flight time from New York is 18 hours to Singapore, then another two hours to Jakarta.

Malaysia **Malaysia Airlines,** the national carrier, offers a direct flight, with one stop in Tokyo, from Los Angeles to Kuala Lumpur. Flying time is 17 hours from Los Angeles, 21 hours from Chicago, and 23 hours from New York. **Northwest,** with its reliable schedule, is often more convenient for departures originating from the United States.

Philippines **Philippine Airlines,** the national carrier, offers a direct flight, with one stop in Honolulu, from San Francisco to Manila. Flying time is 16 hours from San Francisco, 20 hours from Chicago, and 22 hours from New York. **United Airlines** has a 17-hour flight from San Francisco to Manila, changing in Seoul. The flight time from New York is 23 hours.

Singapore **Singapore Airlines,** the national carrier, offers direct, one-stop flights from Los Angeles to Singapore. **Northwest,** with its superior frequent-flyer program, and **United,** winning a reputation for its Connoisseur (business) class, have direct one-stop flights from Los Angeles, San Francisco, and Seattle, and connecting flights (one stop, with a change in Tokyo) from New York and Chicago. Flying time is 18 hours from Los Angeles, 20 hours from San Francisco, 20 hours from Chicago, and 22 hours from New York. **Finnair** out of New York via Helsinki takes 18 hours.

Thailand **Thai Airways International,** the national carrier, known for its exceptional service, offers direct, one-stop flights from Los Angeles to Bangkok. Three times a week Thai Airways International flights also originate from Toronto en route to Bangkok via Seattle and Tokyo. **United Airlines** offers direct, one-stop flights from San Francisco and Seattle to Bangkok. **Northwest Airlines** has has the most gateways to Bangkok, with flights from Dallas, Detroit, Chicago, Los Angeles, New York, San Francisco, Seattle, and Washington, DC, with a stop and change of planes in Tokyo. The airline offers the lowest total travel time between the United States and Bangkok: 16 hours from Seattle, 20 hours from Chicago, and 22 hours from New York. **Finnair** takes 17 hours from New York with one change in Helsinki.

Stopovers For independent travelers, most airlines, including **United, Northwest,** and **Thai Airways International,** offer special "Circle Pacific" fares. These allow four stopovers at no extra charge, but must be purchased 14–30 days in advance and carry cancellation penalties. You usually can add extra stopovers, including Australian and South Pacific destinations, for a nominal charge (about $50). In addition to its six-stopover "Circle Pacific" fare, **Cathay Pacific** offers a "Super Discovery" fare. This is the lowest possible fare for any Cathay Pacific itinerary but is restricted to a very limited number of seats and should be booked well in advance. Flying on the eastbound route with **Finnair** permits a stopover in Helsinki and side trips to Moscow and St. Petersburg.

Several airlines work together to offer "Around the World" fares. Sometimes these are not much more expensive than the "Circle Pacific" fares, but you must follow a specific routing itinerary and you cannot backtrack. "Around the World" itineraries usually include several Southeast Asian destinations before continuing through Asia and Europe.

Discount Because of the great number of air miles covered, fares are expen-
Flights sive, but it is possible to save some money off regular coach tickets. The key is to start with a flexible schedule and to make your reservations as far in advance as possible. Discounted, advance-purchase seats are limited and tend to sell out quickly. Compared to full economy fare, travel is cheaper through a tour operator.

If you are not already participating in the airline's frequent-flyer program, join. Membership is free, and all it takes is a simple application. Traveling halfway around the world will add about 22,586 km (14,000 mi) to your account. Many programs will give you additional bonus miles if you travel within a certain time period following your application submission. Some foreign airlines are partners in American Airlines' frequent-flyer programs. For example, if you fly on Cathay Pacific, your miles are added to your American Airlines frequent-flyer account and can be used toward future American Airlines flights.

Cutting Costs The Sunday travel section of most newspapers is a good source of deals. When booking, particularly through an unfamiliar company, call the Better Business Bureau and your local or state Consumer Protection Bureau to find out whether any complaints have been registered against the company, pay with a credit card if you can, and consider trip-cancellation and default insurance (*see* Insurance in Before You Go, *above*).

Promotional Airfares Less expensive fares, called promotional or discount fares, are round-trip and involve restrictions, which vary according to the route and season. You must usually buy the ticket—commonly called an APEX (advance purchase excursion) when it's for international travel—in advance (seven, 14, or 21 days is usual), although some of the major airlines have added no-frills, cheap flights to compete with new bargain airlines on certain routes.

With the major airlines the cheaper fares generally require minimum and maximum stays (for instance, over a Saturday night or at least seven and no more than 30 days). Airlines generally allow some return date changes for a $25 to $50 fee, but most low-fare tickets are nonrefundable. Only a death in the family would prompt the airline to return any of your money if you cancel a nonrefundable ticket. However, you can apply an unused nonrefundable ticket toward a new ticket, again with a small fee. The lowest fare is subject to availability, and only a small percentage of the plane's total seats will be sold at that price. Contact the U.S. Department of Transportation's Office of Consumer Affairs (I–25, Washington, DC 20590, tel. 202/366–2220) for a copy of "Fly-Rights: A Guide to Air Travel in the U.S."

Consolidators Consolidators or bulk-fare operators—"bucket shops"—buy blocks of seats on scheduled flights that airlines anticipate they won't be able to sell. They pay wholesale prices, add a markup, and resell the seats to travel agents or directly to the public at prices that still undercut the airline's promotional or discount fares (higher than a charter ticket but lower than an APEX ticket and usually without the advance-purchase restriction). Moreover, some consolidators sometimes give you your money back. Carefully read the fine print detailing penalties for changes and cancellations. If you doubt the reliability of a company, call the airline once you've made your booking and confirm that you do, indeed, have a reservation on the flight.

Discount Travel Clubs Travel clubs offer members unsold space on airplanes, cruise ships, and package tours at as much as 50% below regular prices. Membership may include a regular bulletin or access to a toll-free hot line giving details of available trips departing from three or four days to several months in the future. Most also offer 50% discounts off hotel rack rates, but double-check with the hotel to make sure it isn't offering a better promotional rate independent of the club. Clubs include **Discount Travel International** (114 Forrest Ave., Suite 203, Narberth, PA 19072, tel. 215/668–7184; $45 annually, single or family), **Entertainment Travel Editions** (Box 1014, Trumbull, CT 06611, tel. 800/445–4137; price, depending on destination, $25–$48), **Great American Traveler** (Box 27965, Salt Lake City, UT 84127, tel. 800/548–2812; $49.95 annually), **Moment's Notice Discount Travel Club** (425 Madison Ave., New York, NY 10017, tel. 212/486–0503; $45 annually, single or family), **Privilege Card** (3391 Peachtree Rd. NE, Suite 110, Atlanta GA 30326, tel. 404/262–0222 or 800/236-9732; domestic annual membership $49.95, international, $74.95), **Travelers Advantage** (CUC Travel Service, 49 Music Sq. W, Nashville, TN 37203, tel. 800/548–1116; $49 annually, single or family), and **Worldwide Discount Travel Club** (1674 Meridian Ave., Miami Beach, FL 33139, tel. 305/534–2082; $50 annually for family, $40 single).

Publications Both "Consumer Reports Travel Letter" (Consumers Union, 101 Truman Ave., Yonkers, NY 10703, tel. 914/378–2562 or 800/234–1970; $39 a year) and the newsletter "Travel Smart" (40 Beechdale Rd., Dobbs Ferry, NY 10522, tel. 800/327-3633; $37 a year) have a wealth of travel deals and tips in each monthly issue. *The Official Frequent Flyer Guidebook* by Randy Petersen (4715-C Town Center

Dr., Colorado Springs, CO 80916, tel. 719/597–8899 or 800/487–8893; $14.99, plus $3 shipping and handling) yields valuable hints on getting the most for your air travel dollars, as does *Airfare Secrets Exposed*, by Sharon Tyler and Matthew Wonder (Universal Information Publishing, $16.95 in bookstores). Also new and helpful is *202 Tips Even the Best Business Travelers May Not Know* by Christopher McGinnis (Box 52927, Atlanta, GA 30355, tel. 404/659–2855; $10 in bookstores).

Enjoying the Flight
Flights to destinations in Southeast Asia are long and trying. Because of time difference, jet lag and fatigue are nearly inevitable. Fly at night if you're able to sleep on a plane. Because the air aloft is dry, drink plenty of fluids while on board. Drinking alcohol contributes to jet lag, as do heavy meals. Bulkhead seats, in the front row of each cabin—usually reserved for people who have disabilities, are elderly, or are traveling with babies—offer more legroom, but trays attach awkwardly to seat armrests, and all possessions must be stowed overhead.

Smoking
British Airways and Cathay Pacific have banned smoking. Since February 1990, smoking has been banned on all U.S. domestic flights of less than six hours' duration; the ban also applies to domestic segments of international flights aboard U.S. and foreign carriers. On U.S. carriers flying to Southeast Asia and other destinations abroad, a seat in a no-smoking section must be provided for every passenger who requests one, and the section must be enlarged to accommodate such passengers if necessary as long as they have complied with the airline's deadline for check-in and seat assignment. If smoking bothers you, request a seat far from the smoking section.

Foreign airlines are exempt from these rules but do provide no-smoking sections, and some nations, including Canada as of July 1, 1993, have gone as far as to ban smoking on all domestic flights; other countries may ban smoking on flights of less than a specified duration. The International Civil Aviation Organization has set July 1, 1996, as the date to ban smoking aboard airlines worldwide, but the body has no power to enforce its decisions.

From the United Kingdom by Plane

British Airways and **Singapore Airlines** fly to Singapore, **British Airways** and **Malaysia Airlines** serve Kuala Lumpur, **British Airways** and **Thai Airways International** travel to Bangkok, and **Cathay Pacific, Virgin Atlantic,** and **British Airways** fly to Hong Kong. Check **Time Out** magazine and the Sunday papers for charters. **Thomas Cook** or **Trailfinders** can often book you on inexpensive flights.

From North America by Ship

Some cruise lines, including **Cunard** (tel. 800/221–4770) and **Royal Viking** (tel. 800/426–0821), call at major Southeast Asian ports as part of their around-the-world itineraries. Plan on spending at least four weeks cruising from the west coast of the United States to Southeast Asia, as these ships usually visit ports in the Pacific and Australia along the way. Or you can take a slow boat to China by booking passage on a freighter from Long Beach, California, to Hong Kong and Taiwan. The round-trip takes approximately 70 days. The freighters hold only 12 passengers and often are sold out a year in advance. For more information, contact **Freighter World**

Cruises (180 South Lake, #335, Pasadena, CA 91101, tel. 818/449–3106).

Staying in Southeast Asia

Getting Around

By Plane   Most of your international travel within the region is likely to be by air. Distances are long and fares are commensurately pricey. For example, the distance between Hong Kong and Singapore is more than 1,500 air miles, and the one-way fare can reach several hundred dollars. You can save money with excursion fares, which require a round-trip but usually allow some stopovers. Some excursion fares require minimum and maximum stays.

Another option is to purchase open-connection tickets through airlines such as **Thai Airways International**, which has flights to all Asian capitals, and special multidestination fares in conjunction with other national carriers. For traveling within Southeast Asia, these tickets allow flexible departure times as long as you retain the order of the cities visited. These work well if you know you want to visit Singapore, Penang, and Bangkok, for example, but are not sure how long you want to stay in each city. Tentative reservations are highly recommended, however, as these flights are often booked well in advance.

You can purchase tickets to fly within the region from travel agents in your Southeast Asian city. (Bangkok is generally reckoned to be the best source of low-cost tickets within Asia.) This allows even more flexibility in your schedule, but be aware that this will take time away from seeing the sights you came halfway around the globe to visit. Pay close attention to make sure the tickets you receive are the ones promised. Note any expiration dates that may invalidate the ticket.

By Car   Driving within the city limits of major Southeast Asian destinations probably is best left to the cabbies and chauffeurs who rule the roads here. For the adventuresome who like to explore the countryside on their own, local and international car rental agencies, including **Avis** (tel. 800/331–1084) and **Hertz** (tel. 800/654–3001), are located in the major cities. Many Asian countries require (or would like you to have) an International Driver's License.

Generally, self-drive car rental is recommended only with caution. In certain locations such as Bali (Indonesia), the east coast of Malaysia, or Phuket (Thailand), renting cars is common practice, but in other locales traffic conditions and poor roads can make driving hazardous. Hiring a car with a driver is usually reasonably inexpensive in Asia, and can be arranged through your hotel on arrival. Even less expensive and perhaps preferable are organized tours or day trips with car and guide, which will give you a chance to see the countryside and still enjoy the convenience of city facilities (including air-conditioning) on your return at night.

By Train   Some countries have excellent rail systems; others are not as well equipped. International rail travel is at present limited to the Singapore–Thailand express—a delightful two-day trip, especially if you like to watch passing scenery as well as your fellow passengers. There are first-and second-class air-conditioned coaches as well as second-and third-class non-air-conditioned coaches. These trains have restaurant service with good Malay and Thai food. Don't forget to take along a good book and a sweater—the air-conditioning is often on full blast.

Since late 1992, the deluxe **Eastern & Oriental Express** has traveled between Singapore and Bangkok once a week. The journey takes 41 hours over two nights. A stop in Butterworth (Malaysia) permits an excursion to Penang. Carriages are restored masterpieces furnished with Thai and Malaysian artifacts; dining is gourmet. For information in the United States, tel. 800/524–2420.

By Public Transport Most Asians don't own cars, so public transport is actually far more developed in Asia than in America, but it is, of course, crowded. In Singapore it is excellent everywhere. The main problem is language; in many countries signs are not in Roman letters. City buses can be very confusing, so get written instructions from your hotel clerk to show the driver. In your free time, buses can give you very cheap sightseeing tours.

Dining

Hotels usually have several restaurants, from coffee shops serving both Western and Oriental cuisine to posh places staffed by famous European chefs. At the other end of the scale are the outdoor stalls and markets where you can eat happily for a song.

Note: Though wine is available in Southeast Asia, it is relatively expensive. Furthermore, wine is not always the best accompaniment to local cuisines—whiskey or beer is often preferred. Mekong from Thailand is an excellent rice whiskey, and Thailand's Singha and Singapore's Tiger beers win international awards. If you are dining on European fare, consider Australian wines. If you want wine with Cantonese fare, check the wine list for Chinese wine (be sure that it is made from grapes and not rice)—Dynasty, for example, is a reasonable white Chablis-type wine.

Chinese The best-known regional Chinese cuisine is **Cantonese,** with its fresh, delicate flavors. Characteristic dishes are stir-fried beef in oyster sauce, steamed fish with slivers of ginger, and deep-fried duckling with mashed taro.

Though the cooking of the **Teochew** (or Chao Zhou), mainly fisherfolk from Swatow in the eastern part of Guangdong Province, has been greatly influenced by the Cantonese, it is quite distinctive. Teochew chefs cook with clarity and freshness, often steaming or braising, with an emphasis on fish and vegetables. Oyster sauce and sesame oil—staples of Cantonese cooking—do not feature much in Teochew cooking.

Characteristic Teochew dishes are *lo arp* and *lo goh* (braised duck and goose), served with a vinegary chili-and-garlic sauce; crispy liver or prawn rolls; stewed, preserved vegetables; black mushrooms with fish roe; and a unique porridge called *congee*, which is eaten with small dishes of salted vegetables, fried whitebait, black olives, and preserved-carrot omelets.

The **Szechuan** style of cooking is distinguished by the use of bean paste, chilies, and garlic, as well as a wide, complex use of nuts and poultry. The result is dishes with pungent flavors of all sorts, harmoniously blended and spicy hot. Simmering and smoking are common forms of preparation, and noodles and steamed bread are preferred accompaniments. Characteristic dishes are hot-and-sour soup, sautéed chicken or prawns with dried chilies, tea-smoked duck, and spicy string beans.

Pekingese cooking originated in the Imperial courts. It makes liberal use of strong-flavored roots and vegetables, such as peppers, garlic, ginger, leeks, and coriander. Dishes are usually served with noodles or dumplings and baked, steamed, or fried bread. The most famous Pekingese dish is Peking duck: The skin is lacquered with aromatic honey and baked until it looks like dark mahogany and is crackly crisp.

The greatest contribution made by the many arrivals from China's **Hainan** island, off the north coast of Vietnam, is "chicken rice": Whole chickens are poached with ginger and spring onions; then rice is boiled in the liquid to fluffy perfection and eaten with chopped-up pieces of chicken, which are dipped into a sour-and-hot chili sauce and dark soy sauce.

Fukien cuisine emphasizes soups and stews with rich, meaty stocks. Wine-sediment paste and dark soy sauce are used, and seafood is prominent. Dishes to order are braised pork belly served with buns, fried oysters, and turtle soup.

Hunanese cooking is dominated by sugar and spices and tends to be more rustic. One of the most famous dishes is beggar's chicken: A whole bird is wrapped in lotus leaves and baked in a sealed covering of clay; when it's done, a mallet is used to break away the hardened clay.

Hakka food is very provincial in character and uses ingredients not normally found in other Chinese cuisines. Red-wine lees are used to great effect in dishes of fried prawns or steamed chicken, producing delicious gravies.

Indian   **Southern Indian** cuisine is generally chili-hot, relies on strong spices like mustard seed, and uses coconut milk liberally. Meals are very cheap, and eating is informal: Just survey the cooked food displayed, point to whatever you fancy, then take a seat at a table. A piece of banana leaf will be placed before you, plain rice will be spooned out, and the rest of your food will be arranged around the rice and covered generously with curry sauce. The really adventurous should sample fish-head curry, with its hot, rich, sour gravy.

Generally found in the more posh restaurants, **northern Indian** food blends the aromatic spices of Kashmiri food with a subtle Persian influence. Northern food is less hot and more subtly spiced than southern, and cow's milk is used as a base instead of coconut milk. Northern Indian cuisine also uses yogurt to tame the pungency of the spices and depends more on pureed tomatoes and nuts to thicken gravies. The signature northern Indian dish is tandoori chicken (marinated in yogurt and spices and cooked in a clay urn) and fresh mint chutney, eaten with *naan, chapati,* and *paratha* (Indian breads).

Malay and   Malay cuisine is hot and rich. Turmeric root, lemongrass, coriander, **Indonesian**   *blachan* (prawn paste), chilies, and shallots are the ingredients used most often; coconut milk is used to create fragrant, spicy gravies. A basic method of cooking is to gently fry the *rempah* (spices, herbs, roots, chilies, and shallots ground to a paste) in oil and then, when the rempah is fragrant, add meat and either a tamarind liquid, to make a tart spicy-hot sauce, or coconut milk, to make a rich spicy-hot curry sauce. Dishes to look for are *gulai ikan* (a smooth, sweetish fish curry), *telor sambal* (eggs in hot sauce), *empalan* (beef boiled in coconut milk and then deep-fried), *tahu goreng* (fried bean curd in peanut sauce), and *ikan bilis* (fried, crispy anchovies). The best-known Malay dish is *satay*—slivers of marinated beef, chicken, or mutton threaded onto thin coconut sticks, barbecued, and served with a spicy peanut sauce.

Indonesian food is very close to Malay; both are based on rice, and both are Muslim and thus do not use pork. A meal called *nasi padang*—consisting of a number of mostly hot dishes, such as curried meat and vegetables with rice, that offer a range of tastes from sweet to salty to sour to spicy—originally comes from Indonesia.

Nonya When Hokkien immigrants settled on the Malay Peninsula, they acquired the taste for Malay spices and soon adapted Malay foods. Nonya food is one manifestation of the marriage of the two cultures, which is also seen in language, music, literature, and clothing. Nonya cooking combines the finesse and blandness of Chinese cuisine with the spiciness of Malay cooking. Many Chinese ingredients are used—especially dried ingredients like Chinese mushrooms, fungus, anchovies, lily flowers, soybean sticks, and salted fish—along with the spices and aromatics used in Malay cooking.

The Nonya cook uses preserved soybeans, garlic, and shallots to form the rempah needed to make *chap chay* (a mixed-vegetable stew with soy sauce). Other typical dishes are *husit goreng* (an omelet fried with shark's fin and crabmeat) and *otak otak* (a sort of fish quenelle with fried spices and coconut milk). Nonya cooking also features sourish-hot dishes like *garam assam*, a fish or prawn soup made with pounded turmeric, shallots, *galangal* (a hard ginger), lemongrass, shrimp paste, and preserved tamarind, a very sour fruit.

Thai Thai cuisine, while linked with Chinese and Malay, is distinctly different in taste. On first tasting a dish, you may find it stingingly hot (tiny chilies make the cuisine so fiery), but the taste of the fresh herbs will soon surface. Not all Thai food is hot. A meal is designed to have contrasting dishes, some of which are spicy hot while others are mild and often sweet. The Thais do not use salt in their cooking. Instead, *nam pla* (salted fish sauce) is served on the side, which you add to suit your taste. Thai food's characteristic flavor comes from fresh mint, basil, coriander, and citrus leaves; extensive use of lemongrass, lime, vinegar, and tamarind keeps the sour-hot taste prevalent.

Thai curries—such as chicken curry with cashews, salted egg, and mango—use coconut milk and are often served with dozens of garnishes and side dishes.

Popular Thai dishes include *mee krob*, crispy fried noodles with shrimp; *tom yam kung*, hot and spicy shrimp soup (few meals start without it); *gai hor bai toey*, fried chicken wrapped in pandanus leaves; and *pu cha*, steamed crab with fresh coriander root and a little coconut milk. For drinks, try Singha beer, brewed in Thailand, or *o-liang*, the national drink, which is very strong, black iced coffee sweetened with palm-sugar syrup.

Lodging

Accommodations in Southeast Asia range from shoebox rooms with community or seatless toilets to five-star luxury. Every major city (except Yangon) and important resort has at least one and probably several luxurious, international-style hotels (many are part of such international chains as Sheraton, Regent, Hyatt, Hilton, Holiday Inn, and Inter-Continental) that are famous for their service and amenities. If you can afford to splurge, this is the place to do it, for the prices of even the very top hotels are still far lower than comparable digs in Europe.

Most bottom-end accommodations are clustered in a particular area of the city, and you will probably want to see your room before committing to stay there—and comparison-shop for the best deal. Also, plan on spending more time getting from the cheaper hotels to the major sights. They are usually not on the beaten tourist path.

In Hong Kong, the budget and moderate-range accommodations can be found in Kowloon; the mass transit railway provides a fast journey beneath the harbor from Kowloon to Hong Kong Island. In Bangkok, try the Banglampoo section of town, especially along Khao San Road. In Kuala Lumpur, try the Jalan Tuanku Abdul Rahman. In Manila, look in the Ermita and Quiapo sections. In Singapore, try Bencoolen Street and Beach Road.

You can find budget dormitory and hotel accommodations at the YMCAs in Bangkok, Hong Kong, Kuala Lumpur, Manila, and Singapore, or at hostels in Hong Kong, Thailand, the Philippines, Indonesia, and Malaysia. They vary greatly in quality but are generally inexpensive and clean. For more on hostels and Y's, *see* Student and Youth Travel in Before You Go, *above.*

You will also find some interesting Asian alternative lodging opportunities. In Sarawak, Malaysia, for example, you can stay in tribal longhouses and observe the native lifestyle, joining in meal preparation and evening entertainments. In northern Thailand, stays in village huts are part of many overnight treks to the hill tribes. For more, *see* the individual chapters.

Reservations A good rule is to reserve your hotel rooms at least two months prior to arrival. This is especially true in December and January, in autumn, at Chinese New Year, and over Easter, the busiest times. The international chains have U.S. reservations offices. If you do arrive in an Asian capital without a hotel reservation, you will generally find a reservations desk at the airport that may be able to provide an immediate booking. This service is usually efficient and free, and often special discounts are available.

Apartment and Villa Rentals If you want a home base that's roomy enough for a family and comes with cooking facilities, a furnished rental may be the solution. It's generally cost-wise, too, although not always—some rentals are luxury properties (economical only when your party is large). Home-exchange directories do list rentals—often second homes owned by prospective house swappers—and some services search for a house or apartment for you (even a castle if that's your fancy) and handle the paperwork. Some send an illustrated catalogue and others send photographs of specific properties, sometimes at a charge; up-front registration fees may apply.

Among the companies are **Property Rentals International** (1 Park West Circle, Suite 108, Midlothian, VA 23113, tel. 804/378–6054 or 800/220–3332) and **Villas International** (605 Market St., Suite 510, San Francisco, CA 94105, tel. 415/281–0910 or 800/221–2260).

Shopping

Some people travel to Southeast Asia exclusively to shop. Finely tailored clothing and unique handcrafts, such as graceful ceramics, colorful textiles, and intricately engraved silver, can be found at rock-bottom prices here.

Although prices in department stores are generally fixed, be prepared to bargain with the smaller shopkeeper. It is the accepted practice in this land of few set prices. If you have time, comparison-shop for similar items in several stores to get a feel for the cost of the items. The final price will depend on your bargaining skill and the shopkeeper's mood, but generally will range from 10% to 40% off the original price.

If you can, carry the items with you instead of trusting the shop-keepers and postal services to ship them safely home. If you're shopping for larger items, such as ceramic vases or furniture, the upscale shops are generally reliable. Some credit card companies, such as American Express, guarantee that items purchased with their card will arrive home safely.

With any purchase, make sure you get a receipt for the amount paid, both for potential returns and for Customs. Also, check on Customs and shipping fees to make sure your bargain doesn't turn into a costly white elephant.

The following is a quick rundown of some of the most popular purchases in individual Southeast Asian countries.

Hong Kong: custom-tailored clothing, designer clothing, electronics, jewelry

Indonesia: batik, rod shadow puppets, handicrafts such as wood masks and statues from Bali

Macau: jewelry, electronics

Malaysia: batik, pewterware, gold jewelry, silver, woven fabrics

Philippines: traditional clothing such as the barong Tagalog, bamboo furniture, rattan baskets, and brassware

Thailand: silk, jewelry, ready-to-wear clothing, such handicrafts as lacquerware, pottery, and silverwork

Sports

Western-style participant sports and unique Southeast Asian spectator sports are becoming more popular with travelers to the region. The following will give you an idea of which countries provide facilities for your chosen sport.

Bicycling: Singapore

Deep-sea fishing: Pattaya (Thai Gulf), Ranong and Phuket (Indian Ocean in Thailand)

Golf: Thailand, Singapore, Philippines

Kite-fighting: Thailand (in March and April)

River rafting: Indonesia

Scuba/Snorkeling: Thailand (Phuket and several marine national parks), Philippines (Batangas, Bohol, Cebu, Palawan), Malaysia (Langkawi)

Tennis: Singapore, Philippines

Windsurfing: Thailand, Philippines

Beaches

Southeast Asia has some of the world's most exotic beaches, ranging from remote volcanic stretches in the Philippines to resort-strewn sites on Bali. The following is a brief rundown of the best beaches in each country. (*See* individual chapters for more information.)

Indonesia: The island of Lombok (a 20-minute flight from Bali) has a warm, dry climate and lovely unspoiled beaches. Surfers frequent the waves at Kuta Beach in Bali, where an annual festival is held with local and Australian participation.

Malaysia: The Batu Ferringhi strip on Penang Island has fine, golden-sand beaches, often shaded by willowy casuarina and coconut trees. Pangkor and Langkawi islands, off Malaysia's northwest coast, offer more remote stretches of sand, while Tioman Island (where the movie *Bali Hai* was filmed) provides idyllic scenery and water-sports facilities.

Philippines: This tropical archipelago of more than 7,000 islands has an abundance of beaches, from pebble-strewn coastlines and black volcanic stretches to shady white expanses. Some of the most picturesque spots are on the smaller islands, particularly on Boracay, Iloilo, Bohol, and Cebu. Puerto Galera on Mindoro Island has several good beaches and is four hours from Manila by bus and ferry.

Thailand: With its long coastlines and warm waters, Thailand offers many opportunities for beach lovers. Ko Samet, a popular Thai vacation spot, has many fine-sand beaches dotted with bungalows and cottages. (There are no big luxury resorts on the island.) Phuket, though much more commercial, boasts long, sandy beaches, cliff-sheltered coves, waterfalls, mountains, and waters that are excellent for scuba diving. Ko Samui in the Gulf is yet another excellent choice.

Key to Our Listings

Throughout this book, the following credit-card abbreviations are used in hotel and restaurant reviews: AE, American Express; DC, Diners Club; MC, MasterCard; V, Visa.

Price ranges in the Dining sections are based on one appetizer, one main course, and dessert, but not taxes, tips, or drinks.

In the Lodging sections, prices are based on a double room in high season.

Highly recommended establishments are indicated by a star ★.

Great Itineraries

The itineraries that follow suggest ways in which destinations can be combined and give an idea of reasonable (minimum) amounts of time needed in various destinations.

Elements from different itineraries can be combined to create an itinerary that suits your interests.

The Capitals Tour

Southeast Asia is more diverse than Europe, yet there is a temptation on a first visit to cover the entire area on one European-style Grand Tour. Such a trip is physically and mentally taxing and cannot begin to do justice to the complexities of Asian cultures. However, as time is often limited, this whirlwind tour encompasses the capitals and a few of the highlights of Southeast Asia in three weeks.

Begin the tour in Hong Kong, or, if you are arriving from Europe, in Singapore. Both are easy places to begin adjusting to the Orient, with a leisurely round of sightseeing interspersed with shopping. We begin in Hong Kong, visit Macau, then fly to Thailand for a look at Bangkok and the ancient capitals. We then stop in Singapore before heading on to Bali and Manila.

Length Three weeks

Transportation Be aware that stopping in all the major regions of Southeast Asia requires the use of different airlines. Coming from the United States, you may want to consider using Thai Airways International, a first-rate airline, or United Airlines, a U.S. airline that covers all the capital cities in Southeast Asia, as your major carriers. Coming from Great Britain, British Airways covers many of Asia's capital cities.

Itinerary **Four nights.** Be sure to take the tram up to the Peak on Hong Kong
Hong Kong Island to get your bearings. Explore Kowloon, the New Territories, and Hong Kong Island and its marvelous southern coastline, including Aberdeen Harbour and Repulse Bay. Spend a day visiting Macau, using the hovercraft to cross there and back from Hong Kong, and another day shopping in Hong Kong.

Bangkok **Four nights.** Take an early morning flight to Bangkok. Explore Thailand's capital city with a look at some of its 300 temples. Go on a morning tour to Damnoen Saduak's floating market and a full-day tour to explore Ayutthaya, Thailand's ancient capital.

Chiang Mai **Two nights.** Fly to Chiang Mai. (Alternatively, take the night train the evening before from Ayutthaya.) Visit the major temples in and around town, including Doi Suthep. Spend a morning at the elephant training camp at Mae Sa and an afternoon browsing the craft showrooms and workshops along San Kamphaeng Road.

Singapore **Three nights.** Fly, by way of Bangkok, to Singapore. You may want to give yourself the morning in Chiang Mai for a little extra shopping time. Once in Singapore, explore the various ethnic neighborhoods—Chinatown, Little India, the Arab district—take an evening stroll along the Padang, the heart of colonial Singapore, check out the myriad shops on Orchard Road, and dine sumptuously on Singapore's multiethnic cuisines. Make a day excursion to Malaysia to visit the historic city of Malacca.

Bali **Four nights.** Fly to Bali. You'll want more than three days to explore the temples, the craft shops, and the town of Ubud, and more than one day on the beaches, so make plans to return next year.

Manila **Three nights.** Fly to Manila. Explore the Philippine capital, especially Intramuros, the walled city. Take an afternoon to visit Corregidor Island, the famous World War II battle site, or the natural beauty of Lake Taal, or the gardens of the Hidden Valley.

The Chinese Syndrome with an Iberian Flavor

Hong Kong, Macau, and the Philippines may be linked together as a two-week excursion or may be divided into separate vacation itineraries for each country.

Start in Hong Kong with a leisurely round of sightseeing interspersed with shopping and dining. Explore Hong Kong Island,

Kowloon, and the New Territories. Include an overnight trip to Macau, unique for its Portuguese-influenced architecture and just steps away from the People's Republic of China. Visit Hong Kong's outlying islands.

Then take a trip over to the Philippines. In Manila, you'll feel the presence of the Spanish colonial past, and outside the capital, you'll experience the beauties of its nature. Next, make excursions first to the north, then to the south.

Hong Kong Length of Stay: One week

Transportation Cathay Pacific is the Hong Kong–based carrier. United Airlines flies into Hong Kong from the United States, British Airways from Great Britain.

Itinerary **Hong Kong: four nights.** Begin your stay with a tram ride to the Peak to get your bearings, and then explore Hong Kong Island, starting at Central and working your way around the island to include Aberdeen Harbour, Stanley, and Repulse Bay. Use one morning to explore Kowloon (Nathan Road, Typhoon Harbour) on foot, and be sure to spend an afternoon out on Lamma or Lantau islands. Take another day to tour the New Territories.

Macau: one night. Take the hovercraft to this Portuguese colony with its casinos and colonial architecture.

Hong Kong: one night. Return to Hong Kong for last-minute shopping.

Fly to Manila, Philippines.

Philippines Length of Stay: 7–10 days

Transportation Philippines Airlines is the national carrier, United Airlines is the leading U.S. carrier, and British Airways flies in from London.

Itinerary **Manila: three nights.** Tour the Philippine capital and visit Malacañang Palace, the Manila Cathedral, and, especially, Intramuros, the walled city built in the 16th century. Exploring out of the Tourist Belt, you'll want to visit the 16th-century Quiapo Church, famed for its black Nazarene statue of Jesus, and nearby Quiapo market, with its colorful and exotic produce. You will surely pass the Coconut Palace, a white elephant and pet project of Imelda Marcos. Farther afield are the Pagsanjan Falls, the cascading drama of which was used in the film *Apocalypse Now.* You'll also want to visit the caldera Lake Taal with its baby volcano pushing up from the crater's languid waters. The charm of Villa Escudero, a coconut plantation with a unique museum, and the nearby tropical gardens of Hidden Valley, will also draw you.

Baguio: three nights. Leave Manila and make the six-hour overland trip by bus or car, or take the 45-minute PAL flight, to north Luzon and the highlands. Use the vacation and provincial capital city of Baguio as your base. If you desperately need a beach, there are the resorts of Bauang with fine sandy beaches, and the hour's drive there is panoramic and thrilling. If you have an extra couple of days, make the eight-hour drive to the Banaue Rice Terraces, which look like giant steps to the sky. Nearby are the Ifugao villages with pyramid-shape huts perched on rocky crags. On the way back, pass through the tribal villages of the Bontoc, who still wear their traditional tasseled G-strings and little else.

Cebu City: two nights. Via Manila, fly to Cebu City, the capital of the Visayas and base for visiting the southern provinces, which can include a trip to explore Zamboanga City and time to relax on the beach on Santa Cruz Island. If you can take a few extra days, head to Boracay Island, which has the Philippines' most beautiful beaches.

Hitting the Beaches

Increasingly Southeast Asia is becoming a sun and beach center. Each destination could be the entire vacation. However, you could cover several beaches in one three-week trip.

The Andaman Sea is known for its crystal-clear turquoise waters. From south Thailand to northern Malaysia, beaches beckon on the shoreline and hundreds of islands offshore offer Robinson Crusoe–style exploring.

Length   Three weeks

Transportation   Thailand is served by Thai Airways International and Northwest Airlines from the United States, and Thai Airways International and British Airways from Great Britain. With the exception of a visit to Langkawi, all travel is by plane. To reach Langkawi from the Phuket area take a bus, via Hattyai, into Malaysia. (There are flights from Phuket to Hattyai and Penang.) You may also travel the whole distance from Bangkok to Singapore by combinations of rail, bus, and ferry.

Itinerary   **Two nights.** Arrive in Thailand and spend at least one day exploring
Bangkok   the capital city.

Phuket   **Five nights.** Fly to Phuket. Enjoy the island's 12 beaches, but do take a cruise out to Phang Nga Bay and "James Bond" island.

Phi Phi   **Three nights.** Take the morning boat to Phi Phi island and the cruise around the islands where you can snorkel and scuba dive.

Hattyai   **One night.** Cross by ferry to Krabi and take the bus to Hattyai and into Malaysia. Cross over to Langkawi. You may want to stay overnight in Hattyai.

Langkawi   **Three nights.** Spend a couple of days beachcombing, soaking up the sun, and cooling off in the warm waters of this tropical island retreat.

Penang   **Four nights.** Return to the mainland and travel south to cross to the island of Penang, where you can mix sightseeing with relaxing on the beach.

Singapore   **One night.** Fly to this island republic and take advantage of the shopping, delicious foods, and creature comforts.

Return home.

2 Portraits of Southeast Asia

Southeast Asia at a Glance: A Chronology

20,000 BC	First evidence of human settlement in the Philippines.
6000	Rice cultivation begins in Southeast Asia.
3000	Use of bronze begins in Thailand.
c. AD 150	Coastal Indonesians establish direct trade with South India.
	Early Malayan rulers adopt Indian Sanskrit.
c. 400	Chinese inscriptions from Province Wellesley (along the coast of Malay Peninsula) indicate presence of Mahayana Buddhism.
638–700s	Empire of Srivijaya emerges on Sumatra and power extends to Malay Peninsula and small archipelagoes to the south; West Java and southwest Borneo are influenced. Eighth-century inscriptions attest to "Old Malay," earliest-known use of national language in Southeast Asia.
c. 775–856	Under Sailendra dynasty the Central Java region prospers; great monuments are built in devotion to Mahayana Buddhism.
1000–1100	Suryavarman I of Angkor conquers area that is now Thailand and Laos. Old Javanese literature flourishes.
1100–1200	Singapore Island becomes prosperous trading center, while Kediri is chief political center in East Java. Khmer temples are built at Lopburi (the region now occupied by Thailand and Laos).
1230	Theravada Buddhist becomes ruler of Ligor (now Malaysia).
1291	Marco Polo arrives in Pasai, in northern Sumatra.
1292–93	Mongols attack Java. Northern Sumatran states adopt Islam.
1293	Majapahit, near present-day town of Modjokerto, is founded as capital of eastern Javanese kingdom.
1350–78	Siamese kingdom of Ayutthaya is founded and shortly thereafter conquers state of Sukhothai.
1364	Nagarajertagama (Old Javanese survey of Indonesian culture) is completed.
1402–1500	Malacca, located along southwestern coast of Malay Peninsula, becomes greatest international trading center in eastern world and is greatest diffusion center of Islam; Islam spreads throughout Sumatra and eastward. Buddhist reforms begin in Burma region.
1431	Brahman political advisors are brought to Ayutthaya (capital of Siam), and king becomes divine monarch; Siamese sack Angkor.
1511	The Portuguese conquer Malacca.
1521	Ferdinand Magellan, on the first voyage to circumnavigate the globe, reaches what is now the Philippines; he is slain in battle by a local chieftain, Lapu-Lapu.
1525–36	Spanish expeditions, under Charles V, claim Philippines.
1596	The Dutch arrive in Indonesia.
1600–1700	Ayutthaya becomes principal port of Far East. The French, under Louis XIV, exchange embassies with Siam; European influence on Southeast Asia increases.

1633 The Dutch blockade Malacca, but do not gain control until 1641, when the Portuguese surrender the city.

1688 Siam enters a period of comparative isolation, not to be broken until the 19th century.

1767 The Burmese destroy Ayutthaya, and Sino-Siamese, Phy Tak Sin, becomes monarch; Siam's capital moves to Thonburi.

1781 The Philippines enter time of prosperity as the state holds monopoly on cultivation, manufacture, and tobacco sales.

1782 The Chakri Dynasty is established in Siam.

1795 Great Britain takes over Malacca.

1807 Organized by Herman Willem Daendels (governor general), Indonesian highway is constructed across the length of northern coast of Java.

1811 British troops occupy Java.

1819 Under East India Company, Singapore becomes new British port south of Malacca.

1824 Britain returns Indonesia to the Dutch.

1826–32 Singapore joins with Penang and Malacca (both in present-day Malaysia) to form Straits Settlements; the territory then becomes seat of government.

1834 After years of clandestinely trading sugar, abaca, and other tropical produce with Europe, Manila enters the world trade market.

1839 At outbreak of Opium War, British merchants withdraw from Canton to Hong Kong.

1842 Hong Kong's cession to Britain is confirmed by signing of Treaty of Nanking.

1851 Siam's King Rama IV begins to reestablish previously severed diplomatic relations with Western powers.

1896–1901 The Philippines experience a countrywide revolt led by Katipunan Society; General Emilio Aguinaldo declares the Philippines independent of Spain; instead of independence, sovereignty changes hands and United States takes control. Though Aguinaldo's troops refuse to recognize transfer, United States forces collapse of Filipino resistance.

1907–1909 Siam cedes Laos and Cambodia to France, and recognizes British control over Kedan, Kelantan, Perlis, and Trengganu.

1916 The Philippines adopt bicameral legislature.

1922 Singapore chosen as principal base for defense of British interests in Far East.

1932 Western-educated minority stages revolution in Siam, sparking what will be years of change in political power but little change in policy.

1935 Primary education is made compulsory throughout Thailand.

1941–42 Japan occupies most of Southeast Asia (Malaya, the Philippines, Hong Kong, Singapore, Taiwan, Burma, Indochina).

1945–49 Indonesia stages resistance against Dutch and declares independence. Singapore liberated from Japanese by Great Britain. Great Britain regains possession of Hong Kong.

1946 Straits Settlements are disbanded and Singapore becomes separate colony; Malacca and Penang are incorporated into Malaya. Republic of the Philippines becomes independent. U.S. economic assistance to Thailand begins. (More than $2 billion of aid sent between 1950 and 1975.)

1947–57 Thailand enters time of political unrest and flux of government policy until finally, in 1957, a state of national emergency is declared; Field Marshal Phibun is ousted and new elections are held.

1947–66 Indonesia's Communist party becomes increasingly powerful, with several coup attempts; in 1965, political tension climaxes with coup that leads to more than 100,000 deaths. Sukarno replaced by Suharto (present-day leader), and Indonesia's Communist Party is banned.

1948–60 Federation of Malaya is proclaimed; Malaya enters 12-year state of emergency as Malayan Communist Party begins widespread terrorist campaign and attacks police stations, plantations, communication facilities; thousands murdered including High Commissioner Sir Henry Gurney in 1951.

1953–57 Ramon Magsaysay elected as president of Philippines; defeats Communist insurgents, the Huks.

1954 In hope of presenting a united front to forestall Communist aggression, Southeast Asia Treaty Organization (SEATO) is formed. Singapore's People's Action Party (PAP) is established under leadership of Lee Kuan Yew.

1958–63 Despite dissension among leading politicians, Thailand's economy grows under Generals Sarit Thanarat and Thanom Kittikachorn.

1959 Lee Kuan Yew wins general elections (agreed upon by Great Britain in 1957) and becomes Singapore's first prime minister.

1963 Malaysia established, joining together the Federation of Malaya, Singapore, Sabah, and Sarawak. Association of Southeast Asian Nations (ASEAN) is formed.

1963–65 The people of Singapore vote heavily in favor of becoming part of Malaysia; after two years Singapore secedes.

1965 Ferdinand Marcos takes office as president of the Philippines. Singapore leaves the Federation of Malaysia and becomes independent sovereign state.

1972 Martial law, imposed by Philippine president Marcos, stifles dissent but increases armed insurgency. The country prospers for a while but by the 1980s falls into deep recession.

1973–76 Continual student demonstrations, strikes, and political assassinations occur in Thailand.

1974 Unrest erupts in Indonesia when students stage street demonstrations against the visit of Japan's premier.

1977 SEATO is disbanded.

1978 Vietnam invades Cambodia, ousting Pol Pot and Khmer Rouge.

1979 Elections for lower house of bicameral legislature are held in Thailand.

1983 Benigno Aquino, Jr., Philippines' opposition leader, is assassinated when he returns from exile; Marcos's downfall begins.

1984 Great Britain agrees that Hong Kong will revert to China in 1997.

1986 In a bloodless, four-day February Manila uprising known as "People Power," the Marcoses are forced into exile. The popular Corazon C. Aquino, widow of Benigno Aquino, Jr., wins victory as president, and democratic rule is restored.

1989 Burma changes name to Myanmar.

1990 Powerful earthquake causes major destruction in Philippines.

1991 Military coup d'état in Thailand.

1992 Thais take to the streets in bloody demonstrations against military junta, forcing the junta out of power and the return of democratic elections.

In the first freely held presidential elections since 1969, Fidel V. Ramos succeeds Corazon Aquino as president of the Philippines.

1994 United States lifts its embargo on Vietnam, and the two countries begin to normalize diplomatic relations.

Religion in Southeast Asia

L
ike the shifting patterns in a kaleidoscope, the rituals, ceremonies, prayers, and customs of all the world's major religions meet the eye of a visitor to Southeast Asia. Intrepid tourists will spend many hours "doing temples," and their weary feet will them carry up hundreds of steps and through miles of courtyards. Their cameras will click unceasingly, recording images of Buddha, of Jesus, of Rama, and the pantheon of Hindu and Chinese gods. They will take pictures of mosques with golden domes and of minarets festooned with loudspeakers. Probably they will view at least one procession, perhaps in Bali, where graceful women bear elaborate towers of bamboo and blossoms, baked rice cakes, and colored sugar to the temple. At night, if they are in Malaysia or Indonesia, they may turn on the TV and listen to a Koran-reading competition.

Mosque and church; wat and temple; the wheel and the lotus, crescent and cross; Hindu and Buddhist, Muslim and Christian live side by side in Southeast Asia. All are imported faiths, and each has undergone some subtle changes in transition.

A quick glance at the calendar in Singapore demonstrates the impact of multiple faiths on a modern society. The government of multiracial Singapore is basically Chinese. The only holiday when these hardworking people close up shop altogether is Chinese New Year. Nevertheless, the government recognizes holidays sacred to four religions. Not only the Chinese New Year, but also important Buddhist, Islamic, and Hindu occasions are public holidays.

Even the date of the year is not the same for everyone. After all, the fact that it is 1,995 years after the birth of Christ is not a meaningful date for most Asians. Muslims date the era from the year of Muhammad's hegira in AD 622. The Buddhist year goes back to 563 BC. Christian dating, like the English language, is used for business, banking, and all international transactions. Many Asian calendars are bilingual, with Arabic numerals and Christian dates on one side and Chinese, Buddhist, or Islamic dates on the other. In Thailand, the cornerstones of important buildings usually carry two dates.

The calendar plays an important part in the lives of the people, because elements of astrology (both Hindu and Chinese) are taken into consideration when making important decisions. Statesmen, kings, and peasants refer to astrologers or *bomohs* or *dukuns* for help. The Chinese and Thai, for example, attach great importance to the year of a person's birth according to a 12-year cycle. Each year is represented by an animal: 1993 was the Year of the Chicken, 1994 the year of the dog, 1995 the year of the Wild Boar, and so on. In considering marriage it is wise to know the birth year of your intended, because certain combinations are said to be fraught with difficulties.

In most of Asia, time is regarded as cyclical, whereas for most Occidentals it is linear. For people in the JudeoChristian tradition (and in Islam, which evolved from that tradition), each individual life is an entity—a unit—created at a specific moment in time. Death is considered the termination of the physical life of that individual, while the soul may continue to exist through eternity. The conditions of the afterlife, according to Christian and Muslim belief, depend in large part on the behavior of the individual during his or her earthly sojourn. Christians, according to most dogmas, believe in resurrection, but nowhere do you find any reference to the idea of reincarnation. And here is where the great schism between Eastern and Western thought begins. Hindu and Buddhist beliefs assume that life, as well as time, is cyclical. The soul may endure over the course of many lives. Often the conditions of the new life depend on the behavior of the soul in its previous body. A Christian seeks eternal life through the teaching of Christ. A Buddhist seeks *nirvana*, or eternal nothingness, and follows the teachings of Buddha as set forth in his sermon "Setting in Motion the Wheel of Righteousness."

Buddhism

The cyclical notion of time and the idea of reincarnation were taken over by Buddhists from older Hindu and Vedic beliefs. Indeed, Buddha was born a Hindu prince, and much of his teaching was aimed at a reform of the structure and complexities of Hinduism. For example, Buddha, like another great Indian religious reformer, Gandhi, deplored the Hindu caste system.

The "historical Buddha" (the term "buddha" actually refers to an awakened or enlightened being) was born Siddhartha Gautama about 563 BC near the border of Nepal. A wealthy prince, he lived in luxury, married happily, and had a son. Like many people of his class, he had been protected from viewing the harsher aspects of life. Legend says that one day he went out from the palace and for the first time saw poverty, sickness, and death. Overwhelmed by these realities, he renounced his worldly position and became a wandering mendicant, seeking the meaning of life. After years of fasting, begging, and traveling, he sat down under a bodhi tree and sank into a deep meditation lasting 49 days. At last he achieved enlightenment, and Siddhartha became a Buddha.

The answer he found after his contemplation was that to escape from suffering and misery, human beings must eliminate desire and attachment. In this world, maintains Buddha, evil is caused by desire, which grows from ignorance caused by wrong thought and misdirected action. Thus, in order to achieve nirvana, an individual must extinguish desire by renouncing evil action and atoning for wrongs already done, either in this or in a previous life. Each life an individual goes through is another chance to escape the wheel. If he or she ignores opportunities for thinking and right action, in the next incarnation he or she will have to pay for past mistakes. The Five Precepts in Buddhist teaching resemble the Ten Commandments and prescribe guidelines for right living. They are: not to kill, steal, do sexual wrong, lie, or use any intoxicants. Thus, a devout Buddhist should be both a pacifist and a vegetarian.

As it spread from northern India throughout Asia, Buddhism branched into many schools and sects. The basic divisions are Theravada Buddhism (sometimes called Hinayana, or "Lesser Vehicle," Buddhism), Mahayana ("Greater Vehicle") Buddhism, and Tantric Buddhism. The Theravada school is closest to the original Buddhism of Gautama. It emphasizes that each person must seek salvation through enlightenment, attained by prayer, fasting, and the rigorous avoidance of temptation and evil. Theravada is a monastic religion, and people enter religious communities (the *sangha*) for mutual guidance and support.

Myanmar (formerly called Burma) and Thailand are both Buddhist countries where religion forms an integral part of life. In Thailand, for example, it is customary for every young man who is able to spend at least three months of his youth as a monk, when he will eat only the food he has received as "merit" offerings by the people early in the morning. The remainder of the day is spent in study, prayer, and meditation. Buddhist monks appear at every official function, whether it be the opening of a village school or the inauguration of a military airfield.

Mahayana Buddhism originated in India but developed most fully in China, Korea, and Japan. The Greater Vehicle is so called because it acknowledges that most people do not have the fortitude to achieve enlightenment on their own. Believers in Mahayana sects such as the Pure Land School call upon the aid of saints to help them to salvation. These saints, called bodhisattvas, are fully enlightened beings who have voluntarily postponed their own entry into nirvana to help others along the way. In Southeast Asia, most Mahayana temples, such as the famous Ayer Hitam Temple in Penang (Malaysia), were founded by Chinese immigrants. These temples are filled with images of Kuan Yin, the Goddess of Mercy, and other bodhisattvas, which have become objects of devotion among the faithful.

Tantric Buddhism is a subsect of Mahayana Buddhism; it in turn has divided into various sects that are found most prominently in Tibet, but also in northern Burma as well as in China and Japan. Tantric Buddhism is also centered on monasteries, and emphasizes secret rituals designed to combat demons and overcome evil.

Buddhism, being a nontheistic religion, is tolerant of other faiths and beliefs. Thus elements of older religions turn up in the practices and customs of Buddhists in Southeast Asia. For instance, in Sri Lanka, which, it is believed, Buddha visited three times, the conversion to Buddhism occurred in 247 BC, when Mahinda, missionary son of Emperor Asoka of India, converted Devanampiyatissa, King of Anuradhapura; to this day, however, it can be seen that the rudiments of demon and cobra worship still survive, along with Hindu influences.

In Thailand, pre-Buddhist animistic notions are widely held. The most visible is the spirit house, a tiny replica of a temple perched on a pole, which serves as a dwelling place for the Phra Phum, or guardian spirit of the land. Every day this spirit, or *phi*, as the Thais say, is presented with an offering of food, incense, and candles. On special occasions, such as New Year or the anniversary of the Phra Phum's installation, grander food offerings are made. As resident phi, he helps the family in time of trouble or difficulty.

Not all phi are friendly. Some are ghosts of people who died suddenly and violently or for whom there were no proper funeral ceremonies. Other phi are demons or fairies from other realms who have come to earth to do mischief. These must be appeased. Help comes from angelic beings borrowed from the Hindu pantheon.

Hinduism

Hindu-Brahmanic influence, which can be seen throughout Southeast Asia from Burma to the island of Java in Indonesia, is a relic of historical kingdoms that came under Indian influence in the 6th to 10th centuries. In Thailand some of these Hindu traditions came from the great Khmer kingdom that flourished in the 9th to 12th centuries. (The most spectacular example of the Khmer glories, of course, is the Angkor Wat complex of temples in Cambodia.) Thai royalty retains several court Brahman priests as a holdover from the times when they advised the king on heavenly omens so that he might rule more wisely. In modern times, these priest-astrologers advise only on special matters affecting the royal family and for public ceremonies such as the Annual Opening of the Plowing Season, held in Bangkok on the Pramane Ground.

The Hindu influence in Indonesia dates back to the powerful Srivijaya kingdom, which controlled much of Sumatra and the Malay Peninsula in the 10th century. In Java, a succession of empires combined several aspects of Hindu and Buddhist traditions so that in some instances Shiva, the Hindu god of destruction and regeneration, became merged with Buddha—as can be seen in the temple at Prambanan near Yogyakarta.

The grounds of the Prambanan temple provide the setting for performances of a modern dance-drama based on the *Ramayana* and held during the summer months. One of two great Sanskrit epics (the other being the *Mahabharata*), the *Ramayana* narrates the life and adventures of Rama, an incarnation of Vishnu descended to earth in human form to subdue the demon Ravanna. The *Ramayana* theme is present in dance, painting, and sculpture throughout Southeast Asia.

The advent of Islam in the 16th century, and its rapid spread thereafter, extinguished Hinduism in Indonesia except on the island of Bali. Balinese religion, which encompasses all aspects of life from work to play, from birth to death, is a rich mixture of Hindu mythology, animist beliefs, and an underlying awe of nature and God as manifest in the great volcano Gunung Agung. The Balinese, who accept the Hindu concept of Kali Yug—the last of the four great epochs before the end of the world—believe that in such times as these it is imperative to maintain a proper reverence for all the gods and spirits who dwell on the island, for their anger can be very destructive. Many Balinese believe that both the eruption of the volcano in 1963 and the wave of killings during the civil unrest in 1965 occurred because of religious improprieties.

The two most famous local deities of Balinese Hinduism are the witch Rangda and her adversary, the lionlike beast called Barong. The Barong Kris Dance performed daily at Batubulan is a modern, secular version of the very sacred *calonerang* exorcistic dance-drama that is used by the Balinese to protect their villages from evil; calonerang is rarely seen by outsiders, because it is performed at midnight at village crossroads and in graveyards. Both versions depict a struggle between Rangda, the personification of darkness and evil, and the protective Barong; the struggle always ends in a draw, because in the mortal world neither good nor evil can completely triumph.

Balinese Hinduism has absorbed so many local island deities as well as mystic practices from Java that it has very little in common with Hinduism as observed by other communities in Southeast Asia. During the 19th century many Indians, especially from the southern part of India, emigrated to the Malay Peninsula and the Indonesian archipelago. They brought their religion with them, but some of its more rigid rules, such as the caste system, were relaxed in the course of the journey.

Hindu belief in reincarnation forms the basis of religious practice and faith. Unlike the Buddhist concept of nirvana, the Hindu concept is one of attained deliverance. The Hindu dogma teaches that the soul can be released from the wheel of life only by the observance of dharma—doing one's duty according to one's position in life. The aim of each existence is to perform the dharma of that life so correctly that the soul will be rewarded with a higher station in the next life.

The Hindu godhead consists of a holy trinity: Brahma the Creator, Vishnu the Preserver, and Shiva the Destroyer. Each god appears in a number of different forms, or incarnations, and has a consort and many minor deities attached to his worship. Brahma is usually depicted with four heads to indicate his creativity and intellect. Vishnu is usually pictured with four arms, stressing his versatility and strength. His consort is the popular goddess of wealth and fortune, Lakshmi. Shiva is probably the most popular of the three, and the most widely worshiped. As he is the god of both destruction and regeneration, he is thought to be sympathetic to the human condition. In his incarnation as Shiva Nataraja, Lord of the Dance, he dances continuously to keep the world in existence. His consort, who is known by many names and is worshiped in several forms, is a source of comfort and inspiration. Her more familiar names are Kali, Parvati, or Dewi. Shiva has two sons: Ganesha, the elephant-headed god of knowledge and "remover of obstacles," and Subramaniam, god of war. Worship of the deities takes place daily in the home and in the temple on festival days. Thaipusam, which pays homage to Subramaniam, is celebrated widely in Singapore and Kuala Lumpur. The other major Hindu holiday is Deepavali, the autumn festival of lights.

Islam

Despite its long cultural and historical role, Hinduism is a minority religion in Southeast Asia today. The reason for this was the great Islamic expansion during the 15th and 16th centuries, when part of the Malay Peninsula (including the four southernmost provinces of Thailand), all of the Indonesian archipelago (with the exception of Bali), and the southern islands of what is today the Philippines became Muslim.

Islam, which is monotheistic (believing in one god), exclusive, and highly moralistic, came as quite a contrast to the pantheism of the Hindu and Buddhist religions it replaced. With the advent of Islam, the way of life in these areas changed. Some of the more obvious changes were in the calendar, the status of women, and the role of the state in regulating citizens' behavior.

The Islamic calendar is divided into 12 lunar months, as is the Chinese, so that all festivals move forward every year. Unlike the Chinese calendar, however, the Muslim lunar calendar does not attempt to make any accommodation to the solar year by adding "leap months" (7 months during the course of every 19 years). Muslim holidays, therefore, move forward 11 days each year, which explains why Muslims do not celebrate a fixed New Year's Day. Coincidentally, this system ensures that the month of fasting, Ramadan, rotates through the seasons and therefore is never confused with local planting or harvest festivities, which hark back to pagan customs and would be considered taboo for orthodox Muslims.

Islam is often seen in the West as a religion that oppresses women. Muslims, however, contend that men and women are treated differently but equally. In Islam's Arabian homeland, the laws of the Koran regarding women were designed mainly to protect their personal dignity and legal rights. Women were expected to cover their hair (but *not* necessarily to wear a veil; that is a later development that varies widely in the Islamic world according to local custom) and to be modest in their dealings with outsiders. They were also given the legal right to own property, and protection from arbitrary divorce. Muslim men may have up to four wives, if they can afford them and treat them all equally. A man may divorce his wife by saying "I divorce thee" three times, but both law and custom require a waiting period for the divorce to become final, and a woman who has borne a son may not be divorced except for grave, and legally specified, causes.

On the other hand, Islamic law clearly also makes women both separate and inferior. The Koran says: "Men have authority over women because God has made the one superior to the other

. . . so good women are obedient." Among some orthodox groups in Southeast Asia, unmarried women are strictly segregated from men in schools and social organizations, and married women are expected to avoid any dealings with men outside their own families. But other groups have adapted Islamic law to local custom; among the Minangkabau of Sumatra and Malaysia, for example, women own most of the property and have a strong voice in community affairs. In other cases, women have received some protection from the strictness of Islamic law through parliamentary women's-rights legislation.

In Southeast Asia, Malaysia and Brunei are avowedly Islamic nations; Indonesia has no official religion, but the population is overwhelmingly Muslim. Government departments include a bureau of religious affairs. Indonesia's constitution requires that every citizen must profess belief in a single deity. This law is inconvenient for the Chinese and Balinese, who have been forced rather artificially to add a "supreme deity" to their elaborate pantheons. In recent years many Chinese have become Christian to avoid harassment.

Islam, like Christianity, is based on a specific holy scripture: the Koran, or Qu'ran, which is a collection of the words of God as revealed to his prophet, Muhammad. To a devout Muslim the book is the holy of holies, and much time is spent reading and studying it. The book must be treated with reverence, never handled carelessly, and should never be placed beneath any other books. One should never drink or smoke while the Koran is being read aloud, and it should be heard in respectful silence. In many villages children are taught to memorize great numbers of verses, and Koran competitions are annual events.

The Koran and Muslim tradition set forth the Five Pillars of Islam: the Profession of Faith, the Five Daily Prayers, the obligation to fast, the obligation to make the pilgrimage, and the obligation to give alms. The Profession of Faith is the familiar doctrine of the Unity of God, which is heard in every mosque and from every minaret: There is no God but God; Muhammad is the messenger of God.

The Five Daily Prayers are made at specific times of day: at dawn, at noon, in the afternoon, at sunset, and at night. The Muslim tradition gives specific instructions on how to say prayers: kneeling and bowing in the direction of Mecca (of course, in this part of the world to "face Mecca" means to turn west, not east). Because the Koran demands cleanliness before prayer (preferably a total bath, but if this is not possible then a ritual cleansing of face, hands, and feet), you will see tanks and basins of water outside all mosques.

The third Pillar of Islam is fasting. The ninth month of the year, Ramadan, is set aside for ritual fasting. For 30 days all adult Muslims are enjoined against taking any food, drink, or cigarettes from dawn to dusk. During this month, as one would expect, work efficiency tends to drop, because in addition to being hungry and thirsty, many Muslims are also sleepy because they have stayed up much of the night eating. Adherence to the tradition is quite strict, and in some villages special police prowl the streets looking for secret munchers. The Koran does, however, give dispensation to the sick and to those who must take a meal in the course of their work. The end of Ramadan is the great feast, Hari Raya Puasa. After a morning visit to the mosque, the family returns home for a memorable feast that more than makes up for the month of deprivation.

The fourth Pillar is the duty to make a pilgrimage to Mecca. Obviously for many Muslims in Southeast Asia this is an expensive and long journey, and therefore the pilgrimage is obligatory only for those who can afford it. Nevertheless, because of the honor and prestige accorded to those who have made the journey and because the pious regard it as a religious duty, every year thousands of men and women, many of them old, board pilgrim ships and planes for the long, arduous journey to the west. Those who return are addressed as Haji (or Hijah for women), indicating that they have fulfilled their obligation. The last Pillar is almsgiving, similar to the Christian custom of tithing. In Malaysia this money is collected by the Department of Religious Affairs and is used for welfare projects for the poor.

Christianity

Because of its claims to universal validity and the simplicity of its faith, Islam swept through the islands of Southeast Asia up to the Philippines, where it ran head-on into the Spanish Catholic Church. With the establishment of Spanish authority in Manila on June 3, 1571, Islam encountered a nearly impenetrable barrier to further expansion.

The Filipinos often pride themselves on having the only Christian country in Asia, as well as the most westernized. Before the 16th century, the myriad islands that make up the Philippines had never reached the advanced stage of civilization of their western neighbors. The Filipinos accepted the Catholic teaching eagerly for a variety of reasons. In the first place, Catholicism did not have to contend with an organized, established religion because most of the indigenous beliefs involved ancestral spirits and nature gods; they offered neither a systematic theology nor a firm promise of salvation. So for the Filipino, acceptance of the new religion did not involve any deep traumatic rejection of old ways. In fact, many of the older customs were absorbed into Catholic ritual. The second factor was the language problem. The islands were a hodgepodge of languages and dialects. Catholic schools, which taught Spanish as well as the catechism, gave the Spanish colonial authorities a means of unifying the country both religiously and linguistically. Furthermore, the church offered protection from marauding pirates and outlaw gangs—one of the terms for new Christians was "those who live under the bells."

As you travel through the Philippine countryside, you will come across some huge, stark, very un-Roman-looking cathedrals.

These are the churches of an indigenous Christian faith, the Iglesia ni Kristo, which incorporates nationalistic feelings into a Protestant liturgy. It is estimated to have almost a million members.

Elsewhere in Southeast Asia, Christian missionaries, both Catholic and Protestant, followed the colonizing European powers. The lovely churches in Macau, Malacca, and parts of Indonesia and along the coastal regions of Sri Lanka, where nearly all the fisherfolk are Catholic, are remnants of the Portuguese presence.

Missionary work in Southeast Asia did not disappear with the departure of the colonial powers. Indeed, in certain areas proselytizing church groups are more active than ever. Much current missionary effort is directed toward the tribal peoples living in remote mountains and jungles, where pagan practices still prevail. Though Islam is Malaysia's national religion, the East Malaysian states are predominantly Christian.

Changing Times

Religion in Southeast Asia no longer plays the role it once did, when personal identity was established by an individual's spiritual tenets. Educational, national, and professional ties have superseded the bonds that rituals in the home and ceremonies in the community once forged. Overcrowding in the cities has pushed people closer together, sometimes with unfortunate results, when vastly different customs clash with one another. The Call to Prayer, when amplified over a loudspeaker, becomes noise pollution to some ears; the clanging cymbals accompanying a Chinese funeral are equally unwelcome to the ears of others.

In today's universities boys and girls of different faiths study together—and sometimes fall in love! Marriages outside the religious community, while still not as numerous as in the West, have become a reluctantly accepted part of life.

In rural areas change comes more slowly. Nevertheless, modern communication techniques have brought once-remote villages into the 20th century almost overnight. An illiterate old farmer may not understand helicopters and moving-picture shows or the news that man has landed on the moon, but he is aware that these phenomena exist.

But just as people in the West have become aware of the value of tradition, so in the East old customs and rituals are undergoing a reassessment in terms of cultural identity as well as spiritual sustenance. During these transitional times a visitor to Southeast Asia has a unique opportunity to observe and participate in the customs, rituals, and ceremonies of many different religions. He can visit a mosque or a Hindu temple, and he is as welcome in a Buddhist wat as in a Christian church. Old taboos about strangers have been relaxed, so that visitors may find themselves overwhelmed by hospitality. Nevertheless, sensitivity and good manners are essential. Do not persist in trying to enter a religious building if the people within ask you not to. Do not intrude on or photograph people at prayer. Remove your shoes when entering a mosque, and wear a waist sash when entering a Balinese temple. Dress modestly, as you would want strangers to dress if they visited your own church or synagogue.

Throughout Southeast Asia, religion has remained a more important feature of day-to-day social activity than it has in most of the West. Although the form and nature of this religious feeling vary widely within the region, a large proportion of the population is actively involved in it. There is still a strong sense of traditional values, reflected in fundamental social attitudes.

3 Hong Kong and Macau

Hong Kong

Most people's first reaction to Hong Kong is a gasp as their airplane dips in its final approach to Kai Tak Airport, seemingly missing the rooftops and harbor by a hairsbreadth. At night the territory appears suddenly, in a blaze of a billion lights; during the day there is some warning, from the clusters of new towns in outlying districts and the crisscrossing wakes of countless vessels serving one of the world's busiest ports.

Once on the ground, visitors have no time to come to terms with the place—they are is at once overwhelmed by the sights, sounds, smells, and physical crush of this community of 6 million. Few arrivals can avoid being swept up in the energy, excitement, and apparent confusion. This vibrancy is just as much a visitor attraction as the tens of thousands of shops selling the world's luxuries duty-free.

The colony (a now unpopular term) consists of 51.5-sq-km (32-sq-mi) Hong Kong Island, the 5.6 sq km (3.5 sq mi) of mainland Kowloon, and the assorted islands and hinterland of the New Territories, which cover about 588 sq km (365 sq mi). Some agricultural areas—with fruit orchards, piggeries, and vegetable and duck farms—can still be found; however, large stretches of rural land have been covered over by multistory factories and vast high-rise housing estates.

The key to Hong Kong's existence, however, remains the port. Here the world's busiest container terminal, with the very latest automation systems, handles a major share of China's trade, as well as the huge shipments of Hong Kong textiles, electronics, toys, watches, and other goods—and does it 24 hours a day.

The deep, sheltered harbor was the reason for Hong Kong's becoming a part of the British Empire in 1841. Previously British traders had their offices in Canton (145 km, or 90 mi, along the coast), where they traded opium and European manufactured goods for tea, silk, and porcelain. The Chinese attempted to ban the import of opium, and a brief war ensued, ending with a British victory and the prize of strategically located Hong Kong.

From the beginning it was an international entrepôt, with a government appointed by London and devoted to the principles of laissez-faire, which meant maintaining law and order and a protective garrison while allowing traders and entrepreneurs total freedom to prosper or fail. The multiracial population—Europeans, Americans, Australians, Japanese, Indians, and Southeast Asians, as well as the predominant Chinese—increased from 4,000 in 1841 to 23,000 by 1847 and by 1941 had reached 1.4 million, inflated by floods of refugees who fled to Hong Kong during times of unrest in China. Following the 1949 revolution, the colony found itself swamped with another 2 million people, who brought the capital and skills that created most of Hong Kong's manufacturing industries. The influx has continued, especially during the Cultural Revolution, and today the population (now 98% Chinese) approaches the 6-million mark.

On June 30, 1997, the British government will leave and the territory will revert to Chinese sovereignty, in accordance with the Sino-British Agreement of September 1984. Beijing has promised that Hong Kong will become a Special Administrative Region, with its own economic, educational, and judicial system for a guaranteed 50 years after the handover.

China describes this as its "one country, two systems" policy (to be applied one day perhaps to Taiwan) and is currently putting togeth-

Hong Kong Territory

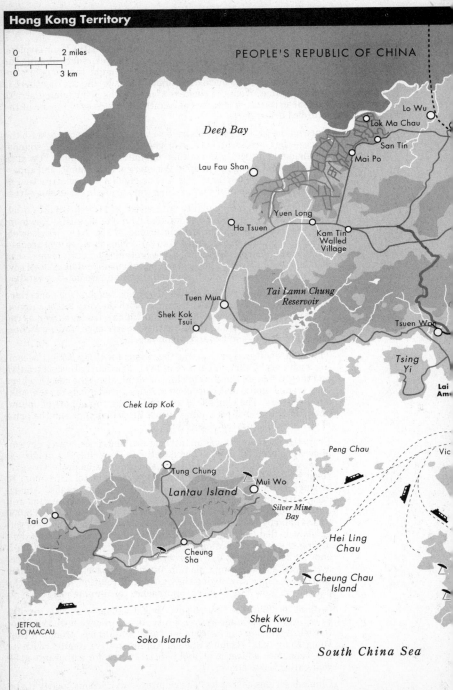

0 — 2 miles
0 — 3 km

PEOPLE'S REPUBLIC OF CHINA

Deep Bay

Lo Wu

Lok Ma Chau

San Tin

Mai Po

Lau Fau Shan

Yuen Long

Ha Tsuen

Kam Tin
Walled
Village

*Tai Lamn Chung
Reservoir*

Tuen Mun

Shek Kok
Tsui

Tsuen Wan

*Tsing
Yi*

Lai
Am

Chek Lap Kok

Peng Chau

Vic

Tung Chung

Mui Wo

Lantau Island

*Silver Mine
Bay*

Tai O

*Hei Ling
Chau*

Cheung
Sha

Cheung Chau
Island

JETFOIL
TO MACAU

*Shek Kwu
Chau*

Soko Islands

South China Sea

Crooked Island

Sheung Shut

Fanling

Wu Kau Lang

Plover Cove Reservoir

Grass island

Tolo Channel

Taipo

Kam Shan

Pan Chung

Tolo Harbour

NEW TERRITORIES

Chek Keng

Shatin

Sai Kung

Ho chung

Kau Sai Chau

High Island

Sung Dynasty Village

Lai Chi Kok Amusement Park

Port Shelter

Basalt Island

KOWLOON

Kai Tak Airport
Kowloon Bay

Yau Tong

Tai Wan Tau

Victoria

Victoria Harbour

Junk Bay

Tei Tong Tsui

HONG KONG

Tung Lung Chau

Stanley

Repulse Bay

Lamma Island

Stanley Peninsula

Po Toi Islands

KEY

- - - - Kowloon/Canton Railway (KCR)

——— Mass Transit Railway (MTR)

Ferry

er—with British government representatives and some Hong Kong citizens—a constitution. Meanwhile, most Hong Kong residents look ahead without enthusiasm. Thousands of skilled young people have emigrated, and many more have applied for visas at the Canadian, American, and Australian consulates. Britain has made it clear that it will not permit Hong Kong passport holders to settle in the United Kingdom. The bulk of the population, however, will remain after 1997, with no great confidence in China's promises or ability to administer a place of Hong Kong's sophistication. Still, the people continue to work hard, invest, obey the law—and hope for the best. In fact, Hong Kong has become a kind of boomtown, with frenetic economic and social activity, as people indulge in a last fling before the end of an era.

Staying in Hong Kong

Important Addresses and Numbers

Visitor Information

Information centers are located just beyond customs at Hong Kong International Airport; on the Star Ferry Concourse in Kowloon; and in the basement of Jardine House on Hong Kong Island. For help by phone, try the **multilingual telephone information service** (tel. 2801-7177, open Mon.–Fri. 8 AM–6 PM, weekends and holidays 9 AM–5 PM). If you prefer to get help by fax, try the **24-hour facsimile information service** (2177–1128). Dial by voice first for the menu.

Consulates and Commissions

U.S. Consulate (26 Garden Rd., Hong Kong Island, tel. 2523–9011, fax 2845–0735). **U.K. Commission** (Overseas Visa Section, Hong Kong Immigration Dept., Wanchai Tower, 7 Gloucester Rd., Hong Kong Island, tel. 2824–6111, fax 2724–2333). **Canadian Commission** (Tower 1, Exchange Sq., 11th–14th Floors, 8 Connaught Pl., Hong Kong Island, tel. 2810–4321, fax 2810–8736).

Emergencies

Police, fire, or **ambulance** (tel. 999).

Royal Hong Kong Police Visitor Hot Line (tel. 2527–7177). English-speaking police wear a red shoulder tab.

Business Information

The **Hong Kong Trade Development Council** (38th Floor, Office Tower Convention Plaza, 1 Harbour Rd., Hong Kong Island, tel. 2584-4333, telex 73595 CONHK HX, cable CONOTRAD HONG KONG, fax 2824–0249) has 35 overseas offices, including six in the United States and one in the United Kingdom. You may also contact the **Hong Kong General Chamber of Commerce** (United Centre, 22nd Floor, Queensway, Hong Kong Island, tel. 2529–9229, telex 83535 TRIND HX, cable CHAMBERCOM, fax 2527–9843), **American Chamber of Commerce in Hong Kong** (1030 Swire House, Chater Rd., Central, Hong Kong Island, tel. 2526–0165, telex 83664 AMCC HX, fax 2810–1289), or **British Chamber of Commerce** (Shui On Centre, 17th Floor, 8 Harbour Rd., Wanchai, Hong Kong Island, tel. 2824–2211, telex 82789 BRIT HX, fax 2824–1333).

Getting Around

A helpful guide to the excellent system of public transport linking Hong Kong's islands and its chunk of the Chinese mainland is the leaflet *Places of Public Interest by Public Transport*, published by the Hong Kong Tourist Association (HKTA, tel. 2801–7177).

By Car

It is unlikely you will want to rent a car in Hong Kong. The driving conditions are difficult, traffic is constantly jammed, and parking is usually impossible. Public transportation is excellent and the taxis are inexpensive. If you do decide to rent a car, take one *with* a driver. Several operators offer such services, which can be arranged through your hotel. Charges are HK$800–HK$1200 for the first four hours (depending on car model) and HK$200–HK$300 for each subsequent hour.

If you are determined to drive yourself, you'll need an international driver's license. Try **Avis** (tel. 800/331–1084, 800/879–2847 in Canada, 2890–6988 in Hong Kong), **Holiday Rental** (tel. 2713–0113 in Hong Kong), **National Car Rental** (tel. 2525–1365 in Hong Kong), and **Fung Hing Hire Co.** (tel. 2572–0333 in Hong Kong).

By Subway The **Mass Transit Railway** (MTR, tel. 2750–0170) is a splendid, air-conditioned subway that links Hong Kong Island to the shopping area of Tsim Sha Tsui and to parts of the New Territories. Trains are frequent, safe, and easy to use (there are only four lines). Station entrances are marked with a simple line symbol resembling a man with arms and legs outstretched. There are clearly marked ticket machines inside the station; change is available at the HK$1 and HK$2 machines or at the Hang Seng Bank counters inside the stations. Fares range from HK$3.50 to HK$9, and there is a special **Tourist Ticket** for HK$25 which can save you money. Another possibility is the **Stored Value Ticket,** which also allows travel on the overground Kowloon Canton Railway (KCR). Tickets may be purchased for HK$70, HK$100, and HK$200.

By Taxi Taxis in Hong Kong are usually red and have a roof sign that lights up when the taxi is available. Fares in the urban areas are HK$11.50 initially and HK$1 per 0.20 kilometer. There is a surcharge of HK$4 per large piece of baggage and a HK$20 surcharge for driving through the Cross-Harbour Tunnel. Aberdeen Tunnel carries a surcharge of HK$5, and the Lion Rock Tunnel toll is HK$6. Most people give a small tip, either odd change or HK50¢–HK$1 for a large fare. Taxis are usually reliable in Hong Kong, but if you have a complaint—about overcharging, for example—call the special hot line (tel. 2577–7177). Be sure to have the taxi license number, which is usually on the dashboard.

It is difficult to find taxis from 3:30 to 6 PM. Most taxi drivers speak some English, but to avoid problems, get someone at your hotel to write out your destination in Chinese.

By Minibus These 14- to 16-seat yellow vehicles with single red stripes travel all over Hong Kong. They are quicker and slightly more expensive than ordinary buses and stop almost anywhere on request. Their destination is written on the front, but the English-language characters are small. Wave the minibus down when you see the one you want. Since fares are adjusted throughout the journey, you could pay as little as HK$2 or as much as HK$6. Visitors who want to travel from Central to Causeway Bay for shopping should look for the minibus marked "Daimaru," the name of a big store in Causeway Bay.

By Maxicab These look the same as minibuses but have single green stripes and run fixed routes. They go from beside the parking lot at the Star Ferry, Hong Kong side, to Mid-Levels and Ocean Park (Route 1, fare HK$5.20); and from HMS Tamar (just beyond City Hall at Star Ferry) they run to Victoria Peak. Fare is HK$6. The most popular route goes from Star Ferry Kowloon to Tsim Sha Tsui East for HK$1.60–HK$2.

By Tram Visitors should ride a street tram at least once. Take your camera and head for the upper deck. The trams run along Hong Kong Island's north shore from Kennedy Town in the west all the way through Central, Wanchai, Causeway Bay, North Point, and Quarry Bay, ending in the former fishing village of Shaukiwan. There is also a branch line that turns off in Wanchai toward Happy Valley, where horse races are held during the season. Destinations are marked on the front; the fare is HK$1.20, HK60¢ children. Avoid rush hours.

By Peak Tram This funicular railway dates back to 1888 and rises from ground level to **Victoria Peak** (1,305 feet), offering a panoramic view of Hong Kong. Both residents and tourists use the tram, which has five stations. The fare is HK$12 one way or HK$19 round-trip (children under 12, HK$4 one way or HK7$ round-trip). The tram runs every 10–15 minutes daily from 7 AM to midnight. There is a free shuttle bus to and from the Star Ferry.

By Rickshaw Rickshaws are operated by a few old men who take tourists on a token ride and pose for pictures for which they charge heavily. Rates are supposed to be around HK$50 for a five-minute ride, but the rickshaw men are merciless. A posed snapshot costs from HK$10 to HK$20. Make sure the price is agreed upon before you take the photo; if not, an unpleasant scene may follow.

By Train The **Kowloon-Canton Railway** (KCR) has 13 commuter stops on its 34-km (22-mi) journey through urban Kowloon (from Kowloon to Lo Wu) and the new cities of Shatin and Taipo on its way to the Chinese border. The main station is at Hunghom, Kowloon, where you can catch the express trains to China. Adult fares range from HK$7.50 to HK$30 (children HK$3.75 to HK$15.00, under 3 years old ride free). The crossover point with the MTR is at Kowloon Tong Station (tel. 2606–9606 or 2606–7799).

By Ferry The **Star Ferry** (contact the HKTA, tel. 2801–7177, or Star Ferry Harbor Cruises, tel. 2366–2576 or 2845–2324 for information) is one of Hong Kong's landmarks. These double-bowed, green-and-white vessels cross the harbor between Central on Hong Kong Island and Tsim Sha Tsui in Kowloon. The ferries cross every few minutes from 6:30 AM to 11:30 PM. The cost for the seven-minute ride is HK$1.50 upper deck and HK$1.20 lower deck (children HK$1–HK$1.20). The Star Ferry also runs a service to Hunghom between 7 AM and 7:20 PM at 10- to 20-minute intervals for HK$1.50–HK$1.80 (HK$1–HK$1.50 children). The newest Star Ferry service is between Wanchai and Tsim Sha Tsui (check the destination over the stairs) from 7:30 AM to 11 PM (HK$1.50).

The ferries of the **Hong Kong Ferry Company (HKF)** go to Hong Kong's beautiful outer islands. There are two-and three-deck ferries; the ones with three decks have an air-conditioned first-class section on the top deck, with magnificent views from the outside deck. Ferries go regularly to Lantau, Lamma, Cheung Chau, and Peng Chau. The HKF ferries leave from the Outlying Islands Pier, a 10-minute walk west of the Star Ferry Pier on Hong Kong Island. Get ferry schedules from the HKTA, or contact the Hong Kong Ferry Company (tel. 2542–3082). Return fares vary from HK$7 to HK$23. Most trips take about an hour and are very scenic. **Hoverferries** (Hong Kong Ferry Co., tel. 2542-3082 for schedules) travel from Central to Tsuen Wan for HK$6–HK$7.50 and to Tsim Sha Tsui East for HK$4.

By Limousine Most of the best hotels have their own limousines. The Mandarin and the Peninsula hotels have chauffeur-driven Rolls-Royces for rent.

On Foot If you're not defeated by the heat, it is pleasant to stroll around Hong Kong. On Hong Kong Island you can enjoy a walk through the very traditional Western district, where life has not changed much over the years. If you are a very keen walker and relish the idea of a self-guided tour, you can go for a long stroll in the New Territories or on Lantau Island. Contact the **HKTA** (tel. 2801–7177) for walking-tour guides to these distinct areas of Hong Kong. Each includes a map and detailed instructions for getting from place to place.

Telephones

Local Calls Use a HK$1 coin for pay phones. Although there are a growing number of these, the tradition is to pop into any store and ask to use the telephone. Many small stores keep their telephone on the counter facing the street, hoping your eyes will browse while your ear and mouth are occupied.

International Calls Many hotels offer direct dial, as do many business centers, but always with a hefty surcharge. Call 013 for assistance with direct dialing. Call 010 for operator-assisted calls to most countries, including the United States, Canada, and the United Kingdom. Dial 011 for international conference calls or outgoing collect calls. Long-distance calls can also be made from **Hong Kong Telecom International** (Exchange Square, Central, tel. 2845-1281, and TST Hermes House, Kowloon, tel. 2732–4243). You can dial direct from specially marked silver-colored phone booths that take **phonecards,** available from the Hong Kong Telephone Companies retail shops and Seven Eleven convenience stores located throughout the island. The cards come in values of HK$25, 50, and 100 and have no expiration date. Multilingual instructions are posted in the phone booths. AT&T's USADirect service allows direct calls to the United States from coin-operated phones by using their access code from Hong Kong (tel. 800–1111). To reach an MCI operator, dial 800–1121; Sprint's access number is 800–1877.

Information Dial 1081 for directory assistance from English-speaking operators. If a number is constantly busy and you think it might be out of order, call 109 and the operator will check the line. Call 013 for international inquiries.

Mail

Postal Rates Postcards and letters under 10 grams for North America or Europe cost HK$2.40 and HK$1.10 for each additional gram. Aerograms are HK$1.90.

Receiving Mail Travelers can receive mail at the **American Express** office (16–18 Queen's Rd., Central; Ground Floor, New World Tower, Central, tel. 2844–0688) Monday–Friday 9 AM–5:30 PM and Saturday 9 AM–12:30 PM. This service is available only for AMEX cardmembers or traveler's check holders. Mail should be addressed c/o Client Mail Service at the office listed above.

Currency

The units of currency in Hong Kong are the Hong Kong dollar ($) and the cent. There are bills of 1,000, 500, 100, 50, 20, and 10 dollars. Coins are 5, 2, and 1 dollars and 50, 20, and 10 cents. At press time the Hong Kong dollar was fixed at 7.8 dollars to the U.S. dollar, 6.52 to the Canadian dollar, and 12.5 to the pound sterling.

What It Will Cost

There is no sales or VAT tax, except for a 5% hotel room tax and airport departure taxes.

Sample Prices Cup of coffee, from 62¢ at McDonald's to $3 or more at a hotel coffee shop; hamburger, from $1.18 at McDonald's to $6.50 at a hotel; soft drink, from 45¢ at a coffee shop to $3 at a hotel bar; beer, $2–$6 at bars; mixed drink in a bar, $3–$6; movie ticket, $3.85–$5.80; ticket to Hong Kong Philharmonic, about $3–$38; theater ticket, $13–$64; dinner at Chinese restaurant, about $10–$32; dinner at Western-style restaurant, $38–$64.

Language

The official languages of Hong Kong are English and Chinese. The most commonly spoken Chinese dialect is Cantonese, but Mandarin is gaining popularity because it is the official language of China. In hotels, major restaurants, shops, and tourist centers, almost everyone speaks fluent English. However, this is not the case with taxi drivers and workers in small shops and market stalls. In a local street café, you may not find anyone who speaks English, or an English-language menu, and you will have to resort to pointing at the food on someone else's table.

Opening and Closing Times

Most banks are open 9 AM to 4:30 PM, but some open in the evening, and major ones are open 9 AM to 12:30 PM on Saturday, and even on Sundays for special purposes. Office hours are more or less the same as in the West, 9 AM–5 or 6 PM, but shops usually open about 10 AM and stay open until 9 or 9:30 PM, especially in the tourist and residential areas.

National Holidays

The following are national holidays (Chinese festival days change each year according to the lunar calendar): January 1, Chinese New Year (three days in February), Good Friday, Easter Saturday, Easter Monday, Ching Ming (April), Queen's Birthday (June 11), Dragon Boat Festival (June), Mid-Autumn Festival (September), Chung Yeung Festival (October), December 25–26. Offices and banks are closed on these days, but except for Chinese New Year, many shops are open.

Tipping

Hotels and major restaurants add a 10% service charge. In the more traditional Chinese restaurants, a waiter will bring small snacks at the beginning of the meal and charge them to you, even if you did not order them. This money is in lieu of a service charge. It is customary to leave an additional 10% tip in all restaurants, and in taxis and beauty salons.

Guided Tours

If your time is limited or you prefer to relax and leave tour organization to professionals, you can choose from a wide variety of tours. Unless otherwise stated, the tours listed here can be booked at major hotels or through any HKTA office.

The **Hong Kong Island** tour is a three-to four-hour trip that departs from all the major hotels daily in the mornings and afternoons. Routes vary, but the following areas are generally covered: Victoria Peak, Wanchai, Aw Boon Haw Gardens, Repulse Bay and Deep Water Bay, Aberdeen, the University of Hong Kong, and Western and Central districts. Cost by bus runs about HK$165 for adults, HK$75–HK$125 for children under 12, HK$600–HK$700 by private car.

The **Kowloon and New Territories** tour usually takes in sights as varied as Kwai Chung Container Terminal, the Castle Peak fishing village, a Taoist temple, the town of Yuen Long, the Chinese border at Lokmachau, and the Royal Hong Kong Golf Club at Fanling. The three- to four-hour tour has morning and afternoon departures from all major hotels and costs HK$150–HK$165 (HK$75–HK$125 for children under 12) by coach and HK$600–HK$700 by car. A slight variation is the six-hour "Land Between Tour"(HK$290, HK$245 children and senior citizens), which offers a glimpse of rural Hong Kong.

Highlights for First-time Visitors

Star Ferry (*see* Tour 1)

Man Mo Temple (*see* Tour 1)

Hong Kong Park (*see* Tour 1)

Victoria Peak (*see* Tour 1)

Peninsula Hotel (*see* Tour 2)

Kansu Street Jade Market (*see* Tour 2)

Precious Lotus Monastery (*see* Tour 5)

Exploring Hong Kong

Tour 1: Hong Kong Island

Numbers in the margin correspond to points of interest on the Tours 1 and 2: Hong Kong and Kowloon map.

Until 1841, when it was ceded by the Chinese, Hong Kong Island was home to a few fishing communities and a haven for pirates. It had no fresh-water source and very little vegetation. Little wonder that, on hearing of this latest addition to the British empire, the foreign minister dismissed it as "that barren island." Today it contains some of the most valuable real estate in the world (much of it on reclaimed land) and a population of more than 1.5 million, as well as reservoirs and well-forested hills. Over the years the entire northern coast has become a series of interlocking townships, which are beginning to challenge the preeminence of **Central District** as a place to do business, thanks to lower rents and convenient MTR connections.

Central, as everyone calls it, features some of Hong Kong's most eye-catching skyscrapers. In close proximity to one another, they soar to the skyline with steel, stone, and glass of all colors and shapes.

More and more high rises are appearing in **Western District** and **Kennedy Town,** to the west of Central, as well as to the east, where

Wanchai and Causeway Bay grow upward with new blocks containing offices, shops, restaurants, theaters, and hotels.

Central and
Western
Districts
1

Star Ferry is the logical place to start your tour of Central District.
Since 1898, the ferry terminal has been the gateway to the island for
visitors and commuters crossing the harbor from Kowloon. Crossing
the harbor on the Star Ferry and riding around Hong Kong Island on
a two-decker tram are two musts for first-time visitors. The charge
is minimal: the Star Ferry charges HK$1.50 first class, HK$1.20 second class, and the tram from Central to Causeway Bay and beyond is
HK$1. In front of the terminal you will usually see a few red rick-
shaws. Once numbering in the thousands, these two-wheel, man-
powered "taxis" are all but gone. Also in front of the terminal is one
of the Tote (off-track betting offices). To the right, as you face in-

2 land, are the main Post Office and the towering **Jardine House,** which
is easy to spot with its many round windows. Jardine House, formerly Connaught Centre, was completed in 1973 and was one of Central's first skyscrapers.

3 Farther to your right is the futuristic **Exchange Square,** with its
three gold-and silver-striped glass towers. This complex is home to
the Hong Kong Stock Exchange (call 522–1122 to arrange a tour
during trading hours, Mon.–Fri. 10 AM–12:30 PM and 2:30 PM–3:30
PM), and contains some of the most expensive rental space on the island. In good weather, local office workers like to buy take-out food
from the various epicurean establishments in the square, including
Häagen-Dazs, and picnic around the life-size bronze water buffalo between the towers. Go up the escalator to the lobby of Exchange Square
1 to see the rotunda, which has exhibitions of contemporary art.

Take a good look at the harbor from Exchange Square, because in a few
years the view will be gone. You can see the construction taking place
on a major land reclamation project, which will create new land for
more development. Much of the prime real estate in Hong Kong sits on
land created this way; at one time Des Voeux Road, where the trams
run through Central, was waterfront property.

4 The **City Hall complex** (between Edinburgh Pl. and Connaught Rd.,
tel. 9–221–2840) faces out over Queen's Pier and the harbor. Almost
any afternoon, you can stroll through the garden and see at least one
or two wedding parties going on. The registry at City Hall is the
territory's most popular spot for weddings, with over 6,500 couples
exchanging vows there each year. In addition to municipal offices, it
contains a theater, a concert hall, and several libraries. Many of the
events in the annual International Arts and Film Festival are held
here. *Library hours: Mon.–Thurs. 10–7, Fri. 10–9, Sat. 10–5, and*
Sun. 10–1. Closed on holidays.

5 The **HMS Tamar** next to the City Hall complex, is not a ship but the
28-story headquarters of the British Army and Royal Navy. The
area gets its name from a ship once anchored in the harbor.

6 **Statue Square** is a small oasis of green between Connaught Road
Central and Chater Road. Filled with shaded walks and fountains, it
is popular with office workers during lunchtime and a favorite weekend gathering spot for hundreds of housemaids from the Philippines. The square is surrounded by some of the most important
buildings in Hong Kong, and it is near the Central MTR station.

A modern building bordering the square houses the **Hong Kong**
Club, one of the last social bastions of the fading British colonial system. Next door is the **Legislative Council** building, with its domes
and colonnades. Formerly home to the Supreme Court, it is one of

the few remaining grand Victorian-style buildings left in this area. Until recently the council had no real power, but since 1991 it has had a majority of elected members who now challenge the administration at sessions held every Wednesday. Its position after 1997, when the Crown Colony reverts to Chinese rule, is uncertain. In front of the Council building is the **Cenotaph** monument to all who lost their lives in the two world wars.

The modern glass-and-steel-structure at the end of the square is the headquarters of the **Hongkong and Shanghai Bank.** Known simply as the Bank, this is the largest and most powerful financial institution in Hong Kong. Just to the left is the old **Bank of China** building, easy to spot by the two Chinese stone lions guarding the front doorway. Built by Chinese Nationalists after World War II, this building was 20 feet higher than the Hongkong and Shanghai Bank building until the latter built its imposing new edifice in the early 1980s. Not to be outdone, the Bank of China commissoned I. M. Pei to design the even more impressive Bank of China Tower, which was completed in 1989. It sits across the street and a few doors east of the two venerable institutions, on Queen's Road Central.

❼ Directly across from the Bank of China Tower is a small park, **Chater Garden** (Chater and Jackson Rds.), former home of the Hong Kong Cricket Club.

Head west and follow the tracks of the double-decker trams that pass in front of the Hongkong Bank. This will take you along **Des Voeux Road,** which is lined with elegant shops and tall office buildings.

❽ **The Landmark** (Des Voeux Rd. and Pedder St., Central) is a rather overwhelming shopping complex with an atrium and European-style cafés. Here you'll find Gucci, Tiffany, and all of the same top designer boutiques that line Fifth Avenue and the Champs-Elysées, though often with higher prices because of stratospheric retail rents here. Concerts, and other events are presented here free of charge.

Follow Pedder Street, beside the Landmark, and turn west on **Queen's Road Central,** one of the main shopping arteries. Narrow lanes on either side are lined with tiny shops and stalls filled with inexpensive clothes and leather goods.

❾ **Central Market** (Queen's Rd. Central and Queen Victoria St.) is the city's largest public food market. More than 300 stalls offer every type of food—fish on the first floor, meat on the second, fruits and vegetables on the third. Next to Central Market is **Jubilee Street,** which is packed with food stalls offering bowls of noodles, rice dishes, and a wide variety of snacks.

From Central Market you can take a detour and ride the half-mile of escalators and walkways that go through the steep incline between Central and **Mid-Levels.** If you want to try this painless uphill climb, which offers an interesting view of small Chinese shops and gleaming residential high rises, go between 10:20 AM and 10 PM. After 10, the escalators shut down, and in the mornings, from 6 to 10, they reverse course and move downhill, so that commuters living in Mid-Levels can get to work in Central.

If you continue along Queen's Road Central, you'll begin to find some of the best local color within the urban jungle. You can find some fascinat-

❿ ing traditional items for sale on **Wing Lok Street,** lined with Chinese shops selling rattan goods, medicines, and engraved seals called chops.

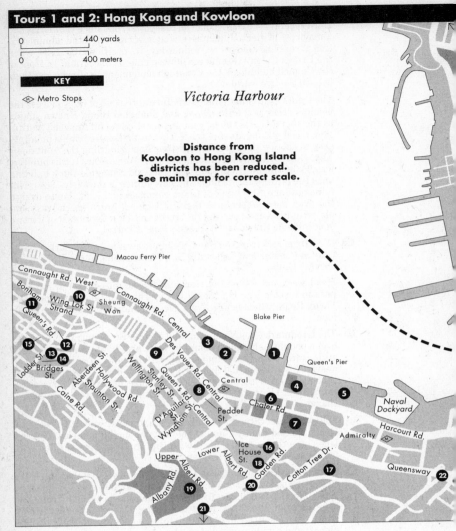

Victoria Harbour

**Distance from
Kowloon to Hong Kong Island
districts has been reduced.
See main map for correct scale.**

KEY

◈ Metro Stops

2 Queen's Road
Central, **16**

Academy for
Performing Arts, **26**

Arts Centre, **25**

Aw Boon Haw (Tiger
Balm) Gardens, **34**

Bird Market, **49**

Bonham Strand East
and West, **11**

Cargo Handling
Basin, **28**

Causeway Bay
Typhoon Center, **30**

Causeway Centre, **24**

Central Market, **9**

Chater Garden, **7**

City Hall complex, **4**

Excelsior Hotel, **29**

Exchange Square, **3**

Happy Valley Race
Course, **35**

HMS Tamar, **5**

Hollywood Road, **13**

Hong Kong Museum of
Art, **40**

Hong Kong Cultural
Centre, **37**

Hong Kong Science
Museum, **43**

Hong Kong Park, **17**

Hong Kong
Convention and
Exhibition Centre, **27**

Hopewell Centre, **23**

Jardine House, **2**

Kansu Street Jade
Market, **47**

Kowloon Park, **45**

Kwun Yum Temple, **33**

Man Mo Temple, **14**

Nathan Road, **44**

Peak Tram, **20**

Peninsula Hotel, **38**

Queen's Road East, **22**

Queen's Road West, **12**

Regent Hotel, **41**

Space Museum, **39**

St. John's
Cathedral. **18**

Star Ferry, **1**

Star Ferry Pier, **36**

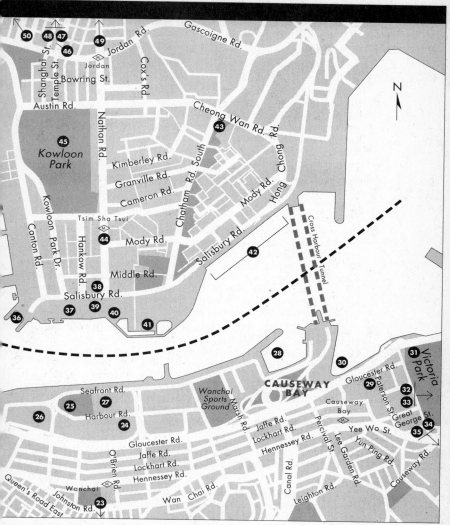

Queen's Road Central now forks to the left, but you should continue straight ahead to Bonham Strand East. **Man Wa Lane** is a tiny street off Bonham Strand East where you'll find more chop carvers.

Take a detour up to **Western Market,** at 323 Connaught Road West, the busy highway that faces the harbor. Built in 1906, it has been totally renovated along the lines of London's Covent Garden, with arcades, wide galleries, and a variety of shops.

⑪ Bonham Strand East and West is an area left relatively untouched by the modern world. The streets are lined with traditional shops, many open-fronted. Among the most interesting are those selling live snakes, both for food and medicinal use. Bonham Strand West is famous for traditional Chinese medicines and herbal remedies.

At the western end of Bonham Strand West is **Des Voeux Road West**—you'll recognize it by the tram tracks. On the left side of the street as you continue west, you will find all kinds of shops selling preserved foods such as dried and salted fish, black mushrooms, and vegetables. This is a good area for lunchtime dim sum.

⑫ Queen's Road West is filled with embroidery shops selling richly brocaded wedding clothes and all types of embroidered linens, clothing, and household goods. There are also more Chinese medicine shops, a few bird shops selling mynah birds and parrots, and shops where colorful items are made and sold for burning at Chinese funerals. Houses, cars, furniture, and TV sets—all made of paper and bamboo—are among the items believed necessary to ensure the departed a good life in the hereafter.

⑬ Funerals are also the theme for some shops along **Hollywood Road.** Here you will find traditional Chinese coffins and more of the elaborate ceremonial items needed for a funeral. Farther along you will find shops selling different grades of rice, displayed in brass-banded wood tubs. Look to the left for a sign saying "Possession Street." This was where Captain Charles Elliott of the British Royal Navy stepped ashore in 1841 and claimed Hong Kong for the British Empire. It is interesting to note how far today's harbor is from this area, which was once on the water's edge—the result of a century of massive land reclamation.

Farther east along Hollywood Road are many antiques, curio, and junk shops, as well as shops selling every type of Asian art and handicraft.

⑭ Man Mo Temple is also on Hollywood Road, in the midst of the antiques and curio shops. Built in 1847, it is Hong Kong Island's oldest temple and is dedicated to Man, the god of literature, and Mo, the god of war. The statue of Man is dressed in green and holds a writing brush. Mo is dressed in red and holds a sword. To their left is a shrine to Pao Kung, god of justice, whose face is painted black. To the right is Shing Wong, god of the city. Coils of incense hang from the roof beams, filling the air with a heavy fragrance. The temple bell, cast in Canton in 1847, and the drum next to it are sounded to attract the attention of the gods when a prayer is being offered.

⑮ To reach **Upper Lascar Row,** also known as **Cat Street,** walk down the steps of Ladder Street, just across from Man Mo Temple. In the days before wheeled traffic, most of the steep, narrow lanes on the hillside were filled with steps. Cat Street is a vast flea market.

Continue downhill and you will return to **Queen's Road Central.** Along this section are shops selling many different kinds of tea and traditional Chinese art supplies, including writing brushes, paper, and ink. Here, too, you can buy fans or have a calligrapher write a good luck message for you on an item you purchase.

Heading back along Queen's Road Central, toward Central Market, you will see a number of street markets in the stepped lanes to your right. On the left is the ornate facade of the **Eu Yan Sang Medical Hall** (152 Queen's Central), which has a collection of traditional Chinese medicines on display in glass cases, in addition to the reindeer antlers, dried fungi, ginseng, and other standard medicinal items for sale. You can browse for hours throughout this area, walking past market stalls and shops selling strange and wonderful goods, streets filled with the aroma of exotic foods, and lined with ornate old buildings that seem to be begging to be explored.

From Central to the Peak ⑯ The best place to start seeingthis area is at **2 Queen's Road Central,** diagonally across the street from Chater Garden. You'll be heading toward the Peak, towering above the harbor and the city. But don't worry, you don't have to walk all the way.

Queen's Road Central was once the seafront, and site of the old military parade grounds. Most of the important colonial buildings of the Victorian era were within easy reach of this area. Walking around this part of Central is a bit tricky because of a series of pedestrian tunnels and overpasses.

⑰ **Hong Kong Park** (between Garden Rd. and Cotton Tree Dr.) is a 25-acre marvel in the heart of Central. It contains lakes, gardens, sports areas, a rain forest aviary with 500 species of birds, and a greenhouse filled with 200 species of tropical and arid-region plants. Also here is **Flagstaff House,** the city's oldest colonial building (built in 1846) and former official residence of the commander of the British forces. The house is now the **Museum of Tea Ware,** and holds displays on everything connected with the art of serving tea from the 7th century onward. *Cotton Tree Dr., tel. 2869–0690. Admission free. Open 10–5. Closed Wed.*

⑱ From here you start climbing up into the steep part of Central that merges into Mid-Levels. On Garden Road is **St. John's Cathedral,** an Anglican (Episcopal) church completed in 1849, is constructed of Canton bricks in the shape of a cross and is a good example of Victorian-Gothic and Norman architecture. *Open daily 9–5. Sunday services open to the public.*

Government House, a handsome white building up the hill from the cathedral, is the official residence of the governor. It was built in 1891 (Upper Albert Rd.).

⑲ A visit to the **Zoological and Botanical Gardens** is a delightful way to escape the city's traffic and crowds. In the early morning, people come here to practice *t'ai chi ch'uan* (the ancient art of shadow-boxing). The quiet pathways are lined with semitropical trees, shrubs, and flowers. The collection of animals in the zoo is small, although there are some exotic ones, such as leopards and jaguars. There is also an aviary with more than 300 species of birds, including flocks of cranes and pink-and-white flamingos. *Upper Albert Rd., opposite Government House, tel. 2530–0155. Admission free. Open daily 6:30 AM–7 PM.*

⑳ A short walk from the Zoological Gardens is the Lower Peak Tram Terminus where you will find the **Peak Tram,** the steepest funicular railway in the world. It passes five intermediate stations en route to the upper terminal, 1,805 feet above sea level, and was opened in 1880 to transport people to the top of Victoria Peak, the highest hill overlooking Hong Kong Harbour. Before the tram, the only way to get to the top was to walk or take a bumpy ride up the steep steps in a sedan chair. The tram has two 72-seat cars that are hauled up the hill by cables attached to electric motors. A free shuttle bus to the Peak Tram leaves from next to City Hall, at Edinburgh Place. *Between Garden Rd. and Cotton Tree Dr. Fare: Adults HK$12 one-way, HK$19 round-trip; senior citizens 50% of regular adult fares; children HK$4 one-way, HK$7 round-trip. Open daily 7 AM–midnight. Trams run every 10–15 min.*

㉑ The Chinese name for **Victoria Peak** is *Tai Ping Shan* (Mountain of Great Peace). It might also be called Mountain of Great Views, for the panorama is breathtaking. On a clear day you can see across the islands to the People's Republic of China. The area is a popular picnic spot and filled with beautiful walking paths that circle the peak.

The new **Peak Galleria** is a shopping mall with a wide selection of restaurants and boutiques selling souvenirs, clothes, and one-of-a-kind gifts. Just below the summit is a lookout pavilion that was once part of a former governor's residence. The original gardens and country walks remain and are open to the public.

As an alternative to taking the Peak Tram down the hillside, you can catch Bus 15 or a cab to Central. This will take you on a trip as beautiful as the one on the tram, through the steep roads of the residential areas of Mid-Levels.

Wanchai Wanchai was once one of the five "wan," or areas that the British set aside for Chinese residences. Today, in addition to the old section with its bars and massage parlors made famous in Richard Mason's novel *The World of Suzie Wong*, it is a mixture of office buildings, restaurants, apartment buildings, and shops. The old waterfront is now well inland, and a whole new area occupies the reclaimed harborside.

A good point to start a circular walking tour is at the junction of Queensway and Queen's Road East. This is a 10-minute ride from Central by tram or on Bus 5. Get off just past the Marriott Hotel.

㉒ **Queen's Road East** is a busy shopping street. Heading east you pass rice and food shops and stores selling rattan and traditional furniture, paper lanterns, and materials for Chinese calligraphy. Farther along, on the right, is the **Tai Wong Temple.** You can see its altar from the street and smell the scent of smoldering joss sticks.

㉓ **Hopewell Centre** (Queen's Rd. East and Spring Garden La.) is 66 stories high and was Hong Kong's tallest structure until the Bank of China building was completed. There is a revolving restaurant (Revolving 66, tel. 2862–6166) at the top with superb views. Continue along Queen's Road East and turn left onto **Wanchai Road,** a busy market area selling a variety of foods as well as clothing and household goods. To the left are several small lanes leading to **Johnston Road,** where you'll see the tram lines again. There are a number of traditional shops here, including some selling household pets. Turn left on Johnston Road, and follow the edge of **Southorn Playground,** a popular meeting place, especially for those looking for a game of cards or Chinese checkers.

Luard Road, with its cross streets—Hennessy, Lockhart, and Jaffe roads—is in the heart of Old Wanchai. At night this area is alive with multicolored neon signs and a lively trade at the bars, pubs, massage parlors, and restaurants. **Hennessy Road,** which roughly follows the line of the original harbor frontage, is one of the better shopping streets. For more good browsing, walk east on Hennessy Road to Fleming Road. Turn north, crossing Harbour Road, to the **Chinese**

Arts and Crafts department store (26 Harbour Rd., tel. 2332–2548, open daily 9 AM–9:30 PM).

 The nearby **Causeway Centre** building houses the **Museum of Chinese Historical Relics.** The collection covers 1,000 years of Chinese history and culture, with all types of art and crafts on display. *28 Harbour Rd., tel. 2827–4692. Admission free. Open weekdays 10–6, Sat. 1–6. Closed Jan. 1, Chinese New Year, Oct. 1 (Chinese National Day), and during the setting up of new exhibitions.*

To the east of Causeway Centre is the **Wanchai Sports Grounds** (Harbour and Tonnochy roads), opened in 1979 to provide world-class facilities for competitive sports. It has a soccer field, a running track, a swimming pool, and an indoor games hall.

Within walking distance of the Sports Grounds are the **Arts Centre** and the **Academy for Performing Arts,** in two adjacent buildings that serve as the venue for the heart of Hong Kong's cultural activities. They have excellent facilities for both exhibitions and the performing arts. You can get information on the busy schedule of activities from local newspapers or the ticket reservations office. The Academy for Performing Arts was financed with horse-racing profits donated by the Royal Hong Kong Jockey Club. While you're at the Arts Centre, visit the **Pao Gallery,** which hosts international and local exhibitions. *2 Harbour Rd., Academy, tel. 2802–0662. Admission free. Open daily 10–8.*

Walk east on Harbour Road to 1 Harbour Road, a huge block containing the **Hong Kong Convention and Exhibition Centre,** which opened in 1988 and is one of the largest and best-equipped meeting facilities in the world. It is adjoined by an office tower, a block of service apartments, and two hotels: the Grand Hyatt and the New World Harbour View.

From here you can taxi back to your hotel, catch the MTR at Admiralty Station, or continue walking along the harborfront to Wanchai Ferry Pier for a ferry back to Kowloon. East of the pier is the **Cargo Handling Basin** (Hung Hing Rd. near Wanchai Stadium), where you can watch the unloading of boats bringing cargo ashore from ships anchored in the harbor.

Causeway Bay, Happy Valley, and North Point

Causeway Bay, one of Hong Kong's best shopping areas, also has a wide range of restaurants and a few sightseeing attractions. Much of the district can be easily reached from Central by the tram, which runs along Hennessy Road, or by the MTR to Causeway Bay Station. If you come by taxi, a good starting point is the Excelsior Hotel (281 Gloucester Rd.), which overlooks the harbor.

The **Excelsior Hotel** and **Noonday Gun** are a fun part of any tour of Causeway Bay. ". . . In Hong Kong they strike a gong and fire off a noonday gun," wrote Noel Coward in his song, "Mad Dogs and Englishmen." They still fire that gun, exactly at noon each day, in a small enclosure overlooking the Yacht Club Basin and Typhoon Shelter, opposite the Excelsior Hotel and the World Trade Centre. The gun itself, with brasswork polished bright, is a 3-pound Hotchkiss dating from 1901.

At the western end of the **Causeway Bay Typhoon Shelter** is a boat basin that used to house a community of sampan dwellers. As the number of fishing families who live in their boats has dwindled, the basin has filled with pleasure craft.

You can still see a few sampans amidst the sleek sailboats and restored junks.

③① **Victoria Park,** reached by passing under the elevated highway at the end of Gloucester Road, offers a delightful escape from the crowds, traffic, and concrete canyons of the city. Beautifully landscaped with trees, shrubs, flowers, lawns, the park has an aviary and recreational facilities for swimming, lawn bowling, tennis, roller skating, even go-cart racing. The Lantern Carnival is held here in midautumn, with the trees a mass of colored lights. Just before Chinese New Year, the park features a huge flower market.

③② On the southeast side of the park, **Tin Hau Temple** is on a street of the same name off Causeway Road, behind Park Cinema. It is one of several temples in Hong Kong dedicated to the goddess of the sea and is notable for its decorative roof and old stone walls. Walk south along Tung Lo Wan Road, a busy street of commercial shops, to where the road turns west, and you will find Lin Fa Kung Street **③③** West. Turn left here and you will come to the **Kwun Yum Temple,** dedicated to the goddess of mercy. A temple has stood on this site for 200 years, but this one dates from 1986. The temple is very popular with local devotees and is open daily 9 till nightfall.

Left of Tung Lo Wan Road is **Jones Street,** which has some fine, traditional Chinese houses. From here continue uphill on Tai Hang **③④** Road (a 15-minute walk, or a brief ride by taxi or Bus 11) to **Aw Boon Haw (Tiger Balm) Gardens.** Built in 1935 with profits from sales of a popular menthol balm, the gardens were the pet project of two Chinese brothers, who also built their mansion here. Eight acres of hillside are covered with grottoes and pavilions filled with garishly painted statues and models of Chinese gods, mythical animals, and scenes depicting fables and parables. There is also an ornate sevenstory pagoda containing Buddhist relics and the ashes of monks and nuns. *Tai Hang Rd., Happy Valley. Admission free. Open daily 9:30–4.*

③⑤ Every Wednesday night and one afternoon each weekend from September to mid-June, you can bet on the horses at the **Happy Valley Race Course.** It is for members only, but you can get a special visitor's admission if you have been in Hong Kong for less than three weeks and are 18 or over. Your passport with the tourist visa stamp is required as proof. *Royal Hong Kong Jockey Club, 2 Sports Rd., Happy Valley, tel. 2837–8111 or 2837–8345. Cost: HK$50 for entrance badge.*

The area east of Victoria Park offers very little for the first-time visitor. **North Point** and **Quarry Bay** are both undeniably the "real" Hong Kong, which means tenements and factories.

Tour 2: Kowloon

Kowloon is a peninsula jutting out from mainland China, directly across Victoria Harbour from Central. Legend has it that Kowloon was named by a Chinese emperor who fled here during the Sung Dynasty (960–1279). He counted eight hills on the peninsula and called them the Eight Dragons—so the account goes—but a servant reminded him that an emperor is also considered a dragon, and so the emperor called the region *Gau-lung* (nine dragons), which became Kow-loon in English.

Kowloon is home to most of Hong Kong's hotels. In the Old Tsim Sha Tsui district is the Victorian-era clock tower of the old Kowloon-Canton Railway station, the new Hong Kong Cultural Centre, the Peninsula Hotel, and the bustling Nathan Road area. The Tsim Sha Tsui East district is on land reclaimed from the harbor and contains many luxury hotels and shopping centers, the Space Museum, and a waterfront esplanade. It is here that you will find the new railroad station.

Today visitors can take a taxi through the Cross-Harbour Tunnel from Causeway Bay or Central to Kowloon, or ride the MTR from Central to Kowloon in minutes. The Star Ferry, however, is still unquestionably the most exciting way to cross the harbor.

36 **Star Ferry Pier** is a convenient starting place for any tour of Kowloon. Here you will also find the bus terminal, with traffic going to all parts of Kowloon and the New Territories. On your left, as you face the bus station, is **Ocean Terminal,** where luxury cruise ships berth. Inside this terminal, and in the adjacent **Harbour City,** are miles of air-conditioned shopping arcades.

To the right of the Star Ferry is the **Victoria Clock Tower,** all that is left of the Kowloon-Canton Railway Station, which once stood on this site. The new station, for travel within China, is a mile to the east.

Head east along **Salisbury Road,** and immediately on your left is **Star House,** where you'll find one of the best branches of the **China Arts and Crafts** department store. Crossing Canton Road, you'll see a tree-covered hill to your left, headquarters of the **Marine Police** (Canton and Salisbury Rds.). Taking the underpass across Kowloon Park Drive, you will come to the **YMCA** (41 Salisbury Rd.).

37 Follow Salisbury Road past the **Hong Kong Cultural Centre.** This is a stark and architecturally controversial building with tiled walls inside and out, sloped roofs, and no windows—an irony, since the view is superb. It houses a concert hall and two theaters. The next block
38 on the left contains the sumptuous **Peninsula Hotel** (Salisbury Rd.). Outside are its fleet of Rolls-Royce taxis, and doormen in white uniforms.

39 Across from the Peninsula, the dome-shaped **Space Museum** houses one of the most advanced planetariums in Asia. It also contains the **Hall of Solar Science,** an **Exhibition Hall,** and a **Space Theatre,** with Omnimax movies on space travel, sports, and natural wonders. *10 Salisbury Rd., tel. 2734–2722. Admission: HK$10 adults, HK$5 children and students (children under 6 not admitted). Open Mon. and Wed.–Fri. 11–9, Sat.–Sun. and holidays 10–9; closed Tues. 7 shows daily, first at 2:30 PM, last at 8:30 PM*

40 The new **Hong Kong Museum of Art** occupies its own building behind the Space Museum. Inside are five floors of well-designed galleries. *10 Salisbury Rd., tel. 2734–2167. Admission: HK$10 adults, HK$5 students, senior citizens, and children. Open Mon.–Wed. and Fri.–Sat. 10–6, Sun. and holidays 1–6; closed Thurs.*

41 The **Regent** (Salisbury Rd.) is among Hong Kong's finest luxury hotels. Its lobby has windows offering panoramic views of the harbor, making it the perfect place for a drink at sunset.

42 Farther east on Salisbury Road is the area called **Tsim Sha Tsui East,** part of the land reclamation now occupied by a parade of luxury hotels, restaurants, and entertainment and shopping complexes.
43 At the corner of Cheong Wan Road and Chatham Road is the **Hong Kong Science Museum.** It houses more than 500 science and technology exhibits that emphasize interactive participation. *2 Science Museum Rd., tel. 2732–3232. Admission: HK$25 adults, HK$15 children and students. Open Tues.–Fri. 1–9, Sat.–Sun. and holidays 10–9.*

44 **Nathan Road,** the "Golden Mile," runs north for several miles and is filled with hotels and shops of every description. To the left and right are mazes of narrow streets lined with even more shops crammed with every possible type of merchandise.

45 Just off Nathan Road is **Kowloon Park,** a restful, green oasis featuring a Chinese Garden with lotus pond, streams, a lake, and an aviary with a colorful collection of rare birds. On the south end of the park, near the Haiphong Road entrance, is the **Jamia Masjid and Islamic Centre,** Hong Kong's main mosque, built in 1984 with four minarets, decorative arches, and a marble dome.

The **Hong Kong Museum of History** offers a journey through Hong Kong's history with life-size dioramas showing prehistoric times, the original fishing village, a 19th-century street, the Japanese occupation, and modern Hong Kong, all complete with sounds and smells. *Haiphong Rd., tel. 2367–1124. Admission: HK$10 adults, HK$5 students, children, and senior citizens. Open Mon.–Thurs. and Sat. 10–6, Sun. and holidays 1–6; closed Fri.*

46 Continue north on Nathan Road three blocks to Jordan Road, make a left and a right onto **Temple Street,** which becomes an **open-air market** in the evening filled with street doctors offering cures for almost any complaint, fortune-tellers, and, on most nights, Chinese opera. The best time to visit is between 8 and 11 PM.

47 North is the **Kansu Street Jade Market.** You'll get there by following Temple Street to Kansu Street and turning left. The daily jade market carries everything from fake jade pendants to precious carvings. The best time to visit is from 10 to noon.

48 **Tin Hau Temple** (Market St., one block north of Kansu St.) is a colorful sight, with its curved tile roofs designed to deter evil spirits. One of Kowloon's oldest temples, it is filled with incense and crowds of worshipers.

49 **Hong Lok Street,** two blocks from Nathan Road, at the Mong Kok MTR stop, is where you'll find the famous **Bird Market,** where old-timers sell antique cages and porcelain, besides, of course, little brown songbirds and colorful talking parrots. See the Bird Market now, as the 50-year old site is slated be torn down for development at the end of 1995.

50 To go back in history hundreds of years, visit the **Sung Dynasty Village,** northwest of Kowloon city. Take the MTR line that is red on the maps to the Mei Foo station. From here it is a short walk along Lai Wan and Mei Lai roads. The village re-creates the life of a Sung Dynasty village 1,000 years ago. There are faithful replicas of the houses, shops, restaurants, and temples of the period. You can watch craftspeople at work and see people dressed in costumes of the time. The easiest way to see the village is to take an organized tour, which can be arranged through your hotel tour desk. *Sung Dynasty Village, tel. 2741–5111. Admission: HK$120 adults, HK$60 children. Open Mon.–Sun. 10–8:30 PM.*

Tour 3: The South Side

The easiest way to tour the south is on a four-hour organized bus tour, but this will show you only a few highlights. If you have time, take a city bus or taxi from Central, and stop at the following points of interest along the way.

Starting in Central and passing through Western, the first major point of interest is **Hong Kong University.** Established in 1911, it has a total of almost 10,000 undergraduate and postgraduate students. Most of its buildings are spread along Bonham Road. In this area you will also find the **Fung Ping Shan Museum.** This museum contains an excellent collection of Chinese antiquities—ceramics and bronzes dating from 3,000 BC, fine paintings, lacquerware, and carvings in jade, stone, and wood. *94 Bonham Rd., tel. 2859–2114. Admission free. Open Mon.–Sat. 9:30–6. Closed Sun. and major holidays.*

Continuing around the western end of the island, you come to two huge housing developments: privately owned **Pok Fu Lam,** and government-sponsored **Wah Fu Estate.** Both overlook Lamma Island and are complete with shops, recreational facilities, and banks. They are typical of Hong Kong's approach to mass housing. From here you ride downhill to Aberdeen, an area deserving exploration.

Aberdeen, named after an English lord, not the Scottish city, got its start as a refuge for pirates some 200 years ago. After World War II, Aberdeen became fairly commercial as the *Tanka* (boat people) attracted tourists to their floating restaurants. Many still live afloat, but others have moved ashore.

You can still see much of traditional Aberdeen, such as the **Aberdeen Cemetery** (Aberdeen Main Rd.), with its enormous gravestones and its glorious view of the bay.

Also in Aberdeen is the famous **Tin Hau Temple,** whose ancient, original bell and drum are still used at its opening and closing each day. Although rather shabby, this is one of several shrines to the goddess of the sea that become very colorful during the Tin Hau Festival in April and May, when hundreds of boats converge along the shore.

You can continue on to **Apleichau (or Duck's Tongue) Island,** which can be reached by a bus across the bridge or by sampan. The island has a boat-building yard where junks, yachts, and sampans are constructed, almost all without formal plans. Look to your right when crossing the bridge for a superb view of the harbor and its countless junks. On your left is a view of boats belonging to members of the Marina Club and the slightly less exclusive Aberdeen Boat Club, as well as the famous floating **Jumbo Restaurant.**

East of Aberdeen are the **Ocean, Water World,** and **Middle Kingdom** theme parks. Ocean Park is on 170 acres of land overlooking the sea and is one of the world's largest oceanariums, attracting thousands of visitors daily. On the "lowland" side are gardens, parks, and a children's zoo. A cable car, providing spectacular views of the entire south coast, takes you to the "headland" side and to Ocean Theatre, the world's largest marine mammal theater, with seats for 4,000 people. Here, too, are various rides including one of the world's largest roller coasters. The adjacent, 65-acre Water World is an aquatic fun park with slides, rapids, pools, and a wave cove. Middle Kingdom is a theme park depicting architecture, arts, crafts, and industry through 3,000 years of Chinese history. There are cultural shows, souvenir shops, and restaurants. *Wong Chuk Hang Rd., Ocean Park, tel. 2873–8888. Admission to both Ocean Park and the Middle Kingdom theme park (tel. 2870–0268): HK$130 per adult includes 1 child under 12, HK$65 per child otherwise. Open daily 10 AM–6 PM. Water World, tel. 2555–6055. Admission: HK$60 adults, HK$40 children, HK$30 students. Open May–Oct. daily 10 AM–6 PM.*

Deep Water Bay (Island Rd.) is just to the east of the theme parks. This was the setting for the film *Love Is a Many-Splendored Thing,* and its deep coves are still beautiful.

The waterside road continues to **Repulse Bay,** named after the British warship HMS *Repulse* (not, as some local wags say, after the pollution of its waters). The famed Repulse Bay Hotel was demolished in 1982 and has been replaced with a luxury residential building, but replicas of its **Repulse Bay Verandah Restaurant** and **Bamboo Bar** are run by the same people who operated the original hotel. For a pampered colonial feeling, go to the restaurant for British high tea. The hotel gained notoriety in December 1941 when invading Japanese clambered over the hills behind it and entered its gardens, which were being used as headquarters by the British. After a brief battle, the British surrendered.

Another reminder of World War II is **Stanley Bay** (Wong Ma Kak Rd.). It became notorious as the home of the largest Hong Kong prisoner-of-war camps run by the Japanese. Today, Stanley is known for its picturesque beaches and its market, where casual fashions are sold at wholesale prices. Hong Kong has dozens of shops offering similar bargains, but it's more fun shopping for them in the countrified atmosphere around Stanley. You can also find ceramics, paintings, and books.

Shek O, the easternmost village on the south side of the island, is filled with old houses, great mansions, a superb golf course and club, a few simple restaurants, a pretty beach, and fine views.

You can hike through **Shek O Country Park** in under two hours. Look here for birds that are hard to find in Hong Kong, such as Kentish plovers, reef egrets, and black-headed gulls, as well as the colorful rufus-backed shrike and the bulbul. From Shek O, the round-island route continues back to the north, to the housing and industrial estate of **Chai Wan** (Chai Wan Rd.). From here you have a choice of a fast journey back to Central on the MTR, or a slow ride to Central on the two-decker tram.

Tour 4: New Territories

The visitor who has explored Hong Kong and Kowloon should go one step farther and spend at least a day in the **New Territories.** Here you can look across the border into the People's Republic of China, enjoy panoramas of forested mountainsides, and visit some of the ancient temples and clan houses of the area.

Only about 25 km (15 mi) separate Kowloon's waterfront from the People's Republic of China. The New Territories is often referred to as "the land between," because it is the area between Kowloon and the Chinese border. It is called the New Territories because it was the last area of land claimed by the British in extending their Hong Kong colony. Although most of the original farmland has given way to cities just as densely populated as much of Hong Kong Island, you will be surprised at the village flavor that has been retained in many areas, with small "wet-markets" (so named because the ground beneath is always wet) selling fresh produce and live chickens and fish and small fishing towns along the water. The New Territories also has vast areas of country park, including Tai Po Kou, a forest that has wild monkeys, near the Tai Po Kowloon–Canton Railway stop. The easiest way to see the region is by taking a tour organized by the Hong Kong Tourist Association. *Book through your hotel tour desk or an HKTA Information Center. For information, tel. 2801–7177.*

Below is a brief description of the highlights of a New Territories tour, circling clockwise out of Kowloon.

Chuk Lam Sim Yuen, translated "The Bamboo Forest Monastery," is one of Hong Kong's most impressive monasteries. It has three large statues of Buddha, and on festival days it is packed with worshipers.

Ching Chung Koon Taoist Temple is near the town of Tuen Mun. This huge temple has room after room of altars, all filled with the heady scent of incense burning in bronze holders. On one side of the main entrance is a cast-iron bell with a circumference of about 5 feet. On the other side of the entrance is a huge drum that was used to call the workers back from the rice fields in the evenings. The grounds are beautiful, with plants and flowers, hundreds of dwarf shrubs, ornamental fish ponds, and pagodas.

Tuen Mun has a population of almost a half million and is one of Hong Kong's "new towns"—independent, small cities created to take the spillover of population from the crowded areas of Kowloon and Hong Kong Island. They provide both industrial areas and living accommodations for the workers and their families. Other new towns are Tsuen Wan, Yuen Long, Shatin, Taipo, Fanling, and Junk Bay. By the end of 1995 the seven towns are expected to house 3 million people, or 41% of Hong Kong's projected population of 7.3 million.

Miu Fat Buddhist Monastery, on Castle Peak Road near Tuen Mun, is a popular place for a vegetarian lunch. The monastery itself is ornate, with large, carved-stone animals guarding the front. Farther on is the village of **Yuen Long,** now completely redeveloped as an industrial and residential complex.

Lau Fau Shan is a village famous for its fish market. Here you will find people selling freshly caught fish, dried fish, salted fish, and shellfish. Make your selection, then take it to one of the village's many restaurants, and have it cooked to order. This is the oyster capital of Hong Kong, but don't eat them raw.

Kam Tin Walled Village, a regular stop on most tours, was was built in the 1600s as a fortified village belonging to the Tang clan. There are actually six walled villages around Kam Tin, but **Kat Hing Wai** is the most popular. The original walls are intact, with guardhouses on the four corners and arrow slits for fighting off attackers. The image of antiquity is somewhat spoiled now by the modern homes and their TV antennas looming over the ancient fortifications.

Next stop is the town of **Lok Ma Chau,** where the big attraction is the view. You can stand on a hill and look down on vast fields and the Sham Chun River winding through them. Across the river, barely a mile away, is the People's Republic of China. Unless you plan a tour into China, this is as close as you will get. Elderly "models" here demand HK$1 before you can photograph them.

Fanling is a town that combines the serene atmosphere of the Royal Hong Kong Golf Club with the chaos of rapid growth. The nearby **Luen Wo Market** is a traditional Chinese market, well worth visiting.

Taipo means "shopping place" in Chinese and every visitor here discovers that the town more than lives up to its name. In the heart of the region's breadbasket, Taipo has long been a trading and meeting place for local farmers and fishermen. It is now being developed as an industrial center, with new housing and highways everywhere you look.

South of Taipo is the **Chinese University.** The Art Gallery, in the university's Institute of Chinese Studies building, is well worth a visit. It has large exhibits of paintings and calligraphy from the Ming period to modern times. There are also important collections of bronze seals, carved jade flowers, and ceramics from South China. *Take the KCR to University Station and then take a campus bus or taxi. 12 Miles Taipo Rd., Shatin, New Territories, tel. 2609–7416. Admission free. Open Mon.–Sat. 10–4:30, Sun. and holidays 12:30–4:30; closed between exhibitions and on major holidays.*

About a 15-minute walk from the University along Taipo Road is the Ma Liu Shui ferry pier, the starting point for a ferry tour of **Tolo Harbour** and **Tap Mun Island.** It makes many stops, and if you take the 8:30 AM ferry, you'll have time to hike around Tap Mun Island. *Call the HKTA for ferry schedule, tel. 2801–7111.*

Take a detour east from Tai Po to the **Tai Po Kau Nature Reserve.** You can get there by bus from the Tai Po KCR stop or take Bus 70 from Nathan Road at Jordan. You can follow well-marked trails through the reserve's rain forest vegetation and along its small meandering river. The reserve is as safe as any wood, but you are advised to wear sturdy hiking boots and not to try to get too close to the monkeys.

To the west of Tai Po, the **Sai Kung Peninsula** consists mostly of park land. **Clearwater Bay Road,** past Kai Tak Airport, will take you into forested areas and land that is only partially developed. Take the MTR to Choi Hung and then Bus 92 or Minibus 1 to Sai Kung Town, or take a taxi along Clearwater Bay Road. Stroll along the waterfront and you'll see some of the most unusual marine life ever—in tanks, outside restaurants.

Rent a *kaido* (small boats run by private operators) for about HK$130 round-trip to cruise around the harbor, stopping at tiny **Yim Tin Tsai Island,** which has a rustic Catholic mission church built in 1890. **Sai Kung Country Park** has one of Hong Kong's most spectacular hiking trails, through majestic hills overlooking the water.

Whether you enter **Shatin** by road or rail, you will be amazed to find this metropolis in the middle of the New Territories. Another of the "new towns," Shatin underwent a population explosion that took it from a town of 30,000 to one of more than a half million in 10 years. It is home to the **Shatin Racecourse,** Hong Kong's largest. Nearby is the huge **Jubilee Sports Centre,** a vast complex of tracks and training fields designed to give Hong Kong's athletes space to train under professional, full-time coaches for international competition. Shatin is also home of **New Town Plaza,** the most extensive shopping complex in the New Territories.

You have to climb some 500 steps to reach the **Temple of Ten Thousand Buddhas,** nestled among the foothills of Shatin, but a visit is worth every step. Inside the main temple are nearly 13,000 gilded clay statues of Buddha, all virtually identical. They were made by Shanghai craftsmen and donated by worshipers. From this perch you can see the famous **Amah Rock.** Amah means "nurse" in Chinese, and the rock, which resembles a woman with a child on her back, is popular with female worshipers. To the west of the temple is **Tai Mo Shan,** Hong Kong's highest peak, rising 3,230 feet above sea level.

Tour 5: The Outer Islands

The outer islands are the "Other Hong Kong," with an unspoiled natural beauty that is as much a part of Hong Kong as Kowloon's crowded tenements or Hong Kong Island's concrete canyons. Unfor-

tunately most visitors miss the opportunity to see this side of the territory.

In addition to Hong Kong Island there are 235 islands under the control of the British—at least until 1997. The four that are most accessible by ferry—Lantau, Lamma, Cheung Chau, and Peng Chau—have become popular residential areas and welcome visitors. The largest, Lantau, is bigger than Hong Kong Island; the smallest is just a few square feet of rock. Most of them are uninhabited. Others are gradually being developed.

Visiting the outer islands is a wonderfully escapist experience after the people, noise, traffic, and frantic activity of the city. Try to go on a weekday; on weekends, Hong Kongers flock to them and pack the ferries. You can reach the islands by scheduled ferry services operated by the Hong Kong Ferry Company (HKF). The ferries are easy to recognize by the large HKF letters painted on their funnels. *Leave from the Outlying Districts Services Pier, Central. Tel. 2 542–3081 for schedule. Round-trip fare: HK$14–$43 depending on day and class.*

Lantau covers 143 sq km (55 sq mi) and is almost twice the size of Hong Kong Island. However, Lantau's population is only 20,000, compared with Hong Kong Island's 1.5 million. Lantau is well worth a full day's visit, even two. The ferry will take you to **Silvermine Bay,** which is being developed as a commuter's suburb of Hong Kong Island.

The island's private bus services link the main ferry town, **Mui Wo** on Silvermine Bay, with **Tung Chung,** which has a Sung Dynasty fort; **Tai O,** an ancient fishing village and the capital of Lantau; and **Po-Lin (Precious Lotus) Monastery.** The monastery, gaudy and exuberantly commercial, has the world's tallest outdoor bronze statue of Buddha—it is more than 100 feet high and weighs 275½ tons. The temple refectory here is known for its vegetarian meals.

Time Out   Allow time to stop for a meal at either of Lamma's two ferry villages—**Sok Kwu Wan** and **Yung Shue Wan.** In both villages, lines of inviting open-air harborside restaurants, some with amazingly diverse wine lists, offer feasts of freshness that put many restaurants on Hong Kong Island to shame.

Dining out is also a joy on **Cheung Chau,** which lies south of Lantau, about one hour from Central by ferry. Almost every Western visitor's favorite Hong Kong island, it has dozens of good open-air cafés on either side of its crowded sandbar township—both on the **Praya Promenade** along the waterfront and overlooking the main public beach at **Tung Wan.**

Cheung Chau is Hong Kong's most crowded outlying island, with about 22,000 people, most of them living on the sandbar that connects the dumbbell-shaped island's two hilly tips. It has a Mediterranean flavor to it that has attracted artists and writers. The entry into Cheung Chau's harbor, through lines of gaily bannered fishing boats, is an exhilarating experience. Also colorful is the island's annual springtime **Bun Festival,** one of Hong Kong's most popular community galas. There is also history on Cheung Chau—pirate caves, ancient rock carvings, and a 200-year-old temple built to protect the islanders from the twin dangers of plagues and pirates.

What to See and Do with Children

Cityplaza (Taikoo Shing, Hong Kong Island) has roller- and ice-skating rinks, as well as the "World of Whimsy" arcade, with games and rides.

Free **cultural shows** are performed at Ocean Terminal, The Landmark, New World Centre, and Cityplaza, under the auspices of the Hong Kong Tourist Association (HKTA).

Hong Kong Science Museum (*see* Tour 2).

Ocean Park and **Water World** theme parks (*see* Tour 3).

Space Museum (*see* Tour 2).

Sung Dynasty Village (*see* Tour 2).

Zoological and Botanical Gardens (*see* Tour 1).

Shopping

Is Hong Kong still a "shopper's paradise" and the world's bargain basement? The answer is a qualified yes. On the credit side, such goods as cameras, sound systems, computers, precious gems and metals, fabrics, and furs are brought into the territory, in large quantities, free of import duties. Another plus is the high standard of craftsmanship found in Hong Kong, which accounts for its being the manufacturer of fashion garments and jewelry, under license, for the world's leading houses as well as local stores.

On the debit side, shop rents in Hong Kong have soared in recent years, and wages have risen, forcing up prices, especially in Central and Tsim Sha Tsui. As a result, many smaller stores, and those selling goods with low markups, have moved—usually to be replaced by brand-name boutiques and jewelry stores, most of which seem to survive on infrequent sales of very expensive items.

The best bargains in clothing are found in the increasing number of factory outlets for seconds and overruns, in the lanes between Queens Road Central and Des Voeux Road, on the side streets of Tsim Sha Tsui, and in Stanley market.

Most stores selling cameras, electronics, sound equipment, jewelry, and high fashion accept major credit cards, although not for the best discounts. A little bargaining can be productive in these shops; a lot of bargaining is expected in the lanes and markets. Department stores and larger shops will pack and ship goods overseas.

For bilingual addresses of the territory's most recommended shops, see the HKTA's *Shopping Guide*.

Shopping Centers Hong Kong Island
Admiralty (Queensway, Central, MTR: Admiralty). This complex is comprised of a large selection of shops clustered in four shopping centers that are connected to one another by elevated covered walkways: **Queensway Plaza, United Centre, Pacific Place,** and **Admiralty Centre.**

Cityplaza I & II (1111 Kings Rd., Taikoo Shing, MTR: Taikoo Shing). This is one of Hong Kong's busiest shopping centers, popular with families because of its ice- and roller-skating rinks, bowling alley, and weekly cultural shows. The more than 400 shops include plenty of clothing stores for men, women, and children and a number of toy stores.

The Landmark (Des Voeux Rd. and Pedder St., Central, MTR: Central). One of Central's most prestigious shopping sites, the multistoried Landmark is home to Celine, Loewe, D'Urban, Gucci, Joyce, Hermès of Paris, and other chichi designer boutiques. There are also art galleries and fine jewelry shops. A pedestrian bridge links the Landmark with shopping arcades at the Swire House, Jardine House, Prince's Building, Mandarin Oriental Hotel, and Nine Queen's Road.

Shun Tak Centre (200 Connaught Rd.; MTR: Sheung Wan). Emerging from the MTR you'll find yourself at the Shun Tak Centre Shopping Arcade (at Macau Ferry Terminal), where a selection of boutiques feature clothing, handbags, toys, and novelties.

Kowloon **Harbour City** (Canton Rd., Tsim Sha Tsui, next to the Star Ferry Terminal; MTR or Star Ferry to Tsim Sha Tsui) is Hong Kong's, and one of the world's, largest shopping complexes. Harbour City houses **Ocean Terminal, Ocean Centre, Ocean Galleries,** and the **Hong Kong Omni Hotel.** At last count there were some 50 restaurants and 600 shops, including 36 shoe stores and 31 jewelry and watch stores.

New World Shopping Centre (18 Salisbury Rd., Tsim Sha Tsui; MTR: Tsim Sha Tsui, then walk to Salisbury Rd.). This shopping center (next to the New World Hotel) has four floors of fashion and leather boutiques, jewelry stores, restaurants, optical shops, tailors, hi-fi stores, arts and crafts shops, and the Japanese **Tokyu Department Store.** The **Regent Hotel Shopping Arcade** (Salisbury Rd., Tsim Sha Tsui), featuring mostly designer boutiques, can be reached through the Center.

Tsim Sha Tsui East (minibus from the Kowloon Star Ferry, or Hovercraft ferry from Central Star Pier). This area east of Chatham Road is home to hotels, offices, and 15 different shopping plazas, including **Wing On Plaza, Tsim Sha Tsui Centre, Empire Centre, Houston Centre, South Seas Centre,** and **Energy Plaza.** Prices are reasonable, and the atmosphere is lively.

Department Stores *Chinese* The various Chinese-product stores give shoppers some of the most unusual and spectacular buys in Hong Kong—often at better prices than are found in China. Whether you are looking for pearls, gold, jade, silk jackets, fur hats, Chinese stationery, or just a pair of chopsticks, you cannot go wrong with these stores. Most are open seven days a week but are crowded on Saturdays, Sunday sale days, and during weekday lunchtimes. These shopkeepers are expert at packing, shipping, and mailing goods abroad.

Chinese Arts & Crafts (Prince's Bldg., Central; Pacific Place, Admiralty; 26 Harbour Rd., Wanchai; Star House, Silvercord Centre, and 233 Nathan Rd., Tsim Sha Tsui; tel. 2523–3933 for information). This chain is particularly good for silk-embroidered clothing, jewelry, carpets, and art objects. **Chinese Merchandise Emporium** (92–104 Queen's Rd., Central, tel. 2524–1051) serves a bustling local clientele. The fabric, toy, and stationery departments are particularly good here. **Chung Kiu Chinese Products Emporium** (18 Peking Rd., Tsim Sha Tsui, tel. 2376–1911; 530 Nathan Rd., Yau Ma Tei, tel. 2780–2351) specializes in arts and crafts but also has a good selection of traditional Chinese clothing and fine silk lingerie. **China Products Company** (19–31 Yee Wo St., Causeway Bay, next to Victoria Park, tel. 2890–8321; 488 Hennessy Rd., Causeway Bay, tel. 2577–0222) offers an excellent selection of goods, including household items.

Japanese Japanese department stores are very popular in Hong Kong. Stock in these stores includes more upscale Western items than Japanese products, but if you're looking for Japanese cosmetics, inventive gift departments, and exotic food halls, these stores—especially Jumbo Sogo in Causeway Bay and Seibu in Pacific Place—are terrific. Japanese department stores in Causeway Bay include: **Daimaru** (Fashion Square, Paterson St., tel. 2576–7321), **Matsuzakaya** (Causeway Bay Store, Paterson St., tel. 2890–6622), **Mitsukoshi** (500 Hennessy Rd., tel. 2576–5222), and **Jumbo Sogo** (East Point Centre, 555 Hennessy Rd., tel. 2833–8338). In Taikoo Shing, try **UNY** (Cityplaza II, 18 Taikoo Shing Rd., tel. 2885–0331). At Admiralty, go to **Seibu** (The Mall, Pacific Place, Admiralty, tel. 2877–3627). On the Kowloon side, **Isetan** (Sheraton Hong Kong Hotel, 20 Nathan Rd., Tsim Sha Tsui, tel. 2369–0111) is smaller but packed with boutiques carrying Hunting World, Swatch, Dunhill, and Dior. Opposite, in the New World Centre, is **Tokyu Department Store** (24 Salisbury Rd., Tsim Sha Tsui, tel. 2722–0102).

Western Of the department stores that stock large selections of Western goods at fixed prices, the oldest and largest chains are **Wing On** (main branch: 211 Des Voeux Rd., Central, tel. 2852–1888; 12 other branches), **Sincere** (173 Des Voeux Rd., Central, tel. 2544–2688; 37K Yen Chao St., Kowloon, tel. 2394–0261), and **Shui Hing** (23 Nathan Rd., Tsim Sha Tsui, tel. 2721–1495). **Lane Crawford** is the most prestigious department store of all, with prices to match. The main store (70 Queen's Rd., Central, tel. 2526–6121) is the best. Branches are in Windsor House, Causeway Bay; Times Square, and Pacific Place on the Hong Kong side; and Mansion House, 74 Nathan Road, and Ocean Terminal in Kowloon.

Markets These give you some of the best of Hong Kong shopping—good bargains, exciting atmosphere, and a fascinating setting.

Jade Market (Kansu St., off Nathan Rd., Yau Ma Tei) has jade in every form, color, shape, and size. Some trinkets are reasonably priced, but unless you know a lot about jade, don't be tempted into buying expensive items.

Li Yuen Streets East and West (between Queen's and Des Voeux Rds., Central) offers some of the best bargains in fashions, with or without famous brand names. Many of the shops also sell trendy jewelry and accessories. You can also find traditional Chinese quilted jackets. Bags of every variety, many in designer styles, are particularly good buys here. Watch out for pickpockets in these crowded lanes.

Stanley Village Market (take Bus 6 or 260 from the Central Bus Terminus) is a popular haunt for Western residents and tourists looking for designer fashions, jeans, T-shirts, and sportswear, all at factory prices and in Western sizes. **Stanley's Selection** (11B New St.) usually has a good selection of sportswear, as does **Fashion Shop** (53 Stanley Main St.), which is always piled high with jeans. Also interesting are the shops selling curios and household items from throughout Asia. A variety of arts and crafts shops stock mostly Chinese products, such as rosewood boxes, porcelain dolls, and traditional tea baskets. **Oriental Corner** (125A Stanley Main St.) has Chinese wedding boxes and other carved items. Stanley Market is also a good place to buy linen.

Temple Street, in Kowloon (near the Jordan MTR station), is a night market, filled with a colorful collection of clothes, handbags, electrical goods, gadgets, and all sorts of household items. Cantonese opera competes with pop music, and there's the constant chatter of

vendors' cries and shoppers' bargaining. The market stretches for almost a mile and is one of Hong Kong's liveliest nighttime shopping experiences.

Specialty Stores
Antiques

Bargains and discoveries are much harder to find these days than they were a few years ago. If you want to be sure your purchase is authentic, patronize shops such as **Altfield Interiors** (Prince's Bldg., Central, tel. 2524–7526; 45 Graham St., Central, tel. 2524–4867), **Charlotte Horstmann and Gerald Godfrey** (Ocean Terminal, Tsim Sha Tsui, tel. 2735–7167), and **Eileen Kershaw** (Peninsula Hotel, Tsim Sha Tsui, tel. 2366–4083).

If you have more curiosity than cash, **Hollywood Road** is a fun place to visit. Treasures are hidden away among a jumble of old family curio shops, sidewalk junk stalls, slick new display windows, and dilapidated warehouses.

C. L. Ma Antiques (43–55 Wyndham St., Central, tel. 2523–7584) has Ming Dynasty–style reproductions. **Eastern Dreams** (47A Hollywood Rd., Central, tel. 2544–2804; 4 Shelley St., Central, tel. 2524–4787, by appointment only) has antique and reproduction furniture, screens, and curios. **Honeychurch Antiques** (29 Hollywood Rd., Central, tel. 2543–2433) is known especially for antique silver jewelry from Southeast Asia, China, and England. **Yue Po Chai Antique Co.** (132–136 Hollywood Rd., Central, tel. 2540–4374) is one of Hollywood Road's oldest shops, and has a vast and varied stock. **Schoeni Fine Arts** (27 Hollywood Rd., Central, tel. 2542–3143) sells Japanese, Chinese, and Thai antiques; Chinese silverware, such as opium boxes; and rare Chinese pottery. **Cat Street Galleries** (38 Lok Ku Rd., Sheung Wan, Western, tel. 2541–8908) has a collection of antiques dealers all under one roof.

Art

At a time when recession has caused most of the high-profile art buyers of Japan and the West to fade into the background, Hong Kong's economic boom has made the city a hot spot for art collecting. The **Pao Gallery at the Arts Centre** (2 Harbour Rd., Wanchai, tel. 2865–6029) and the **Hong Kong Museum of Art** (Salisbury Rd., Tsim Sha Tsui, tel. 2734–2167) host exhibitions of masters from East and West. There is also a lively contemporary gallery scene in Central and the Lan Kwai Fong area, much of it concentrating on the best work coming out of China and Southeast Asia. If you're interested in gallery-hopping, try **Alisan Fine Arts Ltd.** (Prince's Bldg., Central, tel. 2526–1091), **Galerie La Vong** (1 Lan Kwai Fong, 13th Floor, Central, tel. 2869–6863), **J. R. Guettinger Gallery** (2 Lower Albert Rd., Central, tel. 2537–1482), **Ho Gallery** (California Tower, 24–26 Lan Kwai Fong, 6th Floor, Central, tel. 2521–0933), **Plum Blossoms Gallery** (One Exchange Sq., Central, tel. 2521–2189), and **Touchstone Gallery** (47 Wyndham St., Central, tel. 2524–3078).

Cameras, Lenses, and Binoculars

Many of Hong Kong's thousands of camera shops are clustered in the Lock Road–lower Nathan Road area of Tsim Sha Tsui, in the back streets of Central, and on Hennessy Road in Causeway Bay. Two well-known and knowledgeable dealers are **Williams Photo Supply** (Prince's Bldg., tel. 2522–8437; Furama Kempinski Hotel, 1 Connaught Rd., tel. 2522–1268) and **Photo Scientific Appliances** (6 Stanley St., tel. 2522–1903).

If in doubt about where to shop for such items, stick to the HKTA member shops. Pick up the HKTA shopping guide at any of its information centers or authorized dealers. All reputable dealers should give you a one-year, worldwide guarantee.

Carpets and Rugs Regular imports from China, Iran, India, Pakistan, Afghanistan, and Kashmir make carpets and rugs a very good buy in Hong Kong. There are also plenty of carpets made locally. Though prices have increased in recent years, carpets are still cheaper in Hong Kong than they are in Europe and the United States. For Chinese carpets, branches of **China Products** and **Chinese Arts & Crafts** give the best selection and price range. For locally made carpets, **Tai Ping Carpets** (Hutchison House, 10 Harcourt Rd., 1st Floor, Central, tel. 2522–7138; Wing On Plaza, 62 Mody Rd., Tsim Sha Tsui East, tel. 2369–4061) is highly regarded, especially for custom-made rugs and wall-to-wall carpets.

Computers All of the big names sell in Hong Kong. If you are going to buy, make sure the machine will work on the voltage in your country; an IBM personal computer sold in Hong Kong will work on 220 volts, while the identical machine in the United States will work on 110 volts. Servicing is a major concern, too.

The real bargains in computers are the locally made versions of the most popular brands. But be forewarned: Even though the prices are lower than in Europe and the United States, you may have trouble getting your Hong Kong computer past customs on your return.

There are four shopping centers crammed with small computer shops. On Hong Kong Island try the **Ocean Shopping Arcade** (128 Wanchai Rd., Wanchai), the **Hong Kong Computer Centre** (54 Lockhart Rd., Wanchai), and **Vicwood Plaza** (199 Des Voeux Rd., Central). The **Golden Shopping Centre** (Shamshuipo, Kowloon) is more difficult to reach. Take the MTR to Shamshuipo Station and use the Fuk Wah Street exit.

Factory Outlets Hong Kong's days as the factory-outlet center of the world are long gone, but you can still find samples and overruns in the territory's many outlets. Discounts generally run a mere 20%–30% off retail, but comb through everything, and more often than not you'll be able to bag at least one fabulous bargain. Check garments carefully for damage and fading.

The **Pedder Building** (12 Pedder St., Central) contains five floors of small shops. Not all offer anything resembling factory-outlet prices, but most are worth at least a quick look. The small area of Central made up of **Lan Kwai Fong** and its intersecting streets is another good place to outlet-shop. In Kowloon, there are a number of outlets worth visiting within a few blocks of the **Laichikok** MTR station.

Furniture and Furnishings The home decor market has boomed tremendously in Hong Kong in recent years, and manufacturers of furniture and home furnishings have been quick to increase production. **Design Selection** (39 Wyndham St., Central, tel. 2525–8339) has a variety of Indian fabrics. **Interiors** (43–55 Wyndham St., Central, tel. 2525–0333) stocks handcrafted items from Southeast Asia and the United Kingdom. **The Banyan Tree** (Prince's Bldg., Central, tel. 2592–8721; Ocean Galleries, Harbour City, Tsim Sha Tsui, tel. 2730–6631) sells ready-made or made-to-order rattan furniture and some antique Chinese, Korean, and Filipino pieces. **Queen's Road East,** in Wanchai, has several furniture shops specializing in rattan.

Rosewood furniture is a very popular buy in Hong Kong. **Queen's Road East,** in Wanchai, the great furniture retail and manufacturing area, offers everything from full rosewood dining sets in Ming style to furniture in French, English, or Chinese styles. Custom-made orders are accepted in most shops here. **Choy Lee Co. Ltd.** (1 Queen's Rd. E, tel. 2527–3709) is the most famous.

Handicrafts and Curios The traditional crafts of China include a fascinating range of items: lanterns, temple rubbings, screen paintings, paper cuttings, seal engravings, and wooden birds. The HKTA publishes a useful pamphlet, *Culture*, listing places where you can buy these specialty items; it is available at all HKTA information centers.

The **Welfare Handicrafts Shop** (Jardine House, 1 Connaught Pl., Central, tel. 2524–3356; Salisbury Rd., Tsim Sha Tsui, tel. 2366–6979) stocks a good collection of inexpensive Chinese handicrafts for both adults and children. All profits go to charity. Small and inexpensive curios from other parts of Asia are sold at **Amazing Grace Elephant Co.** (Excelsior Hotel, Gloucester Rd., Causeway Bay, tel. 2890–2776; Ocean Centre, Harbour City, Tsim Sha Tsui, tel. 2730–5455). **Mountain Folkcraft** (12 Wo On La., Central, tel. 2525–3199) offers a varied collection of fascinating curios. **Kinari** (Anson House, 61 Wyndham St., Central, tel. 2869–6827) sells crafts and antiques from all over Southeast Asia. For Indonesian silver, crafts, and batiks, visit **Folkways** (Silvercord Centre, 30 Canton Rd., Tsim Sha Tsui, tel. 2987–9111) and **Vincent Sum Designs Ltd.** (15 Lyndhurst Terr., Central, tel. 2542–2610).

Jewelry Jewelry is the most popular item among visitors to Hong Kong. It is not subject to any local tax or duty, so prices are normally much lower than they are in most other places. Turnover is fast, competition fierce, and the selection fantastic.

Famous international jewelers with shops in Hong Kong include **Van Cleef & Arpels** (Peninsula Hotel, Tsim Sha Tsui, tel. 2368–7648; Jumbo Sogo, Causeway Bay, tel. 2831–8459), **Cartier** (Prince's Bldg., Central, tel. 2522–2964; Peninsula Hotel, Tsim Sha Tsui, tel. 2368–8036), and **Ilias Lalaounis** (The Landmark, Central, tel. 2524–3328; Regent Hotel, Tsim Sha Tsui, tel. 2721–2811). Other opulent and reputable jewelers include **Kevin** (Holiday Inn, 50 Nathan Rd., Tsim Sha Tsui, tel. 2367–1041), **Larry Jewelry** (The Landmark, Central, tel. 2521–1268; Pacific Place, Central, tel. 2868–3993; Ocean Terminal, Harbour City, Tsim Sha Tsui, tel. 2730–8081), **Dickson Watch and Jewellery** (The Landmark, Central, tel. 2521–4245; The Peninsula, Tsim Sha Tsui, tel. 2369–8264; Holiday Inn Golden Mile, 50 Nathan Rd., Tsim Sha Tsui, tel. 2722–6256), **S.P.H. De Silva** (The Mall, Pacific Place, Central, tel. 2522–5807, fax 2845–1547), and **Manchu Gems** (402 Asian House, 1 Hennessy Rd., Wanchai, tel. 2861–0896).

For modern jewelry with an Oriental influence, take a look at the fabulous designs by **Kai-Yin Lo** (The Mall, Pacific Place, Central, tel. 2840–0066; Peninsula Hotel, Tsim Sha Tsui, tel. 2723–2722). **Chinese Arts & Crafts** stores have a wide selection of jade, pearls, and gold as well as porcelain, jewelry, and enamelware.

As one of the world's largest diamond-trading centers, Hong Kong offers these gems at prices that are at least 10% lower than world-market levels. When buying diamonds, check the "Four C's": color, clarity, carat (size), and cut. Shop only in outlets listed in the Hong Kong Tourist Association's shopping guide (available in HKTA centers). For information or advice, call the **Diamond Importers Association** (tel. 2523–5497).

Pearls, another good buy, should be checked for color against a white background. Shades include white, silvery white, light pink, darker pink, and cream. Cultured pearls usually have a perfect round shape, semibaroque pearls have slight imperfections, and baroque pearls are distinctly misshapen. Jewelry shops with a good selection of pearls include **Trio Pearl** (Peninsula Hotel, Tsim Sha Tsui, tel. 2367–9171), **Gemsland** (Mandarin Oriental Hotel, Central, tel. 2525–2729), and **K.S. Sze & Sons** (Mandarin Oriental Hotel, tel. 2524–2803).

Hong Kong's most famous stone, jade comes not only in green but in shades of purple, orange, yellow, brown, white, and violet. Although you will see "jade" trinkets and figurines everywhere in Hong Kong, high-quality jade is rare and expensive. Translucency and evenness of color and texture determine jade's value.

If you are wary of spending your money at the Kansu Street Jade Market (*see* Markets, Bazaars, and Alleys, *above*), visit Tsim Sha Tsui's **Jade House** (162 Ocean Terminal, Tsim Sha Tsui, tel. 2736–1232). **Chow Sang Sang** (229 Nathan Rd., Tsim Sha Tsui, tel. 2730–0111, and 17 smaller branches around town) and **Chow Tai Fook** (29 Queens Rd., Central, tel. 2523–7128, and 15 branches) are also good places to shop for fine jade.

Kung-Fu Supplies   The two most convenient places to buy your drum cymbal, leather boots, sword, whip, double dagger, studded wrist bracelet, Bruce Lee kempo gloves, and other kung-fu exotica are **Kung Fu Supplies Co.** (188 Johnston Rd., Wanchai, tel. 2891–1912) and **Shang Wu Kung Fu Appliance Centre** (366 Lockhart Rd., Wanchai, tel. 2893–4535).

Leather   Leather items are high on the list for the Hong Kong shopper. The best and most expensive leather goods come from Europe, but locally made leather bags in designer styles go for a song on Li Yuen streets East and West, in Central, and in other shopping lanes. Some good buys can also be found in the factory outlets in Hunghom, Kowloon.

Linens, Silks, Embroideries   Pure silk shantung, silk and gold brocade, silk velvet, silk damask, and printed silk crepe de Chine are just some of the exquisite materials available in Hong Kong at reasonable prices. The best selections are in the **China Products Emporiums, Chinese Arts & Crafts,** and **Yue Hwa** stores. Ready-to-wear silk garments, from mandarin coats and cheongsams to negligees, dresses, blouses, and slacks are good buys at **Chinese Arts & Crafts.**

Irish linens, Swiss cotton, Thai silks, and Indian, Malay, and Indonesian fabrics are among the imported cloths available in Hong Kong. Many of them can be found on **Wing On Lane** in Central. **Vincent Sum Designs** specializes in Indonesian batik. Fabrics from India are available from **Design Selection** (75 Wyndham St., Central, tel. 2525–8339).

The best buys from China are hand-embroidered and appliquéed linens and cottons. You can find a magnificent range of tablecloths, place mats, napkins, and handkerchiefs in the **China Products Company** and **Chinese Arts & Crafts** stores, and in linen shops in **Stanley Market.**

Optical Goods   There are a vast number of optical shops in Hong Kong, and some surprising bargains, too. Soft contact lenses, hard lenses, and frames for glasses go for considerably less than in many other places. **The Optical Shop** (main branch: Prince's Bldg., Central, tel. 2523–8385) is the fanciest and probably the most reliable store.

Sporting Goods   Hong Kong is an excellent place to buy sports gear, thanks to high volume and reasonable prices. You can find a good range of equipment and clothing at **World Top Sports Goods Ltd.** (Pacific Place, Admiralty, Central, tel. 2845–9811; 49 Hankow Rd., Tsim Sha Tsui, tel. 2376–2937) and in the many outlets of **Marathon Sports** (Tak

Shing House, Theatre La., 20 Des Voeux Rd., Central, tel. 2810–4521; Ocean Terminal, Harbour Centre, Tsim Sha Tsui, tel. 2730–6160).

Stereo Equipment Hennessy Road in Causeway Bay has long been a mecca for those in search of stereo gear, although many small shops on Central's Queen Victoria and Stanley streets and on Tsim Sha Tsui's Nathan Road offer a similar variety of goods. Be sure to compare prices before buying, as they can vary widely. Also make sure that guarantees are applicable in your own country.

Tailor-Made Clothing For a suit, overcoat, or jacket, give the tailor plenty of time—at least three to five days, and allow for a minimum of two proper fittings plus a final one for finishing touches. Shirts can be done in a day, but you will get better quality if you allow more time. Some shirtmakers like to give one fitting. Women will find that tailors do their best work on tailored suits, coats, and dresses and do not do as well with more fluid styles or knit fabrics.

There are a number of reputable and long-established tailors in Hong Kong. **Sam's** (Burlington House, 94 Nathan Rd., Kowloon, tel. 2367–9423), for men and women, has been in business since 1957. **Ascot Chang** (Prince's Bldg., Central, tel. 2523–3663; Peninsula Hotel, Tsim Sha Tsui, tel. 2366–2398; Regent Hotel, Tsim Sha Tsui, tel. 2367–8319) has specialized in making shirts for men since 1949. **W. W. Chan & Sons** (Burlington House, 92–94 Nathan Rd., Tsim Sha Tsui, tel. 2366–9738) is known for top-quality classic cuts for men and has bolts and bolts of fine European fabrics to choose from. Top women's tailors include **Irene Fashions** (Burlington House, 92–94 Nathan Rd., Tsim Sha Tsui, tel. 2367–5588), the women's division of W. W. Chan, and **Mode Elegante** (Peninsula Hotel, Tsim Sha Tsui, tel. 2366–8153).

TVs and Videocassette Recorders Color TV systems vary throughout the world, so it's important to be certain the TV set or videocassette recorder you purchase in Hong Kong has a system compatible to the one in your country. Hong Kong, Australia, Great Britain, and most European countries use the PAL system. The United States uses the NTSC system, and France and Russia use the SECAM system. The HKTA has a useful brochure called *Shopping Guide to Video Equipment*.

Sports and Fitness

Participant Sports

Golf Three Hong Kong golf clubs allow visitors with reciprocal privileges from a club at home to play their courses.

The **Clearwater Bay Golf and Country Club,** in the New Territories, has five outdoor and two indoor tennis courts, three indoor squash courts, and two indoor badminton courts, as well as an outdoor pool, a health spa, and an 18-hole golf course. *Clearwater Bay Rd., Saikung Peninsula, tel. 2719–1595 (HKTA tour, tel. 2801–7177). Greens fees: HK$1,000 for 18 holes. Cart, club, and shoe rentals available; no lessons.*

The **Discovery Bay Golf Club** on Lantau Island has an 18-hole course that is open to visitors on weekdays. *Tel. 2987–7271 or 987–7273. Take the ferry from Star Ferry Pier in Central. Costs: greens fees HK$700, club rental HK$150, golf cart rental HK$150, and shoe rental HK$50. Lessons HK$500 per hr.*

The **Royal Hong Kong Golf Club** allows visitors to play on its nine-hole pitch-and-par course at Deep Water Bay, Hong Kong Island, or on its three 18-hole courses at Fanling, New Territories. *Fanling, tel. 2670–1211 for bookings, 670–0647 for club rentals (HK$ 300). Greens fees: HK$1,300 for 18 holes. Deep Water Bay, tel. 2812–7070. Weekdays only. Greens fees: HK$400 for 18 holes, HK$550 for 36 holes. Lessons at both locations for nonmembers on weekdays only; HK$250–HK$400 per half hr.*

Hiking Hong Kong's well-kept and reasonably well-marked hiking trails, never more than a few hours away from civilization, are one of its best-kept secrets. You can hike through any of the territory's country parks and around any of the accessible outlying islands. A day's hike (or two days if you're prepared to camp out) takes a bit of planning, but it's well worth the effort. Before you go, pick up trail maps at the **Government Publications Centre** (Central Post Office Bldg., near the Star Ferry pier, tel. 2523–5377). Ask for the blueprints of the trails and the Countryside Series maps. The HM20C series are handsome four-color maps, but not very reliable.

Jogging Visitors who are experienced runners can join members of the **Hong Kong Running Clinic** every Sunday morning at 7. Newcomers are especially welcome and looked after. These runs are in the tradition of conversation-speed jogging—if you can't talk to your neighbor, you must be running too fast. *Meet in front of Adventist Hospital, 40 Stubbs Rd., Happy Valley, tel. 2574–6211, ext. 888 (ask for director of health).*

Victoria Park at Causeway Bay has an official jogging track.

Squash Squash is very much a club activity in Hong Kong. However, there are public courts at the **Harbour Road Indoor Games Hall, Hong Kong Squash Center,** and **Victoria Park** in Central, and **Laichicok Park** in Kowloon. Bookings can be made up to 10 days in advance; book as early as possible. Bring a passport for identification. *Harbour Road Indoor Games Hall, 27 Harbour Rd., Wanchai, tel. 2827–9684. Hong Kong Squash Centre, Cotton Tree Dr. (across from Peak Tram Terminal), Central, tel. 2521–5072. Victoria Park, Hing Fat St., Causeway Bay, tel. 2570–6186. Laichikok Park, Lai Wan Rd., Kowloon, tel. 2745–2796. Cost: HK$46 per hr. Call the Hong Kong Urban Council, tel. 2521–5077, for further information and other locations.*

Tennis If you want to play tennis, you will probably either have to get someone who is a member of a private club to take you or have reciprocal privileges through your home club. Although there are a limited number of public tennis courts, they are usually completely booked far in advance. To book a public tennis court you will need identification such as a passport. *Victoria Park, Causeway Bay, tel. 2570–6186, 14 courts; Bowen Rd., Happy Valley, tel. 2528–2983, 4 courts; Wongneichong Gap, Happy Valley, tel. 2574–9122, 17 courts; and Kowloon Tsai Park, Kowloon Tong, tel. 2336–7878, 8 courts.*

Water Sports **Junking**—dining on the water aboard large junks that have been converted to pleasure craft—is unique to Hong Kong. This leisure activity has become so popular in the colony that there is now a fairly large junk-building industry that produces highly varnished, plushly appointed, air-conditioned junks up to 80 feet long.

These floating rumpus rooms serve a purpose, especially for citizens living on Hong Kong Island who need to escape through a day on the water. Because so much drinking takes place, the junks are also known as "gin-junks," commanded by "weekend admirals." They also serve as platforms for swimmers and waterskiers. If anyone so much as breathes an invitation for junking, grab it. You can also rent a junk. The HKTA recommends **Simpson Marine Ltd.** (Aberdeen Marina Tower, 8 Shun Wan Rd., Aberdeen, tel. 2555–7349), whose junks, with crew, can hold up to 33 people and cost between HK$2,000 and HK$2,200 for a four-hour evening trip and from HK$2,500 to HK$5,500 for an eight-hour day trip, depending on the season. The pilot will take you to your choice of the following outer islands: Cheung Chau, Lamma, Lantau, Po Toi, or the islands in Sai Kung Harbour.

To go **sailing** you must belong to a yacht club that has reciprocal privileges with one in Hong Kong. Contact the **Royal Hong Kong Yacht Club** (tel. 2832–2817) to make arrangements.

Swimming is extremely popular with the locals, who have dozens of beaches to choose from. Pollution is a problem in Hong Kong waters, however, so don't swim if a red flag—indicating either pollution or an approaching storm—is hoisted, or if you see trash floating on the water.

Windsurfing is certainly not unique to Hong Kong, but the territory has welcomed it with open sails. Windsurfing centers at **Stanley Beach** on Hong Kong Island and **Tun Wan Beach** on Cheung Chau island offer lessons and board rentals. The cost for lessons is about HK$250 for four hours (spread over two days); board rental costs around HK$55 per hour. Other beaches that have stands where you can rent boards are the small beach opposite the main beach at **Shek O,** Hong Kong Island; **Tolo Harbour,** near Taipo in New Terrorities; and **Sha Ha Beach,** in front of the Surf Hotel at Sai Kung, also in the New Territories. For further information, call the **Windsurfing Association of Hong Kong** (tel. 2866–3232).

Spectator Sports

Horse Racing and Gambling

Horse racing is the nearest thing in Hong Kong to a national sport. It is a multimillion-dollar-a-year business, employing thousands of people and drawing crowds that are almost crazed in their eagerness to rid themselves of their hard-earned money.

The Sport of Kings is run under a monopoly by the Royal Hong Kong Jockey Club, one of the most politically powerful entities in the territory. Profits go to charity and community organizations. The season runs from September or October through May. Some 65 races are held at two racecourses—**Happy Valley** on Hong Kong Island and **Shatin** in the New Territories. Shatin's racecourse is only a few years old and is one of the most modern in the world. Both courses have huge video screens at the finish line so that gamblers can see what is happening each foot of the way.

Races are run at one track on Wednesday night and at one or the other on either Saturday or Sunday. Even if you're not a gambler, it's worth going just to see the crowds. You can view races from the Members' Stand at both tracks by showing your passport and paying HK$50 for a badge.

In a place where gambling has developed into a mania, it may come as a surprise to learn that most forms of gambling are forbidden. Excluding the stock market, which is by far the territory's biggest single gambling event, the only legalized forms of gambling are horse racing and the lottery. Nearby Macau is another story—there you can get your fill of casino gambling (*see* Macau *below*).

Dining

By Jack Moore

Revised by Jane Lasky

Nowhere in the world is the cooking more varied than in this city, where Cantonese cuisine (long regarded by Chinese gourmets as the most intricate and sophisticated in Asia) is augmented by cookery from many other parts of China and virtually every other culinary region on earth. French, German, Italian, Portuguese, Japanese, Korean, Indian, Indonesian, Thai, and even specialty American food is served up by literally thousands of restaurants. Be advised, however, that while Hong Kong contains some of Asia's best restaurants, it also contains some of the worst—so don't expect just any old neighborhood restaurant to turn out to be a gourmet's dream.

While in Hong Kong, you *must* try two things: Peking duck (nowhere will you find better) and dim sum—tasty hors d'oeuvres served as a meal between breakfast and late afternoon.

Highly recommended restaurants are indicated by a star ★.

Category	Cost*
$$$$	over HK$500 (US$64)
$$$	HK$300–HK$500 (US$38–US$64)
$$	HK$100–HK$300 (US$13–US$38)
$	under HK $100 (US$13)

per person, not including 10% service charge

In more traditional Chinese restaurants, tips are not expected. However, it is customary to leave small change.

Although major credit cards are widely accepted, many smaller establishments do not accept them. Ask before you sit down.

American
$$–$$$
★

San Francisco Steak House. For more than 20 years, this mock Barbary Coast eatery has been pleasing both locals and travelers with a combination of casual Bay Area atmosphere—dark paneled walls, red flock wallpaper, and replicas of Powell Street cable cars—and American fare. The clam chowder is an original Boston recipe, and the cioppino is what you'd expect at Fisherman's Wharf. American Angus steaks are treated with the respect good meat deserves. Also excellent is the Canadian salmon, served as a whole baked baby coho. You can always ask for a burger, they're the best in town. All portions are very generous. *Harbour City, Canton Rd., Tsim Sha Tsui, Kowloon, tel. 2735–7576. Reservations advised. Dress: casual. AE, DC, MC, V.*

$–$$

Beverly Hills Deli. Service here is rushed in the middle of the day and not much better at dinnertime, but the food keeps people coming back. You'll find all the usual deli specials and a kosher-style menu with imported ingredients. Still, don't expect New York–quality matzo-ball soup or bagels—they just don't make the grade. Other menu items include chili con carne, superb frozen yogurts, cheese blintzes, and gargantuan overstuffed sandwiches. Try the pastrami, it's great. *55 New World Centre, 2nd level, Tsim Sha Tsui, Kowloon, tel. 2369–8695. Reservations advised. Dress: casual. AE, DC, MC, V.*

Chinese
$$$$

The Chinese Restaurant. It takes some nerve to call your establishment *the* Chinese restaurant in Hong Kong, but this one gets away with it. The postmodern interior design offers a new take on the traditional 1920s teahouse, and subdued lighting creates a mellow atmosphere. The talented kitchen staff's innovative Cantonese cooking is what makes the the place a standout. The menu changes seasonally, though some oft-ordered items—papaya soup, crispy chicken skin, and stewed goose in brown ginger gravy—are always available and well worth tasting. The Peking duck here is out of this world, as is the braised abalone on a bed of artichoke hearts. *Hyatt Regency Hotel, 67 Nathan Rd., Tsim Sha Tsui, Kowloon, tel. 2311–1234. Reservations advised. Jacket and tie advised. AE, DC, MC, V.*

$$$$ **Lai Ching Heen.** The name of this truly luxurious Cantonese restau-
★ rant means, quite appropriately, "In the Regent, where you'll be very happy." Tucked away in the lower level of the Regent Hotel, the subtly decorated dining room has a stunning view of the harbor near sea level. Opulent table settings include ivory chopsticks and curved jade spoons. The food here is some of the most highly regarded by Hong Kong's culinary critics. Each patron is welcomed with a complimentary appetizer that represents the yin and yang: Mild slivers of deep-fried fish are dressed with tart vinegar, the contrasting but complementary tastes signifying balance and harmony. There are special menus for each month of the Chinese lunar calendar, always featuring fresh steamed seafood dishes and seasonal Chinese fruits and vegetables. The most popular dishes are braised abalone with oyster sauce, deep-fried scallops and pears, and braised shark's fins in brown sauce. *Regent Hotel, 18 Salisbury Rd., Tsim Sha Tsui, Kowloon, tel. 2721–1211. Reservations required. Jacket and tie advised. AE, DC, MC, V.*

$$ **Bodhi Vegetarian.** The three branches of this restaurant offer the some of the best Chinese vegetarian meals in Hong Kong. The diverse selection of dishes will probably be a pleasant surprise to Westerners, whether vegetarian or not. A wide array of vegetables, dozens of varieties of mushrooms, bird's nests, and noodles, are often combined with tofu, which can be prepared to suggest meat or fish. Try the deep fried taro (a bland potato-like vegetable) or the stir-fried Chinese vegetables. The Buddhist scrolls that decorate the walls emphasize the philosophical roots of the menu. No alcohol is served. *384–388 Lockhart Rd., Wanchai, Hong Kong Island, tel. 2739–2222; 56 Cameron Rd, Tsim Sha Tsui, Kowloon, tel. 2739–2222; 2–6 Tak Wah St., Tsuen Wan, New Territories, tel. 2415–0113. Dress: casual. AE, DC, MC, V.*

$$ **Yung Kee.** For more than half a century, this massive (five floors
★ hold some five thousand guests), multistory eatery has offered very good Cantonese food amid riotous Chinese decor featuring writhing golden dragons. Convenient to hotels and the Central business district, the restaurant attracts a varied clientele—from office workers to visiting celebrities—all of whom receive the same cheerful, high-energy service. Roast goose is the specialty, the skin beautifully crisp. Seafood fanciers should try the sautéed fillet of pomfret with chili and black bean sauce. *32–40 Wellington St., Central, Hong Kong Island, tel. 2522–1624. Reservations advised. Dress: casual. AE, DC, MC, V.*

$ **American Restaurant.** Despite the name, the cuisine here is from Pe-
★ king, which means hearty, stick-to-the-ribs dishes suitable for the chilly climate of northern China. An overdecorated restaurant full of red and gold fixtures, the American has been a gastronomic amenity in Hong Kong for over 40 years. Favorites here include the hot-and-sour soup, fried and steamed dumplings, noodle dishes, delicious hot pots in the winter, and excellent beggar's chicken that's cooked in clay and lotus leaves. Every meal starts with complimentary peanuts and sliced cucumber in vinegar. Don't confuse this place with the American Cafe, which has branches all over town and is merely a

Hong Kong and Kowloon Dining and Lodging

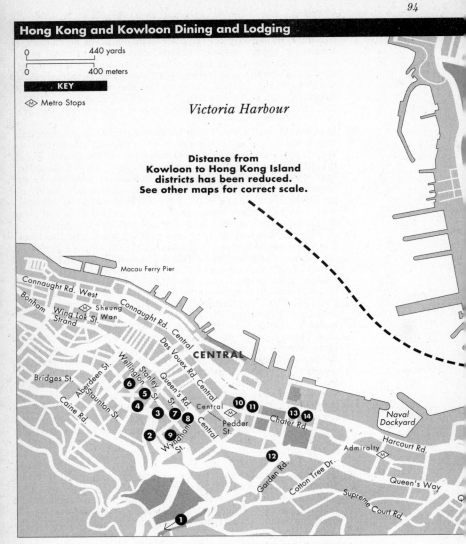

Victoria Harbour

Distance from Kowloon to Hong Kong Island districts has been reduced. See other maps for correct scale.

0   440 yards
0   400 meters

KEY

Ⓜ Metro Stops

Macau Ferry Pier

Connaught Rd. West

Bonham Strand

Wing Lok St.

Sheung Wan Ⓜ

Connaught Rd. Central

Des Voeux Rd. Central

CENTRAL

Bridges St.

Aberdeen St.

Staunton St.

Caine Rd.

Wellington St.

Stanley St.

Queen's Rd.

Queen's Rd. Central

Central Ⓜ

Pedder St.

Chater Rd.

Wyndham St.

Naval Dockyard

Harcourt Rd.

Admiralty Ⓜ

Queen's Way

Garden Rd.

Cotton Tree Dr.

Supreme Court Rd.

Dining

American Restaurant, **16**
Au Trou Normand, **36**
Bentley's Seafood Restaurant and Oyster Bar, **11**
Beverly Hills Deli, **37**
Bodhi Vegetarian, **23, 33**
Café Deco, **1**
The Chinese Restaurant, **39**
Gaddi's, **40**

Hugo's, **39**
Il Mercato, **24**
Indochine, **8**
Jimmy's Kitchen, **7, 45**
La Brasserie, **46**
Lai Ching Heen, **38**
Luk Yu Tea House, **6**
Papillon, **4**
Pierrot, **10**
Sagano Restaurant, **30**
San Francisco Steak House, **44**
Spice Island Gourmet Club, **5**

Tandoor Restaurant, **2**
Three-Five Korean Restaurant, **42**
Valentino Ristorante Italiano, **35**
Vietnam City, **31**
Wyndham Street Thai, **9**
Yung Kee, **3**

Lodging

Bangkok Royal, **48**
Booth Lodge, **51**
Century, **22**
Concourse, **53**
Excelsior, **25**
Furama Kempinski, **14**
Grand Tower, **52**
Grand Hyatt, **20**
Harbour View International House, **18**

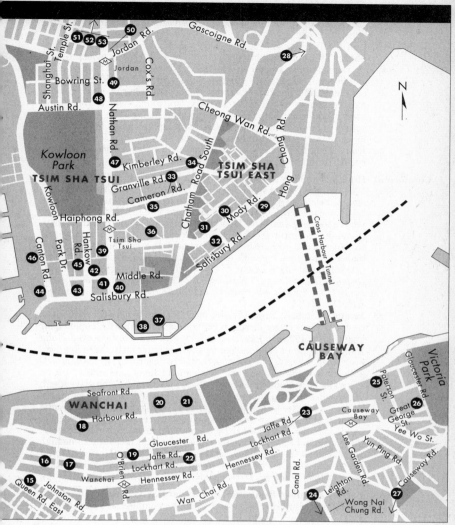

Hilton, **12**
Holiday Inn Crowne Plaza Harbour View, **29**
Hyatt Regency, **39**
Kowloon, **44**
Kowloon Shangri-La, **32**
Luk Kwok, **19**
Majestic, **50**
Mandarin Oriental, **10**
Miramar, **47**

New World Harbour View, **21**
Omni Hongkong , **41**
Park Lane, **26**
Peninsula, **40**
Prudential, **49**
Ramada Hotel Kowloon, **34**
Regal Airport, **28**
Regal Hongkong Hotel, **27**
The Regent, **38**

Ritz-Carlton, **13**
Salisbury YMCA, **43**
The Wesley, **15**
Wharney, **17**

fast-food chain. *20 Lockhart Rd., Wanchai, Hong Kong Island, tel. 2527–7277 or 527–7770. Weekend reservations required. Dress: casual. No credit cards.*

$ **Luk Yu Tea House.** The food here takes a backseat to the atmosphere. This unofficial historical monument is a living museum with extraordinary character. It's been in business for more than 60 years and lets you catch a rare glimpse of old colonial Hong Kong. The decor, including handsome carved wood doors, hardwood paneling, marble facings, and, unfortunately, spittoons (which are noisily used by the clientele), is definitely worth seeing. The morning dim sum is popular with Chinese business people, though the fare is no more than standard Cantonese. *24–26 Stanley St., Central, Hong Kong Island, tel. 2523–5464. Reservations impossible unless you speak Cantonese. Dress: casual. No credit cards.*

Continental **Hugo's.** The Hyatt Hotel's showpiece restaurant since it opened in
$$$$ 1969, Hugo's is a big space, elegant and sophisticated, that still manages to be cozy. Open trellises and fine pieces of antique armor decorate the constantly bustling dining room. The food is renowned, for very good reasons. The lobster bisque and prime rib are exceptional. Even better are the baked rack of lamb in an onion-and-potato crust with juniper-berry cream and the salmon and scallops baked in flaky pastry with mango and spinach. Go for the romantic candlelight at night or one of the terrific Sunday brunches. *Hyatt Regency Hong Kong, 67 Nathan Rd., Tsim Sha Tsui, Kowloon, tel. 2311–1234. Lunch reservations advised. Jacket and tie required. AE, DC, MC, V.*

$$ **Jimmy's Kitchen.** Probably the most famous—and still one of the
★ best—of the territory's restaurants, this institution first opened for business in 1928. It has been catering to a deeply devoted Hong Kong clientele in one location or another (currently there are two) ever since. Nicely, but not spectacularly decorated, it has comfortable booths, dark woodwork, lattice partitions, and brasswork on the walls. The food is as charmingly old-fashioned as the place itself: Where else in Hong Kong can you find corned beef and cabbage? Other specialties, including borscht, stroganoff, goulash, and bangers and mash, are accompanied by the restaurant's traditional pickled onions. The rhubarb tart is must for dessert. Unfortunately, the Kowloon branch, on Ashley Road, does not meet the same high standards as the Wyndham Street location. *South China Bldg., 1 Wyndham St., Central, Hong Kong Island, tel. 2526–5293. Lunch reservations required. Dress: casual. AE, DC, MC, V.*

English **Bentley's Seafood Restaurant and Oyster Bar.** One flight down from
$$$ the Prince's Building office and shopping complex, is an exact copy
★ of a well-known swank London restaurant, with cream-colored walls, floral carpet, Dickensian prints, and the overall feeling of an exclusive English club. There are even English oysters from Colchester in season and oysters from many other places in the world as well. They are served up raw or cooked at the oyster bar or your table. Choose from oysters Imperial with champagne sauce, oysters Bentley with tomato and curry sauces, and oysters Kilpatrick with tomato, chili, and bacon. The seafood here is some of the best in town, grilled simply with lemon and butter. The house fish pie is classic English cooking at its rare best. *Prince's Bldg., 10 Chater Sq. (enter off Statue Sq.), Central, Hong Kong Island, tel. 2868–0881. Lunch reservations required. Jacket and tie advised. AE, DC, MC. Closed Sun.*

French
$$$$
★

Gaddi's. The classiest lunch or dinner venue in Hong Kong for the last 40 years, and completely refurbished in 1994, this restaurant's reputation is as grand as the hotel in which it thrives. The decor includes huge chandeliers made in Paris and salvaged from wartime Shanghai, ankle-deep Tai Ping carpets that exactly match the napery, and a priceless Chinese coromandel screen, made in 1670 for the emperor's summer palace in Beijing and on semipermanent loan from one of the hotel's owners, Lord Kadoorie. The service is superlative, and the menu changes frequently. Soufflés are always offered and are exquisite; a favorite is orange-flavored and liberally laced with Grand Marnier. There's a magnificent wine list and low-key live music played nightly. *Peninsula Hotel, Salisbury Rd., Tsim Sha Tsui, Kowloon, tel. 2366–6251, ext. 3989. Reservations required. Jacket and tie required. AE, DC, MC, V.*

$$$$

Pierrot. A specially commissioned ceramic clown welcomes you to this theatrical restaurant whose windows, framed with ornate plum and gold drapes, overlook the quintessential Hong Kong Harbour panorama. The service is flawless. The management often invites visiting European chefs to prepare their specialties as part of food promotions. The regular menus change seasonally. Both lunch and dinner menus are small but feature exquisitely crafted dishes such as ravioli of scampi with white curry sauce, and the restaurant has one of the most extensive and best-chosen wine lists in this part of the world. An added attraction is the bar with a selection of caviars. *Mandarin Oriental Hotel, 5 Connaught Rd., Central, Hong Kong Island, tel. 2522–0111. Reservations required. Jacket and tie required. AE, DC, MC, V. No lunch weekends.*

$$$
★

Au Trou Normand. For a quarter of a century this place has offered diners a chance to hide away in a typical French farmhouse—not an easy thing to arrange in the middle of bustling Tsim Sha Tsui. Redchecked tablecloths, a dark wood mantlepiece, and candlelight on shiny copper utensils create the atmosphere. You can be certain you're getting a series of authentic Gallic tastes. The tournedos Rossini is topped with Strasbourg pâté, the rack of lamb comes in a tangy Dijon mustard sauce, and there's an excellent chicken in Madeira sauce. Also among the many selections are long-established favorites such as super smooth mousses, savory terrines, and veal and kidney dishes. *6 Carnarvon Rd., Tsim Sha Tsui, Kowloon, tel. 2366–8754. Reservations advised. Jacket and tie advised. AE, DC, MC, V.*

$$$
★

Papillon. Down a dead-end alley in the heart of Central, this intimate restaurant, reminiscent of a small bistro in the south of France, sets the stage for a romantic meal. Although thoroughly French in presentation, Asian ingredients add an exotic touch to the cuisine. Especially enjoyable are the salmon ravioli and chilled watercress and cucumber soup. If you don't have time to make a reservation in this tiny place, ask to dine at the bar: It offers a perfect vantage point for people-watching. *8 Wo On La., Central, Hong Kong Island, tel. 2526–5965. Dress: casual. AE, DC, MC, V.*

$$–$$$
★

La Brasserie. What might have been a boring basement coffee shop has here been cleverly changed into a charming French bistro, with lots of plants, etched glass, and framed prints of cartoon chefs engaged in various antics. Live music is supplied by an accordionist, and the chef's daily menu is written on a huge mirror that's wheeled to your table. French provincial cooking is the draw here. The fresh crabmeat ravioli or salmon marinated in lime and olive oil are good starters, and the outstanding bouillabaisse features local seafood. Strangely enough, this is one of the better places in town to find California wine. *Omni Marco Polo Hotel, Harbour City, Canton Rd., Tsim Sha Tsui, Kowloon, tel. 2736–0888, ext. 113. Reservations advised. Dress: casual. AE, DC, MC, V.*

Indian
$$–$$$
★
Tandoor Restaurant. This upstairs eatery, one of the classiest venues in town for Indian food, is exotically decorated with mirrors, Indian paintings, colorful cloth hangings, and musical instruments. A glass-fronted kitchen allows you to watch the chef at work. There's a rose for every lady and a cheroot for every gentleman after a dinner that is likely to be superb. There are almost 100 dishes to choose from, but don't miss the tandoor (clay oven) specialties, the roast lamb *sagwalla* (covered with tasty spinach), and the lamb *rogan josh*, swimming in Kashmiri spices. There are no fewer than 14 kinds of Indian bread on the menu, all worth tasting. *19 Wyndham St., Central, Hong Kong Island, tel. 2845–2299. Reservations required. Dress: casual. AE, DC, V.*

$
★
Spice Island Gourmet Club. This is a "club" because the place has no back door and thus was unable to qualify for a restaurant license. This means you have to join (it's free) and get your membership card before you're properly qualified to sample one of the best Indian buffets in the city. The place is small, but there's elbow room. The basic decor is livened by some interesting old Victorian lithographs. There's a different buffet at lunch and dinner, each offering a variety of Indian chicken, lamb, and seafood dishes. The club is in the old district, just west of the business core. *63 Wellington St., Central, Hong Kong Island, tel. 2522–8706. Reservations advised. Dress: casual. MC, V. Closed Sun.*

Italian
$$–$$$
★
Valentino Ristorante Italiano. This romantic hideaway right in the middle of the otherwise-bustling Tsim Sha Tsui district exists behind a marble facade and a doorway flanked by potted cedar trees. The pastel decor includes framed posters of Valentino, and there is plenty of room between tables—a rare commodity in Hong Kong. There's a wide selection of pizzas and pastas; try the fettuccine with scallops. Also tempting are the Macau sole grilled in lemon butter and Italian herbs, any of the tempting veal dishes, and the chef's daily specials. *16 Hanoi Rd., Tsim Sha Tsui, Kowloon, tel. 2721–6449. Reservations advised. Dress: casual. AE, DC, MC, V.*

$
★
Il Mercato. The best place in town for American-style pizza, this tiny 24-seat place (with room for a few more on an outdoor patio) is hidden away in bustling Stanley Market. It's often found by accident by delighted visitors who simply weren't expecting an Italian eatery in that location. The menu is unpredictable, changing every three days, but there's usually an excellent tagliatelle alla Bolognese with ground beef and fresh tomato, and wonderful roast chicken flavored with rosemary. *Stanley Main St., Stanley Village, Hong Kong Island, tel. 2813–9090. Reservations required. Dress: casual. AE, MC, V.*

Japanese
$$$$
★
Sagano Restaurant. Impeccable service, a panoramic view of Hong Kong Harbour, a sushi bar with fresh fish imported exclusively from Japan, and a teppanyaki counter where chefs chop and cook on the spot have made this into what is probably the most popular Japanese restaurant in Hong Kong. The Kansai cuisine, from the region around Kyoto, is characterized by light sauces and the use of fresh ingredients. Seasonal dishes should always be considered. Save some room for the special house dessert, plum sherbet, and sample the liqueured ginger cocktail. *Hotel Nikko, 72 Mody Rd., Tsim Sha Tsui, Kowloon, tel. 2739–1111. Reservations required. Dress: casual. AE, DC, MC, V.*

Korean
$
★
Three-Five Korean Restaurant. A genuine treasure, this tiny but impressive eatery is tucked away on a minor Tsim Sha Tsui street. Inside it's sparsely decorated, spotlessly clean, and a trifle cramped; but the food makes up for any of the other shortcomings. The best

dishes are the Korean barbecues of beef, ribs, chicken, or fish, which you cook yourself at the table. These are accompanied by many small dishes of Korean specialties, such as bean curd, marinated vegetables, dried anchovies, bean sprouts, and the traditional *kimchi* (cabbage preserved in brine, with black beans, red peppers, and more than enough garlic to make it a good idea for everybody in the party to sample some). *6 Ashley Rd., Tsim Sha Tsui, Kowloon, tel. 2376–2993. Reservations difficult to make (they don't always have someone who speaks English) but advised anyway. Dress: casual. No credit cards.*

Pan-Asian
$$$
Cafe Deco. If you're in Hong Kong on a clear day, take the Peak tram up to the top to dine at this spiffy, double-decker restaurant overlooking the city. It's worth the trek. The decor is art deco to the hilt. You can choose from a menu of Chinese, Indian (there's a tandoor in the kitchen), and Italian dishes, or eat at the oyster bar or in the ice cream parlor. *The Peak Galleria, 1st level, 118 Peak Rd., Victoria Peak, Hong Kong Island, tel. 2849–5111. Reservations advised. Dress: smart casual. AE, DC, MC, V.*

Thai
$$$
Wyndham Street Thai. Nothing will have prepared you for this Thai experience, so throw out all past memories. You are greeted at the front door by a beautifully spotlit golden Buddha. A screamingly pink curved wall to the left leads you inside to walls of softer green and blue. The rest of the decor is austere in comparison: black leather chairs and stark white tablecloths. The menu consists of strikingly new interpretations of traditional Thai dishes. Try the crispy fish with pork cubes in lime juice or the crab, bean sprouts, coriander, sweet basil, lemongrass, peanuts, and fish sauce wrapped in betel nut leaves. Another favorite is the stir-fried asparagus with chili jam, snow peas, and shiitake mushrooms. Ask your waiter for help with the wine list, which is decidedly exotic and includes many Australian vintages. *38 Wyndham St., Central, Hong Kong Island, tel. 2869–6216. Dress: smart casual. AE, DC, MC, V.*

Vietnamese
$$$
Indochine. Recently opened in this midst of Hong Kong's trendiest area, this restaurant offers a contemporary version of Vietnamese cuisine—a kind of cross between the cooking styles of Saigon and Southern California. The deep-fried soft-shelled crabs are to die for. The airy eatery is filled with potted palms and has huge French windows looking out onto the street. *California Tower, Lan Kwai Fong, Central, Hong Kong Island, tel. 2869–7399. Reservations advised. AE, DC, MC, V.*

$$
Vietnam City. This is one of the most attractive and popular of the Vietnamese restaurants that have appeared in Hong Kong in recent years. Located in one of the frenzied office blocks of east Tsim Sha Tsui, it is spacious and cheerful, with plenty of rattan and bamboo, a friendly staff, and a large menu that includes garlic bread and spring rolls as well as coconut seafood stew, crab in beer, prawns on sugarcane, beef seven ways, and other favorites. *Energy Plaza, 92 Granville Rd., Tsim Sha Tsui, Kowloon, tel. 2366–7880. Reservations advised. Dress: casual. AE, MC, V.*

Lodging

Until the early 1960s, Hong Kong didn't have a single international hotel. Today the territory accommodates some 6 million visitors each year in more than 90 hotels, with a combined total of more than 35,500 rooms. And these figures only include hotels and lodging facilities that belong to the Hong Kong Tourist Association (HKTA). The HKTA publishes the *Hotel Guide*, a listing of their hotel members and daily rates, services, and facilities. The brochure is published twice a year, so it is usually one price hike behind the current situation. The HKTA does not arrange hotel reservations. The Hong Kong Hotel Association (HKHA) does, at no extra charge, but only through its reservations office at Kai Tak International Airport, which is immediately beyond the Customs area.

As might be expected of one of the world's most important financial centers, Hong Kong is a business executive's paradise. Most of the major hotels have business centers, which provide secretarial, translation, courier, telex, fax, and printing services—even personal computers. For an overview of Hong Kong meeting, convention, and incentive facilities, contact the **Convention and Incentive Department** (Hong Kong Tourist Association, 35th Floor, Jardine House, Central, Hong Kong Island, tel. 2801–7177).

Book your rooms in advance for a trip to Hong Kong. Even with the rash of new hotels, rooms can prove scarce, especially during the high season of September through early December.

Choosing where to stay in Hong Kong depends on the purpose of your visit. Thanks to the two tunnels that run underneath the harbor, the Star Ferry, and the Mass Transit Railway (MTR) subway, it no longer matters whether you stay "Hong Kong–side" or "Kowloon-side": The other side will be only minutes away by MTR.

The 800 numbers listed are for use in the United States.

Highly recommended lodgings are indicated by a star ★.

Category	Cost*
$$$$	over HK$1,500 (US$192)
$$$	HK$1,000–$1,500 (US$128–US$192)
$$	HK$700–$1,000 (US$90–US$128)
$	under HK$700 (US$90)

All prices are for a double room, not including 10% service charge and 5% tax.

Hong Kong Island

If you need to be near the city's financial hub, you'll prefer the Central district on Hong Kong Island. Central is as busy as New York City on weekdays, but it is quiet at night and on weekends. Wanchai, east of Central, was once a sailor's dream of "Suzie Wongs" and booze. Although it is still one of the city's more entertaining nightlife areas, land reclamation has given it an array of new harborfronting skyscrapers. Causeway Bay, farther east, is an ideal area for shopping or trying lots of different restaurants. Happy Valley is near the racetrack and the colony's largest sports stadium.

$$$$ **Grand Hyatt.** No expense was spared in building this opulent hotel, which adjoins the Hong Kong Convention Centre. On the Wanchai waterfront, the facility has fabulous views. The hotel's restaurants are notable, including Grissini, with its superb northern Italian food; One Harbour Road, possibly the most elegant Cantonese garden-style restaurant in town; and Kaetsu, for Japanese Edo cuisine. The restaurants are very popular with locals, who also line up to get into JJ's, the nightclub and disco. Art deco touches give panache to the marble-clad, greenery-filled lobby and the ballroom, which is

reminiscent of Old World Europe. Seventy percent of the guest rooms have harbor views, while the remaining rooms overlook the pool and garden. The Hyatt and the New World Harbour View share a vast recreation deck on the 11th floor with pools, gardens, a golf driving range, tennis courts, and health club facilities. *1 Harbour Rd., Wanchai, tel. 2588–1234 or 800/233–1234, fax 2802–0677. 572 rooms. Facilities: 4 restaurants, lounges, disco/nightclub, ballroom, health club, pool, golf driving range, 2 tennis courts, beauty salon, florist. AE, DC, MC, V.*

$$$$ ★ **Hilton.** The extensive business facilities, six executive floors, and Central district location make this elegant hotel an attractive choice for business travelers. The hotel also boasts tennis courts, a swimming pool, and its own 110-foot brigantine, which makes regular lunch, cocktail, and dinner cruises and is available for weekend island picnics or private hire. Modern guest rooms are decorated in pastels and have well-stocked minibars and large marble baths. A massive renovation in 1992 created a spiffy, marble-laden lobby. Sketti's, the hotel's most casual restaurant, has a California-style menu that includes such offbeat dishes as chicken curry pizza, crabmeat popcorn, and truffled mashed potatoes with teppanyaki vegetables and roast veal. *2 Queen's Rd., Central, tel. 2523–3111 or 800/445–8667, fax 2845–2590. 750 rooms. Facilities: 9 restaurants, health club with heated outdoor pool, business center, 2 no-smoking floors, beauty salon, barbershop, gift shop, shopping arcade, florist. AE, DC, MC, V.*

$$$$ ★ **Mandarin Oriental.** Much touted by travel writers from all over the globe as one of the world's great hotels, the Mandarin Oriental is representative of the high end of Hong Kong accommodations. For more than 30 years, it has catered to the well-to-do and business travelers with hefty expense accounts. The vast lobby, decorated with Asian antiques, has a live jazz ensemble (with singer) afternoons and evenings. The comfortable guest rooms are decorated with antique maps and prints, and a complimentary plate of fresh fruit welcomes you upon your arrival. Mah Wah, on the 25th floor, serves Cantonese cuisine in a genteel atmosphere; the Pierrot serves fine French food. Centrally located beside the Star Ferry concourse, the Mandarin is definitely a place to spot visiting celebrities and VIPs. *5 Connaught Rd., Central, tel. 2522–0111 or 800/526–6566, fax 2810–6190. 489 rooms, 58 suites. Facilities: 4 restaurants, 3 bars, health club with heated indoor pool, business center, beauty salon, barbershop, gift shop, shopping arcade, florist. AE, DC, MC, V.*

$$$$ **Regal Hongkong Hotel.** Opened in 1993, this 33-story hotel has a slightly overdone decor with European overtones, including masses of marble and a dramatic lobby with high windows, Louis XIV furniture, and a huge mural depicting a scene from the Mediterranean. Gilded elevators lead to nicely appointed guest rooms with maple-inlay furniture crafted by local artisans, walls and carpets in muted earth tones, and brightly colored bedspreads. Bathrooms are spacious, with triangular tubs. The hotel is near the Happy Valley Race Course and Hongkong Stadium and overlooks Victoria Park. *88 Yee Wo St., Causeway Bay, tel. 2890–6633, or 800/222–8888, fax 2881–0777. 425 rooms. Facilities: 4 restaurants, bar, health club, business center, disco/karaoke club, shopping arcade, swimming pool, function rooms, 3 no-smoking and 4 executive floors. AE, DC, MC, V.*

$$$$ **Ritz-Carlton.** Opened in 1993, the Ritz occupies the prime block between Chater Road and Connaught Road in Central, right next to the Furama Kempinski. If you can't find the edifice, just look for a near imitation of the Empire State Building; it's similar in shape.

The interior of the property has an elegant, refined atmosphere created by European antiques and reproductions mixed with a few Oriental accents. Everything from the Chippendale-style furniture to the gilt-frame mirrors is spotless and shining. The large guest rooms, all with marble bath, honor bar, and Colonial-style rosewood furniture, overlook either Victoria Harbour or Chater Garden. The main restaurant, Tuscano, serves northern Italian cuisine. There are also Chinese and Japanese restaurants; Cossacks, a vodka bar; and a lounge serving breakfast, lunch, and high tea. *Connaught Rd., Central, tel. 2877–6666 or 800/241–3333, fax 2877–6778. 189 rooms, 27 suites. Facilities: 4 restaurants, bar, pool, fitness center, ballroom, executive floor, 3 no-smoking floors, gift shop, florist. AE, DC, MC. V.*

$$$ **The Excelsior.** In Causeway Bay, overlooking the Royal Hong Kong
★ Yacht Club marina, the Excelsior offers not only great views, but a good selection of restaurants and entertainment. You can spend evenings dining in the Excelsior Grill (Continental) or Cammino (Italian), then listening to live jazz in the basement bar or dancing at the rooftop disco. Rooms are decorated in shades of terra-cotta and purple or purple, and many (80%) have harbor views. Extras for the fitness-minded include the rooftop tennis courts and the jogging track in adjacent Victoria Park. Business travelers are provided with many service amenities, and the World Trade Centre can be reached by a quick stroll through an air-conditioned walkway. *281 Gloucester Rd., Causeway Bay, tel. 2894–8888, fax 2895–6459. 875 rooms, 22 suites. Facilities: 4 restaurants, business center, no-smoking floors, beauty salon, barbershop, gift shop, shopping arcade, florist. AE, DC, MC, V.*

$$$ **Furama Kempinski.** A contemporary, elegant hotel in the heart of the Central district, the Furama is the Asian flagship of Germany's Kempinski management group. Guest rooms have beautiful views of either Chater Garden and the Peak or City Hall and Victoria Harbour. Ask for a room above the 17th floor. The rooftop revolving restaurant and bar offers the ultimate panorama, as well as a spectacular dinner buffet of Chinese, Japanese, and Western dishes. On the ground floor, a bakery sells delicious snacks to famished shoppers. *1 Connaught Rd., Central, tel. 2525–5111 or 800/426–3135, fax 2845–9339. 474 rooms, 43 suites. Facilities: 5 restaurants, health club, business center, 2 no-smoking floors, beauty salon, barbershop, gift shop, shopping arcade, florist. AE, DC, MC, V.*

$$$ **Luk Kwok.** This contemporary hotel-and-office tower desiged by Hong Kong's leading architect Remo Riva has replaced the Wanchai landmark of the same name immortalized in Richard Mason's novel *The World of Suzie Wong.* This place garners its appeal from its proximity to the Convention Centre, the Academy for Performing Arts, and the Arts Centre. Room decor is clean and simple, with contemporary furniture; rooms on the higher floors afford mountain or city views. The hotel's facade and lobby were renovated in 1993 and are fresh and sleek. *72 Gloucester Rd., Wanchai, tel. 2866–2166, fax 2866–2622. 198 rooms. Facilities: 2 restaurants, business center, 2 no-smoking floors. AE, DC, MC, V.*

$$$ **New World Harbour View.** Sharing the Convention Centre complex with the Grand Hyatt is this more modest, but just as attractive, hotel. Guest rooms are moderately sized and have a modern decor. Amenities include excellent Chinese and Western restaurants, a cozy bar, and the pools, gardens, driving range, tennis courts, and health-club facilities found on the recreation deck between the two hotels. The free-form pool here is Hong Kong's largest, complete with lagoons and an alfresco dining area. *1 Harbour Rd., Wanchai, tel. 2802–8888 or 800/227–5663, fax 2802–8833. 862 rooms. Facili-*

ties: *3 restaurants, 2 bars, pool, recreation center, business center, beauty salon, barbershop, florist, shopping arcade, some no-smoking rooms. AE, DC, MC, V.*

$$$ Park Lane. This elegant hotel, opposite Victoria Park and in the midst of the small shops and department stores of Causeway Bay, is in the center of Hong Kong Island's busiest shopping, entertainment, and business area. All the rooms have luxurious marble bathrooms, elegant yet comfortable furniture reminiscent of an English mansion, and marvelous views of the harbor and/or Victoria Park. Color schemes range from beige to salmon. The rooftop restaurant serves Continental cuisine, while the Cafe is known for its mixture of Asian and Western specialties (you can order a hamburger if you're homesick, but we suggest the roast beef). Two lounges—the Gallery Bar, where guests are serenaded by a six-piece jazz band every evening, and George & Co.—offer a variety of beer, wine, cocktails, and snacks. *310 Gloucester Rd., Causeway Bay, tel. 2890–3355, fax 2576–7853. 790 rooms, 25 suites. Facilities: 3 restaurants, 2 lounges, health club, business center, beauty salon, shopping arcade, florist, no-smoking floors. AE, DC, MC, V.*

$$ Century. This 23-story Wanchai hotel, opened in 1992, is ideal for conventioneers—and anyone else—looking for a moderately priced place to stay. It's a five-minute walk by covered overpass (a lifesaver in the steamy summer months) from the convention center and the MTR. Rooms are modern, with wooden furniture painted in pastels. One restaurant and the bar are designed to take advantage of the building's corner location, with picture windows on two sides looking out at the Star Ferry and the convention center. *238 Jaffe Rd., Wanchai, tel. 2598–8888, fax 2598–8866. 486 rooms, 25 suites. Facilities: 4 restaurants, bar, gift shop, pool, health club, business center. AE, DC, MC, V.*

$$ Wharney. Within walking distance of the Convention Centre, this no-frills hotel is designed to appeal to the budget-conscious business traveler. It's not impressive, but it does have two restaurants, a health club, and a pub that's popular with locals. *57–73 Lockhart Rd., Wanchai, tel. 2861–1000, fax 2865–6023. 335 rooms. Facilities: 2 restaurants, pub, indoor heated pool, health club, business center. AE, DC, MC, V.*

$ Harbour View International House. On the Wanchai waterfront, this
★ YMCA property offers clean, inexpensive accommodations. The best rooms face the harbor. The hotel provides free shuttle service to Causeway Bay and the Star Ferry. *4 Harbour Rd., Wanchai, tel. 2802–0111, fax 2802–9063. 320 rooms. Facilities: restaurant. AE, DC, MC, V.*

$ The Wesley. Opened in 1992 on the site of the old Soldiers and Sailors Home, this 21-story, moderately priced hotel is a short walk from the Convention Centre, the Academy for Performing Arts, and the MTR. It has a tram stop outside the door, and Pacific Place is close by, as are the bars of Wanchai. *22 Hennessy Rd., Wanchai, tel. 2866–6688, fax 2866–6633. 251 rooms. Facilities: Chinese restaurant, Western coffee shop, 251 rooms accessible to wheelchair users. AE, DC, MC, V.*

Kowloon

Most of the hotels in Hong Kong are on the Kowloon peninsula, which includes "Old" Tsim Sha Tsui, Tsim Sha Tsui East, Harbour City, and the districts north of Tsim Sha Tsui to the border of the New Territories. The fabled shopping "Golden Mile" of Nathan Road runs through Old Tsim Sha Tsui. Backstreets are filled with restaurants, stores, and hotels.

Tsim Sha Tsui East is a grid of modern office buildings (many with restaurants or nightclubs) and luxury hotels. This area has been created on land reclaimed from the harbor in the last decade, so none of these hotels is very old.

There are three luxury hotels (all members of the Omni hotel chain) in Harbour City, on the western side of the Tsim Sha Tsui promontory. This area next to the Star Ferry is one of Asia's largest air-conditioned shopping and commercial complexes.

Northern Kowloon contains more of the moderately priced, smaller, older hotels. Most are on or very near to Nathan Road and are probably the best bets for economy-minded visitors. Excellent bus service and the MTR make it possible to reach the center of Old Tsim Sha Tsui quickly.

$$$$ **Kowloon Shangri-La.** Billed as one of the top 10 hotels in the world,
★ this waterfront hotel, now managed by Shangri-La International, caters to the international business traveler. Twenty-one stories above the lobby is the executive floor, with 24-hour business and concierge services, personalized stationery, and complimentary breakfast and cocktails. The modern, pastel rooms are large by Hong Kong standards, and a variety of in-house restaurants, lounges, a bar, and a nightclub offer a range of live entertainment, including string quartets and harp and piano music. Views are of Victoria Harbour or the city. *64 Mody Rd., Tsim Sha Tsui East, tel. 2721–2111 or 800/942–5050, fax 2723–8686. 689 rooms, 29 suites. Facilities: 5 restaurants, health club with indoor pool, business center, no-smoking floor, barbershop, gift shop. AE, DC, MC, V.*

$$$$ **Peninsula.** The "Pen," the grand old lady of Hong Kong hotels, was
★ built in 1928, when travelers from London took many weeks (and many trunks) to reach Hong Kong by boat and then by train. This is the ultimate in colonial class. The Pen's good taste and Old World style is in evidence everywhere: the columned and gilt-corniced lobby, the fleet of Rolls-Royces, the spacious bedrooms, the attentive room valets, and the designer French soaps. Gaddi's, the hotel's French restaurant, is one of Hong Kong's most distinguished gourmet institutions. The new 30-story tower, completed in 1994, includes 132 spacious new guest rooms and suites, a business center, banquet and meeting facilities, a sundeck, a health club, a Romanesque-swimming pool, and a rooftop restaurant, Felix, designed by superstar French architect Phillipe Starck. *Salisbury Rd., Tsim Sha Tsui, tel. 2366–6251, fax 2722–4170. 246 rooms, 54 suites. Facilities: 6 restaurants, business services, beauty salon, barbershop, gift shop, health club, swimming pool, shopping arcade, florist. AE, DC, MC, V.*

$$$$ **The Regent.** This elegantly modern hotel on the most southern tip of
★ Tsim Sha Tsui offers luxurious guest rooms and spectacular harbor views. The view can also be enjoyed from the restaurants or the cocktail lounge, where windows rise 40 feet above the polished granite floor. The Lai Ching Heen restaurant has some of the best Cantonese dishes in Hong Kong; Plume, serving French and Italian fare, is ultra-exclusive. Yü is the hotel's newest restaurant and has an aquatic decor to match its seafood menu. A wide range of features, such as a health spa with masseur, fine Oriental art displays, an oversize outdoor pool, and a computer system that stores information about guests' preferences, will appeal to those who want the best and are prepared to pay for it. *18 Salisbury Rd., Tsim Sha Tsui, tel. 2721–1211 or 800/545–4000, fax 2739–4546. 508 rooms, 94 suites. Facilities: 5 restaurants, health club with heated outdoor*

pool, business center, beauty salon, barbershop, shopping arcade, florist. AE, DC, MC, V.

$$$ **Holiday Inn Crowne Plaza Harbour View.** At the eastern end of Tsim Sha Tsui East, this luxury hotel has an unobstructed harbor view from more than half its rooms. The hotel is well known locally for its restaurants, particularly the Mistral, which serves Italian cuisine. Taxis or limousines provide more convenient transportation than the MTR or Star Ferry, which are on the other side of the peninsula. The large rooms, done in warm earth tones, have finely crafted wood furniture. *70 Mody Rd., Tsim Sha Tsui East, tel. 2721–5161 or 800/ 465–4329, fax 2369–5672. 574 rooms, 18 suites. Facilities: 4 restaurants, health club with heated outdoor rooftop pool, business center, beauty salon, shopping arcade, florist. AE, DC, MC, V.*

$$$ **Hyatt Regency.** Major renovations in 1995 will give the Hyatt a face-
★ lift, transforming the dramatic marble and teak lobby and plush, earth-toned guest rooms. The hotel has a gallery of Oriental antiques and the award-winning Chinese Restaurant. Gourmets will also want to sample the classic Continental fare at Hugo's. The hotel is five minutes away from the Star Ferry, beside an MTR station. *67 Nathan Rd., Tsim Sha Tsui, tel. 2311–1234 or 800/233–1234, fax 2739–8701. 706 rooms, 17 suites. Facilities: 4 restaurants, business center, no-smoking rooms, beauty salon, barbershop, gift shop, shopping arcade, florist. AE, DC, MC, V.*

$$$ **Miramar.** In the middle of the Golden Mile, across the street from Kowloon Park, the Miramar has a vast lobby with a dramatic stained-glass ceiling, several opulent banquet rooms, plus a convention center. Guest rooms are exceptionally large and are done in muted tones and light wood. *130 Nathan Rd., Tsim Sha Tsui, tel. 2368–1111, fax 2369–1788. 550 rooms. Facilities: 4 restaurants, health club with heated indoor pool, business center, beauty salon, barbershop, gift shop, shopping arcade, florist. AE, DC, MC, V.*

$$$ **Omni Hongkong.** All three of the Omni hotels on the western side of
★ Tsim Sha Tsui (the Omni Marco Polo and Omni Prince are the other two) are part of the enormous Harbour City hotel, entertainment, and shopping complex. The Hongkong is especially popular with business travelers due to its excellent reputation for efficiency. It is also noted for its first-class Taipan Grill and the Gripps bar, with close-up, sixth-floor views of the harbor, drinks and meals, and live entertainment at night. Rooms here are pleasant but plain, which is only a problem if you aren't assigned one with an ocean view. The Star Ferry and bus terminals are next door, and Old Tsim Sha Tsui is just a short walk away. *Harbour City, Tsim Sha Tsui, tel. 2736– 0088 or 800/843–6664, fax 2736–0011. 665 rooms, 84 suites. Facilities: 7 restaurants, heated outdoor pool, business center, no-smoking floor, beauty salon, barbershop, shopping arcade, florist. AE, DC, MC, V.*

$$$ **Regal Airport.** A three-minute stroll through an air-conditioned walkway takes you from this hotel to the customs area of the airport. It's the perfect place to stay if you're moving on quickly or have airport-related business. The best rooms face the airport, as does the romantic top-floor restaurant. All rooms are fully soundproofed. There is a half-price day-use discount for transit passengers. *30 Sa Po Rd., tel. 2718–0333 or 800/222–8888, fax 2718–4111. 400 rooms, 20 suites. Facilities: 3 restaurants, pool, business center, no-smoking floors, beauty salon, barbershop, shopping arcade. AE, DC, MC, V.*

$$ **Grand Tower.** This hotel gives tourists a sense of the real Hong Kong. Bird Street (where many Chinese walk and talk, together with their caged birds) and the Women's Market are a short walk away, as is the Mongkok MTR. Rooms are clean and functional. *627–*

641 Nathan Rd., Mongkok, tel. 2789–0011, fax 2789–0945. 536 rooms, 13 suites. Facilities: 4 restaurants, business center, beauty salon, barbershop, gift shop, shopping arcade, florist. AE, DC, MC, V.

$$
★ **Kowloon.** A shimmering mirrored exterior and a chrome, glass, and marble lobby reflect the Kowloon's high efficiency and hi-tech amenities. Rooms are incredibly compact, similar to what you would find in a Japanese business hotel. Computerized TVs offer information on shopping, events, flights, and your bill. The location, on the southern tip of Nathan Road's Golden Mile, puts you just minutes away from the Star Ferry and even closer to the MTR. You have a choice of restaurants and can use the facilities of the Peninsula hotel across the street. *19–21 Nathan Rd., Tsim Sha Tsui, tel. 2369–8698, fax 2739–9811. 704 rooms, 34 suites. Facilities: 3 restaurants, business center, no-smoking rooms, beauty salon, barbershop, gift shop, shopping arcade, florist. AE, DC, MC, V.*

$$ **Majestic.** This hotel opened in 1992 on the site of the old Majestic Cinema on upper Nathan Road. It's managed by the Furama, so standards are higher than the price range suggests. The sparsely furnished rooms have contemporary furniture, and all suites are equipped with fax machines. There is an elegant bar-nightclub and a superior Western restaurant. In the same complex are two cinemas, shops, and several Chinese restaurants. *348 Nathan Rd., tel. 2781–1333, fax 2781–1773. 387 rooms. Facilities: restaurant, bar, business center, shops, cinemas, no-smoking floor. AE, DC, MC, V.*

$$ **Prudential.** Rising from a busy corner in upper Nathan Road, with an MTR station underneath, this is a hotel is a great find for travelers on a modest budget. Rooms are spacious and offer interesting city views. It shares a building with a lively shopping mall, and has its own pool, sauna, and gym. *222 Nathan Rd., tel. 2311–8222, fax 2367–6537. 434 rooms. Facilities: coffee shop, lounge, pool, gymnasium, sauna, shops, business center. AE, DC, MC, V.*

$$ **Ramada Hotel Kowloon.** This modern hotel is relatively small and tries to appeal to travelers with a home-away-from-home ambience. A fireplace in the lobby and comfortably furnished rooms with natural woods throughout create a cozy atmosphere. *73–75 Chatham Rd., South Tsim Sha Tsui, tel. 2311–1100 or 800/854–7854, fax 2311–6000. 205 rooms, 1 suite. Facilities: 2 restaurants, business center, gift shop, florist. AE, DC, MC, V.*

$ **Bangkok Royal.** Just off Nathan Road and steps away from the Jordan MTR, this hotel offers rooms that are sparse and somewhat scruffy. There are no bars, lounges, or live entertainment, but there is a good Thai restaurant off the lobby, and you are within walking distance of the restaurants and entertainment of Nathan Road. *2 Pilkem St., Yau Ma Tei, tel. 2735–9181, fax 2730–2209. 70 rooms. Facilities: 2 restaurants. AE, DC, MC, V.*

$ **Booth Lodge.** This pleasant contemporary retreat, built in 1985 near the Jade Market, is operated by the Salvation Army. But don't be turned off—the facilities are not of the donated kind. In fact, everything is clean, bright, and new, from the crisply painted walls to the starched sheets on the double beds. The lobby is a study in minimalism and has an officelike atmosphere. *11 Wing Sing La., Yau Ma Tei, tel. 2771–9266, fax 2385–1140. 53 rooms. Facilities: restaurant. AE, MC, V.*

$ **Concourse.** One of the Hong Kong's nicer budget hotels, the Concourse was opened in 1991 by the China Travel Service in Mongkok, reasonably close to public transportation and active nightlife. There is a Chinese as well as a Korean restaurant on the premises. Cheers is the name of their karaoke lounge. *20 Lai Chi Kok Rd., tel. 2397–*

6683, fax 2381–3768. 435 rooms, 5 suites. Facilities: 2 restaurants, coffee shop, karaoke lounge. AE, DC, MC, V.

$ **The Salisbury YMCA.** The most popular of Hong Kong's Ys, the Salisbury occupies a huge, sterile-looking block. Although the rooms are decorated circa 1960, the location is convenient to the Star Ferry and a few minutes walk from the MTR. The Airbus stops opposite. *41 Salisbury Rd., Tsim Sha Tsui, tel. 2369–2211, fax 2739–9315. 380 rooms. Facilities: 3 restaurants, 2 pools, fitness center, squash courts. AE, DC, MC, V.*

The New Territories and the Outer Islands

Tsuen Wan's 1,026-room Kowloon Panda has helped alleviate the shortage of first-class accommodations in the fast-developing New Territories and has been welcomed by visitors involved in manufacturing here. Accommodations are still limited on the outlying islands, although some of them (such as Cheung Chau) have a booming business in rooms to rent, with agents displaying photographs of available rentals on placards that line the waterfront opposite the ferry pier.

$$ **Kowloon Panda.** This massive hotel is the first of its size in the western New Territories. Located close to the MTR in bustling Tsuen Wan, it offers a pool, a health club, business and meeting facilities, and a variety of restaurants. The decor is reminiscent of hotels in Tokyo's Ginza district, with lots of open-plan lounges and very contemporary rooms, some with harbor views. There is a department store on the premises. *3 Tsuen Wah St., Tsuen Wan, tel. 2409–1111, fax 2409–1818. 1,026 rooms. Facilities: 4 restaurants, 3 lounges, pool, health club, business center, 2 executive floors, 1 no-smoking floor, airport transfers, florist. AE, DC, MC, V.*

$$ **Regal Riverside.** In one of the territory's new towns, this large, modern hotel overlooks the Shing Mun River in the foothills of Shatin. Rooms, which have harbor and garden views, are done in pastel colors and have contemporary furniture. The Riverside has Hong Kong's largest hotel disco and a health club that's home to Hong Kong's only float capsule, purported to soothe away the day's pressures. Be prepared to spend at least 20 minutes getting to the Kowloon shopping district. *Tai Chung Kiu Rd., Shatin, tel. 2649–7878 or 800/222–8888, fax 2637–4748. 786 rooms, 44 suites. Facilities: 3 restaurants, pool, business center, no-smoking floor, beauty salon, barbershop, shopping arcade. AE, DC, MC, V.*

$$ **Royal Park.** This hotel adjoins Shatin's Town Plaza, which contains shops, restaurants, cinemas, and the train station. The rooms are basic, but clean and pleasant. *8 Pak Hok Ting St., Shatin, tel. 2601–2111, fax 2601–3666. 448 rooms. Facilities: 3 restaurants, pool, health center, business center. AE, DC, MC, V.*

$ **Cheung Chau Warwick.** This eight-story hotel overlooks Tung Wan Beach. The tennis court, beach, and swimming pool, and the fact that there are no cars on this island, which is only an hour by ferry from Hong Kong Island, has made this a popular getaway for Hong Kong families. *East Bay, Cheung Chau, tel. 2981–0081, fax 2981–9174. 70 rooms. Facilities: 2 restaurants, swimming pool, tennis court. AE, DC, MC, V.*

The Arts and Nightlife

The best daily calendar of cultural events is the daily arts and culture page of the *South China Morning Post* newspaper. You can read previews in the *Sunday Post*. The *Hong Kong Standard* also lists events. Weekly listings are in the *TV and Entertainment Times*, which comes out on Thursday, as well as in the biweekly *HK Magazine*, a free newspaper available in many restaurants, stores, and bars.

City Hall (by Star Ferry, Hong Kong Island) has posters and huge bulletin boards listing events and ticket availability, and booths where tickets can be purchased, although finding the right booth can be a bit confusing. **URBTIX** outlets are the easiest place to purchase tickets for most main performances. There are branches at City Hall and the Hong Kong Arts Centre (tel. 2734–9009 for information).

The Arts

Performance Halls
Hong Kong Island

City Hall (Edinburgh Pl., by Star Ferry, Central, tel. 2522–9928). This complex has a large auditorium, a recital hall, and a theater. Classical music, plays, and films are presented here.
Hong Kong Academy for Performing Arts (1 Gloucester Rd., Wanchai, tel. 2584–1500). This arts school has two major theaters each seating 1,600 people, plus a 200-seat studio theater and outdoor theater. Performances include local and international theater, and modern and classical dance.
Hong Kong Arts Centre (2 Harbour Rd., Wanchai, tel. 2582–0200). Here you will find 15 floors of auditoriums, rehearsal halls, and recital rooms. Local and visiting groups perform here.
Hong Kong Fringe Club (2 Lower Albert Rd., Central, tel. 2591–1347). This locally run club hosts some of Hong Kong's most interesting visiting and local entertainment and art exhibitions.
Queen Elizabeth Stadium (18 Oi Kwan Rd., Wanchai, tel. 2575–6793). Although this is basically a sports stadium with a seating capacity of 3,500, it frequently presents ballet, orchestra concerts, and pop concerts.

Kowloon

Hong Kong Coliseum. (Hunghom Railway Station, Hunghom, tel. 2765–9233). This stadium has the capacity to seat more than 12,000 and presents everything from basketball to ballet, and from skating polar bears to international pop stars.
Hong Kong Cultural Centre (Salisbury Rd., tel. 2734–2009). This venue for shows and conferences contains the Grand Theatre, which seats 1,750, and a concert hall, which accommodates 2,100. The center is used by visiting and local artists, ranging from opera to ballet to orchestral music..

The New Territories

Shatin Town Hall (New Town Plaza, Shatin, tel. 2694–2536). This impressive building, attached to an enormous shopping arcade, hosts cultural events, including dance, drama, and concerts.
Tsuen Wan Town Hall (Tsuen Wan, tel. 2414–0144; take the MTR to Tsuen Wan Station). Although it's off the beaten track, this auditorium has a constant stream of performers. Groups include everything from the Warsaw Philharmonic to troupes of Chinese acrobats.

Festivals and Seasonal Events

Hong Kong Arts Festival (Jan.–Feb.). This includes four weeks of music and drama from around the world. Information abroad can be obtained through HKTA offices.

Hong Kong Fringe Festival (Jan.–Feb.). Running simultaneously with the Arts Festival, this festival starts off with Sunday street theater in Central and continues with shows at the Fringe Club, near Star Ferry pier, and just about everywhere.

Hong Kong International Film Festival (Apr.). This includes two weeks of films from virtually every country in the world. Call URBTIX at 734–9009 for information.

Chinese Opera Fortnight (Sept.). This is two weeks of Cantonese, Peking, Soochow, Chekiang, and Chiu Chow opera presented in City Hall Theatre, Concert Hall, and Ko Shan Theatre.

Festival of Asian Arts (Oct.–Nov.). Perhaps Asia's major cultural festival, this draws over 150 artistic events (dance, music, and theater) from as far afield as Hawaii, Bhutan, and Australia. It occurs biennially, in even-numbered years, and will next occur in 1996.

Performing-Arts Ensembles

Hong Kong Philharmonic Orchestra. More than 100 artists from Hong Kong, the United States, and Europe perform everything from classical to avant-garde to contemporary music by Chinese composers. Performances are usually on Friday and Saturday at 8 PM in City Hall or recital halls in the New Territories (tel. 2721–2030 for ticket information).

Hong Kong Chinese Orchestra. Created in 1977 by the Urban Council, this group performs only Chinese works. Weekly concerts are given throughout Hong Kong (tel. 2853–2622 for further information).

Chinese Opera

Cantonese Opera. There are 10 Cantonese opera troupes in Hong Kong, as well as many amateur singing groups. These groups perform "street opera," as in the Shanghai Street Night Market on Sunday, while others perform at temple fairs, in City Hall, or in playgrounds under the auspices of the Urban Council. In this highly complex and extremely sophisticated art form, every gesture has its own meaning. In fact, there are 50 different gestures for the hand alone. It is best to have a local friend translate the gestures, since the stories are so complex that they make Wagner or Verdi librettos seem almost simplistic.

Peking Opera. Another highly stylized musical performance, this venue of opera employs higher-pitched voices than Cantonese opera. This is an older opera form and more respected for its classical traditions. Several troupes visit Hong Kong from the People's Republic of China each year. They perform in City Hall or at special temple ceremonies.

Dance

Hong Kong Dance Company (tel. 2853–2638). The Urban Council created the Hong Kong Dance Company in 1981 to promote the art of Chinese dance and to present newly choreographed works on Chinese historical themes.

Hong Kong Ballet (tel. 2573–7398). This is Hong Kong's first professional ballet company and vocational ballet school. It is Western-oriented, both classical and contemporary, with the dancers performing at schools, auditoriums, and various festivals.

City Contemporary Dance Company (tel. 2326–8597). This group is dedicated to contemporary dance inspired by Hong Kong and has very innovative programs. Performances are usually held at the Hong Kong Arts Centre (*see above*).

Drama

The Fringe Club (tel. 2521–7251). An enormous amount of alternative theater, ranging from one-person shows to full dramatic performances, is presented by this low-key club.

Zuni Icosahedron (tel. 2893–8419). The most well-known avant-garde group in the territory puts on new drama and dance in Cantonese and English at various locations.

Nightlife

Cabaret and Nightclubs The ballroom of the **Hilton** (2 Queen's Rd., Central, tel. 2523–3111) is the major dinner-theater destination, often featuring short seasons of British theater companies staging three-act comedies for nostalgic British expatriates.

The biggest and best old-fashioned nightclub-restaurants are Chinese. The cuisine is Cantonese, and so are most of the singers. Big-name local balladeers and "Cantopop" stars make guest appearances. Though modest by Las Vegas standards, the shows can be entertaining, as are those at the massive **Ocean City Restaurant & Night Club** (New World Centre, Tsim Sha Tsui, tel. 2369–9688).

Post 97 (8–11 Lan Kwai Fong St., Central, tel. 2810–9333) is a small, smoky, usually crowded nightclub. It is open from 11 PM to 3 AM or later, as long as there are customers. The club charges HK$50 admission on Friday and Saturday.

Cocktail and Piano Bars Harbor-gazing is the main attraction at the Island Shangri-La's **Cyrano** music lounge (2 Pacific Pl., 88 Queensway, Hong Kong, tel. 2820–8591), the Kowloon Shangri-La's **Tiara Lounge** (64 Mody Rd., Tsim Sha Tsui East, 21st floor, tel. 2721–2111), and the Sheraton's **Sky Lounge** (20 Nathan Rd., Tsim Sha Tsui, 18th floor, tel. 2369–1111; go up in the bubble elevator—try to get there at sunset), and the Excelsior's **Talk of the Town** (281 Gloucester Rd., Causeway Bay, tel. 2894–8888), where you'll be greeted by a 270° vista of Hong Kong Harbour.

Feeling pampered is the pleasure at the Peninsula's clublike **Verandah** (Salisbury Rd., Tsim Sha Tsui, tel. 2366–6251) or the Mandarin Oriental's mezzanine **Clipper Lounge** (5 Connaught Rd., Central, tel. 2522–0111). The socially aware go to the Peninsula's **Lobby** or Regent's two lobby lounges to see and be seen.

Pubs Off-duty Central business folks flock to the pirate-galleon **Galley** at Jardine House (in front of Star Ferry Terminal, Central, tel. 2526–3061) for pub grub. In Central, the oak-beamed, British-managed **Bull & Bear** (10 Harcourt Rd., tel. 2525–7436) draws all types—a large share of whom are English expats—serves standard pub fare, and is known to get a little rowdy on weekends. Another popular spot is **The Jockey Pub,** tucked away in Swire House (2nd-floor shopping arcade, Chater Rd., tel. 2526–1478). The uppity British pub atmosphere draws a yuppish crowd.

In Wanchai, **The Horse & Groom** (161 Lockhart Rd., tel. 2893–2517) and its neighboring **Old China Hand Tavern** (104 Lockhart Rd., tel. 2527–9174) are reliable starting points. End up at the Excelsior Hotel's **Dickens Bar** (281 Gloucester Rd., tel. 2837–6782), where there's live music most nights and jazz sessions on a Sunday afternoons.

Cool off at an outdoor table at Causeway Bay's **King's Arms** (Sunning Plaza, Sunning Rd., tel. 2895–6557), one of Hong Kong's few city-center "beer gardens." The other hot spot in this part of town is **China Jump** (463 Lockhart Rd., Wanchai, tel. 2832–9007), where bartenders toss bottles and concoct some strange brews—consider the FBI, a combination of ice cream and vodka.

Over in Tsim Sha Tsui, a diverse, happy crowd frequents the Aussie-style **Kangaroo Pub** (35 Haiphong Rd., tel. 2312–0786), which has good pub food and interesting views of Kowloon Park. The **Blacksmith's Arms** (16 Minden Ave., Tsim Sha Tsui, tel. 2369–6696) is a cozy gathering place. **Rick's Cafe** (4 Hart Ave., Tsim Sha Tsui, tel.

2367–2939), a local hangout, is a restaurant-pub decorated à la *Casablanca*, with potted palms, ceiling fans, and posters of Bogie and Bergman. Neighboring **Grammy's Lounge** (2A Hart Ave., tel. 2368–3833) features Filipino-led sing-alongs and attracts a rowdy crowd. **Ned Kelly's Last Stand** (11A Ashley Rd., Tsim Sha Tsui, tel. 2376–0562) is Aussie-style, with beer and filling grub.

Discos The latest "in" nightspot is **JJs** (Grand Hyatt, 1 Harbour Rd., Hong Kong, tel. 2588–1234), the Grand Hyatt's entertainment center. It contains a disco, a nightclub, and a pizza lounge with a pool table and a dart board. The **Catwalk** in the New World Hotel (22 Salisbury Rd., Tsim Sha Tsui, tel. 2369–4111) has a disco, live band, and karaoke lounges. **Joe Bananas** (23 Luard Rd., Wanchai, tel. 2529–1811) is a high-ceilinged, American-style disco-café that's busiest when the fleet's in town.

Topless Bars With a few notable exceptions, most topless bars are scruffy dives. A beer may seem reasonably priced, at around HK$25, but the "champagne" the women drink is not. Charges for conversational companionship can also be unexpected extras.

Bottoms Up (14 Hankow Rd., Tsim Sha Tsui, tel. 2721–4509) was immortalized by its use in the James Bond film *The Man with the Golden Gun*. Cozy circular bar counters are tended by topless women. This place is so respectable that visiting couples are welcomed. A popular cluster of Wanchai haunts are to be found on and off Wanchai's Fenwick Street—stick your nose in **An-An, Crossroads, Club Mikado, Club Pussycat,** and, of course, the **Suzie Wong Club.**

Hostess Clubs **Club BBoss** is the grandest and most boisterous, in Tsim Sha Tsui East's Mandarin Plaza (tel. 2369–2883). Executives, mostly locals, entertain here, tended by a staff of more than 1,000. If one's VIP room is too far from the entrance, one can hire an electrified vintage Rolls and purr around an indoor roadway. Along the harbor, in New World Centre, are **Club Cabaret** (tel. 2369–8431) and **Club Deluxe** (tel. 2721–0277), both luxurious dance lounges.

Macau

By Shann Davies

Revised by Jane Lasky

The voyage from Hong Kong to Macau is a pleasant progress between hilly green islands, some belonging to Hong Kong, some Chinese, and most uninhabited. As it appears on the skyline, Macau jolts the imagination. Hills crowned with a lighthouse and church spire, a blur of pastel buildings, and tree-lined avenues all confirm that this is a bit of transplanted Iberia, settled in 1557 by the Portuguese as Europe's first outpost in China.

Macau is 144 km (90 mi) south of Canton (now Guangzhou), the traditional port for China's trade with foreign "barbarians." In the 16th century, however, its traders were forbidden by the emperor to deal with Japan, whose shogun had imposed a ban on China trade. The Portuguese saw their chance and soon were making fabulous fortunes from their command of trade between the two Asian countries and Europe. Among the cargoes that passed through Macau were silk, tea, and porcelain from China, silver and lacquerware from Japan, spices and sandalwood from the East Indies, muslin from India, gems from Persia, wild animals and ivory from Africa, foodstuffs from Brazil, and European clocks, telescopes, and cannons.

Macau's golden age came to an abrupt end with the closure of Japan and the loss of Portugal's mercantile power to the Dutch and English. The northern Europeans and the Americans sent their Indiamen and clipper ships to Macau to barter ginseng, furs, woolens, and opium for tea and silk. Their merchants treated the city as their own but, with their rents and customs duties, helped Macau survive. Then, in the mid-19th century, Hong Kong was founded and the merchants moved out, leaving Macau a backwater.

In the early part of this century, Macau was cast by movie producers and novelists as a den of sin, sex, and spies. True, it had casinos, brothels, opium divans, and secret agents; but, in fact, it was a small, pale shadow of Shanghai or even Hong Kong. Today, any traveler in search of wild and wicked Macau will be disappointed, and so will romantics looking for a colonial twilight. As you approach through the ocher waters of the silt-heavy Pearl River estuary, the reality of modern Macau is unavoidable. High-rise apartments and office blocks mask the hillsides, multistory factories cover land reclaimed from the sea, and construction hammers insist that this is no longer a sleepy old town.

The modern prosperity comes from taxes on gambling and the export of textiles, toys, electronics, furniture, luggage, and ceramics. Like Hong Kong, Macau is a duty-free port where anyone can set up a business with minimal taxation or government restrictions. As a result, there is little evidence of city planning and many of the new skyscrapers are grotesque. However, some building projects have benefited Macau. These include the University of Macau and the racetrack on Taipa Island, a handsome handful of good hotels, and a number of superbly restored or re-created historical buildings.

Relations with China have never been better, with ever-increasing two-way trade and joint ventures in Zhongshan, the neighboring Chinese county. Following the Sino-British agreement to hand Hong Kong back to China in 1997, the Portuguese negotiated the resumption of Chinese sovereignty over Macau, which will take place on December 20, 1999.

Macau has a population of about 450,000, and most live in the 6.5 sq km (2.5 sq mi) of the mainland peninsula, with small communities on the mostly rural islands of Taipa and Coloane. About 95% of the inhabitants are Chinese, many of them of long-standing residence. About 7,000 people speak Portuguese as their first language, but only a few come from Portugal, the others being Macanese from old established Eurasian families. Although Portuguese is the official language, and Cantonese the most widely spoken, English is generally understood in places frequented by tourists.

Important Addresses and Numbers

Tourist Information In Macau, the **Department of Tourism** offers information, advice, maps, and brochures about the territory. It has an office at the arrival terminal (open daily 9–6 daily). The main office is in Leal Senado Square (tel. 315–566, open daily 9–6).

Generally more helpful is the **Macau Tourist Information Bureau** in Hong Kong. It has a wide range of maps, brochures, and up-to-the-minute information on hotels and transportation. The office is in Room 3704 at the Shun Tak Centre (tel. 2540–8180) and is open weekdays 9–5, Saturday 9–1. In addition, there is a Macau information desk in Room 336 of the Shun Tak Centre (tel. 2857–2287) and at Hong Kong's Kai Tak Airport, just outside the Arrivals Hall. Both are open daily, 8 AM–10 PM.

National Holidays

Macau celebrates all major Catholic holidays, Chinese New Year, other important festival days, plus historic occasions, such as Portugese Republic Day (Oct. 5) and Independence Day (Dec. 1). Offices and banks close for these holidays, but most shops stay open.

Festivals and Seasonal Events

June: The **Dragon Boat Festival** derives from an ancient Chinese festival in which fishing communities would compete in long, shallow boats with dragon heads and tails, in honor of a poet who drowned himself to protest official corruption. (His friends took to boats and pounded their oars in the water while beating drums to scare away the fish who would have eaten the poet's body.) The races are held in the Outer Harbour, where the waterfront provides a natural grandstand. Teams from all over the world compete in gaily decorated boats, accompanied by drum beating and firecrackers.

Nov.: The **Macau Grand Prix** takes place on the third or fourth weekend in November. From the beginning of the week, the city is filled with the sound of supercharged engines testing the 6-kilometer (3.8-mi) Guia Circuit, which follows the city roads along the Outer Harbour to Guia Hill and around the reservoir. The Grand Prix was first staged in 1953 and the standard of performance has now reached world class. Today cars achieve speeds of 224 kph (140 mph) on the straightaways. The premier event is the Formula Three championship, with cars brought in from around the world. Hotel bookings during the Grand Prix are made far in advance; the weekend should be avoided by anyone not interested in motor racing.

Currency

The official currency unit in Macau is the pataca, which is divided into 100 avos. Bank notes come in five denominations: 500, 100, 50, 10, and 5 patacas; coins are 5 and 1 patacas and 50, 20, and 10 avos. The pataca is pegged to the Hong Kong dollar (within a few cents). Hong Kong currency circulates freely in Macau but not vice versa, so remember to change your patacas before you return to Hong Kong.

What It Will Cost

Prices in Macau for hotels, restaurants, and merchandise are anywhere from a third to a half lower than those in Hong Kong.

Travel Documents

Visas are *not* required for Portuguese citizens or nationals of the United States, Canada, the United Kingdom, Australia, New Zealand, France, West Germany, Austria, Belgium, the Netherlands, Switzerland, Sweden, Denmark, Norway, Italy, Greece, Spain, Japan, Thailand, the Philippines, Malaysia, South Korea, Ireland, Singapore, Brazil (up to a six-month stay), or Hong Kong residents. There is unlimited stay for Chinese, 20 days for non-Chinese. Other nationals need visas, available on arrival: HK$175 for individuals and HK$88 for group members.

Language

Portuguese is the official language, though since 95% of Macau's residents are Chinese, most speak Cantonese. English is widely understood.

Telephones

Telephone service is a bit erratic, with numbers constantly being changed; however, international calls are handled efficiently. Macau's country code is 853.

Information Call 121 for directory assistance. Operators speak English.

Mail

The **General Post Office** (Largodo Senado, tel. 2574–491) and most hotels supply stamps—much in demand by collectors—and provide telex, cable, and facsimile services. Airmail letters start at 3.30 patacas; postcards and aerograms, 2.50 patacas.

Receiving Mail Macau's General Post Office offers Poste Restante, but there are no American Express or other mail holding offices.

Arriving and Departing from Hong Kong

By Boat The majority of ships to Macau leave Hong Kong from the Macau Terminal in the Shun Tak Centre (200 Connaught Rd.), a 10-minute walk west of Central. In Macau, ships use the new (1994) three-story ferry terminal, which has separate arrival and departure levels and is near the Mandarin Oriental Hotel. Information can be hard to obtain over the phone, as the operators don't speak English; it's best to call the MTIB (tel. 2540–8180), whose operators do.

A fleet of Boeing Jetfoils provides the most popular service between Hong Kong and Macau. Carrying about 260 passengers, these craft ride comfortably on jet-propelled hulls at 40 knots and make the 64-km (40-mi) trip in about an hour. Jetfoils depart every 15 minutes from 7 AM to 8 PM, with less frequent sailings between 8 PM and 7 AM. The top deck of each vessel is first class, and there are no-smoking sections on both decks. Fares for first class are HK$126 on weekdays, HK$113 on weekends and public holidays, and HK$158 on the night service. Lower-deck fares are HK$111 weekdays, HK$119 weekends, and HK$138 at night.

Hong Kong Macau Hydrofoil Company (HMH) operates jet-propelled catamarans called Jetcats, which carry 215 passengers and make the trip in about 70 minutes. Six round-trips a day depart from the Macau ferry terminal. Fares are HK$70 on weekdays, HK$78 on weekends. The HMH also operates Jumbocats—called Super-Shuttles—which carry 306 passengers and take just over an hour. They sail every 30 minutes from 8 AM to 5:30 PM. One-way fares are HK$80 on weekdays, HK$88 on weekends.

The largest vessels on the Macau run are high-speed ferries, which take about an hour and a half and make five round-trips daily between 8 AM and 8 PM (7:30 AM–8:30 PM Sunday and public holidays). These sleek, comfortable craft have a sundeck and first-class lounge. One-way fares are HK$93 first class; HK$78 tourist; HK$59 economy weekdays; HK$116, HK$101, and HK$81 weekends and public holidays. Bookings can be made at Ticketmate and the ferry terminal.

There is also catamaran service from from the China Terminal on the Kowloon peninsula. The two-deck vessels hold 433 passengers and take an hour to cross the South China Sea. One-way fares are $9 weekdays; $11 weekends and public holidays.

All tickets between the two territories carry departure taxes: $HK26 from Hong Kong; 22 patacas from Macau.

By Air   Macau's first international airport, with runways on an artificial island in Macau Harbor, is scheduled for completion by the end of 1995, but details were not available at press time. Helicopter service is available from the Macau Terminal, with at least eight round-trips daily. The 20-minute flights cost HK$986 weekdays, HK$1,086 weekends and public holidays, excluding taxes. Book through the Shun Tak Centre (tel. 2859–3359) or the terminal in Macau (tel. 572–983).

Getting Around

The old parts of town and the shopping areas lend themselves to walking. Here the streets are narrow, often under repair, and invariably crowded with vehicles weaving between sidewalk vendors and parked cars. Otherwise transport is varied, convenient, and often fun.

By Pedicab   This tricycle-drawn, two-seater carriage has been in business as long as there have been bicycles and paved roads in Macau, and a few look like originals. They cluster at the ferry terminal and near hotels around town, their drivers hustling for customers and usually offering guide services. In the past it was a pleasure to hire a pedicab for the ride downtown, but no longer. Construction along the Outer Harbour and the outrageous prices asked by today's drivers make it a hassle. To appreciate the pedicab, especially on a sunny day, take one along the Praia Grande and admire the avenue of ancient trees and the seascape of islands and fishing junks. The city center is not a congenial place for pedicabs, and the hilly districts are impossible. You have to haggle, but you shouldn't pay more than HK$30 for a trip to a nearby hotel.

By Taxi   There are usually plenty of taxis at the terminal, outside hotels, and cruising the streets. All are metered and most are air-conditioned and reasonably comfortable, but the cabbies speak little English and probably won't know the English or Portuguese names for places. It is highly recommended that you carry a bilingual map or name card in Chinese. The base charge is 6.50 patacas for the first 1,600 m (about 1 mi), and 80 avos for each additional 480 m (about 0.3 mi). Drivers don't expect more than small change as a tip. For trips to Taipa there is a 5-pataca surcharge, and to Coloane 10 patacas. Expect to pay about 7.0–8.8 patacas for a trip from the terminal to downtown.

By Bus   The public buses that run around Macau are cheap—no more than 1.5 patacas within the city limits—and convenient. Most useful for visitors are services from the terminal: the 3A passes the Lisboa, Beverly Plaza, Sintra, and Metropole hotels before proceeding down the main street to the Inner Harbour; the 28C passes the Lisboa, Guia, and Royal hotels, Lou Lim Ioc Gardens, and Kun Iam Temple en route to the border. All routes are detailed on posts at bus stops. Other buses commute between the city and the islands. For information on all bus service call 555–686, ext. 3004.

By Bicycle   Bicycles are available for rent at about 10 patacas an hour from shops near the Taipa bus station.

By Hired Car   You can rent mokes, little jeeplike vehicles, which are fun and ideal for touring. Driving is on the *right* side. International and most national driver's licenses are valid. Rental rates are HK$280 for 24 hours weekdays and HK$320 weekends, plus HK$50 insurance and a HK$1,000 deposit. Hotel packages often include special moke-rental deals. In Hong Kong, contact **Macau Mokes** (tel. 2543–4190) or any of the 11 Ticketmate offices; in Macau there's an office (tel. 378–851) at the terminal.

Guided Tours

Traditional and customized tours, for individuals and groups, by bus or car, are easily arranged in Macau, and cover the most ground in the shortest time.

There are two basic tours available. One covers mainland Macau with stops at the Chinese border, Kun Iam Temple, St. Paul's, and Penha Hill. It lasts about 3½ hours and costs from HK$62 to HK$150 per person, depending on the number of people in the group and on whether you travel by car or by bus. The other typical tour consists of a two-hour bus trip to the islands across the bridge to see old Chinese villages, temples, beaches, the Jockey Club, and the University of East Asia. This tour costs HK$15 each for four or more.

The most comfortable way to tour is by chauffeur-driven luxury car. For a maximum of four passengers it costs HK$100 an hour. Regular taxis can also be rented for touring.

Most people book tours with Macau agents while in Hong Kong or through travel agents before leaving home. If you do it this way, you will have transport from Hong Kong to Macau arranged for you and your guide waiting in the arrival hall. There are many licensed tour operators in Macau. Among those specializing in English-speaking visitors, and who have offices in Hong Kong, are **Able Tours** (Hoi Kwong Building, Travessa do Pe. Narciso, Macau, tel. 89798; in Hong Kong, 8 Connaught Rd. W, tel. 2545–9993; **Estoril Tours** (Lisboa Hotel, Macau, tel. 573–614; in Hong Kong, Macau Terminal, tel. 2559–1028); **International Tourism** (9 Travessa do Pe. Narciso, Macau, tel. 975–183; in Hong Kong, Cheong Tai Commercial Bldg., 60 Wing Lok St., tel. 2541–2011); **Macau Star** (511 Tai Fung Bank Bldg., 34 Ave. Almeida Ribeiro, Macau, tel. 558–855; in Hong Kong, 18 Cheong Ning Bldg., Tsuen Wan, New Territories, tel. 2417–4600); **Macau Tours** (35 Ave. Dr Mario Soares, Macau, tel. 385–555; in Hong Kong, 387 Des Voeux Rd., tel. 2542–2338); and **Sintra Tours** (Sintra Hotel, Macau, tel. 85878; in Hong Kong, Macau Terminal, tel. 2540–8028).

Exploring Macau

Numbers in the margin correspond to points of interest on the Macau map.

Tour 1: The Outer Harbour

❶   The history of Portuguese Macau almost came to an end at the **Outer Harbour** in 1622, when the Dutch fleet landed a large invasion force to capture the rich port. From here the troops attacked Guia and Monte forts, only to be defeated by a ragtag army of Jesuit priests, Portuguese soldiers, and African slaves.

Today the harbor is designed to welcome all arrivals. On the mile-long avenue from the terminal are the Mandarin Oriental,

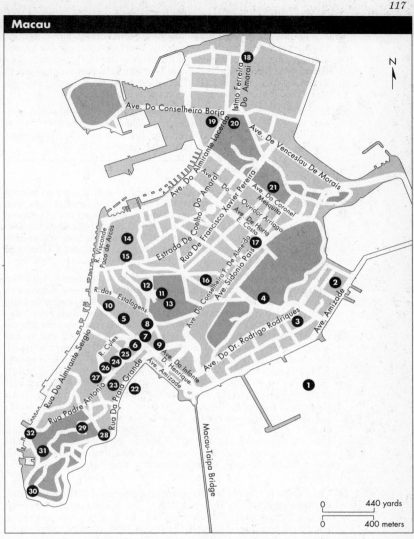

Macau

A-Ma Temple, **31**
Avenida Almeida
  Ribeiro, **5**
Bela Vista Hotel, **28**
Bishop's Palace, **29**
Camões Grotto and
  Garden (Casa
  Garden), **14**
Canidrome, **19**
Dom Pedro V, **24**
Guia Hill, **4**

Jai Alai Stadium, **2**
Kun Iam Temple, **21**
The Leal Senado, **6**
Lin Fung Miu, **20**
Lou Lim Ieoc
  Garden, **16**
Macau Forum, **3**
Maritime Museum, **32**
Memorial Home of Dr.
  Sun Yat-sen, **17**
Monte Fort, **13**

Monte Hill, **11**
Old Protestant
  Cemetery, **15**
Outer Harbour, **1**
Palacio, **23**
Portas do Cerco, **18**
Post Office, **9**
Pousada de São
  Tiago, **30**
Praia Grande, **22**

Rua Cinco do
  Outubro, **10**
St. Augustine, **25**
St. Lawrence, **27**
St. Paul's, **12**
Santa Casa da
  Misericordia, **7**
São Domingos, **8**
Seminary of St.
  Joseph's, **26**

Presidente, New World Emperor, Kingsway, Holiday Inn, and Lisboa hotels; the **Jai Alai Stadium,** casino, and entertainment center;
❸ the **Macau Forum** for conferences and sports events; and the grandstand for the annual motor and motorcycle Grand Prix events. The
Grand Prix Museum opened in the Tourism Activity Center adjacent
to the Macau Forum in 1994. The tallest building in the city, the 38-
story Bank of China tower, is next to the Lisboa.

❹ Overlooking the harbor are the slopes of **Guia Hill,** embossed with
new homes, a convent, and a hospital. The hill is topped with a fort
that dates from the 1630s, the oldest lighthouse on the China coast
(built in 1865), and a small whitestone chapel built in 1707.

Tour 2: Downtown

For a relatively straightforward introduction to the many-layered
and often contradictory character of the city, you can stroll the mile
❺ or so of the main street, **Avenida Almeida Ribeiro,** generally known
by its Chinese name, **Sanmalo.** It begins a short walk from the Lisboa and ends at the floating casino in the inner harbor. Within this
short distance you find colonial Portugal, traditional China, and
modern Asia locked in architectural and social embrace.

Like a European city, the focal point of this downtown is a large
square with a fountain and plaza surrounded by several impressive
buildings. The square was given a new look in 1994. Patterned tile
paving, seating among the trees, and a lighted fountain spruce it up.
The multicolored tiles were imported and set by masons from Portu-
❻ gal. **The Leal Senado** (Loyal Senate) building is a superb example of
colonial architecture, constructed in the late 18th century to house
the senate of leading citizens—who were at the time far more powerful than the governors—while they served their short terms before
returning to Portugal. Today the senate, with some elected and
some appointed members, acts as the municipal government, with
its president holding the same power as a mayor. Inside the building, a beautiful stone staircase leads to a wrought-iron gate and a
charming garden. The original national library is also housed within
the Leal Senado. A superb copy of Mafra, the classic Portuguese library, it contains possibly the best collection of books in English
about China's history, society, economy, and culture. *Open Mon.–
Sat. 1–7.*

❼ The Senate president is by tradition the president of the **Santa Casa
da Misericordia** (Holy House of Mercy), the oldest Christian charity
on the China coast. Founded in 1569, its headquarters occupy a
handsome baroque building in the square, and its offices administer
homes for the elderly, kitchens for the poor, clinics, and a leprosari-
❽ um. Behind the Santa Casa is the **São Domingos** church, with a magnificent baroque altar.

❾ The central **Post Office** and telephone exchange, as well as some
handsome old commercial buildings with arcades at street level, are
also in the square. (One of them has been restored to house the Government Tourist Office.) The São Domingos produce market, its narrow streets packed with stalls selling fruit, vegetables, and
wholesale-price clothing from local factories, leads off the square.

Sanmalo has some clothing stores, but the majority of shoppers
come here for gold jewelry, watches and clocks, Chinese and Western medicines, brandy, biscuits, and salted fish. Interspersed are
banks, lawyers' offices, and the Central Hotel. Now a rather dingy,
inexpensive place to stay, the Central used to contain the city's only

casinos, where the *fan-tan* (button game) attracted the high rollers and the top-floor brothel did a thriving business.

The heart of the old red-light district was Rua da Felicidade ("Street of Happiness"), which runs off Sanmalo. Few brothels have survived the competition from sauna and massage parlors; most have been replaced by budget hotels and restaurants. The area does preserve the atmosphere of a prewar China-coast community, especially in the evening. After sunset, food stalls with stools and tiny tables are set out. Lights blaze from open-front restaurants, laundries, tailor shops, and family living rooms.

⑩ Another side street off Sanmalo worth a detour is **Rua Cinco do Outubro,** which contains one of the best-looking traditional Chinese medicine shops anywhere. The Farmacia Tai Ning Tong has an elaborately carved wood facade and a cavernous interior, its walls lined with huge apothecary jars of medicinal roots, deer horn, and other assorted marvels. In a corner are mortars and pestles for making potions to order.

Tour 3: The Old Citadel

The most remarkable early buildings in Macau were situated on **⑪** **Monte Hill.** Built by the Jesuits, they included a fort, a college, and **⑫** the collegiate church of the Mother of God, commonly known as St. Paul's. The church was built between 1602 and 1627 by exiled Japanese Christians and local craftsmen under the direction of the Jesuits, and it was declared the most magnificent in Asia. The college, the first Western-style university in Asia, attracted such scholars as Matteo Ricci and Adam Van Schall, who studied here before going to the court in Peking.

Today this area is the heart of old Macau for visitors and is easily reached from Senate Square via Rua da São Domingos. The college was used as army housing until it was destroyed in a disastrous fire in 1835, and the ruins of the fort are now a quiet belvedere. Of the church, only the great stone facade remains, but it is less a ruin than a dramatic symbol of Macau; it is certainly the leading attraction.

Traditional craftsmen, still in business carving camphorwood chests and family shrines, hand-beating metal utensils, making barrels and mattresses, and weaving birdcages, still occupy the jumble of narrow streets below the church. Tercena and Estalagens are the most interesting streets.

⑬ **Monte Fort,** on the hill overlooking St. Paul's, was also built by the Jesuits and completed in 1623. The year before it was completed, the fort was the scene of Macau's most famous battle. The Dutch invaded the territory, which was protected by a small force of soldiers, African slaves, and priests. A lucky cannon shot, fired by one of the priests, hit the Dutch powder supply, and the enemy was driven back to sea. In 1626, the first full-time governor of Macau evicted the Jesuits from the fort. For the next century and a half it was the residence and office of Macau's governors. The fort's buildings were destroyed in the 1835 fire, but the great walls remain, along with their cannon. *Admission free. Open 7 AM to dusk.*

⑭ Following either Rua de São Paulo or Tercena, you reach Praça Luis de Camões and the **Camões Grotto and Garden (Casa Garden).** Macau's most popular public park, it was named for Portugal's greatest poet, who spent some years in Macau. The garden was originally the home of the former Camões Museum and now houses the Casa Garden Orient Foundation offices. The foundation restored the

18th-century house here, which was once home to the British East India Company and part of which now serves as a museum for the Camões collection. *Admission free. Gardens open dawn–dusk; house open daily 9:30 AM–6 PM.*

⑮ The **Old Protestant Cemetery,** a "corner of some foreign field" for more than 150 Americans and British, is opposite the entrance to the garden. It is a tranquil retreat where tombstones recall the troubles and triumphs of Westerners in 19th-century China. Some of the names are familiar: George Chinnery; Captain Henry Churchill, great granduncle of Sir Winston; Joseph Adams, grandson of John Adams, the second U.S. president; Robert Morrison, who translated the Bible into Chinese; Thomas Beale, the opium king; and traders James B. Endicott and Samuel Proctor.

Tour 4: Restoration Row

Conservation and common sense don't always go together, but there is an outstanding example of such a match in Macau's Restoration Row. Actually it is a row of houses built in the 1920s in symmetrical arcadian style, on the **Avenida do Conselheiro Ferreira de Almeida,** a block or so from the Royal hotel. The owners of the houses were persuaded to forgo huge profits and sell to the government. The houses were then converted into homes for the Archives, the National Library, the Education Department, a contemporary-art center, and university offices. The exteriors were extensively repaired and the interiors transformed.

⑯ Continuing along the avenue, you come to Estrada de Adolfo Loureiro and the **Lou Lim Ieoc Garden,** a classic Chinese garden modeled on those of old Soochow. Built in the 19th century by a wealthy Chinese merchant, the enclosed garden is a miniaturized landscape with miniforests of bamboo and flowering bushes, a mountain of sculpted concrete, and a small lake filled with lotus and golden carp. A traditional nine-turn bridge zigzags (to deter evil spirits, which can move only in straight lines) across the lake to a colonial-style pavilion with a wide veranda. *Admission: 1 pataca. Open daily dawn–dusk.*

⑰ Another place of interest in this area is the **Memorial Home of Dr. Sun Yat-sen.** Sun, father of the 1911 Chinese revolution, worked as a physician in Macau from 1892 to 1894, and some of his family stayed here after his death. The memorial home, in strange mock-Moorish style, was built in the mid-1930s. It contains some interesting photographs, books, and souvenirs of Sun and his long years of exile in different parts of the world. *1 Rua Ferreira do Amaral. Admission free. Open weekdays (except Tues.) 10–1, weekends 10–1 and 3–5.*

Tour 5: On the Doorstep of China

⑱ **Portas do Cerco** (The Border Gate) marks the traditional boundary of Macau. Beyond is the Chinese border town of Gongbei. The present gate was built in 1870 and bears the arms of Portugal's navy and artillery, along with a quotation from Camões, which reads, in translation: "Honor your country for it looks after you." Today there is a steady flow of vegetable farmers, businesspeople, and tourists at the gate. *Open daily 7 AM–midnight.*

⑲ ⑳ Close by the border are two very different attractions. On one side is the **Canidrome,** where greyhound races are enthusiastically followed. On the other side of the road is the **Lin Fung Miu,** or Temple of the Lotus. This superb temple, dedicated to both Buddhist and

Taoist deities, was built in 1592 and used for overnight accommodations by mandarins traveling between Macau and Canton. It is famous for its facade of intricate clay bas-reliefs depicting mythological and historical scenes and an interior frieze of colorful writhing dragons. *Open daily dawn–dusk.*

㉑ **Kun Iam Temple,** nearby on the Avenida do Coronel Mesquita, should not be missed. It has a wealth of statuary and decoration, and in the courtyard is a stone table where the first Sino-American treaty was signed in 1844 by the Viceroy of Canton and President John Tyler's envoy, Caleb Cushing. *Open daily dawn–dusk.*

Tour 6: Peninsula Macau

The narrow, hilly peninsula stretching from the main street to Barra Point and the Pousada de São Tiago is quintessential Macau, very Portuguese and very Chinese, ancient and uncomfortably mod-
㉒ ern. It is bounded on one side by the **Praia Grande** and its extension, Avenida da Republica, a graceful, banyan-shaded boulevard where people fish from the sea wall or play Chinese chess. Unfortunately, parts of the promenade have been taken over by parked cars, but there are also plenty of benches, and the traffic is well diluted by pedicabs.

The cargo and fishing wharfs of the inner harbor, with their traditional Chinese shop houses—the ground floors occupied by ship's chandlers, net makers, ironmongers, and shops selling spices and salted fish—are on the opposite side of the peninsula. In between there are several areas of historic or scenic interest. One is Largo de Sto. Agostinho, or St. Augustine Square, which is reached by climbing the steep street next to the Senate, or from the Praia Grande and
㉓ the pink-and-white **Palacio,** which houses government offices.

Take the Travessa do Paiva to the right of the Palacio, turn right along Rua de São Lourenco to the dimple-stone ramp to the square, which looks as if it came all of a piece from 19th-century Portugal. To
㉔ the left is the **Dom Pedro V** theater, built in 1859 in the style of a European court theater. Renovated recently by the Orient Foundation, it is now in use again. Opposite is the imposing baroque build-
㉕ ing of the church of **St. Augustine,** and next door is Casa Ricci, offices for one of the most active Catholic charities in Macau. Across the
㉖ square is the **Seminary of St. Joseph's,** home of preeminent local historian and living legend Father Manuel Teixeira and a collection of religious art by 17th-century European and Japanese painters. The baroque chapel is now open to the public Thursday–Tuesday 10–4. The entrance is on Rua do Seminario.

Retracing your steps down the ramp and continuing along the Rua
㉗ de São Lourenco, you reach the elegant twin-tower church of **St. Lawrence** and the Salesian Institute, a technical school that stands on part of the site of the headquarters of the British East India Com-
㉘ pany. From here you can take the Rua do Pe. Antonio to the **Bela Vista Hotel** or return to the Praia Grande and follow it to the Calcada do Bom Parto. Either way, you'll pass the Bela Vista, a century-old landmark hotel that reopened in 1992 as a luxury inn and restaurant.

Farther up the hill is one of the best lookouts in Macau, the court-
㉙ yard of the **Bishop's Palace** and Penha Chapel. The palace is always closed, but the chapel is open daily 10–4. The present building was constructed in 1935 on the site of the original 1622 structure and is dedicated to Our Lady of Penha, patroness of seafarers.

③⓪ At the far end of the peninsula is Barra Point, with the **Pousada de São Tiago,** a Portuguese inn built into the ruined foundations of a
③① 17th-century fort; the **A-Ma Temple,** Macau's oldest and most venerated place of worship (which gave its name to Macau); and the
③② **Maritime Museum.** This gem of a museum has been a consistent favorite since its doors opened at the end of 1987. It is ideally located where the first Chinese and later first Portuguese made landfall. The new four-story building resembles a stately ship and is considered one of the foremost maritime museums in Asia. The adjacent dock was restored to provide a pier for a fishing junk, tug, dragon boat, sampan, and a working replica of the pirate-chasing lorchas. Inside are displays on the local fishing industry, models of historic vessels, charts of great voyages by Portuguese and Chinese explorers, models of 17th-century Macau and the A-Ma Temple, navigational aids, and much, much more. *Tel. 595–481. Admission free. Open Wed.–Mon. 10–6.*

Tour 7: Taipa Island

Linked to the city by a graceful 1.6-mile bridge, as well as by a secondary bridge from the Outer Harbour to the airport, Taipa can be reached by bus (especially popular are the open-top double-deckers) or taxi. Up until the end of the 19th century, Taipa was two islands and provided a sheltered anchorage where clipper ships and East India–men could load and unload cargoes, which were then carried by junks and barges to and from Canton. Gradually the islands were joined by river silt and land reclamation, but Taipa Praia, with its mansions—one of which now houses a museum—offers a reminder of the old days.

Taipa and Coloane, its neighbor, are Macau's New Territories, having been ceded by China only in 1887. Until the building of the bridge, both islands led a somnolent existence, interrupted only by occasional pirate raids. Taipa's economy depended on the raising of ducks and the manufacture of firecrackers. The duck farms have given way to apartment blocks while the courtyarded firecracker factories have closed, unable to compete with China.

The **village of Taipa** is a tight maze of houses and shops in the traditional mold. It is changing, due to the island's new prosperity, and now boasts banks, a two-story municipal market, air-conditioned shops, and several excellent restaurants. Below the church of Our Lady of Carmel is the **Taipa House Museum.** This finely restored 1920s mansion contains authentic period furniture, decorations, and furnishings that recapture the atmosphere and lifestyle of a middle-class Macanese family in the early part of the century. *Taipa Praia, tel. 327–088. Admission free. Open Tues.–Sun. 9–1 and 3–5.*

Another restored building worth a visit is the **Pou Tai Un Temple,** a short walk from the Hyatt Regency. It is famed for its vegetarian restaurant (the vegetables are grown in an adjoining garden) and has been embellished with a new yellow tile pavilion and statue of the Buddhist goddess of mercy.

For Buddhists, Taoists, and Confucians, Taipa is a favored last earthly address. They are buried or their bones stored in the massive **United Chinese Cemetery,** which covers the cliff on the northeastern coast of the island. It is lavishly decorated with colored tiles and assorted religious images. Offshore you can see the site of the Macau International Airport.

The northeast section of Taipa provides a stunning contrast, thanks to a recent building boom. Just across the bridge is the luxurious Hyatt Hotel, the equally impressive New Century Hotel, and the hilltop **University of Macau.** Directly facing the bridge is a monument sculpted with images from Macau's history. On the western side of the island is the raceway of the **Macau Jockey Club,** 50 acres of reclaimed land with an ultramodern five-story grandstand and tracks.

Tour 8: Coloane Island

Situated at the end of a 2.4-km (1.5-mi) causeway from Taipa, the larger, hillier island of Coloane has so far been spared from development. About a 25-minute drive from the city, it is generally considered to be remote. This makes it a popular spot for relaxed holidays, especially at the attractive 22-room **Pousada de Coloane.** There is a long beach below the Pousada and another at **Hac Sa** (Black Sands). Both are clean, although the water is Pearl River ocher. There are plenty of cafés for food and drink. The luxury hotel and championship golf course of the **Westin Resort,** which opened in 1993, overlooks Hac Sa beach.

The village of Coloane, with its old tile-roof houses, the Tam Kong Temple, and the **Chapel of St. Francis Xavier,** are interesting to overseas visitors. The picturesque chapel, with its cream-and-white facade and bell tower, was built in 1928. Outside its door is a monument surrounded by cannonballs commemorating the local defeat of a pirate band in 1910, Macau's last encounter with old-style pirates.

Coloane Park, on the west coast of the island, is one of Macau's natural preserves. Its centerpiece is a walk-in aviary containing more than 200 species of birds, including the rare Palawan peacock and the crested white pheasant. Nearby is a pond with black swans, a playground, a restaurant, a picnic area, and a nature trail around the hillside. Developed by the Forestry Department, the park has an impressive collection of exotic trees and shrubs. *Tel. 569–684. Admission charge for aviary. Open daily 9–7.*

Spectator Sports

Greyhound Racing Races are held in the scenic, open-air Canidrome, close to the Chinese border. Most dogs are imported from Australia, with some from Ireland and the United States. The 10,000-seat stadium has rows and rows of betting windows and stalls for food and drink. *Ave. General Castelo Branco. Races held weekends, Tues., Thurs., and holidays at 8 PM.*

Horse Racing The raceway, built for Asia's first trotting track, is located on reclaimed land close to the Hyatt Regency Hotel. The Macau Trotting Club spared no expense: The five-story grandstand accommodates 15,000 people, 6,000 of them in air-conditioned comfort. There are restaurants, bars, and some of the most sophisticated betting equipment available. Unfortunately, trotting races did not bring in sufficient revenue and so the Macau Jockey Club was formed. These local and Taiwan interests enlarged and improved the track for flat racing. Meetings are held September to April on one day each midweek—when there are no races in Hong Kong.

Stadium Sports A variety of sporting events are held at the **Macau Forum**'s multipurpose hall, including the world table-tennis championships. Call the Macau Forum (tel. 568–711), or the Tourism Department for a schedule of events.

Dining

By the time the Portuguese arrived in Macau, they had adopted many of the ingredients grown and used in the Americas and Africa—peanuts, green beans, pineapples, lettuce, sweet potatoes, shrimp paste, and a variety of spices—and brought them to China. In China, the Portuguese discovered tea, rhubarb, tangerines, ginger, soy sauce, and the Cantonese art of fast frying to seal in flavor.

Over the centuries a unique Macanese cuisine developed, with dishes adapted from Portugal, Brazil, Mozambique, Goa, Malacca, and China. A good example of Macanese food is the strangely named Portuguese chicken, which consists of chunks of chicken baked with potatoes, coconut, tomato, olive oil, curry, olives, and saffron. Extremely popular family dishes include *minchi* (minced pork and diced potatoes panfried with soy), pork baked with tamarind, and duckling cooked in its own blood, all of which are served with rice.

The favorites of Portuguese cuisine are regular menu items. The beloved *bacalhau* (codfish) is served baked, boiled, grilled, deep fried with potato, or stewed with onion, garlic, and eggs. Portuguese sardines, country soups such as *caldo verde* and *sopa alentejana*, and dishes of rabbit are on the menus of many restaurants. Sharing the bill of fare are colonial favorites: from Brazil come *feijoadas*, stews of beans, pork, spicy sausage, and vegetables; from Mozambique, African chicken, baked or grilled in fiery *piri-piri* peppers. In addition, some kitchens prepare baked quail, curried crab, and the delectable Macau sole that rivals its Dover cousin. And then there are the giant prawns that are served in a spicy sauce—one of Macau's special dining pleasures.

Not surprisingly, Chinese restaurants predominate in Macau. In addition, there are several restaurants offering excellent Japanese, Thai, Korean, Indonesian, and even Burmese meals. One of the best bargains in Macau is wine, particularly the delicious Portuguese *vinho verde*, a slightly sparkling wine, and some reds and whites, such as the Dao family of wines.

All restaurants are open every day of the year except, for some, a few days after Chinese New Year. Dress is informal, and nowhere are jackets and ties required. The Department of Tourism's brochure, "Eating Out in Macau," is very useful.

Highly recommended restaurants are indicated by a star ★.

Category	Cost*
$$$	over 150 patacas
$$	70–150 patacas
$	under 70 patacas

per person including service

Macanese-Portuguese
$$$

Fortaleza. The setting of this exquisite restaurant would be reason enough to dine here. Located in the traditional Portuguese inn built into the 17th-century Barra fortress, it offers vistas, between the branches of gnarled trees, onto an idyllic seascape of green islands and sailing junks. The decor and atmosphere recall the days of the Portuguese empire, with crystal lamps, hand-carved mahogany furniture, blue and white tiles, and plush drapes. The food is almost as marvelous, with a good selection of classic Macanese dishes, such as baked codfish, quail, and spicy prawns, and Continental dishes, too. Service is attentive, and prices expensive only by Macau standards. *Pousada de Sao Tiago, Ave. Republica, tel. 781–111. Dinner reservations advised. AE, DC, MC, V.*

$$$ **Hotel Bela Vista.** A slice of heaven up a winding staircase in a landmark hotel (*see* Lodging, *below*), this is a romantic place to dine, especially when you sit outside on the charming Colonial balcony overlooking the city. The decor is understated, and the chef's style is innovative and contemporary. His uptown cuisine is nouvelle Macanese and is lighter than the conventional fare. There isn't a dish that is bad, but the seafood dishes in particular are terrific (try the grilled garoupa with mango in banana leaf) as are the desserts (like the Portuguese tartlets or the traditional rice pudding with cinnamon). Their cappuccinos, which are to die for, come in huge white China cups and last forever. There is an extensive wine list. *8 Rua Do Comendor Kou Neng, tel. 965–333. Reservations strongly advised. AE, DC, MC, V.*

$$ **Afonso's.** This is one of the most attractively designed restaurants in Macau. It is horseshoe-shaped, with Portuguese tiles on the wall, Cantonese tiles on the floor, floral cushions on the rattan chairs, spotless table linen, and dishware made to order in Europe. Picture windows frame the gardens outside. The imaginative menu features a good balance of Macanese favorites, such as spicy prawns, and regional Portuguese dishes, including *açorda* bread, seafood soup, and *frango na pucara* (chicken in a clay pot). There is an excellent wine list, the Portuguese coffee is terrific, and the service is cheerful and efficient. *Hyatt Regency Hotel, Taipa Island, tel. 831–234. Reservations advised. AE, DC, MC, V.*

$$ **A Galera.** This is an elegant, handsomely decorated restaurant, with blue-and-white-tile wall panels, black-and-white-tile floors, pearl-gray table linen, Wedgwood dishware, a bar with high-back armchairs, and views of the S. Francisco fortress. Try such main dishes as *bacalhau a bras* (codfish cooked in a skillet with rice, olives, egg, and onion) and squid stuffed with spiced meat, any of the rich, homemade soups, and the dessert soufflés. As for wine, there is *vinho verde* and reds and whites for 60 patacas a bottle. *Lisboa Hotel, 3rd floor of new wing, tel. 577–666, ext. 1103. Reservations not necessary. AE, DC, MC, V.*

$$ ★ **A Lorcha.** This Portuguese restaurant near the Maritime Museum has become a firm favorite with demanding locals. Come here for casseroles, codfish, chicken giblets, and *pudim* (a cream, egg, and sugar dessert) with first-class service and extremely reasonable prices. *289 Rua do Almirante Sergio, tel. 313–193. Reservations advised. MC, V. Closed Tues.*

$$ ★ **Balichao.** In the city's northern suburbs, this Portuguese restaurant is, by general consent, the most originally elegant in town, with a tented ceiling, antique-filled walls, rattan furniture, and Canton floor tiles. The menu is equally unusual, with great casseroles and dishes served with "balichao" shrimp paste. Try the rice with red beans, the codfish cakes, and the mango pudding. This is a favorite eatery among locals. *Hoi Fu, Est. de Cacilhas 93, tel. 566–000. Reservations advised. AE, MC, V.*

$$ **Fat Siu Lau.** Dating to 1903, this is the oldest European restaurant in Macau and one that has maintained high standards of food and service. Years ago it looked like the average Chinese café, but now each of its three floors is elegantly furnished and decorated—although somewhat kitschy. The ground floor seems to have been transported from Portugal. The walls of bare brick are partly cov-

ered with white stucco, blue tiles, and green vines. There is also a false half-roof with Cantonese tiles. The menu is tried and true. Regulars automatically order the roast pigeon Fat Siu Lau made famous. Other favorites are African chicken, sardines, and ox breast with herbs. A large carafe of wine runs 35 patacas. *64 Rua da Felicidade, tel. 573–580. Reservations not necessary. No credit cards.*

$$ **Fernando's.** You have to know where to find this great, country-style Portuguese restaurant located next to Hac Sa beach, because the entrance looks like a typical Chinese café (although local cabbies usually know how to find it). Inside it's red brick with huge windows and ceiling fans. The clams in garlic are the best in town, and the *bacalhau* (codfish) is hard to beat. There is a pavilion-style bar and courtyard. Local diners tend to sit in the front of the restaurant, while tourists dine in the more spacious back area, which overlooks the sandy beach. Since the menu is only in Portuguese, you may need the aid of eccentric owner Fernando Gomes, who's always happy to translate. *Hac Sa Beach 9, Coloane Island, tel. 328–531. Reservations not usually necessary. No credit cards.*

$$ **Galo.** This new restaurant proves what can be done, with flair and dedication, to transform a traditional Taipa village house into a delight for all the senses. The owners—he was with the Portuguese military, she (his wife) is Macanese—gutted the two-story building. Then they decorated it in bright Iberian colors and added Macanese touches, such as Chinese rattan hats for lamp shades and big porcelain plant pots, plus a fireplace and country-style bar. The food is also country style. One specialty is from Madeira and consists of chunks of orange-flavored lamb on a suspended skewer; others include *pipis*, rice with chicken in a hot sauce, codfish salad with tomatoes and green olives, and curry crabs. Topping off the pleasure of dining here are scenes of village life viewed through the lattice windows. *47 Rua do Cunha, Taipa Island, tel. 377–318. Reservations not necessary. No credit cards.*

$$ **Henri's Galley.** Situated on the banyan-lined waterfront, this is a favorite with local residents and visitors from Hong Kong. The decor reflects owner Henri Wong's former career as a ship's steward. There is a coiled blue-rope pattern on the ceiling, pictures of old ships on the walls, and red and green lights to keep passengers on an even keel. The food is consistently good, with probably the biggest and best spicy prawns in town, delicious African and Portuguese chicken, Portuguese soups, Macau sole, and fried rice, complete with hot Portuguese sausage. *4 Avenida da Republica, tel. 556–251. Reservations advised, especially on weekends. MC, V.*

$$ **Pinocchio's.** This was the first Macanese/Portuguese restaurant on Taipa, and it's still one of the best. It began with one room, then expanded to fill a large, covered courtyard. Now the owner has expanded to a neighboring modern block. Favorite dishes are curried crab, baked quail, grilled king prawns, and steamed shrimp. If you order ahead you can have delectable roast lamb or suckling pig. *4 Rua do Sol, Taipa Island, tel. 327–128 or 327–328. Reservations advised on weekends. MC, V.*

$$ **Pousada de Coloane.** This is 20 minutes by car from the city, by Macau standards a long, long way to go for a meal, but many residents and Hong Kong regulars consider it well worth the trip. The setting is fine, with a large open terrace outside the restaurant. Inside, the restaurant is reminiscent of many in Lisbon, with darkwood panels, colorful tile floors, and folk-art decorations. Service can be rather haphazard, but the food is usually excellent. Among the specialties are feijoadas, grilled sardines, and stuffed squid. Best of all is the Sunday buffet, with a great selection of Macanese

dishes for only 90 patacas per person. *Praia de Cheoc Van, Coloane Island, tel. 328–143. Reservations not necessary. MC, V.*

$$ **Praia Grande.** Wonderfully situated on the Praia Grande, this classic Portuguese restaurant was cleverly created from an ordinary corner building. Decor is simple with white arches, terra-cotta-tile floors, and wrought-iron furniture. The menu has such imaginative items as Portuguese dim-sum appetizers, although the not-so-unusual chocolate cake is terrific too. *10A Lobo d'Avila, Praia Grande, tel. 973–022. Reservations required for lunch. AE, MC, V.*

$ **Riquexo.** This self-service café was created by and for lovers of authentic Macanese food at family prices. Each day half a dozen dishes are prepared in private kitchens and delivered to the *Riquexo* (Portuguese for rickshaw and pronounced the same) in large tureens, which are kept heated in the restaurant. Beer and wine (regulars have their own bottles in the big refrigerator) are offered at little more than shop prices, as well as soups, salads, and desserts. The place is bright and basic, with the atmosphere of a family get-together. The staff doesn't speak much English but is very helpful. *69 Sidonio Pais, tel. 565–655. No reservations. No credit cards. No dinner.*

Lodging

Highly recommended lodgings are indicated by a star ★.

Category	Cost*
$$$	800–1,400 patacas
$$	300–800 patacas
$	under 300 patacas

per room, not including 10% service charge and 5% tax

$$$ **Bela Vista.** Originally built in the 1880s on a hill overlooking Praia Grande Bay, this landmark hotel has been extensively renovated and upgraded by the new managers, Mandarin Oriental Hotels, and is now a deluxe inn with suites. The Bela Vista veranda has been famous among visitors to Macau for decades, and a new lounge and open-air terrace are now open for barbecues. *Rua do Comendador Kou Ho Neng 8, tel. 965–333, fax 965–588; in Hong Kong, tel. 2548–7676. 8 suites with bath. Facilities: restaurants, bar. AE, DC, MC, V.*

$$$ **Holiday Inn.** Opened in 1993 and part of the international chain, this spiffy hotel is the latest addition to the rapidly developing Outer Harbour area, minutes from the new Ferry Terminal and within walking distance of the town center. Each of the rooms has contemporary decor and a built-in window seat with a city or sea view. Dining choices include the glass-enclosed restaurant Frascati, serving Italian cuisine in an alfresco setting; the Dragon Court, for Cantonese specialties; and the VIP Cafe, with its harbor view. At street level is Macau's first pub, Oskar's, complete with a pool table and video games. *Rua Pequin, tel. 783–333, fax 782–321; in the U.S., tel. 800/465–4329. 450 rooms, 6 suites. Facilities: 3 restaurants, bar, casino, fitness center, pool, steam bath, Jacuzzi. AE, MC, V, DC.*

$$$ **Hyatt Regency and Taipa Island Resort.** Rooms here conform to
★ Hyatt Regency's high standards, with all the modern conveniences and attractive furnishings. The public areas combine the best of Iberian architecture and Chinese decor. The foyer is a spacious lounge with white arches, masses of potted plants, and fabulous Chi-

nese lacquer panels. Beyond is the coffee shop, an aptly named Greenhouse salon, a hideaway bar, and Afonso's Portuguese restaurant. A small casino is located off the lobby. The Taipa Resort, which adjoins the hotel, has a complete health spa with different baths and massage and beauty treatments; facilities for tennis, squash, and ball games; a large pool and botanical garden; a jogging track; and the Flamingo Macanese veranda restaurant. *Taipa Island, tel. 831–234, fax 830–195; in Hong Kong, tel. 2559–0168; in the U.S., tel. 800/233–1234; elsewhere Hyatt Hotels Reservations. 365 rooms with bath. Facilities: restaurants, bars, casino, health spa and gym, outdoor pool, 2 squash courts, 4 tennis courts, beauty parlor/barber. AE, DC, MC, V.*

$$$ **Mandarin Oriental.** Built on the site of the old Pan Am seaplane ter-
★ minal, with marvelous views of the Pearl River and islands, this is a beautifully designed and furnished hotel. Its lobby features reproductions of Portuguese art and antiques, the Grill Room has a wood ceiling inlaid with small oil paintings, and the Cafe Girassol could have been transported from the Algarve. The new Italian restaurant, Mezzaluna, serves excellent pastas and has a wood-burning pizza oven. The Bar da Guia is probably the most elegant drinking spot in town, and the casino is certainly the most exclusive. Recreation facilities consist of two pools, tennis and squash courts, and a health club, all overlooking the outer harbor. The guest rooms have marble bathrooms and teak furniture. *Avenida da Amizade, tel. 567–888, fax 513–303; in Hong Kong, tel. 2881–1688; in the U.S., tel. 800/526–6566. 438 rooms with bath. Facilities: restaurants, bars, casino, 2 outdoor pools, 2 tennis courts, 2 squash courts, gym, sauna, massage, beauty parlor. AE, DC, MC, V.*

$$$ **New Century.** Opened on a site between the university and the Hyatt Regency, this sumptuously appointed hotel has quickly joined the industry leaders. The atrium lobby is breathtaking, and the huge pool terrace offers splendid views of the city and Taipa. Rooms are standard luxurious, with minibars, hair dryers, writing desks, in-house movies, and other thoughtful touches. It has a wide range of dining options, including a wooden deck with Caribbean-style cabanas for parties. The Prince Galaxie is an excellent entertainment center. *Estrada Almirante Marques Esparteiro, Taipa Island, tel. 831–234, fax 830–195; in Hong Kong, tel. 2548–2213; in the U.S., tel. 800/233–1234. 599 rooms with bath. Facilities: restaurants, bar, outdoor pool, health spa, tennis and squash courts, bowling, casino. AE, DC, MC, V.*

$$$ **Pousada de São Tiago.** This is as much a leading tourist attraction as
★ a place to stay. It is a traditional Portuguese inn that was built, with enormous imagination and dedication, into the ruins of a 17th-century fortress. The ancient trees that had taken over the fort were incorporated into the design, and the position of their roots dictated the shape of the coffee shop and terrace. Furnishings, made to order in Portugal, include mahogany period furniture, blue-and-white-tile walls, and crystal lamps, plus terra-cotta floor tiles from China and carpets woven in Hong Kong. The entrance is the original entry to the fort, and natural springs have been trained to flow down the rocky wall in tile channels on either side of the staircase. There is also a swimming pool, sun terrace, meeting room, and superb restaurant. Each of the rooms, complete with four-poster beds and marble bathrooms, has a balcony for great views with breakfast or cocktails. Book well in advance. *Avenida da Republica, tel. 378–111; in Hong Kong, tel. 2810–8332 or 2739–1216. 23 rooms with bath. Facilities: restaurant, bar, terrace, outdoor pool, chapel. AE, DC, MC, V.*

Orchard - Center Rd
④ Dynst. Hotel

① Maxim Trip included
②

Raza Singapore
Newton Circus

S

① Nat'l Mus.   monday closed.??
② Bot. Gardens
③ Empress Place Mu
④

RENAISSANCE CRUISES℠

Raffles Hotel

Printed in U.S.A.

<u>Dress</u> — informal

① No ties, except Maxim

1, 38 Sin to 1 dollar

$$$ Pousada Ritz. This handsome inn opposite the Bela Vista commands fine views of Praia Grande Bay from balconied rooms and the spacious dining terrace. The restaurants serve Chinese and Continental meals. Recreational facilities include an indoor pool and gym, as well as a games room with billiards and darts. *Rua Comendador Kou Ho Neng, tel. 339–955, fax 317–826; in Hong Kong, tel. 2739–6993, 2540–6333, or 2367–3043. 12 rooms, 19 suites. Facilities: sauna, pool, gym, restaurants. AE, DC, MC, V.*

$$$ Royal. The Royal has an excellent location, with fine views of Guia, the city, and Inner Harbour. It has a marble-clad lobby with a marble fountain and lounge, plus some excellent shops. In the basement are the health club, squash court, sauna rooms, and a karaoke bar. Upstairs is the glass-roof swimming pool and four restaurants: the Royal Canton for Chinese food, the Japanese Ginza, the Portuguese-Continental Vasco da Gama, and the coffee shop. The hotel has shuttle bus service to the casinos. *2 Estrada da Vitoria, tel. 552–222, fax 563–008; in Hong Kong, 2540–6333; elsewhere, Dai-Ichi Hotels reservations offices. 380 rooms with bath. Facilities: restaurants, bar, lounge, indoor pool, squash court, sauna, gym, shuttle bus to casino. AE, DC, MC, V.*

$$$ Westin Resort. This marvelous facility opened in 1993 on a headland overlooking Hac Sa Beach on Coloane Island. The hotel rooms are built around the bluff and have huge terraces that overlook the beach and water. The Macau Golf and Country Club has a clubhouse in the building, with the course laid out behind it. There are also tennis and squash courts, indoor and outdoor pools, a health club, Cantonese and international restaurants. *Hac Sa Beach, Coloane Island, tel. 871–111, fax 871–122; in Hong Kong, tel. 2803–2015; in the U.S., tel. 800/228–3000. 208 rooms with bath. Facilities: restaurants, bars, golf, 2 pools, 8 tennis courts, 2 squash courts, health club, shops, banquet rooms. AE, DC, MC, V.*

$$ Beverly Plaza. Located in the new suburb behind the Lisboa, this hotel is managed by the China Travel Service, which has offices in the building. The hotel also has a shop with goods at bargain prices. The hotel's lobby bar has become a popular rendezvous. *Avenida Dr. Rodrigues, tel. 782–288, fax 780–684; in Hong Kong, tel. 2739–9928. 300 rooms. Facilities: Chinese and Western restaurants, bar. AE, DC, MC, V.*

$$ Guia. Situated on Guia Hill, this small hotel with a pleasant atmosphere and breathtaking views is an excellent value. *1 Estrada Engenheiro Trigo, tel. 513–888, fax 559–822. 89 rooms. Facilities: Chinese restaurant, coffee shop, disco, karaoke bar. AE, DC, MC, V.*

$$ Lisboa. Rising above a two-story casino, with walls of mustard-color tiles, frilly white window frames, and a roof shaped like a giant roulette wheel, you can't miss this monstrosity. The main tower of the Lisboa has, for better or worse, become one of the popular symbols of Macau and is an inescapable landmark. One wing houses the Crazy Paris Show, the superb A Galera restaurant, a nightclub, and billiards hall, plus an ostentatious collection of late Ching Dynasty art objects and a small, lobby-level exhibition area. The original tower has restaurants serving some of Macau's best cuisine of Chiu Chow province, Japan, and Shanghai. *Avenida da Amizade, tel. 377–666, fax 567–193; in Hong Kong, tel. 2559–1028. 1,050 rooms with bath. Facilities: restaurants, bars, casino, games rooms, disco, theater, bowling, sauna, outdoor pool. AE, DC, MC, V.*

$$ Metropole. This centrally located hotel is managed by the China Travel Service. It has pleasant, comfortable rooms and an excellent Portuguese-Macanese restaurant. The hotel is popular with business travelers and China-bound groups. *63 Rua da Praia Grande,* *tel. 388–166, fax 330–890; in Hong Kong, tel. 2833–9300. 109 rooms with bath. Facilities: restaurant, coffee shop, supper club. MC, V.*

$$ New World Emperor. This 1992 addition to the Outer Harbour district is handy to casinos and the wharf and is a smart value. It has a fine Cantonese restaurant and popular Bistro. *Rua de Xangai, tel. 781–888, fax 728–287; in Hong Kong, tel. 2724–5622; elsewhere, New World Hotels International. 405 rooms with bath. Facilities: restaurants, bar, sauna, shuttle bus to city center. AE, DC, MC, V.*

$$ Pousada de Coloane. This *pousada* is a small, delightful resort inn that was upgraded in 1993. Among the delights are the huge terrace overlooking a good sandy beach, a pool, and a superb restaurant serving excellent Macanese and Portuguese food. The rooms have good-size balconies and honor bars, and, since the renovation, roomy bathtubs, too. This is a place for lazy vacations and, in summer it's usually packed with families from Hong Kong as well as singles who want an inexpensive getaway. *Praia de Cheoc Van, Coloane Island, tel. 328–144, fax 552–735; in Hong Kong, tel. 2540–8180. 22 rooms with bath. Facilities: restaurant, bar, terrace, outdoor pool. MC, V.*

$$ Presidente. The Presidente has an excellent location and is very popular with visitors from Hong Kong. It offers an agreeable lobby lounge, European and Chinese restaurants, the best Korean food in town, a sauna, and a great disco with a skylight roof. *Avenida da Amizade, tel. 553–888; in Hong Kong, tel. 2526–6873; elsewhere, Utell International reservations offices. 340 rooms with bath. Facilities: restaurants, sauna, nightclub/disco. AE, DC, MC, V.*

$$ Sintra. A sister hotel of the Lisboa, the Sintra is, in contrast, quiet, with few diversions apart from a sauna, nightclub, and European restaurant and bar. It is ideally located, overlooking the Praia Grande bay and within easy walking distance of the Lisboa and downtown. *Avenida Dom Joao 1V, tel. 710–111, fax 510–527; in Hong Kong, tel. 2540–8028. 236 rooms with bath. Facilities: 2 restaurants. AE, DC, MC, V.*

$ Central. In the very heart of town, this was once the home of Macau's only legal casino and best brothel. Now it is a budget hotel with clean but basic rooms and an excellent Chinese restaurant. *Avenida Almeida Ribeiro, tel. 378–888. 160 rooms with bath. Facilities: restaurant. AE, MC, V.*

$ Grande. A pre–World War II hotel geared for the gamblers who frequent the nearby casinos, the Grande has a European atmosphere and good restaurants. *146 Avenida Almeida Ribeiro, tel. 921–111. 90 rooms. Facilities: restaurants, nightclub/disco. No credit cards.*

$ Ko Wah. Located in a modern building in the Felicidade entertainment district, this guest house is clean and comfortable. *Rua Felicidade, tel. 75452; in Hong Kong, 2540–8180. 30 rooms. No credit cards.*

$ Peninsula. Situated in a harborside block that also contains restaurants and a nightclub, with the floating casino next door, this small hotel has some rooms with great views of the Inner Harbour. *Rua das Lorchas, tel. 318–899; in Hong Kong, 2833–9300. 123 rooms. No credit cards.*

Nightlife

According to old movies and novels about the China coast, Macau was a city of opium dens, wild gambling, international spies, and slinky ladies of the night. It might come as a letdown to some visitors to find the city fairly somnolent after sunset. Most people spend their evenings at the casinos or over long dinners.

Casinos There are eight casinos in Macau: those in the **Lisboa, Mandarin Oriental, Kingsway, and Hyatt Regency** hotels, the **Jai Alai Stadium,** the **Jockey Club,** the **Kam Pek,** and the **Palacio de Macau,** usually known as the floating casino. No one under 18 is allowed in, although identity cards are not checked. Although there are posted betting limits, high rollers are not discouraged by such things. There are 24-hour money exchanges, but most gamblers use Hong Kong dollars.

Discos The **Skylight** is a disco and nightclub, with floor shows three times nightly by English striptease artists. *Presidente Hotel, Ave. da Amizade, tel. 780–923. Admission: 60 patacas; includes one drink. Open 6 PM–4 AM.*

The Lisboa's **Savoy** nightclub is a sleek, slinky place with hostesses, high-tech lighting, and a lively crowd. *Lisboa Hotel, new wing, tel. 577–666. Drink minimum 200 patacas. Open 6 PM–4 AM.*

China City, the most upscale nightclub in Macau, in the Jai Alai Stadium, attracts wealthy local and visiting Hong Kong businessmen and Japanese tourists. The club employs more than 300 hostesses (35 patacas for about 10 minutes of their company in the club) and has a live band and a dance floor. *Jai Alai Stadium, tel. 312–333, drink minimum 200 patacas. Open 6 PM–4 AM.*

The Tonnochy Nightclub is a new rival to China City. It is a sophisticated nightspot in the heart of town, with elegant hostesses, live music for dancing, and private rooms for karaoke parties. *7/F Si Toi Building, 73 Rua da Praia Grande, tel. 372–211. Open 6 PM–4 AM.*

For those who want to dance and maybe have a meal without strobe lights and deafening music, there is the **Portos do Sol** in the Lisboa. It is an attractive room with a live band 8 PM–midnight, later on weekends. The minimum charge is 45 patacas on weekdays, 55 patacas on weekends. There is occasionally a floor show.

Theater **Mona Liza Theater** (Lisboa Hotel). Apart from a few concerts by visiting performers or shows by local artists, theater in Macau means the Crazy Paris Show at the Lisboa, first staged in the late 1970s. The stripper-dancers come from Europe, Australia, and the Americas. The show is very sophisticated and cleverly staged. *Lisboa Hotel, 2nd floor, Avenida da Amizade, tel. 577–666. Daily shows at 8:30 and 10 PM, with additional show on Sat. at 11:30 PM. Admission: HK$90 weekdays, HK$100 weekends and holidays. Tickets available at hotel desks, Hong Kong and Macau ferry terminals, and the theater.*

4 Indonesia

By Nigel Fisher and Lois Anderson

The sheer size of Indonesia is mind boggling. This nation of 165 million people covers 13,677 islands (more than half of them uninhabited) stretching for 5,120 km (3,200 mi) from the Pacific to the Indian Ocean. From north to south, the islands form a 1,760-km (1,100-mi) bridge between Asia and Australia.

The size and diversity of Indonesia are what make the country so fascinating. A visitor has the option of relaxing in one of Bali's luxury resorts or taking a river trip through the jungles of Borneo. Since tourism is a new priority for Indonesia, infrastructure is sporadic. Only in areas slated for tourist development can travelers expect to find services approaching international standards. Elsewhere, expect only modest accommodations and casually scheduled transport. Patience is a key to enjoying Indonesia.

Because of its fertile lands, Java has supported some of Indonesia's mightiest kingdoms. For the same reason, the island has become overcrowded, accounting for 60% of the nation's population. At least 13 million people live in and around Jakarta, the capital. Jakarta already has a range of international hotels, and more are under construction. Efforts are being made to improve the museums, whose displays do not do justice to their wealth of treasure. Offshore, in the Java Sea, Pulau Seribu (Thousand Islands) has resort hotels. Excursions are available to Krakatau (Krakatoa), the island whose volcano erupted with such violence in 1883. Within a two-hour drive of Jakarta are hill towns offering an escape from the tropical heat, tea plantations, botanical gardens, and the volcanic crater of Tangkuban near Bandung, a pleasant university town in the mountains.

As a tourist destination, Jakarta doesn't hold a candle to the rest of the country, but it serves as a convenient gateway to other Indonesian destinations. Central Java, for example, has the architectural wonders of the 9th-century Buddhist Borobudur and Hindu Prambanan temples. Both are within a short drive of Yogyakarta and Solo (Surakarta), towns rich in culture and handicrafts.

Across a 2-mile strait from East Java is the magical island of Bali, with a proud, smiling people whose religion is a unique form of Hinduism blended with Buddhism and animism. Here, distinctive architecture and holy mountains compete for attention with surf-swept beaches and sophisticated hotels.

From Bali, islands stretch eastward like stepping-stones. There is Lombok, offering virgin beaches and the hospitality of Balinese Hindus and Sasak Muslims. The tiny island of Komodo—home to the world's largest reptile, the Komodo dragon—is part of the Lesser Sundas island group, which includes the predominantly Catholic island of Flores, with wonderfully unspoiled physical beauty and crystal-clear waters.

Northeast of Bali is Sulawesi, home to the Bugis, who for centuries have sailed their stout *prahus* (boats) on the Java Sea. Part of the island is inhabited by the Toraja, whose unique animist culture celebrates death as the culmination of life.

West of Sulawesi is Kalimantan, which shares the island of Borneo with Brunei and the Malaysian states of Sabah and Sarawak. Home to the Dayaks, tribal peoples whose generous hospitality is shadowed only by their recent past as headhunters, Kalimantan is for the most part traversed by river.

Farther west is Sumatra, with the popular resort at Lake Toba, where on Samosir Island the Batak people have ornately carved tra-

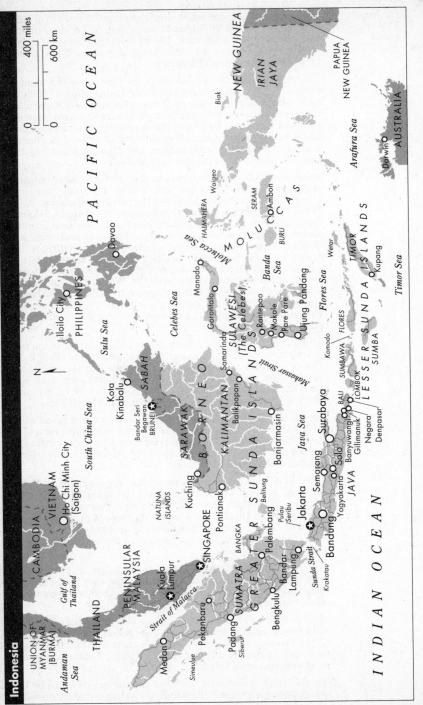

Indonesia

ditional houses built on poles, with high, saddle-shaped roofs. To the south, around Bukit Thinggi, a quiet hill town north of Padang, the Minangkabau live in distinctive houses with buffalo-horn-shaped roofs.

East of Sulawesi are the Moluccas, a group of islands no less fascinating and beautiful than the rest, with jungle-clad volcanoes, beaches, and coral gardens, but virtually ignored by tourists. From the Moluccas, it is less than an hour's flight to Irian Jaya, former Dutch New Guinea. Irian Jaya is rough and mountainous but offers anyone willing to hike along narrow paths from one village to the next the rare opportunity of meeting primitive cultures confronting the 20th century.

From Jakarta's tall steel-and-glass office buildings to Irian Jaya's thatched huts, Indonesia embraces an astonishing array of cultures. The national motto—Unity in Diversity—reflects the proud individualism of the many ethnic groups, who continue to preserve their culture. Today Indonesia's 165 million people—Asmats, Balinese, Bataks, Dayaks, and on down through the alphabet—speak as many as 300 languages, though a national language, Bahasa Indonesia, is officially recognized as a means of binding the population together.

Staying in Indonesia

Getting Around

By Plane Under the current restructuring of government-owned airlines, **Garuda Indonesia Airways** will hand over many of its domestic flights to **Merpati Airlines.** Garuda will retain the routes between major airports, but for shorter hauls Merpati—using either jets or propeller planes—will be the government carrier. A new private airline, **Sempati,** is challenging both Garuda and Merpati with better service and lower fares. **Bouraq,** a quasi-government airline, flies to smaller towns. The airports at Bali, Jakarta, Medan, and Surabaya have been opened to foreign airlines, and the best choice is a foreign carrier, such as Singapore Airlines, into one of these cities.

Reservations are strongly advised on popular routes—between Jakarta and Yogyakarta, for example. Expect delays, especially during the monsoon rains, which can make air travel impossible. You can save up to 60% on domestic flights by buying your tickets in Indonesia instead of overseas. However, if you don't use these tickets, you will not receive a full refund. Garuda offers a **Visit Indonesia Pass** to a minimum of three destinations within Indonesia for US$300 and an additional US$100 for each additional destination.

By Train Only Java has a useful passenger railroad, running east–west across the island. It offers three travel classes, with air-conditioned sleepers available for trips between Jakarta and Yogyakarta and on to Solo and Surabaya. Southern Sumatra has train service between Panjang and Palembang. Except for the Jakarta–Yogyakarta and the Jakarta–Bandung expresses, trains can be slow (and late), and they're not always air-conditioned. You can get schedules and tickets at hotel travel desks, travel agencies, or train stations; schedules are also available at tourist offices.

By Bus The main means of land travel in Indonesia, buses offer varying degrees of comfort. Long-distance expresses are air-conditioned and have reclining seats; some even show video programs. Local buses can be crowded and steaming hot. It's an inexpensive means of transport—the 14-hour trip between Jakarta and Yogyakarta, for instance, costs Rp 17,500 on an air-conditioned express. Tickets and schedules are available from terminals, travel desks, or travel agencies. Tourist offices also provide schedules. For Java and Sumatra, contact **Antar Lintas Sumatra** (Jln. Jati Baru 87A, Jakarta, tel. 021/320970). For Java, Bali, and Sumatra, **PT. ANS** (Jln. Senen Raya 50, Jakarta, tel. 021/340494).

By Boat Ferries run between many of the islands. Hotel travel desks and travel agencies have schedules; you buy your tickets at the terminals. For longer trips, **Pelni,** the state-owned shipping company, serves all the major ports with ships accommodating 500 to 1,000 passengers in four classes. First-class cabins are air-conditioned and have private bathrooms. Schedules and tickets are available from Pelni's head office (Jln. Angkasa 18, Jakarta, tel. 021/416262) or at travel agencies.

By Car Rentals Self-drive rental cars are available only in Jakarta, Yogyakarta, and Bali—and only for use in the vicinity. You'll need an international driver's license. Elsewhere, and for long-distance trips, your rental car includes a driver. A helpful hint: Indonesians love to talk. If your driver gets too chatty, feign sleep so he'll concentrate on the road. But do talk to him occasionally or suggest rest stops to keep him awake and alert.

Road Conditions Indonesia's main roads are in fairly good condition, but side and back roads can be poor. Tourist areas often get very congested, with small trucks, bemos, scooters, bicycles, and pedestrians adding to car traffic.

Rules of the Road Driving is on the left, as in Great Britain. Road signs reading *hati hati* mean "warning."

Gasoline Gas prices are higher than in the States. Stations are few and far between, so don't set out with less than a quarter tank.

By Taxi Registered taxis and hired cars may be hailed on city streets—look for the yellow, number plates. Except in Jakarta and Surabaya and at most airports, you negotiate the fare with the driver before setting out. Most hotels have taxi stands.

By Bajaj Popular in Jakarta, this three-wheeled, two-passenger motor vehicle is less comfortable and less expensive than a taxi but can be faster, since it can scoot amid the traffic. They are hailed on the street, and you negotiate the fare.

By Becak These three-wheeled pedicabs are useful for short distances. In Jakarta they are permitted only in the outlying neighborhoods, but elsewhere in Indonesia they are plentiful. Becak drivers are tough bargainers, but if one doesn't meet your price, another may.

By Bemo A bemo is a converted pickup truck or minivan—a standard form of transport for short trips. Most bemos follow regular routes and will stop anywhere along the way to pick up or discharge passengers. You pay when you get out. Try to learn the fare (they vary according to distance) from another passenger; otherwise you'll be overcharged. An empty bemo will often try to pick up Western travelers, but beware: Unless you clarify that it's on its regular route, you will be chartering it as a taxi.

By Horse Cart Horse-drawn carts are disappearing fast, but they remain popular in Padang and other tourist areas. The cost depends on your bargaining skill.

Telephones

Jakarta's telephone system has improved, and most business establishments have phones, but the rest of the country is less well endowed. In most cases you are best off using hotel phones despite the small surcharges; that way you don't need to amass quantities of coins, and an operator can help with translation and information.

Older public phones take Rp 100 coins, but the newer ones accept only phone cards—a recent introduction restricted to the larger cities and tourist areas. Your best chance of finding a phone is in hotel lobbies. For local calls, three minutes costs Rp 100. For long distance, dial the area code before the number; remember to omit the initial "0" when dialing from overseas.

International Calls Major Indonesian cities are now hooked into the International Direct Dialing (IDD) system via satellite. If you want to avoid using hotel phones, the most economical way to place an IDD call is from the nearest **Kantor Telephone & Telegraph** office. For towns without the IDD hookup, go through the operator (in tourist destinations many speak English). You may make collect calls to Australia, Europe, and North America; for other countries, you need a telephone credit card. Reduced rates on international phone calls are in effect 9 PM–6 AM daily. When calling the States you can also use AT&T's cheaper **USADirect Service.** Dialing 008–0110 will put you in touch with an ATT operator. For information, tel. 412/553–7458, ext. 914, or 800/874–4000, ext. 314. If you're outside the United States, call collect—AT&T will pick up the tab.

Information For operator and directory assistance dial 108 for local calls, 106 for the provinces, and 102 for international.

Mail

Postal Rates Two kinds of airmail are available: regular *(pos udara)* and express *(kilat)*. Kilat rates to the United States or the United Kingdom are Rp 1,200 and Rp 1,300 respectively for postcards and Rp 1,600 and Rp 1,700 for 1 gram (.035 oz) letters.

Receiving Mail In Jakarta, have letters sent to the main post office (open Mon.–Thurs. 8–4, Fri. 8–11 AM, Sat. 8 AM–12:30 PM) addressed to you c/o Central Post Office, Jalan Pos Utara, Jakarta, and marked *poste restante.* Your surname should be written in underlined capitals, with only the initial of your given name, to avoid misfiling. Major post offices outside Jakarta also accept *poste restante.*

Travelers can also use the services of **American Express** (Arthaloka Bldg., Jln. Merdeka Selatan 17, Jakarta, tel. 021/5703310). The office is open weekdays 8:10 AM–midnight, Saturday 8:15 AM–11 PM. You should be a cardholder or be using American Express traveler's checks.

Currency

Indonesia's unit of currency is the rupiah. Bills come in denominations of 100, 500, 1,000, 5,000, 10,000, 20,000, and 50,000 Rp, coins in 5, 10, 25, 50, 100, 500, and 1,000 Rp. Exchange rates at press time were Rp 2,000 = US $1, Rp 3,100 = £1.

What It Will Cost

Prices in Indonesia depend on what you're buying: The basic cost of living is low and domestic labor is cheap, but you pay a premium for anything imported. Thus, renting a car is expensive, hiring a driver is not; camera film is expensive, food is not. Regionally, costs rise in direct relation to tourism and business development. Prices in Bali and Jakarta are relatively high, particularly at deluxe hotels and restaurants. Sumatra and Sulawesi, by contrast, are bargains. In general, Indonesia's prices are comparable to Malaysia's and lower than Thailand's.

Taxes **Hotels** and formal **restaurants** add a 7.5% government tax and a 10% service charge to their bills. In Lombok, the tax is 11%. Departing passengers on international flights pay an **airport departure tax** of Rp 11,000. For domestic travel, airport taxes vary from Rp 3,500 at the smaller airports to Rp 6,500 at Jakarta.

Sample Prices Continental breakfast at hotel, $3; bottle of beer at hotel, $2.50; bottled water, 75¢; Indonesian dinner at good restaurant, $15; 1-mile taxi ride, 75¢; double room, moderate $50–$75, very expensive over $115 ($250 in Jakarta and Bali).

Language

Although some 300 languages are spoken in Indonesia, Bahasa Indonesia has been the national language since independence. English is widely spoken in tourist areas.

Opening and Closing Times

Banks are open from either 8 or 8:30 AM to noon or 2 PM. Bank branches in hotels stay open later. **Government offices** are open Monday–Thursday 8–3 and Friday 8–11:30 AM. Some are also open on Saturday 8–2. **Business offices** have varied hours; some are open weekdays 8–4, others 9–5. Some offices work a half day on Saturday. Most **museums** are open Tuesday–Thursday and weekends 9–2 (although some larger museums stay open until 4 or 5), Friday 9–noon. Most **shops** are open Monday–Saturday 9–5.

National Holidays

The following are national holidays (some are tied to the Muslim or Buddhist calendar, hence the dates vary from year to year): New Year's Day, Jan. 1; Isra Miraj Nabi Mohammed (Mohammed's Ascension), Feb./Mar.; Good Friday; Ascension Day, 40 days after Easter; Lebaran, the last two days of Ramadan (May); Waicak, Birth of Buddha, variable (May); Haji, commemorating Mecca pilgrimages, variable (July); Independence Day, Aug. 17; Birth of Mohammed, variable (Oct.); Christmas Day, Dec. 25.

Festivals and Seasonal Events

Festival dates depend on the type of calendar prevalent in the region where they take place. Most of Indonesia uses the Islamic calendar; the Balinese use a lunar calendar. The **Indonesia Calendar of Events,** with listings for the entire archipelago, is available at Garuda airline offices, or contact the tourist information offices.

Early spring: Galungan, Bali's most important festival, celebrates the creation of the world, marks a visit by ancestral spirits, and honors the victory of good over evil. Celebrants make offerings in family shrines and decorate their villages. On the 10th and last day they bid farewell to the visiting spirits with gifts of *kuningan*, a saffron-yellow rice.

Around Mar. 22: Nyepi, the Balinese New Year, falls on the vernal equinox. New Year's Eve is spent exorcising evil spirits, which are first attracted with offerings of chicken blood, flowers, and aromatic leaves, then driven away with noise as masked youths bang gongs and tin pans. The island falls silent: No fires or lamps may be lit, and traffic is prohibited.

May: Waicak Day, a public holiday throughout Indonesia, celebrates the Buddha's birth, death, and enlightenment.

May: Idul Fitri, two days marking the end of Ramadan (a month of fasting during daylight), is the most important Muslim holiday. Festivals take place in all the villages and towns of Muslim Indonesia.

May–Oct: The **Ramayana Ballet Festival** is held at the Prambanan temple near Yogyakarta during the full-moon week each month. A cast of 500 performs a four-episode dance-drama of the *Ramayana* epic.

Aug. 17: Independence Day is celebrated throughout Indonesia with flag-raising ceremonies, sports events, and cultural performances.

Mid-Oct.: The town of Pamekasan on Java holds **bull-racing finals.** A jockey stands on skids slung between two yoked bulls. The animals are decorated, and there's mass dancing before they run. The winner is judged by which bulls' front feet cross the finish line first.

October: Sekaten commemorates the birth of Mohammed. In Yogyakarta the sultan's antique *gamelan*—a unique Indonesian musical instrument—is played only on this day. The concert is performed in the gamelan pavilion of the *kraton*, the sultan's palace complex. Then the celebrants form a parade, carrying enormous amounts of food from the kraton to the mosque, where they distribute it to the people.

Dec.–Jan.: Kesodo ceremonies are held by the Hindu Tenggerese at the crater of Mt. Bromo on Java.

Tipping

Most **hotels** add a 10% service charge. Some **restaurants** do as well; if not, tip 10%. **Porters** at the airport should receive Rp 500 per bag. **Taxi drivers** are not tipped except in Jakarta and Surabaya, where Rp 300, or the small change, is the minimum. For a driver of a **hired car,** Rp 1,000 for half a day would be the minimum tip. **Private guides** expect a gratuity, perhaps Rp 5,000 per day.

Shopping

Arts and crafts in Indonesia are bargains by U.S. standards. From **Java** the best buys are batik cloth and garments, traditional jewelry, leather *wayang* puppets, and leather accessories. In **Bali,** look for batiks, stone and wood carvings, bamboo furniture, ceramics, silverwork, traditional masks, and wayang puppets. **Sumatra** is best for thick handwoven cotton cloth; carved-wood panels and statues, often in primitive, traditional design; and silver and gold jewelry. From **Sulawesi,** there's filigree silverware, handwoven silks and cottons, hand-carved wood panels, and bamboo goods. Be aware that machine-produced goods are sometimes sold to tourists as handcrafted.

Bargaining Major cities have shopping complexes and department stores where prices are fixed. At small shops, bargaining is necessary. Offer half the asking price, even a third in the tourist areas. You will finish somewhere in between. Shops with higher quality merchandise are likely to take credit cards, but payment in cash puts you in a better bargaining position.

Sports and Beaches

Swimming pools, health clubs, tennis, badminton, and sometimes squash and racquetball are available at the major hotels. There are golf courses near the larger cities. Special adventure tours can be arranged through tour operators.

Scuba Diving Scuba diving is becoming popular, and licensed diving clubs have sprung up around the major resort areas. Flores and North Sulawesi have some of the world's best diving; there is diving also at Pulau Seribu, off Jakarta. For information, call the Indonesian diving organization **Possi** (Jln. Prapatan No. 38, Jakarta, tel. 021/348685).

Spectator Sports Traditional sports include **bull races** in Madura, Java; **bullfights** (bull against bull) at Kota Bharu, near Bukit Thinggi, Sumatra; and **cockfighting** (though it is illegal) in Java, Bali, and Sulawesi.

Beaches **Bali, Lombok, Flores,** and **North Sulawesi** have some of the most beautiful beaches in the world. Bali's Kuta Beach is popular with surfers.

Dining

Warungs are Indonesian street food stalls, sometimes with benches and tables in the open, under canvas, or sheltered by a sheet of galvanized tin. The food here—usually rice dishes and *soto ayam*, the native chicken soup—varies from drab to tasty but is always cheap: You can eat well for Rp 1,000. Warungs are often clustered together at a *pasar malam*, or night bazaar.

Rumah makans are just like warungs, only with fixed walls and roofs. Another step up is the *restoran*, a very broad category. Most are Chinese-owned and serve both Indonesian and Chinese cuisine. The dining rooms of tourist hotels generally offer Chinese, Indonesian, and Western fare; the native specialties are usually toned down. If you enjoy spicy food, you'll be happier at more authentic eateries.

Rice *(nasi)* is the staple of the Indonesian diet. It's eaten with breakfast, lunch, and dinner, and as a snack. But it normally serves as a backdrop to an exciting range of flavors. Indonesian food can be very hot. Your first sample might be *sambal*, a spicy relish made with chilis that is placed on every restaurant table. Indonesians cook with garlic, shallots, turmeric, cumin, ginger, fermented shrimp paste, soy sauce, lime or lemon juice, lemongrass, coconut, other nuts, and hot peppers.

Naturally, fresh fish and shellfish abound throughout Indonesia. Fish *(ikan)* is often baked in a banana leaf with spices, grilled with a spicy topping, or baked with coconut. Shrimp come cooked in coconut sauce, grilled with hot chilis, made into prawn-and-bean-sprout fritters, or, in Sulawesi, with butter or Chinese sweet-and-sour sauce.

For dessert, Indonesians eat fresh fruit: papaya, pineapple, rambutan, salak, and mangosteen. Because this is a mostly Muslim country, wine and alcohol are expensive additions to a meal; beer is your best bet.

Even in Jakarta, you will see well-dressed Indonesians eating with their fingers. Most food comes cut into small pieces, and finger bowls are provided. Tourists normally receive forks.

Drink only bottled water, and avoid ice in any beverage. It's best to steer clear of raw, unpeeled fruits and vegetables.

Throughout this chapter, the following restaurant price categories apply:

Category	Cost*
$$$	over Rp 40,000 (US$20)
$$	Rp 20,000–Rp 40,000 (US$10–US$20)
$	Rp 10,000–Rp 20,000 (US$5–US$10)
¢	under 10,000 (US$5)

per person, not including tax or service

Highly recommended restaurants are indicated by a star ★.

Lodging

Most Indonesian towns offer a range of hotels and three types of rooming houses: *penginapan, losmen,* and *wisma.* Theoretically, the penginapan is cheapest, with thin partitions between rooms, and the wisma most expensive, with thicker walls. The term "losmen" is often used generically to mean any small rooming house. Facilities vary widely: Some Bali losmen are comfortable and social, others dingy and dirty.

The government classifies hotels with star ratings, five stars being the most luxurious. Its criteria are somewhat random, though. No hotel without a garage gets four stars, for example, and most tourists don't need a garage. In general, upkeep and cleanliness correlate with room rates.

You'll find superb resorts—such as the Bali Oberoi and Mandarin Oriental in Jakarta—that cost half what you would expect to pay in Europe. At the bottom range in the less touristed areas, you get a clean room with shower and Asian toilet for less than $2.50 a night.

Category	Cost*
$$$$	over Rp 300,000 (US$150)
$$$	Rp 200,000–RP 300,000 (US$100–US$150)
$$	Rp 150,000–Rp 200,000 (US$75–US$100)
$	Rp 80,000–Rp 150,000 (US$40–US$75)

All prices are for a standard double room, not including 7.5% tax (11% in Lombok) and 10% service charge.

Highly recommended lodgings are indicated by a star ★.

Jakarta

Indonesia's capital is a place of extremes. Modern multistory buildings look down on shacks with corrugated-iron roofs. Wide boulevards intersect with unpaved streets. Elegant hotels and high-tech business centers stand just a few blocks from overcrowded kampongs. BMWs accelerate down the avenues while pedicabs plod along the back streets.

Although the government is trying to prepare for the 21st century, Jakarta has trouble accommodating the thousands who flock to it each year from the countryside. Because of the number of migrant workers who come to the city each day, it is difficult to accurately estimate the city's population. The census reports 7 million, but the true number is closer to 13 million. The crowds push the city's infrastructure to the limit. Traffic grinds to a standstill, and a system of canals, built by the Dutch to prevent flooding in below-sea-level Jakarta, cannot keep pace with the heavy monsoon rains, so the city is sometimes under water for days. The heat and humidity take getting used to. But air-conditioning in the major hotels, restaurants, and shopping centers provides an escape. Early morning and late afternoon are the best times for sightseeing.

As a tourist destination, Jakarta has a limited number of sights, but the government is intent on creating attractions for the overseas visitor, and private enterprise is building new luxury hotels, opening varied and good restaurants, and initiating an entertaining nightlife.

Important Addresses and Numbers

Tourist Information The main branch of the Indonesian tourist office, at Dimas Pariwisata (Jln. Kuningan Baroat 2, Jakarta 12710, tel. 021/511073, fax 021/510738) is difficult to find, and the assistance given is minimal. But the **City Visitor Information Centre** has brochures and maps locating city sights and hotels. You can also get information here on bus and train schedules to other Java destinations. *Jakarta Theatre Bldg., Jln. M.H. Thamrin 9, tel. 021/354094; open Mon.– Thurs. 8–3, Fri. 8–11:30 AM, Sat. 8–2.*

The more comprehensive Falk City Map of Jakarta is available at bookstores for Rp 9,200. The *Jakarta Program*, available at most hotel newsstands for Rp 4,000, is a monthly magazine listing attractions and events.

Embassies Most nations are represented in Jakarta, including the United States (Jln. Medan Merdeka Selatan 5, tel. 021/360360, open weekdays 8–2), United Kingdom (Jln. M.H. Thamrin 75, tel. 021/330904, open weekdays 8:15–4), and Canada (Jln. Jend. Sudirman Kav. 29, 5th floor, Wisma Metropolitan 1, tel. 021/510709, open weekdays 8–2:45).

Emergencies Consult your hotel concierge, if possible, for advice in English. Call 110 for **police,** 119 for **ambulance service,** 118 in **traffic accidents.** For emergency transport, however, **Blue Bird Taxi** (tel. 021/325607) may be more reliable.

Doctors English-speaking staff are available at the 24-hour clinic and pharmacy **SOS Medika Vayasan** (Jln. Prapanca Raya 32–34, tel. 021/ 771575 or 021/733094). A group practice clinic, **Bina Medica** (Jln. Maluku 8–10, tel. 021/344893) provides 24-hour service, ambulance, and English-speaking doctors. **Doctors-on-Call** (tel. 021/683444,

021/681405, or 021/514444) has English-speaking doctors who make house calls. Payment in cash is required.

Dentists Dental services are provided at the **Metropolitan Medical Centre** (Wisata Office Tower, 1st floor, Jln. M.H. Thamrin, tel. 021/320408) and **SOS Medika Clinic Service** (Jln. Prapanca Raya 32–34, Kebayoran Baru, tel. 021/733094).

English-Language Bookstores Major hotel shops carry magazines, newspapers, paperbacks, and travel guides in English. For a larger book selection, try **PT Indira** (Jln. Melawi V/16, Blok M, tel. 021/770584, open Mon.–Sat. 8 AM–8:30 PM) or the **Family Book Shop** (Kemang Club Villas, Jln. Kelurahan Bangka, tel. 021/799–5525, open daily 9:30–8:30). The largest selection is at the **Times Bookshop** on the lower floor of Plaza Indonesia (Jln. M.H. Thamrin 28–30, tel. 021/570–6581).

Late-Night Pharmacies **SOS Medika Vayasan** (Jln. Prapanca Raya 32–34, tel. 021/771575 or 021/733094) is open 24 hours. **Melawai Apotheek** (Jln. Melawai Raya 191, tel. 021/716109) has a well-stocked supply of American medicines.

Travel Agencies Travel agencies arrange transportation, conduct guided tours, and can often secure hotel reservations more cheaply than you could yourself. **Natourin** (18 Buncit Raya, Jakarta 12790, tel. 021/799–7886) has extensive facilities and contacts throughout Indonesia. Three large government-owned travel agencies with branch offices at most Indonesian tourist destinations are **Nitour** (Duta Merlin, Jln. Gajah Mada 3–5, tel. 021/346346), **Pacto** (Jln. Surabaya 8, tel. 021/332634), and **Satriavi** (Jln. Prapatan 32, tel. 021/380–3944).

Arriving and Departing by Plane

Airport and Airlines Jakarta's airport, **Soekarno Hatta,** is a modern showpiece, with glass-walled walkways and landscaped gardens. While most of the area is not air-conditioned, it's breezy and smartly clean. There is a small duty-free shopping area. Terminal A handles international flights and Terminal B serves domestic routes. Between the two terminals, a Visitor Information Centre (tel. 021/550–7088) is open 8 AM–10 PM, closed Sunday and when they feel like it. In both terminals there are **Indotel** desks (tel. 021/550–7179) where hotel reservations may be made, often at discounted rates. There is an airport tax of Rp 17,000 for international departures, Rp 6,600 for domestic departures.

The national carrier is **Garuda Indonesia Airways** (tel. 021/588707). But most people, including Indonesians, prefer a foreign carrier, such as **Singapore Airlines** (tel. 021/587441), **Thai International** (tel. 021/320607), or **Qantas** (tel. 021/326707). Garuda and **Merpati** (tel. 021/348760) cover all 27 provinces. The privately owned **Sempati** (tel. 021/809–4407) flies to many tourist destinations at better prices.

Between the Airport and Center City The airport is 35 km (20 mi) northwest of Jakarta. A toll expressway takes you three-quarters of the way to the city quickly, but the rest is slow going. To be safe, allow a good hour for the trip on weekdays.

By Taxi Taxis *from* the airport add a surcharge of Rp 2,300 and the road toll (Rp 4,000) to the fare on the meter. The surcharge does not apply going *to* the airport. **Blue Bird Taxi** (tel. 021/325607) offers a 25% discount on the toll charge either way. The average fare to a downtown hotel is Rp 17,000. On request, some hotels, such as the Mandarin Oriental, will arrange to have a chauffeur-driven car waiting for you. The cost is Rp 43,200.

By Bus Air-conditioned buses, with DAMRI in big letters on the side, operate every 20 minutes between the airport and six points in the city, including the Gambir Railway Station, Rawamangun Bus Terminal, Blok M, and Pasar Minggu Bus Terminal. The cost is Rp 3,000.

Hotels have stopped offering transfer service, but a **shuttle bus** leaves from the airport to most of the larger hotels. If you are not staying at one of them, catch the shuttle to the hotel nearest yours and take a taxi for the remaining distance. Shuttle bus cost is Rp 4,000.

Arriving and Departing by Train and Bus

By Train Use the **Tanah Abang Railway Station** (Jln. KH Wahid Hasyim, southwest of Merdeka Sq., tel. 021/340048) for trains to Sumatra. All other trains—to Bogor and Bandung or to the east Java cities of Semarang, Yogyakarta, Solo, Surabaya, Madiun, and Malang—start from the **Kota Railway Station** (Jln. Stasiun Kota, south of Fatahillah Square, tel. 021/678515 or 021/679194) or the **Gambir Railway Station** (Jln. Merdeka Timur, on the east side of Merdeka Sq., tel. 021/342777 or 021/348612). Make sure you have the correct station: The Bima train for Yogyakarta, for example, departs from Kota, but the Sinja Maya departs from Gambir.

Tickets may be purchased at the station at least an hour before departure for long distance trains, or from travel agencies, including **Carnation** (Jln. Menteng Raya 24, tel. 021/344027) and **P.T. Bhayangkara** (Jln. Kebon Sirih 23, tel. 021/327387).

By Bus All three bus terminals are off Merdeka Square. **Pulo Gadang** (Jln. Perintis Kemerdekaan, tel. 021/489–3742) serves Semarang, Yogyakarta, Solo, Surabaya, Malang, and Denpensar. Use **Cililitan** (Jln. Raya Bogor, tel. 021/809–3554) for Bogor, Sukabumi, Bandung, and Banjar. **Kalideres** (Jln. Daan Mogot) is the depot for Merak, Labuhan, and major cities in Sumatra. Buy tickets at the terminals or at travel agencies.

Getting Around

By Car Though self-drive rental is available, it is not advised. Traffic congestion is horrendous and parking is very difficult. Cars may be rented from **Avis** (Jln. Doponegoro 25, tel. 021/331974), **Hertz** (Jln. Tenku, C.K. Ditoro 11E, tel. 021/332610), or **National** (Hotel Kartika Plaza, Jln. M.H. Thamrin 10, tel. 021/333423).

By Taxi A cheap and efficient way of getting around, Jakarta's metered taxis charge Rp 900 (47¢) for the first km and Rp 400 (21¢) for each subsequent 100 m. Taxis may be flagged on the streets, and most hotels have taxi stands. Be sure that the meter is down when you set off, and avoid taxis with broken or no meters or you will be seriously overcharged. For a radio-dispatched taxi, call **Blue Bird Taxi** (tel. 021/325607 or 021/799–9000).

By Bus Non-air-conditioned public buses charge a flat Rp 350; the (green) air-conditioned buses charge Rp 500. All are packed during rush hours, and pickpockets abound. The routes can be labyrinthine, but you can always give one a try and get off when the bus veers from your desired direction. For information, contact these companies: **Hiba Utama** (tel. 021/413626 or 021/410381), **P.P.D.** (tel. 021/881131 or 021/411357), or **Mayasari Bhakti** (tel. 021/809–0378 or 021/489–2785).

By Chauffeured Car Air-conditioned, chauffeur-driven cars can be hired for a minimum of two hours, at hourly rates of Rp 11,375 for a small Corona or Rp 21,000 for a Mercedes. Daily charters cost Rp 105,000 and Rp 210,000, respectively. Try **Blue Bird** (tel. 021/325607) or **Hertz** (*see* By Car, *above*).

By Bajaj, Becak, and Bemo: *See* Getting Around in Staying in Indonesia, *above*.

Guided Tours

Gray Line (tel. 021/639–0008) covers most of Jakarta and surrounding attractions. Tourists who show up at the city's tour center at Lapangan Binteng, Bantung Square (open 8 AM) may join any of the tours operating that day, usually at a discounted rate. Hotel tour desks will book the following tours or customize outings with a chauffeured car.

Orientation **City Tour.** This six-hour tour covers the National Monument, Pancasila Monument, Beautiful Indonesia in Miniature Park, and Museum Indonesia.

Indocultural Tour. This five-hour tour visits the Central Museum, Old Batavia, the Jakarta Museum, and a batik factory.

Beautiful Indonesia Tour. This three- to four-hour afternoon tour takes you by air-conditioned bus through the Beautiful Indonesia in Miniature Park (*see* Tour 3), where the architecture and customs of different regions are displayed.

Jakarta by Night. This five-hour trip around the city includes dinner, a dance performance, and a visit to a nightclub.

Excursions Tours beyond Jakarta include the following: a nine-hour trip to **Pelabuhanratu,** a former fishing village that is now a resort; an eight-hour tour to the **safari park** at **Bogor** and the **Botanical Gardens,** 48 km (30 mi) south of Jakarta at a cool 183 m (600 ft) above sea level, and to **Puncak Mountain Resort;** and a two-day tour into the highlands to visit **Bandung** and its volcano, with stops at **Bogor** and **Puncak.**

Highlights for First-time Visitors

Beautiful Indonesia in Miniature Park (*see* Tour 3)

Dunia Fantasi at Ancol (*see* Tour 3)

Fatahillah Square (*see* Tour 1)

Merdeka Square, with the National Monument and National Museum (*see* Tour 2)

Pasar Ikan and Sunda Kelapa Harbour (*see* Tour 1)

A shadow puppet performance at the Museum Wayang (Puppet Museum; *see* Tour 1)

Exploring Jakarta

At Jakarta's center is the vast, parklike Merdeka Square, where Sukarno's 433-foot Monas Monument is topped with a gold-plated flame symbolizing national independence. Wide boulevards line the square, and the Presidential Palace (Suharto does not live here), army headquarters, City Hall, Gambir Railway Station, National Museum, and other government buildings have addresses here.

The square and the area immediately south along Jalan M.H. Thamrin (*jalan* means "street") comprise the Menteng district. This is the downtown of new Jakarta, home to most banks, large corporations, and international hotels. New Jakarta extends southwest, continuing through the district known as Kebayoran to Blok M, where many expatriates live.

North and west of Merdeka Square, around the port of Sunda Kelapa at the mouth of the Ciliwung River, is the Kota area. This is "old town," where the Portuguese first arrived in 1522. A century later, in 1619, the Dutch secured the city, renamed it Batavia, and established the administrative center for their expanding Indonesian empire.

Dutch rule came to an abrupt end when, in World War II, the Japanese occupied Batavia and changed its name back to Jayakarta. The Dutch returned after Japan's surrender, but by 1949 Indonesia had won independence and, abbreviating the city's old name, established Jakarta as the nation's capital.

We deal with the old and the new areas as separate tours, followed by exploration of Jakarta's parks, offshore islands, and other attractions within easy reach.

Numbers in the margin correspond to points of interest on the Jakarta map.

Tour 1: Old Batavia

The heart of the old city, or Kota, as it is known, is **Fatahillah Square,** which is cobbled with ballast stones from old Dutch trading ships. The fountain at its center is a reproduction of one originally built in 1728. This was the last object seen by the criminals who were beheaded in the square while their judges watched from the nearby Town Hall balconies. Just to the north is an old Portuguese cannon whose muzzle tapers into a clenched fist. The clenched fist is a Javanese fertility symbol, and childless women have been known to straddle the cannon.

Around the square are three noteworthy museums, to which we will return. For now, walk up Jalan Cengken, the street leading off from the north side of the square, to the **Pasar Ikan** (fish market). This market is in full swing early in the morning. It's colorful, noisy, smelly, and slimy, and if you can take it, there are great photo opportunities.

Walk through the back of the fish market onto the wharf of **Sunda Kelapa Harbour,** and save the entrance fee, or walk out of the market and enter the port through the main gate. Lined up at oblique angles to the piers are Makassar and Bugis sailing ships (called *prahus*). They look like beached whales, but they sail the Indonesian waters as they have for centuries, trading between the islands. You can negotiate a small boat (punt) for about Rp 1,500–2,000 for a 30-minute tour of the harbor. Because the government plans to develop a tourist marina here and moor the trading ships elsewhere, this scene may soon change. *Admission charge to enter the port. Open daily 8–6.*

On the way back to Fatahillah Square on Jalan Pasar Ikan are two former Dutch East Indies warehouses that have been restored to house the **Maritime Museum** (Museum Bahari). One warehouse contains ancient maps and documents that tell the history of the spice trade; the other is devoted to models of Indonesian sailing vessels.

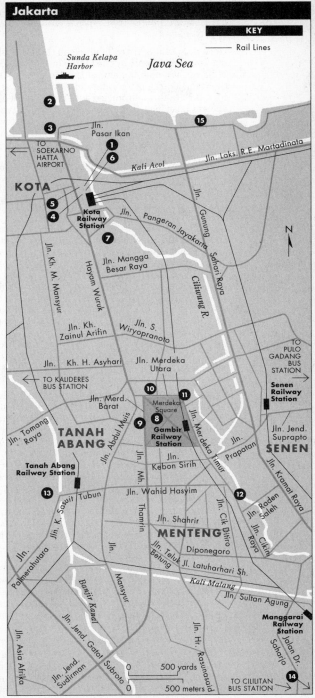

Jakarta

KEY

—— Rail Lines

Neither exhibit is very thorough. *Jln. Pasar Ikan 1, tel. 021/669–0518. Admission charge. Open Tues.–Thurs. 9–2, Fri. 9–11, Sat. 9–1, Sun. 9–3.*

Once in Fatahillah, you'll notice on the south side of the square the old Town Hall, built by the Dutch in 1707. Preserved as a historical building, it's now the site of the **Museum of Old Batavia** (Museum Sejarah Jakart), often referred to as the Jakarta Museum. The history of Batavia is chronicled with antique maps, portraits, models of ancient inscribed Hindu stones, antique Dutch furniture, weapons, and coins. Unfortunately, the exhibits have few explanations in English, and the museum is rather gloomy. Beneath the halls are the dungeons where criminals once awaited trial. Prince Diponegoro, the Indonesian patriot who nearly managed to evict the Dutch from Java in 1830, was imprisoned here on his way to exile in Menado. All you see of the dungeons are the double-barred basement windows along Jalan Pintu Besar. *Jln. Taman Fatahillah No. 1, tel. 021/679101. Admission charge. Open Tues.–Thurs. 9–2:30, Fri. 9–noon, Sat. 9–1, Sun. 9–3.*

On the west side of Fatahillah Square, in a former Protestant church, is the **Puppet Museum** (Museum Wayang). It contains an extensive collection of traditional Indonesian *wayang kulit* (intricately cut leather shadow puppets used to perform stories from the Hindu epics *Ramayana* and *Mahabarata*) and *wayang golek* (wood puppets used to play Arabic folk tales or stories of Prince Panji, a legendary Javanese prince associated with the conversion of Java to Islam), as well as puppets from Thailand, China, Malaysia, India, Cambodia, and elsewhere. Abbreviated wayang kulit shadow plays are performed on Sunday morning. Also on display are puppets used for social education, including wayang kulit used in the Yogyakarta family planning program. *Jln. Pintu Besar Utara No. 27, tel. 021/679560. Admission charge. Open Tues.–Thurs. and Sun. 9–2, Fri. 9–11, Sat. 9–1.*

On the east side of the square is the **Jakarta Fine Art Gallery** (Belai Seni Rupa Jakarta), in the former Palace of Justice, built between 1866 and 1870. The permanent collection includes paintings by Indonesia's greatest artists; contemporary works, such as wood sculptures; and the Chinese ceramic collection of Adam Malik, a former Indonesian vice-president. (A museum in the southeast of the Menteng district, the **Adam Malik Museum,** Jalan Diponegoro No. 29, tel. 021/337400 or 021/337388, has a larger display of his collection.) *Jln. Taman Fatahillah No. 2, tel. 021/676090. Admission charge. Open daily 9–2.*

Time Out The **Fatahillah** café (Jln. Taman Fatahillah No. 14, tel. 021/23842), on the north side of the square, is a friendly place for Indonesian hors d'oeuvres or ice cream and has interesting bric-a-brac for decor.

Behind the Old Town Hall, on Jalan Pangeran Jayakarta opposite the Kota Railway Station, is the oldest church in Jakarta. The exterior is plain, but inside you'll see 17th-century carved pillars, copper chandeliers, solid ebony pews, and plaques commemorating prominent Dutch administrators.

Glodok is Old Batavia's Chinatown. Much of this district has been demolished. But wander around Glodok Plaza (a shopping center and office building—the landmark of the area), and you can still find small streets crowded with Chinese restaurants and shops selling Chinese herbal medicines. Glodok is also a night entertainment district, but unless you know your way around, it's better left to the locals.

Tour 2: New Jakarta

Modern Indonesia is celebrated by Merdeka Square and the towering **National Monument** (Monumen Nasional, or Monas). Local wags call it "Sukarno's last erection," and many have scoffed at this Russian-built phallic symbol commemorating Indonesia's independence. The World Bank supplied funds for 77 pounds of pure gold to coat the "flame of freedom" atop the column while most Indonesians starved. But the monument now stands for Indonesia's impressive economic development. For the visitor it serves as a useful landmark. Take its interior elevator up to just below the flame for a bird's-eye view of the city. *Admission charge.*

In the basement of the monument is the **Museum of National History,** with a gallery of 48 dioramas illustrating Indonesia's history and struggle for independence. The Hall of Independence contains four national treasures: the flag raised during the independence ceremony in 1945; the original text of the declaration of independence; a gilded map of the Indonesian Republic; and the Indonesian coat of arms, which symbolizes the five principles of the Indonesian Republic (belief in one supreme god; a just and civilized humanity; unity of Indonesia; consensus arising from discussion and self-help; and social justice). *Jln. Silang Monas, tel. 021/681512. Admission charge. Open Tues.–Sat. 9–2:30 (Fri. 9–11:30).*

On the west side of Merdeka Square stands the **National Museum** (Museum Nasional), recognizable by the bronze elephant in front—a gift from the King of Thailand in 1871. The museum has the most complete collection of Indonesian antiquities and ethnic artwork in the country. There are five sections: Hindu and Buddhist stone carvings from the 7th to 15th centuries; an exhibit of prehistoric skulls, weapons, and cooking utensils dating back 4,000 years; Indonesian ethnic crafts; a treasure room with gold trinkets, jeweled weapons, and Buddhist statues; and one of the largest collections of Chinese ceramics outside China. If you can time your visit to coincide with one of the free tours given in English—Tuesday, Wednesday, and Thursday at 9:30 AM—you'll appreciate the museum a thousand times more. On Sunday morning there is Javanese or Sundanese gamelan music from 9:30 to 10:30. To the right, as you face the museum, is the museum shop, selling artifacts such as wayang golek or wayang kulit (*see* the Puppet Museum, *above*)—made for tourist sale, but of good quality—and books on Indonesia. *Jln. Merdeka Barat No. 12, tel. 021/360976. Admission charge. Open Tues.–Thurs. 9:30–2, Fri. 9:30–11, Sat. 9:30–1, Sun. 9:30–3.*

From the museum, you may want to make a circle around the square in a taxi. Traveling clockwise, you'll pass the **Presidential Palace** on the northwest corner; the **Istiqlal Mosque** (Jln. Veteren), Indonesia's largest mosque (guided tours are available); and **Emmanuel Church** (Jln. Merdeka Timor 10), a classical Dutch Protestant church built in 1835.

Keep the taxi and continue south down Jalan Cikini Raya to the **Jakarta Cultural Center** (Taman Ismail Marzuki), or TIM. (If you walk, it's about 15 minutes from the south side of the square.) There is something happening here from morning to midnight. Most evenings, either the open-air theater or the enclosed auditorium stages some kind of performance, from Balinese dance to imported jazz, from gamelan concerts to poetry readings. Your hotel will have a copy of the monthly program. Two art galleries display paintings, sculpture, and ceramics. Also within the complex are an art school, an art workshop, a cinema, a planetarium, and outdoor cafés. *Taman Ismail Marzuki, Jln. Cikini Raya No. 73, tel. 021/342605. Admission charge. Open daily 8–8. Shows at the planetarium are Tues.–Sun. 7:30, and Sun. 10, 11, and 1.*

⑬ Directly west from TIM and about 10 minutes by taxi is the **Textile Museum** (Museum Tekstil), with a collection of more than 327 kinds of textiles made in Indonesia and a small workshop demonstrating the batik-making process. It will give you an idea of what to expect by way of design and quality in the fabrics you'll come across when traveling in the country. *Jln. K. Sasuit Tubun No. 4, tel. 021/ 365367. Admission charge. Open Tues.–Thurs. 9–2, Fri. 9–11, Sat. 9–1, Sun. 9–2.*

Tour 3: Green Parks

⑭ About 12 km (7 mi) southeast of Merdeka Square and 30 minutes by taxi is the **Beautiful Indonesia in Miniature Park** (Taman Mini Indonesia Indah). Its 250 acres hold 27 full-size traditional houses, one from each Indonesian province. The Batak houses of North Sumatra, the Redong longhouses of the Kalimantan Dyaks, the cone-shape huts of Irian Jaya, and the Toraja houses of South Sulawesi are all represented. There are even miniature Borobudur and Prambanan temples.

Other attractions include a 30-minute movie, *Beautiful Indonesia*, shown daily from 11 to 5; the Museum Indonesia, with traditional costumes and handicrafts; a stamp museum; the Soldier's Museum, honoring the Indonesian struggle for independence; the Transportation Museum; and Museum Asmat, highlighting the art of the master carvers of the Asmat people of Irian Jaya. The park also has an orchid garden, an aviary, a touring train, cable cars, horse-drawn carts, paddleboats, and places for refreshment. English-speaking guides are available, if you call in advance. *12 km (7 mi) south of central Jakarta, off Jagorawi Toll Rd., tel. 021/849525. Admission charge. Museums open daily 9–3; outdoor attractions open daily 9–5.*

⑮ North of Kota and along the bay stretching east is **Dunia Fantasi at Ancol** on 1,360 acres of land reclaimed in 1962. Billed as Southeast Asia's largest recreation area, it provides entertainment round the clock. A village unto itself, it has hotels, nightclubs, shops, and amusement centers, including an oceanarium with dolphin and sea lion shows, a golf course, a race-car track, swimming pools, and water slides. Here Africa is represented by a comedy of mechanized monkeys, America by a Wild West town, Europe by a mock Tudor house, and Asia by buildings from Thailand, Japan, India, and Korea. Rides, shooting galleries, and food stalls surround these attractions. Because Ancol is near Kota, you may want to spend the afternoon here after touring Old Batavia. Avoid coming on weekends, however, when it is thronged with Jakarta families. *Tel. 021/ 681512. Admission charge. Open daily 24 hrs.*

Short Excursions from Jakarta

The Highlands You can explore some of the lovely countryside around Jakarta in a day trip. The sprawling, smoky city of **Bogor,** 60 km (36 mi) south of the capital, hides several attractions. Travel agents can arrange a visit of the former **presidential palace.** Behind the white-porticoed

building are the **Botanical Gardens** (Kebun Raya Bogor), founded in
1817 by the first English governor-general of Indonesia, maintained
by the Dutch, and adopted by Sukarno. The 275-acre garden has
15,000 species of plants, hundreds of trees, an herbarium, cactus
gardens, and ponds with enormous water lilies. The monument in
the park is of Olivia Raffles, first wife of Sir Stanford Raffles, who
died here at the Bogor Palace. Guides are available at Rp 6,000 an
hour. *Admission charge. Open daily 9–5.*

The road from Bogor winds through tea plantations and rain forests,
past waterfalls and lakes. This is the **Puncak** region, where on clear
days you'll get views of the Gede, Pangrango, and Salak mountains.
If you wish to take a tour, try Panen Travel (Jln. Kyai Caringin 3,
tel. 021/601–0344). At the **Safari Park,** 75 km (46 mi) from Jakarta on
the road to Puncak, you can fondle lion cubs, ride elephants, and
watch other animals roam. *Admission charge. Open daily 9–5.*

Krakatau You'll need to make an overnight trip to see the famous **Krakatau**
(Krakatoa) volcano, in the Sunda Strait between Sumatra and Java.
This Krakatau is actually the son of the volcano that erupted in 1883,
killing 36,000 people and creating marvelous sunsets around the
world for the next two years. The **Carita Krakatau Beach Hotel** (tel.
0254/21043; Jakarta res. tel. 021/314–0252) at Carita Beach, near
Labuan, 150 km (95 mi) west of Jakarta, will arrange trips (including the two-hour sea crossing) to the volcano and is a destination in
itself (*see* Beaches, *below*). Boats leave around 8 AM; the trip takes
2½ hours on speedboats, four hours on slower boats. You'll have two
hours on Anok Krakatoa. Count on spending Rp 100,000 for the speedboats. **Warning:** Don't venture out if the seas are up—the waters get
rough, and some boats never return. You can travel from Jakarta to
Carita Beach by public bus, but the minivans of **P.J. Krakatau**
(Unjung Kulon Tours, Hotel Wisata International, tel. 021/314–
0252) are a lot more comfortable.

Bandung At the turn of the century the Dutch escaped the heat of Jakarta
(Batavia) at Bandung. Situated on a plateau at 760 m (2,500 ft),
enshadowed by majestic volcanoes, Bandung became an oasis of Holland as the Dutch superimposed their culture on the Sundanese. European architects put up Art Deco buildings, and café society
adopted fashions from Paris and Amsterdam. Bandung became the
cultural and intellectual heart of Indonesia, and there was even
speculation that the capital might be transferred to this mountain-
fresh hill town.

The city's status waned after World War II; with independence the
political focus shifted to the tightly centralized government in Jakarta. The Sundanese lifestyle reasserted itself, and now Bandung
is an appealing mix of European and Asian cultures. With overcrowding burdening Jakarta's infrastructure, Bandung is starting
to attract high-tech businesses with its intellectual environment
and its universities, which include the prestigious Institut
Teknologi Bandung.

Getting There Though there are flights from Jakarta, the 187-km (120-mi) train
trip—approximately three hours from Gambir Station, with nine
departures daily—is more scenic: The train travels through flat rice
lands before climbing through the mountains along curving track
and over tressled bridges built by the Dutch in 1884. The road offers
equally spectacular views, and many minibuses make the trip each
day—though fretful passengers may spend more time watching the
next curve than the scenery.

Exploring While the brochures exaggerate the attractions of the city, it does have a pleasant climate—warm days and cold nights—and it's small enough to cover on foot. In the days when Bandung called itself the "Parijs van Java," Jalan Braga was the "Rue St. Honoré." There aren't many remnants of these glory days, but the classic Art Deco **Savoy Homann Hotel** (*see* Lodging, *below*) has been restored at great pains by its current owners. Nearby on Jalan Asia-Africa is the **Gedung Merdeka** (Freedom Building), where in 1955 Chou Enlai, Ho Chi Minh, Nehru, Nassar, and U Nu attended the famous Asia-Africa Conference of nonaligned nations. Walking north back past the Savoy Homann, you'll reach the *alun-alun,* the heart of Bandung; it's a little drab and derelict now, but with the current rejuvenation the alun-alun may soon regain its rightful place.

Continue north along Jalan Braga for 2 km (1¼ mi), passing rather forlorn-looking colonial buildings, until you reach the **Geological Museum** (Jln. Diponegoro; admission free; open daily 9–5). Here you'll find replicas of the fossils of Java Man (*Australopithecus*). Farther north is the **Institut Teknologi Bandung,** designed by Maclaine Pont, a proponent of the Indo-European integrated style, exemplified here by the *Minangkabau* (Sumatran) upturned roofs. Beyond the institute is the **Dago Tea House** and the nearby waterfall with its splendid panorama of the city.

Outside the The highlands surrounding Bandung are known as **Parahyangan**
City (Abode of the Gods) and are sacred to the Sundanese. The first stop on a tour of this area is usually **Lembang,** 16 km (10 mi) north of Bandung. Used by the Dutch as a hill resort, the Lembang Grand Hotel (1926) still stands and offers simple accommodation, with swimming pool and tennis courts, for around $30 (Jln. Raya Lembang 228, tel. 022/82393). Ten km (6 mi) beyond the town is **Tangkuban Perahu Nature Reserve,** featuring the only active volcano in Indonesia whose rim is accessible by car: From the entrance, the narrow road winds 4 km (2½ mi) up to the crater's edge. The souvenir stands and hawkers are a nuisance, but the crater, shaped like an upturned boat and boiling and seething with sulfurous steam, is dramatic. Several kilometers away is **Ciater Hot Springs,** with public baths that visitors may use to soothe nervous tension and cure skin problems. Also near Lembang is **Maribaya,** where families from Bandung come on the weekend to picnic and wander the park's nature trails.

In many nearby villages, Sunday morning is the time for the weekly *adu domba* (ram fights). Facing off two at a time, the prize rams bang, crash, and lock horns until one contestant decides that enough is enough and scampers off. It's as much a social event as a serious sport (though the wagerers take it seriously) and shouldn't be missed if you're around on the weekend.

From Bandung, travelers can continue on to Yogyakarta by air or rail (eight hours). The night train has second-class compartments with reclining seats, air-conditioning, and blankets. The day train lacks these amenities, and sometimes it lacks second-class carriages. The optimal way to get from Bandung to Yogyakarta is to hire a car with a driver, which costs approximately US$100 and may be arranged through your hotel.

What to See and Do with Children

Beautiful Indonesia in Miniature Park *(see* Tour 3)

Fantasy World (Dunia Fantasi at Ancol) *(see* Tour 3)

The **planetarium** at the Jakarta Cultural Center *(see* Tour 2) has astronomy shows. *Jln. Cikini Raya No. 73, tel. 021/342605. Admission charge. Show times Tues.–Sun. at 7:30 PM, Sun. also at 10 AM, 11 AM, and 1 PM.*

Indonesian zoos are notorious, but the **Ragunan Zoo & Botanical Gardens** is better than most—not very comprehensive, but pleasant. Joggers make use of it in the mornings and evenings. *Jln. Harsomo R.M., Pasar Minggu, tel. 021/780–6164. Admission charge. Open daily 7 AM–6 PM.*

Shopping

Markets **Jalan Surabaya Antiques Stalls** (Pasar Barang Antik Jalan Surabaya, in the Menteng residential area), the "flea market" of Jakarta, has mundane goods at either end, but in the middle you might find delftware, Chinese porcelain, old coins, old and not-so-old bronzes, and more. You *must* bargain. *Open daily 9–6.*

Pasar Melawai (Blok M, Jln. Melawai) is a series of buildings and stalls with everything from clothing to toys, cosmetics, and fresh foods. English is spoken. *Open daily 9–6.*

Department Stores Jakarta's largest department store, **Pasaraya** (Jln. Iskandarsyah 1½ in Blok M, tel. 021/7390170), tempts you to visit its multistory complex to see Indonesia's latest in women's fashions and handicrafts by paying your taxi fare if you are staying at a five-star hotel. Check with your hotel's concierge for a coupon. The city's newest shopping center is **Plaza Indonesia** (Jln. M.H. Thamrin, tel. 021/310–7540), under the Grand Hyatt and across the square from the Mandarin Oriental. Among its 250 stores are upscale boutiques, art and antiques galleries, bookshops, travel agents, Sogo's food store, and restaurants.

Specialty Stores
Antiques For serious antique shopping, try Jalan Paletehan I (Kebayoran Baru), Jalan Maja Pahit and Jalan Gajah Mada (Gambir/Kota), Jalan Kebon Sirih Timur and Jalan H.A. Salim (Mentang), and Jalan Ciputat Raya (Old Bogor Rd.). Some reliable shops are **NV Garuda Arts, Antiques** (Jln. Maja Pahit No. 12, Kota, tel. 021/342712), **Madjapahit Art and Curio** (Jln. Melawai III/4, behind Sarinah Jaya Department Store, tel. 021/715878), and **Alex Papadimitiou** (Jln. Pasuruan No. 3, Meteng, no sign, tel. 021/348748). For antique Chinese porcelain, visit **Cony Art Antiques** (Jln. Malawai Raya 180E, tel. 021/716554) in the Kebayoran district.

Handicrafts The **Sarinah** department store's third floor is devoted entirely to handicrafts (Jln. M.H. Thamrin 11, Menteng, tel. 021/323705), which you can also find in abundance at its larger sister store, Pasaraya (*see above*).

Textiles **Batik Mira** (Jln. MPR Raya No. 22, tel. 021/761138) has expensive but excellent-quality batik. Its tailors will do custom work, and customers can ask to see the factory at the rear of the store.

Batik Semar (Jln. Tornang Raya 54, tel. 021/567–3514) has top-quality batik with many unusual designs. **Batik Danar Hadi** (Jln. Raden Saleh No. 1A, tel. 021/342748) carries a large selection of batik. **Bin House** (Jln. Panarukan No. 33, tel. 021/335941) carries Indonesian handwoven silks and cottons, including ikat, plus antique textiles and objets d'art. Iwan Tirta is a famous designer of batik fabrics and clothing for men and women. His company and shop go by the name **PT Ramacraft** (Jln. Panarukan No. 25, tel. 021/333122). At the **Pla-**

za Indonesia shopping complex (*see* Department Stores, *above*), especially on the first floor, there are chic, fashionable batiks for sale.

Sports and Fitness

Diving   **Jakarta Dive School and Pro Shop** (Hilton Hotel, Bazaar Shop No. 32, Jln. Jend. Sudiman, tel. 021/583051, ext. 9008) offers open-water lessons and equipment rental. **Dive Indonesia** (Borobudur Hotel, Jln. Lapangan Banteng Selatan, tel. 021/370108) specializes in underwater photography and arranges trips to Flores and Sulawesi islands. On Pulau Sepa is the **Thousand Island Resort and Diving Center** (Jln. Kalibesar Barat 29, tel. 021/678828).

Golf   Jakarta has two well-maintained 18-hole golf courses open to the public, both extremely crowded on weekends: the **Ancol Golf Course** (Dunia Fantasi at Ancol, tel. 021/682122), with pleasant sea views, and **Kebayoran Golf Club** (Jln. Asia-Afrika, Pintu No. 9, tel. 021/582508).

Health and Fitness Centers   You can get a good workout in Jakarta whenever you need one. The **Clark Hatch Physical Fitness Center** has two facilities with up-to-date equipment plus massage, heat treatment, sauna, and whirlpool (Hotel Borobudur Intercontinental, Jln. Lapangan Banteng Selatan, tel. 021/370108, and Jakarta Hilton Hotel, Jln. Jend. Gatot Subroto, tel. 021/583051). Other gyms include the **Medical Scheme** (Setiabudi Bldg. L., Jln. H.R. Rasuda Said, Kuningan, tel. 021/515367), **Pondok Indah Health and Fitness Centre** (Jln. Metro Pondok Indah, tel. 021/764906), and **Executive Fitness Centre** (ground floor, south tower, Kuningan Plaza, Jln. H.R. Rasuda Said, tel. 021/578–1706).

Jogging   The **Hash House Harriers/Harriettes,** an Australian jogging club, has a chapter in Jakarta. Men run Monday at 5 PM, women Wednesday at 5 PM, and there's socializing in between. For meeting places and running routes, write to Hash House Harriers/Harriettes (HHH Box 46/KBY, Jakarta, tel. 021/799–4758).

Racquetball   The **Borobudur Hotel** (Jln. Lapangan Bateng Selatan, tel. 021/370108) has courts.

Squash   Nonguests can play squash at three top hotels when the courts are not fully booked: **Borobudur Hotel** (Jln. Lapangan Banteng Selatan, tel. 021/370108), **Jakarta Hilton International** (Jln. Jend. Gatot Subroto, tel. 021/583051), and **Mandarin Oriental** (Jln. M.H. Thamrin, tel. 021/321307).

Swimming   Most of Jakarta's tourist hotels have pools. **Dunia Fantasi at Ancol** has a four-pool complex with a wave pool (*see* Tour 3).

Beaches

The Thousand Islands   North of Jakarta in the Java Sea are the little **Pulau Seribu,** or Thousand Islands—a misnomer, because there are only 250 of them (*pulau* means island). Their white-sand beaches, covered with coconut palms, offer a retreat from the heat and bustle of the capital. For a day trip, you can hop over to **Kepulauan Seribu** by motorboat from Marina Jaya Ancol (tel. 021/681512), or take a hovercraft (the port is at Jln. Donggala 26A, Tanjun Priok, tel. 021/325608). Several islands have rustic getaways, such as the Kotok Island Resort, with 42 unspoiled acres of coconut groves and tropical foliage, plus good scuba diving and snorkeling (*see* Lodging, *below*). Accommodations are also available on Pulau Patri, Pulau Melinjo, Pulau Bidadari, and Pulau Onrust.

For island bookings, contact **PT Pulau Seribu Paradise** (Setiabudi Bldg. 1, ground floor, block C1, tel. 021/515884), **PT Seabreeze** (Marina Ancol, tel. 021/680048), **PT Sarotama Prima Perkasa** (Jln. Ir. H. Juanda III/6, tel. 021/342031), or **Pulau Seribu Marine Resort PT Pantara** (Wisata Jaya Rm., 6/7 Borobudur Hotel, Jln. Lapangan Banteng Selatan, tel. 021/370108).

Carita Beach Quiet and unspoiled, Carita Beach lies 150 km (95 mi) west of Jakarta. The **Carita Krakatau Beach Hotel** (tel. 0254/21043, fax 0254/330846) has equipment for all water sports and arranges trips to the Krakatau volcano, a four-hour (round-trip) boat ride away (*see* Short Excursions from Jakarta, *above*). Air-conditioned buses leave daily from the hotel's reservation office in Jakarta (ground floor arcade, Hotel Wisata International, Jln. M.H. Thamrin, tel. 021/320252 or 320408, ext. 125). Those who take the bus get a 25% discount on their first night's stay at the hotel.

Dining

All the major hotels have Western and Indonesian restaurants; many of the Indonesian restaurants also offer Chinese food. Outside the hotels, dining options range from restaurants providing formal atmosphere to inexpensive street stalls. The following terms appear frequently on Indonesian menus:

bakmi goreng—fried noodles with bits of beef, pork, or shrimp, tomatoes, carrots, bean sprouts, cabbage, soy sauce, and spices
dendeng ragi—thin squares of beef cooked with grated coconut and spices
gudeg—chicken with jackfruit
ikan—fish
kelian ayam—Sumatran chicken curry
nasi champur—steamed rice with bits of chicken, shrimp, and vegetables with sambal
nasi goreng—fried rice with shallots, chilies, soy sauce, and ketchup; at breakfast, likely to be topped with a fried egg; at other meals, may include pork (in Bali), shrimp, onions, cabbage, mushrooms, or carrots
nasi rames—a miniature rijstaffel
rijstaffel—literally, "rice table"; steamed rice with side dishes such as sayur lodeh, gudeg, or kelian ayam
sambal—a spicy, chili-based relish
satay—grilled skewered *ayom* (chicken), *babi* (pork), *daging* (beef), *kambing* (lamb), or ikan, with a spicy peanut sauce
sayur lodeh—a spicy vegetable stew
soto ayam—chicken soup, varying from region to region but usually including shrimp, bean sprouts, spices, chilies, and fried onions or potatoes.

$$$
Chinese
★
The Spice Garden. The Taiwanese chef at this elegant, high-ceilinged restaurant prepares 160 spicy Szechuan specialties, including sliced braised chicken with hot pepper oil and abalone soup with fermented black beans. You'll also have the opportunity to try an excellent bird's nest soup and stir-fried lobster in a hot black bean sauce. The crimson-and-gold decor includes batik wall hangings by renowned designer Iwah Tirta. *Mandarin Oriental Hotel, Jln. M.H. Thamrin, tel. 021/321307. Reservations advised. Dress: semiformal. AE, DC, MC, V.*

$$$
Continental
Oasis. The Oasis—after decades, still the most popular restaurant among Western visitors—serves international cuisine as well as a traditional rijstaffel. A specialty is medallions of veal Oscar, in a

Jakarta Dining and Lodging

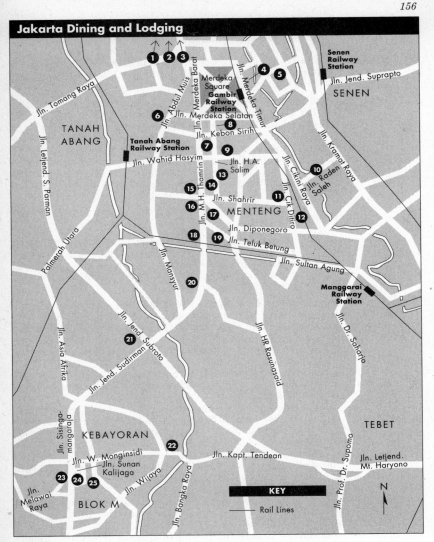

Dining

The George and Dragon/George's Curry House, **19**

Green Pub, **7**

Handayani, **6**

In the Streets of Jakarta, **21**

Le Bistro, **9**

Manari, **20**

Mira Sari, **23**

Natrabu, **8**

Oasis, **10**

Omar Khayyam, **12**

Paregu, **24**

Pondok Laguna, **2**

Sari Kuring, **4**

The Spice Garden, **17**

Tora-Ya, **13**

Lodging

Grand Hyatt, **15**

Hotel Borobudur Intercontinental, **5**

Hotel Indonesia, **16**

Hotel Wisata International, **18**

Interhouse, **25**

Jayakarta Tower, **3**

Kebayoran Inn, **22**

Kotok Island Resort, **1**

Mandarin Oriental, **17**

Marcopolo, **11**

President Hotel, **14**

cream sauce with mushrooms, crabmeat, and asparagus. The atmosphere lives up to the cuisine in this lovely old house decorated with tribal art and textiles. A combo alternates with Batak singers to provide music nightly. *Jln. Raden Saleh No. 47, tel. 021/326397. Reservations necessary. Dress: semiformal. AE, DC, V. Closed Sun.*

$$$
French
Le Bistro. Candlelit and intimate, with checked tablecloths and copper pots, the decor here puts you in the mood for the classic Provençal menu—simple food, prepared with herbs, from the south of France. Try the roast chicken with rosemary and thyme. At the back of the dining room is a circular piano bar where you can have an after-dinner liqueur and maybe persuade one of the hostesses to sing. *Jln. K.H. Wahid Hasyim 75, tel. 021/364272. Reservations recommended. Jacket and tie suggested. AE, DC, V.*

$$$
Japanese
Tora-Ya. Some say this is Jakarta's best Japanese restaurant. The several attractive small dining rooms, each with a clean, spare decor, reflect the Japanese aesthetic. The service is low-key and very good. Both sushi and *kaiseki* (banquet) cuisine are offered. *Jln. Gereja Theresia No. 1, tel. 021/310–0149. Reservations suggested. Jacket and tie required. AE, DC, V.*

$$
British
The George and Dragon. For a change from rice dishes, try this restaurant for fish-and-chips or steak, kidney, and mushroom pie. The atmosphere is informal, and the bar, the first British pub in Jakarta, is very friendly. The decor is warm and cozy, with lots of wood. **George's Curry House** next door is under the same management and serves Indian, Sri Lankan, and Sumatran curries. Specialties include *tandoori murk*, chicken marinated in yogurt and spices, then charcoal-roasted. *Jln. Teluk Betung No. 32, tel. 021/325625. Reservations advised for weekends at George's Curry House. Dress: casual. AE, V.*

$$
Indonesian
Handayani. This is a true neighborhood restaurant, with friendly service and some English-speaking help. Decor is not its strong point—lines of tables and chairs in a bare room. But Handayani is popular with locals for its Indonesian food. The extensive menu offers such dishes as chicken bowels steamed in banana leaves, beef intestine satay, and goldfish fried or grilled, along with lobster-size king prawns cooked in a mild chili sauce. The *nasi goreng Handayani* is a special version of the Indonesian staple. *Jln. Abdul Muis No. 35E, tel. 021/373614. Reservations not necessary. Dress: casual. DC, V.*

$$
Indonesian
In the Streets of Jakarta. Around the pool on Friday night, the Hilton hotel creates a completely "safe" version of the food stalls found throughout the city, with satays, Indonesian fried chicken, and various rice dishes. Since the Hilton is in the expatriate district, you'll see many Europeans dropping in for Friday night dinner. *Jakarta Hilton International, Jln. Jend. Gatot Subroto, tel. 021/583051. Reservations advised for Fri. night. Jacket and tie suggested. AE, DC, MC, V.*

$$
Indonesian
Manari. The menu at this popular restaurant, where locals often take their foreign guests, is primarily Indonesian, with additional selections from China (Canton) and Thailand. But it's not for food that Manari is known so much as for its varied dinnertime cultural performances—dances and songs from Indonesia's multi-ethnic heritage. *Jln. Jend. Gatot Subroto No. 14, tel. 021/516102. Reservations advised. Dress: smart casual. AE, MC, V.*

$$
Indonesian
Mira Sari. Regional Indonesian specialties are served in the air-conditioned dining room, in the garden, or on the terrace. Comfortable rattan chairs with soft pillows, fresh flowers on the tables, and warm, friendly service make this a congenial spot. The menu includes a very good version of Indonesian chicken soup, excellent

spiced grilled fish, prawns grilled with spices and chilies, and roast or fried spiced chicken. *Jln. Patiunus 15, tel. 021/771621. Reservations required. Jacket and tie suggested. No credit cards.*

\$\$ **Natrabu.** Decor at this popular Padang restaurant is minimal: bare
Indonesian tabletops and side booths, red Sumatran banners hanging from the ceiling, and a model of a Minangkabau house set in a corner. Waiters wearing Padang headscarves deliver bowls of food from the moment you sit down. You can order, or you can select from the dishes they bring you—you pay for the ones you try. *Jln. H.A. Salim (often called Jln. Sabang) 29A, tel. 021/335668. No reservations. Dress: casual. MC, V.*

\$\$ **Pondok Laguna.** This is one of Jakarta's most popular restaurants.
Indonesian The large dining room, divided by water pools and falls, is always
★ crowded with families and young couples. The noise level is fairly high and the service casual. Some of the staff speak English; all are anxious to help foreign guests. Primarily fish is served—either fried or grilled and accompanied by different sauces ranging from hot to mild. Whatever you choose, the fish is fresh and cooked to perfection. *Jln. Batu Tulis Raya 45, tel. 021/359994. Reservations accepted for parties of 8 or more. Dress: casual. AE, DC, MC, V.*

\$\$ **Sari Kuring.** This restaurant near Merdeka Square serves very good
Indonesian Indonesian seafood, especially the grilled prawns and fried Thai-
★ land fish "à la Sari Kuring," marinated in spices, then quickly fried. The restaurant is large, but on many levels connected by stone steps, so there is a feeling of some intimacy. If you are unable to secure a table here, try next door at **Sari Nusantara** (tel. 021/352972). The fare is similar except for a slight Chinese influence in the cooking and fewer spices in the sauces. *Jln. Silang Monas Timur 88, tel. 021/352972. Reservations suggested. Dress: casual. AE, V.*

\$\$ **Green Pub.** The Green Pub is recommended not only for its Mexican
Mexican food but for live country-western music (6:30–9) and jazz (9:30–1). The decor is somewhere between a Western saloon and a Mexican ranch, with tapestries adorning the walls. The burritos and enchiladas are quite authentic. Recently the menu has added Tex-Mex dishes, such as barbecued spare ribs. *Jakarta Theatre Bldg., Jln. M.H. Thamrin 9, tel. 021/359332, or Jln. H.R. Rasuna Said, Setia Budi Bld. 1, tel. 021/517983. No reservations. Dress: casual. AE, V.*

\$\$ **Paregu.** This is the place for the best Vietnamese food in town and
Vietnamese top-notch service. The decor is simple with Oriental embellishments. Try the Vietnamese version of spring rolls; fried rice with scrambled eggs, chicken, shrimp, and a blend of herbs and spices; and the herbed seafood. *Jln. Sunan Kalijaga No. 64, tel. 021/774892. Reservations suggested. Dress: casual. No credit cards.*

\$ **Omar Khayyam.** In addition to an Indian buffet lunch, there is an ex-
Indian tensive menu of specialties, including very good curries and tandoori dishes. The restaurant's decor gives homage to the eponymous Persian poet: Some of his poetry is inscribed on the walls. Try the chicken *tikka makhanwalla*, boneless tandoori chicken with tomato, butter, and cream sauce; or the marinated fish, wrapped in a banana leaf and deep-fried. *Jln. Antara No. 5–7, tel. 021/356719. No reservations. Dress: casual. No credit cards.*

Lodging

Jakarta has some world-class accommodations, with all the modern amenities. Most international hotels are south of Merdeka Square. Besides the Mandarin Oriental, the Grand Hyatt, and the Borobudur Intercontinental, the other leading hotels are the Jakarta Hilton, between the new center and Blok M, and the Hyatt Aryaduta, near Gambir Station. A recent spate of openings, including the Shangri-La high rise and the Regent, has brought a surfeit of five-star hotels—which means that actual rates should be far better than the published ones.

$$$$ **Grand Hyatt.** Glitter and shining-marble modernity characterize this 1992 hotel. You enter the four-story atrium lobby and mount a palatial staircase (or take the escalator) to the reception area. One more short flight up brings you to the expansive Fountain Lounge, where you can watch the stalled traffic on Jalan M.H. Thamrin. On the fifth floor is the pool garden, an extensive area of greenery with a patio restaurant. The hotel is rather overwhelming and lacks the personal touches of its neighbor, the Mandarin Oriental. Rooms are spacious, each with two bay windows; bathrooms have a separate shower stall and toilet. Furnishings are in the ubiquitous pastels, but pleasant nonetheless. Beneath the Hyatt is the Plaza Indonesia (*see* Shopping, *above*), with restaurants and nightclubs in addition to 250 shops: In a city that sprawls without a center, this proximity to a "social center" is an advantage. *Jln. M.H. Thamrin, Jakarta 10230, tel. 021/390–1234 or 021/310–7400, fax 021/334321. 413 rooms, 47 suites. Facilities: 5 restaurants (Cantonese, Indonesian, Japanese, Western, seafood), outdoor pool, 6 lighted tennis courts, 2 squash courts, business center, fitness center, jogging track, massage. AE, DC, MC, V.*

$$$$ **Hotel Borobudur Intercontinental.** Billed as "your country club in Jakarta," this large, modern hotel complex boasts 23 acres of landscaped gardens and excellent facilities. Floor-to-ceiling windows at the back of the Pendopo Lounge look out onto the tropical gardens, which makes the lounge a delightful place for afternoon tea, cocktails, or snacks. The guest rooms, except those on floors nine and 16, have been renovated to conform to a modern Javanese design. These rooms are quite compact. The Garden Wing has suites with kitchens. The Music Room disco has the feel of a private club. Restaurants include the Toba Rotisserie for Continental cuisine, the Keio Japanese Restaurant, the Nelayan Seafood Restaurant, and the Bogor Brasserie for informal meals and snacks. Reserve a room overlooking the gardens and the swimming pool, not facing the car park. *Jln. Lapangan Banteng Selatan, Box 329, Jakarta 10710, tel. 021/380–5555, fax 021/359741. 852 rooms, including 140 suites in the Garden Wing. Facilities: 4 restaurants, tea/cocktail lounge, disco, 24-hr room service, Olympic-size pool, 8 tennis courts, 5 squash courts, racquetball, badminton court, jogging track, minigolf course, fitness center, business center, children's play area, conference and banquet facilities. AE, DC, MC, V.*

$$$$ **Hotel Indonesia.** Built for the Asian Games in 1962, the Hotel Indonesia was Jakarta's first high rise. It offers comfort, if not luxury; the big lobby, with a shopping arcade to the side, is cold and unwelcoming. Room decor is modern, with spare hotel furniture, but with Indonesian-patterned bedcovers and framed batik on the walls. The rooms are utilitarian, with color TV and minibar. *Jln. M.H. Thamrin, Box 54, Jakarta 10310, tel. 021/390–6262, fax 021/321508. 600 rooms. Facilities: 2 restaurants, bar, large outdoor pool, conference facilities. AE, DC, MC, V.*

$$$$ **Mandarin Oriental.** This is the most sophisticated hotel, with the
★ best service, in Jakarta. The circular, elegant lobby has three tall, beautifully carved Batak roofs, each housing a Sumatran statue. An open mezzanine above the lobby provides comfortable seating for tea or cocktails and some elegant shops, including a gallery for Ida Bagus Tilem, Bali's master wood-carver. The guest rooms are spacious and have top-quality furnishings: thick russet carpeting, floral bedspreads, off-white draperies on the picture windows, and dark

wood furniture. Complimentary afternoon tea and hors d'oeuvres are delivered to your room. Most of the rooms are "executive" (deluxe), with butler service. (A nominal extra fee gives you use of the executive lounge for concierge assistance, and complimentary breakfast and cocktails.) The location is central, and with the Plaza Indonesia shopping complex and the Hyatt across the square, there are shops, restaurants, and bars within a two-minute walk. Restaurants include Pepe's, with classic Italian cuisine, the Spice Garden (*see* Dining, *above*), the Clipper Lounge for light meals, the Pelangi Terrace for breakfast or buffet lunch by the pool, and the Captain's Bar. *Jln. M.H. Thamrin, Box 3392, Jakarta 10310, tel. 021/321307, fax 021/324669; U.S. reservations, tel. 800/526–6566. 455 rooms. Facilities: 4 restaurants, cocktail bar, 24-hr room service, health center, outdoor pool, sauna, business center, meeting and conference rooms. AE, DC, MC, V.*

$$$ **Hotel Wisata International.** Ranked as a three-star hotel by the government, the ungainly Wisata is off Jakarta's main thoroughfare. Corridors are long and narrow, guest rooms compact but clean. Each room has a king-size bed; a television and safe take up most of the remaining space. Rooms on the executive floor are only marginally larger. Still, the price, the convenient restaurant off the lobby, and the central, safe location make the Wisata a reasonable choice. *Jln. M.H. Thamrin, Jakarta 10230, tel. 021/320308, fax 021/315–0578. 181 rooms. Facilities: 24-hr coffee shop, lounge bar, meeting rooms. AE, DC, MC, V.*

$$$ **Kotok Island Resort.** On 42 unspoiled acres of coconut groves, this resort two hours from Jakarta by boat owns all the island except the eastern tip, which belongs to a private Japanese club. The resort has 22 bungalows with bamboo walls and basic bamboo furniture, plus a tiled shower bathroom. Eight units are air-conditioned, but thanks to the sea breezes, the rest are comfortable with just an overhead fan. This is a back-to-nature environment, and the accommodations are rustic, with primitive plumbing. The dining room—an open-air pavilion over the water—serves well-prepared Indonesian specialties, especially grilled fresh fish. Licensed instructors give scuba-diving courses. The resort provides a launch service from Jakarta. *The reservation office is at the Duta Merlin Shopping Arcade, 3rd floor, Jln. Gajah Mada 3–5, Jakarta, tel. 021/362948. 22 rooms. Facilities: restaurant, bar, boutique, diving center (diving packages available). No credit cards, unless you book through a travel agent.*

$$$ **President Hotel.** Like many other hotels in the Japanese Nikko Hotel group, the President has a spare, utilitarian atmosphere but is equipped with all the modern amenities. Guest rooms are simple, with blue-and-navy striped fabrics and plain wood furniture. The bathrooms are small. The President offers good Japanese food at its Ginza Benkay restaurant, Japanese and Indonesian at the Kahyangan, and Chinese at the Golden Pavilion. *Jln. M.H. Thamrin 59, Jakarta 10350, tel. 021/320508, fax 021/333–6310. 354 rooms. Facilities: 3 restaurants, cocktail lounge, coffee shop, banquet and conference facilities. AE, DC, MC, V.*

$$ **Jayakarta Tower.** This tourist-class hotel is within walking distance
★ of Kota. The marble lobby is accented with hand-blown chandeliers and carved-wood panels. The coffee shop's menu includes Western and Indonesian specialties, but ask to see the special Thai menu. Guest rooms are spacious. Each has a double or two twin beds, with Javanese patterned spreads, plus a table and two chairs and a vanity/desk. Only executive rooms have minibars. Restaurants include the Munakata, a branch of a Tokyo restaurant, and the Dragon, a Chinese restaurant with a separate Thai menu—the better choice. Next door, and affiliated with the hotel, is the Stardust Disco-

theque. The hotel is now affiliated with KLM's Golden Tulip hotels, and reservations may be made through the airline. *Jln. Hayam Wuruk 126, Box 803, Jakarta 11001, tel. 021/629–4408, fax 021/626–5000. 435 rooms. Facilities: 2 restaurants, coffee shop, 24-hr room service, disco, large outdoor pool, health center, meeting and banquet rooms. AE, DC, MC, V.*

$ **Interhouse.** Centrally located in Kebayoran—the expatriate neighborhood and shopping district—this hotel offers comfortable, though not large, air-conditioned rooms with pleasant, homey furnishings and usually a pastel decor. *Jln. Melawai Raya No. 18–20, Box 128/KBYB, Jakarta, tel. 021/720–6694, fax 021/706988. 130 rooms. Facilities: restaurant. AE, V.*

$ **Kebayoran Inn.** Just south of the center of Jakarta, this is a quiet, residential-type lodging. The clean, air-conditioned rooms are simply decorated, with an Indonesian batik or ikat here and there. *Jln. Senayan 87, Jakarta 12180, tel. 021/775968, fax 021/560–3672. 61 rooms. Facilities: restaurant. AE, V.*

$ ★ **Marcopolo.** This basic and economical hotel caters to businesspeople and tourists alike. Often you will find businesspeople here who were unable to obtain a reservation at a five-star hotel. The staff is helpful, and while the carpeted rooms are plainly decorated, they are clean, adequate, and fully air-conditioned. The restaurant serves good Chinese and European food. *Jln. T. Cik Ditiro 19, Jakarta 10350, tel. 021/325409, fax 021/310–7138. 181 rooms. Facilities: restaurant/coffee shop, outdoor pool, nightclub. AE, V.*

Bandung $$ ★ **Savoy Homann.** It's neither the priciest nor the most up-to-date in town (for that, try the Grand Hotel Preager), but the Savoy Homann is loaded with character. Built in the 1880s, it acquired its Art Deco design in 1930. In the evening, guests gather at the bar in the central courtyard to listen to the band. The superior rooms are the size of small suites, usually with a sitting area, and look onto either the street (windows are double-glazed) or the courtyard. The English-speaking staff is very friendly. *Jln. Asia-Afrika 112, Bandung 40261, tel. 022/432244, fax 022/436187. 153 rooms. Facilities: restaurant, bar, coffee shop. AE, DC, MC, V.*

$$ **Sheraton Inn.** Though it's in a residential neighborhood 15 minutes by taxi from downtown, many travelers—especially business travelers—prefer the modern facilities, the well-trained staff, and the quiet of this hotel. The best of the rooms overlook the circular courtyard and its pool. Dining is a relaxed affair, either on the circular terrace facing the pool or inside with air-conditioning. The Sheraton-style architecture and ambience are more American than Indonesian. *Jln. Ir. H. Juanda 390, Box 6530, Bandung 40065, tel. 022/210303, fax 022/210301; U.S. reservations tel. 800/325–3535. 111 rooms. Facilities: restaurant with Indonesian and Western fare, 2 lighted tennis courts, business center. AE, DC, MC, V.*

The Arts

For information on Jakarta art events, good sources to check are the *Indonesian Observer* and the City Visitor Information Centre (tel. 021/354094). *Jakarta Week*, which lists forthcoming entertainment, can be found at your hotel. Where necessary, your concierge can make reservations.

Plays, music and dance performances, art shows, and films are held at the **Taman Ismail Marzuki** arts center. Monthly schedules of events are distributed to hotels. *Jln. Cikini Raya No. 73, tel. 021/342605.*

Jakarta Hilton Cultural Program (Indonesia Bazaar, Hilton Hotel, Jln. Jend. Sudirman, tel. 021/583051). Programs of regional dance are offered weekly. Every afternoon from 4 to 6, the famous and very old Cakra Delam Raya Gamelan orchestral set is played.

At the **Bharata Theater** (Jln. Kalilio, no phone), regular performances of traditional *wayang orang* (dance-dramas), depicting stories from the *Ramayana* or *Mahabharata* epics, are staged from 8:15 to midnight every night but Monday and Thursday. Sometimes the folk play *Ketoprak*, based on Javanese history, is also performed.

Wayang kulit (leather shadow-puppet plays, depicting stories from the *Ramayana* or *Mahabharata)* or wayang golek (wood puppet plays, usually depicting Islamic legends) are performed twice a month at the **Museum Nasional** (Jln. Merdeka Barat No. 12, tel. 021/360976).

The **Wayang Museum** (Jln. Pintu Besar Utara No. 27, tel. 021/679560) also offers puppet performances. Check with the museum for dates and times.

Beautiful Indonesia in Miniature Park (off Jagorawi toll rd., tel. 021/849525) offers various regional dances on Sunday and holidays from 10 to 2. (*Also see* Tour 3 in Exploring Jakarta, *above*).

Batik Berdikari (Jln. Masjid in Palmerah, southwest of Merdeka Sq., tel. 021/5482814), a shop with a factory on the premises, presents various types of Indonesian batik, and displays the ways batik is made, either hand-drawn or printed. *Open daily 9–4.*

Nightlife

Across from the Sarinah department store, the long-established **Jaya Pub,** located in the Jaya Building, has a piano bar with lively music and vocalists at night. It's very popular with expatriates and Indonesians alike, in part because the owners are two former Indonesian movie stars, Rimi Melati and Frans Tumbuan. *Jln. M.H. Thamrin No. 12, tel. 021/327508. Open daily noon–2 AM.*

The **Captain's Bar** offers a comfortable, relaxed evening of music by a small international or local group. *Mandarin Oriental Hotel, Jln. M.H. Thamrin, tel. 021/321307. Open nightly 8 PM–1 AM.*

The dimly lit **Tanamur** has good jazz and soft rock and is usually the most crowded disco in town, with a bevy of aging hostesses ready to dance and drink with guests. *Jln. Tanah Abang Timur 14, tel. 021/353947. Open nightly 9 PM–2 AM.*

The **Pit Stop** nightclub/disco is a favorite for Filipino bands. *Hotel Sari Pacific, Jln. M.H. Thamrin, tel. 021/323707. Open nightly 9 PM–2 AM.*

The **Hard Rock Café** offers the same pleasures here as at its other venues. Lunch is American fare. In the evening, live music starts at about 9 PM. The stage has a huge stained-glass window depicting Elvis Presley as a backdrop. *Sarinah Bldg., 2nd floor, Jln. M.H. Thamrin No. 11, tel. 021/390–3565. Open daily 11 AM–1 AM.*

The **Ebony Videotheque** is a lively, posh two-floor disco with a large screen for viewing old movies and a Saturday-night floor show. Waitresses are dressed in Nubian attire. *Kuningan Plaza, Jln. Rasuna Said No. C11–14, tel. 021/513700. Open Sun.–Thurs. 9 PM–2 AM, Fri. and Sat. 9 PM–3 AM.*

The **Stardust,** housed in a former theater, claims to be Asia's largest disco. *Jayakarta Tower Hotel, Jln. Hayam Wuruk 126, tel. 021/629–4408. Open nightly 9 PM–2 AM.*

The Regent Space Palace is popular with executive types, especially for its sci-fi decor. It's suitable for single men or couples—but not for single women. There is a Rp 20,000 entrance fee. *Glodok Saya Bldg., 21 Hayam Wuruk, tel. 021/600–0685.*

The **Green Pub** (*see* Dining, *above*) is another a local expat pub where you can sit at the bar or take a table and listen to music performed by local singers and bands.

The **Fire Discotheque** incorporates the newest gadgetry: 12-color laser lighting and a huge video screen. Up the spiral staircase, in the balcony lounges, the decor and noise are slightly more subdued. *Plaza Indonesia L3–003, Jln. M.H. Thamrin, tel. 021/330639.*

For variety entertainment, try the **Blue Ocean Restaurant and Nite Club,** with seating for 2,000. Shows vary from magicians to acrobats and singers. *Jln. Hayam Wuruk 5, tel. 021/366650. Admission: Rp 25,000.*

The **Dynasty** is another popular nightspot, with shows and hostesses. *Glodok Plaza, 8th floor, Jln. Pinangsla, tel. 021/628–3988.*

For a downscale disco bar with bar girls, try **Tigakuda.** *105, Jln. Cikini Raya, tel. 021/325543. Admission: Rp 7,500.*

Central Java

Central Java nurtured some of Indonesia's great Indian kingdoms in the 8th and 9th centuries, including the Buddhist Sailendras, who built the Borobudur temple, and the Hindu Sanjayans, who made Prambanan their religious center. Today tourists use Yogyakarta (also called Yogya) as a base for visiting these temples, the best-known architectural and cultural sites of Indonesia. Yogyakarta, a city of some 300,000 on a fertile plain in the shadow of three volcanoes, has many hotels, restaurants, and shops. The ancient city of Solo, 64 km (40 mi) to the east, is quieter and less commercial, but also a cultural center.

Important Addresses and Numbers

Tourist Information
Yogyakarta's **Tourist Information Office** (Jln. Malioboro 16, tel. 0274/66000) has maps, schedules of events, bus and train information, and a helpful staff. (Open Mon.–Sat. 8–8.) There is also a tourist booth at the railway station. In Solo, the Tourist Information Office is at Jalam Slamet Riyadi 275, tel. 0271/46501. (Open Mon.–Sat. 8–5.)

Emergencies
Police, tel. 110; **fire,** tel. 113; **ambulance,** tel. 118, for Solo and Yogyakarta.

Travel Agencies
Yogya and Solo's three main companies are **Nitour** (Jln. K.H.A. Dahlan 71, tel. 0274/3450), **Pacto** (Hotel Ambarrukmo Palace, Jln. Adisucipto, tel. 0274/88488, ext. 711), and **Satriavi** (also at Hotel Ambarrukmo Palace, tel. 0274/88488, ext. 505). The locally operated **Setia Tours** (Natour Garuda Hotel, Jln. Malioboro, tel. 0274/86353, ext. 151) is also helpful.

Arriving and Departing by Plane

Airports and Airlines
From Jakarta's Soekarno-Hatta Airport, **Garuda** (Jakarta tel. 021/ 334425, Yogyakarta tel. 0274/4400–5184) offers several daily flights to **Adisucipto Airport,** 10 km (6 mi) east of Yogyakarta. Flights take about 45 minutes. They fill up quickly, so reservations are essential. There are also flights into Yogya from Denpasar (Bali) and Surabaya (Java) on both **Merpati** and **Sempati.**

Between the Airport and Center City
A minibus runs until 6 PM from the Adisucipto Airport to the terminal on Jalan Senopati for Rp 250; from there you can catch a becak to your hotel. Taxis to or from downtown charge Rp 5,500. The major hotels send their own minibuses to the airport.

Arriving and Departing by Car, Train, and Bus

By Car
The distance between Jakarta and Yogyakarta is 618 km (371 mi). Although the scenery may be beautiful, the drive is slow going and service areas are few and far between. It is advisable to hire a driver when traveling through Indonesia.

By Train
Trains from the Gambir and Kota railway stations in Jakarta leave several times daily for Yogya. The trip takes seven–12 hours and costs Rp 6,700–Rp 21,500, depending on whether the train is an express or a local and on the class of ticket. The most comfortable trip is via the *Bima Express*, which leaves Gambir at 3:19 PM and arrives in Yogya at 1:15 AM. The train has sleeping compartments, and you can have someone from your hotel meet you at the station. There are also day and night trains from Bandung (an eight-hour trip) and from Surabaya (seven hours).

By Bus
Night buses from Jakarta take about 14 hours and cost about Rp 12,250. Buses also run from Denpasar on Bali (12 hours), Bandung (seven hours), and Surabaya (eight hours). (*See* Getting Around by Bus in Staying in Indonesia, *above.*) For information contact **Antar Lintas Sumatra** (Jln. Jati Baru 87A, Jakarta, tel. 021/320970) or **PT. ANS** (for Java, Bali, and Sumatra), Jalan Senen Raya 50, Jakarta, tel. 021/340494.

Getting Around

By Becak
Yogya has 25,000 becak, and they are the main form of public transportation. Prices need serious negotiation. The proper fare is about Rp 500 per kilometer.

By Taxi
Catch taxis in front of the larger hotels, such as Garuda or Mutiara; in general, they do not cruise the streets. Taxis are not metered; there are hourly charges, averaging Rp 7,500 per hour within the city, with a two-hour minimum. There's little bargaining leeway within Yogya; drivers will negotiate more for out-of-town trips.

By Bicycle
Bicycles may be rented for Rp 1,000 a day from the **Hotel Indonesia** (Sosromenduran IV), the **Restaurant Malioboro** (Jln. Malioboro 67), and from other shops.

By Motor Scooter
These cost about Rp 8,000 a day and may be rented from **Yogya Rental** (Jln. Pasar Kembang 86) and **A.A. Rental** (Jln. Pasar Kembang 25, tel. 0274/4489).

Guided Tours

Hotels and travel agencies can arrange the following tours, either in a private chauffeured car or as a group tour by bus:

Yogya City A three-hour tour including the sultan's palace, Sono Budoyo Museum, Kota Gede silverworks, and batik and wayang workshops.

Borobudur An eight-hour tour of Yogyakarta, the countryside, and the Borobudur, Mendut, and Pawon temples.

Prambanan A three-hour tour of the temple complex.

Yogya Dieng Plateau A 10-hour tour of the Dieng Plateau, with its spectacular scenery, sulfur springs, and geysers, plus a visit to Borobudur.

Art and Handicrafts A five-hour tour of the local craft centers for leather puppets, wood carving, silverwork, batik, and pottery.

Exploring Central Java

Numbers in the margin correspond to points of interest on the Central Java map.

Tour 1: Yogyakarta

1 Every Indonesian has a soft spot for **Yogyakarta,** or Yogya. It is in many respects the heart of Indonesia. Students from Yogya's Gajah Mada University account for some 20% of the city's population. Dance and choreography schools, wayang troupes, and poetry workshops make it an artist's mecca. Every evening classical drama and dance performances are staged somewhere in the city. Leading Indonesian painters and sculptors display their work in numerous galleries, and crafts shopping is a major preoccupation. The batik here and in Solo is said to be superior even to Bali's.

Yogya sprawls. Unless you stay at the Garuda or one of the less expensive city hotels, chances are you will be a few kilometers from Jalan Malioboro. This thoroughfare is where the action is, day and night. It is the main shopping street, not only for established shops but also for sidewalk vendors. These set up cardboard stands selling handicrafts until about nine in the evening, then convert to food stalls serving Yogya's specialties: *nasi gudeg* (rice with jackfruit in coconut milk) and *ayam goreng* (marinated fried chicken). Malioboro is a fascinating street to stroll, and if you arrive by 8 PM, you can catch both the shops and the food. But even with intensive bargaining, prices are high. You can find better deals at the new indoor market, **Pasar Beringharjo,** at the top of the street; it's worth visiting just to see the stacked merchandise—everything from jeans to poultry.

At the southern end of Malioboro stands the **kraton,** or sultan's palace. The large, grassy square in front of the kraton—a walled city within the city—is the **alun-alun,** where the townspeople formerly gathered to trade, gossip, and hear the latest palace news.

The Yogya kraton has special significance to Indonesians as the bastion against Dutch colonialism. During the War of Independence (1945–49), Yogya's Sultan Hamengku Buwono allowed the Indonesian freedom fighters—including guerrilla commander Suharto, now the nation's president—to use the kraton as a military base. Built in 1756, it is a vast complex of pavilions and buildings, part of which—strictly off-limits to the public—is home to the present sultan. The complex is protected by 400 guardians (in blue shirts) and 1,000 servants (in red shirts).

At the center of the green-trimmed white palace is the **Golden Pavilion** (Bengsal Kengono), an open hall with carved teak columns and a black-and-gold interior, where weddings, cremations, and corona-

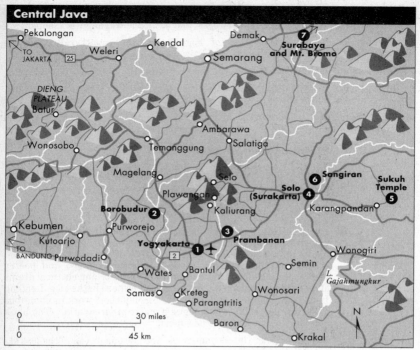

Central Java

Pekalongan
TO JAKARTA 25
Weleri
Kendal
Demak
Semarang
Surabaya and Mt. Bromo 7

DIENG PLATEAU
Batur
Wonosobo
Temanggung
Ambarawa
Salatiga
Magelang
Selo
Solo (Surakarta) 4
Sangiran 6
Sukuh Temple 5
Borobudur 2
Plawangan
Kaliurang
Karangpandan
Kebumen
Purworejo
Yogyakarta 1
Prambanan 3
Wonogiri
Kutoarjo
TO BANDUNG
Purwodadi
Wates
Bantul
Semin
L. Gajahmungkur
Samas
Kreteg
Wonosari
Parangtritis
N
Baron
Krakal

0   30 miles
0   45 km

tions are held. The complex includes a gallery exhibiting a collection of gamelan instruments. Try to time your visit to catch the Sunday classical dance rehearsal (10:30 and noon, except during Ramadan). In another pavilion is a collection of sedan chairs. The last one was used in 1877; now a Rolls-Royce transports the sultan on ceremonial occasions. *No phone. Admission charge. Open Sun.–Thurs. 8:30–1, Fri. and Sat. 8:30–11:30.*

Behind the kraton is the recreational **Water Palace** (Taman Sari), constructed by the same sultan who built the kraton. A large artificial lake, sunken bathing pools, underground passageways, and towers where gamelan orchestras serenaded the royalty were all part of this noble retreat. It was abandoned in the 18th century and fell into ruin; the restored sections give a sense of what the privileged enjoyed. Visit the ornate bathing pools used by the princesses, the underground mosque, and the tower from which the sultan watched his concubines lounge by the water. *No phone. Admission charge. Open Sun.–Thurs. 8–1, Fri. 8–11.*

Of Yogya's several museums, the most interesting and well-maintained is the **Sono Budoyo Museum** on the square before the kraton. Inside this traditional Javanese-style building is a collection of crafts and batiks from Java and Bali. Its archaeological treasures include a small gold Buddha, and the display of *wayang golek*, the wood puppets used in Muslim theater, is charming. *Tel. 0274/2775. Admission charge. Open Tues.–Thurs. 8–1, Fri. and Sun. 8–11, Sat. 8–noon.*

Out toward the airport, about 8 km (5 mi) southeast of Yogya, is the **Affandi** museum, the home and studio of Indonesia's best-known painter (1907–1990). A permanent collection of his works, along with paintings by young artists, is exhibited in an oval, domed extension to the traditional paddy-field house. *Jln. Laksda, Adisucipto 67, no phone. Admission free. Open daily 9–5.*

Sasono Wirotomo was the residence of Prince Diponegoro, who rebelled against the Dutch occupation and led a bloody guerrilla battle in the Java War (1825–30). The house is now a museum, displaying the prince's krises, lances, and other revered possessions. *Tegalrejo (4 km [2.5 mi] west of Yogyakarta), tel. 0274/3068. Donation. Open by appointment only.*

Tour 2: Borobudur

You can take guided coach tours from Yogya hotels or hire a minibus and guide (usually more informed) from a Yogya travel agency. Or take the public bus toward Samarung, then change at Muntilan for the Ramayana bus to **Borobudur.**

That Borobudur took perhaps 10,000 men 100 years to build becomes credible the moment you set eyes on the temple's cosmic structure, in the shadow of the powerful volcanoes that the Javanese believe are the abode of God. Borobudur is about 42 km (26 mi) from Yogyakarta. Try to go early in the morning—plan to end your two-to three-hour visit before noon—while the temperature is still relatively cool.

Borobudur was abandoned soon after completion (AD 850), and the forest moved in. The man who founded modern Singapore, Thomas Stamford Raffles (then the English lieutenant-governor of Java), and his military engineer, H.C.C. Cornelius, rediscovered the temple in 1814. A thousand years of neglect had left much of it in ruins, and the temple has undergone two mammoth restorations, first from 1907 to 1911, and then from the 1960s to the 1980s with the help of UNESCO and US$25 million.

The temple is a giant stupa: Five lower levels contain 1,500 relief carvings depicting the earthly life of Siddhartha in his passage to enlightenment. Start at the eastern staircase on the first level and walk clockwise around each gallery to follow the sequence of Lord Buddha's life.

Above the reliefs are 432 stone Buddhas. Even higher, above the square galleries, are three circular terraces with 72 latticed stupas that hide statues depicting the Buddha's departure from the material world and existence on a higher plane. The top stupa symbolizes the highest level of enlightenment. Looking out at the surrounding mountains from the upper level of Borobudur, you feel some of the inspiration that created this grand monument. If you go around each of the nine galleries, you will have walked 4.8 km (3 mi) closer to heaven. On weekends the complex is fairly crowded—another reason to come early. In 1990, a museum opened on the grounds of Borobudur, charging additional admission that its contents do not justify. *No phone. Admission charge. Open daily 6:15–5.*

About 1.5 km (1 mi) east of Borobudur, on the way back to the main road, is a small temple, **Candi Pawon,** built around the same time as Borobudur. It is thought that worshipers purified themselves here on their way to Borobudur. Another kilometer or so farther east is the small 9th-century temple **Mendut.** The exterior of this friendly temple is superbly carved with some 30 large relief panels depicting scenes from the Buddha's previous incarnations. Inside stands a magnificent 3-m (10-ft) statue of Buddha, flanked by the bodhisattvas Avalokitesvara and Vajrapani. *No phone. Admission charge. Open daily 9–5.*

Tour 3: Prambanan

③ **Prambanan** is a half-hour drive (16 km, or 10 mi) from Yogyakarta via the Solo road. If you book through a tour agency, you can combine a visit to Prambanan with a visit to Borobudur, or you can combine Prambanan with a trip to Solo, 46 km (29 mi) farther from Yogya. Minibuses go out to Prambanan from the Jalan Solo terminus in Yogya. If you hire a taxi, the round-trip will cost Rp 35,000.

When the Sanjayan kingdom evicted the Buddhist Sailendras, the Sanjayans wanted to memorialize the return of a Hindu dynasty and, supposedly, undermine Borobudur. Toward this end, they built Prambanan. When the 9th-century complex was rediscovered in 1880, it had fallen into ruin from centuries of neglect and enveloping vegetation. In 1937 reconstruction began, and the work continues today.

The temple was built with an outer stage for commoners, a middle stage for high-ranking nobility, and a main temple area for royalty. Of the original 244 temples, eight major and eight minor temples are still standing, in the highest central courtyard of the Prambanan plain.

The center temple, dedicated to Shiva the Destroyer, is the highest (47 m, or 155 ft) and the best-restored; Vishnu's is to the north, and Brahma's, to the south. Originally the temples were painted— Shiva's red, Brahma's white, Vishnu's a dark gray—but only traces of the paint remain. To the east of these temples are three smaller ones, which contained the "vehicles" of each god: Shiva's bull, Vishnu's elephant, and Brahma's goose. Only the bull is extant.

In part because the complex was dedicated to Shiva, and in part because Shiva's temple is the best restored, this is where you will want to focus. Over the entrance is the head of Kali, a protection against evil from land. On the balustrade, the *naga* (serpent) guards against evil from the sea. The base is decorated with medallions with lions (an imported figure) and half-bird, half-human figures flanked by trees of good hope. Above these, on the outer balustrade, are carvings of classical Indian dancers and celestial beings.

The inner wall of the balustrade is carved with lively, sometimes frivolous, reliefs telling the story of the *Ramayana*. From the east gate, walk around the temple clockwise to follow the story in sequence. The reliefs show free-flowing movement, much humor, and a love of nature. In contrast to Borobudur's reliefs, these carvings combine a celebration of the pleasures and pains of earthly life with scenes from Hindu mythology. They are more fun to look at (monkeys stealing fruit and bird-women floating in air), but the drama they portray—the establishment of order in the cosmos—is just as serious.

In the main chamber, at the top of the east stairway, a four-armed statue of Shiva the creator and destroyer stands on a lotus base. In the south chamber, Shiva appears as divine teacher, with a big beard and big stomach. The statue in the western chamber is Ganesha, Shiva's elephant-headed son. And in the northern chamber, Shiva's consort, Durga, kills the demon buffalo. An archaeological museum (separate admission) was opened in 1990, but its contents do not add much to the imposing architecture of the temples. However, you may want to stop at the information desk at the entrance to clarify any questions you have about the complex. Within walking distance of Prambanan is a theater complex where performances of the Ramayana epic are given in the evening, either at the Ramayana Theatre (open-air) or the Trimurti Theatre (indoor). *No phone. Admission charge. Open daily 6–5*.

The numerous other Buddhist and Hindu temples between Yogya and Prambanan are in various states of ruin but merit at least a day of exploring. A great way to see them is to rent a bike and pack a lunch. Signs on the Yogya–Solo road point the way to the temples. Most are off the road, down small paths, and charge a small admission. **Candi Sambisari,** a small temple located off the highway and two miles back toward Yogya, is set in a sunken garden and usually deserted—ideal for a quiet rest.

Tour 4: Solo

4 Minibuses leave for **Solo** throughout the day (7–5) from Yogyakarta's Terminal Terban (Rp 1,500) or may be caught along Jalan Sudirman or Jalan Solo. From Solo's **Gilligan bus terminal,** take a bemo (Rp 300) or a becak (Rp 750) the 3 km (1.8 mi) into town. A shared taxi from Yogya to Solo costs Rp 2,500 per person. The train from Yogya, invariably behind schedule, takes one hour; third-class fare is only Rp 500.

Just 60 km (38 mi) east of Yogyakarta, Solo (also known as Surakarta or Sala) is less Westernized than Yogya, with fewer tourists and much less hustling. Solo has its own traditional batik designs and its own style of dance. And while its people are devoutly Muslim, their daily life is less religious.

There are two kratons, or sultan's palaces, in Solo. On the west side of town is the **Mangkunegaran Palace,** a complex of carved, gilded teak pavilions. The outer center pavilion, or *pendopo*, serves as the audience hall and is typical of a Javanese royal building. The Italian marble floor, laid in 1925, guardian lions from Berlin, and 50-ft roof supported by teak pillars make the pendopo very grand. Its ceiling is painted with a flame motif bordered by symbols of the Javanese zodiac, designed with the eight mystical colors (yellow to ward off sleep, green to subdue desire, purple to keep away bad thoughts, etc.). The effect is gaudy but dramatic.

The museum, in the ceremonial pavilion just behind the main pendopo, displays dance ornaments, masks, jewelry, chastity belts for men and women, and wayang kulit and wayang golek. At center stage is the enclosed bridal bed (originally a room reserved for offerings to the rice goddess). To the left of the museum are the official reception rooms: a formal dining room, with a Javanese-style stained-glass window (made in Holland) and an ivory tusk carved with depictions of the wedding of Arjuna, one of the heroes of the Mahabharata; a mirrored parlor area; and a "bathing" room for royal brides. *No phone. Admission charge. Open Mon.–Thurs. and Sat. 9–noon, Fri. 9–11 AM*.

From the palace, return to Solo's main street, Jalan Slamet Riyadi, via Jalan Diponegoro. Just off Diponegoro is Pasar Triwindu, Solo's daily flea market, where hundreds of stalls sell everything from junk to old coins to batik. Bargain like crazy!

Walk north about five blocks and take a left onto Gladak to reach Solo's other palace, **Kraton Kasuhunan** (sometimes called Kraton Solo). This kraton suffered terrible damage from a fire in 1985 that gutted the elaborate ceremonial pavilion. Now the palace is being rebuilt. The museum—one of Central Java's best—was unharmed by the fire. It contains a priceless collection of silver and bronze Hindu figures and Chinese porcelain, but the real treat is three royal carriages given to the sultanate by the Dutch in the 18th century. The English-speaking guide will help you appreciate the collection. *Tel. 0271/44046. Admission charge. Open Sat.–Thurs. 9–noon.*

Excursions from Solo

5 **Sukuh Temple** stands 35 km (21 mi) east of Solo. A hired car (cost: Rp 15,000) is the most convenient way to get there; the journey takes a good hour along winding, hilly roads. You can also reach it by bus, but it requires three changes: At Tertomoyo catch the bus to Tawangmangu, then get off at Karangpandan for a minibus to Sukuh.

Sukuh contains elements of Hinduism, Buddhism, and animism. Looking like an abbreviated pyramid, the delightful temple is full of cult symbols and objects with erotic suggestions. The temple dates back to the 15th century, but no one knows who built it or what cults were celebrated. Because few tourists make it here, the place has a mystical atmosphere, enhanced by the lush surrounding rice terraces. *Admission charge. Open daily 9–4.*

6 **Sangiran** is where Eugene Dubois discovered Java Man (or *Homo erectus*, as the species is now known) in 1891. (It is not to be confused with Sanggarahan, a village just outside Yogya known for its pleasure houses.) The museum contains a replica of Java Man's cranium and models of *Homo sapiens'* ancestors who lived some 250,000 years ago, plus fossils of other forms of life, such as now-extinct elephants. You can get to Sangiran, 15 km (9 mi) north of Solo, by taking a bus to Kaliso, then walking 30 minutes to the site; or have a taxi take you from Solo for Rp 15,000 round-trip. *No phone. Admission charge. Open Mon.–Sat. 9–4.*

Tour 5: Surabaya and Mt. Bromo

7 **Surabaya,** 258 km (150 mi) northeast of Solo, isn't on the traditional tourist route, but with a rapidly expanding business and industrial base—it now ranks as the nation's third-largest city—it is looking for visitors. Hope springs eternal in the human breast! Surabaya does not offer exotic attractions. It was virtually leveled on November 10, 1945, when the Dutch and their allies tried to reclaim the city after the Japanese surrender. The Surabayans resisted, and the day came to symbolize the country's determination to throw off the colonial yoke; it is now celebrated throughout Indonesia as Revolutionary Heroes' Day.

There are flights to Surabaya on Garuda, Merpati, and Sempati airlines from most Javanese cities as well as from Bali and Lombok. There is also train service from Jakarta, Yogyakarta, and Solo. Another train line links Surabaya to Banyuwangi, on the eastern tip of Java; from there ferries depart every 30 minutes for the 20-minute crossing to Bali. This is a slow train, though, and most non-air travelers to Bali prefer the night express buses.

Beyond serving as a port for ferries to the little-visited islands of Madura (famous for its bullfights and the adroitness of its women) and Sulawesi (*see below*) and international flights to Singapore, Hong Kong, and Japan, Surabaya is a good base from which to visit Mt. Bromo. While there are monuments to see in the old town, you may want to use the city simply for a night's rest before traveling on.

The usual way to visit **Mt. Bromo,** an active volcano, is on an organized tour that will place you at the rim of the caldera just before dawn. You can either leave Surabaya in the afternoon and catch a short night's rest in a small bungalow hotel, or leave in the wee hours of the morning and return by lunchtime. Either way, you'll have a walk in the chilly predawn hours, so take a sweater.

The largest tour agency is **Orient Express** (Jln. Jend. Basuki Rakhamat 78, Surabaya 60262, tel. 031/515253, fax 031/511811), which will meet you at the airport or anywhere else in Surabaya. Tours depart at 3 PM for the Bromo Cottages in Tosari, where the accommodation is simple, modern, and clean. You then rise at 3:30 AM and travel by jeep up Mt. Penanjakan (2,770 m, or 9,088 ft) for views of the spectacular sunrise. Afterward the jeep takes you to the sea of sand and the stairway to the rim of the Bromo crater; then it's back to the cottages for breakfast before returning to Surabaya. *Cost: US$85 per person. Tours departing 1 AM (these do not include a sleep at the Bromo Cottages): US$40 per person.*

You can also rent a chauffeured car and do the trip independently for about Rp 100,000, plus the fee for a jeep on the last leg of the journey. Try **P.T. Zebra Nusantart** (Jln. Tegalsari 107, Surabaya, tel. 031/511777; the firm also has a representative at the Surabaya Hyatt.

If you prefer public transport, take the bus from Surabaya's Bungurasih Bus Station to Probolinggo and change for a bemo up to Pasuruan; from there take a minibus up to Tosari. To get from Tosari to the crater's rim, another 7½ km (4½ mi), you can rent a jeep (about US$25) or walk (if you're fit—it's a two-hour uphill trudge). If you go by jeep, after the sun has risen ask the driver to take you to the sand sea and walk back from there to Tosari or to Cemoro Lawang. At Cemoro Lawang, a popular base from which to hike up to the northern rim of the caldera—it takes a couple of hours—there are jeeps down to Ngadisari, where minibuses ply the route to Probolinggo. In Probolinggo you can board buses for Banyuwangi, Bali, or back to Surabaya.

Shopping

Yogyakarta and Solo are a shopper's dream, but be selective—there's a lot of tacky merchandise alongside the treasures—and bargain gracefully. After you have offered your next-to-last price, walk away; you will probably be called back. There are any number of scams to lure you into shops—for instance, the claim that a student art exposition is being held and the works are being sold without commercial profit. Don't believe it!

Shopping Streets — **Jalan Malioboro** in Yogya is lined with shops; the handicraft stalls turn into food stalls around 9 PM. Most of the merchandise is junk, but it's worth picking through. This is a convenient area to buy T-shirts or shorts, but prices are better at the new indoor market, **Pasar Beringharjo,** at the top end of the street. This fascinating market contains endless spices and foodstuffs, as well as pots and pans, clothes, and transistors.

Solo's main shopping street is **Jalan Secoyudan.** In addition to a score of goldsmiths, you'll find antiques stores selling curios from the Dutch colonial days, as well as krises and other Javanese artifacts. **Jalan Slamet Riyadi** also has antiques shops.

Specialty Shops *Batik* — The patterned Indonesian textiles called batik—made by drawing on fabric with wax, then dyeing the unwaxed parts—can be found in all the stalls in Yogyakarta. Many prints with batik design are machine-made, however, so beware. Before you buy, try to visit the batik factories, where you can watch the process and shop in the show-rooms. One such place is Yogya's **Batik Plentong** (Jln. Tirtodipurun No. 28, tel. 0274/2777), which has everything from yard goods to pot holders and batik clothing, hand-stamped and hand-drawn. Also visit **Iman Batik Workshop** (Jln. Dagen 76B, just off Jln. Malioboro), where Iman Nuryanto, the owner, holds visiting exhibitions of local artists. Don't pay more than 50% of the asking price. The **Koperasi (Cooperative) Fine Arts School** (Jln. Kemetiran Kidul, no phone), south of the railway station, has batik designed by talented arti-sans, but be sure to bargain well.

Solo has its own batik style, often using indigo, brown, and cream, as opposed to the brighter colors of Yogya's batiks. Prices are better in Solo, and you have some 300 batik factories to choose from. Aside from the shops along Jalan Secoyudan, visit **Pasar Klewer,** a huge ba-tik market just outside the Kraton Solo with a fine selection of goods on the second floor. An established shop that sells batik and demon-strates the batik-making process is **Dinar Hadi Batik Shop** on Jalan Dr. Rajiman (no phone).

Handicrafts   Handicrafts in Yogyakarta include batik "paintings," batik-pat-terned T-shirts and other apparel or household items, small hand-tooled leather goods, pottery (items decorated with brightly col-ored elephants, roosters, and animals from mythology are made in Kasongan, just south of Yogya), and wayang kulit (leather) and wayang golek (wood) puppets. All the shops and stalls on Jalan Malioboro and around the kraton sell puppets and other handicrafts. The **Yogyakarta Handicrafts Center** on Jalan Adisucipto (no phone), not far from the Ambarrukmo Palace Hotel, sells work by artisans with disabilities.

Leather   Leather is a great buy in Yogyakarta. The shops and stalls on Jalan Malioboro offer a wide variety of goods, but you'll get better quality and design at **Kusuma** (Jln. Kauman 50, parallel to Malioboro, tel. 0274/5453). There's room for modest bargaining, but no credit cards are accepted.

Silver   Many silversmiths have workshops and salesrooms in **Kota Gede**, 6 km (3½ mi) southeast of Yogya. The largest, **Tom's Silver** (Jln. Kota Gede 3-1 A, tel. 0274/3070 or 0274/2818), offers quality workman-ship. Also try **MD Silver** (Jln. Keboan, tel. 0274/2063).

Dining

Yogyakarta   **The Floating Restaurant.** This restaurant looks Moroccan, with a pa-
$$$ vilion overlooking gardens, and low tables—with ikat-covered floor cushions—as well as Western-style tables. At the center is a copious buffet of Indonesian specialties, which may include *gudeg* (chicken with jackfruit), the most famous dish of central Java, and *pepes ikan* (marinated fish baked with coconut). An Indonesian singer and in-strumentalist provide background music. The place also has a bar-becue buffet with Western dishes such as pasta carbonara, as well as Indonesian specialties, accompanied by native dance-drama. *Ambarrukmo Palace, Jln. Laksda Adisucipto, tel. 0274/88488. Reservations advised. Dress: casual. AE, DC, MC, V.*

$$ **Pesta Perak.** Smartly decorated with wrought-iron furniture and a sultan-costumed maître d', Pesta Perak has excellent Javanese cui-sine. Its rijstaffel includes satays, gudeg, and fish wrapped in ba-nana leaves. An à la carte menu is also offered, but customers rarely choose this. A gamelan trio plays traditional music. Use a becak to get there and have it wait for you; the fare from Jalan Malioboro, including waiting time, is less than Rp 2,500. *Jln. Tentura Rakyat*

Mataran 8, tel. 0274/86255. Reservations accepted. Dress: smart casual. MC, V.

$$ **Pringsewu Garden Restaurant.** For relaxed alfresco dining at tables tucked between shrubs and trees, this new restaurant offers some of the best fare in the region served by a friendly staff attired in colorful batiks. The cooking is from West Sumatra. Try the *ayam goreng mantega* (fried chicken with a butter sauce) or the *ikan mas baket* (grilled golden fish in ginger sauce). *Jln. Magelang Km 6, tel. 0274/64993. Reservations accepted. Dress: casual. AE, DC, MC, V.*

$$ **Sintawang.** Though the tables are Formica, the restaurant is clean and offers a wide range of outstanding seafood, either cooked Javanese-style or grilled for Western palates. Try the *udang bakar* (marinated and grilled prawns), *pais udang* (prawns spiced and grilled in a banana leaf), or *ikan asam manis* (fish in a sweet-and-sour sauce). *Jln. Magelang 9, tel. 0274/2901. No reservations. Dress: casual. AE, DC.*

$ **Legian Garden Restaurant.** Choose a table next to the open windows at the edge of its terrace and watch fellow tourists *jalan jalan* (amble around) on the street below. Since the food is pretty average (primarily Western, with a few Indonesian alternatives), you may just want to stop by for a beer. *Jln. Perwakilan 9 (off Jln. Malioboro), 1st floor, tel. 0274/64644. No reservations. Dress: casual. No credit cards.*

$ ★ **Ny Suharti.** People come here for the best fried chicken in Java, perhaps in all of Indonesia. Order one for two people, with rice on the side. The chicken is boiled, marinated in spices, then fried to a crisp. Forget charm or atmosphere, but diners can sit outside on the veranda. *Jln. Laksda Adisucipto, Km 7, tel. 0274/5522. No reservations. Dress: casual. No credit cards.*

Solo **Kasuma Sahid.** Without a doubt this is the place to dine in Solo. Part
$$ of the Prince Hotel, this formal restaurant is light and airy, with white linen and polished silver. The menu, offering Indonesian specialties, features chicken with jackfruit and fish wrapped in banana leaves, with the restaurant's own special blend of spices. Western dishes with a nouvelle French influence and Indonesian accent are featured as well. *Jln. Sugiyopranoto 20, Solo, tel. 0271/46356. No reservations. Dress: casual. AE, DC, MC, V.*

$$ **Kusuma Sari.** This spotless restaurant is excellent for Indonesian fare, be it ayam goreng or a snack such as *resoles ragout* (chicken wrapped in a soft pancake). The tile floors, glass-topped wood tables, and plate-glass windows don't offer a lot of atmosphere, but choose a table by the window and watch the flow of pedestrians and becaks on the town's main street. *Jln. Slamet Riyadi 111, Solo, tel. 0271/37603. No reservations. Dress: casual. No credit cards. Open daily until 11 PM.*

Lodging

Although there are some full-service hotels in Yogyakarta and Solo that meet international standards, many hotels and guest houses do not have such facilities as private bath and air-conditioning. The ones listed below do. Should you decide to seek budget accommodation, a good selection of small hotels is to be found off Jalan Malioboro, across from the Hotel Garuda and two blocks from the railway station. So many hotels have opened of late (with more to come, including the Conrad Hilton and Yogyakarta Sheraton) that good discounts—as much as 50%—are there for travelers who ask.

Yogyakarta
$$$
★

Ambarrukmo Palace. Yogyakarta's premier tourist hotel is built on the grounds of the former royal country retreat. The lobby is spacious. Guest rooms are large, decorated with light Indonesian-pattern fabrics and mahogany furniture, and equipped with all the amenities, including color TV and minibars. The best rooms have balconies overlooking the gardens. Some are a little worn, so don't be reluctant to ask for another. This is an active hotel, popular with American tour groups. Every evening offers a different event, usually dances from the *Ramayana. Jln. Laksda Adisucipto, tel. 0274/ 88488, fax 0274/63283. 266 rooms. Facilities: 3 restaurants, bar, 24-hr room service, large outdoor pool, travel agencies, shopping arcade. AE, DC, MC, V.*

$$

Hotel Garuda. The newer rooms in this imposing old hotel in the center of town are much better than the older ones (which have a slight odor), but they've all suffered from the steady stream of tour groups leaving black scrape marks on the walls and stains on the carpets. It's the hotel's location that makes it the number-one choice. The standard guest rooms are plainly furnished but have all the latest conveniences, including color TV with VCR and minibar. The restaurant offers Indonesian and Western food and dinner performances from the *Ramayana.* Specify when you register whether you wish your room rate (approximately US$110) to include the price of dinner and the show (US$18). *Jln. Malioboro 60, tel. 0274/ 66353, fax 0274/63074. 120 rooms. Facilities: 2 restaurants, coffee shop, tennis court, outdoor pool, fitness center, business center, travel desk. AE, DC, MC, V.*

$$

Hotel Santika. This relatively characterless 1992 hotel—a 10-minute walk from the bustle of Jalan Malioboro—is built around a courtyard with pool. The carpeted guest rooms (just under $100 for a double), furnished in deep rose fabrics, are uniform but clean and efficient. The choice ones face the courtyard; those on the street can be noisy. The spacious lobby and lounge area is designed to receive tour groups; the coffee shop is a convenient place to wait for traveling companions. The hotel's freshness makes it a more comfortable choice than its chief competitor, especially since discounts are usually negotiable. *Jln. Jend. Sundiman 19, tel. 0274/63036, fax 0274/ 62047. 148 rooms. Facilities: Indonesian and Chinese restaurant, 24-hr Western-style coffee shop, pool, fitness center, travel/tour desk, meeting rooms, shops. AE, DC, MC, V.*

$

Batik Palace Hotel. For modest accommodations in the center of Yogyakarta, this hotel offers worn but clean rooms, each with twin beds, table, and chair. The lobby, decorated with batiks and crafts, is a comfortable place to relax. *Jln. Mangkubumi 46, Box 115, tel. 0274/62229, fax 0274/62149. 38 rooms. Facilities: restaurant, outdoor pool. V.*

$

Mutiara. In the heart of Yogya on Jalan Malioboro, this downtown hotel consists of two buildings. The rooms in the older one are somewhat worn and musty. The newer building has fresher rooms that, in spite of their pale-green-and-orange-flecked decor, are worth the extra $5. Cracked plaster and stained carpets notwithstanding, all the rooms are swept clean, fresh towels supplied through the day, and the cheerful staff is always ready to give advice. The restaurant serves meals throughout the day, but stick to the breakfast. A small combo on the ground floor plays every evening. *Jln. Malioboro 18, tel. 0274/63814, fax 0274/61201. 109 rooms. Facilities: restaurant, coffee shop, outdoor pool and pool bar, 24-hr room service. AE, DC, MC, V.*

$

Rose Guest House. The rooms here are very modest but they do have private baths and either air-conditioning or overhead fans. The tariff includes breakfast and airport transfer, so this hotel is an extremely good value. *Jln. Prawirotaman 22, tel. 0274/27991. 29 rooms. Facilities: small restaurant, outdoor pool. No credit cards.*

Solo
$$
★

Kusuma Sahid Prince Hotel. Three two-story buildings and outlying bungalows are set on 5 acres of landscaped gardens. The lobby veranda—the original *pendopo agung* (prince's courtyard)—is a wonderful place for tea or a cooling drink. Most guest rooms have twin beds, a couple of upholstered chairs, and a desk; the best overlook the pool. The bathrooms are pristine, and hot water is usually available. The dining room offers excellent Indonesian and Western food at reasonable prices. This is by far the nicest place to stay in the Yogyakarta–Solo area, and it's cheaper than the Yogyakarta hotels. *Jln. Sugiyopranoto 22, tel. 0271/46356, fax 0271/44788. 103 rooms. Facilities: restaurant, bar, 24-hr room service, large outdoor pool, travel desk, drugstore and shops, banquet/meeting rooms. AE, DC, MC, V.*

$

Mangkunegaran Palace Hotel. Adjacent to the palace and owned by Prince Mangkunegoro, this hotel has great potential, but it desperately needs renovation that is being performed only intermittently. Inspect your room before signing in. If you don't mind cracked plaster and a musty smell, the Mangkunegaran is the least expensive palace you are ever likely to stay in. The most appealing room is the dining room, which has a batik-painted ceiling just like the palace's. *Istara Mangkunegaran, tel. and fax 0271/35683. 50 rooms. Facilities: restaurant, outdoor pool, free admission to the palace. AE, DC, MC, V.*

$

Wisata Indah. Though the plastered walls have hand smudges and the bathrooms are the bucket-dip (*mundi*) style, the hot water is hot and the sheets freshly laundered, and the staff is friendly and helpful. Outside each room are tables and chairs for breakfast (included in the rate) and meals that may be ordered from the bellboys. Negotiate on the room rate before you sign in. *Jln. Slamet Riyadi 173, tel. 0271/43753. 27 rooms. No restaurant. MC, V.*

Surabaya
$$$

Hotel Majapahit. Built in 1910 in the center of town, this is one of Indonesia's few heritage hotels. Its expansive courts and green lawns became derelict after World War II, but some of their colonial serenity remains. In 1994, the Mandarin Oriental Hotel Group, who manage such distinguished properties as the Oriental in Bangkok, took over, and they have begun massive restoration. At the grand reopening in 1995, the Majapahit may have more character than any other hotel in Surabaya. *Jln. Tunjungan 65, Box 199, Surabaya 60275, tel. 031/43351, fax 031/43599. 105 rooms. Facilities: Indonesian and Western restaurant, bar/lounge, Saturday-evening barbecue, business services. AE, DC, MC, V.*

$$$

Hyatt Regency Surabaya. With competition from the new Shangri-La and Hilton, the Hyatt has refurbished its 11-story wing and added the 27-story Regency Tower with Regency Club rooms, meeting rooms, two business centers, and offices. An added convenience is a new airline ticketing office. Rooms are typical Hyatt—comfortable, beige, fairly large, and furnished with wooden cabinets, king-size beds, and ferns in huge clay pots. The main lobby is a popular spot for locals who come to drink and listen to a trio playing sentimental favorites. Expats gather in the Tavern for drinks and light meals. A new extension has 300 executive rooms with concierge service. *Jln. Jend. Basuki Rakhmat 124-8, Surabaya 60275, tel. 031/511234, fax 031/521508; U.S. reservations tel. 800/233–1234. 500 rooms. Facilities: 2 restaurants, 24-hr coffee shop, pool with swim-up bar, fitness center, business center, airline offices, shops. AE, DC, MC, V.*

The Arts

Eight-hour wayang kulit performances of the full *Ramayana* or *Mahabharata* are usually held every second Saturday of the month at **Sasono Hinggil,** just south of Yogya's kraton, on the opposite side of the alun-alun. These plays begin at 9 PM and last until dawn. Shorter versions of two to three hours are given at other times. Your hotel should have the schedule, or check at the information booth outside the theater.

Actors perform stories from the *Ramayana* nightly at the **People's Park** (Taman Hiburan Rakyat, Jln. Brig. Jen. Katamso, Yogyakarta). Shows last about two hours.

At the **Yogyakarta Crafts Center,** called Ambar Budaya, hour-long wayang kulit performances take place every Monday, Wednesday, and Saturday at 9:30 PM (Jln. Laksda Adisucipto, opposite the Ambarrukmo Palace Hotel).

The *Ramayana* ballet is performed outdoors before the Prambanan temple complex at various times through the year. From January through March, performances are usually once a week on Thursday. April through June and October through December, there are at least three performances (Tuesday, Wednesday, and Thursday). July through September features up to five performances a week— always on Tuesday, Wednesday, and Thursday, and usually on Saturday and Sunday. Hotel tour desks can arrange tickets and transportation, or you can share a taxi from the Tourist Information Center (Jln. Malioboro 12) at 6:30. Public buses pass by the theater's entrance, but they can be unreliable, and the drivers tend to gouge foreigners. This is an elaborate presentation with scores of dances, a full-blown orchestra, and armies of monkeys strutting around the stage. *Jln. Raya Yogya-Solo Km 16, Prambanan, Yogyakarta, tel. 0274/63918. Admission: Rp 15,000.*

At Solo's **Mangkunegaran Palace,** a gamelan orchestra performs each Saturday from 9 to 10:30 AM. Dance rehearsals are held on Wednesday from 10 to noon and on Monday and Friday afternoon.

Bali and Lombok

The "magic" of Bali has its roots in the fact that the island is religiously distinct from the rest of Indonesia: Unlike their Muslim neighbors, the Balinese are Hindus. Their faith also contains elements of Buddhism and of ancient animist beliefs indigenous to the archipelago. To the Balinese, every living thing contains a spirit; when they pick a flower as an offering to the gods, they first say a prayer to the flower. All over the island, from the capital city of Denpasar to the tiniest village, plaited baskets filled with flowers and herbs lie on the sidewalks, on the prows of fishing boats, and in markets. These offerings are made from dawn till dusk, to placate evil spirits and honor helpful ones. Stone figures guard the entryways to temples, hotels, and homes. The black-and-white-checked cloths around the statues' waists symbolize the balance between good and evil. Maintaining that harmony is the life work of every Balinese.

Hindu culture came to Bali as early as the 9th century; by the 14th century, the island was part of the Hindu Majapahit empire of east Java. When that empire fell to Muslim invaders, Majapahit aristocrats, scholars, artists, and dancers fled to Bali, consolidating Hindu culture and religion there.

tremely good value. *Jln. Prawirotaman 22, tel. 0274/27991. 29 rooms. Facilities: small restaurant, outdoor pool. No credit cards.*

Solo
$$
★

Kusuma Sahid Prince Hotel. Three two-story buildings and outlying bungalows are set on 5 acres of landscaped gardens. The lobby veranda—the original *pendopo agung* (prince's courtyard)—is a wonderful place for tea or a cooling drink. Most guest rooms have twin beds, a couple of upholstered chairs, and a desk; the best overlook the pool. The bathrooms are pristine, and hot water is usually available. The dining room offers excellent Indonesian and Western food at reasonable prices. This is by far the nicest place to stay in the Yogyakarta–Solo area, and it's cheaper than the Yogyakarta hotels. *Jln. Sugiyopranoto 22, tel. 0271/46356, fax 0271/44788. 103 rooms. Facilities: restaurant, bar, 24-hr room service, large outdoor pool, travel desk, drugstore and shops, banquet/meeting rooms. AE, DC, MC, V.*

$
Mangkunegaran Palace Hotel. Adjacent to the palace and owned by Prince Mangkunegoro, this hotel has great potential, but it desperately needs renovation that is being performed only intermittently. Inspect your room before signing in. If you don't mind cracked plaster and a musty smell, the Mangkunegaran is the least expensive palace you are ever likely to stay in. The most appealing room is the dining room, which has a batik-painted ceiling just like the palace's. *Istara Mangkunegaran, tel. and fax 0271/35683. 50 rooms. Facilities: restaurant, outdoor pool, free admission to the palace. AE, DC, MC, V.*

$
Wisata Indah. Though the plastered walls have hand smudges and the bathrooms are the bucket-dip (*mundi*) style, the hot water is hot and the sheets freshly laundered, and the staff is friendly and helpful. Outside each room are tables and chairs for breakfast (included in the rate) and meals that may be ordered from the bellboys. Negotiate on the room rate before you sign in. *Jln. Slamet Riyadi 173, tel. 0271/43753. 27 rooms. No restaurant. MC, V.*

Surabaya
$$$

Hotel Majapahit. Built in 1910 in the center of town, this is one of Indonesia's few heritage hotels. Its expansive courts and green lawns became derelict after World War II, but some of their colonial serenity remains. In 1994, the Mandarin Oriental Hotel Group, who manage such distinguished properties as the Oriental in Bangkok, took over, and they have begun massive restoration. At the grand reopening in 1995, the Majapahit may have more character than any other hotel in Surabaya. *Jln. Tunjungan 65, Box 199, Surabaya 60275, tel. 031/43351, fax 031/43599. 105 rooms. Facilities: Indonesian and Western restaurant, bar/lounge, Saturday-evening barbecue, business services. AE, DC, MC, V.*

$$$
Hyatt Regency Surabaya. With competition from the new Shangri-La and Hilton, the Hyatt has refurbished its 11-story wing and added the 27-story Regency Tower with Regency Club rooms, meeting rooms, two business centers, and offices. An added convenience is a new airline ticketing office. Rooms are typical Hyatt—comfortable, beige, fairly large, and furnished with wooden cabinets, king-size beds, and ferns in huge clay pots. The main lobby is a popular spot for locals who come to drink and listen to a trio playing sentimental favorites. Expats gather in the Tavern for drinks and light meals. A new extension has 300 executive rooms with concierge service. *Jln. Jend. Basuki Rakhmat 124-8, Surabaya 60275, tel. 031/511234, fax 031/521508; U.S. reservations tel. 800/233–1234. 500 rooms. Facilities: 2 restaurants, 24-hr coffee shop, pool with swim-up bar, fitness center, business center, airline offices, shops. AE, DC, MC, V.*

The Arts

Eight-hour wayang kulit performances of the full *Ramayana* or *Mahabharata* are usually held every second Saturday of the month at **Sasono Hinggil,** just south of Yogya's kraton, on the opposite side of the alun-alun. These plays begin at 9 PM and last until dawn. Shorter versions of two to three hours are given at other times. Your hotel should have the schedule, or check at the information booth outside the theater.

Actors perform stories from the *Ramayana* nightly at the **People's Park** (Taman Hiburan Rakyat, Jln. Brig. Jen. Katamso, Yogyakarta). Shows last about two hours.

At the **Yogyakarta Crafts Center,** called Ambar Budaya, hour-long wayang kulit performances take place every Monday, Wednesday, and Saturday at 9:30 PM (Jln. Laksda Adisucipto, opposite the Ambarrukmo Palace Hotel).

The *Ramayana* ballet is performed outdoors before the Prambanan temple complex at various times through the year. From January through March, performances are usually once a week on Thursday. April through June and October through December, there are at least three performances (Tuesday, Wednesday, and Thursday). July through September features up to five performances a week— always on Tuesday, Wednesday, and Thursday, and usually on Saturday and Sunday. Hotel tour desks can arrange tickets and transportation, or you can share a taxi from the Tourist Information Center (Jln. Malioboro 12) at 6:30. Public buses pass by the theater's entrance, but they can be unreliable, and the drivers tend to gouge foreigners. This is an elaborate presentation with scores of dances, a full-blown orchestra, and armies of monkeys strutting around the stage. *Jln. Raya Yogya-Solo Km 16, Prambanan, Yogyakarta, tel. 0274/63918. Admission: Rp 15,000.*

At Solo's **Mangkunegaran Palace,** a gamelan orchestra performs each Saturday from 9 to 10:30 AM. Dance rehearsals are held on Wednesday from 10 to noon and on Monday and Friday afternoon.

Bali and Lombok

The "magic" of Bali has its roots in the fact that the island is religiously distinct from the rest of Indonesia: Unlike their Muslim neighbors, the Balinese are Hindus. Their faith also contains elements of Buddhism and of ancient animist beliefs indigenous to the archipelago. To the Balinese, every living thing contains a spirit; when they pick a flower as an offering to the gods, they first say a prayer to the flower. All over the island, from the capital city of Denpasar to the tiniest village, plaited baskets filled with flowers and herbs lie on the sidewalks, on the prows of fishing boats, and in markets. These offerings are made from dawn till dusk, to placate evil spirits and honor helpful ones. Stone figures guard the entryways to temples, hotels, and homes. The black-and-white-checked cloths around the statues' waists symbolize the balance between good and evil. Maintaining that harmony is the life work of every Balinese.

Hindu culture came to Bali as early as the 9th century; by the 14th century, the island was part of the Hindu Majapahit empire of east Java. When that empire fell to Muslim invaders, Majapahit aristocrats, scholars, artists, and dancers fled to Bali, consolidating Hindu culture and religion there.

Although the island is only 140 km (84 mi) long by 80 km (48 mi) wide, a week would not be enough to appreciate Bali's beaches, temples, volcanoes, and towns. With Indonesia's most developed tourist infrastructure, Bali has three main beach areas on the southern coast, where 90% of its visitors stay. Each has its distinctive appeal, and the three are within easy reach of one another.

Kuta has one of the world's most splendid golden-sand beaches. The first resort to be developed on Bali, it is now extremely commercial—and somewhat tawdry. It appeals mainly to young Australians on package holidays that (even with airfare) cost less than a beach vacation at home. Kuta's main street, just two blocks from the beach, is crammed with boutiques, Western fast-food chains, bars, discos, and, after hours, hustling ladies of the night. But the sunsets are as spectacular as ever, and as you walk east along Kuta to Legian, the beach becomes less crowded. Legian Beach is a little quieter and less congested; it's for those who like to be close to the action but not right in it—though both Kuta and Legian are for 24-hour partying, not peace. Just to the south of Kuta—really part of Kuta Bay—is another area of hotels, promoted under the name Tuban and designed to attract families and those looking for quieter vacations.

Sanur Beach, 9 km (5 mi) east of Denpasar, was Bali's second beach resort. Its hotels, restaurants, and shops are more spread out, so the pace here is less hectic than in Kuta. The beach is less dramatic, too: Instead of wild waves, there's a coral reef that keeps the water calm—especially appealing to windsurfers.

Nusa Dua, a former burial ground, consists of two tiny islands linked to the mainland with a reinforced sand spit. Unlike Kuta and Sanur, this is an entirely planned resort, with no indigenous community. Its large, self-contained hotels include a Grand Hyatt, a Sheraton, and a Hilton. Visitors who stay here must travel inland to see the real Bali, but Nusa Dua's beaches are wide and peaceful, and its hotels luxurious.

Few tourists miss the sunset at Tanah Lot, on the southwest coast. This pagodalike temple sits on a small, rocky islet, surrounded by water at high tide and otherwise accessible by a ramp. Though it's packed with visitors and souvenir stalls, the temple is still venerated as a holy site; it is believed to be guarded by snakes in the rock holes. Despite the commercialism, few sights anywhere match the view of the sun dropping behind the sea and silhouetting the temple—though the wonder may soon disappear if Meridien is permitted to open a hotel close by.

Another popular destination is Ubud, an artists' colony that has grown into a center of art galleries and crafts shops. Ubud offers several good hotels and guest houses to fit all budgets for those who come here more for Balinese culture than for the beaches. It's also cooler here than to the south.

Most of Bali's cultural attractions are inland, to the north and east of Denpasar, Bali's capital. Tourists do not normally stay in this busy market town of about 20,000 people, but Denpasar is worth a half-day visit.

Important Addresses and Numbers

Tourist Information **Dipardi Bali** (Jln. Raya Puputan Renon, Denpasar, tel. 0361/238184). In Kuta, there is the **Government Tourist Information Cen-**

ter (Jln. Legian, tel. 0361/753540). Helpful in Ubud is **Ubud Tourist Information** (Jln. Raya Ubud, tel. 0361/976285).

Emergencies **Police,** tel. 110; **ambulance,** tel. 118; **fire,** tel. 113.

Should you lose your **American Express** card, contact the Amex division of **Pacto Travel Agency** at the Bali Beach Hotel (tel. 0361/788449, ext. Pacto). For **Diners Club:** Jln. Veteran 5, Denpasar, tel. 0361/34771. For **MasterCard** and **Visa:** Jln. Raya Kuta, tel. 0361/751412).

Australian Consulate (146 Jln. Raya Sanur, Denpasar, tel. 0361/235092). **U.S. Consular Agency** (Jln. Sanur Ayu, Sanur, tel. 0361/288478).

Pharmacies **Bali Farma Apotik** (Jln. Melatig, Denpasar, tel. 0361/22878) and **Indonesia Farma Apotik** (Jln. Diponegoro, Denpasar, tel. 0361/27812) provide reliable service and advice.

Arriving and Departing by Plane

Airport and Airlines Bali's airport, **Ngurah Rai,** is 13 km (8 mi) southwest of Denpasar, at the southern end of the island between Kuta and Sanur. **Garuda Indonesia** is the main carrier, with flights from Los Angeles, Hong Kong, Kuala Lumpur, Jakarta, Yogyakarta, Ujung Pandang, and other domestic airports. **Qantas** flies to Bali from Australia, **Singapore Airlines** flies in from Singapore, and **Thai Airways International** from Bangkok. Departure tax is Rp 14,000 for international flights, Rp 6,000 for domestic.

Between the Airport and Hotels Most hotels have a car or minivan waiting to meet arriving planes, and certainly will if you let them know in advance. Otherwise, order a taxi at the counter outside customs; the fixed fare varies from Rp 5,000 to Rp 10,000, depending on the location of your hotel (Rp 6,500 for Kuta; Rp 10,000 for Legian; Rp 15,000 for Sanur; Rp 34,000 for Ubud).

Arriving and Departing by Boat and Bus

From Java **Ferries** make the 35-minute crossing frequently between Ketapang in eastern Java and Gilimanuk in western Bali. Inquire at the pier.

Buses from Yogyakarta to Denpasar (16 hours) use the ferry; an air-conditioned bus costs Rp 16,500. Bus service is available also from Jakarta and Surabaya. Tickets may be purchased through any travel agent.

From Lombok Two ferries a day make the four-hour crossing from Lembar, south of Ampenan in Lombok, to Padangbai, east of Denpasar (fare: Rp 5,000). Bemos provide transport from Padangbai to Denpasar. The major travel agencies will be able to tell you about schedules.

In 1994 a new hydrofoil service, the **Mabua Express,** was introduced between Benoa, just north of Nusa Dua, and Lembar on Lombok (schedules, tel. 0361/772370 on Bali, 0364/37224 on Lombok). It currently makes two round-trips a day—morning and afternoon—at a one-way price of $25 for the upper deck and $17.50 for the lower.

Getting Around

By Taxi Taxis are available in the main tourist areas. They are unmetered, but fares within the Kuta–Sanur–Nusa Dua area are fixed. The 15-minute ride from Kuta to Nusa Dua, for example, is Rp 9,000; from Sanur to Nusa Dua, Rp 15,000. Taxis hailed in the street usually charge 40% less than those hired at a hotel, since these drivers are open to negotiation. For longer journeys, rates are more negotiable—count on about Rp 15,000 per hour.

By Bemo Bemos ply the main routes from Denpasar to Sanur and Kuta and from Kuta to Ubud.

By Car Renting cars or jeeps in Bali is convenient and popular. Daily rates vary from Rp 90,000 at Avis to Rp 36,000 at a small operator, including insurance (with a Rp 540,000 deductible) and unlimited mileage. Legally you have to have an international driver's license, though some agencies will not ask for it. Be aware, if you rent from an upscale hotel, that the cost of the car will be considerably higher than if you rent off the hotel property. Though determined by the places you wish to visit (and the distance covered), a car with driver runs about $65 per 12 hours.

Two companies to try are **Lina Biro Jasa** (Jln. Bakungsari, Kuta, tel. 0361/51820) and **Avis** (Jln. Danau Tamblingan, Sanur, tel. 0361/289138; also at the Bali Hyatt, Sanur, tel. 0361/8271; Nusa Dua Beach Hotel, tel. 0361/71210; and Hotel Sanur Beach, tel. 0361/288011).

Guided Tours

The best way to explore Bali is with a private car and a knowledgeable guide. Without a guide, you may miss much of what is so intriguing about Bali. A car, driver, and guide can be hired from most travel/tour agencies or from your hotel travel desk. The following standardized tours take groups in buses or vans virtually every day and will usually collect you from your hotel:

Denpasar City Tour (three hours) includes the Art Centre and the Bali Museum. **Kintamani Tour** (eight hours) includes the Barong and kris dance performance; silversmith-and-goldsmith, wood-carving, and painting villages; the sacred spring at Tampaksiring; and Kintamani, with its view of Batur volcano and Lake Batur.

Sangeh and Mengwi Tour (four hours) visits the Bali Museum in Denpasar, Sangeh and the sacred monkey forest, and the Pura Taman Ayun temple at Mengwi. **Ubud Handicraft Tour** (five hours) visits the handicraft villages north of Denpasar; Ubud, the artists' center; the museum in Ubud; and Goa Gajah, the elephant cave.

Besakih Temple Tour (seven hours) offers fantastic views on the way to the temple on the slopes of Mt. Agung and includes the ancient hall of justice in Klungkung and the bat cave. A full-day (10-hour) tour includes Besakih and Kintamani, the handicraft villages, Ubud, and other temples.

Afternoon Tanah Lot Sunset Tour (five hours) includes the monkey forest, the temple at Mengwi, and sunset at Tanah Lot.

Turtle Island Tour (four hours) goes by fishing boat from Suwung, near Benoa harbor, to Serangan, an island just off the coast of Sanur, to watch the giant sea turtles.

One established company is **Satriavi Tours & Travel** (Jln. Cemara 27, Semawang, Sanur, tel. 0361/287494); it also maintains a desk at the Nusa Dua Beach Hotel (tel. 0361/971210, ext. 719) and at Hotel Sanur Beach (tel. 0361/288011). This agency offers the most comprehensive selection of tours and also arranges custom tours. One new tour is a day's trek through villages that are off the beaten track. Since Satriavi is a subsidiary of Garuda Indonesia Airlines, it is better equipped to handle onward flight reservations, too. Other reliable tour operators include **Nitour** (Jln. Veteran 5, Denpasar, tel. 0361/736096) and **Pacto** (Jln. Tanjung Sari, Sanur, tel. 0361/788449). For a personal guide, contact **I Made Ramia Santana** (Jln. Planet No. 9, Denpasar, tel. 0361/725909).

Exploring Bali

Numbers in the margin correspond to points of interest on the Bali map.

Tour 1: Denpasar

You can book city tours through your hotel, or you can see Denpasar on your own, by taxi or bemo. A good place to begin is **Pasar Banjung,** the liveliest market in town. It is busiest in the early morning but continues until early afternoon. The large, two-story covered market, near the bridge off Jalan Gajahmada, is packed with spice vendors and farmers selling vegetables, meats, and flowers. The little girls who volunteer to guide you around the market get commissions from any vendor you patronize; of course, your price is raised accordingly.

If you come to Denpasar in the evening, head for the **night market** in the riverside parking lot of the multilevel shopping center at Kusumasari. The market is a gathering place for locals, who come to chat, shop, and feast on Balinese food.

At the center of the crossroads where Jalan Gajahmada intersects with Jalan Veteran is a large statue of Brahma. Its four faces look in the cardinal directions. To the left on Jalan Veteran is the **Hotel Bali** (Jln. Veteran 3, tel. 0361/5681), in a building dating from the Dutch colonial period.

Continue through this intersection past Puputan Square—a park on the right-hand side, with its Sukarno-inspired heroic statue of the common man—to reach **Pura Agung Jagatnatha,** Bali's state temple. To find the entrance, go right at the end of the park onto Jalan Letkol, and it's on your left.

The temple's center stupa is surrounded by a moat and rises eight levels; at the top is a statue of Shiva with flames coming out of his shoulders. The stupa is supported by the cosmic turtle (on whose back the real world symbolically sits) and protected by a huge carved face with a red-cloth tongue. *Nagas* (serpents) entwine the base; around the bottom are relief carvings.

You must wear a sash to enter any Balinese temple; one can be rented on-site for a few rupiah. As shorts are considered improper temple attire, avoid them or borrow a sarong when visiting any holy place.

Farther down Jalan Letkol is the **Bali Museum,** with Balinese art dating from present times back to the prehistoric. The buildings are excellent examples of Balinese temple and palace architecture. *Jln. Letkol. Wisnu, tel. 0361/2680 or 0361/5362. Admission charge. Open Tues.–Thurs. and Sun. 8–2, Fri. 8–11 AM, Sat. 8 AM–12:30 PM.*

Another Denpasar attraction is **Abiankapas,** a large art complex. In the summer, dance performances are held in its auditorium. During the rest of the year, it offers temporary exhibits of modern paintings, batik designs, and wood carvings. *Jln. Abiankapas, no tel. Admission charge. Open daily 10–4.*

Tour 2: Inland to Ubud

The main route leading north to Ubud from Denpasar passes through several villages, each known for a different craft. None is more than 8 km (5 mi) from the next. Ubud itself gained fame as an art colony and has since become a popular shopping area and base for exploring the interior of Bali. To the east are important Hindu temples and the holy mountain of Agung.

❶ The first village out of Denpasar is **Batubulan,** famous for the stone carvers whose workshops and displays line the road. Their wares range from the classic guardian figures that stand before Balinese temples and houses to smaller statues. At 9:30 each morning, dance-dramas are performed at each of the village's three theaters. The same show is performed at all three (*see* The Arts, *below*).

❷ Next comes **Celuk,** the village of the silver- and goldsmiths, then
❸ **Suka Wati,** the cane-weaving village. Both have lots of workshops
❹ and salesrooms. **Batuan,** farther north, is a weaving and painting village. An excellent art gallery, **Jati,** carries a vast array of Balinese arts (*see* Shopping, *below*).

Before leaving Batuan for Mas, visit the 10th-century **temple of Brahma** (Pura Puseh Pura Desa). The brick-and-sandstone temple has three parts. You enter the outer courtyard through a classic Balinese split gate. The bell tower, in the second courtyard, is hung with the ubiquitous black-and-white-checked cloth. In the main courtyard, a stone screen protects the temple from bad spirits: Because a bad spirit can't turn a corner, it can't go around the screen.

In one corner of the main courtyard is a shrine to Brahma, where a hermaphroditic figure is guarded by two nagas. This is the main shrine and, as in every Balinese temple complex, it faces the home of the gods, Mt. Agung. (Oddly for an island people, the Balinese have always turned inward, toward the land—the sea is full of demons.) Nearby, another shrine has three roofs representing the god's three manifestations. The face over the gate entrances, known as Boma, guards against evil from the earth, the nagas against evil from the sea.

❺ Just before Mas, you'll come to the village of **Kemenuh,** where the **home of Ida B. Marka,** a famous wood-carver, is open to the public. The sales showroom is in front; there is no pressure to make a purchase. Behind is a courtyard and a cluster of buildings that serve as the family complex. The centerpiece is the building used for weddings and other rites of passage; this is where the oldest family member sleeps. Other structures include the family temple, a granary, and a cooperative workshop where other villagers help carve and polish. This is a rare opportunity to look inside a Balinese home.

❻ The next stop is **Mas,** the wood-carvers' village. **Ida Bagus Tilem,** often called Bali's top wood-carver, lives here. His work, which has been exhibited internationally, is sold in his small shop.

After Mas, take a right turn on the road toward Pejeng and Gianyar.
❼ A parking lot on the right indicates the entrance to the **Elephant Cave** (Goa Gajah). Discovered in 1923 by a farmer cultivating his field, the cave temple is thought to have been built in the 11th century. In the courtyard, water spouts from the hands of six stone nymphs into two pools. It is believed that worshipers would purify themselves here before passing through the mouth of the giant Boma face carving on the entrance. The Balinese consider the face protective even though it contains the same symbolic features as the

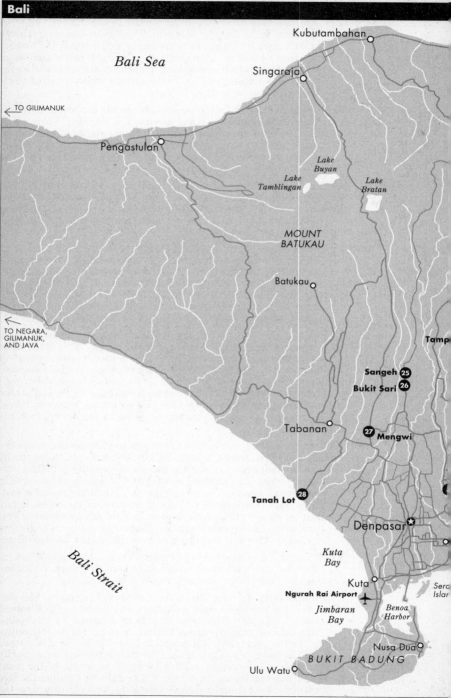

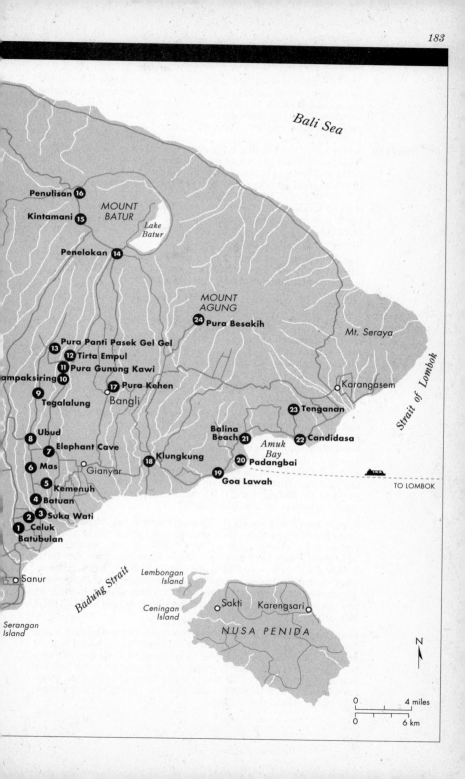

Kali face found at other Hindu temples. To enter the cave, worshipers must pass through her mouth.

The cave itself is pitch dark—hope that your guide has a flashlight. To the left is a niche with a statue of Ganesha, the elephant-headed god and son of Shiva. In the center, to the right of a crumbled statue, are three *linga* (upright carved stones symbolizing male fertility), each with three smaller *yoni* (female forms).

Time Out At the top of the hill, above the cave, is a pleasant restaurant, **Puri Suling** (no phone, no credit cards). A terrace looks out over the rice fields and down to the cave area. In addition to dull Western food, the restaurant serves excellent Indonesian specialties.

8 Beyond Mas is the artist-colony town of **Ubud.** For an overview of Balinese and Indonesian painting, visit the **Neka Gallery,** at the east end of the main street; it also shows works by Western artists who have lived in Bali. *Open daily 9–4.*

Another gallery worth visiting is the **Rudana Gallery** (tel. 0361/26564), which exhibits collectors' pieces of hand-painted batik as well as more affordable prints. *Open daily 9–7.*

Ubud also has its own style of wood carving, slightly more ethereal than you'll find in Mas. A good place to see both old and newer work is the **Nyana Tilem Gallery** (no phone) on the Mas Road.

The **Puri Lukisan Museum**—set in a garden at the west end of the main street, with rice paddies and water buffalo in the background—exhibits only modern Balinese art. The work is arranged chronologically, so you can follow the development from formal religious art to more natural, realistic depictions of dances, festivals, and rice harvesting.

Ubud's main street is lined with shops selling art, textiles, clothing, and other handicrafts. On most days you'll also find a street market. In the center of town is **Puri Saren,** a prince's palace that is also a hotel. The complex is beautiful, but not very well maintained. The prince's living quarters are at the end of the courtyard; guest accommodations are in surrounding buildings. One contains an old tiger costume from the Barong dance, and a peacock walks the grounds. On Monday and Friday dances are performed in the courtyard; the dancers rehearse on Sunday.

Across from Puri Saren is the **Monkey Forest Road,** which in recent years has filled up with souvenir and T-shirt shops and inexpensive restaurants. (Farther along are small hotels, losmen, and homestays where you can find simple accommodation for under US$20 a night.) Keep walking and you'll reach the **Monkey Forest,** where a small donation will get you a close-up view of monkeys so accustomed to tourists that the little monsters will lift items from your pocket or tear jewelry off your neck and scamper off with their loot into the trees.

Ubud has become a major tourist center for those who care about Balinese culture. Every day dance performances are held here or nearby, and artists still have their workshops in this region. However, with hotels, restaurants, shops, and souvenir stalls multiplying monthly, Ubud has lost its tranquil character. To find that, you'll need to take one of the many trails that lead through the surrounding countryside to small villages.

Tour 3: Inland from Ubud

The road north from Ubud passes through lovely countryside with patchwork rice fields in different stages of cultivation. Men ankle-deep in mud plant and weed, while ducks paddle and dip for their lunch. Out in the fields stand shrines to Dewi, the goddess of rice, and stilted, roofed structures for the farmers to rest or eat in. In the village of **Tegalalung,** artisans carve intricate flower designs into wood. In the town of **Tampaksiring,** follow the sign to **Pura Gunung Kawi,** a monument to an 11th-century ruler and one of the oldest in Bali. From the access road, a stone stairway leads down to a lush green valley. Pass through a stone archway to the canyon floor and two rows of memorial temples, carved in niches in the face of two cliffs. According to legend, the giant Kebo Iwa carved these niches in one night with his fingernails.

Beyond the village of Tampaksiring, the road forks. To the right is the famous temple at **Tirta Empul.** People from all over Bali come to bathe in the holy spring, said to have been created when the god Indra pierced a stone to produce magical waters that revived his poisoned army. At the **Pura Panti Pasek Gel Gel** holy spring, a few kilometers farther north, the hawkers are less demanding, and fewer tourists interrupt the sanctity of the temple. The temple is dedicated to Vishnu, whose many responsibilities include water and irrigation. The main shrine stands in the center of a pool filled with holy water and fat goldfish. Bathing pools are segregated by sex and age.

North of Sebatu, the vanilla-and-clove-bordered road climbs quickly. Roadside stalls sell fruits and vegetables, replacing the souvenir and handicraft kiosks of the lower altitudes. **Penelokan,** a village at the edge of the old crater of 1,450-m (4,757-ft) Mt. Batur, affords a great view of the lake inside the vast crater, where a new volcano has arisen.

Time Out | Except when the low clouds move in, as they often do later in the day, two restaurants offer superb views of the crater: **Puri Salera** (tel. 0361/88226, no credit cards), about a kilometer out of Penelokan toward Batur, and the **Batur Garden** in Batur. The local fare is reasonably good, but you pay for the view.

Along the road on the rim of the crater are two other villages, **Kintamani**—a quiet town with losmen used by hikers—and **Penulisan.** Here, an old stairway leads up a hill to the ancient temple **Pura Sukawana.** Most of the decaying sculptures are from the 11th century, but look closely and you will find older, pagan phallic symbols. The view, which stretches across Bali to the Java Sea, is breathtaking, especially at sunrise.

The drive south from Penelokan to Bangli is a quick run downhill. On the outskirts of Bangli is an S-curve; here take a left, and at the foot of the hill is **Pura Kehen,** a 12th-century temple dedicated to Shiva. A great flight of steps leads up to this terraced temple. In the first courtyard is a giant holy banyan tree with a bell tower used to summon the villagers for ceremonies and other events. The entrance to the inner courtyard is up two steep, parallel flights of steps. At the top center are the "closed gate" and the Boma face, blocking evil spirits. Within the inner courtyard, the main shrine sits on a cosmic turtle, symbolizing the spiritual world, entwined by nagas, symbolizing the material. Material binds the spiritual—another example of Balinese harmony. The Meru in the center has 11 roofs, the highest honor to the gods.

Besakih, on the slopes of Mt. Agung, is about a 40-minute drive northeast from Bangli, but you may want to call it a day at this point and return to Ubud or the beach. We have combined Besakih with Klungkung in the next excursion.

Tour 4: Eastern Bali

⑱ Klungkung, To the southeast of the main road between Ubud and Denpasar is a former dynastic capital. In the center of town stands the **Kerta Gosa** (Hall of Justice), built in the late 18th century. The raised platform in the hall supports three thrones—one with a lion carving for the king, one with a dragon for the minister, and one with a bull for the priest. The accused brought before this tribunal could look up at the painted ceiling and contemplate the horrors in store for convicted criminals: torches between the legs, pots of boiling oil, decapitation by saw, and dozens of other punishments to fit specific crimes. To the right of the Hall of Justice is the **Bale Kambang** (Floating Pavilion), a palace surrounded by a moat. It, too, has a painted ceiling, this one of the Buddhist *Suta Sota*.

⑲ Heading east out of Klungkung, the road drops south to run along the coast and through the area of Kusamba, speckled with the thatched roofs of salt-panning huts. Just beyond is **Goa Lawah,** the bat cave. Unless you long to see thousands of bats hanging from the ceiling, you may not want to subject yourself to the aggressive hawkers, postcard sellers, and young girls who throw you a flower, then angrily demand payment when you leave. The cave is said to lead all the way to Mt. Agung.

⑳ Continuing east along the coast will take you to **Padangbai**—the **㉑** port for the ferry to Lombok—and then to **Balina Beach,** a quiet area with a deserted strand and small hotel complexes offering sportfishing and diving facilities.

㉒ Candidasa, once a budget traveler's escape from Kuta, now boasts a dozen small hotels and restaurants. The waters here are gentle because of a reef 270 m (300 yd) offshore—good for snorkeling—but at high tide the sea swallows the beach.

㉓ On the western side of Candidasa, a road turns inland to **Tenganan,** an ancient walled village of the Balinese who preceded the Majapahit. The village consists of two parallel streets lined on either side with identical walled compounds. Inside the compounds, houses face each other across a grassy central strip, where the public buildings stand. Tenganan keeps to its traditions—it is, for example, the only place in Indonesia where double ikat is still woven—and people seldom marry outside the village.

Return to the main coast road at Candidasa, where a left turn leads to Amlapura. Here the road splits; take the road to Rendang, then turn right to climb the 11 km (7 mi) to Besakih.

㉔ Pura Besakih, known as the mother temple of Bali, is the most sacred of them all. Situated on the slopes of Mt. Agung, the complex has 30 temples—one for every Balinese district—on seven terraces. It is thought to have been built before Hinduism reached Bali and subsequently modified. The structure consists of three main parts, the north painted black for Vishnu, the center white for Shiva, and the south red for Brahma. You enter through a split gate.

Much of the temple area was destroyed in 1963 when Mt. Agung erupted, killing 1,800 believers, but diligent restoration has repaired most of the damage. Visitors are not allowed into the inner courtyard, but there is enough to see to justify the 2-km-long (1¼ mi) walk from the parking lot through souvenir stands and vendors. From Besakih, return the 8 km (5 mi) to the main road, then continue straight to Klungkung or go right for Bangli. Denpasar is 60 km (35 mi) away.

Tour 5: Western Bali

Much of western Bali, from Gilimanuk, where the ferries leave for Java, as far east as the Tabanan district west of Denpasar, is made up of valleys twisting below volcanic peaks. Few tourists visit this area, but if you have time, its temples, forests, and black-sand beaches are fascinating. In the following one-day excursion, you drive north from Denpasar to Sangeh, then back south to Mengwi, turn west toward Tabanan, and finally head south for sunset at the coastal temple at Tanah Lot.

㉕ **Sangeh,** 20 km (12 mi) north and slightly west of Denpasar, is a pleasant temple town where the community decided to put an end to aggressive hawkers: Vendors are barred from stepping onto the street to lure in customers (a regulation we'd like to see implemented throughout Bali). According to the Balinese version of the *Ramayana,* Hanuman, on his way to crush the evil Rawana between two halves of the holy mountain, dropped a huge chunk of the mountain—including some of his soldiers—at Sangeh; the soldiers have **㉖** propagated ever since at the nearby Monkey Forest, **Bukit Sari.** And a precocious band of little buggers they are: They will lift, in a flash, any shining item from your person. They don't shy from grabbing at earrings, and lately they've taken to dipping into trouser pockets for rupiah notes. *So don't wear or carry anything that can be lifted.* On the way to the moss-covered temple, **Pura Bukit Sari,** note the large grove of tall nutmeg trees. The nutmeg is not native to Bali, and no one knows how these got here—a mystery that has made them sacred to the Balinese and adds to the mystical feeling of the forest.

㉗ Returning from Sangeh, head south for **Mengwi** to visit the state temple of **Pura Taman Ayun,** just off the main road. Built in 1634 and renovated in 1937, this serene, moat-encircled structure—once the main temple of the western kingdom—has wonderfully executed stone carvings in its inner courtyard. Notice the half-face of Boma on each side of the split gate. (The nearby Water Palace restaurant, overlooking the moat, is a good place for refreshment.)

Head south from Mengwi for 3 km (1½ mi), then turn west; before you reach Tabanan—a prosperous market town with little to see— **㉘** take a left (south) at the well-signposted road for **Tanah Lot.** Though tourists come here in droves for the postcard-like setting, the Balinese revere this pagoda-style temple as deeply as they do the mountain shrines. It has the added mystery of snakes that secret themselves in the rock holes and are said to guard the spirits residing at Tanah Lot. The temple stands on a small rocky islet accessible (except at high tide) by a small causeway. (Some of the isolation may be lost if a new Meridien hotel opens as planned in 1995 within sight of the temple.)

Ideally, you should arrive at Tanah Lot an hour before sunset, which will give you enough time to inspect the snakes; entering the caves on the shore, you can usually find a sleepy reptile resting in the cool. Cross the causeway to the temple, then return to the shore to watch it become silhouetted against the burning sky as the sun goes down. Not even the hawkers and the lines of snapping cameras can spoil the vision.

Tour 6: Lombok

The island of Lombok lies 45 km (27 mi) east of Bali. You can take a 20-minute flight to the island, spend the day exploring, and return by nightfall—though Lombok really deserves more time. The beaches are superior to those of Bali and the level of commercialism is substantially less. Also, Lombok has a climate considerably drier than Bali's, which is a distinct advantage during the rainy season, from December through May.

Merpati and **Sempati** airlines run a shuttle service, with flights every hour beginning at 7 AM, from Denpasar to Lombok's Mataram airport. The last flight is at 3 PM. Purchase tickets (Rp 62,000 one-way) at the airport an hour before departure. Returning from Lombok to Denpasar, you can only reserve a seat if you have a connecting flight. Flights have a tendency to be late, and are frequently cancelled. The recently introduced 248-passenger hydrofoil, the **Mabua Express,** does the run in 2½ hours. In addition, two ferries make the crossing daily, in four hours. (*See* Arriving and Departing by Boat and Bus, *above.*) Since the ferry docks some distance from the tourist centers on both Bali and Lombok (it takes three bemos to travel from Lembar Harbor to Senggigi), a bus/ferry package—between Ubud, Kuta, or Sanur on Bali and Mataram or Senggigi on Lombok—is a better alternative. **Perama Travel** (tel. 0364/51561) organizes the packages, and most small travel agents can make the booking. Fares are reasonable—e.g., Rp 13,000 from Kuta to Senggigi.

Public transport on Lombok consists of crowded bemos (minibuses) and the *cidomo,* a horse-drawn cart that seats four or five and costs approximately Rp 500 per kilometer. Taxis are available from the airport and hotels; a taxi from the airport to Senggigi should cost less than Rp 7,000 (though you'll be asked for at least Rp 10,000 initially). Rental cars cost about Rp 45,000 a day or Rp 75,000 with driver. **Satriavi Tours & Travel** has an office at Senggigi Beach Hotel (tel. 0364/23430, ext. 8602) and organizes different tours of the island.

Lombok is rather like Bali was 30 years ago, before the onslaught of hotel developers. That's changing fast, though: Senggigi Beach is now a crowd of hotels, the beaches on the Gil coral atolls are lined with inexpensive bungalows, and the Indonesian president's son has bought up the beautiful beaches to the south to make way for a Nusa Dua–type megaresort of impersonal international hotels.

Lombok, meaning chili pepper in Javanese, is home to two cultures, the Balinese Hindu and the Sasak Moslem. Most of the Balinese, who ruled the island until 1894, live on the western side of the island around Ampenan, Mataram (the provincial capital), and Cakranegara (known for its handwoven textiles). Here you will find Balinese temples of interest, though none are as fully developed as in Bali. Lombok's most famous temple-palace complex is **Narmada Taman,** built in 1727 in Narmada. The temple is notable for its man-made lagoons symbolizing the lakes of the holy mountain, Mt. Rinjani, in the north of Lombok.

En route to Narmada from Mataram and Senggigi Beach, stop in Cakranegara to see the **Taman Mayura,** once a Balinese royal palace, now a large artificial pool filled with lotus. In the center of the pool is Balé Kembang, a floating pavilion that is similar to but smaller and less ornate than the one in Klungkung, Bali. At **Sweta,** the main market on Lombok, you can shop for spices and beautifully made cane baskets that entrepreneurs buy and take back to Bali to sell at in-flated prices.

Five km (3 mi) north of Narmada is **Lingsar Temple,** built in 1714 by the first migrating Balinese and reconstructed in conjunction with Sasak Moslems as a symbol of their unity. Nearby is **Suranadi,** a cool hill town with a Hindu temple, especially venerated for its spring water and eels. Both promise good fortune to the pilgrim.

The south of the island is scattered with small Sasak villages. On the road to Kuta, stop at the government "protected village," **Rambitan.** The long sloping thatched roofs of traditional Sasak houses are clustered together, and a few of the villagers sell batik sarongs at ridiculously low prices. Try to get a glimpse into the houses. Each house has two main areas: The outer area is where the men sleep; the inner area is reserved for the women.

Kuta is a tiny village on the shores of the Indian Ocean. The curving sandy beach is virtually deserted, frequented only by a few hardy travelers staying at the two losmen on the other side of the road. The better of the two is **Arja,** with its small restaurant, for Rp 10,000 a night. Farther east along the coast is the horseshoe-shaped **Tanjung An,** the most beautiful beach on Lombok. With its fine, soft, white sand, the beach is postcard-perfect—and usually deserted, except for two hopeful vendors selling watermelons.

A 30-minute drive north of Senggigi are three small coral atolls, all of which have small cottage bungalows popular with backpackers. **Gil Air** is closest to shore and requires only a quick 10-minute sea crossing in a motorized prahu. Here dazzling white sand meets crys-tal-clear water, which is home to brightly colored tropical fish. Bring snorkeling equipment since there is none to rent on the island. For even more pristine waters, the next atoll, **Gil Meno,** has an abun-dance of sea life—red-lined triggerfish, starfish, five-line damsel, and the occasional shark—and, for scuba divers, there is unique blue coral 50–80 feet below the surface. Visibility isn't what it was 10 years ago, however, and during the rains (January–March) it can di-minish to 50 feet.

For shopping, go to the market at Sweta for spices and handwoven baskets. In Cakranegara, the handwoven textiles are well known; visit **Pertenunan Rinjani** (Jln. Pejanggik 46, tel. 0364/23169) on the town line of Mataram for handwoven ikat. The public market in Cakranegara is good for silver and gold and for straw baskets. To see ikat made and to buy the cloth, head for the village of Sukare.

Shopping

Though there are countless stores in Kuta, Sanur, and Ubud, the best places for shopping are the craft villages north of Denpasar, where you usually buy right at the workshop. Workshop prices should be better, but you must always bargain: The tourist asking price is at least 25% higher than normal. Also remember that most guides get a commission on your purchases. If your guide stops at every shop along the road, speak up—there is too much to see in Bali to spend all your time this way. For shopping in Lombok, *see* Tour 6.

Art For the best of Batuan—Bali's painting center—ask any local to di-rect you to the studios of **Mokoh, I. Made Budi,** or **Wayan Darmawan.** The **Jati Art Gallery** (Batuan Sukawati Gianyar) sells paintings and artifacts, including antique wayang kulit, old masks and temple or-naments, handwoven ikat, batiks, wood carvings, and new puppets.

In Ubud, first visit the **Neka Art Gallery** (*see* Tour 2, *above*) to get an overview of Balinese fine art, then head for the **Rudana Gallery** for its collection of batiks and paintings at more affordable prices. Once you have grasped the concepts behind Balinese art, get directions to the workshops of **A.A. Gd. Sobart, Gusti Ketut Kobot, I.B. Made Poleng, Mujawan, Sudiarto,** or **I. Bagus Nadra.**

The Grace Shop (Jln. Legian Tengah 435, Kuta, tel. 0361/752003) offers a range of Balinese antiques. For Asmat art from Irian Jaya and other village artifacts, take a look at the wares in **Asmat** (Jln. Tunjung Mekar 55, Kuta, no phone).

Baskets and Cane The village of **Sukawati** is known for its cane weaving and for wind chimes. Stalls lining the road sell baskets, hats, and some furniture.

Batik Balinese batiks tend to be more colorful than the traditional Javanese style, and the designs are more floral than geometric. You'll find selections all over Kuta, Sanur, and Ubud. A good source of hand-drawn batiks is **Popiler** (tel. 0361/36498) in Tohpati village, just north of Batubulan. If you pay cash instead of using a credit card, you may increase your bargaining power by around 20% for the yard goods, paintings, garments, and household items here. Behind the shop, you're invited to watch girls outlining the designs with wax.

Furniture Look for handcrafted furniture, one of the best buys on Bali, at **Mario Antiques** (Peninjauan Sukawati, Gianyar, tel. 0361/98541), just outside Ubud.

Ikat The town of **Tenganan** (*see* Tour 4, *above*) is the only place in Indonesia where double ikat fabric is still woven. The design is dyed on individual threads of both the warp and the filling before being woven (in single ikat, the dye goes only on the warp threads).

Silver and Gold **Celuk,** north of Denpasar, is the gold-and-silversmiths' village. In the workshops behind the stores, you can watch boys working the silver and setting semiprecious stones. As a rule, the jewelry you find here is 90%–92% silver, the tableware 60%–70%. If you have time, you can custom-order pieces.

One shop with a large selection is **Dewi Sitha** (no phone), on the left side of the road going north. Remember that with a smile and a murmur you might drive the cost of a $125 bracelet down to $80. Especially where price tags are in dollars, bargaining is the rule.

Stone Carving **Batubulan,** the first village on the road north from Denpasar, is the source of virtually every guardian figure in Bali. On each side of the road you'll see workshops where boys chip at the soft sandstone, and sculptures are for sale out front. Most workshops make small carvings for tourists. **I. Made Sura** is one of the better shops; it also carries some wood carvings, old wood ornaments, and carved doors.

Wayang Kulit The hand-cut, painted shadow puppets for sale on Bali are usually new. You can buy antiques at the **Jati Art Gallery** in Batuan (*see* Art, *above*) and at the **Mega Art Gallery** in Denpasar (Jln. Gajahmada), which also sells new puppets, wood carvings, and paintings.

Wood Carving There are some 4,000 wood-carvers on Bali, and most of them are in Mas. Just outside the village are the home and studio of **Ida B. Marka,** where you can see works in progress and buy finished examples (*see* Tour 2, *above*). In Mas itself is the home of **Ida Bagus Tilem,** Indonesia's most famous wood-carver (tel. 0361/6414–*also see* Tour 2). Mask-carvers have shops in the back lanes; the masks, which make great wall hangings, range in price from $2 to $50, depending on their size and complexity. The **Taman Harum Cottages** (Box 216,

Denpasar, tel. 0361/35242) in Mas, with 17 compact adjoining duplexes, offers wood-carving classes to its guests and has its own
shop, the **Tantra Gallery,** with the works of master carver Nyana.
Another gallery worth searching out is the **Tinem Gallery** (tel. 0361/
35136), with the works of Nyana's brother, Ida Bagus Nyana. For
toys, try the **Joger Handcraft Center** in Kuta Beach (Jln. Raya Kuta,
tel. 0361/53959).

Sports, Fitness, Beaches

Beaches   The tourist enclaves at Kuta/Legian, Sanur, and Nusa Dua all boast
very different beaches (*see above* for complete descriptions). Off the
beaten track, try **Balina Beach** and **Candidasa** in eastern Bali (*see*
Tour 4, *above*).

Boating   For yacht charters, contact **Jet Boat Tours** (Jln. Pantai Karang 5,
Sanur, tel. 0361/28839). Sanur's **Bali Hyatt** has two deep-sea fishing
boats.

Cockfighting   Although cockfighting is technically illegal in Indonesia, the Balinese incorporate the sport into their temple ceremonies, and many
men keep cocks for playing and betting. These rituals are not meant
for tourists, but any local you befriend will know where the next
fight is scheduled.

Golf   The 18-hole **Bali Handera Kosaido Country Club** (tel. 0361/788994)—
possibly the only course anywhere that's set in a volcanic crater,
with beautiful landscaped gardens on the sides of the fairways—is
at Bedugul, one hour north of Denpasar. Daily greens fees are $45
on weekends and $30 during the week. Caddies, both male and fe-
male, are $4.50 a round, and there are accommodations, decorated
with modern Balinese furniture and batiks, available for $70–$120 a
double. The **Bali Hyatt** in Sanur (tel. 0361/8271) has a three-hole
course. The new 18-hole course (to be expanded to 36 holes over the
next two years) of the **Bali Golf & Country Club,** on the Bukit Peninsula near the hotels of Nusa Dua, offers $77 greens fees and $27 club
rental (Box 12, Nusa Dua, tel. 0361/871791).

Rafting   It takes 2½ hours to drift and bump through gorges and rapids down
the Ayung River, ending in the gentle valley near Ubud. Several
outfits organize rubber raft trips for around $55, including the reli-
able Australian outfit **Bali Adventure Rafting** (Jln. Tunjung Mekar,
Legian, tel. 0361/751292).

Tennis and   Several hotels have tennis courts; the **Nusa Dua Beach** also has
Squash   squash courts.

Water Sports   Personnel at all beach hotels can direct you to facilities for surfing,
diving, windsurfing, and deep-sea fishing. The **Balina Diving Association** (Balina Beach, tel. 0361/80871) also arranges dives. You can
get scuba equipment and a ride out to the reef at Sanur from **Bali
Marine Sport** (Jln. Bypass Ngurah Rai, Sanur, tel. 0361/87872) or
Ocean Dive Centre (Jln. Bypass, Ngurah Rai, Sanur, tel. 0361/
88652). Windsurfers can be rented at the beach market in Sanur.

Nusa Lembongan, the island opposite Sanur beach and next to Nusa
Penida, offers surfing and diving. But for the best surfing, head to
Ulu Watu, on the western side of the Bukit Peninsula at Bali's south-
ern tip.

Dining

Kuta and Sanur offer a fairly wide range of restaurants. In Nusa Dua, most of the dining is at hotels. Western food abounds in Kuta, though mostly of the fast-food variety. Hotels offer better Western cooking.

Kuta/Legian
$$$

Oberoi. In an open pavilion with a bamboo ceiling, you dine around a pool with a fountain surrounded by trees and flowers. A Swiss chef and Balinese sous-chef turn out both an Indonesian buffet and an à la carte menu with a Continental flair. Try the crepe "le Oberoi," with its filling of crabmeat, cream, onions, and white wine, or the coconut-breaded shrimp, deep-fried and served with a ginger cream sauce. The Oberoi also prepares Indian specialties. *Legian Beach, Jln. Kayu Aya, tel. 0361/751061. Reservations suggested during busy season. Jacket suggested. AE, DC, MC, V.*

$$

Glory Bar & Restaurant. There are dozens of seafood restaurants in Kuta all offering the same fare. What puts the Glory a cut above is the freshness of its fish, mud crabs, and lobster. The atmosphere is convivial, and prices are fair. The wide-ranging Indonesian buffet on Wednesday night includes corn soup, fried chicken, sweet-and-sour pork, batter-fried fish, satay, and noodles. *Jln. Legian Tengah 529, Legian, tel. 0361/751091. No reservations. Dress: casual. AE, DC. MC, V.*

$$

Indah Sari. On Kuta's main drag, this seafood-and-barbecue restaurant serves well-prepared dishes, from prawns to grouper, that you can order either spicy or bland. The open-fronted restaurant can get boisterous, but the freshness of the food makes up for the lack of personal service and intimacy. *Jln. Legian, Kuta, tel. 0361/751834. No reservations. Dress: casual. AE, MC, V.*

$$

Poppies. A high wall surrounding the garden and well-spaced tables that permit you to hear your dining companions make this one of the few spots where you can escape the beer-chugging revelries of Kuta. The relaxed alfresco atmosphere is the drawing card; the food, mostly Western dishes, is average to good. *Poppies La., off Jln. Legian, Kuta, tel. 0361/52574. No reservations. Dress: casual. MC, V.*

$$

Warung Kopi. Five marble-topped tables facing the street and another ten in the rear garden provide an oasis from the surrounding honky-tonk scene. The menu is eclectic: Indonesian fish, vegetable, and rice dishes; Indian curries; Western beef and lamb. It's also fine for just a beer and an appetizer or coffee and dessert. *Jln. Legian Tengah 427, Legian, tel. 0361/753602. No reservations. Dress: casual. MC, V.*

$

Bakung Mas Garden. This peaceful and romantic restaurant belongs to the Segara Village Hotel. There are only six tables under the thatched roof, and a tiny bar in case you have to wait. The food has a Chinese influence: Try the stir-fried vegetables with pork or the *semur daging* (thinly sliced beef with a rich sauce of mushrooms and onions). *Jln. Bakung Sari, Kuta, tel. 0361/788407. No reservations. Dress: casual. No credit cards.*

Nusa Dua
$$$

Kertosa Restaurant. This formal Continental restaurant has the atmosphere of a European hotel, despite the Balinese stone sculptures on pedestals. The menu is international with a French flavor, and there's an extensive wine list—a costly luxury in Bali. With the opening of the Grand Hyatt and the Hilton, the Kertosa now faces some stiff competition. *Nusa Dua Beach Hotel, tel. 0361/977120. Reservations suggested. Jacket suggested. AE, DC, MC, V.*

Bali Dining and Lodging

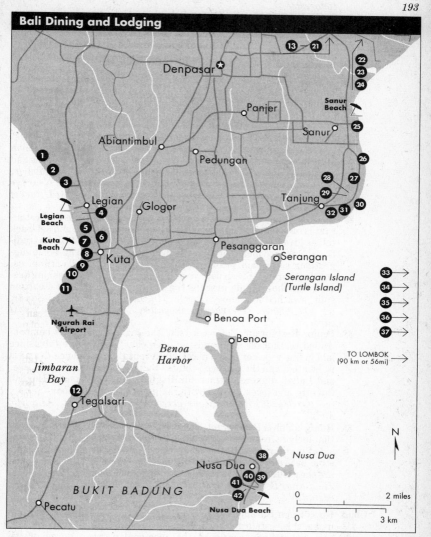

Dining

Ananda Cottages, **13**
Bakung Mas Garden, **10**
Glory Bar & Restaurant, **5**
Indah Sari, **6**
Kertosa, **38**
Kupu Kupu Barong, **14**
Le Gong, **29**
Lotus Café, **15**
Murni's Warung, **16**
Oberoi, **1**
Penjor, **27**

Poppies, **8**
Ronny's Pub & Restaurant, **31**
Spice Islander, **30**
Telaga Naga, **28**
Warung Kopi, **4**

Lodging

Agung Raka, **17**
Amandari, **18**
Amankila, **24**
Ananda Cottages, **13**
Bali Dynasty, **11**
Bali Hilton International, **41**

Bali Hyatt, **30**
Bali Imperial, **2**
Balina Beach, **22**
Buala Club, **42**
Four Seasons Resort, **12**
Graha Beach, **36**
Grand Hyatt Bali, **40**
Hotel Sanur Beach, **32**
Intan Laguna, **35**
Kul Kul Beach Resort, **34**
Kupu Kupu Barong, **14**
Kuta Palace Hotel, **3**
Oberoi, **1**

Pondok Senggigi, **33**
Puri Buitan Cottages, **23**
Sari Yasa Samudra Bungalows, **7**
Segara Village, **25**
Sehati, **19**
Senggigi Beach Hotel, **37**
Sheraton Lagoon Nusa Dua, **39**
Sheraton Senggigi Beach Resort, **34**
Tandjung Sari, **26**
Tjampuhan, **20**
Ubud Village Hotel, **21**

Sanur
$$$
★
Spice Islander. The elegant Balinese decor, with gilded table bases and heavy rattan chairs, is a great setting in which to get acquainted with Balinese cuisine. A rijstaffel buffet with no fewer than 30 dishes—all labeled with their ingredients—is laid out on a lotus altar in the center of the room. Among the delicacies: *crancam ayam* (chicken soup with ginger), *kalio hati dengan kentang* (spicy chicken livers with potato), *opar sapi* (beef in coconut curry sauce), *satay lilit* (skewered pork and beef), and *gudeg yogya* (a dish made of jackfruit). *Bali Hyatt, Sanur, tel. 0361/88271. Reservations suggested during busy season. Jacket suggested. AE, DC, MC, V.*

$$$
Telaga Naga. With a name meaning "dragon's pond," this is the best Chinese restaurant in Bali. Two lily ponds create a floating pavilion atmosphere, and the Singaporean chef specializes in Cantonese and Szechuan cuisine. Try the minced chicken with chili and cucumber, followed by fried lobster with chili and black bean sauce. *Near the Bali Hyatt, Sanur, tel. 0361/88271. Reservations required. Jacket suggested. AE, DC, MC, V.*

$$
Le Gong. The gong hangs in a central garden, and while the restaurant is on Sanur's main street, its woven bamboo walls and set-back tables give it a relaxing atmosphere. To make the most of the traditional Balinese menu, order a few dishes and share them. Some suggestions: soto ayam, prawns in butter sauce, fish grilled with spices, and nasi goreng. Fresh papaya or pineapple makes a refreshing dessert, but the coup de grâce is the Balinese equivalent of a banana split, swathed in a honey treacle. *Jln. Legong, Semawang-Sanur, tel. 0361/88066. Reservations suggested. Dress: casual. No credit cards.*

$$
Penjor Restaurant. Set back from the main street, this bamboo-walled restaurant surrounds an open courtyard where tables are laid in fine weather. Each night a different Balinese dance-drama is presented, and the set menu rotates Balinese, Indonesian, Chinese, and Indian dinners. Owner Ida Bagus Ketut Oka speaks English fluently and loves to chat with his guests. *Batu Jumbar, Sanur, tel. 0361/88226. Reservations accepted. Dress: casual. AE, DC, MC, V.*

$$
Ronny's Pub & Restaurant. For a choice of primarily Western dishes that include fresh fish, sirloin steaks, and nonspicy satay, this open-sided restaurant is better than most of the stops along the Sanur strip between the Hyatt and Sanur Beach hotels. Especially good are the grilled prawns served with butter rice and fresh vegetables. *Jln. Sanur Beach, Sanur, tel. 0361/978370. No reservations. Dress: casual. V.*

Ubud
$$$
★
Kupu Kupu Barong. Perched on a terrace in the hotel of the same name, this restaurant—which has been newly refurbished, retiled, and rethatched—overlooks the spectacular green gorge of the Ayung River. Marble-top tables and rattan chairs add charm. The best views are from the upstairs dining room, though it takes longer for drinks to arrive from the bar. The menu includes Indonesian and international fare. Try the smoked duck with Balinese side dishes; the pan-fried lobster topped with shallots, mushrooms, and coriander; or the fish grilled on bamboo skewers and served with a light peanut sauce. *Kedewatan, Ubud, tel. 0361/923172. Reservations suggested during busy season. Jacket suggested. AE, V.*

$$
Ananda Cottages. Part of the Ananda Cottages hotel, this open-air restaurant is surrounded by rice paddies. Its menu lists Western and Indonesian specialties, including *satay pusut* (skewered meat in a spicy peanut sauce) and *betutu bebek* (Balinese duck). *Ananda Cottages, Box 205, Denpasar, tel. 0361/958001. No reservations. Dress: casual. No credit cards.*

$$ **Lotus Café.** Owned and managed by a Balinese and his Australian wife, this peaceful and charming restaurant has blue-and-white-tile-topped tables in a small garden with a Hindu temple at the back. The menu is creative and refreshing. Try the avocado with diced peanuts, or perhaps the roasted chicken. The homemade pasta is remarkably good, too. *Jln. Raya, Ubud, no phone. No reservations. Dress: casual. No credit cards.*

$$ **Murni's Warung.** On the side of a small ravine, this simple terraced restaurant with bamboo furniture offers both Indonesian and Western cooking. The duck *tu tu* is a Balinese specialty of duck stuffed with spices and thoroughly baked so that the meat falls off the bones. The restaurant has two dining rooms: One is at street level and bustles with activity; the other, a steep flight down, is often empty and has the best views of the waterfall 50 feet away. *Campuan, Ubud, tel. 0361/995233. No reservations. Dress: casual. No credit cards.*

Lodging

More hotels open every year in Bali's popular areas; the Sheraton group manages three of the dozen or so resorts. On the edge of Nusa Dua, the Four Seasons and Amanusa opened in 1994. On the beaches of Kuta/Legian, the most notable new hotel is the Bali Imperial. Ubud has yet to have mammoth hotels (thank goodness), but the number of smaller hotels (20–50 rooms) multiplies every year. Development is now taking place on the east coast; Amankila, a sister property to the Amandari, has set the pace with its luxurious villas. And Lombok is no longer the "undiscovered Bali": Hotels are opening every month, though the Sheraton Senggigi Beach Resort is still the smartest. The following are just some of the many options for travelers. Mailing addresses are given rather than street locations.

**Balina Beach/
Candidasa
$$$$**

Amankila. Luxury thatched-roof pavilions are positioned on a hillside looking out across the Bandung Straits to Lombok. Each includes an outdoor terrace with large daybed, table, and chairs; a bedroom with a canopied king-size bed; and a bathroom with a sunken tub and separate shower. All pavilions are identical; the price (US$330–US$550) varies with the view. The pool is built into the hillside, forming a terrace of its own, while the beach is a stiff downhill climb away. The restaurant takes in the view of the straits. *Manggis, near Candidasa, tel. 0366/21993, fax 0366/21995; U.S. reservations, tel. 800/447-7462; U.K. reservations, tel. 0800/ 282684. 35 suites. Facilities: restaurant, pool with separate restaurant, water sports, private beach. AE, DC, MC, V.*

$ **Balina Beach.** Popular among scuba and snorkel enthusiasts for its diving club, this hotel has one- and two-story thatched cottages scattered near the sandy beach 3 km (1.8 mi) west of Candidasa. The best rooms, upstairs in the two-story bungalows, have sitting rooms and porches. All have private baths and ceiling fans; their rattan decor is simple. *Partai Buitan, Manngis Karang Asem, tel. 0361/8777. 41 rooms. Facilities: restaurant, bar, diving club. V.*

$ **Puri Buitan Cottages.** Opened in late 1988, the Puri Buitan has recently added to its bungalow capacity. The beach here is very quiet, and a reef keeps the sea perfect for swimming. Rooms are simple and clean, with the first-floor units good for families. *Box 464, Denpasar 80001, no phone. 34 rooms. Facilities: restaurant, outdoor pool. V.*

**Kuta/Legian
$$$$
★**

Oberoi. Among the luxurious Oberoi's assets is its location, at the far western end of Legian Beach away from the crowds. Its 33 acres offer tranquillity and privacy, with thatched cottages and private villas spaced among gardens of bougainvillea, hibiscus, and frangi-pani. The lobby and lounge building, with a coral exterior and pol-ished stone floors inside, faces the sea. Rooms are beautifully furnished in dark wood, with ikat bedcovers and draperies. Each cottage has its own veranda; the villas have balconies and garden courtyards. The luxurious villas have private pools and traditional Balinese inner courtyards. Service is personal and friendly, and Ba-linese dance is performed on most evenings in an amphitheater. *Box 451, Denpasar 80001, tel. 0361/751061, fax 0361/752791; U.S. reser-vations, tel. 800/5–OBEROI. 63 cottages, 12 villas. Facilities: res-taurant (see Dining), beachfront café, poolside bar, water sports, tennis, 24-hr room service, jeep rental, shopping arcade, laundry service. AE, DC, MC, V.*

$$$ **Bali Imperial.** Set beyond the crowds along the Kuta/Legian strip but within a 10-minute walk of the action, this 1994 resort is a quiet oasis. The relaxed, expansive lobby is glass and marble. Guest rooms have high ceilings, light wood furniture, shining wood floors, either two twins or one king-size bed, balconies looking onto either the sea or the garden, and marble bathrooms with separate shower stalls. Butler service brings complimentary coffee or tea. The resort is under the same management as the Imperial Hotel in Tokyo—hence the emphasis on service; with a staff-to-guest ratio of three to one, attention is immediate. *Box 384 (Jln. Dhyanapura), Legian Beach, Denpasar 80001, tel. 0361/754545, fax 0361/751545; U.S. res-ervations, tel. 212/692–9001; U.K. reservations, tel. 0171/355–1775. 138 rooms (including 17 bungalows). Facilities: 2 restaurants, karaoke bar, 24-hr room service, 2 pools, 2 tennis courts, CNN, travel desk, shuttle bus to Kuta. AE, DC, MC, V.*

$$–$$$ **Kul Kul Beach Resort.** Opened in 1989, Kul Kul is architecturally the
★ most interesting and attractive hotel on Kuta beach. The sundeck is built over rocks on one side of the pool, and you clamber down boul-ders to have a dip or get a drink. Accommodations consist of modern bungalows that include sitting rooms and bedrooms furnished in Ba-linese style—rattan and bamboo—with deluxe bathrooms. The at-tentive service of the staff adds to the sense of harmony guests feel amid the resort's Balinese architecture. The restaurant has a com-prehensive menu ranging from Italian pasta dishes to New Zealand lamb and beef to fresh fish to Indonesian rice dishes. In the evening, a wayang kulit performance is given in English, an Indonesian sing-er entertains in the bar, and a video is shown on a wide screen. *Jln. Pantai Kuta, Legian Kelon, Kuta, tel. 0361/752921, fax 0361/ 752519. 76 rooms. Facilities: European/Indonesian restaurant, poolside bar, disco. AE, MC, V.*

$$ **Bali Dynasty.** Tuban has more than enough restaurants, shops, and nightclubs, but it's still less congested than nearby Kuta. At the Dy-nasty, two wings branch out from the main building to house the guest rooms. These have a standard rectangular layout with a dou-ble or twin beds against one wall and a writing table along the other, and a couple of easy chairs; an extra $10 gets you a garden view. The pool is close to the beach. There is a Western-style restaurant and a particularly good Chinese restaurant, the Golden Lotus, whose Singaporean chef has a sure hand with spices. *Box 2047, Jln. Kartika Plaza, Tuban 80361, tel. 0361/752403, fax 0361/752402; U.S. res. 800/942–5050; U.K. res. 0181/747–8485. 225 rooms, 12 suites. Facilities: 2 restaurants, 2 bars, disco, pool, travel desk, TV with CNN, tennis court. AE, DC, MC, V.*

$$ **Kuta Palace Hotel.** Set on 11 acres on Legian beach, this hotel consists of two-story buildings surrounding a courtyard with gar-dens and pools. Rooms are simply but pleasantly decorated in Bali-nese-patterned fabrics and a cream-and-rust color scheme. All have

air-conditioning, refrigerators, and views. *Box 3244, Denpasar 80001, tel. 0361/751433, fax 0361/752948. Facilities: restaurant, outdoor pool, 24-hr room service, tennis, laundry service. AE, DC, MC, V.*

$ **Sari Yasa Samudra Bungalows.** Across the road from Kuta beach, this collection of cottages offers bare-bones accommodations with ceiling fans and only limited hours of hot water in the private baths. It's virtually without aesthetic appeal but cleaner and newer than its sister property, Yasa Samudra, next door. *Box 53, Denpasar 80001, tel. 0361/751562, fax 0361/752948. 31 rooms. Facilities: restaurant, bar, pool. No credit cards.*

Lombok **Intan Laguna.** A vast, lagoon-shape swimming pool is this hotel's fo-
$$–$$$ cal point. The design of the bungalows is a modern interpretation of Balinese architecture; guest rooms are spacious with tile floors and unadorned walls. These may crowd the property and detract from the feeling of openness that it now has. The open-air dining room, cooled by the sea breezes, offers some of the best fare on the island. *Intan Laguna, Box 50, Mataram, Lombok 83125, tel. 0364/23680. Reservations also through Intan International, Box 1089, Tuban 80361, Bali, tel. 0361/52191, fax 0361/52193. 52 bungalows. Facilities: 2 restaurants, poolside bar, outdoor pool, 2 tennis courts, small fitness center, shops. AE, DC, MC, V.*

$$–$$$ **Senggigi Beach Hotel.** The location of this hotel, on a small peninsula jutting into the Lombok Strait, will always make this a choice resort; sunsets are particularly splendid. Thatched roof cottages— with several rooms per building—are scattered over 25 acres of grass and coconut trees. White sandy beaches form the perimeter. The open-sided dining room, overlooking the pool, serves mostly buffet-style meals both for breakfast and dinner. Guest rooms are modest: Most have twin beds, with scant furniture other than a table, chairs, and a television. Bathrooms have showers only. *Senggigi, Box 1001, Mataram 83125, Lombok, tel. 0364/93210, fax 0364/93200. Reservations also through Hotel Sanur Beach in Bali. 150 rooms. Facilities: restaurant, 24-hr room service, outdoor pool, tennis, badminton, windsurfing, snorkeling, outrigger-boat sailing, tour desk, drugstore/souvenir shop. AE, DC, MC, V.*

$$–$$$ **Sheraton Senggigi Beach Resort.** Rooms at this new (1992) resort are in three-story buildings around a compact enclave of landscaped gardens with a free-form pool as the central focus. An island stage in the pool is used for dance performances. All rooms look onto the gardens and pool, and many offer a glimpse of the beach beyond. The main restaurant offers indoor and outdoor dining, and the reception and lounge areas are open. Rooms are slightly larger and newer than at the Senggigi Beach Hotel. *Jln. Raya Senggigi, Box 156, Mataram, Lombok, tel. 0364/93333, fax 0364/93140; U.S. res. tel. 800/325–3535. 158 rooms. Facilities: Indonesian and Western restaurant, pool, 2 tennis courts, Clark Hatch fitness center (extra charge), water sports, travel desk. AE, DC, MC, V.*

$ **Graha Beach.** Set on the beach, this is one of the best of several inexpensive hotels and losmen in Senggigi. The facilities are limited to a restaurant serving primarily local food, though a few Western and Chinese dishes are offered. Air-conditioned rooms, with twin beds, are clean but Spartan, although each has a private shower and toilet. There is a small souvenir shop and money exchange. Tours of the island can be arranged—prices are negotiable. *Senggigi Beach, Mataram, Lombok, tel. 0364/25331. 29 rooms. Facilities: restaurant, tours and car rental available. No credit cards.*

$ **Pondok Senggigi.** It's usually filled with budget travelers, who stream in around 6 PM. The Rp 15,000 rooms are the first to go, then the slightly larger Rp 20,000 ones. Both have twin beds and private bathrooms with Western-style showers. The Rp 10,000 rooms have *mundi* toilets (a tank with a dipper). All rooms are clean, with fresh sheets. The restaurant and bar, open all day, serve as the lounge area. A band plays Western music in the evening. *Senggigi Beach, Senggigi, Lombok, tel. 0364/93275. 45 rooms. Facilities: restaurant (mostly Western fare), bar. No credit cards.*

Nusa Dua
$$$–$$$$

Bali Hilton International. A spectacular floodlit waterfall sets the scene at this huge property. Five-story buildings on either side of the vast open-sided reception area create a U around a courtyard filled with lagoons. It takes 10 minutes to walk from the reception area to the buildings closest to the beach, though if you have a car you can drive. Most rooms look onto the lagoon courtyard rather than the sea. The Executive Court rooms are slightly larger and have separate showers. *Box 46, Nusa Dua 80361, Bali, tel. 0361/ 771102, fax 0361/771199; U.S. reservations, tel. 800/HILTONS. 537 rooms. Facilities: 4 restaurants, 24-hr coffee shop, Balinese theater, pool, tennis and squash courts, fitness center, in-room safes, meeting rooms. AE, DC, MC, V.*

$$$–$$$$

Four Seasons Resort. This extravagant 1994 resort set on 35 acres is a village of luxury bungalows rising from the shore some 45 meters up the hill. The most elevated bungalows have the best view of Jimbaran Bay, but they're also the ones farthest from the public areas, including the beach and pool. Never fear: There's an electric taxi to beat the hike. Each one-bedroom bungalow consists of three thatched-roof pavilions: an open-sided living/dining area, an air-conditioned bedroom, and a bathroom with a large tub and, in an adjacent garden, an outdoor shower—not to mention a private sundeck and a 12-meter plunge pool. (Eight larger bungalows have two bedrooms.) The pool down by the beach spills over a 20-foot waterfall into a free-form soaking pool below. The Four Seasons is very much a self-contained resort; there are no villages within a couple of miles, and the nearest building is the Bali InterContinental a mile or so down the beach. The quoted rate is expensive—about $300 a night—but standard discounts usually put it closer to half that amount. *Jimbaran, Denpasar 80361, tel. 0361/771288, fax 0361/ 771280. 147 bungalows. Facilities: 2 restaurants, pool, tennis program, complimentary windsurfing, sailing, canoeing, and snorkeling equipment, spa, massage. AE, DC, MC, V.*

$$$–$$$$

Grand Hyatt Bali. You need a map to find your way around the four compounds of hotel rooms, let alone the beach. Each compound has its own small lagoon or swimming pool so that all guest rooms have water views. Rooms are large, with king-size beds facing small sitting enclaves with banquette seats. The bathrooms, with separate shower stalls, have wooden shutters that may be opened to the bedrooms, creating a greater sense of space. Regency rooms (15%–20% costlier) offer separate lounge areas where complimentary breakfasts and evening cocktails are served. The hotel is designed to seem Balinese, from a temple to a night market of food stalls to a fish restaurant using Balinese fishing nets for decor. The complex's size is attractive to large groups and package tours. *Box 53, Nusa Dua 80361, Bali, tel. 0361/777–1188, fax 0361/777–2038, U.S. res. tel. 800/233–1234. 750 rooms. Facilities: 5 restaurants (Chinese, Indonesian, Italian, Japanese, Western), coffee shop, Balinese theater, 6 pools, tennis and squash courts, fitness center, in-room safes, meeting rooms. AE, DC, MC, V.*

$$$–$$$$

Sheraton Lagoon Nusa Dua. Much smaller than most hotels on Nusa Dua, the Sheraton Lagoon forms a U facing the sea. The central courtyard is a series of connected swimming lagoons and waterfalls;

rooms face either these lagoons (the ones at ground level have swimming ladders from the balcony and a 20% higher tariff) or the gardens. The excellent service employs the butler concept, whereby one staff member is responsible for all a guest's wants. Most of the restaurants and activities are close to the beach. *Box 2044, Nusa Dua 80361, tel. 0361/771327, fax 0361/771326, U.S. reservations, tel. 800/325–3535. 276 rooms including 65 suites. Facilities: 4 restaurants, pool, children's pool, 2 tennis courts, fitness center, tour desk, in-room safes, business center, Balinese theater. AE, DC, MC, V.*

$$$ **Buala Club.** At the southern end of Nusa Dua beach, this quiet hotel offers an all-inclusive vacation, with free activities and personalized service. Accommodations are in a two-story Balinese-style building surrounded by gardens. Rooms are simple but pleasant, with ikat-patterned fabrics; all have a private balcony or veranda. *Box 6, Nusa Dua 80363, tel. 0361/771310, fax 0361/771313. 50 rooms. Facilities: 3 restaurants, bar, outdoor pool, private beach, horseback riding, water sports, boutique, drugstore, conference rooms. AE, DC, MC, V.*

Sanur **Tandjung Sari.** This unique hotel is a peaceful "village" of Balinese-
$$$$ style bungalows set in tropical gardens that hide small stone temples and statues. The lobby is an open pavilion decorated with carvings. Bungalows have split bamboo walls and are furnished with handwoven fabrics, an antique or two, and a minibar. Most of the bathrooms have skylights. Prawns, curries, fritters, and a dozen other items—and, on Wednesday night, a superb rijstaffel—are served in a romantic setting just back from the beach. *Box 25, Denpasar 80001, tel. 0361/288441, fax 0361/235157. 24 bungalows. Facilities: restaurant, private beach, beach bar, outdoor pool, water sports. No credit cards.*

$$$ **Bali Hyatt.** The queen of Sanur, this hotel sits on 36 acres of gardens along the beach. The open lobby has a soaring roof thatched with elephant grass; from the ceiling hang chandeliers of gilded carved coconut. Built in 1973, the hotel had started to show signs of age and closed in 1994 for a year of remodeling; it should be back in full swing by the spring of 1995, with the same attentive staff (Hyatt kept them all on payroll) and its splendor restored. This Hyatt, in contrast to the Grand Hyatt at Nusa Dua, focuses on the individual traveler rather than groups. *Box 392, Denpasar 80001, tel. 0361/288271, fax 0361/271693. 387 rooms. Facilities: 5 restaurants, 4 bars, disco, 2 outdoor pools, boating, golf, tennis, water sports, function rooms. AE, DC, MC, V.*

$$$ **Hotel Sanur Beach.** Most of the action takes place around the pools, the beach, and the patio bars. The best rooms face the pool. All rooms have a private balcony, and most have huge double beds, though a few in the older wing have twins. There are also 26 self-contained bungalows for more privacy. Classical Balinese dance performances and buffet dinners are offered most nights. *Box 3279, Denpasar 80001, tel. 0361/288011, fax 0361/287566. 298 rooms and 26 bungalows. Facilities: 3 restaurants, 24-hr coffee shop, dance performances, 2 outdoor pools, tennis, badminton, sailing, windsurfing, games room, and function rooms. AE, DC, MC, V.*

$$$ **Segara Village.** At the north end of Sanur Beach, this small, family-owned hotel offers Balinese-style thatch-roof cottages. The open lobby houses both of the hotel's restaurants, so it can be busy. Rooms are air-conditioned and have a balcony or veranda and private bath. Decor is very simple, but the hospitality is genuine. *Box 91, Denpasar 80001, tel. 0361/288407, fax 0361/287242. 40 rooms.*

Facilities: 2 restaurants, 4 bars, room service 6 AM–10 PM, 2 outdoor pools, tennis, games room, drugstore, bike rental. AE, DC, MC, V.

Ubud
$$$$

Amandari. Owned by the same Indonesian who has the Amanpuri in Phuket, Thailand, this boutique hotel employs the same formula for success—luxury and elegance in a modern architectural style that reflects local custom. The Amandari, like the Kupu Kupu Barong, overlooks the rice terraces of the lush Ayung gorge. The service here is more professional (though the staff suffers from intimidation by the management), the furnishings more modern, the pool larger, and the prices some 15% higher than at the Kupu Kupu. The formality is somewhat stiff, and the architecture lacks the ideal Balinese warmth and the harmony—the feeling is of sharp angles rather than the flowing balance of nature. *Box 33, Ubud 80571, tel. 0361/975333, fax 0361/975335; U.S. reservations, tel. 800/447–7462; U.K. reservations, tel. 0800/282684. 40 rooms. Facilities: restaurant, outdoor (salt-water) pool, bar, and tour services. AE, DC, MC, V.*

$$$$
★

Kupu Kupu Barong. The loveliest of Bali's country lodgings, this beautiful and intimate hotel sits on the precipice of a deep valley, with glorious views of rice terraces and the Ayung River below. You approach the dining room via a path trellised with banana leaves, hibiscus, and clove trees. The rooms vary; all require stout legs, since they're built into the hillside. The older bungalows are individually designed to blend with the hilly landscape, with woven rattan or stone-face walls and unique crafted furnishings. The duplexes, with Indonesian wood paneling and luxuriously large bathrooms, have a modern freshness. The restaurant is delightful. (The food and beverage manager is an avid collector of Balinese art with plenty of advice on shops.) Children are not welcome. *Box 7, Jln. Kecubung 72, Denpasar, tel. 0361/795478, fax 0361/795079; U.S. res. tel. 310/568–0009; U.K. res. tel. 0171/742–7780. 54 rooms. Facilities: restaurant, outdoor pool, tennis. AE, DC, MC, V.*

$$

Tjampuhan. On the main road just out of Ubud, atop a ravine overlooking a holy river, Tjampuhan was once an artists' colony and still includes the former house of German painter Walter Spies. The lobby is no more than an open terrace off the road, with paths leading to the bungalows. These have carved and gilded wood doors, woven bamboo walls, bamboo furniture, and handwoven fabrics and batik as decorations. During the rainy season, the rooms tend to be a little damp; because of the terracing, small children can take quite a tumble. You ring for breakfast with bamboo bells. *Box 15, Denpasar, tel. 0361/728871, fax 0361/795155. 40 bungalows. Facilities: restaurant, bar, outdoor pool, tennis, car and bike rental. MC, V.*

$
★

Agung Raka. Four of the guest rooms at this lodging in a developing area off Monkey Forest Road are duplexes: Downstairs is a covered patio and a small lounge area; up steep wooden stairs is the main bedroom with a canopied bed and a small balcony overlooking the rice fields. The bathroom and shower are outside, enclosed but open to the sky. The rate—about US$50—includes breakfast. The remaining rooms, which cost about a quarter less, are in small two-story houses; the ground-floor ones have patios, the upstairs ones balconies. The duplexes are the better value. *Pengoseken, Ubud, tel. 0361/975757, fax 0361/975546. 12 rooms. Facilities: small restaurant, small pool. MC, V.*

$

Ananda Cottages. This friendly, relaxed hotel is set in the rice paddies in Campuhan, up the hill outside Ubud. The open-air lounge and lobby surround a central garden; the "cottages" are thatch-roof, brick bungalows with two units above and two below. Room decor is simple, with rattan furniture and ikat bedcovers. The upper rooms have better views and baths. *Box 205, Denpasar, no phone, telex*

35428 Ubud IA. 30 rooms. Facilities: restaurant, bar, outdoor pool. No credit cards.

$ **Sehati.** A cross between a homestay and guest house (there are any number of both in Ubud), Sehati offers six double rooms, each with a private bathroom with a hot water shower, for about $20 a night. The choice room, No. 5, has a fine veranda facing a small forested ravine. A light breakfast is included in the room charge. *I Wayan Jembawan 7 (behind the post office), Ubud 80571, tel. 0361/975460. 6 rooms. No restaurant. No credit cards.*

$ **Ubud Village Hotel.** The two-story buildings surrounding an attractive garden and pool are in Ubud's busy central area, but set back from the road. Rooms are comfortable, clean, and well maintained if you can stand the occasional chip in the bathtub's enamel. The preferred ones are on the upper floors; they catch the breezes from the rice paddies and offer a little more privacy than the fan-cooled ground-floor rooms. There is a small restaurant, and Continental breakfast is included in the rates. *Jln. Monkey Forest, Ubud 80571, tel. 0361/795571, fax 0361/795069. 32 rooms. Facilities: restaurant, pool. MC, V.*

The Arts

Dance Dance is everywhere in Bali: at celebrations, temple rituals, weddings, birthdays, processions to the sea, tooth-filing and purification ceremonies, and, occasionally, exorcisms. The dances performed at hotels are often commercially adapted and shortened; the ones at the theaters listed below will be more genuine. Even better is a local performance on a village green: Nearly every evening some village will be having a celebration. These aren't publicized, but ask around and you might get lucky.

The dancers move low to the ground, with bent knees, arched backs, and controlled steps, arms at right angles with elbows pointing up and fingers spread wide. The female dancers flutter their long-nailed fingers. They'll move slowly across the stage, then turn quickly but precisely with a staccato movement. Head movements are staccato, too, without facial expression except for their darting and flashing eyes. They wear petaled or gold headdresses. The men have to do battle and get killed, and their movements are more varied.

Most dances are accompanied by the traditional *gamelan* orchestra of gongs, drums (mostly hand-beaten), a type of xylophone with bronze bars, two different stringed instruments, and a flute. Balinese dancing is far more exuberant than Javanese, and the Balinese gamelan is sharper, with more crescendo. Behind every dance is a legend with a moral theme.

The **Barong** is a dance of Good versus Evil. The Good is Barong, a dragon with a huge, bushy, lionlike head and a long flower-bedecked beard. Bells ring as he snaps his head. The two dancers inside use complicated motions to make Barong humorous and good natured, but ferocious when he meets Evil, in the form of the witch Rangda. Rangda's horrifying mask is white, with bulging eyes and tusks extending from her mouth. Her long braided hair sweeps down to the floor amid evil red mirrored streamers. She rushes threateningly back and forth across the stage. There are also beautiful female dancers with petaled headdresses, tasseled girdles, and gold-and-green sarongs, and male warriors whose prince is crowned with gold and flowers. Rangda forces the warriors to turn their kris blades on themselves, but Barong's powers keep the blades from harming them. A bird dancer enters and is killed—the required sacrifice to the gods; and Rangda is banished.

The **Legong** is a glittering classical dance. The story involves a young princess kidnapped by an enemy of her father. Three young girls in tight gold brocade and frangipani headdresses perform several roles. Their movements are rapid and pulsating; they punctuate the music with quick, precise movements and flashing eyes. It is an exacting dance—girls start training for the roles at 5 and retire before they are 15.

The dramatic **Kecak,** the Monkey Dance, depicts the monkey armies of Hanuman, who rescued Rama and his love, Sita, from the forests of Ceylon in the *Ramayana*, the great Hindu epic. No gamelan is used; all sound comes from the chorus, who, in unison, simulate both the gamelan and the chattering, moaning, bellowing, and shrieking of monkeys. This dance is always performed at night under torchlight. The dark figures, again in unison, make wild arm gestures and shake their fingers. (The Kecak is not a classical dance but a product of this century.)

At least 200 dances, with a story for every occasion, have been handed down from generation to generation: the **Keris,** an ancient temple dance performed by two bare-chested men in a trance who continually stab themselves (the blades don't pierce their skin); the **Joged,** a social dance in which a female dancer selects a partner from the audience who dons a sash and joins her; the **Sanghyang,** a sacred dance to ward off epidemics caused by demons; the **Janger,** a lively women's dance to songs accompanied by flute and drum; and the **Baris,** a warrior dance accompanied by the full gamelan orchestra.

Consult the *Bali Tourist Guide* and the *Bali Guide to Events* for current schedules. Usually Legong is performed at the **Peliatan Stage** (2 km, or 1¼ mi, from Ubud) every Friday 6:30–8, and at **Puri Saren** in Ubud every Monday 7:30–9. Other dances may be seen at **Pengosaka** in Ubud every Thursday 7:30–9. The Kecak is performed at the **Ayodya Pura Stage,** Tg. Bungkak, Denpasar, daily 6–7; at the **Padang Tegal** in Ubud, Sunday at 6; and at **Sari Wisata Budaya** on the Ngurah Rai bypass outside of Kuta, daily at 6:30. The Barong is performed in the theaters at **Batubulan** daily at 9 AM.

Nightlife

Tourist life on Bali focuses on sightseeing and beach activities; by late evening, most areas quiet down, with one exception: Kuta Beach. Here the activity begins with drinks at cafés (one of the most consistently popular is **Poppies;** *see* Dining, *above*) in the early evening, which may continue well into the night or shift to the discos. Most of these have a modest cover charge of Rp 2,000–Rp 3,000, though there's none at the **Hard Rock Café** (Jln. Legian 204, Kuta, tel. 0361/755661) unless a live band is billed. Generally, the action starts rolling at 9 PM and grinds down at 2 AM.

Gado-Gado (Jln. Dhyana Puru, tel. 0361/775225; open Wed.–Sun.) is an open-air disco near the ocean. **Kayu Api** (no phone), at the intersection of Jalan Legian and Jalan Melasti, has live music, often of international caliber. **Koala Blu** (Jln. Kuta) attracts mostly Australians. The popularity and life span of the other Kuta/Legian discos swing like a pendulum. For informality, drop in at the **Kuta Jaya Jazz Corner** (Jln. Raya. Pantai Kuta, tel. 0361/752308).

There's a karaoke bar at the **Kul Kul Beach Resort** (tel. 0361/51952) on Jalan Pantai Juta at the boundary of Kuta and Legian townships.

Here, on an open-sided stage, a small band plays the top 20 interspersed with large-screen video. A delightful veranda lounge offers a lower noise level. Another popular karaoke bar is at the Bali Dynasty's **Karaoke & Waves Discotheque** in Tuban (tel. 0361/752403).

In Sanur, the largest disco is **Subee** (Jln. Danau Tamblingen 21, tel. 0361/288888). Most hotels here have some form of entertainment with a live band. One lively spot is the Bali Hyatt's plush **Matahari** (tel. 0361/88271). In Nusa Dua, the hotels all offer evening entertainment, either Balinese dance or a live band playing current international favorites. Try **Soarrosa** at the Bali Resort Palace hotel in nearby Tanjung Benoa for glittering action.

Sulawesi

To the north and east of Bali and Java is the island of Sulawesi, formerly called the Celebes. Four long peninsulas radiate from a central mountainous area, giving the island an orchid shape. Its geography is dramatic—from rice fields to rain forests and mountains to hidden bays, from which Bugis pirates once raided merchant ships. As if cast off in some strange upheaval, Sulawesi has become the last home of such unique animals as the babirusa (a pigdeer with upward-curving tusks) and the anoa (a pygmy buffalo). At present, Sulawesi is virtually unspoiled, and its tourist infrastructure is confined mostly to the main city, Ujung Pandang, and to Tanatoraja (Torajaland).

The Toraja live in the northern mountains of south Sulawesi, practicing an ancient animist religion alongside Christianity. With their traditional clan houses—the carved and painted *tongkonans*—built on piles and topped by a massive roof shaped like a ship or buffalo horns, and their public sacred rituals, the Toraja offer the visitor a fascinating glimpse of Indonesia's multifaceted population.

The Toraja comprise only a small minority of Sulawesi's inhabitants, however. The Makassarese and the Bugis are more numerous, and the journey from Ujung Pandang to Tanatoraja passes through Bugis country. Though many now have settled on land to cultivate rice, the seafaring Muslim Bugis still ply the Asian seas in their sailing ships, called *prahus*, trading among Indonesia's islands.

Most visitors fly into Ujung Pandang and use it as a starting point for travel in Sulawesi. The city, called Makassar by the Dutch, is a bustling commercial center. Although it's the fifth-largest Indonesian city, Ujung Pandang has little to hold the tourist's attention.

The Toraja people are Sulawesi's prime attraction. Tourism has affected the Toraja, but their customs, rituals, and social structure have survived the centuries. Perhaps the only obvious change in the last 500 years is that now buffalo and pigs are sacrificed instead of humans.

Tanatoraja's two main towns are Makale, the administrative center, and Rantepao, the commercial and tourist center with the best selection of hotels. You'll need at least three days to visit Tanatoraja, plus two to get there and back. Plan on a longer stay if you want to get off the beaten track to the remote villages. The best time for a trip is at the beginning or end of the dry season, April through October. Vast numbers of Europeans descend in June and July, so try to avoid those months.

Because the country between Ujung Pandang and Rantepao is fascinating, the ideal way to visit Tanatoraja is to make the outbound journey by road and return by air.

Important Addresses and Numbers

Tourist Information In Ujung Pandang, the **South Sulawesi Tourist Office** (Jln. Sultan Alauddin 105 B, tel. 0411/83897) is open Monday–Thursday and Saturday 7–2, Friday 7–11 AM. For most tourist information, the tourist office is not worth much; your hotel can supply as much, if not more, information.

Emergencies **Police,** tel. 110 or 7777; **ambulance,** tel. 118.

Arriving and Departing by Plane

Airports and Airlines **Garuda** flies to Ujung Pandang from Jakarta and Surabaya on Java, and from Denpasar on Bali. Garuda also has service from Ambon, Biak, and Jayapura. The smaller **Merpati, Bouraq,** and **Mandala** also serve Ujung Pandang.

Merpati Airlines flies between Ujung Pandang and Rantepao's simple airport in Tanatoraja three times a week. The runway can become unserviceable in the rainy season, causing frequent flight cancellations. The airport is 24 km (15 mi) from town.

Between the Airport and Downtown Taxis from the Ujung Pandang airport cost about Rp 9,000. Purchase a coupon inside the terminal, next to the baggage claim. In Rantepao, a cab to town costs Rp 15,000.

Arriving and Departing by Ship

Pelni ships from Surabaya (tel. 031/21041) or Ambon (tel. 0311/3161–2049) pass through Ujung Pandang every seven days and moor at Pelabuhan Hatta Harbor, a short becak ride from the center of town. Because Ujung Pandang is the gateway to eastern Indonesia, many other shipping companies take passengers from here aboard freighters to the Moluccas and other eastern islands and to Kalimantan, on Borneo. Pelni also has a subsidiary, **Perintis,** which serves many of the outer ports of Indonesia. For information, contact Pelni at one of the above numbers, or call the head office in Jakarta (tel. 021/416262).

Getting Around

By Taxi You can hail cruising cabs in Ujung Pandang or find them waiting outside hotels. Taxis are unmetered; you negotiate the fare. Two large companies are **Mas. C.V.** (tel. 0411/4599) and **Omega** (tel. 0411/22679).

By Bus A large company, with the newest buses serving towns outside Ujung Pandang, is **Liman Express** (tel. 0411/5851).

The bus to Tanatoraja from Ujung Pandang takes nine hours, plus an hour lunch break. There are morning and evening departures in both directions. At Rp 12,500, it's an economical way to go. Since the countryside is not to be missed, make sure to make one trip during daylight.

By Bemo In Ujung Pandang, bemo minivans run along Jalan Jend. Sudirman/Ratulangi; Jalan Hasnuddin/Cendrawash; and Jalan Bulusaraung/Mesjid Raya to Maros (sometimes detouring to the airport). Public minibuses to towns outside Ujung Pandang leave from Jalan Sarappo whenever they're full.

By Becak For journeys less than 3¼ km (2 mi), bicycle rickshaws are popular. Bargain hard—a trip in town should cost about Rp 1,000, even if the driver begins by asking Rp 5,000.

By Car Self-drive rental cars are not available—or permitted—on Sulawesi.

By Tour Bus Travel agencies either take clients one way from Ujung Pandang to Rantepao by minibus and fly them back, or go both ways by minibus. The advantage of such a tour is the guide. (*See* Guided Tours, *below*, for tour companies in Ujung Pandang.)

Guided Tours

Ramayana Tours (Jln. Bulukunyi 9A, tel. 0411/81791) is particularly good for tours into Torajaland because many of its guides come from there. It also offers excursions to the southeast peninsula, famous for boatbuilding and a reclusive Muslim village, and arranges customized tours, such as a jeep trip across the island and a canoe visit to the weavers of Galumpang in central Sulawesi.

Other agencies include **Intravi** (Jln. Urip Sumoharjo 225, tel. 0411/311442) and **Pacto Ltd.** (Jln. Jend. Sudirman 56, tel. 0411/83208).

Exploring Ujung Pandang

The principal site is **Fort Rotterdam,** now officially called Benteng ("fort") Ujung Pandang, though most people still use its old name. Located by the harbor in the center of the old city, it began as a fortified trading post for the Sulawesi Goanese dynasty and a defense against pirates. The fort was first captured and rebuilt by the Portuguese in 1545, then captured by the Dutch in 1608 and reinforced again. On Saturday night at 8, dance performances are often held here. Personnel at your hotel should know whether any are scheduled. *Fort admission free. Open daily 8–5.*

The fort includes the **Galigo Museum** (the Ujung Pandang State Museum), divided into ethnology and history sections. The ethnographic museum is the more interesting, with a large collection of artifacts from different areas of Sulawesi. *Admission charge to each museum. Open Tues.–Thurs. 8 AM–1 PM, Fri. 8 AM–10 AM, Sat.–Sun. 8–4.*

Just 3¼ km (2 mi) north of Ujung Pandang is Paotare, a harbor where the Bugis prahus come to unload their cargo, mend their sails, and prepare for their next passage. Sunsets from here are marvelous, but the pier has missing planks and gaping holes, so watch where you step.

Exploring Tanatoraja

The four-hour drive north to Pare Pare, halfway between Ujung Pandang and Rantepao, is through flat countryside of rice fields, with the Makassar Strait on the left. The area is inhabited by Bugis, whose houses, on stilts and with crossed roofbeams, line the road. In some you'll see fish hanging from the rafters, curing in the sun. **Pare Pare** is a city of 90,000 and Sulawesi's second-largest town. From its port, boats cross the Makassar Sea to Kalimantan. There is little to see in Pare Pare, but it has two decent restaurants.

Time Out **Bukit Indah** is a smart restaurant with six hotel rooms and a view of the bay. Perched on a hill, it catches a breeze, and everything is pristinely clean. To reach Bukit Indah, take a right turn up the hill from the main street just before entering downtown Pare Pare. The crab and corn soup is delicious, as are the fried frogs' legs. Clean, simple rooms are available if you wish to stay the night. *$*.

Sempurna (149 Jln. Bau Massepe, tel. 0421/21573), on the main street, is a clean, Formica-furnished, air-conditioned restaurant that serves tasty Indonesian and Chinese food. Try the sweet-and-sour shrimp.

From Pare Pare the road twists and turns inland, leaving the sea to the west as it climbs into limestone hills forested with tropical pine and palms. Shimmering in the distance are the steely blue mountains that locked out intruding cultures for centuries. Not until 1980 was the road paved. Before then, the rutted, stony track took hours to cover. Dominated by Bamba Buang mountain, the scenery becomes increasingly dramatic. According to legend, the souls of the Torajan dead assemble here to journey to the "gate of God." As the road continues into the mountains of Tanatoraja, look to the right across the small valley and you'll recognize the **"Lady Mountain,"** where two ridges split off, suggestive of a woman's legs. In the distance is **Rura,** said to be the very first Toraja village.

Time Out Located 248 km (153 mi) from Ujung Pandang and 54 km (32 mi) before Makale is a roadside restaurant, **Puntak Lakawan,** with a terrace affording spectacular views—an exciting introduction to Tanatoraja. Travelers stop here for the views, the strong coffee, and the "tourist only" Western toilet facilities—not for the food.

Finally, the road leads through carved gates, announcing the entrance into Tanatoraja. Bypass Makale and head for Rantepao, the center of travel and the hub of the network of roads that peel off into the countryside to the Toraja villages.

Numbers in the margin correspond to points of interest on the Torajaland map.

❶ **Rantepao** is a small, easygoing town. Its big event occurs every sixth day, when the "weekly" market at the town crossroads attracts just about everyone from the surrounding villages. Even on off days, the market shops sell wood carvings, cloth, and other Toraja-crafted goods. Rantepao also has small restaurants and inexpensive hotels. The more comfortable accommodations are a bit out of town, however, either back on the road to Makale or on the road east toward Marante.

If you have time, the ideal way to experience Tanatoraja is by hiking through the hills along small paths from one village to the next. Visiting them by bus is possible, with short hikes, but it is slow going. You can also hire a minivan or four-wheel-drive jeep with a guide. Wear strong, ankle-supporting shoes, because you'll do some walking over rutted tracks or roads. Each tour guide has his favorite villages for visiting. He should be able to learn about any scheduled ceremonies. Encourage him to do so, for witnessing one is an event you won't forget.

The **funeral ceremony** is the most important event in the life of a Toraja. Though families traditionally gave as lavish a funeral as possible to demonstrate the prestige of the dead to the gods, a competition for status has now entered the ceremony. Wealth is measured in

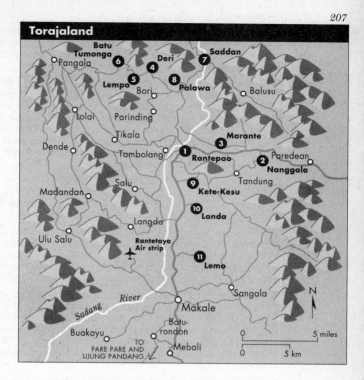

Torajaland

buffalo: The more buffalo sacrificed at the funeral, the more honor to the dead, the family, and the clan. Even Toraja who have converted to Christianity continue the funeral ritual to show prestige, keep tradition, and make sure the dead have plenty of influence with the gods.

When a clan erects a new tongkonan, there's a large **housewarming** ceremony with the whole clan present, which may mean hundreds of people. Buffalo and pigs are sacrificed—again to display prestige.

Of the hundreds of villages in Tanatoraja, the following are some of the more accessible. To varying degrees, they give the visitor a chance to see aspects of animist culture and architecture. Most villages on the regular tourist route require a donation of Rp 1,500 or more. In theory, this helps the villagers maintain their buildings.

2 To the east of Rantepao is **Nanggala,** a quiet village and one of the best examples of traditional Toraja life. The tongkonan and other houses are built on poles with soaring prow-shaped roofs, lined up facing north (whence the ancestors came); *lumbung* (granaries or rice barns, smaller than the houses but similar in shape) stand opposite. The tongkonan is cared for by the clan leader. A noble clan may decorate all the walls with carved and painted designs symbolizing the buffalo, the sun, and important crops. A middle-ranking clan is permitted to decorate only the front gable. When you see a wood buffalo head or the horns of sacrificed buffalo affixed to the front pole of the house, you're looking at the house of a noble clan.

3 Also to the east of Rantepao is **Marante,** where you'll find burial caves in a limestone cliff. The remnants of poles used to support hanging coffins and some old carved coffins are here. There is also a funeral bier shaped like a traditional house—a ship to carry the deceased to the next life. At one end of the village is a modern home with a prow projecting from the roof and a wood buffalo head attached to its front post—a fabulous anachronism.

④ ⑤ ⑥ A drive north from Rantepao to **Deri, Lempo,** and **Batu Tumonga** provides spectacular scenery—mountains, rice terraces, and rain forest. A right turn off the road to Deri leads to the weaving center **⑦** of **Saddan** (a blue sign points the way). Here, Toraja women weave and sell their colorful designs, which use mainly primary colors in geometric patterns. You can also purchase the beautiful vegetable-dyed ikat textiles from Galumpang, an area north and west of Tanatoraja known for its weaving.

⑧ On the road back to Rantepao from Saddan is the very old village of **Palawa,** where hundreds of horns of sacrificed buffalo hang on the houses and where eight traditional homes contain shops selling Toraja carvings, textiles, old coins, and junk.

⑨ The more heavily traveled tourist villages, such as **Kete-Kesu,** **⑩ ⑪** **Londa,** and **Lemo,** lie south of Rantepao. Some are the sites of limestone burial caves with *tau taus*, wood effigies carved for noble Toraja and placed on a balcony at the cave. The spirit of the ancestor honored thus will help the descendants enjoy a better life.

These are just a few of the villages nestling in the valleys throughout Tanatoraja. The farther you go from Rantepao and Makele, the fewer tourists the inhabitants have seen, and the more welcoming they are. If you have time and spirit, head into the northwestern or eastern part. These areas are the least infiltrated. Most of the inhabitants will know a few words of Bahasa Indonesia, but no English.

Evening entertainment is minimal in Rantepao. Some hotels offer cultural shows, but they are generally a waste of time.

Dining

The Makassarese and Bugis are famous seafarers, so you can expect good seafood in Sulawesi, but the best kitchens are often run by local Chinese. In Tanatoraja, you will probably wish to eat at your hotel, though the café/restaurants in the center of Rantepao offer good, basic Chinese fare.

Rantepao **Pondok Torsina.** Set in the rice fields a few kilometers south of
$ Rantepao, this small hotel and restaurant serves good Indonesian food on a veranda overlooking the paddies. Try the asparagus soup, shrimp in spicy butter sauce, and grilled fish. The Toraja owner is very helpful in filling in the information gaps left by your guide. *Tikunna Malenong, tel. 0423/21293. No reservations. Dress: casual. No credit cards.*

$ **Restaurant Rachmat.** Near the traffic circle with a model of a Toraja house, this Chinese-operated restaurant offers tasty Indonesian and Chinese dishes. *Jln. Abdul Sari 8. No reservations. Dress: casual. No credit cards.*

Ujung **Restaurant Surya.** Super Crab, as this restaurant is called, serves
Pandang some of the best seafood in Ujung Pandang. It is always crowded,
$$ and you will probably have to wait for a table. The proprietor, Jerry, speaks English, so you won't have any problem with the menu. The large, bright room has no decor or atmosphere, but the crab-and-asparagus soup is delicious, as are the gigantic prawns. *Jln.*

Nusakambangan 16, tel. 0411/7066. No reservations. Dress: casual. No credit cards.

Lodging

Rantepao
$$
★

Hotel Misiliana. Make sure to book rooms in the new part of this hotel, where a courtyard garden has a row of traditional houses with rice barns opposite. Guest rooms surround the courtyard in two- or four-unit bungalows designed to complement the houses. The rooms are spotless, furnished with twin beds in colorful native covers, and have modern tile bathrooms. Breakfast and dinner are included in the room price, and both meals offer a fixed menu—Europeanized Indonesian fare of no distinction. The cultural show in the evening is not worth the entrance fee. *Jln. Raya Makele, Box 01, tel. 0423/ 21212, fax 0423/21512. 80 rooms. Facilities: restaurant, art shop. DC, V.*

$$
★

Toraja Cottages. Just 3 km (2 mi) east of Rantepao, and set among tropical gardens, this hotel consists of rows of attached cottages terraced around the main building. The guest rooms, with twin beds, are small but clean. Westernized Indonesian food is served in an open veranda restaurant with rattan furniture, and, amusingly, a model of the Statue of Liberty on a corner table. A small bar off the lobby functions as a gathering place at this popular tourist hotel, which has a variety of activities and services available, including tours and gift shops. *Kamp. Bolu, tel. and fax 0423/21268. Reservations and information: Jln. Johar 17, Jakarta Pusat, Jakarta, tel. 021/321346; or Jln. Somba Opu 281, Ujung Pandang, tel. 0411/ 84146. 158 rooms. Facilities: 2 restaurants, bar, outdoor pool. AE, DC, V.*

$

Pondok Torsina. This small hotel, set in the rice fields, is utilitarian but clean. Its owner is knowledgeable about Toraja culture, and the restaurant serves good Indonesian food. No activities are arranged and the walk to town is over a mile, so you need to make your own arrangements to get around Tanatoraja. *Rantepao Tikunna Maenong, tel. 0423/21293. Reservations: Elly 6, Tondirerung, Do. S. Tangka 19, Ujung Pandang, tel. 0411/4985. 10 rooms, 6 with private bath. Facilities: restaurant. No credit cards.*

Ujung Pandang
$$$
★

Makassar Golden Hotel. This hotel at the harbor sports Toraja-style roofs on its main building. Most rooms face the sea and have wall-to-wall carpeting, with beige decor and woven bedcovers in a Toraja design. Makassar also has cottages facing the sea. All rooms have private bath, minibar, and TV with video programs. The elegant Losari Restaurant serves French food. *Jln. Pasar Ikan 50, tel. 0411/ 314408, fax 0411/317999. 115 rooms. Facilities: 2 restaurants, banquet hall, conference hall, disco, art shop, Olympic-size outdoor pool. AE, DC, MC, V.*

$$

Makassar City Hotel. Toraja-style carved-wood panels are the theme here. The hotel, which is competitive with the Makassar Golden Hotel, is centrally located; its lounge has crushed-velvet sofas and soft leather chairs. The coffee shop serves Western and Indonesian dishes. Rooms are spacious, with sitting areas, king-size beds, color TV, and minibar. *Jln. Khairil Anwar 28, tel. 0411/317955, fax 0411/ 311818. 100 rooms. Facilities: restaurant, bar, outdoor pool, conference room. AE, DC, MC, V.*

$

Hotel Ramayana. Between the airport and Ujung Pandang, this place is clean but purely utilitarian. It's conveniently located across from the Liman Express office, which runs buses to Torajaland. *Jln. G. Bawakaraeng 121, tel. 0411/324153, fax 0411/324165. 35 rooms. Facilities: restaurant, travel desk. No credit cards.*

5 Malaysia and Brunei

By John W.
English

Updated by
Nigel Fisher

Malaysia is, for one thing, an extraordinary olfactory experience. In the cities, the acrid smell of chilies frying in street-vendor stalls mingles with the sweetness of incense wafting out of Indian shops, the pungency of curry powders from spice merchants, the delicate scents of frangipani and other tropical flowers that bloom everywhere, and the diesel fumes from taxis and buses. The jungle has a heavy, damp, fermenting aroma that will haunt your imagination long after you've returned to comfortable, everyday life at home.

Malaysia is composed of two parts. East Malaysia comprises the states of Sabah and Sarawak on the island of Borneo, which includes the Indonesian state of Kalimantan as well as the republic of Brunei. West Malaysia, the southern portion of the Malay Peninsula (which also includes part of Thailand), is also called peninsular Malaysia or Malaya, as the country was known before the addition of the East Malaysian states in 1963.

Though East Malaysia has a larger landmass, it is mostly jungle, and 80% of the nation's population lives on the peninsula. This population—some 15.6 million—is about 56% indigenous Malays, 34% ethnic Chinese, 9% Indians, and 1% others, including the Kadazan, Dayak, and other tribes of East Malaysia. While Malaysia is officially a Muslim country, some Malays remain animists, the Chinese are mostly Buddhists and Christians, and most Indians are Hindu. The East Malaysian states are primarily Christian, due to the 20th-century missionaries who helped develop the area.

This mix of cultures is one of Malaysia's main fascinations. It confronts visitors especially in the cities, where, interspersed with businessmen in Western garb and teenagers in T-shirts and jeans, you'll see Malay women in floral-print sarongs, Muslim women with traditional head coverings, Chinese in the pajama-type outfits called *samfoo*, and Indian men in dhotis. It manifests itself in a lively and varied street-food scene, with a proliferation of vendors selling everything from exotic fruits and juices to Hokkien noodles to Malay satay to fish grilled with pungent Asian spices. And it proclaims itself joyously in the street festivals and religious ceremonies that these different cultures celebrate throughout the year.

Malaysia is also topographically diverse, offering some of the world's best coral reefs, long stretches of white-sand beaches (both developed, with plenty of water-sports facilities, and deserted), the highest mountain in Southeast Asia, hill resorts that provide recreation and escape from the tropical sun, spectacular limestone outcroppings (at Ipoh), vast areas of primary jungle, and networks of rivers perfect for white-water rafting.

On the west coast of the peninsula is Kuala Lumpur, Malaysia's capital and the gateway through which most visitors enter the country. It is a sprawling, clamorous, modern city that nevertheless retains many reminders of the past, though perhaps not a lot of charm. The island of Penang, on the other hand, is an exciting combination of beach resort area and university town, with charm to spare. It is a wonderful place to tool around on a bicycle through streets lined with lively shops and graceful colonial architecture. North of Penang is the duty-free island of Langkawi, whose idyllic setting has attracted the attention of resort hotel developers. For a sense of Malaysia's colonial history, a visit to Malacca, with ruins and restored buildings from successive European colonizers, is a must.

The peninsula's east coast is less developed, allowing a glimpse of a quieter Malaysia. The area around Kuantan offers excellent beaches and some first-rate resorts; Mersing, to the south, is the jumping-off

West Malaysia

THAILAND

Langkawi

Kangar

George Town
Penang

Butterworth

Taiping

Ipoh

Telok Anson

Cameron
Highlands

Fraser's
Hill

Kuala
Lumpur

Klang

Port Dickson

Pengkalan Kempas

Malacca

0   100 miles
0   150 km

N

Kota Bharu

South China Sea

MALAYSIA

Kuala
Trengganu

Kuala Lipis

Cherating

Pancing
Caves

Kuantan

Genting
Highlands

NEGRI
SEMBILAN

Sri
Menanti

Seremban

Gemas

Segamat

S. Pahang

Pekan

Tioman
Island

Mersing

Keluang

Strait of Malacca

Johore
Bahru

Desaru

SINGAPORE   Singapore   Strait

SUMATRA

Pakanbaru

INDONESIA

point for Tioman Island, where the film *South Pacific* was shot. The scenery is as idyllic today as it was then, and a resort hotel offers a perfect base for a water-sports and jungle-hiking island vacation. Much of the rest of the peninsula is covered with rubber estates, oil palm plantations, and cool hill stations.

Sabah and Sarawak, on Borneo, deliver all the adventure that the word *Borneo* promises, including trips through dense jungle by backpack and longboat to visit the descendants of headhunters at their longhouses, where you can stop over for the night—a rare opportunity to learn about a culture so very different from what you've left at home.

Over the past five years, efforts have been made to woo tourists to Malaysia. More facilities are available for the international traveler, though the major destinations remain Malacca, Kuala Lumpur, Penang, and Langkawi on the west coast; Kuantan and Tioman Island on the east coast; Cameron and Genting highlands in the center; Kota Kinabalu in Sabah; and Kuching in Sarawak.

A Brief History
The earliest inhabitants of the Malay Peninsula were neolithic Negrito peoples whose descendants—the Orang Asli—still live simply in jungle uplands. Several waves of progressively more Mongoloid groups brought Iron and Bronze cultures to the peninsula and spread out over the entire archipelago. Later, with the emergence of the Java-based Majapahit, the Malay Peninsula came under the influence of a Hindu-Javanese empire that exerted little political control but strong cultural influence. This can be seen in the *wayang kulit* (shadow puppet) plays—a form of oral storytelling—still performed in villages, and in many ceremonies and customs that remain in practice.

In the 15th century, Islam entered Malaya from northern Sumatra and became the official religion of the powerful state of Malacca during the reign of Sultan Iskandar Shah. Islam solidified the system of sultanates, in which one person and his family provided both political and religious leadership. (Today Malaysia still has nine sultans; every five years one is elected to serve a term as constitutional monarch. The head of government in this parliamentary democracy is the prime minister.)

For the next 200 years the peninsula was a hornets' nest of warring sultanates, marauding pirate bands, and European adventurers who, searching for spice and gold, introduced guns and cannons. The Portuguese conquered Malacca, followed by the Dutch, who established a stronghold in Java and outposts in Sumatra and Malacca. British settlements in the Straits of Malacca, Singapore, and Penang flourished. In 1824 a treaty with the British separated Malaya from Dutch-held Sumatra, and the two regions, so similar in historical development, cultural traditions, and religious customs, began to split and follow the lead of the new European colonists.

In the middle of the 19th century, millions of Chinese fled from war and famine in their homelands and sought employment in Malaya's rapidly expanding tin industry. Soon after their arrival, another new enterprise developed: rubber. Rubber requires intensive labor, and workers were again brought in from outside—this time from India. Other groups came from India to trade, open shops, or lend money. The British in India had also trained many civil servants and professionals, and they, too, came to Malaya to practice.

The Indian community maintained strong ties with home. Even today it is not unusual for an Indian to request a bride or groom from his or her ancestral village—many marriages are still arranged—and Indians often return to their native land at retirement, something the Chinese can no longer do.

These patterns of life in Malaya were well established until World War II. Malays continued their traditions in *kampongs*, or communal villages, where time flowed slowly. The sultans prospered under British protection, combining the pleasures of East and West. The Chinese, growing ever more numerous and powerful, became the economic backbone of the peninsula, with the Indians performing various middleman roles. The British maintained a benevolent rule. Each community flourished separately, with little cultural interchange.

The war had little impact on life in Malaya until the Japanese attack on Pearl Harbor and subsequent invasion of Malaya threw the complacent population into turmoil. Japanese forces landed in the northern state of Trengganu and moved rapidly down through the jungle, taking Singapore in March 1942. Life on the Malay Peninsula changed overnight.

The British, of course, had farthest to fall. Many women and children were evacuated to Australia, but the men remained. Former planters, bankers, executives, and soldiers were suddenly thrust from a life of ease into hardship or jail. Many prisoners perished constructing the infamous "Death Railway" in Siam. The survivors had to endure the indignities of captivity, which completely undermined their image as "superior" whites.

The Chinese received particularly harsh treatment from their Japanese conquerors. They faced constant harassment from Japanese forces, who jailed and executed thousands. Many Chinese fled to the jungle, where, aided by remnants of the British army, they formed guerrilla bands. As in Europe, those most adept at underground organization were Communist-trained. By the end of the war, Communist influence among the Chinese was much enhanced by the years spent in the jungle fighting the Japanese.

The war left the people floundering in economic uncertainties. Until independence under a federation of Malayan states was declared in 1957, politics consisted mostly of power struggles between the two major racial groups. The Malays, realizing that independence would remove British protection and leave the Chinese in control, became politically active. The Chinese, despite their economic clout and with their ranks decimated by the occupation, failed to organize politically. Thus, the years of separatism took their toll on national unification and development. Bitter disputes raged among the local leadership. In 1948 the Chinese guerrilla forces began a campaign of terrorism, harassing plantation workers, owners, and managers. Travel along the jungle roads was hazardous, and many Malays and British were killed in ambush. The insurgents were gradually pushed back into the jungle, and in 1960 the emergency was lifted.

Such ethnic factionalism plagued the new federation until 1963, when the nation of Malaysia was created. It included two British protectorates in northern Borneo—Sabah and Sarawak—that were to serve as an ethnic balance against the power of the Chinese in Singapore. Indonesia, however, viewed Malaysia as a threat, and President Sukarno declared Confrontation—a sort of miniwar that finally fizzled out in 1967.

Today Malaysia's racial and political power balance is still delicate. In spite of legislation to promote "Bumiputra," or numerically dominant ethnic Malay interests, the Chinese still control much of Malaysia's commerce and industry. Much has been done to defuse tensions among the ethnic groups, but pressures continue, as evidenced in the movements to strengthen Muslim law (for example, by arresting Muslims who break the Ramadan fast) and give greater emphasis to the Malay language. Over the last few years, the press has been increasingly muzzled and criticism of politicians suppressed; citizens are becoming more careful about what they say, and to whom.

Staying in Malaysia

Getting Around

By Plane　**Malaysia Airlines** flies to 35 towns and cities in Malaysia. Domestic flights are relatively inexpensive and often fully booked, especially during school holidays and festivals. You must confirm reservations a day or so beforehand. Malaysia Airlines offers a **Discover Malaysia Pass** that enables international visitors to travel on domestic routes for about half the normal fare. You may make flight reservations and purchase tickets overseas or in Malaysia. You will be required to show your international airline tickets to prove that you are a bona fide visitor.

By Train　**Malayan Railways,** known as KTM, offers cheap and relatively comfortable service on the peninsula. Beginning at Singapore, one branch leads northwest to Butterworth, the Penang station, via Kuala Lumpur; at Butterworth, a connection can be made with the International Express to Bangkok (which runs thrice weekly) or a local train to Hat Yai, Thailand. Another branch leads to Kota Bharu, at the northeast tip of peninsular Malaysia; at Pasir Mas, a trunk line connects KTM with the Thai railway, 23 km (14 mi) to the north. Both express and local service, and both air-conditioned and non-air-conditioned cars, are available. Passengers with tickets for distances over 200 km (124 mi) can stop off at any point on the route for one day per 200 km traveled: *The stationmaster must endorse the ticket immediately upon arrival at the stopoff station.* On long trips movies are shown, but the passing scenery is always more interesting. In some sections the route goes through jungle and you may see wild monkeys. Sleepers are available on overnight service for a supplemental charge. Dining-car food is simple, cheap, and tasty. For information on the rail line in Sabah, *see* Getting Around by Train in East Malaysia, *below.*

Rail Passes　A foreign tourist can buy the KTM Railpass, permitting unlimited travel for 10 days (M$85) or 30 days (M$175), at main railway stations in Malaysia and in Singapore.

By Bus　Bus service is extensive and cheap, but only coaches traveling between major cities are air-conditioned. Local buses are usually crowded, noisy, and slow, but it's a great way to peoplewatch and sightsee at the same time.

By Boat　**Feri Malaysia** (tel. 03/238–8899) operates the cruise ship *Muhibah* between Kuantan (on the east coast of peninsular Malaysia), Singapore, Kuching (Sarawak), and Kota Kinabalu (Sabah). The ship offers air-conditioned cabins and suites, restaurants, a cinema, a disco, a gym, and a swimming pool. In port cities there's regular **ferry service** to the islands. To get to Pangkor, catch the ferry in Lumut; for Langkawi, in Kuala Perlis or Penang. Launches serve Tioman Island from Mersing and Pulau Gaya from Kota Kinabalu.

By Taxi Taxi operators near bus terminals call out destinations for long-distance, shared-cost rides; drivers leave when they get four passengers. Single travelers who want to charter a taxi pay four times the flat rate and leave whenever they want. The quality of service depends on the condition of the vehicle and bravado of the driver. In general, the cost is comparable to that of a second-class train ticket or non-air-conditioned bus fare.

City taxis are plentiful and relatively cheap. Rates in peninsular Malaysia are metered. Those in Sabah and Sarawak are not—set the fare with the driver in advance. Air-conditioned or late-night rides cost 20% more than what's on the meter.

By Car Rentals The largest car-rental operation in Malaysia, **Avis** has offices all over the mainland; rates range from M$40 to M$125 a day with unlimited mileage. Special three-day rates are available. The main office is in Kuala Lumpur (40 Jln. Sultan Ismail, tel. 03/242–3500). **Budget** (tel. 03/242–5166) has offices in Kuala Lumpur and counters at Subang and Penang airports. **Hertz** (tel. 03/243–3433) has offices in Kuala Lumpur, Penang, and Johore Bahru. **Mayflower** (tel. 03/261–1136) is part of Acme Tours, with a counter at the Ming Court Hotel in Kuala Lumpur. One-way rentals are popular and the surcharge is very modest. **Thrifty,** which often offers the best one-way rates, has offices in Kuala Lumpur (tel. 03/293–2388), Kuantan (tel. 09/528–400), Penang (tel. 04/830–958), and Singapore (tel. 02/272–2211).

Road Conditions The only superhighway in the country runs from Kuala Lumpur to Malacca and on to Johore Bahru. It is lightly traveled because of the tolls. The two-lane trunk road between Kuala Lumpur and Penang has heavy traffic day and night. Slow-moving trucks, motorcycles, and bicycles make it somewhat treacherous. Back roads are narrow but paved, and the pace is relaxed—you'll weave around dogs sleeping in the road. Mountain roads are often single-lane, and you must allow oncoming cars to pass.

Rules of the Road Tourists are urged to get an international driver's license in addition to a valid permit from home. Seat belts are compulsory for drivers and front-seat passengers, and stiff fines are imposed on those caught without them. Driving is on the left side of the road. Some common traffic signs: *AWAS* (caution), *jalan sehala* (one way), *kurangkan laju* (slow down), and *ikut kiri* (keep left). Directions are *utara* (north), *selatan* (south), *timur* (east), and *barat* (west).

Parking In the cities, on-street parking is plentiful, and meters are closely monitored. Public lots are also available. In some areas of Kuala Lumpur, you are expected to pay young hoodlums to "protect" your car while you are away; if you don't, they may vandalize your car. Locals believe it's worth a few coins for such insurance.

Gas Stations charge about M$5 per gallon and offer full service. Except for a few 24-hour stations in cities, most places are closed at night.

Breakdowns Car-rental agents in most cities will assist with problems. The **Automobile Association of Malaysia** (Hotel Equatorial, KL, tel. 03/261–3713 or 03/261–2727) can also offer advice in case of a roadside emergency.

Telephones

Local Calls Public pay phones take 10-sen coins (time unlimited on local calls). Remember to press the release button, which allows your coins to drop down, when the person you call picks up the receiver.

International
Calls
You can direct-dial overseas from many hotel-room phones. If you want to avoid the hotel charges, local phone books give pages of information in English on international calling, rates, and locations of telephone offices. Public phones using telephone cards are found at strategic locations throughout the country. There are two types of cards: **Kadfon**, good only for Telekom phone booths, and **Unicard**, for Uniphone booths. Instructions are displayed in the phone booths. The cards come in denominations of M$3 to M$50 and can be purchased at airports, Shell and Petronas petrol (gas) stations, and most 7-11 and Hop-In stores.

AT&T's **USADirect** service (tel. 800–0011)allows you to call collect or charge calls from abroad to your AT&T calling card; either way, you pay AT&T rates and speak to an English-speaking operator. For information at home, tel. 412/553–7458, ext. 314 (call collect if you are abroad) or 800/874–4000. MCI has a similar system for calls to the United States (tel. 800–0012). To use AT&T's **UKDirect** to Britain, dial 800–0044. Public phones require you to deposit a coin or use a phone card.

To call Malaysia from overseas, dial the country code, 60, and then the area code, omitting the first 0.

Information Dial 104 for directory information.

Mail

Postal Rates Stamps and postal information are generally available at hotel front desks. **Postcards** cost 40 sen to Europe, 55 sen to the Americas; **airmail letters** M$2.20 (½ oz). **Aerograms** are the best value of all, at 40 sen.

Receiving
Mail
American Express (Bangunan MAS, 5th Floor, Jln. Sultan Ismail, KL) will hold mail for 30 days at no charge, as long as you can produce identification and either an American Express card or American Express traveler's checks.

Currency

Malaysian ringgit, also called Malaysian dollars, are issued in denominations of M$1, M$5, M$10, M$20, M$50, M$100, M$500, and M$1,000. The units are called sen (100 sen equals M$1) and come in coins of 1, 5, 10, 20, and 50 sen. Exchange rates at press time were M$2.70 = US$1 and M$4.10 = £1.

What It Will Cost

The Malaysian ringgit has lost some of its value in recent years, and since prices have remained relatively stable, Westerners get more for their money. As might be expected, prices in the cities are higher than elsewhere, Kuala Lumpur being the most expensive. But generally Malaysia offers much more value for lodging, meals, and shopping than, for example, neighboring Singapore.

Taxes A 5% tax is added to **hotel** and **restaurant** bills, along with a 10% service charge, in a system that the locals call "plus plus." (You'll see the "++" symbols where this applies.) **Airport departure tax** varies depending on destination. For domestic flights it's M$3; for flights to Singapore and Brunei, M$5; for other international flights, M$15.

Sample Prices
(in US$)
Cup of tea in hotel coffee shop, $1.30; cup of tea in open-air *kedai*, 60¢; Chinese dim sum breakfast, $3; hotel breakfast buffet, $6; bottle of beer at a bar, $2; bowl of noodles at a stall, $1.10; 1-mile taxi

ride, 75¢; typical bus fare, 19¢; double room, $30 budget, $50 moderate, $100 luxury ($150 in Kuala Lumpur).

Language

The official language is Bahasa Malaysia, but English is widely spoken in government and business and is the interracial lingua franca. The Chinese speak several dialects, including Cantonese, Teochew, Hakka, and Hokkien. The Indians are primarily Tamil speakers. In the countryside, most people use a kampong version of Malay, even in Sabah and Sarawak, where native languages (Kadazan and Iban) predominate.

Opening and Closing Times

Shops are generally open 9:30 AM–7 PM; **department stores** and **supermarkets,** 10–10. Many places are closed Sunday, except in the states of Johor, Kedah, Perlis, Kelantan, and Terengganu, where Friday is the day of rest. **Banks** are open weekdays 10–3 and Saturday 9:30 to 11:30 AM. **Government office hours** are Monday–Thursday 8–12:45 and 2–4:15, Friday 8–12:45 and 2:45–4:15, and Saturday 8–12:45.

National Holidays

The major national public holidays include Chinese New Year; Labor Day, May 1; Hari Raya Puasa, usually mid-May; King's Birthday, June 1; Hari Raya Haji, usually late July; Maal Hijrah, August 14; National Day, August 31; Prophet Muhammad's Birthday, October 23; Deepavali, November 8; and Christmas, December 25. Museums and government offices may be closed on state holidays as well.

Festivals and Seasonal Events

Malaysia's multiracial society celebrates numerous festivals, since each ethnic community retains its own customs and traditions. The dates of some holidays are fixed, but most change according to the various religious calendars.

Jan. or Feb.: During **Chinese New Year,** Chinese families visit Buddhist temples, exchange gifts, and hold open house for relatives and friends.

Jan.–Feb.: The Hindu festival **Thaipusam** turns out big crowds for a street parade in Penang and a religious spectacle at the Batu Caves near Kuala Lumpur. Indian devotees of the god Subramaniam pierce their bodies, cheeks, and tongues with steel hooks and rods.

Mar.–June: Hari Raya Puasa, a major holiday, the date of which varies according to the Muslim lunar calendar, marks the end of Ramadan, the fasting month. It is a time of feasting and rejoicing and often includes a visit to the cemetery, followed by mosque services. Tourists are welcome at the prime minister's residence in Kuala Lumpur during open-house hours.

Mid-May: The **Kadazan Harvest Festival** is celebrated in Sabah with feasting, buffalo races, games, and colorful dances in native costumes.

May–June: Gawai Dayak, a week-long harvest festival, is celebrated in Sarawak with dances, games, and feasting in the longhouses.

Early June: The **Dragon Boat Festival** features boat races off Gurney Drive in Penang.

June 3: Every state marks the **King's Birthday** (Yang Di-Pertuan

Agong) with parades. In Kuala Lumpur's Merdeka Stadium, a trooping of the colors is held.

Aug. 31: Merdeka Day is Malaysia's Independence Day. Arches are erected across city thoroughfares, buildings are illuminated, parades are arranged, and in Kuala Lumpur there is a variety show in Lake Gardens.

Aug.–Sept.: On **All Soul's Day,** or the **Feast of the Hungry Ghosts,** Chinese honor their ancestors by burning paper objects (for the ancestors' use in the afterlife) on the street. Chinese opera is performed in various locations in Penang and other cities.

Oct.–Nov.: During **Deepavali,** the Hindu festival of lights that celebrates the triumph of good over evil, houses and shops are brightly decorated.

Late Dec.: During the **Chingay Procession,** Malaysian Chinese parade through the streets of Penang and Johore Bahru doing stunts with enormous clan flags on bamboo poles, accompanied by cymbals, drums, and gongs. It's a noisy, colorful, folksy pageant.

Dec. 25: Christmas is widely celebrated, with decorations, food promotions, music, and appearances of Father Krismas.

Tipping

Tipping is usually unnecessary, since a 10% service charge is automatically added to restaurant and hotel bills. You'll know that's the case when you see the + + symbol on menus and rate cards. Tip porters one ringgit per bag. It would be insulting to tip less than 50 sen. Malaysians usually tip taxi drivers with their coin change. Otherwise, when you want to acknowledge fine service, 10% is generous—not expected.

Shopping

For an overview of Malaysian goods, check out the Central Market and the Karyaneka Handicraft Centre in Kuala Lumpur.

Malaysia's hand-printed batiks, with layers of rich colors and elaborate traditional designs, have become high fashion worldwide. Shirts and simple skirts and dresses can be purchased off the rack in most sizes, or you can buy lengths of fabric and have garments made at home.

Pewter is another Malaysian specialty, since it's made from one of the country's prime raw materials, tin. The best-known manufacturer is Selangor Pewter, which markets its goods through its own showrooms as well as department stores, gift shops, and handicraft centers throughout the country.

Malaysian handicrafts, especially those from Sarawak in East Malaysia, are well made and appealing, such as rattan baskets in pretty pastels and handwoven straw goods and handmade silver jewelry from Kelantan. The Dayak people in Sarawak create weavings called *pua kumbu*, which use primitive patterns and have a faded look like that of an antique Persian carpet. Tribal sculptures have an allure similar to their African counterparts. Perhaps the most unusual handcrafted material is *kain songket*, an extraordinary tapestrylike fabric with real gold threads woven into a pattern.

Prices in most shops and larger stores are fixed, but you can discreetly ask for a discount. In street markets, flea markets, and antiques stores, bargaining is expected.

Sports and Beaches

Beaches and Water Sports There are good beaches along the Batu Ferringhi strip on Penang Island. The resort hotels that line most of the beachfront offer rental equipment for windsurfing, sailing, waterskiing, and parasailing. Pangkor and Langkawi islands, off the northwest coast, have good golden-sand beaches and are not yet as developed, although both do offer resorts and water-sports facilities. On the east coast, Kuantan, Desaru, and Tioman Island offer resort life; north of Kuantan, miles of quiet and lovely sandy beaches and picturesque villages await those willing to swap luxuries for a more traditional Malay experience. In East Malaysia, the Damai is the best beach in Sarawak, and the pristine islands off Kota Kinabalu in Sabah offer fine snorkeling and beaches. As elsewhere in Southeast Asia, you should find out whether there are stinging jellyfish in the water before you wade in.

Diving Sipadan Island, off Sabah's east coast in the Celebes Sea, is the best dive spot in Malaysia, and one of the best in the world. Coral reef and green sea turtles are among the attractions. Tioman Island is located on coral fringes and has diving facilities.

Golf Golf is part of the British legacy in Malaysia, and you'll find excellent courses throughout the country. Among the best are the **Royal Selangor Golf Club** in Kuala Lumpur and the **Bukit Jambul Golf and Country Club** in Penang. Ask the MTPB for its *Golf Handbook*.

Hiking The best climb in Southeast Asia is Mt. Kinabalu in Sabah. Paths through a park at its base offer rewarding but less arduous walking. Jungle trekking can be arranged in Taman Negara, a national park north of Kuala Lumpur. For leisurely hikes in cooler temperatures, try the hills of the highland resorts (ask the MTPB for its hill resorts booklet).

East Malaysia specializes in hiking, either full-scale backpacking through dense jungle or shorter hiking trips combined with road and river transport.

River Rafting Sabah's scenic white-water rivers guarantee exciting outdoor adventures.

Dining

Surprisingly, "real" Malay food is not as widely available in Malaysia's restaurants as Chinese or even American fast-food fare, including Kentucky Fried Chicken and A&W. Restaurants in major hotels offer a range of international dining styles, including Japanese, Korean, French, Italian, and Continental. Kuala Lumpur and Penang are Malaysia's culinary stars, with excellent restaurants and a variety of cuisines.

Street food is a main event throughout Malaysia; locals share tables when it's crowded. Look at what others are eating, and if it looks good, point and order. One favorite is the *popiah*, a soft spring roll filled with vegetables. The *meehon* and *kweh teow* (fried noodles) are especially tasty and cheap. Pay each provider for the individual dish he or she makes. Be cautious with the *nasi kandar*, a local favorite, for the chilies rule the spicy prawns and fish-head curry.

As a general rule, food handlers are inspected by health-enforcement officers, but the best advice is to patronize popular places: Consumers everywhere tend to boycott stalls with a reputation for poor hygiene.

Because fruit is so plentiful and delicious, Malaysians consume lots of it, either fresh from the ubiquitous roadside fruit vendors or fresh-squeezed—try especially star fruit or watermelon juice. Mangoes, papayas, rambutans, mangosteens, and finger-size bananas are widely available. The "king" of fruits is the durian, but be prepared: The smell is not sweet, even though the taste is. Hotels have strict policies forbidding durians in guest rooms, so most buyers select a fruit, have the seller cut it open, then eat the yellow flesh on the spot (it's sort of like vanilla pudding).

Category	Cost*
$$$$	over M$80 (US$30)
$$$	M$50–M$80 (US$19–US$30)
$$	M$20–M$50 (US$7–US$19)
$	under M$20 (US$7)

per person without tax, service, or drinks, based on 3 dishes shared between 2 people

Highly recommended restaurants are indicated by a star ★.

Lodging

In the cities you will find international-class hotels affiliated with such global chains as Hilton, Holiday Inn, Hyatt, Regent, and Shangri-La. Regional and local hotel groups, such as Merlin and Ming Court, also run luxury operations. Beach resorts at Penang's Batu Ferringhi, Pangkor, and Langkawi islands off the peninsula's west coast, and Port Dickson near Kuala Lumpur also range from quiet and simple to world-class facilities. Cherating, on the quieter east coast, has a Club Med (tel. 800/258–2633 in the U.S.).

Nightlife in Malaysia revolves around the major hotels, which may offer cultural shows, lounges and bars with live entertainment, discos, and restaurants from coffee shops to supper clubs. All top city hotels have fully equipped business centers and health clubs.

Bathrooms in the city generally offer Western-style commodes, whereas Asian-type squat facilities are common in rural areas. Better hotels have in-house movies available on color television. The government censors the media, so there is only limited satellite programming, and only a half-dozen hotels are permitted to broadcast CNN.

Inexpensive Chinese hotels abound in Malaysia, though they are often a bit down at heel. Rest houses, a British legacy in which government bungalows are rented out to officials on duty in the area, are available to tourists at low rates when government officers aren't using them, but they are difficult to book in advance, and you can count on their being full during school holidays. To check their location and availability, write or visit any Malaysian Tourist Promotion Board office. **Youth Hostels Association** (Box 2310, 9 Jln. Vethavanam, off 3½-mi Jln. Ipoh, KL, tel. 03/660872) operates hostels throughout Malaysia. For a complete list of accommodations, ask the MTPB for a copy of its Hotel List. Also, Utell International (tel. 800/44–UTELL in the U.S.) represents more than 30 hotels in Malaysia.

Throughout the chapter, the following hotel price categories will apply.

Category	Cost*
$$$$	over M$300 (US$111)
$$$	M$225–M$300 (US$83–US$111)
$$	M$150–M$225 (US$56–US$83)
$	under M$150 (US$56)

All prices are for a double room; add 5% tax and 10% service charge.

Highly recommended lodgings are indicated by a star ★.

Kuala Lumpur

Kuala Lumpur (KL) is a city of contrasts. Gleaming new skyscrapers sit next to century-old, two-story shophouses. On six-lane super-highways, rush hour traffic often appears to be an elongated parking lot, but nearly a quarter of the population still lives in *kampongs* within the city, giving KL as much a rural feel as urban.

KL was founded by miners who discovered tin in this spot where the Kelang and Gombak rivers formed a broad delta. Those pioneers were a rough, hardy lot, and the city retains some of that early boomtown character. Despite its bustling, cosmopolitan style, KL is at heart an earthy place, where people sit around the *kedai kopi* (coffeehouse) and talk about food, religion, and business. It also is the center of the federal government, and since government is dominated by Malays and business by Chinese, the tone of the city is as much influenced by the easygoing Malays as by the hyperactive Chinese.

While not one of the world's great destination cities, KL does offer first-rate hotels, excellent and varied cuisines, a lively blend of cultures, a rich mix of architectural styles from Moorish to Tudor to International Modern, a generally efficient infrastructure, and the lowest prices of any major Asian city.

Important Addresses and Numbers

Tourist Information The **KL Visitors Centre** (3 Jln. Hishamuddin, tel. 03/230–1369) is open weekdays 8–4:15, Saturday 8–12:45 PM. It supplies city maps, directions, and assistance in finding hotels. The **Malaysian Tourist Promotion Board** (MTPB, 26th Floor, Menara Dato Onn, Putra World Trade Centre, Jln. Tun Ismail, tel. 03/293–5188) has information on all of Malaysia. It is open Monday–Thursday 8–12:45 and 2–4:15, Friday 8–noon and 2:30–4:15, and Saturday 8–12:45 PM. There is also an information counter at the airport and the main railway station.

Embassies **Australia High Commission** (6 Jln. Yap Kwan Seng, tel. 03/242–3122). **British High Commission** (Wisma Damansara, 5 Jln. Semantan, tel. 03/254–1533). **Canadian High Commission** (Plaza MBF, 5th Floor, Jln. Ampang, tel. 03/261–2000). **United States Embassy** (376 Jln. Tun Razak, tel. 03/248–9011).

Emergencies For **police, ambulance,** and **fire,** dial 999.

Doctors The telephone directory lists several government clinics, which treat walk-in patients for a cash fee; these are open during normal business hours.

English-Language Bookstores Because English is widely used in Malaysia, reading material is easy to find, especially on Jalan Tuanku Abdul Rahman, in the 100-block area, and in the Sungei Wang Plaza on Jalan Sultan Ismail.

Travel Agencies **American Express** (MAS Bldg., 5th Floor, Jln. Sultan Ismail, tel. 03/261–0000). **Thomas Cook** (Wisma Bouftead, Jln. Raja Chulan, tel. 03/241–7022). *Also see* Guided Tours, *below.*

Arriving and Departing by Plane

Airports and Airlines **Subang Airport,** 26 km (16 mi) southwest of downtown, is the gateway to Malaysia. In addition to international flights, domestic routes are served by **Malaysia Airlines** (MAS; tel. 03/261–0555). Among the many other airlines that serve Subang are **British Airways** (tel. 03/242–6177), **Northwest Orient** (tel. 03/238–4355), **Qantas** (tel. 03/238–9133), **Royal Brunei** (tel. 03/242–6511), **Singapore Airlines** (tel. 03/292–3122), and **Thai Airways International** (tel. 03/293–7100). During the day both MAS and Singapore Airlines fly hourly between Kuala Lumpur and Singapore; you can cut the fare in half by buying a standby air-shuttle ticket at the airport.

Between the Airport and Downtown
By Taxi Taxi service to city hotels runs on a queue-and-coupon system. You buy the coupon outside customs from the kiosk near the queue, paying by zone; prices run M$20–M$25 to the downtown area. Beware of unscrupulous drivers trying to lure you into private "taxis"—before you get in, look for a license posted on the dash of the passenger side and a meter.

By Bus Public bus 47 runs between the airport and the central bus station downtown, where you can catch another bus to your final destination. Fares are cheap, but the "hourly" service is erratic and unavailable after midnight, when international flights often arrive. Buses to the airport start running at 6 AM. Travel time is about 45 minutes, depending on traffic.

Arriving and Departing by Car, Bus, and Train

By Car The roads into and out of KL are clearly marked, but traffic jams are legendary. It's best to avoid the morning and late-afternoon rush hours if possible.

By Bus Regional buses bring passengers to the main **Pudu Raya terminal** on Jalan Pudu, across from the new Maybank skyscraper, where you can get a taxi or local bus to your city destination. Kuala Lumpur–Singapore express buses cost M$17; Kuala Lumpur–Butterworth, M$15.50. For Kota Bahru and other destinations on the east coast, buses and shared taxis use the Putra Bus Station opposite the Putra World Trade Centre.

By Train All trains from Butterworth and Singapore deposit passengers at the main railway station (tel. 03/274–7435) on Jalan Sultan Hishamuddin, a short distance from the city center. There are always cabs at the taxi stand. The second-class air-conditioned train fare to Kuala Lumpur from either Singapore or Butterworth is M$28.

Getting Around

Walking is the best way to get around the city center's three main areas, called the Golden Triangle. For short distances you can always hop a minibus or hail a taxi.

By Bus Bus service covers most of the metropolitan area. Fares are based on distance, 20 sen for the first kilometer and 5 sen for each additional 2 kilometers. Just tell the conductor where you want to go, and have small change ready, because ticket sellers don't like to break large bills. Minibuses charge 50 sen for rides of any distance. Before you get on, ask the driver whether his route serves your destination. Bus stops are usually marked. Bus companies serving KL include **Foh Hup** (tel. 03/238–2132), **Sri Jaya Kenderaan** (tel. 03/442–0166), and **Toon Foong** (tel. 03/238–9833). The two major bus stations are **Pudu Raya** on Jalan Pudu and the **Kelang** terminal on Jalan Sultan Mohamed.

By Taxi Taxis are plentiful in KL. You can catch them at stands, hail them in the street, or request them by phone (pickup costs extra). Radio-dispatch taxi companies include **Kuala Lumpur Taxi Assn.** (tel. 03/221–4241), **Comfort Radio Taxi** (tel. 03/733–0495), and **Teletaxi** (tel. 03/221–1011). Taxis are metered. Air-conditioned cabs charge 20% more (M$1.50 first 2 km, 10 sen each additional 200 m). You can hire a cab by the hour for M$15 the first hour and M$10 per hour afterward. A 50% surcharge applies between midnight and 6 AM, and extra passengers (more than two) pay an additional 20 sen each per ride. Luggage, if placed in the trunk, is and additional M$1. Most taxi drivers speak passable English, but make sure they understand where you want to go and know how to get there before you get in. Be sure the meter is activated when you take off so there won't be any dispute over the fare when you arrive.

Guided Tours

The MTPB maintains a list of all licensed tour operators; you can also get brochures in most hotel lobbies and information from local travel agents. One of the biggest operators is **Mayflower Acme Tours**, with a main office at 18 Jalan Segambut Pusat (tel. 03/626–7011) and a desk at the Ming Court Hotel lobby (tel. 03/261–1120). The other major tour operator is **Reliance** (3rd Floor, Sungei Wang Plaza, Jln. Sultan Ismail, tel. 03/248–0111).

Highlights for First-time Visitors

National Museum

National Art Gallery

Lake Gardens

Central Market

Sultan Abdul Samad building and Selangor Club

Coliseum Cafe

Karyaneka Handicraft Centre

Pudu Prison mural

Bank Bumiputra building

Exploring Kuala Lumpur

In this walking tour, we cover the area known as the Golden Triangle. The walk can be done in a couple of hours, but you'll get more out of it if you linger along the way. Don't hesitate to talk to the locals—they are, by and large, open and friendly.

Numbers in the margin correspond to points of interest on the Kuala Lumpur map. Note: the Friday afternoon prayer break usually lasts from 12:15 to 2:45.

❶ The ideal place to begin is Malaysia's **National Museum** (Muzim Negara), a short walk from the Visitors Centre. The museum's distinctive architecture makes it easily identifiable; the building is modeled after an old-style Malay village house, enlarged to institutional size. On its facade are two large mosaic murals depicting important moments in history and elements of Malay culture.

A number of exhibits are located behind the museum. The **transportation shed** displays every form of transport used in the country, from a Malacca bullock cart, with its distinctive upturned roof, to pedaled trishaws, still in use in Penang, to the newest symbol of national pride, the Malaysian car called the Proton Saga, coproduced with Japan's Mitsubishi Motor. Don't miss the Malay-style house, called **Istana Satu** ("first palace"). Built on stilts, the simple little wood structure is open and airy—perfectly adapted for the tropics—and features decorative wood carvings. Burial totem poles from Sarawak line the path to the museum.

The cultural gallery, to the left as you enter the museum, emphasizes Malay folk traditions. One exhibit explains *wayang kulit*, the shadow plays performed with puppets cut out of leather and manipulated with sticks. You can see how a simple light casts the images on the screen, though the exhibit doesn't capture the theatrical magic the storyteller creates as he spins out rich folk legends. You'll also see a tableau of an elaborate Malay wedding ceremony and exhibits on etiquette, top spinning, Islamic grave markers, colorful cloth headdresses, and a martial-arts form called *silat*. Chinese culture in Malaysia is highlighted at the far end of the gallery. A model Nonya (Peranakan, or straits-born Chinese) home shows classical Chinese furniture, such exquisite antiques as carved canopy beds, and a table-and-chair set with pearl inlay.

The historical gallery has models of regional-style homes and a collection of ceramic pottery, gold and silver items, and other artifacts, plus traditional costumes, now seen only at festivals or on hotel doormen. Exhibits trace the stages of British colonization from the old East India Company in the late 18th century to its withdrawal in the mid-20th. Photos and text outline the Japanese occupation during World War II and Malaysia's move toward federation status in 1948 and independence in 1957. A natural-history exhibit upstairs is devoted to indigenous wildlife, with stuffed flying lemurs, birds, insects, and poisonous snakes. *Jln. Damansara, tel. 03/238-0255. Admission free. Open daily 9-6; closed for Fri. prayers, 12:15-2:45 PM.*

❷ Behind the museum are the scenic **Lake Gardens,** where you can enjoy a leisurely stroll and join city dwellers relaxing, picnicking, and boating on the lake. Also in the park is the **National Monument,** a bronze sculpture dedicated to the nation's war dead, and an **orchid garden** with more than 800 species.

❸ Next door to the Visitors Centre is the **National Art Gallery.** The four-story building was the old Majestic Hotel until its conversion into a museum in 1984. The permanent collection serves as an aesthetic introduction to Malaysia and its people. It also reflects native artists' visions and concerns. They tend to work in contemporary modes—conceptual pieces, pop images, bold sculptures, humorous graphics, and realistic landscapes. The gallery is a bit funky, with its ceiling fans, linoleum-covered floors, and some dimly lit rooms,

Kuala Lumpur

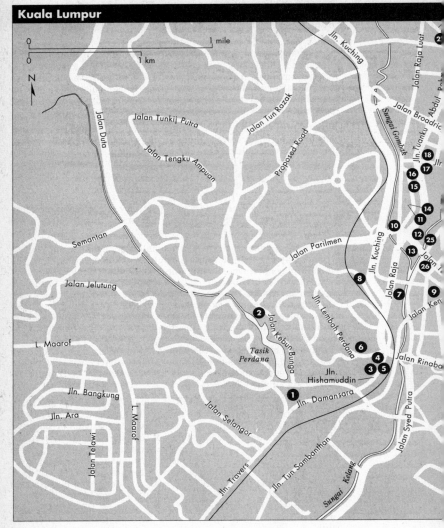

N

0 — 1 mile
0 — 1 km

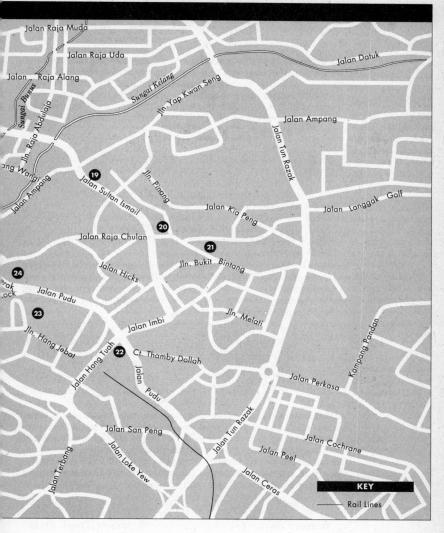

Jalan Raja Muda
Jalan Raja Uda
Jalan Raja Alang
Jalan Datuk
Sungai Burus
Sungai Kelang
Jln. Raja Abdulaja
Jln. Yap Kwan Seng
Jalan Ampang
Jalan Tun Razak
ang Wangi
Jalan Ampang
19
Jalan Sultan Ismail
Jln. Pinang
Jalan Kia Peng
Jalan Langgak Golf
20
Jalan Raja Chulan
21
Jalan Hicks
Jln. Bukit Bintang
24
Jalan Pudu
Jln. Melati
Kampang Pandan
rak
ock
23
Jalan Imbi
Jln. Hang Jebat
22
Ct. Thamby Dollah
Jalan Hang Tuah
Jalan Perkasa
Jalan Pudu
Jalan San Peng
Jalan Cochrane
Jalan Tun Razak
Jalan Peel
Jalan Terbang
Jalan Loke Yew
Jalan Ceras

KEY
—— Rail Lines

but it's still a treat. The museum shop sells witty posters, prints and cards, and artsy T-shirts at reasonable prices. *1 Jln. Sultan Hishamuddin, tel. 03/230–0157. Admission free. Open daily 10–6, except for the Fri. prayer break.*

4 5 The imposing Moorish structures next door and across the street are the **main railway station** and the administrative **offices of KTM** (Kereta-api Tanah Melayu), the national rail system. Built in the early 20th century and renovated since, they were designed by a British architect to reflect the Ottoman and Mogul glory of the 13th and 14th centuries. The KTM building blends Gothic and Greek designs and distinctive, wide exterior verandas.

6 Up Jalan Sultan Hishamuddin is the **National Mosque** (Masjid Negara), currently undergoing restoration and expansion. Its contemporary architecture features a towering minaret spire (240 ft), purple roof, and geometric-patterned grillwork. Though not the largest mosque in Asia, it can accommodate 10,000 worshipers. The entrance is on Jalan Lembah Perdana. Signs remind visitors to dress modestly and to remove their shoes when entering, and that certain areas are off-limits, especially during prayer times. The mosque complex also houses a library and a mausoleum. *Open Sat.–Thurs. 9–6, Fri. 2:45–6.*

7 At Jalan Cenderasari, go under the road via the pedestrian walkway to the impressive **Dayabumi Complex** (Kompleks Dayabumi). Constructed in 1984, it has three parts—the main post office building, the spectacular gleaming white office tower with its lacy Islamic motif, and the plaza connecting the two.

In the post office, philatelists can buy colorful and exotic stamps. Around the corner from the main lobby is a tiny **Stamp Museum** (Galeri Setem), which will be opened for viewing if you ask. Inside, series of stamps spotlight native musical instruments, animals, butterflies, and orchids. The stamp exhibit also promotes nationalistic spirit, with early series focusing on historical events, royalty, and the military. *Post office open weekdays 8–6, Sat. 8–noon.*

At the center of the two-level plaza area is a huge fountain. From the upper level, you can get a good view of the commercial district. One landmark on the horizon is the Hindu temple **Sri Mahamariamman,** in Jalan Bandar. The ornate structure, with images of numerous deities in tile, gold, and precious stones, was rebuilt in 1985 by craftsmen from India and houses a tall silver chariot that is part of a procession to the Batu Caves each Thaipusam.

Stroll through the glistening red-marble lobby of the Dayabumi tower, the major tenant of which is Petronas, the national oil company. Occasionally, art exhibits in the lobby feature local work. On the shopping-arcade level is a host of shops, including the **Pasaraya Supermarket** and the trendy **Rupa Gallery** (lot 158), which specializes in architectural artworks (*see* Shopping, *below*).

8 Across the plaza in the other direction is the **British Council,** on a hill beyond the main road. The public reading room has all sorts of English books and magazines and is a pleasant place to rest. *Jln. Bukit Aman, tel. 03/298–7555. Open Tues.–Fri. 10–6:30, Sat. 10–4:45.*

9 On the town side of the plaza, cross the pedestrian bridge to the **Central Market,** a lively bazaar in the heart of Kuala Lumpur. Housed in a renovated Art Deco building that used to be the city's produce market, it was converted into a series of stalls and shops in 1986. Now the 50-year-old market, painted apricot and baby blue, is the commercial, cultural, and recreational hub of downtown from 10 to 10 daily. Some 250 tenants do business within the two-story, block-long market. Demonstrations of such disappearing arts as batik block printing, Kelantan silversmithing, and the weaving of *kain songket*—a lush (and expensive) fabric made with gold threads—draw crowds to an area called the kampong. Cultural programs are presented daily, highlighting such Malaysian fare as wayang kulit, gamelan orchestras, Chinese opera, lion dances, and traditional Malay dances. Major festivals always include programs here. Free shows are held outdoors on a stage next to the Kelang River most nights (*see* The Arts, *below*).

The Central Market gives visitors a chance to study the whole gamut of Malaysian goods. It has local cakes called *kuih*, herbal products used as medicines and for cooking, Malaysian kites, batik clothing, jewelry, antiques, copper relief pictures, rattan baskets, and wood and bamboo crafts. Young artists produce watercolors of rustic village life, and tile painters will custom-make a tile for you in pop or romantic designs. The portrait corner, where artists do both caricatures and realistic sketches in colored charcoal, always attracts a crowd.

In addition, some 40 food vendors serve Malaysian dishes at reasonable prices. This is a great place to sample new dishes. Or, in the evening, drop by the small Riverbank Restaurant for light Continental fare and live jazz.

Exit either the way you came in or via the other side door onto a street called Leboh Pasar Besar, which means "big market." Cross the river and go up a block to the corner, where you will see the pa-
⑩ dang, or playing field, of the **Selangor Club,** a private club in a rambling Tudor-style building. The padang covers an underground parking lot for the central business district.

⑪ The massive **Sultan Abdul Samad building,** constructed in 1897 with Moorish arches, copper domes, and clock tower, is considered the center of the old city. Preservationists fought to have it restored in the early 1980s. Originally occupied by the state secretariat (Dewan Bandaraya), it now houses the judicial department and high courts, along with a handicrafts museum called **Infokraf Malaysia,** a branch of the national handicrafts center. *Cnr. of Jln. Tun Perak Museum, tel. 03/293–4929. Admission free. Open Sat.–Thurs. 9–6.*

Three major religious centers surround the old Dewan, as the build-
⑫ ing is called. **St. Mary's Anglican Church,** pristine with its red-tile roof and manicured grounds, offers services in Tamil and English.
⑬ **Masjid Jamek Bandaraya,** on a point where the Kelang and Gombak rivers flow together, is the city's oldest mosque. Its two minarets are only slightly taller than the coconut palms on the grounds. A vendor beside the main gate sells tape recordings of those hypnotic
⑭ prayer chants. **Masjid India,** a modern Indian Muslim mosque, is the centerpiece of Little India. One attraction here is the street vendors selling local *ubat* (medicine) or *jamu* (cosmetics) with all the theatricality of old carnival barkers and snake-oil salesmen. They lure potential customers with elaborate stories and "magic" acts in which audience members participate.

Heading north up Jalan Tuanku Abdul Rahman, note the few remaining turn-of-the-century, two-story shophouses, with decorative flourishes along the roofline. Walking through these often-crowded streets and peeking into the shops is exciting, but there are many steps to negotiate, and the pavement is uneven and can be treacherous.

At Jalan Melayu, an Indian vendor runs a tidy **newsstand** that reeks of incense. A fun souvenir is a Malay comic book called *Gila Gila* ("crazy"), a local version of *Mad* magazine.

Along this strip of "Batu Road," as the locals call Jalan Tuanku Abdul Rahman, are a number of colorful sari shops, bookstores, stationery shops, Indian Muslim restaurants, and stores of an indeterminate nature. If you enjoy seeing local films when you travel, drop by the **Coliseum Theatre,** which showcases the best of Malaysian and Indonesian cinema. Tickets are inexpensive, and all seats are reserved. Note that the cheap seats are downstairs in front and first class is in the balcony—the reverse of what you might expect. These movies usually have only Chinese subtitles, but you can usually figure out what's going on because they are quite action-oriented. Around the theater's parking lot are public toilets *(tandas)*, near the traffic signal, and a number of American fast-food outlets, where the homesick can gorge on burgers, fries, and fried chicken.

Across the road from the theater on Jalan Bunus, lots of little shops and vendors press on in the shadow of the bustling Mun Loong department store. Outside Mun Loong is a bank of telephones.

Time Out The **Coliseum Cafe** (98–100 Jln. Tuanku Abdul Rahman, tel. 03/292–6270; *see* Dining, *below*) is another city landmark. Built in 1921, the Coliseum is known for two things: It has the best steak in town, and it's the favorite watering hole for rowdy locals. The delightfully seedy atmosphere exudes history, so with a little imagination you can conjure up visions of British rubber planters in the 1930s ordering a *stengah*, or half-pint of ale. A sizzling steak with all the trimmings costs about M$13.50, a great value. The place is usually crowded and doesn't take reservations, but waiting in the pub can be an event in itself.

Coliseum owners Wong Chin-wan and Loi Teik-nam sit behind the bar working and chatting with customers: young Europeans traipsing around Asia on a student budget, and regulars—a mix of expatriates, Chinese, Indians, and Malays, including a number of journalists and a cartoonist nicknamed Lat. Lat is an institution: His cartoons—which appear in the *New Straits Times* and have been collected into nearly a dozen books—often reflect the national mood.

Walking north on Batu Road, you can stop for a frosty mug of root beer at the **A&W** or a bowl of steaming noodle soup at one of the open-air coffee shops with marble-top tables and bentwood chairs. In the daytime, shopping families fill the streets while a troupe of blind musicians with bongo drums and electric piano entertains passersby. After midnight the street life changes dramatically, as *pondans* (transvestites) chat up men who cruise by in cars.

Farther along Batu Road is the **Peiping Lace Shop** (No. 223), which features Chinese linens, lace, jewelry, and ceramics. **China Arts,** next door, is a branch of Peiping Lace that sells furniture; the rambling shop is filled with decorative coromandel screens, carved writing desks, teak and camphor chests, and antique vases.

The **Selangor Pewter showroom** (No. 231) has a full range of pewter products, which have been made in Malaysia for more than 100 years. Most designs are simple and of superior quality. A few items, such as a photo frame encrusted with Garfield the Cat, are pure kitsch. In its Heritage Collection, Selangor has replicas of *caping*, fig leaf–shape "modesty discs" that nude children once wore to cover their genitals; now teenagers wear them on chains as pendants. In the back of the shop you can see a demonstration of the process of pewter making.

18 At the meeting of Jalan Dang Wangi and Jalan Tuanku Abdul Rahman, the Odeon Theatre occupies one corner, and the huge **Pertama Kompleks** another. Pertama ("first") is typical of most town shopping centers: clothing, shoe, appliance, and record shops, plus several recreational spots, including a video-games room, a pool hall, and a nightclub.

Continue up Jalan Dang Wangi and turn left onto Jalan Ampang, where the auto dealership shows various models of the Proton Saga.

19 Turn right at the next corner and you'll see the **Concorde Hotel** (formerly the Merlin), the coffee shop and lobby lounge of which are popular meeting spots. In front of the hotel, in the early morning, a makeshift stand hawks Malaysia's favorite breakfast dish, *nasi lemak*—a bundle of rice with salt fish, curry chicken, peanuts, slices of cucumber, and boiled egg—for one ringgit.

The next stretch of "gold coast," with its high-rise luxury hotels and modern skyscraper offices, argues convincingly that Malaysia is a nation emerging into modernity. Another confirmation of that fact comes when you get into a taxi and the driver tells you that you can make a local phone call for about a quarter—and hands you a mobile phone.

Caution: Watch your handbag or shoulder bag while walking in this district. Snatch thieves on motorcycles are known to ride up alongside strollers, snatch their goods, and buzz off. Police advise walkers to carry bags under the arm, on the side away from the street, to forestall such incidents.

20 Turn right on Jalan Raja Chulan. In the next block you'll see a row of outdoor food stalls along Jalan Kia Peng, just behind the Hilton Hotel in the parking lot. Locals insist that this hawker area, **Anak Ku,** is among the best in the city.

21 The **Karyaneka Handicraft Centre** is a campus of museums and shops that sell regional arts and crafts. Each of 13 little houses is labeled with the name of a Malaysian state. Inside, goods from that area are on display and demonstrations are conducted by local artisans. The main building, shaped like a traditional Malay house, stocks goods from the entire country, including a wide selection of rattan baskets and straw purses and mats; batik-design silk shirts, dresses, scarves, and handkerchiefs; delicate silver jewelry; native sculpture from Sarawak; and lengths of kain songket. *186 Jln. Raja Chulan, tel. 03/243–1686. Admission free. Open Sun.–Fri. 9–6, Sat. 9–6:30.*

Behind the center, across a little stream, are two small museums. The **Crafts Museum** has changing exhibits. The **International Crafts Museum** nearby has a modest collection of work from other parts of the world. The **botanical gardens** that border the little stream offer a quiet spot to rest and reflect.

As you leave the center, turn left and head for the next block, which is Jalan Bukit Bintang, then turn right. A couple of blocks along on the left you'll find the **Kuala Lumpur Shopping Centre,** and across the street, the **Regent Hotel.** Two shopping complexes at the next intersection, the **Bukit Bintang Plaza** in front and the **Sungai Wang Plaza** behind it, form one of the largest shopping areas in the city. Among the tenants are boutiques, bookshops, and the **Metrojaya** and **Parkson** department stores, possibly the city's finest. The atrium area almost always has an exhibition of some sort—comic books, fitness equipment, whatever.

Outside, across from the taxi stand, are racks of a strange green produce that resembles a porcupine more than a fruit: the Malaysian durian, which grows in the jungle and is prized highly by city dwellers (*see* Dining in Staying in Malaysia, *above*). Hereabouts, as elsewhere, hawkers contribute to the atmosphere with the pungent smell of chilies frying and peanuts steaming. At night, crowds often gather around a pitchman selling medicines.

Jalan Bukit Bintang is a jumble of modest hotels, goldsmiths and other shops, and finance companies. Past the Federal Hotel, in front of the Cathay and Pavilion cinemas, the vendors hawk the usual candies and some unusual drinks, such as coconut water or crushed sugarcane juice, pressed as you wait.

②② Head east up Jalan Pudu one block. On the corner at Jalan Imbi stands the **Pudu Prison** with its beautifully painted tropical-landscape wall—topped with barbed wire. The mural, painted by inmates, is the longest in the world, according to the *Guinness Book of World Records*. You'll also note a warning that death is the mandatory sentence for drug trafficking in Malaysia, and the news reports will confirm that the law is enforced. Turn around and head back down Jalan Pudu.

②③ The **Pudu Raya bus station** has all the rough-and-tumble of any big-city bus station. The area is beset by a severe litter problem, despite government fines. Air pollution, too, can be a problem because of the incessant traffic jams and the continued practice of using leaded gasoline.

②④ On the imposing hill just ahead is the new **Maybank Building,** designed to resemble the handle of a *kris* (an ornately decorated dagger), the national emblem. Up the escalators, you can enter and walk around the soaring five-story bank lobby during banking hours. The new **Numismatic Museum,** which exhibits Malaysian bills and coins from the past, can supply information on the nation's major commodities, and adjoins a gallery of contemporary art. *Tel. 03/280–8833, ext. 2023. Museum admission free. Open daily 10–6; closed public holidays.*

Beyond Pudu Raya, Jalan Pudu becomes Jalan Tun Perak, with several of the ubiquitous kedai kopi offering simple, refreshing snacks. Beyond Leboh Ampang you'll come again to the Kelang River. To **②⑤** your right is the **Bank Bumiputra,** built in the shape of a kampong house. On the other side of Jalan Tun Perak is Wisma Batik, with the **②⑥** **Batik Malaysia Berhad** (BMB) on the first and second floors. This shop has a wide selection of batik fabrics, shirts, dresses, and handicrafts upstairs. At the next intersection the loop of our tour is completed.

②⑦ A unique attraction about 11 km (7 mi) north of the city is the **Batu Caves,** vast caverns in a limestone outcrop discovered in 1878 by American naturalist William Hornaday in one of his forays for new species of moth larvae. The caves are approached by a flight of 272 steps, but the steep climb is worthwhile. A wide path with an iron railing leads through the recesses of the cavern. Colored lights provide illumination for the stalagmites and other features and formations. It is here that the spectacular but gory Thaipusam festival (held around February) takes place in its most elaborate form. In the main cave is a Hindu Temple dedicated to Lord Subramaniam. Behind the Dark Cave lies a third cave called the Art Gallery, with elaborate sculptures of figures from Hindu mythology. The caves are staggering in their beauty and immensity: The Dark Cave is 366 m (1,200 ft) long and reaches a height of 122 m (400 ft). The caves are open daily 7 AM–9 PM. To reach the caves, take a taxi for about M$25 round-trip, or a local bus from Pudu Raya Bus Terminal.

Off the Beaten Track

Near the Turf Club's old racetrack on Jalan Ampang is a little arts and design center called **10 Kia Peng.** In the renovated stables of an old mansion there, 14 prominent sculptors, painters, wood-carvers, calligraphers, and printers hold workshops and sell their art at reasonable prices. A gallery has regular exhibitions, and hawker stalls provide snacks. *Off Jln. P. Ramlee and Jln. Pinang, tel. 03/248–5097. Open daily 10–6.*

Shopping

Malaysia offered few bargains until duty-free shopping reduced prices a few years ago. Now most quality radios, watches, cameras, and calculators are slightly cheaper in Kuala Lumpur than in Singapore; look for a duty-free sticker in shop windows. Fashion, too, has come to KL, and at prices far better than in Singapore. You can also pick up inexpensive clothing, from jeans to shirts, for much less than in the United States and Europe.

If you can't find a particular product or service, call **Infoline** (tel. 03/230–0300), a telemarketing company that will try to steer you in the right direction. It also gives advice on restaurants and nightspots.

Many of the following shops and centers are discussed in greater detail in Exploring, above.

Shopping Centers **The Mall** on Jalan Putra is the largest in Southeast Asia. Its anchor tenant is the **Yaohan** department store, but it has numerous specialty shops as well. **The Weld** on Jalan Raja Chulan is one of the decidedly upscale malls in Kuala Lumpur: It has a marble interior and an atrium, and its shops include Crabtree & Evelyn, Benetton, Bruno Magli, and Etienne Aigner.

The most popular shopping centers are the **Bukit Bintang Plaza, Sungai Wang Plaza,** and **KL Plaza,** all in the same vicinity on Jalan Bukit Bintang and Jalan Sultan Ismail. All have major department stores, such as **Metrojaya** and **Parkson,** plus bookstores, boutiques, and gadget shops. Also worth a visit are **Yow Chuan Plaza,** on Jalan Tun Razak, and the **Pertama Kompleks** at Jalan Tuanku Abdul Rahman and Jalan Dang Wangi (*see* Exploring, *above*).

Street Markets At KL's street markets, crowded hawker stalls display everyday goods, from leather handbags to pocketknives to pop music cassettes. Bargaining is the rule, and only cash is accepted. Two major night markets operate daily. The largest is on **Petaling Street** in Chinatown; the other is **Chow Kit** on upper Jalan Tuanku Abdul Rahman. On Saturday night, between 6 and 11, **lower Jalan Tuanku Abdul Rahman** near the Coliseum Theatre is closed for a market, where you'll find everything from the latest bootleg tapes to homemade sweets. In the **Kampung Baru** area on Sunday, another openair bazaar (called *pasar minggu*) offers Malay handicrafts and local food.

Specialty Stores
Antiques For Nonya antiques, try **Le Connoisseur** in Yow Chuan Plaza. The shop is open only in the afternoon, but call Mrs. Cheng to visit at other times (tel. 03/241–9206). For Chinese arts and crafts, look in at

Peiping Lace Co. (223 Jln. Tuanku Abdul Rahman, tel. 03/298–3184) or **China Arts** (tel. 03/292–9250) next door. For Nonya and colonial antiques, visit the **Treasure Chest** (Jaya Supermarket, Petaling Jaya, tel. 03/755–3942).

Art The **Rupa Gallery** (Dayabumi Shopping Centre, tel. 03/755–9142) specializes in architectural artwork, including delightful watercolor-print notecards of shophouses and line-drawing prints of Kuala Lumpur landmarks by Victor Chin. Watercolors and portraits finished or in progress can be found at the **Central Market.**

Handicrafts The best buys are Malaysian handicrafts, which are simple and attractive. For rattan baskets, straw handbags, wood carvings, Kelantan silver jewelry, and batik fashions, try **Karyaneka Handicrafts Centre** (tel. 03/241–3704) on Jalan Raja Chulan. The stalls of the **Central Market** (Jln. Cheng Lock, tel. 03/274–6542) offer handicrafts as well as a wide range of other souvenirs, including portraits, painted tiles, jewelry, and antiques. The best selection of batik fabric and fashions is at **Batik Malaysia Berhad** (tel. 03/291–8606) on Jalan Tun Perak.

Traditional and modern pewterware designs are available at the **Selangor Pewter** showrooms (231 Jln. Tuanku Abdul Rahman, tel. 03/298–6244). Other fine gift shops are at **Metrojaya** in Bukit Bintang Plaza and **Plaza Yow Chuan** on Jalan Ampang. You can also visit the **Selangor Pewter Factory,** a few miles north of the city in the suburb of Setapak. In its showroom, visitors can see how pewter is made from refined tin, antimony, and copper, and formed into products such as pitchers and candelabras. Duty-free souvenirs can be bought here, too. *4 Jln. Usahawan 6, Setapak, tel. 03/422–3000. Open Mon.–Sat. 8:30–4:45, Sun. 9–4.*

Jewelry Try **Jade House** (tel. 03/241–9640) on the ground floor of KL Plaza or **Jewellery by Selberan,** with showrooms in KL Plaza (tel. 03/241–7106) and Yow Chuan Plaza (tel. 03/243–6386).

Sports and Fitness

Golf Hotels can make arrangements for guests to use local courses, including the **Selangor Golf Club** (tel. 03/984–8433), which enjoys the best reputation.

Jogging Two popular places to run are the **parcours** in Lake Gardens and around the **racetrack area** on Jalan Ampang.

Spectator Sports

The sports pages of the newspapers list many sporting events at **Merdeka Stadium** (on Jalan Stadium).

Horse Racing Malaysians, especially the Chinese, have a passion for horse racing, and a regional circuit includes race days in Kuala Lumpur, Penang, Ipoh, and Singapore. Races are held on Saturday and Sunday year-round.

Martial Arts In some cultural shows (*see* The Arts, *below*), you can see men performing *silat*, a traditional Malay form of combat and self-defense.

Beaches

The beach nearest Kuala Lumpur is at Port Dickson, about an hour and a half away. Intercity buses from Pudu Raya station take passengers to the terminal in Port Dickson; local buses there will drop you off anywhere you want along the coast road. Alternatively, you can charter a limousine for M$200. The beach stretches for 16 km (10 mi), from the town of Port Dickson to Cape Rachado, with its 16th-century Portuguese lighthouse. A good place to begin a beach walk is the fifth milestone from town. On the coast road, stalls offer fruits of the season.

Dining

By Eu Hooi Khaw

Eu Hooi Khaw has worked as a journalist and restaurant reviewer in Malaysia for many years.

Though Kuala Lumpur is not a coastal city, it reaps the ocean's benefits. Seafood is the rage among locals, who wash it down with ice-cold beer, and outdoor restaurants serving both have sprung up in the city and on its fringes.

The lack of purely Malay restaurants is offset by the hotels, which serve Malay buffets and à la carte dishes. Food festivals featuring regional specialties from the different Malaysian states are also frequently held. Three styles of Indian cooking—southern Indian, Mogul, and Indian Muslim (a blend of southern Indian and Malay)—can be found in Kuala Lumpur. Eating Indian rice and curry with your hands on a banana leaf, as is done in the southern Indian restaurants, is an experience to be savored.

Thai and Japanese restaurants are legion, and the cuisine of the Nonya, or straits-born Chinese—a combination of Malay, Chinese, and Thai tastes—is gaining popularity. A few restaurants, such as Nonya Heritage, distinguish themselves through their authenticity: Their cooking methods are traditional and laborious, but the result is outstanding eating.

The increasingly affluent city population is growing fond of fine Continental restaurants, found mostly in the four-and five-star hotels. Traditional steakhouses, such as the Coliseum Cafe, also draw crowds. But for some of the best Chinese and other cuisines, you may want to venture out of Kuala Lumpur into Petaling Jaya, a suburb 12 km (7.5 mi) southwest and just 20 minutes by cab.

Eating out almost anywhere is informal. Jackets and ties are seldom worn, except at the swankiest five-star hotels. Most places accept credit cards. The more expensive restaurants add a 10% service charge and 5% sales tax, in which case tipping is not necessary. Lunch is normally served from 11:30 AM to 2:30 PM, dinner from 6:30 to 11. Seafood restaurants are usually open from 5 PM to 3 AM.

The following terms appear throughout this section:

asam—sour, a reference to the sourness of the *asam* fruit, used in some curries

dim sum—Chinese snacks, eaten at breakfast or lunch, made with meat, prawns, or fish and usually steamed or deep-fried

garoupa—a local fish with tender flesh and a sweet flavor

green curry—a Thai curry with fewer chilies than Indian, made with small green *brinjals* (eggplants) and meat

ice kacang—shaved ice heaped over red beans, jelly, sweet corn, and green rice-flour strips, flavored with syrup or coconut sugar

kacang (pronounced "ka-chang")—signals the presence of beans or nuts

kaya—a jam made from steaming a mixture of eggs, sugar, and coconut cream

kerabu—a hot-and-sour Thai salad of chicken, jellyfish, mango, squid, beef, or almost anything else, dressed with onions, lemongrass, lime juice, and small chilies

Nonya—Chinese born in Malaysia who have assimilated and adapted Malay customs

rendang—meat simmered for hours in spices, chilies, and coconut milk until nearly dry

roti—bread

sambal—a thick, hot condiment of chilies, local roots and herbs, and shrimp paste

tandoori—meat or seafood roasted in a clay oven, northern-Indian style

tomyam—Thai soup cooked with seafood or meat in asam juice, sometimes very hot and sour

$$$$
Chinese
★

Lai Ching Yuen. Master Chef Choi Wai Ki came from Hong Kong to establish Kuala Lumpur's foremost Cantonese restaurant. The extensive menu draws on shark's fin, bird's nest, abalone, pigeon, chicken, and duck, as well as barbecue specialties; the drunken prawns are superb. The dining room is designed as two Chinese pavilions, with illuminated glass etchings, modern Chinese art, silver panels, a Burmese teak ceiling, and silver-and-jade table settings creating an elegant ambience. Traditional music on Malay instruments accompanies dinner. *The Regent, 126 Jln. Bukit Bintang, tel. 03/241–8000. Reservations suggested. Jacket and tie required. AE, DC, MC, V.*

$$$$
French

Lafite Restaurant. Named for France's finest vineyard, Lafite serves classic European cuisine in a romantically lit setting with pastel-hued wallpaper and upholstery. Oil paintings and fine crystal are on display, and an impressive wine cellar is the dining room's centerpiece. Specialties include rabbit loin with figs and port wine, trio of seafood in yellow-pepper sauce, and poached pear with almond cream. The Table Surprise Lafite is a lavish Continental dinner buffet. *Shangri-La Hotel, 11 Jln. Sultan Ismail, tel. 03/232–2388. Reservations advised. Jacket and tie preferred. AE, DC, MC, V.*

$$$$

Melaka Grill. In a setting designed to re-create an ancient Chinese courtyard, this restaurant has a unique, colorful ambience accented by crisp linens, elegant crockery, and sparkling crystal. The style of cooking is European, though ingredients are primarily fresh local products, such as tiger prawns. An excellent value is the one-price luncheon where, for M$45, guests may select four courses from a number of options—a duck liver parfait with Kalahari truffles for an appetizer perhaps, followed by a lobster bisque soup, and then sukiyaki in a seashell for the main course; dessert is selected from the trolley. For dinner, there is a seven-course *menu dégustation* for M$68, as well as an extensive à la carte menu. *Kuala Lumpur Hilton, Jln. Sultan Ismail, tel. 03/242–2122. Reservations suggested. Jacket and tie required. AE, DC, MC, V.*

$$$$

Regent Grill. Choosing between Shangri-La's Lafite, the Hilton's Melaka Grill, or the Regent Grill is a gourmet dilemma. The Grill is new, aims to impress, and is a little more expensive than the other two. Wood paneling, leather upholstery, and stark earth-color walls make the white German Schenwald china and Schoff Zweisel crystal stand out. The menu varies, but frequent items are lamb chops served on a bed of herbs, medallions of venison, and a pumpkin and scallop soup or goose liver terrine to start. The wine list is comprehensive—there are some 300 selections, many of which are surprisingly affordable, though you may be tempted by the Château Margaux 1929 at M$7,800. *The Regent, 160 Jln. Bukit Bintang, tel. 03/241–8000. Reservations suggested. Jacket and tie required. AE, DC, MC, V.*

$$$ **Terrace Garden.** Soothing shades of green and gray, white walls,
Continental black-framed windows, and pale green trellis dividers blend well in
this restaurant converted from a house. Dolly Lim runs the place
sweetly and efficiently; Dolly Augustine sings evergreen numbers
for entertainment. The chef recommends U.S. tenderloin stuffed
with spinach leaves and smoked salmon; the lobster Thermidor is
the best around. Finish with mocca Bavaria, a three-layer cream
custard with Tía Maria sauce, or the blueberry pie. On Friday and
Saturday there's a barbecue in the open-air extension. *308 Jln.
Ampang, tel. 03/457–2378. Reservations advised on weekends.
Dress: casual. AE, DC, MC, V.*

$$$ **Chikuyo-tei.** Despite the rather dismal entrance into the basement
Japanese of an office complex, Chikuyotei—the oldest Japanese restaurant in
the city—has a warmly lit, woody interior with tatami rooms and
sectioned-off dining areas. It serves excellent *unagi kabayaki*
(grilled eel) and *nigirisushi*, a variety of sushi made with tuna, her-
ring, salmon eggs, and squid. The *teppanyaki*—meat, seafood, and
vegetables sliced, seasoned, and cooked on a hot plate in front of
you—is popular. *See Hoy Chan Plaza, Jln. Raja Chulan, tel. 03/
230–0729. Reservations advised. Dress: casual. AE, DC, MC, V.
No lunch Sun.*

$$ **Bon Ton.** Though this bistro-style restaurant with Southeast Asian
Asian artifacts lining its walls also serves European dishes, the Nonya set
meal, with chicken and lamb, is an excellent way to experience the
native cuisine. The Indian blackened fish with tandoori yogurt and
cucumber relish is also well worth trying. The ambience is quiet and
relaxed, though the small chairs and paper napkins can become un-
comfortable if you linger too long. *7 Jln. Kia Peng, tel. 03/241–3611.
Reservations advised. Dress: smart casual. AE, MC, V.*

$$ **Happy Hour Seafood Restaurant.** Strings of lights drape the front of
Chinese this restaurant, and its tables spill out onto the walkway, which has
Seafood a little more atmosphere than the brightly lit, functional room indoors. Steamed, baked, or fried crabs filled with rich red roe are the
specialty. Other good choices are the prawns steamed with wine and
ginger, and the deep-fried garoupa. *53 Jln. Barat, off Jln. Imbi, tel.
03/248–5107. Reservations not necessary. Dress: casual. AE, DC,
V. No lunch.*

$$ **Restoran Makanan Laut Selayang.** This excellent restaurant is very
Chinese plain: Food, not decor, is its raison d'être. You can eat outside, under
Seafood a zinc roof, or in a simple air-conditioned room that seats 30 at three
★ large, round tables. One great dish here is black chicken—a small
Malaysian bird with black skin and white feathers—steamed in a co-
conut. Also good are the deep-fried soft-shell crabs and the prawns
fried with butter, milk, and chilies. Adventurous diners can try
steamed river frogs and soups of squirrel, pigeon, or turtle. The
house specialty is fatt thieu cheong ("monk jumps over a wall"), a
soup of shark's fin, sea cucumber, dried scallops, mushrooms, and
herbs, which must be ordered in advance. *Lot 11, 7½ mi Selayang,
tel. 03/627–7015. Reservations not necessary. Dress: casual. AE,
V.*

$$ **Coliseum Cafe.** The aroma of sizzling steak—the house specialty—
Continental fills the air in this old café established before World War II. A nostal-
gic, slightly seedy colonial ambience prevails, with the waiters'
starched white jackets a bit frayed and the walls cracked and brown
with age. Steaks are served with brussels sprouts, chips, and salad.
Another favorite here is crab baked with cheese. The Sunday lunch,
or *tiffin*, of light curry dishes, is not to be missed. *Also see* Exploring, *above. 98–100 Jln. Tuanku Abdul Rahman, tel. 03/292–6270.
No reservations. Dress: casual. No credit cards.*

Kuala Lumpur Dining and Lodging

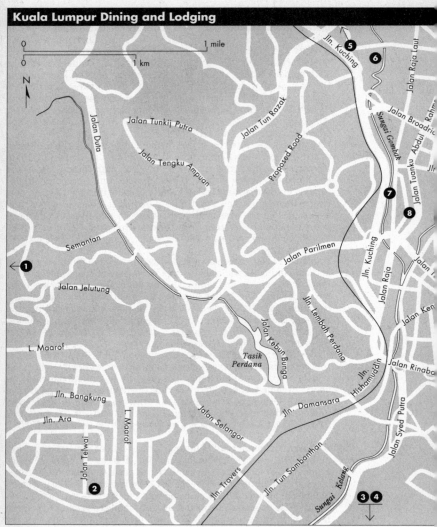

Dining
Ala'din, **2**
Bon Ton, **13**
Chikuyo-tei, **19**
Ciao, **30**
Coliseum Cafe, **8**
Happy Hour Seafood
Restaurant, **28**
Kedai Makanan Yut
Kee, **9**
Lafite Restaurant, **10**
Lai Ching Yuen, **20**

Lotus Restaurant, **3**
Melaka Grill, **16**
Nonya Heritage, **21**
Regent Grill, **20**
Restoran Makanan
Laut Selayang, **5**
Satay Anika, **22**
Teochew
Restaurant, **26**
Terrace Garden, **31**
Yazmin, **29**

Lodging
Carcosa Seri Negara, **1**
Cardogan Hotel, **23**
Concorde Hotel, **12**
Equatorial, **15**
Federal Hotel, **24**
Holiday Inn City
Centre, **7**
Holiday Inn on the
Park, **14**

Hotel Istana, **18**
Kuala Lumpur
Hilton, **16**
Lodge Hotel, **17**
P. J. Hilton, **4**
Pan Pacific, **6**
Park Avenue, **25**
Regent, **20**
Park Royal of Kuala
Lumpur, **27**
Shangri-La, **11**

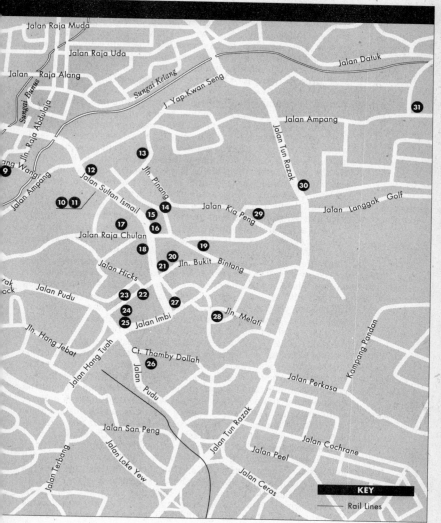

Jalan Raja Muda

Jalan Raja Uda

Jalan Datuk

Jalan Raja Alang

Sungai Kelang

Sungai Burns

Jln. Raja Abdulah

J. Yap Kwan Seng

Jalan Ampang

Jalan Tun Razak

31

ng Wangi

9

Jalan Ampang

12

Jalan Sultan Ismail

13

Jln. Pinang

30

Jalan Langgak Golf

10 11

14

Jalan Kia Peng

29

15

17

Jalan Raja Chulan

16

18

19

Jalan Hicks

20

21

Jln. Bukit Bintang

rak
ock

Jalan Pudu

23 22

27

28

Jln. Melati

24

25   Jalan Imbi

Jln. Hang Jebat

Ct. Thamby Dollah

26

Kampang Pandan

Jalan Hang Tuah

Jalan Pudu

Jalan Perkasa

Jalan San Peng

Jalan Tun Razak

Jalan Terbang

Jalan Loke Yew

Jalan Peel

Jalan Cochrane

Jalan Ceras

KEY

Rail Lines

$$ **Ciao.** The owner, Leo Spadavecchia, will enthusiastically guide you
Italian   to a table and talk you through the menu. Listen well, because the
choicest items often aren't written down. Follow the *antipasto
rustico* with one of the pasta dishes. For the main course, consider
the hearty, traditional veal marsala or, for lighter fare, the fresh
fish with tomatoes baked in foil. *428 Jln. Tun Razak, tel. 03/986–
2617. Reservations advised. Dress: casual. AE, MC, V. Closed
Mon.; no lunch weekends.*

$$ **Yazmin.** Good Malay food in pleasant surroundings is hard to find, so
Malay   this restaurant in a white colonial bungalow on shady, sprawling
★   grounds is worth a visit. Guests dine in an airy upstairs hall with
front windows overlooking a bamboo grove. Evocative black-and-
white photographs taken by a sultan grace the walls, and the owner/
hostess is Raja Yazmin, a Malay princess. Especially recommended
are the *rendang tok* (beef simmered with spices and coconut), *roti
canai* (unleavened bread), and *rendang pedas udang* (prawns
cooked in coconut, chilies, and herbs). If you prefer, you can have
your buffet lunch or dinner on a cozy, village-style timber terrace
with a dried-palm roof. High tea is served daily, there's a Sunday
brunch, and traditional Malay dances are performed every night. *6
Jln. Kia Peng, tel. 03/241–5655. Reservations advised. Dress: casual. AE, DC, MC, V. Closed 4 days at end of Ramadan.*

$$ **Nonya Heritage.** White lace curtains and ethnic wood carvings grace
Nonya   this cozily lit restaurant, which serves hot-and-sour, spicy, and rich
cuisine. The Nonya Golden Pearl, a deep-fried ball of minced prawns
and fish with a salted egg yolk in the middle, is a good start. Then
try the spicy fried rice in a pineapple, the *melaka sotong* (squid)
with chilies, the asam fish-head curry, or the kerabu. *44–4 Jln. Sul-
tan Ismail, tel. 03/243–3520. No reservations. Dress: casual. AE.*

$$ **Ala'din.** The deep pink table settings in this cozy place contrast with
Northern   creamy white walls; trellis screens separate the tables; sitar music
Indian   soothes the senses. The curries (with yogurt and cream, rather than
coconut) are served with various Indian breads, and the chicken,
crab, and rabbit tandooris are popular. Another winner is mutton
karai—meat simmered in a clay pot with coriander, black pepper,
and capsicums. For dessert there's *rasmalai*, a rich custard with
semolina and almonds. *6 Jln. Telwai Empat, Bangsar Baru, tel. 03/
255–2329. No reservations. Dress: casual. AE, DC, MC, V.*

$$ **Lotus Restaurant.** The fun here is eating from a banana leaf with
Southern   your hands. Heaped on the leaf are rice, pickles, and such spicy
Indian   goodies as chili-hot crabs and mutton curry. Try also the *dosai*, a
thin, crisp Indian pancake with a hint of sourness. *Badam halva*, an
almond-and-milk drink, takes away the curry sting, as does the res-
taurant's cool cream-and-sky-blue interior. Mind how you close up
the banana leaf after eating: Folding it toward you means you en-
joyed the meal, folding it away from you shows you were displeased.
*15 Jln. Gasing, Petaling Jaya, tel. 03/792–8795. No reservations.
Dress: casual. No credit cards. Open 7 AM–11 PM.*

$$ **Teochew Restaurant.** Spanning two shop buildings, this restaurant
Teochew   is soothingly decorated in cream and brown, with well-spaced tables
Chinese   and screened-off private dining rooms. It's popular on weekends and
holidays, when 100 varieties of dim sum are served for breakfast and
lunch. Typical Teochew specialties include noodles made entirely of
fish; sea cucumber stuffed with scallops, crab, mushrooms, and water chestnuts; and sizzling prawns. Try also the *oh wee*, a sweet yam
dessert with ginkgo nuts, served with tiny cups of bitter Teochew
tea. *270–272 Jln. Changkat Thamby Dollah, off Jln. Pudu, tel. 03/
241–5851. Reservations advised. Dress: casual. MC, V.*

$ **Kedai Makanan Yut Kee.** This 60-year-old family-run coffee shop/
Hainanese restaurant is one of the few that has not been torn down in the name
★ of progress. Big and airy but rather noisy from the city traffic, the
place boasts marble-topped tables and regular customers who insist
on their favorite seats. Recommended are *roti babi*, a sandwich with
pork filling dipped in egg and deep-fried, and asam prawns. The
black coffee is the best around, and the Swiss roll filled with kaya
makes a fine dessert. *35 Jln. Dang Wangi, tel. 03/298–8108. No reservations. Dress: casual. No credit cards. Open 7 AM–6 PM. Closed
Mon.*

$ **Satay Anika.** Meat marinated with spices, threaded on sticks like a
Satay kebab, grilled over charcoal, and served with a nutty, spicy sauce
used to be a delicacy found only in street stalls. Now you can enjoy it
in the cool comfort of a restaurant in Kuala Lumpur's busiest shopping complex. Plainly furnished and well lit, Satay Anika is owned
by a family that has been cooking satay for four generations. A portion of beef, mutton, chicken, or beef liver satay is 10 sticks. Wash it
down with Malaysian fruit juices, and try the ice kacang for dessert.
(A number of other restaurants on this floor offer a wide range ethnic dishes from Malay to Chinese.) *Lower ground floor, Bukit
Bintang Plaza, Jln. Bukit Bintang, tel. 03/248–3113. Reservations
advised. Dress: casual. No credit cards.*

Lodging

Almost all the tourist hotels are north of the train station, with the
best concentrated near the intersection of Jalan Sultan Ismail and
Jalan Bukit Bintang, the heart of the commercial district and one
corner of the Golden Triangle. The range is broad. Those at the top
level can compete with the world's best in terms of luxury and service; at the lower level, you can find nearly unbeatable prices—for
example, at the Meridian International Youth Hostel on Jln. Hang
Kasturi (tel. 03/232–5819), where US$7 will get you a clean room for
the night. For a map pinpointing hotel locations, *see* Dining, *above.*

$$$$ **Carcosa Seri Negara.** These two adjacent colonial mansions on an estate 7 km (4 mi) from downtown once housed the Governor of the
Straits Settlement. There are seven suites in Carcosa, the main
house, and six in Seri Negara, the guest house, with a golf-cart
shuttle (or an eight-minute walk) between the two. Suites vary in
size, grandeur, and price, but all are appointed with late-19th-cen-
tury furniture. They can be stiff and slightly dreary, but those with
a veranda have streams of light pouring in. They're not for families
or scene makers, but they're ideal for anyone seeking genteel Victorian accommodation. The dining room is one of KL's best. And if
you don't stay or dine here, then come for the Seri Negara's afternoon tea. *Taman Tasik Perdana, 50480 Kuala Lumpur, tel. 03/282–
1888, fax 03/282–7888. 13 suites. Facilities: restaurant, tea lounge,
pool, 2 tennis courts, sauna, massage, gym, business center. AE,
DC, MC, V.*

$$$$ **Kuala Lumpur Hilton.** Though dated, KL's first high-rise luxury hotel still maintains its world-class standards for service and quality.
The mood of crisp elegance is set in the lobby, with fresh flowers and
glowing chandeliers. The pastel-decorated rooms have bay windows, sitting areas, and desks. Rooms with the best views look down
onto the hotel's pool and the Turf Club's racetrack. The Aviary Bar,
just off the lobby, is a popular meeting lounge, and the Melaka Grill
features gourmet dining. The Cantonese restaurant, Tsui Yuen, is
one of the city's best. The Hilton's cosmopolitan reputation is further enhanced by an English pub and Japanese and Korean restau-

rants. *Box 10577, Jln. Sultan Ismail, 50718 KL, tel. 03/242–2122 or 800/HILTONS, fax 03/244–2157. 581 rooms, including executive suites. Facilities: restaurants, 24-hr coffee shop, shopping arcade, squash and tennis courts, fitness center, pool, business center, conference facilities. AE, DC, MC, V.*

$$$$ **Pan Pacific.** This 1986 hotel stands next to the Putra World Trade Centre and across from The Mall shopping complex—a location more suited to conventioneers than to tourists. Its multilevel lobby includes exposed-glass elevators and live music in the lounge. The rooms are richly appointed with comfortable furniture. The VIP floor has butler service. *Box 11468, 50746 KL, tel. 03/442–5555 or 800/937–1515, fax 03/443–1167 or 03/441–7236. 600 rooms, with executive floor and suites. Facilities: 24-hr coffee shop, 3 restaurants (Chinese, Japanese, Continental), health club, pool, business center. AE, DC, MC, V.*

$$$$ **Park Royal of Kuala Lumpur.** Because of its location near the shopping district, this 21-story hotel is a popular meeting place, especially the serene garden lounge off the lobby. Despite the presence of many tour groups, the staff is exceptionally good-humored and helpful, and the room rate is less than at other hotels in this category. The Grill is extremely popular for its European fare (baked duck breast, roast prime rib) and for its unique flap fans, which sway backward and forward. *Jln. Sultan Ismail, 50250 KL, tel. 03/242–5588 or 800/835–SPHC, fax 03/241–5524. 360 rooms. Facilities: 3 restaurants, shopping arcade, business center, health club. AE, DC, MC, V.*

$$$$ **P.J. Hilton.** Located in Petaling Jaya near the industrial zone, this luxury hotel caters to visiting executives who wish to be near many of Kuala Lumpur's multinational corporations. Its rooms and public areas are less grand than the Hilton's, but the accommodations are quite spacious. The sedate lobby lounge is as comfy as a living room. *2 Jln. Barat, 46200 Petaling Jaya, tel. 03/755–9122 or 800/HILTONS, fax 03/755–3909. 398 rooms. Facilities: 3 restaurants, fitness center, squash, tennis, golf, pool, disco. AE, DC, MC, V.*

$$$$ ★ **Regent.** This hotel, located across from the KL Plaza Shopping Centre, opened in 1990. Spacious guest rooms with natural woods and pastel fabrics, and opulent marble bathrooms with huge tubs and separate glass-enclosed showers, create a feeling of spaciousness, and there is plenty of light. The large atrium lobby is stepped, with each level separated by flower boxes. Marble and mirrors, attactive hostesses, and deep-seated chairs in the lounge all spell out glamour and high style. The fifth-floor pool looks over the city and a crowded public pool across the avenue. The Regent Grill and the Lai Ching Yuen vie for top culinary honors with the Hilton's and Shangri-La's European and Chinese restaurants. *126 Jln. Bukit Bintang, 55100 KL, tel. 03/241–8000 or 800/545–4000, fax 03/242–1441. 454 rooms. Facilities: pool, Cantonese, European, and Japanese restaurants, tea lounge, a coffee shop with Malay/Continental food, health club, sauna, Jacuzzi, squash courts, 24-hr business center, meeting and function rooms. AE, DC, MC, V.*

$$$$ **Shangri-La.** Centrally located, this is the most expensive of Kuala Lumpur's hotels. Glamorous people parade through its spacious and opulent lobby, while businesspeople keep up with stock prices and Reuters news with a Beriteks interactive videotext unit. All guest rooms are large, decorated with pastel furnishings and equipped with every amenity. The higher floors are quieter. When all is said and done, however, the glitz is wearing a little thin next to the smooth sophistication of the Regent. *11 Jln. Sultan Ismail, 50250 KL, tel. 03/232–2388 or 800/44–UTELL, fax 03/230–1502. 722 rooms. Facilities: health club, pool, squash, tennis, English pub,*

disco, convention ballroom accommodating 2,000, 13 function rooms, 24-hr business center, 3 restaurants (Cantonese, Japanese, French), garden coffee shop. AE, DC, MC, V.

$$$ Equatorial. This 16-story hotel near the Hilton doesn't have a warm or appealing layout, but it serves well the businessperson on a budget. The deluxe rooms are spacious and equipped with such amenities as a hair dryer and telephone in the bathroom. Rooms in the rear are quieter. The basement café serves a "hawker" buffet of authentic local dishes, and the reasonably priced lunches at its Japanese restaurant, the Kampachi, have developed a well-deserved reputation. *Jln. Sultan Ismail, 50250 KL, tel. 03/261-7777 or 800/44-UTELL, fax 03/261-9020. 300 rooms. Facilities: 4 restaurants (Swiss, local, Chinese, Japanese), pool, business center, shopping arcade, ballroom, function rooms. AE, DC, MC, V.*

$$$ Federal Hotel. This Nikko hotel in the heart of the shopping district is distinguished by a revolving rooftop restaurant and an 18-lane bowling alley downstairs. The front of the hotel, with its street-level coffee shop, is decidedly urban, but the landscaped pool area is tropical in atmosphere. The guest rooms have large windows and the usual amenities. *35 Jln. Bukit Bintang, 55100 KL, tel. 03/248-9166 or 800/44-UTELL, fax 03/248-2877. 450 rooms, including executive and VIP suites. Facilities: pool, disco, Chinese restaurant, poolside buffet, coffee shop, shopping arcade, convention halls. AE, DC, MC, V.*

$$$ Holiday Inn City Centre. Alongside the Gombak River, this 18-story hotel faces a major thoroughfare, so the atmosphere is urban. Its central location is a prime asset. The hotel's lobby is compact and busy. Guest rooms have refrigerators and minibars, along with the usual amenities. *12 Jln. Raja Laut, Box 11586, 50750 KL, tel. 03/293-9233 or 800/HOLIDAY, fax 03/293-9634. 250 rooms. Facilities: business center, shopping arcade, pool, health center, squash court, Chinese restaurant, local coffee shop, bar. AE, DC, MC, V.*

$$$ Holiday Inn on the Park. Just off the main drag, this 14-story hotel is surrounded by trees and is the smarter of the two Holiday Inns in KL. Many guest rooms are decorated in ghastly corporate green-and-white, but they do offer complimentary extras such as in-room movies and coffee- and tea-making facilities. One of its restaurants, the Satay Station, is created from an old railway coach. The continuous passage of tour groups has taken its toll on the furnishings, however. *Box 10983, Jln. Pinang, 50732 KL, tel. 03/248-1066 or 800/HOLIDAY, fax 03/248-1930. 200 rooms. Facilities: small pool, shopping arcade, 4 restaurants (Thai, Italian, pizza, coffee shop), fitness room, sauna, tennis court. AE, DC, MC, V.*

$$$ Park Avenue. Formerly the Prince, this high-rise hotel is near the major shopping district. Its rooms were renovated when the hotel changed hands in 1989. An 18th-floor restaurant serves Western fare. *Jln. Imbi, 55100 KL, tel. 03/242-8333, fax 03/242-6623. 300 rooms. Facilities: 3 restaurants (Chinese, Western, coffee shop), business center, pool, disco. AE, MC, V.*

$$ Cardogan Hotel. It's mainly a business hotel with few frills, but the rooms are clean, smart, and equipped with air-conditioning, television, and minibars. The staff is cheerful, and the coffee shop is good for a quick meal. Best of all is the Golden Triangle location, close to many restaurants and hawker stands. *64 Jln. Bukit Bintang, 55100 KL, tel. 03/244-4856, fax 03/244-4865. 61 rooms and suites. Facilities: coffee shop, business center, health center. MC, V.*

$$ Concorde Hotel. Once the government-owned Merlin Hotel, this large, centrally located building has been completely—and impersonally—refurbished. But the rooms are bright and fresh and the price is right. Pay more for the concierge floor if you want more per-

sonalized service, including complimentary breakfasts. The large
lobby is often filled with tour groups. *2 Jln. Sultan Ismail, 50250
Kuala Lumpur, tel. 03/244–2200, fax 03/244–1628. 600 rooms and
suites. Facilities: 3 restaurants (Malay, Continental, Chinese), coffee shop, 3 concierge floors, pool, fitness center, parking. AE, DC,
MC, V.*

$ **Lodge Hotel.** Across from the Hilton in the Golden Triangle, this ho-
tel offers basic air-conditioned accommodation. Everything is a little shabby—carpets have stains and bathrooms need some plaster
repair—but the rooms are clean and service is friendly. The swimming pool is tiny, but the coffee shop stays open, albeit sleepily, 24
hours a day. *Jln. Sultan Ismail, 50250 KL, tel. 03/242–0122, fax 03/
241–6819. 50 rooms. Facilities: 24-hr coffee shop, bar, and outdoor
pool. DC, V.*

The Arts

A free monthly guide called "This Month," published by the Kuala
Lumpur Tourist Association, is available at hotels and MTPB offices. The Metro Diary column in the daily *The Star* also lists cultural events, including films, seminars, and clubs.

Most government-sponsored cultural events are in the folk rather
than the fine-arts vein. Traditional cultural programs are regularly
presented on Friday evening from 8 to 9 on Level 2 of the Putra
World Trade Centre. Free performances are held nightly at 7:45 at
the **Central Market's** outdoor stage. Contemporary offerings sometimes include fashion shows or jazz concerts. The schedule of events
is published in a monthly brochure distributed to hotels.

Nightlife

Hotel Lounges At the lounges and clubs of the major hotels, the atmosphere is international, the tabs pricey. Most have entertainment nightly except Sunday. The **Aviary Lounge** at the Hilton (Jln. Sultan Ismail,
tel. 03/242–2222) becomes darkly romantic when its highly regarded
jazz combo, the Jazzmates, play Monday through Saturday. The
Lobby Lounge of the Pan Pacific Hotel (Jln. Putra, tel. 03/442–5555)
has a piano bar with singer. The Federal Hotel (35 Jln. Bukit
Bintang, tel. 03/248–9166) features nostalgic tunes in its **Sky Room
Supper Club** and live popular music in its **Lobby Bar.** The **Casablanca
Club** at the Holiday Inn City Centre (Jln. Raja Laut, tel. 03/293–
9233) has pop singers. The **Blue Moon Lounge** of the Equatorial Hotel (Jln. Sultan Ismail, tel. 03/261–7777) offers a live combo.

Pubs and Bars Pubs are modeled after their British counterparts, while bars are
American-style, with country-and-western, blues, jazz, or pop bar
bands. The main problem with either type is location, which is frequently in the suburbs and difficult to find, even for taxi drivers.

Spuds (ground floor, Annex Bldg., Jln. Raja Chulan, tel. 03/248–
5097) is a wine bar with live music that stays open until 2 AM. The
timber and rattan interior is comfortable for a drink or a bite of local or
Western food. In the Damansara vicinity, the **Eighty Eight Pub** (84
Jln. SS21/39, Damansara Utama, tel. 03/717–5403) has live music
nightly, and the **DJ Pub,** part of the Executive Club (37 Jln. SS22/19,
Damansara Jaya, tel. 03/717–0966), opens at 4:30 PM and often has
bands. **Riverbank** (tel. 03/274–6652) and **Network** (tel. 03/232–5734)
at the Central Market are currently popular meeting places. The
Hard Rock Cafe (Wisma Concorde, 2 Jln. Sultan Ismail, tel. 03/244–
4062) has come to KL; it's in the building adjacent to the Concorde

Hotel. The quirkiest spot may be the **Anglers Pub** (22 Jln. SS2/67 in Petaling Jaya), which shows fishing videos in the early evening, with musical entertainment afterward. A number of the major hotels have pubs—they are more expensive, of course.

Discos While pubs close around 11 PM, the action at the discos only cranks up about then and continues until 2 AM. Some discos have live bands as well as platter-spinning. Some places have a cover and others may have a drinks minimum. Ask locals which discos are hot at the moment, but at press time the Hilton's **Tin Mine** (Jln. Sultan Ismail, tel. 03/242–2222), long a hot spot for Malaysian film, TV, and fashion celebrities, remains the premier spot. Its main competitors are **Club Oz** at the Shangri-La Hotel (Jln. Sultan Ismail, tel. 03/232–2388) and **Reflections** at the P.J. Hilton (Jln. Barat in Petaling Jaya, tel. 03/755–9122). The **Hippodrome** (tel. 03/261–2562), on the roof of the Ampang Park Shopping Complex, has a floor show with Chinese singers from Taiwan, live music, high-tech lighting, and a seating capacity of 2,500. If this is too expansive, **Hearts** (tel. 03/242–2222) is in the same building complex. At both establishments, there is a MS$20 per hour fee for female company.

Nightclubs and Cabarets *Kelab malam,* as these places are known, seem stuck in the 1950s, with variety acts, floor shows, and bands with singers. The two best-known nightclubs are **Pertama,** in the Pertama Complex (Jln. Tuanku Abdul Rahman, tel. 03/298–2533) and the **Nite Club** (tel. 03/232–1695) at Pudu Raya.

Excursions from Kuala Lumpur

Malacca

Once the most important port in Southeast Asia, Malacca (Melaka) is now a relatively sleepy backwater. Created as the capital of a Malay sultanate, it was captured in 1511 by the Portuguese, who built fortifications and held it until 1641, when the Dutch invaded and took possession. The British took over in Victorian times and remained in control until Malay independence in 1957. In this, Malaysia's most historic town, you'll find impressive buildings and ruins dating from all these periods of colonial rule. These sights are brought to life nightly in a sound-and-light show, in which the city's history is told to the accompaniment of Malay music, sound effects, and illuminated monuments. (Admission charge to outdoor seating area. Narration in Bahasa Melayu, 8:30 PM; in English, 10:30 PM.)

Tourist Information The **Melaka Tourist Information Centre** is in the heart of the city on Jalan Kota (tel. 06/236538).

Getting There By Car The superhighway between Kuala Lumpur and Johore Baru has an exit for Melaka, which is about 147 km (91 mi) south of Kuala Lumpur. Several local tour operators organize day trips to Melaka in an air-conditioned limousine for M$200. Day tours by coach are about M$70. These may be arranged through your hotel.

By Train Malacca does not have a train station, but train travelers can get off in Tampin, 38 km (24 mi) north of the city. From Tampin, take a taxi to Malacca (about M$3). For information, call the KTM office (tel. 06/223091 in Malacca) or the train station in Tampin (tel. 06/411034).

By Bus Express bus service from Kuala Lumpur to Malacca is offered by **Jebat Express** (tel. 03/282202 in Kuala Lumpur or 06/222–222503 in Malacca) for M$6.50. You can take other buses from Malacca to Port Dickson (Barat Express, tel. 06/249937), Butterworth (Ekspress Nasional, tel. 06/220687), or Singapore (Melaka–Singapore Express, tel. 06/224470). The one-way fare to Singapore is M$11.

By Taxi A taxi from Kuala Lumpur to Melaka costs approximately M$70 (a shared taxi costs M$17.50). A round-trip is less than double, but a Kuala Lumpur taxi driver is unlikely to know his way around Melaka. To order a taxi from Melaka to Kuala Lumpur, phone 06/223630.

Guided Tours

The best-known travel guide in Malacca is Robert Tan Sin Nyen (256-D Jln. Parameswara, 75000 Melaka, tel. 06/244857). You can take a river tour of the city (45 or 90 minutes) from the dock (tel. 06/236538) on Jalan Quayside, behind the information center.

Exploring

One of the oldest of Malacca's Portuguese ruins, dating from 1521, is **St. Paul's Church,** atop Residency Hill. In 1753 the site became a burial ground. The statue at the summit commemorates St. Francis Xavier, who was buried here before being moved to his permanent resting spot in Goa, India, where he began his missionary career. The **Church of St. Peter**—built in 1710 and now the church of the Portuguese Mission under the jurisdiction of the bishop of Macao—is interesting for its mix of Occidental and Oriental architecture. It is about a half mile east of the city center, on Jalan Bendahare.

The only surviving part of the 1511 Portuguese fortress, **A Famosa,** is the impressive Porta de Santiago entrance gate, which has become the symbol of the state of Malacca. Near the gate, the **Muzium Budaya,** a museum with collections on Muslim culture and royalty, is housed in a re-creation of a traditional wood palace. *Admission charge.*

The Dutch influence in Malacca is more palpable today. **Christ Church** was built in 1753 of bricks brought from Zeeland (Netherlands) and faced in red laterite. Across the street is the imposing **Stadthuys,** thought to be the oldest remaining Dutch architecture in the Orient. This complex of buildings was erected between 1641 and 1660 and used until recently as government offices. Now it houses the **Malacca Historical and Literary Museums,** which feature such exhibits as Dutch furniture, Chinese and Japanese porcelain, Straits Chinese embroidery, and numerous photographs. *Tel. 06/ 220769. Admission charge. Open daily 9–6.*

Malacca's history, of course, predates the arrival of the Western colonialists. Six centuries ago, a Ming emperor's envoy from China set up the first trade arrangements in the ancient Malay capital; a daughter of the emperor was sent to Malacca as wife to Sultan Mansor Shah. She and her 500 ladies-in-waiting set up house on **Bukit China** (Chinese Hill). The early Chinese traders and notables who lived and died in Malacca were buried on this hill, and their 17,000 graves remain, making Bukit China the largest Chinese cemetery outside China.

The **Chinese quarter**—narrow streets lined with traditional shophouses, ancient temples, and clan houses (note the intricately carved doors)—reflects the long Chinese presence. **Cheng Hoon**

Teng Temple is one of the city's oldest temples; you'll recognize it by its ceremonial masts, which tower over the roofs of the surrounding old houses, and by the porcelain and glass animals and flowers that decorate its eaves. Built in the Nanking style, the temple embraces three doctrines: Buddhist, Taoist, and Confucian. You can tell the monks apart by their robes; Taoists expose their right shoulder. On your way out, you can buy sandalwood (the scent that permeates the temple) as well as papier-mâché houses and cars and symbolic money ("hell money") burned as offerings during funeral ceremonies.

Close by on Temple Street are the papier-mâché doll makers, who fashion legendary figures from Chinese mythology. Wander on, turning right into Jalan Hang Lekiu and right again into Jalan Hang Jebat (often referred to by its old name, Jonker Street), loaded with stores selling antiques and collectibles. You'll also find good pork satay at No. 83 and several coffee shops selling wonderful noodles.

From Jalan Hang Jebat take a left into Jalan Kubu, then another left into Jalan Tun Tan Cheng Lock. This street was once called "Millionaires Row" for its glorious mansions, built by the Dutch and then taken over by wealthy Babas in the 19th century. Don't miss **Baba Nyonya Heritage,** two 19th-century mansions in the Straits-born Chinese style, whose intricate woodwork is as impressive as their elegant antique Chinese furnishings. Built by a Chinese millionaire named Chan, the museum is today run by a fifth-generation family member. *48 Jln. Tun Tan, Cheng Lock, tel. 06/231272. Admission charge. Open daily 10–12:30 and 2–4:30.*

Near the **Padang Pahlawan** (where you'll find Malacca-style bullock carts that you can ride in or pose beside, for a fee), in a building that was once the old Malacca Club, the **Proclamation of Independence Memorial** documents events leading up to the nation's independence with photographs, maps, and more. *Tel. 06/241231. Open Tues.– Sun. 9–6 (except closed Fri. noon–3).*

Several attractions are near the 810-acre **Ayer Keroh Recreational Forest** (Utan Rekreasi, tel. 06/328401), which offers cabins and camping. **Mini-Malaysia Cultural Village,** 15 km (9 mi) from Malacca, showcases 13 model houses built in styles representing different states and decorated inside with regional arts and crafts. Cultural shows and native games are performed outdoors. *Tel. 06/328498. Admission charge. Open weekdays 10–6, weekends and holidays 9–7.*

Adjacent to Ayer Keroh Lake is the open-plan **Melaka Zoo,** with species from Southeast Asia and Africa displayed in environments approximating their native habitats. (At the nearby **Melaka Reptile Park,** you can see snake races as well as exhibits.) *Tel. 06/324054 or 06/228229. Admission charge. Open daily 10–6. Tours are given after 4:30 on weekdays and throughout the day on weekends.*

Off the Beaten Track

For a change of locale, cross over to Indonesia. A ferry service makes the four-hour crossing to **Dumai** on Sumatra every Thursday at 10 AM. Malaysians and Indonesians cross back and forth for shopping; the ferry is an inexpensive way from one country to the other. You must have a visa. The return trip is on Saturday, arriving back in Melaka at 2 PM. Reservations are made through **Hadai Shipping** (321A Jln. Tun Ali, Melaka, tel. 06/240671). You can also spend a day picnicking on the little tropical isle of **Pulau Besar,** 3 mi off the mainland in the Straits of Malacca. A boat service operates from Umbai Jetty (M$4 per person), or you can charter a boat for around M$35.

Shopping

A number of antiques shops line **Jonker Street** (now known as Jalan Hang Jebat). For local souvenirs, try the row of stalls just behind the restaurants along Jalan Taman, which used to be the waterfront road before land reclamation.

The most unusual souvenir in town is a pair of 3-inch brocade slippers made by **Yeo Sing Guat** (92 Jln. Hang Jebat, no phone), for Chinese women whose feet were bound when they were children to create tiny "lotus feet," a symbol of beauty during the Ming Dynasty. Mr. Yeo says only a handful of elderly women still wear his shoes; most of his purchasers are tourists. A pair costs about M$50.

Dining

It would be a shame to leave the city without trying some of its spicy cuisine, both Nonya and Portuguese fare. If you visit Portuguese Square, where descendants of the original community still live (a cultural show is held here at 7:30 each Saturday night), try the **Restoran De Lisbonz** (tel. 06/248067) and the **Restoran De Portugio** (tel. 06/243156).

Summerfield's Coffee House. This 24-hour café, a popular meeting place, serves both Western and local dishes. Snacks range from a bowl of noodles to an ice-cream sundae. *Ramada Renaissance, Jln. Bendahara, tel. 06/248888. No reservations. Dress: casual. AE, DC, MC, V. $$*

Trading Post. Try the daily buffet of spicy local dishes, such as rendang, at this garden restaurant. Barbecues by the pool are held in the evening. *Malacca Village Resort, Ayer Keroh, tel. 06/323600. No reservations. Dress: casual. AE, DC, MC, V. $$*

Nyonya Makko Restaurant. This modest restaurant has such Nonya specialties as curried fish. For dessert, cool off with *gula Melaka*, a sago pudding with coconut milk and palm syrup. *123 Taman Melaka Jaya, tel. 06/240737. No reservations. Dress: casual. No credit cards. $*

Lodging

Malacca Village Resort. Located on 7 acres just off the superhighway between Kuala Lumpur and Singapore, this luxury resort is lushly landscaped and well equipped. Its distance from the city may be a problem for those without a car, but it is within walking distance of the zoo, Mini-Malaysia, and the forest. Recreational facilities are plentiful, including a small lake across the road and nearby golf course. Rooms have a tropical atmosphere, with tile and shutters. *Ayer Keroh, 75450 Malacca, tel. 06/323600 or 800/44–UTELL, fax 06/325955. 147 chalets. Facilities: 3 restaurants, 2 bars, boating. AE, DC, MC, V. $$$*

Ramada Renaissance. Business travelers choose this 24-story hotel, built in 1984, for its central location, its spacious rooms equipped with refrigerators, and its many amenities. Under the helm of a German general manager, this is the most efficiently run hotel in Melaka. Everything works, and the coffee shop is the most popular dining spot for European food in town. *Jln. Bendahara, Box 105, 75720 Melaka, tel. 06/248888 or 800/228–9898, fax 06/249269. 295 rooms, including 16 suites. Facilities: 4 restaurants, 2 lounges, disco, large pool, gymnasium, Jacuzzi, squash courts, billiards, convention facilities, nearby golf course. AE, DC, MC, V. $$$*

Tapa-Nyai Island. On the small island of Pulau Besar is this bungalow-style resort with air-conditioned guest rooms in either single-story chalets or the main building. Though Malacca is only 45 minutes away by ferry, Tapa-Nyai is more of a resort at which to relax, golf the nine-hole course, swim, or walk along the island paths. It's more popular with Singaporeans and weekenders from KL than with Westerners on a tour of Southeast Asia. *Pulau Besar, tel. 06/242088, fax 06/243588. 143 rooms. Facilities: 2 restaurants (Chinese/seafood, Malay/Western), pool with pool bar, tennis, health center, meeting rooms. AE, DC, MC, V. $$$*

Emperor Melaka. Rooms here are a trifle tatty, but the facility offers full service and good value. *Jln. Munshi Abdullah, 75100 Melaka, tel. 06/240777, fax 06/238989. 243 rooms and suites. Facilities: pool, billiards, squash, roller skating, shopping center next door, 2 restaurants, lounge, disco. AE, DC, MC, V. $$*

Penang and Langkawi

Called the Pearl of the Orient for its natural beauty as well as for its charming and graceful colonial architecture, Penang respects tradition but is neither stodgy nor sleepy. The island's beaches—in particular the glorious stretch at Batu Ferringhi—may have made it justly famous as a beach-vacation destination, but its capital city, George Town, is a vibrant university town that is the intellectual center as well as the conscience of the country, a place where ideas are generated and venerated. It is also a great place to tour on foot, by bicycle, or by trishaw, stopping off frequently to sample the many fun shops and world-famous cuisine that are found around every corner.

The population is primarily Hokkien Chinese, with a sizable Indian community living downtown and Malays residing in the countryside. Batu Ferringhi has all the resort activity you could wish for, yet is never overcrowded. The airport is in the southeast of the island and George Town is in the northeast. The north coast has the most popular beaches and the resort hotels. (Don't plunge into the sea unless it's clear of jellyfish; the tide sometimes brings them in along the coast, and their sting can be serious.)

Important Addresses and Numbers

Tourist Information The **Penang Tourist Association** distributes information from centers on level 3 of the Komtar building (tel. 04/614461) and downtown near Fort Cornwallis, at the intersection of Leboh Pantai and Leboh Light (tel. 04/616663). Both booths are open weekdays 8–noon and 2–4, and Saturday 8–12:30. The **MTPB** has a counter at the airport (tel. 04/830501; open weekdays 8:30–4:45, Sat. 8:30–1) and an office in Komtar (tel. 04/620066).

Emergencies For **police, fire,** or **ambulance** service, dial 999. The **Penang Adventist Hospital** (tel. 04/373344) also sends ambulances.

Doctors Contact the **Hospital Besar** (tel. 04/373333), on Jalan residency at Hospital Road, on the edge of downtown, or the **Specialists Centre** (tel. 04/368501) at 19 Jalan Logan.

English-Language Bookstores The **Times Bookstore** is on the first floor of the Penang Plaza shopping complex (126 Jln. Burmah, tel. 04/23443). Bookshops on Leboh Bishop include **City Book Center** (No. 11, tel. 04/51593) and **Academic** (No. 23, tel. 04/615780).

Travel Agencies **American Express** (8 Greenhall, 3rd Floor, tel. 04/368317). **Thomas Cook** (1 Pengkalan Weld, tel. 04/610511). **Malaysia Airline System**

(MAS) is on the ground floor at Komtar, and next door is **Ace Tours & Travel** (Kompleks Tun, Abdul Razak, Penang Rd., 10000 Penang, tel. 04/611205), which often sells airline tickets for less than MAS. Ask for Mr. Joe Y.C. Ng.

Arriving and Departing by Plane

Airports and Airlines The **Penang International Airport** (tel. 04/831373), located in Bayan Lepas, about 18 km (11 mi) from George Town, is served by **MAS, Singapore Airlines, Garuda, Cathay Pacific,** and **Thai Airways International.** All departing passengers pay an airport tax: M$15 for international flights, M$5 to Singapore, and M$3 for domestic destinations. Penang is about a 40-minute flight from Kuala Lumpur.

Between the Airport and Hotels *By Bus* Airport **taxis** use a coupon system with fixed fares. A one-way ride into the city costs M$17; to Batu Ferringhi it's M$25. A **public bus** (Yellow No. 66) just outside the airport entrance will take you to the terminal in the city center for less than a ringgit. Buses run hourly at night, more frequently during the day.

Arriving and Departing by Bus, Car, Ferry, and Train

By Bus The **main bus station** (tel. 04/344928) for intercity service is on the Butterworth side near the ferry terminal. Coach service to Singapore can be booked through **MARA Express** (tel. 04/361192) or **Hosni Express** (tel. 04/617746). The fare from Kuala Lumpur is M$15.50.

By Car You can either drive across the Penang Bridge from Butterworth (M$7 toll) or bring your car across on the ferry (M$4–M$6, depending on the size of your vehicle; passengers pay 40 sen). The ferry operates 24 hours, but service after midnight is infrequent.

By Ferry There are now two ferries that ply between Penang and Medan in Sumatra. They depart daily from Penang at noon and arrive at Medan's port of Belawan at 4 PM (no visa required for American and British citizens). The return trip departs Belawan on Tuesday, Thursday, and Sunday at 9 AM, arriving in Penang at 3 PM. The one-way fare is M$90. The terminal office is next to the Tourist Information Office on Leboh Pantai, near Fort Cornwallis.

By Train The train station serving Penang is at the ferry terminal on the Butterworth side. You can buy a ticket at the **Butterworth station** (tel. 04/347962) or at a booking station at the **ferry terminal** (Weld Quay, tel. 04/610290). It's not a long walk from Butterworth station to the ferry, but you'll have to carry your own luggage. On the Penang side, porters and taxi drivers will help.

Getting Around

You can walk to most places in downtown George Town.

By Taxi Taxi stands are located near many hotels. Two taxi companies are **Syarikat George Town Taxi** (tel. 04/613853) and **Island Taxi** (tel. 04/625127). A convenient 24-hour taxi stand, where you can reserve ahead, is **Jade Auto** (25 Jln. Burmah, tel. 04/23220). The minimum charge is M$3, more for air-conditioned cars. Though taxis have meters, they are rarely used. Establish the price before you get in.

By Bus Five bus companies operate in the Penang area. Each is identified by a different bus color and serves a different route. All buses operate out of a central terminus on Jalan Prangin, a block from Komtar. Passengers buy tickets from conductors on the bus and pay according to the distance traveled. For information on routes and schedules, call 04/629357.

By Car Avis (tel. 04/373964 or 04/811522), **Hertz** (tel. 04/374914), and other major companies have counters at the airport and next to the E & O Hotel in George Town. **Sintat** (tel. 04/830958) has an airport counter only.

By Trishaw Not just tourists but some city residents, mainly elderly Chinese women, rely on trishaws—large tricycles with a carriage for passengers and freight—for transport around town. The pace is pleasant, and it's a relatively inexpensive way to sightsee. Negotiate the route and fare before you get in. A short trip is likely to cost only 5 ringgits. If you want to hire a trishaw for longer, the usual hourly rate for one person riding on a nice day would be about M$10. The driver will, of course, ask for more, but negotiate.

Guided Tours

Local companies offer a number of general tours. The most popular is a 73-km (45-mi), 3½-hour drive around the island. From Batu Ferringhi it goes through Malay kampongs, rubber estates, and nutmeg orchards, stops at the Snake Temple, cruises past the Universiti Sains Malaysia campus and through George Town, and returns via the beach road.

Major tour companies are **Tour East** (Golden Sands Hotel, Batu Ferringhi, tel. 04/811662, or Penang Plaza, 4th Floor, tel. 04/363215) and **Mayflower Acme Tours** (Shangri-La Inn on Jln. Magazine, tel. 04/623724, or Tan Chong Building, 23 Pengkalan Weld, tel. 04/628196). Both will arrange private car or limousine tours at additional cost and offer side trips to Langkawi Island, Cameron Highlands, and Pangkor Island. Most tours run just under three hours and cost M$90 per car.

Boat Tours Tour agents can arrange harbor cruises with **Waterfront Sdn. Bhd.**, which runs a sunset dinner cruise, a waterfront and Penang Bridge trip, and a Monkey Beach excursion.

Special-Interest Tours The principal tour companies offer such excursions as Penang Hill and Temples, City and Heritage, and Penang by Night, in addition to trips to the world's largest butterfly farm (at Telok Bahang), and the Botanical Gardens.

Exploring George Town

Numbers in the margin correspond to numbered points of interest on the George Town map.

1 Just in front of the Tourist Information Office, near the Swettenham Pier, stands a **Victorian clock tower,** donated to the city by a Penang millionaire to commemorate the diamond jubilee of Queen Victoria. The tower is 60 feet tall, 1 foot for every year of her reign up to 1897.

2 Head from the tower up Jalan Tun Syed Barakbah past **Fort Cornwallis,** the harborside site where city founder Captain Sir Francis Light of the British East India Company first landed on the island in 1786. On the outside, the 1810 compound's moss-encrusted ramparts and cannons give the impression of a mighty fortress, but it never saw any real action. On the inside are an open-air amphitheater, shade trees, and public toilets, as well as some annoying local hustlers offering to serve as guides.

George Town

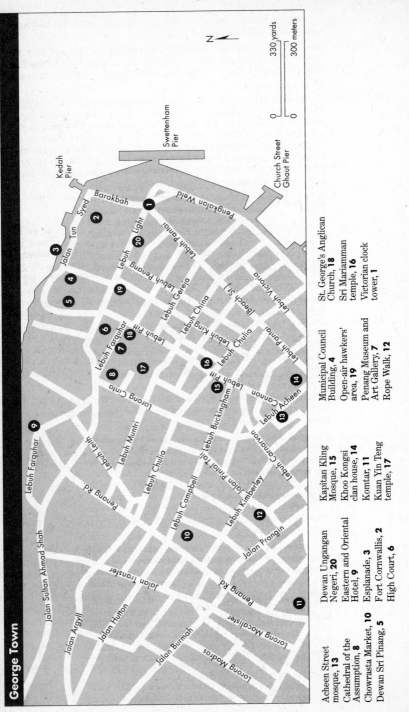

330 yards

300 meters

Kedah Pier

Swettenham Pier

Church Street Ghaut Pier

Acheen Street mosque, **13**
Cathedral of the Assumption, **8**
Chowrasta Market, **10**
Dewan Sri Pinang, **5**

Dewan Ungangan Negeri, **20**
Eastern and Oriental Hotel, **9**
Esplanade, **3**
Fort Cornwallis, **2**
High Court, **6**

Kapitan Kling Mosque, **15**
Khoo Kongsi clan house, **14**
Komtar, **11**
Kuan Yin Teng temple, **17**

Municipal Council Building, **4**
Open-air hawkers' area, **19**
Penang Museum and Art Gallery, **7**
Rope Walk, **12**

St. George's Anglican Church, **18**
Sri Mariamman temple, **16**
Victorian clock tower, **1**

③ The **Esplanade**—an open, grassy field next door—is a pleasant site for a stroll, especially in the evening, when the sea breezes roll in and the hawkers set up their mobile stands. The padang is often used for recreational sports and festival events. A monument surrounded by palms honors soldiers who died in World War I.

Penang's center used to be Beach Street near the ferry terminal, the heart of the banking district. But since the construction of the Penang Bridge in the mid-1980s reduced pedestrian traffic, the city center has gravitated toward Komtar, the tallest building in Malay-
④ sia. The **Municipal Council Building,** a stately turn-of-the-century structure with arched windows, no longer houses the city government, which moved to Komtar several years ago. The building is now
⑤ used for special exhibitions. The **Dewan Sri Pinang** next door is the city's major auditorium, seating some 1,300 for concerts, theater, and other events. Coming cultural activities are posted on a billboard in front. The **Penang Library** is on the first floor.

⑥ The colonial structure across the street houses the **High Court.** Malaysia uses the British legal system, and the courts conduct much of their business in English. Cases are open to the public, and visitors are free to wander in and immerse themselves in a local legal drama. Inside the compound is a marble statue dedicated to James Richardson Logan, a lawyer and newspaper editor who devoted his life to public service, advocating freedom of speech, law, and order.

⑦ Behind the High Court, on Lebuh Farquhar, is the **Penang Museum and Art Gallery.** The statue outside the 1821 building, which was used as the Penang Free School for more than a century, is of Sir Francis Light. On the first floor is a small museum packed with old photographs, maps, and relics of the city's past. An art gallery upstairs constantly changes exhibits, which range from contemporary works to traditional Malaysian art. *Admission free. Open daily 9–5 (closed Fri. 12:15–2:45).*

⑧ Next door is the **Cathedral of the Assumption,** one of the oldest Roman Catholic churches in Malaysia. Past the City Bayview Hotel is
⑨ the **Eastern and Oriental Hotel,** commonly known as the E&O. Its reputation as one of Asia's early grand hotels, in the tradition of Raffles in Singapore and the Strand in Rangoon, has long since faded, but it's still a pleasant place to visit. The palm-shaded poolside garden is right on the waterfront, a delightful spot to stop for a rest and a cool drink, and the Anchor Pub, a vestige of colonial days, is ideal for afternoon tea.

The E&O entrance looks down Penang Road, the city's main shopping area. In the first block is a series of handicraft and antique shops, all carrying a variety of Asian jewelry and gift items, such as Thai and Indonesian wood carvings. In the next block, in front of the Continental, Malaysia, and Ambassador hotels, you'll find a number of trishaw drivers—mostly older men—who will solicit you aggressively. A suggested trishaw sightseeing route: Head up Lebuh Muntri past some of the city's best examples of traditional architecture, turn left onto Love Lane, up to Farquhar Street again, and then turn left onto Leboh Leith past the 18th-century Cheong Fatt Tse Mansion, one of the oldest remaining Chinese homes in Asia.

At Lebuh Chulia, you'll see lots of young European, Australian, and American travelers of the nouveau hippie genre, who seek out the cheap hotels and seedy bars in this area. The next street is Lebuh Campbell, another main drag for shopping. The shops here sell fabrics, shoes and clothing, costume jewelry, and inexpensive bags and luggage.

⑩ The next block of Penang Road takes you to the **Chowrasta Market,**
an indoor market selling all sorts of local produce. In front of the entrance, shops sell more produce, plus pickled and dried nutmeg, papaya and mango, and candies made from gingerroot, coconut, and
durian. The durian cake, called *dodol,* is sold in little triangular
pieces or foot-long rolls.

Time Out Near the market, across the road from the Choong Lye Hock movie
theater, is an old-fashioned coffee shop with marble-top tables. The
Teik Hoe Cafe is nearly hidden by the souvenir vendor who works
the sidewalk out front. Although the place looks scruffy, it's a great
spot to people-watch over a cup of local coffee (pronounced "ko-pee"
in Malay). The blend is strong, with a smooth mocha flavor. The parade of shoppers and passersby makes fine entertainment.

In the labyrinth of stalls in the alley next door to the **Penang Bazaar**
(a dry-goods market), you'll find such basics as underwear, belts,
and handbags. At the corner, a street hawker sells *chendol,* a local
dessert that looks bad—wormlike strands of green jelly served in
coconut milk over ice—but tastes good.

Across the plaza, in front of the Capitol Theatre, street vendors ped-
dle luxury knockoffs. Fake Gucci watches sell for about M$24; ersatz
Polo cologne and Chanel No. 5 perfume go for half that. Pirated pop
and country cassette tapes sell for a little more than M$2.70 each.
The concession stand for the theater is outside, so the confections
Asians enjoy are available: Try the dried cuttlefish, called the chewing gum of the Orient. And the young portrait artist who often
works here does good charcoal likenesses for just over M$27.

⑪ The Tower of the East, as **Komtar** was dubbed, is now the second-
tallest building in the ASEAN region (recently surpassed by the
OUB Plaza tower in Singapore), and totally out of scale with the di-
minutive neighboring buildings. The long flight of stairs you see
leads up to a food court on the fifth floor. On the lower levels is a
shopping complex named after the country's second prime minister,
Tun Razak. At **Chin's Art Gallery,** next to an MAS office, you can
have a stone chop (seal) engraved with your initials for M$54–
M$135, depending on the stone size and quality. Among the tower's
busiest tenants are hip young tailors with trendy haircuts and smart
outfits who scurry about fitting customers with garments cut from
the bolts of fabric they stack in every corner of their tiny shops.
Their creations have original flourishes, even such common items as
jeans or military-style shirts. They often toil late at night, long after
the rest of the shopkeepers have gone home.

In the center of the mall are a number of fast-food outlets serving
hamburgers, fried chicken, and pizza. One of the best Chinese restaurants in the city, Supertanker, is on the upper level (*see* Dining,
below).

A two-lane street and pedestrian walkway runs through the ground
floor of Komtar. Here you'll notice the **Centre Point** pool parlor—not
your typical smoke-filled dive. The teenage boys who surround the
tables are practicing for tournaments, when they dress in black bow
ties and vests and compete before hushed, well-mannered crowds.
On the 58th floor is the **Tower Tourist Centre,** an observation deck
with cultural performances at 8:30 and 9:15 every evening but Monday. Buy the M$5 ticket on the ground floor, and hold onto it—you
can redeem it for beverages. A **duty-free shop** is one floor down; one
floor up is the **Tower Palace Restaurant** (tel. 04/622222), which offers

buffet lunches, dinner dances, and a karaoke bar. The Shangri-La Penang (*see* Lodging, *below*) is also here.

(12) A number of antiques stores have congregated around **Rope Walk,** on Jalan Pintal Tali. Turn right onto Lebuh Kimberly, then, past a row of highly decorated shophouses with elaborately carved doors, turn left onto Carnarvon Street, and then right on Acheen. At the next corner is the **Tang Lee Trading Co.,** which manufactures the **(13)** cheap summer sandals called flip-flops. On the right is the **Acheen Street mosque,** the oldest in Penang. To enter, you must get permission from officials. Turn left and you'll be on Cannon Street.

(14) On the right, look for a small sign posted above an entrance to an alley, which announces the **Khoo Kongsi clan house,** a complex of structures that may be the most elaborately decorated in Malaysia. Recently restored, the **Leong San Tong** (Dragon Hall) temple is a showcase of Chinese architecture and art, constructed by 19th-century master craftsmen from China. Virtually no surface is unadorned. Notice the relief sculptures depicting Chinese legends and the heavily gilt dragons. The open theater across the square is used for opera performances. Visitors are welcome weekdays 9–5, Saturday 9–1. Permission to enter must be obtained from the office.

(15) Pitt Street is often called the street of harmony, because all four major religions are represented along its few blocks. The **Kapitan Kling Mosque** is at the Lebuh Buckingham intersection. Built in the early 1800s, the mosque has been recently renovated and continues to serve the Indian Muslim community. You need permission to enter.

Along this section of Pitt Street is a row of small jewelry shops run by the Indians who deal in gold and semiprecious stones. Many are also licensed money changers. These street bankers can handle almost any type of foreign currency and work much longer hours than regular banks. Some are also numismatists who sell to collectors.

(16) Past the gates of the **Teochew Association house,** on the corner of Pitt and Lebuh Chulia, is the **Sri Mariamman temple** on Queen Street, in the heart of the Indian district. The entranceway is topped by a *gopuram,* a tower covered with statues of Hindu deities. Inside, the ceiling features the symbols for the planets and signs of the zodiac. The most prized possession of the faithful is a statue of Lord Subramaniam, which is covered with gold, silver, diamonds, and emeralds. The statue is paraded about during the Thaipusam festival. Visitors can enter the temple, with permission.

(17) The **Kuan Yin Teng temple,** dedicated to the goddess of mercy, Kuan Yin, is the busiest in the city, perhaps because it's associated with fertility. Built in 1800, this temple serves the Cantonese and Hokkien communities. In the next block, on Farquhar Street, is **(18)** stately **St. George's Anglican Church,** with its gracious flowering trees and gazebo. Built in 1818 by convicts, this symbol of the British role in Penang's early history is now attended mostly by Indians.

(19) Turn right at Bank Negara on the corner of Lebuh Light. At King Street, at an **open-air hawkers' area,** old-Chinese men often bring their caged pet birds when they come for a cup of coffee and a breath of morning air. In this area, you may also note elderly men writing letters on old portable typewriters. These public scribes serve clients who need help dealing with the bureaucracy or illiterates who simply want to write a friend.

At Penang Street and Lebuh Light is **Pashnis Restaurant,** one of the few places to get Malay food in this Chinese city. Try a satay snack: charcoaled strips of beef, chicken, or goat dipped in a peanut sauce.

㉚ On the right you'll see the **Dewan Ungangan Negeri,** a majestic colonial building with massive columns. This is the state assembly, and
the luxury cars parked out front belong to its illustrious members.
You're now across from Fort Cornwallis again—near the ferry if
you're hopping back to the mainland and a waterfront cab ride away
from the beach hotels.

What to See and Do with Children

At the **Penang Botanical Gardens,** about 8 km (5 mi) from the city
center on Jalan Waterfall, relatively tame monkeys live amid the
tropical plants. *Admission free. Open daily 10–6.*

The **Penang Bird Park,** located in Perai near Butterworth on the
mainland, makes another fine outing. Take the ferry across the harbor and a taxi to the park, a ride of about 13 km (8 mi). A huge walk-
in aviary contains all sorts of exotic fowl and beautiful flowers. *Tel.
04/399899. Admission charge. Open daily 10–7.*

Off the Beaten Track

Kek Lok Si is reputedly the largest and most beautiful Buddhist
temple in Malaysia. It's worth the trip to the suburb of Air Itam to
absorb the temple's serene atmosphere, especially when the monks
chant their morning prayers. The century-old hilltop pagoda blends
Chinese, Thai, and Burmese architectural influences. The shopping
stalls along the route to the temple offer some excellent bargains.

In Air Itam, joggers or walkers may also want to explore the **track**
around the reservoir, where Penang gets its drinking water. The
path cuts through a tropical forest and across the dam. There is no
bus service up to the area, so getting there is a workout in itself. It's
best as an early morning outing.

Shopping

Don't hesitate to bargain, but remember that shopkeepers play the
game full-time. You'll see signs for duty-free prices on certain
goods. Most shops are open 10–10.

Shopping
Districts
Penang Road is the main shopping area, with Leboh Campbell and
Jalan Burmah as offshoots. Look for antiques and junk in the **Rope
Walk** district, now listed on maps as **Jalan Pintal Tali.**

Department
Stores
Yaohan, Super Komtar, and **Pulau Pinang** are in the Komtar complex. **GAMA** is across the road on Jalan Dato Keramat, and **Super** is a
couple of blocks up Jalan Burmah.

Markets
The **Chowrasta Market** on Penang Road (*see* Exploring, *above*) is an
indoor wet market with shops and stalls outside. On Sunday morning, a **flea market,** offering a mixture of junk and antiques, is held on
Jalan Pintal Tali.

Specialty
Stores
Antiques
The **Saw Joo Ann** antiques shop, on the corner of Lebuh Hong Kong,
has high-quality Malaysian artifacts. If it's not open during normal
business hours, ask at the coffee shop next door and someone will
come to let you browse.

Crafts
On Upper Penang Road, shops sell crafts from Malaysia, Thailand,
Indonesia, China, and India. **Selangor Pewterware** (tel. 04/366742)
has a showroom next to the E&O Hotel on Lebuh Farquhar. The
best selection of batik prints is at the **BMB** shop (tel. 04/621607) in

Komtar. **Penang Butterfly Farm** (803 Mk. 2, Jln. Taluk Bahang, tel. 04/811253) sells artifacts from all of Southeast Asia.

Sports and Fitness

Beaches and Water Sports The **Batu Ferringhi Beach,** with fine, golden sand shaded by casuarina and coconut trees, has made Penang one of the best-known holiday islands in Southeast Asia. Public facilities, such as showers and changing rooms, are nonexistent. Hotel guests can use hotel lounge chairs on the beach.

Bicycling Several small bicycle-rental firms operate across the road from the major hotels in Batu Ferringhi, but be aware that the traffic often drifts quite close on the narrow roads.

Golf Penang has two 18-hole golf courses open to the public—**Batu Gantung** and **Bukit Jambul.** For information, fees, and tee times, call the golf section of the Penang Turf Club (tel. 04/362333) or the Bukit Jambul Country Club (tel. 04/842255).

Hiking For jungle hiking, the best bet is the Recreational Forest (called Rima Rekreasi in Malay), 1½ km (1 mi) past the village of Telok Bahang. The tropical forest also has a museum, a children's playground, and picnic tables. A **Malayan Nature Society brochure** with six other treks around the hills of Penang is available at tourist information centers.

Horseback Riding For information about trail or beach rides, contact the **Bay Riders** (tel. 04/373390).

Dining

For elegant dining with attentive service, the major hotels are your best bet, but reserve one evening for dining alfresco along Guerney Drive. For about 2 km (1.2 mi), the sea laps one side of the road and restaurants and hawkers' stalls line the other. Seafood, understandably, is the specialty. Most of the cooking is Hokkien, though there are also good Malay hawker stalls. There are other hawker centers are at Lebuh Campbell, the Esplanade, and Jalan Macalister; don't miss them. Local specialties include *char koay teow,* flat rice noodles fried smooth and soft with bean sprouts, prawns, and eggs; chicken curry *kapitan,* spicy chicken cooked with ginger, coconut milk, and lemon juice; Hokkien mee noodles, beans and sprouts in a spicy shrimp soup topped with fried onions; *inchee kabin,* deep-fried chicken pieces marinated with coconut milk, ginger, chili, and spices; *chandol,* a dessert of green bean noodles and kidney beans in fresh coconut milk and ice; and *bubur cha cha,* a Nonya dessert of sweet potatoes, yams, and beans in fresh coconuts.

$$$ Continental ★ **Brasserie.** Candles and fresh flowers on the tables soften the sophisticated French decor of wood-paneled walls, lace curtains, and black-and-white floor tiles. At lunch you select your main course (seafood or meat) from the menu and then help yourself from the buffet for appetizers, soups, salads, and dessert. For dinner, the menu takes the nouvelle approach to European gourmet cooking, with small, attractive portions of lamb, duck, steak, or tiger prawns. Try the frog-leg ravioli and the sherbet with cassis. *Shangri-La Inn, Jln. Magazine, tel. 04/622622. Reservations suggested. Dress: formal. AE, DC, MC, V.*

$$$ Italian **Il Ritrovo.** This Italian bistro, cozily decorated with travel posters and candles in wine bottles, draws locals and tourists alike. Its excellent three-course meal is good value. Chef Luciano does a perfect *antipasti tutti mare* (seafood antipasto), followed by an impressive range of pasta, veal, lamb, and chicken dishes and classic Italian *dolci*. A Filipino band enhances the atmosphere by playing requests. *Casuarina Beach Hotel, Batu Ferringhi, tel. 04/811711, ext. 766. Reservations suggested. Dress: casual. AE, DC, MC, V. Closed Mon.*

$$$
Italian
La Farfalla. Farfalla's swank decor includes a white grand piano and a different ice sculpture every night. It overlooks the pool and sea, but the place is so pretty you may not notice the view. Try the *carpaccio d'agnello con zucchine* (thin strips of lamb with zucchini) or the *saltimbocca alla Romana* (veal stuffed with cheese and ham). You may be more impressed by the chic setting and the presentation than the creativity of the chef. *Penang Mutiara, Telok Bahang, tel. 04/812828. Reservations suggested. Dress: formal. AE, DC, MC, V.*

$$$
Seafood
Eden Seafood Village. This open-air beachfront restaurant caters to tourists with a nightly cultural show. Its Chinese-style specialties include crab cooked in a spicy chili-tomato sauce, steamed prawns dipped in ginger sauce, lobster, and fried squid. *Batu Ferringhi, tel. 04/811852. Reservations suggested. Dress: casual. AE, DC, MC, V.*

$$
Chinese
Prosperous. This busy restaurant serves some 200 Cantonese and Hainanese dishes. Specialties include barbecued pork ribs and sweet-and-sour fish. *25 Jln. Gottlieb, tel. 04/27286. Reservations not necessary. Dress: casual. AE, DC, MC, V.*

$$
Chinese
Supertanker. The noise and crowds at Supertanker are its testimonials: Locals love the food and the prices. Favorites on its Teochew menu are the crisp roast suckling pig and the porridges. *Komtar, tel. 04/616393. Reservations not necessary. Dress: casual. AE, MC.*

$$
European
★
Eden. A downtown restaurant with a funky decor, Eden makes fresh oxtail soup every day and does a magnificent Tunisian saddle of lamb. The lunch menu caters to Westerners, with sandwiches, salads, and ice cream sundaes. *15 Jln. Hutton, tel. 04/377263. Reservations not necessary. Dress: casual. AE, DC, MC, V.*

$$
Nonya
Dragon King. People come here for the food, not the atmosphere or modest decor. This is a good place to sample Nonya cuisine, a spicy local blend of Malay and Chinese food. Try the spicy curried chicken and the kerabu salad. *9 Lebuh Bishop, tel. 04/618035. Reservations not necessary. Dress: casual. AE, MC, V. Closes at 9 PM.*

$
Chinese
E. T. Steamboat. At this restaurant named after the do-it-yourself Chinese stew, waiters bring vegetables, seafood, tofu, and a fondue pot full of rich broth to your table; you custom-cook your own dinner. For variety, try *lowbak* (pork rolls) or *tom yom*, a spicy Thai soup. *Two locations: Komtar and 4 Jln. Rangoon, tel. 04/366025. Reservations not necessary. Dress: casual. AE, MC.*

$
Indian Muslim
Hameediyah. This simple downtown restaurant excels with its *nasi kandar* (rice with mutton), fish and chicken curry, or *murtabak*, an Indian-style pizza filled with spicy mutton and onions. *164 Lebuh Campbell, tel. 04/611095. No reservations. Dress: casual. No credit cards. Closed Fri.*

$
Malay
Golden Phoenix. Once you claim your table in this hawker-stall area, remember its number so the different vendors will know where to deliver your food. The open-air accommodations are somewhat primitive, but the food is authentic, and you get a fine sea breeze from across the road. Try *laksa asam* (a sour soup made with local fish), or *chien* (a fried oyster omelet), or the crisp roast duck. You can wash it down with juices made from starfruit and watermelon. *Gurney Dr., no phone. No reservations. Dress: casual. No credit cards. Open nightly until 2 AM.*

$
Malay
★
Minah. This simple open-air restaurant is in Minden, near the university. You fill your plate by pointing to what you want as it goes by: curry dishes, satay, beef rendang, or sambal. Try the *goreng*

pisang (fried bananas) for dessert. *Glugor Rd., tel. 04/881234. No reservations. Dress: casual. No credit cards.*

Lodging

The two main locations for tourist accommodations are George Town and the beach, either at Tanjung Bungah or farther out at Batu Ferringhi.

$$$$ **Equatorial Hotel.** Close to the airport, the industrial zone, and the golf course, but far from town and the beaches, this hotel has a unique 10-story atrium garden with bubble elevators. Its restaurant, the View, offers a range of Western dishes with a smattering of Asian ones; the view, by the way, is of the ships moving through the straits. *1 Jln. Bukit Jambul, 11900 Bayan Lepas, Penang, tel. 04/838000 or 800/44–UTELL, fax 04/848000. 415 rooms and suites. Facilities: 3 restaurants, coffee shop, tennis, squash, health club, ballrooms, function rooms. AE, DC, MC, V.*

$$$$ **Penang Mutiara.** This luxury resort at the end of Batu Ferringhi
★ beach opened in late 1988 and has set a new standard for glitz and glitter in Malaysia. All rooms have an ocean view and are decorated with rattan furniture, batik wall prints, and Malay-pattern rugs. Balconies drooping with bougainvillea, ceiling fans, and shutters give additional tropical flavor. The sparkling-white marble lobby features fountains and waterfalls and floor-to-ceiling windows. Restaurants include La Farfalla for Italian fare (*see* Dining, *above*) and a seafood restaurant aptly named Catch. *Jln. Teluk Bahang, 11050 Penang, tel. 04/812828 or 800/44–UTELL, fax 04/812829. 443 rooms. Facilities: 2 swimming pools, health club, tennis, water sports, 5 restaurants, 2 lounges, disco. AE, DC, MC, V.*

$$$$ **Shangri-La Penang.** The glitziest hotel in George Town is next to the Komtar complex downtown. Its efficient rooms are comfortably decorated with large floral drapes and bedspreads and offer great views of the city. The Shang Palace, a Cantonese restaurant, serves dim sum daily. Guests are a mix of tourists and business travelers seeking modernity rather than the Old World charm of the E&O. *Magazine Rd., 10300 Penang, tel. 04/622622 or 800/44–UTELL, fax 04/626526; U.S. res. 800/942–5050; U.K. res. 081/747–8485. 426 rooms, 16 suites. Facilities: 3 restaurants, coffee shop, lobby lounge, business center, health club, pool, disco. AE, DC, MC, V.*

$$$ **Merlin Penang.** The impressive gray marble facade of this hotel, which opened in 1985, gives it architectural distinction, but the effect of the grand staircase in the lobby is diminished by the coffee shop right underneath. The rooms are done in pastel colors. *126 Jln. Burmah, 10050 Penang, tel. 04/376166 or 800/44–UTELL, fax 04/376615. 283 rooms and suites. Facilities: restaurant, lounge, buffet, pool, disco, convention rooms. AE, DC, MC, V.*

$$$ **Shangri-La Golden Sands.** The beachfront Golden Sands has lush tropical landscaping around two pools and an open-air lounge and café, with a spectacular indoor-outdoor garden effect. Each room is decorated in soft pastels accented with cane and has a private balcony with a view of sea or hills. Such activities as jungle walks and sandcastle-building competitions are arranged, and special poolside events, such as Chinese buffet dinners or barbecues, are held most nights. The hotel's most popular restaurant, Peppino, serves a wide variety of antipasti, pizzas, and nine types of pasta. *Batu Ferringhi Beach, 11100 Penang, tel. 04/811911 or 800/44–UTELL, fax 04/811880. 310 rooms. Facilities: 2 restaurants, 24-hr coffee shop, 2 pools, outdoor Jacuzzi, children's pool with slide, bar, poolside bar, water sports. AE, DC, MC, V.*

$$$ **Shangri-La Rasa Sayang.** This is the top of the luxury hotels that line overcrowded Batu Ferringhi Beach. Between the main building and beach is a large pool that is turned into a fountain floodlit by colored lights in the evening. The hotel has programmed activities day and night. Popular with Japanese tourists, it offers a restaurant with teppanyaki, sushi bar, and tempura, as well as a European and a Chinese restaurant. *Batu Ferringhi Beach, 11100 Penang, tel. 04/ 811811 or 800/457–5050, fax 04/811984; U.S. res. 800/942–5050; U.K. res 081/747–8485. 520 rooms. Facilities: 3 restaurants, disco; bar; 24-hr coffee shop; putting green; water sports; 2 pools; tennis; squash; volleyball; fully equipped fitness center with sauna, massage, and steam room; convention facilities. AE, DC, MC, V.*

$$ **Casuarina Beach Hotel.** Large, cozy rooms, a low-key pace, and attentive service make this established resort a favorite. Named for the willowy trees that mingle with palms along the beach, this hotel has a pleasant pool area and offers champagne brunches and country-and-western music nights. *Batu Ferringhi, 11100 Penang, tel. 04/811711 or 800/44–UTELL, fax 04/812155. 179 rooms. Facilities: 3 restaurants, lounge, pool bar, water sports. AE, DC, MC, V.*

$$ **Eastern & Oriental Hotel.** Known as the E&O, this delightful small
★ hotel was opened in 1885 by the Sarkie brothers (of Singapore's Raffles). Although some of the colonial tropical charm was lost in renovation after the war, a sense of that era pervades every room. The waterfront gardens and pool area are Victorian gems, and the wood-paneled dining room with austerely dressed waitresses and waiters is terribly British. The Anchor Bar has the well-worn comfort of a reading room, and it's lovely for a spot of afternoon tea or as an evening watering hole. The guest rooms have a mixture of old furniture that makes the modern television look out of place. Some bathrooms are as large as a bedroom and the groaning pipes emit steaming hot water. The junior suites are palatial. *10 Farquhar St., tel. 04/ 635322, fax 04/634833. 100 rooms. Facilities: pool, 1885 Grill, Anchor Bar. AE, DC, MC, V.*

$$ **Holiday Inn Penang.** This seven-story hotel surrounds a large pool right on the beach. Popular with Australians, it offers such activities as bike rides and jungle walks, snooker and ping-pong tournaments, and tennis and windsurfing lessons. Day rates available. *Batu Ferringhi Beach, 11100 Penang, tel. 04/811611 or 800/HOLIDAY, fax 04/811389. 54 rooms. Facilities: 3 restaurants, 3 bars. AE, DC, MC, V.*

$ **Bellevue.** Located atop Penang Hill, this little hotel is reachable only by funicular railway. Its attractions are spectacular views, an aviary and pretty gardens, cool air, and privacy. *Bukit Bendera, 11300 Penang, tel. 04/892256. 12 rooms. Facilities: restaurant, bar. No credit cards.*

$ **Lone Pine.** The best bargain on the beach, this hotel is a bit scruffy, with no pool and few amenities, but its beachfront area is shaded and pleasant. The air-conditioned rooms are spacious if Spartan; all have bath, TV, and fridge. Rates include breakfast and morning tea. *97 Batu Ferringhi Beach, 11100 Penang, tel. 04/811511. 54 rooms. Facilities: restaurant, bar. AE, DC, MC, V.*

$ **Malaysia.** All the rooms in this hotel, conveniently located downtown on upper Penang Road, have bath, TV, and fridge. *7 Penang Rd., 10000 Penang, tel. 04/363311. 130 rooms. Facilities: coffeehouse, bar, disco. AE, MC, V.*

The Arts

Eden Seafood Village (tel. 04/811852) in Batu Ferringhi holds a cultural show for diners most evenings. The show features gentle Ma-

lay dancers, Indians laden with bells, and noisy Chinese lion dancers. Beyond Batu Feriringhi is the **Pinang Cultural Centre** (Jln.
Teluk Bahang, tel. 04/811175), which re-creates a kampong with a
balai (community center), an Orang Ulu longhouse, a padang for
outdoor activities, and an exhibition hall. There are three 45-minute
cultural performances daily (10:15, noon, and 3:15) with dances and
traditional music. *Admission charge. Open daily 9:30–5.*

Arts events held at the City Hall auditorium downtown are adver-
tised with posters and in the newspapers. Festivals include street
events, such as Chinese opera.

Nightlife

Penang's nightlife revolves around the major hotels, where discos
cater to the trendy set and sedate lounges host those who enjoy listening to live music while chatting over a drink. Combos tend to
stick to "Candy Man" and "Feelings."

Lounges A favorite spot is the Merlin Hotel's **Sri Pinang Lounge** (Jln. Larut,
tel. 04/376166), where a singer and band entertain after 8:30 PM. The
Penang Mutiara's serene **Palmetto Lounge** (Telok Bahang, tel. 04/
812828) has a resident pianist. In the downtown Shangri-La Hotel's
Lobby Lounge (Jln. Magazine, tel. 04/622622), a string quartet—
playing everything from classical pieces to waltzes to pop—alternates evenings with a Latin combo. For a drink with a panoramic
city view, head for the revolving restaurant atop the **City Bayview
Hotel** (Farquhar St., tel. 04/23301). For listings of who is playing
where, check the Nightspots column in *The Star*.

Discos The **Cinta** in the Rasa Sayang Hotel (Batu Ferringhi, tel. 04/811800,
ext. 1151) draws an international crowd nightly. **Street One** in the
Shangri-La (Jln. Magazine, tel. 04/622622) features the latest lighting effects and sound equipment from London, with special events
most nights. **Cinnamon Tree** (Orchid Hotel, tel. 04/803333) is the
current spot for the young and hip.

Bars Downtown George Town still has seedy bars, with dim lights and ladies of indeterminate age and profession. Try the **Hong Kong Bar** on
Lebuh Chulia (tel. 04/619796), or ask the young hippies who flock to
the cheap Chinese hotels in the vicinity. One or two bars, such as the
Liverpool Bar (Lebuh Bishop, tel. 04/612153) and **Sumn's** (Lebuh
Pantai, tel. 04/610193) in the central business district, attract an expatriate crowd for lunch and darts in the evening. At the **Cheers
Beer Garden** (22 Jln. Argyll, tel. 04/637971), Ken and Pat run their
pub with an eye to assisting the traveler. The most venerable bar is
the **Anchor Bar** at the E&O hotel.

Langkawi

The hottest resort destination in Malaysia is currently Langkawi,
an archipelago of 101 islands at low tide (99 at high tide). Pulau
Langkawi, the largest island, houses the airport, the ferry terminal, and the major hotel resorts.

Arriving and Malaysia Airlines has daily flights from Kuala Lumpur and Penang
Departing (the flight from Penang is M$40). A ferry departs at 8 AM daily from
From Malaysia Penang for the five-hour crossing (fare: M$25). However, a better ferry
leaves from Kuala Perlis on the mainland, making six crossings a day
that take under two hours; a hovercraft from Kuala Perlis takes 35 minutes. To reach Kuala Perlis from Penang, either use a hired car or take

the bus/shared taxi from Butterworth—a seven-hour trip in either case.

From Thailand   There is now ferry service to and from Satul on the southwestern Thai coast. It takes about 90 minutes, departing from Langkawi at approxminately 9 AM and 3 PM and from Satul at approximately noon and 4:30 PM. If you travel to Satul by the morning ferry, a minibus from Hat Yal will get you to Krabi, Phuket, or Ko Samui by the end of the day.

Exploring   In contrast to Penang's resort-cluttered north coast, Langkawi is an unspoiled spot where relaxation is the only game in town. Commercialism may be arriving soon: Envious of islands like Bali and Phuket, Malaysia is in a rush to develop Langkawi as a big foreign exchange earner. To encourage development and tourism, Langkawi has been made a tax-free island. For the tourist, this means the cost of a beer and whiskey is much less than on the mainland, but there is limited shopping beyond that. The scene is changing rapidly, though. By 1995, a dozen new hotels (including the Mahsuri Westin, the Berjaya Langkawi Beach Resort, and Hotel Grand Continental) will have been added to the existing half dozen. Langkawi is losing its serenity, but for a few years yet it will remain a sun-and-sea haven with a lovely slow pace. (Its first and only traffic light was installed in 1993.)

It doesn't take much more than three hours to explore and to learn the local legends (Langkawi is being promoted as "the Isles of Legends"); after that, all that's left is to explore the beaches of Pulau Langkawi and the other 100 islands. There are boats for hire, and the major resorts rent snorkeling equipment; there are also organized trips to the other islands for picnics and diving. Take a boat, find your island, snorkel, dive, and laze away the day on your own beach!

Lodging   The choice is varied, from luxurious resorts priced at US$300 a night to local hotels with fan-cooled rooms that cost about US$10.

★   **Datai.** Tucked away on the northwestern tip of the island (a 40-minute drive from most of the other attractions), fronting the turquoise Andaman Sea and backed by a tropical rain forest, this 1994 hotel ranks as one of the world's finest hideaways. Many a tree that a cruder architect would have had uprooted has been left standing; the result is a beautiful blend with the environment. The large open-air main building, which serves as a reception area and lounge, perches at the top of a small valley that carves its way steeply down to the beach, a 10-minute walk away. Open-air corridors link the lobby to the 54 rooms, 40 villas, and 14 suites, laid out in a V, with the majority of guest rooms looking down into the valley. The large rooms are decorated in silk and red balau, a warm Malaysian hardwood that shines from the floors to the walls; each boasts a bedroom with a king-size bed, a living room with bar, writing desk, and two daybeds for lounging, and a grand bathroom with two vanities, shower, bath, and luggage space. Villas and suites are almost twice as big and include a private deck with a sun lounge and elevated veranda. Food here is of a high standard—not innovative, but well orchestrated. The open-air Pavilion, set among the treetops and amidst the evening sea breezes, serves Thai food. The Dining Room is cozily candlelit. Lunch and evening snacks are served on the beach. *Jln. Teluk Datai, 07000 Pulau Langkawi, tel. 604/950–2500, fax 604/959–2600; KL res. 603/245–3515, fax 603/245–3540; U.S. res. 800/447–7462; U.K. res. 0800/181–535. 108 villas, rooms, and suites. Facilities: 2 restaurants, beach bar, 2 pools, 2 tennis courts,*

18-hole golf course, mountain bike rental, 2 meeting rooms, health club, water sports facilities. AE, DC, MC, V. $$$$

Pelangi Beach Resort. The service, amenities, architecture, and ambience are tops for a large Malaysian resort. The intent throughout the 51 one-and two-story buildings on 25 acres of beachfront is to create the atmosphere of a kampong. But the primary feeling is of a vacation resort with pool, swim-up bar, and so forth. The beach is not spectacular, but at low tide you can wade across to a nearby island for privacy. In the center of the large lobby is a relaxing lounge bar for tea and cocktails. Guest rooms are rather small, and the extensive use of (compressed) wood and heavy carpeting makes them seem smaller; fortunately, they come with balconies, as well as both air-conditioning and fans. About a third face the sea, another third a man-made lake, and the remainder the back lot; room rates reflect these locations. *Pantai Cenang, 07000 Pulau Langkawi, Kedah, tel. 04/911001, fax 04/911122; KL office tel. 03/261–0393; Singapore office tel. 235–7788. 357 rooms, including 55 suites. Facilities: 2 restaurants and beach barbecue, 24-hr room service, outdoor pool, 3 tennis and 2 squash courts, fitness center, sauna, tour desk (all cost extra). AE, DC, MC, V. $$$*

East Malaysia: Sabah and Sarawak

Sabah and Sarawak, Malaysia's eastern states, share the northern third of the island of Borneo with Brunei, which is sandwiched between them. Each state has a large landmass—much of it primary jungle, with majestic tropical forests and abundant wildlife—and a relatively small population. Borneo's forbidding interior made it far less attractive to early traders and explorers than neighboring countries. Sabah and Sarawak remained uncolonized by the British until the mid-19th century, and they were annexed to the independent state of Malaysia only in 1963. Thus the native peoples—the Iban, Bidayuh, Kadazan, and other tribes—have little in common with West Malaysians, who absorbed much European and Chinese culture. The ancient languages, arts and crafts, and social customs of Sabah and Sarawak remain relatively intact. Some tribes still live in traditional longhouses, communal bamboo structures that house from 10 to 40 families under one roof.

Borneo is among the last wildernesses in Southeast Asia. Rain forest and jungle, threaded by numerous rivers and rapids, cover most of the land, and intrepid travelers explore it on foot, by jeep, or by longboat. Because the tourist industry is only now being developed, you won't trip over other tourists, and native lifestyles are for the most part uncorrupted and authentic. You can trek through the jungle interior, ride a longboat upriver, and stay overnight in a tribal longhouse. At the same time, the capital cities and beach resorts offer considerable luxury, with gourmet restaurants, water sports, and tennis courts.

A visitor taking a trip up one of the rivers for a night or two in a longhouse will find the "forest primeval." Insects hum, invisible creatures croak and grunt, water gurgles and sighs. Equally mysterious are the groaning and screeching of trees that, burdened by age and debris, finally crash through the jungle growth.

Sabah, known as the Land Below the Wind because it lies below the typhoon belt, occupies the northern tip of the island. Its primary re-

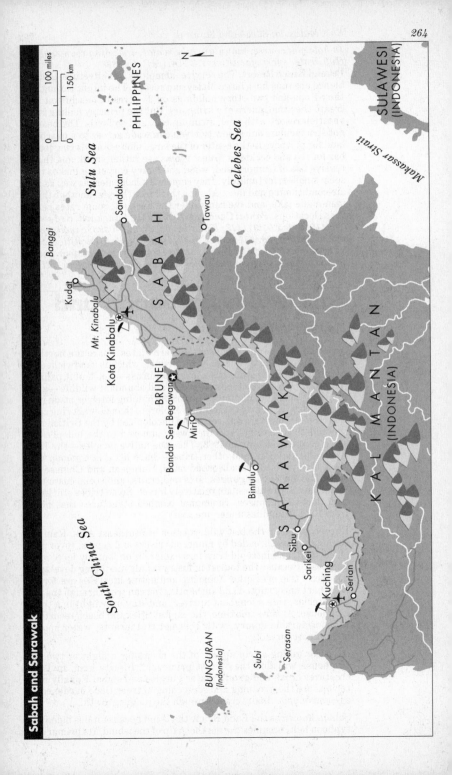

Sabah and Sarawak

source is its vast timber operations, on which fortunes have been built. With an area of some 77,700 sq km (30,000 sq mi), the state has about 1 million people, of which the Kadazans are the largest ethnic group. The Bajaus, who live along the west coast, are seafarers; many also farm and raise ponies. Chinese make up about a quarter of the population. Most Sabahans are Christians, so there is some religious tension between the Islamic state and its citizens. Sabah's capital, Kota Kinabalu, is a relatively new town, rebuilt after the Japanese destroyed it during the Second World War. It contains little to interest the tourist but serves as a jumping-off point and transportation hub for exploring the state.

Most travelers to Sabah visit Mt. Kinabalu, the legendary mountain in the primitive interior. This is the highest peak in Southeast Asia, at 4,100 m (13,500 ft). From a national park at its base, climbers can make the ascent in two days. For beachcombers, the seas around Sabah offer a kaleidoscope of marine life: You can snorkel, scuba dive, or putter about the reefs in glass-bottom boats.

Sarawak's modern history began in 1846, after Sir James Brooke settled a dispute between the local raja and the Sultan of Brunei. Establishing peace and bringing relief from marauding pirate bands, Raja Brooke instituted a benevolent family regency that lasted more than a century, until the arrival of the Japanese. Their intrusion was deeply resented by the tribal people, who eagerly resumed their practice of head-hunting, which had been banned by the Brooke rajas. But Sarawak has otherwise remained for the most part peaceful, unspoiled, and serene.

Sarawak is bigger and poorer than Sabah, with some 1.5 million people inhabiting its 125,000 sq km (48,250 sq mi). About 360,000 live around the capital city of Kuching, a pleasant and fairly modern town that still retains many of its Victorian buildings and Chinese shophouses. About 80% of Sarawak's population is Chinese or Malay; as in Sabah, Christians outnumber Muslims.

Sarawak's principal tourist attractions are the Dayak and Iban longhouses upriver from Kuching. The guided trips give travelers a sense of river life as well as of the richness and power of the jungle. You can visit longhouses for a day or stay over for a night or more, sharing communal meals and admiring native dances. Another fascinating destination is the Niah Caves, which have yielded a wide range of archaeological finds, including human remains believed to date from 40,000 years ago.

Important Addresses and Numbers

Tourist Information — **Sabah Tourist Association** (Level 1, International Airport, Kota Kinabalu, tel. 088/211484, ext. 335). **MTPB** (Block L, Lot 4, Bangunan STPC, Bandaran Sinsuran, Box 136, 93100 Kota Kinabalu, tel. 088/211698).

Sarawak Tourist Association (Main Bazaar, 93000 Kuching, tel. 082/240620; airport counter, tel. 082/456266). **MTPB** (AIA Building, 2nd Floor, Jln. Song Thian Cheok, Kuching, tel. 082/246575).

In Singapore: **Sarawak Tourism Centre** (268 Orchard Rd., #08–07 Yen San Bldg., Singapore 0923, tel. 736–1602; the staff is not very helpful).

Emergencies — Dial 999.

Arriving and Departing by Plane

Note: Sabah and Sarawak have separate immigration-control systems from those in West Malaysia. American visitors need valid passports but are not required to get a visa. Travelers on business or with student passes can stay up to three months.

Airports and Airlines Malaysia Airlines is the primary carrier to Sabah and Sarawak. In addition, **Royal Brunei** flies into both the **Kota Kinabalu International Airport** (tel. 088/54811) and Sarawak's **Kuching International Airport** (tel. 082/454242) and **Philippine Airlines, Singapore Airlines,** and **Cathay Pacific** fly into Kota Kinabalu.

Between the Airport and Center City A taxi ride from the Kota Kinabalu airport to city center costs M$10.20. Purchase the taxi voucher from the counter designated "Tarsi." Kuching's spacious airport is about 11 km (7 mi) south of town, and the unmetered taxis charge M$12 for the trip.

Arriving and Departing by Ship

The cruise ship *Muhibah* (contact **Feri Malaysia,** Menara Utama UMBC, Jln. Sultan Sulaiman, 5000 Kuala Lumpur, tel. 03/238–8899) makes regular runs to these eastern states from Port Kelang and Kuantan in West Malaysia.

Getting Around

By Bus Public bus companies serve the cities and the countryside, but poor road conditions make intercity travel rough. Kota Kinabalu's main terminal is in front of the port. **Leun Thung Transport Co.** (tel. 088/762655) goes from city center to Tanjung Aru, and **Tuaran United Co.** (tel. 088/31580) stops at all the villages along the road to Tuaran.

In Kuching, the main terminal is on Mosque Road, where a posted map displays the routes. Among the companies serving the area are **Kuching Matang Transport** (tel. 082/422814) and **Sarawak Transport** (tel. 082/242579).

By Car Four-wheel-drive vehicles are recommended for driving in the interior. Drivers can be hired, too. For rentals in Kota Kinabalu, try **Avis** (tel. 088/56706), **Kinabalu** (tel. 088/23602), or **E&C** (tel. 088/57679). In Kuching, local rental companies have counters at the airport; Avis and Hertz are not represented. Prices are high—at least M$175 a day. Try **Makena Rent-a-Car** (tel. 082/411970).

By Ferry In Sarawak, ferries and riverboats are the popular form of transport. At least four ferries a day depart from Kuching for Sibu, where you can transfer onto a riverboat for destinations inland. From Sabah, there are high-speed ferries that make the 2½-hour run to Labuan from Kota Kinabalu.

By Taxi In Kota Kinabalu you can always find a cab near the Hyatt downtown; in Kuching, drivers gather in front of the Holiday Inn. Outside these cities, taxis are not plentiful. Ask personnel at your hotel to call one for you, or inquire in the street about the location of the nearest taxi stand. Summoning cabs by telephone isn't very reliable, but you can try 088/51863 or 088/25669 in Kota Kinabalu.

Cabs are more expensive here than in peninsular Malaysia, and they are unmetered. Ask at your hotel about the usual fares to various destinations; agree on the price with your driver before setting out. To hire a car with driver for three hours to see the main sights costs about M$40.

By Train **Sabah State Railways** (tel. 088/54611) runs a scenic rail line from Kota Kinabalu south to Tenom. The 49-km (31-mi) stretch between Beaufort and Tenom passes through the spectacular Crocker Range and Padas Gorge, takes 1½–2 hours, and costs M$12.20 first class, M$4.25 economy. Sarawak has no rail service.

Other Transportation **Shared taxis** and **minibuses** congregate near the bus terminals, and **boat taxis** and **chartered launches** have kiosks along the waterfront.

Guided Tours

Sabah Tour operators in Kota Kinabalu include **Api Tours** (Bandaran Berjaya, tel. 088/221230), **Bakti** (Hyatt Hotel, Jln. Datuk Salleh Sulong, tel. 088/534426), and **Popular Express Travel** (33 Jln. Tugu, 88305 Kota Kinabulu, tel. 088/214692). The **Marina** (Tanjung Aru Beach Hotel, tel. 088/214215) specializes in island trips and water sports.

Orientation A Kota Kinabalu city tour covers the highlights in just two hours (note that the mosque and Sabah Museum are closed Friday). A countryside tour stops at Mengkabong, a stilted village of Bajau fisherfolk 30 km (19 mi) out of Kota Kinabulu, driving past rice fields and rural kampongs and the township of Tamparalim, reached by a rope suspension bridge. Other excursions include the Sunday market at Kota Belud, a day trip to Tenom, and the Sepilok orangutan sanctuary.

Diving Trips The diving season lasts from mid-February to mid-December; in August and September, the green sea turtles come ashore to lay their eggs. **Borneo Divers** (Bag 194, Kota Kinabulu, tel. 088/421371) arranges dive excursions to Sipadan and the reefs of Tunku Rahman National Park; the company also offers packages with Malaysia Airlines.

Rafting and Jungle Treks **Api** and **Marina** have white-water rafting as well as hiking safaris into the interior, including visits to native villages.

Sarawak Four travel agencies in Kuching offer a variety of tours throughout the state. You'll find the itineraries and prices comparable at **Interworld Travel Service** (85 Jln. Rambutan, Box 1838, Kuching, tel. 082/252344), **Sarawak Travel** (70 Padungan Rd., tel. 082/243708), and **Borneo Island Tours** (Jln. Borneo, tel. 082/423944). **Borneo Adventure** (1st Floor, Padungan Arcade, Jln. Song Thian Cheok, tel. 082/245175) specializes in backpacking tours but has longhouse and hotel-based excursions as well.

Orientation It takes about three hours to cover Kuching's historic sites, including a drive past the central market and a Malay village, with a stop at the Sarawak Museum.

Nature You can take guided nature walks to the orangutan sanctuary, a crocodile farm, or the Bako National Park and Matang area. Tour organizers also arrange backpacking and spelunking excursions into mountain regions, national parks, and ancient caves.

Exploring Sabah

Kota Kinabalu The capital, called Jesselton when Sabah was the British crown colony of North Borneo, was razed during World War II, thus its local name Api-Api ("fires"). It was renamed in 1963, when Sabah and Sarawak joined independent Malaysia. Little of historic interest remains—the oldest part of the city is vintage 1950s. The multistory shophouses sell hardware and other practical goods; the upper floors are residences. The central market on the waterfront sells produce and handicrafts. Next to the central market is a smaller collection of stalls selling produce from the Philippines.

Kota Kinabalu's main draw is the **Sabah Museum,** on a hilltop off Jalan Penampang about 3 km (2 mi) from city center. The building resembles a traditional longhouse, and its contents are a good introduction to local history, archaeology, botany, and ethnography. One exhibit features innumerable varieties of the large ceramic *tajau,* a household jar common throughout Asia. Another displays the many ingenious uses of bamboo in toys, animal traps, musical instruments, and farm tools. A third gallery is devoted to head-hunting. *Bukit Istana Lama, tel. 088/53199. Admission free. Open Sat.– Thurs. 9–6.*

Excursions A favorite destination is **Mt. Kinabalu National Park,** 113 km (68 mi)—about two hours—from Kota Kinabalu. Nature lovers can walk miles of well-marked trails through jungle dense with wild orchids, carnivorous pitcher plants, bamboo, mosses and vines, and unusual geologic formations. The wildlife is shy, but you are likely to see exotic birds and possibly a few orangutans.

For some, the main event is scaling **Mt. Kinabalu,** at 4,100 m (13,500 ft) the highest mountain in Southeast Asia—and thus a place of spiritual significance for the Kadazan people. Climbers can reach the peak in two days without too much exertion, and the view from the summit on a clear morning is worth every step. Climbers get their second wind at the overnight rest house at Penar Laban (3,350 m, or 10,988 ft) before leaving at 2 AM to reach the summit by dawn. Rooms cost about M$28; bunk beds in the nearby mountain shelters go for M$5. (These should be reserved ahead at Kota Kinabalu.) Mountain guides are equipped with mobile telephones, and the park has a helipad.

To reach Mt. Kinabalu, take the minibus departing Kota Kinabalu for Ranau at 8 AM and noon (fare: M$10); it passes the park's entrance. You can stay at the **Kinabalu Lodge** in the park (deluxe room M$300, twin-bedded room M$50, dormitory accommodation M$10). Make reservations before you arrive at the Mt. Kinabalu Park Office (ground floor, Lot 3, Block A, Complex Sinsuran, Kota Kinabalu, tel. 088/211585). Day and overnight tours can be arranged through **Popular Express Travel** (33 Jln. Tugu, Kampung Air, 88805 Kota Kinabalu, tel. 088/214692, fax 088/225140).

Three seas converge at the northern tip of Borneo, and their shores are all easily accessible from Kota Kinabalu. You can make a day trip to picnic and snorkel among the reefs at the little park on **Pulau Gaya,** in the South China Sea, or join a boat excursion to a **turtle park** and **crocodile farm** off the east coast, in the Sulu Sea. Divers will find some of the world's richest reefs off **Sipadan Island** in the Celebes Sea farther south.

The small coastal trading town of Sandakan, reached by sea or air, is 21 km (13 mi) from the **Sepilok Orang Utan Rehabilitation Centre**—a jungle habitat for these near-human primates. (From Sandakan, buses go out several times a day—you'll have to walk 2 km, or 1.2 mi, from the entrance to the center. For schedules, tel. 088/215106.) Here, illegally captured animals are prepared for a return to the wild. There's no guarantee that you'll see the apes in this vast forest, but there's enough to make the trip worthwhile if you don't—including waterfalls, cool streams for swimming, and other rain-forest wildlife. *Tel. 089/214179 or 660811. Admission free. Open daily 9–4.*

Arrange any of these trips through one of the tour companies listed under Guided Tours, *above.*

Exploring Sarawak

Kuching suffered little damage during the Second World War, and a walk around town will give the visitor some feeling for its history. You'll note the gentle, unhurried pace as you walk along the newly landscaped waterfront, where there are benches, food stalls, and a small stadium in which dancers perform. The town's oldest building is the 1840s **Tua Pek Kong** Chinese temple, downtown on Jalan Tuanku Abdul Rahman and Padungan Road. You can watch worshipers lighting incense and making paper offerings to the god of prosperity. Among the colonial buildings worth seeing is the **Court House,** the former seat of the British White Rajahs, with its portico and Romanesque columns (the clock tower was added in 1883). This remains the venue for any event of pomp and circumstance. Behind the Court House on Jalan Tun Haji Openg stands the **Pavilion building,** where, behind an elaborate Victorian facade, the Education Department now does its business.

Across the river is **Fort Margherita,** built in 1879 by Raja Charles Brooke. Today it's a police museum displaying cannons and other colonial weapons. The nearby **Astana** was the Brooke palace, built in 1870—three bungalows, complete with military ramparts and tower. Today Astana is the official residence of Sarawak's head of state and is not open to the public.

The highlight of the city is the **Sarawak Museum,** one of the best in Southeast Asia—comprehensive and beautifully curated. In addition to exhibits of local insects and butterflies, sea creatures, birds, and other wildlife, there are displays on Dayak body tattoos, burial rites, face masks, and carvings. In the new building across the road is a delightful exhibit on cats *(kuching* means "cat" in Malay), a model of the Niah Caves showing how nests are gathered, a movie theater, an art gallery, and a crafts shop. *Jln. Tun Haji Openg, tel. 082/ 244232. Admission free. Open Mon.–Thurs. 9:15–5:30, Sat. and Sun. 9:15–6.*

For beach action, head for **Damai,** 35 minutes by taxi from Kuching. The Holiday Inn there (*see* Lodging, *below*) can supply all the amenities you need for relaxing on the white powdery sands. You can also wander over to the 20-acre **Sarawak Cultural Village** (Santubong, tel. 082/422411), a new venture created by the government to display the lifestyles of the seven major tribes indigenous to the region. Here you can see demonstrations of the arts of top spinning, kite flying, and using a blowpipe. *Admission charge. Open daily 9–12:30 and 2–5:30.*

Excursions   Few tourists come this far without making a trip to a tribal **longhouse.** Some are as close as a 1½-hour drive from Kuching; others involve longer rides and boat trips. You can visit for a day or stay for as long as a week. Either way, your hosts welcome you with a mixture of hospitality and polite indifference. While accommodations are spartan, guest quarters usually include mosquito netting, flush toilets, and running water. The attraction here is seeing—and sharing—a lifestyle that has changed little in centuries. Tour operators give advice on dress and comportment.

One overnight trip goes to the **Skrang River.** A car or bus takes you through pepper plantations, run mostly by Chinese families, to the town of Serian, where you board a canoe for a beautiful ride through the jungle on the clear, green river. A longhouse awaits you at the end of the journey.

The **Niah Caves,** an archaeologist's mecca, are 109 km (68 mi) from the port town of Miri, a 40-minute flight from Kuching. (A taxi from Miri costs M$20.) The caves contain stone, bone, and iron tools; primitive paintings and drawings; and Chinese ceramics. The caves were occupied for thousands of years and are still used as a commercial resource by the local people, who gather guano from the cave floors for fertilizer and collect birds' nests from the ceilings for bird's-nest soup—a Chinese delicacy. Adventurous travelers can go through the caves with a guide. To reach the caves you must walk over a long path of 10-inch-wide boards. This trip is not for the lazy, but greatly rewarding. In the Niah National Park, there's a hostel (contact the National Parks Office, tel. 085/33361 or 36637).

About 22 km (14 mi) from Kuching is the **Semonggok Wildlife Rehabilitation Centre,** where orangutans, other monkeys, honey bears, and hornbills formerly in captivity are prepared for return to their natural habitat. You can get a visitor's permit through the Forestry Department (Mosque Rd., Kuching, tel. 082/248739). *For tour arrangements, tel. 082/423111, ext. 1133. Admission charge. Open weekdays 8–4:25, Sat. 8–12:45.*

Shopping

Sabah   Sabah handicrafts are less elaborate than Sarawak's, but they do have character. Two Kota Kinabalu shops specializing in local products are **Borneo Handicrafts** (ground floor, Lot 51, Jln. Gaya, tel. 088/714081) and **Sabah Handicraft Centre** (ground floor, Lot 49, Bandaran Berjaya, tel. 088/221230). Borneo Handicrafts also has an outlet at the airport (tel. 088/230707).

For other shopping in Kota Kinabalu, cruise through **Kompleks Karamunsing** off Jalan Kolam or the **Matahari Superstore** (tel. 088/214430) in the Segama district near the Hyatt. For jewelry, try **Ban Loong** (tel. 088/217126) or **Yun On Goldsmiths** (tel. 088/219369) in the Wisma Merdeka building.

The **night market** in Kota Kinabalu usually sets up about 7 PM in front of the central market. One portable souvenir is mountain-grown Sabah tea.

Sarawak   The handicrafts in Sarawak are among the most fascinating in the world. Especially distinctive are the handwoven blankets, or *pua kumbu,* whose intricate tribal designs have ceremonial significance. Baskets, hats, and mats are made from a combination of rattan, palm leaves, and reeds; their designs vary according to the ethnic group. The wood carvings often bear the motif of the hornbill, the national emblem. Pottery designs show a Chinese influence, as do brassware and silver objects. The crafts shop next to the **Sarawak Tourist Information Center** in Kuching has a large selection of all kinds of handicrafts, and other shops around the city stock similar goods.

A **Sunday market** in the parking lot of Bank Bumiputra on Jalan Satok sells everything from fruit to heirlooms. For antiques, try along Wayang Street, Temple Street, and the Main Bazaar. Bargaining is expected.

Sports, Fitness, Beaches

Sabah Beaches The best beaches are on the islands of the **Tuanku Abdul Rahman National Park,** a 15-minute speedboat ride from the pier in downtown Kota Kinabalu. Here serenity and privacy prevail. Pretty coral formations and exotic marine life attract snorkelers and divers. Tour operators will arrange a picnic lunch for an outing. Some camping facilities and a few cabins are available for overnight stays.

Golf Kota Kinabalu has two private golf courses that can be used by visitors who make arrangements in advance through their hotels. The 18-hole course at **Bukit Padang** is run by the Sabah Golf and Country Club; the nine-hole course at **Tanjung Aru** is under the auspices of the Kinabalu Golf Club.

Health and Fitness Centers The **Likas Sports Complex** is a 300-acre facility behind Signal Hill, a few kilometers east of Kota Kinabalu on Jalan Kompleks Sukan, with an Olympic-size pool, a track, eight tennis courts, and a weight-training gym. Also open to the public are the **International** in Bandaran Berjaya (tel. 088/212586) and **Merigaya** at the Hyatt Hotel (tel. 088/210407).

Water Sports You can snorkel, scuba dive, windsurf, and sail off the beach at **Tanjung Aru,** only a few minutes from Kota Kinabalu, and on small islands accessible through the major hotels.

Sarawak Beaches Idyllic **Damai Beach** is about 20 km (12 mi) northwest of Kuching, at the foot of Santubong Mountain. The Holiday Inn resort there provides facilities for such water sports as windsurfing, catamaran sailing, kayaking, and waterskiing.

Other picturesque but undeveloped beaches in Sarawak include **Brighton Beach** and **Tanjong Lobang** in Miri, and **Tanjong Batu** and **Tanjong Kidurong** in Bintulu.

Boating Recreational boating is available at the **Holiday Inn Damai Beach** resort (tel. 082/411777).

Golf The **Sarawak Golf and Country Club** (tel. 082/23622) at Petra Jaya is open to guests of major hotels. The **Holiday Inn Damai Beach** (tel. 082/411777) has a new 18-hole course.

Jogging Runners in Kuching use the **Holiday Inn course** or head to the stadium at Petra Jaya. Australia's **Hash House Harriers** (tel. 082/411133) have open runs on Tuesday for men and on Wednesday for women.

Squash The **Sarawak Golf and Country Club** has squash courts; make arrangements through your hotel.

Swimming There's a public pool on Padungan Road (tel. 082/51354).

Dining

Kota Kinabalu **Gardenia Steak and Lobster Bar.** This elegant restaurant has a Western-style menu listing lobster as well as New Zealand lamb with mint sauce. Business travelers and government officials eat here. *55 Jln. Gaya, tel. 088/54296. Reservations required during holidays. Dress: smart casual. AE, DC, MC, V. $$$*
Garden Terrace Restaurant. The Tanjung Aru's open-fronted restaurant, decorated with antique overhead fans and rattan furniture, serves traditional Italian food in a setting made romantic by candlelight and the chirping of tropical creatures in the surrounding gardens. (The resort's casual Garden Room offers delectable seafood and grills.) *Tanjung Aru Beach Resort, Jln. Aru, tel. 088/58711. No reservations. Dress: casual. AE, DC, MC, V. $$$*

Nam Hing. The locals who patronize this Chinese restaurant order the dim sum, but there are also tasty seafood dishes—chili crab, squid, and prawns. The noise and gusto of the clientele provide a lively distraction from the bland decor. *32 Jln. Haji Saman, tel. 088/51433. No reservations. Dress: casual. No credit cards. $$*

Tioman. Across from the Capitol Theatre, this restaurant features 30 types of noodle dishes, some in soups, some dry, and others fried. Also on the menu are 20 varieties of *congee* (rice porridge) and three delicious creamy dessert puddings—peanut, almond, and sesame. *56 Bandaran Berjaya, tel. 088/219734. No reservations. Dress: casual. AE, DC, V. $*

Kuching **Beijing Riverbank.** The food—light refreshments and drinks downstairs, a more elaborate Cantonese and Western menu upstairs—is acceptable, but what draws people to this modest pagoda is its situation overlooking the river. *Kuching Waterfront, tel. 088/234126. No reservations. Dress: casual. MC, V. $$*

Lok Thian. This large restaurant, located near the Dewan Mesayakat, is renowned for its Cantonese barbecue. *319 Jln. Padungan, tel. 088/3130. No reservations. Dress: casual. AE, DC, V. $$*

Meisan Szechuan. This gaudily decorated Chinese restaurant overlooks the Sarawak River. Waiters deliver 23 varieties of dim sum—all you can eat. *Holiday Inn Kuching, Jln. Tuanku Abdul Rahman, tel. 082/423111. Reservations suggested on Sun. morning. Dress: casual. AE, DC, MC, V. $$*

Tsui Hua Lau. Cantonese and Szechuan dishes highlight an extensive menu at this brightly lit, two-story restaurant. The unusual entrées include braised turtle, sea cucumber, and bird's nest soup (a bowl for 10 costs M$100). The barbecued duck and Szechuan-style shredded beef meet high standards. *22 Ban Hock Rd., tel. 082/414560. No reservations. Dress: casual. AE, DC, V. $$*

Waterfront Cafe. On the river, this serene ground-floor coffee shop has a good view of the wharf and the water traffic. Its menu features Malay, Chinese, and Indian favorites plus Western specialties. The noodle dishes are delicious; the service is fine. *Kuching Hilton, Jln. Tuanku Abdul Rahman, tel. 082/248200. No reservations. Dress: casual. AE, DC, MC, V. $$*

Lodging

Sabah **Hyatt Kinabalu.** The Hyatt, which appeals especially to business travelers, is anxious to keep its leading position downtown, so there has been considerable refurbishment, and a new extension has been added. Between the hotel and the waterfront is a pool in an Astroturf garden. Rooms are spacious and comfortable; many have views of the port and nearby islands. The top two floors have Regency Club (concierge) rooms. The Semporna Grill is good for fresh seafood, and the Phoenix Court serves Szechuan and Cantonese fare. In the evening, a *pasar malam* has hawker food stalls. The 24-hour coffee shop is a magnet for late-night revelers. *Jln. Datuk Salleh Sulong, 88994 Kota Kinabulu, tel. 088/221234 or 800/223–1234, fax 088/225972. 315 rooms, including 26 suites. Facilities: business center, 2 bars, 3 restaurants, pool. AE, DC, MC, V. $$$$*

★ **Tanjung Aru Beach Hotel.** This premier luxury resort, run by Shangri-La International, is near the airport and 10 minutes from downtown (a bus shuttles guests downtown five times a day). No longer a quiet getaway, it has become a major resort hotel that bustles with activity when it is fully occupied. For all the publicity the place receives, the rooms are rather ordinary, though the wicker furniture gives an airy feel, and each has a private balcony overlooking the hotel's 57 landscaped acres and the sea and islands beyond. The leisure center teaches and arranges windsurfing, scuba diving, waterskiing, sailing, white-water rafting, and glass-bottom boat rides. For dining, the buffet of local specialties at the Garden Terrace restaurant has well-prepared Western (particularly Italian) food, and there are the Shang Palace for Cantonese and the Ristoran Pulau Bayu for seafood. Extensions in 1994 added 200 rooms and another pool. *Locked Bag 174, 88999 Kota Kinabulu, tel. 088/225800 or 800/942–5050, fax 088/244871. 500 rooms and suites. Facilities: 3 restaurants, lounge, disco, 4 lighted tennis courts, golf course nearby, business center, fitness center, 2 pools, Jacuzzi. AE, DC, MC, V. $$$$*

Hotel Perkasa. It stands on a hilltop facing Mt. Kinabalu, to which excursions can be arranged. Its rooms offer a mountain view as well as heaters—a rarity in the tropics—to warm the brisk mountain air. But that's the extent of the luxury. The hotel is a 2½-hour drive from the airport. *W.D.T. 11, 89300 Ranau, tel. 088/889511, fax 088/889101. 74 rooms. Facilities: restaurant and lounge, secretarial service, sightseeing desk, tennis court, fitness center, golf nearby. AE, DC, MC, V. $$*

Way May Hotel. In the center of Kota Kinabulu is a Chinese hotel that keeps its small twin-bedded rooms clean and offers friendly welcomes to its guest. It offers no more, but the price is good. For meals, there are plenty of local restaurants a street or two away. *36 Jln. Haji Saman, 88000 Kota Kinabulu, tel. 088/266118, fax 088/266122. 24 rooms with bath. MC, V. $*

Sarawak   **Batang Ai Longhouse.** Brand new in late 1994, this resort, designed on the lines of a traditional Iban timber longhouse, stands on a small island in Batang Ai Lake surrounded by mountains and rain forests. Guest rooms are simply, comfortably furnished with native woods. Another longhouse contains a large dining room with a terrace overlooking the lake. Evening meals are buffet-style. Batang Ai National Park is close by, and trekking tours and longboat excursions to Iban communities are the main options for daily activities. The resort is a four-hour drive, then a five-minute boat ride, from Kuching; Hilton International will make travel arrangements through a local tour operator. *Reservations: Kuching Hilton, Jln. Tuanku Abdul Rahman, Box 2396, 93748 Kuching, tel. 082/248200 or 800/HILTONS, fax 082/428984. 100 rooms. Facilities: restaurant, excursions. AE, DC, MC, V. $$$$*

★   **Kuching Hilton.** This 15-story luxury hotel on the Sarawak River, just across from Fort Margherita, has become a landmark for quality service and fine dining. The bleached furniture in its spacious rooms includes a desk with a view. One "Penthouse Floor" and two executive floors offer special amenities: separate check-in, a personal butler, and a private lounge. The views—and all the restaurants have them—are far better than the ones at the newer Riverside Majestic next door. *Jln. Tuanku Abdul Rahman, Box 2396, 93748 Kuching, tel. 082/248200 or 800/HILTONS, fax 082/428984. 322 rooms and 3 floors of suites. Facilities: 4 restaurants, cocktail lounge, fitness center, pool, executive business center, convention and banquet rooms. AE, DC, MC, V. $$$$*

Holiday Inn Damai Beach. Except for the rather primitive accommodations at Santubong Fishing Village or at Santin, this is the only beach resort in Sarawak. (There may be some new ones in late 1995.) Set on 90 acres in a tropical rain forest, it's about 24 km (15 mi) from Kuching on a lovely stretch of beach on the South China Sea. (A shuttle bus connects the two Holiday Inn properties.) Rooms are large and well furnished, with an outdoor feeling created by glass patio doors. The hotel offers water sports, jogging, and jungle treks among its plentiful opportunities for recreation. The word *damai* means "harmony and peace," but to find it one must walk away from all the activity—though an additional 80 deluxe rooms and 20 suites in the longhouse style have opened on the breezy hill slopes adjacent to the main part of the hotel, and they're quieter and more attractive. *Box 2870, 93756 Kuching, tel. 082/411777 or 800/HOLIDAY (0171/722–7755 in the U.K.), fax 082/428911. 302 rooms, including suites, studios, and chalets. Facilities: 3 restaurants, disco, 2 tennis courts, 2 squash courts, 18-hole golf course, minigolf, large pool, poolside snack bar, water-sports equipment, bicycle rental, sauna, fitness center, game room, business center, convention and banquet rooms, children's playground with minizoo, aviary, child-care center. AE, DC, MC, V. $$$*

Holiday Inn Kuching. The first international hotel on the river seems to bustle all the time, perhaps because it's next to a major shopping arcade, but also because it receives most of the tour groups that come to Kuching. Arrangements can be made to split one's stay between this Kuching property and the Holiday Inn on Damai Beach. The rooms are compact, with typical Holiday Inn furniture along with the standard amenities. The view of the road is rather depressing, so request a room that looks out over the Sarawak River. A new executive floor has rooms with newer furniture and a shared lounge with a splendid view of the river. *Jln. Tuanku Abdul Rahman, Box 2362, 93100 Kuching, tel. 082/423111 or 800/HOLIDAY (0171/722–7755 in the U.K.), fax 082/426169. 305 rooms, including executive suites. Facilities: 24-hr coffeehouse, 2 restaurants, bake shop, bar, disco, sauna, fitness center, lighted tennis court, pool, business center, children's playground, in-house movie channel. AE, DC, MC, V. $$–$$$*

Aurora. This well-located Asian hotel is clean, and a good value. Its large rooms are cheaply furnished but have air-conditioning, TV, phone, and private bath. *McDougall Rd., Box 260, Kuching, tel. 082/240281, fax 082/425400. 86 rooms. Facilities: coffeehouse, 2 restaurants, terrace. No credit cards. $$*

Hotel Longhouse. The city-center location does mean some street noise, but the cleanliness and the helpful staff make this place a good budget choice. *Jln. Abell, Padungan, 93100 Kuching, tel. 082/410333, fax 082/323690. 26 rooms. Facilities: coffeehouse. MC, V. $–$$*

The Arts and Nightlife

The international hotels offer East Malaysia's most sophisticated entertainment. Local culture is most evident during harvest festivals—May in Sabah and June in Sarawak.

Sabah A year-round opportunity to see Kadazan culture and taste its food is now available at a **folk village** at **Karambunai,** about 16 km (10 mi) out of Kota Kinabalu via the Tuaran Road. The village opened in 1990, and more native houses are under construction to permit artisans to make and sell their traditional crafts. Cultural shows at the model kampong are presented by the Kadazan Cultural Association (tel. 088/713696). The **Tanjung Aru Beach Hotel's** Garden Terrace restaurant (tel. 088/58711) has cultural shows every Saturday at 8:30 PM. At the Sunday **market** in **Kota Belud,** visitors can watch Bajau dancing, pony riding, and cockfights.

Among the modern nightclubs recommended in Kota Kinabalu are the **Mikado** (Hyatt Hotel lower level, tel. 088/219888), **Tiffany Disco**

and Music Theatre (9 Jln. Karamunsing, tel. 088/210645), and the **Bistro Showcase and Discotheque** (Wisma Budaya, Jln. Tuanku Abdul Rahman, Kg. Air, tel. 088/225877). Most nightspots are small, seedy, dark rooms with disco music blaring through mega-watt sound systems. On occasion the pace slows down and local danc-es—such as the Kadazan *sumazou*—are requested. Most places have hostesses to chat and dance with; you are expected to buy them drinks in return for their company.

Sarawak The new **Cultural Village and Heritage Centre** at Damai runs twice-weekly programs of such folk arts as dancing, kite flying, and handi-craft production. A restaurant serves local dishes and delicious rum punches, and plans call for a longhouse-style accommodation for tourists. The Sarawak Economic Development Corporation directs the project, but call the Damai Beach Resort (tel. 082/411777) for de-tails.

The Holiday Inn Kuching has a small cultural show every Monday, Thursday, and Saturday evening at 7:30. A troupe of gong players and pretty female dancers perform a variety of dances from the state's different ethnic groups.

For nightlife in Kuching, the most popular local clubs include **White Swan, Silver Star, Starlight Disco,** and the **Aquarius** in the Holiday Inn.

Brunei

Nestled between Sabah and Sarawak is a tiny nation different from any other in Southeast Asia. Since 1929, when oil was discovered off its shores, the sultanate of Brunei Darussalam—no larger than the state of Delaware, and with a population of only 245,000—has devel-oped into the second-richest country in the world. While Brunei shares with its neighbors a blend of Malay and Muslim traditions, a tropical climate, and a jungle terrain, its people enjoy a standard of living unmatched except by that in preinvasion Kuwait. In the 16th century, Brunei dominated an empire reaching as far south as Ma-nila, but the nobility was cruel and unpopular, and its power was gradually eroded by internal politics and revolts. Partly to protect the primitive tribes of the interior—and partly to exploit the weak-ness of the Brunei throne—the first British White Rajah, James Brooke, took over the region in 1839. Brunei became a British pro-tectorate in 1888, and the money started flowing when the oil did, about 40 years later. Britain helped quell a rebellion against the sul-tanate in 1962; political stability followed, and Brunei was granted full independence in 1984.

Brunei's 29th sultan has ruled since 1967, when his father abdicated. Like his predecessors, he takes seriously his role as a guardian of Islamic values. For instance, he mandated whippings for criminals convicted of crimes ranging from vandalism to rape. His fabulous wealth also makes him a major player in global politics: His US$10 million contribution to the Nicaraguan rebels linked his name with the Iran-Contra arms scandal. Bragging about his extravagance—his passion for polo ponies, Italian sports cars, and London fash-ions—is a national pastime. He is famous also for his beneficence. His government spends its oil revenues on public education, health care, and cultural programs. And his investments abroad have en-sured that Brunei's prosperity will continue long after its oil and gas are exhausted.

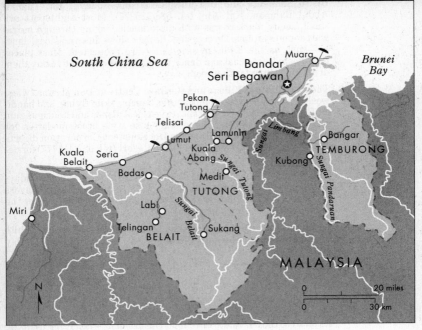

Because the country doesn't need foreigners' hard currency and generally disdains foreign values and customs, tourism is not a highly developed industry, although recently Brunei has been promoting ecotourism with trips to the interior. (More than 80% of the country is forest, mostly primary rain forest dominated by giant dipterocarp trees, with eagles, ospreys, bears, wildcats, bats, and monkeys of all kinds—plus ants, snakes, and some of the other less attractive jungle dwellers.) Visitors can also be comfortably accommodated in the modern capital, Bandar Seri Begawan (BSB). The city, situated on a wide, lovely river, and the Kampung Ayer (water village), where many of its citizens dwell in houses built on stilts, are well worth a stop.

Important Addresses and Numbers

Tourist Information Brunei has no official agency to handle visitors. The **Economic Development Board** (State Secretariat Office, BSB, tel. 02/231794) can provide general information, and a booth at the airport distributes city maps and hotel brochures.

Emergencies Dial 02/222333 for **police**, 02/222366 for an **ambulance**, and 02/222555 in case of **fire**.

Passports and Visas

Americans need a visa to enter Brunei. Canadian and British citizens, and those from neighboring Asian countries, can visit for two weeks without a visa.

When to Go

Brunei's tropical temperatures don't vary much from one season to the next: It's hot and humid year-round, and the equatorial sun is fierce. Even during the December–January monsoon, be prepared for blasts of heat between downpours. There is no peak tourist season.

Festivals and Seasonal Events

The widely observed Muslim religious holidays vary according to the Islamic calendar. Chinese, Hindu, and Christian holidays are also observed, some on fixed dates. (*See* Festivals and Seasonal Events in Staying in Malaysia, at the beginning of this chapter.) In addition, Brunei celebrates **National Day** (Feb. 23), the **anniversary of the Royal Brunei Army** (May 31), and the **sultan's birthday** (July 15).

Currency

Brunei dollars are issued in notes of B$1, B$5, B$10, B$50, B$100, B$500, and B$1,000. Coins come in denominations of 1, 5, 10, 20, and 50 cents. The Brunei dollar is at par with the Singapore dollar, which also circulates in Brunei; at press time B$1.50 = US$1, B$2.25 = £1.

What It Will Cost

Sample Prices Breakfast of toast, eggs, and coffee, B$10–B$15; taxi ride, B$4 for first mile, B$2 per mile thereafter; double room, B$230 expensive, B$100–B$145 moderate.

Language

The official language is Bahasa Malaysia, but English and the Hokkien Chinese dialect are widely spoken.

Telephones

You can direct-dial international calls from the major hotels or from the Central Telegraph Office on Jalan Sultan. The country code for Brunei is 673; the area code for Bandar Seri Begawan is 02 (omit the "0" when dialing from overseas). Pay phones use phone cards in values of B$10, B$20, B$50, and B$100, on sale at Telecom offices and post offices.

Mail

Receiving Mail The only means of receiving letters in Brunei is at your hotel. American Express and Thomas Cook do not have offices, and the GPO will not hold mail. Overseas postcards require a B$.25 stamp.

Arriving and Departing by Plane

Airport and Airlines The national carrier, **Royal Brunei Airlines** (tel. 02/242222), has routes throughout Southeast Asia. **Malaysia Airlines** flies from Kuching in Sarawak and Kota Kinabalu in Sabah, though not daily. **Singapore Airlines, Cathay Pacific,** and **Thai Airways International** also serve Brunei.

Brunei International Airport, near Bandar Seri Begawan, is sleek, modern, and efficient. Departing passengers pay an airport tax of B$12 on international flights, B$5 to Singapore or Malaysia.

Between the Airport and Center City
The only way to get downtown from the airport is via taxi. Taxis are unmetered, but the fare is fixed at B$20. If you have a flight after 8 PM, be sure to order your taxi beforehand. Taxis are never plentiful even during the day and many stop working early in the evening.

Arriving and Departing by Car, Bus, and Boat

A paved road links Kuala Belait, 112 km (70 mi) southwest of Bandar Seri Begawan, with the Malaysian town of Miri in Sarawak. It's slow going and involves two river crossings by ferry and two immigration-control stops. Shared taxis charge about B$30 for the ride. Brunei's **Sharikat Berlima Belait** runs daily buses on this route; the fare is B$16.

You can get to Brunei from Limbang in northern Sarawak via a riverboat that takes half an hour and costs about B$14. A ferry also runs between Bandar Seri Begawan and the island of Labuan in Sabah in two hours; fare is B$15.

Getting Around

By Car Two rental agencies have counters at the airport—**Avis** (tel. 02/242284) and **National** (tel. 02/224921).

By Taxi You can hire a private taxi for sightseeing, but drivers often speak little English. Hotels will arrange such service for B$45 an hour, often with a minimum of three hours.

By Bus Bus service in Bandar Seri Begawan is erratic. Buses leave only when full, so there may be a long wait. The central bus terminal is behind the Brunei Hotel on Jalan Pemancha—also where you catch the bus to Seria.

By Boat Water taxis—small, open boats—to the Kampung Ayer areas are available near the market off Jalan Sungai Kianggeh. Bargain with drivers for fares; a complete hour tour should cost between B$20 and B$25.

Guided Tours

Sunshine Borneo Tours & Travel (Box 2612, No. 205, 1st Floor, Bangunan Awang Mohd Yussuf Shopping Complex, 2682 Jln. Tutong, tel. 02/441790) organizes tours of the capital, as well as river trips and tours to Iban longhouses both in Brunei and across the border in Sarawak. The enthusiastic owner, Cany, will customize a tour to meet your interests.

Exploring Bandar Seri Begawan

Unlike most Asian cities, where imposing modern offices and hotels dominate the skyline, Brunei's capital city has a traditional look. Its buildings are appealing and well landscaped, but few are more than six stories tall. This low profile makes the mosque's stately minarets and huge golden dome—the first thing you see as you drive into Bandar Seri Begawan—all the more impressive. You can easily walk to the main attractions of this clean little city in a day: Most are near the mosque in the central district.

The **Sultan Omar Ali Saifuddin Mosque** may be the most beautiful in Southeast Asia. This superb example of modern Islamic architecture was built in 1959 of imported white marble, gold mosaic, and stained glass—all made possible by petrodollars. It's partly surrounded by a lagoon, where a religious stone boat called the **Mahaligal** floats year-round, as elegant and ornate as the mosque itself. *Cnr. Jln. Elizabeth II and Jln. Stoney. Open to the public Sat.–Wed. 8–noon and 1:30–4:30, Fri. 4:30–5:30.*

Across from the mosque on Jalan Elizabeth II, note the mosaic mural on the facade of the **Language and Literature Bureau,** depicting scenes from village life. Walk away from the mosque to Jalan Sultan, where a left turn will take you past the **Parliament House,** a gilted and tiled building now used mainly for ceremonial purposes, and a new mosque.

Backtrack on Jalan Sultan and turn left toward the river on Jalan Cator. Along the riverbank here is the town market, where women come daily to buy and sell fresh produce and other necessities. Merchandise is spread on mats on the ground, and everybody bargains. Walking along the riverfront, you'll come to Jalan Residency and the **Arts and Handicrafts Centre** (tel. 02/440676). The new, eight-story building, shaped like the scabbard of a kris, contains workshops for silversmithing, brassmaking, weaving, and basketware. The silver goods—including such oddities as miniature cannons and boats—are exquisitely made. Crafts are for sale in the showroom, but prices are steep. *Open Sat.–Thurs. 7:45–12:15 and 1:30–4:30.*

On the river near the Brunei Hotel, you can board a boat for a tour of the Kampong Ayer (*see* Getting Around by Boat, *above*). More than a third of the city's population lives in these river communities, in modern homes built on stilts in the water. Schools, clinics, and small mosques stand among the houses, which all sport TV antennae. Such artisans as boatbuilders, weavers, and brassworkers earn their living in these communities, but most residents commute by water taxi or private boat to work on terra firma. And while most women shop at the market across the river, you'll still see the older generation in paddleboats on the water selling food and household goods.

Two attractions lie short distances from the central district of Bandar Seri Begawan. The **sultan's palace** (called Istana Nurul Iman, or "Palace of Righteous Light") is about 3 km (2 mi) west on Jalan Tutong. Although the palace is officially closed to the public, impromptu tours are sometimes given if you ask, and there's a three-day open house during the Hari Raya Puasa festival in late spring. Built in the shape of a Borneo longhouse at a cost of US$500 million, this is the largest and most opulent home in the world. The sultan, his first wife, and their children actually inhabit the palace, which boasts 1,788 rooms and a throne room that seats 2,000. If you can't visit the interior, drive by just to glimpse the massive arched roofs, gold domes, and expanses of imported marble. Near the palace wall is a sculpture garden, a permanent ASEAN exhibit that features modern works from neighboring countries, all based on the theme "Harmony in Diversity."

Several other palaces have been newly constructed by members of the royal family, including one built by the sultan for his second wife. Be sure to ask your guide/driver to show you some of these magnificent buildings; they stand in rich contrast to the houses of Kampong Ayer.

About 6 km (4 mi) from town on the Kota Batu road is the **Brunei Museum,** set on 120 acres near the river. The brassware, silver, Chinese bronzes, ivory, and gold collections are magnificent. A natural history gallery displays stuffed animals and mounted insects; another exhibit showcases ancient ceramics, traditional tools and weapons, and other artifacts of Borneo life. The museum has an entire section, sponsored by Shell Petroleum, devoted to the local oil industry. Here, too, is the relocated **Churchill Memorial.** The late sultan, educated at Sandhurst in Britain, revered Winston Churchill and built this memorial to instill the statesman's values in the children of Brunei. The museum here houses the largest collection of Churchilliana outside Britain, including a series of hats symbolizing his many roles: soldier, patriot, scholar, and polo player. Other exhibits are memorabilia from the last days of Britain's Far Eastern empire, displays and videos commemorating Brunei's independence, and documents tracing the history of its constitution. A building nearby houses the **Museum of Malay Technology,** which emphasizes native ingenuity in coppersmithing, loom weaving, hunting, fishing, and extracting juice from sugarcane. This and the Churchill Memorial are the two most interesting museums in Bandar Seri Begawan. *Jln. Subok, tel. 02/444545. Admission free. Open Tues.–Sun. 9:30–5.*

Shopping

The showroom at the **Brunei Arts and Handicrafts Centre** (*see* Exploring Bandar Seri Begawan, *above*) has the best selection of local work, but its prices—especially for the finely worked silver—are high. Popular items include *karis* (ornamental daggers) and *kain songket,* a cloth containing gold or silver thread.

Gold jewelry (24 karat) is popular among Brunei's citizens, so goldsmiths offer a wide selection. Try **Chin Chin Goldsmith** (33 Jln. Sultan, tel. 02/222893) or **Million Goldsmith & Jewelry** (Mile 1, Teck Guan Plaza, Jln. Sultan, tel. 02/429546).

The **Plaza Abdul Razak** shopping complex on Jalan Tutong (tel. 41536) is anchored by the **Yaohan** department store. Less than a kilometer from city center, the high-rise structure includes office units, apartments, a music center, restaurants, and shops. Stores close at 9:30 PM. But the most fun place to browse is the **open market** alongside the Kianggeh River.

Sports and Fitness

The Sheraton Utama publishes a jogger's guide, which features a 20-minute run up to Tasek Park to see the waterfall, or a 35-minute hilly route through Kampong Kianggeh. Joggers are urged to run early in the morning to avoid the heat and traffic. Also at the Sheraton is a fitness center with aerobics classes.

Dining

Bandar Seri Begawan is not a great place for eating out, although it has a few noteworthy restaurants. Hotel coffee shops are popular with locals as well as visitors. Restaurants close at 10:30 PM. If you enjoy low-cost hawker food, visit the **open-air stalls** near the Edinburgh Bridge and along the river on Jalan Kianggeh, near Jalan Pemancha.

Deal's. The Sheraton's formal dining room offers the only respectable European fare beyond the coffee-shop variety. In a small, personable room with Regency-style decor, the German chef serves Dover sole, U.S. prime beef, and New Zealand lamb as well as local seafood. Recipes are simple but professionally executed. *Sheraton Utama, Jln. Tasek, tel. 02/444272. Reservations suggested. Dress: smart casual. AE, DC, MC, V. $$$*

Lucky Restaurant. In a shopping complex close to the Supreme Court, this second-floor restaurant is popular with local Chinese and expatriates. White tablecloths, lazy Susans, and bare, wood-paneled walls are the extent of the decor. The cuisine is Cantonese and, for Western tastes, uses too much corn starch, but offers an array of dishes. The best choices are those made with duck—very crisp yet succulent. *107–110 H.H. Princess Amal Shophouses, Jln. Tutong, tel. 02/220181. No reservations. Dress: casual. AE, DC, MC, V. $$*

Rasa Sayang. On the fifth floor of a Central Business District office/shopping complex, the Rasa Sayang has excellent dim sum at lunch time. The Malaysian waitresses are happy to help you select a variety of dishes, from steamed buns to barbecued ribs. For something more substantial, the fish dishes (particularly pomfret with onions and a soy-based sauce) are better than the beef. *Top floor, Bangunan Guru 2 Melayu, tel. 02/223600. No reservations. Dress: casual. AE, DC, V. $$*

Lodging

Because Brunei is ambivalent toward tourists, accommodations are not plentiful and advance reservations are advised. Apart from the Sheraton, most hotels are plain, but clean and comfortable. All listed here have a private bath, air-conditioning, and a TV in each room.

Sheraton Utama. Despite the opening of the **Riverview Inn** (tel. 02/221900) under the sponsorship of the Sultan's family, the Sheraton Utama in the Central Business District is, after its recent refurbishment, the smartest and most professionally managed hotel in Brunei. The light fabrics and furnishings help overcome the limited light from the small windows. Bathrooms have been retiled but are still functional rather than luxurious, though toiletries and bathrobes are supplied. Superior rooms, with two queen-size beds or a large king, are worth the extra B$20. Two- and three-room suites are available; rooms overlooking the pool have the best view. The hotel's Deal's restaurant is excellent for European cuisine. The more casual Café Melati serves a buffet breakfast, lunch, and dinner from 7 AM to 10:30 PM. On most evenings, there is a barbecue or fondue dinner served poolside. The bar is a friendly meeting place. *Box 2203, Jln. Tasek, 1922 BSB, tel. 02/244272, fax 02/221579. Reservations in the U.S., tel. 800/325–3535; in the U.K., tel. 0800/353535. 156 rooms, including 10 suites. Facilities: 2 restaurants and bar, business center, outdoor pool, gift shop, exercise area. AE, DC, MC, V. $$$$*

Ang's Hotel. Ang's offers modest air-conditioned rooms with queen-size beds, color televisions, and en suite bathrooms. At half the room rates of the Sheraton, this hotel does not have the smartness or professionalism or the amenities of its neighbor. The staff is polite but abrupt. The bar is a watering hole for expats under contract in Brunei. *Jln. Taser Lama, Box 49, 1900 BSB, tel. 02/243553, fax 02/227302. 80 rooms, including 3 suites. Facilities: coffee shop, dining room, bar, outdoor pool, beauty parlor. AE, DC, MC, V. $$$*

Brunei Hotel. In the heart of the Central Business District, this hotel has neat, clean, minimally furnished but pleasant rooms with oak trim. The Coffee Garden restaurant serves local and Western food (seafood is the best thing to order); there's usually a theme buffet in the evening. The VIP Room offers classic Cantonese fare. *Box 50, 95 Jln. Pemancha, 1900 BSB, tel. 02/242372, fax 02/226196. 75 rooms. Facilities: restaurant. AE, DC, V. $$$*

6 Philippines

By Luis H.
Francia

*Born and
raised in
Manila and
now a New
York resident,
Luis H.
Francia is a
poet and
playwright,
film
critic/curator,
and a
freelance
writer for
such
publications
as the* Village
Voice,
Asiaweek,
and
Cinemaya, *a
film quarterly
based in New
Delhi.*

Filipinos are often referred to as the "Latins of the East," and, indeed, this archipelago of 7,100 islands extending between Taiwan to the north and Borneo to the south sometimes seems like a misplaced Latin American country. While the dominant racial stock is Malay—akin to the indigenous populations of Indonesia, Borneo, and Malaysia—people's names are Hispanic and their faith Roman Catholic (the Philippines is the only Christian nation in Asia). To add to this cultural mix, English is widely spoken here, making the Philippines the fourth-largest English-speaking nation in the world after the United States, the United Kingdom, and India. Furthermore, the government is headed by a democratically elected president. These features reflect four centuries of Spanish and American colonization. As a celebrated Filipino writer put it, the Philippines spent more than 300 years in a convent and 50 in Hollywood.

Historically, this cultural potpourri began around the 9th to the 15th century, when the native Malays intermarried with Arab, Indian, and Chinese merchants who came to trade. Then, in 1521, Ferdinand Magellan, landing on the island of Mactan off the coast of Cebu, claimed the country for Spain. The intrepid Portuguese navigator was killed shortly thereafter by Lapu-Lapu, a native chieftain. Spanish rule was uneasy, periodically interrupted by regional revolts that culminated in 1896 in a nationwide revolution, the first of its kind in Asia. Nationalist aspirations were aborted, however, when the United States, after defeating Spain in the Spanish-American War, took over in 1898 but not without a bitter, five-year guerrilla war.

American rule lasted until July 4, 1946, when Manuel Roxas took over as the first postcolonial president. Since then, except during the dictatorial rule of Ferdinand Marcos from 1972 until 1986 (when he was ousted by the bloodless four-day "People Power" revolution), the government has been a democratically elected one, with a new constitution adopted in 1987 under President Corazon C. Aquino. Elections in 1992 to determine her successor resulted in Fidel V. Ramos winning the presidency.

Because of its colonial history and its people's innate warmth, the Philippines today is a country open to strangers and tolerant of cultural idiosyncrasies. Filipinos are a gregarious, fun-loving people whose hospitality is legendary. "No" is a word frowned upon; a Filipino will find countless ways to decline a request without sounding negative, smoothing over a potentially disruptive moment. Westerners should be aware that insistent straightforwardness is not necessarily prized and can be counterproductive.

Filipinos love to joke and tease and have a natural sense of the absurd. These qualities come in handy in a society full of paradoxes and contradictions, where Catholic values coexist with tropical hedonism; a freedom-loving people still contends with such feudal practices as private armies; and poverty persists amid sunshine and rich natural resources.

A nationwide Communist insurgency more than two decades old—with its roots in agrarian unrest and social injustice—has been compounded by a Muslim secessionist movement in southern Mindanao. And while there have been several coup attempts on the part of the military, you can rest easy; no Beirut-like scenarios exist here. Except for in some remote areas, the chances of being caught in a cross fire are virtually nil.

The Philippines, with three island groupings—Luzon (the largest), the Visayas, and Mindanao—has twice the coastline of the continental United States and offers diverse attractions. Luzon has cosmopolitan, historic Metro Manila—with its vibrant nightlife—the breathtaking mountain ranges to the north, and Spanish-era architecture and churches. The Visayas has some of the country's best beaches, charming cities, and music-loving inhabitants, while Mindanao has a number of minority tribes, a sizable Muslim population, and rare flora and fauna. All three regions have warm, translucent seas, inviting tropical beaches, highland treks, and unusual physical features. And the traveler will find in all three that dining well, especially on seafood, is an inexpensive treat.

The Philippines may not have world-class museums or a monumental ruin at every turn, but the outstanding beauty of the land, the many picturesque towns and villages, and the hospitality, music, and gaiety of its people more than compensate.

Staying in the Philippines

Getting Around

By Plane   **Philippine Air Lines (PAL)**, the nation's flag carrier, serves 42 cities and towns in the archipelago. **Manila Domestic Airport** is the country's biggest hub; next is Cebu City's **Mactan International Airport**, used mainly for domestic flights and chartered international flights from Tokyo, Australia, and Singapore. There are also direct flights from Taiwan to **Laoag International Airport** in northern Luzon.

PAL changes its flight schedule every quarter, though the changes don't usually affect major routes. It's always wise to confirm your flight at least two days in advance. The 24-hour PAL reservation line in Manila is 2/816–6691.

Smaller, privately owned charter companies, such as **Aerolift** (tel. 2/817–2369 or 2/818–4223) and **Pacific Air** (tel. 2/832–2731, 2/832–2732, or 2/833–2390), have regular flights to some cities and resorts, mainly in the south. Both offer light-aircraft and helicopter charters.

By Train   Only Luzon has a railway system, the **Philippine National Railways** (PNR, tel. 2/210–011 or 2/561–1125), a single-rail system that has seen better days. Lines run to San Fernando in Pampanga Province, north of Manila, and as far south as Iriga, Camarines Sur in the Bicol region. (There are plans to extend rail service farther north, to La Union, and farther south, to Legazpi City.) Fares are slightly lower than those for bus travel, but trips take longer.

By Bus   The Philippines has an excellent bus system, with 20 major bus lines covering the entire archipelago. Service between major destinations is frequent, often on an hourly basis. This is a cheap way to travel, and it's generally safe. It's possible to go island-hopping through a combination of buses and island ferries. These routes are usually limited to islands close together, though today one can travel from Manila in Luzon to Davao City in Mindanao, on the Philtranco line, in 44 hours.

Outside Manila, most bus terminals are adjacent to the public markets. In Manila, the most convenient terminals are along the Epifanio de los Santos Highway. Bus companies serving major routes have coaches with or without air-conditioning. The former offer films on videotape, but the quality is hideous. Some of the bigger bus lines are **Philtranco** (tel. 2/833–5061 to –5064), **BLTB** (tel. 2/

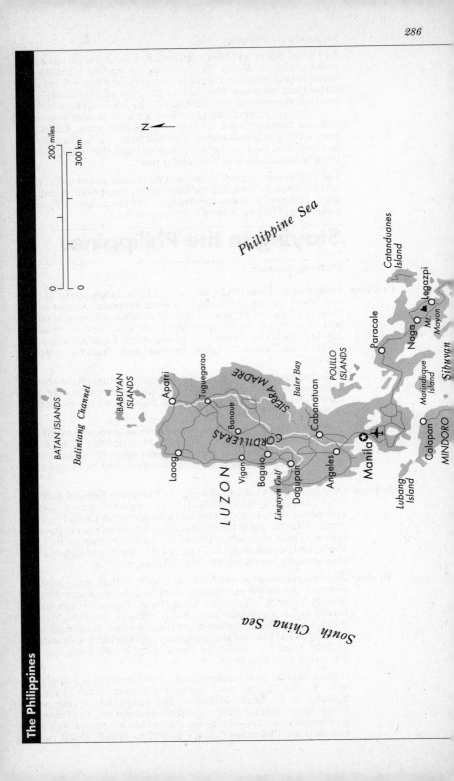

The Philippines

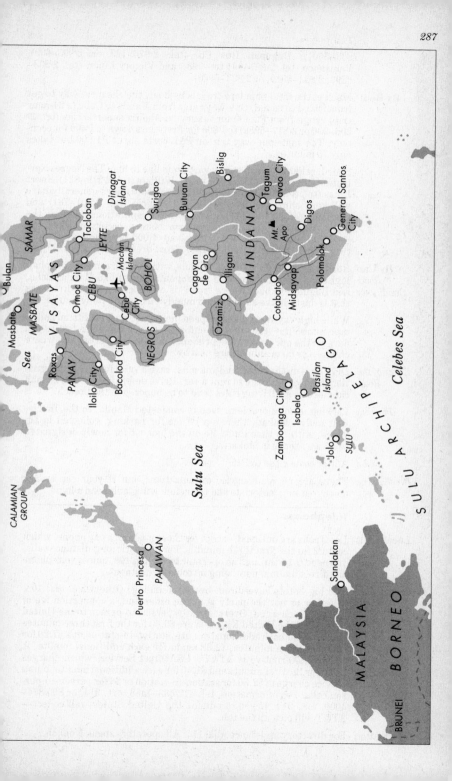

833–5501), **Dagupan Bus Co.** (tel. 2/976–123 or 2/995–639), **Pantranco** (tel. 2/997–091 to –098), and **Victory Liner,** (tel. 2/833–0293, 2/833–5019, or 2/833–5020).

By Boat Much of the local populace travels by boat, the cheapest way to get from island to island. One-way rates from Manila to Cebu (a 24-hour trip) range from P2,400 for luxury on **Aboitiz** superferries (tel. 2/206–990 or 2/817–5986) to P800 for first-class down to P400 for economy. The same one-way trip on PAL costs about P1,600 but takes only 70 minutes.

Speed, reliability, and safety vary from line to line: The **Negros Navigation** (tel. 2/816–3481 or 856–986), **William** (tel. 2/219–821), **Sweet Lines** (tel. 2/263–544), and **Aboitiz** (*see above*) lines generally have well-kept ships and good records. **Sulpicio** (tel. 2/201–781) and **Gothong** (tel. 2/213–611) lines have lesser reputations. Possibly the worst maritime disaster in modern history occurred when the Sulpicio Line's *Doña Paz,* with about 4,000 passengers on board (way above the limit), sank in 1987. Most drowned.

By Car Road conditions vary from excellent, with smooth cement or asphalt
Road highways (generally around metropolitan areas like Manila, Cebu,
Conditions and Baguio), to bad, where "road" is a euphemism for a dirt track that is dusty in the summer and muddy during the rainy season.

While highway signs display speed limits—60 mph maximum and 35 mph minimum—they are not enforced, so you can go as fast as you dare on the open road. Use prudence in populated areas and where children or farm animals are nearby.

Rules of the Driving is on the right, and you must have a valid foreign or interna-
Road tional driver's license to rent a car. Drive defensively—this is not a car culture, so driving rules tend to be honored in the breach.

Parking Parking is not a problem, even in congested Manila. In the Tourist Belt and in Makati, there's a P7 fee for parking, collected in advance, with no time limit. Be on the lookout for newly designated tow-away zones in Makati.

Gas A liter costs close to P15.

Breakdowns There are no road-service organizations, but if your car breaks down, passing motorists and townsfolk will gladly lend a hand.

Telephones

Local Calls Local calls are untimed, except for those made on a pay phone, which cost P2 for the first three minutes. For domestic long-distance calls, you need to go through an operator by dialing 109, unless your phone has direct dialing, now being introduced in stages.

International The big hotels have direct overseas dialing. Otherwise, dial 108.
Calls Whether or not the party is at the other end, a connection fee of about $1 is charged. Overseas rates person-to-person to the United States and the United Kingdom are $9.60 for the first three minutes and $2.32 for each additional minute; station-to-station, it's $7.20 for the first three minutes, $2.32 again for each additional minute. A cheaper alternative is AT&T's **USADirect Service,** which charges $3.25 for the first minute and $1.40 for each additional minute, plus a service charge of $2.50 for station-to-station or $6 for person-to-person calls. For information, tel. 412/553–7458, ext. 914, or 800/874–4000, ext. 314. If you're outside the United States, call collect—AT&T will pick up the tab.

Information For directory assistance, dial 114. All operators speak English.

Mail

Postal Rates To most Western countries, stamps are P8 for a letter and P5 for a postcard or an aerogram.

Receiving Mail Letters sent c/o Poste Restante at the General Post Office in Manila (Plaza Lawton, Manila, tel. 2/471–411) will be held for you. Otherwise, have your mail addressed to you c/o American Express, Ground Floor, PhilamLife Building, United Nations Avenue, Ermita, Manila.

Currency

The unit of currency is the peso, made up of 100 centavos. Bills come in denominations of P2, P10, P20, P50, P100, P500, and P1,000. Coins range from 5 centavos to P2. The exchange rate at press time was P27=$1; P40=£1.

What It Will Cost

The Philippines remains a bargain, with low inflation. Predictably, Metropolitan Manila is the most expensive destination. Other urban areas, such as Cebu City in the Visayas and Baguio in northern Luzon, are less expensive, and the surrounding provincial areas are cheapest of all.

Taxes The international airport departure tax is P500, while domestic airports charge P50. Hotels add a 10% service charge (as do most restaurants) and a government tax of 13.7%. Value Added Tax (VAT) is 10%.

Sample Prices Cup of instant coffee, 25¢; fresh-brewed native coffee, 35¢–50¢; bottle of beer, 50¢–80¢; Coca-Cola, 25¢; hamburger, $1.50–$2.50; 1-mile cab ride, $2; double room, $10–$15, budget; $16–$60, moderate; $61–$120, expensive; above $120, luxury.

Language

The Philippines is an English-speaking country, a legacy of its years as a U.S. colony. Communicating is rarely a problem, either in the cities or in the countryside. A second lingua franca is Pilipino, which is based on the regional language of Tagalog.

Opening and Closing Times

Banks are open 9–3; **supermarkets,** 9:30–7:30; **public markets,** dawn to dusk; **museums,** 9–noon and 1–5.

National Holidays

New Year's Day, Jan. 1; Holy Week, Maundy Thursday through Easter Sunday; Labor Day, May 1; Day of Valor, May 6; Independence Day, June 12; All Saints' Day, Nov. 1; Andres Bonifacio Day, Nov. 30; Christmas, Dec. 25; José Rizal Day, Dec. 30. Except for Holy Week, most shops remain open during holidays, though banks close. Museums close on holidays and Sunday.

Festivals and Seasonal Events

The most spectacular festivals are in honor of Jesus Christ, either as the Holy Infant (Santo Niño) or the martyred Son of God, and the Virgin Mary.

Jan.: Three orgiastic, dancing-in-the-streets carnivals take place this month: the **Ati-Atihan** (the third weekend of the month, in Kalibo, Aklan), the **Sinulog** (the third weekend in January, in Cebu City), and the **Dinagyang** (the last weekend in January, in Iloilo City). In all three, the Holy Infant is the object of veneration. Kalibo's Ati-Atihan, the oldest and most popular, is also the noisiest, as competing town bands thump enthusiastically night and day. All three cities get crammed to the gills, and plane, ship, and room reservations must be made two or three months in advance. In contrast, on January 9, the **Black Nazarene** procession of the Quiapo district in Manila is a more somber but equally intense show of devotion, as the faithful compete to pull the carriage holding a statue of Christ that is believed to be miraculous.

Late Mar.–early Apr.: Christ's final sufferings are remembered during the last week of Lent, Holy Week. In the provincial towns of Bulacan and Pampanga, in central Luzon, masked and bleeding flagellants atoning for their sins are a common sight in the streets. Small groups of old women and children gather at makeshift altars and chant verses describing Christ's passion. The **Turumba** in Pakil, Laguna (held the second Tuesday and Wednesday after Holy Week) honors Our Lady of Sorrows. Devotees dance through the streets trying to make her smile.

Mar.–June: With the **Hari Raya Puasa,** the date of which varies according to the lunar calendar, Muslims celebrate the end of the month-long period of fasting and abstention known as Ramadan.

May: All over the country, the **Santacruz de Mayo** commemorates St. Helen's discovery of the Holy Cross in 1324. The celebrations include colorful processions, complete with floats of each town's patron saint, beautifully gowned young women acting as May queens, and local swains dressed in their Sunday best. One of the more unusual feasts is in Lucban, Quezon Province, where multicolored rice wafers, called *kiping*, are shaped into window ornaments, usually in the form of fruits and vegetables.

Sept.: The **Peñafrancia** (third weekend in September) is the biggest festival in the Bicol region, drawing as many as 10,000 spectators to Naga City in southern Luzon. A procession of floats on the river honors the Virgin of Peñafrancia.

Dec.: 'Tis the season for carolers, midnight masses, and such feasts as the **Maytinis** festival of the town of Kawit, Cavite—a 90-minute drive from Manila. Christmas Eve is celebrated with 13 colorful gigantic floats. Be there by 6 PM to get a good view.

Tipping

Tipping is now an accepted practice, and 10% is considered standard for waiters, bellboys, and other hotel and restaurant personnel; many restaurants and hotels tack on a 10% service charge. When there is a service charge, tipping becomes optional, but it is customary to leave loose change. At Ninoy Aquino International Airport, arrivals pay P30 per cart, and **porters** expect P10 for each piece of luggage (in addition to P10 per piece paid to the porter office). **Hotel doormen** and **bellboys** should get about the same. For **taxi drivers,** P5 is fine for the average 1½-mile ride.

Shopping

The Philippines can yield great bargains if you know what to look for and where. There are handicraft stores all over the country, usually near the public market in small- to medium-size cities and towns and in shopping centers in such large urban areas as Manila, Cebu, and Baguio. Because Manila is the commercial capital of the country, regional goods are available there, though prices are not usually advantageous. Focus on handicrafts special to the region you're visiting. For example, look for handwoven rattan baskets and backpacks from northern Luzon; handwoven cloth from northern Luzon, Iloilo City, and southern Mindanao; shellcraft from Cebu City and Zamboanga City; handwoven pandan mats with geometric designs from Zamboanga City and Davao City; brassware from southern Mindanao; bamboo furniture from central Luzon; gold and silver jewelry from Baguio City and Bulacan province; and cigars from Baguio City and the Ilocos region.

Bargaining is an accepted and potentially profitable way of shopping in public markets, flea markets, and small, owner-run stores. Department stores and big shopping areas have fixed prices.

Tax In addition to a 4% sales tax, a value added tax (VAT) of 10% is charged by all businesses.

Sports and Beaches

Beaches and Water Sports The Philippines has an abundance of beaches, from pebble-strewn coastlines and black volcanic stretches to brilliant white expanses. The advantage of being on a tropical archipelago (remember, 7,100 islands!) is that you're never far from the sea.

The tropical waters are ideal for a variety of water sports, from snorkeling to waterskiing. A number of resorts in different regions offer equipment and facilities. Some of the loveliest beaches are in the Visayas region, such as Boracay, Panay, Bohol, and Cebu. Palawan is possibly the least developed island and the wildest in terms of flora and fauna.

Diving The country has some of the best dive sites in the world, with more than 40 known spots, most concentrated around Palawan, the Visayas, and Batangas Province. Many more wait to be discovered. Most resorts rent out snorkeling equipment; the tonier ones have scuba gear as well. Philippine Air Lines allows divers an extra 30 kilograms free of charge on domestic flights and will issue a permit card good for one year. For more information, contact the Philippine Commission on Sports Scuba Diving (tel. 2/585–857 or 2/503–627).

Golf There are 26 golf courses in the country, 13 in Luzon alone.

Mountain Climbing/Trekking The Cordilleras, Mt. Mayon in southern Luzon, Mt. Hibok-Hibok on Camiguin Island, and Mt. Apo in Mindanao are all good sites for mountain climbing and trekking. For more information, call the Department of Tourism (tel. 2/501–703) or PAL Mountaineering Club (tel. 2/586–712).

Surfing Surfers have discovered the Philippines, though there are still only a handful of surf centers. Most are on the island of Catanduanes off southern Luzon, on the Pacific coast. Call the Philippine Commission on Sports Scuba Diving (tel. 2/503–627) or the Department of Tourism (tel. 2/501–703).

Dining

For a discussion of Philippine cooking in general, *see* the introduction to Manila's Dining section, *below*. Also, as prices vary widely from area to area, *see* the Dining sections of cities and regions, *below*, for price charts.

Lodging

Manila and the larger cities offer accommodations ranging from luxury hotels to spartan lodgings. The major establishments routinely add a 10% service charge. All add a government tax of 13.7%.

During the peak season, from October through April, prices quoted are prices charged. In the off-season, however, some of the higher-priced hotels in the big cities offer discounts ranging from 30% to 50%. In other regions, prices are firm—and low.

As prices vary widely from location to location, *see* the Lodging section of cities and regions, *below*, for price charts.

Metro Manila

The urban sprawl that is Metropolitan Manila (made up of the cities of Manila, Makati, Pasay, Quezon, Caloocan, plus 13 towns) is a fascinating, even surreal combination of modernity and tradition. In Manila's streets you'll see horse-drawn *calesas*, or carriages, alongside sleek Mercedes-Benzes, Japanese sedans, passenger buses, and the ubiquitous passenger jeepneys—usually converted World War II jeeps.

It is also a city of stark contradictions and a microcosm of Philippine society. At the upper end of the scale is Makati, the country's financial center, with its wide, well-kept boulevards, high-rise apartment and office buildings, ultramodern shopping centers, and the well-guarded walled enclaves of the often fabulously rich. In contrast to the Makati mansions—the aesthetics of which range from the sublime to the ridiculous—is the large slum of Tondo, dominated by a huge pile of garbage known as "Smoky Mountain" for the endless burning of trash fires. Here the poor live in cardboard shanties and scavenge for a living.

For all that, the "noble and ever loyal city"—as Manila was described by its Spanish overlords—and its 10 million inhabitants have a joie de vivre that transcends their day-to-day battles for survival. The fortuitous blend of Latin and Southeast Asian temperaments makes for an easygoing atmosphere, where fun is as important as business. Manilans bear their burdens with humor and a casual grace. If, like New Yorkers, they love to complain about their considerable hardships, it doesn't prevent them from crowding the city's myriad restaurants, bars, and clubs. The nightlife here may well be Asia's liveliest. Manila has discotheques, coffeehouses, nightclubs, massage parlors, topless bars, music lounges, and beer gardens. Certainly its bands—rock, Latin, or jazz—have the reputation for being the finest in Southeast Asia.

The city was built by the Spanish conquistadors in 1571 as Intramuros, a fortified settlement on the ashes of a Malay town. Manila spread outward over the centuries, so that the oldest districts are those closest to Intramuros. Yet very few buildings attest to the city's antiquity, since it suffered extensive destruction during World War II. Among the older districts are Ermita and Malate.

Fronting Manila Bay, they make up the so-called Tourist Belt because of their central location and the density of hotels, clubs, restaurants, boutiques, and coffee shops.

Like most other Third World cities, Metro Manila has its share of congestion, pollution, haphazard planning, and poverty. But its flamboyance and spontaneity can be insanely marvelous.

Important Addresses and Numbers

Tourist Information
The **Department of Tourism** has a Tourist Information Center on the ground floor of its main offices at the Tourism Building (Agrifina Circle, Rizal Park, Manila, tel. 2/599–031, ext. 146, or 2/501–728). Other counters: mezzanine and arrival mall at Ninoy Aquino International Airport (NAIA; tel. 2/832–2964); Manila Domestic Airport (tel. 2/832–3566); Nayong Pilipino Reception Unit at the Nayong Pilipino Complex (tel. 2/832–3767 or 2/832–3768), Airport Road, NAIA. The Tourist Security Division (tel. 2/501–728 or 2/501–660, 24 hours) can assist in cases of theft, missing luggage, or other untoward incidents.

Embassies
Australia (16th Floor, Bank of the Philippine Islands, cnr. Ayala Ave. and Paseo de Roxas, Makati, tel. 2/817–7911). **Canada** (9th Floor, Allied Bank Center, 6754 Ayala Ave., Makati, tel. 2/815–9536 to –9541). **United Kingdom** (Electra House, 115–117 Esteban St., Makati, tel. 2/853–002 to –009). **United States** (1201 Roxas Blvd., Manila, tel. 2/521–7116).

Emergencies
The **Metropolitan Police Command** now has one line for all emergencies: tel. 166.

Emergency Rooms
Makati Medical Center (2 Amorsolo St., cnr. De La Rosa, near Ayala Ave., tel. 2/815–9911 to –9944). **Manila Doctors' Hospital** (667 United Nations Ave., Ermita, near the UN stop on the LRT, tel. 2/503–011).

Dental Clinics
Call **Philippine Dental Association** (tel. 2/818–6144) for referrals.

Medical Clinics
Call the **Philippine Medical Association** (tel. 2/974–974 or 2/992–132) for referrals.

Late-Night Pharmacies
Mercury Drug Store, a citywide chain, has 24-hour branches in Cubao, Quezon City (tel. 2/781–746); Quiapo, Plaza Miranda (tel. 2/401–617); and Guadalupe Commercial Center, Makati, (tel. 2/864–327). **College Pharmacy** (1458 Taft Ave., tel. 2/593–683) is also open 24 hours.

English-Language Bookstores
National Book Store is a popular chain. In the Tourist Belt, try the branch at Harrison Plaza (cnr. M. Adriatico and Vito Cruz Sts., tel. 2/572–179); in Makati, try the Quad Arcade at the Makati Commercial Center (tel. 2/865–766 or 2/865–771). **Solidaridad** (531 Padre Faura, Ermita, tel. 2/591–241) is frequented by Manila's literati and offers political, literary, and popular titles.

Travel Agencies
In addition to **American Express** (Ground Floor, PhilamLife Bldg., United Nations Ave., tel. 2/506–480 or 2/521–9492) and **Thomas Cook** (Ayala Ave., Makati, tel. 2/816–3701 or 2/818–5891), you might try **Baron Travel Corp.** (Pacific Bank Bldg., Ayala Ave., Makati, tel. 2/817–4926) and **Manila Sightseeing Tours** (500 United Nations Ave., tel. 2/521–7093 or 2/521–2060).

Arriving and Departing by Plane

Airports and Airlines Metropolitan Manila is served by the **Manila Domestic Airport** (tel. 2/832–0991 or 2/832–0932), cheek-by-jowl with **Ninoy Aquino International Airport** (tel. 2/832–3011 or 2/832–1901). In light traffic, it's a 30-minute ride to Makati's hotels; getting to the Tourist Belt takes close to an hour. The domestic airport is used almost exclusively by PAL.

Between the Airport and Downtown

Manila Domestic Airport This is essentially a one-building affair, with cabs lined up on the driveway. Though metered, they are available on a pre-agreed basis for P100–P300, depending on your destination. But a scant 15 meters away is the busy Domestic Airport Road, where you can hail a passing cab and pay lower, metered rates.

Ninoy Aquino International Airport The major hotels provide shuttles to and from the international airport, so look around for one before using another means of transport.

By Taxi Normally a metered cab ride to Makati should cost no more than P50, and to the Tourist Belt in Manila, P75. But airport taxi drivers charge a higher, agreed-upon price. **Avis** (tel. 2/833–7897) has a taxi-coupon service, with rates averaging P300. It's best to go to the departure area on the third level and flag a taxi that has just brought departing passengers.

By Limousine Limousine service is available for $40–$50. Check at the arrivals hall.

By Car **Hertz, Avis,** and **National** have booths in the arrival area.

By Bus To the right of the airport building at the end of the driveway are stops for public buses, such as the **Love Buses** (tel. 2/951–203), that pass by the Tourist Belt via Makati. Public buses leave every 15 minutes. Though inexpensive, they're not recommended if you have a lot of luggage, and they make many stops.

Arriving and Departing by Car, Train, and Bus

By Car The best routes for leaving or entering the city are the Epifanio de los Santos Highway (EDSA), the South Expressway, and the EDSA-North Diversion link. EDSA is the main artery connecting Pasay, Makati, Mandaluyong, Quezon, and Caloocan. The North Diversion begins in Caloocan, at a junction of EDSA, and leads to points north. The South Expressway originates in Manila, passes through Makati with EDSA as a junction, and leads to points south.

By Train The main terminal, **Tutuban Station** (tel. 2/210–011), is in the Tondo district of Manila. Two other stations are in the Paco and Makati districts. Commuter trains operate on a north–south axis during rush hours, from Paco, in Manila, to Alabang, a southern suburb. Minimum commuter fare is P1.50.

By Bus There are about 20 major bus companies in the Philippines and almost as many terminals in Manila. Those closest to downtown Manila and Makati can be found at Plaza Lawton (now called Liwasang Bonifacio, but bus signboards still use "Lawton") and along a portion of EDSA in Pasay City, not far from Taft Avenue. Another important terminal is farther north on EDSA, on the corner of New York Street, in the district of Cubao, Quezon City.

American Express offers Travelers Cheques built for two.

Cheques *for Two*℠ from American Express are the Travelers Cheques that allow either of you to use them because both of you have signed them. And only one of you needs to be present to purchase them.

Cheques *for Two* are accepted anywhere regular American Express Travelers Cheques are, which is just about everywhere. So stop by your bank, AAA* or any American Express Travel Service Office and ask for Cheques *for Two*.

So, you're getting away from it all.

Just make sure you can get back.

AT&T Access Numbers
Dial the number of the country you're in to reach AT&T.

AMERICAN SAMOA	633-2-USA	**INDONESIA♦**	**001-801-10**	*PHILIPPINES		**105-11**
AUSTRALIA	**1800-881-011**	*JAPAN	0039-111	**SAIPAN†**		**235-2872**
CHINA, PRC♦♦	**10811**	**KOREA**	**009-11**	SINGAPORE		800-0111-111
COOK ISLANDS	09-111	**KOREA◊◊**	**11 ✱**	SRI LANKA		430-430
GUAM	**018-872**	MACAO	0800-111	*TAIWAN		**0080-10288-0**
HONG KONG	**800-1111**	*MALAYSIA	800-0011	THAILAND♦		0019-991-1111
INDIA♦	**000-117**	NEW ZEALAND	000-911			

Countries in bold face permit country-to-country calling in addition to calls to the U.S. **World Connect℠** prices consist of **USADirect®** rates plus an additional charge based on the country you are calling. Collect calling available to the U.S. only. *Public phones require deposit of coin or phone card. ♦Not available from public phones. ♦♦Not yet available for all areas. ◊◊From public phones only, push the red button, wait for dial tone and then dial. †May not be available from every phone. ©1994 AT&T.

Here's a travel tip that will make it easy to call back to the States. Dial the access number for the country you're visiting and connect right to AT&T. It's the quick way to get English-speaking AT&T operators and can minimize hotel telephone surcharges.

If all the countries you're visiting aren't listed above, call **1 800 241-5555** for a free wallet card with all AT&T access numbers. Easy international calling from AT&T. **TrueWorld Connections.**

AT&T

Some companies: **Philtranco** (EDSA and Apelo Cruz St., Pasay City, tel. 2/833–5061 to –5064); **Victory Liner** (EDSA, Pasay City, tel. 2/833–0293, 2/833–5019, or 2/833–5020); **BLTB** (EDSA, Pasay City, and at Plaza Lawton, tel. 2/833–5501); **Pantranco** (325 Quezon Blvd. Ext., Quezon City, tel. 2/997–091 to 098); and **Dangwa** (1600 Dimasalang, Sampaloc, tel. 2/731–2859). The only way to get tickets is to go to the terminal; you can purchase tickets in advance.

Getting Around

Manila isn't a city for walking, though you can do so within certain areas, particularly in the Tourist Belt and in some parts of Makati. Sidewalks are generally narrow, uneven, and sometimes nonexistent. Instead, choose from a vast array of transportation, public and private, from horse-drawn carriages to elevated trains.

By Car Between the frustration and the smoke emissions, traffic jams in Manila can reduce drivers to tears. If you don't have to drive within the city, don't. Public transportation is plentiful and cheap.

If you do drive, improvisation—such as sudden lane changing—is the rule rather than the exception. Many of the nonarterial roads are narrow and become clogged during morning (7:30–10) and afternoon (3:30–7:30) rush hours. On the other hand, a car gives you flexibility, parking isn't a problem, and you don't have to deal with cabs, the meters of which may run faster than a speeding bullet. Some car-rental agencies: **Avis** (tel. 2/741–0394 or 2/878–497), **Car Express** (tel. 2/876–717), **Dollar** (tel. 2/883–134 or 2/883–138), **Hertz** (tel. 2/832–5325, 2/868–685, or 2/831–9827), **National** (tel. 2/818–8667 or 2/833–0648).

By Elevated Railway The **Light Rail Transit** (LRT, tel. 2/832–0423) is an elevated, modern railway, with 16 stops on a north–south axis. It's the fastest, cleanest, and safest mode of transport in the city. The southern terminal is at Baclaran in Pasay City, the northern at Monumento in Caloocan City. Most stops are in Manila. Hours of operation are from 4 AM to 9 PM. Fare between any two stations is P6.50. Each station displays a guide to the routes.

By Bus and Jeepney Public bus and jeepney routes crisscross Metropolitan Manila and, for areas not served by the LRT, are the cheapest form of travel. The average fare ranges from 10¢ to 25¢. An excellent means of transport is the **Love Bus** (tel. 2/951–203), a fleet of air-conditioned coaches that make fewer stops than the regular, non-air-conditioned ones. Fares average P15. Buses make sense for longer trips, while jeepneys are best for short ones. For example, a bus is recommended to reach Quezon City from Ermita, but within Ermita, or from one district to the next, take a jeepney. The latter can accommodate 12 to 15 passengers and is perhaps the city's most colorful form of public transport, gaudily decorated and with the driver's favorite English slogan emblazoned in front.

By Taxi Taxis are not as cheap as other means of public transport but they're still cheap; a metered 2-mile cab ride should cost about P75, plus tip. However, while rates are theoretically standard, a number of cab companies tolerate their drivers' tampering with the meters. **R & E** (tel. 2/341–464) has a reputation for reliability and honesty. If you feel the fare registered is exorbitant, say so politely. Often the driver will allow you to pay less than what's shown.

Try to take a taxi from the better hotels, where cabs are always waiting and hotel doormen note down the taxi number, which is useful in case of problems.

By Limousine	The major hotels have limousine service and use mostly Mercedes-Benzes. Also try **Filipino Transport** (tel. 2/581–493), which charges P1,600 for eight hours and P180 per additional hour. Outside Manila, rates vary. For instance, Manila to Baguio overnight costs P5,000, and P2,000 per additional day. At least 24-hour notice is required.
By Caretela or Calesa	Good for short hops within a neighborhood are the horse-drawn carriages called *caretelas* (the larger size) and *calesas*. They are available mostly in the older neighborhoods, such as Chinatown, and are very inexpensive (about P5–P10 a ride).
By Pedicab	These motorcycles with attached cabs are found everywhere and are also good for inexpensive (P5) short hops.

Guided Tours

Orientation	The average city tour takes four hours and can be arranged by any of the travel agencies listed above.
Boat	**Sun Cruises** (tel. 2/522–3636 or 2/522–3613) offers daily cruises to Corregidor—the famous World War II battle site and island fortress at the mouth of Manila Bay. Cruise boats leave weekdays at 9 AM, weekends at 8 AM and 11 AM, from a dock right by the Cultural Center of the Philippines.
Personal Guides	English-, Spanish-, Japanese-, French-, Italian-, German-, Indonesian-, and even Hebrew-speaking guides are available. The Department of Tourism will provide a list. Guides charge P350 for the standard city tour. Guides for day tours to nearby Tagaytay and Pagsanjan charge P650 and P850 (with lunch) respectively.

Highlights for First-time Visitors

Bamboo Organ (*see* Short Excursions from Manila)

Coconut Palace (*see* Tour 2)

Intramuros (*see* Tour 1)

Malacañang Palace (*see* Tour 1)

Pagsanjan Falls (*see* Short Excursions from Manila)

Quiapo Church (*see* Tour 2)

Rizal Park (*see* Tour 1)

Villa Escudero/Hidden Valley (*see* Short Excursions from Manila)

Exploring Manila

Metropolitan Manila is roughly crescent-shape, with Manila Bay and the scenic Roxas Boulevard, which runs along it, forming the western boundary. Forming the eastern border is the Epifanio de los Santos Highway (EDSA). The Pasig River bisects the city into north and south, with the oldest districts, including the ancient walled city of Intramuros, near where the river empties into Manila Bay.

By using Roxas Boulevard and Taft Avenue as the western and eastern limits, respectively, and Intramuros and Vito Cruz Street as the north and south parameters, a visitor should get a pretty good idea of Ermita and Malate, or the Tourist Belt. On the boulevard are nightclubs, the Cultural Center of the Philippines complex, hotels, restaurants, apartment buildings, the huge Rizal Park, and Intramuros. On Taft Avenue are the Light Rail Transit, universities, shops, retail stores, and several hospitals. In between are bars and cocktail lounges, the infamous go-go joints (especially on M.H. Del Pilar and A. Mabini streets), massage parlors, coffeehouses, more restaurants and hotels, office buildings, boutiques, and shopping malls.

Numbers in the margin correspond to points of interest on the Manila and Intramuros maps.

Tour 1: Historic Manila

❶ We begin at **Malacañang Palace,** former seat of the Spanish governor-generals and the colonial American administrators. Today it is the official residence of Philippine presidents—the Philippine White House—though Corazon Aquino preferred to live in the guest house, a symbolic gesture meant to disassociate her from the dictatorial Ferdinand Marcos. Now open to the public, Malacañang's colonial Spanish architecture and interior decor are worth seeing, especially the three chandeliers in the reception hall, the beautiful hardwoods used for the grand staircase, the portraits of former presidents, and the exquisite music room. The Marcoses' personal effects, which included Ferdinand's dialysis machine and Imelda's infamous hoard of shoes and bulletproof bra, have been replaced by selected memorabilia of past presidents. *J.P. Laurel St., tel. 2/407–775. Admission charge. Open Tues.–Thurs., guided tours only, 9–3:30; Fri.–Sat., general viewing, 9–3.*

❷ A half-hour drive from Malacañang Palace, on the other side of the Pasig River, is **Paco Park.** At the intersection of San Marcelino and General Luna streets, this petite but beautiful circular park of moss-covered stone—with a picturesque chapel in the middle—was a cemetery until it was declared a national park in 1966. Its two concentric walls served as burial niches for the Spanish elite. No burials have been performed here since 1912. Free concerts are offered on Friday at 6 PM. *Tel. 2/502–011 or 2/590–956. Admission charge. Open daily 8–5.*

❸ West of Paco Park and 30 minutes away by foot is the 128-acre **Rizal Park,** named after the national hero José Rizal. He was, among other things, a doctor, linguist, botanist, novelist, poet, educator, and fencer. Executed by the Spanish in 1896 because of his reformist views, he was originally buried at Paco Park but now lies under the Rizal Monument, designed by Swiss artist Richard Kissling and erected in 1912. Rising above the statue is a stately 50-foot obelisk. The 24-hour guards, like honor guards everywhere, try to be as impassive as possible. A nearby marble slab set into an octagonal wall is inscribed with Rizal's poem *Mi Ultimo Adios*, composed just before his death, in the original Spanish and in several other languages including English. Nearby is the Chinese Garden (admission charge), a pleasant enclosure.

❹ A short stroll from the monument is the doyen of Philippine hotels, the **Manila Hotel** (Rizal Park, tel. 2/470–011), built in 1912. This is where General Douglas MacArthur lived during much of the American colonial era (Ernest Hemingway also stayed here once). The lobby is spacious without making you feel lost, and gracious in that Old World style. Note the ceiling and woodwork, made entirely of precious Philippine hardwoods, the floors of Philippine marble, and the mother-of-pearl and brass chandeliers.

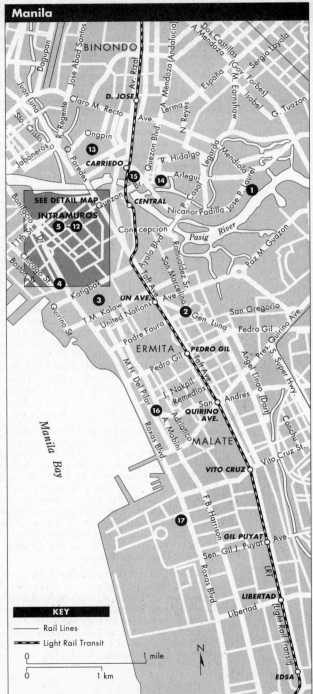

Time Out The hotel has an airy, pleasant poolside coffee shop, **Café Ylang-Ylang** (tel. 2/470–011). The menu is quite good, offering native and Continental cuisine and sumptuous desserts.

❺ Across from the hotel is **Intramuros,** Manila's ancient walled city. Built by the Spaniards in the 16th century on the site of a former Malay settlement, Intramuros is a compact 7.5 sq km (3 sq mi). Within were churches, schools, convents, offices, and residences. In its heyday it must have been a magnificent sight to visiting galleons. The walls are still formidable, 9 m (30 ft) thick, with cannon emplacements and a strategic location facing the bay. It had seven drawbridges and an encircling moat, filled in by the Americans and now used as a golf course.

Exploring Intramuros on foot should take about three hours, or you can rent a caretela for about P300, which can carry several persons.
❻ You can hire one from within **Fort Santiago,** a stone fort off Aduana Street, previously used by the Spanish, Americans, and Japanese
❼ and now a pleasant park. Other key points are **Plaza Roma,** where
❽ bullfights were once staged, and the Romanesque **Manila Cathedral** (a reconstruction of the original 1600 structure). Three arched door-ways form an imposing facade: The middle one is made of bronze, with eight panels portraying the cathedral's history. Inside, the clerestory's stained-glass windows depict the history of Christianity in the Philippines. Underneath the main altar is a crypt where the remains of the former archbishops are entombed. On General Luna
❾ Street is **San Agustin Church,** the second-oldest stone church in the country, with 14 side chapels and a trompe l'oeil ceiling. Up in the choir loft, note the hand-carved 17th-century seats of molave, a beautiful tropical hardwood. Adjacent to the church is a small museum run by the Augustinian Order, featuring antique religious vestments and religious paintings and icons.

❿ The **Barrio San Luis Complex** is made up of several shops and the splendid **Casa Manila,** a re-creation of a 19th-century Spanish patrician's three-story domicile, complete with carriage entrance, inner courtyard, and grand stairway.

⓫ Be sure to explore the walls and the fortified gates—the **Puerta Isabel,** the chambers of which house a display of baroque floats bearing
⓬ statues of saints, and the **Puerta Real** are fine examples. Gray, stately, and defiant, the walls give you a feeling of invincibility. *Tel. for Intramuros: 2/487–325 or 2/461–195. Admission free to Puerto Isabel. Casa Manila, tel. 2/496–793 or 2/483–275. Admission: P15, P10 students. Open daily 9–6.*

Tour 2: Colorful Neighborhoods and a Palace

Forbidden by the Spanish from living in Intramuros, Chinese merchants and their families settled north of the Pasig River, and a siza-
⓭ ble community—now known as **Binondo,** Manila's Chinatown—grew up here in the 18th century. Bounded by the river, Claro M. Recto Avenue, Del Pan Street, and Avenida Rizal, the district is a jumble of narrow streets packed with jewelry shops, sporting-goods and clothing stores, apothecaries, kung fu schools, movie houses showing Hong Kong flicks, magazine stalls, seedy hotels, brothels, and restaurants that usually offer Amoy and Fukienese cuisine. Simply stroll about, especially on Ongpin, the main street, or stop a calesa and have the driver take you around. The 16th-century **Binondo Church** (at the Plaza Calderon de la Barca, on Paredes Street), still with its original stone walls, is worth visiting. Note the

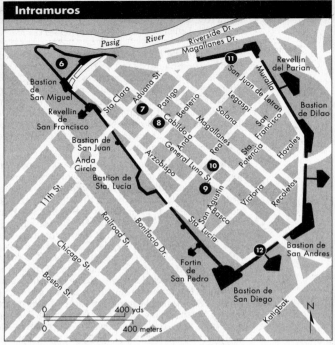

Intramuros

replica of St. Peter's dome at the main altar and the Madonna encased in glass. The first Filipino saint, Lorenzo Ruiz, started here as an altar boy.

East of Binondo, not far from the foot of Quezon Bridge and fronted by Plaza Miranda, is **Quiapo Church.** The church (built in the 16th century and later enlarged) and its crowded environs are as close to an authentic Philippine neighborhood as you can get in Manila. On the side streets are vendors from whom you can buy amulets or herbal cures for a wide variety of ailments. The church is home to the famed **Black Nazarene,** a dark statue of Jesus of Nazareth made by a Mexican craftsman and brought from Mexico in the 18th century. Its devotees claim that praying to the statue can produce miracles. It isn't unusual to see supplicants crawling on their knees from the entrance to the altar.

In Plaza Miranda, orators of varying skills and persuasions harangue passersby. Toward Quezon Bridge and the river is the **Quiapo Public Market.** Here, especially in the sections below Quezon Bridge, one can find handicrafts, from handwoven mats to rattan baskets and straw brooms, at bargain prices. Be mindful of your wallet or bag, because this is a crowded section and a favorite of pickpockets. Be especially wary of persons wanting to buy your dollars.

Moving south across the river into the **Malate** district, you'll come to **Malate Church,** on the corner of Remedios and M.H. Del Pilar streets. The gray stone church is an intriguing mixture of Romanesque and Baroque styles. Photographers love to shoot its picturesque, well-kept facade. Its interior, however, is unremarkable.

Between the church and Roxas Boulevard is **Rajah Sulayman Park,** the centerpiece of which is a statue of Rajah Sulayman, a pre-Spanish (16th-century) ruler of Manila.

Time Out Around Malate Church are innumerable places for lunch. You can walk eastward on Remedios Street—i.e., away from the bay—and choose from several cafés around Remedios Circle. **Cafe Adriatico** (1790 Adriatico St., tel. 2/584–059) serves good hamburgers and Continental or Philippine entrées. **Penguin Cafe** (Remedios St., cnr. Bocobo St., tel. 2/521–2088) has a nice outdoor patio and serves homemade pasta, salads, and Viennese-style desserts. The 24-hour **Aristocrat** (Roxas Blvd., cnr. San Andres St., tel. 2/507–671) is a popular choice with everyone from gangsters to businesspeople; prices are reasonable and the food is decent.

17 A 10-minute drive from the church south on Roxas Boulevard is a $10 million project of former first lady Imelda Marcos, the **Coconut Palace,** so named because more than 70% of the construction materials were derived from the coconut tree. This grandiose structure, located within the Cultural Center Complex, faces Manila Bay and was constructed for Pope John Paul's visit in 1981 (he refused to stay there). Each of the seven (the Marcoses' lucky number) palatial suites is named and styled after a different region of the country. The Ilocos Room, for instance, has chairs with mother-of-pearl inlay and a coffee table laminated with tobacco leaves, while the Zamboanga Room features brassware and handwoven mats. Many of the bathroom fixtures are 24-karat gold. Several of Imelda's jet-set friends stayed here at one time or another, among them Van Cliburn, Cristina Ford, and Brooke Shields. *Cultural Center Complex, tel. 2/832–0223. Admission charge. Open Tues.–Sun. 9–11:30 and 1–4:30.*

Short Excursions from Manila

Tagaytay Ridge and the Bamboo Organ A 60-km (37-mi) drive that begins on the South Expressway and takes you along tree- and flower-lined roads, with rice fields on either side, brings you to Tagaytay Ridge, 750 m (2,500 ft) above sea level. Here you can view what may be the world's smallest volcano, Taal Volcano, actually a volcano within a volcano. With cool temperatures and scenic vistas, Tagaytay provides welcome relief from Manila's heat and congestion. On the way you can detour to Las Piñas to view the world's only bamboo organ, housed in the 18th-century San José Church. The organ, built in 1795, has 121 metal pipes, 832 bamboo pipes, 22 registers, and a five-octave manual. Not far from the church is the Sarao Motor Works, largest manufacturer of the ubiquitous and gaudy jeepney.

Getting There To get to San José Church, go south on Roxas Boulevard, turn left on Airport Road, turn right on Quirino Avenue, and continue until you get to Las Piñas. For Tagaytay, backtrack to Roxas, go north, turn right after Baclaran Church onto Redemptorist Road. This will take you to EDSA. Take the South Expressway, and get off at the Carmona exit. From there, clearly marked signs will take you to Tagaytay.

Pagsanjan Falls About an hour and a half southeast of Manila, the town of Pagsanjan was used by Hollywood director Francis Ford Coppola for his epic film *Apocalypse Now* (the older residents complain the town hasn't been the same since). It is known for its river rapids and the numerous waterfalls that empty into the Magdapio River, with the last, the Magdapio Falls, cascading from a height of about 30 m (100 ft).

Visitors begin downstream, in small boats guided through the rapids by skillful oarsmen. A raft trip under the Magdapio Falls into a cave caps off the ride. This exhilarating trip offers a glimpse of rural life: villagers bathing and laundering in the river as well as an occasional water buffalo (*carabao* in Pilipino) cooling off. Be sure to dress appropriately, and wrap your camera and watch in plastic. Life preservers aren't provided, so you might want to think twice about bringing children along. The round-trip takes 2½–3 hours. The fee is P500 for two, or P250 per head. Although not obliged to, passengers are expected to tip the boatmen; P50 to P60 each is a reasonable sum.

Getting There To get to Pagsanjan, take the South Expressway to the end, then turn left to Calamba (there will be signs). Turn right at the first major intersection and follow the signs to Pagsanjan.

Villa Escudero/ Hidden Valley If the sight of smiling children in traditional dress serenading you with native instruments doesn't warm your heart, nothing will. These friendly children greet visitors to Villa Escudero (tel. 2/593–698 or 2/521–0830), a working 1,600-acre rice-and-coconut plantation with its own river and man-made falls, only a 90-minute drive from Manila. After being serenaded you can explore the **Escudero Museum,** with an eclectic and colorful collection that includes war memorabilia (such as cannons and tanks, which children always seem to enjoy), antique religious artifacts and altars, paintings, stuffed animals, and celadon. At the popular **Hidden Valley** resort (tel. 2/531–0995), the emphasis is on springs and lush tropical miniforests. Overnight cottages are available.

Getting There To drive to Villa Escudero, start on the South Expressway and go all the way to the end. Turn right toward Lucena City, and bear left at the Santo Tomás intersection. You will be on the road to San Pablo City, passing through Alaminos. As soon as you approach the archway signaling the end of Laguna Province and the start of Quezon Province, slow down. The entrance to Villa Escudero is immediately after the archway, on your left, while Hidden Valley is on your right, before the archway.

What to See and Do with Children

Manila Zoo. This small zoo in the Tourist Belt has the usual assortment of wild animals, including such local species as the tamaraw (a peculiar water buffalo), the rare mouse deer, and the Palawan pheasant. *Quirino Ave., cnr. Adriatico St., tel. 2/586–216. Admission charge. Open daily 7 AM–6 PM.*

Matorco Ride. This is a scenic drive by Manila Bay in open-air, double-decker buses on Roxas Boulevard that starts and ends at the Rizal Monument. *Tel. 2/597–177 or 2/711–1585. Fare: P6 round-trip. Buses run 6–10 PM.*

Off the Beaten Track

A ride on the LRT. The Light Rail Transit (LRT) is an excellent means of getting beyond the usual tourist sights. For only P6.50 you can take in the heart of Manila. Begin at the Baclaran Terminal, not far from Baclaran Church, which is packed with devotees for special services every Wednesday. From Baclaran, there are 15 stops; a round-trip takes about 1¼ hours. You pass through congested neighborhoods and can often peer into offices, apartments, and backyards. It's worth getting off at the R. Papa station, taking a pedicab, and visiting the remarkable Chinese Cemetery (there's a small entrance fee). The mausoleums are virtual mansions with architectural styles that range from Chinese classical to baroque, a reminder that wealth makes a difference even in death. At the last stop, Monumento, walk a short distance to the monument marking the spot where Filipino revolutionaries began their struggle against Spain. *LRT hrs: 4 AM–9 PM.*

The Tabacalera Tour. La Flor de Isabela, Compañía General de Tabacos de Filipinas (Flower of Isabela, General Company of Philippine Tobacco), with a well-deserved reputation for fine cigars, will show visitors the time-honored process of making a cigar. Cigars and humidors can be purchased and even personalized. Call the factory in advance for a free tour. *900 Romualdez St., cnr. United Nations Ave., tel. 2/508–026, loc. 273 or 274. Open Mon.–Sat. 9–5.*

Cockfights. This national pastime, in which two cocks equipped with razor-sharp spurs fight to the death, can involve betting sums ranging from the petty to the astronomical. A fight can last less than a minute if uneven, longer if the combatants are well matched. This is obviously not for animal lovers. Sometimes the winner may be barely alive at the end and will wind up, like the loser, on the owner's dinner table. The prefight ceremonies are fascinating: Oddsmakers patrol the noisy and often cigarette-smoke-filled cockpit taking bets, and handlers prepare their feathered charges with time-honored methods.

In the metropolitan area, cockfights are usually held on Sunday. The big arenas are La Loma Cockpit (68 Calavite St., tel. 2/731–2023) and the Pasay Arena (Dolores St., Pasay City, tel. 2//861–746).

Shopping

As the nerve center of the country, Manila has all the shopping options, from sidewalk vendors and small retail stores to market districts and shopping centers. Both local and foreign goods are readily available in different precincts.

Nothing beats shopping in the market districts for color, bustle, and bargains—in a word, for atmosphere. Here haggling is raised to a fine art. Located in the older areas of the city, each encompasses several blocks and is a neighborhood unto itself. Crowds can be intense, and as in any urban area, they include pickpockets. Don't be paranoid, just alert. Shopping malls are found in relatively newer areas, such as Makati's commercial center, and in Quezon City. The malls are better organized and easier to get to, making up in convenience what they lack in charm. Prices are fixed here, so bargaining is pointless.

Market Districts
Divisoria
North of Binondo, this is the largest district, with everything from fresh produce, fruit, and cooking utensils to hardware, leather goods, and handicrafts. Savvy Manilans come to browse among the assorted stalls, emporia, and department stores until they see what they want at the right price.

Baclaran
The many stalls on Roxas Boulevard near Baclaran Church specialize in ready-to-wear clothing. Prices are supposedly lowest on Wednesday, when the weekly devotions to Our Lady of Perpetual Help are held at the church. The disadvantages of Wednesday shopping are the crowds and worse-than-usual traffic jams.

San Andres Market
In the Tourist Belt, this market is noted for its tropical and imported fruits. Bright and neatly arranged, the piles of mangoes, watermel-

ons, custard apples, and jackfruit are above average. It's pricey, but you can bargain.

Shopping Malls
Pistang Pilipino

Innumerable stalls here sell all types of Philippine handicrafts, from woven rattan baskets and woodcraft to brassware, shellcraft, and tribal clothing and jewelry. The quality ranges from kitsch to classic. If you're traveling to other parts of the country, it might be a good idea to look at that region's goods here to get an idea of what's available and the price range. Crafts are bound to be cheaper in their region of origin. And you can always come back once you return to Manila. *M.H. Del Pilar St., cnr. Pedro Gil, Ermita. Open daily 9 AM–7:30 PM.*

Harrison Plaza

This huge center has department stores, supermarkets, jewelers, drugstores, boutiques, record and electronics shops, video rentals, restaurants and snack bars, and four movie houses. *In the Tourist Belt, adjacent to the Century Park Sheraton, on Adriatico and Vito Cruz Sts. Opening hours vary, but all shops close at 7:30 PM, except the fast-food shops, which are open until 8:30.*

Shopping Centers
Makati Commercial Center

Bounded by Makati Avenue on the west, Ayala Avenue on the north, Epifanio de los Santos Highway on the east, and Pasay Road on the south, this is the biggest such center in the country, including several shopping malls and such gigantic department stores as Shoemart and Landmark, two hotels, sports shops, money changers, etc. There are small plazas where the weary can rest and watch humanity stream by. Nearby, on EDSA between Shaw Boulevard and Ortigas Avenue, three gigantic air-conditioned shopping malls—Robinson's, Shangri-La, and SM—have been erected. *Opening hours vary, but most shops close at 8 PM. Restaurants close at 10.*

Specialty Stores

For antiques and small handicraft stores, a good street for shopping is A. Mabini in the Tourist Belt. Some of the more reputable stores are **Bauzon Antiques** (1219 A. Mabini, tel. 2/504–542), **Tesoro's** (1325 A. Mabini, tel. 2/503–931), **T'boli Arts and Crafts** (1362 A. Mabini, tel. 2/586–802), **Terry's Antiques** (1401 A. Mabini, tel. 2/588–020), **Via Antica** (1411 A. Mabini, tel. 2/507–726), **Likha Antiques** (1475 A. Mabini, tel. 2/598–125), and **Goslani's** (1571 A. Mabini, tel. 2/507–338).

Sports and Fitness

Golf

Golf courses in the metropolitan area open to the public include **Capitol Hills Golf Club,** Quezon City, 18 holes (tel. 2/976–691 to –694); **Intramuros Golf Club,** Intramuros, 18 holes right beside the historic walls of Intramuros (tel. 2/478–470); and **Puerto Azul Beach and Country Club,** Ternate, Cavite, a championship 18-hole course in a tropical resort by the sea and a 90-minute drive from Manila (tel. 2/574–731 to –740).

Jogging

The best places to go jogging are along Roxas Boulevard by the sea wall; at Rizal Park; on the grounds of the Cultural Center complex; Rizal Memorial Stadium; and at the Ayala Triangle Park, corner of Ayala Avenue and Paseo de Roxas.

Swimming

All the major hotels have swimming pools open to nonguests for a fee. Other public pools are at **Pope Pius X Catholic Center** (United Nations Ave., Ermita, tel. 2/573–806 or 2/590–484) and **Rizal Memorial Sports Complex** (Vito Cruz St., Malate, tel. 2/509–556, 2/585–909, or 2/582–136).

Tennis

The city's numerous tennis courts include **Club Intramuros** (Intramuros, tel. 2/477–754), **Philippine Plaza Hotel** (Cultural Center Complex, tel. 2/832–0701), **Rizal Memorial Stadium** (Vito Cruz St., Malate, tel. 2/583–513), and **Velayo Sports Center** (Domestic Airport Rd., tel. 2/832–2316).

Spectator Sports

Basketball Basketball is the Philippines' premier sport, an enduring legacy of the American colonial era. Tournaments are held by the professional Philippine Basketball Association (tel. 2/833–4103) as well as by the NCAA, the University Athletic Association of the Philippines (UAAP), and the Philippine Amateur Basketball League (PABL). The major courts are at the Ultra Center in the town of Pasig, Rizal Coliseum in Malate, and the Cuneta Astrodome in Pasay City.

Cockfights *See* Off the Beaten Track, *above.*

Horse Racing The Santa Ana Race Track (tel. 2/879–951) and the San Lazaro Hippodrome (tel. 2/711–125) feature races on Tuesday and Wednesday evenings and Saturday and Sunday afternoons.

Beaches

In spite of its magnificent bay, Manila has no beaches to speak of. There are, however, several beach areas from two to five hours' drive from the city.

Puerto Galera Located on the nearby island of Mindoro, five hours away by bus and ferry, Puerto Galera is very popular with Western travelers, especially single men, many of whom bring along bar girls (*see* Nightlife, *below*). At times the scene here is overly commercial and crowded, but the approach by ferry is beautiful, with coconut-tree-lined shores and dramatic inlets. There are about six beach areas, but La Laguna, Talipanan, and White Beach are best for swimming and snorkeling along the small reefs. Accommodations in general are basic, with prices for cottages ranging from P350 up per night.

Hundred Islands North of Manila on the west coast of Luzon, this aggregate of small islands (the largest being Governor's and Quezon)—part of the Hundred Islands National Park—has good to spectacular beaches and some good snorkeling. There are no commercial establishments, so bring food and refreshments. Some of the islands have no shade, and some have snakes; the boatmen will know which ones are which. You board boats in the town of Lucap, a 4½-hour drive from Manila.

Dining

By Doreen G. Fernandez

A professor of communication at Ateneo de Manila University, Doreen G. Fernandez is the author of several books.

Philippine food may puzzle the visitor, including as it does both patently Asian and Western sides. History is responsible; for, starting with a Malay matrix of dishes kin to the rest of Southeast Asia's, Chinese traders input their culinary culture; Spanish colonizers added theirs, as well as Mexico's (through which the islands were governed); Indian and Arab interaction influenced the food of Mindanao; and, finally, American colonization brought in American popular culture.

The indigenous cuisine consists of seafood or meat broiled, steamed, cooked in vinegar (*paksiw* or *adobo*, for preserving without refrigeration), or stewed in broth soured with tamarind or tomato (*sinigang* or *tinola*, which are cooling in hot weather) or in other liquids like coconut water (*pinais*) or coconut milk (*laing*). Coconut is prominent—as vegetable (the bud, the heart of palm), as drink (juice of young coconut, *tuba* from the sap, *lambanog* when distilled), as coco milk or cream in which to cook fruits and vegetables (*ginataan*), as flesh grated into desserts and sweets.

Rice is the staple, background, and shaper of other tastes. It is also ground into flour and made into a myriad varieties of cake for snacks and festive occasions. One such is *bibingka*, baked in a clay oven with charcoal above and below, and topped with freshly grated coconut, salted duck's egg, and slices of white cheese; another is leaf-wrapped *suman*, sticky rice cooked with coconut milk and eaten with ripe mangoes.

The Chinese connection is apparent in such foods as vegetable- or pork-filled *lumpia* (spring rolls), and especially in *pansit*, noodles (rice, mung bean, wheat, fresh or dried, fat or thin) sautéed with vegetables, pork, sausages, or seafood—the ingredients used differ from region to region.

Spanish dishes are the stuff of fiestas: *lechon*, spit-roasted suckling pig; chicken *relleno* stuffed with pork, sausage, and spices; *paella* rich with crabs, prawns, sausage, ham, and clams; *pochero*, a beef stew Filipinized with a vegetable relish; *callos* (tripe) with chick-peas and pimentos; *caldereta*, goat or beef stew with olive oil, bell peppers, and olives.

The American regime, which began in 1898, brought in convenience (sandwiches and salads), quick cooking (fried chicken, hamburg-ers), and a new food culture. The East-West range is therefore wide, but Filipinized through time by local ingredients, dipping sauces (*patis* and *bagoong*, *calamansi* and chilies, vinegar, and garlic), cooking styles, and general fine-tuning.

In a nation whose 7,100 islands are home to some 90 ethno-linguistic groups, there are, of course, regional variations. The food of the Bicol people is chili-hot; so is that of some Muslims, like the Maranaws, whose food has a kinship with Indonesian cooking. Keep an eye out for the Bicol *pinangat* (shrimp or pork wrapped in taro leaves, cooked with coco cream and ginger, and chili-embellished) or the Maranaw catfish (cooked with turmeric, coco milk, and chilis).

The Ilocano north favors vegetable stews flavored with the salty shrimp or fish sauce called *bagoong*, often with the bitter-sweetness of *ampalaya* (bitter melon). Try *pinakbet*, which has become the pan-Philippine vegetable dish. Leyte and Samar have many dishes cooked in coconut milk (like chicken with ginger, or prawns). Taga-log dishes lean toward a controlled sourness, as in beef, pork, or chicken *sinigang*. Pampango food is one of the richest regional cui-sines, including a plethora of sweets and such exotica as stuffed frogs (*betute*).

Almost all of these regional—and most international—cuisines can be sampled in Metro Manila restaurants, as well as in food malls, markets with *turo-turo* ("point-point" arrays to choose from), and street stalls. But venturing into the provinces is the way to get a real taste of the Philippines.

Most restaurants can accommodate diners who drop in, but reserva-tions are a good idea on holidays and weekends. Most places close only on Christmas, New Year's Day, and Good Friday. Few require formal dress; jackets or the long-sleeved *barong tagalog* for men suf-fice for even the most expensive establishments, and most others draw the line only at athletic shorts, tank tops, and slippers. Lunch hours are normally noon to 2:30, dinner 7 to 11, and some restau-rants are open as well for breakfast (7 to 10) and *merienda* (4 to 6). Restaurants apply a 4.2% tax on food and an 8.7% tax on alcohol.

Ask if a service charge is included; it often is not, in which case a 10%–15% tip would be expected.

Highly recommended restaurants are indicated by a star ★.

Category	Cost*
$$$$	over P500 ($18)
$$$	P275–P500 ($10–$18)
$$	P165–P275 ($6–$10)
$	under P165 ($6)

per person without tax, service, or drinks

$$$$ **Champagne Room.** The dining room of the grand old Manila Hotel (*see* Lodging, *below*) is decorated with wrought-iron tracery and glass palm trees. The cuisine is French, the wine list reasonable in range, and the staff attentive. On the menu are both classics (Chateaubriand, rack of lamb) and inventions: black tiger prawns carpaccio, veal tenderloin with forest fruits, crispy mango feuillantine. Strolling musicians play light classical music and Philippine *kundiman*. *Manila Hotel, Rizal Park, Manila, tel. 2/470–011. Reservations required. Jacket and tie or long-sleeved barong tagalog required. AE, DC, MC, V. Closed Sat. lunch, Sun. dinner, and holidays.*

$$$ **Ben Kay.** Among Manila's Japanese restaurants, this one stands out. It is the signature outlet of a Japanese-owned hotel, with decor, chefs, and foodstuffs imported from Japan. At the sushi bar, in private rooms, and at *teppanyaki* tables you can order the usual popular dishes: tempura and soba and udon noodles, as well as *bento* (a meal in a lacquer tray), *nabe* (hot pot), and such fish as *gindara* (cod) and *hamachi* (yellowtail). *Nikko Manila Garden Hotel, Makati Commercial Center, EDSA and Arnaiz Ave., Makati, Metro Manila, tel. 2/810–4104. Reservations advised. Dress: smart casual. AE, DC, MC, V.*

$$$ **La Tasca.** One of the restaurants that gave Manila its well-deserved
★ fame for the best Spanish cuisine in Asia. The basic menu has such favorites as *sopa de ajo* (garlic soup), *paella* Valenciana or marinera (all seafood), *fabada asturiana* (bean stew with bacon), *bacalao a la vizcaina* (codfish), and desserts like *canonigo* (meringue, mangoes, and syrup). There are also changing specials and excellent staples, including pepper steak and prawns in garlic sauce. *Legazpi St., Greenbelt Park, Makati, Metro Manila, tel. 2/893–8586 or 2/819–5435. Reservations advised. Jacket advised. AE, DC, MC, V. Closed Sun.*

$$$ **Sea Food Market.** Take a cart, and then choose your seafood, meat, and vegetables from a long counter. (A guide suggests dishes and condiments.) The ingredients are then cooked by chefs in full view of the street. Try crabs of all shapes and sizes (*curacha* from Zamboanga, coconut crab from Marinduque), lobsters, and marine and freshwater fish, prepared in Chinese, Filipino, or Continental style. *7829 Makati Ave., Makati, Metro Manila, tel. 2/815–4237, 2/850–361, or 2/862–107; 1190 J. Bocobo St., Ermita, Manila, tel. 2/521–4351 or 2/505–761; Araneta Center, cnr. of EDSA and MacArthur Ave., Cubao, Quezon City, tel. 2/922–8765 or 2/922–6148. Dress: casual. AE, DC, MC, V.*

$$$ **Tin Hau.** An elegant Cantonese restaurant, with ranks of personnel in formal wear or Chinese costume providing excellent service in a setting of paneling, Chinese paintings, and mirrors. The 150-item

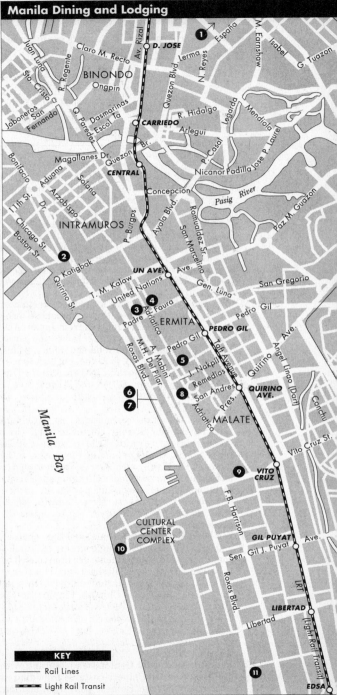

Manila Dining and Lodging

Dining

Aristocrat, **7**
Ben Kay, **18**
Bistro Remedios, **8**
Café Intermezzo, **14**
Flavours and Spices, **15**
Gene's Bistro, **25**
Kamayan, **1, 3, 12**
La Tasca, **16**
Le Soufflé, **17**
Sea Food Market, **4, 22, 24**
SM Megamall Food Court, **23**
Tin Hau, **21**
Via Mare, **13**

Lodging

Admiral Hotel, **6**
Adriatic Arms, **5**
Century Park Sheraton, **9**
Hyatt Regency, **11**
Mandarin Oriental, **21**
Manila Hotel, **2**
Manila Peninsula, **20**
Nikko Manila Garden, **18**
Philippine Plaza, **10**
Shangri-La Manila, **19**

KEY

— Rail Lines
▪▪▪ Light Rail Transit

menu includes Peking duck (three ways), soya pigeon, whole abalone in oyster sauce, steamed live garoupa or shrimps, stir-fried live crab with roe, vegetarian dishes, and double-boiled bird's nest in coconut milk. Dim sum is served at lunch, and there is a Sunday brunch. *Mandarin Oriental Hotel, Makati Ave., Makati, Metro Manila, tel. 2/816–3601. Reservations advised. Dress: smart casual. AE, DC, MC, V.*

$$$ **Via Mare Seafood Specialty Restaurant.** This is an institution—a
★ gracious setting for seafood in many guises. Fat live oysters are flown in daily to the Oyster Bar from the Visayas. At the main restaurant, prime seafood, foreign and local (salmon and trout, blue marlin and *maliputo* or Taal Lake cavalla, scallops and lobsters), is prepared in such international and Filipino dishes as timbale of salmon and sole, seafood grillades, pompano *en papillote*, and calamares en su tinta. *Greenbelt Sq., Paseo de Roxas, Makati, Metro Manila, tel. 2/893–2306, 2/893–2746, or 2/815–1918. Reservations not required. Dress: smart casual. AE, DC, MC, V. No lunch Sun.*

$$ **Bistro Remedios.** Pampanga regional cooking is served here in a set-
★ ting of traditional furniture and paintings of Philippine landscapes. Taste the local culture through *betute* (stuffed frog), *gising-gising* (chopped chili with minced pork in coconut cream), *adobong palos* (freshwater eel in coconut milk, *kamias*, and chili), crisp-fried beef ribs, cooling *guinumis* (gelatin, tapioca, coco milk, and shaved ice), or a breakfast of garlic rice, eggs, sausages, and a cup of thick hot chocolate. *1903 Adriatico St., cnr. Remedios St., Malate, Manila, tel. 2/521–8097. Reservations advised. Dress: casual. AE, DC, MC, V. Open daily 7 AM–midnight.*

$$ **Café Intermezzo.** The place for Cal-Ital—California-Italian cuisine, emphasizing fresh vegetables, fruits, and seafood (from Philippine growers and fishermen). Pastas include black fettuccine with tuna roe, green fettuccine with smoked *tanguingue* (Spanish mackerel) and mangoes, and angel hair with crabmeat and mushrooms. Prawns, *lapu-lapu* fillets, blue marlin, and pampano come with such sauces as cilantro lime butter or tomato or mango vinaigrette, and others. End it with the unique Seasons Decadent Chocolate Cake. *Legazpi St., cnr. Greenbelt Dr., Makati, Metro Manila, tel. 2/819–7286. Dress: smart casual. AE, DC, MC, V. Open daily 11:30–11, till 1 AM Fri. and Sat.*

$$ **Flavours and Spices.** The first of the city's many Thai restaurants, this is also a store for spices and condiments. Try the popular favorites: *tom yam* soup, chicken in *pandan* leaf, red/green/yellow curries, catfish salad with green mango, *phad thai* noodles, little *takho* cakes, crushed-ice desserts like *tub tim grob* or *ruam-mit*, and also the less usual *tom-kha-gai*, chicken soup with ginger, lemongrass, and coconut milk. *Garden Sq., Greenbelt Commercial Center, Makati, Metro Manila, tel. 2/815–3029, 2/819–1375, or 2/819–0690. Reservations advised. Dress: casual. AE, DC, MC, V.*

$$ **Kamayan Restaurant.** The name means "to eat with the hands," picnic- or provincial-style. At these four restaurants, your food is served on leaf-lined wooden plates; forks are optional. Selections range through regional cuisines: *lechon de leche*, whole roast suckling pig; sautéed crab with a sauce of its own coral; *kinulob na kitang*, butterfish wrapped in banana leaf with onions and tomatoes; prawns in crab fat. You get all this in a setting of paneled walls, *capiz*-shell windows, and staff in stylized Philippine costumes. *47 Pasay Rd., Makati, Metro Manila, tel. 2/815–1463 or 2/883–604; 207 EDSA, Greenhills, Mandaluyong, tel. 2/795–504, 2/709–224, 2/704–308, or 2/704–610; 532 Padre Faura, cnr. M. Adriatico, Ermita, Manila, tel. 2/521–9490 or 2/582–537; 15 West Ave., Quezon*

City, tel. 2/989–470. Reservations advised. Dress: casual. AE, DC, MC, V.

$$ **Le Soufflé Restaurant and Wine Bar.** The three chefs who own and
★ operate this restaurant, where large picture windows overlook a
public garden, have designed a light, fresh cuisine, generally Medi-
terranean but with salutes to Asia and eclecticism. If they have the
ingredients, they'll accommodate requests not on the menu. Special-
ties range from pan-fried fresh goose liver in raspberry sauce to
shiitake mushroom salad, baked salmon in phyllo pastry, and Straw-
berry Fields, a fruit dessert with Grand Marnier and black pepper.
*2F Josephine Bldg., Greenbelt Dr. cnr. Makati Ave., Makati, Metro
Manila, tel. 2/812–3287. Reservations advised. Dress: casual but
neat. AE, DC, MC, V.*

$ **Aristocrat Restaurant.** The Aristocrat has been in operation since
1936, run by four generations of the Reyes family, and although
there are five other branches, this one beside the bay is the signa-
ture outlet. Popular dishes include chicken or pork barbecue with
Java rice, satay sauce, and papaya pickles; *pansit luglog*, fat rice
noodles with a shrimp and duck-egg sauce; chicken honey; and a na-
tive breakfast of rice, dried beef or marinated milkfish, and coffee or
chocolate. *432 San Andres, cnr. Roxas Blvd., Malate, Metro Ma-
nila, tel. 2/507–671 to –679. Dress: casual. AE, MC, V. Open 24 hrs.*

$ **Gene's Bistro.** Euro-Philippine cuisine, which flourished at the turn
of the century in the now-vanished Pampanga town of Sulipan, is the
specialty here: French white soup with custard cubes, ox tongue
with a mushroom velouté, *lapu-lapu* poached in wine with a spinach
puree. The rest of the menu consists of owner/chef Gene Gonzalez's
creations, which include ube (purple yam) vichyssoise hot or cold,
wild boar sausage with mustard sauce, fried Laguna cheese with
fruit purees, and 56 hot and cold coffees, decaf or otherwise. *243
Tomas Morato Ave., Quezon City, tel. 2/921–5193. Dress: casual.
AE, MC, V.*

$ **SM Megamall Food Court.** In the air-conditioned basement of the
largest shopping mall in Metro Manila, some 40 food stores ring the
tables, presenting a spectrum of current popular taste. The offer-
ings include Filipino food: *bibingka* at **Ferino's,** lechon at **Lydia's,**
pansit and regional dishes at **Aristocrat** and **Casa Ilongga;** Chinese
vegetarian food at **Bodhi,** Cantonese food at **Golden Cantonese,** dim
sum at **Maxim's;** Japanese food at **Moshi-Moshi;** Korean at **Kimchi;**
Mexican at **El Burrito;** and American-style pizzas, hamburgers,
fried chicken, pies, cookies, and salads. *SM Megamall Bldg. A,
EDSA and Julia Vargas St., Pasig, Metro Manila, tel. 2/633–5012 to
5016. Dress: casual. No credit cards. Open weekdays 10–9, week-
ends 10–9:30.*

Lodging

Manila has lodgings for every type of traveler, from the hedonists
with deep pockets to the backpackers who must count their pennies.
Almost all the hotels are in two areas: the so-called Tourist Belt
(Malate and Ermita districts) in downtown Manila, and Makati,
Manila's Wall Street and fashionable residential enclave. The former
has more lodging options, while Makati has mainly upscale hotels.

Unless otherwise noted, rooms in all listed hotels have private
baths. For a map pinpointing hotel locations, *see* Dining, *above.*

Highly recommended hotels are indicated by a star ★.

Category	Cost*
$$$$	over P5,600 ($200)
$$$	P3,640–P5,600 ($130–$200)
$$	P1,680–P3,640 ($60–$130)
$	under P1,680 ($60)

All prices are for a standard double room; add 10% service charge and 13.7% government tax.

Ermita/Malate The advantages of staying in the Tourist Belt are Manila Bay, with its fabled sunsets, and the assortment of restaurants, bars, clubs, coffeehouses, and shops. The Cultural Center of the Philippines is right on Roxas Boulevard, the scenic main road flanking the bay.

★ **Century Park Sheraton.** The sunny, six-story lobby brings the outdoors in, with an aviary and artfully arranged tropical foliage. A string quartet serenades lobby loungers every evening from 4 to 8. The hotel seems popular with Asian guests. The rooms, done in muted but cheery tones, are spacious. Best are those facing the bay; worst are those with a view of the adjacent parking lot and shopping complex, although you still see part of the bay. *Vito Cruz, cnr. Adriatico St., tel. 2/522–1011, fax 2/521–3413. 500 rooms. Facilities: 8 restaurants, a coffee shop, deli, nightclub, bar, fitness center, business center, grand ballroom, outdoor swimming pool. AE, DC, MC, V. $$$$*

Manila Hotel. The doyen of Manila's hotels, this is where General MacArthur made his headquarters before World War II. Other luminaries have stayed here, including Ernest Hemingway and Douglas Fairbanks. The magnificent lobby exudes an Old World feeling, with floors of Philippine marble, narra and mahogany hardwood ceilings, and mother-of-pearl and brass chandeliers. The MacArthur Club, reached by private elevator, serves complimentary breakfast. Room decor re-creates the colonial era. Best rooms face the bay and the pool. *Rizal Park, tel. 2/470–011, fax 2/471–124. 570 rooms. Facilities: outdoor pool, 2 tennis courts, grand ballroom, 7 restaurants, bar, business center, gym. AE, DC, MC, V. $$$$*

★ **Philippine Plaza.** Luxurious and grand—a veritable resort sans beachfront—the Plaza has an enormous lobby with two levels, the lower one graced by a carp pool and a waterfall. The huge circular swimming pool, with slides for the kids and a snack bar smack in the middle, is one of Asia's best. All rooms have terraces with views of Manila Bay. The furniture is rattan and the decor has a beige-and-white color scheme. *Cultural Center Complex, Roxas Blvd., tel. 2/832–0701, fax 2/832–3485. 673 rooms. Facilities: outdoor pool with bar/restaurant, 4 tennis courts, minigolf course, ballroom and function rooms, 24-hr fitness center, 8 restaurants, nightclub, lounge, business center. AE, DC, MC, V. $$$$*

Hyatt Regency. Right on the boulevard. The spare but elegant lobby, graced by *capiz* (mother-of-pearl) chandeliers, never seems crowded. The rooms—all with views of the bay—are done in native style, with wood and straw headboards and cane chairs. *2702 Roxas Blvd., tel. 2/833–1234, fax 2/833–5913. 265 rooms. Facilities: outdoor pool, 3 restaurants, nightclub, bar, business center, function rooms, gym. AE, DC, MC, V. $$$*

Admiral Hotel. Fronting the bay, this businesslike place is unpretentious but efficient, with a quiet café in its small, informal lobby. Rooms are air-conditioned, neat, and modern but a bit small. Best are those with a view of the bay. The staff is friendly and attentive. *2138 Roxas Blvd., tel. 2/572–081 to –093, fax 2/522–2018. 110* *rooms. Facilities: pool, disco, restaurant, coffee shop. AE, DC, MC, V. $$*

Adriatic Arms. This small, cozy European-style hotel, with armchairs in the lobby and a combination coffee shop/deli, is in the heart of Malate in the Tourist Belt. The rooms are tastefully, if simply, furnished. *Adriatico and Nakpil Sts., tel. 2/521–0736, fax 2/588–014. 28 rooms. Facilities: coffee shop. AE, DC, MC, V. $*

Makati   This district, the business capital of the country and neighbor to the airport, is relatively new and uncongested. The streets and sidewalks are wide, making it easier than elsewhere to walk around, and the hotels are concentrated around the gigantic Makati Commercial Center, which has everything from movie houses to money changers.

Mandarin Oriental. The ambience here is discreet and elegant, with a small but stately lobby done in black marble with a cut-crystal chandelier, and luxurious room decor. A favorite with businesspeople. *Makati Ave. and Paseo de Roxas St., tel. 2/816–3601, fax 2/817–2472. 470 rooms. Facilities: outdoor pool, ballrooms and function rooms, 4 restaurants, bar/nightclub, bake shop, gym, business center. AE, DC, MC, V. $$$$*

★ **Manila Peninsula.** The Pen, as Manilans call it, exudes an informal elegance, expressed in the wide lobby—divided by a grand aisle with floral decor—and the understated furnishings and color schemes of the well-kept and spacious rooms that are more like suites. *Makati and Ayala Aves., tel. 2/819–3456, fax 2/815–4825. 535 rooms. Facilities: outdoor pool, 4 restaurants, nightclub, bar, deli, business center. AE, DC, MC, V. $$$$*

Shangri-La Manila. It's huge, with a luxurious, soaring, light-filled lobby. The spacious rooms, however, disappoint with their bland decor. *Ayala Ave. cnr. Makati Ave., tel. 2/813–8888, fax 2/813–5499. 703 rooms. Facilities: 4 restaurants, bar, deli, disco, outdoor pool, gym, business center. AE, DC, V, MC. $$$$*

Nikko Manila Garden. Smack in Makati Commercial Center, with snack bars, restaurants, bookstores, cinemas, boutiques, and department stores, the Manila Garden has an uninspired and somewhat cluttered lobby but extremely helpful staff. Rooms are a bit cramped; the decor is modern and cheerful. The Japanese restaurant here is among Manila's best. *Makati Commercial Center, tel. 2/857–911, fax 2/817–862. 523 rooms. Facilities: outdoor pool, gym, 5 restaurants, nightclub, bar, 6 banquet and conference rooms, business center, medical and dental clinic. AE, DC, MC, V. $$$*

The Arts

Good guides to the city's cultural life are the *Expat Weekly* and *What's on in Manila*, distributed free by major hotels, restaurants, and tourist information centers. Check the entertainment pages of the dailies, particularly the Sunday editions.

At the entrance to the offices of the Cultural Center of the Philippines (tel. 2/832–1125 to –1139), you can pick up a monthly calendar of the center's offerings. The government-run center emphasizes music, theater, dance, and the visual arts and has a resident dance company and theater group. The center also hosts internationally known artists and musicians, sometimes in cooperation with the various cultural arms of the foreign embassies. The center's two art galleries display figurative and abstract art.

Concerts   Free concerts are given at **Rizal Park** on Sunday beginning at 5 PM, usually featuring a program of popular Western and Philippine music.

Well-known singers and musicians are featured. **Paco Park** and **Puerta Real** in Intramuros offer similar programs, at 6 PM on Friday and Saturday respectively.

Dance   The Cultural Center of the Philippines has a resident dance company, **Ballet Philippines** (tel. 2/832–3675), and provides offices for **Bayanihan Dance Company** (tel. 2/832–3688), a world-famous folkdance group. The ballet company is the Philippines' best, with guest dancers from around the world.

Film   Metro Manila has many cinema houses, but most of the English-language films are the substandard B type.

Free films are presented at **Rizal Park**'s open-air theater at 5 PM on Saturday afternoon and after the concert on Sunday evening. The **Goethe House** (687 Aurora Blvd., Quezon City, tel. 2/722–4671), the **University of the Philippines Film Center** (Diliman campus, Quezon City, tel. 2/962–722), and the **Thomas Jefferson Library** (395 Buendia Ave. Ext., tel. 2/818–5484) regularly offer free film screenings, ranging from silent classics to contemporary movies. During the two-week **Metro Manila Film Festival** in June and December, only Philippine films are shown in the cinemas.

Museums   The **National Museum** (Padre Burgos St. at Rizal Park, tel. 2/494–450), once the site of Congress, has varied displays, ranging from archaeological treasures to paintings, including an impressive array of the 19th-century artist Juan Luna's works.

Art Galleries   Metropolitan Manila's best galleries include **Ateneo de Manila Gallery** (tel. 2/998–721) in Loyola Heights, Quezon City, with its display of modern art; **Heritage Art Center** (tel. 2/700–867) in Cubao, Quezon City, which exhibits both traditional and nontraditional art; **Luz Gallery** (Makati Ave. at Ayala Ave., tel. 2/815–6906), a famous venue for well-established modern artists; and **Hiraya Art Gallery** (tel. 2/594–223) in Ermita, which favors up-and-coming artists.

Nightlife

Metropolitan Manila is a pleasure-seeker's paradise with a catholic array of night activities, from the soothing to the sinful. You can listen to jazz or rock, have a drink at a bar while ogling topless female dancers, dance madly at a disco, or have a snack and cappuccino in one of the lively coffeehouses.

Cafés   The largest concentration is in the Malate district, in and around Remedios Circle. **Penguin Cafe** (Remedios and Bocobo Sts., tel. 2/521–2088), which doubles as an art gallery, has the best outdoor patio, an artistic crowd, and good homemade pasta. **Cafe Adriatico** (1790 Adriatico St., tel. 2/584–059) features classical music, Philippine food, and a more subdued atmosphere. Tiny **Cafe Mondial** (Adriatico St. cnr. Pedro Gil, tel. 2/598–946) serves fresh fruit shakes, delicious crepes, and finger sandwiches. **Blue Cafe** (Nakpil St. cnr. Bocobo, tel. 2/581–725) serves no food but has a cash bar, a gay ambience, and excellent sounds. In Quezon City there's the **Cine Cafe** (76-C Roces Ave., tel. 2/969–421), a gay gathering spot with offbeat, often experimental, films on video monitors.

Folk and Rock Houses   **Your Father's Mustache** (2144 M.H. Del Pilar St., tel. 2/521–8543) and **Hobbit House** (1801 A. Mabini St., tel. 2/506–573 or 2/521–7604) feature a regular roster of folk singers. Freddie Aguilar, who's famous throughout Southeast Asia, performs twice a week at the Hobbit House, where midgets wait on you. **Mayric's** (1320 Espana St., in front of the University of Santo Tomas, tel. 2/732–3021) has bands that alternate between punk and grunge. In Quezon City, the **'70's Bistro** (46 Anonas St., tel. 2/922–0492) has a mix of students and professionals listening to folk-rock bands, while **Club Dredd** (570 EDSA cnr. Tuason St., tel. 2/912–8464) favors hard-core rock.

Discos Manila discos tend to be cavernous. The beat is generic and follows Western fashions. Some of the trendier ones are **Altitude 49** (Nikko Manila Garden, tel. 2/857–911); the **Billboard** (7838 Makati Ave., tel. 2/876–727), a favorite of expatriates; **Euphoria** (Hotel Intercontinental, Ayala Ave., tel. 2/815–9711), a hangout for yuppies; **Faces** (2 San Lorenzo Dr., Makati, tel. 2/818–6592 or 2/810–7513); **Pulse** (1030 Pasay Rd., tel. 2/818–5288); and the **Cellar Disco** (Century Park Sheraton Hotel, Vito Cruz, tel. 2/501–201). In Quezon City, a popular gay disco is **Club 69** (690 Amoranto St. at Biak-na-Bato St., tel. 2/712–3662), with shows featuring dancers and impersonators.

Bars and Lounges There are really two types of bars: those with skimpily attired dancers and those without. The former play disco music, while the latter have more varied fare. There used to be a large concentration of "girlie" bars in the Tourist Belt, but the current mayor has had them shut down. Most have moved to Pasay City, along Roxas Boulevard.

Nongirlie bars and music lounges are spread out in Makati and the Tourist Belt. In the Tourist Belt try **Tap Room** (Manila Hotel, tel. 2/470–011), **Siete Pecados** (Philippine Plaza Hotel, tel. 2/832–0701), **Oar House** (A. Mabini St., cnr. Remedios, tel. 2/595–864), **Remembrances** (1795 A. Mabini, tel. 2/521–7605), and **Guernica's** (1856 Bocobo St., Malate, tel. 2/521–4415). In Makati, try **Nina's Papagayo** (1 Anza St., tel. 2/887–925), **Sirena** (Manila Peninsula, Ayala Ave., tel. 2/819–3456), **Chez Moi** (5347 General Luna St., tel. 2/885–038), and **Intramuros Bar** (Nikko Manila Garden, tel. 2/857–911).

Nightclubs Manila nightclubs offer floor shows that vary from performances of well-known bands and cultural presentations to highly choreographed "model" shows, in which a lot of skin is bared. **Pistang Pilipino** (Pedro Gil, cnr. Mabini, tel. 2/521–2209) and **Zamboanga** (1619 Adriatico St., tel. 2/572–835) serve Philippine cuisine and present regional folk dances. **Lost Horizon** (Philippine Plaza, tel. 2/832–0701) usually has a lively pop band, while **Top of the Century** (Century Park Sheraton, tel. 2/522–1011) and **La Bodega** (Manila Peninsula, tel. 2/819–3456) are more intimate, with well-known jazz singers and ensembles.

Casinos Manila has two government-run casinos, one at the **Silahis International Hotel** (Roxas Blvd., tel. 2/573–811) occupying the whole mezzanine, with a room reserved for high rollers, and the other at the **Manila Pavillion Hotel** (United Nations Ave., tel. 2/573–711).

Northern Luzon

The Philippines is justly acknowledged for its beautiful waters and beaches, though the fact that the country is essentially mountainous is sometimes overlooked. In northern Luzon are the rugged Cordillera and the Sierra Madre ranges, with breathtaking views at elevations of 3,000 to 9,500 feet, and the narrow but beautiful coastal plains of the Ilocos region. It can be chilly at night, especially from November through February. Rains are torrential during the wet season (mid-June through October) and can cause rock slides and impassable roads.

This is where one finds the ancient highland cultures—referred to collectively as Igorots and less Westernized than their lowland counterparts—whose origins can be traced to migratory groups older than the Malays. Over the centuries there has been the inevitable intermingling of highland and lowland cultures through commerce, religion, education, and conflict. Nowhere is this more evident than in the charming city of Baguio: A good number of its inhabitants are lowlanders (businesspeople, retirees, artists), so you're as likely to hear Pilipino as Ilocano, the regional tongue. The city also has several universities, attracting students from all over Luzon. Sitting at 1,500 m (5,000 ft) above sea level among pine-covered slopes, Baguio is a lovely respite from the lowland heat and serves as a base from which to explore the rice terraces of Banaue or the towns and churches of the Ilocos region—especially the area around Vigan and Laoag. A combination of rugged terrain and coastal plains, Ilocos is known for its neat towns, its hardworking, thrifty natives, and its gorgeous Spanish-era churches.

Important Addresses and Numbers

All the places noted here are in Baguio City, unless otherwise specified. The area code for Baguio is 74.

Tourist Information **Department of Tourism** (Governor Pack Rd., tel. 74/442–5415 or 74/442–5416) or the **Cordillera Autonomous Region** (tel. 74/442–6708).

Emergencies **Police,** tel. 74/21–11; **fire,** tel. 74/311–3222.

Hospitals **Benguet General Hospital** (La Trinidad, tel. 74/221–06). **St. Louis University Hospital** (Assumption Rd., tel. 74/442–5701).

Late-Night Pharmacies **Mercury Drug Store** (Session Rd., tel. 74/442–4310) is open until 9 PM.

Arriving and Departing by Plane

Airports and Airlines Philippine Air Lines (tel. 74/832–3166) has daily 45-minute flights from Manila Domestic Airport to Loakan Airport in Baguio, and Monday, Wednesday, and Friday flights to Laoag Airport, farther north. A cab ride to Baguio City should cost between P80 to P100. There are public jeepneys available at Laoag Airport.

Arriving and Departing by Car and Bus

By Car From Manila it's a mostly smooth six-hour drive to Baguio via the North Diversion highway, which begins at EDSA, links up to the MacArthur Highway, and leads to the zigzagging Kennon Road. (In case Kennon is closed for repairs, you can take Naguilian Road or the Marcos Highway [which has a Mt. Rushmore–like bust of the late dictator], farther north along the coast. Add an extra hour for these routes to Baguio.)

By Bus A number of bus companies run daily trips from Manila to Baguio on an hourly basis, plus numerous daily trips to Vigan and Laoag. Among them are **Pantranco** (tel. 2/997–091 to –098), **Victory** (tel. 2/835–5019), **Dangwa** (tel. 2/731–2859), and **Dagupan Bus Co.** (tel. 2/976–123 or 2/995–639).

Getting Around

By Car On the coastal plains and around the cities of Baguio, Vigan, and Laoag, the roads range from good to excellent. Northeast of Baguio, however, deeper into the Cordilleras, they can be very bad, and public transportation is a better bet.

By Bus Buses are used to get from one town to the next, and they are numerous and cheap. Terminals are located near the public markets. Baguio has two terminals, one in front of the public market on Magsaysay Avenue and the other on Governor Pack Road near the corner of Session Road.

By Taxi The region's only cabs are in Baguio. They are small Japanese models, and cheap: Rides within the central part of town average $1.

By Jeepney Plentiful and good for short routes, jeepneys begin and end their routes at or near the public market. They can also be hired for out-of-town trips. The average cost of a ride is a mere P2.

Guided Tours

Manila travel agents can arrange northern tours (*see* Guided Tours in Metro Manila, *above*). In Baguio, consult the Department of Tourism (tel. 74/442–5415 or 74/442–5416) or the Cordillera Autonomous Region (tel. 74/442–6708) for local operators.

Exploring Northern Luzon

Numbers in the margin correspond to points of interest on the Northern Luzon map.

Tour 1: Baguio

❶ Billed as the "summer capital of the Philippines," **Baguio** was developed during the American colonial administration and is now the commercial, educational, and recreational hub of the Cordilleras. The air here—at 1,500 m (5,000 ft) above sea level—is crisp, invigorating, and laden with the fragrance of pine trees. Avoid the city during the Christmas holidays and Easter week, when both the population of 150,000 and prices practically double. A day tour could begin at the Department of Tourism (*see* Important Addresses and Numbers, above), where you can pick up maps and suggestions. Then move on to the **Baguio–Mt. Province Museum,** at Camp John Hay, which houses an excellent collection of artifacts, tribal clothing, weaponry, and dioramas. *Tel. 74/442–7902 to –7908. Admission charge. Open daily 8–5.*

A 10- to 15-minute drive from Session Road, the city's main downtown artery, is **Mines View Park,** a promontory from which you can gaze at the surrounding mountains and abandoned silver mines. (Below the promontory, local children wait for you to toss coins.) Souvenir stalls sell wood carvings, brassware, walking sticks, jewelry, native blankets, and bamboo flutes.

A short drive from the park, back toward the city center, is **Mansion House,** built in 1908 as the summer residence of the American governor-generals and now the getaway of Philippine presidents. Visitors enter through gates that replicate those of Buckingham Palace in London. Across the road is the **Pool of Pines,** a carp pool 100 m (109 yds) long that's bordered by pine trees. From the vine-covered stone trellis at the far end, steps lead down to **Wright Park,** where horses can be rented. You can ride out of the park to different parts of the city, but only with a guide.

A stroll away is the **Baguio Botanical Park.** Here you will find sculptures of *anitos* (native gods) and examples of dwellings used by the

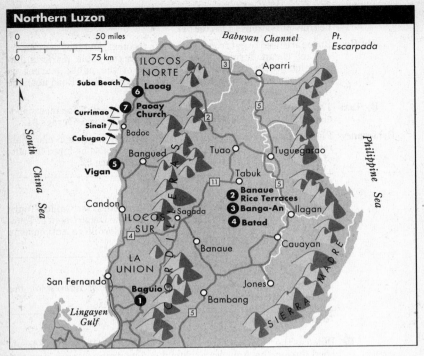

Northern Luzon

different highland ethnic groups. For a small fee, natives dressed in traditional tribal finery will pose for photos.

Baguio Cathedral, just off Session Road, may be the world's only cathedral painted a light, cheery pink. With its hints of Norman architecture, the cathedral won't inspire raves, but it is a good perch from which to get a panoramic view of Baguio and of Mt. St. Tomás, its highest peak. On one side of the cathedral is a long flight of steps leading to **Session Road,** downtown Baguio's half-mile-long main street, with bazaars, restaurants, movie houses, offices, and cafés.

South of Session Road is **Burnham Park.** Named for American landscape architect Daniel Burnham, the park's spacious grounds are perfect for an idyllic stroll. There's boating on the artificial lake, and bicycles can be rented. North of the park and at the bottom of Session Road is the **Baguio Public Market.** Set between a hill and Magsaysay Avenue, the market is an indispensable part of the Baguio experience. A series of alleys with stalls on either side, it has sections devoted to fish and meat; fresh vegetables and strawberries, for which Baguio is famous; dry goods, from Igorot blankets and loincloths to army surplus; regional handicrafts, with an emphasis on rattan backpacks, silver jewelry, and tribal ornaments; tailor shops; and antiques. The money changers here give a better rate than you'll find at hotels or banks.

Tour 2: Banaue

② The **Banaue Rice Terraces** are spectacular, man-made rice paddies terraced into the mountainsides of Mayaoyao and Carballo by the Ifugao, a highland tribe, more than 2,000 years ago. Looking like giant steps to the sky, these terraces would extend for 22,500 km (14,000 mi) if placed end to end, or halfway around the world. Banaue is an eight-hour drive from either Baguio or Manila. The area is also good for trekking, and guides can be hired at pre-agreed fees. Expect to pay about P200.

Some of the terraces can be seen from Banaue itself, but the best views are in the countryside. Start at **Viewpoint,** a 1½-hour trek (ask for directions) or a 20-minute drive from the town proper. This promontory offers a panoramic view of the terraces. Wizened Ifugao women in native dress will pose for a little money.

❸ Even more spectacular Ifugao villages are **Banga-An** (an hour's
❹ drive away on rough roads or three hours on foot) or **Batad** (1½-hour drive, four to five hours on foot), both set among the terraces. Along the way you'll see pine-covered slopes, green valleys dwarfed by clouded peaks, far-off, pyramid-shape Ifugao huts improbably perched on crags, and mountain streams irrigating the terraces. You can't drive into these villages; to get there, you must walk. There life goes on pretty much as it has for centuries: Rice is still planted in age-old rituals and plowed regularly with the help of the ubiquitous water buffalo. Dogs, pigs, and ducks wander about and under the native huts, which are elevated on wood posts. Handicrafts—rattan backpacks, baskets, and ornaments—are sold for low prices.

Tour 3: Vigan and Laoag

The respective capitals of the Ilocos Sur and Ilocos Norte provinces, the small, coastal cities of Vigan and Laoag date to the early years of Spanish colonization. Both—but especially Vigan—have some of the best-preserved Spanish-influenced architecture in the country, suggesting how Manila's Intramuros would have looked had it not been destroyed during World War II. The towns between these two cities are noteworthy for their ancient churches and bell towers.

❺ In **Vigan,** a 3½-hour scenic drive from Baguio City, you can explore the old quarter in a couple of hours. (An excellent guide to the area is Ric Favis, tel. 77/722–2286, who owns a home in Vigan's ancestral quarter. His rates average $10 per hour.) The **Ayala Museum** (Burgos St., tel. 77/855–316; open Tues.–Sun. 9–noon and 1–5; admission charge) is a collection of dioramas, artifacts, and paintings relating to the area's history. From there it's about a 10-minute walk to the town's main landmark, the 16th-century **Vigan Cathedral** (also known as the Cathedral of St. Paul), a massive, whitewashed brick-and-wood structure with a tile roof. Chinese lions guard the portals and the gleaming silver altar within. It's a short stroll northwest of the cathedral to the old quarter. The buildings have whitewashed brick walls, tile roofs, sliding *capiz* (mother-of-pearl) windows, and lofty interiors. **General Luna, Crisologo, De los Reyes,** and **Bonifacio streets** have row upon row of these edifices—perfect for Philippine Westerns or Gothic films, for which, in fact, they have been used.

❻ **Laoag** (a 1½-hour ride from Vigan) isn't as interesting as Vigan, though the **Laoag Cathedral** and its **Sinking Bell Tower** are worth visiting. The 17th-century cathedral is heavily buttressed (a protection against earthquakes), with two exterior stone stairways, urn ornamentation, and foliate capitals. North of the church is a bell tower that has sunk about 1 m (1.09 yds), so that its portal is barely visible.

Between Vigan and Laoag are towns whose churches are fine examples of what a local writer once termed Filipino Baroque—unique, even rococo combinations of Western and Asian styles. Among the most impressive are **Santa Maria,** with its stately broad steps; **Magsingal,** with a small but intriguing museum nearby; and the majestic **Paoay Church** in **Paoay,** a sleepy town about 15 minutes south of Laoag. The frontal crenellations and turrets, massive curlicued buttresses, exterior stairways, and niches give the impression of a Javanese temple. Beside this splendid fusion of styles is a belfry made of limestone, which was used as an outpost during the revolution of 1896 and by guerrillas during the Japanese occupation in World War II.

Off the Beaten Track

Sagada, northeast of Baguio, is a small, tightly knit community deep in the central Cordilleras among the rice terraces. A favorite with adventurous backpackers, the town has several burial caves with hanging coffins, an underground river, waterfalls, limestone formations, and hiking trails. There are no cinemas, no discos, no shopping malls, and no pollution. This is a wonderful place to visit, but be respectful of local customs. The trip from Baguio is a dusty, eight-hour bus ride on narrow winding roads but is more than compensated for by breathtaking mountain vistas. Dangwa buses (tel. 74/442–4150 or 74/442–2449) leave in the early morning from the terminal in front of the Baguio public market.

The **Batanes** are the country's northernmost islands, closer to Taiwan than to Luzon. The rugged cliffs, rolling grassy fields akin to the Scottish moors, scenic coastline, and idyllic towns with unique stone-walled homes make for great treks. The crime rate is nil. It's best to visit between November and May, as these isles are in the middle of the typhoon belt. PAL flies to Basco, the capital, thrice weekly. Be sure to book your flight well in advance, as it is a popular destination with the locals.

Shopping

Baguio Check out the handicraft section of the **Baguio Public Market** and the antiques shops right above it. **Tucucan** (tel. 74/442–4169) has unusual artifacts, from baskets to beads. For items made of *ikat* (an indigenous woven cloth), try **Narda's** at its main shop on Kilometer 5, Trinidad Valley (tel. 74/432–2362). Easter Weaving School (Easter Rd., a 10-minute drive from Session Rd.) offers highland blankets and clothing woven on the premises. At **Munsayac's Handicraft** (21 Leonard Wood Rd., tel. 74/442–2451), good wood carvings, brass, and silverware can be found. Off Session Road there's the **St. Louis Silver Shop** (tel. 74442–7136), with conventional but high-quality artisanship.

Banaue Besides the town market, souvenir stands at the most popular scenic spots carry local handicrafts, including tribal spears.

Vigan/Laoag Other than the town markets, there's the *burnay*, or potters' district, of Vigan, about a 15-minute walk from the cathedral, where jars and urns can be bought for low prices from the potters themselves. The Old Quarter has antiques shops, such as **Ciudad Fernandina** (888 Plaza Burgos, tel. 77/722–2888), while in the town of Santiago, south of Vigan, there's **Cora's Ethnic Handwoven,** where the prized local weave is available.

Beaches

The route between Baguio and Vigan consists mainly of a coastal highway by the South China Sea. Numerous small resorts dot the coast, especially in the province of **La Union,** the first province you enter descending from Baguio via Naguilian Road. Accommodations tend to be basic. Between Vigan and Laoag are good beaches—most of which have no resorts—near the towns of **Cabugao, Sinait, Currimao,** and **Pangil.** Sinait's beach, **Pug-os,** is a picture-pretty white-sand beach used by local fishermen to store their boats and nets. Some four hours by bus north of Laoag is the fishing village of **Pagudpud,** with coves and beaches popular with the locals.

Dining and Lodging

Dining. On the Ilocos coast, seafood dishes are the specialty. Try fried squid, fresh shrimp marinated in vinegar and peppers, and grilled catch of the day. In Vigan's plaza, you can taste the local delicacy, *empanada* (a turnover) stuffed with vegetables. In the Cordilleras, vegetables and meat, particularly pork and chicken, are favored. Also worth trying are *ipon*, delicious teeny fish caught seasonally, and *pinakbet*, a vegetable dish with bits of pork and tiny shrimp, flavored with *bagoong*, a salty shrimp paste (also used as a condiment).

Restaurants in the region are open every day and do not require reservations or formal dress. However, most do not tolerate shorts or sandals.

Highly recommended restaurants are indicated by a star ★.

Category	Cost*
$$$$	over P450 ($16)
$$$	P250–P450 ($9–$16)
$$	P112–P250 ($4–$9)
$	under P112 ($4)

per person, not including 10% VAT; 10% service charge usually added

Lodging. Baguio City has a wide range of accommodations, from medium-size hotels to pension-style lodgings. The other cities offer mostly family-run hotels, short on amenities but generally well maintained and clean, with the staff invariably courteous and helpful.

Highly recommended hotels are indicated by a star ★.

Category	Cost*
$$$$	over P1,680 ($60)
$$$	P1,120–P1,680 ($40–$60)
$$	P420–P1,120 ($15–$40)
$	under P420 ($15)

All prices are for a double room, not including 10% service charge and 13.7% government tax.

Baguio
Dining

★ **Mario's.** This restaurant has a first-rate Caesar salad, good steaks, seafood, and daily chef's specials. Its success has spawned two branches in Metro Manila. *Session Rd., tel. 74/442-4241. AE, DC, MC, V. $$$*

★ **Cafe by the Ruins.** An airy place with a patio setting, this café serves excellent home-cooked Philippine cuisine, including delicious tiny fried fish, fish roe steak, and vegetarian spring rolls. The café makes its own pastas and bread. *23 Chuntug St., tel. 74/442-5041. No credit cards. $$*

Star Cafe. This bright, busy Chinese restaurant has an extensive menu of tasty dishes, most of which are reasonably priced. *Session Rd., tel. 74/442-3148. AE, DC, MC, V. $$*

Bonuan. This one specializes in seafood and Philippine cuisine. *10-B Happy Glen Loop, tel. 74/442-5175. AE, V. $*

Lodging **Benguet Prime Hotel.** Right in the heart of busy downtown, this hotel has no lobby to speak of but is clean and convenient. Rooms are spacious, though the decor is plain. *Session Rd. at Calderon, tel. 74/442-7066. 51 rooms. Facilities: 24-hr room service, fast-food restaurant. AE, DC, V. $$*

Burnham Hotel. The rooms in this small hotel near Session Road, the heart of downtown Baguio, are clean and wood-paneled. The rooms on the ground floor can be noisy. *21 Calderon Rd., tel. 74/442-2331 or 74/442-5117, fax 74/442-8415. 18 rooms. Facilities: restaurant, room service. AE, DC, V. $$*

Mountain Lodge. A cozy establishment with a lobby fireplace and local artifacts as decor, the lodge is in a quiet area. The rooms are clean and simply furnished. Service is adequate. *27 Leonard Wood Rd., tel. 74/442-4544. 21 rooms. Facilities: restaurant, bar. DC, MC, V. $$*

Munsayac Inn. This is a small, family-run hotel with good ambience. Long patronized by missionaries, the inn will appeal to those who like their lodgings on the quiet side. *124 Leonard Wood Rd., tel. 74/442-2451. 20 rooms. Facilities: restaurant, handicraft shop, lounge. AE, DC, MC, V. $$*

★ **Casa Amapola.** Located in a quiet neighborhood, this pension—once a family residence—retains a family-style informality. What was once the living room is now a lounge where guests meet informally, and there's a terrace where you can breakfast while watching the fog lift from the surrounding hills. In addition to the regular rooms, three three-story chalets with verandas and kitchens are available for those who like more privacy. *46 First Rd., Quezon Hill, tel. 74/442-3406. 13 rooms, 3 chalets. Facilities: dining room, garden. AE, V. $-$$*

Banaue
Dining

★ **Banaue Hotel Restaurant.** This is an informal but excellent restaurant serving both Continental food and such Philippine regional dishes as *pinakbet* (vegetable stew with pork in a salty sauce). The room is large and airy, with bright red decor, native wall hangings, and a view of the hotel gardens. Service is superb. *Banaue Hotel, Banaue, tel. 73/386-4007. AE, DC, MC, V. $$$*

Lodging **Banaue Hotel.** Each room at this semiluxury hotel has a good view of the town and valley, a terrace, and decor reminiscent of a country lodge. *Banaue, tel. 73/386-4007; in Manila, tel. 2/810-4741 to -4745, fax 2/817-9566. 90 rooms. Facilities: outdoor pool, restaurant, handicraft shop. AE, DC, MC, V. $$$$*

Sanafe Lodge. Near the city market, Sanafe is a combination dormitory and hotel. The small lobby overlooks rice terraces; the rooms are small but clean. Dorm rooms—which sleep eight—are spartan but also clean, and cheaper. The resident manager is a gold mine of information concerning the area. *Banaue; for reservations in Manila, tel. 2/721–1075. 14 rooms (8 with bath) and 2 dorms. Facilities: restaurant. No credit cards. $–$$*

Laoag **Pamulinawen.** Wood-paneled and spacious, Pamulinawen serves
Dining very good Philippine cuisine, including *pinakbet* and beef *tapa*
★ (cured, dried strips of meat served with a vinegar-and-garlic sauce),
and some Continental dishes. *Fort Ilokandia Hotel, near Laoag Airport, tel. 77/221–166. AE, DC, MC, V. $$$*

Lodging **Fort Ilokandia.** This sprawling hotel is made up of several two-story
★ buildings whose style and room decor suggest Vigan's old residences. Tiled walkways connect the buildings, which are nestled
among sand dunes. The hotel has a good black-sand beach. *Near
Laoag Airport, tel. 77/221–166 to –170, fax 77/422–356. 250 rooms.
Facilities: restaurant, pool, banquet rooms, disco, bar, gift shops.
AE, DC, MC, V. $$$*

Vigan **Cool Spot.** In a wide, airy thatch-and-bamboo hut, regional dishes
Dining are served. *Burgos St., tel. 77/722–2588. No credit cards. $*

Lodging **Cordillera Inn.** This is a colonial-era building with broad stairways
and good views of the old quarter. The rooms are on the bare side but
clean. *General Luna St., cnr. Crisologo St., tel. 77/722–2526. 23
rooms. Facilities: restaurant, handicraft shop. No credit cards, but
traveler's checks accepted. $$*
Villa Angela. A lovely turn-of-the-century home and garden converted into a pension, with period furniture. The living room has
family memorabilia on display. Meals have to be ordered in advance.
*Quirino Blvd., cnr. Liberation St., tel. 77/722–2755 or 77/722–2766.
No credit cards. $*

The Arts

Baguio has a lively arts scene, with the arts collective, the **Baguio
Arts Guild** (tel. 74/442–8489), and other civic groups organizing the
biannual *Baguio Arts Festival* in late November. Poetry readings,
art exhibits, dance, music, and performance art constitute a cornucopia of activity. And there is the **Phoenix Art Gallery** (tel. 74/442–
5041) adjacent to Cafe by the Ruins. Of course there are also the different handicraft stores throughout the region, the **Ayala Museum**
(tel. 77/855–316) in Vigan, and the **Juan Luna Museum**—the home of
a well-known 19th-century Filipino artist—in the sleepy town of
Badoc, near Laoag (no phone; admission charge; open 9–noon and
1–4). Festivals are occasions for traditional performances, including
native dances. The **Banaue Hotel** puts on a free cultural show of
Ifugao dances for its guests nightly at 8, or after dinner. After the
performance, the dancers try to get the guests to join in for an impromptu session.

Nightlife

Baguio has some nightclubs (concentrated mainly on Abanao
Street, not far from the public market), a disco, and a casino. Vigan
closes down around 8 PM, while Laoag has a disco and a casino.

Pub Luz. Folk and rock bands play here on weekends. *12 Chuntug
St., Baguio City, across from City Hall, no phone.*
Rumors. A low-key bar and lounge with tasty appetizers; you can
also hear live music here from time to time. *55 Session Rd., Baguio
City, no phone.*

Songs. This club features jazz or folk music; patrons are of all ages. *181 Session Rd. at Carlu St., Baguio City, tel. 74/442–4963.*

Spirits. This is a pleasant, lively disco in a rambling colonial-era gingerbread-style wooden house that is itself worth a close look. *22 Otek St. at Burnham Park, Baguio City, tel. 74/442–3097.*

The Visayas, Mindanao, and Palawan

Geographically, the Visayas are the center of the Philippines. Bound on the north by Luzon and on the south by Mindanao, this group of islands has some of the best beaches and resorts in the country, unusual natural attractions, and Muslim and other non-Hispanicized minority cultures.

The land and seas are especially fertile, so while northerners are known for their industry and frugality, southerners are easygoing, gregarious, and musical (the best guitars come from this area). Yet some of the worst pockets of poverty are also found here, arising out of centuries-old feudalism, an overdependence on cash crops, and the often tragic effects of militarization in areas where the New People's Army is active. It bears repeating that travelers need not worry about being caught up in the conflict: Armed clashes almost always occur in remote rural areas.

Except for Cebu City, there isn't much nightlife in the region. To really enjoy the south, one has to appreciate the affectionate, fun-loving ways of its people, explore the beaches and beautiful scenery, and take in the charm of small towns and cities, with their old Spanish homes.

Cebu City, the "Queen City of the South" and capital of Cebu Island, is where Ferdinand Magellan claimed the country for Spain in 1521. The first Philippine settlement colonized by the Spanish, Cebu is the oldest city in the country. This small but strategically important port has the advantages of a big city—restaurants, shops, lodgings, schools, and businesses—but few of its drawbacks. Pollution so far isn't a problem.

Cebu City's airport provides a crucial link between Manila and Mindanao and between the western and eastern parts of the Visayas. It makes sense to use Cebu as a focal point for exploring the southern Philippines. Most regional destinations—such as charming Iloilo City, rich in old mansions and baroque churches—are only a 30-minute flight away. Zamboanga City in southwest Mindanao, only 45 minutes away by plane, is an intriguing mix of Christian and Muslim cultures. An hour away by plane are bustling Davao City—possibly the nation's most ethnically diverse city—and Puerto Princesa on Palawan Island.

Important Addresses and Numbers

All numbers are in Cebu City unless noted otherwise. Area codes: Cebu, 32; Iloilo, 33; Zamboanga, 62; Davao, 82; Palawan, 4821.

Tourist Information

Department of Tourism. Cebu City: Fort San Pedro, tel. 32/915–03. Davao City: Magsaysay Avenue at Magsaysay Park, tel. 82/221–6798 or 82/221–6955, fax 82/221–0070. Iloilo City: Sarabia Hotel, General Luna St., tel. 33/754–11, fax 33/270–245. Puerto Princesa:

	Provincial Capitol, tel. 4821/2983. Zamboanga City: Lantaka Hotel, Valderrosa St., tel. 62/991–0217 or 62/991-9218, fax 62/991–1626.
U.S. Consulate	Fourth Floor, IBAA Building, Gorordo Avenue, tel. 32/795–10, 32/520–44, or 32/707–25.
Emergencies	**Police and medical:** tel. 32/956–76 or 32/746–42.

Arriving and Departing

By Plane Philippine Air Lines (tel. 32/832–3166) has daily flights from Manila to major cities in the region, with six to Cebu City's **Mactan International Airport** (on Mactan Island and 45 minutes from the city proper), five to Iloilo City, and two to Zamboanga. In the summer, PAL also has flights from Tokyo to Cebu. **Singapore Airlines** (tel. 32/548–49) has direct flights from Singapore to Cebu. Smaller **Lahug Airport**—30 minutes from Cebu City—is used by charter lines, such as **Aerolift** (tel. 32/928–54) and **Varona Aero Services** (tel. 32/702–29). Flights are available from Mactan Airport to most cities in the region, including Iloilo, Zamboanga, Davao, and Palawan.

By Ship Cebu is a busy port and a primary stop for interisland ships. All the major lines have trips between Cebu and ports all over the archipelago. The Cebu–Manila voyage takes 21 hours; Cebu–Davao, 12 hours. Some Cebu offices: **Aboitiz Shipping** (Osmeña Blvd., tel. 32/754–40 or 32/930—75; in Manila, tel. 2/276–332), **Escaño Lines** (Reclamation Area, tel. 32/772–53 or 32/621–22), and **Negros Navigation** (Port Area, tel. 32/943–07; in Manila, tel. 2/816–3481 or 2/856–986).

Getting Around

By Car Roads in the urban areas, especially in Iloilo City, are in good shape. While having a car gives you freedom and privacy, rates for taxis and jeepneys are inexpensive, and local drivers know the area better than you do. Car-rental agencies in Cebu: **Avis** (tel. 32/745–11 or 32/998–23), **Cattleya** (tel. 32/730–74 to –76), and **Hamilcars** (tel. 32/924–31). In Iloilo it's **Avis** (tel. 33/271–171), while in Davao try **Guani** (tel. 82/221–5000). In Puerto Princesa, try **Labuyo** (tel. 4821/2606 or 4821/2580.)

By Bus As elsewhere in the Philippines, bus is the main form of transport between towns. Buses usually begin and end their routes in the vicinity of the public market. Get to the market early in the morning to secure a good seat. Most buses are not air-conditioned.

By Taxi Taxis in Cebu are metered, while in Iloilo, Zamboanga, and Davao prices are agreed upon beforehand. The average taxi ride in Cebu costs P50. Trips to the airport and to out-of-town destinations start at P150. In Davao, a ride to the airport averages P60. In Puerto Princesa, motorized pedicabs are available for as low as P20.

By Jeepney Jeepneys also begin and end their trips at the public market. Fares are very low: A 2-mile ride within Cebu City, for example, costs only P2.

Guided Tours

Tours can be arranged in Manila (*see* Travel Agencies in Metro Manila, *above*). You can also consult the local Department of Tourism office (*see* Important Addresses and Numbers, *above*) for suggestions and a list of guides. The larger hotels usually house tour operators.

Exploring the Visayas, Mindanao, and Palawan

*Numbers in the margin correspond to points of interest on the
Visayas and Mindanao map.*

Tour 1: Cebu City

❶ **Cebu City** is the country's oldest city—founded by the Spanish con-
quistador Miguel Lopez de Legazpi in 1571. Little is left of the original settlement. Combined with other attractions, though, there's
enough for a fascinating and rewarding day-long tour. Most of the
historical sights are within walking distance of one another in the
downtown area near the ports.

We begin at **Fort San Pedro,** the oldest and smallest fort in the country, built in 1565. The Department of Tourism office is located here.
You may want to drop in first, ask questions, and pick up maps before exploring the fort and the city. The three bastions with turrets
for cannon give the fort its triangular shape. The parapets afford a
good view of the sea—a necessity in the days when the settlement
was a target of pirate raids. *Port Area, tel. 32/965–18. Admission
charge. Open daily 8–noon and 1–5.*

From the fort it's a 10-minute walk to **Magellan's Cross,** brought
over by the famed Portuguese navigator in 1521. You won't see the
original; because residents believe the cross is miraculous and used
to take slivers from it, it has been encased (for protection) in a hollow
wooden cross that is suspended from the ceiling of an open-sided
domed pavilion on Magallanes Street.

Opposite the cross are the **Santo Niño** and **Basilica Minore.** The
18th-century basilica (closed daily noon–2 PM), done in typical Spanish baroque style, houses the oldest Catholic image—that of the Holy
Infant or Santo Niño—brought over by Magellan and presented to
Queen Juana of Zebu. Enshrined in glass and ornamented with gold
and precious stones, the icon stands atop a side altar, venerated by a
constant stream of devotees. Outside the church stand candle-bearing
middle-aged women who, for a donation, will pray and dance to the
Santo Niño on your behalf.

A short stroll from the basilica is the oldest street in the country,
named after Cristóbal Colón, otherwise known as Christopher Colum-
bus. Formerly the heart of the Parian District (or Chinatown), **Colón
Street** is now downtown Cebu's main drag. Here modernity crowds
in on you in the form of movie houses, restaurants, department
stores, and other commercial establishments.

Time Out Of the many eateries on Colón Street, try **Snow Sheen** (tel. 32/767–
69), the **International Rice House** (tel. 32/719–10), or **Ding How Dim
Sum House** (tel. 32/937–00 or 32/617–24). These busy, unpretentious places serve inexpensive but tasty Chinese food.

From the eastern end of Colón Street, it's a short walk to **Casa
Gorordo,** former residence of Cebu's first bishop, Juan Gorordo.
Now restored, the century-old wood house has a tile roof, mother-of-
pearl windows, a wide veranda, and a fine collection of household
furnishings from the last century. *Lopez Jaena St., tel. 32/945–76.
Admission charge. Open daily 9–noon and 2–6.*

From Casa Gorordo it's a 20-minute walk to the **University of San
Carlos Museum,** which has an extensive collection of seashells, fauna, and anthropological relics: local prehistoric stone and iron tools,

The Visayas and Mindanao

Romblon
Odiongan
*Tablas
Island*
*Sibuyan
Island*
Catarman
Laoang
Palapag
Masbate
Uson
Balud
MASBATE
SAMAR
Calbayog
City
Catbalogan
Boracay Island
T H E   V I S A Y A S
Kalibo
Roxas
City
*Visayan
Sea*
*Biliran
Island*
Culast
PANAY
Sicogon Island
*Bantayan
Island*
Escalante
Ormoc
City
Baybay
Burauen
LEYTE
*Leyte
Gulf*
Passi
Cadiz
City
Silay City
Talisay
Iloilo City
2
Bacolod
City
San Carlos
City
CEBU
*Matcan
Island*
Hilongos
*Dinagat
Island*
Miagao
Guimaras
Island
Guimaras
*Panay
Gulf*
Cebu City
1
Naga
Carcar
Maasin
*Panaon
Island*
Kabankalan
Strait
Strait
Cauayan
Sipalay
NEGROS
Badian
Island
Bohol
BOHOL
Chocolate Hills
8
Surigao City
*Mindanao
Sea*
Cabadbaran
1
Hinob-an
Bais City
Tanjay
Tagbilaran
City
Bayawan
Santa Catalina
Dumaguete
City
*Panglao
Island*
Camiguin
Island
7
Butuan
City
6
Palawan
*Siquijor
Island*
*Sulu
Sea*
Dapitan City
Dipolog City
Cagayan
de Oro City
Gingoog
City
1
Oroquieta
City
7
Iligan
City
M I N D A N A O
Marawi
City
Valencia
Pagadian
City
*Lake
Lanao*
Quezon
Tagum
Zamboanga Peninsula
N
Parang
Cotabato City
Sultan Kudarat
Mt. Apo
Magpet
3
Davao
City
5
4
Taluksangay
*Moro
Gulf*
Dinaig
Pikit
Kidapawan
3
Zamboanga City
Santa Cruz Island
Lamitan
Isabela
*Basilan
Island*
5
*Davao
Gulf*
Malita
Celebes Sea
N
Polomolok
General
Santos City
Glan
N

0   100 miles
0   150 km

burial jars, and pottery. Another section focuses on traditional clothing and ornaments of various tribal minorities. *Cnr. Rosario and Junquera Sts., tel. 32/724–10. Admission charge. Open 9–noon and 3–6, weekends and holidays by appointment.*

Incongruously located in an expensive suburb known as Beverly Hills is the **Taoist Temple,** dedicated to the teachings of the 6th-century BC Chinese philosopher Lao-tzu. You can get here by taxi (referred to as a P.U., for "public utility") for about P60. A flight of 99 steps leads to it from the road. Come for the panoramic views of the city, the colorful and ornate Chinese architecture, and to have your fortune read. *Beverly Hills, tel. 32/936–52. Admission free. Open daily until dark.*

Tour 2: Iloilo City

This city, capital of Iloilo Province on the island of Panay, is a half-hour flight from Cebu City, with Iloilo airport just 10 minutes from the center. A small and gracious aggregate of six districts, **Iloilo** (pronounced "*ee*-lo-*ee*-lo") has a genteel air and loads of southern charm. As always, it's a good idea to visit the Department of Tourism office (Sarabia Hotel, General Luna St., tel. 33/754–11 or 33/277–511) to pick up maps, brochures, and tips.

In the city and surrounding area are several churches worth visiting. In the city itself are **Molo Church** and the **Jaro Cathedral.** The former, a twin-spired Gothic structure erected in the late 19th century, sits in a pleasant park and has an intricate facade, with a kind of domed pergola, complete with Greek columns. The larger Jaro Cathedral also shows Gothic influences. In front is an open-air balcony with a statue of the Virgin Mary that locals consider miraculous. Across the street is the church's reconstructed belfry. Take some time to walk around the district and look at the grand, colonial-type residences, with their intricate grillwork and mother-of-pearl windows.

The 200-year-old **Miagao Fortress Church,** 8 km (5 mi) south of the city, has two differently designed bell towers—erected by two different friars—that also served as watchtowers against invasions by Muslim pirates. If you promise to be careful, the bell ringer will let you climb one of the towers. The sandstone facade depicts, amid floral designs, St. Christopher planting a coconut tree.

Time Out Try the seafood or Continental dishes on the breezy terrace of the **Igmaan** restaurant (tel. 33/271–171) at Hotel Del Rio (M.H. Del Pilar St.), by the broad Iloilo River. Note the bamboo fish pens on the water.

Closer to the city center and across from the provincial capitol building is the **Museo Iloilo.** The museum has an excellent collection of pre-Hispanic artifacts dug up mainly on Panay Island. These include fossils, Stone Age flake tools, and gold death masks. Other exhibits focus on liturgical art and the treasures of a British frigate shipwrecked nearby in the 19th century. *Bonifacio Dr., cnr. General Luna St., tel. 33/729–86. Admission charge. Open daily 8–noon and 1–5.*

Tour 3: Zamboanga City

A 45-minute plane ride from Cebu, **Zamboanga City** is famous for its bright flowers (its early name, Jambangan, meant "land of flowers"), which grow profusely in every garden. The roadsides are lined with bougainvillea and the bright-red-flowered *gumamela* bushes. It is also a city with a sizable Muslim population, made up mainly of the Yakan, Badjao, Samal, and Tausug tribes.

Begin exploring the city at **Plaza Pershing,** named after "Blackjack" Pershing, the first American governor of the region formerly known as Moroland. It's a pleasant spot for a stroll. Two blocks southeast of the square is **City Hall,** on Valderrosa Street. Built by the Americans in 1907, it's a curious combination of Arabic and baroque styles.

Heading east on Valderrosa Street you'll come to **Ft. Pilar,** an old Spanish fort not far from the Lantaka Hotel, where the Department of Tourism has its field office (tel. 62/991–0217 or –0218). Beyond the fort is **Rio Hondo,** a small riverine Muslim village with its own mosque. Many of the houses are on stilts. Men wear white skullcaps, and women wear the distinctive *malong,* brightly decorated wraparound clothing.

Time Out **Alavar's** (R.T. Lim Blvd., tel. 62/991–2483), run by a husband-and-wife team (he cooks, she manages), serves wonderful seafood. The specialty is *curacha* crabs in a creamy, sweet-spicy sauce that is the chef's secret. Down your food with refreshing *buko* (young coconut) juice.

❹ A bigger Muslim village on the coast is **Taluksangay,** about 16 km (10 mi) from Zamboanga. At the back of the town's distinctive red-and-white mosque is a prominent Muslim family's burial plot. The community is made up of seaweed gatherers; everywhere piles of seaweed dry in the sun. Stroll along the many catwalks and watch as women weave and sell mats. Remember to bargain; prices quoted at first will be high. On the way back to the city, stop by **Climaco Freedom Park** (named after a beloved mayor slain some years ago) and **Pasonanca Park.** The former's attraction is the Ecumenical Holy Hill: 14 Stations of the Cross on a roadside cliff leading to a giant white cross at the top, where you get good views of the city. The unique offering in Pasonanca is the **Pasonanca Treehouse,** which is available for one or two nights' (bathroomless) lodging if prior notification is given the city—a fun Tarzan-and-Jane experience for couples young at heart.

Tour 4: Davao City

❺ One of the largest cities in the world in terms of area (approximately 1,937 sq km, or 748 sq mi), **Davao City** (Tourism Office: Magsaysay Ave., Magsaysay Park, tel. 82/221–6798 or 82/221–6955.) is busy and booming. It's also probably the most ethnically diverse urban area in the country, with Muslim, Christian, Chinese, and indigenous tribal communities. Visit the **Madrazo fruit district,** famous for its tropical fruits, especially the *durian,* said to "smell like hell and taste like heaven"; the orchid vendors by City Hall; the intricate **Lon Wa Buddhist Temple,** the largest in Mindanao; the banana plantations and orchid gardens around the city; the Muslim fishing village near the wharf; and the breeding center for the majestic Philippine eagle, an endangered species, in Calinan, about 36 km (22 mi) from the city center. For pleasant beaches, there is nearby **Samal Island.** The city is also a good base from which to explore the surrounding countryside, including **Mt. Apo,** at 10,000 feet the tallest peak in the country. The average time for getting to the summit and back is four to five days.

Tour 5: Palawan

❻ Looking like a long dagger, **Palawan** is the archipelago's western-most island and one of its most isolated and least developed, with un-paved roads outside the capital of Puerto Princessa. There are beautiful beaches throughout, with excellent snorkeling and diving spots. North of the capital is a national rain-forest park with the world's longest known underground river, **St. Paul's Underground River.** To the south are the **Tabon Caves,** where remains of the earli-est Philippine inhabitants were unearthed. Palawan has flora and fauna not found elsewhere in the country, such as giant turtles, pea-cocks, mouse deer, scaly anteaters, and seven-color doves. Perhaps the most secluded luxury resorts in the Philippines are **El Nido** (in Manila, tel. 2/810–7291 to –7293, or 2/818–2623) and **Amanpulo** (in Manila, tel. 2/532–4040). Food, transportation, and lodging are all included in the price, which must be prepaid.

As the island has malaria-bearing mosquitoes, take preventive med-ication at least two weeks before making the 90-minute flight from Cebu City or Manila. There is a tourism counter at the airport and a field office at City Hall (tel. 4821/21–54).

Off the Beaten Track

❼ **Camiguin.** A three-hour trip from Cagayan de Oro City on the northwest coast of Mindanao, this lovely unspoiled isle is still heavi-ly forested and has seven volcanoes. Hibok-Hibok, the largest volca-no, can be climbed with a paid guide. The best place to hire guides is Ardent Hot Springs, not far from Mambajao, which is also a good place to begin—and end—the climb. Accommodations are basic but cheap and clean, and the inhabitants friendly. There are hot springs, trekking opportunities, beaches, and waterfalls.

❽ **Chocolate Hills, Bohol Island.** These are about 50 striking limestone hills, with an average height of 36 m (120 ft), that look like over-turned teacups sans handles. About a two-hour bus ride from the market in Tagbilaran City—a half-hour flight from Cebu City—the hills turn chocolate-brown during the dry months (February through May). In July they become green again, their grasses nour-ished by rain.

Mt. Mayon. Legazpi City near the tip of southern Luzon—an hour's flight from either Cebu or Manila—has what may be the world's most symmetrical (and still active) volcano, towering 2,457 m (8,189 ft) over the Bicol countryside. Aside from the lure of the two- to three-day climb, Mt. Mayon has a volcanology/seismography station at about 750 m (2,500 ft), with a rest house offering panoramic views of the volcano and the surrounding terrain. The station has geologi-cal displays relating to volcanoes, earthquakes, and tidal waves. You can also see a seismograph in operation. Just 5 km (3 mi) from Legazpi City are the **Cagsawa Bell Tower and Ruins.** They are rem-nants of a church buried by an 1814 eruption along with more than 1,000 people who had sought refuge there. The Department of Tour-ism office in the city is at Peñaranda Park, Albay District (tel. 5221/4492 or 5221/4026).

Shopping

Cebu City **Colón Street** is a good shopping street, with a number of **Gaisano** de-partment stores, part of a regionwide chain. One of the best handi-craft stores in the city is the **Cebu Display Center** (11–13 Magallanes, at Lapu-Lapu St., tel. 32/522–23 or 32/522–24), which has an excellent collection of regional crafts, particularly shellcraft. Prices aren't inflated for tourists.

Davao City The downtown **Aldevinco Shopping Center** is a complex of neat rows of small stores selling Mindanao tribal crafts, woven mats, Muslim brassware, antiques, batik cloth, and wood carvings. A 15-minute walk away is the **Madrazo fruit district,** where exotic tropical fruits like *lanzones, chico, atis, rambutan,* and durian can be seen, tasted, and bought.

Iloilo City At **Asilo de Molo** (Avancena St., Molo, tel. 33/774–17), an orphanage for girls, the skills of fine embroidery, especially for church vestments, are taught by nuns. Embroidered gowns, dresses, and exquisite *barong tagalogs* are sold at firm prices. **Sinamay Dealer** (Osmeña St., Arevalo, tel. 33/42–21) is a weaving store where fine cloth is spun from pineapple fiber. Shirts and dresses are made from the cloth, then hand-embroidered.

Puerto Princesa Along Rizal Avenue, handicrafts, antiques, and baskets can be purchased at **Mencoco, Culture Shack,** or **Karla's.** The public market is a good source as well. Try **Macawili Handicraft** for baskets and brassware.

Zamboanga City The **City Market** (Alano St., dawn to dark) is one of the most colorful in the country. The handicraft section, especially Row C, has the woven mats for which Zamboanga is noted, along with brassware, antiques, shellcraft, and batik from Indonesia. For tribal weavings prized by Philippine designers, visit the **Yakan Weaving Village,** 5 km (3 mi) from the city on the west coast. The weave is so fine it takes at least a week to finish a meter of cloth. Zamboanga is also famous for shells; the pickings are good at **Zamboanga Home Products** (San José St. at Jaldon, tel. 62/28–74), **San Luis Shell Industries** (San José Rd., tel. 62/24–19), and **Rocan** (San José Rd., tel. 62/24–92).

Beaches

Santa Cruz Island, Zamboanga City. Rent a motorized *banca,* a native canoe fitted with outriggers, from the **Lantaka Hotel** (tel. 62/991–2033 to 2036) for the 20-minute trip to Santa Cruz Island. (Rates are officially set at $7 round-trip.) The small island has a wonderful pink coral beach and a lagoon in the middle. Be sure to bring water and refreshments, as there are no food or beverage stands. At the beach's eastern end is a Muslim burial ground, ornamented with stars, crescents, and tiny boats—to provide passage to the next life. *Admission charge. Open daily 7–4.*

Badian, Cebu. A small island off the southwest coast of Cebu, Badian houses the **Badian Beach Club** (Cebu, tel. 32/613–06), with its lovely beachfront, scenic views of the bay, sailboats, and a variety of water sports, including scuba diving.

Panglao, Bohol. This isle is connected by a bridge to Tagbilaran City on Bohol Island, a 20-minute flight from Cebu, and has three beautiful beach areas: **Bikini Beach, Bolod,** and **Alona Beach.** Bolod has the pricey Bohol Beach Club (Manila tel. 2/522–2301), complete with private beach, cabanas, water sports, pool, and bar. Inexpensive accommodations are available at the other two beaches.

Boracay Island. Famous among Europeans, this bow-tie-shape island off the coast of Panay has one of the Philippines' most beautiful beaches, with sands as fine and smooth as refined sugar. It has accommodations ranging from the expensive to the basic—a few too many, in fact—and is crowded from November to May. Charter flights are available from Cebu or Manila via **Aerolift.**

Guimaras Island. A 45-minute boat ride from Iloilo City, this lush island, famous for mangoes, has secluded resorts, including **Isla Naburot** (tel. 33/766–16), which has native-style cottages, excellent meals, water sports, and diving facilities.

Dining and Lodging

Dining. This region has several specialties, particularly in seafood. *Sinugba* is a Cebu method of grilling fish and shellfish over coals. Zamboangeños like raw fish marinated in vinegar and hot green peppers, steamed crabs, and barbecued meats. Iloilo is well known for its *pancit molo* (pork dumplings in noodle soup), *la paz batchoy* (a tripe stew), and pastries. At all establishments listed, dress is casual and reservations unnecessary.

Highly recommended restaurants are indicated by a star ★.

Category	Cost*
$$$$	over P500 ($18)
$$$	P300–P500 ($11–$18)
$$	P150–P300 ($6–$11)
$	under P150 ($6)

not including 10% VAT; most places add 10% service charge

Lodging. Cebu City, the second-biggest city in the Philippines, has a full range of accommodations, while Iloilo and Zamboanga have mainly mid-range and medium-size hotels. All hotels listed have private baths, unless otherwise noted. Highly recommended hotels are indicated by a star ★.

Category	Cost*
$$$$	over P3,000 ($108)
$$$	P1,500–P3,000 ($53–$108)
$$	P600–P1,500 ($22–$53)
$	under P600 ($22)

All prices are for a standard double room, not including 10% service charge and 13.7% tax.

Cebu City
Dining
★ **Lantaw Seafoods Restaurant.** You can feast on a splendid, well-priced buffet—including seafood—in an open-air, garden setting while enjoying a folk-dance show and scenic views of the city. Seating at long tables is available for groups. *Cebu Plaza, Nivel Hills, Lahug, tel. 32/924–31 to –39. AE, DC, MC, V. $$$*

Ding How Dim Sum. Good light Chinese meals are served here. *Colón St., tel. 32/937–00 or 32/617–24. No credit cards. $*

★ **Vienna Kaffehaus.** Run by an Austrian, the place tries to re-create the ambience of a Viennese coffeehouse, complete with Viennese food, newspapers, and magazines. *Manros Plaza, Maxilom Ave., tel. 32/526–20. No credit cards. $*

Lodging
★ **Cebu Plaza.** A luxurious hotel, the Cebu Plaza has panoramic views, sprawling grounds, and a clientele consisting mainly of Japanese

and Chinese tourists. The best rooms are those with a view of the city. *Nivel Hills, Lahug, tel. 32/212–41, fax 32/531–06. 417 rooms. Facilities: outdoor pool, restaurants, bars, disco, shops, tennis courts, function rooms. AE, DC, MC, V. $$$$*

Montebello Villa. Located in a quiet neighborhood, this hotel has nice gardens and cheerfully decorated rooms. *Banilad, tel. 32/850–21, fax 32/839–20. 142 rooms. Facilities: restaurants, pool, tennis courts, casino, convention rooms, tour offices, gift shop. AE, DC, MC, V. $$*

Park Place Hotel. In the heart of downtown, this neat and cozy establishment is patronized mostly by Westerners. *Puente Osmena, tel. 32/211–131, fax 32/634–7509. 114 rooms. Facilities: restaurant, café, bar, shops, function rooms. AE, DC, MC, V. $$*

Davao City
Dining

Luz Kinilaw. It's on the shore area, where fishermen take their yellowfin tuna catch, for which Davao is famous. The specialties are coal-grilled tail and jaw, and sashimi. *Salmonan, Quezon Blvd., tel. 82/646–12. DC, V. $$*

Molave. Well known for its unique, truly greaseless fried chicken. *Matina District, tel. 82/728–54. No credit cards. $*

Lodging
★

Davao Insular Hotel. Close to the airport and about 3 km (2 mi) from town, the hotel is located on 20 lush acres with coconut groves, gardens, and a beachfront. Nearby is a small settlement of an indigenous tribe, the Mandaya. Twice a day *tuba* (coconut wine) gatherers climb the tall trees to collect the sap. The airy rooms, done in native-style decor, come with verandas. *Lanang, Davao City, tel. 82/234–3050, fax 82/629–59. 153 rooms. Facilities: outdoor pool, tennis and squash courts, restaurants, coffee shop, cocktail lounge, function rooms, gift shops, beachfront. AE, DC, MC, V. $$$$*

Apo View. Located in downtown Davao, with a pleasantly busy lobby and rooms that are comfortably furnished, this place has a regular clientele of locals and businessmen. *J. Camus St., tel. 82/221–6430, fax 82/221–0748. 105 rooms. Facilities: outdoor pool, coffee shop, restaurant, cocktail lounge, gift shop. AE, DC, MC, V. $$$*

Iloilo City
Dining
★

Sunset Terrace. For the money, you get excellent seafood (try the blue marlin and *tanguigue*, or local mackerel, plus scenic views of the river and (if you time it right) a sunset to boot. *Hotel del Rio, M.H. Del Pilar St., tel. 33/755–85. AE, DC, MC, V. $$*

Ihawan. A down-home atmosphere prevails in this friendly place serving good chicken barbecue and other grilled meats. *Yulo St., tel. 33/768–34. No credit cards. $*

Lodging
★

Hotel Del Rio. The place is modest but quiet, appealing, and well run. The spacious, clean rooms get breezes from the Iloilo River, which flows right beside it. *M.H. Del Pilar St., tel. 33/755–85, fax 33/707–36. 57 rooms. Facilities: outdoor pool, restaurants, disco, bar, gift shop. AE, DC, MC, V. $$*

Sarabia Manor. This hotel has a cosmopolitan feel and a friendly, well-informed staff. Rooms are well kept and spacious, but ceilings are rather low. *General Luna St., tel. 33/727–31, fax 33/791–27. 100 rooms. Facilities: outdoor pool, restaurants, cocktail lounge, disco, gift shop. AE, DC, MC, V. $$*

Puerto Princesa
Dining

Café Puerto. Continental cuisine, including seafood and chops, in one of the city's more formal settings. *Rizal Ave., tel. 4821/2266. AE, DC, M, V. $$$*

Ka Lui's. Puerto's free spirits hang out here to dine on fresh seafood and delicious fruit shakes served in an airy bamboo veranda. *Rizal Ave., tel. 4821/2580. No credit cards. $$*

Lodging **Badjao Inn.** A pleasant place, with a veranda. Many of the rooms, however, are cheerless. *350 Rizal Ave., tel. 4821/2761. 26 rooms. Facilities: restaurant, laundry. AE. $$*

Casa Linda. Right behind Badjao and constructed of bamboo, wood, and thatch, this inn has a veranda, as well as a courtyard garden and parrots. *Tel. 4821/2606. 13 rooms. Facilities: restaurant, laundry. AE. $$*

Zamboanga **Alavar's.** Justifiably famous for his seafood, the owner/chef creates
City delicious sauces for crabs. Prawns, clams, blue marlin—you name
Dining it, this restaurant has it—are served in what was once a rambling
★ house. *R.T. Lim Blvd., tel. 62/991-2483. DC, MC, V. $$*

Palmeras. Dine pleasantly in a shaded terrace set in a garden. Service is a bit slow, but the barbecued meats are good. *Santa Maria Rd., tel. 62/991-3284. AE, V. $$*

Lodging **Lantaka.** In the heart of the city and right by the waterfront, Lantaka has well-appointed rooms and gracious service. The terrace abuts the sea, where Badjaos, a tribe of sea gypsies, sell mats and seashells. Watch the sunset and the sea from the lovely open-air Talisay Bar. Unfortunately, the hotel cuisine (which, believe it or not, rarely includes seafood) is mediocre. *Valderrosa St., tel. tel. 62/991-2033, fax 62/991-1626. 112 rooms. Facilities: pool, restaurants, bar, conference room, travel offices, handicraft shop. AE, DC, MC, V. $$*

Zamboanga Hermosa Inn. The rooms are small but comfortably furnished. *Mayor Jaldon St., tel. 62/991-2042. 33 rooms. Facilities: restaurant, laundry service. DC. $*

The Arts

The ground floor of **Casa Gorordo** in Cebu City (Lopez Jaena St., tel. 32/945-76) is used as an art gallery for contemporary works by Filipino artists. Iloilo has a small but fine museum, the **Iloilo Museum** (Bonifacio Dr. at General Luna St., tel. 33/729-86) with dioramas, artifacts from the region, and video and art exhibits. There are two galleries, the **Iloilo Society of Arts Gallery** (2nd Floor, B & C Square, Iznart St., tel. 33/710-26) and **Galeria de Madia-as** (Washington St., Jaro, Department of Tourism, tel. 33/787-01 or 33/745-11), both of which display works by contemporary artists. The **Dabaw Museum** in Davao City (Insular Village, Lanag St., tel. 82/732-96), not far from the Insular Hotel, has fascinating displays of tribal artifacts and costumes. The **Palawan Museum** in Puerto Princesa (Rizal St.) has good ethnographic and crafts displays.

Nightlife

Cebu City is the only place in the region with nightlife to speak of. Iloilo and Davao cities have a few discos and bars, but that's about it. Zamboanga has a few bars. All the following are in Cebu City.

After Six (Osmena Blvd., tel. 32/532-66), an animated disco with live bands, is popular with the young set. The city's fashionable set dances at the strobe-lit **Bai Disco** (Cebu Plaza Hotel, Nivel Hills, Lahug, tel. 32/924-31). At the **Cebu Casino** (Nivel Hills, Lahug, tel. 32/743-61), not far from Cebu Plaza, the action at the tables goes from 5 PM to 5 AM. **Love City** (Osmeña Blvd., tel. 32/940-77) is a raucous downtown bar with a mostly male clientele who come for beer and the go-go dancers. **St. Gotthard** (Fulton St., Lahug, tel. 32/753–76) is a lively disco with waitresses on roller skates. Europeans favor the friendly, informal **St. Moritz Bar** (Gorordo Ave., Lahug, tel. 32/612–40), part of a hotel of the same name.

7 Singapore

By Nigel Fisher

Nigel Fisher is the editor of the monthly travel publication Voyager International. *He has traveled extensively throughout Asia and the world.*

To arrive in Singapore is to step into a world where the muezzin call to prayer competes with the bustle of capitalism; where old men play mah-jongg in the streets and white-clad bowlers send the ball flying down well-tended cricket pitches; where Chinese fortune-tellers and high-priced management consultants advise the same entrepreneur. This great diversity of lifestyles, cultures, and religions thrives within the framework of a well-ordered society. Singapore is a spotlessly clean—some say sterile—modern metropolis, surrounded by green, groomed parks and populated by 2.7 million extremely polite, well-mannered people.

Malays, who have the oldest historical claim to Singapore, today account for 14.9% of its population. Their faith in Allah and their orientation to family and service to the community provide a more relaxed, peaceful, and communal flavor and act as a counterpoint to the entrepreneurial vigor of the Chinese.

Though the Chinese make up approximately 76% of the population, their ranks comprise at least half a dozen different ethnic groups— Hokkien, Teochew, Cantonese, Hakka, Fukien, Hainanese—each with its own language, mythology, and especially cuisine. They came as impoverished immigrants in the 19th century and now hold the economic and political strings.

Singapore's Indian population, who also descend from 19th-century immigrants, are almost as ethnically diverse as the Chinese. While the majority are Hindu Tamils from South India, there are also Muslims from South India and, in smaller numbers, Bengalis, Biharis, Gujeratis, Marathis, Kashmiris, and Punjabis. From Sri Lanka come other Hindu Tamils and the Sinhalese (often mistaken for Indians), who are neither Hindu nor Muslim but follow the teachings of Hinayana Buddhism. Today, Indians, who account for 7% of Singapore's population, remain deeply tied to their community and traditional customs. Hinduism remains a powerful force—Singapore has more than 20 major temples devoted to Hindu gods—and some of the Tamil Hindu festivals, such as Thaipusam, are observed with more feverish ritualism than in India. Indian food, too, remains true to its roots; it has been said that one can eat better curries in Singapore than in India.

While the Malays, Chinese, and Indians account for 97% of Singapore's population, other ethnic groups—from Eurasians to Filipinos, from Armenians to Thais—contribute significantly to the nation's cultural mix. Understandably, the British and the heritage of their colonial stay is profoundly felt even though Singapore became an independent nation in 1965.

In a part of the world where histories tend to be ancient and rich, Singapore is unique in having almost no history at all. Modern Singapore tends to date its history from the early morning of January 29, 1819, when a representative of the British East India Company, Thomas Stamford Raffles, stepped ashore at Singa Pura (Sanskrit for "lion city"), as the island was then called, hoping to establish a British trading settlement on the southern part of the Malay Peninsula. The two sons of the previous sultan, who had died six years earlier, were in dispute over who would inherit the throne. Raffles backed the claim of the elder brother, Tunku Hussein Mohamed Shah, and proclaimed him sultan. Offering to support the new sultanate with British military strength, Raffles persuaded him to grant the British a lease allowing them to establish a trading post on the island in return for an annual rent; within a week the negotiations were concluded. (A later treaty ceded the island outright to the

British.) Within three years, the small fishing village, surrounded by swamps and jungle and populated by only tigers and 200 or so Malays, had become a boomtown of 10,000 immigrants, administered by 74 British employees of the East India Company.

As Singapore grew, the British erected splendid public buildings, churches, and hotels, often using Indian convicts for labor. The Muslim, Hindu, Taoist, and Buddhist communities—swelling rapidly from the influx of fortune-seeking settlers from Malaya, India, and South China—built mosques, temples, and shrines. Magnificent houses for wealthy merchants sprang up, and the harbor became lined with *godowns* (warehouses) to hold all the goods passing through the port.

By the turn of the century, Singapore had become the entrepôt of the East, a mixture of adventurers and "respectable middle classes." World War I hardly touched the island, although its defenses were strengthened to support the needs of the British navy, for which Singapore was an important base. When World War II broke out, the British were complacent, expecting that any attack would come from the sea and that they were well prepared to meet such an attack. But the Japanese landed to the north, in Malaya. The two British battleships that had been posted to Singapore were sunk, and the Japanese land forces raced down the peninsula on bicycles.

In February 1942 the Japanese captured Singapore. Huge numbers of Allied civilians and military were sent to Changi Prison; others were marched off to prison camps in Malaya or to work on the notorious "Death Railway" in Thailand. The 3½ years of occupation was a time of privation and fear; an estimated 100,000 people died. The Japanese surrendered on August 21, 1945, and the Allied military forces returned to Singapore. However, the security of the British Empire was never again to be felt, and independence for British Southeast Asia was only a matter of time.

In 1957 the British agreed to the establishment of an elected 51-member legislative assembly in Singapore. General elections in 1959 gave an overwhelming majority—43 of 51 seats—to the People's Action Party (PAP), and a young Chinese lawyer named Lee Kuan Yew became Singapore's first prime minister. In 1963 Singapore became part of the Federation of Malaysia, along with the newly independent state of Malaysia.

Mainly due to Malays' anxiety over a possible takeover by the ethnic Chinese, the federation broke up two years later and Singapore became an independent sovereign state. The electorate remained faithful to Lee Kuan Yew and the PAP. In 1990, Lee resigned after 31 years as prime minister, though as a senior minister he maintains his strong grip. His firm leadership of the party, his social and economic legislation, and his suppression of criticism led to his reputation as a (usually) benevolent dictator; yet Singaporeans recognize that his firm control had much to do with the republic's economic success and high standard of living. Lee is rumored to be grooming his son for the reigns of the PAP—though the fact that the party is receiving fewer votes than in the past suggests a disaffection with the (virtually) one-party system. In the meantime, Lee's hand-picked successor, Goh Chok Tong, has established a power base of his own during his years as prime minister.

Staying in Singapore

Important Addresses and Numbers

Tourist Information
The most useful address in Singapore is that of the **Singapore Tourist Promotion Board** (STPB, 328 N. Bridge Rd., #02–34 Raffles Hotel Arcade, tel. 800/334–1335, 800/334–1336, or 339–6622 for the main switchboard). The staff here will answer any question that you may have on visiting Singapore and will attend to legitimate complaints. It's open weekdays 8–5, Saturday 8–1. The recent move to Raffles Hotel Arcade seems designed to bring the tourist into this over-priced complex, which was a pet project of the STPB. You may find it more convenient to visit the branch on the second floor (#02–02) of Scotts Shopping Centre, close to the busy intersection of Orchard and Scotts roads (tel. 800/738–3778 or 800/738–3779; open daily 9:30–9:30).

Should you have questions about your visitor's permit or wish to extend your stay beyond the time stamped in your passport, contact the **Immigration Department** (95 S. Bridge Rd., #08–26 South Bridge Centre, tel. 532–2877).

Embassies and Missions
Australia High Commission, 25 Napier Road, tel. 737–9311. Open weekdays 8:30–noon and 2–4. **British High Commission,** Tanglin Road, tel. 473–9333. Open weekdays 9–noon and 2–4. **United States,** 30 Hill Street, tel. 338–0251. Open weekdays 8:30–noon.

Emergencies
Police, tel. 999; **ambulance and fire,** tel. 995.

Doctors and Hospitals
Singapore's medical facilities are among the best in the world, and most hotels have their own doctors on 24-hour call. **Paul's Clinic** (435 Orchard Rd., #11–01 Wisma Atria, tel. 235–2511), a centrally located clinic with several doctors, is open weekdays 9–5. Some government hospitals accustomed to treating overseas visitors are **Alexandra Hospital** (Alexandra Rd., tel. 473–5222), **Kadang Kerbau Hospital** (Maternity–Hampshire Rd., tel. 293–4044), and **Singapore General Hospital** (Outram Rd., tel. 222–3322).

Pharmacies
Pharmaceuticals are available at supermarkets, department stores, and hotels. Registered pharmacists work 9–6. Some pharmacies in the major shopping centers stay open until 10 PM. Prescriptions must be written by locally registered doctors. Hospitals can fill prescriptions 24 hours a day.

Credit Cards
For assistance with lost or stolen cards: **American Express** (tel. 235–8133), **Carte Blanche** (tel. 296–6511), **Diners Club** (tel. 294–4222), **MasterCard** (tel. 244–0444), and **Visa** (tel. 532–3577).

English-Language Bookstores
Since English is the lingua franca, all regular bookstores carry English-language books. Should you have trouble finding a book, try the head office of the **Times Bookstore** (tel. 284–8844), which will tell you whether any of its branches carries the title you want.

Travel Agencies
It is convenient to have your hotel's concierge handle airplane reservations and ticket confirmations, but airline tickets are less expensive if you buy them from a travel agent. Agencies abound in Singapore and will arrange tours, transportation, and hotels in Indonesia, Malaysia, and Thailand—or anywhere else, for that matter.

Two of the better-known international travel agencies are **American Express Travel Services** (#02–02/04 UDL Bldg., 96 Somerset Rd., tel. 235–8133) and **Thomas Cook Travel Services** (#03–05 Sanford

Bldg., 15 Hoe Chiang Rd., tel. 221–0222; #02–04 Far East Plaza, 14 Scotts Rd., tel. 737–0366). For discount airfares from Singapore, try **Dragon Tour** (109 N. Bridge Rd., #05–04 Funan Centre, tel. 338–5454).

Getting Around Singapore

By Subway   The most recent addition to Singapore's public transport system is a superb subway, known as the MRT, consisting of two lines that run north–south and east–west and cross at the City Hall and Raffles Place interchanges. The system includes a total of 42 stations along 67 km (42 mi). All cars and underground stations are air-conditioned, and the trains operate between 5:45 AM and midnight daily.

Tickets may be purchased in the stations from vending machines (which give change) or at a booth. There's a S$2 fine for underpaying, so make sure you buy the right ticket for your destination. Fares start at S$.60 for about two stations; the maximum fare is S$1.50. The fare between Orchard Road Station and Raffles Place Station (in the business district) is S$.70. For information, call 732–4411.

By Bus   Buses are much cheaper than taxis and—with a little practice— easy to use. During rush hours, they can be quicker than cabs, since there are special bus lanes along the main roads. Some buses are air-conditioned, and service is frequent—usually every five to 10 minutes on most routes. Even without the excellent *Bus Guide,* available for S$1 at any bookstore, finding your way around is relatively easy. Bus stops close to sightseeing attractions have signs pointing out the attractions.

The minimum fare is S$.50, the maximum S$1.10 for non-air-conditioned buses, S$.80 to S$1.70 for air-conditioned buses. Exact change is necessary (conductors cannot give change) and should be deposited in the box as you enter the bus. Remember to collect your ticket. Bus numbers are clearly marked, and most stops have a list of destinations with the numbers of the buses that service them. Buses run from 5:30 or 6 AM until around 11:30 PM.

The **Singapore Explorer Bus Ticket,** which may be purchased at most major hotels and tour agencies, lets you travel anywhere on the island on any bus operated by Singapore Bus Service (SBS—the red-and-white buses) or Trans Island Bus Service (TIBS—the orange-and-yellow buses). You may embark and disembark as frequently as you like, flashing your pass as you board. A one-day pass costs S$5 and a three-day pass costs S$12. With this ticket you also receive an **Explorer Bus Map** with color-coded routes showing bus stops and all major points of interest. Explorer Tickets are also available at SBS Travelcentres, located at bus interchanges. For further details, call the Singapore Bus Service Passenger Relations Center (tel. 287–2727).

The recently introduced **Transitlink** farecard functions as a prepaid mass-transit ticket. You can purchase one, for S$12 to S$52 (including a S$2 deposit), from Transitlink sales offices at MRT stations and at bus interchanges. The card lets you travel on the trains and on many buses; the fare for each trip is deducted from the balance on the card. Any unused fare and the deposit can be refunded at Transitlink offices. (Since this is a new system, not all buses have been equipped with validators yet.)

Coming from Malaysia, you can board a public bus at the Johore bus station or, after the Malaysia checkpoint, at the causeway. You get off the bus on the other side of the causeway at the Singapore checkpoint, then reboard the bus for the ride into the city's center. Since you may not be reboarding the same bus—depending on the line at Immigration—do not leave your belongings behind when you get off.

The new **Singapore Trolley** bus service starts at the Botanic Gardens and continues to Orchard Road, Tanjong Pagar, and the World Trade Centre. It's not very convenient, and it's expensive (S$9 adults, S$7 children), but it does make 22 stops and your ticket is good all day for unlimited journeys. You can buy the ticket (you'll need exact change) when you board. A one-ticket point-to-point fare is S$3.

By Taxi There are more than 10,000 taxis in Singapore, strictly regulated and metered. Many are air-conditioned. The starting fare is S$2.20 for the first 1.5 km (0.9 mi) and S$.10 for each subsequent 275 m (900 ft). After 10 km (6 mi) the rate increases to S$.10 for every 250 m (820 ft). Every 45 seconds of waiting time carries a S$.10 charge.

Several surcharges also apply: There is a charge of S$.50 for each additional person (the maximum is four passengers); S$1 is added for every piece of luggage stored in the trunk; trips made between midnight and 6 AM have a 50% surcharge; rides from (not to) the airport carry a S$3 surcharge; and there are "entrance and exit fees" on taxis and private cars going into and out of the central business district, or CBD. Unless a taxi displays a yellow permit, a S$1 surcharge is added to fares from the CBD between 4 and 7 PM on weekdays and noon and 3 PM on Saturday. To the CBD, a S$3 fee applies to rides between 7:30 and 10:15 AM Monday through Saturday.

Taxis may be found at stands or hailed from any curb not marked with a double yellow line. Radio cab services are available 24 hours (tel. 452–5555, 474–7707, or 250–0700); a S$2 surcharge is imposed, and the meter should not be switched on until after you have entered the taxi.

Drivers carry tariff cards, which you may see if you want clarification of your tab. Complaints should be registered with the STPB (*see* Tourist Information, *above*). However, just threatening to complain usually resolves any difficulty, since drivers can lose their licenses if they break the law.

By Ferry One of the pleasures of visiting Singapore is touring the harbor and visiting the islands. Most of the regularly scheduled ferries leave from the World Trade Centre. On weekdays, departures are at 10 AM and 1:30 PM (cost: S$5 round-trip); but on Sunday and holidays, there are eight scheduled departures. Check the return schedule before leaving for the islands.

By Bumboat Bumboats are motorized launches that serve as water taxis. Sailors use these to shuttle between Singapore and their ships. You can hire bumboats to the islands from Clifford Pier or Jardine Steps. The charge is approximately S$30 an hour for a boat that can comfortably accommodate six passengers.

By Car Hiring a chauffeur-driven or self-drive car is not at all necessary in Singapore. Distances are short, and parking, especially in the central business district, is very difficult. Taxis and public transportation are far more convenient and less expensive. Even to visit attractions out of the downtown area, buses or taxis are nearly as convenient and much more economical. And almost everything worth seeing is accessible by tour bus (*see* Guided Tours, below).

The following are some local branches of international agencies. **Avis:** Changi Airport, tel. 542–8833; Shangri-La Hotel, tel. 734–

4169; Liat Towers, Orchard Road, tel. 737–1668. **Hertz:** Changi Airport, tel. 545–8181; Marina Square, tel. 336–5200; Tanglin Shopping Centre, Tanglin Road, tel. 734–4646; Westin Stamford Hotel, tel. 339–5656. **National:** 200 Orchard Boulevard, tel. 737–1668. **Sintat/Thrifty:** Changi Airport, tel. 273–2211.

Rates start at S$90 a day or S$475 a week, with unlimited mileage. A collision-damage waiver (CDW) insurance premium of S$90 per week will cover you for the initial S$2,000 not covered by the insurance included in the basic charge. There is a surcharge for taking the car into Malaysia: Avis, for example, adds S$50 a day or S$300 per week to its base charge for compact cars. The CDW is also higher for cars driven into Malaysia.

If you plan to do an overland drive through Malaysia, you can rent a car from a Singapore agency, but it is significantly less expensive to do so in Malaysia. Take the bus for S$.80 to Johore Bahru and you can save approximately S$50 a day on your car rental. Furthermore, you can make reservations with a rental agency in Johore (for example, Sintat/Thrifty, tel. 03/248–2388) from Singapore, and even be picked up from your Singapore hotel by private car at no extra charge.

Rules of the Road Singapore's **speed limits** are 80 kph on expressways unless otherwise posted, and 50 kph on other roads. One rule to keep in mind: Yield right of way at rotaries. Drive on the left-hand side of the road in both Malaysia and Singapore. Driver's licenses issued in the United States are valid in Singapore. To rent a car, you must be at least 23 years old and have a major credit card.

Gasoline Gas costs S$1.43 per liter in Singapore, significantly less in Malaysia. A new government ruling requires any car passing the causeway out of Singapore to have at least half a tank of gas or be fined; the republic's huge losses in revenue as a result of Singaporeans' driving to Malaysia to gas up cheaply led to the understandably unpopular ruling.

Telephones

Local Calls From a pay phone, the cost is S$.10. To make a call, insert a coin and dial the seven-digit number. There are free public phones at Changi Airport, just past Immigration.

International Calls Direct dialing is available to most overseas countries. The top hotels provide direct-dial phones in guest rooms; smaller hotels have switchboards that will place your calls. In either case, the service charge can be substantial. You can avoid the hotel charge by making international calls from the General Post Office (*see* Mail, *below*) or by using the services at Changi Airport. International cables may also be sent from either of these places.

The direct-dial prefix for Malaysia is 106. For other international calls, dial 104 and the country code. The country code for Singapore (for calls from outside the republic) is 65.

An economical way to call North America or the United Kingdom is to use international Home Countries Direct phones—USA Direct or UK Direct—which put you immediately in touch with either an American or a British telephone operator. The operator will place your call, either charging your telephone credit card or making the call collect. These phones may be found at the GPO and at many of the post offices around the city center, such as the one in the Raffles City shopping complex. You can also use pay phones by first depositing S$.10 and then dialing 8000–111–111 to reach the AT&T operator, 8000–112–112 for the U.S. MCI operator, or 8000–440–440 for the United Kingdom.

Phone Card There are public phones at many post offices and at the airport that accept **Diners Club, MasterCard,** and **Visa** cards. The **Telecoms** phone card can be useful if you'll be making several long-distance calls during your stay in Singapore. The cards, similar to the Foncards used in Great Britain, can be purchased in denominations of S$2, S$5, S$10, S$20, and S$50 and permit you to make local and overseas calls. The price of each call is deducted from the card total, and your balance is roughly indicated by the punched hole in the card. The costs will be the same as if you had made the call from the GPO. Phone cards are available from post offices and Telecoms Customer Services outlets. Telephones that accept the phone card are found in shopping centers, post offices, subway stations, and at the airport. For inquiries, call 288–6633.

Information For directory inquiries, dial 103.

Mail

Most hotels sell stamps and post guests' letters. In addition, there are 87 post offices on the island, most of them open weekdays 8:30–6 (Wednesday until 8) and Saturday 8:30–1. The airport post office and the Orchard Point post office are open daily 8–8. For postal inquiries, contact the **General Post Office (GPO)** in Fullerton Square, off Collyer Quay (tel. 533–6234).

Postal Rates Postage on local letters up to 20 g (0.8 oz) is S$.10. **Airmail** takes about five business days to reach North America and Great Britain. An airmail postcard costs S$.30 to most overseas destinations; a large-format card costs S$.70. A letter up to 10 g (0.4 oz) is S$.35 within Asia, S$.50 to Australia, S$.75 to Great Britain, and S$1 to North America. Printed **aerogram** letters (available at most post offices) are S$.35.

Shops are normally trustworthy in shipping major purchases, but if you prefer to make arrangements yourself, you will find post office staff helpful and efficient. All branches sell "Postpac" packing cartons, which come in different sizes.

Receiving Mail Mail can be sent to you c/o General Delivery, General Post Office, Fullerton Square, Singapore. American Express cardholders or traveler's-check users can have mail sent c/o American Express International, #14–00 UDL Building, Singapore 0923. Envelopes should be marked "Client Mail."

Currency

The local currency is the Singapore dollar (S$), which is divided into 100 cents. At press time, the following exchange rates applied: US$1 = S$1.50, UK£1 = S$2.25, A$1 = S$1.05. Notes in circulation: S$1, S$5, S$10, S$20, S$50, S$100, S$500, S$1,000, S$10,000. Coins: S$.01, S$.05, S$.20, S$.50, S$1.

What It Will Cost

Compared with other world capitals, Singapore is still inexpensive. However, prices have risen over the last five years, and while a gastronomical delight will still cost half what you would pay in Paris, hotel prices are in the New York range. You can keep costs down by eating at the inexpensive but hygienic hawker food centers and using the efficient, clean public transportation system that provides easy, low-cost access around the city of Singapore and the island.

Taxes There is a 4% sales tax in Singapore. This tax is added to restaurant and hotel bills; sometimes a 10% service charge is added as well. There is a S$12 airport departure tax (for travelers to Malaysia, the tax is S$5). It is payable at the airport. To save time and avoid standing in line, you can buy a tax voucher at your hotel or any airline office.

Sample Prices Cup of coffee, 70¢; large bottle of beer, $3; lunch at a hawker stand, $7; dinner at an elegant restaurant, $40; full breakfast at a luxury hotel, $12. The cost of a standard double room: moderate, $125–$150; very expensive, over $240.

Language

Singapore is a multiracial society with four official languages: Malay, Mandarin, Tamil, and English. The national language is Malay; the lingua franca is English. English, also the language of administration, is a required course for every schoolchild and is used in the entrance examinations for universities. Hence, virtually all Singaporeans speak English with varying degrees of fluency. Mandarin is increasingly replacing the other Chinese dialects. However, many Chinese will use SinEnglish, a Singaporean version of English, to converse with other ethnic groups, including other Chinese.

Opening and Closing Times

Businesses are generally open weekdays 9 or 9:30 to 5 or 5:30; some, not many, are also open on Saturday morning.

Banks Banking hours are weekdays 10–3, Saturday 9:30–11:30 AM. Branches of the Development Bank of Singapore stay open until 3 PM on Saturday. The bank at Changi Airport is open whenever there are flights. Money changers operate whenever there are customers in the shopping centers they serve.

Museums Many museums close on Monday; otherwise, they are generally open 9–5.

Shops Shop opening times vary. Department stores and many shops in big shopping centers are generally open seven days a week from about 10 to 9 (later some evenings). Smaller shops tend to close on Sundays, although there is no firm rule now that competition is so intense.

National Holidays

Singapore has 11 public holidays: New Year's Day (Jan. 1), Chinese New Year (two days, Feb. or Mar.), Good Friday (Mar. or Apr.), Hari Raya Puasa (Mar. to June, according to the year), Labor Day (May 1), Vesak Day (May), Hari Raya Haji (July), National Day (Aug. 9), Deepavali (Nov.), and Christmas (Dec. 25).

Festivals and Seasonal Events

Singapore is a city of festivals, from the truly exotic to the strictly-for-tourists. The exact dates vary from year to year according to the lunar or Islamic calendar.

Mid-Jan. During **Ponggal,** the four-day harvest festival, Tamil Indians from South India offer rice, curries, vegetables, sugarcane, and spices in thanksgiving to the Hindu gods. In the evening, the celebration takes place at the temples, where rice is cooked while prayers are chanted to the music of bells, drums, clarinets, and conch shells. The Perumal Temple of Serangoon Road is the best place to view these rites.

Mid-Jan.–Feb. **Thaipusam,** probably the most spectacular—and certainly the most gruesome—festival in Asia, celebrates the victory of the Hindu god Subramaniam over the demon Idumban. After night-long ritual purification and chanting, penitents enter a trance and pierce their flesh with knives, steel rods, and fishhooks, which they wear during the procession. The 8.1-km (5-mi) procession begins at the Perumal Temple on Serangoon Road, passes the Sri Mariamman Temple on South Bridge Road, and ends at the Chettiar Temple.

Chinese New Year is the only time the Chinese stop working. The lunar New Year celebration lasts for 15 days, and most shops and businesses close for about a week.

Feb. The end of the Chinese New Year is marked by the **Chingay Procession.** Chinese, Malays, and Indians all get into the act for this event. Clashing gongs and beating drums, lion dancers lead a procession of Chinese stilt-walkers, swordsmen, warriors, acrobats, and characters from Chinese myth and legend.

Feb. or Mar. The **Birthday of the Monkey God** celebrates this character greatly loved by the Chinese. His birth is marked with a festival twice a year in Chinese temples—once in the spring and again around September. Mediums, with skewers piercing their cheeks and tongues, go into trances. Chinese street operas and puppet shows are usually performed in temple courtyards, and processions are held at the temples along Eng Hoon and Cumming streets.

Apr.–May **Ramadan** is the month of daytime fasting among the city's Muslim population. Food stalls in Bussorah Street and around the Sultan Mosque sell a variety of dishes at the end of the day's fast. The end of Ramadan is marked with a major feast, **Hari Raya Puasa.** Animals are ritually slaughtered and given to the poor; celebrating Muslims, dressed in traditional garb, visit friends and relatives; and nighttime concerts and fairs are held in Geylang.

May or June The **Birthday of the Third Prince** celebrates this child god. The Chinese worship him as a hero and a miracle-worker. A temple in his honor is located at the junction of Clarke Street and North Boat Quay, near Chinatown; on his birthday, it is crowded with noisy worshipers who come to watch the flashy Chinese operas, which begin around noon.

Vesak Day commemorates the Buddha's birth, enlightenment, and death. It is the most sacred annual festival in the Buddhist calendar. Throughout the day, starting before dawn, saffron-robed monks chant holy sutras in all the major Buddhist temples. Captive birds are set free. Candlelight processions are held around some of the temples in the evening.

June The **Dragon Boat Festival** commemorates the martyrdom of Qu Yuan, a Chinese poet and minister of state during the Chou dynasty (4th century BC) who was exiled for speaking out against court corruption and finally threw himself into the river. On seeing Qu Yuan's final and desperate act, local fishermen thrashed the water with their oars and beat drums to prevent fish from devouring their drowning hero. The anniversary of his death is celebrated with a regatta of boats decorated with dragon heads and painted in brilliant colors.

July During the **Birdsong Festival,** owners of tuneful birds hold competitions to see whose chirps best.

When a given month has no traditional festival to attract tourists, the Singapore Tourist Promotion Board is wont to create one. In 1994 the month-long **Food Festival** was inaugurated, meaning lots of publicity but not much more than a series of cooking competitions ("Longest Spring Roll," "Biggest Roti Prata"), usually held at week's end.

Aug. 9 **National Day,** the anniversary of the nation's independence, is a day of processions, fireworks, folk and dragon dances, and national pride. The finest view is from the Padang, where the main participants put on their best show. Tickets for special seating areas are available through the STPB.

Aug.–Sept. For a month each year, during the Chinese **Festival of the Hungry Ghosts,** the Gates of Hell are opened and ghosts are free to wander the Earth. The unhappy ghosts, those who died without descendants, may cause trouble and must therefore be placated with offerings. Imitation money ("Hell money") and joss sticks are burned, and prayers are said at all Chinese temples and in front of Chinese shops and homes. Chinese-opera *(wayang)* performances are held on open-air stages set up in the streets.

Sept. The **Mooncake Festival,** a traditional Chinese celebration, is held on the night of the year when the full moon is thought to be at its brightest. The Chinese have nighttime picnics and carry lanterns through the streets. Mooncakes—sweet pastries filled with red-bean paste, lotus seeds, nuts, and egg yolks—are eaten in abundance.

Sept.–Oct. During the nine-day **Navarathri Festival,** Hindus pay homage to three goddesses: Parvati, consort of Shiva the Destroyer; Lakshmi, goddess of wealth and consort of Vishnu the Protector; and Sarawathi, goddess of education and consort of Brahma the Creator. On all nights, at the Chettiar Temple on Tank Road, there are performances of classical Indian music, drama, and dancing from 7 to 10. On the last evening, the image of a silver horse is taken from its home in the Chettiar Temple and paraded around the streets.

Oct. The Chinese believe that the deities celebrated in the **Festival of the Nine Emperor Gods** can cure illness, bring good luck and wealth, and encourage longevity. They are honored in most Chinese temples on the ninth day of the ninth lunar month; the celebrations are at their most spectacular in the temples on Upper Serangoon Road and at Lorong Tai Seng.

Oct.–Nov. In the **Thimithi Festival,** Indian Hindus honor the goddess Duropadai by walking on fire. According to myth, Duropadai proved her chastity by walking over flaming coals. Today worshipers repeat her feat by walking barefoot over a bed of red-hot embers. See the spectacle at the Sri Mariamman Temple on South Bridge Road.

Deepavali celebrates the triumph of Krishna over the demon king Nasakasura. All Indian homes and temples are decorated with oil lamps and garlands. In Little India the streets are brilliantly illuminated.

Nov. **Merlion Week** is Singapore's version of Carnival, with food fairs, fashion shows, masquerade balls, and fireworks displays. Brochures of the activities are available in every hotel.

Nov.–Dec. Being a multiracial society, Singapore has taken **Christmas** to its commercial heart. All the shops are deep in artificial snow, and a Chinese Santa Claus appears every so often to encourage everyone to buy and give presents.

Tipping

Tipping is not customary in Singapore, and the government actively discourages it. It is prohibited at the airport and not encouraged in hotels that levy a 10% service charge or in restaurants. Hotel **bellboys** are usually tipped S$1 per bag for handling luggage. **Taxi drivers** are not tipped by Singaporeans.

Guided Tours

A wide range of sightseeing tours cover the highlights of Singapore. They are especially convenient for business travelers or others on a tight schedule and can be easily arranged through the tour desks in hotels. The following are a few of the tour operators providing services through major hotels, but there are many others as well. **RMG Tours** (25 Hoot Kiam Rd., tel. 738–7776) organizes nightlife and food tours. **Siakson Coach Tours** (3 Miller St., Siakson Bldg., tel. 336–0288) has daily tours to the zoo and Mandai Gardens, plus excursions to Malaysia. **Tour East International** (163 Tanglin Rd., tel. 235–5205) offers a variety of tours in Singapore and excursions to Malaysia and Indonesia. **Elpin Tours and Limousine Services** (317 Outram Rd., #02–23 Glass Hotel, tel. 235–3111) arranges tours of Sentosa Island.

The itineraries offered by the different tour operators are very similar. Tours can take two hours or the whole day, and prices range from S$16 to S$70. Most are operated in comfortable, air-conditioned coaches with guides and include pickup and return at your hotel. Tour agencies can also arrange private-car tours with guides; these are considerably more expensive.

Orientation
City Highlights These are 3½-hour tours, given in the morning or the afternoon. Itineraries vary slightly, but generally you will be shown some of the major sightseeing and shopping areas, including Orchard Road, the high-rise business district along Shenton Way, and the historic buildings along the Padang. You will also see Chinatown and probably the Thian Hock Keng Temple. A visit to the Sri Mariamman Temple, a stroll through the beautiful Botanic Gardens, a drive up Mt. Faber for a panoramic view of the city, and a visit to a handicraft factory are also likely to be included. A morning city tour usually features the "Instant Asia" cultural show.

City and East If the tour covers the east coast, you'll see the city highlights and
or West Coast visit some rural sights, such as a Malay village and/or the Kuan Yin Temple. You may also visit the infamous Changi Prison and drive through the green coastal area. This tour takes 4½ hours. The west-coast tour includes the Chinese and Japanese gardens and the Jurong Bird Park.

Boat Trips **Water Tours** (70 Clifford Pier, #01–31, tel. 533–9811) operates motorized junks for cruises in the harbor and to Kusu Island. **J & N Cruise** (24 Raffles Pl., #26–02 Clifford Centre, tel. 533–2733) operates the *Equator Dream*, a catamaran that offers lunch, high tea, and dinner cruises (with disco) around the harbor and to the islands. **Island Cruises** (50 Collyer Quay, #01–27 Overseas Union House, tel. 221–8333) offers breakfast, lunch, teatime, and starlight cruises (with strolling musicians) on the sleek new *Singapore Princess*.

Personal Guides Some 500 tourist guides, speaking a total of 26 languages and dialects, are licensed by the STPB. Call the **Registered Tourist Guides Association** (tel. 734–6425 or 734–6472) to make arrangements. These guides are knowledgeable, and if they are unable to answer a question, they will seek out the information and satisfy your curiosity later.

Excursions A number of tour operators arrange trips into Malaysia and Indonesia. These run the gamut: a half-day trip to Johore Bahru for S$19, a full-day trip to Malacca for S$68, a two-day visit to the Riau Islands of Indonesia for S$180, a three-day trip to Tioman Island (off the east coast of Malaysia) for S$370. There are also longer tours, which include Kuala Lumpur and Penang in Malaysia, and Lake Toba on the Indonesian island of Sumatra. Several cruises stopping in at Southeast Asian ports begin and/or end in Singapore.

Highlights for First-time Visitors

Chettiar Temple (*see* Tour 5)

Empress Place (*see* Tour 1)

Kuan Yin Temple (*see* Tour 4)

Pioneers of Singapore/Surrender Chambers (*see* Tour 7)

Raffles Hotel (*see* Tour 1)

Singapore Zoological Gardens (*see* Tour 6)

Sri Mariamman Temple (*see* Tour 2)

Sultan Mosque (*see* Tour 4)

Temple of 1,000 Lights (*see* Tour 3)

Thian Hock Keng Temple (*see* Tour 2)

Exploring Singapore

The main island of Singapore is shaped like a flattened diamond, 42 km (26 mi) east to west and 23 km (14 mi) north to south. At the top of the diamond is the causeway leading to peninsular Malaysia (Kuala Lumpur is less than six hours away by car). At the bottom is Singapore city, the docks, and, offshore, Sentosa and 57 smaller islands—most of them uninhabited—that serve as bases for oil refining or as playground or beach escapes from the city. To the east is Changi International Airport and, between it and the city, a parkway lined for miles with amusement centers of one sort or another. To the west is the industrial city of Jurong and several decidedly unindustrial attractions, including gardens and a bird park. At the center of the diamond is Singapore island's "clean and green" heart, with a splendid zoo, an orchid garden, and reservoirs surrounded by some very luxuriant tropical forest. Of the island's total land area, less than half is built up, with the balance made up of farmland, plantations, swamp areas, and forest. Well-paved roads connect all parts of the island, and Singapore city is served with excellent public transportation.

Tour 1: Colonial Singapore

Numbers in the margin correspond to points of interest on the Tour 1: Colonial Singapore map.

❶ A convenient place to start exploring colonial Singapore is at Clifford Pier and **Collyer Quay,** where most Europeans alighted from their ships to set foot on the island. Walk up Collyer Quay toward the Singapore River; **Change Alley**—once the site of a popular old bazaar and row of money changers—would have been on your left. In 1989 the area was closed down to make way for a modern business complex.

❷ Farther along is the **General Post Office** (GPO), a proud Victorian building of gray stone with huge pillars that's an anachronism in an area of glass-and-steel high rises. Walk down the short, narrow, tree-lined street alongside the GPO and past the riverbank mini–
❸ food center to cross the gracious 1868 iron-link **Cavenagh Bridge,** named after Major General Orfeur Cavenagh, governor of the Straits Settlements from 1859 to 1867.

Should you walk along the south bank of the river before crossing the bridge, you will find a wide towpath, now a paved pedestrian
❹ street, along a section called **Boat Quay**—a highly popular new area for restaurants with both indoor and outdoor dining. It is one of the few places that has not been masterminded by the Singapore Tourist Promotion Board or by a quasi-government real estate developer; instead, local restaurant and café entrepreneurs have created a mélange of eateries to satisfy diverse tastes. Between 7 PM and midnight, the place swells with both locals and tourists, who stroll along the pleasant quay, perhaps stopping to take a meal or refreshment.

Once over the Cavenagh Bridge, take a left onto North Boat Quay. Slightly back from the river is Empress Place, a huge white Victorian building that has been meticulously restored as an exhibition hall. We shall return here shortly, but for now let us proceed a bit farther along
❺ the quay to a **statue of Sir Thomas Stamford Raffles,** who is believed to have landed on this spot early on the morning of January 29, 1819. Once this river was the organ of bustling commercial life, packed with barges and lighters that ferried goods from the cargo ships to the docks.

Now all that seeming mayhem is gone, and the river is close to being the sleepy waterway it was when Raffles first arrived. Cargo vessels are banned from entering the river, and the riverfront shops and two-story godowns were left to deteriorate until recently. Public pressure saved them from destruction, and the Singapore Tourist Promotion Board stepped in to renovate the buildings and rent them out to merchants and restaurants catering to tourists. Promoted as a festival village combining entertainment, food, and shopping plus a heritage-inspired Disney-style adventure, the result, known as
❻ **Clarke Quay** in remembrance of Sir Andrew Clarke, the second governor of Singapore, is in fact a sanitized and regimented area that lacks any real character. Several artificial scenarios are played throughout the day: A tinsmith demonstrates his skill; a band performs in a small gazebo at the central square; stilt-walkers wobble down the pedestrian-only streets. Few Singaporeans make the effort to come out here, but since you are in the neighborhood, you might take time to browse through the shops and have something to eat alongside the river or aboard one of the four *tongkangs* (similar to Chinese junks). Be aware, though, that the prices, both in the shops and at the restaurants, are inflated. You can also board one of the bumboats that offer 30-minute **cruises** along the river and into Marina Bay; you can see as much from the shore as from the water, but it's a pleasant ride, and a respite for tired feet. *Dock kiosk, North Boat Quay, tel. 227–9228. Cost: S$6 adults, S$3 children under 12. Operating times: daily 9–7.*

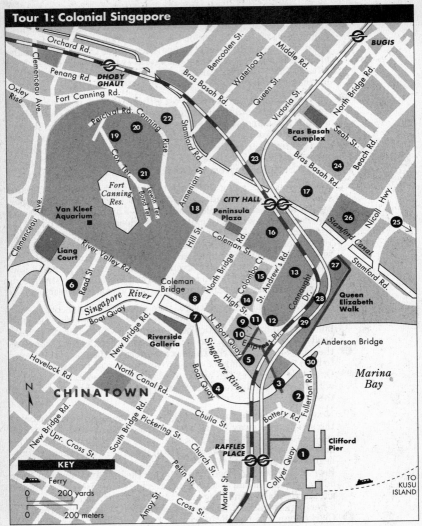

Tour 1: Colonial Singapore

BUGIS

Orchard Rd.

Clemenceau Ave.

Penang Rd.

DHOBY
GHAUT

Oxley
Rise

Fort Canning Rd.

Bencoolen St.

Bras Basah Rd.

Waterloo St.

Middle Rd.

Queen St.

Victoria St.

North Bridge Rd.

Percival Rd.

Canning Rise

Stamford Rd.

Bras Basah
Complex

Seah St.

Beach Rd.

19

20

22

23

24

Fort
Canning
Res.

Cox Ter.

21

Jewin Ter.

Bond Ter.

Armenian St.

CITY HALL

Peninsula
Plaza

17

26

Nicoll Hwy.

25

Van Kleef
Aquarium

18

Coleman St.

16

Stamford Canal

Stamford Rd.

Clemenceau Ave.

River Valley Rd.

Hill St.

Coleman St. Rd.

Connaught Dr.

27

Liang
Court

Read St.

6

Singapore River

Boat Quay

Coleman
Bridge

North Bridge Rd.

Colombo Ct.

St. Andrew's Rd.

15

13

Queen
Elizabeth
Walk

New Bridge Rd.

8

High St.

14

28

Riverside
Galleria

7

N. Boat Quay

Singapore River

9

11

12

29

Havelock Rd.

North Canal Rd.

Empress Pl.

10

Anderson Bridge

CHINATOWN

Boat Quay

5

Marina
Bay

N

Chulia St.

4

3

2

New Bridge Rd.

Upr. Cross St.

South Bridge Rd.

Pickering St.

Church St.

Battery Rd.

Fullerton Rd.

30

Clifford
Pier

RAFFLES
PLACE

1

KEY

Ferry

0   200 yards

0   200 meters

Pekin St.

Amoy St.

Cross St.

Market St.

Collyer Quay

TO
KUSU
ISLAND

Armenian Church, **18**
Boat Quay, **4**
Cavenagh Bridge, **3**
Cenotaph War
Memorial, **28**
City Hall, **15**
Clarke Quay, **6**
Collyer Quay, **1**
Convent of the Holy
Infant Jesus, **23**

Elgin Bridge, **7**
Empress Place, **10**
European
Cemetery, **20**
Fort Canning Park, **19**
General Post Office, **2**
High Street Centre, **8**
Marina Square, **25**
Memorial to Major
Gen. Lim Bo Seng, **29**
Merlion Park, **30**

National Museum and
Art Gallery, **22**
Padang, **13**
Parliament House, **9**
Raffles City, **17**
Raffles Hotel, **24**
St. Andrew's
Cathedral, **16**
Singapore Cricket
Club, **12**

Statue of Sir Thomas
Stamford Raffles, **5**
Supreme Court, **14**
Tomb of Iskandar
Shah, **21**
Victoria Memorial
Hall/Victoria
Theatre, **11**
Victorian Fountain, **27**
War Memorial, **26**

7 Head west along the quay to **Elgin Bridge,** named after Lord Elgin, a governor-general of India. At the bridge, turn right onto North

8 Bridge Road and you'll see the **High Street Centre.** Take the elevator to the top floor of this office-and-shopping complex for one of the best panoramic views of downtown and colonial Singapore—it's free.

Back at street level, continue on to High Street and turn right to pass under a sheltered, colonnaded walkway lined with mostly open-front shops of Indian merchants. Farther down High Street are graceful old buildings housing the attorney general's chambers

9 and **Parliament House,** designed in 1827 by Irishman George Coleman, the architect of many of Singapore's early buildings. Out front is a bronze statue of an elephant—presented by King Chulalongkorn of Siam during his state visit in 1871.

10 Across from Parliament House stands the neoclassical **Empress Place** building seen earlier. Constructed in the 1860s as the new courthouse, it has had four major additions and housed nearly every government body. Now, after a S$22 million renovation, Empress Place has a new lease on life as a cultural exhibition center. Its vast halls, high ceilings, and many columns give a majestic drama to exhibitions from around the world, though most of the major exhibits are art collections from China. *1 Empress Pl., tel. 336–7633. Admission charge. Open daily 9:30–9:30.*

11 The adjacent **Victoria Memorial Hall,** built in 1905 as a tribute to Queen Victoria, and the **Victoria Theatre,** built in 1862 as the town hall, are the city's main cultural centers, offering regular exhibitions, concerts, and theatrical performances of all types. In front of the clock tower is a **bronze statue of Raffles** by Thomas Woolner. (The Raffles statue by the river is a copy of this.)

12 Across the road from the theater is the old **Singapore Cricket Club.** Founded during the 1850s, it became the main center for the social and sporting life of the British community. The club is not open to passing sightseers, but you can sneak a quick look at the deep, shaded verandas around back, from which members still watch

13 cricket, rugby, and tennis matches. The **Padang** (Malay for "field" or "plain")—the playing field on which these matches take place—was originally only half its present size; it was extended through land reclamation in the 1890s. Once called the Esplanade, it was where the colonial gentry strolled, exchanging pleasantries and gossip.

14 15 Looking out over the Padang are two splendidly pretentious, imperial-looking gray-white buildings: the **Supreme Court** and **City Hall.** The Supreme Court was completed in 1939, replacing the famous Hôtel de l'Europe, where Conrad used to prop up on the bar eavesdropping on sailors' tales that he would later use in his novels. The pedimental sculptures of the Grecian temple–like facade portray Justice and other allegorical figures. City Hall, completed in 1929, now houses a number of government ministries. Here the British surrender took place in 1942, followed by the surrender of the Japanese in 1945.

16 Continuing north on St. Andrew's Road, which runs along the Padang, cross Coleman Street toward the green lawns that surround the Anglican **St. Andrew's Cathedral.** The first church was built on this site in 1834; after being struck twice by lightning, it was demolished in 1852. Indian convicts were brought in to construct a new cathedral in the 12th-century English Gothic style. The structure, completed in 1862, with bells cast by the firm that made Big Ben's, resembles Netley Abbey in Hampshire, England. The cathedral's lofty interior is white and simple, with stained-glass windows coloring the sunlight as it enters. Around the walls are marble and brass memorial plaques, including one remembering the British who died in the 1915 Mutiny of Native Light Infantry. Within easy walking distance is the huge **Raffles City** complex, easily recognized by the towers of the two Westin hotels.

From the cathedral, return to Coleman Street and turn right (away from the Padang). Cross Hill Street, and on the right-hand corner is the **Armenian Church** or, more correctly, the Church of St. Gregory the Illuminator, one of the most endearing buildings in Singapore. It was built in 1835, which makes it the oldest surviving church in the republic. A dozen wealthy Armenian families supplied the funds for the ubiquitous Coleman to design this church. It is, perhaps, his finest work.

Behind the church is **Fort Canning Rise.** Seven centuries ago this hill was home to the royal palaces of the Majapahit rulers, who no doubt chose it for the cool breezes and commanding view of the river. Raffles established government house (headquarters for the colonial governor) on the Rise. In 1859, a fort was constructed; its guns were fired to mark dawn, noon, and night for the colony. Little remains of these grand constructions, but **Fort Canning Park** offers a green and peaceful retreat from the city center. On the slope, beneath the ruins of the fort, is an old **European cemetery.** Farther up the slope and to the left is the sacred **tomb of Iskandar Shah.** The government once decided to have the grave opened to determine whether the ruler was actually buried here, but no one would dig it up.

Exit the park via Percival Road to reach the **National Museum and Art Gallery.** Housed in a grand colonial building topped by a giant silver dome, the museum originally opened as the Raffles Museum in 1887. Included in its collection are 20 dioramas depicting the republic's past; the Revere Bell, donated to the original St. Andrew's Church in 1843 by the daughter of American patriot Paul Revere; the 380-piece Haw Par Jade Collection, one of the largest of its kind; ethnographic collections from Southeast Asia; and many historical documents. The Art Gallery displays contemporary works by local artists. *Stamford Rd., tel. 330–9562. Admission charge. Open 9–4:30; closed Mon.*

Leaving the museum, walk east on Stamford Road and turn left onto Victoria Street. On the right, you'll pass the **Convent of the Holy Infant Jesus,** one of Singapore's most charming Victorian buildings.

Turn right onto Bras Basah Road and walk toward the sea. On your left, opposite Singapore's tallest hotel and largest convention center, is the **Raffles Hotel.** The Raffles has had many ups and downs, especially during World War II, when it was first a center for British refugees, then quarters for Japanese officers, then a center for released Allied prisoners of war. After the war the hotel deteriorated. It survived mostly as a tourist site, trading on its heritage rather than its facilities. However, in late 1991, after two years of gutting, rebuilding, and expansion, Raffles reopened as the republic's most expensive hotel. The casual tourist is no longer welcome to roam, but instead is channeled through new (albeit colonial-style) buildings—to a museum of Raffles's memorabilia, a multimedia show (with free performances at 10, 11, 12:30, and 1), or a reproduction of the famous Long Bar, where the Singapore sling was created. (A Raffles Sling now costs S$14.65, which includes service and tax but not the glass—that's another S$7.05.) If you're hungry, there's the new Empress Café; if you want to shop, there are 60 boutiques. By walking to the end of the new attractions and turning left, you can reach the original Tiffin Room and the Bar and Billiard Room. Casual visitors are discouraged from entering the original part of the hotel, but you may want to brazen it out just to see how unlikely it would be to find a Conrad at the tiny and stiff new Writer's Bar.

㉕ Across Nicoll Highway is **Marina Square,** a minicity of its own, with its 200 shops and three smart atrium hotels: the Pan Pacific, the Marina Mandarin, and the estimable Oriental. The whole area is built on reclaimed land. A convention center, Suntec City, and a convention hotel, the Marina Pacific, should be in full swing by 1995. The complex symbolizes much of what Singapore has become: a modern convention city built on landfills and clusters of theme parks to entertain the delegates' spouses.

To return to Collyer Quay and Clifford Pier, recross Nicoll Highway. In a park below Bras Basah Road you'll notice the four 70-m (230-ft) tapering white columns (known locally as "The Four Chop-
㉖ sticks") of the **War Memorial,** which commemorates the thousands of civilians from the four main ethnic groups (Chinese, Malay, Indian, and European) who lost their lives during the Japanese occupation of Singapore. Another tribute to the war dead of all Allied nations is the **Kranji War Memorial,** a meticulously maintained cemetery in the north of the island, off Woodlands Road. This is a touching experience, a small but potent reminder of the greatness of the loss in war.

Farther south on Connaught Drive, across Stamford Road, is an or-
㉗ nate **Victorian fountain,** sculpted with Greek-inspired figures wearing Empire dress. In 1882, the colonial government commissioned it as a memorial to Tan King Seng, a wealthy Chinese who helped provide Singapore with a fresh-water supply.

Time Out Just behind the fountain is a delightful alfresco eating place. It is known as the **Satay Club,** but the open-air stalls offer other local dishes besides satay.

Continuing south, the imposing structure you'll see on the left is the
㉘ **Cenotaph War Memorial** to the dead of the two world wars. From here, you can cross over the grass to join **Queen Elizabeth Walk,** running alongside Marina Bay. It was opened in 1953 to mark the queen's coronation and remains a popular place to take the evening air.

㉙ A few yards farther on is the **Memorial to Major General Lim Bo Seng,** a well-loved freedom fighter of World War II who was tortured and died in a Japanese prison camp in 1944. At the end of Queen
㉚ Elizabeth Walk is Anderson Bridge. On the other side, in **Merlion Park,** stands a statue of Singapore's tourism symbol, the Merlion—half lion, half fish. In the evening, the statue—on a point of land looking out over the harbor—is floodlit, its eyes are lighted, and its mouth spews water. Once over the bridge, you are on Fullerton Road, which eventually becomes Collyer Quay.

Tour 2: Chinatown

In a country where 76% of the people are Chinese, it may seem strange to name a small urban area Chinatown. But Chinatown was born some 170 years ago, when the Chinese were a minority (if only for half a century) in the newly formed British settlement. In the belief that it would minimize racial tension, Raffles allotted sections of the settlement to different ethnic groups. The Chinese immigrants were given the area to the south of the Singapore River. Today, the river is still the northern boundary of old Chinatown, while Maxwell Road marks its southern perimeter and New Bridge Road its western. Before the 1933 land reclamation, the western perimeter was the sea. The reclaimed area between Telok Ayer Street and Collyer Quay/Shenton Way has become the business district, often referred to as Singapore's Wall Street.

Within the relatively small rectangle apportioned to the Chinese, immigrants from mainland China—many of them penniless and half starved—were crammed. Within three years of the formation of the Straits Settlement, 3,000 Chinese had moved in; this number increased tenfold over the next decade.

In the shophouses—two-story buildings with shops or small factories on the ground floor and living quarters upstairs—as many as 30 lodgers would live together in a single room. Life was a fight for space and survival. What order existed was maintained not by the colonial powers but by Chinese guilds, clan associations, and secret societies, which fought for control of various lucrative aspects of community life.

Until recently, all of Chinatown was slated for the bulldozer, to be replaced by uniform concrete structures. However, the government finally recognized not only the people's desire to maintain Chinese customs and strong family ties, but also the important role these play in modern society. Chinatown received a stay of execution, and an ambitious plan to restore a large area of shophouses was set in motion.

Numbers in the margin correspond to points of interest on the Tour 2: Chinatown map.

The only way to appreciate Chinatown is to walk its streets, letting sights and smells guide your feet. The following excursion covers many of the highlights, but let your curiosity lead you down any street that takes your fancy.

We'll begin at Elgin Bridge, built to link Chinatown with the colonial administrative center. At the south end of the bridge, logically enough, South Bridge Road begins. Off to the right is Upper Circular Road, on the left-hand side of which is **Yeo Swee Huat,** at No. 13 (tel. 533–4288). Here, paper models of the necessities of life—horses, cars, boats, planes, even fake money—are made, to be purchased by relatives of the deceased (you can buy them, too) and ritually burned so that their essence passes through to the spirit world in flames and smoke.

Back on South Bridge Road, at the corner of Circular Road, is the **Sam Yew Shop** (21 South Bridge Rd., tel. 534–4638). Here you can have your name—translated into Chinese characters—carved onto an ivory chop, or seal, for about S$60. Continuing down South Bridge Road, you'll pass the **Jamae Mosque**—built in the 1830s by Chulia Muslims from India's Coromandel Coast—before reaching **Sri Mariamman Temple,** the oldest Hindu temple in Singapore. Its pagodalike entrance is topped by one of the most ornate *gopurams* (pyramidal gateway towers) you are ever likely to see. Hundreds of brightly colored statues of deities and mythical animals line the tiers of this towering porch; glazed cement cows sit, seemingly in great contentment, atop the surrounding walls. Inside are some spectacular paintings that have been recently restored by Tamil artisans brought over from southern India.

Tour 2: Chinatown

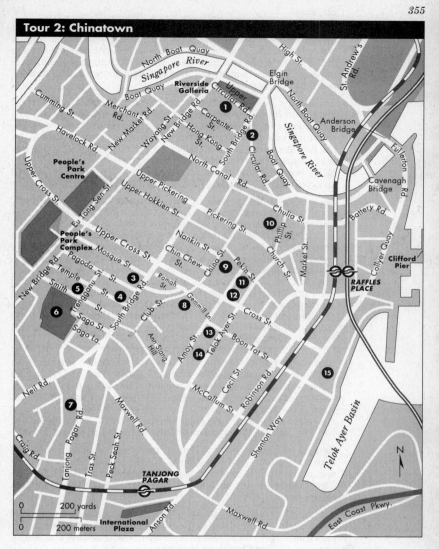

North Boat Quay
High St.
Singapore River
Elgin Bridge
St. Andrew's Rd.
Cumming St.
Upper Circular Rd.
Riverside Galleria
Boat Quay
Merchant Rd.
New Market Rd.
Havelock Rd.
Carpenter St.
New Bridge Rd.
Wayang St.
Hong Kong St.
South Bridge Rd.
Circular Rd.
North Boat Quay
Singapore River
Anderson Bridge
Fullerton Rd.
Cavenagh Bridge
People's Park Centre
Upper Cross St.
Eu Tong Sen St.
Upper Pickering
Upper Hokkien St.
North Canal Rd.
Pickering St.
Chulia St.
Phillip St.
Church St.
Boat Quay
Battery Rd.
Cecil Quay
Clifford Pier
People's Park Complex
Mosque St.
Upper Cross St.
Nankin St.
Chin Chew St.
Pekin St.
Market St.
Pagoda St.
Temple St.
China St.
Ramah St.
New Bridge Rd.
Smith St.
Trengganu St.
South Bridge Rd.
Club St.
Gemmill Ln.
Cross St.
RAFFLES PLACE
Sago St.
Sago La.
Ann Siang Hill
Amoy St.
Telok Ayer St.
Boon Tat St.
Cecil St.
Neil Rd.
McCallum St.
Robinson Rd.
Maxwell Rd.
Tanjong Pagar Rd.
Craig Rd.
Tanjong Rd.
Tras St.
Peck Seah St.
TANJONG PAGAR
Anson Rd.
Maxwell Rd.
Shenton Way
Telok Ayer Basin
East Coast Pkwy.
International Plaza

0 200 yards
0 200 meters

N

Brothel, **5**
Chinatown Centre, **6**
Fuk Tak Chi Temple, **11**
Hakka Clan Hall, **12**
Jamae Mosque, **3**
Jen Foh Medical Hall, **9**
Nagore Durghe Shrine, **13**
Sam Yew Shop, **2**

Say Tian Hong Buddha Shop, **8**
Sri Mariamman Temple, **4**
Tanjong Pagar, **7**
Telok Ayer Market, **15**
Thian Hock Keng Temple, **14**
Wak Hai Cheng Bio Temple, **10**
Yeo Swee Huat, **1**

At the junction of Trengganu and Temple streets, notice the old building on the corner. Reliable sources say this was a famous **⑤ brothel** in its time. Opium dens and brothels played important roles in the lives of Chinese immigrants, who usually arrived alone, leaving their families behind, and worked long days, with little time for relaxation or pleasure.

You are now in the core of Chinatown, an area known as Kreta Ayer, **⑥** dominated by **Chinatown Centre,** mobbed inside and out with jostling shoppers. At the open-air vegetable and fruit stands, women—toothless and wrinkled with age—sell their wares. Inside, on the first floor, hawker stalls sell a variety of cooked foods, but it is the basement floor that fascinates: Here you'll find a wet market (so called because water is continually sloshed over the floors), where an amazing array of meats, fowl, and fish are bought and sold.

Leaving the market, walk up **Sago Street** to South Bridge Road, then turn right and head for the intersection of Tanjong Pagar and Neil roads. On the left of Neil Road you'll notice The Inn of the Sixth Happiness, a small hotel with several good cafés and a huge dragon **⑦** draped over its roof. Cross the square and continue down **Tanjong Pagar,** the center of redevelopment in Chinatown. More than 50 restored shophouses now hold teahouses, restaurants, and shops.

Time Out For casual refreshments, you'll find small restaurants and a food court of fancy hawker stands at **51 Neil Road.** For snacks (or even Teochew smoked turkey), try the **Delicious Kitchen** (24–28 Tanjong Pagar, tel. 226–0607), next door to the intriguing **Hua Tuo Herbal Products** (tel. 221–2432).

Also worth visiting are the renovated shophouses on Duxton Road off Tanjong Pagar, and the **Pewter Museum** at No. 49A, which houses a private collection of 75 pewter items and the tools that were used to make them (admission free; open daily 9–5:30). Off Duxton Road is Duxton Hill, a short street with several lively bars and eating establishments: the **Flag and Whistle** at No. 10, **Barnacle Bill's** at No. 10A, and the **Chicago Bar & Grill** (for blues and jazz) at No. 8.

Retrace your steps to South Bridge Road. Just beyond Sago Street, take a right onto Ann Siang Road. On the left, at No. 3, is a shop selling superb lion-head costumes and other masks. A left up Club Street takes you past old buildings that continue to house many clan associations.

A right off Club Street takes you to Gemmill Lane and several small shops where sculptures of deities are carved from sandalwood. Clients from all over Southeast Asia place orders for statues and temple **⑧** panels at the **Say Tian Hong Buddha Shop,** at No. 6. Continue along Club Street and turn left onto Ramah Street, where, at No. 12, paper-thin pancakes are cooked on a griddle and sent to restaurants to be turned into spring rolls. On the other side of Cross Street, Club Street becomes China Street. Here, at another pancake shop, **Chop Chuan An,** you can watch spring rolls being made—and sample the finished products. To the left off China Street are Chin Chew, Nankin, and Hokkien streets; all have a number of well-preserved shophouses selling coffees, Chinese wines, birds' nests, herbal medicines, candy, and funeral paper.

⑨ Back on China Street, opposite Nankin Street, is the **Jen Foh Medical Hall,** where salespeople are very helpful in suggesting cures for diseases or inadequacies you never knew you had. Where China Street ends, turn right onto Church Street, then take the first left

⑩ onto Phillip Street. Here you'll find the **Wak Hai Cheng Bio Temple,** built between 1852 and 1855 by Teochew Chinese from Guangdong Province and dedicated to the goddess of the sea. The wonderfully ornate roof is covered with decorations—including miniature pagodas and human figures—depicting ancient Chinese villages and scenes from opera.

⑪ Retrace your steps to Telok Ayer Street. On the next block is the Taoist **Fuk Tak Chi Temple,** built by Hakka and Cantonese immigrants. Show deference to the two sinister gods on the left as you enter or risk losing your spirit to them. In front of you are small statues representing some of the many Chinese deities. In the far right corner is one of Tua Pek Kong, to whom this temple is dedicated. Represented as a bearded sailor dressed in mourner's sackcloth, this deity is appealed to by those hoping for a prosperous and safe voyage.

⑫ Continue south on Telok Ayer; at Cross Street, notice the **Hakka Clan Hall** (Ying He Hui Guan), on the right-hand corner. It is set in a courtyard and features intricate wood carvings on its gables. At No. 134 is **Meow Choon Foh Yit Ken,** a store well known for traditional medicines.

⑬ Past the **Nagore Durghe Shrine,** an odd mix of minarets and Greek columns built by southern Indian Muslims between 1828 and 1830, is **⑭** the **Thian Hock Keng Temple** (Temple of Heavenly Happiness), completed in 1841 to replace a simple shrine built 20 years earlier. This Chinese temple is one of Singapore's oldest and largest, built on the spot where, prior to land reclamation, immigrants stepped ashore from their hazardous journey across the China Sea. In gratitude for their safe passage, the Hokkien people dedicated the temple to Ma Chu P'oh, the goddess of the sea.

Thian Hock Keng is richly decorated with gilded carvings, sculptures, tile roofs topped with dragons, and fine carved-stone pillars. Outside, on either side of the entrance, are two stone lions. The one on the left is female and holds a cup, symbolizing fertility; the other, a male, holds a ball, a symbol of wealth. Inside, a statue of a maternal Ma Chu P'oh, surrounded by masses of burning incense and candles, dominates the room. On either side of her are the deities of health and of wealth. The two tall figures are her sentinels: One can see for 1,000 miles, the other can hear for 1,000 miles. The gluey black substance on their lips—placed there by devotees in days past—is opium, to heighten their senses. While the main temple is Taoist, the temple at the back is Buddhist and dedicated to Kuan Yin, the goddess of mercy. She has many arms, to represent the way she reaches out to all those who suffer on earth.

⑮ Return to the Nagore Durghe Shrine and take a right on Boon Tat Street. Crossing Robinson Road you'll soon see the **Telok Ayer Market,** the largest Victorian cast-iron structure left in Southeast Asia. A thriving fish market in 1822, it was redesigned as an octagonal structure by George Coleman in 1894. Now it has reopened as a planned food court, with hawker stalls offering the gamut of Asian fare. By day it's busy with office workers. After 7 PM Boon Tat Street closes to traffic and the mood turns festive: The hawkers wheel out their carts and musicians give street performances until midnight. Only time will tell whether the high prices will drive away the locals.

From Telok Ayer, S$.60 will take you on the MRT subway one stop north to Raffles Place on Collyer Quay; another S$.10 will get you up to Orchard Road.

Tour 3: The Indian District

Indians have been part of Singapore's development from the beginning. While Singapore was administered by the East India Company, headquartered in Calcutta, Indian convicts were sent here to serve their time. Other Indians came freely to seek their fortunes as clerks, traders, teachers, and moneylenders.

The area Raffles allotted to the Indian immigrants was north of the British colonial district. The heart of this area—known today as Little India—is Serangoon Road. A good starting point for a tour is the junction of Serangoon and Sungei roads. As you walk along Serangoon, your senses will be sharpened by the fragrances of curry powders and perfumes, by tapes of high-pitched Indian music, by jewelry shops selling gold and stands selling garlands of flowers. Other shops supply the colorful dyes used to mark the *tilak*—the dot seen on the forehead of Indian women.

In the first block on the left is **Zhu Jiao Centre,** one of the largest wet markets in the city. The array of fruits, vegetables, fish, herbs, and spices is staggering. On the Sungei Road side of the ground floor are food stalls that offer Chinese, Indian, Malay, and Western foods. Upstairs are shops selling brass goods, "antiques," porcelains, and textiles. On the right, just past Hastings Street, is **P. Govindasamy Pillai,** at No. 48/50, famous for Indian textiles, especially saris. Farther along, after Dunlop Street, at No. 82, is **Gourdatty Pillai,** with baskets filled with spices of every kind.

The streets to the right off Serangoon Road—Hastings Road, Campbell Lane, and Dunlop Street—are also filled with shops, many of them open-fronted, selling such utilitarian items as pots and pans, plus rice, spices, brown cakes of palm sugar, and every other type of Indian grocery item imaginable. Along Buffalo Road, to the left off Serangoon, are shops specializing in saris, flower garlands, and electronic equipment. Also along this short street are a number of moneylenders from the Chettiar caste—the only caste that continues to pursue in Singapore the role prescribed to them in India.

Continuing down Serangoon Road, you'll pass poster shops; the **Mi Ramassy Flour Mill** (at No. 92), where customers come for freshly ground flour; and shops selling silver charms and flower garlands. Down Cuff Road on the right, simple restaurants serve superb chicken, mutton, or fish curries, often on banana leaves with great mounds of boiled rice and an assortment of condiments.

A little farther down Serangoon Road on the left (opposite Veerasamy Road) you'll notice the elaborate gopuram—adorned with newly repainted sculptures—of the **Sri Veeramakaliamman Temple,** built in 1881 by indentured Bengali laborers working the lime pits nearby. It is dedicated to Kali the Courageous, a ferocious incarnation of Shiva's wife, Parvati the Beautiful. Inside is a jet-black statue of Kali, the fiercest of the Hindu deities, who demands sacrifices and is often depicted with a garland of skulls. More cheerful is the shrine to Ganesh, the elephant-headed god of wisdom and prosperity. Unlike the other temples, which are open all day, this one is open 8 AM–noon and 5:30–8:30 PM. At these times, you will see Hindus going in to receive blessings: The priest streaks devotees' foreheads with *vibhuti*, the white ash from burned cow dung.

Continue along Serangoon to Race Course Road and the Sakya Muni Buddha Gaya Temple. It is popularly known as the **Temple of 1,000 Lights** because, for a small donation, you can pull the switch that lights countless bulbs around a 15-m (50-ft) Buddha. The entire temple, as well as the Buddha statue, was built by the Thai monk Vutthisasala, who, until he died at the age of 94, was always in the temple, ready to explain Buddhist philosophy to anyone who wanted to listen. The monk also managed to procure relics for the temple: a mother-of-pearl-inlaid cast of the Buddha's footstep and a piece of bark from the bodhi tree under which he received Enlightenment. Around the pedestal supporting the great Buddha statue is a series of scenes depicting the story of his search for Enlightenment; inside a hollow chamber at the back is a re-creation of the scene of the Buddha's last sermon.

Across the road is the charming **Leong San See Temple.** Its main altar is dedicated to Kuan Yin—also known as Bodhisattva Avalokitesvara—and framed by beautiful ornate carvings of flowers, a phoenix, and other birds. Backtrack on Race Course Road to Perumal Road; to the left is the **Sri Srinivasa Perumal Temple.** Dedicated to Vishnu the Preserver, the temple is easy to recognize by the 18-m-high (60 ft) monumental gopuram, with tiers of intricate sculptures depicting Vishnu in the nine forms in which he has appeared on earth. From Sri Perumal, head back down Serangoon, exploring the side streets, or take a five-minute taxi ride to the Arab District.

Tour 4: The Arab District

Long before the Europeans arrived, Arab traders plied the coastlines of the Malay Peninsula and Indonesia, bringing with them the teachings of Islam. By the time Raffles came to Singapore in 1819, to be a Malay was also to be a Muslim. Traditionally, Malays' lives have centered on their religion and their villages, known as *kampongs*. These consisted of a number of wood houses, with steep roofs of corrugated iron or thatch, gathered around a communal center, where chickens and children would feed and play under the watchful eye of mothers and the village elders while the younger men tended the fields or took to the sea in fishing boats. The houses were usually built on stilts above marshes and reached by narrow planks serving as bridges. If the kampong was on dry land, flowers and fruit trees would surround the houses.

The area known as the Arab District, or Little Araby, while not a true kampong, remains a Malay enclave, held firmly together by strict observance of the tenets of Islam. At the heart of the community is the Sultan Mosque, or Masjid Sultan, originally built with a grant from the East India Company to the Sultan of Jahore. Around it are streets whose very names—Bussorah, Baghdad, Kandahar— evoke the fragrances of the Muslim world. This is a place to meander, taking time to browse through shops or enjoy Muslim food at a simple café. This tour begins at the foot of Arab Street, just across Beach Road from the Plaza Hotel.

The first shops on Arab Street are bursting with baskets of every description, either stacked on the floor or suspended from the ceiling. Farther along, shops selling fabrics—batiks, embroidered table linens, rich silks and velvets—dominate. However, don't go all the way up Arab Street yet. First turn right onto Baghdad Street (with more shops) and watch for the dramatic view of the Sultan Mosque when Bussorah Street opens up to your left. On Bussorah Street itself, on the right-hand side, are some interesting shops, including a Malay bridal shop, purveyors of batiks and Arab-designed cushion covers, and an importer of leather goods from Yogyakarta (Indonesia).

The first mosque on the site of the **Sultan Mosque** was built early in the 1820s with a S$3,000 grant from the East India Company. The current structure, built in 1928 by the same architects who designed the Victoria Memorial Hall, is a dramatic building with golden domes and minarets that glisten in the sunlight. The walls of the vast prayer hall are adorned with green and gold mosaic tiles on which passages from the Qur'an are written in decorative Arab script.

Two blocks east of the mosque, on Sultan Gate, is **Istana Kampong Glam,** the sultan's Malay-style palace. Rebuilt in the 1840s on a design by George Coleman, it is in a sad state of repair today. Next door, faring only slightly better, is another grand royal bungalow: the home of the sultan's first minister. Notice its gateposts surmounted by green eagles. Neither building is open to the public, but through the gates you can get a glimpse of the past.

Baghdad Street becomes Pahang Street at Sultan Gate, where several traditional Chinese stonemasons create statues curbside. At the junction with Jalan Sultan, turn right and, at Beach Road, left, to visit the endearing **Hajjah Fatimah Mosque.** The minaret is reputedly modeled on the spire of the original St. Andrew's Church in colonial Singapore, but it leans at a 6° angle. No one knows whether this was intentional or accidental.

Return to Jalan Sultan and take a right. Past Minto Road is the **Sultan Plaza.** Inside, dozens of traders offer batiks and other fabrics in traditional Indonesian and Malay designs, and one store on the third floor (No. 26) sells handicrafts from the Philippines. Return to North Bridge Road and take a right back to Arab Street. North Bridge Road is full of fascinating stores selling costumes and headdresses for Muslim weddings, clothes for traditional Malay dances, prayer beads, scarfs, perfumes, and much more. Across Arab Street, Haji Lane, Shaik Madereah Lane, and Clyde Street offer a maze of small shops to explore. As you walk southeast along North Bridge Road you'll start seeing fewer signs in Arabic and fewer Malay names. Rochor Road is an unofficial boundary of the Arab District. The next right will bring you to **Bugis Street**—until recently, the epitome of Singapore's seedy but colorful nightlife.

Tourists (and Singaporeans, too, for that matter) used to delight in Bugis Street's red lights and bars, where transvestites would compete with the most attractive women for attention and favors. The government was *not* delighted, though, and so the area was razed to make way for a new MRT station. So strong was the outcry that Bugis Street has been re-created, approximately 150 yards from its original site, between Victoria and Queen streets, Rochor Road, and Cheng Yan Place. The shophouses have been resurrected; hawker food stands compete with open-front restaurants (Kentucky Fried Chicken has a dominant corner). The streets in the center of the block are closed to traffic. But pedestrians look in vain for the old Bugis: Plainclothes security staff make sure that the drunken brawls and general sleaziness remain things of the past. The area has failed to attract the night revelers and performers, and trade hasn't boomed as anticipated. Still, it's convenient for lunch or an early-evening meal, though hardly worth a special trip.

Three blocks beyond where Bugis Street becomes Albert Street— past the **Fu Lu Shou** shopping complex (mostly for clothes) and the food-oriented **Albert Complex**—is Waterloo Street. Near the corner is the **Kuan Yin Temple,** one of the most popular Chinese temples in Singapore. The dusty, incense-filled interior, its altars heaped with hundreds of small statues of gods from the Chinese pantheon, transports the visitor into the world of Chinese mythology.

Tour 5: Orchard Road

If "downtown" is defined as where the action is, then Singapore's downtown is Orchard Road—an ultra-high-rent district that is very modern and very, very flashy, especially at night, when millions of lightbulbs, flashing from seemingly every building, assault the senses. Here are some of the city's most fashionable shops, hotels, restaurants, and nightclubs, plus a number of sights with which to break up a shopping trip.

Leaving the MRT station Dhoby Ghaut, with the **Plaza Singapura** shopping complex on your right, you'll see the enormous **Istana**, once the official residence of the colonial governor and now that of the president of the republic. It is open to the public only on National Day. On the first Sunday of each month, there's a changing-of-the-guard ceremony: The new guards leave Bideford Road at 5:30 PM and march along Orchard Road to the Istana, reaching the entrance gate punctually at 6.

On the other side of Orchard Road and a few steps on Clemenceau Avenue is the lovely old **Tan Yeok Nee House,** built around 1885 for a wealthy merchant from China. Whereas most homes built in Singapore at that time followed European styles, this town house was designed in a style popular in South China—notice the keyhole gables, terra-cotta tiles, and massive granite pillars. Since 1940 the Salvation Army has made the place its local headquarters. *207 Clemenceau Ave., tel. 734-3358. Admission free. Open weekdays 8:30–4:30, Sat. 9–noon, Sun. 8:30–6.*

Turn onto Tank Road and continue to the **Chettiar Temple,** which houses the image of Lord Subramaniam. The temple is a 1984 replacement of the original, built in the 19th century. The 21-m-high (70 ft) gopuram, with its many colorful sculptures of godly manifestations, is astounding. The chandelier-lit interior is lavishly decorated; 48 painted-glass panels are inset in the ceiling and angled to reflect the sunrise and sunset. *Open daily 8–noon and 5:30–8:30.*

Return to Orchard Road and continue until you reach Cuppage Road, with a **market** (open every morning) known for imported and unusual fruit and a row of shops with a good selection of antiques.

Time Out For a quick break, try the **Cuppage Food Centre,** next to the Centrepoint shopping complex. Many of the stalls open out onto an attractive tree-lined walkway. The **Selera Restaurant** is famous for its Hainanese curry puffs.

Returning once more to Orchard Road, you'll pass the block-long **Centrepoint;** immediately after it is **Peranakan Place,** a celebration of Peranakan (also called Straits-born Chinese, or Baba) culture. This innovative blending of Chinese and Malay cultures emerged in the 19th century as Chinese born in the Straits Settlements adapted Malay fashions, cuisine, and architectural style to their own satisfaction. At Peranakan Place, six old wooden shophouses, with fretted woodwork and painted in pastel colors, have been beautifully restored. Notice the typical Peranakan touches, like the distinctive use of decorative tiles and unusual fence doors.

Inside the buildings, ranged around a cobblestone forecourt, are shops selling Baba crafts; **Ba Chik's Foto Saloon,** where you can have taken a sepia-toned print of yourself, dressed in Peranakan clothing; and two restaurants serving Nonya food, the distinctive cuisine of the Straits-born Chinese, both with outdoor tables. Costumed guides conduct tours through the **Peranakan Place** museum, a re-creation of a turn-of-the-century Peranakan home. The unique mixture of Malay, Chinese, and European styles that characterizes Peranakan decor is represented by such furnishings as a Malay bed, a large Chinese altar, and an English sporting print. *180 Orchard Rd., tel. 732–6966. Admission free. Show House Museum tour: S$4 adults, S$2 children under 12. Open daily 11–6:30.*

Time Out In **Bibi's** colonial-style dining room one floor up, overlooking Peranakan Place, the S$15 buffet luncheon is a good way to experience the marriage between Chinese and Malay cuisines. *Tel. 732–6966. Open daily noon–3 and 6:45–11. AE, DC, V.*

Continue past the **Lucky Plaza** shopping center, packed with camera, electronic, and watch shops, to the corner of Orchard and Scotts roads. You are now at the heartbeat of downtown Singapore. Here, in the lobby of the **Dynasty Hotel,** you'll find a very special attraction: two facing walls of magnificently executed murals. These are 24 gigantic panels of intricately carved teakwood, each 1.2 m (4 ft) wide and three stories high. Viewed as a whole, they present a vast panorama of 4,000 years of Chinese history and legend. The carving was done in China by 120 master carvers, mostly between 60 and 75 years old, on teak imported from the Burma-Thai border. (A book called *Tales of the Carved Panels* is available at the desk.)

Cross over Scotts Road by the pedestrian bridge, and continue up Orchard Road. Things quiet down a bit now. Walk on the right-hand side of the street past the **Liat Towers** complex (Hermès and Chanel are here), the **Far East Shopping Center,** the **Hilton** and its gallery of boutiques, and the **Ming Court Hotel.** At the Ming Court, veer left onto Tanglin Road, another main thoroughfare. Past the **Tudor Court Shopping Gallery** is the **Singapore Handicraft Centre,** with more than 40 shops showcasing the crafts of Asia, both contemporary and traditional. On Wednesday and from Friday through Sunday (6:30–10) a *pasar malam* ("night bazaar") is held here. The mall and courtyard are jammed with stalls selling souvenirs and sundry wares.

Tour 6: Around the Island

Using the republic's excellent public transportation system, you can make an East Coast tour, a West Coast tour, and a Center Island tour. Each can easily be accomplished in a morning or an afternoon. Alternatively, you can join one of the many organized tours that cover the attractions that interest you.

Numbers in the margin correspond to points of interest on the Tours 6 and 7: Singapore Island map.

West Coast Near the satellite city of **Jurong,** Singapore's main industrial area, are a number of attractions.

❶ **Haw Par Villa** (Tiger Balm Gardens), on the West Coast Highway, reopened in late 1990 as a completely new theme park. This spot was once an unusual landscaped garden with a bizarre series of displays, sculpted in cement and brightly painted, illustrating scenes from Chinese mythology, folk stories, and more. Now at a cost of S$80 million, a local soft-drink company has redeveloped it as a Chinese Mythological Theme Park on 24 acres of terraced land. The park is designed for family outings; allow half a day to see it all, and expect large crowds on weekends. *423 Pasir Panjang Rd., tel. 774–0300. Admission: S$16 adults, S$10 children under 16. Open daily 9–6. A taxi from Orchard Rd. will run S$10, or you can take Bus 143 from Orchard Rd. or Bus 10 or Bus 30 from the Padang.*

Three popular west-coast attractions, relatively close to one another, are the Chinese Garden, the Japanese Garden, and the Jurong Bird Park. The easiest way to get to them is by air-conditioned express bus. The **Bird Park/Road Runner Service,** operated by Journey Express (tel. 339–7738), departs twice daily, in the morning and afternoon, from hotels along Orchard and Havelock roads. The round-trip fare is S$10 for adults, S$6 for children; there is also a shuttle service three times daily between the Bird Park and the Chinese Garden. Alternatively, you can take either the MRT (get off at Clementi Station) or the public bus (take the No. 10 or No. 30 from Clifford Pier or the No. 7 from Orchard Road to the Jurong Interchange; from the Interchange, you can walk to the gardens or take the No. 240, 242, or 406 bus). A taxi costs about S$12 to the Bird Park or the gardens from Orchard Road.

❷ The 34.6-acre **Chinese Garden** (Yu Hwa Yuan) reconstructs an ornate Chinese imperial garden, complete with temples, courtyards, bridges, and pagodas. It is beautifully landscaped, with lotus-filled lakes, placid streams overhung by groves of willows, and twin pagodas. *Off Yuan Ching Rd., Jurong, tel. 265–5889. Admission charge. (Combined ticket with Japanese Garden available.) Open Mon.–Sat. 9–7, Sun. 8:30–7.*

❸ Adjacent to the Chinese Garden and connected to it by a walkway is the **Japanese Garden.** This delightful formal garden is one of the largest Japanese-style gardens outside Japan. Its classic simplicity, serenity, and harmonious arrangement of plants, stones, bridges, and trees induces tranquillity. *Off Yuan Ching Rd., Jurong, tel. 265–5889. Admission charge. Open Mon.–Sat. 9–7, Sun. 8:30–7.*

❹ Across the water from the gardens is the **Singapore Science Centre,** dedicated to the space age and its technology, which are entertainingly explored through audiovisual aids and computers that you operate. *Science Centre Rd., off Jurong Town Hall Rd., tel. 560–3316. Admission charge. Open Tues.–Sun. 10–6.*

❺ The **Jurong Bird Park,** on 50 landscaped acres, boasts the world's largest walk-in aviary, complete with a 30-m-high (100 ft) man-made waterfall that cascades into a meandering stream. More than 3,600 birds from 365 species are here, including the colorful, the rare, and the noisy. If you get to the park early, try the breakfast buffet (from 9 to 11) at the Song Bird Terrace, where birds in bamboo cages tunefully trill as you help yourself to sausages, eggs, and toast. From there you can walk over to the Free Flight Show (held at 10:30), featuring eagles and hawks. In the afternoon, at 3:30, you might catch the Parrot Circus, complete with bike-riding bird gymnasts. *Jurong Hill, Jalan Ahmad Ibrahim, tel. 265–0022. Admission charge. Open daily 9–6. Take Bus 250, 251, or 253 from the Jurong Interchange.*

❻ Next to the bird park is the **Jurong Crocodile Paradise.** At this 5-acre park you'll find 2,500 crocs in various environments—in landscaped streams, at a feeding platform, in a breeding lake. You can feed the crocodiles, watch muscle-bound showmen (and a show*lady*) wrestle crocodiles, or buy crocodile-skin products at the shop. You can also watch the beasts through glass, in an underwater viewing gallery.

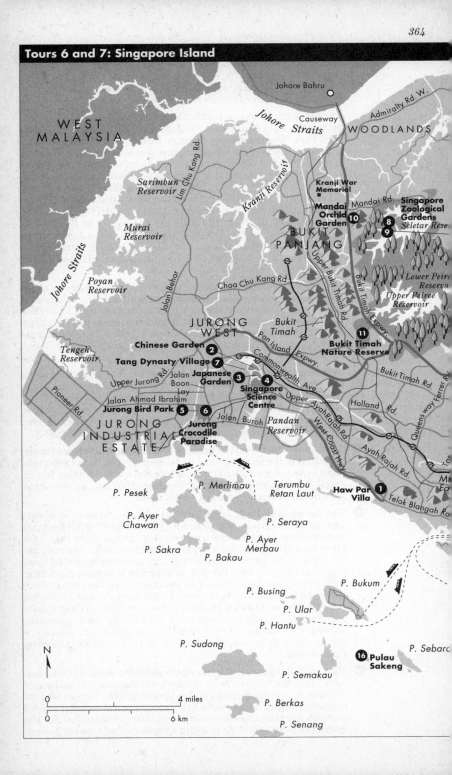

Tours 6 and 7: Singapore Island

WEST MALAYSIA

Johore Bahru

Causeway

Johore Straits

Admiralty Rd. W.

WOODLANDS

Sarimbun Reservoir

Lim Chu Kang Rd.

Kranji Reservoir

Kranji War Memorial

Mandai Orchid Garden ❿

Mandai Rd.

Singapore Zoological Gardens

Seletar Rese

❽
❾

Murai Reservoir

BUKIT PANJANG

Poyan Reservoir

Jalan Behar

Choa Chu Kang Rd.

Upper Bukit Timah Rd.

Bukit Timah Expwy

Lower Peirc Reserv

Upper Peirce Reservoir

Johore Straits

JURONG WEST

Bukit Timah

Pan Island Expwy.

❶❶

Bukit Timah Nature Reserve

Tengeh Reservoir

Chinese Garden ❷

Tang Dynasty Village ❼

Commonwealth Ave.

Bukit Timah Rd.

Upper Jurong Rd.

Jalan Boon Lay

Japanese Garden ❸

❹

Singapore Science Centre

Upper Ayah Rajah Rd.

Holland Rd.

Queensway Ferrer Rd

Pioneer Rd.

Jalan Ahmad Ibrahim

Jurong Bird Park ❺ ❻

Jalan Buroh

Pandan Reservoir

West Coast Hwy.

Ayah Rajah Rd.

JURONG INDUSTRIAL ESTATE

Jurong Crocodile Paradise

P. Pesek

P. Merlimau

Terumbu Retan Laut

Haw Par Villa ❶

Telok Blangah Ra

Tre

Mi Fa

P. Ayer Chawan

P. Seraya

P. Sakra

P. Ayer Merbau

P. Bakau

P. Busing

P. Bukum

P. Ular

P. Hantu

N

P. Sudong

P. Sebard

❶❻ **Pulau Sakeng**

P. Semakau

0   4 miles
0   6 km

P. Berkas

P. Senang

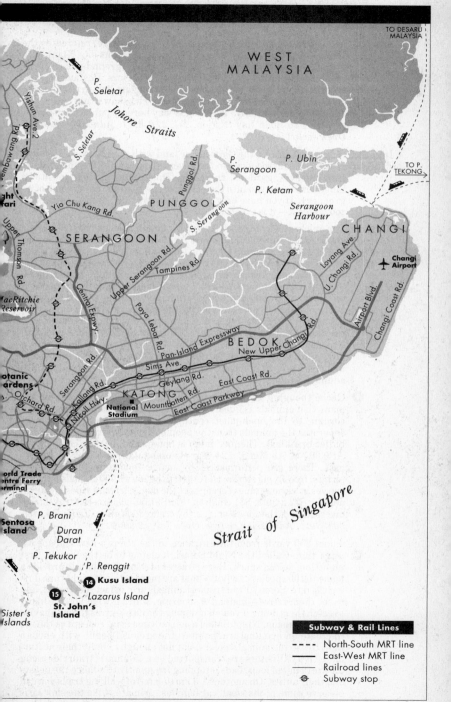

TO DESARU
MALAYSIA

WEST
MALAYSIA

P. Seletar

Johore Straits

Yishun Ave 2

S. Seletar

**ght
fari**

Yio Chu Kang Rd.

PUNGGOL

P. Serangoon

P. Ubin

P. Ketam

Serangoon Harbour

CHANGI

TO P.
TEKONG

Punggol Rd.

SERANGOON

S. Serangoon

Loyang Ave.

U. Changi Rd.

Changi
Airport

Upper Thomson Rd.

Upper Serangoon Rd.

Tampines Rd.

Airport Blvd.

Changi Coast Rd.

Central Expwy.

Paya Lebar Rd.

Pan-Island Expressway

BEDOK

New Upper Changi Rd.

U. Changi Rd.

MacRitchie
Reservoir

Serangoon Rd.

Sims Ave.

Geylang Rd.

East Coast Rd.

otanic
ardens

Orchard Rd.

Kallang Rd.

Nicoll Hwy.

KATONG

Mountbatten Rd.

East Coast Parkway

East Coast Parkway

**National
Stadium**

Strait of Singapore

**orld Trade
entre Ferry
rminal**

P. Brani

*Duran
Darat*

**Sentosa
sland**

P. Tekukor

P. Renggit

⑭ **Kusu Island**

⑮ *Lazarus Island*

**St. John's
Island**

*Sister's
slands*

Subway & Rail Lines

- - - - North-South MRT line
——— East-West MRT line
——— Railroad lines
⊖ Subway stop

241 Jalan Ahmad Ibrahim, tel. 261–8866. Admission charge. Open daily 9–6.

7 Yet another theme park, the **Tang Dynasty Village,** re-creates the 7th-century Chinese village of Chang'an (present-day Xian) with pagodas, gilded imperial courts, and an underground palace of the royal dead guarded by 1,000 terra-cotta warriors. Restaurants and entertainment facilities are modern intrusions, but artisans make and sell traditional wares, and acrobats, rickshaws, and oxcarts all add to the authenticity. The easiest way here by public transport is the MRT to Boon Lay Station. *Tel. 271–6111. Admission charge. Open daily 9 AM–10 PM.*

Into the Garden Isle Singapore is called the Garden Isle, and with good reason. Obsessed as it is with ferroconcrete, the government has also established nature reserves, gardens, and a zoo. This excursion from downtown Singapore takes you into the center of the island to enjoy some of its greenery. If you have only a little time to spare, do try to fit in the zoo, at least—it is exceptional.

The quickest way to reach the zoo is a 20-minute taxi ride (the fare is about S$11). Bus 171 *(Singapore Explorer)* from Orchard Boulevard or Bus 137 from Upper Thomson Road will take you to the zoo in under 40 minutes for S$.80 any time of the day; other buses connect the nearby tourist sites. Alternatively, the air-conditioned **Zoo Express** bus (tel. 235–3111 or 732–2133) takes about 30 minutes, depending on which hotel you're picked up from, and includes a short stopover at the Mandai Orchid Garden. The bus makes two runs a day, starting at 8:30 AMand at 1 PM. Cost (including round-trip and admission to the zoo and the Mandai gardens) is S$30 adults, S$20 children under 12. The **Zoo Road Runner Service** (tel. 339–7738) makes three runs a day, picking up at seven hotels. It also takes about 30 minutes and includes a stop at Mandai Orchid Garden. Cost (bus fare only): S$10 adults, S$6 children under 12.

8 Cliché though it may be, at the **Singapore Zoological Gardens,** humans visit animals as guests in their habitat. The zoo is designed according to the open-moat concept, wherein a wet or dry moat separates the animals from the people. Try to arrive in time for the buffet breakfast. The food itself is not special, but the company is. At 9:30 AM, Ah Meng, a 24-year-old orangutan, comes by for her repast. There are performances by snakes, monkeys, fur seals, elephants, free-flying storks, and other of the zoo's 1,700 animals from 160 species at various times throughout the day. Elephant rides are available for S$2 adults, S$1 children. For S$1.50, visitors can travel from one section of the zoo to another by train. *80 Mandai Lake Rd., tel. 269–3411. Admission charge. Open daily 8:30–6.*

9 About 250 yards from the entrance to the zoo is a new and special attraction. Called the **Night Safari,** it claims to be the world's first nighttime wildlife park. Here 80 acres of secondary jungle provide a home to 100 species of wildlife that are more active at night than during the day. Some 90% of tropical animals are, in fact, nocturnal, and to see them active—instead of snoozing, which is what you are likely to catch them doing if you visit during the day—gives their behavior a new dimension. Night Safari uses the same moat concept as the zoo to create an open natural habitat; the area is floodlit with enough light to see the animals' colors, but not enough to limit their nocturnal activity. Visitors are transported on a 45-minute tram ride along 3.2 km (2 mi) of loop roads, stopping frequently to admire the beasts and their antics. On another 1.3 km (0.8 mi) of walking trails you can observe some of the small cat families, primates (like the slow loris and tarsier), and the pangolin, or scaly anteater. Larger animals include the Nepalese rhino (the largest of rhinos, with a mammoth single horn) and the beautifully marked royal Bengal tigers—which are somewhat intimidating to the nearby shy mousedeer, babirusa (pig deer with curled tusks protruding through the upper lip), gray gorals (wild mountain goats), and bharals (mountain sheep). *80 Mandai Lake Rd., tel. 269–3411. Admission: S$15 adults, S$10 children. Open daily 6:30–midnight.*

⑩ The **Mandai Orchid Garden,** a half-mile down the road from the zoo (Bus 171 links the two), is a commercial orchid farm. The hillside is covered with the exotic blooms, cultivated for domestic sale and export. There are many varieties to admire, some quite spectacular. *Mandai Lake Rd., tel. 269–1036. Admission charge. Open weekdays 9–5:30.*

⑪ For those who prefer their nature a little wilder than what the carefully manicured parks around the city can offer, the **Bukit Timah Nature Reserve** is the place to go. In these 148 acres around Singapore's highest hill, the tropical forest runs riot, giving a feel for how things were before anyone besides tigers roamed the island. Wandering along structured, well-marked paths, you may be startled by flying lemurs, civet cats, or long-tailed macaques. The view from the hilltop is superb. Wear good walking shoes—the trails are not smooth gravel but rocky, sometimes muddy, paths. *Km 12, Upper Bukit Timah Rd., no tel. Admission free. Open dawn to dusk. From the zoo or the Mandai Orchid Garden, take Bus 171. The same bus departs from the Orchard and Scotts Rds. intersection.*

⑫ Back toward the city center are the **Botanic Gardens,** an ideal place to escape the bustle of downtown Singapore (and only a short bus ride away). They began in Victorian times as a collection of tropical trees and plants. The beautifully maintained gardens are spread over some 74 acres, with a large lake, masses of shrubs and flowers, and magnificent examples of many tree species, including 30-m-high (98 ft) fan palms. An orchid bed boasts specimens representing 250 varieties, some of them very rare. *Cnr. of Napier and Cluny Rds., tel. 474–1163. Admission free. Open weekdays 5 AM–11 PM, weekends 5 AM–midnight. Via Bus 7, 14, 105, 106, or 107, it's a 10-min ride to the Botanic Gardens from Orchard Rd.*

Tour 7: The Islands

Sentosa In 1968, the government decided that Sentosa, the Isle of Tranquil-
⑬ lity, would be transformed from the military area it was into the Disney-type resort playground it is, with museums, parks, golf courses, restaurants, and hotels. A tremendous amount of money has been poured into the island's development, and some Singaporeans find Sentosa an enjoyable place to spend some of their free time. Though Sentosa is certainly not a must-see in Singapore, there are two good reasons to go: the visual drama of getting there and the fascinating wax museum.

To reach Sentosa, take either the 1.8-km (1.1-mi) cable car (the more dramatic method, with gondolas holding four passengers each), the ferry, or the causeway via shuttle bus or taxi. The **cable car** picks up passengers from the Cable Car Towers, next to the World Trade Centre, and the Mt. Faber Cable Car Station. Since the trip from Cable Car Towers starts at the edge of the sea and is a bit shorter, it does not afford the panoramic views you get swinging down from Mt. Faber. At 113 m (377 ft), Mt. Faber is not particularly high, but it offers splendid views. There is no bus to the Mt. Faber station, and it's a long walk up the hill, so a taxi is the best way to get there. The Towers station *is* accessible by bus: from Orchard Road, take Bus 10 or 143; from Collyer Quay, Bus 10, 20, 30, 97, 125, or 146. *Off Kampong Bahru Rd., tel. 270–8855. Cost: S$6.50 round-trip, S$5 one way. Open Mon.–Sat. 10–7, Sun. and public holidays 9–9.*

To reach Sentosa by land, take a bus to the World Trade Centre—Bus 10, 97, 100, or 125 from Shenton Way, or Bus 65 or 143 from Orchard Road—and transfer from there onto a **shuttle bus** across the causeway. The S$5 round trip fare includes admission onto the island. The shuttle operates 7 AM–11 PM (midnight on the weekend). You can also get to Sentosa by **taxi** (there's a $S6 toll in addition to the fare), but only between 7 PM and 10 AM, and cabs may drop or collect passengers only at the two island hotels, the Beaufort and the Rasa Sentosa. (An unofficial method of reaching Sentosa is to take the shuttle bus from the Shangri-La Hotel off Orchard Road to its sister hotel, the Rasa Sentosa.)

Ferries ply between Jardine Steps at the World Trade Centre and Sentosa every 15 minutes from 7:30 AM, seven days a week; the crossing takes four minutes. The last ferry back from Sentosa departs at 11 PM Monday through Thursday. From Friday through Sunday and on public holidays, there are two extra return ferries, at 11:15 PM and midnight. Cost: S$2 one way.

While at the World Trade Centre, you may want to visit the **Guinness World of Records Exhibition,** where record-breaking feats from the famed book are displayed by the hundreds. *02–70 World Trade Centre, tel. 271–8344. Admission charge. Open daily 9–5:50.*

Also at the World Trade Centre is the **Singapore Maritime Showcase,** designed to entertain and enlighten visitors on the past, present, and future of Singapore's shipping industry with high-tech interactive exhibits and displays. *Admission free. Open daily 9–5.*

Once on Sentosa, there is a **monorail** system—the first of its kind in Southeast Asia—whose six stations cover most of the major attractions (operates daily 9 AM–10 PM). Unlimited rides are included in the price of the admission ticket—you may get on and off at any of the stations at will. A free bus (daily 9–7) also provides transportation to most of the attractions. A small train runs along the island's south coast for 3.2 km (2 mi). Bicycles are available for rent at kiosks throughout the island.

There are two main types of all-day (8:30 AM–10 PM) admission passes to the island, plus cheaper evening-only (5–10 PM) versions of the same. The **Day Charges Ticket** covers round-trip ferry or shuttle bus over the causeway, unlimited monorail and beach train rides, swimming in the lagoon, and admission to the fountain shows and the Maritime Museum. Cost: S$6 adults, S$4 children under 12. The **Sentosa Saver** (a day's package) includes the above, plus admission to the Pioneers of Singapore/Surrender Chambers, the Coralarium, and Fort Siloso. Cost: S$9.50 adults, S$5 children under 12. Alternatively, you can pay for each individual attraction you visit. (S$1–S$2.50 each for adults). Call if you need further information (tel. 270–7888).

In front of the ferry terminal are the **Fountain Gardens;** several times each evening, visitors are invited to dance along with the illuminated sprays from the fountains to classical or pop music. **Asian Village,** a new addition adjacent to the ferry terminal, is yet another theme park containing three independent "communes" representing East Asia, South Asia, and Southeast Asia. In each village, street performances, demonstrations, merchandise, and food stalls do what they can to add life to a Disneyfied mix. *Admission: S$4 adults, S$2 children. Open daily 10–9.*

The one Sentosa attraction that stands out from all the rest is the **Pioneers of Singapore/Surrender Chambers** wax museum. A series of galleries traces the development of Singapore and portrays the characters whose actions profoundly influenced the island's history. The second part of the museum is the Surrender Chambers, with wax tableaux depicting the surrender of the Allies to the Japanese in 1942 and the surrender of the Japanese in 1945. Photographs, documents, and audiovisuals highlight significant events in the Japanese occupation and the battles that led to the eventual defeat. *Open daily 9–9.*

A three-hour guided tour of Sentosa covers the major attractions, including the Pioneers of Singapore, **the Maritime Museum, Fort Siloso,** and the **Coralarium.** These tours depart daily at 10:30 AM. Tickets may be purchased at the Sentosa Cable Car Station ticket booth. You can certainly do as well on your own, however. A recording on the monorail points out sights as you pass, and audiovisual displays accompany many exhibits in the museums. You may also want to visit the **Rare Stone Museum,** the **Butterfly Park and World Insectarium,** and **Underwater World Sentosa.**

In addition to historical and scientific exhibitions, Sentosa offers a nature walk through secondary jungle, a night market with 40 stalls (Fri.–Sun. 6–10 PM), campsites and tent rentals by the lagoon, and a wide range of recreational activities. (For detailed information on Sentosa's recreational offerings, *see* Participant Sports, *below.*)

The intent has been to make Sentosa a resort destination, not just an afternoon's outing, and with that in mind the 175-room **Beaufort Hotel** (tel. 275–0331; $$$) and the slightly less expensive **Rasa Sentosa** (tel. 275–0100; $$$) have opened. Should you wish to visit either for lunch, there's a frequent shuttle bus between the hotels and Sentosa's ferry terminal. The Beaufort is the quieter and more refined, with an excellent luncheon restaurant next to its attractive pool; the larger Rasa Sentosa, popular with families, has one of the better island beaches.

Kusu
⑭
Kusu is approximately 30 minutes by ferry from the Singapore Cruise Centre at the World Trade Centre, or you can take a day cruise on a junk or a luxury boat (*see* Guided Tours, *above*). Also known as Turtle Island, Kusu is an ideal retreat (except on weekends) from the traffic and concrete of Singapore. There is a small coffee shop on the island, but you may want to bring a picnic lunch to enjoy in peace on the beach.

Next to the coffee shop is a small, open-fronted Chinese temple, **Tua Pek Kong,** built by Hoe Beng Watt in gratitude for the birth of his child. The temple is dedicated to Da Bo Gong, the god of prosperity, and the ever-popular Kuan Yin, goddess of mercy. This temple has become the site of an annual pilgrimage. From late October to early November, some 100,000 Taoists bring exotic foods, flowers, joss sticks, and candles and pray for prosperity and healthy children. The Chinese believe in covering all bases, so while they are here, they will probably also visit the **Malay shrine** on top of the hill. To reach the shrine (called a *keramat*), you must climb 122 steps.

St. John's
⑮
St. John's is the most easily reached island for beach activities, and the one to which Singaporeans go for weekend picnics. The same ferries that go to Kusu go to St. John's. The trip takes an hour from the Singapore Cruise Centre at the World Trade Centre. St. John's was

first a leper colony, then a prison camp for convicts. Later it became a place to inter political enemies of the republic, and now it has become an island for picnicking and overnight camping. Without any temples or particular sights, it is quieter than Kusu.

Off the Beaten Track

A special Sunday-morning treat is to take breakfast with the birds at a **bird-singing café**. Bird fanciers bring their prize specimens to coffee shops and hang the intricately made bamboo cages outside for training sessions: By listening to their feathered friends, the birds learn how to warble. One place to try is the coffee shop on the corner of Tiong Bahru and Seng Poh roads—get there around 9 AM on Sunday.

16 **Pulau Sakeng** is off the tourist track. Indeed, no public ferries cross to the island. You'll need to hire a bumboat from Jardine Steps for the 45-minute passage. The islanders have resisted change; the Malay fishing village on stilts is much as it was a century ago. About 150 families live in the kampong. Aside from a small, simple mosque to visit and local crafts to buy, there is little to do but enjoy the warmth and hospitality of the villagers. It is possible to go swimming off the shore, but there are no facilities. If you're changing on the beach, do remember to respect the Malays' sense of propriety.

Shopping

Singapore is a shopping fantasyland. What makes it so is not the prices but the incredible range of goods brought in from all over the world to be sold in an equally incredible number of shops. The prices, unfortunately, are no longer competitive with places like Kuala Lumpur, Bangkok, or even Hong Kong. Best buys are items indigenous to the region—leather, batiks, Oriental antiques, and silks. Watch for the Singapore Tourist Promotion Board logo—a gold Merlion (a lion's head with a fish tail) on a red background. This signifies that the retailer is recommended by the STPB and the Singapore Retail Merchants Association.

Electrical Goods Singapore's current is 220–240 volts at 50 cycles, similar to Australia's, Great Britain's, and Hong Kong's. Canada, Japan, and the United States use 110–120 volts at 60 cycles. When buying electrical equipment, verify that you can acquire special adapters, if required, and that these will not affect the equipment's performance.

Imitations Singapore has recently tightened its copyright laws: It is illegal either to sell or to buy counterfeit products. (It's also illegal to bring them back to the States.) There are still street stalls and bargain stores offering Rolexes, LaCoste shirts, and Gucci purses at ridiculously low prices, but you can be certain they're fakes.

Bargaining Bargaining is widely practiced in Singapore; the type of store determines the potential "discount." Only department store prices are fixed—it's a good idea to visit one first to establish the base price of an item, then shop around. If you do not like to bargain, the department stores usually have the lowest initial ("first") price. Shops in upscale complexes tend to give a 10%–15% discount on clothes. However, at a jewelry store, the discount can be as high as 50%. At less-upscale complexes, the discounts tend to be greater, especially if they view you as a tourist—that will boost their initial asking price.

How to Pay All department stores and most shops accept credit cards and traveler's checks. Except at the department stores, paying with a credit card will mean that your "discounted price" will reflect the commission the retailer will have to pay the credit card company. Check the exchange rates before agreeing to any price—some store owners try to skim extra profit by giving an unfair rate of exchange.

Guarantees Make sure you get international guarantees and warranty cards with your purchases. Check the serial number of each item against its card, and don't forget to mail the card in. Sometimes guarantees are limited to the country of purchase.

Complaints Complaints about either a serious disagreement with a shopkeeper or the purchase of a defective product should be lodged with the STPB (#01–19 Raffles City Tower, Singapore 0617, tel. 339–6622).

Shopping Districts

Throughout the city are complexes full of shopping areas and centers. Many stores will have branches carrying much the same merchandise in several of these areas.

Orchard Road The heart of Singapore's preeminent shopping district, Orchard Road is bordered on both sides with tree-shaded tile sidewalks lined with modern shopping complexes and deluxe hotels that house exclusive boutiques. It is known for fashion and interior design shops with unusual Asian bric-a-brac.

Chinatown Once Singapore's liveliest and most colorful shopping area, Chinatown lost a great deal of its vitality when the street stalls were moved indoors (into the **Kreta Ayer Complex,** off Neil Road; the **Chinatown Complex,** off Trengganu Street; and the **People's Park Centre,** on Eu Tong Sen Street), but it is still fun to explore. South Bridge Road is the street of goldsmiths, specializing in 22K and even 24K gold ornaments in the characteristic orange color of Chinese gold. You *must* bargain here. On the same street are art galleries, such as the **Seagull Gallery** (#62B, tel. 532–3491) and the **Wenian Art Gallery** (#95, tel. 538–3750), and seal carvers in the **Hong Lim Shopping Centre** will carve your name into your own personal chop.

Little India Serangoon Road is affectionately known as Little India. For shopping purposes, it begins at the **Zhu Jiao Centre,** on the corner of Serangoon and Buffalo roads. Some of the junk dealers and inexpensive-clothing stalls from a bazaar known as Thieves Market were relocated here when the market was cleared out. All the handicrafts of India can be found here: intricately carved wood tables, shining brass trays and water ewers, hand-loomed table linens, fabric inlaid with tiny mirrors, brightly colored pictures of Hindu deities, and even garlands of jasmine for the gods. At dozens of shops here you can get the six meters of voile, cotton, Kashmiri silk, or richly embroidered Benares silk required to make a sari. For the variety, quality, and beauty of the silk, the prices are very low.

Arab Street The area really begins at Beach Road, opposite the Plaza Hotel. A group of basket and rattan shops first catches your eye. There are quite a few jewelers and shops selling loose gems and necklaces of garnet and amethyst beads. The main business is batiks and lace.

Holland Village Holland Village, 10 minutes from town by taxi, is the place to browse for unusual and inexpensive Asian items. Many shops specialize in Korean chests. Behind the main street is Lorong Mambong, a street of shophouses jammed with baskets, earthenware, porcelain, and all sorts of things from China and Thailand. The **Holland Village Shopping Centre** on Holland Avenue has quite a few shops, including **Lim's Arts and Crafts** (tel. 467–1300), selling inexpensive gifts and

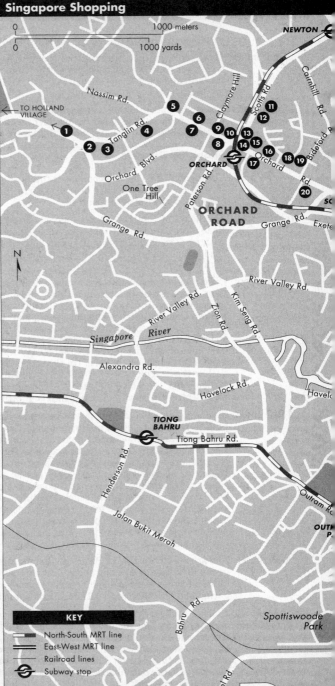

Singapore Shopping

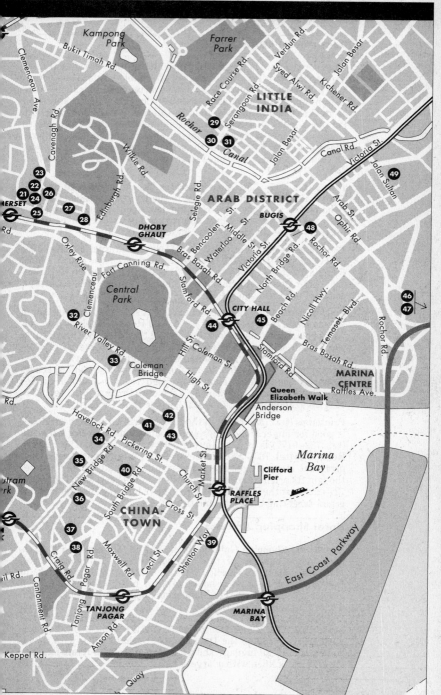

souvenirs; there always seems to be something out of the ordinary to pick up here.

Department Stores

Singapore has two homegrown chains. **Metro** stores are of two types: regular Metros offer a wide range of affordable fashions and household products, and Metro Grands focus on upmarket fashion. Metro designs are up-to-the-minute, and the prices are unbelievably good by international standards. Look for Metros in Far East Plaza, the Paragon, and the Holiday Inn Building (25 Scotts Rd.); Metro Grands are in the Scotts Shopping Centre and in Lucky Plaza. **Klasse** department stores put the accent on budget buys but are best for Chinese imports. The most interesting one is at Lucky Plaza (tel. 235–0261).

Tang's (tel. 737–5500), also known as Tang's Superstore or C.K. Tang's, has just one branch, next to the Dynasty hotel on Orchard Road (#320). It looks upmarket but has some of the best buys in town. Its fashions are, at best, improving, but its accessories are excellent—especially the costume jewelry.

The **Chinese Emporium** (tel. 737–1411) in the International Building (360 Orchard Rd.) and the **Overseas Emporiums** in the People's Park Complex (tel. 535–0555) and the People's Park Centre (tel. 535–0967) offer Chinese silk fabric, silk blouses, brocade jackets, crafts, children's clothes, and china.

Singaporeans enjoy Japanese department stores, such as **Isetan**, in Wisma Atria (tel. 733–7777), the Apollo Hotel (Havelock Rd., tel. 733–1111), Shaw House (350 Orchard Rd., tel. 733–1111), and Parkway Parade (Marine Parade Rd., tel. 345–5555); **Daimaru** (tel. 339–1111), in Liang Court; **Yaohan**, whose biggest store is in Plaza Singapura (tel. 337–4061), by far the most popular chain, especially for appliances and audio equipment; **Sogo** (tel. 339–1100), in Raffles City; **Takashimaya**, in Ngen An City (391 Orchard Rd., tel. 738–1111); and **Meitetsu** (tel. 732–0222), at the Delfi Orchard.

Printemps (tel. 733–9722), in the Hotel Meridien on Orchard Road, is good for lingerie and other women's fashions. **Galeries Lafayette** (tel. 732–9177) is at Liat Towers (541 Orchard Rd.). The English **Robinsons** (tel. 733–0888), in Centrepoint, is Singapore's oldest department store. It recently shed its fuddy-duddy image and rethought its pricing and is once again one of the best. **John Little** (tel. 727–2222), at the Specialists Centre, has a full range of offerings but is now targeting the young and trendy.

Hotel Shopping Arcades

The **Hilton Shopping Gallery,** in the Hilton (581 Orchard Rd.), is home to a number of top designer names—Giorgio Armani, Matsuda, Valentino, Gucci, Davidoff, Vuitton, L'Ultimo, Daks of London, Dunhill—and a boutique with many other Italian and French fashion houses. The **Mandarin Shopping Arcade,** in the Mandarin Singapore (333 Orchard Rd.), has Courrèges, Givenchy, Ungaro, Versace, Hermès, A. Testoni, Bally, and Ferraud, plus two shops that offer a selection of haute couture names. Other hotels with arcades include the **Dynasty** (320 Orchard Rd.), with a boutique for Porsche luggage and accessories, and the **Hyatt Regency** (10–12 Scotts Rd.), with a large shop for Lanvin.

Markets

Food Markets Stalls crowd upon stalls in a covered, open space to make a hectic, colorful scene where everything edible is sold. The range of foodstuffs is staggering, and some of the items may turn your stomach. The live animals eyed by shoppers will tug at your heartstrings. Usually a food market is divided into two sections: the dry market and the wet market. In the latter, where squirming fish, crawling turtles, strutting chickens, and cute rabbits are sold for the pot, the floors are continually sluiced to maintain hygiene. The wet market at the **Chinatown Centre** is the most fascinating, while **Cuppage Centre** (on Cuppage Rd., off Orchard Rd.), where the flower stalls are particularly appealing, is best for the squeamish.

Street Markets In the **Sungei Road area,** site of the once-notorious Thieves Market, a few street vendors creep back each weekend. The stalls sell mainly inexpensive shirts, T-shirts, children's clothes, and underwear, as well as odds and ends such as inexpensive watches, costume jewelry, and sunglasses. The **Kreta Ayer** complex in Chinatown may be modern, but it has all the atmosphere of a bazaar. Some of Chinatown's elderly junk peddlers refuse to leave the streets. In the afternoon, they line up along **Temple Street** and lay out a strange variety of goods—old bottles, stamps, bits of porcelain or brass, old postcards, etc.—on cloths in front of them. The bazaar at the **Singapore Handicraft Centre,** held from 6:30 to 10 PM on Wednesday and from Friday through Sunday, is a good place to buy souvenirs. There are new evening markets at **Bugis** and **Telok Ayer,** but the merchandise tends to be overpriced.

Specialty Shops

Antiques At the Tanglin Shopping Centre, try **Antiques of the Orient** (tel. 734–9351), specializing in maps, ceramics, and furniture; **Funan Selected Works of Art** (tel. 737–3442), with Buddhas and other religious items; and **Moongate** (tel. 737–6771), for porcelain. Off Orchard Road on Cuppage Road is a row of restored shophouses. Here, **Babazar** (31A–35A Cuppage Terr., tel. 235–7866) has jewelry, furniture, clothes, art, knickknacks, and antiques; **Aizia Discoveries** (29B Cuppage Rd., tel. 734–8665) has yet more antiques. **Keng of Tong Mern Sern** (226 River Valley Rd., tel. 734–0761), near the Chettiar Temple, is a rabbit warren full of antiques. For primitive art and antique Indonesian batik and ikat (a woven fabric of tie-dyed yarns), there is **Tatiana** (tel. 235–3560) in the Tanglin Shopping Centre. For museum-quality Asian antiques, visit **Paul Art Gallery** (62–72 Greenleaf Rd., tel. 468–4697).

Art Singapore has more than its share of fine artists. For a range of art, try **Art Forum** (tel. 737–3448) and **Raya Gallery** (tel. 732–0298), both in the Promenade; for local Singapore artists, **Sun Craft** (tel. 737–1308), in the Tanglin Shopping Centre, and **Collectors Gallery** (tel. 339–8007), in Raffles City. There are also many galleries on South Bridge Road in Chinatown (*see* Chinatown, *above*).

Batik A traditional craft item of Singapore, Malaysia, and Indonesia, batik is now also important in contemporary fashion and interior design. **Blue Ginger** (tel. 235–6295) and **Design Batik** (tel. 235–5468), both in the Handicraft Centre, sell clothes and fabrics in modern designs. Traditional batik sarong lengths can be bought in the shops on **Arab Street** and in the **Textile Centre** on Jalan Sultan—try **Eng Leong Seng** (#01–37, tel. 294–4945). **Tang's** sells inexpensive batik products, including a good range of men's shirts.

Cameras Photo equipment may not be the bargain it once was, but the range can be matched only in Hong Kong. All department stores carry cameras, and there are so many in Lucky Plaza that you can do all your comparison-shopping in one spot. **Cost Plus Electronics** (#B1–21 Scotts Shopping Centre, tel. 235–1557), something of a supermarket of cameras and electronics, has low listed prices, and no further discounts are given. For more personalized service, try **Bobby O Store** (43 Stamford Rd., tel. 337–2191), near Raffles City.

Carpets Afghan, Pakistani, Persian, Turkish, and Chinese carpets—both antique and new—are very attractively priced in Singapore. In the Handicraft Centre, try **Chinese Carpets** (tel. 235–6548) or **Oriental Carpet Palace** (tel. 235–8259).

Curios Curio shops sell a fascinating variety of goods, mainly from China, including reverse-glass paintings, porcelain vases, cloisonné, wood carvings, jewelry, ivory carvings, embroidery, and idols. These shops—such as the International Building's **Asia Arts** (#01–02, tel. 737–3631), Orchard Towers' **Chen Yee Shen** (#01–12, tel. 737–1174), and the **Ivory Palace** (tel. 737–1169)—are great places for those who seek the unusual.

Fun Fashion In department stores and small boutiques all over the island—but especially on Orchard Road—locally made ladies' fashions and Japanese imports sell for a song. Three of the better-known boutiques are **Mondi** (#02–13 Scotts, tel. 235–1812; #03–36 Centrepoint, tel. 734–9672), **Man and His Woman** (#02–07 The Promenade, tel. 737–9492), and **Trend** (Centrepoint, tel. 235–9446; Plaza Singapura, tel. 337–1038).

High Fashion Singapore has its own designers: **Tan Yoong** has his shop in Lucky Plaza (tel. 734–3783), **Lam** has his in Liang Court (tel. 336–5974), and **Benny Ong** (who is based in London) sells through Tang's and China Silk House (*see* Silk, *below*). For European couture, check the arcades of the **Regent** hotel, the **Hilton International,** and the **Mandarin,** as well as the more fashionable shopping centers. Men's and women's fashions may be found at **Kenzo** (tel. 734–4738) in Galleries Lafayette in Liat Towers. Men's fashions are represented by such names as **Dunhill** (tel. 737–8174) in the Hilton; **Mario Valentino** in the Scotts Shopping Centre (tel. 235–0876); **Hermès** (tel. 734–1353) in Liat Towers; **Ralph Lauren** (tel. 732–0608) in the Promenade; and **Melwani** (tel. 339–6075) in the Metro department store at Marina Square.

Jewelry Singapore is a reliable place to buy jewelry, and there are so many jewelers that prices are competitive. Never accept the first price offered by any jeweler, no matter how posh the store. All jewelers give enormous discounts, usually 40% or more, but some only when pressed.

In Chinatown, particularly along South Bridge Road and in People's Park, there are dozens of Chinese jewelers selling 22K gold. Many of these, such as **Poh Heng** (27/28 N. Canal Rd., tel. 535–4933), are old family firms. On Orchard Road, the jewelry shops are often branches of Hong Kong firms or are local firms modeled along the same lines. They sell 18K set jewelry, often in Italian designs, as well as loose investment stones. **Larry's** (tel. 734–8763), with branches in Orchard Towers and Lucky Plaza, is one popular store. One of the many other small jewelers in Lucky Plaza is **The Hour Glass** (tel. 734–2420), which carries a large selection of designer watches.

Luggage and Accessories Luggage is a bargain in Singapore. Every complex boasts several stores carrying all the designer names in luggage and leather accessories. **Dunhill** (tel. 737–8174) is in the Hilton; **Etienne Aigner** is in Shaw Centre (tel. 737–6141), Scotts Shopping Centre (tel. 235–2742), and Delfi Orchard (tel. 732–9700); **Louis Vuitton** (tel. 737–5820) is in the Hilton; **Hermès** is at Liat Towers (541 Orchard Rd., tel. 734–1353) and at Daimaru in Liang Court, (tel. 339–1111); and **Charles Jourdan** (tel. 737–4988) is in the Promenade. The **Escada** boutique (tel. 734–7624) at Delfi Orchard has a range of accessories and custom-made luggage.

Pewter and Dinnerware Malaysia is the world's largest tin producer, and pewter is an important craft item in the region. **Selangor Pewter,** the largest pewter concern in Singapore, has a great product range displayed at the main showrooms in the Singapore Handicraft Centre (tel. 235–6634) and Raffles City (tel. 339–3958). The main office is at 7500 A Beach Road (tel. 293–3880).

Reptile-Skin Products Check the import restrictions on these goods. Singapore issues no export certificate for these or for ivory. The price of alligator, crocodile, and snake skins is lower here than anywhere else except Hong Kong. In the old shops around the Stamford Road–Armenian Street area, hard bargaining will yield dividends. The range is widest at big stores, such as the showroom at the **Crocodilarium** (730 East Coast Pkwy., tel. 447–3722) and **Nan Hen** (Bright Chambers, 108 Middle Rd., tel. 338–3702).

Silk Indian silk, in sari lengths, is found in the dozens of sari shops in the Serangoon Road area at a fraction of what you would pay elsewhere. Try **Maharanee's** (Blk. 664, #01–05 Buffalo Rd., tel. 294–9868) and **P. Govindasamy Pillai** (48/50 Serangoon Rd., tel. 337–2050). Chinese silk is found in all the emporiums. **China Silk House** (Tanglin Shopping Centre, tel. 235–5020, and Centrepoint, tel. 733–0555) has a wide range of fabrics in different weights and types, plus silk clothing. Thai silk comes in stunning colors by the meter or made up into gowns, blouses, and dresses. **Design Thai** (tel. 235–5439) in the Tanglin Shopping Centre is one of the largest shops.

Tailoring Tailors who offer 24-hour service rarely deliver, and their quality is pretty suspect. Allow four to five days for a good job. **Justmen** (tel. 737–4800) in the Tanglin Shopping Centre is one of a number of excellent men's tailors. For ladies, shops such as the Tanglin branch of **China Silk House** (tel. 235–5020) and the Specialists Centre's **M.B. Melwani** (tel. 737–5342) and **Bagatelle Shoppe** (tel. 737–7090) offer good tailoring.

Participant Sports

Golf Some of the top Singapore hotels, including the Oriental, have arrangements for guests at local golf clubs, or you can make your own. Ask the STPB for its brochure on clubs.

Jurong Country Club (9 Science Centre Rd., tel. 560–5655) has an 18-hole, par 71 course on 120 acres. **Keppel Club** (Bukit Chermin, tel. 273–5522) is the nearest 18-hole course to the city. **Seletar Country Club** (Seletar Airbase, tel. 481–4746, Tues.–Fri. only) is considered the best nine-hole course on the island. **Sembawang Country Club** (17 Km Sembawang Rd., tel. 257–0642) is an 18-hole, par 70 course known as the commando course for its hilly terrain. There are also squash courts available. **Sentosa Golf Club** (tel. 275–0022) permits visitors to play on the 18-hole, par 71 Tanjong course on the southeastern tip of the island. **Singapore Island Country Club** (180 Island

Rd. or 240 Sime Rd., tel. 459–2222 or 466–2244) permits visitor use of its four 18-hole, par 71 courses—two at Upper Thomson Road and two (including the world-class Bukit course) on Sime Road—on weekdays.

Horseback Riding Arrangements may be made through the **Singapore Polo Club** (Thomson Rd., tel. 256–4530) or the **Saddle Club,** which is associated with the Singapore Turf Club (Bukit Timah Rd., tel. 469–3611, ext. 295).

Hotel Health Facilities Several of the hotels have health and fitness facilities. For addresses and telephone numbers, *see* Lodging, *below.*

Jogging Singapore has numerous parks, and a number of leading hotels offer jogging maps. Serious joggers can tackle the 10-km (6.2-mi) **East Coast Parkway track,** then cool off with a swim at the park's sandy beach. One of the most delightful places to run is the **Botanic Gardens** (off Holland Rd. and not far from Orchard Rd.), where you can jog on the paths or the grass until 11 PM.

Scuba Diving Though the waters near Singapore aren't great for diving, there are some good spots around the outlying islands. Both the **Great Blue Dive Shop** (Holland Rd. Shopping Centre, 211 Holland Ave., tel. 467–0767) and **Asia Aquatic** (#07–37 Cuppage Centre, tel. 738–8158) organize trips offshore.

Squash and Racquetball Several hotels have their own squash courts (*see* Lodging, *below*), and there are numerous public squash and racquetball courts available, including **East Coast Recreation Centre** (East Coast Pkwy., tel. 449–0541), **Kallang Squash and Tennis Centre** (National Stadium, Kallang, tel. 348–1258), and **Singapore Squash Centre** (Fort Canning Rise, tel. 336–0155).

Swimming *See* Beaches and Water Parks, *below.*

Tennis Several public clubs welcome visitors, including **Alexandra Park** (Royal Rd. off York Rd., tel. 473–7236) and **Changi Courts** (Gosport Rd., tel. 545–2941). Also try the **Singapore Tennis Centre** (1020 East Coast Pkwy., tel. 442–5966) and **Tanglin Tennis Courts** (Minden Rd., tel. 473–7236).

Waterskiing The center of activity for waterskiing is Ponggol, a village in northeastern Singapore. **Ponggol Boatel** (17th Ave., Ponggol, tel. 481–0031) charges S$60 an hour for a boat with ski equipment. Some of the local boats are for hire at considerably lower rates. Make sure the proper safety equipment is available.

The Kallang River, where the recent world championships were held, is also popular. Try **Bernatt Boating and Skiing** (62C Kg Wak Hassan, tel. 257–5859), where S$25 buys you six runs along a slalom course.

Windsurfing **East Coast Sailing Centre** (1210 East Coast Pkwy., tel. 449–5118) has sailboard rentals and lessons. Windsurfing is also available on **Sentosa Island.**

Spectator Sports

In addition to the sports listed below, international matches of golf, tennis, cycling, formula motor racing, swimming, badminton, and squash are held on and off. Most events are detailed in the newspapers; information is also available from the **National Sports Council** (tel. 345–7111).

Cricket From March to September, games take place on the Padang grounds in front of the old **Cricket Club** (tel. 338–9271) every Saturday at 1:30 PM and every Sunday at 11 AM. Entrance to the club during matches is restricted to members, but you can watch the game from the sides of the playing field.

Horse Racing The **Singapore Turf Club** (Bukit Timah Rd., tel. 469–3611), about 10 km (6 mi) from the city center, is set in lush parkland, and its facilities are superb. Races are usually held on Saturday, beginning at about 1:30 PM. Gambling on the tote system (automatic gambling organized by track operators) is intense. For the S$5 admission price, you can watch the action either live or on a huge video screen.

You can get to the races easily by way of an organized tour. An air-conditioned coach picks you up from selected hotels and takes you to the club for a buffet lunch, followed by an afternoon of races and a guided tour of the paddock. Passports are required for the tour. *RMG Tours, tel. 738–7776; Singapore Sightseeing, tel. 737–8778. Cost (both): S$68.*

Polo The **Singapore Polo Club** (Thomson Rd., tel. 256–4530) is quite active, with both local and international matches. Spectators are welcome to watch Tuesday, Thursday, Saturday, and Sunday matches, played in the late afternoon.

Rugby Rugby is played on the Padang grounds in front of the Singapore **Cricket Club.** Kickoff is usually at 5:30 PM on Saturday from September through March.

Soccer Soccer is the major sport of Singapore. Important matches take place in the **National Stadium** at Kallang (Sept.–Mar.).

Beaches and Water Parks

CN West Leisure Park. This huge complex boasts a flow pool, a baby pool with slide, a wave pool, and a 50-m (164-ft) water slide. Also here are amusement rides, such as minicars and a minijet merry-go-round. *9 Japanese Garden Rd., Jurong, tel. 261–4771. Admission charge. Open Tues.–Fri. noon–6, weekends and holidays 9:30–6.*

East Coast Park. Here you'll find an excellent beach and a lagoon where you can rent sailboards, canoes, and sailboats. The Aquatic Centre has four pools—including a wave pool—and a giant water slide called The Big Splash. *East Coast Pkwy., tel. 449–5118. Admission charge. Open Mon., Tues., Thurs., Fri. noon–6; weekends 9–6.*

Sentosa Island. Sentosa offers a range of recreational facilities, including a reasonable beach and a swimming lagoon, with changing and refreshment facilities, as well as rowboats, sailboards, and canoes for rent. You can camp here, play golf or tennis, or roller-skate.

Offshore Islands. The islands of Kusu and St. John's have reasonable small beaches and swimming facilities.

Desaru, Malaysia. The best beach area near Singapore is on peninsular Malaysia, 100 km (60 mi) east of Johore Bahru. Lots of resort-type activities on the water, as well as an 18-hole golf course, are available. You can charter a taxi from Johore Bahru for about M$60 (US$23), but it's easier to take the 450-passenger/80-vehicle catamaran *Tropic Chief*, which makes a 45-minute run between the Marine Terminal at Changi and Tanjung Belungkar; from there, a coach makes the 32-km (20-mi) run to Desaru (Ferrylink, Changi Ferry Rd., tel. 545–3600; S$15 one-way; reservations strongly advised).

For overnight accommodations, Desaru has two hotels and several chalets (the Desaru View Hotel will collect you from Singapore).

Dining

By Violet Oon

Singapore offers the greatest feast in the East, if not in the world. Here you'll find excellent restaurants specializing in a wide variety of foods from all corners of the earth. Historically, immigrants from China and India added their culinary cultures to the native Malay cuisine. The Chinese, in Singapore since 1819, created the home-grown fare known as Nonya, or Peranakan, cuisine. To these rich traditions, you can add the foods of Indonesia, Thailand, Vietnam, Korea, Japan, France, Germany, Mexico, Cambodia, Italy, Britain, and the United States. At the hawker centers—semioutdoor markets with as many as 200 vendors selling wonderfully cooked, authentic foods—you can sample most of these cuisines in the same meal!

With the **Chinese** making up about 76% of Singapore's population, their varied cuisines predominate. While Cantonese chefs are the most numerous in the restaurants, the earthy cooking of Teochew, spicy-hot Szechuan, refined Pekingese (known for its crackly crisp ducks), chickens poached with ginger, garlic, and onions from Hainan, soups and stews from Fukien, rustic foods from Hunan, and the provincial food of the Hakkas are all represented.

Hot and spicy food is found at restaurants owned by southern **Indians,** while their northern compatriots make greater use of aromatic spices to create less hot dishes, the most popular of which is tandoori chicken (marinated in yogurt and spices and cooked in a clay urn).

Malay cuisine is hot and rich, using turmeric root, lemongrass, coriander, prawn paste, chilies, shallots, and coconut milk. Nonya cooking is a mixture of Malay and Chinese, combining the finesse of the latter with the spiciness of the former. (All spicy foods are popular in Singapore, and the cusines of Thailand, Indonesia and Malaysia are rated very highly by the population.)

Seafood here is generally very inexpensive (though elegant and expensive seafood meals featuring delicacies like shark's fin, dried abalone, and lobster are served in some Chinese restaurants). The **Seafood Centre** on the East Coast Parkway offers no less than eight restaurants in terracelike pavilions looking out toward the sea. Dishes marked "market price" on the menu are the premium items. Before ordering, be sure to find out exactly how much each dish will cost.

The many **Continental** restaurants have impeccable service and high-quality food. Perhaps the most important gastronomic gift from France is its famous visiting chefs, who have raised Singapore's standard of French cooking—classic or nouvelle—to great heights. Italian food is the great European culinary discovery of the '90s, and a great number of Italian restaurants have just sprung up.

While some cultures consider atmosphere, decor, and service more important than food, in Singapore, a good meal means good food cooked with fresh ingredients. Gourmet cooking can be found as easily in small, unpretentious, open-front coffee shops as in the most elegant restaurants in the world, with service that's second to none. Most of the latter are located in hotels—Singaporeans love to make a grand entrance through a sparkling, deluxe hotel lobby.

At the other end of the scale are the **hawker centers,** agglomerations of individual vendor-chefs selling cooked foods in the open air. These vendors originally traveled from door to door selling their wares from portable stalls. Some years ago, Singapore decided to gather them in food centers for reasons of hygiene. (And these new centers *are* all perfectly clean—the health authorities are very strict.) Visitors and locals alike find these centers a culinary adventure. You can check out each stall—see the raw materials and watch the cooking methods—then choose whatever strikes your fancy from as many different stalls as you like. Find a seat at any of the tables, note the number of your table so you can tell the hawkers where to deliver your orders, and then sit down and wait for the procession of food to arrive. Someone will come to your table to take your drink order. You pay when the food is delivered. Most dishes cost S$4 or slightly more; for S$12, you can get a meal that includes a drink and a slice of fresh fruit for dessert.

The most touristy center is **Newton Circus.** Many people find Newton *the* place to see life at night—it's raucous and noisy, and the mood is really festive. Go to Newton if you must for the experience, but avoid the seafood stalls: They are known to fleece tourists. Feast, instead, at stalls offering the traditional one-dish meals, such as fried Hokkien noodles, roast-duck rice, *rojak,* or Malay *satay* (*see* Glossary of Food Terms, *below*). These stalls have prices displayed prominently in the front. When you place your order, specify whether you want a S$2, S$3, or S$4 order.

Other hawker centers include **Lau Pa Sat**, in the city; **Lagoon,** on the East Coast Parkway; **Telok Ayer Food Centre,** on Shenton Way in the financial district; and **Bugis Square,** at Eminent Plaza (this one's open 7 AM–3 AM). An excellent covered center at **Marina South** has hundreds of stalls offering a vast selection of Chinese and Malay foods. You need a taxi to get there, but the ride is only about S$8 from Orchard Road.

Another experience in Singaporean dining is the **stir-fry stalls,** fondly called "wok-and-roll" by Americans. These stalls, most half restaurant and half parking lot, can be found in abundance on Geylang and Changi roads. They are characterized by open kitchens and a stream of waiters yelling and running about. As a rule of thumb, always follow the crowd to the busiest place. The most popular dish at the stir-fry stalls is fried noodles, followed closely by prawn-paste chicken, deep-fried baby squid, and steamed prawns or fish. There is certainly no elegance here—just good, fresh food cooked according to tried-and-true recipes. Prices are very reasonable. Stalls open at 5 PM.

Dim sum—called *dian xin* ("small eats") in Singapore—is a particularly Cantonese style of eating. Featured are a selection of bite-size steamed, baked, or deep-fried dumplings, buns, pastries, and pancakes, with a variety of savory or sweet flavorings. The selection, which may comprise as many as 50 separate offerings, may also include such dishes as soups, steamed pork ribs, and stuffed green peppers. Traditionally, dim sum are served three on a plate in bamboo steamer baskets on trolleys that are pushed around the restaurant. You simply wait for the trolleys to come around, then point to whichever item you would like. Dim sum is usually served for lunch from noon to 2:30 PM, though in some teahouses in Chinatown, it is served for breakfast from 5 to 9. An excellent place for dim sum is the **Wah Lok Restaurant** (76 Bras Bahah Rd., tel. 338–8333) in the Carlton Hotel. **Tung Lok Shark's Fin Restaurant** (Liang Court Complex, 177 River Valley Rd., tel. 336–6022) has a vast selection. For a dim sum breakfast, try the **New Nam Thong Tea House** (*see below*).

High tea has become very popular in Singapore, and in many hotels, such as the **Goodwood Park Hotel** and the **Holiday Inn Park View,** is accompanied by light Viennese-style music. Though British-inspired, the Singapore high tea is usually served buffet style and includes dim sum, fried noodles, and other local favorites in addition to the regulation finger sandwiches, scones, and cakes. Teas are usually served between 3 and 6 PM.

Glossary of Food Terms   The following are dishes and food names you will come across often at the hawker centers.

char kway teow—flat rice noodles mixed with soy sauce, chili paste, fish cakes, and bean sprouts and fried in lard.

Hokkien prawn mee—fresh wheat noodles in a prawn-and-pork broth served with freshly boiled prawns.

laksa—a one-dish meal of round rice noodles in coconut gravy spiced with lemongrass, chilies, turmeric, galangal, shrimp paste, and shallots. It is served with a garnish of steamed prawns, rice cakes, and bean sprouts.

mee rebus—a Malay version of Chinese wheat noodles with a spicy gravy. The dish is garnished with sliced eggs, pieces of fried bean curd, and bean sprouts.

rojak—a Malay word for "salad." Chinese rojak consists of cucumber, lettuce, pineapple, *bangkwang* (jicama), and deep-fried bean curd, tossed with a dressing made from salty shrimp paste, ground toasted peanuts, sugar, and rice vinegar. Indian rojak consists of deep-fried lentil and prawn patties, boiled potatoes, and deep-fried bean curd, all served with a spicy dip sweetened with mashed sweet potatoes.

roti prata—an Indian pancake made by tossing a piece of wheat-flour dough into the air until it is paper-thin and then folding it to form many layers. The dough is fried until crisp on a cast-iron griddle, then served with curry powder or sugar. An ideal breakfast dish.

satay—small strips of meat marinated in fresh spices and threaded onto short skewers. A Malay dish, satay is barbecued over charcoal and eaten with a spiced peanut sauce, sliced cucumbers, raw onions, and pressed rice cakes.

thosai—an Indian rice-flour pancake that is a popular breakfast dish, eaten with either curry powder or brown sugar.

Dress   Except at the fancier hotel dining rooms, Singaporeans do not dress up to eat out. An open-neck shirt and a jacket represent the upper limit of formality. Generally, though, shorts, thongs, and tracksuits are not considered appropriate.

Hours   Most restaurants are open from noon to 2:30 or 3 for lunch and from 7 to 10:30 (last order) for dinner. Seafood restaurants are usually open only for dinner and supper, until around midnight or 1 AM. Some hotel coffee shops (and the Indian coffee shops along Changi Road) are open 24 hours a day; others close between 2 AM and 6 AM. At hawker centers, some stalls are open for breakfast and lunch, while others are open for lunch and dinner. Late-night food centers like Eminent Plaza in Jalan Besar are in full swing until 3 AM.

Taxes and Charges   Hawker stalls and small restaurants do not impose a service charge. Most medium-size and larger restaurants, however, add a 10% service charge as well as a 4% government tax to the bill. Most Chinese restaurants also automatically add a charge of S$2 per person for tea, peanuts, pickles, and rice.

Tipping Do not tip in restaurants and hawker centers unless you really feel the service deserves an extra bit of recognition. (The 10% service charge is shared by a restaurant's staff.)

Alcohol Liquor is very expensive in Singapore. A bottle of wine in a restaurant costs about S$36; a cocktail, S$6–S$8.

Smoking Smoking is banned in air-conditioned restaurants and banquet/meeting rooms.

Highly recommended restaurants are indicated by a star ★.

Category	Cost*
$$$$	over S$70 (US$46)
$$$	S$35–S$70 (US$23–US$46)
$$	S$10–S$35 (US$7–US$23)
$	under S$10 (US$7)

per person, excluding tax, tip, and drinks

Chinese:
Cantonese
$$$–$$$$
★

Li Bai. Its dining room evokes richness without overindulgence: deep maroon wall panels edged with black and backlighted, elaborate floral displays that change with the seasons, jade table settings, ivory chopsticks. The service is very fine, as is the cooking, which is modern and innovative, yet deeply rooted in the Cantonese tradition. The chef's unusual creations include deep-fried diamonds of egg noodles in a rich stock with crabmeat and mustard greens; fried lobster in black bean paste; and double-boiled shark's fin with Chinese wine and *jinhua* ham. The extensive menu also features barbecued sliced duckling with fresh mango; suckling pig on prawn toast; and Monk Jumps over the Wall with abalone, mushrooms, fish maw, sea cucumber, Chinese herbs, and shark's fin. The restaurant is small, seating fewer than 100 people. *Sheraton Towers Hotel, 39 Scotts Rd., tel. 737–6888. Reservations advised. Dress: smart casual to elegant. AE, DC, MC, V.*

$$–$$$ **Lei Garden.** This is one of Singapore's most respected Chinese restaurants, and it has built up a devoted following. The food represents the nouvelle Cantonese style with its pristine tastes and delicate textures. One old-fashioned item is the soup of the day, cooked just the way mother did—assuming that mother had the time to stew a soup lovingly for many hours over low heat. The menu also offers a long list of double-boiled tonic soups (highly prized by the Chinese), barbecued meats, seafoods, and a variety of shark's fin dishes. Dim sum is available; recommendations include Peking duck, grilled rib-eye beef, and fresh scallops with bean curd in black bean sauce. The decor is beautifully ascetic, with well displayed Chinese art. *Boulevard Hotel, Basement 2, 200 Orchard Blvd., tel. 235–8122. Reservations advised. Dress: smart casual to elegant. AE, DC, MC, V.*

$$–$$$ **Xin Cuisine.** The most innovative Chinese food in Singapore. The chefs do their best to come up with unusual dishes, all with a Cantonese base. (Recent experiments have included a romantic tryst with Chinese herbal dishes and the addition of gold leaf to the food.) The cooking is excellent, the service full of finesse, the setting cloistered and restful with elegant overtones; and you can be sure of getting a good meal. Dishes change regularly; watch for the monthly specials. We can recommend the wok-fried salmon with shiitake and pickled ginger. The steamed fish is a good bet, and the desserts are all good for you—they either improve your complexion or cool you

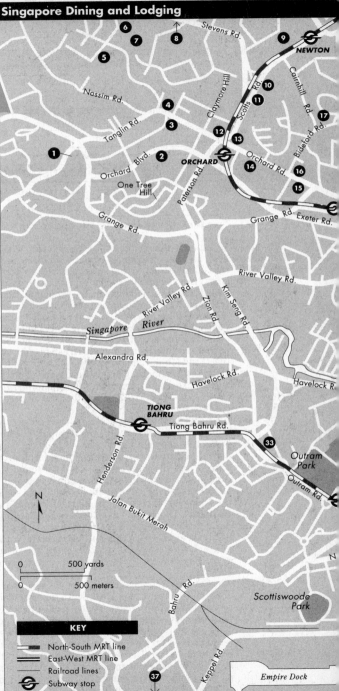

Singapore Dining and Lodging

Dining

Alkaff Mansion, **37**
Aziza's, **21**
Banana Leaf Apollo, **19**
Bintang Timur, **11**
Chang Jiang, **10**
Cherry Garden, **30**
Dragon City, **8**
Fratini La Tratoria, **34**
Gordon Grill, **10**
Ivin's Restaurant, **18**
La Brasserie, **1**
L'Aigle d'Or, **35**
Latour, **7**
Lei Garden, **2**
Li Bai, **12**
Madras New Woodlands, **20**
Min Jiang, **10**
New Nam Thong Tea House, **31**
Pine Court, **15**
Sukmaindra, **12**
Sushi Nogawa, **14, 16**
Tandoor, **22**
Thanying, **36**
UDMC Seafood Centre, **28**
Xin Cuisine, **33**

Lodging

Bencoolen, **25**
Boulevard, **2**
Cairnhill, **17**
Carlton, **26**
Duxton, **35**
Dynasty, **13**
Goodwood Park, **10**
Hilton International, **3**
Inn of the Sixth Happiness, **32**
Ladyhill, **5**
Mitre, **23**
Omni Marco Polo, **1**
Orchard, **4**
Oriental, **30**
Raffles, **27**
RELC International House, **6**
Shangri-La, **7**
Sheraton Towers, **9**
Singapore Peninsula, **29**
YMCA International House, **24**

NEWTON

Stevens Rd.

Nassim Rd.

Claymore Hill

Scotts Rd.

Cairnhill Rd.

Tanglin Rd.

Orchard Blvd.

ORCHARD

Orchard Rd.

Paterson Rd.

Brideford Rd.

One Tree Hill

Grange Rd.

Grange Rd. Exeter Rd.

River Valley Rd.

River Valley Rd.

Zion Rd.

Kim Seng Rd.

Singapore River

Alexandra Rd.

Havelock Rd.

Havelock R.

TIONG BAHRU

Tiong Bahru Rd.

Outram Park

Outram Rd.

Henderson Rd.

Jalan Bukit Merah

N

0   500 yards
0   500 meters

Scottiswoode Park

Bahru Rd.

Keppel Rd.

Empire Dock

KEY

North-South MRT line
East-West MRT line
Railroad lines
Subway stop

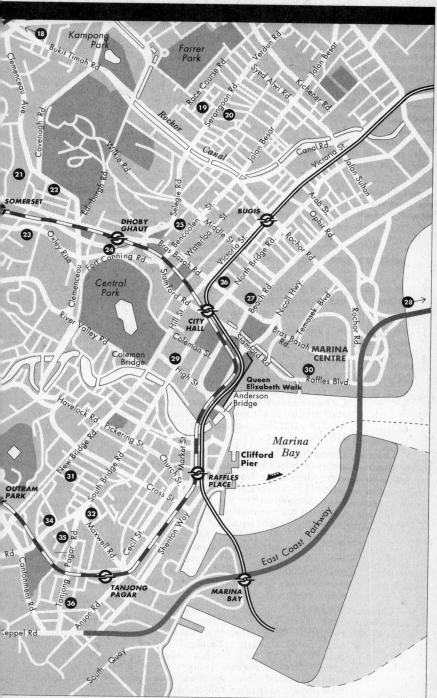

down. Double-boiled bird's nest, Chinese herbal pudding, and double-boiled *hasma* (snow frog jelly) with gingko nuts are just some of
the endings to sample. *Concorde Hotel, 317 Outram Rd., tel. 733–
0188. Reservations advised. Dress: smart casual. AE, DC, MC, V.*

$ **New Nam Thong Tea House.** An absolutely inelegant but totally au-
thentic teahouse in Chinatown. Breakfast here between 5 and 9:30
for a view of real Singapore life. Older folk, mainly men, congregate
daily to meet and gossip with friends and read the Chinese papers.
Situated above an open-front shophouse, the teahouse is not air-
conditioned and can be muggy, but it serves hearty, giant-size dim
sum—*char siew pow* (steamed barbecued pork buns), *siew mai*
(prawn-and-minced-pork dumplings), and other assorted dishes.
Wash it all down with piping-hot Chinese tea. They don't understand
English here, so just point. *8–10A Smith St., tel. 223–2817 or 226-
0718. No reservations. Dress: casual. No credit cards.*

Chinese: **Cherry Garden.** The Cherry Garden restaurant is a beautiful setting
Hunanese for a meal: A wood-roofed pavilion with walls of antique Chinese
$$$ brick encloses a landscaped courtyard. Artworks are tastefully cho-
★ sen and displayed. The service is impeccable, and the food is a wel-
come change from the usual Cantonese fare. An unusual dish is the
steamed rice in woven bamboo baskets. Also try the minced-pigeon
broth with dry scallops steamed in a bamboo tube, or, in season,
served in a fragrant baby melon; the superior Yunnan honey-glazed
ham served between thin slices of steamed bread; or the camphor-
smoked duck in a savory bean curd crust. *Oriental Hotel, 6 Raffles
Blvd., Marina Square, tel. 338–0066. Reservations advised. Dress:
smart casual to elegant. AE, DC, MC, V.*

Chinese: **Pine Court.** Baked tench, marinated lamb, and fried dry scallops are
Pekingese just a few of the dishes that distinguish the cooking of the Pine
$$$ Court. The restaurant's Peking duck is famed for its crisp, melt-in-
your-mouth skin and delicate pancake wrapping. Dinner is the Pine
Court's best meal; the more economical lunch (frequently a buffet) is
less inspired. The carved-wood wall panels create the ambience of a
Chinese mansion; the award-winning service is fine and caring, by a
staff dressed in Chinese style. *Mandarin Hotel, 333 Orchard Rd.,
tel. 737-4411. Reservations advised. Dress: smart casual. AE, DC,
MC, V.*

Chinese: **Chang Jiang.** Meals in this stylish restaurant are served Western-
Shanghainese style—portions are presented on dinner plates, and patrons do not
$$$$ serve themselves from a central platter. The kitchen staff was
trained by the chef of Shanghai's leading restaurant, Yang Zhou.
Recommended dishes are the chicken and goose surprise, fresh
crabmeat in a yam basket, baby kale with scallops, lion's head in con-
sommé, and sliced beef fillet stir-fried and served with leeks. Presentation is an art here. Even the chopsticks are gold-plated.
Children are not welcome—the management wants to preserve the
valuable furnishings and the serene atmosphere. If you must bring
your child, he or she will add a cover of S$25. *Goodwood Park Hotel,
22 Scotts Rd., tel. 737-7411. Reservations advised. Dress: casual.
AE, DC, MC, V.*

Chinese: **Dragon City.** Singaporeans consider Dragon City the best place for
Szechuan Szechuan food. Set in a courtyard and entered through a flamboyant
$$–$$$ red moongate door, the restaurant is a large room that looks Chinese
★ but is not particularly appealing. The food is where all the artistry
is. Choose from such Szechuan staples as *kung po* chicken and
prawns, in which the meat is deep-fried with whole dried chili peppers and coated with a sweet-and-sour sauce; or try the delicious
minced-pork soup in a whole melon, steamed red fish with soybean

crumbs, or smoked Szechuan duck. The service is fast. If you don't quite know how to order your meal, ask for Mr. Wang Ban Say, the restaurant's manager and one of the owners. *Novotel Orchid Inn, Plymouth Wing, 214 Dunearn Rd., tel. 254–7070. Reservations advised. Dress: smart casual. AE, DC, MC, V.*

$$ **Min Jiang.** Housed in a Chinese pavilion on the grounds of the Goodwood Park, Min Jiang is always packed, thanks to its delicious food, fast service, and reasonable prices. The decor is very Chinese in a mellow, resplendent style. The camphor-smoked duck, kung po chicken, and long beans fried with minced pork are favorites. *Goodwood Park Hotel, 22 Scotts Rd., tel. 737–7411. Reservations advised. Dress: smart casual. AE, DC, MC, V.*

Continental **Latour.** Floor-to-ceiling windows provide a spectacular view of
$$$$ the palm-fringed swimming pool and the garden of the Shangri-La
★ Hotel. Inside, an eclectic luxury reigns: salmon-pink walls, comfortable rattan chairs, batik paintings, and Austrian chandeliers, plus elegant crystal, china, and silver table settings. The food is French-based nouvelle cuisine. Thinly sliced beef marinated in lemon pepper à la Cipriani, cream of smoked salmon soup, fresh warm goose-liver salad enhanced with truffles, and deboned rack of lamb with herbed morello sauce are some of the star dishes. At lunch (about S$35 per person), appetizers and desserts are offered buffet-style while the main course is ordered à la carte from a small but well-chosen menu. The wine list is one of the best in town and includes a fine selection from France's Château Latour. *Shangri-La Singapore, 22 Orange Grove Rd., tel. 737–3644. Reservations required. Dress: smart casual to elegant; no jeans. AE, DC, MC, V.*

$$$ **Gordon Grill.** The Scottish country/hunting lodge look, with heavy draped curtains, is lightened with celadon and soft apple greens, light-wood chairs and accents, and glass panels etched with delicate drawings of Scottish lairds. The Goodwood Park's restaurant has changed decor and location within the hotel many times, but tradition is served up here very much as it always has been, including excellent roast beef, perfect steaks, and the best sherry trifle in town. The service is also very good. *Goodwood Park Hotel, 22 Scotts Rd., tel. 737–7411. Reservations advised. Dress: smart casual. AE, DC, MC, V.*

French **L'Aigle d'Or.** Glittering crystal contrasts with gaily decorated floral
$$$ plates at this small, cheerful restaurant in the Duxton Hotel (in the Tanjong Pagar area of Chinatown). A five-course *menu dégustation* for about S$70 may include chestnut soup, sautéed fresh foie gras, a delicate fillet of sea bass in a basil sauce, and a panfried medallion of veal. Desserts come in pairs; you'll rave about the chocolate cake in licorice sauce. *83 Duxton Rd., tel. 227–7678. Reservations advised. Dress: smart casual. AE, DC, MC, V.*

$$–$$$ **La Brasserie.** Often named as the favorite French restaurant in Sin-
★ gapore, this is an informal place, with garçons clad in traditional ankle-length aprons serving hearty traditional fare like French onion soup, émincé de veau à la crème (sliced veal with mushrooms in cream sauce), and fluffy lemon pancakes with vanilla ice cream. Here you'll dine on the spirit of Paris as well as the food: Red-checkered tablecloths, antique wrought-iron lamps, exuberant French art, lace curtains, gleaming copper pans, and two very attractive bar counters bring this brasserie to life. *Omni Marco Polo Hotel, Tanglin Rd., tel. 474–7141. Reservations advised. Dress: smart casual. AE, DC, MC, V.*

Indian
$$$
★

The Tandoor. The food has a distinctly Kashmiri flavor at this luxurious restaurant, where Indian paintings, rust and terra-cotta colors, and Indian musicians at night create the ambience of the Moghul court. The clay oven, seen through glass panels across a lotus pond, dominates the room. After you place your order for tandoori chicken, lobster, fish, or shrimp—marinated in yogurt and spices, then roasted in the oven—sit back and watch the chef at work. Also cooked in the oven is the northern Indian leavened bread called *naan*; the garlic naan is justifiably famous. The tender spice-marinated roast leg of lamb is a favorite of the regulars. Spiced masala tea at the end of the meal seems to wash down the richness of the meal perfectly. Service is exceptionally attentive. *Holiday Inn Park View, 11 Cavenagh Rd., tel. 733–8333. Reservations advised. Dress: smart casual. AE, DC, MC, V.*

$
★

Banana Leaf Apollo. Along Race Course Road are a host of southern Indian banana-leaf-type restaurants. The food is served on rectangles of banana leaves, the specialty is fish head curry (S$18 and above), and the taste is gutsy and chili-hot. Recently this down-home cafeteria-style restaurant has undergone a transformation, and it's now posh and stylish. The food itself is fabulous, though you may end up crying yourself through the fiery, southern-Indian-style meals. Each person is given a large piece of banana leaf; steaming-hot rice is spooned into the center; then two *papadam* (deep-fried lentil crackers) and two vegetables, with delicious spiced sauces, are arranged neatly around the rice. *56/58 Race Course Rd., tel. 298–5054. No reservations. Dress: casual. No credit cards.*

$
★

Madras New Woodlands Restaurant. Locals have formed an allegiance to this simple restaurant in the heart of Little India. The zesty food is vegetarian, combining northern (Punjabi) and southern styles. For a full meal, order a *thali*—a set of dosa (thosai) served with three assorted spiced vegetables, curd, dhal, *rasam* (sour and hot soup), sambar, sweet raita, and papadams. The dosas are superb. Ask for the paper dosa, which comes in an enormous roll and is served with two ground coconut sauces and a rasam. Or ask for the masala dosa, rava, onion, or udipi. Or ask for the fluffy bhatura. They're all wonderful enough to make a meal on their own. *14 Upper Dickson Rd., tel. 297–1594. No reservations. Dress: casual. No credit cards.*

Italian
$$

Fratini La Trattoria. These days the trend is away from splendid hotel dining rooms and toward intimate establishments, like this exciting new restaurant in Tanjong Pagar. The chef is Gabriel Fratini himself, and his traditional cuisine has established a strong following. The antipasto selection is always splendid, especially the thinly sliced veal in a tuna sauce. Make sure you order one of the fabulous pastas or pizzas. For dessert, there's a splendid tiramisu. *51 Neil Rd., tel. 323–2088. Reservations advised. Dress: smart casual. AE, DC, MC, V.*

Japanese
$$$
★

Sushi Nogawa. Chef Nogawa himself presides, and his clientele is so discerning that he is able to fly in tons of fresh Japanese produce throughout the year. The best dishes are seasonal (hence it's difficult to say what to expect). The small original restaurant, where aficionados sit cheek by jowl, is in the Crown Prince Hotel; the new, larger branch, at Takashimaya Shopping Centre on the opposite side of Orchard Road, offers more egalitarian food. If you're nervous, you can order the superb sushi or sashimi. The adventurous can leave it all to the restaurant manager and hope to be surprised. Prices are steep, but you can expect the best. There's *dobinmushi* (teapot soup) as well as tempura, more unusual stews, and even a fish-head dish. Over at Takashimaya, in addition to the incomparable sushi and sashimi selections, you can choose from a selection of set menus, including the most elegant of Japanese meals, the *kaiseki* banquet. *Crown Prince Hotel, 270 Orchard Rd., tel. 732–3053; Level 4, Takashimaya Shopping Centre, 391 Orchard Rd., tel. 735–5575. Reservations advised. Dress: smart casual. AE, DC, MC, V.*

Malay
$$$

Alkaff Mansion. Once the estate of wealthy merchants, this 19th-century house on Mt. Faber Ridge opened as a restaurant in 1991. You can sit inside under twirling fans or out on a veranda decorated to reflect the diverse tastes of the old Arab traders. Downstairs there's a huge Malay-Indonesian dinner buffet; on the upstair's balconies, 10 sarong-clad waitresses serve a multicourse *rijsttafel*. Western food is also offered, from the S$32 three-course luncheon to a more elaborate à la carte menu (from steaks to seafood bordelaise) at dinner. Overall, the delightful turn-of-the-century ambience (something hard to find in Singapore) and the presentation are more rewarding than the food. *10 Telok Blangah Green, tel. 278–6979. Reservations advised. Dress: smart casual. AE, DC, MC, V.*

$$

Aziza's. Hazizah Ali has brought elegant Malay cooking out of the home and into her intimate street-front restaurant on the charming Emerald Hill Road, just up from Peranakan Place. It's the spicy cooking of the Malay Peninsula you get here—lots of lemongrass, galangal, shallots, pepper, coriander, cloves, and cinnamon. Try the beef *rendang* (stewed for hours in a mixture of spices and coconut milk), *gado gado* (a light salad with a spiced peanut sauce), or *bergedel* (Dutch-influenced potato cutlets). The oxtail soup is especially delicious. Ask for *nasi ambang* and you'll get festive rice with a sampling of dishes from the menu. The Orchard Road location and the friendly setting make this an easy place to experiment with Malay food. *36 Emerald Hill Rd., tel. 235–1130. Reservations advised for dinner. Dress: casual. AE, DC, MC, V.*

$$

Sukmaindra. Moorish arches and marble columns support a sculptured geometric ceiling. (There is something almost awesome in the amount of marble present.) The atmosphere is a trifle cold, but this is the poshest Muslim restaurant in town. Dishes to sample include oxtail soup stewed in a light blend of spices, satays, and *kepala ikan* (fish-head curry). For dessert, *chendol* (a sort of stringlike jelly) served with palm sugar and coconut milk is a delight. No alcoholic beverages are served. *Royal Holiday Inn Crowne Plaza, Level 3, 25 Scotts Rd., tel. 732–4677. Reservations advised. Dress: smart casual. AE, DC, MC, V.*

$–$$

Bintang Timur. A very pleasant restaurant done up in green and light wood, with a good view from picture windows. It serves Malay food with a touch of Indonesian and Arab influences. Try the deep-fried satay *goreng*, the prawn satay, the fish-head curry (cooked Malay-style, with lots of fresh root spices, such as galangal and lemongrass), or the *ikan pepes* (flaked fish mixed with a ground hot-spice paste, wrapped in banana leaves, then grilled over charcoal). The tastes are rather sharp. *Far East Plaza (#02–08/13), Ground Floor, 14 Scotts Rd., tel. 235–4539. No reservations. Dress: casual. AE, DC, V.*

Nonya
$$

Ivin's Restaurant. Housed in the remote high-class suburb of Bukit Timah, beyond the Turf Club (you'll need a cab to get there), this casual restaurant serves traditional Nonya food à la carte. Specialities include *ayam buah keluak*, a spicy, sour gravy made with chicken and a black Indonesian nut that has a creamy texture and the smokiness of French truffles; *babi pongteh*, pork stewed in soy sauce and onions; *udang masak nanas*, prawns cooked with pineapple; and *pong tauhu* soup, a prawn soup with julienned bamboo shoots and minced chicken, prawn, and bean curd dumplings. Prices are reasonable. *19/21 Binjai Park, tel. 468-38-3060. Reservations advised. Dress: casual. AE, DC, MC, V.*

Seafood
$$-$$$

UDMC Seafood Centre. You *must* visit this place at the East Coast Parkway, near the entrance to the lagoon, to get a true picture of the way Singaporeans eat out, as well as real value (prices here are generally cheaper than in other seafood restaurants). Walk around the eight open-fronted restaurants before you decide where to eat. Chili crabs, steamed prawns, steamed fish, pepper crabs, fried noodles, and deep-fried squid are the specialties. *East Coast Pkwy. Restaurants include Chin Wah Heng, tel. 444-7967; Gold Coast Seafood, tel. 242-7720; Golden Lagoon Seafood, tel. 448-1894; Jumbo Seafood, tel. 442-3435; Kheng Luck Seafood, tel. 444-5911; Lucky View Seafood Restaurant, tel. 241-1022; Ocean Park Seafood Restaurant, tel. 242-7720; and Red House Seafood Restaurant, tel. 442-3112. No reservations. Dress: casual. AE, DC, MC, V. Dinner only (5-midnight).*

Thai
$$-$$$

Thanying. Possibly the best Thai restaurant in Singapore (the owners and chefs are Thai), the Thanying is decorated in exquisite Thai noble taste, and the food—redolent of kaffir lime leaves, sweet basil, mint leaves, ginger, and coriander leaves—is cooked in the best palace tradition. As with Chinese food, you normally order one dish per person with one extra. Try the *gai kor bai toey* (chicken marinated and chargrilled to perfection), an exquisite Thai salad like *yam sam oh* (shredded pomelo tossed with chicken and prawns in a spicy lime sauce), *pla khao sam rod* (garoupa deep-fried until it's so crispy you can practically eat the bones), and one of the Thai curries. And of course, don't miss out on the sour and hot *tom yam* soup. *Amara Hotel, Level 2, 165 Tanjong Pagar Rd., tel. 222-4688. Reservations advised. Dress: smart casual. AE, DC, MC, V.*

Lodging

Tourists and business travelers are flocking to Singapore in record numbers. In 1993, hotels were recording 70% to 80% occupancy rates and were sometimes fully booked, but since then more have opened—the total number of rooms has risen from 24,404 to 30,785—and discounting rates has become popular again. Indeed, no one ever pays the published price. If you're willing to take the gamble and arrive without reservations, then (except perhaps during the busiest periods in August and at Christmas, or during a large convention) you are likely to find hotels willing to offer instant discounts. The Singapore Hotel Association maintains two reservations counters at Changi Airport and can set you up with a room—and often a discount during a slow period—upon your arrival. There is no fee charged for the booking.

The best of Singapore's hotels are equal to the best anywhere else in the world and certainly offer more value for the money than most. The staff goes to great lengths to meet guests' needs. Guest rooms are spacious and fitted out with the latest amenities, from bedside computer control panels to marble-tiled bathrooms with telephone extensions and speakers for the television. Many hotels offer business and fitness centers loaded with the latest technology and equipment.

Perhaps because Singapore's top hotels set such high standards, less expensive properties appear to work harder. Indeed, a major reason why Singapore makes such a convenient and comfortable base from which to explore Southeast Asia is the overall high quality of its lodgings. If all you're looking for is a bunk, there are dormitory-type guest houses on Bencoolen Street where you can sleep for no more than S$15 a night.

Your choice of hotel location may be influenced by your reason for visiting Singapore. Certainly the Orchard and Scotts roads area favors the shopper and evening reveler. Marina Square would be the logical choice for those attending conventions in the complex or who like the openness of space the area offers. For those doing business in the financial district, a hotel close to Shenton Way is ideal; likewise, hotels along the Singapore River are convenient for anyone making trips to the industrial city of Jurong. But location should not be overemphasized. Singapore is a relatively compact city, and taxis and public transportation, especially the new subway, make travel between one area and another a matter of minutes. No hotel is more than a 30-minute cab ride from Changi Airport.

For a map pinpointing locations, *see* Dining, *above*. Highly recommended hotels are indicated by a star ★.

Category	Cost*
$$$$	over S$400 (US$266)
$$$	S$300–S$400 (US$200–US$266)
$$	S$200–S$300 (US$133–US$200)
$	S$100–S$200 (US$66–US$133)
¢	under S$100 (US$66)

*All prices are for a standard double room, excluding 4% tax and 10% service charge.

$$$$ **Goodwood Park.** Ideally located just off Scotts Road and within min-
★ utes of Orchard Road, the Goodwood Park has a tradition of hospitality that dates back to 1900, when it began life as a club for German expatriates. Guests are remembered and greeted by name, high tea is accompanied by a string quartet, and guest rooms are furnished in the style of a country house. All rooms offer the latest in amenities; many look onto the garden and pool area. Each of the Parklane split-level suites has a separate bedroom and living-dining room; though intended for long-term stays, they can be rented for one or two days as well, and at less than what a double costs in the main hotel. *22 Scotts Rd., Singapore 0922, tel. 737–7411 (U.S. res. 800/ 323–7500), fax 732–8558. 235 rooms, including 64 suites. Facilities: 4 restaurants, 24-hr coffee shop, lounge for afternoon tea and light meals, 24-hr room service, beauty salon, business center with laptop computers, baby-sitting, tour desk, 3 outdoor pools, 5 function rooms. AE, DC, MC, V.*

$$$$ **The Oriental.** Within this triangular Marina Square hotel, architect John Portman has created a 21-story atrium with interior balconies stepped inward as they ascend. Through the center of the atrium, glass elevators glide from floor to floor. The Oriental is smaller than many of the modern deluxe hotels in Singapore; this permits the staff to give personalized attention to each guest. All the guest rooms are decorated in soft hues of peach and green; hand-woven carpets and paintings of old Singapore add to the feeling of understated elegance. The Italian-marble-tile bathrooms offer separate tubs and showers, a telephone extension, radio and television speakers, and an array of toiletries, including terry-cloth bathrobes. One-bedroom suites have elegant sitting rooms and a separate guest washroom. *6 Raffles Blvd., #01–200, Singapore 0103, tel. 338–0066 or 800/526–6566, fax 339–9537. 640 rooms. Facilities: 5 restaurants, 24-hr room service, outdoor pool, jogging track, tennis and squash courts, fitness center with sauna and massage, travel desk, arrangements for golf, business center, banquet and function rooms. AE, DC, MC, V.*

\$\$\$\$ Raffles Hotel. The Sarkies brothers opened Raffles in 1887, and—embellished by the visits of Conrad, Kipling, and Maugham—the hotel became the belle of the East during its heyday in the '20s and '30s. After World War II it fell on hard times. True to form, Singapore has taken the noble old place and spent millions (S\$160 million in this case) to make it fit a desired self-image. In the process, the charm of the original has been sanitized beyond recognition. The new Raffles is a glistening showpiece, especially from the outside; inside, it's sterile (*see* Tour 1: Colonial Singapore, *above*). The polished marble lobby seems cold. All guest suites have teak floors, 14-foot ceilings, overhead fans, central air-conditioning, and '20s-style furnishings that can be a little stiff. The rectangular layout, with a small living room facing directly into the bedroom and the bathroom beyond, is awkward. For this you pay S\$750 (S\$650 if you'll accept a suite facing the busy street). *1 Beach Rd., Singapore 0718, tel. 337–1886, fax 339–7650. 104 suites. Facilities: restaurants, 24-hr room service, outdoor pool, small fitness center, small business center, shopping arcade. AE, DC, MC, V.*

\$\$\$\$ ★ Shangri-La. This hotel has consistently ranked as one of the top three in Singapore since it opened in 1971. The most spacious rooms are in the newer Valley Wing, with its own entrance, check-in counter, concierge, and boardrooms. Rooms in the main building have been upgraded, and the lobby has been sparklingly redesigned. Set amid 15 acres of gardens in a residential area at the top of Orchard Road, the Shangri-La is a pleasant 10-minute walk from the shopping areas; taxis are always on call for those in a hurry. *22 Orange Grove Rd., Singapore 1025, tel. 737–3644 or 800/457–5050, fax 733–7220. 821 rooms (136 in the Valley Wing). Facilities: restaurants, 24-hr room service, tennis and squash courts, fitness center, indoor and outdoor pools, poolside bar, putting green, live evening entertainment (jazz and contemporary music), disco, 24-hr business center, meeting and banquet rooms. AE, DC, MC, V.*

\$\$\$ ★ The Dynasty. The 33-story, pagoda-inspired Dynasty is a landmark dominating Singapore's "million-dollar corner"—the Orchard and Scotts roads intersection. It is the one hotel in Singapore that celebrates the island's Chinese heritage to the hilt. Depending on your taste, the three-story lobby in rich, deep red—the Chinese color for good fortune—is either opulent or garish. Notice especially the 153-bulb crystal chandelier and 24 remarkable carved-teak wall panels, each 4 feet wide and 40 feet high. The guest rooms seem more Western: light gray carpets, pink-and-gray upholstery, glass coffee tables, and marble-floored bathrooms. A terrace pool and garden, with trickling waters, palms, and bamboo, give the feeling of an imperial Chinese courtyard. Given its location and its room rates at the low end of this category, the Dynasty is a good choice for tourists wanting to be in the middle of things. *320 Orchard Rd., Singapore 0923, tel. 734–9900 (U.S. res. 800/777–4182), fax 733–5251. 374 rooms, including 21 suites. Facilities: restaurants, 24-hr coffee shop, 24-hr room service, business center, fitness center, Twilight disco, outdoor pool with poolside bar, ballroom, function rooms. AE, DC, MC, V.*

\$\$\$ Hilton International. It may be short on dazzle, but its renovated rooms have all the amenities of a modern deluxe property, and for what it offers, the rates are highly competitive. The most prestigious lodgings are the Givenchy suites, each designed by Hubert de Givenchy and serviced by a personal valet. The hotel's strongest suit is its shopping arcades, which have some of Singapore's most exclusive boutiques. *581 Orchard Rd., Singapore 0923, tel. 737–2233 or 800/445–8667, fax 732–2917. 435 rooms. Facilities: 4 restaurants, 2 bars, 24-hr room service; outdoor rooftop pool; health club with sauna, steambath, whirlpool, and massage; shopping arcade; business center; large ballroom; 10 function rooms. AE, DC, MC, V.*

$$$ **Omni Marco Polo.** Set on 4 acres in a high-rent residential district five minutes by taxi from Orchard Road, this hotel has undergone several changes since it opened in 1968. The most recent renovation has given the lobby and lounge areas a modern ambience that blends with the hotel's traditional European atmosphere. The guest rooms in the Continental Wing have been refurbished with Chippendale reproductions and marble-tile bathrooms. New in 1994 is the Continental Club concierge floor, with a split-level lounge for complimentary breakfast and cocktails and a separate business center. At night, a basement bar turns into a private-membership disco open to hotel guests. *Tanglin Rd., Singapore 1024, tel. 474–7141 (U.S. res. 800/843–6664), fax 471–0521. 603 rooms, including 30 suites. Facilities: 3 restaurants, lobby lounge and bar, disco, hair dryers, minibars, coffee- and tea-making facilities, 24-hr room service, landscaped outdoor pool, fitness center, business center, function rooms. AE, DC, MC, V.*

$$$ **Sheraton Towers.** Service at this hotel, which opened in 1985, is a key
★ attraction (it continually receives Singapore's "Hotel of the Year" award). For example, guests are asked upon arrival if they'd like their suits pressed at no charge, and complimentary early morning coffee or tea is delivered with your wake-up call. The pastel guest rooms have all the deluxe amenities, including a small sitting area with sofa and easy chairs. The hotel's dramatic visual is the cascading waterfall—the rocks are fiberglass—seen through a 30-foot glass panel from the Terrazza restaurant (especially welcoming for a superb high tea). *39 Scotts Rd., Singapore 0922, tel. 737–6888 or 800/325–3535, fax 737–1072. 406 rooms. Facilities: 3 restaurants, 24-hr coffee lounge, 24-hr room service, health center with sauna and massage, outdoor pool, poolside snack bar, business center, disco, ballroom, function rooms. AE, DC, MC, V.*

$$ **Boulevard Hotel.** Located at the top end of Orchard Road, the Boulevard is within easy walking distance of the Singapore Handicraft Centre and the main Orchard Road area. It has two wings: the old one, with renovated rooms, and the 15-story Orchard Wing, with a large, airy atrium lobby dominated by a floor-to-ceiling sculpture. The emphasis is on the traveling executive. Guest rooms include large work desks, minibars, IDD telephones, and pantries with coffee-making facilities. The 72 "executive suites" each have a lounge area. *200 Orchard Blvd., Singapore 1024, tel. 737–2911 or 800/421–0536, fax 737–8449. 528 rooms. Facilities: 3 restaurants (American, Japanese, northern Indian), 24-hr coffee shop, 24-hr room service, fitness center, 2 outdoor pools, business center, hairdresser, drugstore, disco, tour desk, shops. AE, DC, MC, V.*

$$ **Carlton Hotel.** Near Raffles City, between Orchard Road and the financial district of Shenton Way, this stark, pristine hotel lacks personality. However, everything is up-to-date and modern, and compared with other hotels in its class, this one's rates are reasonable. Guest rooms have individually controlled air-conditioning, minibars, IDD telephones with bathroom extensions, and coffee- and tea-making facilities. The upper five stories are concierge floors, with express check-in and complimentary breakfast and evening cocktails. *76 Bras Basah Rd., Singapore 0718, tel. 338–8333 or UTELL International reservations 800/448–8355, fax 339–6866. 420 rooms, including 53 suites. Facilities: 2 restaurants (Cantonese and Continental), 24-hr coffee shop, wine bar, lounge bar, outdoor pool with poolside grill and bar, 24-hr room service, fitness center, business center, function rooms. AE, DC, MC, V.*

\$\$ The Duxton Hotel. In a city of high-rise accommodations, Singapore's first boutique hotel—eight smartly converted shophouses in the Tanjong Pagar district of Chinatown—is a breath of fresh air. It's furnished with colonial reproductions. The standard rooms, at the back, are small; you may prefer spending the extra S\$50 for one of the small duplex suites. Since windows aren't double-glazed, there is some street noise (including a few alley cats). Breakfast is included, and afternoon tea is served in the lounge. The excellent French restaurant, L'Aigle d'Or (*see* Dining, *above*), is off the lobby. *83 Duxton Rd., Singapore 0208, tel. 227–7678 (U.S. res. 800/272–8188; U.K. res. 0181/876–3419), fax 227–1232. 48 rooms. Facilities: restaurant, secretarial service. AE, DC, MC, V.*

\$\$ Orchard Hotel. The small lobby and public areas can become congested with arriving and departing tour groups, but otherwise this hotel offers comfortable accommodations close to the bustle of Orchard Road. Rooms in the older Orchard Wing have been refurbished. The slightly larger (and more expensive) rooms in the new Claymore Wing have in-room safes and bathrooms with separate stall showers; there are concierge "executive" rooms on the top four floors. *442 Orchard Rd., Singapore 0293, tel. 734–7766, fax 733–5842. 679 rooms. Facilities: 24-hr coffee shop, 4 restaurants, terrace pool and poolside bar, business center, tour desk, disco. AE, DC, MC, V.*

\$ Cairnhill Hotel. Once an apartment block, this hotel is a 10-minute walk from Orchard Road. While the building is not particularly attractive, its location on a hill does allow many of its guest rooms a good view of downtown Singapore. Its Cairn Court restaurant serves Pekingese and Szechuan food, as well as regional fare. *19 Cairnhill Circle, Singapore 0922, tel. 734–6622, fax 235–5598. 220 rooms. Facilities: 24-hr coffee shop, business center, fitness center, pool with drink service, shopping arcade, small function room. AE, V.*

\$ The Inn of the Sixth Happiness. The stretch of shophouses on Erskine Road at the top end of Tanjong Pagar in Chinatown has been converted into a hotel that pays tribute to Singapore's Chinese heritage with original Chinese paintings, rosewood furniture, and antiques from the mainland. Standard rooms aren't overdecorated, but they're spacious; all rooms tend to be a little dark. Prices are quite reasonable if you negotiate a discount, though the location and the atmosphere are the main reasons people stay here. The Heritage suites (S\$300) have pure silk sheets and hand-embroidered pillows on rare opium blackwood beds, and bathtubs large enough for two to soak. *33–35 Erskine Rd., Singapore 0106, tel. 223–3266, fax 223–7951. 44 rooms. Facilities: restaurant, coffee shop, pub, nightclub. AE, DC, MC, V.*

\$ ★ Ladyhill Hotel. Ladyhill emphasizes home comforts and relaxation; the feeling is more of a resort than a city hotel. Located in a residential area a good 10-minute walk uphill from Orchard Road (a hotel bus shuttles the weary back and forth), the complex consists of a main building and a series of cottages surrounding a pool. In the main building are the intimate Swiss-style restaurant Le Chalet, a cozy split-level bar with a Filipino band in the evenings, and some guest rooms. Guest rooms have been refurbished in earth tones and pastels, and the lobby has been refitted. The "superior" rooms in the cottages around the pool are spacious enough that an extra bed may be added for children. Usually in the evening there is a poolside barbecue. *1 Ladyhill Rd., Singapore 1025, tel. 737–2111 or 800/421–0536, fax 737–4606. 171 rooms. Facilities: coffee shop, outdoor pool, bar/cocktail lounge with live band, 2 small conference rooms. AE, V.*

$ ★ **RELC International House.** This is less a hotel than an international conference center often used by Singapore's university for seminars. However, the upper floors of the building are guest rooms and offer one of the best bargains in Singapore. The centrally air-conditioned rooms are large and furnished with the basic comforts. The building is in a residential neighborhood, a stiff 10-minute walk from the Orchard and Scotts roads intersection. Because of its good value, it is often booked, so reservations are strongly advised. *30 Orange Grove Rd., Singapore 1024, tel. 737–9044, fax 733–9976. 128 rooms. Facilities: coffee shop, laundry facilities. No credit cards.*

$ **Singapore Peninsula Hotel.** Near the Padang and between the fashionable areas of Orchard Road and Singapore's commercial district, this hotel offers the basic creature comforts. The fairly spacious guest rooms are clean—the best are on the newly refurbished 17th floor—though one may have to tolerate water stains in the bathtub. All rooms have TVs with Teletext, minibars, and safes. The lobby is small. *3 Coleman St., Singapore 0617, tel. 337–2200, fax 339–3580. 315 rooms, including 4 suites. Facilities: 24-hr coffee shop, cocktail lounge, nightclub with floor shows and hostesses, outdoor pool, fitness center with sauna and massage, 24-hr room service. AE, MC, V.*

¢ **Hotel Bencoolen.** On the commercial street that leads from Orchard Road to Little India, this hotel has air-conditioned rooms with IDD phones. Usually one can negotiate a discount on the room rate, making the Bencoolen a fine value, especially with its central location and helpful staff. *47 Bencoolen St., Singapore 0718, tel. 336–0822, fax 336–4384. 86 rooms. Facilities: rooftop restaurant and garden. MC, V.*

¢ **Mitre Hotel.** Overhead fans whirl in sparsely furnished bedrooms; downstairs, in the lounge/lobby bar, old-timers ruminate on how life used to be. If you are looking for staff who can manage pidgin English at best and a Conradesque atmosphere, the Mitre is for you. It does not have modern amenities, nor is it listed with the Singapore Tourist Promotion Board, so you may be the only Westerner. *145 Killiney Rd., Singapore 0923, tel. 737–3811. 19 rooms with shared bath. Facilities: count only on breakfast and drinks at the bar. No credit cards.*

¢ **YMCA International House.** This well-run YMCA at the bottom end of Orchard Road offers hotellike accommodation, with double (S$70) and single (S$45) rooms, plus dormitories for budget travelers (S$20). (S$5 will buy you temporary YMCA membership.) All rooms have private baths and come with color TVs and direct-dial phones. In addition to an impressive gym, there are squash and badminton courts and a rooftop pool. And there's a McDonald's at the entrance. *1 Orchard Rd., Singapore 0923, tel. 336–6000, fax 337–3140. 60 rooms. Facilities: pool, gym, 2 squash courts. AE, DC, MC, V.*

The Arts and Nightlife

The Arts

The Singapore Tourist Promotion Board (STPB) has listings of events for the current month. You can also find the schedules of major performances in the local English-language newspaper, the

Straits Times, or in the free monthly *Arts Diary* brochure (available at most hotel reception desks).

Chinese, Indian, and Malay events are limited to sporadic performances and to festivals, but some commercial shows drawing on Asian culture are given nightly for tourists. Indian music, drama, and dance performances are staged during the major festivals at the more important temples. Themes are from the ancient epics—tales of gods, demons, and heros.

The best of what there is in the area of serious international theater and classical concerts may be found at the **Victoria Theatre and Memorial Hall,** in two adjoining Victorian buildings. This is the home of the 85-member **Singapore Symphony Orchestra,** which was founded in 1979 and has built an excellent reputation for its wide repertoire, including popular classics as well as works by local and Asian composers. Also presented here from time to time are Chinese opera and Indian classical dance, as well as performances by Singapore's various theatrical and operatic societies and festivals featuring music and dance groups from throughout Southeast Asia.

Concerts   The **Singapore Symphony Orchestra** gives concerts on Friday and Saturday evenings twice a month at the Victoria Theatre (*see above*). Tickets may be reserved by telephone between noon and 8 PM (tel. 339–6120; AE, V). Three times a year, the **Chinese Orchestra of the Singapore Broadcasting Corporation** performs Chinese classical music, also at the Victoria (tel. 338–1230 or 256–0401, ext. 2732).

Theater   **Theatreworks** (tel. 280–0188) is a professional drama company focusing on contemporary works. **Act 3** (tel. 734–9090) concentrates on children's plays. **Stars** (tel. 468–9145) is a community theater that offers performances of family shows, such as American musicals and Christmas specials, as well as classic and modern dramas. **Hi! Theatre** (tel. 468–1945) is Singapore's theater of the deaf; its mask, mime, black-light, and sign-language performances appeal as much to the hearing.

Dance   Performances are given throughout the year by the **Singapore Ballet Academy** (tel. 737–5772) and by the **Sylvia McCully** dance group (tel. 457–6995), who perform ballet and jazz.

Cultural Shows   **"ASEAN Night"** at the Mandarin Hotel offers traditional songs and dances from the various countries of ASEAN. The shows are held at poolside, and dinner is available. *333 Orchard Rd., tel. 737–4411. Tues.–Sun. Dinner starts at 7, the show at 7:45. Cost: dinner and show, S$47; show only, S$26.*

"Cultural Wedding Show" is a 45-minute re-creation of a Peranakan wedding ceremony. The presentation is part of a three-hour immersion in the culture of Straits-born Chinese that includes a tour of Peranakan Place's Show House Museum and dinner at Bibi's restaurant, serving Nonya food. *Peranakan Place, 180 Orchard Rd., tel. 732–6966. Weeknights 6:30 PM. Cost: S$36 adults, S$18 children.*

"Instant Asia" is a 45-minute revue of Chinese, Indian, and Malay dance. At the end of the show, members of the audience are invited onto the stage to participate. The show is clichéd and commercial, but fun if you've never seen this kind of thing before. *Singa Inn Seafood Restaurant, 920 East Coast Pkwy., tel. 345–1111. Weeknights at 7:30 PM. Free to diners. Daytime version performed at Cockpit Hotel, tel. 345–1111. Show at 11:45 AM. Admission: S$5 adults, S$2 children.*

"Malam Singapura" is the Hyatt Regency's colorful 45-minute show of song and dance (mostly Malay) performed at poolside with or without dinner. *10–12 Scotts Rd., tel. 733–1188. Nightly. Dinner starts at 7, the show at 8. Cost: dinner and show, S$38; show only, S$18.*

Chinese Opera Chinese operas—called *wayangs*—are fascinating. Usually they are performed on temporary stages set up near temples, in market areas, or outside apartment complexes. Wayangs are staged all year but are more frequently seen in August and September, during the Festival of the Hungry Ghosts. Gongs and drums beat, maidens weep, devils leap, and heros reap the praise of an enthusiastic audience. The characters are weirdly made up and gorgeously costumed.

Nightlife

Music clubs, offering everything from serious listening to jazz to the thumping of discos, are becoming more popular as Singaporeans take up the Western custom of dating. The increasingly popular *karaoke* bars, where guests take microphones and sing along to the music track of a video, offer chronic shower singers the opportunity to go public.

Nightclubs with floor shows are also popular, and the feeling seems to be that the bigger the place is, the better—some accommodate as many as 500 guests. Often these clubs have hostesses (affectionately called public relations officers, or PRO's) available for company. Companionship is remunerated by either a flat hourly fee (the term used is "to book the hostess") or a gratuity given at the end of the evening.

At nightclubs or music bar/lounges, there is usually a cover charge or first-drink charge (cover plus one free drink) of about S$15 weeknights and S$25 weekends. At the nightclubs where there are floor shows and hostesses, the common practice is to buy a bottle of brandy, which may cost as much as S$300. You are advised to let your "hostess" drink from your bottle, rather than order her own.

Prostitution is not exactly legal, but certain areas, such as Geylang, do have red-light districts. The bars along Keppel Road are not recommended. Ladies have been known to slip sleeping draughts into men's drinks.

Dance and Theater Nightclubs The most popular nightclubs among Singaporeans are those with floor shows and hostesses. You are not under any obligation to select a hostess, however. The cost of going to these clubs is in the bottle of brandy you are expected to buy (if you don't mind losing face, you can forgo the brandy and order whatever you want from the bar). There are also "dinner theater" evenings held from time to time at the Hilton, Hyatt, and Shangri-La hotels. Dinner and a show at the **Shangri-La,** which often has some good comedians, runs about S$85.

Kasbah. The decor is Moroccan in this long-established, tiered nightclub where, on occasion, good artists from abroad entertain. Dancing is both fast and slow, and the music allows for conversation. The crowd, too, is more subdued and "properly" dressed. *Mandarin Hotel, Orchard Rd., tel. 737–4411. Open nightly 9–2.*

Marco Polo. A four-piece band plays popular dance music to which diners can take a turn on the floor between courses in the formal and elegant split-level Le Duc Continental restaurant in the Marco Polo Hotel. *Tanglin Rd., tel. 474–7141. Dinner for 2: approximately S$70. Open nightly 8–11.*

Neptune. This sumptuous two-story establishment, designed as an

Oriental pavilion, is reputed to be the largest nightclub in Southeast Asia. Cantonese food is served, and there is a gallery for nondiners. Local, Taiwanese, and Filipino singers entertain in English and Chinese; occasionally a European dance troupe is added to the lineup. *Overseas Union House, Collyer Quay, tel. 224–3922; for show information and reservations, tel. 737–4411. Open nightly 8–2.*

Discos and Dance Clubs

Caesars. The decor and the waitresses dressed in lissome togas give this disco an air of decadent splendor. DJ-spun music plus imported live bands make it a hot venue. *Orchard Towers front block (#02–36), 400 Orchard Rd., tel. 235–2840. Open Sun.–Thurs. 8–2, Fri. and Sat. 8–3.*

Celebrities. Having moved from Centrepoint to Orchard Towers, this establishment is now considered a sophisticated nightspot. Dance music spun by a DJ is interspersed with live pop music; one of the key attractions is the all-girl band Heaven Knows. There is ample room to drink at the 150-foot-long bar. *Orchard Towers rear block (#B1–41), 400 Orchard Rd., tel. 734–5221. Open Sun.–Thurs. 8–2, Fri. and Sat. 8–3.*

Chinoiserie. This is currently the in place for yuppies. Outside, lines of people wait to enter and be entertained by a variety of musical groups. *Hyatt Hotel, 10–12 Scotts Rd., tel. 733–1188. Open nightly 8–3.*

Fire. One of Singapore's steady favorites, with live music and a lively crowd. You pay for drinks by coupons, so work out the cost of what you want before making the purchase. *Orchard Plaza, tel. 235–0155. Drink prices higher on weekends. Open nightly 9–2.*

Rumours. One of the largest discos in Singapore, this is a favorite among the younger crowd. The two-level dance floor is designed to make you feel as though you are dancing in space; the play of mirrors adds to the distortion. *Forum Galleria (#03–08), 483 Orchard Rd., tel. 732–8181. Open Sun.–Thurs. 8–2, Fri. and Sat. 8–3.*

Shock! Odyssey. Using the latest high tech and robots to startle the senses, this ultramodern disco with live entertainment is the newest night place. *Orchard Hotel, 442 Orchard Rd., tel. 734–7766. First drink charges vary, but highest weekends. Open nightly 8–2.*

Xanadu. With the pull of a switch, the American Western scene of a moment ago becomes a tropical-island night. Gimmicky, perhaps, but it works; each time the switch is pulled (twice an evening), to the amused surprise of the clientele, the ambience at this popular yuppie nightclub changes. *Shangri-La Hotel, 22 Orange Grove Rd., tel. 737–3644. Open nightly 9–3.*

Pubs and Beer Gardens

Brannigans. Decorated with knickknacks from around the world to celebrate the adventures of Captain David Brannigan, British wanderer, this popular watering hole is often used as a convenient meeting spot before an evening of revelry or as a friendly place for an evening nightcap. *Hyatt Regency, 10–12 Scotts Rd., tel. 733–1188. Open daily 11 AM–1 AM.*

Champions. There are 20 Champions in the United States, but only one existed elsewhere (in Dubai) until Singapore's became the second. In a room dominated by video sports and decorated with sports uniforms, posters, equipment, and photographs, drinks and snacks are served to enthusiastic fans. *Marina Mandarin Hotel, 6 Raffles Blvd., Marina Sq., tel. 331–8567. Open Mon.–Sat. 5–2; closed Sun.*

The Coolies' Pub. The Inn of the Sixth Happiness, in the newly renovated Tanjong Pagar area of Chinatown, has devoted the top floors of four shophouses to this friendly, casual café. Light music is played on most evenings. *Erskine Rd., tel. 223–3266. Drinks from S$8. Open nightly 7–midnight.*

Dickens Tavern. At this pub/lounge, regulars listen to bands while being served by friendly waitresses (not hostesses). It's a good place to visit if you do not want to have a raucous and expensive evening. *Parkway Parade (#04–01), 80 Marina Parade Rd., tel. 440-0215. No cover. Open nightly 8–2.*

Flag & Whistle. Down in the renovated area of Chinatown, this English-style pub chatters with expat conversations lubricated by beer and fortified by British snacks. *10 Duxton Hill, tel. 223-1126. Open daily 11 AM–midnight.*

Hard Rock Café. The mood is casual, young, and festive, with a bar, booths, and a souvenir shop. Hamburgers and light fare are served, and a band plays in the evenings. *50 Cuscaden Rd. (#02–01), tel. 235-5232. Cover charge. Open nightly 6–1.*

Jim's Pub. Try this cozy bar, owned and managed by pianist Jimmy Chan, for an evening of light music from a vocalist or instrumentalist. *Hotel Negara, 15 Claymore Dr., tel. 737-0811. Open nightly 7–1.*

Jazz **Saxophone.** At this club, which offers both jazz and popular rock, the volume is loud and the space is compact, with standing room only. However, there is a terrace outside where you can sit and still hear the music. *23 Cuppage Terr., tel. 235-8385. Open nightly 6–1.*

Somerset Bar. The New Orleans–style jazz played here has attracted a loyal following over the past four years. With a larger space than the Saxophone, it offers room to sit and relax, making it more popular with the older crowd. *Westin Plaza, 4 Stamford Rd., 3rd Floor, tel. 338-8585. Open nightly 5–2.*

Country-and-Western **Golden Peacock Lounge.** The star attraction is Matthew Tan, Singapore's own singing cowboy, who has a unique vintage country twang. *Shangri-La Hotel, 22 Orange Grove Rd., tel. 737-3644. Open nightly 8–2.*

Comedy **Boom Boom.** Don't expect the delightful unsavoriness of old Bugis Street, but this comedy house usually offers a few belly laughs with its twice-nightly schedule. A DJ spins discs between shows. *Bugis Village, tel. 339-8187. Admission varies from around S$15. Open Tues.–Sun. 8 PM–2 AM; closed Mon.*

8 Thailand

By Nigel Fisher

Thailand is unique among Southeast Asian nations in having developed its culture independently of Western colonialism, and the Thais are proud of their history. The kingdom's Buddhism is the purest in the region. Its language, which is like no other, is enormously rich, with an extraordinary capacity for exact expression of the nuances of human relationships, a sign of the importance Thais place on dealing with one another peaceably and with dignity. Contrasts abound in the country, both geographically and socially. In a land the size of France, beach resorts run the gamut from sleazy Pattaya to dignified Hua Hin. Idyllic island hideaways of virgin beaches sheltered by palm groves and lapped by gentle waters contrast with the frenetic capital.

Bangkok is a sensory kaleidoscope in which temples and palaces of amazing beauty stand alongside ramshackle homes on the banks of evil-smelling *klongs* (canals); appetizing odors of exotic street food mix with the earthy pungency of open drains; and graceful classical dancers perform on stages next door to bars where go-go girls gyrate in clinical nakedness. BMWs stall in traffic jams while *tuk-tuks* (three-wheel cabs) scoot between them; deluxe hotels share the same block with tin-roof stalls; and designer boutiques compete with street vendors hawking knockoff Pierre Cardin shirts.

Chiang Mai, Thailand's second-largest city, is in the mountainous north. Older than Bangkok—in fact, older than the Thai kingdom—Chiang Mai has a cultural heritage that reflects those of its neighbors, Burma (now Myanmar) and Laos, as much as it does Thailand's. The surrounding hills are dotted with small villages of a people collectively known as the hill tribes, whose way of life has, until the last two decades, remained independent from Thailand's national development and the 20th century.

At the northern tip, the Golden Triangle, once notorious for opium trafficking, is still famous for mountain scenery spread over three countries—Thailand, Burma, and Laos. The small, sleepy market towns of Sukhothai and Ayutthaya contain restored ruins that bear witness to their might as past capitals of the Thai kingdom.

Thailand has no fewer than 50 national parks. Phu Kradung in the northeast, for example, is 155 sq km (60 sq mi) of tableland covered with pine trees and tropical flora. Just south of Bangkok, the province of Kanchanaburi is filled with breathtakingly lush forests and cascades. Forest cover, though, is declining, down from 57% in 1961 to 30% today. The mighty elephant, which used to work the great teak forests, has joined the ranks of the unemployed. What work he picks up nowadays is performing for tourists a charade euphemistically called "Elephants at Work."

Just as tourism has given elephants a new lease on life, so has it created alternative opportunities for a population that is 70% agrarian. More than 4 million visitors flock to Thailand each year to seek a quick fix of the exotic at bargain prices. Their demands and willingness to pay top dollar for their pleasures have changed the Thai view of the foreigner. No longer a guest, the visitor is something akin to a one-armed bandit: If the Thai can jerk the tourist just right, he will hit the jackpot. Because the Thai does this with a smile, the foreigner keeps coming back for more. This is not the Thai heritage. In the past, making money for its own sake was frowned upon. Important to the Thai was social harmony and the simple goal of enough "fish in the rivers and rice in the fields" for everybody—an idyllic state associated with the 13th-century founding of the kingdom.

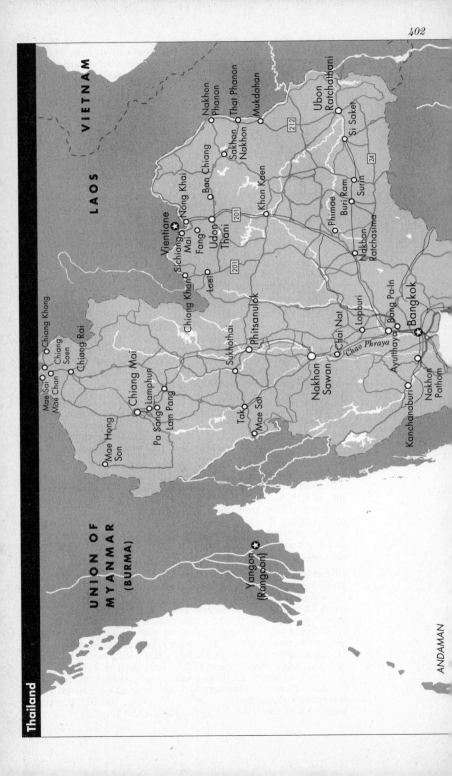

402

UNION OF
MYANMAR
(BURMA)

Yangon
(Rangoon)

ANDAMAN

VIETNAM

LAOS

Nakhon
Phanon

That Phanon

Mukdahan

Ubon
Ratchathani

Si Saket

212

24

Surin

Buri Ram

Phimae

Nakhon
Ratchasima

Ban Chiang

Sakhon
Nakhon

Khon Kaen

Nong Khai

Vientiane

Schiang
Mai

Fang

Udon
Thani

201

201

Loei

Chiang Khan

Sukhothai

Phitsanulok

Chai Nat

Lopburi

Bang Pa-In

Bangkok

Chao Phraya

Nakhon
Sawan

Ayutthaya

Nakhon
Pathom

Chiang Khong

Chiang
Saen

Chiang Rai

Mae Sai
Mae Chan

Chiang Mai

Lamphun

Pa Sang

Lam Pang

Mae Hong
Son

Tak

Mae Sot

Kanchanaburi

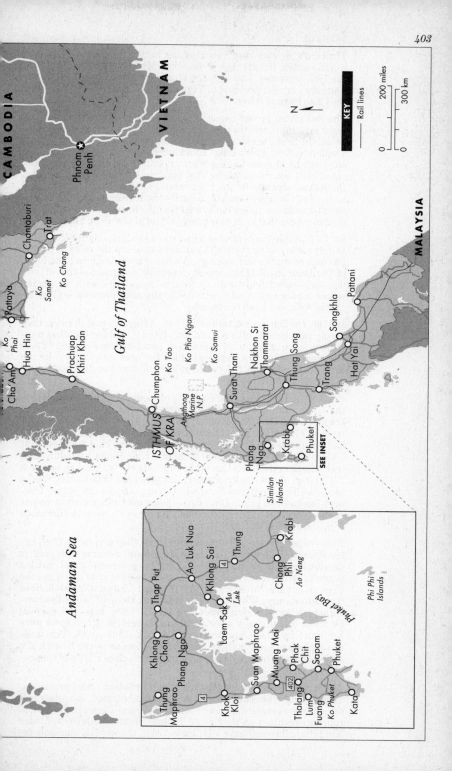

CAMBODIA

VIETNAM

Phnom Penh

Chantaburi

Trat

Pattaya

Ko Samet

Ko Chang

Ko Phai

Hua Hin

Cha'Am

Prachuap Khiri Khan

Gulf of Thailand

Ko Tao

Ko Pha Ngan

Ko Samui

ISTHMUS OF KRA

Chumphon

Angthong Marine N.P.

Surat Thani

Nakhon Si Thammarat

Thung Song

Songkhla

Pattani

Trang

Hat Yai

MALAYSIA

Phang Nga

Krabi

Phuket

SEE INSET

Similan Islands

KEY

— Rail lines

N

0   200 miles

0   300 km

Andaman Sea

Thung Maphrao

Khlong Chon

Phang Nga

Thap Put

Ao Luk Nua

Khlong Sai [4]

Thung

Krabi

Khok Kloi [4]

Laem Sak

Ao Luk

Chong Phli

Ao Nang

Suan Maphrao

Muang Mai

Phuket Bay

Phak Chit

Sapam

Thalang [402]

Lum

Fuang

Ko Phuket

Phuket

Kata

Phi Phi Islands

Thailand's origins may reach as far back as 5,600 years, to the world's oldest Bronze Age civilization. Much later, from the 6th to the 13th centuries, known as the Dvaravati period, people from the southern Chinese province of Yunnan moved into the fertile basin of the Chao Phraya River.

The Sukhothai period began when two Siamese chieftains banded together, captured the Khmer outpost of Sukhothai, and established the first Thai kingdom in 1238. Early in the Sukhothai period, Thailand's first great king, Ramkhamhoeng, came to power. Not only was he an outstanding warrior, but he made two lasting and significant contributions to Thai culture. He revised and adapted the Khmer alphabet to the requirements of the Thai language, and he invited Ceylonese monks to purify the Khmer-corrupted Theravada (sometimes called Hinayana) Buddhism and establish the religion in a form that is, for the most part, still practiced today.

By 1350, Sukhothai's strength had waned sufficiently for the rising and dynamic young state of Ayutthaya to usurp the reins of power. For four centuries and 33 kings, Ayutthaya was the heart and brain of Thailand. In the 1650s, the city's population exceeded that of London and—according to many foreign travelers—with its golden spires, waterways, and roads, it was the most glorious capital not just in Asia, but in all the world.

In 1766, the Burmese attacked the city. After a 15-month siege, they finally captured Ayutthaya and plundered it. Golden Buddhas were melted down, treasuries ransacked, and buildings burned. Thais who were unable to escape were killed or sent into slavery; by the time the Burmese left, Ayutthaya's population had dropped from 1 million to 10,000.

Under General Taksin, the Thais regrouped, established a capital on the Chao Phraya River at Thonburi (opposite present-day Bangkok), and set about successfully expelling the Burmese from Thailand. In 1782, Chao P'ya Chakri, a supporter of General Taksin, who had briefly been crowned king, became the first king of the current Chakri dynasty. (The present monarch, King Bhumibol Adulyadej, is the ninth in the line.) One of the first acts of P'ya Chakri, or Rama I (all kings of the Chakri dynasty are given the title Rama), was to move the Thai capital to Bangkok. During the past 200 years, Thailand has had two prime concerns: staving off foreign encroachment on its sovereignty and restructuring its society to meet the demands of modern industrialism.

Western powers were first welcomed when they arrived in 1512, but the French (from whom the Thai word *farang*, meaning foreigner, is derived) tried to overthrow the legitimate government and install a puppet regime. The result was that the Thais not only threw out the French, but also closed their doors to all outsiders until the middle of the 19th century. When the West again threatened Thailand's sovereignty, King Mongkut (Rama IV, 1851–1868) kept the colonial forces at bay through a series of adroit treaties. His efforts were continued by King Chulalongkorn (Rama V, 1868–1910). Thai independence was eventually secured by the cession to the British of a little of what is now Malaysia and to the French of a little of Cambodia.

Thailand's other concern was adapting to modern social pressures. Under King Chulalongkorn, slavery was abolished, hospitals and schools were established, and some upper-class Thais received a European education so they could replace Western advisers. Under King Prajadhipok (Rama VII, 1925–1935), the world's economic depression brought its share of discontent to Thailand. The pressure for sweeping reform ended in 1932 with the military demanding the establishment of a constitutional monarchy on lines similar to that of Great Britain. Since then, quasi-military governments and a strong bureaucracy have administered the country. Changes in government have been by coup as often as by election. Despite such occasional upheavals, the nation's policies have been remarkably consistent in fostering the expansion of the industrial economy. But in their increasing affluence, Thais are developing a desire for pluralistic representation and accepting less the dictates of unelected officials.

Up to now, the Thais' strong belief in Buddhism (except in the south, where most of Thailand's 2 million Muslims live) has accounted for their tolerant attitude, which can be summed up by their expression *mai pen rai* ("never mind, it does not matter"). The Thais' respect and deference for the monarchy (it is an indictable offense to slander the monarch) has fostered an acceptance of political authority, and a coup is treated with the attitude of mai pen rai. Whether the resilience of the Thai culture can withstand the pressures of the late-20th century is the current question.

Thailand's attraction rests with the people. Proud of their independence, the Thais believe in accommodation rather than confrontation, and that there is, or at least should be, a way to resolve differences politely and amicably. Demands, displays of anger, and any behavior that upsets harmony are frowned upon. The Thais communicate by smiles, which have many meanings, some of which we are probably better off not knowing.

Staying in Thailand

Getting Around

By Plane   The major domestic carrier is **Thai Airways International** (485 Silom Rd., Bangkok, tel. 02/234–3100). Its planes connect Bangkok with all major cities and tourist areas in Thailand with one exception. The closest Thai Airways flies to Ko Samui is Surat Thani, a two-hour bus-and-ferry ride from the island. For direct flights to Ko Samui, call **Bangkok Airways** (tel. 02/253–4014), which has three scheduled daily flights between Bangkok and Ko Samui, using 40-seat planes. Bangkok Airways also has two daily flights to Phuket and one to Hat Yai. Thai Airways offers a travel package called the **Discover Thailand Pass.** For $239 you can take four flights to any of the airline's Thailand destinations. You must purchase the pass outside Thailand. Virtually all planes go through Bangkok, though Thai Airways has recently initiated daily nonstop service between Chiang Mai and Phuket. On popular tourist routes during peak holiday times, flights are often fully booked. Make sure you have reservations, and make them well in advance of your travel date. Flights should be reconfirmed when you arrive in Thailand. Get to the airport well before departure time. Recently, the airlines have started to give away the reserved seats of late passengers to standby-ticket holders. Thai Airways has a good record for keeping to schedule. During the rainy season, however, you may experience delays due to the weather.

By Train   The State Railway of Thailand has three lines, all of which terminate in Bangkok. The Northern Line connects Bangkok with Chiang Mai, passing through Ayutthaya and Phitsanulok; the Northeastern

Line travels up to Nong Khai, near the Laotian border, with a branch that goes east to Ubon Ratchathani; and the Southern Line goes all the way south through Surat Thani—the stop for Ko Samui—to the Malaysian border and on to Kuala Lumpur and Singapore, a journey that takes 37 hours. (There is no train to Phuket, though you can go as far as Surat Thani and change to a scheduled bus service.)

Most trains offer second- or third-class tickets, but the overnight trains to the north (Chiang Mai) and to the south offer first-class sleeping cabins. Couchettes, with sheets and curtains for privacy, are available in second class. Second-class tickets are about half the price of first-class, and since the couchettes are surprisingly comfortable, most Western travelers choose these. Do not leave valuables unguarded on these overnight trains.

Tickets may be bought at the railway stations. Travel agencies can also sell tickets for the overnight trains. Reservations are strongly advised for all long-distance trains. Train schedules in English are available from travel agents and from major railway stations. The State Railway of Thailand offers two types of rail passes. Both are valid for 20 days of unlimited travel on all trains in either second or third class. The **Blue Pass** costs B1,500 (children B750) and does not include supplementary charges such as air-conditioning and berths; for B3,000 (children B1,500), the **Red Pass** does. Currently, a special discounted rate, available for nonresidents of Thailand, gives a reduction of B1,000 for the Red Pass and B400 for the Blue Pass. For more information, call **Bangkok Railway Station,** Advance Booking Office (tel. 02/223–3762).

Fares are reasonable. An air-conditioned, second-class couchette, for example, for the 14-hour journey from Bangkok to Chiang Mai is B530; first class is B980.

By Bus Long-distance buses are cheaper and faster than trains, and there are buses into every corner of the country. A typical fare for the nine-hour trip between Chiang Mai and Bangkok is B300. The level of comfort depends on the bus company. Air-conditioned buses are superior, but the air-conditioning is always turned on full blast, and so you may want to take along an extra sweater. The most comfortable long-distance buses are operated by private travel/tour companies. For the most part, these private buses serve only resort destinations. Travel agents have the bus schedules and can make reservations and issue tickets.

By Car Cars are available for rent in Bangkok and in major tourist destinations. If your current driving license is not written in English, an international driving license is required. Driving is on the left; speed limits are 60 kph (37 mph) in cities and 90 kph (56 mph) outside. With a significant surcharge over the basic one day's rental cost of B1,500 for a 1.6-liter car, Avis permits one-way rentals with drop-offs in most major cities. If Thai driving intimidates you, you may wish to hire a driver. The additional cost is small, and the peace of mind great. If a foreigner is involved in an automobile accident, he—not the Thai—is likely to be judged at fault.

In Chiang Mai, Ko Samui, Pattaya, and Phuket, hiring a jeep or motorcycle is a popular and convenient way to get around. Be aware that many rentals, especially those from small companies, are not covered by insurance, and you are liable for any damage to the vehicle, regardless of who is at fault. **Avis** (16/23 N. Sathorn Rd., Bangkok, tel. 02/251–1131) and **Hertz** (1620 Petchburi Rd., Bangkok, tel. 02/252–4903) are more expensive, but tend to offer better insurance coverage. Also be aware that motorcycles skid easily on gravel roads or on gravel patches on the pavement. In Ko Samui, a sign posts the year's count of foreigners who never made it home from their vacation!

The major roads in Thailand tend to be very congested, and street signs are often in Thai only. But the limited number of roads and, with the exception of Bangkok, the straightforward layout of cities combine to make navigation relatively easy. Driving at night in rural areas, especially north and west of Chiang Mai and in the south beyond Surat Thani is not advised, as highway robberies have been reported.

By Taxi Most Bangkok taxis now have meters installed, and these are the ones tourists should take. In other cities, fares are still negotiated. Taxis waiting at hotels are more expensive than those flagged down while cruising. Never enter the taxi until the price has been established. Most taxi drivers do not speak English, but all understand the finger count. One finger means B10, two is for B20 and so on. Ask at your hotel what the appropriate fare should be. Never pay more than what the hotel quotes, as they will have given you the high price. If in doubt, accept 65%–75% of the cabbie's quote.

With any form of private travel, never change your initial agreement on destination and price unless you clearly establish a new "contract." Moreover, if you agree to the driver's offer to wait for you at your destination and be available for your onward or return journey, you will be charged for waiting time, and, unless you have fixed the price, the return fare can be double the outbound fare.

By Samlor Usually called tuk-tuks for their spluttering sound, these three-wheel cabs are slightly less expensive than taxis and, because of their maneuverability, the most rapid form of travel through congested traffic. All tuk-tuk operators drive as if your ride will be their last, but, in fact, they are remarkably safe. Tuk-tuks are not very comfortable, though, and subject you to the polluted air, so they're best used for short journeys.

By Songthaew Songthaews seat passengers on side bench seats and can serve as minibuses or as private taxis. If they travel as a minibus, they will follow a fixed route and the fare is set. If they are used as a taxi, the fare must be negotiated.

By Bicycle Rickshaw For short trips, bicycle rickshaws are a popular, inexpensive form of transport. They become expensive for long trips. Fares are negotiated. It is imperative to be very clear with these drivers about what price is agreed upon. They have a tendency to create a misunderstanding leading to a nasty scene at the end of the trip.

Telephones

Public telephones are available in most towns and villages and take B1 coins or both B1 and B5 pieces. Long-distance calls can only be made on phones that accept both B1 and B5 coins. For a long-distance call in Thailand, dial the area code and then the number. When telephoning Thailand from overseas, the country code is 66, and the "0" at the beginning of the area code is omitted. To make overseas calls, you are advised to use either your hotel switchboard—Chiang Mai and Bangkok have direct dialing—or the overseas telephone facilities at the central post office and telecommunications building. You'll find one in all towns. In Bangkok, the overseas telephone center, next to the general post office, is open 24 hours; up-country, the facilities' hours may vary, but they usually open at 8 AM and some stay open until 10 PM. Some locations in Bangkok, including the tele-communications building next to the general post office, have **AT&T USADirect** phones. These phones place you in direct contact with an AT&T operator, who will accept your AT&T credit card or place the call collect. You can also use those public phones which accept both B1 and B5 coins to reach AT&T USADirect by dialing 0019–991–1111. First, deposit a coin. It will be returned after the call. For **MCI's Call USA**, dial 001–999–1–2001; ask the operator at that number for customer service. If you wish to receive assistance for an overseas call, dial 100/233–2771. For local telephone inquiries, dial 100/183, but you will need to speak Thai. In Bangkok, you can dial 13 for an English-speaking operator.

Mail

Thailand's mail service is reliable and efficient. Major hotels provide basic postal services. Bangkok's central general post office on Charoen Krung (New Road) is open weekdays 8–6, weekends and public holidays 9–1. Up-country post offices close at 4:30 PM.

Airmail postcard rates to the United States are B9; B8 to the United Kingdom. The minimum rate for airmail letters is B14.50 to the United States and B12.50 to the United Kingdom. Allow about two weeks for your mail to arrive at its overseas destination. If you want to speed that process, major post offices offer overseas express mail services (EMS), where the minimum rate (200 g or 8 oz) is B230.

You may have mail sent to you "poste restante." Usually, there is a B1 charge for each piece collected. Thais write their last name first, so be sure to have your last name written in capital letters and underlined.

Currency

The basic unit of currency is the baht. There are 100 satang to one baht. There are five different bills, each a different color: B10, brown; B20, green; B50, blue; B100, red; and B500, purple. Coins in use are 25 satang, 50 satang, B1, B5, and the recently introduced B10. One-baht coins and B5 coins both come in different sizes and can be easily confused—get the feel of them quickly. The new B10 coin has a gold-colored center surrounded by silver.

The baht is considered a stable currency whose rate of exchange is pegged to the U.S. dollar. All hotels will convert traveler's checks and major currencies into baht, though exchange rates are better at banks and authorized money changers. The rate tends to be better in Bangkok than up-country and is better in Thailand than in the United States. Major international credit cards are accepted at most tourist shops and hotels.

At press time, B25 = US $1, B37 = £1, B17.75 = C$1.

What It Will Cost

The cost of visiting Thailand is very much up to you. It is possible to live and travel quite inexpensively if you do as Thais do—eat in local restaurants, use buses, and stay at non-air-conditioned hotels. Once you start enjoying a little luxury, prices jump drastically. For exam-ple, crossing Bangkok by bus is a 14¢ ride, but by taxi the fare may run to $10. Prices are typically higher in resort areas catering to for-eign tourists, and Bangkok is more expensive than other Thai cities. Anything purchased in a luxury hotel is considerably more expen-sive than it would be if purchased elsewhere. Imported items are heavily taxed. A 7% Value Added Tax is built into the price of all goods and services and is essentially not refundable.

Sample Prices Continental breakfast at a hotel, $8; large bottle of beer at a hotel, $6, but in a local restaurant it will be under $3; dinner at a good restaurant, $15; 1-mile taxi ride, $1.50; double room, $20–$60 inexpensive ($), $60–$100 moderate ($$), $100–$160 expensive ($$$).

Language

Thai is the country's national language. As it uses the Khmer script and is spoken tonally, it is confusing to most foreigners. What may sound to a foreigner as "krai kai kai kai" will mean to a Thai, said with the appropriate pitch, "who sells chicken eggs?" In polite conversation, a male speaker will use the word "krap" to end a sentence or to acknowledge what someone has said. Female speakers use "ka." It is easy to speak a few words, such as "sawahdee krap" or "sawahdee ka" (good day) and "khop khun krap" or "khop khun ka" (thank you). With the exception of taxi drivers, Thais working with travelers in the resort and tourist areas in Bangkok generally speak sufficient English to permit basic communication.

Some words that may be useful to know in Thailand are:

Bot: The main chapel of a wat (*see below*), where ordinations occur and the chief image of the Lord Buddha is kept.
Chedi: A pagoda built in Thai style with a bell-shaped dome tapering to a pointed spire, often where holy relics are kept.
Farang: Foreigner.
Klong: Canal.
Ko (often written *Koh*): Island.
Nam: Water, often used to mean river.
Prang: A chedi built in the old Khmer style with an elliptical spire.
Soi: Small street, or lane, often assigned a number and described in conjunction with the abutting main street.
Stupa: Another word for chedi.
Viharn: The large hall in a wat where priests perform religious duties.
Wat: The complex of buildings of a Buddhist religious site (monastery), or a temple.

Opening and Closing Times

Thai and foreign **banks** are open weekdays 8:30–3:30, except for public holidays. Most **commercial concerns** in Bangkok operate on a five-day week and are open 8–5. **Government offices** are generally open 8:30–4:30 with a noon–1 lunch break. Many **stores** are open daily 8–8.

National Holidays

The following are national holidays: New Year's Day, January 1; Chinese New Year, January 31; Magha Puja, February, on the full moon of the third lunar month; Chakri Day, April 6; Songkran, mid-April; Coronation Day, May 5; Visakha Puja, May, on the full moon of the sixth lunar month; Queen's Birthday, August 12; King's Birthday, December 5. Government offices, banks, commercial concerns, and department stores are usually closed on these days, but smaller shops stay open.

Festivals and Seasonal Events

The festivals listed below are national and occur throughout the country unless otherwise noted. Many events follow the lunar calendar, so dates vary from year to year.

Dec. 31–Jan. 2: New Year celebrations are usually at their best around temples. In Bangkok, special ceremonies at Pramanae Ground include Thai dances.

Feb.: Magha Puja commemorates the day when 1,250 disciples spontaneously heard Lord Buddha preach the cardinal doctrine on the full moon of the third lunar month.

Feb.–Apr.: Kite-flying contests are held (in Bangkok, see them at the Pramanae Ground). Barbs attached to kite strings are used to destroy the other contestants' kites.

Apr. 6: Chakri Day. This day commemorates the enthronement of King Rama I, founder of the present dynasty, in 1782.

Mid-Apr.: Songkran. This marks the Thai New Year and is an occasion for setting caged birds and fish free, visiting family, dancing, and water-throwing, in which everyone splashes everyone else in good-natured merriment. The festival is at its best in Chiang Mai with parades, dancing in the streets, and a beauty contest.

May: Plowing Ceremony. At the Pramanae Ground in Bangkok, Thailand's king and queen take part in a traditional ritual that serves to open the rice-planting season.

May 5: Coronation Day: The king and queen take part in a procession to the Royal Chapel to preside over ceremonies commemorating the anniversary of their coronation.

May: Visakha Puja: On the full moon of the sixth lunar month, the nation celebrates the holiest of Buddhist days—Lord Buddha's birth, enlightenment, and death. Monks lead the laity in candlelit processions around their temples.

Aug. 12: Queen's Birthday. Queen Sirikit's birthday is celebrated with religious ceremonies at Chitralda Palace.

Nov.: Loi Krathong Festival. Held on the full moon of the 12th lunar month, this is the loveliest of Thai festivals. After sunset, people throughout Thailand make their way to a body of water and launch small lotus-shaped banana-leaf floats bearing lighted candles. The aim is to honor the water spirits and wash away one's sins of the past year.

Nov.: Golden Mount Festival. Of all the fairs and festivals in Bangkok, this one at the Golden Mount is the most spectacular, with sideshows, food stalls, bazaars, and crowds celebrating.

Nov.: Elephant Roundup. Held at Surin in the northeast, this is a stirring display of 100 noble animals' skills as traditional beasts of war, bulldozers, and even soccer players.

Dec. 5: King's Birthday. A trooping of the colors is performed in Bangkok by Thailand's elite Royal Guards.

Tipping

In Thailand, tips are generally given for good service, except when a price has been negotiated in advance. A **taxi driver** is not tipped unless hired as a private driver for an excursion. With metered taxis in Bangkok, however, the custom is to round the fare up to the nearest 5 baht. **Hotel porters** expect at least a B20 tip, and **hotel staff** who have given good personal service are usually tipped. A 10% tip is appreciated at a **restaurant** when no service charge has been added to the bill.

Shopping

Thailand offers some of the world's best shopping, and Bangkok and Chiang Mai are the best shopping cities. The critical factor in successful shopping is to know the product, especially if it is a precious stone or an antique. Another requirement for a successful buy is bargaining. It's a process that takes time, but it saves you money and wins respect from the vendor.

Thailand produces several specialties to tempt shoppers:

Antiques The Thai government has very strict regulations on the export of antiques and religious art. Images of the Lord Buddha are not permitted to be exported. By law, no antique may leave the country, and even reproductions not sold as antiques may need an export permit issued by the Fine Arts Department. A reputable dealer can obtain these permits in about one week.

Bronzeware Uniquely handcrafted bronzeware can be bought in complete table services, coffee-and-tea and bar sets, letter openers, bowls, tankards, trays, and candlesticks. Lately, the designs have become modern and simple. Traditional methods are still used, but a silicone coat is added to prevent tarnishing. Chiang Mai is a good source for this product.

Carved Wood Teakwood carvings, in the form of boxes, trays, or figures, are popular. Beware, there is a very convincing technique that makes carvings into instant antiques! You'll find wood carving all over Thailand, but Chiang Mai is its main center.

Dolls The more expensive dolls come dressed in Thai silk and represent classical Thai dancers or mythological characters.

Jewelry Thailand's third-largest export is jewelry, and buying it here saves all the import fees and markups. The range of what is offered is vast, from chunky bracelets made by the northern hill tribes to refined pieces in gold settings. Handcrafted gold chains, pendants, and earrings are available in abundance in hundreds of gold shops in Bangkok, but be persnickety in what you purchase, making sure that the workmanship is professional. And bargain well.

Lacquerware Lacquerware, which is usually made into small tables or boxes, is lightweight and commonly comes in a gold-and-black color scheme. You'll find the better pieces are made in Chiang Mai.

Nielloware This special kind of silver with its inlaid design, which looks black when held against the light at an angle and white when looked at straight on, is also available with color inlays. Nielloware comes as cuff links, jewelry, ashtrays, cream-and-sugar sets, and a host of other articles. Bangkok and the southern province of Nakhon Si Thammarat are good places to buy it.

Precious Stones Rubies and sapphires are associated with Thailand. These can be bought loose or in jewelry. Unless you are a gemologist, you may wish to make your purchases from a Tourism Authority of Thailand–approved store. You should also get a guarantee and receipt written in English.

Rattan and Wickerwork A wide variety of both furniture and decorative objects such as jewelry boxes is available in rattan and wicker. Most companies will arrange to ship the large items to your home.

Thai Celadon The ancient art of making this type of ceramic has been revived, and the ware can be found mostly around Chiang Mai, though some can be purchased in Bangkok. Also made in the Chiang Mai area is

Sukhothai stoneware. Near Bangkok, the kilns produce a very fine blue-and-white porcelain.

Thai Silk Through the efforts of Jim Thompson (*see* Tour 2 in Bangkok), Thai silk has become a much-sought-after luxury fabric. The prices are fairly high, but they are much less than what you would pay at home. Be aware that the weights and quality do differ. Most yardage comes 40 inches wide and may be bought by the yard or as ready-made goods. Rivaling Thai silk are the handwoven cottons made in the Chiang Mai area and in I-san.

Aside from traditional crafts, Thailand offers a host of other good buys, ranging from local handicrafts to ready-made clothes to designer knockoffs. There are also knockoff watches with designer names. A "Rolex" can be purchased for $20, though the emblem may be a little crooked. Pirated cassettes are another phenomenally inexpensive item. However, be aware that it is illegal to import pirated goods into the United States. Beauty is a big business in Thailand, and walk-in beauty parlors are ubiquitous. For 40¢ to $2, you can have a manicure or pedicure; facials, permanents, and massages can be had at correspondingly low prices.

Prices are fixed in department stores. In fashion boutiques, there is no harm in asking for a small discount. In stores selling artifacts, price is open to negotiation, and in bazaars and street-side stalls, bargaining is essential.

Sports

Spectator Sports With so many rivers, Thailand has many kinds of boat racing. Teams from various towns and provinces vie for honors in colorful paddle-powered boats. Annual races are held in Bangkok, Pichit, Ayutthaya, and Nan.

Boat Racing

Horse Racing Races are held at tracks in Bangkok.

Kite-fighting This sport dates back hundreds of years. Elaborate kites armed with barbs, designated *pakpao* (female) or *chula* (male), struggle for dominance, trying to ensnare or cut the opponent's line. A good place to watch this is at Bangkok's Pramanae Ground near the Royal Palace, particularly in March and April.

Motorcycle Racing With the opening of the Bira Pattaya Circuit, on Route 36 between Pattaya and Rayong, international motorcycle events are held regularly.

Takro This sport involves passing a small rattan ball back and forth as long as possible before it falls to the ground. All parts of the body may be used. The more complicated the pass, the better it is judged. Other forms of takro require a hoop or net.

Thai Boxing Thai boxing, known locally as *muay Thai*, allows boxers to use their feet, knees, thighs, and elbows, as well as their gloved fists, to hit an opponent. Moreover, all parts of the opponent's body can be struck, and points are awarded for any blow. Thai boxing requires years of training, and prior to each bout, boxers indulge in ritual praying that involves complicated maneuvers designed to limber up the body.

Participant Sports More than 50 excellent golf courses are spread around the kingdom, though the majority are in the Bangkok region. Three of the best are Navatanee golf course, site of the 1975 World Cup tournament, the Rose Garden course, and the Krung Thep Kreta course.

Golf

Hiking and Trekking	Hiking is especially popular in the north, where groups go in search of hill-tribe villages and wildlife. The main center for northern treks is Chiang Mai. But with dozens of national parks around the country, you may hike in tropical jungles and isolated highlands alike. Contact the Tourism Authority of Thailand for information on bungalow-style accommodations in the national parks.
Horseback Riding	Though some of the beach resorts may have horses, only Pattaya has a permanent stable, where horse treks into the countryside are available to the public.
Water Sports	With its long coastline and warm waters, Thailand offers splendid opportunities for all sorts of water sports, including waterskiing, surfing, windsurfing, and parasailing. It is possible to rent power boats, water scooters, and sailboats. Scuba diving and snorkeling in the clear waters are also available, especially in Ko Samui and Phuket, where rentals, instruction, and trips to uninhabited islands may be arranged. Big-game fishing is a feature at Bang Saray, near Pattaya.

Beaches

The beaches of Thailand, both on the Gulf of Siam (the south and east coasts) and on the Andaman Sea (the southwest coast) are popular with Westerners. Full-scale resort areas have been developed on both coasts—Pattaya, Hua Hin and Cha' Am on the Gulf, Phuket on the Andaman Sea. New resort areas are developing all the time. Ko Samui on the Gulf is becoming increasingly crowded, as is Ko Phi Phi off Phuket. For those who like idyllic havens of beaches and no people, the area around Krabi facing the Andaman Sea is paradise, Ko Pha Ngan and Ko Tao off Ko Samui are tiny islands with idyllic bays, Ko Samet on the Gulf (near Pattaya) has a number of small beaches with bungalows for rent, and Ko Chang near the Cambodian border, with its beautiful bays and coves, is just being discovered. The waters around Bangkok are tropical, warm, and inviting, but do check on two factors before you plunge in: the undertow and the presence of stinging jellyfish. You should also steer clear of those little cone shells. Some varieties are venomous; their sting not only hurts but can lead to heart failure if untreated. Sand tends to be golden in color and slightly coarse. Scuba diving and snorkeling are best off Ko Samui and among the Similan Islands off Phuket.

Dining

Thai cuisine is distinctive, often hot and spicy, and perfumed with herbs, especially lemongrass and coriander. It is influenced by the cooking styles of China, India, Java, Malaysia, and Portugal. Rice, boiled or fried, forms the basis for most Thai meals, though noodles can also play this role. Meats, poultry, and seafood are highly seasoned with herbs and chilies. Soups are also important in Thai cuisine and are usually spiced with lemongrass and chilies. All courses of a Thai meal are served at the same time.

Each region has its own specialties. The northeast favors sticky rice served with barbecued chicken and shredded green papaya mixed with shrimp, lemon juice, fish sauce, garlic, and chilies. In the north, a local sausage, *naem*, is popular, while in the south there is an abundance of fresh seafood. Dessert is usually exotic fresh fruit or sweets made of rice flour, coconut milk, palm sugar, and sticky rice. Singha beer and Mekong whiskey (made from rice) are the usual beverages. Western food is available in most hotels and at many restaurants in resort areas. Thai fruit is not to be missed. The mangoes, especially *Nam doc mai*, are exceptional. And there's the exotic durian. It has such a strong odor when cut that restaurants do not serve it, but aficionados will kill for a taste.

Among the myths that just won't die is that all Thai food is hot. There are plenty of pungent dishes, of course, but most Thai recipes are not especially aggressive. Indeed, many Thais do not care for very spicy food and tend to avoid it. A normal Thai meal is composed of several dishes, including a hot and spicy one—a curry, perhaps, or a hot stir-fried dish—that is balanced with a bland soup, a salad, and a vegetable dish or stuffed omelet.

Thai food is eaten with a fork and tablespoon, with the spoon held in the right hand and the fork used like a plow to push food into the spoon. Chopsticks are used only for Chinese dishes, such as noodle recipes. After you have finished eating, place your fork and spoon on the plate at the 5:25 position; otherwise the server will assume you would like another helping.

Because the English translations, when they are provided at all, can be bizarre, it is not a bad idea to be armed with a few food-related words in Thai when you take to the streets in search of an authentic meal. This short list will give you a head start.

jued ("jood," sounding like "good")—bland. A *kaeng jued* is a clear soup without chili, often with clear vermicelli noodles and wood-ear mushrooms added for texture.
kaeng (pronounced "gang")—curry, although the term covers many thin, clear, souplike dishes that are very different from what most Westerners think of as curry.
kaeng khio waan ("gang khee-yo wahn")—a rich curry made with coconut cream and a complicated mixture of spices and other flavorings as well as eggplant and meat or fish (chicken, beef, shrimp, and a fish ball called *luuk cheen plaa krai* are the most common) pounded into a paste. The Thai name means "green, sweet curry," but it is very rarely sweet. "Green, hot curry" is more like it.
nam plaa ("nahm plah")—fish sauce used instead of salt in Thai cooking.
phad ("pot")—stir-fried.
phad bai kaphrao ("pot by ka-*prow*")—stir-fried with fresh basil, hot chili, garlic, and other seasonings.
phad phed ("pot pet")—popular dishes in which meat or fish is stir-fried with hot chili, sweet basil, onion, garlic, and other seasonings. They can be *very* phed; so watch it.
phed or **phet** ("pet")—spicy hot.
phrik ("prik")—any hot chili pepper. The notorious, nuclear-strength bird chilies are called *phrik kee noo*, and you can always find them on the table in a Thai restaurant, cut into pieces and steeping in *nam plaa (see above)*. They should be approached with respect.
thawd ("taught")—deep-fried.
tom khaa ("tome khah")—a rich soup made with coconut cream, lime, hot chilies, *khah* (a root spice related to ginger), and chicken (or, less commonly, shrimp).
tom yam ("tome yom")—a semiclear hot-and-sour soup based on lime juice and small hot chilies, with lemongrass, mushrooms, and fresh coriander. Popular versions are made with shrimp, chicken, or fish.
yam ("yom")—a hot-and-sour saladlike dish, served cold and flavored with hot chilies, lime juice, and onions.

Highly recommended restaurants are indicated by a star ★.

Except in the Bangkok Dining section, the following dining price categories apply throughout this chapter:

Category	Cost*
$$$$	over B500 ($20)
$$$	B250–B500 ($10–$20)
$$	B100–B250 ($4–$10)
$	under B100 ($4)

per person, including service charge

A 7% government tax (VAT) is added to restaurant bills.

Lodging

Every town of reasonable size offers accommodations. In the smaller towns, the hotels may be fairly simple, but they will usually be clean and certainly inexpensive. In major cities or resort areas, there are hotels to fit all price categories. At the high end, the luxury hotels can compete with the best in the world. Service is generally superb—polite and efficient—and most of the staff usually speak English. At the other end of the scale, the lodging is simple and basic—a room with little more than a bed. The least expensive places may have Asian toilets (squat type with no seat) and a fan rather than air-conditioning.

All except the budget hotels have restaurants and offer room service throughout most of the day and night. Most will also be happy to make local travel arrangements for you—for which they receive commissions. All hotels advise that you use their safe-deposit boxes.

During the peak tourist season, October–March, hotels are often fully booked and charge peak rates. At special times, such as December 30–January 2 and Chinese New Year, rates climb even higher, and hotel reservations are difficult to obtain. Weekday rates at some resorts are often lower, and virtually all hotels will discount their rooms if they are not fully booked. Don't be reticent about asking for a special rate. Breakfast is never included in the room price. Hotel rates tend to be lower if you reserve through a travel agent (in Thailand). The agent receives a reduced room rate from the hotel and passes some of this discount on to you.

A 7% government tax (VAT) is added to all hotel bills. In addition, deluxe hotels often add a 10%–15% service charge.

Highly recommended lodgings are indicated by a star ★.

Throughout this chapter, the following price categories apply:

Category	Cost*
$$$$	over B4,000 (over $160)
$$$	B2,500–B4,000 ($100–$160)
$$	B1,500–B2,500 ($60–$100)

$	B500–B1,500 ($20–$60)
¢	under B500 ($20)

per double room, including service and tax

Bangkok

A foreigner's reaction to Bangkok is often as confused as the city's geography. Bangkok has no downtown, and the streets, like the traffic, seem to veer off in every direction. The oldest quarter clusters around the eastern bank of the Chao Phraya River, which winds between Bangkok and Thonburi, where the Thais first established their capital after the fall of Ayutthaya in 1767.

Even Bangkok's name is disconcerting. Foreigners call the city Bangkok, but Thais refer to their capital as Krung Thep, the City of Angels. When Thailand's capital was Ayutthaya, to the north of present-day Bangkok, foreign vessels would reach there by the Chao Phraya. After the fall of Ayutthaya, King Rama I decided in 1782 to move his capital from Thonburi to a new site across the river. Foreigners looked at their navigational charts and understood the capital to be where the village of Bangkok was marked.

In the last 20 years, the face of Bangkok has changed. Before the Vietnam War, and before Bangkok became the R & R destination for American servicemen, the city had a population of 1.5 million. Then, the flaunting of U.S. dollars attracted the rural poor to the city. Within two decades, it grew to 6 million, 40 times the size of any other city in Thailand. Space in which to live and breathe is inadequate. Air pollution is the worst in the world (policemen directing traffic are now required to wear masks). Traffic jams the streets from morning to evening, and no cure is in sight. Use the pedestrian crosswalks—the traffic will stop if you insist—or use the pedestrian flyovers.

Yet, while hurtling headlong into the world of modern commercialism and technology, Bangkok strangely gives a sense of history and timelessness, even though it is only some 200 years old. This is perhaps because King Rama I was determined to build a city as beautiful as the old capital of Ayutthaya had been before the Burmese ransacked it. Bangkok requires an adjustment on our part, but we soon come to appreciate the gentle nature of the Thai people and their respect for others.

Important Addresses and Numbers

Tourist Information The **Tourist Authority of Thailand (TAT;** 372 Bamrung Muang Rd., Pom Prap, Bangkok 10100, tel. 02/226–0060) tends to have more in the way of colorful brochures than hard information, but it can supply useful material on national parks and various transportation routes to out-of-the-way destinations. The problem is that the TAT office is in an extremely inconvenient location—not far from the Golden Mount and adjacent to the Metropolitan Water Tower—where the stalled traffic comes close to gridlock. There is also a TAT branch at the international terminal at Don Muang airport (tel. 02/ 523–8973, open 8 AM–midnight).

Thai International Airways has an office at 485 Silom Road (tel. 02/ 233–3810).

Telephone information from an English-speaking operator is available by dialing 13.

Immigration Division (Soi Suan Sathorn Tai Rd., tel. 02/286–9176) is the place to go for a visa extension. Visas are not required for many nationalities, but tourists are permitted to stay only 15 days in the country without an extension. If you go beyond your specified stay by a few days, don't worry. You can simply pay a B100 per diem fine as you exit through emigration at Bangkok's airport.

Embassies Most nations maintain diplomatic relations with Thailand and have embassies in Bangkok. Should you need to apply for a visa to another country, the consulate hours are usually 8–noon: **Australian Embassy** (37 Sathorn Tai Rd., tel. 02/287–2680); **British Embassy** (1031 Wireless Rd., tel. 02/253–0191); **United States Embassy** (95 Wireless Rd., tel. 02/252–5040).

Emergencies **Tourist Police** (509 Vorachak Rd., tel. 02/221–6209), with headquarter post located opposite the Dusit Thani hotel in Lumpini Park, are available daily 8 AM–midnight. You're advised to contact the Tourist Police rather than the local police in an emergency—dial 195.

Police, tel. 191; **fire,** tel. 199; **ambulance,** tel. 02/246–0199.

Hospitals **Chulalongkorn Hospital** (Rama I Rd., tel. 02/252–8181), **Police Hospital** (Rajdamri Rd., tel. 02/252–8111).

Lost Credit Cards To report lost or stolen credit cards: American Express, tel. 02/273–3660; Diners Club, tel. 02/238–3660; MasterCard and Visa, tel. 02/246–0300.

English-Language Bookstores The English-language dailies, the *Bangkok Post* and *The Nation*, are available at newsstands. **Asia Books** (221 Sukhumvit Rd., Soi 15, tel. 02/252–7277 and in the Peninsula Plaza, adjacent to the Regent Hotel, tel. 02/253–9786) has a wide selection, as does DK Books or, more properly, **Duang Kamol Bookshop** (244–6 Siam Sq., tel. 02/251–6335).

Pharmacies There is no shortage of pharmacies in Bangkok. Compared to the United States, fewer drugs require prescriptions, but should you need them, you must have a prescription written in Thai. Be aware that over-the-counter drugs are not necessarily of the same chemical composition as those in the United States.

Travel Agencies In virtually every major hotel, a travel desk books tours in and around Bangkok. Smaller travel agencies sometimes do not live up to their promises, and so for significant purchases and arrangements, you may want to select a larger and more established agency, such as **Diethelm** (544 Phoenchit Rd., tel. 02/252–4041) or **World Travel Service** (1053 New Charoen Krung Rd., tel. 02/233–5900).

Arriving and Departing by Plane

Airports and Airlines Bangkok's Don Muang Airport international terminal, adjacent to what is now the domestic terminal, has relieved passenger congestion and presents international passengers with modern efficiency on arrival. As you exit customs, you'll find an array of information desks where you can make arrangements for taxis into Bangkok and transport to other destinations; a reservation desk for Bangkok hotels (no fee); and a TAT (Tourist Authority of Thailand) desk that has a large selection of free brochures and maps. Both terminals have luggage-checking facilities (tel. 02/535–1250).

There is a tax of B200 for international departures and B20 for domestic departures.

Thai Airways International is the national airline, and most of its flights come in and out of Don Muang. Thai International has direct flights from the West Coast of the United States and from Toronto in Canada. The airline also has daily flights to Hong Kong, Singapore, Taiwan, and Japan, and direct flights from London.

The major U.S. carrier that covers the most Asian capitals with the most frequent service is **Northwest Airlines** (tel. 800/447–4747). It has direct service through Tokyo (with a minimal stopover) from New York, Detroit, Seattle, Dallas, San Francisco, and Los Angeles and a comprehensive domestic service to connect with these cities. Northwest also has a round-Asia fare, which, in conjunction with local airlines, permits hopping from one capital city to another. **Singapore Airlines** flies in from Singapore, **British Airways** flies in from London, and **Finnair** actively promotes the eastbound route out of New York via Helsinki. In total, 35 airline companies have flights to and from Bangkok, and more are seeking landing rights.

Getting Into Town
By Taxi
Don Muang is 25 km (15 mi) from the city center. The road is often congested with traffic. Be prepared for a 90-minute journey by taxi, though there are times when it can take less than 40 minutes. Obtain a taxi reservation at the counter (at either terminal) and a driver will lead you to the taxi. The fare for downtown Bangkok depends on the exact location and, to some extent, the time of day. Count on B300–B350 from the international terminal and B250 from the domestic. Taxis to the airport from downtown Bangkok are, with negotiation, approximately B130.

By Riverboat Shuttle
Really for the benefit of guests at the Oriental, the Royal Orchid Sheraton, and the Shangri-La hotels, a bus-and-boat service runs every 30 minutes. The bus takes passengers between the airport and the river, where they transfer to boats for the half-hour run to the hotels. Fare is $28; overall time is under an hour.

By Helicopter
The quickest way downtown is the helicopter that lands at the Shangri-La Hotel. Mostly, guests staying there, at the Royal Orchid Sheraton, or at the Oriental use it, but anyone who will pay the $200 fare is welcome aboard.

By Minibus
Thai Airways has a minibus service between the airport and Bangkok's major hotels. The minibuses depart when they are full. Cost: B100.

By Bus
Bus No. 4 goes to the Rama Garden Hotel, Indra Regent, Erawan, Hyatt, and Dusit Thani hotels, and down Silom Road. (The last bus comes at 8 PM.) Bus No. 10 goes to the Rama Garden Hotel, the Northern Bus Terminal, the Victory Monument, and the Southern Bus Terminal (last bus at 8:30 PM). Bus 13 goes to the Northern Bus Terminal, Victory Monument, and down Sukhumvit Road to the Eastern Bus Terminal (last bus at 8 PM). Bus 29 goes to the Northern Bus Terminal, Victory Monument, Siam Square, and Bangkok's main railway station, Hualamphong (last bus at 8:30 PM). Buses are air-conditioned. Cost: B15.

By Train
The **Bangkok Airport Express** trains make the 35-minute run every 90 minutes from 8 AM to 7 PM. Check the schedule at the tourist booth in the arrival hall. Fare: B100. You can also take the regular trains from 5:30 AM to 9 PM. The fare is B5 for a local train, B13 for an express.

Arriving and Departing by Train and Bus

By Train
Hualamphong Railway Station (Rama IV Rd., tel. 02/223–7461) is the city's main station and serves most long-distance trains. There is

also **Bangkok Noi** (Arun Amarin Rd., tel. 02/411–3102) on the Thonburi side of the Chao Phraya River, used by local trains to Hua Hin and Kanchanaburi.

By Bus Bangkok has three main bus terminals. **Northern/Northeast Bus Terminal** (Phaholyothin Rd., tel. 02/279–4484 for air-conditioned buses, tel. 02/279–6222 for non-air-conditioned buses) is for Chiang Mai and the north. **Southern Bus Terminal** (Pinklao-Nakomchaisri Rd., Talingchan, tel. 02/434–5557), on the Thonburi side of the river, is for Hua Hin, Ko Samui, Phuket, and points south. **Eastern Bus Terminal** (Sukhumvit Rd., Soi 40, Ekimae, tel. 02/391–2504 for air-conditioned buses, tel. 02/392–2391 for non-air-conditioned buses), often simply referred to as Ekimae, is for Pattaya and points southeast, to Rayong and Trat province.

Getting Around

There is no subway, and the horrendous road traffic is made even worse by the ongoing construction of intersection overpasses. Allow twice the normal travel time during rush hours, 7–10 AM and 4–7 PM.

By Bus Though buses can be very crowded, they are convenient and inexpensive for getting around. For a fare of only B3.50 (any distance) on the ordinary city non-air-conditioned buses and B6 to B16 on the less frequent air-conditioned buses, you can travel virtually anywhere in the city. Buses operate from 5 AM to around 11 PM. The routes are confusing, but usually someone at the bus stop will know the number of the bus you need to catch. You can pick up a route map at most bookstalls for B35. Be aware of purse snatchers on the buses.

By Taxi For years it has been necessary to bargain before climbing into the unmetered Bangkok taxis, but in 1993, meters were installed in more than half of them (not in tuk-tuks). The tariff for the first 2 km (1.2 mi) is set at B35 and then increases a baht for about every 50 m. If the speed drops to under 6 kph, there is a surcharge of one baht per minute. A typical journey of about 5 km (3 mi) runs about B60. (At press time taxi drivers were demonstrating for B50 for the first 2 km.)

By Samlor Tuk-tuks are slightly cheaper than taxis and best used for short trips in congested traffic.

By Boat Water taxis and express (ferry) boats ply the Chao Phraya River. For the express boats, the fare is based on zones, but B5 will cover most trips that you are likely to take. You'll also have to pay a B1 jetty fee. The jetty adjacent to the Oriental Hotel is a useful stop. In about 10 minutes, you can travel up the river, making half a dozen stops, to the Grand Palace, or farther up to the other side of Krungthon Bridge in about 15 minutes. It is often the quickest way to travel in a north–south direction.

Long-tailed (so called for the extra-long propeller shaft that extends behind the stern) boats may be hired for about B300 an hour.

Guided Tours

Numerous tours cover Bangkok and its environs. Each tour operator offers some slight variation, but, in general, they cover the following itineraries.

Floating Market Tour. This is a tour to the floating market at Damnoen Saduak, south of Bangkok.
Grand Palace and Emerald Buddha Tour. Because you can easily

reach the palace by taxi or public transport and hire a guide on the spot, you may want to visit these sights independently.

City and Temples Tour. In half a day, you can visit some of Bangkok's most famous temples: Wat Po with the reclining Buddha; Wat Benjamabopit, famous for its marble structure; and Wat Traimitr, with the 5-ton golden Buddha. This tour does not include the Grand Palace.

Thai Dinner and Classical Dance. This evening tour includes a buffet-style Thai dinner with a show of classical dancing. You can manage it just as well on your own.

Highlights for First-Time Visitors

Ferry ride on the Chao Phraya River (*see* Off the Beaten Track)

Grand Palace and **Wat Phra Keo (Temple of the Emerald Buddha)** (*see* Tour 1)

Jim Thompson's House (*see* Tour 2)

National Museum (*see* Tour 2)

Thai dance performance (*see* Tour 2)

Wat Po (Temple of the Reclining Buddha) (*see* Tour 1)

Wat Traimitr (Temple of the Golden Buddha) (*see* Tour 1)

Exploring

Because confusion is part of Bangkok's fascination, learning your way around is a challenge. It may help to think of Bangkok as an isosceles triangle with the base abutting the *S* curve of the Chao Phraya and the apex, pointing east, ending down Sukhumvit Road, somewhere around Soi (Lane) 40.

Sukhumvit, at the apex of this conceptual triangle, was once a residential neighborhood. In the last decade, it has developed into a district of hotels, shops, nightclubs, and restaurants while retaining some of its warm, residential atmosphere. In this area, the new Bangkok Conference Centre has opened and will attract more hotels and commercial enterprises. Indeed, ever since Ramkhamhaeng University opened in the 1970s, Bangkok has sprawled even farther east. Now the area known as Bangkapi has become a satellite town, attracting industry and residential complexes.

Westward, toward the Chao Phraya, you come to spacious foreign embassy compounds, offices of large corporations, and modern international hotels. Slightly farther west, stores, offices, and more hotels are more closely packed. Now you reach the older sections of Bangkok. On the southern flank is Silom Road, a shopping and financial district. Parallel to Silom Road is Suriwongse Road, with more hotels, and between the two is the entertainment district of Patpong. Continue farther and you reach two of the leading hotels on the riverbank: the Oriental and the Shangri-La.

Traveling down Rama I Road in the center of the triangle, you pass the Siam Square shopping area and the National Stadium. Continue in the direction of the Hualamphong Railway Station. Between Hualamphong and the river is Chinatown, a maze of streets with restaurants, goldsmiths, and small warehouses and repair shops.

In the northern part of the triangle, moving westward, you pass through various markets before reaching Thai government buildings, the Victory Monument, Chitlada Palace, the Dusit Zoo, the

National Assembly, the National Library, and, finally, the river. Slightly to the south of this route are the Democracy Monument, the Grand Palace, and the Temple of the Emerald Buddha.

Knowing your exact destination, its direction, and approximate distance are important in negotiating taxi fares and planning your itinerary. Crossing and recrossing the city is time-consuming—many hours can be spent in frustrating traffic jams. Above all, remember that Bangkok is enormous and distances are great; it can take a half hour or more to walk between two seemingly adjacent sites.

Tour 1: The River Tour

Numbers in the margin correspond to points of interest on the Bangkok map.

Start the tour with breakfast on the terrace of the **Oriental Hotel,** overlooking the Chao Phraya River. The hotel itself is a Bangkok institution. To the side of the Oriental's entrance, a small lane leads to the river and a landing stage for the river buses that ply it. Take the river bus upstream to the Grand Palace and Wat Phra Keo.

❶ The **Grand Palace** is Bangkok's major landmark. This is where Bangkok's founder, King Rama I, built his palace and walled city in 1782. Subsequent Chakri monarchs enlarged the walled city, though today the buildings are used only for state occasions and royal ceremonies. The compound—but not all of the buildings—is open to visitors.

The official residence of the king—he actually lives elsewhere, at Chitlada Palace in Bangkok—is the Chakri Maha Prasart palace. Occasionally, its state function rooms are open to visitors, but most of the time only the exterior can be viewed. To the right of Chakri Maha Prasart is the Dusit Maha Prasart, a classic example of Thai royal palace architecture. To the left of the palace is the Amarin Vinichai Hall, the original audience hall built by King Rama I and now used for the presentation of ambassadors' credentials. Note the glittering gold throne.

Visit this compound first, because none of these buildings excites such awe as the adjoining royal chapel, the most sacred temple in the **❷** kingdom, the **Temple of the Emerald Buddha** (Wat Phra Keo). No other wat in Thailand is so ornate and so embellished with murals, statues, and glittering gold. For many, it is overly decorated, and as your wat experience grows, you may decide that you prefer the simplicity of the lesser known wats, but you'll never quite get over the elaborate richness of Wat Phra Keo.

As you enter the compound, take note of the 6-m-tall (20 ft) helmeted and tile-encrusted statues in traditional Thai battle attire standing guard and surveying the precincts. They set the scene—mystical, majestic, and awesome. Turn right as you enter, and notice along the inner walls the lively murals (recently restored) depicting the whole *Ramayana (Ramakien* in Thai) epic. The main chapel, with its gilded, glittering, three-tiered roof, dazzles the senses. Royal griffins stand guard outside, and shining gold stupas in the court establish serenity with their perfect symmetry. Inside sits the Emerald Buddha.

Carved from one piece of jade, the ¾-m-high (31 in) figure is one of the most venerated images of the Lord Buddha. No one knows its origin, but history places it in Chiang Rai, in northeast Thailand, in 1464. From there it traveled first to Chiang Mai, then to Lamphun, and finally back to Chiang Mai, where the Laotians stole it and took

Bangkok

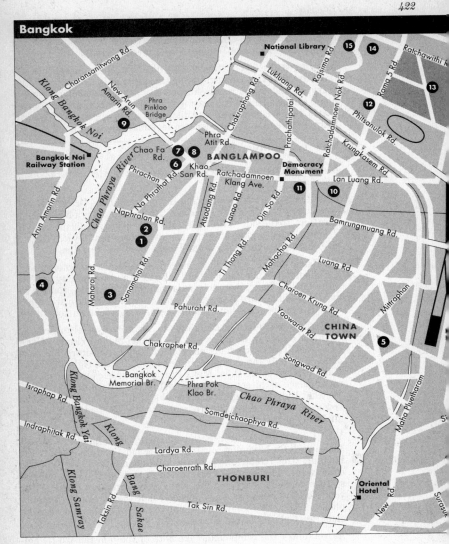

National Library

Charansanitwong Rd.

New Arun Amarin Rd.

Klong Bangkok Noi

Phra Pinklao Bridge

Bangkok Noi Railway Station

Chao Fa Rd.

Phrachan

Na Phrathat Rd.

Naphralan Rd.

Arun Amarin Rd.

Maharaj Rd.

Sonamchai Rd.

Atsadang Rd.

Tanao Rd.

Chao Phraya River

Phra Atit Rd.

Khao San Rd.

BANGLAMPOO

Ratchadamnoen Klang Ave.

Democracy Monument

Lan Luang Rd.

Chakraphong Rd.

Lukluang Rd.

Ratsima Rd.

Prachathipatai

Ratchadamnoen Nok Rd.

Phitsanulok Rd.

Krungkasem Rd.

Rama 5 Rd.

Ratchawithi

Din So Rd.

Mahachai Rd.

Luang Rd.

Bamrungmuang Rd.

Ti Thong Rd.

Pahuraht Rd.

Charoen Krung Rd.

Yaowarat Rd.

CHINA TOWN

Mitraphan

Chakraphet Rd.

Bangkok Memorial Br.

Phra Pok Klao Br.

Israphap Rd.

Klong Bangkok Yai

Klong Bang Sakae

Indraphitak Rd.

Somdejchaophya Rd.

Chao Phraya River

Songwad Rd.

Maha Phetharam

Lardya Rd.

Charoenrath Rd.

THONBURI

Klong Samray

Taksin Rd.

Tak Sin Rd.

Oriental Hotel

New Rd.

Surasak

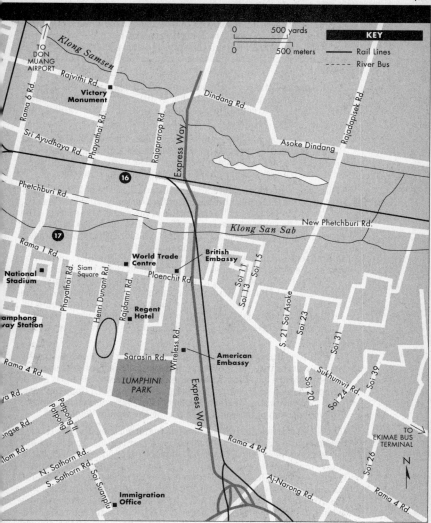

KEY

Rail Lines

- - - - River Bus

0   500 yards

0   500 meters

Klong Samsen

TO
DON
MUANG
AIRPORT

Rajvithi Rd.

Victory
Monument

Dindang Rd.

Rama 6 Rd.

Phayathai Rd.

Rajaprarop Rd.

Express Way

Asoke Dindang

Rajadapisek Rd.

Sri Ayudhaya Rd.

Phetchburi Rd.

16

Klong San Sab

New Phetchburi Rd.

Rama 1 Rd.

17

World Trade
Centre

British
Embassy

Siam
Square

Ploenchit Rd.

Soi 11

Soi 15

National
Stadium

Phayathai Rd.

Henri Dunant Rd.

Rajdami Rd.

Regent
Hotel

Soi 13

S. 21 Soi Asoke

Soi 23

Soi 31

amphong
ay Station

Wireless Rd.

Sukhumvit Rd.

Soi 39

Rama 4 Rd.

Sarasin Rd.

American
Embassy

Soi 20

Soi 24 Rd.

ya Rd.

LUMPHINI
PARK

Express Way

Soi 26

TO
EKIMAE BUS
TERMINAL

ongse Rd.

Patpong II
Patpong I

Rama 4 Rd.

Aj-Narong Rd.

Rama 4 Rd.

lom Rd.

N. Sathorn Rd.

S. Sathorn Rd.

Soi Suanplu

Immigration
Office

N

it home with them. Eventually, the Thais sent an army into Laos to secure it. The statue reached its final resting place when King Rama I built the chapel. The statue is high above the altar, and visitors can see it only from afar. Behind the altar and above the window frames are murals depicting the life and eventual enlightenment of the Lord Buddha.

At the back of the royal chapel you'll find a scale model of Angkor Wat. As this complex, in Cambodia, is difficult to reach nowadays, this is a chance to sense the vastness of the old Khmer capital. *Admission charge. Open daily 8:30–11:30 and 1–3:30.*

Just to the east of the Grand Palace compound is the City Pillar Shrine that contains the foundation stone (Lak Muang) from which all distances in Thailand are measured. The stone is believed to be inhabited by a spirit that guards the well-being of Bangkok.

 When you leave the Grand Palace, walk south to the oldest and largest temple in Bangkok, the **Temple of the Reclining Buddha** (Wat Po, or Wat Phya Jetuphon). Much is made of the size of this statue—the largest in the country, measuring 46 m (151 ft) in length. Especially noteworthy are his 3-m-long (10 ft) feet, inlaid with mother-of-pearl designs depicting the 108 auspicious signs of the Lord Buddha. Walk beyond the chapel containing the Reclining Buddha and enter Bangkok's oldest open university. A hundred years before Bangkok was established as the capital city, a monastery was founded to teach classical Thai medicine. The school still gives instruction in the natural methods of healing. Around the walls are marble plaques inscribed with formulas for herbal cures, and stone sculptures squat in various postures demonstrating techniques for relieving muscle pain.

Don't be perturbed by the sculpted figures that good-naturedly poke fun at farangs (Westerners). Referred to as Chinese rock sculptures, they are gangling 3.6-m-high (12 ft) figures, the most evil of demons, which scare away all other evil spirits. With their top hats, they look farcically Western. In fact, they were modeled after the Europeans who plundered China during the Opium Wars.

These tall statues guard the entrance to the northeastern quarter of the monastery and a very pleasant three-tier temple. Inside are 394 seated Buddhas. Usually, a monk sits cross-legged at one side of the altar, making himself available to answer your questions (you will need to speak Thai or have a translator). On the walls, bas-relief plaques salvaged from Ayutthaya depict stories from the *Ramayana*. Around this temple area are four tall *chedis* (Thai-style pagodas where holy relics are kept), decorated with brightly colored porcelain, each representing one of the first four kings of the Chakri (present) dynasty. *Admission charge. Open daily 7–5.*

Time Out   The monks of Wat Po still practice ancient cures and have become famous for their massage technique. The massage lasts one hour, growing more and more pleasurable as you adjust to the technique. Masseurs are available 7–5. Cost: B150. When you're ready for refreshment, there is a pleasant snack bar in the northeastern compound, where the fare includes delicious chilled coconut milk.

From Wat Po, if you walk halfway back to the Grand Palace and then cut down to the river past a small market, you'll reach the jetty, Tha Thien, for the ferry to cross over the Chao Phraya to **Wat Arun** on the western bank of the river.

Wat Arun means "Temple of the Dawn," and at sunrise, it is inspiring. It is even more marvelous toward dusk, however, when the setting sun casts its amber tones. Within the square courtyard, the temple's architecture is symmetrical, containing five Khmer-style prangs (stupas). The central prang, towering 86 meters (282 feet), is surrounded by its four attendant prangs in the corners. All of the prangs are covered in mosaics of broken Chinese porcelain. The surrounding grounds are a peaceful haven in which to relax and watch the sun go down. The more energetic climb the steep steps of the central prang for the view over the Chao Phraya River. *Admission charge. Open 8–5:30.*

Wat Arun has a small park around it, and, by the river, is a pleasant spot in which to linger. However, if time is short, cross back to the eastern shore and wander inland through Chinatown. You may want to take a tuk-tuk as far as Pahuraht Road.

The site of Bangkok's first tall buildings, **Chinatown** used to be the prosperous downtown neighborhood, but, as Bangkok has grown, new, taller office buildings have sprung up to the east, and Chinatown, losing some of its bustle and excitement, has become less the hub of activity. Red lanterns and Chinese signs still abound, and modest Chinese restaurants line the streets. Pahuraht Road is full of textile shops, with nearly as many Indian dealers here as Chinese. Farther east and a zigzag to the left, is Yaowarat Road, Chinatown's main thoroughfare, crowded with gold and jewelry shops. Between Yaowarat and Charoen Krung (New Road) is the so-called Thieves Market (Nakorn Kasem), an area of small streets with old wood houses, where you can buy all sorts of items, from hardware to porcelains. Bargains are hard to find nowadays, but these small, cluttered streets are fascinating to walk through, and, who knows, a porcelain vase may take your fancy. Bargain hard!

❺ Farther southeast, Yaowarat Road leads into Charoen Krung. On the opposite corner is **Wat Traimitr** (Temple of the Golden Buddha). The main temple has little architectural merit, but off to the side, next to the money-changing wagon, is a small chapel. Inside is the world's largest solid-gold Buddha image, cast about nine centuries ago. Weighing 5½ tons and standing 3 m (10 ft) high, the statue gleams with such a richness and purity that even the most jaded are inspired by its strength and power. Sculpted in Sukhothai style, the statue is believed to have been brought first to Ayutthaya. When the Burmese were about to sack the city, the statue was covered in plaster. Two centuries later, still in plaster and regarded as just another statue, it was being moved to a new temple in Bangkok, when it slipped from the crane. Leaving the statue in the mud, the workmen called it a day. First thing in the morning, a temple monk, who had dreamed that the statue was divinely inspired, went to see the Buddha image. Through a crack in the plaster, he saw the glint of yellow, and opening the plaster farther, he discovered that the statue was pure gold. *Admission charge. Open daily 9–5.*

Tour 2: Temples, Museums, and Villas

❻ Unless you can get an early start to visit some temples and beat the heat, the **National Museum** should be your first stop. Try to make it on a Wednesday or Thursday, when free, guided, 90-minute tours in English start at 9:30 AM. Volunteers who specialize in different aspects of Thai art explain the complexities of Thai culture and give visitors a general orientation to the vast collection of treasures in the museum. The tours meet at the entrance to the main building, which was originally built in 1783 as a palace for surrogate kings (a position abolished in 1874). The two new wings were added in 1966.

This extensive museum has one of the world's best collections of Southeast Asian art in general, and Buddhist and Thai art in particular. As a result, it offers the best opportunity to trace Thailand's long history, beginning with ceramic utensils and bronzeware from the Ban Chiang civilization, thought to have existed 5,000 to 6,000 years ago. To the left of the museum's ticket counter is an artifact gallery that depicts the history of Thailand. You may want to see this first for a historical overview. Afterward, explore the galleries that portray the early history of Thailand—the Dvaravati and Khmer periods of more than 1,000 years ago. These will prepare you for the complex of galleries displaying the different styles of Thai art from the Sukhothai period (1238–mid-14th century) and later. The majority of the great masterpieces created during the Sukhothai and Ayutthaya periods, as well as those works from the northern provinces, have found their way into the Bangkok National Museum. Consequently, up-country museums are rather bare of fine Thai art, so take the opportunity to see this collection if you can. A cafeteria is centrally located in the museum complex. *Admission charge. Open Wed.–Fri. and weekends 9–noon and 1–4.*

⑦ Next door is the **National Theatre,** where classical Thai dance and drama performances are held (*see* The Arts and Nightlife, *below*).

⑧ Opposite is the **National Art Gallery,** with exhibits, both modern and traditional, by Thai artists. *Chao Fa Rd., tel. 02/281–2224. Admission charge. Open Tues.–Thurs. and weekends 9–noon and 1–4.*

⑨ Walk or take a tuk-tuk across the Phra Pinklao Bridge to the dockyard, where the royal **ceremonial barges** are berthed. The ornately carved barges, crafted in the early part of this century, take the form of famous mythical creatures featured in the *Ramayana*. The most impressive is the red-and-gold royal flag barge, *Suphannahongse* (Golden Swan), used by the king on special occasions. *Admission charge. Open Tues.–Thurs. and weekends 9–noon and 1–4.*

⑩ Back across the river is **Wat Sakret.** It's too far to walk; so take a tuktuk for B20. You'll first pass the tall and imposing Democracy Monument, and at the next main intersection, right across the street, will be Wat Sakret.

Wat Sakret (the Temple of the Golden Mount) is a notable landmark of the old city and was, for a long time, the highest building around. King Rama III started the building of this mound and temple, which were completed by Rama V. To reach the gold-covered chedi, you must make an exhausting climb up 318 steps winding around the mound. Don't even attempt it on a hot day, but on a cool, clear day, the view over Bangkok from the top is worth the effort. Every November, the compound is the site of Bangkok's largest temple fair, with food stalls, stage shows, and merrymaking. *Admission charge. Open daily 8–5.*

⑪ Across from Wat Sakret is **Wat Rachanada,** built to resemble the mythical castle of the gods. According to legend, a wealthy and pious man built a fabulous castle, Loha Prasat, following the design laid down in Hindu mythology for the disciples of the Lord Buddha. Wat Rachanada, built in metal, is meant to duplicate that castle and is the only one of its kind remaining. In its precincts are stalls selling amulets that protect the wearer from misfortune—usually of the physical kind, though love amulets and charms are also sold. They tend to be rather expensive, but that's the price of good fortune. *Admission charge. Open daily 8–6.*

⓬ A short tuk-tuk ride away—no more than B20—is one of Bangkok's most photographed wats, the **Marble Temple** (Wat Benjamabophit), built in 1899. Go north from Wat Rachanada, up Ratchadamnoen Nok Road and past the Tourist Authority of Thailand office, toward the equestrian statue of King Chulalongkorn. Just before the statue is Si Ayutthaya Road. Take a right, and Wat Benjamabophit will be on your right. Statues of Buddha line the courtyard, and the magnificent interior has crossbeams of lacquer and gold, but Wat Benjamabophit is more than a splendid temple. The monastery is a seat of learning that appeals to Buddhist monks with intellectual yearnings. It was here that Thailand's present king came to spend his days as a monk before his coronation. *Admission charge. Open daily 7–5.*

⓭
⓮ Leaving Wat Benjamabophit, you can take another short tuk-tuk ride to Vimarnmek Palace. Ask the driver to go there by way of Rama V Road past **Chitlada Palace,** one of the king's residences. The palace will be on the right. On the left will be the **Dusit Zoo,** a place to visit perhaps when you are exhausted by Bangkok's traffic and want to rest in a pleasant expanse of greenery. *Tel. 02/281–0021. Admission charge. Open daily 8–6.*

⓯ **Vimarnmek Palace,** the largest teak structure in the world, was built by King Rama V, grandfather of the present king, as a four-story suburban palace. Now, with the capital's growth, it's in the center of administrative Bangkok, right next door to the entrance of the National Assembly building. The palace fits its name, "Castle in the Clouds." Its extraordinary lightness is enhanced by the adjacent reflecting pond. King Rama's fascination with Western architecture shows in its Victorian style, but the building retains an unmistakable Thai delicacy. Most of the furniture was either purchased in the West or given as gifts by European monarchs. Some of the exhibits by late-19th-century craftsmen are exquisite—porcelain, handcrafted furniture, and crystal—and some have novelty value, such as the first typewriter to have been brought to Thailand. *Tel. 02/281–1569. Admission charge. Open daily 9:30–4.*

⓰ By way of contrast with Vimarnmek Palace, visit the **Suan Pakkard Palace** next. You'll need a taxi or a tuk-tuk; it's a good B30 ride due east down Ayutthaya Road. Five traditional Thai houses, built high on teak columns, adorn the perfectly kept grounds, which include undulating lawns, shimmering lotus pools, and lush shrubbery. The center of attraction, the Lacquer Pavilion, is at the back of the garden. Inside is gold-covered paneling with scenes from the life of Buddha. On display in the houses are porcelain, Khmer stone heads, old paintings, and statues of Buddha. The serene atmosphere of the houses and grounds makes Suan Pakkard one of the most relaxing places in which to absorb Thai culture. *Tel. 02/245–4934. Admission charge. Open Mon.–Sat. 9–4.*

⓱ Another compound of traditional Thai architecture and Southeast Asian furnishings—**Jim Thompson's House**—is fairly close, no more than a B30 tuk-tuk ride away. Go south on Phayathai Road and then west (right) on Rama I. Bargain lovers may want to make an interim stop at the Praturnam Market, just before the Rama I junction and after the Indra Regent Hotel. Hundreds of stalls and shops jam the sidewalk vying for shoppers' attention. The stacks of merchandise, consisting primarily of inexpensive clothing, are overwhelming, and the prices are irresistible—jeans for $5 and shirts for $4.

The entrance to Jim Thompson's House is easy to miss. Walk down Soi Kasemsong, an unprepossessing lane leading off to the right of

Rama I as you come from Phayathai. At the end of the lane, the entrance is on your left.

American Jim Thompson was once an architect in New York; he joined the OSS in World War II and went to Asia. After the war, he stayed in Thailand and took it upon himself to revitalize the silk industry, which had virtually become extinct. His project and product met with tremendous success. That, in itself, would have made Thompson into a legend, but, in 1967, he went to the Malaysian Cameron Highlands for a quiet holiday and was never heard from again.

Aside from reestablishing the Thai silk industry, Thompson also left us his house. Using parts of old up-country houses, some as old as 150 years, he constructed a compound of six Thai houses, three of which are exactly the same as their originals, including all the details of the interior layout. With true appreciation of Southeast Asian art, Thompson then set out to collect what are now priceless works of art to furnish his home. *Tel. 02/215–0122. Admission charge. Open Mon.–Sat. 9–4:30.*

Off the Beaten Track

A relaxing way to see Bangkok is to hire a motorboat for an hour or two and explore the small canals (klongs). The cost is about B250, and a boat can seat four easily.

Alternatively, you can travel on the Chao Phraya River on the ferryboats. One good trip past waterside temples, Thai-style houses, the Royal Barge Museum, and Khoo Wiang Floating Market starts at the Chang Pier near the Grand Palace and travels along Klong Bangkok Noi and Klong Bangkok Yai. Boats leave every 20 minutes between 6:15 AM and 8 PM and cost B10.

Stroll around the **Banglampoo** section of Bangkok, the area where the backpackers gravitate. It's a source for the latest in travel tips and has many travel agencies that can book inexpensive travel and tours. The main thoroughfare, Khao Sahn Road, is full of cafés, secondhand bookstalls, and inexpensive shops. In the evening, the streets are full of stalls and food stands serving the needs of young Westerners on their grand around-the-world tour.

Visit the **Pratunam night market** at the junction of Phetchburi and Rajaprarop roads. Locals come here for noodles and other tasty dishes after an evening at the movies. It's a good place to meet Thais and eat inexpensive Thai and Chinese food.

Shopping

Shopping Districts The main shopping areas are along Silom Road and at the Rama IV end of Suriwongse for jewelry, crafts, and silk; along Sukhumvit Road for leather goods; along Yaowarat in Chinatown for gold; and along Silom Road, Oriental Lane, and Charoen Krung Road for antiques. The Oriental Plaza and the River City Shopping Centre next to the Sheraton Orchid Hotel have shops with collector-quality goods; the shops around Siam Square and at the new World Trade Centre attract middle-income Thais and foreign shoppers. The Peninsula Plaza, across from the Regent Hotel, has very upmarket shops, and the newest and glitziest shopping complex is Thaniya Plaza, between Silom and Suriwongse roads, near Patpong. You need to know about fabric and cut, but for the knowledgeable, bargains can be found at the fabric merchants and tailors who compete along Pahurat Road in Chinatown and Pratunam off Phetchburi Road.

Duty-Free Shopping
Despite protests from shopkeepers, **TAT** (888 Ploenchit Rd., Lumpini, Patumwan, Bangkok 10330, tel. 02/253–0347) opened a duty-free shop that carries everything from fresh fruits to handicrafts, fashion goods to imported perfumes. Store personnel speak English and other languages. Prices are not particularly low, however, and you miss out on the cultural experience of shopping in a foreign country. Purchasers need their passports and airline tickets. *Open daily 9:30 AM–10:30 PM.*

Street Markets
Bangkok's largest street market is the **Weekend Market,** now at Chaturhak Park (on Paholyothin Road opposite the Northern Bus Terminal), where virtually everything is offered for sale. If you want inexpensive chinaware or a tough pair of boots, this market will suit your needs. *Open weekends 9–9.*

Another lively market for goods that are cheap, but inflated for the tourist, is in **Patpong.** Along Silom Road, stalls are set up in the afternoon and evening to sell tourists everything from "Rolex" watches to leather belts and knockoff designer shirts. **Thieves Market** in Chinatown, at the northwestern end of Yaowarat Road, once a place for bargains in antiques, has become more utilitarian in its wares, but is still fun to browse through. Parallel to Yaowarat Road is **Soi Sampeng,** known for its bargain textile sales. An auctioneer with a microphone announces that everything at a particular stall is to be sold at half price, and the shoppers surge over to buy. **Ta Phra Chan,** near Wat Phra Keo, where the Weekend Market was held before it moved, still has booths selling antiques and assorted goods. At the corner of Wat Mahathat, the sidewalk stands sell amulets and good-luck charms. More antiques (both old and new) are found a block away on Ta Chang Road, where there's also jewelry made by Thailand's northern hill tribes.

Department Stores
Good-quality merchandise may be found at **Robinson Department Store** (459 Rajavithi, tel. 02/246–1624), which has several locations, including one at the top of Silom Road. For Japanese-inspired goods, **Sogo** (Amarin Plaza, Ploenchit Rd., tel. 02/256–9131) presents its wares in modern glitter. However, the locals shop at the **Central Department Store** (306 Silom Rd., tel. 02/233–6930; 1691 Phaholyothin Rd., tel. 02/513–1740; and 1027 Phoenchit Rd., tel. 02/251–9201). Prices are good and the selection is extensive.

Specialty Stores
Art and Antiques
Suriwongse Road, Charoen Krung Road, and the Oriental Plaza (across from the Oriental Hotel) have many art and antiques shops. You will also find quality artifacts in the shops at the **River City Shopping Centre,** next to the Royal Orchid Sheraton Hotel. **Peng Seng** (942 Rama IV, tel. 02/234–1285), at the intersection of Suriwongse Road, is one of the most respected dealers in Bangkok. The price may be high, but the article is likely to be genuine. Thai antiques and old images of Buddha need a special export license.

Clothing and Fabrics
Thai silk gained its world reputation only after World War II, when technical innovations were introduced. Two other Thai fabrics are worth noting: Mudmee (tie-dyed) silk, produced in the northeast of Thailand, and Thai cotton, which is soft, durable, and easier on the wallet than silk.

The Jim Thompson Thai Silk Company (9 Suriwongse Rd., tel. 02/234–4900), begun by Jim Thompson, has become *the* place for silk by the yard and for ready-made clothes. There is no bargaining and the prices are high, but the staff is knowledgeable and helpful. A branch store has opened in the Oriental Hotel's shopping arcade. **Choisy** (9/25 Suriwongse, 02/233–7794) is run by a French woman who offers Parisian-style ready-to-wear dresses in Thai silk. **Design Thai** (304 Silom Rd., tel. 02/235–1553) has a large selection of silk items in all price ranges—a good place for that gift you ought to take home. (It's not standard practice, but you can usually manage a 20% discount here.)

For factory-made clothing, the **Indra Garment Export Centre** behind the Indra Regent Hotel on Rajaprarop Road is where you can visit hundreds of shops selling discounted items, from shirts to dresses.

The custom-made suit in 48 hours is a Bangkok specialty, but the suit often hangs on the shoulders just as one would expect from a rush job. If you want a suit of an excellent cut, give the tailor more time. The best in Bangkok is **Marco Tailor** (430/33 Siam Sq., Soi 7, tel. 02/252–0689), where, for approximately B10,000, your suit will equal those made on Savile Row.

Jewelry   While the government **Narayana-Phand** store (295/2 Rajaprarop, Payatai, tel. 02/245–3293) has a selection of handcrafted jewelry, **Polin** (860 Rama IV Rd., tel. 02/234–8176), close to the Montien Hotel, has jewelry of interesting design, and the **A.A. Company** (in the Siam Centre, tel. 02/251–7283), across from the Hotel Siam Intercontinental, will custom-make jewelry.

Leather   Leather is a good buy in Bangkok, with possibly the lowest prices in the world, especially for custom work. Crocodile leather is popular, but be sure to obtain a certificate that the skins came from a domestically raised reptile; otherwise U.S. Customs may confiscate the goods. For shoes, try **River Booters** at the River City Shopping Centre (tel. 02/235–2966), next to the Sheraton Orchid Hotel.

Silverware,   You may wish to wait until you travel to Chiang Mai for these goods.
Nielloware,   However, **Anan Bronze** (157/11 Phetchburi Rd., tel. 02/215–7739)
Bronzeware   and **S. Samran** (302/8 Phetchburi Rd., tel. 02/215–8849) have good selections at fair prices. Both will arrange for shipping purchases home.

Participant Sports and Fitness

Golf   Although weekend play requires advance booking, tee times are usually available during the week. Three good golf courses are the **Krungthep Sports Golf Course** (522 Gp 10 Huamark, tel. 02/374–0491), with fairways flanked by bougainvillea and pine trees, and elevated greens surrounded by sandtraps; the **Navatanee Golf Course** (22 Mul Sukhaphiban 2 Rd., Bangkapi, tel. 02/374–6127), designed by Robert Trent Jones; and the **Rose Garden Golf Course** (4/8 Soi 3 Sukhumvit, tel. 02/253–0295). Greens fees are approximately B500 weekdays and B1,000 weekends.

Jogging   Because of the heat, the crowds, and the air pollution, the best time to run is early in the morning. For a quick jog, the small running track at many hotels may be the best bet. The **Siam Inter-Continental Hotel** has a track in its parkland gardens, and **Lumphini Park** has paved pathways. **Chatuchak Park,** twice as large, is north of the city, and a third park is **Sanam Luang,** in front of the Grand Palace. In all city parks, stay off the grass; don't run in the parks at night, but women can run alone safely during the day. A **Clark Hatch Athletic Club** has opened in the new Thaniya Plaza (Silom Rd., tel. 02/231–2250). The **Grand Hyatt Erawan** hotel has the best fitness-and-health facilities.

Massages Thailand is known for its different schools of massage; the one you receive in Had Yai is likely to differ from that of Chiang Mai or Bangkok. Even in Bangkok, the massage (B150) given at the famous Wat Po school (*see* Exploring, *above*), is a far cry from a massage at the new Health and Beauty Center (tel. 02/236–0400) of the Oriental Hotel. Here in wood-paneled sophistication you can get facials, hydrotherapy, mud and seaweed wraps, and herbal treatments at prices that start at B3,000 for a "Jet Lag Solution" and go up to US$200 for a full day's pampering.

Spectator Sports

Horse Racing Horse races are held every Sunday at the **Royal Bangkok Sports Club** (02/251–0181) or the **Royal Turf Club** (02/280–0020), alternately. Each meeting has up to 12 races, and public betting is permitted.

Thai Boxing The two main Bangkok stadiums are **Lumphini** (tel. 02/251–4303) on Rama IV Road and **Ratchadammon** (tel. 02/281–4205) on Ratchadammon Nok Road near TAT. The latter has bouts every Monday, Wednesday, and Thursday; Lumphini has bouts every Tuesday, Friday, Saturday, and Sunday. Evening bouts begin at 6 PM, Sunday bouts at 1 PM. Tickets may be purchased at the gates for B100–B500. Understanding the rules of this sport is close to impossible. It's fast and furious, and the playing of traditional music heightens the drama.

Dining

By Robert Halliday

Updated by Nigel Fisher

Thais are passionate about food. In Thailand, seeking out the out-of-the-way food shop that prepares some specialty better than anyone else, then dragging friends off in groups to share the discovery, is a national pastime. Some of Bangkok's best restaurants are in the big hotels, and many visitors will be content to look no further. But the gastronomically curious will be eager to get out and explore. Wonders await those prepared to try out small, informal eating places, but there are also dangers.

As a general rule, steer clear of open outdoor stands in markets and at roadsides. Most of these are safe, but you're far better off sticking to the clean, well-maintained food shops on major roads and in shopping centers. These rarely cause problems and will give you a chance to taste the most popular Thai dishes in authentic versions, and at very low prices.

Water is much less of a problem these days than in the past, but it's best to drink it bottled or boiled; see that the bottle is opened in front of you. Clear ice cubes with holes through them are made with purified water, and most restaurants use them.

A word should also be said about price categories. No restaurant in Bangkok is very expensive in the sense one understands the term in New York, London, or Paris. Even the priciest dining rooms in the city will rarely go above $50 per person, unless one is *determined* to spend more. There are individual luxury dishes like the famous Chinese pot dish *phra kradode kamphaeng* ("monk jumps over the wall"), a mixture of everything expensive—abalone, fancy mushrooms, large shrimp, lobster—that can run to $400 or more for a party of four or five. In the inexpensive places, a large and tasty meal can be had for as little as a dollar or two. Most restaurants stop serving dinner at 10:30 PM.

Highly recommended restaurants are indicated by a star ★. For Bangkok restaurants, the following price categories apply.

Category	Cost*
$$$$	over B1,000 ($40)
$$$	B500–B1,000 ($20–$40)
$$	B100–B500 ($4–$20)
$	under B100 ($4)

per person without tax, service, or drinks

Thai **Sala Rim Naam.** Definitely a tourist restaurant, but with style to spare. This elegant *sala* (room), on the bank of the Chao Phraya River across from the Oriental Hotel, realizes many of the images that come to mind with the word *Siam*. Here some dishes are so beautifully prepared that eating them feels like vandalism. Try some of the hot-and-sour salads, particularly the shrimp version called *yam koong*. There's excellently staged Thai dancing. *Use free boat service from the Oriental Hotel, tel. 02/437–6211. Reservations required on weekends and Oct.–late-Feb. Dress: smart casual; no shorts. AE, DC, MC, V. $$$*

Salathip. Built as a Thai pavilion, with an outside veranda facing the Chao Phraya River, the restaurant provides an ambience that guarantees a romantic evening. Be sure to reserve a table outside. Though the Thai cooking may not have as much hot chili as some like, the food hasn't been adulterated to suit Western tastes. On Sundays, the restaurant offers possibly the best buffet in Bangkok, allowing customers to sample some of the finest Thai cuisine in the country. *Shangri-La Hotel, 89 Soi Wat Suan Phu, New Rd., tel. 02/236–7777. Reservations are essential for a veranda table. Dress: casual but neat. No lunch. AE, DC, MC, V. $$$*

Seafood Market. This vast restaurant still feels like the fish supermarket it used to be. You take a cart and choose from an array of seafood—crabs, prawns, lobster, clams, oysters, flatfish, snapper-like fish, crayfish—and vegetables. The waiter takes it away and cooks it any way you like. Typically one's eyes are bigger than one's stomach, so order your selections with prudence and not gusto. While the ambience of the dining room with its fluorescent lighting is that of a giant canteen, people pack the tables because the prices are reasonable and the fish is fresh. *388 Sukhumvit Rd., 02/258–0218. No reservations. Dress: casual. AE, DC, MC, V. $$$*

Tumnak Thai. The biggest restaurant in the world, according to the *Guinness Book of World Records*, Tumnak Thai seats 3,000 and is so extensive that the staff once used to zip around on roller skates. A few still do, but these are mostly students doubling as waiters during vacation time. Well worth trying are dishes based on rare freshwater fishes, which are now being farmed in Thailand. The bizarre *plaa buek*, a type of firm-fleshed, white, slightly sweet-flavored catfish that also makes the *Guinness Book* as the world's biggest freshwater fish, is featured in several dishes, including a tasty *tom yam* salad. Also worth trying is the sweet-fleshed *plaa yeesok* fish. Several of the pavilions overlook a small artificial lake with a stage, where classical Thai dance is sometimes performed. Be forewarned that fame has pushed the prices up and made the service brusque. Come for fun with a group of friends rather than for a romantic dinner for two. *131 Rajadapisek Rd., tel. 02/274–6420. No reservations. Dress: casual. AE, DC, MC, V. $$–$$$*

Ban Chiang. The decor of this restaurant is turn-of-the-century Bangkok, with painted walls adorned with prints, photographs, and artifacts including a pendulum clock. The menu is extensive and can be quite spicy. The roast-duck curry and the shrimp-and-vegetable herb soup, for example, are zesty. The fried fish cakes and the grilled prawns are milder as is the chicken marinated in coconut milk, then baked in pandanus leaves. The service is not the strong point, and you need to know your way around a Thai menu to be able to order a balanced set of dishes. *14 Srivieng Rd., tel. 02/236–7045. Reservations accepted. Dress: casual. MC, V. $$*

Ban Khun Phor. If you're in the area of Siam Square, try this popular bistro located diagonally across from the Novotel. The decor consists of wooden tables and a mix of European Victoriana and Thai artifacts. The menu is varied, with such standard favorites as *tom khaa gai* (lemongrass coconut soup with chicken), and also roast duck with red curry, and even spicy stir-fried boar's meat. The best dish is the spicy crab soup. *458/7–9, Soi 8, Siam Sq., tel. 02/250–1733. No reservations. Dress: casual. MC, V. $$*

Cabbages & Condoms. Don't be misled by the restaurant's name or disconcerted by the array of birth-control devices on display for sale. C&C is a fund-raiser for Thailand's birth-control program, Population & Community Development Association. Once you accept this strange association with fine dining, you'll find the Thai food here excellently prepared, with such items as chicken wrapped in a pandanus leaf, crisp fried fish with a chili sauce, and shrimp in a mild curry sauce. Aside from the simply decorated dining room, there is a pleasant garden with bench tables shaded by trees—one of the few places in Bangkok to sit outside without being overwhelmed by noise and air pollution. *10 Sukhumvit Soi 12, tel. 02/251–0402. Reservations advised. Dress: casual. AE, DC, MC, V. $$*

Lemongrass. Elegance and a certain adventurousness have made this restaurant a favorite with both Thais and resident Westerners. Embellished with Southeast Asian antiques, the dining rooms and the outdoor-garden dining area all have plenty of atmosphere. Among regional specialties, two southern Thai favorites are the notoriously hot fish curry, *kaeng tai plaa*, a good point of departure for those ready to explore, and the *kai yaang paak phanan*, a wonderfully seasoned barbecued-chicken-type dish. Be sure to try a glass of *nam takrai*, the cold, sweet drink brewed from lemongrass. *5/1 Sukhumvit Soi 24, tel. 02/258–8637. Reservations advised. Dress: casual. AE, DC, MC, V. $$*

My Choice. Middle-class Thais with a taste for their grandmothers' traditional recipes flock to this restaurant throughout the day. Particularly popular is *ped aob*, a thick soup made from beef stock, but foreigners may prefer the *tom khaa tala*, a hot and-sour dish with shrimp served with rice. The interior decor is plain and simple, and the outside tables face the parking lot. *Soi 33 Sukhumvit, tel. 02/258–5726. No reservations. Dress: casual. AE, DC, MC, V. $$*

★ **Sanuknuk.** Named for one of the oldest surviving works of Thai literature, Sanuknuk was originally conceived as a drinking place for the city's intellectual community, particularly writers and artists. Its unique menu includes dishes that had been virtually forgotten until they were resurrected by the owner and his wife through interviews with old women in up-country areas. The eccentric decor—which features original work by the artist owner and many others among the city's most prominent creative figures—is of near-museum quality. Sanuknuk's writer-artist crowd drinks a good deal and keeps things lively. Go with a Thai friend if you can, as the menu—a series of cards in a tape cassette box—is written only in Thai. Especially good are the many types of *nam phrik* and the soups like *tom khaa gai*, chicken with coconut cream, chili, and lime juice. *411/6 Sukhumvit Soi 55 (Soi Thong Law) at the mouth of Sub-soi 23, tel. 02/390–0166 or 392–2865. Reservations advised on weekends.*

Bangkok Dining and Lodging

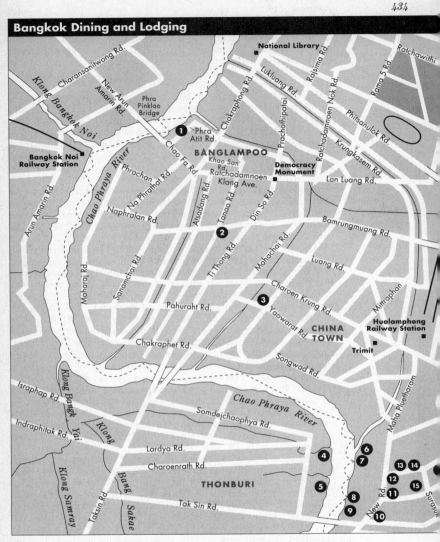

Dining
Ban Chiang, **18**
Ban Khun Phor, **23**
Cabbages &
Condoms, **43**
Coca Noodles, **24**
Genji, **33**
Himali Cha Cha, **11**
Hok Thean Lauo, **4**
Le Dalat, **46**
Lemongrass, **51**
Le Normandie, **8**

Mandalay, **42**
My Choice, **50**
Pan Pan, **34, 49**
Prachak, **10**
The Regent Grill, **28**
River City Bar B-Q, **6**
Royal Kitchen, **30**
Sala Rim Naam, **5**
Salathip, **9**
Sanuknuk, **54**
Saw Ying Thai, **2**

Seafood Market, **48**
Soi Polo Fried
Chicken, **36**
Spice Market, **28**
Sweet Basil, **53**
Thai Room, **26**
Thong Lee, **45**
Ton Po, **1**
Tumnak Thai, **47**

Lodging
Airport Hotel, **20**
Ambassador Hotel, **41**
The Atlanta, **37**
Bel-Air Princess, **40**
Century Hotel, **32**
Dusit Thani, **29**
The Executive
House, **14**
First House, **21**
Grand China
Princess, **3**

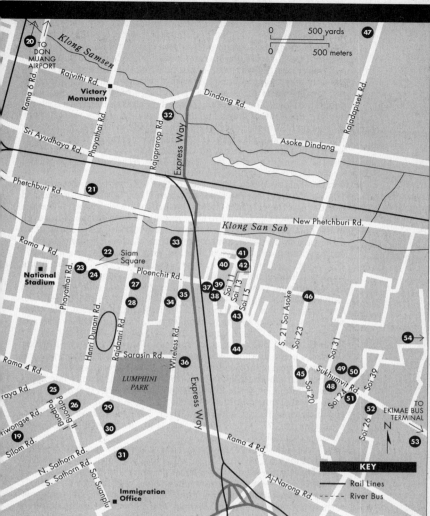

Grand Hyatt
Erawan, **27**

Imperial Hotel, **35**

Landmark Hotel, **38**

Manohra Hotel, **13**

Mermaid's, **44**

Montien, **25**

Narai Hotel, **19**

New Trocadero, **12**

Oriental Hotel, **8**

Park Hotel, **39**

The Regent, **28**

La Residence, **16**

Royal Orchid
Sheraton, **7**

Shangri-La Hotel, **9**

Siam Inter-
Continental, **22**

Silom Plaza Hotel, **15**

Sukhothai, **31**

Tara Hotel, **52**

Tower Inn, **17**

Dress: very casual. DC, MC, V. Dinner only, but open until mid-night. Closed 3rd and 4th Sun. of each month. $$

★ **Spice Market.** Here is Thai home cooking as it was when domestic help was cheap. The decor re-creates a once-familiar sight—the interior of a well-stocked spice shop, with sacks of garlic, dried chilies, and heavy earthenware fish-sauce jars lined up as they were when the only way to get to Bangkok was by steamer. The authentic recipes are prepared full-strength; a chili logo on the menu indicates peppery dishes. The Thai curries are superb, and there is a comprehensive selection of old-fashioned Thai sweets. From mid-January to the end of March, try the *nam doc mai* (Thai mango) with sticky rice and coconut milk; foreign businessmen arrange trips to Bangkok at this time of year just for this dessert. *Regent of Bangkok Hotel, 155 Rajadamri Rd., tel. 02/251–6127. Reservations advised on weekends. Dress: casual. AE, DC, MC, V. $$*

★ **Ton Po.** This is open-air riverside dining without tourist trappings. Ton Po (Thai for the Bo tree, of which there is a large, garlanded specimen at the entrance) takes the form of a wide, covered wooden veranda facing the Chao Phraya. To get the breeze that blows even in the hottest weather, try to wangle a riverside table. Many of its dishes are well-known, none more so than the *tom khlong plaa salid bai makhaam awn*, a delectable but very hot-and-sour soup made from a local dried fish, chili, lime juice, lemongrass, tender young tamarind leaves, mushrooms, and a full frontal assault of other herbal seasonings. Less potent but equally good are the *kai haw bai toei* (chicken meat wrapped in fragrant pandanus leaves and grilled) and *haw moke plaa* (a type of curried fish custard, thickened with coconut cream and steamed in banana leaves). *Phra Atit Rd., no phone. No reservations. Dress: casual. AE, DC, MC, V. $$*

River City Bar B-Q. Seated on the roof of the River City Shopping Centre, guests do their own cooking. Waiters bring the burner and hot plate, and a mound of different meats and vegetables. Guests use their chopsticks to grill the foods to their liking. Order some appetizers to nibble on while dinner is cooking—the northern Thai sausage is excellent. Request a table at the edge of the roof for a romantic view of the Chao Phrao River. *5th Floor, River City Shopping Centre, tel. 02/237–0077, ext. 240. Reservations accepted. Dress: casual. MC, V. $–$$*

Saw Ying Thai. Unless you speak Thai or are accompanied by a Thai friend, it may not be worth your while to track down this place. Saw Ying Thai has been open for almost 60 years and has an extremely devoted clientele, many of whom have been regulars for decades. It is rare to find a tourist at Saw Ying Thai, and the circle of even long-term expatriate customers is small. The menu, written on placards on the wall, is in Thai only, and none of the staff speaks English. If you do go, be sure to order the *kai toon*, a chicken soup with bamboo sprouts; *plaa du thawd krawb phad phed*, crisp-fried catfish stir-fried with curry spices and herbs; and *khai jio neua puu*, an omelet full of crabmeat. For many years, the decor consisted of long-out-of-date posters on the walls. Recently, it has been spiffed up, but the charm remains the same. This restaurant would rate a star were it more accessible. *Cnr. of Bamrungmuang and Tanao Rds., no phone. No reservations. Dress: casual. No credit cards. $*

★ **Soi Polo Fried Chicken.** Although its beat-up plastic tables, traffic noise, and lack of air-conditioning make this small place look like a sure thing for stomach trouble, it is one of the city's most popular lunch spots for nearby office workers. The reason: its world-class fried chicken flavored with black pepper and plenty of golden-brown, crisp-fried garlic. The chicken should be sampled with sticky rice and perhaps a plate of the restaurant's excellent *som tam* (hot-

and-sour raw papaya salad, a hydrogen bomb of a hot coleslaw from the northeast). Try to get there a bit before noon, or landing a table will be a problem. *Walk into Soi Polo from Wireless Rd. (the restaurant is the last in the group of shops on your left as you enter the soi), no phone. No reservations. Dress: very casual. No credit cards. No dinner. $*

Thong Lee. This small but attractive shophouse restaurant has an air-conditioned upstairs dining area. Although prices are very low, Thong Lee has a devoted upper-middle-class clientele. The menu is not adventurous, but every dish has a distinct personality—evidence of the cook's artistry and imagination. Almost everyone orders the *muu phad kapi* (pork fried with shrimp paste); the *yam hed sod* (hot-and-sour mushroom salad) is memorable but very spicy. *Sukhumvit Soi 20, no phone. No reservations. Dress: casual. No credit cards. $*

Non-Thai Asian
Genji. Bangkok has many good Japanese restaurants, although a number of them give a chilly reception to those not of the city's insular Japanese community. Genji is a happy exception. Although culinary purists may wince to learn that it is located in a large international hotel, they would be wrong to stay away. There is an excellent sushi bar and several small private rooms. Try some of the sushi, especially the succulent grilled eel. Set menus for lunch and dinner are well conceived. Japanese breakfasts are also served. *Hilton International, 2 Wireless Rd., tel. 02/253–0123. Reservations advised. Dress: casual. AE, DC, MC, V. $$$*

★ **Royal Kitchen.** Perhaps the most elegant of Bangkok's many Chinese restaurants, the Royal Kitchen consists of a number of small, atmospherically decorated dining rooms where everything, right down to the silver chopsticks on the tables, has been carefully considered. The menu is a reference resource for southern Chinese delicacies, including such offerings as *Mieng nok*, with finely minced, seasoned pigeon served on individual fragrant leaves. At lunchtime, dim sum is served, and it, too, is probably Bangkok's best, as beautiful to look at as it is subtle in taste. *N. Sathorn Rd., opposite YWCA and Thai Oil, tel. 02/234–3063. Reservations required. Jacket and tie suggested. AE, DC, MC, V. $$$*

Hok Thean Lauo. A shuttle boat runs guests across the Chao Praya from the River City Shopping Centre to one of Bangkok's top Cantonese restaurants. Decor is with Chinese lanterns, but the best sight is outside; people sit at tables by the window, watching the streams of rice barges labor up and down the river. Hok Thean Lauo is known for its dim sum lunches, especially on Sunday (be sure to make a reservation). Waiters continually pass your table offering you small baskets of delicacies. Be selective; otherwise you're likely to overindulge and spoil your appetite for the next two days. *762 Ladya Rd., Klongsam, tel. 02/437–1121. Reservations advised. Dress: casual. AE, DC, MC, V. $$–$$$*

Sweet Basil. It is worth making the long trek down Sukhumvit to Soi 62 (Ekimae) for absolutely splendidly presented Vietnamese fare in a fresh, crisp setting of white tablecloths, glistening silver and glassware, and ferns and flowers. The cooking is professional—try the *bo la lat* (brochettes of beef wrapped in a pungent leaf) and the *ban cuon tom* (dumplings stuffed with shrimp and mushrooms) or the more usual but delicious salads and crispy *cha gio* (spring rolls with a sweet, tangy sauce). This is a smart restaurant where you find Thais dressing up for a special meal. *23 Soi 62, tel. 02/176–5490. Reservations advised. Dress: smart casual. AE, DC, MC, V. $$–$$$*

Himali Cha Cha. Cha Cha, who prepares the food at this popular Indian restaurant, was once Nehru's cook. He serves up northern Indian cuisine in a pleasantly informal setting with the usual decor. Far from usual, however, is the quality of the food, which has kept the place a favorite for a decade. The tandoori chicken is locally famous, and there are daily specials that Cha Cha himself will recommend and explain. Always good are the breads and the fruit-flavored *lassis* (yogurt drinks—the mango ones are especially successful). *1229/11 New Rd., tel. 02/235–1569. Reservations advised for dinner. Dress: casual. AE, DC, MC, V. $$*

★ **Le Dalat.** Once a private home and now a very classy Vietnamese restaurant, Le Dalat consists of several intimate and cozily decorated dining rooms. Much Vietnamese cuisine is based on flavor juxtapositions striking to the Western palate, and here it's all served up with style. Try *naem neuang*, which requires you to take a garlicky grilled meatball and place it on a round of *mieng* (edible thin rice paper used as a wrapper), then pile on bits of garlic, ginger, hot chili, star apple, and mango, spoon on a viscous sweet-salty sauce, and wrap the whole thing up in a lettuce leaf before eating. The restaurant has become a favorite with Bangkok residents. Its branch in Patpong I has a similar menu, but the decor is by no means as attractive. *51 Sukhumvit Soi 23, opposite Indian Embassy, tel. 02/258–4192. Reservations advised. Dress: casual. AE, DC, MC, V. $$*

★ **Mandalay.** One of only two Burmese restaurants in Thailand, Mandalay offers food that looks similar to Thai, but tastes very different indeed. Many of the highly seasoned, saladlike dishes are real surprises. One marvel called *lo phet* (made from marinated young tea leaves, peanuts, sesame, garlic, toasted coconut, and several aromatic herbs) is a stunner, but remember the caffeine content of the tea leaves—too much will keep you awake. Also available are excellent, very thick beef and shrimp curries and an unusual pork curry called *hangle*. On the walls are Burmese antiques from the owner's famous shop, Elephant House, and taped Burmese popular music plays in the background. An unusual touch is a plate of Burmese cheroots and lumps of coconut sugar placed on the table after the meal. *77/5 Soi Ruamrudee [Soi 11] Sukhumvit (behind the Ambassador Hotel), tel. 02/250–1220. Reservations advised on weekends. Dress: casual. AE, DC, MC, V. $$*

Coca Noodles. This giant, raucous restaurant is as high-spirited as any in town. On evenings and weekends, it is full of Chinese families eating a daunting variety of noodle dishes with noisy gusto. Both wheat- and rice-based pastas are available in abundance, in combination with a cornucopia of meats, fish, shellfish, and crunchy Chinese vegetables. Try some of the green, wheat-based noodles called *mee yoke*, topped with a chicken thigh, red pork, or crabmeat. Also, on a gas ring built into the table, you can prepare yourself an intriguing Chinese variant of sukiyaki. *In Siam Square Shopping Center facing 461 Henri Dunant Rd., tel. 02/251–6337 or 02/251–3538. Another branch is on Suriwongse Rd., tel. 02/236–0107. Reservations advised on weekends. Dress: casual. No credit cards. $*

Prachak. Known for its duck, this simple, no-nonsense, tile-floor and bare-walls restaurant has superb roast duck (*ped*) and red pork (*moo daeng*). Families from wealthy neighborhoods send their maids here to bring back dinner, and by 6 PM there's often no duck or pork left. Don't come here if you're squeamish about rolls of toilet paper for napkins, the occasional water beetle, and tables wiped down with a shirt sleeve. But if the lack of refinement doesn't bother you, two can dine well for $6. *1415 Charoen Krung (New Road), Silom Bansak, tel. 02/234–3755. No reservations. Dress: casual. No credit cards. $*

Western

★ **Le Normandie.** Perched atop the Oriental Hotel, this legendary Bangkok restaurant commands a panoramic view across the Chao Phraya River. Periodically, it persuades the most highly esteemed chefs in France to temporarily abandon their three-star restaurants and take over in the kitchen. Michelin three-star chef Georges Blanc is the restaurant's permanent consultant. These artists usually import ingredients from home, and at such times the restaurant's patrons enjoy what is literally the finest French food in the world. Even when no superstar chef is on the scene, the cuisine is unforgettable, with the menu often including rare dishes taught to Le Normandie's own master chef by the visiting chefs. *48 Oriental Ave., tel. 02/234–8690. Reservations required 1 or 2 days in advance. Jacket and tie required. AE, DC, MC, V. No lunch on Sun. $$$$*

The Regent Grill. This is a strikingly designed, high-fashion French restaurant. Appearing on the menu from time to time are such memorable dishes as fresh goose liver in raspberry vinegar (this can be specially prepared if requested a day or so in advance). Excellent endive salads and lobster dishes, one with a subtle goose liver sauce, are regularly featured on the menu. In addition to changing its name from Le Cristal, the Regent Grill has been enlarged to encompass an outdoor terrace overlooking the imaginatively landscaped grounds of the Regent of Bangkok Hotel, where it is located. The renovated restaurant is now putting more emphasis on grilled dishes. *155 Rajadamri Rd., tel. 02/251–6127. Reservations required. Jacket and tie required. AE, DC, MC, V. Dinner only on weekends. $$$$*

Pan Pan. The two branches of this Italian-food-and-ice-cream chain are among the most popular restaurants in Bangkok. They are pleasingly decorated with Italian kitchen items and spices. Tables are comfortable, and the relaxed feeling in both places invites long, intimate talks. The long list of pasta includes generous and delicious dishes: linguine with a sauce of salmon, cream, and vodka that is a taste of high-calorie heaven; or "Chicken Godfather," with its cream-and-mushroom sauce, which is similarly disappointment-proof. But save room for the ice cream. It is of the thick, dense Italian type, and there is a fine durian-flavored one for those who dare. The branch on Sukhumvit Road offers a buffet-style antipasto and a large selection of extremely rich desserts. *6–6/1 Sukhumvit Rd., near Soi 33, tel. 02/258–9304 or 258–5071; or 45 Soi Lang Suan, off Ploenchit Rd., tel. 02/252–7104. Reservations advised. Dress: casual. AE, DC, MC, V. $–$$*

Thai Room. A time capsule that has remained virtually unchanged since it opened during the Vietnam War, in 1966, the Thai Room was usually packed in the evening with GIs on R&R. Not a molecule of the decor has changed since then, and it is not unusual to see a veteran of that war quietly reminiscing. Around him, however, will be local residents and tourists in from the tawdry riot of Patpong. The Mexican food is a peculiar hybrid of Mexican and Thai cuisines, and the result is not unpleasing. Some of the Italian items, like the eggplant parmigiana, are very good by any standard, however, and the Thai food can be excellent. Local clients feel great affection for this one-of-a-kind restaurant, which stays open until midnight. *30/37 Patpong 2 Rd. (between Silom and Suriwongse Rds.), tel. 02/233–7920. No reservations. Dress: casual. AE, DC, MC, V. $*

Lodging

The past surge in tourism taxed Bangkok's hotels to the limit, but the situation has considerably improved in the last two years with

the opening of new hotels. Also, a decline in the number of tourists
has made hotels more competitive, slowing their spiraling rates.
Nevertheless, during peak season, from November through March,
you may find the hotel of your first choice fully booked unless you
have made reservations in advance.

You will often find that, in all but the very expensive ($$$$) category, hoteliers have not reinvested their profits in refurbishment.
Carpets tend to have stains, plasterwork is patched, and, if your
room faces the street, the only way to deaden the traffic noise is to
hope the air conditioner works and that its clanking will be loud
enough to do the trick. With the opening of new properties and in-
sufficient hotel schools to supply the staff for them, service may fal-
ter for a few years even in the top hotels.

That said, Bangkok hotel prices are still lower than in Singapore and
Hong Kong and are not expensive by European standards. The deluxe hotels are superb, offering unparalleled comfort and service.
Indeed, in the past, the Oriental Hotel has been rated by some as the
world's best hotel, and the Shangri-La, the Royal Orchid Sheraton,
and the Dusit Thani are also in the running for that position. Such
hotels are about $250 for a double. An equivalent hotel in Paris
would be close to $450.

There are many hotels in the $80–$100 range, and these, too, have
every modern creature comfort imaginable, with fine service, excellent restaurants, health centers, and facilities for businesspeople.
For $50, you can find respectable lodgings in a hotel with an efficient
staff. Rooms in small hotels with limited facilities are available for
around $10, and, if you are willing to share a bathroom, guest houses
are numerous.

The four main hotel districts are next to the Chao Phraya and along
Silom and Suriwongse roads; around Siam Square; in the foreign-
embassy neighborhood; and along Sukhumvit Road. Other areas,
such as Khao San Road for inexpensive guest houses favored by
backpackers, and across the river, where modern high-rise hotels
are sprouting up, are not included in the following list. The latter
are inconveniently located, and finding a room in Khao San, especially in the peak season, requires going from one guest house to another in search of a vacancy—which is best done around breakfast,
as departing residents check out.

$$$$ **Dusit Thani.** At the top end of Silom Road, this low-key 23-story ho-
★ tel with distinctive, pyramid-style architecture is the flagship property of an expanding Thai hotel group. An extensive shopping
arcade, a Chinese restaurant, and an elegant Thai restaurant are at
street level. One floor up is the lobby, reception area, and a delightful sunken lounge, especially pleasant for enjoying afternoon tea
while listening to piano music and looking out over a small courtyard
garden. The pool area is within a central courtyard filled with trees
and serves as a peaceful oasis amid Bangkok's frenzy. Rooms are
stylishly furnished in pastels, and the higher floors have a panoramic view over Bangkok. The Dusit Thani is particularly noted for the
spaciousness and concierge service of its Landmark suites, and for
the tremendous attention paid to every possible need. On request, a
personal fax machine is installed in your room. The public areas
were totally refurbished in 1992 and the 30 Thai Heritage suites are
furnished in classical Thai tradition with handcrafted furniture.
*Rama IV Rd., Bangkok 10500, tel. 02/233–1130, 800/223–5652, or in
NY, 212/593–2988; fax 02/236–0450. 525 rooms, including 15 suites.
Facilities: 7 restaurants, 24-hr coffee shop, disco, cocktail lounge,*

small pool, health center, business center, in-room videos, meeting and banquet rooms, shopping arcade. AE, DC, MC, V.

$$$$ Grand Hyatt Erawan. The Grand Hyatt is built on the site of the old Erawan Hotel and next to the much-revered Erawan shrine. In typical Hyatt style, the lobby is a four-story atrium with a domed, stained-glass roof. It's smart, impressive, and decorated with an extensive art collection. Service is swift and efficient. Guest rooms are large, with a window bay area for a desk and a couple of chairs. The wood floors are strewn with area rugs, and each room has original art. Messages are displayed on a television monitor, and the bathrooms have separate showers, oversize tubs, and separate dressing areas. The three Regency floors offer concierges and other services. The rooms with the best view look over Lumphini Park and the racetrack, though the traffic on Rajdamri Road can be heard. Restaurants abound. The Italian fare at the Spasso developed by a Milanese chef is especially creative. The outdoor pool terrace area is covered with ferns and plants to shade the brilliance reflected from the building. The elaborate fitness center is managed by a trained physical therapist. *494 Rajdamri Rd., Bangkok 10330, tel. 02/254–1234, fax 02/253–5856; U.S. reservations, tel. 800/233–1234. 389 rooms and suites. Facilities: 3 restaurants, lounge, pool and poolside snack bar, tennis and squash courts, fitness center, 24-hr business center, meeting rooms, garage. AE, DC, MC, V.*

$$$$ Landmark Hotel. Calling itself Bangkok's first high-tech hotel, it has created an ambience suggestive of a grand European hotel by the generous use of teak in its reception areas. Guest rooms are unobtrusively elegant, geared to the international business traveler, and include a good working desk and a TV/video screen that can be tuned into information banks linked to the hotel's business center. With a staff of 950 to manage this 450-room hotel, service is swift and attentive. Its Hibiscus restaurant has a view of the city to accompany European fare and an elegant setting. The Huntsman Pub has a jazz trio to accompany drinks and light meals. *138 Sukhumvit Rd., Bangkok 10110, tel. 02/254–0404, fax 02/253–4259. 395 rooms and 55 suites. Facilities: 4 restaurants, 24-hr coffee shop, pool with snack bar, fitness center, 2 squash courts, sauna, shopping complex, business center, meeting rooms. AE, DC, MC, V.*

$$$$ Oriental Hotel. ★ Often cited as the best hotel in the world, the Oriental has set the standard toward which all other Bangkok hotels strive. Part of its fame stems from its past famous guests, and today's roster features heads of state and film personalities. The location on the Chao Phraya is unrivaled; the original building, now the Garden Wing, looking out on the gardens and the river, has been refurbished, and the rooms here—and the main building's luxury suites—are the hotel's best. The hotel has several well-known restaurants, including the China House, Sala Rim Naam, across the river, renowned for its Thai food, and Le Normandie, which ranks as the best French restaurant in Bangkok. In addition, the hotel has a riverside barbecue every night. The Oriental radiates elegance and provides superb service, though in recent years some of the crispness and panache have disappeared, perhaps because the staff is continually wooed away by other hotels. The Oriental instituted a Thai cooking school, afternoon seminars explaining Thai culture, and, more recently, a smart spa across the river (next to the Sala Rim), where you can indulge in all sorts of luxurious treatments. The hotel, in conjunction with the Royal Orchid Sheraton, has a helicopter service ($200) to and from the airport and a bus-riverboat shuttle ($28) that's faster than a taxi in the daytime traffic. *48 Oriental Ave., Bangkok 10500, tel. 02/236–0400, fax 02/236–1939; U.K. reservations, tel. 0171/537–2988; U.S. reservations, tel. 800/526–*

6566. 398 rooms. Facilities: 3 restaurants, 2 tennis courts, jogging track, golf practice nets, 2 squash courts, health club, disco/night-club, business center, boat landing. AE, DC, MC, V.

\$\$\$\$ **Royal Orchid Sheraton.** This 28-story palace rivals its neighbors, the Oriental and the Shangri-La, for top marks in riverfront luxury. All rooms face the river and are well appointed—the namesake flowers are everywhere—and the public rooms, done in low-key peaches and creams, are well laid out and soothing to the eye. The restaurants are almost too numerous to mention, but the Thai one is memorable, with subtle classical music accompanying your meal as you sit on a raised platform with your feet in a sunken box. You could equally well choose Japanese, Indian, or Italian cuisine. A glassed-in bridge leads to the River City Shopping Center next door, and if the heat is getting you down, try the beautiful free-form pool or the lushly land-scaped pool next door at the Portuguese embassy. *2 Captain Bush La., Bangkok 10500, tel. 02/234–5599 or 02/237–0022, fax 02/236–8320, 02/236–6646, and 02/237–2152. 771 rooms. Facilities: 9 restau-rants and bars, ballroom, 8 conference and meeting rooms, busi-ness services, boat landing, helicopter service, riverboat shuttle parking, shops, tennis courts, fitness center, children's pool. AE, DC, MC, V.*

\$\$\$\$ **Shangri-La Hotel.** For decades the Oriental could safely claim to be
★ Bangkok's finest hotel, but the 25-story Shangri-La successfully challenges this position. Service is excellent (many top staff from the Oriental were enticed to the Shangri-La). The facilities are impecca-ble, and the open marble lobby, with crystal chandeliers, gives a feeling of spaciousness that is a relief from the congestion of Bang-kok. The lobby lounge, enclosed by floor-to-ceiling windows, looks over the Chao Phraya River. The gardens are a peaceful oasis, inter-rupted only by the river boat traffic. The spacious guest rooms are decorated in pastels. In the opulent Krungthep Wing, a separate tower across the gardens, all guest rooms have balconies looking over the river. Primarily designed for businesspeople, all rooms have fax outlets. The hotel now has helicopter service to the airport as well as the \$28 bus-riverboat shuttle. *89 Soi Wat Suan Phu, New Rd., Bangkok 10500, tel. 02/236–7777, fax 02/236–8579. 808 rooms and 60 suites. Facilities: 16 restaurants and bars, shops, 2 pools, tennis and squash courts, extensive fitness center, business center. AE, DC, MC, V.*

\$\$\$\$ **Sukhothai.** On 6 landscaped acres off Sakthorn Road (a high-traffic area with no tourist attractions), this 1991 hotel attempts to recap-ture the glory of Thailand's first kingdom in its architecture and am-bience, but does not quite succeed. It does, however, offer quiet; with its numerous courtyards, the clutter and chaos of Bangkok seem a world away. The hotel's Thai restaurant is attractively set in a pavilion in an artificial lake, but for all the elegance, it feels a bit stiff and pretentious. Public areas have stern pillars, sharp right an-gles, and prim little tables laid for tea. The dining room for Conti-nental and grilled fare is comfortable, but prices are high. Standard rooms are spacious but not exceptionally well-furnished, and the price is \$200. The one-bedroom suites (\$350) have splendid oversize, teak-floor bathrooms with "him and her" washbasins and mirrors. Most of the guest rooms face one of the pond-filled courtyards. *13/3 South Sathorn Rd., Bangkok 10120, tel. 02/287–0222, fax 02/287–4980. 212 rooms, including 76 suites. Facilities: 2 restaurants, pool, fitness center with sauna and massage, 2 squash courts, floodlit tennis court. AE, DC, MC, V.*

\$\$\$ **Airport Hotel.** If you need to stay within walking distance of the air-port, this is your only option. The hotel is modern and utilitarian, with a helpful staff. In contrast to the exotic surroundings of Thai-

land, however, it is a bit boring. Rooms are functional and efficient.
The daytime rate for travelers waiting for connections is B450 for
stays up to three hours between 8 AM and 6 PM, and video screens in
the public rooms display the schedules of flight arrivals and departures. *333 Chert Wudhakas Rd., Don Muang, Bangkok 10210, tel.
02/566–1020, fax 02/566–1941. 440 rooms. Facilities: 2 restaurants,
24-hr coffee shop, disco, pool, free shuttle bus to town, conference
rooms. AE, DC, MC, V.*

$$$ **Ambassador Hotel.** This hotel, with three wings of guest rooms, a
complex of restaurants, and a shopping center, is virtually a mini-
city, which perhaps explains the impersonal service and limited
helpfulness of the staff. Milling convention delegates contribute to
the businesslike atmosphere. Guest rooms are compact, decorated
with standard pastel hotel furnishings. There is plenty to keep you
busy at night: the Dickens Pub garden bar, the Flamingo Disco, and
The Club for rock music. The 5,000-room Ambassador City on
Jontien Beach, Pattaya, is a sister hotel. *171 Sukhumvit Rd., Soi
11–13, Bangkok 10110, tel. 02/254–0444, fax 02/253–4123. 1,050
rooms, including 24 suites. Facilities: 12 restaurants, 24-hr coffee
shop, 24-hr room service, pool with poolside snack bar, health center
with massage, 2 tennis courts, business center with secretaries, 60
function rooms. AE, DC, MC, V.*

$$$ **Imperial Hotel.** After a major renovation in 1989, the Imperial be-
 came the smartest hotel in this price category. The restored lobby's
grand, high ceiling is magnificent, and the staff is friendly and eager
to please. Located on 6 acres in the embassy district, the hotel is
separated from the main road by expansive lawns. The inner gardens surround the pool and arcades. Guest rooms facing the garden
are preferred. The rooms are decorated with pale cream walls accented by bright, often red, bedspreads and draperies. *Wireless
Rd., Bangkok 10330, tel. 02/254–0023, fax 02/253–3190. 400 rooms.
Facilities: 4 restaurants (Chinese, Japanese, Thai, Western), tennis court, 2 squash courts, pool, fitness center, sauna, putting
green, shops. AE, DC, MC, V.*

$$$ **Montien.** Across the street from Patpong, this hotel has been re-
markably well-maintained over its two decades of serving visitors,
especially those who want convenient access to the corporations
along Silom Road. The concierge is particularly helpful. The guest
rooms are reasonably spacious, though not decoratively inspired.
They do, however, offer guests private safes. Prices are slightly
higher than you would expect, but the hotel will give discounts. It's
also the only hotel with in-house fortune-tellers who will read your
palm or stars in the evening for B250. *54 Suriwongse Rd., Bangkok
10500, tel. and fax 02/234–8060. 500 rooms. Facilities: 2 restau-
rants, 24-hr coffee shop, disco with live music, pool with pool bar,
business center, banquet rooms. AE, DC, MC, V.*

$$$ **Narai Hotel.** Conveniently located on Silom Road near the business,
shopping, and entertainment areas, this friendly, modern hotel of-
fers comfortable, utilitarian rooms, many of which are decorated
with warm, rose-colored furnishings. At the low end of this price
category, the hotel is a good value, given its cheerful rooms and high
level of service. The most distinguishing feature is Bangkok's only
revolving restaurant, La Rotunde Grill, on the 15th floor. *222 Silom
Rd., Bangkok 10500, tel. 02/257–0100, fax 02/236–7161. 500 rooms,
including 10 suites. Facilities: 3 restaurants, 24-hr coffee shop,
nightclub, pool, small fitness center, business center. AE, DC, MC,
V.*

$$$ **The Regent.** Long one of Bangkok's leading hotels, the Regent is in
what was once the embassy district and is now the geographical cen-
ter of the city. You enter from the palatial steps into a formal lobby

where local society meets for morning coffee and afternoon tea. The decor is sophisticated luxury, with Thai classical art to add serenity. Service is exemplary. A special delight is the courtyard to the left, around which are shops and restaurants, including the popular Spice Market (*see* Dining, *above*). Guest rooms are spacious and equipped with all the creature comforts, but the ones with a view of the racetrack are the best. *155 Rajdamri Rd., Bangkok 10330, tel. 02/251–6127, fax 02/253–9195. 400 rooms. Facilities: 3 restaurants, pool, business center, shops, satellite TV, including CNN. AE, DC, MC, V.*

$$$ **Siam Inter-Continental.** In the center of Bangkok on 26 landscaped acres, the Siam Inter-Continental has a soaring pagoda roof. The lobby, with its lofty space and indoor plantings and cascades, echoes the pagoda roof and the gardens. Its modern Thai-style architecture and feeling of space make this hotel stand out from all others in Bangkok. Each of the air-conditioned rooms is stylishly decorated with teak furniture and trim, upholstered wing chair and love seat, and a cool, blue color scheme. Especially attractive are the teak-paneled bathrooms with radio, telephone extension, and built-in hair dryer. *967 Rama I Rd., Bangkok 10330, tel. 02/253–0355, fax 02/ 253–2275. 411 rooms and suites. Facilities: 4 restaurants, 2 bars, conference rooms, 24-hr room service, pool, .8-km (½-mi) jogging track, putting green and driving range, outdoor gym with workout equipment. AE, DC, MC, V.*

$$ **Bel-Air Princess.** Two hundred yards down Soi 5 from bustling Sukhumvit is this quiet, well-managed hotel. It gets its fair share of tour groups, but for the most part the lobby and lounge area are cool and peaceful, and the coffee shop restaurant is a good place to relax over a light meal. Indian cooking is served in the formal restaurant, the Tiffin Room. The carpeted guest rooms, with two queen-size beds or a single king, are large enough for a round coffee table and chairs as well as the standard TV-cabinet/desk. A personal safe, in-house movies, hair dryer, and tea/coffee-making facilities are pluses, and the complimentary bowl of fruit on each landing is a nice touch. *16 Sukhumvit Rd., Soi 5, Bangkok 10110, tel. 02/253–4300, fax 02/255–8850. 160 rooms. Facilities: coffee shop/restaurant, Indian restaurant, pool with poolside bar, fitness center. AE, DC, MC, V.*

$$ **Century Hotel.** The hotel's location in the northern part of downtown is convenient for those who are only staying overnight in Bangkok and don't want to risk a long drive to the airport in the morning. The rooms, though neat and clean, are small and dark. The coffee shop/bar is open 24 hours, a plus for travelers with early morning flights. *9 Rajaprarop Rd., Bangkok 10400, tel. 02/246–7800. 240 rooms. Facilities: 24-hr coffee shop/bar/restaurant, pool. AE, DC, MC, V.*

$$ **Grand China Princess.** There are two good reasons for staying in Chinatown: First, it's the center of old Bangkok and has far more exotic turn-of-the-century Asian ambience than the new areas along Sukhumvit. The second reason is this new hotel, which opened in October 1993. It occupies the top two-thirds of a 25-story tower from which the guest rooms have panoramic views of the city. Room 2202, for example, gives you a wonderful sight in the morning of the Temple of Dawn, the Golden Mount, and Wat Tuk in one sweep of the eyes. Since the rooms form a segment of a circle, they are not rectangular; the window wall is narrower than the back wall, so the side walls seem to converge. The furnishings are unexciting but functional, and all the rooms have safes and satellite television. The bathrooms are on the small side. Service is wonderfully friendly, and the reception floor (10th) has a welcoming bar, lounge, and coffee shop.

The main restaurant, Siang Ping Loh (serving Chinese fare), is one floor down. *215 Corner of Yaowaraj and Ratchawongse Rd., Samphantawongse, Bangkok 10100, tel. 02/224–9977, fax 02/224–7999. 155 rooms. Facilities: restaurant, coffee shop, business center, fitness center. AE, DC, MC, V.*

$$ **La Residence.** You would expect to find this small town house–type hotel on the Left Bank of Paris, not in Bangkok. Though a little over-priced, La Residence suits the frequent visitor to Bangkok looking for a low-key hotel. The staff members, however, can be abrupt at times. The guest rooms are small, but the furnishings, from light-wood cabinets to pastel draperies, give them a fresh, airy feel. The newness of the hotel, which opened in 1989, adds to the freshness. The restaurant serves Thai and European food, and, since there is no lounge or lobby, it often acts as a sitting area for guests. *173/8–9 Suriwongse Rd., Bangkok 10150, tel. 02/233–3301. 23 rooms. Facilities: restaurant, laundry service. AE, DC.*

$$ **Manohra Hotel.** An expansive marble lobby characterizes the pristine efficiency of this hotel located between the river and Patpong. Rooms have pastel walls, rich patterned bed covers, and dark-green carpets. If you can take Bangkok's polluted air, there is a roof garden for sunbathing. For evening action, there is the Buccaneer Night Club. A word of caution: If the Manohra is fully booked, the staff may suggest its new sister hotel, the Ramada (no relation to the American-managed Ramada), opposite the post office at 1169 New Road (tel. 02/234–897). Unless you are desperate, decline. The Ramada is overpriced and has small, poorly designed rooms. The Manohra, on the other hand, is attractive and well run, with a helpful, friendly staff. *412 Suriwongse Rd., Bangkok 10500, tel. 02/234–5070, fax 02/237–7662. 230 rooms. Facilities: 2 restaurants, coffeehouse, nightclub, indoor pool, meeting rooms. AE, DC, MC, V.*

$$ **Park Hotel.** After its 1992 renovation, the hotel has a fresh crispness to it not often found in this price category. The lobby area, lounge, and bar are far from being designer decorated, but there is adequate room for checking in and comfortable seating. Adjacent to the bar lounge is a small pool in the garden. Ample light makes the guest rooms cheerful. The deluxe doubles are slightly larger, to give space for a writing desk. Bathrooms are small and clean. *Sukhumvit Soi 7, Sukhumvit Rd., Bangkok 10110, tel. 02/255–4300, fax 02/255–4309. 139 rooms. Facilities: restaurant, coffee shop, bar, pool, travel desk. MC, V.*

$$ **Silom Plaza Hotel.** Opened in 1986 in the shopping area on Silom Road, this hotel has an open lobby area with a lounge; upstairs are compact rooms with modern decor in soft colors. The more expensive rooms have river views. The hotel caters to business travelers who want to be close to Silom Road. Service is quick. The facilities are limited, but nearby is all the entertainment you could wish for. *320 Silom Rd., Bangkok 10500, tel. 02/236–0333, fax 02/236–7562. 209 rooms. Facilities: Chinese restaurant, coffee shop, 24-hr room service, indoor pool, poolside bar, gym, sauna, 4 function rooms. AE, DC, MC, V.*

$$ ★ **Tara Hotel.** Built in 1989, the Tara is in the developing restaurant-and-nightlife section of Sukhumvit Road. Guests register in a check-in lounge, with tea or coffee served while the formalities are completed. The lobby is spacious, lined with teakwood carving. Guest rooms, which are on the small side, are decorated with pastels, and many overlook the eighth-floor terrace garden with swimming pool. *Sukumvit Soi 26, Bangkok 10110, tel. 02/259–0053, fax 02/259–2900. 200 rooms and 20 suites. Facilities: restaurant, 24-hr coffee shop, pool with poolside bar, banquet room. AE, DC, MC, V.*

$$ Tower Inn. For a reasonably priced room, centrally located, consider the Tower Inn. The hotel's name is appropriate; it is a tall skinny building on Silom Road between the Thai International Airways office and the new Holiday Inn Crown Plaza. The top floor has a fitness center and a swimming pool, from which you can glimpse the Chao Phraya River. The reception desk, a bar, and a small lounge are on the ground floor, and the coffee shop (Thai and Continental food) is on the second floor. The rooms are as spacious as rooms at the Shangri-la, with plenty of light flooding in from the picture windows. The furnishings, mind you, are ordinary and utilitarian—two queen-size beds and a cabinet that holds the television and serves as a writing desk. The bathroom is smallish—not one to linger in. You can usually negotiate a 30% discount with no trouble at all, which brings the room rate down to B1,335 ($53). *533 Silom Rd., Bangkok 10500, tel. 02/237–8300, fax 02/237–8286. 150 rooms. Facilities: restaurant, pool, fitness center, travel desk, cable and CNN TV. AE, DC, MC, V.*

$ The Executive House. Though it offers only limited services, this hotel has a friendly staff at the reception desk who will help with travel questions and a coffee shop that will deliver food to your room until midnight. The rooms are spacious for the price, the air-conditioning works, and, even if the decor is drab and a bit run-down, the rooms on the upper floors have plenty of light. The penthouse rooms—on the 16th–18th floors—are spacious and include small kitchens; they're also flooded with light. Rooms with a river view are B200 more than those with a city view. Over the last few years, room prices have steadily increased, with no improvement of facilities. While the rate is still good value for the size of the rooms, the lack of tourist services makes this hotel more suited for visitors already familiar with Bangkok. The hotel is next to the Manohra Hotel, down a short driveway. *410/3–4 Suriwongse Rd., Bangkok 10500, tel. 02/235–1206, fax 02/236–1482. 120 rooms. Facilities: coffee shop, small business center. AE, DC, MC, V.*

$ First House. Tucked behind the Pratunam market on a soi off Phetchburi, the First House offers excellent value for a full-service hotel in this price range. The small lobby/sitting area serves as a meeting place where guests can read the complimentary newspapers. Off to the left, the Saranyuth coffeehouse/restaurant, open 24 hours, serves Thai and Western dishes. The compact rooms are carpeted and amply furnished but so dark as to be depressing during the day. Bathrooms are clean, though patches of rough plaster and drab fixtures don't encourage leisurely grooming. However, the reasonable rates, the security, and the helpfulness of the staff all contribute to making this hotel worth noting. *14/20–29 Petchburi Soi 19, Pratunam, Bangkok 10400, tel. 02/254–0303. 84 rooms. Facilities: 24-hr coffee shop and tour desk. AE, DC, MC, V.*

$ New Trocadero. This hotel, between Patpong and the Chao Phraya River, has been a Westerner's standby for six decades. Recently refurbished, it offers queen-size-plus beds in smallish rooms and clean bathrooms. Service is friendly, with a helpful travel/tour desk in the lobby. *343 Suriwongse Rd., Bangkok 10500, tel. 02/234–8920, fax 02/236–5526. 130 rooms. Facilities: 24-hr coffee shop, small pool. AE, DC, MC, V.*

¢ The Atlanta. This hotel began life in the '30s as a chemistry lab, but gradually the present owner's father started taking in guests, and the Atlanta became a budget stopover for visiting academics and scholars. Now Charles Henn, a part-time professor of humanities, caters to mature frugal travelers who come for more than Bangkok's cheap whiskey and ribald nightlife. The dining room and the lobby lounge, with its lovely oval staircase, are straight out the 1950s, with leatherette banquettes and a circular sofa; it's often used for fashion shoots. The accommodations are simple and without TV, but clean and very spacious for the rock-bottom rates. Some rooms have air-conditioning, some have fans and ventilators, and some have balconies; most have personal safes. Ask for a room on the quiet side. The hotel's big plus is the dining room, where classical music is heard before 5 and jazz thereafter. The lady chef, who speaks English, produces superb Thai fare, and an informative menu explains the ingredients of each dish (Charles Henn is a food critic in his own right). *Sukhumvit Soi 2, Bangkok 10110, tel. 02/252–1650 or 02/252–6069, fax 02/255–2151. 59 rooms. Facilities: restaurant, travel desk, pool. No credit cards.*

¢ **Mermaid's.** Down a small, partly residential street off Sukhumvit Road near the Ambassador Hotel, this Scandinavian-owned hotel seems more like a guest house. The value is good, even if the staff's attitude is a little perfunctory at times. Rooms are clean and neat, and each of the more expensive ones has a private balcony. *39 Sukhumvit Soi 8, Bangkok 10110, tel. 02/253–3410. 70 rooms with fan or air-conditioning, some with private bath. Facilities: restaurant, lounge with video, small pool, travel desk. AE, DC.*

In the neighborhood of Khao San Road, there are hundreds of small guest houses where the price of a room and shared bathroom is about B60. The **C&C Guest House** (12 Wisut Kasat Rd., Bang Khunprom, Bangkok 10200, tel. 02/282–4941) is located near Wat In and has clean rooms, a coffee lounge, a small garden, and a friendly staff. The same can be said for the **Shanti Lodge** (37 Sri Ayutthaya, Bangkok 10200, tel. 02/281–2497), located behind the National Library.

The Arts and Nightlife

The English-language newspapers, the *Bangkok Post* and *The Nation,* have good information on current festivals, exhibitions, and nightlife. TAT's weekly *Where* also lists events.

The Arts Thai classical dance is the epitome of grace. Themes for the dance
Classical drama are taken from the *Ramayana* (*Ramakien* in Thailand). A se-
Thai Dance ries of controlled gestures uses eye contact, ankle and neck movements, and hand and finger gestures to convey the stories' drama. The accompanying band consists of a woodwind instrument called the piphat, which sounds like an oboe, and percussion instruments.

Thai dance drama comes in two forms, the *khon* and the *lakhon.* In khon, the dancers (originally all men) wear ferocious masks, and in the lakhon, both male and female roles are played by women. In the old days of the courts of Siam, the dance drama would last for days, taking 720 hours and some 311 actors to perform. Now, seen mostly at dinner shows in hotels, only a few selected scenes are presented about how Rama (a reincarnation of Vishnu) battles with the demon king Ravana and how he frequently has to rescue the beautiful princess Sita. In 1994, dance drama received a shot in the arm, with support from private industry and the donation by King Rama VII of the Chalermkrung Royal Theatre (66 New Rd., tel. 02/222–0434). A troupe of 170 dancers now performs the Khon Masked Dance, with stunning light effects and high-tech sophistication. English translations are printed in the programs and on screens above the stage. Performances are held Tuesday and Thursday at 8 PM; your hotel can make seat reservations.

Occasionally, you may find a performance of *nang taloung*, a form of shadow puppet theater using silhouettes made from buffalo hide. These plays are similar to those found in Java and Bali, Indonesia.

Various restaurants, such as the **Baan Thai** (Soi 22, Sukhumvit Rd., tel. 02/258–5403) and the **Sala Rim Naam** (Oriental Hotel, 489 Charoen Nakom Rd., tel. 02/437–6211), offer a classical dance show with dinner. At the **National Theatre** (Na Phra That Rd., tel. 02/221–5861 or 02/224–1342), performances are given most days at 10 AM and 3 PM, and special performances are held also on the last Friday of each month at 5:30 PM.

Nightlife Most of Bangkok's nightlife is geared to the male tourist. Unfortunately, tourism has propagated its most lurid forms. Live sex shows, though officially banned, are still found in Patpong and other areas. Expect to be ripped off if you indulge. A classic trick is for the hustler outside to promise you B60 beer and no cover charge, but when the bill comes, the beer is perhaps B200 and the service charge is B500. When you dispute the charge, large burly men appear, and since you have little cash, you then pay with a credit card. The establishment secretly makes several imprints of your card, which it later fills in for large amounts, forging your signature from the one you signed.

Cabaret Most of the nightlife will be found on three infamous side streets that link Suriwongse and Silom roads. Patpong I and II are packed with go-go bars with hostesses by the dozen. The obscene club acts are generally found one flight up and, despite promises to the contrary by touts, usually require a hefty cover charge. Patpong III caters to homosexuals. Patpong is quite safe, well patrolled by police, and even has a night market where Thai families shop. A quieter version of Patpong is Soi Cowboy, off Sukhumvit Road at Soi 22, where bars have more of a publike atmosphere. Nana Plaza, at Soi 4 off Sukhumvit Road, is another party area, with 20 bars that cater mostly to the spirited male, but also a few geared more to the family-oriented visitor. The largest troupe of performing transvestites is reputed to be on stage at the **Calypso Garden** (688 Sukhumvit Rd., between Soi 24 and 26, tel. 02/258–8987) with nightly shows at 8:15 and 10. For less ribald entertainment with live bands and internationally known nightclub artists, try the **Tiara** penthouse restaurant at the Dusit Thani Hotel.

Bars Just beyond Soi Cowboy in the curving side streets (Soi 23 to Soi 31) off Sukhumvit are several small, pleasant bars, often with a small live band playing jazz or country music. **Rang Phah** (16 Sukhumvit 23 Soi, tel. 02/258–4321) is a restaurant with excellent Thai food, but you can sit in the garden outside the marvelous Thai house and drink, eat a little, and gaze at the stars. **September** (120/1 Sukhumvit 23, tel. 02/258–5785), another restaurant, is designed in a Victorian Thai style with a heavy teak bar. **Fred and Barts** (123/1 Sukhumvit, tel. 02/258–4541), a modern bar with stainless-steel furnishings, has enthusiastic hostesses if you need companionship. Around the corner the friendly and cozy **Drunken Duck Pub** (59/4 Soi 31, Sukhumvit Road, tel. 02/258–4500) has a three-piece band playing popular jazz. A country-and-western band plays at the nearby **Trail Dust** (43/2 Sukhumvit 31, tel. 02/258–4590), a large tavern with tables both in its patio garden and inside.

Friendly pubs and cafés, popular with yuppie Thais and expats, can be found along Sarasin Road (north of Lumphini Park). The three best are **Brown Sugar** (231/20 Soi Sarasin, tel. 02/250–0103), which has a clutter of small rooms humming with animated conversation;

the **Old West Saloon** (231/17 Soi Sarasin, tel. 02/252–9510), which re-creates the atmosphere of America's Old West aided by a four-piece band; and the **Burgundy Pub** (231/18 Soi Sarasin, tel. 02/250–0090), good for conversation and relaxation. **The Hemingway Bar & Grill** (159/5 Sukhumwit, Soi 55, tel. 02/392–3599) is popular with Thais and expats for an evening of fellowship in log cabin–style ambience. For those who want to snack on Western while listening to live music in the evenings, there's always the **Hard Rock Cafe** (Siam Sq., tel. 02/251–0792). An oasis in Patpong is the British-style bar **Bob-bies Arms** (Car Park Blvd., Second Level, Patpong 2 Rd., tel. 02/233–6828), where you can get a decent pint of beer (chilled) with convivial chatter and pub grub. On weekends, a live band plays and various excuses are made for a party—anything from St. Patrick's Day to St. George's Day.

At **Summertime** (133/19 Kesorn Rd., Rajprasong, near the Erawan Hyatt, tel. 02/253–7604), which has a solid-mahogany bar and fea-tures Italian food, the collectibles decorating the walls are for sale. Across the street is the seafood restaurant **Moon Shadow** (tel. 02/253–7553), which features live jazz in an upstairs lounge, in addition to excellent fresh fish served in a publike setting. **Witch's Tavern** (Soi Thonglor, Sukhumvit Rd., tel. 02/391–9791) offers classical jazz in a cozy Victorian atmosphere where you can order just a beer or hearty English fare.

Discos   Most of the large hotels have their own disco/nightclubs. Two of the best known are **Juliana's of London** at the Hilton and **Diana's** at the Oriental, which is said to be Bangkok's most extravagant club. Late-ly the sparklingly refurbished **Bubbles,** at the Dusit Thani (tel. 02/233–1130), attracts the Thai BMW set. If you wish to venture else-where, head for **Silom Plaza** (320/14 Silom Rd., tel. 02/234–2657 and nearly opposite the Patpong District), the hot new disco and pub center. Discos, such as the **Virgin,** and bars thumping out music from loud stereos line either side of the plaza both at ground level and one story up. In the center of the plaza are tables where you can also drink and eat while watching the comings and goings of young Thais swinging to the latest beat.

Dinner Cruises   Strictly for tourists are the dinner cruises on the Chao Phraya Riv-er. Boats such as the *Wan Foh* (tel. 02/433–5453)—built to look like a traditional Thai house—start at the Mae-Nam Building near the Shangri-La Hotel. During the two-hour trip, a Western/Thai dinner is served. Your hotel staff will make reservations. The difference be-tween one ship and another is marginal. Cost: B450 per person.

Cultural Shows   **Silom Village** (286 Silom Rd., tel. 02/234–4448) may perhaps be rather touristy, but its appeal also reaches out to Thais. The block-size complex, open 10 AM–10 PM, has shops, restaurants, and perfor-mances of classical Thai dance. A couple of the restaurants feature chefs cooking tasty morsels in the open, and you may select from them what takes your fancy or order from a menu. The best cultural show is at the dinner restaurant **Ruan Thep** (reservations, tel. 02/234–4581). Dinner starts at 7 and showtime is at 8:20. Cost: dinner and show, B350; show only, B200.

Excursions from Bangkok

Damnoen Saduak and Nakhon Pathom

Don't bother visiting the floating market in Bangkok; instead, head for Damnoen Saduak, 109 km (65 mi) southwest of Bangkok in the province of Rajburi. The colorful floating market there, with its multitude of vendors paddling their small boats, is a photographer's fantasy. About 30 minutes from Damnoen Saduak is Nakhon Pathom, the oldest city in Thailand. The bridge over the River Kwai at Kanchanaburi is another worthwhile stop, though Kanchanaburi Province is so full of natural beauty that you may want to visit the area and the famous bridge during separate excursions.

Getting There
By Taxi You can also arrange to be picked up by a private car or taxi, which is far superior to a tour bus because you can reach the Damnoen Saduak market by 9 AM, before the tours arrive. It is cheaper to negotiate with a car firm outside your hotel. Speak to the concierge "on the quiet"—nine times out of 10, he or she will have a good resource. The cost for two people will be no more than the tour bus. Round-trip fare from Bangkok to Damnoen Saduak can be as low as B600. If you keep the car to visit both Nakhon Pathom and Kanchanaburi in a one-day excursion, the cost will be about B1,000.

By Bus Public buses, some air-conditioned, leave from the Southern Bus Terminal on Charan Sanitwong Road for Damnoen Saduak every 20 minutes from 6 AM. The fare on an air-conditioned bus is B50; B30 for a non-air-conditioned one. From the Damnoen Saduak Bus Station, walk for 1½ km (1 mi) on the path running along the right-hand side of the canal, or take a taxi boat at the pier to the nearby floating market for B10. Buses are also available to Nakhon Pathom.

By Train Trains from the Bangkok Hua Lunphong and Bangkok Noi stations stop in Nakhon Pathom.

Guided Tours All the major hotels have arrangements with a tour operator who organizes morning trips to Damnoen Saduak for about B700. This tour may be combined with a visit to the Rose Garden, or Kanchanaburi (*see below*) and the Bridge over the River Kwai.

Exploring Once at Damnoen Saduak, hire a *ruilla pai* (sampan) for about
Damnoen B300—an outrageous sum, but so many tourists will pay the price
Saduak that you cannot negotiate a much lower rate. Then, for an hour or more, lazily travel the canal. If you think Bangkok traffic is bad, witness true gridlock from a sampan in the middle of a mess of boats, each trying to shove its way along the *klong* (canal). The traffic jams of sampans, with vendors selling fresh vegetables, meats, and clothes, are a memorable sight. Farmers' wives dressed in baggy pants, long-tailed shirts, and straw hats sell their produce from their sampans, paddling back and forth, or rather pushing and barging their way through the congestion. Other women, cooking tasty treats on their little stoves, sit ready to ferry sustenance to the hungry, either in other boats or on the shore. It's an authentic and colorful slice of Thai life.

If you want to rest, a wharf alongside the klong has tables and chairs. Buy your drinks from the stall and your food from any one of the ruilla pai. By 11 AM, you will have seen the best of Damnoen Saduak; any longer and the novelty of exotica wears thin and the irritation of the vendors' commercialism sets in.

Nakhon Nakhon Pathom is reputed to be Thailand's oldest city, dating from
Pathom 150 BC. Its main attraction is **Phra Pathom Chedi,** the tallest Buddhist monument in the world—at 127 m (417 ft), it stands a few feet higher than the Shwe Dagon Chedi of Burma. The first *chedi* (Thai pagoda where holy relics are kept) on this site was erected in the 6th century, but today one sees a larger chedi, built in 1860, that encases the ruins of the original. Phra Pathom Chedi also marks the

first center of Buddhist learning on the Thai peninsula, established here about 1,000 years ago.

The man responsible for reconstructing the chedi was King Monghut, when he was a monk, saw the Phra Pathom Chedi as crucial to the establishment of Buddhism in Thailand. Believing that the chedi, then in a state of disrepair, contained Buddha's holy ashes, he ordered the existing chedi to be incorporated into the new one. In the outer courtyard are four *viharn* (halls) facing in different directions and containing images of Buddha in various postures. The eastern viharn depicts Buddha beneath a boa tree; the western viharn shows Lord Buddha in a reclining position (symbolizing his imminent death), surrounded by his disciples; in the southern viharn, Buddha is being protected by a Naga; and in the northern viharn, Buddha is standing. At the base of this image are the ashes of King Vajiravudh. The terraces around the temple complex are full of fascinating statuary, including a Dvaravati-style Buddha seated in a chair, and the museum contains some interesting Dvaravati (6th–11th century) sculpture. Occasionally classical Thai dances are performed in front of the temple, and during the Lai Krathong festival, bazaars and a fair are set up in the adjacent park. *Museum open Wed.–Sun. 9–noon and 1–4.*

Sanan Chan Palace, just west of Phra Pathom Chedi, was built during the reign of King Rama IV. The palace is closed to the public, but the surrounding park is a lovely place to relax in between Damnoen Saduak and Bangkok.

Rose Garden Tour. On Bangkok Road, 20 km (12 mi) east of Nakhon Pathom, is a complex that commercially replicates a Thai village. Amid flowers and gardens containing 20,000 rosebushes, there are traditional Thai houses and a stage where a "cultural show" of dance, Thai boxing, sword fighting, and a wedding ceremony are performed at 2:15 and 3:15. The park also contains hotels, restaurants, swimming pools, and other playground activities. Though this afternoon tour is popular, the Rose Garden is a sterile tourist resort. Should you wish to go there independently, reserve through the *Rose Garden booking office, 26414 Siam Sq., tel. 02/253–0295.*

Equally commercial are the elephant roundups and crocodile shows at the neighboring **Samphran Elephant Ground & Zoo.** The elephants are hard to resist, however, as they perform dutifully every day at 1:45 and 3:30; an additional performance is given at 11 AM on weekends. Less appetizing are the crocodile wrestling demonstrations, during which trainers put their heads into the open mouths of well-behaved crocodiles each day at 12:45, 2:40, and 4:20. *Tel. 02/284– 1873 for reservations. Admission charge. Grounds and zoo open daily 9–6.*

Kanchanaburi

The movie *The Bridge Over the River Kwai*, adapted from Pierre Boulle's novel, gave the area of Kanchanaburi a certain fame—or, more accurately, the Japanese gave the area the dubious distinction of being the site of the Death Railway. Even without this publicity, however, Kanchanaburi province would attract tourists. Lush tropical vegetation and rivers with waterfalls and gorges make it one of the most beautiful national parks in Thailand. The town of Kanchanaburi has little architectural merit, but its location, situated where the Kwai Noi and Kwai Yai rivers meet to form the Mae Khlong River, is splendid.

Tourist Information The TAT office (Saeng Chuto Rd., Kanchanaburi, tel. 034/511–200) has good maps and brochures, as well as a knowledgeable and helpful staff. If you wish to take a minibus tour, daily guide services are available from B.T. Travel (Saeng Chuto Rd., Kanchanaburi, tel. 034/511–967), next door to the TAT.

Getting There
By Train From Bangkok's Noi Thonburi Station (tel. 02/411–3102), the train for Kanchanaburi leaves at 8 AM and 1:55 PM. The State Railway of Thailand also offers a special excursion train every Saturday, Sunday, and on holidays; it leaves Hualumpong Railway Terminal at 6:15 AM and returns at 7:30 PM. On the program are stops at Nakhon Pathom, the River Kwai Bridge, and Nam-Tok, from which point minibuses continue on to Khao Phang Waterfall. Tickets for this full-day, round-trip outing may be purchased at Bangkok Railway Station (tel. 02/223–3762), and advance booking is recommended. Cost: B75 for adults, B40 for children.

By Bus Air-conditioned and non-air-conditioned buses leave the Southern Transportation Bus Station, at Pinklao-Nakomchaisri Road, Talingchan (tel. 02/434–5557), every half hour. The journey takes about 2½ hours.

Getting Around Attractions around Kanchanaburi town are accessible either on foot or by *samlor* (small three-wheel cabs). A hired car with a driver is the most convenient means of transportation. Buses leave from the town's terminal on Saeng Chuto Road (tel. 034/511–387) every 30 minutes to most of the popular destinations.

By Raft For rafting on either the Kwai Yai or Mae Khlong rivers, make advance reservations through the TAT office or a travel agent. These trips, which take at least a full day, let you experience the tropical jungle in a leisurely way. The rafts, which resemble houseboats, are often divided into sections for eating, sunbathing, and diving. If you decide to go for a swim, be careful—the currents can have a whirlpool effect that will suck a swimmer down. For one-day rafting trips, the cost is approximately B300. Longer trips are also offered. If you book through a responsible travel agent, you may have to pay a bit more, but you'll also be more likely to get a raft in good condition and a skipper familiar with the currents.

Guided Tours **Kanchanaburi and the Bridge over the River Kwai.** Usually a full day is necessary to travel the 140 km (87 mi) to Kanchanaburi to visit the Allied war cemeteries, the infamous bridge over the river, and to tour the lush tropical countryside. Speak to your hotel tour desk or any operator in Bangkok to arrange a visit.

Exploring One may forgive, but one cannot forget, the inhumanity that caused the death, between 1942 and 1945, of more than 16,000 Allied prisoners of war and 49,000 impressed Asian laborers. Forced by the Japanese, under abysmal conditions, to build a railway through the jungle from Thailand into Burma, one person died for every railway tie on the track.

A reconstruction of the now famous bridge (it was successfully bombed by the Allies toward the end of the war) stands just north of the small, sleepy town of Kanchanaburi. Nearby are two Allied war cemeteries with the remains of 8,732 POWs. To reach the bridge, go through town on Saeng Chuto Road, the main street.

Kanchanaburi War Cemetery is on the left. In row upon row of neatly laid-out graves rest 6,982 American, Australian, British, and Dutch prisoners of war. A commemorative service is held every April 25. After the cemetery, take the next road to the left and make a right at the T junction. Notice the **Japanese War Memorial Shrine** at the junction. Be sure to read the plaque—it has an English translation.

Just up the street from the memorial, the road opens out to a plaza—**the bridge** is on the left. Built with forced labor toward the end of the war, the bridge has steel girders, the center spans of which were knocked out by Allied bombs and replaced after the war with girders made in Japan. The other steel spans are the original ones. You can walk across the bridge to the opposite bank. The wooden bridge associated with the movie was located 2–3 km (1–2 mi) downstream.

Restaurants, souvenir shops, and jewelry stores are located in the plaza before the bridge. Blue sapphires from the Bor Ploy mines, 45 km (28 mi) north of Kanchanaburi, are generally a good buy, but prices are marked up at these shops. You're better off buying the sapphires at the small shops in the center of town.

Upriver, on the road leading back to town, is the **JEATH War Museum** ("JEATH" is an acronym for Japan, England, America, Australia, Thailand, and Holland). Founded by a monk from the adjoining temple, the museum consists of a reconstructed bamboo hut—the type used to house the POWs—and a collection of utensils, railway spikes, clothing, aerial photographs, newspaper clippings, and illustrations designed to show the conditions the POWs lived under during the construction of the Death Railway. *Admission charge. Open daily 8–5.*

Another Allied burial ground, the **Chong-Kai War Cemetery,** lies across the river. To get there, take the ferry from the pier below the park off Patana Road.

A 1-km (½-mi) walk inland from Chong-Kai is **Wat Thum Khao Pun,** one of the best cave temples in the area. A small temple stands outside and a guide entices you into the cave, where serene images of Buddha sit between the stalagmites and stalactites.

If you want to visit some of the spectacular countryside of Kanchanaburi province, the **Erawan Waterfall,** perhaps the most photographed waterfall in Thailand, is worth the trip. Located in the beautifully forested Khao Salop National Park, the falls are at their best in early autumn. To reach the falls, located 65 km (40 mi) from Kanchanaburi on the Kanchanaburi–Srisawat Highway (Route 3199), either take a tour bus from Kanchanaburi or use the public bus. Buses (No. 8170) leave every hour for the 90-minute journey; it's a 1½-km (1-mi) walk or taxi ride to the foot of the falls.

Allow two hours to climb up all seven levels of the Erawan Waterfall, and wear tennis shoes or similar footwear. The rock at the top of the falls is shaped like an elephant, hence the name Erawan, which means elephant in Thai.

Five km (3 mi) farther up the road from the Erawan Waterfall is the 91-m (300-ft) **Sri Nakharin Dam** and a hydroelectric power station. Behind the dam is a vast reservoir. A tour boat makes a two-hour excursion from here to the **Huay Khamin Falls.**

The most memorable trip, though, is to another waterfall, **Sai Yok Noi** (also called Kao Phang) because you travel the 77 km (46 mi) on the Death Railway (notice the wood crosses at the side of the track). The train leaves Kanchanaburi each day at 10:33 AM, passing through lush jungle landscape and by rushing waterfalls as it clings to the mountainside for a two-hour run that is not for the faint-hearted. From Nam-Tok, the last stop, it's a 1½ km (1 mi) walk to Sai Yok Noi. A lot smaller than Erawan, this waterfall offers pools for swimming during the rainy season (May–Aug.), the best time to visit. On weekends, the area is packed with Thai families. There is a bus back to Kanchanaburi that takes half the time of the train, with half the strain on the nervous system.

Dining and Lodging Most of the restaurants for tourists are situated by the River Kwai Bridge or farther downstream at the confluence of the Kwai Noi and Kwai Yai rivers. The most attractive—and most crowded—is the open-air **River Kwai Floating Restaurant** (tel. 034/512–595), to the right of the bridge. Fish dishes, either cooked with Thai spices or lightly grilled, dominate the menu. The specialty is *yeesok*, a fish found in the Kwai Yai and Kwai Noi rivers. Try to arrive before the tour groups, and request a table alongside the river. For more authentic Thai food, try the **Pae Karn Floating Restaurant** (tel. 034/513–251) at the river confluence. The food is better, though the decor is plain.

Most of the area hotels are located along the riverbanks. A few of the resorts also offer thatched bungalows on the river. These raft houses offer a river view during the day, but tend to be hot and muggy at night. Most foreign visitors only spend a day in Kanchanaburi, so the hotels are designed primarily for Thai families who have come for an inexpensive vacation.

Felix River Kwai Resort. This luxury hotel, completed in 1992, was first managed by Sofitel and then by a Thai group. It is still going through its growing pains, but it does have a tranquil setting along the bank of the river in sight of the bridge. Polished wood floors and wicker headboards give a cool country airiness to the rooms. Each has two queen beds or one king as well as a private safe and four-channel cable TV. A large free-form pool amid the tropical plants sets the scene, and this relaxing hotel is within walking distance to most of Kanchanaburi's attractions. *9/1 Moo 3 Thamakham, Amphur Muang, Kanchanaburi 71000, tel. 034/515–061, fax 034/515–095; Bangkok reservations, tel. 02/255–3410. 83 rooms. Facilities: restaurant, pool, Thai massage, and gym. AE, DC, MC, V. $$$*

Kwai Yai Garden Resort. Located 15 minutes by ferry from Tha Kradan Pier, this small resort offers thatched bungalows, a few raft houses, a small restaurant, and a friendly staff. *125 Moo 2, Tambon Tamakham, Amphoe Muang, Kanchanaburi 71000, tel. 034/513–611; Bangkok reservations, tel. 02/513–5399. 12 rooms and 4 raft houses. Facilities: restaurant, bar, tour desk. MC, V. $$*

River Kwai Hotel. Across the bridge on the banks of the Kwai Yai, this hotel is a small complex of thatched bungalows, including some on rafts. On one raft, the dining room and lounge offer a picturesque view of the bridge. *284/4–6 Saengchuto Rd., Amphoe Muang, Kanchanaburi 71000, tel. 034/511–184. 7 rooms and 9 raft houses. Facilities: restaurant, tour desk. MC, V. $$*

River Kwai Village. Nestled in the heart of the jungle in the River Kwai Valley, this resort village consists of five one-story log cabins. A few guest rooms are also located on rafts. All guest rooms have air-conditioning and are simply furnished, with teak and colored stones embedded in the walls. The cafeteria-style restaurant offers a combination of Thai and Western dishes. More enjoyable is the casual restaurant on one of the anchored floating rafts. The resort will supply transportation from Bangkok and arrange tours of the area. *Amphoe Sai Yok, Kanchanaburi 71150. No phone. Reservations should be made in Bangkok at 1054/4 New Phetchburi Rd., Bangkok 10400, tel. 02/251–7552. 60 rooms and 7 raft houses. Facilities: 2 restaurants, pool, conference rooms. Tours arranged. AE, DC, V. $$*

Ayutthaya and Bang Pa-In

Ayutthaya became the kingdom's seat of power in 1350, and toward the end of the 16th century, Europeans described the city, with its 1,700 temples and 4,000 golden images of Buddha, as more striking than any capital in Europe. Certainly the Ayutthaya period was also Thailand's most glorious. In 1767, the Burmese conquered Ayutthaya and destroyed the temples with such vengeance that little remained standing. The city never recovered from the Burmese invasion, and today it is a small provincial town with partially restored ruins. The site is particularly striking at sunset, when the silhouetted ruins glow orange-brown and are imbued with a melancholy charm.

Getting There Ayutthaya, 72 km (45 mi) north of Bangkok, may be visited either as an excursion from Bangkok or on the way from Bangkok to Thailand's northern provinces. Try to get an early start for Ayutthaya in order to visit as many of the sights as possible before 1 PM, when the heat becomes unbearable. Then take a long lunch and, if you have time, continue sightseeing in the late afternoon and catch the sunset before you leave.

By Train Between 4:30 AM and late evening, trains depart frequently from Bangkok's Hualamphong station, arriving in Ayutthaya 80 minutes later. Halfway between the two cities (in time, not distance) is Don Muang Airport. Many travelers on their way south from Chiang Mai stop at Ayutthaya and then continue by train only as far as the airport, from which they fly to their next destination instead of going all the way back into Bangkok.

By Bus Buses leave Bangkok's Northern Terminal on Phaholyothin Road (tel. 02/271–0101) every 30 minutes between 6 AM and 7 PM.

Guided Tours **Ayutthaya and Bang Pa-In.** This visit to Thailand's former glorious capital and the royal palace of Bang Pa-In takes a full day. Tours may travel either both ways by coach or in one direction by cruise boat and the other by coach. The best combination is to take the morning coach to Ayutthaya for sightseeing before the day warms up, and return down river on the boat, which reduces the three-hour river trip by 30 minutes. The most popular trip is aboard the *Oriental Queen*, managed by the Oriental Hotel (tel. 02/236–0400, ext. 3133; cost B900). The *Oriental Queen* now has some stiff competition, however. The *Ayutthaya Princess* (tel. 02/255–9200), a new boat with an exterior design resembling a royal barge, offers the *Oriental Queen*'s itinerary for the same fare. It departs from both the Shangri-La and Royal Orchid Sheraton piers. To book either of these cruises, contact the respective hotels or any travel agent. Neither the service nor comfort level on the *Oriental Queen* or the *Ayutthaya Princess* matches the quality of service found at their respective hotels.

The **Bang Pa-In Summer Palace** is a popular Sunday excursion for Thais. A tour boat departs from Bangkok's Maharat Pier at 8:30 AM and travels up the Chao Phraya River to Bang Pa-In in time for lunch. On the downriver trip, the boat stops at the Bang Sai Folk Arts and Craft Centre before returning to Bangkok by 5:30 PM. The tour is operated by the Chao Phraya Express Boat Co. (2/58 Aroon-Amarin Rd., Maharat Pier, Bangkok, tel. 02/222–5330).

Getting Around For a three-hour tour of the sights, tuk-tuks can be hired within Ayutthaya for approximately B250; a four-wheel samlor can be rented for about B500. English-speaking guides can be hired around the station.

Exploring Ayutthaya is situated within a large loop of the Chao Phraya River,
Ayutthaya where it meets the Nam Pa Sak and Lopburi rivers. To completely
encircle their capital by water, the Thais dug a canal along the
northern perimeter, linking the Chao Phraya to the Lopburi. Although the new provincial town of Ayutthaya, including the railway
station, is on the east bank of the Nam Pa Sak, most of Ayutthaya's
ancient glory is on the island. An exception is Wat Yai Chai Mongkol,
about a B20 tuk-tuk ride southeast of the railway station.

Wat Yai Chai Mongkol was built in 1357 by King U-Thong for meditation. After King Naresuan defeated the Burmese by killing the
Burmese crown prince in single-handed combat on elephants in
1582, he enlarged the temple. The complex was totally restored in
1982; with the contemporary images of Buddha lining the courtyard
and the neatly groomed grounds, it looks a little touristy, an impression not helped by a souvenir shop, beverage stand, and a host of
tour buses from Bangkok. *Admission charge. Open daily 8–5.*

The road continues to **Wat Phanan Choeng,** a small temple on the
banks of the Lopburi. The temple predates the time when Ayutthaya became the Thai capital. In 1324, one of the U-Thong kings, who
had arranged to marry a daughter of the Chinese emperor, came to
this spot on the river; instead of entering the city with his fiancée, he
arranged an escort for her. But she, thinking that she had been deserted, threw herself into the river in despair and drowned. The
king tried to atone for his thoughtlessness by building the temple.
The story has great appeal to Thai Chinese, many of whom make romantic pilgrimages here. *Admission charge. Open daily 8–6.*

Returning to the main road, go left and cross over the bridge to the
island. Continue on Rojana Road for about 1½ km (1 mi) to the **Chao
Phraya National Museum.** Ayutthaya's more important historical
masterpieces are in Bangkok's National Museum, but if you do visit
the Chao Phraya Museum, find a guide who can highlight the evolu-
tion of Ayutthaya art over four centuries. *Admission charge. Open
Wed.–Sun. 9–noon and 1–4.*

Just beyond the Chao Phraya National Museum, turn right onto Si
Samphet Road. Pass the city hall on the left and continue for 1 km (½
mi) to **Wat Phra Si Samphet,** easily recognizable by the huge parking
lot. The shining white marble temple nearby not only looks modern,
it is. Built in 1956, **Viharn Phra Mongkol Bopitr** houses one of
Thailand's largest bronze images of Buddha, one of the few that escaped the destruction wrought by the Burmese.

Wat Phra Si Samphet was the largest wat in Ayutthaya and the temple of the royal family. Built in the 14th century, in 1767 it lost its
15-m (50-ft) Buddha, Phra Sri Samphet, to the Burmese, who
melted it down for its gold—170 kg (374 lbs) worth. The chedis, restored in 1956, survived and are the best examples of Ayutthaya architecture. Enshrining the ashes of Ayutthaya kings, they stand as
eternal memories of a golden age. Beyond these monuments is a
grassy field where the royal palace once stood. The field is a cool,
shady place in which to walk and picnic. The foundation is all that
remains of the palace that was home to 33 kings. *Open daily 8–5.*

Before you leave, visit some of the stalls in the market behind the
souvenir stands; you'll find a marvelous array of vegetables, fruits,
and other foods. After wandering around, stop at the café at the
viharn end of the market for refreshments—try the chilled coconut
in its shell.

From the large coach park, Naresuan Road crosses Si Samphet Road and continues past a small lake to nearby **Wat Phra Mahathat,** on the corner of Chee Kun Road. Built in 1384 by King Ramesuan, the monastery was destroyed by the Burmese, but a buried treasure chest was found during a 1956 restoration project. The chest contained a relic of Lord Buddha, golden Buddha images, and other objects in gold, ruby, and crystal that are now housed in Bangkok's National Museum. If you climb up what is left of the monastery's 42-m (140-ft) *prang* (Khmer-style pagoda with an elliptical spire), you'll be able to envision just how grand the structure must have been. You can also admire the neighboring **Wat Raj Burana,** built by the seventh Ayutthaya king in memory of his brother.

Continue down Naresuan Road, now called Chao Phnom Road, to the Mae Nam Pa Sak River. Either go left up U-Thong Road to **Chandra Kasem Palace** or right to the bridge that leads to the mainland. The reconstructed 17th-century palace is used as Ayutthaya's second national museum. If you're hungry, take a right on U-Thong Road; at the bridge over the Mae Nam Pa Sak are two floating restaurants. If you have a train to catch, try **Tevaraj,** a good Thai restaurant near the railway station, for tasty freshwater lobster.

For an educational overview of the 400 years of the Ayutthaya period, stop in at the new Ayutthaya Historical Study Centre, located near the Teacher's College and the U-Thong Inn. Financed by the Japanese government, the center functions as a place of national research and as a museum. Models of the city as a royal capital, as a port city, as an administrative and international diplomatic center, and as a rural village depicting lifestyles in the countryside are displayed. *Rotchana Rd., tel. 035/245–124. Admission charge. Open Tues.–Sun. 9–4:30.*

About 5 km (3 mi) north of Ayutthaya is the **Elephant Kraal,** the only intact royal kraal in the country. A stockade of massive teak logs, it was formerly used to hold wild elephants picked to be trained for martial service. The kraal was last used in May 1903, during King Chulalongkorn's reign.

Bang Pa-In A popular attraction outside Ayutthaya is **Bang Pa-In Summer Palace,** 20 km (12 mi) to the south. Minibuses leave Chao Prom Market in Ayutthaya regularly, starting from 6:30 AM. The 50-minute trip costs B10. Boats also make the 40-minute run between Ayutthaya and Bang Pa-In; the fare is B150. Trains regularly travel the 70 km (42 mi) from Bangkok to Bang Pa-In railway station, from which a minibus runs to the palace.

The original palace, built by King Prusat (who ruled from 1630 to 1655) on the banks of the Mae Nam Pa Sak, was used by the Ayutthaya kings until the Burmese invasion. Neglected for 80 years, it was rebuilt during the reign of Rama IV (1851–1868) and became the favored summer palace of King Chulalongkorn (Rama V, 1868–1910) until tragedy struck. Delayed in Bangkok on one occasion, the king sent his wife ahead by boat. The boat capsized and she drowned. She could easily have been saved, but the body of a royal personage was sacrosanct and could never be touched by a commoner, on pain of death. King Chulalongkorn could never forgive himself. He built a pavilion in her memory; be sure to read the touching inscription engraved on the memorial.

King Chulalongkorn was fascinated by Europe and its architecture, and many Western influences are evident in Bang Pa-In. The area's most beautiful building, however, is the **Aisawan Thippaya,** a Thai pavilion that seems to float on the lake. Featuring a series of staggered roofs leading to a central spire, the pavilion has represented the country at worldwide expositions.

In addition to Aisawan Thippaya, four other buildings and well-tended gardens make up this striking architectural complex. **Phra Thinang Warophat Piman,** nicknamed the Peking Palace, stands to the north of the Royal Ladies Landing Place in front of a stately pond. Constructed from materials custom-made in China as a replica of a palace of the Chinese imperial court, it was a gift from Chinese Thais eager to demonstrate their loyalty and persuade the king to look more favorably on them. An exquisite collection of jade and Ming-period porcelain is on display inside.

Take the cable car across the river to the unique wat south of the palace grounds. In his fascination with Western architecture, King Chulalongkorn built this Buddhist temple, **Wat Nivet Thamaprawat,** in the Gothic style. Complete with a belfry and stained-glass windows, it looks as much like a Christian church as a wat. *Admission charge to Bang Pa-In Palace. Open 8–3, closed Mon. and Fri.*

Bang Sai Folk Arts and Craft Centre is 24 km (14½ mi) south of Bang Pa-In on the Chao Phraya River. Set up by the queen in 1976 to employ families with handicraft skills, the center makes products that are sold throughout Thailand at the Chirlada handicraft shops. The handicrafts on sale include fern-vine basketry, wood carvings, dyed silks, and handmade dolls. The park is a pleasant place for a picnic, although it is crowded on weekends with Thai families. It also has a small restaurant.

Dining and Lodging Romantics may want to stay overnight in Ayutthaya to see the ruins at night. Since most tourists arrive from Bangkok around 10 AM and depart at 4 PM, those who stay are treated to genuine Thai hospitality. Don't expect deluxe accommodations or restaurants, however, Ayutthaya boasts only simple Thai hotels.

Dining **Pae Krung Kao.** If you want to dine outdoors and watch the waters of the Mae Nam Pa Sak, this is the better of the two floating restaurants near the bridge. The food is Thai; you can also come here for a leisurely beer. *4 U-Thong Rd., tel. 035/241–555. Dress: very casual. No credit cards. $$*

Tevaraj. For good Thai food that does not spare the spices, it's worth heading to this unpretentious restaurant behind Ayutthaya's railway station. The restaurant is short on decor, but the fish dishes and the *tom khaa* (soup made with coconut milk) are excellent. *74 Wat Pa Kho Rd., no phone. Dress: casual. No credit cards. $*

Lodging **U-Thong Inn.** Until the Holiday Inn Ayutthaya is finished, perhaps in 1996, this is the best hotel in town, but don't expect much more than a modern hotel catering to businesspeople and a few package tours (reserve ahead). It's about 2 km (1¼ mi) out of town, which means you need a taxi each time you step out the door. The hotel's dining room, serving Thai and Chinese food, is the most congenial place to eat in Ayutthaya. (Don't confuse this hotel with the U-Thong Hotel, which is not quite as commodious.) *210 Moo 5, Tambon Rotchana Rd., Amphoe Phra Nakhon Si, Ayutthaya 13000, tel. 035/242–236, fax 035/242–235. 100 rooms. Facilities: restaurant, coffee lounge, bar, tour desk, gift shop. MC, V. $$*

Lopburi

Lying 150 km (94 mi) north of Bangkok is Lopburi, one of Thailand's oldest cities. The first evidence of habitation dates from the 4th century AD. After the 6th century, Lopburi's influence grew under the

Dvaravati rulers, who dominated northern Thailand until the Khmers swept in from the east. From the beginning of the 10th century until the middle of the 13th century, when the new Thai kingdom drove them out, the Khmers used Lopburi as the chief provincial capital to control the region. During the Sukhothai and early Ayutthaya periods, Lopburi's importance declined until, in 1664, King Narai (of Ayutthaya) made the city his second capital to escape the heat and humidity of Ayutthaya. French architects were employed to build King Narai's palace; consequently, Lopburi is a strange mixture of Khmer, Thai, and Western architecture.

Lopburi is relatively off the beaten track for tourists. Few foreigners stay overnight, which perhaps explains why the locals are so friendly and eager to show you their town—and to practice their English!

Getting There Lopburi is another 75 km (47 mi) north of Ayutthaya from Bangkok. While it's possible to visit both towns in one day, the journey would be strenuous. You can spend a night in either Ayutthaya or Lopburi, but don't expect deluxe accommodations. Another option is to visit Lopburi on a day's excursion out of Bangkok or en route to Phitsanulok and/or Chiang Mai. Luggage can be stored at the train station.

By Train Three morning and two afternoon trains depart from Bangkok's Hualamphong station on the three-hour journey to Lopburi. The journey from Ayutthaya takes just over an hour. Trains to Bangkok run in the early and late afternoon. The express sleeper train to Chiang Mai from Bangkok comes through Lopburi at 8:20 PM.

By Bus Buses leave Bangkok's Northern Terminal on Phaholyothin Road (tel. 02/271–0101) every 30 minutes between 6 AM and 7 PM.

Getting Around Although bicycle samlors are available, most of Lopburi's attractions are within easy walking distance.

Exploring At the back of the railway station is **Wat Phra Si Mahathat.** First built by the Khmers, it underwent so many restorations during the Sukhothai and Ayutthaya periods that it's difficult to discern the three original Khmer prangs—only the central one has survived intact. Several Sukhothai- and Ayutthaya-style chedis are also within the compound. *Admission charge. Open 8:30–4:30.*

Walk diagonally through Wat Phra Si Mahathat to **Narai Ratchaniwet Palace.** The preserved buildings, which took 12 years (1665–1677) to complete, have been converted into a museum. Surrounding the buildings are castellated walls and triumphant archways grand enough to admit an entourage mounted on elephants. The most elaborate structure is the **Dusit Mahaprasat Hall,** built by King Narai to receive foreign ambassadors. The roof is gone, but you'll be able to spot the mixture of architectural styles: The square doors are Thai and the dome-shaped arches are Western. *Admission charge. Open Wed.–Sun. 9–noon and 1–4.*

The next group of buildings in the palace compound—the **Chan Phaisan Pavilion** (1666), the **Phiman Monghut Pavilion** (mid-19th century), and the row of houses once used by ladies of the court—are now all museums. The latter houses the **Farmer's Museum,** which exhibits regional tools and artifacts seldom displayed in Thailand.

Heading north across the road from the palace (away from the station), you'll pass through the restored **Wat Sao Thong Thong.** Notice the windows of the viharn, which King Narai changed in imitation of Western architecture. Beyond the wat and across another small street is **Vichayen House,** built for Louis XIV's personal representative, De Chaumont. The house was later occupied by King Narai's infamous Greek minister, Constantine Phaulkon, whose political schemes eventually caused the ouster of all Westerners from Thailand. When King Narai was dying in 1668, his army commander, Phra Phetracha, seized power, attacked these residences, and beheaded Phaulkon. In the attack, the Vichayen House and its ancillary buildings, including a Roman Catholic church, were nearly destroyed. *Admission charge. Open Wed.–Sun. 9–noon and 1–4.*

Walk east along the road separating Wat Sao Thong Thong and Vichayen House to **Phra Prang Sam Yot,** a Khmer Hindu shrine and Lopburi's primary landmark. The three prangs symbolize the sacred triad of Brahma, Vishnu, and Siva. King Narai converted the shrine into a Buddhist temple, and a stucco image of the Lord Buddha sits serenely before the central prang once dedicated to Brahma.

Walk about 250 yards down the street facing Phra Prang Sam Yot, and cross over the railway tracks to the **San Phra Kan shrine.** The respected residents of the temple, Samae monkeys, often perform spontaneously for visitors. These interesting animals engage in the human custom of burying their dead.

Dining and Lodging

Accommodations in Lopburi are used mostly by Thai traveling salesmen. Except for the hotel dining rooms, Lopburi restaurants are sidewalk cafés serving Thai and Chinese food. Menus are written in Thai, but you point to what you want in the glass cases at the front of the restaurant.

Lopburi Inn. Located in the new part of town, this is the only hotel in Lopburi with air-conditioning and modern facilities. Even so, don't expect your room to have much more than a clean bed and a private bath. The dining room serves Thai and Chinese food, and the hotel has achieved a certain fame by having an annual dinner party for the town's resident monkeys. *28/9 Narai Maharat Rd., Lopburi, tel. 036/412–300, fax 036/411–917. 142 rooms. Facilities: dining room, coffee lounge. DC, V. $$*

Northern Thailand

Chiang Mai serves as Thailand's northern capital and, for the tourist, the gateway to the north. Many travelers take lodging for a month or longer and make several excursions, returning to Chiang Mai to rest. The hill tribes around Chiang Mai have been visited so frequently by tourists that they have lost some of their character. Travelers in search of villages untainted by Western commercialism need to go farther afield to areas around Tak to the west and Nan to the east. Even Mae Hong Son, west of Chiang Mai, known for its sleepy, peaceful pace of life and the regular gathering of the area's hill tribes, is developing its tourist trade. A paved highway from Chiang Mai opened up the region in 1965; a new, northern route opened in 1989; and now daily flights connect the two towns.

The Golden Triangle (Sop Ruak in Thai), the area where Thailand, Laos, and Burma (Myanmar) meet, has long captivated the Western imagination. The opium poppy grows here, albeit on a much diminished scale, and the hill tribes that cultivate it are semiautonomous, ruled more by warlords such as Khun Sa than by any national government. Today, the tribes of Laos and Myanmar retain their autonomy, but Thailand's Corner of the Golden Triangle has become a tourist attraction, with the tribes caught up in the tide of commercialism. Guest houses and sophisticated hotels accommodate travelers spilling out of crowded Chiang Mai, and well-worn tracks lead into the tribal villages. The opium trade still flourishes, flowing illegally into southern Thailand en route to the rest of the world. For the tourist, however, the attractions are forested hills laced with rivers, the cultures of the hill tribes, and the cool weather. (Those travelers who also seek the poppy while trekking often find themselves languishing in a Chiang Mai prison.)

Chiang Rai, 180 km (112 mi) northeast of Chiang Mai, is the closest city to the hill tribes and the Golden Triangle. In 1990 Chiang Rai had only one luxury hotel; now there are at least three resort complexes, and two more have even been built at the heart of the Golden Triangle, overlooking Laos and Burma.

Chiang Mai

Chiang Mai is the second most popular city to visit in Thailand. Its rich culture stretches back 700 years. Under King Mengrai, several small tribes banded together to form a new "nation" called Anachak Lanna Thai, and made Chiang Rai (north of Chiang Mai) their capital. In 1296, they moved the capital to the fertile plains between Doi Suthep mountain and the Mae Ping River and called it Napphaburi Sri Nakornphing Chiang Mai.

Lanna Thai eventually lost its independence to Ayutthaya and later, Burma. Not until 1774—when General Tuksin (who ruled as king before Rama I) drove the Burmese out—did the region revert to Thailand. After that, the region developed independently of southern Thailand. Even the language is different, marked by its relaxed tempo. Only in the last 50 years have communications between Bangkok and Chiang Mai opened up. No longer a small, provincial town, it has exploded beyond its moat and gates, and some of its innocence has gone.

Tourist Information TAT (105/1 Chiang Mai-Lamphun Rd., tel. 053/248–604) is now on the far side of the river. Contact **Thai International Airways** (Phra Poklao Rd., tel. 053/241–044), to arrange domestic and international bookings.

Emergencies **Police** and **ambulance** (tel. 191). **Tourist Police** (105/1 Chiang Mai-Lamphun Rd., tel. 053/248–974 or 053/248–130). There is also a tourist police box in front of the Night Bazaar. **U.S. Consulate** (387 Wichayanom Rd., tel. 053/252–629); **U.K. Consulate** (Charoen Rat Rd., tel. 053/222–571).

Hospitals **Lanna Hospital** (103 Superhighway, tel. 053/211–037) has 24-hour service and up-to-date equipment.

English-Language Bookstores **D.K. Books** (234 Tapae Rd., opposite Wat Buparam, tel. 052/235–151) has one of the best selections of English-language books, including guidebooks. **Suriwongse Centre** (54/1–5 Sri Douchai Rd., tel. 053/252–052) also carries a range of English-language books, with a large selection of Thai/English dictionaries.

Travel Agencies For plane, train, or bus tickets, one efficient and helpful agency is **ST&T Travel Center** (193/12 Sridonchai Rd., Amphur Muang, tel. 053/251–922), on the same street as the Chiang Plaza Hotel.

Arriving and Departing *By Plane* Thai Airways International has 10 or more flights daily between Bangkok and Chiang Mai, and direct daily flights between Phuket and Chiang Mai. The Bangkok flight takes about an hour and costs approximately B1,700. During the peak season, flights are heavily booked. The airport is about 10 minutes from the downtown area, about a B70 taxi (fixed price) ride.

By Train The State Railway links Chiang Mai to Bangkok and points south. Trains depart from Bangkok's Hualamphong Railway Station and arrive at Chiang Mai Depot (Charoenmuang Rd., tel. 053/245–563). As the journey from Bangkok takes about 13 hours and there is little to see but paddy fields, the overnight sleeper (departs Bangkok 6 PM, arrives Chiang Mai 7:25 AM) is the best train to take. For the return trip, the train departs Chiang Mai at 5:15 PM and arrives in Bangkok at 6:25 AM. (These departure times are subject to minor changes.) The overnight State Railway trains are invariably well maintained, with clean sheets on the rows of two-tier bunks. The second-class carriages, either fan-cooled or air-conditioned, are comfortable. The fare is approximately B505. First class has only the advantage of two bunks per compartment for twice the price. There is also the Nakhonping Special Express that departs Bangkok at 7:40 PM and arrives at Chiang Mai at 8:25 AM (return trip departs at 9:05 PM and arrives Bangkok at 9:40 AM). This train does not have first-class compartments. Most of the Bangkok–Chiang Mai trains stop at Phitsanulok and Lam Pang. There are hotel booking agents at Chiang Mai railway station. The tuk-tuk fare to the center of town ranges from B20 to B30.

By Bus Numerous companies run buses both day and night between Bangkok and Chiang Mai. The buses are slightly faster than the trains (time is about 11 hours) and less expensive—approximately B300. VIP air-conditioned buses with only 24 seats run about B470. State-run buses leave from Bangkok's Northern Terminal (Phahonyothin Rd., Bangkok, tel. 02/279–4484). Direct buses also connect Chiang Mai with Phitsanulok and Sukhothai. Thais generally prefer the train to the bus, because reports of frequent bus crashes make them fearful of tempting fate! But for bus-miles traveled, the law of averages is actually on your side.

Private tour coach operators have more luxurious buses and cost B30–B60 more. Try **Top North** (tel. 02/252–2967) or **Chan Tour** (tel. 02/252–0349).

Getting Around The city itself is compact and can be explored easily on foot or by bicycle, with the occasional use of public or other transport for temples, shops, and attractions out of the city center.

By Car A car, with a driver and guide, is the most convenient way to visit three of the five key temples located outside Chiang Mai as well as the Elephant Camp and hill tribe villages. For a morning's visit to the 6-km- (3.8-mi-) long craft factory/shopping area, the price for a car should not be more than B100, as the driver will be anticipating commissions from the stores you visit. You can also make private arrangements with a taxi for a day's transportation. The cost for a day is approximately B1,000–B1,400, depending on mileage. Be sure to negotiate the price before you step in the car or, better yet, establish the price the evening before and have the driver collect you from your hotel in the morning. Do not pay until you have completed the trip. More and more tourists are discovering the pleasures of having one's own wheels—and they usually rent four-wheel-drive vehicles. Driving is easier than it may first appear, though pedestrians and unlighted vehicles make it hazardous at night. Rent from a reliable car agency, and make sure you have insurance coverage for both third-party and collision damage. Two major agencies are **Hertz** (90 Sridornchai Rd., tel. 053/279–474) and **Avis** (14/14 Huay Kaew Rd., tel. 053/221–316).

By Motorcycle Motorcycles are popular. Rental agencies are numerous, and most small hotels have their own agency. Shop around to get the best price and a bike in good condition. Remember that any damage to the bike that can be attributed to you will be. This includes theft of the vehicle.

By Songthaew These red minibuses follow a kind of fixed route, but will go else-where at a passenger's request. Name your destination before you get in. The cost is B5.

By Bus The Arcade bus terminal (tel. 053/274–638) serves Bangkok, Sukhothai, Phitsanulok, Udon Thani, and Chiang Rai (and towns within the province of Chiang Rai). The other terminal, Chiang Phuak, serves Lamphun, Fang, Tha Ton, and destinations within Chiang Mai province.

Guided Tours Every other store seems to be a tour agency here; so you'd be wise to pick up a list of TAT-recognized agencies before choosing one. Also, each hotel has its own travel desk and association with a tour opera-tor. **World Travel Service** (Rincome Hotel, Huay Kaeo Rd., tel. 053/221–1044) is reliable, but it is the guide who makes the tour great; so meet yours before you actually sign up. This is particularly impor-tant if you are planning a trek to the hill tribe villages. Prices vary quite a bit, so shop around, and carefully examine the offerings.

For trekking, unless you speak some Thai, know the local geogra-phy, understand the local customs, and are stricken with the ro-mance of adventure, use the services of a certified guide. Dozens of tour operators, some extremely unreliable, set up shop on a Chiang Mai sidewalk and disappear after they have your money. Obtain a list of trekking tour agencies from TAT. **Top North** (15 Soi 2, Moon Muang Rd., tel. 053/278–532) and **Summit Tour and Trekking** (Thai Charoen Hotel, Tapas Rd., tel. 053/233–351) offer good tours at about B350 a day (more for elephant rides and river rafting). Since the individual guide determines the quality of the tour and the vil-lages visited, be sure yours knows several hill tribe languages, as well as good English.

Because areas quickly become overtrekked and guides come and go, the only way to select a tour is to obtain the latest information by talking to travelers in Chiang Mai. What was good six months ago may not be good today. It is imperative, also, that you discuss with your proposed guide the villages and route before setting out. You usually can tell whether the guide is knowledgeable and respects the villagers. It can become very cold at night; so take something warm as well as sturdy hiking shoes. You may also want to take along some strong soap, preferably with disinfectant, in case the sleeping huts are grubby. Otherwise, travel light.

Exploring *Numbers in the margin correspond to points of interest on the Chiang Mai map.*

❶ **Wat Prathat Doi Suthep** is perched high up—1,080 m (3,542 ft)—on Doi Suthep, a mountain that overlooks Chiang Mai. It is a 30-minute drive (16 km, or 10 mi) from Chiang Mai, and then a cable car ride or a steep climb up 290 steps beside a marvelous balustrade in the form of *nagas* (mythical snakes that bring rain to irrigate the rice fields, and then cause the waters to retreat so the crop may be harvested), with scales of inlaid brown and green tiles, to the *chedi* (Thai pagoda where holy relics are kept).

❷ Across from Wat Prathat is **Phuping Palace,** the summer residence of the Thai Royal Family. Though the palace may not be visited, the gardens are open on Friday, Sunday, and public holidays, unless any of the royal family is in residence. The blooms are at their best in January.

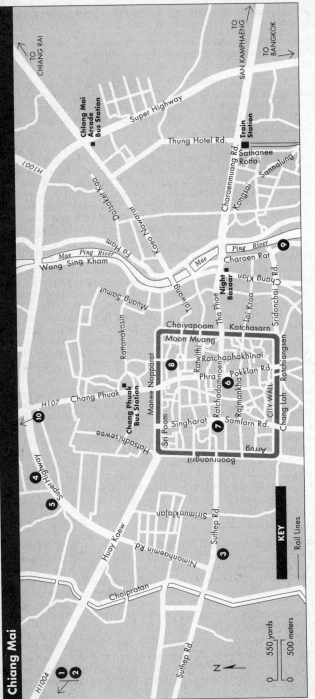

Chiang Mai

TO CHIANG RAI

TO SAN KAMPHAENG

TO BANGKOK

H1001

Super Highway

Chiang Mai Arcade Bus Station

Thung Hotel Rd.

Dusakit Kao

Keo Nawarat

Fa Ham

Charoenmuang Rd.

Train Station

Sathanee Rottai

Kongsai

Sannalung

Mae Ping River

Wang Sing Kham

Muang Samut

Ping River

Mae

Charoen Rat

Night Bazaar

Tha Phae

Taiwang

Loi Kroa

Chang Klan

Sridonchai Rd.

Rattanakosin

Chaiyapoom

Moon Muang

Ratchaphakhinai

Phra

Ratwithi

Pokklan Rd.

Ratchadamnoen

Kotchasarn

Ratchiangsen

CITY WALL

Chang Loh

Manee Nopparat

Chang Phuak

Chang Phuak Bus Station

H107

Singharat

Sri Poom

Samlarn Rd.

Rajmankha

Rajpakinai

Hatsadhisewee

Arrug

Boonruangrit

Suthep Rd.

Sirimunklajan

Nimanhaemin Rd.

Huay Kaew

Super Highway

Cholpratan

Suthep Rd.

H1004

N

KEY
— Rail Lines

0   550 yards
0   500 meters

Elephant Training Centre, **10**
National Museum, **4**
Phuping Palace, **2**
Wat Chaimongkol, **9**
Wat Chedi Luang, **6**

Wat Chiang Man, **8**
Wat Photharam
Maha Viharn, **5**
Wat Phra Singh, **7**
Wat Prathat Doi
Suthep, **1**
Wat Suan Dok, **3**

③ On Suthep Road is **Wat Suan Dok,** one of the largest of Chiang Mai's temples, said to have been built on the site where some of Lord Buddha's bones were found. Some of these relics are reportedly housed in the chedi; the others went to Wat Prathat on Doi Suthep. At the back of the *viharn* (large hall where priests perform religious duties) is the *bot* (main chapel) housing Phra Chao Kao, a superb bronze Buddha made in 1504. In a graveyard alongside the wat, Chiang Mai nobility are buried in stupas.

④ On the superhighway, between its intersection with Huay Kaew Road and Highway 107, is the **National Museum.** In this northern Thai-style building are numerous statues of the Lord Buddha, as well as a huge footprint of Buddha's made from wood and inlaid with mother-of-pearl. The upper floor houses collections of archaeological items, including a bed with mosquito netting used by one of the early princes of Chiang Mai. *Admission charge. Open weekdays 8:30–noon and 1–4:30.*

⑤ From the museum, you can walk to **Wat Photharam Maha Viharn,** more commonly known as Wat Chedi Yot (Seven-Spired Pagoda). Built in 1455, it is a copy of the Mahabodhi temple in Bodh Gaya, India, where the Lord Buddha achieved enlightenment. The seven spires represent the seven weeks that Lord Buddha spent in Bodh Gaya after attaining enlightenment. The sides of the chedi have marvelous bas-relief sculptures of celestial figures.

⑥ Three of the most important temples are within Chiang Mai's city walls, all in easy walking distance of one another. The first is **Wat Chedi Luang** on Phra Pokklan Road just before it crosses Rajmankha Road. In 1411, a vision commanded King Saen Muang Ma to build a chedi to a "height as high as a dove could fly." He died before it was finished, as did the next king, and, during the third succeeding king's reign, an earthquake knocked down 30 m (100 ft) of the 86-m-high (280 ft) chedi. It is now a superb ruin. Don't miss the naga balustrades flanking the entrance steps to the viharn—they are considered the finest of their kind.

⑦ Nearby at the junction of Ratchadamnoen and Singharat roads, in the middle of town, is Chiang Mai's principal monastery, **Wat Phra Singh,** with the Buddha image Phra Singh. The serene and benevolent facial expression of this statue has a radiance enhanced by the light filtering into the chapel. Be sure to note the temple's facades of splendidly carved wood, the elegant teak beams and posts, and the masonry. In a large teaching compound, student monks often have the time and desire to talk.

⑧ **Wat Chiang Man,** Chiang Mai's oldest (1296) monastery, typical of northern Thai architecture, has massive teak pillars inside the bot. Two important images of the Buddha sit in the small building to the right of the main viharn. Officially, they are on view only on Sunday, but sometimes the door is unlocked.

⑨ Each of Chiang Mai's multitude of temples has merit, but the one that counts is the one that inspires you. One that may, for example, is **Wat Chaimongkol,** along the Mae Ping River, near the Chiang Mai Plaza Hotel. It's small, with only 18 monks in residence, and foreigners rarely visit. Though the little chedi is supposed to contain holy relics, its beauty lies in the quietness and serenity of the grounds.

⑩ If you have not visited an "elephant camp" elsewhere in Thailand, visit the **Elephant Training Centre** about 20 km (12 mi) from Chiang Mai at **Mae Sa.** As commercial and touristy as it is, elephants are such magnificent beasts that the show cannot fail to please. Action begins at 9:30. The mahouts bring their beasts to the river for a thorough wash down. The elephants frolic in the water, loving every moment of it. They then stage a dull demonstration of dragging 30-m-long (100 ft) teak logs into the "camp," where the strongest nudge the logs onto a pile. At the end of the show, some tourists choose to ride an elephant around the camp. Far better is riding the elephant on a 2½-hour trek through the jungle to the Mae Sa Valley waterfall (reserve ahead—price is B300), where your driver-guide will meet you with the car. In the valley, lunch at the Mae Sa Valley Resort (tel. 053/251–1662) with well-appointed thatched cottages among beautiful landscaped and flower-filled gardens. Ask the owner for the honey-cooked chicken with chili.

Shopping Always negotiate prices. Even if the shop lists prices, there is room for negotiation. Most of the shops honor major credit cards. A further discount for cash is often possible. One excursion you will surely want to make is along the **Golden Mile**, a 16-km (10-mi) stretch of road from Chiang Mai to San Kamphaeng. On both sides, large emporiums sell crafts and goods for which the region has particular expertise—silverware, ceramics, cottons and silks, wood carvings, hill tribes crafts and artifacts, lacquerware, bronzeware, and hand-painted umbrellas. Most of these emporiums include a factory workshop where you can watch the goods being made, an experience worth the trip whether you buy anything or not. Any taxi driver will happily spend a couple of hours taking you around for about B50 to B100, depending on the level of your intent to buy. If you make purchases, he receives a commission.

Two new modern shopping centers are the Chiang Inn Plaza, across from the Chiang Inn, and the Rimping Superstore Chotana (171 Chang Puak Rd., tel. 053/210–377), where a number of established retailers sell quality goods at fixed prices.

Markets One of Thailand's fullest and most exciting markets is the **Night Bazaar** in the center of town. On the sidewalk on the main street and inside the covered building is a congestion of stalls selling anything from intricately woven Burmese rugs to designer-label shirts made in Thailand. The clothing can be very inexpensive, and, at times, good quality. The "Dior" and "Lacoste" shirts can be excellent at a third of the price of their cousins in the West. Some objets d'art are instant antiques. If you are careful and inspect the goods thoroughly, this is a shopper's heaven for crafts made in the rural villages throughout Myanmar, Laos, and northern Thailand. Be sure to wander to the back of the stalls of the Night Bazaar, which opens up into a sort of courtyard, with restaurants and some good stalls for hill-tribe products. The **Anusan Night Bazaar**, farther down the main street, past the Princess Hotel, has more food outlets, selling both Chinese and Thai fare at reasonable prices.

Specialty Stores **Borisoothi Antiques** (15/2 Chiang Mai–San Kamphaeng Rd., tel. 053/338–460) has a reputation for expertise in Thai and Burmese antiques, though it is always recommended that you have some expertise yourself before you settle on a purchase. Borisoothi also manufactures Ming Dynasty–style furniture.

Siam Celadon (40 Moo 6, San Kamphaeng Rd., Km 10, tel. 053/331–526) has the largest collection of Thai Celadon, a type of ceramicware modeled on the Sawankholoke pottery made hundreds of years ago. Its character comes from the mixture of Chiang Mai and Lumpang clays. The deep, crackled, gray-green glaze is achieved with a wood-ash formula developed a thousand years ago.

Celadon tends to be expensive, but prices are better here than in Bangkok.

Prempracha's Collection (224 Chiang Mai–San Kamphaeng Rd., tel. 053/331–540). In a single 2,000-sq-m (21,600-sq-ft) complex next to Bo Sang (the umbrella village) is displayed an array of products from ceramics, instant antiques, batik, and Thai silk, to wood carvings and bronze statues. Prices tend to be high here, though, and bargaining is discouraged.

Hilltribe and Handicraft Centre, Co, Ltd. (172 Moo 2, Bannong Khong, Chiang Mai-San Kamphaeng District, tel. 053/331–977). Handicrafts and fabrics from the six hill tribes (Meo, Yao, Lisu, Igo, Muser, and Karen) are on display. Goods range from dolls dressed in multicolored traditional costumes to elaborate half-moon necklaces and clothes made from natural hemp.

Pen's House (267/11 Chang Klarn Rd., Ampher Muang, tel. 053/252– 917). To the side, somewhat artificially, are hill-tribe-style houses where craftsmen "perform" their craft. There are also musical instruments, including antique Karen elephant bells, which go for B30,000. Shoulder bags in traditional hill-tribe designs make especially good gifts.

Chiang Mai is fast becoming Thailand's major jewelry center for trinkets, precious stones, and hill tribe ornaments. **PN Precious Stones** (Nai Thawan Arcade, opposite the Rincome Hotel, 95/6–7 Nimmanhemin Rd., tel. 053/212–368) has quality gems. For hill tribe jewelry and ornaments, visit the **Hill Tribe Products Promotion Centre** (21/17 Suthep Rd., near Wat Suan Dok, tel. 053/277–743, and a branch at 100/51–52 Huay Kaew Rd., opposite Chiang Mai University, tel. 053/212–978).

Chiang Mai Laitong (80/1 Moo 3, Chiang Mai–San Kamphaeng Rd., tel. 053/338–237). This shop offers a vast array of lacquerware, ranging from small boxes to tables, and is a good place to see what is available. The shop attendants explain the seven-step manufacturing process, and visitors can watch the artists at work.

BU Leather (Boonkrong Leather Chiang Mai, 9/9 Km 1, Chiang Mai–San Kamphaeng Rd., tel. 053/242–753). The offering here is a variety of bags and shoes made from a range of skins, particularly cow and elephant.

San Kamphaeng (toward the end of the Golden Mile) has the best Thai silk at good prices. **Shinawatra** (on the Golden Mile) has the most stylish silk clothing and fabrics. For cotton, the best merchandise is south of Chiang Mai at **Pa Sang**, near Lamphun.

Jolie Femme (8/3 Chiang Mai–San Kamphaeng Rd., 500 m/1,640 ft beyond the superhighway intersection, tel. 053/247–222) has Thai silk garments designed in the United Kingdom or will custom-make clothes in 24 hours. **Neramit Custom Tailoring** (9½ Ratchawong Rd., tel. 053/236–353) has a solid reputation built upon 30 years of business. For Thai and hill-tribe dolls, pay a visit to **Chiang Mai Doll Making Centre** (187/2 Moo 16, Baen Danf Kilek, tel. 053/248–433).

The silverwork along the Golden Mile is delicate, using close to 100% pure silver (look for the marks certifying percentage). The silversmiths here are known for their bowls with intricate hammered designs depicting stories from the life of the Buddha or scenes from *Ramayana*.

Hill-tribe jewelry is chunky but attractive and can be bought at the villages (that of the Meos has the most variety) or at **Thai Tribal**

Crafts (208 Bamrung Rd., tel. 053/241–043, closed Sun.), a nonprofit store run by church groups.

A fascinating traditional craft still continues at **Bo Sang** (off the Golden Mile). Here villagers make paper umbrellas, beginning by soaking mulberry wood and ending by hand-painting with colorful designs. **Umbrella Making Centre** (111/2 Bo Sang, Chiang Mai, tel. 053/331–324). This manufacturer and retailer has some of the most colorful displays of hand-painted umbrellas and fans.

SA Paper and Umbrella Handicraft Centre (999/16 Ban Nong-khong, Chiang Mai–San Kamphaeng Rd., tel. 053/331–973). At one of the largest manufacturers of handmade paper, umbrellas, and fans, the selection is extensive—the hand-painted fans make an attractive gift.

Modern carvings of all sorts abound, most of which are suitable for the woodpile. An inexpensive, but useful souvenir is a teak salad bowl. Some furniture stores on the Golden Mile have teak furniture carved in incredible detail with jungle and other scenes in deep relief. These *must* be seen. Some also have "antique" wood carvings of the Buddha, but religious carvings need an export certificate.

Dining Continental and Thai cuisines are served in all the top hotels. For Thai food, though, some of the best dining in Chiang Mai is in restaurants without hotel affiliations. A new area with several good bistro-style restaurants, most of which serve northern Thai cuisine, is across from the Rincome Hotel on Nimanhaemin Road, about 1½ km (1 mi) northwest of downtown.

Arun Rai. This is the best-known restaurant in Chiang Mai for northern-Thai cuisine. The restaurant's success has inspired the owner to roof half of what was once only an outdoor restaurant, but you still should not expect great ambience; the focus is on the food. Try the *phak nam phrik* (fresh vegetables in pepper sauce), *tabong* (bamboo shoots boiled then fried in batter), *sai owa* (sausage filled with minced pork and herbs), or the famous frog's legs fried with ginger. The menu is available in English. The Arun Rai often has the delicacy *jing kung* (an insect much like a cricket) that you may want to try. *45 Kotchasarn Rd., tel. 053/276–974. No reservations. Dress: casual. No credit cards. $$*

Baen Suan. This delightful restaurant is off the San Kamphaeng Road (the shopping/factory street) and a B40 tuk-tuk ride from downtown. The northern-style teak house sits in a peaceful garden, and the excellently prepared food is from the region. Try the hot Chiang Mai sausage (the recipe originally came from Burma), broccoli in oyster sauce, green curry with chicken, and a shrimp-and-vegetable soup. *51/3 San Kamphaeng Rd., tel. 053/242–116. Reservations advised. Dress: casual. No credit cards. $$*

Hong Tauw Inn. With the atmosphere of a Thai-style bistro, the Hong Tauw Inn is a relaxing, intimate restaurant where you can linger, trying dishes from northern Thailand and from the central plains. There is an English menu, and the owner speaks fluent English. Excellent Thai soups, *sai oua* (northern sausages), crispy *mee krob* (fried fish with chili), and *nam prik ong* (minced pork with chili paste and tomatoes) are among the popular dishes. The restaurant is just off the Doi Suthep Road, across from the Rincome Hotel, adjacent to a beer garden. *95/17–18 Nantawan Arcade, Nimanhaemin Rd., tel. 053/215–027. Reservations accepted. Dress: casual. MC, V. $$*

★ **Kaiwan.** Not many Westerners come here, but the food is held in high esteem by Thais. The best place to sit is on the second floor at one of the picnic-type tables under the starlit sky. For a not-so-spicy beef curry, try Kaeng Mat Sa Man, and for a zesty fried fish, go for the Pla Tot Na Phrik. *181 Nimmanhemin Rd., near the Rincome Hotel, tel. 053/221–687. Reservations unnecessary. Dress: casual. MC, V. $$*

Nang Nuan. Though this large restaurant has tables indoors, it's pleasant to sit at a table on the terrace facing the Mae Nam Ping. As it's located 3 km (2 mi) south of Chiang Mai, you'll need a tuk-tuk or taxi to reach it, but the *kai tom khaa* (chicken soup with coconut milk) and the *yam nua* (beef salad) are worth the trip. Grilled charcoal steaks and fresh seafood (from display tanks) are also on the menu. *27/2 Ko Klang Rd., Nonghoy, tel. 053/281–955. Reservations accepted. Dress: casual but neat. AE, DC, MC, V. $$*

Riverside. On the banks of the Mae Nam Ping, in a 100-year-old teak house, this restaurant serves primarily Western food given zest by the Thai chef. The owner is a Dutchman, John Vloet, and the Riverside attracts young Thais and Westerners. In the casual, conversation-laden atmosphere, with lots of beer flowing, the food receives only partial attention. The choice tables are on the wood deck jutting out over the river, with views of Wat Phra That on Doi Suthep in the distance. Bands play light jazz or popular music after 7 PM. *9–11 Charoen Rat Rd., tel. 053/243–239. No reservations. Dress: casual. No credit cards. $$*

Ta-Krite. This small, intimate restaurant opens onto the street and is patronized by local Thais. The service and ambience are casual. Cheerful blue tablecloths, wooden beams, and a veranda facing a garden set the tone for the food, which ranges from spicy hot to gently mild. Try the watercress sweet-and-sour soup and the crispy sweet rice noodles with shrimp and egg in a taro basket. For curry, choose the duck for its seasoned sauce, which is tasty without being too hot. *17–18 Samkarn Rd. (it's just off the main road), tel. 053/278–333. No reservations. Dress: casual. No credit cards. $$*

Whole Earth. On the road leading to the Chiang Plaza Hotel, this long-established restaurant serves delicious vegetarian and health foods. On the second floor of an old, attractive Thai house set in a garden, the dining room takes full advantage of any breezes. *88 Sridonchai Rd., tel. 053/282–463. No reservations. Dress: casual. No credit cards. $$*

Lodging With Chiang Mai on every tourist's itinerary, hotels of every persuasion flourish, with new construction making possible many new choices. In high season, however, the better hotels are booked in advance, and some add a surcharge to room rates during January and February, bringing the price of a room close to that in Bangkok. Hotels cluster in four main Chiang Mai districts. The commercial area, between the railway station and the city walls, offers modern accommodations, but in a region that holds little interest for most tourists. The area between the river and the old city walls has the largest concentration of hotels and has the advantage of being close to most of the evening street activity. Within the old city walls are small hotels and guest houses offering inexpensive and simple accommodations, centrally located between markets and temple sites. The west side of town, near Doi Suthep, has attracted the posh hotels, which are quietest but also farthest from points of interest. Several new hotels have opened in the past two years, but they are away from the center of town and you need a taxi or tuk-tuk whenever you leave the hotel.

★ **Chiang Mai Orchid Hotel.** The change of management in 1989 has led to improvements in this leading hotel. The goal is to become the only four-star hotel in the northern capital. So far the new management has added new facilities and renovated the guest rooms. This is a grand hotel in the old style, with teak pillars in the lobby. Rooms are tastefully furnished and trimmed with wood. You can choose among the formal Continental restaurant, Le Pavillon, the new Japanese restaurant, or the informal Thai coffee shop, and find entertainment in the lobby bar or the cozy Opium Den. The suites include the Honeymoon Suite, which, we are told, is often used by the Crown Prince. The drawback is that the hotel is a 10-minute taxi ride from Chiang Mai center. *100–102 Huay Kaeo Rd., Chiang Mai 50000, tel. 053/222–099, fax 053/221–625; Bangkok reservations, tel. 053/245–3973. 267 rooms, including 7 suites. Facilities: 3 restaurants, 2 bars, disco, business center, Clark Hatch fitness center, sauna, rooftop pool with poolside bar, meeting room, beauty salon, drugstore, doctor on call 24 hrs. AE, DC, MC, V. $$$*

Mae Ping Hotel. This high-rise hotel, opened in 1988, has the advantage of a central location. Its rooms are decorated in ever-popular pastels. An executive club floor offers escape from the tour groups massing in the remainder of the hotel. The service staff could use more training. The two restaurants serve Thai and Western food and Italian specialties. *153 Sridonchai Rd., Changklana Muang, Chiang Mai 50000, tel. 053/270–160, fax 053/270–181; Bangkok reservations, tel. 02/232–7712. 400 rooms. Facilities: 2 restaurants, pool with poolside bar, garden terrace, meeting rooms. AE, DC. $$$*

Royal Princess. Formerly the Dusit Inn and still part of the chain, this hotel is ideal if you'd like to step out the front door into the bustle of Chiang Mai's tourist center. The famous Night Bazaar is a block away, and street vendors are even closer. The rooms were refurbished two years ago, but the lack of natural light makes them seem a little dreary. However, the staff are well-trained and helpful, the lobby is pleasant, the cocktail lounge has a pianist in the evenings, and the Jasmine restaurant serves the best Cantonese fare in Chiang Mai. *112 Chang Rd., Chiang Mai 50000, tel. 053/281–033, fax 053/281–044; Bangkok reservations, tel. 02/233–1130. 200 rooms. Facilities: 2 restaurants, small pool with poolside service, airport shuttle service, meeting room. AE, DC, MC, V. $$$*

Chiang Inn. Behind the Night Market and the center of Chiang Mai, the Chiang Inn has offered well-kept guest rooms since it opened in 1980. As the hotel is set back from the main street, the rooms are quiet (the higher the better). Appealingly decorated in light pastels with locally handwoven fabrics produced from homegrown cotton and dyed with purely natural herbs, the rooms are reasonably spacious. For dining, La Grillade serves Thai-influenced French cuisine in a formal atmosphere, or, more casual, the Ron Thong Coffee House serves Thai and Western dishes. The only problem is that the Chiang Inn is usually swamped with tour groups arriving and departing, and its facilities are geared to that kind of traffic. *100 Chang Khlan Rd., Chiang Mai 50000, tel. 053/270–070, fax 053/274–299; Bangkok reservations, tel. 02/251–6883. 170 rooms, including 4 suites. Facilities: 2 restaurants, disco, pool with poolside service, meeting room, travel/tour desk. AE, DC, MC, V. $$*

Melia/Suriwongse. Located around the corner from the Royal Princess and near the Night Bazaar, this hotel has recently undergone a refurbishment that brings it up to first-class standards. Its association with the French hotel chain attracts European tour groups, and the staff makes a game attempt to speak French using some English words and a Thai accent! The Suriwongse offers all tourist facilities, including a pickup point for the airport shuttle bus. The rooms, redecorated in pastels, are bright and cheery. Centrally located, the hotel compares favorably with the Royal Princess. *110 Chang Khlan Rd., Chiang Mai 50000, tel. 053/270–051, fax 053/271–604; Bangkok reservations, tel. 02/251–9883; U.S. reservations, tel. 800/221–*

4542. 170 rooms, including 4 suites. Facilities: restaurant, coffee shop, tour desk, airport shuttle bus stop. AE, DC, MC, V. $$

Grand Apartments. In the old city, this new building offers rooms by the day or by the month, making it a useful place for an extended stay at very reasonable rates (B4,000 per month). The rooms are efficient and clean, and guests have access to telex and fax machines. *24/1 Prapklao Rd., Chang Pluck Gate, Chiang Mai 50000, tel. 053/217–291, fax 053/213–945. 36 rooms. Facilities: café for breakfast and snacks. MC, V. $*

★ **River View Lodge.** Facing the Mae Nam Ping and within an easy 10-minute walk of the Night Bazaar, the lodge is tastefully furnished with wood furniture crafted in the region and rust-colored clay floor tiles. While the furnishings are neither elegant nor luxurious, the rooms have a restful simplicity and are a far cry from the standard uniformity in most of Chiang Mai's high-rise hotels. The more expensive rooms have private balconies overlooking the river. The small restaurant is better for breakfast than for dinner, and the veranda patio is good for relaxing with a beer or afternoon tea. The owner speaks nearly fluent English and will assist in planning your explorations. Some seasoned travelers to Chiang Mai say this is the best place to stay in the city. *25 Charoen Prathet Rd., Soi 2, Chiang Mai 50000, tel. 053/271–109, fax 053/279–019. 36 rooms. Facilities: restaurant, pool. AE, DC, MC, V. $*

★ **Galare Guest House.** On the Mae Ping riverfront, this guest house has many advantages: its good location, within five minutes' walk of the Night Bazaar; friendly service from its staff; small but clean rooms with air-conditioning or fan; and a restaurant. Even though this hotel is in the budget category (¢), it offers more charm and personal service than many of the other city hotels. It is also the best value in town. *7 Charcoplathat Rd., Chiang Mai 50000, tel. 053/273–885, fax 053/279–088. 25 rooms. Facilities: restaurant. No credit cards. ¢*

Lai Thai. On the edge of the old city walls, and a 10-minute walk from the Night Bazaar, this friendly guest house offers rooms around a garden courtyard and a casual open-air restaurant that serves Thai, European, and Chinese food. The rooms are either air-conditioned or cooled by fan. Bare, polished floors and simple furniture give them a fresh, clean look. The rooms farthest back from the road have less traffic noise. *111/4–5 Kotchasarn Rd., Chiang Mai 50000, tel. 053/271–725, fax 053/272–724. 120 rooms. Facilities: restaurant, laundry, tour/travel desk, motorbike rental. MC. ¢*

The Arts and Nightlife Chiang Mai is a good place to experience the art of traditional Thai massage. It has Indian origins, has been practiced since the time of Buddha, and is believed to have curative powers for problems ranging from epilepsy to backaches and simple tension. One place to have a massage is **Patngarm Hat Wast** at the Diamond Hotel (33/10 Charoen Prathet Rd., Chiang Mai, tel. 053/234–153). Another establishment that offers respectable traditional Thai massages with or without herbs is **Suan Samoon Prai** (105 Wansingkham Rd., tel. 053/252–706). The cost is B100 for a simple hour massage and B400 for a two-hour herbal rubdown.

No first visit to Chiang Mai should be without a Khantoke dinner, which usually consists of sticky rice (molded into balls with your fingers for eating), delicious *kap moo* (spiced pork skin), a super spicy dip called *nam prink naw* with onions, cucumber, and chili, and *kang kai*—a chicken-and-vegetable curry. All this is to be washed down with Singha beer.

Often the Khantoke dinner includes performances of Thai and/or hill-tribe dancing. One such "dinner theater" is at the back of the **Diamond Hotel** (tel. 053/272–080), which offers a commercial repertory of Thai dancing in a small, comfortable restaurant-theater setting. Another place for a Khantoke dinner and dance is the **Old Chiang Mai Cultural Centre** (tel. 053/275–097), a complex of buildings just out of Chiang Mai, designed as a hill tribe village. Though the dances at the Cultural Centre are more authentic, perhaps the best venue for watching both hill-tribe and classical Thai dances is the **Khum Kaew Palace** (252 Phua Pok Klao Rd., Chiang Mai, tel. 053/214–315). The symbolism of each dance is given a brief explanation in Thai and English. The building is a distinctive traditional northern Thai house, where you can sit cross-legged on the floor or at long tables with others. The Khantoke dinner is good or bad, depending on whether you like sticky rice, pork crackling, and curry. The price, at B650 for two, is on par with the others. Reservations are necessary. All three places start the evening at 7.

The Hill (92–93 Bumrungburi Rd., tel. 053/277–968), in a large, mostly covered courtyard, is a popular place for Thais to while away the evening (from 7) snacking and drinking while listening to a live band (mostly with Thai vocalists). The bare cement floors are scattered with bench tables, a wooden bridge crosses a stream that divides the cavernous area in two, and a balcony area attracts more demonstrative couples. The focus is an artificial hill, designed with rocks and ferns, where the entertainers perform. You collect your food, beer, and soft drinks (bring your own bottle if you want the hard stuff) from stands at the rear of the courtyard after buying tickets at a kiosk. Tour buses deposit middle-aged Westerners at the **Blue Moon** (5/3 Moon Muang Rd., tel. 053/278–818) for a very routine performance of a dance show that includes a troupe of transvestites.

For more mundane evening entertainment, aside from the "love palaces," of which Chiang Mai has its share, there are several pub restaurants. The **Riverside** (*see* Dining, *above*) is one of the most popular, especially for its location next to the Mae Ping and the small bands that drop in to perform throughout the evening. For a casual evening, with a jazz trio, you may want to stop off at the European-style **Bantone** (99/4 Moo 2, Huay Kaew Rd., tel. 053/224–444).

At the **Cozy Corner** (25 Moon Muang Rd., tel. 053/277–964) the pub atmosphere, chatty hostesses, and beer garden with a waterfall are all popular with the patrons, who come for hamburgers and beer. For those who want to visit each branch of the famous chain, there is a **Hard Rock Cafe** (6 Kotchasarn Rd., Soi 1, near Thape Gate, tel. 053/216–432) in Chiang Mai. Described by *Newsweek* as "one of the world's best bars," **The Pub** (88 Huay Kaew Rd., tel. 053/211–550) can get a little crowded. Still, for draft beer, good grilled steak, and a congenial atmosphere, this place is hard to beat. **Bubbles** (tel. 052/270–099), in the Pornping Tower Hotel, is a lively disco for the young at heart, while **Club 66** (tel. 053/222–099), in the Chiang Mai Orchid Hotel is a little more sophisticated and draws a smarter crowd. **The Domino Bar** (33 Moon Muang Rd., tel. 053/224–766), an English-style pub with snacks, is a meeting place where you may leave messages for fellow travelers.

Excursions from Chiang Mai

To the south and east of Chiang Mai are **Lamphun, Pa Sang,** and **Lam Pang.** A trip to Lamphun, only 26 km (16 mi) from Chiang Mai, is an easy morning or afternoon excursion. Include Pa Sang, and the excursion will take the whole day. If you continue on to Lam Pang, 100 km (62 mi) southwest of Chiang Mai, you will probably want to stay overnight. If you are driving north from Chiang Mai, an interesting excursion is to **Don Inthanon National Park,** whose beauty is characterized by trees, flowers, waterfalls, and tremendous views from Thailand's highest mountain (2,565 m/8,464 ft).

Lamphun Lamphun claims to be the oldest existing city in Thailand (but so does Nakhon Pathom). Originally called Nakorn Hariphunchai, it was founded in AD 680 by the Chamdhevi dynasty, which ruled until 1932, when Thailand changed from a system of city rulers to provincial governors. Unlike Chiang Mai, which has experienced rapid growth over the past two decades, Lamphun remains a sleepy town. Its architectural prizes are two temple monasteries.

Getting There Local trains running between Bangkok and Chiang Mai stop at Lamphun. Local trains are slow, however, and the Lamphun station is 3 km (2 mi) out of town. Bicycle samlors can take you into town for B30. The easiest way to reach Lamphun from Chiang Mai is to take the minibus songthaew (fare is B10), which leaves about every 20 minutes from the TAT office on Lamphun Road.

Exploring Located 2 km (1¼ mi) west of the town's center is **Wat Chama Devi**—often called Wat Kukut (topless chedi) because the gold at its top has been removed. You'll probably want a samlor to take you down the narrow residential street to the wat. Since it is not an area where samlors generally cruise, it's a good idea to ask the driver to wait for you.

Despite the modern viharn to the side of the complex, the beauty of this monastery is in its weathered look. Suwan Chang Kot, to the right of the entrance, is the most famous of the monastery's two chedis. Built by King Mahantayot to hold the remains of his mother, the legendary Queen Chama Devi, the first ruler of Lamphun, the five-tier, sandstone chedi is square; on each of its four sides, and on each tier, are three Buddha images. The higher the level, the smaller the images. All are in the Dvaravati style—8th and 9th century—though many have obviously been restored over the centuries. The other chedi was probably built in the 10th century, though most of what we see today is the work of King Phaya Sapphasit in the 12th century.

The other major attraction, **Wat Phra That Hariphunchai,** is dazzling. Enter the monastery from the river, passing through a large coach park lined with stalls selling mementos. Once through the wat's gates, which are guarded by two ornamental lions, you'll encounter a traditional, three-tier, sloping-roof viharn. This is a replica (built in 1925) of the original, which burned to the ground in 1915. Inside, note the large Chiang Saen–style bronze image of Buddha, Phra Chao Thongtip, and the carved *thammas* (Buddhist universal principals) to the left of the altar.

Leave the viharn by walking to the right past what is reputedly the largest bronze gong in the world, cast in 1860. The 50-m (165-ft) Suwana chedi, covered in copper plates and topped by a golden spire, dates from 847. A century later, King Athitayarat, the 32nd ruler of Hariphunchai, raised its height and added more copper plating to honor the relics of Lord Buddha inside. On top of the chedi, he added a nine-tier umbrella, gilded with 6½ kg (14 lbs) of pure gold. The monk who brought the relics from India is remembered by a gold statue in a nearby chamber. He's also remembered for his potbelly—legend has it that he made himself obese so his youthful passion for women wouldn't prevent him from concentrating on Buddha's teachings.

At the back of the compound—which leads to a shortcut to the center of town—is another viharn with a standing Buddha, a *sala* (an assembly hall in a Buddhist monastery) housing four Buddha footprints, and the old museum. The new museum, just outside the compound, has a fine selection of Dvaravati stucco work and Lamma antiques. *Admission charge. Museum open Wed.–Sun. 8:30–4.*

Downtown Lamphun, a sleepy town where the locals are in bed by 10 PM, consists of a main street with stores, several food stalls, and not much else. For lunch or cold drinks, go back through Wat Hariphunchai to the main road along the Kwang River and choose any one of the string of cafés. Lamphun is also known for its lamyai fruit (a sweet cherry-sized fruit with a thin shell). (In the nearby village of Tongkam, a B10,000 lamyai tree nets its owner that sum in fruit every year.) Buy yourself a jar of lamyai honey; you'll be in for a treat.

Pa Sang Many visitors go to **Pa Sang,** 12 km (7½ mi) down Highway 106 from Lamphun, for the cotton weaving. Songthaews (fare is B10) ply the route all day long. Once in town, you'll find one main street with numerous stores selling cotton goods produced locally. However, in recent years, the better stores have relocated to Chiang Mai, and the selection of goods is not as great as it once was. Most of the shops have clothing with traditional designs and good prices; a shirt with a batik pattern is about B100, while dresses run about B175. More contemporary clothing and household items may be found at **Nandakwang Laicum,** on the right-hand side of the street as you arrive from Lamphun. Five km (3 mi) south of Pa Sang on Highway 106 is **Phra Bhat,** commonly known as the Temple of Buddha's Footprint. While the energetic may mount the 152 steps to the chedi at the top of the hill for the view, the main attraction is the huge imprint of the Lord Buddha's footprint inside the temple that is located to the right of the car park. As you enter the temple, purchase a piece of gold leaf (B20), which you can paste in the imprint and make a wish.

On the return trip to Chiang Mai, about 20 km (12 mi) from Lamphun, is a small road off to the left marked by a Shell station on the corner. Down this road is **Wat Chedi Liem,** a five-tier wat built by King Mengrai in the 13th century and probably copied from Wat Chama Devi in Lamphun. Approximately 3 km (2 mi) past this monastery is the **McKean Leprosarium.** Occupying a small island in the Mae Nam Ping, the institute was created in 1908 to treat sufferers of leprosy, and it has since become internationally recognized as a model of a self-contained community clinic. Don't worry about catching the disease—it requires multiple contacts with a leper to acquire leprosy. The community itself is inspiring: Some 200 patients have their own cottages on 160 secluded acres. In addition to the medical facilities, there are occupational therapy workshops, stores, and a church. A visit here is an ennobling experience. *Donations requested. Open weekdays 8–noon and 1–4, Sat. 8–noon.*

Lam Pang During the reign of Rama VI, horses were imported from England to draw the carriages through the streets of Lam Pang. This charming image, combined with quaint streets, is still promoted by tourism officials. The 20th century has come to Lam Pang, however, and a superhighway connects it to Chiang Mai and Bangkok. Concrete houses and stores have replaced the wooden buildings, and cars and buses have taken over the streets, leaving only a few remaining horses. Today, Lam Pang is a busy metropolis, built on both sides of the Wang River. The confusion and congestion of its streets may deter you from spending the night here, but a few hours visiting the city's impressive temples makes for a pleasant stopover between Chiang Mai and Phitsanulok.

Getting There   **Thai International Airways** has one morning flight between Bangkok and Lam Pang.

From Chiang Mai, the train takes approximately 2½ hours to reach Lam Pang. From Bangkok, it takes 11 hours, and from Phitsanulok, five hours.

Both air-conditioned and non-air-conditioned buses connect Lam Pang to Thailand's northern and northwestern cities. Buses also travel directly to Bangkok's Northern Bus Terminal. The bus ride actually takes less time than the train. The bus station is 3 km (2 mi) out of town—take a samlor into the city—but you can book your ticket at the bus companies' offices in town.

Getting Around   Horse-drawn carriages are available for tourists. The carriage rank is outside the government house, although some carriages are usually waiting for tourists at the train station. The price for a 15-minute tour of central Lam Pang is B30. The hourly rate is approximately B100. The easiest and least expensive way to get around, however, is by samlor.

Exploring   Despite its rush into the 20th century, Lam Pang has some notable Burmese architecture remaining. Opposite the Thai International Airways office is **Wat Phra Fang,** easily recognizable by the green corrugated-iron roof on the viharn and the tall white chedi, decorated with gold leaf, at the top. Surrounding the chedi are seven small chapels, one for each day of the week. Inside each chapel is a niche with images of the Lord Buddha.

The next stop is **Wat Sri Chum,** a well-preserved example of Burmese architecture. Pay particular attention to the viharn: The roof eaves have beautiful carvings, and its doors and windows have elaborate decorations. Inside, gold-and-black lacquered pillars support a carved-wood ceiling, and to the right is a bronze Buddha cast in the Burmese style. Red-and-gold panels on the walls depict country temple scenes.

To the north of town, on the right bank of the River Wang, is **Wat Phra Kaeo Don Tao.** The dominating visual element here is the tall chedi, built on a rectangular base and topped with a rounded spire. Two buildings of more interest, however, are the Burmese-style shrine and the adjacent Thai-style *sala* (assembly hall). The 18th-century shrine has a multitier roof rising to a point; inside are masterfully carved walls with colored-stone inlays, and an ornately engraved ceiling inlaid with enamel. The Thai sala next door has the traditional three-tier roof and carved-wood pediments, which house a Sukhothaistyle reclining Buddha. Legend suggests that the sala was also home to the famous Emerald Buddha (Phra Keo). In 1436, King Sam Fang Kaem was transporting the statue from Chiang Rai to Chiang Mai; when his elephant reached Lam Pang, it refused to go any farther. The statue remained in Lam Pang for the next 32 years until the succeeding king managed to bring it into Chiang Mai.

Farther along the road toward Chiang Mai is **Wat Chedi Sao,** a charming, peaceful monastery named after its 20 small white chedis. It's only worth coming here if you are driving to Chiang Mai or you want a tranquil rural escape.

South of Lam Pang is **Wat Phra That Lampang Luang,** one of the most venerated temples in the north. You'll spot the chedi towering above the trees, but it is the viharn to the left that is most memorable. The carved-wood facade and two-tier roof complement the harmonious proportions of the structure. The intricate decorations around the porticoes are the painstaking work of Thai artisans. The temple compound was once part of a fortified city, which has long since disappeared. Originally founded in the 8th century by the legendary Princess Chama Dewi of Lopburi, the city was destroyed about 200 years ago when the Burmese occupied the city and monastery. Inside the temple museum are excellent wood carvings, but the most revered treasure is a small emerald Buddha, which some claim was carved from the same stone as its counterpart in Bangkok's Royal Palace. *Admission charge. Open 9–4, closed Mon.*

Shopping　Lam Pang is known for its blue-and-white pottery. You'll find shops selling the pottery in the city center, or you can visit any of the 60 factories located throughout Lam Pang. A store with a good selection of ceramics is **Ku Ceramic** (167 Mu 6, Phahonyothin Rd., tel. 054/218–313). Generally, a samlor driver will be happy to take you to these factories for a few baht, hoping you'll give him a commission on what you buy. These goods are sold in Bangkok and Chiang Mai with hefty markups; so do your shopping here.

Dining and　While Lam Pang has lost some of its quaint charm, the city's wats,
Lodging　shops, and few old-style Thai wooden houses are sufficiently pleasant that you may wish to spend the night. Hotels in Lam Pang are the best that you will find between Chiang Mai and Phitsanulok. Your best bet for Western food is at the **Thip Chang** hotel, but for Thai food, the open-sided restaurant on the main street across from the access road to the Thip Chang hotel has an excellent range of dishes. Football fans gather here to dine and drink the evening away while watching international matches on the half dozen television sets suspended from the ceiling. For a formal Thai meal, take a samlor to the popular **Si Wang** (Paholyothin Rd., tel. 054/226–766), a northern-Thai-style house where locals gather to dine in the many small, heavily timbered dining rooms. The price for two is approximately B600. MasterCard is accepted.

Thip Chang. This is the most comfortable hotel in Lam Pang; most rooms have two double beds, a coffee table, and a couple of chairs. Rooms are kept clean, though the furnishings are basic. The hotel boasts the only swimming pool in town. A few of the staff members speak some English. The coffee shop stays open until 1 AM, and the restaurant serves respectable Western, Thai, and Chinese food. Call ahead for reservations; it is sometimes fully booked by tour groups. *54/22 Thakraw Noi Rd., Amphoe Muang, Lam Pang 52000, tel. 054/ 226–501, fax 054/225–362. 120 rooms. Facilities: restaurant, coffee shop, bar, pool. AE, MC. $*
No 4 Guest House is in an old Thai-style teak house with a garden. The friendly owner teaches English at the local school. *54 Pamai Rd., Vieng Nuea, Lam Pang, no phone. 25 rooms. Facilities: Breakfast room. No credit cards. ¢*

Don Inthanon　The turnoff for the park is 57 km (36 mi) north of Chiang Mai. From
National Park　that point, you can either drive the steep, 48-km (30-mi) toll road to the top or rent a minibus from Chom Thong, beyond the park's turnoff. It's a good idea to rent a minibus if you wish to see the Mae Ya waterfall, because the road there, consisting of 12 km (7½ mi) of un-

paved tracks, can be impassable. An easier waterfall to reach is Mae Klang, which has three tiers of falls. The turnoff for Mae Klang is 6 km (3½ mi) after the entrance to the park.

Mae Hong Son

West of Chiang Mai, just inside the Burmese (Myanmar) border, this sleepy market town where villagers trade vegetables and wares is like the Chiang Mai of 30 years ago, but it is developing fast. Already it has two comfortable hotels, several small resorts, and at least a dozen guest houses. Aside from the lush countryside, waterfalls, and caves, the tourist lure is visiting hill-tribe villages, especially that of the Karen Long Necks.

Getting There
By Plane

Thai International (in Bangkok, tel. 02/513–0121 or 02/234–3100) has two flights a day between Chiang Mai and Mae Hong Son. They tend to be fully booked, so make reservations in advance. The cost is amazingly low—B345 one way. Bangkok Airways has a direct daily flight between Bangkok and Mae Hong Son for B2180. The airport is within walking distance of town, though a tuk-tuk costs only B10.

By Bus

An express bus leaves Chiang Mai Arcade Bus Station (tel. 053/242–664) in the morning, and the trip takes eight hours and costs B175. On the return trip from Mae Hong Son, you could disembark from the bus at Mae Taeng and connect with the bus from Chiang Mai that goes to Fang and Tha Thon (the village where boats leave for the river trip to Chiang Rai; *see* Chiang Rai and the Golden Triangle, Arriving and Departing, *below*).

By Car

You can rent a car and drive from Chiang Mai, but unless you hire a driver to return the car, you're forced to make the eight-hour drive twice. The road has arm-wrenching bends but is also very scenic; the shortest and best route is the northern route through Mae Thaeng and Hual Nam Dang. The southern route, Highway 106, through Mae Sariang and Khun Tuan, while easier driving, can take 12 hours.

Getting Around

The actual town of Mae Hong Son is very small; everything is within walking distance, though you may need a tuk-tuk or taxi to take you into town from your hotel. It is usual to take trips to the outlying villages and sights with a guide and chauffeured car. Should you hire a jeep on your own, be sure that its four-wheel drive is in working order. Less expensive, if you want to explore on your own, are motorbikes, which can be rented from one of the shops along the town's main street. Be careful: The main roads have gravel patches, the side roads are rutted, and in the rainy season, you must also contend with mud. The **Thai Tourist Police** has an office at Rajadrama Phithak Rd., tel. 053/611–812.

Exploring

Photographs and postcards of the Karen Long Necks (also called Padong), whose women wear copper bands around their necks, making them exceptionally long, are often used as bait for visits to northern Thailand, but most of the Karen Long Necks are in Myanmar—an estimated 3,000 families. In Thailand, there are only two villages, both outside Mae Hong Son, with a total of 22 Long Neck families, all of whom are accustomed to posing for photographs. There is a B300 fee for entering the village; half of the tax goes to the village, the other half to the local warlord, who uses the money to fund his army.

The easiest village to reach is the one with six families, upriver from Mae Hong Son beyond the village of Nam Pieng Din. By arrangements made through your hotel or a local guide, you travel by boat, with a guide, for the 90-minute trip. Long Neck Karens have a legend that the tribe's first ancestors were descended from the god of wind and a female dragon, and it is thought that the women extend their necks to imitate the dragon. Perhaps it is more true that the copper bands are a sign of wealth. The girls start to wear bands at six, adding another every three years until they are 21. They are never removed, even after death, except for cleaning and in the case of adultery, when the woman's relatives will forcibly take off the bands.

Visiting the other Long Neck village requires a two-hour four-wheel-drive journey to Nai Soi, a Shan village, followed by a 30-minute hike (or a shortcut by motorbike, over a rough trail and a swinging bridge, but only if you are an experienced rider traveling with a guide). You can also continue farther upstream to the Burmese border, but there is little to see except for the jungle.

Aside from the Karen Long Necks, the Shans, Lanna Thais, Karens, and Hmongs (Meo) have villages within a three-hour drive of Mae Hong Son, which are usually visited on guided treks of three or more days. You can leave the choice of village up to the guide—each has his favorites—but you'll need to ascertain whether he speaks the village language and discuss fully with him what is planned and how strenuous the trek is. Since guides come and go, and villages tend to change in their attitude toward foreigners, what is written today is out of date tomorrow. However, one young Shan guide, Robert, speaks English well and knows the trails along the border and up in the north. You can find him at Jean's Guest House (6 Prachautith Rd., tel. 053/611–662), or if he is not there, Jean should be able to recommend another knowledgeable guide.

Mae Hong Son is a serene rural retreat, whose name means "province of the three mists," and it seems as if the outside world does not exist. Tourists usually spend a night, two at the most, here, though a few foreign travelers have embraced the gentle pace and stayed in the region a month or more. If you take a 15-minute walk up the winding stepped path to the top of Doi Kong Mu, Mae Hong Son's highest hill, you will be rewarded first by restful views as you sit in the small shaded pavilion, then by the marvelously varied structures of Wat Phra That Doi Kong Mu, a gleaming white temple inhabited by wonderful white plaster demons with gaping scarlet mouths. A kiosk sells bottled water and film. In town, after you stroll around the lake and look at the two temples, there is little to do but have coffee or eat at one of the restaurants on the main street and observe daily life. A few stores sell hill-tribe jewelry and textiles, but the merchandise is more of the souvenir variety than art. (Art objects are bought by dealers directly from the villages and shipped to Chiang Mai or Bangkok.) In the morning, the local market has a colorful array of fruits, vegetables, and people.

Dining and Lodging

Holiday Inn. This international-style hotel, about 1½ km (1 mi) out of town off the main road to Khun Yuam, bustles with tour groups coming and going; activity focuses around the pool in the daytime, and in the disco at night. Rooms are standard Holiday Inn variety, but clean and well maintained. Many of the staff speak English—the general manager is English. The hotel has its own travel desk and tour guides. *114/5–7 Khumlunprapas Rd., Mae Hong Son 58000, tel. 053/611–390, fax 053/611–524. 144 rooms. Facilities: restaurant (mostly Western fare), pool, disco, river and hill-tribe tours. AE, DC, MC, V. $$*

★ **Tara Mae Hong Son.** This Thai-inspired hotel, owned by the same family who has the Imperial Hotel in Bangkok, is slightly less expen-

sive than the Holiday Inn. The northern Thai architecture, with a
large lobby reception area and huge open porches, gives it an airy
feeling. The restaurant, which serves good Thai food—both northern and Bangkok—has a glassed-in section for chilly mornings and
evenings. It faces the lush terraced valley, as does the beautifully
landscaped pool. Rooms have either two queen-size or one king-size
bed. The decor emphasizes wood with highly polished floors and
bamboo chairs and tables. The service is enthusiastic and helpful.
The hotel is 3 km (2 mi) out of town, slightly beyond the Holiday Inn.
*149 Moo 8 Tambon Peng Moo, Amphur Muang, Mae Hong Son
58000, tel. 053/611–473, fax 053/611–252; in Bangkok, tel. 02/254–
0023. 104 rooms. Facilities: restaurant, pool, river and hill-tribe
tours. AE, DC, MC, V. $$*

Dining **Kai-Mook,** just off the main street, is the best restaurant for alfresco
dining and excellent northern Thai cooking. Of the 10 or so restau-
rants along this street, Kai-Mook has the freshest and tastiest food.
*71 Khunlumpraphas, tel. 053/612–092. No reservations. Dress: ca-
sual. No credit cards. $*

There are also several rustic resort hotels: the **Mae Hong Son Resort**
(24 Bang Huay Dua, tel. 053/611–404, fax 053/611–504 or, in Chiang
Mai, tel. 053/251–217) has 40 rooms, some air-conditioned and some
fan-cooled, at B900 a night, and the **Rim Nam Klang Doi** (Ban Huay
Dua, tel. 053/612–142, fax 053/612–066), on the river, has 24 small
fan-cooled rooms at B450 and 10 larger, air-conditioned bungalows
at B650 a night. Both are approximately 5 km (3 mi) out of town. The
most comfortable guest house is the **Piya Guest House** (Kulum
Prapat, Mae Hong Son, tel. 053/611–260), which is peacefully situ-
ated facing a small lake, and has 11 rooms, at B200 (fan cooled) and
B300 (air-conditioned).

Chiang Rai and the Golden Triangle

**Tourist
Information** The **Tourist Authority of Thailand** (TAT) in Chiang Mai handles the
region, but Chiang Rai also has a small **Tourist Information Center**
(Singhakhlai Rd., tel. 053/711–433), which has a good supply of local
maps and gives helpful advice on which surrounding areas to ex-
plore. You should confirm your outbound flight with the **Thai Air-
ways International** office (tel. 053/711–464).

Emergencies The local police (tel. 053/711–444) provide assistance to visitors. For
medical services, call either the **Chiang Rai Hospital** (tel. 053/711–
300) or the **Over Brook Hospital** (tel. 053/711–366).

**Arriving and
Departing
*By Plane*** **Thai Airways International** offers two nonstop flights daily into
Chiang Rai from Bangkok (B1,820) and two direct flights from
Chiang Mai (B230). Taxis meet incoming flights, but most tourist
hotels have their own shuttle vans waiting for guests.

By Bus Buses run throughout the day from Chiang Mai to Chiang Rai, de-
parting from the Chiang Mai Arcade Bus Station (tel. 053/242–664).
The express bus takes 2½ hours and costs about B80, while the local
bus takes 3½ hours and is even cheaper.

***By Bus
and Boat*** The most exciting way to reach Chiang Rai is via a combination bus
and boat trip. Passengers depart from Chiang Mai at 6:30 AM for a
four-hour trip on a local bus to Tha Ton, north of Fang. An alternative
to the bus is to hire a car and driver for about B1,200 and have him pick
you up from your Chiang Mai hotel at 8 AM. In Tha Thon, take lunch at
the restaurant opposite the landing stage. Long-tailed boats depart at
12:30 PM. Purchase your passage beforehand at the kiosk. These public
boats hold 10 passengers, and the fare is B160 per person. You may hire

your own personal boat for B1,600, something you will have to do if you arrive after 12:30 PM. The trip down the Mae Kok River to Chiang Rai takes five hours and passes through rapids and by a few hill-tribe villages. Bringing bottled water and a sun hat is recommended. The more adventurous visitors can travel to Chiang Rai by unmotorized raft. These raft trips are best taken during October and November, when the water flows quickly; participants stay overnight in small villages on the three-day journey.

Getting Around

Taxis and bicycle samlors are always available in Chiang Rai and in the surrounding small towns. Buses depart frequently for nearby towns (every 15 minutes to Chiang Saen or to Mae Dai, for example), or you can commission a taxi for the day.

Guided Tours

The four major hotels in Chiang Rai (*see* Dining and Lodging, *below*) and the Golden Triangle Resort in Chiang Saen organize minibus tours of the area. Their travel desks will also arrange treks to the hill-tribe villages with a guide. Should you prefer to deal directly with a tour/travel agency, try **Golden Triangle Tours** (590 Phahotyothin Rd., Chiang Rai 57000, tel. 053/711–339).

Exploring

King Mengrai, who founded the Lammu kingdom, built his capital in Chiang Rai in 1256. According to legend, a runaway royal elephant stopped to rest on the banks of the Mae Kok River. Believing the elephant's actions to be auspicious, King Mengrai built his capital where the elephant stopped. In the 15th century the area was overrun by the Burmese, and the Thais were unable to recover the region until 1786. Architecturally, little can be said for this city of two-story concrete buildings. Most of the city's famous old structures are gone: Wat Phra Keo once housed the Emerald Buddha that is now in Bangkok's Royal Palace, and a precious Theravada Buddha image in the 15th-century Wat Phra Singh has long since disappeared. Today, Chiang Rai is a market town that works during the day and is fast asleep by 10 PM. Chiang Rai's raison d'être is as a base for exploring. The Akha, Yao, Meo, Lisu, Lahu, and Karen tribes all live within Chiang Rai province. Each tribe has a different dialect, different customs, handicrafts, costumes, and a different way of venerating animist spirits. Only in the past two decades have the tribes been confronted with 20th-century internationalism and tourism. Now, the villages are learning to produce their handicrafts commercially for eager buyers in exchange for blue jeans and other commodities. Visits to these villages can be done as day trips or as two- to five-day treks to more remote villages. A guide is necessary for these treks. It's important to pick a guide who's familiar with the languages spoken in the villages and who knows which villages are least frequented by tourists. Question a guide thoroughly about his experience before you sign up.

Remarkable for its natural beauty and friendly inhabitants, the Golden Triangle is relatively easy to explore on your own. The following itinerary passes from Chiang Rai to Chiang Saen and up to the focal point of the Golden Triangle, Bop Sop Ruak. Then, following the Burmese border, the route continues to Mae Sai and back to Chiang Rai. You can travel either by hired taxi or public bus, though many people rent Jeeps or motorbikes.

An hour outside Chiang Rai, on the banks of the Mae Khong River, is **Chiang Saen.** Buses from Chiang Rai depart every 30 minutes, or you can take a taxi. Chiang Saen is only a small, one-street town, but in the 12th century, it was home to the future King Mengrai. Only fragments of the ancient ramparts destroyed by the Burmese who dominated northern Thailand after 1588 survived. The remainder was ravaged by fire in 1786, when the Thai army ousted the last Burmese intruders.

Only two ancient chedis are standing. Just outside the city walls is Chiang Saen's oldest chedi, **Wat Pa Sak.** Its name (*sak* means teak) reflects the fact that 300 teak trunks were used to build the structure. The stepped pyramid, which narrows to a spire, is said to enshrine holy relics brought here when the city was founded. Inside the city walls is an imposing octagonal 14th-century chedi, **Wat Luang.** Next door, the **National Museum** houses artifacts from the Lamma period (Chiang Saen style), as well as some archaeological finds dating to Neolithic times. The museum also has a good collection of carvings and traditional handicrafts from the hill tribes, and Burmese lacquerware. *Admission charge. Open Wed.–Sun. 9–4.*

Continuing past the museum, the road comes to the Mae Khong River. If you turn right onto the recently paved road and drive 57 km (35 mi) you'll reach the town of **Chiang Khong.** On the way, there are magnificent views of the Mae Khong. Not too many tourists make the journey to these villages, and the tribes—Hmong and Yao—seem less affected by visitors. Across the river is the Laotian town of Ban Houie Sai, from which beautiful antique Lao textiles and silver jewelry are smuggled to Thailand. After a long period of border confrontation, Laos opened the country to Western tourists (with the appropriate visa), but they are only permitted to cross the Mae Khong at Nong Khai, opposite Vientiane. Only locals are permitted to cross over to Ban Houie Sai; they bring back tiger skins and deer antlers in exchange for salt, sugar, and soap. From Chiang Khong, the road is paved back to Chiang Rai. Once the Chiang Khong-Chiang Saen road is surfaced, you may want to drive directly to Chiang Khong from Chiang Rai and then to Chiang Saen. The wild, rugged, and beautiful scenery following the Mae Khong north from Chiang Khong is, in fact, more dramatic than that around the Golden Triangle.

A left turn at the T junction in Chiang Saen leads 8 km (5 mi) to **Bop Sop Ruak,** the village in the heart of the Golden Triangle where the opium warlord Khun Sa ruled. A decade ago, Thai troops forced him back to Burmese territory, but visitors still flock here to see this notorious region. Now the village street is lined with souvenir stalls to lure tourists from their buses. Worse yet, on a small island in the river, a casino is being built.

Some of the best views over the confluence of the Mae Ruak and Mae Khong rivers, and into the lush hills of Myanmar and Laos, are from the new **Golden Triangle Resort Hotel.** Even if you are not staying at the hotel, visit to check out the view. Another good viewing point is the pavilion along the path leading from behind the police station.

From Bop Sop Ruak, take a minibus—or your car or motorbike— to **Mae Sai,** 60 km (37 mi) west along the Mae Ruak River (its name changes to the Mae Sai). The road is semipaved, dusty, and easy to travel. Mae Sai is a border market town where merchants trade goods with the Burmese from Tha Kee Lek village, on the other side of the river. Visitors need a one-day visa, which is obtainable at the bridge for $10. You can also obtain a seven-week visa for $30 if you wish to travel north to Kengtung. The trip on the unpaved road (163 km/101 mi) takes four to five hours in the dry season and up to eight from June through November. At press time visitors were not permitted to go farther into Myanmar. Kengtung is a quaint town with British colonial structures still remaining alongside the old Buddhist temples. Thais take across household goods and consumer products, and the Burmese bring sandalwood, crafts, raw jade, and rubies. Though you may want to put a foot into Myanmar, the prices and quality of the goods will not be better than in Mae Sai, where prices are better than in Chiang Mai. A good store is **Mengrai Antique** (tel. 053/731–423), located close to the bridge. On the east side of Phaholyothim Road, opposite the Tourist Police, is the **Thong Tavee Jade** factory. If you are in Mae Sai during December or January, be sure to try the area's famous strawberries.

Time Out   To the side of the bridge, the **River Side Restaurant** (tel. 053/731–207) has an open terrace above the Mae Sai that overlooks Myanmar. The Thai food is good, but you can also admire the view with just a Singha beer. Leave time to climb up to **Wat Phra That Doi**—the 207-step staircase starts from behind the Top North Hotel—for the best view.

From Mae Sai, it is a two-hour local bus ride back to Chiang Rai (B14), or you can take an air-conditioned express bus to Chiang Mai (via Chiang Rai) that takes about five hours. If you are traveling back by car or motorbike, drive 5 km (3 mi) from Mae Sai to the **Cheng Dao Cave Temple,** known for its Buddha carvings and monstrous stalactites. Farther up the dirt road is the **Monkey Temple,** where playful monkeys will snatch anything that sparkles with silver.

Back on the road toward Mae Chan and Chiang Mai, look for the right-hand turnoff for Highway 149, a steep, rough road that runs 17 km (11 mi) up to **Phra That Chedi** on Doi Tun, the highest peak in northern Thailand. En route, stop at the Akha Guest House to inquire about road conditions up to Doi Tun. The drive is awe-inspiring; at the summit, mist cloaks monks chanting at the temple, which was built in 911. If you don't feel like driving, you can arrange in Ban Hui Kai (farther down the road toward Mae Chan) for a car to take you.

Dining and   For Western food, stick to the luxury hotels; countless small restau-
Lodging   rants serve Thai food. The local staple is sticky rice, which you will inevitably eat if you stay in any of the hill-tribe villages. The luxury resort hotels are in Chiang Rai and in Chiang Saen (Bop Sop Ruak), and in Mae Sai, a new four-star hotel caters to tourists and businesspeople. Elsewhere, accommodations are in guest houses, usually separate thatched bungalows consisting of a small room (most without bath) and an eating area.

Chiang Rai   **Dusit Island Resort.** Of the three luxury hotels in Chiang Rai, the
★   Dusit Island has the most enviable location. Sitting on an island in the Kok river, which skirts the northern edge of town, the hotel offers guests quick access to town with all the space and amenities of a resort hotel. The 10-story building has three wings permitting all of the guest rooms to have a stunning view of the river. The spacious rooms, decorated in warm pastel colors and furnished in a modern rendition of traditional Thai, have bedside control panels, air-conditioning, and television. The large bathrooms are marble tiled. The corner Landmark suite No. 833 has the most dramatic views up and down the river. The high-ceilinged and spacious lobby/lounge/reception area enhances the hotel's appeal. The formal dining room offers Western cuisine and a panoramic view; a Chinese restaurant offers Cantonese food; and the Cattleya Garden, where a buffet breakfast is served, has Thai and Continental food throughout the day. If you are arriving in Chiang Rai by river, you can have the boatman drop you off at the hotel's pier. *1129 Kraisorasit Rd., Amphur Muang,*

Chiang Rai 57000, tel. 053/715–777, fax 053/715–801; Bangkok reservations, tel. 02/238–4790. 271 rooms. Facilities: 3 restaurants, bar, nightclub, in-room safes, fitness center, pool, games room, shops, Avis car rentals, airport shuttle service, and banquet facilities. AE, DC, MC, V. $$$

Little Duck Hotel. The first luxury resort in Chiang Rai, this hotel screams modernity. Guests, often salespeople on an incentive trip, mill around the huge lobby among the imitation marble pieces, far removed from the world outside. The rooms are bright and cheery, with light-wood fixtures and large beds. Service is brisk and smart, and the travel desk is ready to organize excursions into the neighboring hills. *450 Super Highway Rd., Amphoe, Muang, Chiang Rai 57000, tel. 053/715–620, fax 053/712–639; Bangkok reservations, tel. 02/255–5960. 350 rooms. Facilities: 2 restaurants, 24-hr coffee shop, pool, tennis, travel desk, meeting and banquet rooms. AE, DC, MC, V. $$$*

Rimkok Resort. This hotel opened in early 1991 and has extensive grounds. Because of its location, across the Mae Kok river from Chiang Rai and a 10-minute drive from town, the hotel has more appeal for tour groups than for the independent traveler. The main building is designed in modern Thai style with palatial dimensions—a long, wide lobby lined with boutiques leads to a spacious lounge and dining area. Guest rooms are in wings on both sides of the main building. Rooms have twin or double beds on one side, a table/desk on the other, and a picture window at the far end. *6 Moo 4 Chiang Rai Tathorn Rd., Rimkok Muang, Chiang Rai 57000, tel. 053/716–445, fax 053/715–859; Bangkok reservations, tel. 02/279–0102. 248 rooms. Facilities: 4 restaurants, bar, pool, shops, car rental, and banquet facilities. AE, DC, MC, V. $$–$$$*

Wiang Inn. In the heart of town, this comfortable, well-established hotel features a small outdoor pool, a pleasant sitting area, and a restaurant. Spacious bedrooms, now slightly worn, made this the top hotel in Chiang Rai until the two resort hotels opened; it is still the best hotel within the town itself. *893 Phaholyothin Rd., Chiang Rai 57000, tel. 053/711–543, fax 053/711–877. 260 rooms. Facilities: restaurant with Chinese, Thai, and Western food; pool; nightclub; health club; travel desk. AE, DC, V. $$–$$$*

Golden Triangle Inn. Don't confuse this hotel with the resort at Bop Sop Ruak. This guest house is a backpackers' base for trips into the hills. Rooms have private bathrooms and are either air-conditioned or fan-cooled. The restaurant/lounge offers Thai and Western fare. The owners arrange trips to Chiang Klong, where they have another guest house. *590 Phaholyothin Rd., Chiang Rai 57000, tel. 053/711–339, fax 053/713–363. 20 rooms. No credit cards. ¢*

Chiang Saen **Baan Boran Hotel.** ★ The newest entry in the Golden Triangle is this distinctive resort hotel (now managed by the Meridien group), located off the Mae Sai road 3 km (2 mi) out of Chiang Saen. Situated on a hill, the hotel has panoramic views over the confluence of the Ruak and Mae Khong rivers and beyond into Laos. All the guest rooms share the view, and feature rust-red fabrics and carpet, a corner table/desk, a couch, a coffee table, and a picture window opening onto a balcony. Bedside panels control the television and lights. The central building houses the Yuan Lue Lao restaurant serving Thai and Western fare. For more serious dining, the Suan Fin offers elaborate Thai and European dishes. A lounge and cocktail bar are the evening meeting venues. *Chiang Saen, Chiang Rai 57150, tel. 053/784–078, fax 053/716–702; Bangkok reservations, tel. 02/251–4707. 106 rooms. Facilities: 3 restaurants, bar, in-room safes, pool, tour* desk, car hire, airport shuttle, and banquet facilities. AE, DC, MC, V. $$$

★ **Delta Golden Triangle Resort Hotel.** The views of the forested hills across the rivers are splendid from this resort, located on a rise at the outskirts of Bop Sop Ruak. The architecture is northern Thai, utilizing plenty of wood throughout. The superior (termed "executive") rooms have private balconies overlooking the Golden Triangle, third-floor rooms have the best view. The hotel also has an elegant dining room called the Border View, but it's more fun sitting out on the deck, sipping Mekong whiskey and imagining the intrigues in the villages across the border. Classical Thai dances are performed in the evening. *222 Baan Sobruak, Chiang Saen, Chiang Rai, tel. 053/784–001, fax 053/784–006; Bangkok reservations, tel. 02/512–0392, fax 02/512–0393. 74 rooms. Facilities: 2 restaurants, evening entertainment, pool, tennis, travel/tour desk. AE, DC, MC, V. $$–$$$*

Chiang Saen Guest House. One of several guest houses in Chaen Saen and Bop Sop Ruak, the Chiang Saen was among the first on the scene and is still a gathering point for travelers. Rooms are clean and simple, and guests can eat and socialize in the dining room. The owner is well-informed on trips in the area and is always eager to help. *45 Tambon Wiang, Amphoe Chiang Saen, Chiang Rai 57150, tel. 053/791–242. 18 rooms. No credit cards. ¢*

Mae Sai **Wang Thong.** Cashing in on the relaxing of trade restrictions with Myanmar, this new hotel on the banks of the Mae Sai opened in 1993. Choose a guest room on the river side, and you can spend the day idly watching the flowing waters and the flowing pedestrian traffic across the bridge. The hotel is designed for upmarket business travelers and tourists staying overnight. Its rectangular rooms are modern and functional, and though the restaurant offers no more than average fare, it has Western dishes as well as Thai and Chinese. *299 Paholyotin Rd., Mae Sai, Chiang Rai, tel. 053/733–248, fax 053/733–399. 148 rooms. Facilities: restaurant, coffee shop, pool. MC, V. $$*

Mae Sai Guest House. This is ranked by backpackers as the best guest house in Mae Sai. On the river, 1 km (½ mi) west of the bridge, the guest house offers clean bungalows and some river views. A small garden area surrounds the bungalows, and a casual dining area is located in the office building. *688 Wiengpangkam, Mae Sai, Chiang Rai, tel. 053/732–021. 20 cottages. No credit cards. ¢*

Northern Guest House. When the Mae Sai Guest House is full, this is a good second choice. Located on the way back to town from the Mae Sai, the guest house offers small (there's just enough room for a bed) but clean rooms. A few cottages have their own shower and toilet. The veranda-style dining room is pleasant in the evenings, and the Mae Sai flows at the edge of the garden. The owner of the guest house is always eager to please. *402 Tumphajom Rd., Mae Sai, Chiang Rai, tel. 053/731–537. 26 cottages, a few with bath. Facilities: dining room. No credit cards. ¢*

The Central Plains and I-San

While Bangkok is the economic heart of Thailand, and the south its playground, the soul of Thailand may be said to live in the vast central area that stretches from the Myanmar border to Cambodia. Here are the rice fields, worked by farmers and water buffalo, who toil in the age-old way. In the western part of this region, at Sukhothai, Thailand's first kingdom was established, when the

Khmer empire was defeated. The eastern part, known as the I-San, close to Cambodia and the Khmer capital of Angkor Wat, was slower in being absorbed into the new Thai nation. With its many Khmer ruins it represents a different aspect of Thailand, strongly influenced by the culture of the land that is now Laos.

The shift of power, first to Ayutthaya and then to Bangkok, left both the western and eastern regions of this central area to become rural backwaters. Modern international hotels are few and far between, yet some of Thailand's most fascinating historic sites are here. Sukhothai takes first place, since it was the nation's first capital, but there are other architectural treasures that span half a millennium of Thai history.

Phitsanulok and Sukhothai

For a brief span, **Phitsanulok** was the capital of Siam after the decline of Sukhothai and before the consolidation of the royal court at Ayutthaya in the 14th century. Further back in history, before the Kwae Noi River changed its course, Phitsanulok was a Khmer outpost called Song Kwae—now only an ancient monastery remains. The new Phitsanulok, which had to relocate 5 km (3 mi) from the old site, is a modern provincial administrative seat with few architectural blessings. Two outstanding attractions, however, merit a visit: Phra Buddha Chinnarat and the Pim Buranaket Folklore Museum. Phitsanulok is also the closest city with modern amenities and communications to Sukhothai—Siam's first royal capital—making the city a good base for exploring the region.

An hour from Phitsanulok by car, **Sukhothai** has a unique place in Thailand's history. Until the 13th century, most of Thailand consisted of many small vassal states under the suzerainty of the Khmer Empire in Angkor Wat. But the Khmers had overextended their resources, allowing the princes of two Thai states to combine forces against their overlords. In 1238, one of the two princes, Phor Khun Bang Klang Thao, marched on Sukhothai, defeated the Khmer garrison commander in an elephant duel, and captured the city. Installed as the new king of the region, he took the name Sri Indraditya, founding a dynasty that ruled Sukhothai for nearly 150 years. His youngest son became the third king of Sukhothai, Ram Khamhaeng, who ruled from 1279 to 1299 (or possibly until 1316). Through military and diplomatic victories, he expanded the kingdom to include most of present-day Thailand as well as the Malay peninsula.

The Sukhothai period was relatively brief—a series of only eight kings—but it witnessed lasting accomplishments. The Thais gained their independence, which has been maintained to the present day despite the empire-building of Western powers. King Ram Khamhaeng formulated the Thai alphabet by adapting the Khmer script to suit the Thai tonal language. And, first under the patronage of Ram Khamhaeng and later under his successor, King Lö Thai, Theravada Buddhism was established and became the dominant national religion. In addition, toward the end of the Sukhothai dynasty, a distinctive Thai art tradition grew up that was so wonderful the period is known as Thailand's Golden Age of Art.

By the mid-14th century, Sukhothai's power and influence had waned, permitting its dynamic vassal state of Ayutthaya to become the capital of the Thai kingdom. Sukhothai was gradually abandoned to the jungle, and a new town of Sukhothai was founded 10 km

(6 mi) away. In 1978, a 10-year restoration project costing more than $10 million saw the creation of the Sukhothai Historic Park.

Tourist Information The **TAT office** has useful brochures, including one describing a walking tour. The office is also responsible for tourist information on Sukhothai. *209/7–8 Boromtrailokanat Rd., Amphoe Muang, Phitsanulok 65000, tel. 055/252–742. Open weekdays 9–4:30.* The **Chinawat Hotel** in the center of New Sukhothai (tel. 055/611–385). It has a travel and tour desk.

Emergencies Phitsanulok doesn't have a Tourist Police office, but the local police (tel. 055/240–199) are helpful in an emergency. For medical attention, try the **Phitsanuwej Hospital** (Khun Piren Rd., tel. 055/252–762). There is no Tourist Police, but the local police (tel. 055/611–199) are accustomed to helping foreigners. For medical emergencies, contact the **Sukhothai Hospital** (tel. 055/611–782).

Arriving and Departing With three direct flights each day, **Thai Airways International** connects Phitsanulok with Bangkok (B920) and Chiang Mai (B650). Taxis meet incoming flights.

Phitsanulok

Phitsanulok is about halfway between Bangkok and Chiang Mai. Rapid express trains take approximately six hours from either city. Some trains between Bangkok and Phitsanulok stop at Lopburi and Ayutthaya, enabling you to visit these two historic cities en route. A special express train between Bangkok and Phitsanulok takes just over five hours. Tickets for this service, which cost 50% more than those for regular second-class travel, may be purchased at a separate booth inside the Bangkok and Phitsanulok stations; reservations are essential.

Buses run frequently to Phitsanulok from Chiang Mai, Bangkok, and Sukhothai. Bus service also connects Phitsanulok to eastern Thailand. Long-distance buses arrive and depart from the intercity bus terminal, 2 km (1¼ mi) northeast of town.

Sukhothai The closest airport and railway station to Sukhothai is at Phitsanulok, a 45-minute taxi ride or an hour's bus ride (B16) away. Taxis, which can be rented for the day for about B900, are available at the airport. By 1995 **Bangkok Airways** should be operating direct flights to Sukhothai from Bangkok.

Buses depart from Phitsanulok's intercity bus terminal, located on the northeast edge of town. The Sukhothai bus, however, makes a stop just before the Naresuan Bridge. These buses end their journey in New Sukhothai; you can take the minibus at the terminal to Old Sukhothai.

Buses also travel directly to Sukhothai from Chiang Mai's Arcade Bus Station (tel. 053/242–664); the trip takes five hours and costs B100. The bus trip from Bangkok's Northern Bus Terminal (tel. 02/279–4484) takes seven hours and costs B140.

Getting Around Most sights in Phitsanulok are within walking distance, but bicycle samlors are easily available. Bargain hard for a proper fare—most rides should cost between B10 and B20. Taxis are available for longer trips; you'll find a few loitering around the station.

Phitsanulok

Sukhothai Bicycle samlors are ideal for getting around New Sukhothai, but take either a taxi (B120) or a local bus (B5) to travel the 10 km (6 mi) from New Sukhothai to Old Sukhothai (Muang Kao) and the Historic Park. Buses depart from the local terminal, located 1 km (½ mi) on the other side of Prarong Bridge.

The best means of transportation around the Historic Park is a rented bicycle (B20 for the day). If you don't have much time, you can hire a taxi from New Sukhothai for B250 for a half day. The drivers know all the key sights. Within the park, a tourist tram takes visitors to the major attractions for B20.

Exploring *Phitsanulok* A major street runs from the railway station to the Kwae Noi River. The newer commercial and office area is found along this street and a little farther south, where the TAT office is located. North of this main street is the market and Phitsanulok's most treasured statue of the Lord Buddha. Phra Buddha Chinnarat sits in majesty at the Wat Phra Si Ratana temple, commonly known as **Wat Yai**.

Use a samlor to reach Wat Yai from the railway station or the major hotels, but pay no more than B15. The temple is close to the river, on the city side of Naresuan Bridge. Built in 1357, the temple has developed into a large monastery with typical Buddhist statuary and ornamentation. Particularly noteworthy are the viharn's wooden doors, inlaid with mother-of-pearl at the behest of King Boromkot in 1756. Behind the viharn is a 30-m (100-ft) *prang* (Khmer-style pagoda) that you can climb, though you cannot see the Buddha relics, supposedly resting in a vault.

All this is secondary, however, to what many claim is the world's most beautiful image of the Buddha, **Phra Buddha Chinnarat**. Cast during the late-Sukhothai period in the position of subduing evil, the statue was covered in gold plate by King Eka Thossarot in 1631. According to folklore, the king applied the gold with his own hands. The statue's grace and humility have an overpowering serenity. The black backdrop, decorated with gilded angels and flowers, further increases its strength. It's no wonder that so many copies of this serene Buddha image have been made, the best known of which resides in Bangkok's Marble Temple. The many religious souvenir stands surrounding the *bot* (main chapel) make it hard to gain a good view of the building itself, but the bot has a fine example of the traditional three-tier roof, with low sweeping eaves. This design has the effect of diminishing the size of the walls, accentuating the nave, and emphasizing the image of the Lord Buddha. *Admission free. Open daily 8–6.*

From Wat Yai, walk south along the river past numerous tempting food stalls lining the bank, particularly in the evening. On the far side of the bank are many houseboats, still popular among the Thais, who have an affinity for rivers and fish. The Naresuan Bridge crosses the river, but some Thais still paddle from one bank to another in sampan ferries. Two blocks after the post office and communications building—from which you can make overseas calls—is a small park. Turn left and the railway station is straight ahead.

Phitsanulok also has an unheralded museum that alone justifies a visit to the city. The **Pim Buranaket Folklore Museum** is about a 15-minute walk south of the railway station, on the east side of the tracks. Since the museum is not well known, here are the directions: Turn left at the traffic circle 50 yards in front of the railway station; go down this street (there's a pleasant coffee shop on the right-hand side) and make another left onto the first main road, about 500 yards farther on; cross the railway tracks and turn right at the first traffic light. The museum will be on your right, about 1 km (½ mi) down the road, but there is no sign and seldom any attendant, either. If no one is around, continue for 50 yards to a private house on your left, where Khun Thawee lives. His compound also contains the Burananthai Buddha Image Factory. Ask at the house to visit the folk museum, and you will be let in. In the early 1980s, Sergeant-Major Khun Thawee traveled to small Thai villages collecting traditional tools, cooking utensils, animal traps, and crafts that are rapidly disappearing. His consuming passion for the past is seen in the array of items he has crammed into a traditional Thai house and barn. Nothing has been properly documented, and so you stumble through a Thailand of tiger traps and cooking pots. Thawee is bashful; so encourage him to demonstrate the instruments. He loves to do so, especially the simple wood pipes used by hunters to lure their prey. *Donations requested. Open daily 9–5.*

Sukhothai *Numbers in the margin correspond to points of interest on the Old Sukhothai map.*

New Sukhothai, where all intercity buses arrive, is a small, quiet market town where most inhabitants are in bed by 11 PM. The old historic site of Sukhothai (*Sukhothai* means "the dawn of happiness") is vast—an area of 70 sq km (27 sq mi) with 193 historic monuments, though many of these are little more than clusters of stones. Only about 20 monuments can be classified as noteworthy, of which six have particular importance.

The bus will drop you on the main street, about 500 yards from the museum, just before the park entrance. You should start with the museum, but first you'll probably want to rent a bicycle from a store along the main street.

❶ Most of the significant pieces of Sukhothai art are in Bangkok's National Museum, but the **Ramkhamhaeng National Museum** has a sufficient sampling to demonstrate the gentle beauty of this period. The display of historic artifacts helps visitors form an image of Thailand's first capital city, and a relief map gives an idea of its geographic layout. *Admission charge. Open Wed.–Sun. 9–noon and 1–4.*

The restaurant across the street from the museum is your last chance for refreshment until you reach the food stalls at the center of the Historic Park. It's a good idea to take a bottle of water with you into the park—cycling in the sun is hot work. The park's main entrance is at the east end of the main street, and the terminus for the tourist tram is at this entrance. The admission ticket does not permit re-entry.

❷ For the modern Thai, Sukhothai represents the utopian state, in which man is free, land is plenty, and life is just. The magical and spiritual center of this utopia is **Wat Mahathat.** Sitting amid a tranquil lotus pond, Wat Mahathat is the largest and quite possibly the most beautiful monastery in Sukhothai. Enclosed in the compound are some 200 tightly packed chedis, each containing the funeral ashes of a nobleman. Towering above these minor chedis is a large central chedi, notable for its bulbous, lotus-bud prang. Around the chedi are friezes of 111 Buddhist disciples, hands raised in adoration, walking around the chedi's base. Though Wat Mahathat was probably built by Sukhothai's first king, Sri Indradita, it owes its present form to a 1345 remodeling by Sukhothai's fourth ruler, King Lö Thai. He erected the lotus-bulb chedi to house two important relics—the Hair Relic and the Neck Bone Relic—brought back from Ceylon by the monk Sisatta. Despite its Singhalese origins, the lotus-bulb chedi became the symbol of Sukhothai. Copies of it were made in the principal cities of its vassal states, signifying a magic circle emanating from Sukhothai, the spiritual and temporal center of the empire.

The image of Sukhothai's government is that of a monarchy that served the people, stressing social needs and justice. Slavery was abolished, and people were free to believe in their local religions, Hinduism and Buddhism (often simultaneously), and to pursue their trade without hindrance.

3 In the 19th century, the famous stone inscription of King Ram Khamhaeng was found among the ruins of the **Royal Palace** across from Wat Mahathat. Sometimes referred to as Thailand's Declaration of Independence, the inscription's best-known quote reads: "This Muang Sukhothai is good. In the water there are fish, in the field there is rice. The ruler does not levy tax on the people who travel along the road together, leading their oxen on the way to trade and riding their horses on the way to sell. Whoever wants to trade in elephants, so trades. Whoever wants to trade in horses, so trades." No other political platform appeals to the Thais as much as this one.

4 Possibly the oldest structure of Sukhothai is **Wat Sri Sawai.** The architectural style is Khmer, with three prangs—similar to those found in Lopburi—surrounded by a laterite wall. (Laterite, made from red porous soil that hardens when exposed to air, is the building material used most in Sukhothai.) The many stucco images of Hindu and Buddhist scenes suggest that Sri Sawai was probably first a Hindu temple, later converted to a Buddhist monastery, and Brahmanism probably played an important role throughout the Sukhothai period.

5 Another one of Sukhothai's noteworthy attractions is the striking and peaceful **Wat Sra Sri,** which sits on two connected islands encircled by a lotus-filled lake; the rolling, verdant mountains beyond add to the monastery's serenity. The lake, called Traphong Trakuan Pond, supplied the monks with water and served as a boundary for the sacred area. In classical Sukhothai style, a Singhalese chedi dominates six smaller chedis. A large, stucco, seated Buddha looks down a row of columns, past the chedis, and over the lake to the horizon. Even more wondrous is a walking Buddha by the Singhalese-style chedi. The walking Buddha is a Sukhothai innovation and the most ephemeral of Thailand's artistic styles. The depiction of Buddha is often a reflection of political authority and is modeled after the ruler. Under the Khmers, authority was hierarchical, but the kings of Sukhothai represented the ideals of serenity, happiness, and justice. The walking Buddha is the epitome of Sukhothai's art: Lord Buddha appears to be floating on air, neither rooted on this earth nor placed on a pedestal above the reach of the common people. Later, after Ayutthaya had succeeded as the kingdom's capital, statues of Buddha took on a sternness that characterized the new dynasty.

6 Just beyond the northern city walls is **Wat Phra Phai Luang,** second in importance to Wat Mahathat. This former Khmer Hindu shrine was also converted into a Buddhist temple. Surrounded by a moat, the sanctuary is encircled by three prangs, similar to those at Wat Sri Sawai. Only one of the laterite prangs has remained intact, decorated with stucco figures. In front of the prangs are the remains of the viharn and a crumbling chedi with a seated Buddha on its pedestal. Fronting these structures is the *mondop* (square structure with a stepped pyramid roof, built to house religious relics), once decorated with standing Buddha images in four different poses. Most of these are now too damaged to be recognizable; only the reclining Buddha still has a definite form.

7 The **Wat Si Chum,** southwest of Wat Phra Phai Luang, is worth visiting for its sheer size. Like other sanctuaries, it was originally surrounded by a moat serving as a perimeter to the mondop. The main sanctuary is dominated by Buddha in the posture of subduing Mara. The huge stucco image is one of the largest in Thailand, measuring 11¼ m (37 ft) from knee to knee. Enter the mondrop through the passage inside the left inner wall. Keep your eyes on the ceiling: More than 50 engraved slabs illustrate scenes from the *Jataka* (stories about the previous lives of Lord Buddha).

8 On the east side of the park, the most notable temple is **Wat Traphang Thong Lang.** The square mondop is the main sanctuary, the outer walls of which boast beautiful stucco figures in niches—some of Sukhothai's finest art. The north side depicts episodes of Buddha returning to preach to his wife; on the west side, Buddha is preaching to his father and relatives. Note the figures on the south wall, where the story of Buddha is accompanied by an angel descending from Tavatisma Heaven.

9 Also on the east side of the park is **Wat Chang Lom.** The Ceylonese-style bell-shaped chedi is raised on a square base atop now damaged elephant buttresses. A few of these elephant sculptures have been reconstructed to give visitors an idea of how impressive these supports looked. In front of the chedi is a viharn and solitary pillars; the remains of nine other chedis have been found within this complex.

Off the Beaten Track With its expanse of mown lawns, Sukhothai Historic Park is sometimes criticized for being too well groomed—even the ruins are neatly arranged. **Si Satchanalai,** 57 km (35 mi) north of Sukhothai, offers a complete contrast. Si Satchanalai may be reached either as part of a tour from Sukhothai—Chinawat Hotel offers a day minibus tour—or by local bus. Si Satchanalai was a sister city to Sukhothai, usually governed by a son of Sukhothai's reigning monarch. Its compactness makes it easier to explore than Sukhothai, and its setting on the right bank of the Mae Yom River adds to the site's attraction.

Dining and Lodging Neither Phitsanulok nor Sukhothai has smart restaurants, and so most travelers eat at their hotels. There are numerous cafés and food stalls in both towns; those around Naresuan Bridge in Phitsanulok are particularly tempting, and most items cost only a few baht. In New Sukhothai, across from the bus station, there are a number of good Thai restaurants. Sukhothai also has wonderful ice cream; the **Rainbow Cafe,** in particular, has delicious sundaes. For the best coffee in the province, visit the **Dream Coffee Shop** across from Sawat Phong Hotel on Singhawat Road.

Phitsanulok has a wider range of hotels than Sukhothai. Most travelers staying in Sukhothai more than one night prefer New Sukhothai to Muang Kao (Old Sukhothai) because it offers more evening entertainment. In Si Satchanalai, accommodations are available only at bungalow-type guest houses.

Phitsanulok **Amarin Nakhon.** If a central location is a priority, this is Phitsanulok's best offering. The hotel is a bit dark and worn, but the staff members are helpful and the rooms are clean. Rooms have two queen-size beds, leaving little space for other furniture. The coffee shop stays busy 24 hours a day, serving late-night customers from the hotel's basement disco. U.S. Army personnel use this hotel during visits to the Thai military base on the outskirts of town. *3/1 Chao Phraya Rd., Phitsanulok, tel. 055/258–588, fax 055/258–945. 130 rooms. Facilities: Chinese restaurant, coffee shop, disco. AE, DC, MC, V. $$*

★ **Rajapruk Hotel.** Of the two best hotels in town, this one is quieter and more refined, and has newer furnishings. The owner's wife is American, and many staff members speak a few English words. Guest rooms are decorated with wood and warm colors that accentuate the hotel's feeling of intimacy. The small restaurant off the lobby is good for dining and light meals; a formal restaurant serves Thai and Chinese food. The hotel's main drawback is its location, away from the town center on the east side of the railroad tracks. *99/9 Pha-Ong Dum Rd., Phitsanulok, tel. 055/258–477, fax 055/251–395; Bangkok reservations, tel. 02/251–4612. 110 rooms. Facilities: coffee shop; restaurant serving Thai, Chinese, and Western food; pool; nightclub; beauty salon; car-rental desk. AE, DC, MC, V. $$*

Sukhothai **Pailyn Sukhothai Hotel.** This modern building, opened in 1991, tries to incorporate Thai architecture, but the result is characterless. It is clean and efficiently run for the tour groups who stay here, but it is about 3 km (2 mi) from Old Sukhothai, with no place of interest in the vicinity. *Jarodvithithong, Sukhothai 64210, tel. 055/613–310, fax 055/613–317; Bangkok reservations, tel. 02/215–7110. 238 rooms. Facilities: 3 restaurants, pool, sauna, health club, shuttle bus. MC, V. $$*

Rajhanee Hotel. Just across the Yom River from the center of the new town, this modern hotel is Sukhothai's best. Rooms have twin beds and are furnished in drab greens and browns. Everything is clean, however. The staff speaks a little English, and the bar serves as an evening gathering spot. The dining room offers superior Chinese and Thai food. Western food is served in the coffee shop. *229 Charodwithithong Rd., Amphoe Muang, Sukhothai 64000, tel. 055/611–031, fax 055/612–878. 81 rooms. Facilities: restaurant, coffee shop, souvenir shop. MC, V. $$*

Thai Village House. This compound of thatched bungalows is usually fully booked with tour groups. Consequently, the staff is impersonal and unhelpful. The hotel's advantage is its location—a five-minute bicycle ride from the Historic Park. Guest rooms have two queen-size beds and little else except for private bathrooms. The open-air dining room is pleasantly relaxing when tour groups aren't around. *2/4 Jarodvithitong Rd., Muang Kao, Sukhothai 64000, tel. 055/611–049, fax 055/612–583. 45 rooms with bath. Facilities: restaurant, souvenir shops. MC, V. $$*

Chinawat Hotel. Steps away from the private bus terminal in the center of the new town, this glorified guest house goes the extra mile to help travelers see the region. (Tours to Si Satchanalai are offered.) The restaurant area includes a bake shop and serves Thai food with Western additions. The rooms are Spartan, small, and rather depressing, except for the air-conditioned ones in the newer block; they are clean, however. *1–3 Nikorn Kasem Rd., Sukhothai, tel. 055/611–385. 43 rooms, a few with private bath. Facilities: dining room, tours arranged. No credit cards. ¢*

No. 4 Guest House. In a small Thai home located down a narrow *soi* (lane) on the south side of the river, this guest house is run by a couple of friendly, helpful women. The wood floors and beams and the small garden add to the feeling that this could be your home away from home. No food is offered, but tea and coffee are always available. *234/6 Jarodwitheethong Rd. and Soi Panison, Sukhothai 64000, tel. 055/611–315. 14 rooms, a few with bath. No credit cards. ¢*

The Northeast

The sprawling northeast plateau known as I-San, is rarely visited by tourists. Comprising one-third of Thailand's land area, 17 provinces and four of the kingdom's most populous cities, the Northeast is also the least-developed area and the poorest. Life, for the most part, depends upon the fickleness of the monsoon rains; work is hard and scarce. For many, migration to Bangkok has been the only option. Most tuk tuk drivers in Bangkok are from I-San, and the bars of Patpong are filled with the daughters of I-San, sending their earnings back to their parents.

The people of the Northeast, burned by the scorching sun and weathered by the hard life, are straightforward and direct, passionate and obstinate. Their food is hot and spicy, their festivals are robust, and their regional language reflects their closeness to Laos. I-San has not yet been overrun by tourists. Its attractions are first, the Khmer ruins, which have only been partially restored; national parks; the Mae Khong river; and the traditional rural way of life. And while there are hotels in every town, and an efficient bus service reaches the smallest of hamlets, the accommodations are not deluxe and lack sophisticated amenities.

Travelers in Bangkok who are short on time may want to limit their travels to Nakhon Ratchasima (only four hours away by train), which can serve as a base for visiting nearby Khmer ruins at Phimae and Buri Ram and, perhaps, the Khao Yai National Park. Our itinerary begins in the far north at Nong Khai on the Mae Khong, then loops west via Loei and the national park, to Udon Thani, then back to the Mae Khong at Nakon Phanom. Then it roughly follows the Mae Khong south along the Laotian border to Ubon Ratchathani before turning west along the Mun River and the Kampuchean border through an area full of Khmer ruins. The itinerary ends in Nakhon Ratchasima.

Getting There All air traffic to the Northeast radiates from Bangkok, with daily
By Air flights on Thai Airways International between the capital and Khon
Kaen, Udon Thani, Sakhon Nakhon, and Ubon Ratchathani.

By Train Northeastern Railways has frequent service from Bangkok to
Nakhon Ratchasima, where the line splits. One route runs east,
stopping at Buri Ram, Surin, and Si Saket before terminating at
Ubon Ratchathani; the other line goes north, stopping at Khon Kaen
and Udon Thani, before arriving at Nong Khai. Both routes have
daytime express and local trains and an overnight express train with
sleeping cars. The Ubon Ratchathani sleeper leaves Bangkok at 9 PM
to arrive at 7:05 AM, and departs from Ubon Ratchathani at 7 PM to
arrive in Bangkok at 5:20 AM. The Nong Khai sleeper departs from
Bangkok at 10:30 PM to arrive at 7:30 AM, and on the return trip leaves
Nong Khai at 7 PM to be back in Bangkok at 6 AM.

By Bus Many of the towns in the Northeast are served by direct air-conditioned and non-air-conditioned buses from Bangkok's Northern Bus
Terminal on Phahonyothin Road. The fares are slightly lower than
those for the train. From Phitsanulok there is daily service to Loei
and then on to Khon Kaen and Nong Khai. There are also daily direct
buses that connect Chiang Mai and the major provincial capitals in
the Northeast.

Tourist The **Tourism Authority of Thailand** has offices at 2102–2104
Information Mittraphap Road, Amphor Muang, Nakhon Rathchasima 30000, tel.
044/243427 and at 264/1 Khuan Thani Rd., Ubon Ratchathani 34000,
tel. 038/377008. A branch of the **Tourist Police** at each of these TAT
offices shares the same telephone number.

Getting Between cities, there are buses throughout the day, from about 6 AM
Around to 7 PM. In towns, the bicycle samlors and songthaews are plentiful.
Rental cars, with or without a driver, are available in the provincial
capitals.

Exploring *Numbers in the margin correspond to points of interest on the
Northeast map.*

❶ The delight of **Nong Khai** is its frontier-town atmosphere: Because
Laos has been closed to the world for so long, you feel as if you're at
the end of the line. However, times are changing. Laos is opening
up, seeking cooperation with Thailand as well as encouraging tourist travel. In 1994, the Friendship Bridge across the Mae Khong
opened, joining Nong Khai and Vientiane in a 1-km (.6-mi) sweeping
arc. Previously the only connection was a scurry of ferries from Tha
Sadet, the boat pier, which has a small immigration and customs
shed. Now the traffic crosses the river, switching on the Laotian
side so drivers can change from driving on the right-hand side—as
in Thailand—to the left-hand side, as in Laos. Non-Thais need Laotian visas to cross the river, which, at press time, cannot be obtained
in Nong Khai (and take about three to seven days to secure in Bangkok).

Fanning out from Tha Sadet, the boat pier, on Rim Khong Road, are
market stalls with goods brought in from Laos. Some of the handmade lace may tempt you, or even such oddities as large washbowls
made of aluminum from downed U.S. aircraft. On Nong Khai's main
street, Meechai Road, are old wooden houses showing French colonial influences from Indochina, for example, the governor's residence. **Wat Pho Chai,** the best-known temple, houses a gold image of
Buddha, Luang Pho Phra Sai, that was lost for many centuries in the
muddy bottom of the Mae Khong. Its rediscovery, part of the local
lore, is told in pictures on the temple's walls. **Village Weaver Handi-**

The Northeast

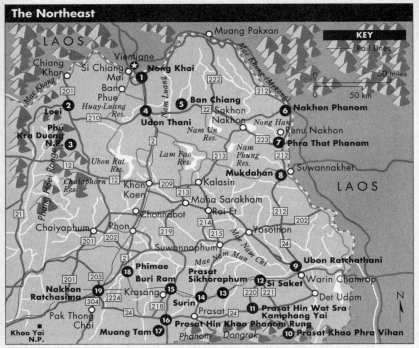

crafts, next to the temple, employs 350 families in the production of indigo-dyed *mudmee* (tie-dyed) cotton. Nong Khai is also a good source for silver. You may want to take a B50 tuk-tuk ride 5 km (3 mi) west of town to visit **Wat Khaek,** something of an oddity created by Luang Pu, a monk, who believes that all religions should work together. The temple's gardens are a collection of bizarre statues representing gods, goddesses, demons, and devils from many of the world's faiths.

Tranquil Nong Khai attracts the philosophical, who watch the flow of the Mae Khong, since there is little else to do. There is a marvelous scenic trip west along the Mae Khong, though, along the old dirt road with your own wheels, or on Highway 211, by bus to **Si Chiang Mai,** 50 km (31 mi) from Nong Khai. This sleepy backwater is famous for its spring roll wrapper production. Everywhere you'll see the white translucent rice flour spread out on mats to dry. Just out of town at kilometer marker 83 is **Wat Hin Maak Peng,** a meditation temple run by *mae chee,* Buddhist nuns, and farther on you'll come to **Than Thong** waterfall, a series of rapids in a stream, where Thais take delight in picnicking and bathing.

After another waterfall at **Sangkhom,** you cross into Loei province and soon reach the town of **Chiang Khan,** where the road turns south to **Loei,** the provincial capital, a major stop on bus routes in all directions. The province's key attraction is **Phu Kra Dueng National Park** (70 km, or 42 mi south of Loei, off the Loei–Khon Khaen highway), a lone, steep-sided mountain topped by a 60-sq-km (23-sq-mi) plateau at 1,360 m (4,462 ft) above sea level. It's wonderfully cool up here, and the profusion of flowers during March and April is brilliant. You reach the plateau by a 9-km (5.6-mi) hike through lightly forested fields of daisies, violets, orchids, and rhododendrons, and on top there are well-marked trails to scenic overhangs at the edge of the escarpment. The park is closed during the rainy season, July through October.

4 From Loei, it's a two-hour bus ride to the rather unattractive **Udon Thani,** due south of Nong Khai. As a major U.S. Air Force base during the Vietnam War, its size and importance grew, and though it's shrunk since then, the American military presence remains in a few glitzy bars and half Thai–half Western young people. A popular hangout for them is the Charoen Hotel on Pho Si Road, where pop singers perform nightly. Udon Thani is known for its *kai yang,* roast chicken, the best of which can be found at the stalls on the corner of Phrajak and Mukkhamontri roads. There is a Western-style shopping center at Jaroensri at the junction of Pho Si and Tahaan roads. At the **Udon Cultural Center** of Udon Teacher's College (Tahaan Road, away from the clock tower), an exhibit of photographs and artifacts illustrates daily life and the regional folkcraft. To buy silk, go to **Ban Na Kha,** a village of silk weavers, about 10 km (6 mi) north on the Nong Khai road.

5 The chief attraction near Udon Thani is **Ban Chiang,** 60 km (36 mi) east of the city, where archaeological finds of "fingerwhorl" pottery, skeletons, jewelry, and flint and iron weapons suggest a civilization here more than 7,000 years ago. The pottery in particular—red-on-cream with swirling geometric spirals—indicates that this civilization was ahead of its time in cultural development, and even more intriguing is that copper bells and glass beads found here are similar to some in North and Central America. This poses the question: Did Asians trade with Americans 7,000 years ago or even migrate halfway around the world? You can reach Ban Chiang from Udon Thani with a car and driver for approximately B600 or on the local bus. Two museum buildings are in the center of the village, and the excavation site is a short walk away at **Wat Pho Si Mai.** The larger of the two museums has English explanations. *Admission charge. Closed Mon., Tues.*

Another attraction out of Udon Thani is the mountain park at **Ban Phue,** 50 km (31 mi) northwest of town (one hour by bus), where you can rent a motorbike (B40) to reach the mountain, 8 km (5 mi) away. The 1,200-acre park is covered with rocks of all sizes, some shaped into Buddhist and Hindu images. At the top of the hill is **Wat Phra Buddha Baht Bua Bok,** named after the replica of Buddha's footprint at its base; its 40-m (131-ft) pagoda copies the style of the revered Wat That Phanom, farther to the east. Take the path to the right of the temple, and within a kilometer, you'll reach a cave with a series of stick-figure and silhouette paintings thought to be 4,000 years old.

Directly south of Udon Thani (110 km/68 mi), about halfway to Nakhon Ratchasima, lies **Khon Kaen,** a rapidly developing town that holds a silk fair in December. This area is known for mudmee silk; in fact, if you are in the neighborhood, you should make the 50-km (30-mi) trip south to the village of Chonnabot to see the silk being processed, from the cocoon through the spinning and dying to the weaving on hand looms.

6 Approximately three hours east of Udon Thani by bus is **Nakhon Phanom,** on the banks of the Mae Khong, a sleepy market town with the best hotel in the area, where you should spend the night before **7** traveling 50 km (31 mi) south to **Phra That Phanom,** northeast Thailand's most revered shrine. Take the bus that goes through to

Mukdahan. No one knows just when Phra That Phanom was built, though archaeologists trace its foundations to the fifth century. The temple has crumbled and been rebuilt several times—it now stands 52 m (171 ft) high, with a decorative tip of gold weighing 10 kg (22 lbs). Though it's impressive, you may be equally moved by the small museum to the left of the grounds that houses its ancient bells and artifacts. Once a year droves of devotees arrive to attend the Phra That Phanom Fair during the full moon of the third lunar month, and the village becomes a minimetropolis, with stalls of market traders and makeshift shelters for the pilgrims.

Ten km (6 mi) back toward Nakon Phanom is the small village of **Renu Nakhon,** which has a row of showrooms and cottage industries along the main street, similar to those at San Kamphaeng in Chiang Mai. They produce and sell an extensive range of products, including cotton and silk dresses, quilted blankets, and ceramics.

8 Continuing south from Phra That Phanom, you come to **Mukdahan,** on the Mae Khong, Thailand's newest provincial capital, opposite the Laotian town of Suwannakhet. It bustles with vendors in stalls and shops all along the riverfront, selling goods brought in from Laos—a fascinating array of detailed embroidery, lace, lacquered paintings, trays, and bowls, cheap cotton goods, and a host of souvenir items. The time out from shopping can be spent promenading along the riverfront, stopping occasionally to sample Thai and Laotian delicacies from one of the numerous food stalls.

9 A three-hour bus ride south takes you to **Ubon Ratchathani,** southern I-San's largest city, whose best-known tourist attraction is the Buddhist-inspired Candle Procession in late July, when huge wax sculptures are paraded through town. At other times, especially after the rainy season, locals make for **Haad Wat Tai Island** in the middle of the Mun River, a site for food stalls. It's connected to the shore by a rope bridge (1 baht) that sends shivers of consternation through those who cross. Try the local favorites: *pla chon,* a fish whose name is often translated as "snakehead mullet," or if your stomach is feeling conservative, the ubiquitous *kai yang* (roast chicken). Temple enthusiasts should visit both the Indian-style pagoda **Wat Nong Bua** and the **Wat Maha Wanaram** (Wat Pa-Yai), which houses a revered Buddha image named Phra Chao Yai Impang, believed to have magical powers.

Turning west from Ubon Ratchathani and traveling parallel to the Cambodian border along the Mun River offers a selection of Khmer ruins. Four deserve more than a special effort to visit: Prasat Khao Phra Vihan on the Cambodian border, southeast of Si Saket; Prasat Wat Sra Kamphang Yai, 25 km (15.5 mi) south of Si Saket; Buri Ram, perhaps the most well-known; and Phimae, northeast of Nakhon Ratchasima.

10 Both Thailand and Cambodia claim that **Prasat Khao Phra Vihan** is on their soil, and the World Court awarded it to Cambodia—but because access from that side requires scaling a cliff, you get to Prasat Khao Phra Vihan from Thailand! Take the bus from Si Saket down Highway 221 to Guntharalak. The temple is on the outskirts of town.

"Prasat," the Thai word for these Khmer complexes, is loosely translated as "castle," though Khmer kings did not live in them. They were used more as Hindu sanctuaries or retreats or as rest stops for travelers en route from Angkor. Prasat Khao Phra Vihan was built during the 12th century, and the sandstone laterite ruins are in a state of neglect, but enough remains in this commanding lo-

cation to let your imagination fly back nine centuries to when the Khmer ruled much of southeast Asia.

⑪ **Prasat Hin Wat Sra Kamphang Yai** (Stone Castle), just outside Ban Sa Kampang, 25 km (15 mi) south of Si Saket, is in better condition. Thailand's Department of Fine Arts has restored it, re-creating what has been lost or stolen over the last 900 years. Particularly marvelous are the lintels of the middle stupa, which depict the Hindu god Indra riding the Erawan (elephant). The main gate, inscribed with Khom letters, is estimated as 10th century and built during the reign of King Suriyaworamann. The temple behind the prasat is a Thai addition, with walls covered with pictures illustrating Thai proverbs.

⑫ With the exception of a brand new Buddhist temple, said to be one of the grandest in the Northeast, the town of **Si Saket** is known more for its pickled garlic, pickled onion, *somtam* (a relish) and, of course, *kai yang* (roast chicken) than its architecture. But in early March, when the colorful lamduan flower blooms, the town comes alive in a riot of yellows and reds, and locals celebrate with the three-day Lamduan Festival. On the main road west, between Si Saket and ⑬ Surin is **Prasat Sikhoraphum,** a five-prang Khmer pagoda built in the 12th century. The central, main structure has wonderfully engraved lintels of Shiva, as well as depictions of Brahma, Vishnu, and Ganesa. Shoppers may want to detour south to Ban Butom, 12 km (7.5 mi) before Surin, where the villagers make straw baskets that are sold in Bangkok. They'll be happy to demonstrate their skill and sell you their wares.

⑭ **Surin** is famous for the celebration of its annual elephant roundup in the third week of November. The roundup is essentially an elephant circus, albeit an impressive one, where elephants perform tricks in a large arena and their mahouts reenact scenes of capturing wild elephants. At other times, if you want to see elephants, you must travel to **Ban Ta Klang,** a village 60 km (37 mi) north of Surin, off Highway 214. This is the home of the Suay people, who migrated from southern Cambodia several centuries ago and whose expertise with elephants is renowned. Until recently, teams of Suay would go into Cambodia to capture wild elephants and bring them back for training. But civil turmoil in Cambodia, the elephants' vast appetites, and the use of heavy machinery to replace them have diminished the beasts and their mahouts to little more than a tourist attraction.

On your return south from Ban Ta Klang, 15 km (10 mi) from Surin a small road leads off to the left to **Ban Choke,** a village once famous for its excellent silk, where now silver jewelry is also made. You can find bargains in bracelets and necklaces with a minimal amount of negotiation.

⑮ Push on to the provincial capital of **Buri Ram,** less than an hour west of Surin by train or bus, for the trip 60 km (37 mi) south to the re-⑯ stored hilltop sanctuary of **Prasat Hin Khao Phanom Rung,** outside the village of Nang Rung. From Buri Ram you take a taxi or a bus to Nang Rung, then transfer to another bus for a 7-km (4.5-mi) ride to Ban Ta Koe on Highway 24, where you can board one of the songthaews (B5) that run back and forth up the mountain.

This supreme example of Khmer art was built in the 12th century under King Suriyaworamann II, one of the great Khmer kings, and restored in the 1980s at a cost of $2 million. It's one of the few Khmer sanctuaries without later Thai Buddhist additions. The approach to the prasat sets your heart thumping—you cross an imposing *naga* bridge (one with snake balustrades), and climb majestic staircases to the top, where you are greeted by the magnificent Reclining Vishnu lintel. This lintel, spirited away in the 1960s, reappeared at the Chicago Art Institute, and after 16 years of protests and negotiations, was finally returned to its rightful place in Thailand. Step under the lintel and through the portal, and you are within the double-walled sanctuary. Intricate carvings in a style similar to those found in Lopburi cover the interior walls, and in the center of the prasat stands the great throne room dedicated to Brahma Lord Siva.

Scattered in the area are other Khmer prasats in various stages of ruin, overgrown by vegetation, with their millennial stones lying where they have fallen. **Muang Tam,** 15 minutes by car south of Prasat Hin Khao Phanom Rung (no public bus makes this trip), 100 years older than its neighbor, has a special aura of forgotten discovery. There are five brick prangs surrounded by holy ponds, engravings that are barely discernible, and collapsed portals. A soft silence envelops the few tourists who come to see these ruins.

At **Phimae,** 58 km (36 mi) north of Nakhon Ratchasima, stands the other great Khmer structure of the Northeast. **Prasat Hin Phimae** was probably built sometime in the late-11th or early 12th century, and though the ruins have been restored, they have not been groomed and manicured. Entering the prasat through the two layers—the external sandstone wall and the gallery—is to step back eight centuries, and by the time you reach the inner sanctuary, you're swept up in the creation and destruction of the Brahman gods engraved on the lintels. Gate towers (*gopuras*) at the four cardinal points guard the entrances, with the main one facing south, the route to Angkor. The central white sandstone prang 19 m (60 ft) tall, flanked by two smaller buildings, one in laterite, the other in red sandstone, make an exquisite combination of pink and white against the darker laterite, especially in the light of early morning and late afternoon. The principal prasat is surrounded by four porches, whose external lintels reflect scenes from the Ramayana and depict the Hindu gods. Inside, the lintels portray the religious art of Mahayana Buddhism. An open-air museum nearby displays a collection of lintels from Phimae and other northeast Khmer sites, which gives you a chance to learn to recognize the different styles of Thai-Khmer art.

You may want to drive about 2 km (1.2 mi) from the ruins to see *Sai Ngam,* the world's largest banyan tree, whose mass of intertwined trunks supports branches that cast a shadow of nearly 1,400 sq m (15,000 sq ft). Some say that it is 3,000 years old. On weekends, the small nearby park has stalls selling *patnee* (noodles) and *kai yang* (roast chicken) for picnics.

Buses leave Phimae for **Nakhon Ratchasima** (called Korat) every 15 minutes between 6 AM and 6 PM. The journey takes one hour and 40 minutes. Most people use **Korat** as a base for visiting Phimae and Buri Ram. It is I-San's major city, with a population of over 200,000, considered the gateway to the Northeast. It also serves as a base to visit **Khao Yai National** Park, which covers 2,168 sq km (833 sq mi) in four provinces, providing fresh air, hiking, and four golf courses for Thais from Bangkok.

A side trip to **Pak Thongchai Silk and Cultural Center,** 32 km (20 mi) south of Korat offers a chance to see the complete silk-making process, from the raising of silk worms to the spinning of thread and weaving of fabric. You can also buy silks at some 70 factories in the area; try, for example, the Srithai Silk showroom, 333 Subsiri Road, in **Pakthongchai** (tel. 044/441588). For ceramics, drive out to the village of **Ban Kwian,** 15 km (10 mi) southwest of Korat. The rust-colored clay here has a tough, ductile texture and is used for reproductions of classic Thai designs. Between 6 and 9 PM, head to the Night Bazaar in the center of town, a block-long street taken over by food stands and shopping stalls. The array of food is more tempting than the mass-produced clothing items. There are outdoor restaurants at either end of the Night Bazaar—you might try **Dot Pub** (tel. 044/236300) across from the Chomsurang Hotel on Thanon Mahattai. Or take a tuk-tuk to **Kung Lung** (Tanon Jomsurangyard, tel. 044/256048) where the Thai food is not as spicy as in a local I-San restaurant.

From Korat, Thailand is your oyster. Bangkok is four hours away by train, via Ayutthaya and Bangkok's Don Muang Airport, and there are direct buses to Bangkok (256 km, 159 mi), Pattaya (284 km, 176 mi), Rayong (345 km, 214 mi), Chiang Rai (870 km, 539 mi), Chiang Mai (763 km, 473 mi), and Phitsanulok (457 km, 283 mi).

Dining and Lodging   With the exception of the new Sima Thani in Nakhon Ratchasima, accommodations in the Northeast are mostly city hotels catering to Thai business travelers. But as more tourists discover the region, hotels are gradually adapting to the needs of the vacationer. Expect polite and friendly service, but do not count on an English-speaking staff or for the hotel to arrange tours. Expect the guest rooms to be mopped clean, but furnished modestly, with faded paint on the walls. In rural areas, expect only basic bathroom facilities, and in budget accommodations, there is no hot water. For Western fare, stay with the hotel restaurant; for Thai food, there is a plenitude of restaurants and stalls. Be prepared for the food to be hot and spicy. You will probably want to stay away from *balah*, a vile-smelling fermented fish sauce. Each province claims to have the best *Kai yang* (roast chicken) and sticky rice but Si Saket and Udon Thani brag the loudest. Pork is popular and *moo pan*, where the pork is beaten flat and roasted over charcoal, is delicious. *Moo yor*, a pork roll wrapped in a banana leaf, is equally delicious, if you like spicy food. *Nua namtok* is lightly grilled beef slices garnished with shallots, rice flour, dried chilies, lemon juice, and fresh mint leaves. Especially popular in Korat is *sai krog I-San*, a sausage filled with minced pork, garlic, and rice, which is cooked and eaten with sliced ginger, dry peanuts, and grilled chilies. It is very spicy, not to say hot.

Nakhon Phanom   **Si Thep Hotel.** Located about 400 yards from the Mae Khong river, this is by far Nakhom Phanom's best hotel. The property is back from a side street off the main road, so all the rooms are quiet. Rooms are standard and the well-used furnishings are slightly depressing, but all is clean, including the bathrooms. The restaurant has a terrace, should you want the evening air instead of air-conditioning. *708/11 Si Thep Rd., Nakhon Phanom, tel. 042/512395, fax 042/511–346. 87 rooms. Facilities: restaurant. MC, V. $–$$*
Windsor Hotel. This basic hotel has little going for it except the price, its central location across from the bus stop for That Phanom, and the friendly staff. Rooms contain little more than a bed. Sheets are well worn and patched. The walls are covered with handprints and smudges, but the floors get mopped each day. The bathroom is Asian-style. *692/19 Bamrungmuang Rd., Nakhon Phanom, tel. 042/511946. 60 rooms. No credit cards. $*

Nakhon Ratchasima (Korat)   **Sima Thani Hotel.** Opened in April 1992 on the outskirts of Korat (a B30 tuk-tuk ride from the Night Bazaar), this sparkling new hotel is I-San's most luxurious and its best place to dine. It is designed ★ around a hexagonal atrium lobby. Furnishings in the guest rooms are not inspired, but are comfortably nonobtrusive. Each room has two queen-size beds, a table and chairs, and a good working desk (except for an inadequate reading lamp). Satellite television provides English-language movies, CNN, and BBC World News. Bathrooms come with hair dryers, telephones, and toiletries. The coffee shop dining room is open 24 hours, the Chinese restaurant is Cantonese, and best of all is the extensive evening buffet outdoors, with musicians and classic I-San dancers every night except Monday. Most of the staff knows some English, and service is extremely professional. *Mittraphap Rd., Tambon Nai Muang, Amphur Muang, Nakhon Ratchasima 30000, tel. 044/243–812, fax 044/251–109. 135 rooms. Facilities: restaurant, coffee shop, buffet with entertainment, piano bar, pool, fitness center, and meeting rooms. AE, DC, MC, V. $$–$$$*

Nong Khai **Phanthawi.** This is Nong Khai's best hotel, but don't expect more than a clean room. The beds suffice rather than being really comfortable, and the furnishings are sparse. The restaurant, on the open-fronted ground floor, serves as a place to sit around in as well as eat. The staff speaks limited English, but enough to direct guests to the appropriate bus stations. *Haisoke Rd., Nong Khai 43000, tel. 042/ 411568. 67 rooms. Facilities: restaurant, air-conditioning or fans. MC, V. $*

Surin **Tharin Hotel.** Surin's newest (and only high-rise) hotel opened in 1990. The lobby and public reception areas are kept shining, and light flooding in through tall glass windows reflects off the polished marble. This is Surin's leading hotel, despite its lack of character and the 10-minute walk from the center of town. Rooms are done in light pastels or burnt browns, have wall-to-wall carpeting, TV, telephones, a table and two chairs. In the evenings, the Darling Cocktail Lounge attracts local swells, and the disco swings at weekends. *60 Sirirat Rd., Surin 32000, tel. 045/514281, fax 045/511580. 160 rooms and 35 suites. Facilities: restaurant, coffee shop, disco, meeting rooms, sauna. AE, MC, V. $–$$*

Petchkasem Hotel. While the newer Tharin Hotel has smarter creature comforts, the Petchkasem has more character and is in the center of town between the bus and railway station. The carpeted guest rooms have air-conditioning, refrigerators, and color TV and not much else. The lobby area is good for lounging and the staff is helpful. In the evening, charming hostesses serve drinks in the relaxing ambience of the Bell Cocktail Lounge. *104 Jitbamroong Rd., Surin 32000, tel. 045/511–274, fax 044/511–041. 162 rooms. Facilities: restaurant, lounge, disco, pool, free parking, meeting rooms. AE, MC, V. $*

Ubon **Patumrat Hotel.** Though the nearby Regent Palace is the newest
Ratchathani four-star hotel in town, the Patumrat's service and personality guarantee its position as Ubon's leading hotel. Its drawback, as is the Regent's, is the location, a 20-minute walk from the center of town. *173 Chayangkun Rd., Ubon Ratchathani 34000, tel. 045/241– 501, fax 045/243–792. 137 rooms. Facilities: restaurant, coffee shop. AE, DC, MC, V. $$*

Rajthani Hotel. This convenient modest hotel used by Thai business travelers and tourists is downtown on the main street. The uncarpeted rooms are simply furnished but clean, and the bathrooms have hot and cold water. The clerks at the reception desk are friendly, but not able to provide much tourist information. *297 Khuan Thani Rd., Ubon Ratchathani 34000, tel. 045/244–388, fax 045/243–561. 100 rooms. Facilities: restaurant. No credit cards. $*

Sri Kamol Hotel. This clean, modern hotel in the center of town, a five-minute walk from the TAT office, has carpeted rooms with twin beds or king-size beds. The furnishings are standard—there's a table with two chairs and a minibar with a small television on top. The staff is welcoming, and a few of them speak good English. You can often negotiate a discount of 25% on the price of a room. *26 Ubonsak Rd., Ubon Ratchathani 34000, tel. 045/255–804, fax 045/243–793. 82 rooms. Facilities: restaurant. No credit cards. $*

The Southern Beach Resorts

Phuket

Backpackers discovered Phuket in the early 1970s. The word got out about its long, white sandy beaches, cliff-sheltered coves, waterfalls, mountains, fishing and seafood, clear waters, scuba diving, and fiery sunsets, rainbow colors shimmering off the turquoise Andaman Sea. Entrepreneurs built massive developments, at first clustering around Patong, and then spreading out. Most formerly idyllic deserted bays and secluded havens now have at least one hotel impinging on their beauty, and hotels are still being built despite a shortage of trained staff and an overburdened infrastructure. Yet, in order to fill the hotels, charter flights are encouraged to bring tourists from Europe, especially Germany, at discounted rates. Nevertheless, Phuket's popularity continues because, with its 20,000 hotel rooms, it is large enough (so far) to absorb the influx.

When to Go Phuket has two seasons. During the monsoon season, from May through October, hotel prices are considerably lower. Though the rain may be intermittent during this time, the seas can make some of the beaches unsafe for swimming. The peak season is the dry period from November through April.

Tourist Information The **TAT office** (73–75 Phuket Rd., Phuket Town, tel. 076/212–213), located near the bus terminal, has information on all Phuket hotels, as well as free maps. The TAT desk at the airport offers limited help.

Emergencies **Police** (tel. 076/212–046); **ambulance** (tel. 076/212–297). **Tourist police** (tel. 076/212–468) are the best officials to seek in an emergency. They are located next to the TAT office. The general emergency number is 199.

Arriving and Departing
By Plane **Thai Airways International** has daily 70-minute flights from Bangkok and 30-minute flights from Hat Yai. The airline also has direct flights from Chiang Mai, from Penang (Malaysia), and from Singapore. **Bangkok Airways** now offers two flights daily between Bangkok and Phuket and one daily flight between Phuket and Ko Samui. A departure tax of B200 on international flights and B20 on domestic flights is charged.

Phuket's airport is at the northern end of the island. Phuket Town is 32 km (20 mi) southeast. Most of the hotels are on the west coast, south of the airport. Many send their own limousine minivans to meet arriving planes. These are not free, just convenient. For Phuket Town or Patong Beach, take a Thai Airways minibus—buy the ticket (B70 and B100, respectively) at the transportation counter in the terminal. Sporadically, songthaews run between the airport and Phuket Town for B20.

By Train The closest station is on the mainland at Surat Thani, where trains connect to Bangkok and Singapore. A bus/coach service links Phuket with Surat Thani. Traveling time between Phuket and Bangkok is five hours on the bus and nine hours on the overnight train (with sleeping bunks). The State Railway of Thailand, in conjunction with Songserm Travel, issues a combined train and bus ticket.

By Bus Non-air-conditioned buses leave throughout the day from Bangkok Southern Bus Terminal. One air-conditioned bus leaves in the evening. Tour companies also run coaches. These are slightly more comfortable, and often the price of a one-way fare includes a meal. **Songserm** (121/7 Soi Chapermla, Phyathai Rd., Bangkok 10400, tel. 02/252–9654) is one such company. The bus trip from Bangkok to Phuket takes 13 to 14 hours.

Getting Fares are, to a large extent, fixed between different destinations. If
Around you plan to use taxis frequently, obtain a fare listing from the TAT
By Taxi office because drivers are not above charging more. A trip from Phuket Town to Patong Beach is B100 and to Promthep Cape is B130.

By Bus Songthaews, the minibuses that seat six people, have no regular schedule, but all use Phuket Town as their terminal. Songthaews to the beaches leave from Rangong Road near the day market and Fountain Circle. They ply back and forth to most beaches, and a few make the trip to the airport. Should you want to travel from one beach to another along the western shore, you will probably have to go into Phuket Town first and change songthaews. Fares range from B10 to B40.

By Rental Car As Phuket has so many different types of beaches, your own trans-
and Scooters port offers the most convenience for exploring. Driving poses few hazards, except for the motor scooter—potholes and gravel can cause a spill, and some minor roads are not paved.

Many hotels have a car/Jeep/scooter rental desk, but their prices are 25%–40% higher than those in Phuket Town. Try the **Pure Car Rent** (75 Rassada Rd., Phuket Town, tel. 076/211–002), where prices for a Jeep start at B770 per day, plus CDW of B120 per day. Motor scooters range up from B150. The larger, 150-cc scooters are safer. Both **Avis** (tel. 076/311–358) and **Hertz** (tel. 076/311–162) have offices at the airport, as well as at some hotels.

Guided Tours Two reputable tour operators on the island are **New World Travel Service** (Hotel Phuket Merlin, tel. 076/212–866, ext. WTS) and **Songserm** (51 Satoon Rd., Phuket Town 83000, tel. 076/222–570, fax 076/214–391), which also operates several cruise boats, air-conditioned buses to Bangkok, and minibuses to Surat Thani, Hat Yai, Penang, and Singapore.

Orientation A half-day Phuket sightseeing tour includes Wat Chalong, Rawai
Tour Beach, Phromtrep Cape, and Khao Rang.

Excursions A full-day boat tour goes from Phuket to Phang Nga Bay on the mainland with visits to other islands. Another full-day tour visits the Phi Phi Islands for swimming and caving. The full-day Ko Hav (Coral Island) tour features snorkeling and swimming. The nine islands of the Similan group offer some of the world's clearest waters and most spectacular marine life. Full-day cruises, costing B1,500, operated by Songserm (tel. 076/216–820), are often available. The luxury cruise ship ***Andaman Princess*** (Siam Cruise Co., 33/10–11 Chaiyod Arcade, Sukhumvit Soi 11, Sukhumvit Rd., Bangkok 10110, tel. 02/255–8950), operates two- and three-night cruises to the islands.

Special- A half-day tour features the Thai Cultural Village, for folk dances,
Interest Tours Thai boxing, and Thai martial arts (Krabea-Krabong). The half-day Naga pearl tour visits cultured pearl farms on Naga Noi Island.

Exploring Shaped like a teardrop pendant with many chips, Phuket is linked to the mainland by a causeway. Typically, tourists go directly to their hotels on arrival and then make day trips to various other beaches. Hence, the exploring section below is less an itinerary than an overview of places to visit.

Phuket Town *Numbers in the margin correspond to points of interest on the Phuket map.*

❶ About one-third of the island's population lives in **Phuket Town,** the provincial capital, but very few tourists stay here. The town is busy, and drab modern concrete buildings have replaced the old Malay-Colonial-influenced architecture. A few hours of browsing through the tourist shops are not wasted, however. Most of the shops and cafés are along Phang-Nga Road and Rasda Road. By bus, you arrive in Phuket on the eastern end of Phang-Nga Road.

Time Out Sidewalk tables in front of the **Thavorn Hotel** on Rasda Road provide a good place to do a little people-watching while sipping a cold beer.

East of the Thavorn Hotel, Phuket Road forks right off Rasda Road. On the left are the TAT office and the Tourist Police. In the opposite direction (west) along Rasda Road, crossing the traffic circle (Bangkok Circle), is Ranong Road. Here, on the left, is the **local market,** Phuket Town's busiest and most colorful spectacle—a riot of vegetables, spices, meats, sellers and buyers, and rich aromas. On the next block down Ranong Road is the Songthaew Terminal for minibus service to Patong, Kata, Kamala, Karon, Nai Harn, and Surin beaches. Songthaews for Rawai and Nai Harn beaches stop at Bangkok Circle. Diagonally across town from Phuket's market is the Provincial Town Hall, which was used as the French Embassy in the movie *The Killing Fields.* Perhaps the most relaxing way to see

❷ Phuket is from the top of **Khao Rang** (Rang Hill) in the northwest of the town. The elevation permits a view of both Phuket Town and the island's interior.

Time Out While enjoying the view from Khao Rang, try the **Tunka Café** (tel. 076/311–5000), which serves good Thai food for lunch and dinner.

The Beaches Starting from the north and working down the west coast, the first

❸ beach is **Mai Khao Beach,** just 5 km (3 mi) from the airport. This beach is the island's largest, often ignored by Western tourists because at low tide it turns slightly muddy, and its steep drop-off makes it unpopular with swimmers. The absence of farangs (foreigners) attracts the Thais, who appreciate the peacefulness of the beach. Giant sea turtles like it, too. They come between November and February to lay their eggs.

❹ **Nai Yang Beach** is really a continuation of Mai Khao—making a 10-km (6-mi) stretch of sand. It curves like a half-moon, with casuarina trees lining the shore. It is also popular with Thais, and now a new resort, Pearl Village, has opened here.

❺ Tucked in the center of a headland is **Nai Thon Beach.** Its rough waters keep swimmers away, and the village remains a peaceful fishing port. South of the headland, the shore curves in to form **Bang Tao Beach,** which had been left undisturbed until recently. First came the smart and attractive Dusit Laguna Resort, and then three more hotels, the latest of which is the Sheraton Grande Laguna, opened in 1993. What was once peaceful beach can now become busy if all of the hotels' 1,000 rooms are occupied.

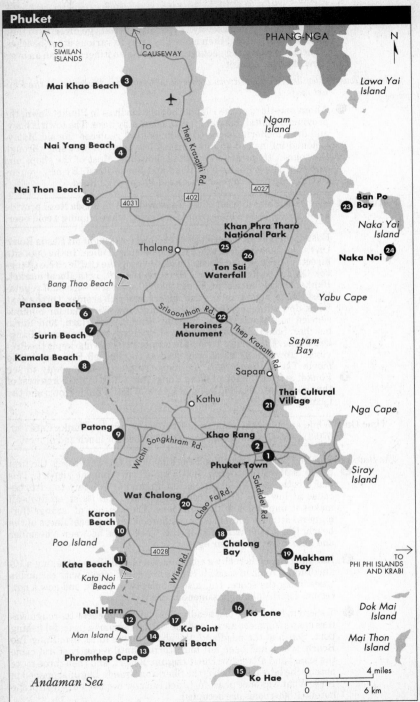

Phuket

PHANG-NGA

N

TO SIMILAN ISLANDS

TO CAUSEWAY

Lawa Yai Island

Mai Khao Beach ③

Ngam Island

Nai Yang Beach ④

Thep Krasatri Rd.

Nai Thon Beach ⑤

4031

402

4027

Ban Po Bay ㉓

Naka Yai Island

Khan Phra Tharo National Park

Thalang ○

㉕

㉖

Naka Noi ㉔

Bang Thao Beach

Ton Sai Waterfall

Yabu Cape

Pansea Beach ⑥

Srisoonthon Rd.

Heroines Monument ㉒

Thep Krasattri Rd.

Surin Beach ⑦

Sapam Bay

Kamala Beach ⑧

Sapam ○

Nga Cape

○ Kathu

Thai Cultural Village ㉑

Patong ⑨

Wichit Songkhram Rd.

Khao Rang

②

Phuket Town ①

Siray Island

Wat Chalong ⑳

Chao Fa Rd.

Sakdidet Rd.

Karon Beach ⑩

Poo Island

4028

⑱

Chalong Bay

⑲ **Makham Bay**

Kata Beach ⑪

TO PHI PHI ISLANDS AND KRABI

Kata Noi Beach

Wiset Rd.

⑯ **Ko Lone**

Dok Mai Island

Nai Harn ⑫

⑰

Ka Point

Man Island

⑭

Rawai Beach

Mai Thon Island

⑬

Phromthep Cape

⑮ **Ko Hae**

Andaman Sea

0 — 4 miles

0 — 6 km

⑥ ⑦ Next in line are **Pansea Beach** and **Surin Beach,** with the island's most elegant resort, Amanpuri. Tucked in a small cove with a complete feeling of privacy, the hotel blends into the cliffside. Surin Beach, despite a long stretch of golden sand, is not good for swimming because of strong currents. On the headland south of Surin are several small intimate and romantic coves. Each requires a climb down a cliff. Surrounded by palms and rocks, the tiny beach is, with luck, your personal haven.

⑧ After the headland is **Kamala Beach,** a small curving strip of sand with coconut palms and a few bungalows rented by Krathomtip Cottages. Unfortunately, a new Sheraton Hotel has been built here. A small dirt road leads on from Kamala Beach to Patong—passable, but very tricky and not advised if it's your first time on a motor scooter. If you don't use this dirt road, drive inland to join the main road before turning west again for Patong.

⑨ **Patong** is Phuket's mini-Pattaya, complete with German restaurants, massage parlors, hustlers selling trinkets, and places like Tatum's, a combined coffeehouse, disco, and go-go dance floor. The 90 hotels, ranging from deluxe to small cottages, with their more than 6,000 double rooms, attest to Patong's popularity among the charter groups flying into Phuket. From about 7 PM on, the main street is lined for about 3 km (2 mi) with stalls selling everything from T-shirts to watches. Down the side streets restaurants offer seafood and Western-style food, and beyond these, one bar crowds out another. Special buses bring hotel guests to Patong for the evening, allowing time for dinner, shopping, and a turn around the café bars, which are full of hostesses of both sexes.

Time Out In the evening, check out **Doolie's Place** (82/51 Soi Bangla, Patong, tel. 076/321–275), where an American proprietor serves steaks, hamburgers, barbecued chicken, and pizza. The restaurant's garden is a minizoo, with monkeys in the majority.

⑩ Beyond Patong is **Karon Beach,** which is divided into two areas. Karon Noi, a small bay surrounded by verdant hills, is truly beautiful but virtually taken over by Le Meridien Hotel, a huge 470-room resort with a meandering swimming pool, many restaurants and shops, plus a cavernous central lobby, ever processing the next batch of holidaymakers. Occasionally, cruise ships anchor offshore from this beach, doubling the crowds. Because of its good swimming and surfing, the other part, Karon Yai, is becoming increasingly popular, and several hotels and a minitown have sprung up to join the first of the luxury hotels.

⑪ **Kata Beach** is the next beach south, 17 km (10.2 mi) southwest of Phuket Town. The sunsets are as marvelous as ever, but the peace and quiet are fading fast. Club MediterrÃ©e has moved in, but there are still stretches of sand with privacy, and the center of town has only a modest number of bars. Nearby is **Kata Noi Beach** (*noi* means small) in the shelter of a forest-clad hill. A few inexpensive bungalows share the quiet beach with the Kata Thani Hotel that's popular with tour groups.

⑫ The road beyond Kata cuts inland across the hilly headland to drop into yet another gloriously beautiful bay, **Nai Harn.** Protected by Man Island, the deep-water bay has been a popular anchorage for international yachtsmen. On the north side, a huge, white stucco, stepped building, the Phuket Island Yacht Club, rises from the beach in stark contrast to the verdant hillside. From the Yacht Club's terrace, the view of the sun, dropping into the Andaman Sea behind Man Island, is superb. The beach is good for sunning and swimming in the dry season, but beware of the steep drop-off.

⑬ From Nai Harn, the road swings around to climb up to **Phromthep Cape.** Its panorama includes Nai Harn Bay, the island's coastline, and the far-off horizon of the Andaman Sea. At sunset, the view is supreme. This evening pilgrimage has become so popular that policemen organize parking, and a row of souvenir stands lines the parking lot. But, once away from this congestion, you can find space enough to enjoy the colors of the setting sun in contemplative solitude.

⑭ Down from Phromthep is **Rawai Beach.** The shallow, muddy beach is not so attractive, but the shoreline, with a fishing village set in a coconut grove, has the charm you may have expected in all of Phuket.

⑮ Cruise boats leave Rawai for **Ko Hae** (Coral Island), 30 minutes from
⑯ shore. North of it is **Ko Lone.** Both are choice islands for snorkeling and sunbathing. Ko Hae has a couple of cafés and receives more visitors than Ko Lone. *Boat fare: B750.*

At the southern end of Rawai Beach is a small gypsy village. The inhabitants are descendants of the original tribes living on Phuket. Called Chao Nam (Water People) by the Thais, they tend to shy away from the modern world, preferring to stay among their own. They are superb swimmers, able to fish at 27-m (90-ft) depths in free dives. One of the three tribes of the Chao Nam is believed to have been the sea gypsies who pirated 17th-century trading ships entering the Burmese-Singapore waters. Of the three Chao Nam villages on Phuket, the one at Rawai Beach is the easiest to visit.

⑰ East of Rawai is **Ka Point,** where most of the promontory is owned by the huge Phuket Island Resort, virtually a small township, with several restaurants, two swimming pools, and a minibus to take
⑱ guests from one facility to another. Along the coast is **Chalong Bay,** with several good inexpensive outdoor seafood restaurants—try Kanning II for delicious crabs and prawns. To the southeast of
⑲ Chalong Bay is the peninsula with **Makham Bay,** the place to catch the ferry boat to the Phi Phi Islands and Krabi.

Inland and Pearl Island   Turning inland from Chalong Bay, rather than take the main road to Phuket Town, take the road at the traffic circle to **Wat Chalong.** Phu-
⑳ ket has 20 Buddhist temples—all built since the 19th century—but Wat Chalong is the largest and most famous. It enshrines the gilt statues, wrapped in saffron robes, of two revered monks who helped quell an 1876 rebellion by Chinese immigrants.

㉑ North of Phuket Town, toward the airport, is the **Thai Cultural Village.** In a 500-seat amphitheater, it presents various aspects of southern Thai culture, including classical Thai dance, shadow puppets, exhibition Thai boxing, sword fighting, an "elephants-at-work" show, and more. *Thepkasati Rd., tel. 076/214–860. Admission charge. Show times: 10:15, 11, 4:45, 5:30.*

Farther north on the airport road, you'll notice a statue of two women; they rallied the Thais in 1785 to ward off a siege by the Burmese, who had sacked Ayutthaya four years earlier. A right turn (east) at
㉒ ㉓ this crossroads of the **"Heroines Monument"** leads to **Ban Po Bay,**
㉔ where you can take a 20-minute boat ride over to **Naka Noi,** the Pearl Island. A small restaurant offers refreshments after you tour the facilities and perhaps look in at the Pearl Extracting Show given at 11 AM. Overnight lodging is also available (tel. 076/212–901, ext. 117).

㉕ Turning inland from Ban Po, the road traverses **Khan Phra Tharo National Park,** the last remaining virgin forest on Phuket. You may
㉖ want to stop at **Ton Sai Waterfall,** a few minutes off the road. It's a popular picnic spot all year, but the falls are best during the rainy season.

Dining   Restaurants on Phuket serve all types of cuisine, including versions of Western. Fresh seafood is the specialty.

Amanpuri. The dining room here is beautiful, with a thatched Thai roof and modern bamboo furniture. The once-French cuisine is now really more Continental with a definite Italian accent, and a meal here is still a treat. Try the fresh fish on a bed of vegetables topped with a sauce sparked with fresh ginger and lemongrass. Make a special effort to visit, even if only for a drink, this split-level Thai building with spectacular sea views. *Pansea Beach, tel. 076/311–394. Reservations advised. Dress: casual but neat. AE, DC, V. Open 11:30–2 and 6–10. $$$*

Phuket Yacht Club. Though the exterior of this hotel may be an eyesore, the main restaurant, the Chart Room, is lovely. With one side completely open, the restaurant has a panoramic view of the bay and islands. The menu now has the choice of European and Thai dishes with an emphasis on seafood, though steaks are available. Try the baked fresh fish stuffed with prawns in a tasty mixture of Thai spices. For entertainment, classical Thai dancers perform. *Nai Harn Beach, tel. 076/381–156. Reservations advised. Dress: casual but neat. AE, DC, V. $$$*

Baan Rim Pa. For classical Thai cooking, come to this restaurant sitting on the cliff at the north end of Patong Beach. The large open-terraced setting is one of the most attractive on Phuket, and the food is prettily presented in traditional style. In fact, the head chef started the Thai Cooking School and has constructed set menus in order to make ordering simpler for non-Thais. Therein lies the warning: If you like hot and spicy Thai fare, you may be disappointed. *100/7 Kalim Beach Rd., Patong, tel. 076/340–789. Reservations accepted. Dress: casual. AE, MC, V. $$*

Coral Beach Hotel. Perched on a bluff overlooking the Andaman Sea and the beach at Patong, the Chao Lay open-front restaurant is in an ideal location to enjoy fantastic views and Thai cooking. Dishes include *tom kha gai* (slightly spicy chicken soup made with coconut milk), *mae krob* (Thai noodles), spring rolls, and grilled seafood. Should you prefer Italian fare, the hotel has recently opened La Gritta, one floor down from the Chao Lay, also with spectacular views. *104 Moo 4, Patong Beach, tel. 076/321–106. Reservations advised. Dress: casual but neat. AE, DC, MC, V. $$*

Kan Eang. There are now two Kan Eang restaurants in Chalong Bay. Thais make a point of going to Kan Eang 1; the food is more authentic and spicier than at nearby Number 2. At Number 1, choose a table next to the sea wall and under the coconut palms to order seafood. Choose spicy dishes carefully, and be sure that your waiter understands whether you want Thai *pet* (spicy hot) or to farang taste. Include the succulent and sweet crabs in your order. *Chalong Bay, tel. 076/381–323. Reservations accepted. Dress: casual. AE, MC, V. $$*

Latitude 8. This pub/restaurant is the base for sailors who come to Phuket with their yachts. You'll find them clustered around the bar from sunset to midnight exchanging seafaring stories. It's a congenial place where conversation flows along with the beer. Simple food, both Thai and Western, is served, from paad thai to steaks, but it's the kind to satisfy the appetite rather than excite the taste buds.

Chalong Bay, tel. 076/214–372. No reservations. Dress: casual. No credit cards. $$

Mallee's Seafood Village. An international array of cuisines is offered at this restaurant in the center of Patong. Two Thai dishes worth trying are the charcoal-grilled fish in banana leaves and the steamed fish in a tamarind sauce. If you want Chinese food, try the shark steak in a green-pepper sauce; for European fare, consider the veal sausage with potato salad. On the other hand, you may simply want to sit at one of the sidewalk tables and indulge in pancakes with honey. *94/4 Taweewong Rd., Patong, tel. 076/321–205. No reservations. Dress: casual. AE, DC, MC, V. $$*

On the Rock. Perched on the rocks overlooking Karon Beach, this 100-seat restaurant occupying three different levels has a wonderfully romantic setting surrounded by tropical bushes. In an aquarium tank, three baby reef sharks lazily glide, glancing at the diners. Fresh seafood is the specialty: mackerel with fresh tomato and onion and *her thalee kanom khrok* (a mixture of seafood with coconut milk, spiced with chili pepper) for appetizers, and for the main course *pla goh tod na phrik* (snapper in a pepper and chili sauce) with rice. Those not partial to this Thai fare for farang tastes can choose Italian pasta dishes. *Marina Cottages, south end of Karon Beach, tel. 076/381–625. Reservations accepted. Dress: casual. AE, MC, V. $$*

Lodging Phuket has accommodations of every variety in virtually all of its main beach areas. You can choose from the most elegant resorts, such as Amanpuri, to modest, thatch-roof bungalows that are a fraction of the price. In all, approximately 160 hotels or cottages offer various levels of hospitality. Hotel prices fluctuate widely, depending on season, day of the week, and holiday periods, when they can more than double.

★ **Amanpuri.** For relaxation amid tasteful and elegant surroundings, there is no finer place in Thailand—nor is any place quite as expensive. The most basic accommodation costs $304, but since that is at the property's entrance and has a view of only trees, you'll want a room with a better view, for example No. 105, and that's $814. The main building is completely open, with polished floors, modern bamboo furniture and pitched, thatch roofs. Guests stay in individual pavilions, staggered up the hillside from the beach. The architectural style is distinctly Thai, adapted with flair to accommodate modern creature comforts and to maximize cooling breezes from the sea. Furnishings are handcrafted with local woods, and each suite has its private sundeck. A split-level bar perches on the hill, affording a romantic view of the sun setting into the Andaman Sea. Meals are prepared by an enthusiastic French chef, whose culinary delights will tempt you to return. The swimming pool is up from the beach, and the beach itself is secluded. Thirteen privately owned villas, each with several bedrooms and a private pool, are also rented out. Should you wish even more privacy, arrangements may be made for an overnight stay on one of the uninhabited islands. *Pansea Beach, Phuket 83110, tel. 076/324–333, fax 076/324–100; Bangkok reservations, tel. 02/287–0226; U.S. reservations, tel. 800/447–7462. 40 pavilions and 13 villas. Facilities: 2 restaurants, bar, pool, 2 tennis courts, water sports, custom tours arranged, gift shop, and drugstore. AE, V. $$$$*

★ **Phuket Yacht Club.** Set in a picturesque westward-facing bay, this stepped, modern luxury hotel looks like an ambitious condominium complex. The architecture aside, its comfort, service, amenities, and secluded location make the Phuket Yacht Club extremely pleasant. Service and attention to detail had declined in recent years, but now it is under the Mandarin Oriental group's umbrella, which should bring new enthusiasm to the staff and investment in new furnishings. Whether you stay here or not, make a point of dining in the open-sided restaurant that overlooks the bay. Furnishings in the guest rooms are modern and stylish, but, like the exterior, lack any identification with the environment. Guest rooms are large and have separate sitting areas and private balconies overlooking the beach and the small islands. If you have a room on the upper floors, your huge private balcony is completely private from other eyes. *Nai Harn Beach, Phuket 83130, tel. 076/381–156, fax 076/381–164; Bangkok reservations, tel. 02/251–4707; U.K. reservations, tel. 071/ 537–2988; U.S. reservations, tel. 800/526–6566. 108 rooms, including 8 suites. Facilities: 2 restaurants, pool and poolside bar, 2 tennis courts, fitness center, water sports arranged, and tour desk. AE, DC, MC, V. $$$$*

Boathouse Inn & Restaurant. With all 33 rooms looking on to Kata Beach, an excellent Thai restaurant facing the Andaman Sea, and a relaxing beach bar, this small hotel is a very comfortable retreat. The Thai-style architecture adds a traditional touch to the otherwise modern amenities, such as bedside control panels and a Jacuzzi pool. Guest rooms are furnished in reds and browns and have individually controlled air-conditioning, private safes, and bathrooms with bath and a massage shower. Though there is an air-conditioned restaurant, it's best to sit on the veranda listening to gentle music from a small band. Try the *kung thot keeow:* fried shrimp paste with green curry, full of herbs and spices, served on thin crisp pastry shells, and garnished with basil leaves and strips of red chili. The Boathouse is now under the management of the Oriental group, which will probably prevent the occasional overbooking that has occurred in the past. *Kata Beach, Phuket 83100, tel. 076/381–557, fax 076/381–561; Bangkok reservations, tel. 02/253–9168; U.K. reservations, tel. 071/537–2988; U.S. reservations, tel. 800/526–6566. 33 rooms. Facilities: restaurant, bar, beauty salon, tour desk. AE, DC, MC, V. $$$*

Diamond Cliff Hotel. North of town, away from the crowds, this is one of the smartest and architecturally most pleasing resorts in Patong. The beach across the road has mammoth rocks that create the feeling of several private beaches. The swimming pool is built on a ledge above the main part of the hotel, providing an unobstructed view of the coast and the Andaman Sea. Rooms are spacious, full of light, and decorated in pale colors to accentuate the open feel of the hotel. Dining is taken seriously, with the fresh seafood cooked in European or Thai style. Guests may dine indoors or on the restaurant's terrace looking out to sea. *61/9 Kalim Beach, Patong, Kathu District, Phuket 83121, tel. 076/321–501, fax 076/321–507; Bangkok reservations, tel. 02/246–4515. 140 rooms. Facilities: restaurant, cocktail/tea lounge, pool with pool bar, water sports arranged, tour desk, and pharmacy. AE, MC, V. $$$*

★ **Dusit Laguna.** Facing a mile-long beach and flanked by two lagoons, this resort hotel is on beautiful Bang Thao Bay. The two new hotels (including the Sheraton Grande Laguna) that now flank the Dusit on either side spoil the seclusion, but they provide alternatives for dining and entertainment. The rooms, with picture windows opening onto private balconies, have modern pastel decor and commodious bathrooms. The hotel is popular with upmarket Thais seeking refuge from the more commercial areas of Patong. It offers barbecue dining on the terrace, and after dinner, dancing to the sounds of the latest discs. European fare is served at the Junkcelyon; Thai cuisine, to the tune of traditional Thai music, is served in the Ruen Thai restaurant. Evening entertainment changes nightly and may consist of a song and dance troupe of transvestites or classical Thai dance. *390*

Srisoontorn Rd., Cherngtalay District, Amphur Talang, Phuket 83110, tel. 076/311–320, fax 076/311–174; Bangkok reservations, tel. 02/236–0450. 240 rooms, including 7 suites. Facilities: 4 restaurants, pool, 2 tennis courts, water sports, putting green, tour desk, meeting rooms. AE, DC, MC, V. $$$

Metropole. If you should come to Phuket Town on business, the best and newest hotel is the Metropole. A sparkling crisp marble lobby greets you as you enter; a spacious lounge bar is on your left—for air-conditioned comfort during the day. The very handsome Chinese restaurant, the Fortuna Pavilion, offers dim sum lunch. For Western food in a steak-house atmosphere, try the Metropole Café. Guest rooms are bright with picture windows and furnishings in soft pastel colors. *1 Soi Surin, Montri Rd., Phuket Town, 83000, tel. 076/254–8197, fax 076/215–990. 248 rooms. Facilities: 2 restaurants, lobby bar, karaoke bar, pool, fitness center, business center, and conference rooms. AE, DC, MC, V. $$*

Paradise Hotel. Of the many similar moderately priced hotels in Patong, this one on the strip facing the beach has more appeal than those in the thick of the restaurants, shops, and bars. The Paradise has reasonably large rooms and clean bathrooms, a pool in its grounds, and a coffee shop/dining room for light Thai and Western fare. *93 Taweewong Rd. (next to the Holiday Inn), Patong 83121, tel. and fax 076/340–172. 16 rooms. Facilities: restaurant, pool, tour desk. MC, V. $$*

Phuket Cabana. This hotel's attraction is its location, in the middle of Patong, facing the beach. Laid-back and casual describe guests as well as staff, but the basic resort amenities are here, with a good tour desk and a reputable dive shop to arrange outings. Modest rooms are in chalet-type bungalows furnished with rattan tables and chairs. The Charthouse restaurant serves grilled Western food and a modest selection of Thai dishes. *80 Taweewong Rd., Patong Beach, Phuket 83121, tel. 076/342–138, fax 076/340–178; Bangkok reservations, tel. 02/278–2239. 80 rooms. Facilities: restaurant, outdoor pool, airport bus, tour desk, dive shop. AE, MC, V. $$*

★ **Marina Cottages.** The 50 small cottages here, straddling the divide between Karon and Kata beaches, all have an ocean view, although those closer to the beach are more spacious than those up the hill. All rooms have air-conditioning, tiled floors, balconies, and private bathrooms. The pool, nestled among rock outcroppings, is surrounded by tropical foliage. Reservations are necessary during high season. *Box 143, Phuket 83000, tel. 076/330–625, fax 076/330–516. 104 rooms. Facilities: 2 restaurants, pool, scuba diving with PADI instructors. AE, MC, V. $–$$*

Friendship Bungalows. In Kata, a four-minute walk from the beach, two rows of single-story buildings house modest, sparsely furnished, but spotlessly clean rooms, each with its own bathroom (there is usually hot water). The owners are extremely hospitable and encourage guests to feel at home. The small restaurant/bar on a terrace offers good Thai food; Western food is also available. What you leave will probably be enjoyed by the two monkeys on the restaurant's wall that play throughout the day. *6/5 Patak Rd., Kata Beach, Phuket 83130, tel. 076/330–499. 30 rooms. Facilities: restaurant. No credit cards. ¢*

Excursions from Phuket

The Similan Islands With some of the world's most interesting marine life, these islands are renowned for snorkeling and diving. No hotels are permitted, though there are camping facilities. The underwater sights rival those of the Seychelles and the Maldives, and visibility ranges from

18 to 36 m (60 to 120 ft). You'll dive in water 3 m (10 ft) deep down to about 36 m (120 ft). The most comfortable way to visit the islands is to take a cruise boat with a sleeping cabin. The boat trip takes about 10 hours from Phuket or about four hours from Thap Lamu Port, two hours north. **Songserm Travel Agency** organizes excursions from both ports. **Marina Divers** (Karon Villa Hotel, Karon Beach, tel. 076/381–625) runs diving trips to the islands. You may also wish to contact PIDC Divers (1/10 Viset Rd., Chalong Bay, tel. 076/381–219), which operates the 66-ft MV *Andaman Seafarer* for four- and six-day live-aboard dive excursions that cost approximately $520 and $720, respectively.

Ko Phi Phi
The Phi Phi islands were idyllic retreats, with secret silver-sand coves, unspoiled beaches, and limestone cliffs that drop precipitously into the sea. Now, tourists come from Phuket to escape its commercialism only to bring that very commercialism to Phi Phi. Several comfortable air-conditioned hotels have been built, and a number of more modest bungalow accommodations are available for the budget traveler. In some ways, Phi Phi has become the poor man's Phuket.

Getting There
Boats leave Makham Bay twice a day for the two-hour journey. **Songserm Travel Agency** (tel. 076/222–570) is the best one.

Exploring
Of the two main islands, Phi Phi Don and Phi Phi Lae, only Don is inhabited. Shaped like a butterfly, Phi Phi Don has two hilly land portions linked by a wide sandbar, 2 km (1¼ mi) long. Most accommodations and the main mall with its shops and restaurants are on this sandbar, where boats come into Ton Sai. No vehicles are allowed on the island; you can disembark at the hotels, on the north cape if you wish. In the evening, visitors stroll up and down the walkway along the sandbar, where numerous small restaurants display the catch of the day on ice in big bins outside. There are no bars or discos on the island. Even though it has been discovered, Ko Phi Phi is still very laid-back.

The most popular way to explore is by either a cruise boat or a long-tailed boat that seats up to six people. One of the most visually exciting trips is to Phi Phi Lae. The first stop along the way is **Viking Cave,** a vast cavern of limestone pillars covered with what look like prehistoric drawings, but are actually only a few centuries old, depicting Portuguese or Dutch cutters. The boat continues on, gliding by cliffs rising vertically out of the sea, for an afternoon in **Maya Bay.** Here the calm, clear waters, sparkling with color from the live coral, are ideal for swimming and snorkeling. Another worthwhile trip is the 45-minute journey by long-tailed boat to **Bamboo Island,** roughly circular and with a superb beach around it. The underwater colors of the fish and the coral are brilliant. The island is uninhabited, but you can spend a night under the stars if you like.

Dining and Lodging
Restaurants on Phi Phi consist of a row of closely packed one-room cafés down the narrow mall. The menus offer mostly fish dishes—you choose your fish from the ice bin outside, and the chef cooks it according to your instructions. Prices are well under B200 for two people, including a couple of Singha beers. The open-air restaurants to the left of the pier cost more, but the food is essentially the same. The two more luxurious accommodations are off by themselves, 15 minutes by boat or a stiff 45-minute hike from the isthmus.

P.P. International Resort. On the north cape of Laemthong, this isolated retreat has standard double rooms and larger deluxe rooms in bungalows with sea views at twice the price. All rooms are air-conditioned and have small refrigerators and color TV. The terraced restaurant has splendid views of the sea, and the fish is absolutely fresh. *Cape Laemthong, Phi Phi. Reservations in Bangkok, tel. 02/ 250–0768; in Phuket, tel. 076/214–297; in Ko Samui, tel. 077/421– 228. 120 rooms. Facilities: restaurant serving Thai and European cuisines, water sports and island tours arranged. AE, V. $$$*

Pee Pee Cabana and Ton Sai Village. Facing the sea amid coconut palms, these two adjacent hotels are owned by the same management company and offer the best accommodations in the center of Phi Phi. Abutting cliffs, Ton Sai Village is about a 10-minute walk from the ferry docks, and it is the quieter of the two. Rooms are slightly larger than those at Pee Pee Cabana. Both have either air-conditioned or fan-cooled rooms, and their outdoor restaurants offer food similar to that found in the village, but costing twice as much. *Reservations: Pee Pee Marina Travel Co., 201/3–4 Uttarakit Rd., Amphoe Muang, Krabi 81000, tel. 075/611–496, fax 075/612–196. 100 rooms. Facilities: restaurant. No credit cards. $$*

Pee Pee Island Village. In the same vicinity as P.P. International Resort, this hotel offers more modest accommodations in small thatched bungalows. It provides the same water sports and tours as its neighbor, but the service is more casual and the atmosphere more laid-back. Views from the hotel are less impressive, however, although guests do have panoramas of the sea and palm-clad hills. *Cape Laemthing, Phi Phi. Reservations in Bangkok, tel. 02/277– 0038; in Phuket, tel. 076/215–014. 65 rooms. Facilities: restaurant, water sports, island tours arranged. AE, V. $$*

Krabi Pee Pee Resort. In the center of the isthmus, this collection of small bungalows in a coconut grove offers clean, simple, fan-cooled rooms with private Asian-style squat toilets and showers. The complex faces Lohdalum Bay, though only a few of the thatched, palm-woven bungalows have views. Guests don't seem to frequent the restaurant, but they do hang around the bar, which faces the bay. Compared with the overpriced costs of other accommodations on the island, this "resort" is the best value. *Lohdalum Bay, Phi Phi. Reservations in Krabi, tel. 075/611–484. 60 rooms. Facilities: restaurant, bar, dive shop. No credit cards. $*

Pee Pee Resort. This hotel consists of two rows of tiny, thatched, palm-woven huts facing the beach, each with its own Asian-style toilet. A mosquito net is supplied. A small café, attractively located on a small headland, offers basic Thai food. *Phi Phi. No phone. 40 rooms. No credit cards. ¢*

Krabi and Ao Phra Nang
On the mainland, 43 km (27 mi) east of Ko Phi Phi, is Krabi, the provincial capital of the region. Once a favorite harbor for smugglers bringing alcohol and tobacco from Malaysia, it has become a fishing port and gateway to the province's islands and famed beaches, particularly Ao (Bay) Phra Nang.

Getting There
Two to four ferries a day make the two-hour run between Krabi and Phi Phi. Bookings can be made on Phi Phi Don; the fare is B150. Air-conditioned buses depart from Bangkok's Southern Bus Terminal at 7 PM and 8 PM for the 290-km (180-mi) journey (fare B290) to Krabi.

To reach Ao Phra Nang, take a songthaew for B20 from Krabi. If you book accommodations for Ao Phra Nang in Krabi, transportation will probably be arranged for you.

Guided Tours
Chan Phen Tour (145 Uttarakit Rd., Krabi, tel. 075/612–404, fax 075/612–629), a café/restaurant next to the Bangkok Bank, has a travel desk. Ms. Lee, the owner, speaks excellent English. **Lao Ruam Kij** (11 Khongka Rd., Krabi, tel. 075/611–930) or one of the many travel shops on Uttarakit Road can also custom-design trips around the area.

Exploring Krabi is a pleasant, low-key town. Most visitors, however, only stop here to do some shopping, cash traveler's checks, arrange onward travel from one of the travel shops, and catch up on the news with fellow travelers idling at the many restaurants on main street, Uttarakit Road.

Ao Phra Nang, less than 20 minutes by road from Krabi, is in the process of being discovered by land speculators. Aside from a few hotels, accommodations consist of rustic bungalows, in which time is measured only by the sunrise and sunset. The beaches have fine sand and calm waters, backed by verdant green jungles inland and sheltered by islands. In fact, the waters are often too calm for enthusiastic sailors. Days are spent on the beach or exploring the islands by boat, particularly Turtle Island and Chicken Island for snorkeling. You can rent boats from the local fishermen or from the Krabi Resort. Pretty soon, beachcombers may have to renew the search for another idyllic area untouched by developers!

Between Krabi and Ao Phra Nang is **Susan Hoi** (Shell Cemetery Beach), aptly named for the 75-million-year-old shells that have petrified to form bizarre-shaped rock slabs. Farther up from Ao Phra Nang Bay is another beach known as **Haad Noppharat Thara,** famed for its rows of casuarina trees. You can walk out to the little rocky island at low tide, but don't linger there too long. When the tide comes in, so does a current. For total seclusion, hire a long-tailed boat to take you (15 minutes) to empty beaches on Pai Pong or Rai Lee.

Dining In Krabi you have the choice of small Thai restaurants, European breakfast food at the cafés along main street, or more elaborate Thai food at the **Isouw** (*see below*). Two basic Thai hotels serve businesspeople in town, while guest houses and resort hotels for tourists are mostly located around Ao Phra Nang.

Isouw. Right on the main street of Krabi Town, this restaurant stands on stilts over the water. It is a wonderful place in which to sit, enjoy lunch, and watch the river traffic. The restaurant specializes in grilled fish with sweet-and-sour sauce, and the *mee krob* (fried Thai noodles) here has an abundance of fresh, sweet shrimp. *256/1 Uttarakit Rd., Krabi, tel. 075/611–956. No reservations. Dress: casual. No credit cards. $$*

Lodging **Dusit Rahwadee.** A true retreat, marvelously laid out on 26 land-
★ scaped acres, this resort is accessible only by boat (20 minutes from Krabi Town, 70 minutes from Phuket, and 10 minutes from Ao Prang Bay), and its gardens and coconut groves lead down to white-sand beaches on three sides. The modern Thai-style pavilions are circular, with spacious living rooms downstairs and spiral staircases to the magnificent bedrooms and sumptuous bathrooms with huge round tubs. The use of highly polished wood floors throughout adds to the cool luxury. Because nearly all the pavilions are between the two beaches that flank the headland, you are never more than a five-minute walk from a beach—you can hear but not see the waves roll in. Krua Pranang, the memorable Thai restaurant in a breezy pavilion one floor up, serves food as exciting as it is delicious. For an appetizer, try the *puk kana* (Thai broccoli leaves filled with mixed lime, chili, shallots, and ginger) or the fried sweetened beef and papaya salad served with steamed rice. For entrées, the steamed fish with pickled plum and the *tom kha gai* (chicken curry in coconut milk) are two tasty choices. A few other properties share the beach—for example the Sand Sea Bungalow (tel. 075/611–944)—offering very basic fan-cooled accommodations (about B300) and café/restaurants. *67 Moo 5 Susan Hoy Rd., Tambol Sai Thai, Krabi 81000, tel. 075/*

620–740, fax 075/620–630. Bangkok reservations, tel. 02/238–4790. 98 pavilions. Facilities: 2 restaurants, bar, satellite TV, video (complimentary tapes), in-room safes, coffee and tea makings, pool with snack bar. AE, DC, MC, V. $$$$

Krabi Resort. A small collection of thatched cottages on Ao Phra Nang has now mushroomed into a large resort, where modern rooms in the new concrete addition are often preferred. There is also a pool in the garden, though the beach has greater attraction. Dinners are often feasts, with steaks or steamed fish in soy sauce; you can work off the calories later, in the disco lounge. *Ao Phra Nang. Reservations: 55–57 Pattana Rd., Amphoe Muang, Krabi 81000, tel. 075/ 611–389, fax 075/612–160. Bangkok reservations, tel. 02/251–8094. 80 rooms. Facilities: restaurant, pool, disco, boat rental. DC, MC, V. $$$*

Ao Nang Villa. Along the same beach as the Krabi Resort are these more modest bungalows. Rooms vary from tiny and fan-cooled (B300) to reasonably spacious with twin beds and air-conditioning (B850). *113 Phra Nang Beach, Krabi 81000, tel. 075/612–728, fax 075/611–837. 42 rooms. Facilities: restaurant. MC, V. $*

Emerald Bungalows. On the quiet, sandy beach of Haad Noppharat, just north of Ao Phra Nang, this hotel offers the option of tiny bungalows with no bath or larger bungalows with a private bath. Those fronting the beach are the best and the most expensive (B500). The restaurant specializes in seafood and is the place for socializing and reading under the lights. *Haad Noppharat Beach, Moo 4, Tambol Ao Phra Nang. Reservations: 2/1 Kongca Rd., Krabi 81000, tel. 075/ 611–106. 36 rooms. Facilities: restaurant. No credit cards. $*

Grand Tower Guest House. This new guest house is extremely popular with backpackers. The rooms are clean and the facilities modern. The café serves basic Western fare, and the tour desk is knowledgeable. Also, many of the long-distance private bus companies stop here. *73/1 Uttarakit Rd. Amphur Muang, Krabi, tel. 075/611–741. 27 fan-cooled rooms. Facilities: restaurant, travel desk. MC, V. $*

Phang Nga Bay Halfway between Krabi and Phuket is Phang Nga Bay, made famous by the James Bond movie *The Man with the Golden Gun*. Caves and outcroppings of limestone, some rising 270 m (900 ft) straight up from the sea, are a unique sight.

Getting There Frequent bus service links Phang Nga Town with Krabi and Phuket. Phang Nga Town is 10 km (6¼ mi) from the bay; most people come here simply to arrange transportation to nearby islands, generally driving or taking a bus straight to the bay.

Guided Tours Guided tours of Phang Nga Bay usually begin from Phuket. **World Travel Service,** with travel desks at the Phuket Yacht Club (tel. 076/ 214–020 ext. WTS) and the Phuket Merlin (tel. 076/212–866 ext. WTS), offers one of the most comprehensive tours.

Exploring At the bay, hire a long-tailed boat to tour the islands. Most tourists come to the bay from Phuket and don't arrive until 11 AM. If you can get into the bay before then, it will be more or less yours to explore, with a boatman as your guide. In order to make an early start, you may want to stay overnight (*see below*). The key sights to visit are **Ko Panyi**, with its Muslim fishing village built on stilts; **Ko Phing Kan**, now known as James Bond Island; **Ko Tapu**, which looks like a nail driven into the sea; **Tham Kaeo grotto**, an Asian version of Capri; and **Tham Lot**, where a large cave has been carved into an archway large enough to allow cruise boats to pass through. You really need two days to see everything and to appreciate the sunsets, which are particularly beautiful on **Ko Mak.**

Lodging **Phang Nga Bay Resort.** This modern hotel's sole raison d'être is as a base for exploring the nearby islands and rocks. Located on an estuary 1½ km (1 mi) from the coast, it does not have panoramic views, but the rooms are comfortable and modern, the bathrooms are clean and large, and the dining room offers reasonable Chinese, Thai, and European food. *20 Thaddan Panyee, Phang Nga 82000, tel. 076/ 411–067; fax 076/411–057. Bangkok reservations, tel. 02/259–1994. 88 rooms. Facilities: restaurant, coffee shop, tennis, pool, and boat hire. AE, MC, V. $$*

Ko Samui

Five hundred km (310 mi) from Bangkok and 30 km (18½ mi) off Surat Thani, in the Gulf of Siam, lies Ko Samui. Backpackers discovered the island several years ago; now, vacationing tourists regard it as an alternative to Phuket. It has already become too commercialized for some people, but there are far fewer hotels, restaurants, and café/bars than on Phuket, and Ko Samui is a veritable haven of tranquillity compared with the seediness of Pattaya.

Ko Samui is half the size of Phuket, and it can be easily toured in a day. But tourists come for the sun and beach, not for sightseeing. The best beaches, those with glistening white sand and clear waters, are on the island's east coast. Beaches on the other coasts either have muddy sand or rocky coves. Already the waters around Ko Samui are less clear than they were years ago. The sea surrounding the small islands nearby is still crystal clear, however, and the tiny islets to the north of Ko Samui that make up the Angthong Marine National Park are superb for snorkeling and scuba diving. Ko Samui has a different weather pattern from Phuket, on the west coast. Typhoons hit Ko Samui in November and December; in Phuket, the monsoon season extends from May through November. Off-season prices are 40% lower than those during peak season (January–June).

Tourist The provincial **TAT** office, on the mainland (5 Talat Mai Rd., Surat
Information Thani 84000, tel. 077/281–828), sells a useful map of Ko Samui (B35) and provides information about guest houses and ferry connections.

Many travel agencies operate out of Surat Thani and Ko Samui's main town, Na Thon. **Songserm Travel Center** (64/1-2 Na Thon, Ko Samui, tel. 077/421–316) operates many of the interisland boats. You can also contact Songserm at its offices in Bangkok (tel. 02/251–8994), Surat Thani (tel. 077/272–928), and Ko Pha Ngan (tel. 077/281–639). A useful travel agency on the east coast of Ko Samui is the **International Air Agency** (63/2 Chaweng Rd., Chaweng Beach, Ko Samui, tel. 077/421–551; fax 077/431–544). For fishing and diving trips, **Fantasia Diving and Yachting** (21 Nathon, Moo 3, Ko Samui, tel. 077/421–289) offers one- to three-day offshore excursions.

Emergencies The **Tourist Police** (Surat Thani, tel. 077/281–300; Na Thon, tel. 077/ 421–281) are the people to call. The **Surat Thani Hospital** is on Surat-Phun Phin Road (tel. 077/272–231).

Warning: Be sure to wear something to protect your feet when wading among the coral. Nasty abrasions can result, and an element in the coral hinders the healing process. Rusty nails in planks of old wood are another hazard.

Arriving and Ko Samui has a small airport, served by the 37-seat planes of **Bang-**
Departing **kok Airways** (in Bangkok, tel. 02/253–4014; in Ko Samui, tel. 077/
By Plane 421–483), which runs five flights daily between Bangkok and Ko Samui (B2,080) and between Phuket and Ko Samui (B1,300). Reser-

vations are crucial during peak periods. **Thai Airways International** (tel. 077/273–355) flies to Surat Thani on the mainland, from which you must travel by car and then ferry to Ko Samui.

The airport is on the northeast tip of the island. Taxis meet arrivals; their price is fixed—with little room for negotiation—to various parts of the island. The most common price is B200. Some hotels have a limo/van service at the airport, but these cost the same as a taxi. Songthaews sporadically travel between the airport and Ko Samui's main town, Na Thon, for B30.

By Train Many express trains from Bangkok's main railway station, Hualamphong (tel. 02/223–7461), pass through Surat Thani on their way south. The journey takes about 12 hours, and the best trains are the overnighters that depart Bangkok at 6:30 PM and 7:20 PM, arriving in Surat Thani soon after 6 AM. The State Railway of Thailand offers a combined ticket that includes rail fare, a couchette in air-conditioned second class, bus connection to the ferry, and the ferry ride for B514. Passengers arrive at Ko Samui at about 10 AM the following day. First-class sleeping cabins are available only on the 7:20 PM train. Two express trains make the daily run up from Trang and Hat Yai in southern Thailand.

By Bus Buses leave Bangkok from the Southern Bus Terminal (tel. 02/411–0112 for air-conditioned buses; tel. 02/411–4978 for non-air-conditioned ones). Buses cost less than the train (about B225 for air-conditioned buses), and they're a bit faster (11 hours), but they are also less comfortable. Buses do have the advantage of going directly to the ferry terminal. Private tour companies use more comfortable, faster buses; try **Chok Anan** (Ratchadamnoen Klang Ave., tel. 02/281–2277). Express buses also travel to Surat Thani from Phuket (5 hours), from Krabi (4 hours), and from Had Yai (7 hours).

By Ferry Two ferries cross to Ko Samui from Surat Thani. Songserm's express boat leaves for Na Thon on Ko Samui from its new terminal 8 km (5 mi) out of town (use the Songserm bus service that collects passengers from the row of travel agencies along Surat Thani's waterfront). Half the ferry ride is down the river's estuary and the other half across the open water, taking, in all, about two hours. (The Songserm ferry goes on to Ko Pha Ngan.) The other ferry leaves from the pier at Donsak at the mouth of the river, 45 minutes by bus from Surat Thani and arrives at New Port, a ferry dock 6½ km (4 mi) south of Na Thon. This ferry takes about 90 minutes to make the sea passage. A combined bus-ferry ticket is available from one of the many tour/bus companies in Surat Thani. The last ferry to Ko Samui leaves around 4 PM, and the last ferry from Ko Samui departs at 3 PM. Times vary, so be sure to check the schedule.

Getting Around
By Songthaew Na Thon on the west coast is the terminus for songthaews (minibuses), which seat 10 people and two or three more standing on the back platform. They take either the north route around the island to Chengmon on the northeast tip and Chaweng on the east coast, or the southern route to reach Lamai on the southeast coast. Between Chaweng and Lamai is a transfer point where you can change songthaews for either the northern or southern route. The fare from Na Thon to Chaweng, the most distant point, is B30. Songthaews making the northern trip start from the waterfront north of the pier; those making the southern trip start south of the pier.

Songthaews may also be rented as private taxis. The price from Na Thon to Chaweng is about B250.

By Rental Car
and Scooters

If you want to explore Ko Samui, it's best to rent your own transportation. Jeeps are expensive (around B1,200 plus B175 for CDW), but they're the safest, although most people choose motor scooters, which can be obtained for about B175 per day. Gravel, potholes, and erratic driving make riding dangerous, and each year some travelers return home with broken limbs. Some never return at all.

Exploring *Numbers in the margin correspond to points of interest on the Ko Samui map.*

1
2
The ferry from Don Sak on the mainland arrives at **New Port**, 5 km (3 mi) south of Ko Samui's main town, **Na Thon**. Unless a hotel van is waiting for you, take a songthaew first to Na Thon, and then another to reach your final destination. The express boat from Surat Thani docks at Na Thon.

Compared with the other sleepy island villages, Na Thon is a bustling town with its shops and restaurants. Most of the restaurants and travel shops are along the waterfront. Commercial shops and banks line the parallel street one block from the waterfront. Though Na Thon has a hotel, tourists seldom stay in town.

3
On the north coast east of Na Thon, the first major tourist area is **Maenam**. Its long, curving, sandy beach is lapped by gentle waters that are great for swimming. Inexpensive guest houses and Dusit's new luxury Santiburi resort hotel can be found along the 5-km (3-mi) stretch of sand. A small headland separates Maenam from the next

4
bay, **Bophut** (Big Buddha). The sand is not as fine at Bophut and becomes muddy during the rainy season, but the fishing village has become a popular gathering spot for backpackers—numerous village homes have become crash pads, some of which might even be called guest houses. The dramatic sunsets attract photographers and romantics.

5
Rather than cutting across the island on the main, paved road to Chaweng, continue along the north shore to **Ko Fan,** a little island with a huge sitting Buddha image covered in moss. Try to visit at sunset, when the light off the water shows the Buddha at its best.

6
Continue east along the north coast to **Haad Chengmon** (*haad* means beach), dominated by the headland Laem Rumrong. This is the end of the road for the few songthaews that take this route. Few tourists come here because it's off the beaten track. Several guest houses are scattered along the shoreline, as well as Ko Samui's most elegant retreat, the Tongsai Bay Cottages, but you can still find peace and tranquillity.

7
8
If you have your own transportation—and don't mind bumping over rutted unpaved roads—the road continues around the peninsula for 6 km (3¾ mi) to **Chaweng Beach.** Of the 11 beach areas of Ko Samui, Chaweng has the finest glistening white sand. It is also Ko Samui's most congested beach, crammed with guest houses and tourists. Chaweng is divided into four parts: Northern **Chaweng Yai** (*yai* means large) is separated from **Chaweng Noi** (*noi* means little) to the south by a small point, Laem Koh Faan. Chaweng Yai is further divided by a reef into two sections, of which the northern one is Ko Matland, a quiet area popular with backpackers. The main part of Chaweng Yai is congested with hotels, tanned, scantily clad youths, and bulbous-breasted German hausfrauen. (Thais find it offensive that Western women sunbathe topless, and while they usually say nothing, they give a scornful smile.) Here you will find anything you want, from water-scooter rentals to money changers and nightclubs, like the currently popular Reggae Pub (tel. 077/422–331).

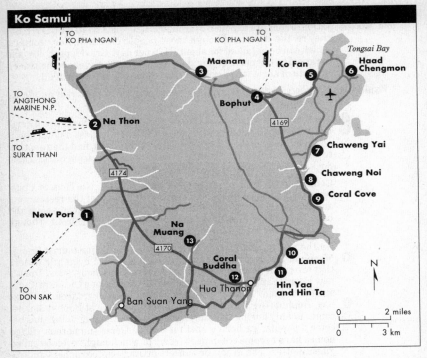

Ko Samui

9 Beyond the Imperial Samui Hotel is **Coral Cove,** popular among scuba diving enthusiasts. But you don't even have to be a diver to enjoy the underwater scenery: Just walk waist high into the water and look through a mask to see the amazing colors of the coral. For a Thai seafood lunch, walk up the rocks to Coral Cove Bungalows, where you also can rent snorkeling equipment.

South of this busy beach is Chaweng Noi, which is only partially developed. It is quieter than Chaweng Yai, and the salt air has yet to be tainted by the odor of suntan oil. At the end of this beach is the island's second-smartest resort, the Imperial Samui Hotel.

10 A rocky headland separates Chaweng from Ko Samui's second most popular beach, **Lamai.** The beach does not have the glistening white sand of Chaweng, but its clear water and rocky pools made this attractive area the first to be developed on Ko Samui. Lamai has a different feel than Chaweng; tourists mingle freely with one another at the local restaurants and bars.

11 Every visitor to Ko Samui makes a pilgrimage to Lamai for yet another attraction. At the point marking the end of Lamai beach stand two rocks, named **Hin Yaa** (Grand Mother Rock) and **Hin Ta** (Grand Father Rock). Erosion has shaped the rocks to resemble weathered and wrinkled intimate private parts.

12 Turn inland, heading back for Na Thon. Two km (1¼ mi) up this road is the **Coral Buddha,** carved by years of erosion. Continue farther on the main road to the village of Baan Thurian, where the road to the right climbs up into the jungle-clad hills to the island's best water-

13 fall, **Na Muang.** The falls are spectacular, especially after the rains, as they tumble from a limestone cliff to a small sandy pool. You can bathe in the pool, getting cooled by the spray and warmed by the sun. For a thrill, swim through the curtain of falling water; you can sit on a ledge at the back to catch your breath.

Back on the main highway, about 4 km (2½ mi) from Na Thon, the road turns off to the right, twisting for about 1½ km (1 mi) until it reaches a track leading up a steep hill. You'll have to walk this track, huffing and puffing, for about an hour, but you'll be rewarded at the top with magnificent views and refreshments.

At least one day should be given to a trip out to the 40 islets that make up the **Angthong Marine National Park,** which covers some 250 sq km (90 sq mi). The waters, the multicolored coral, and the underwater life are superb. Above water, the rocky islets form weird and wonderful shapes. Songserm operates daily boat trips, departing from Na Thon at 8:30 AM, to the islands for snorkeling and scuba diving; the cost is B250.

Dining and Lodging
Ko Samui's notable dining is found at the major hotels—Thai food at Santiburi, Mediterranean fare at Baan Taling Ngam, and Thai and European fare with magnificent views at the Imperial Tongsai Bay. The greatest number of local restaurants are in Chaweng, but there is little to distinguish one from another. Just look to make sure that the seafood, always the specialty, is fresh. Now, besides guest houses, full-fledged hotels have sprung up to meet every budget. Chaweng is the most developed, with Lamai, Maenam, and Bophut not far behind. The TAT has a list of guest houses on the islands. Most travel agencies in Bangkok, Surat Thani, and Ko Samui can make reservations at the hotels and at some guest houses.

Baan Taling Ngam. The newest luxury hotel on Ko Samui is this member of the Mandarin Oriental group. Its name in Thai means "home on a beautiful cliff," which eminently suits this small and appealing hotel set dramatically on the side of a cliff facing west across the sea. Sunsets are phenomenal—be sure that you make it here for a sundowner at least once. The swimming pool is equally stunning, set a couple of hundred feet above the sea. Its water flows over one side to disappear (seemingly) over the cliff. The guest rooms are also built into the cliff side, each with a private terrace looking out to sea. The contemporary furnishings are given warmth by a generous use of wood paneling. Down by the beach are seven suites that are reached by a shuttle-cart service, while above the main part of the hotel are some private villas that the hotel leases for two-bedroom hideaways. Baan Taling Ngam is secluded, but some may find it inconveniently far from most of the island's attractions—you'll need transport whenever you leave the property. *295 Moo 3, Taling Ngam, Ko Samui 84140, tel. 077/423–019, fax 077/423–220; U.K. reservations, tel. 071/537–2988; U.S. reservations, tel. 800/526–6566. 40 rooms, 7 beach suites, 42 villas. Facilities: 2 restaurants (Asian and Mediterranean), pool, fitness center, 2 tennis courts, travel desk. AE, DC, MC, V. $$$$*

Imperial Tongsai Bay Hotel. Although the Imperial Samui Hotel is the leading hotel on the island, its sister property, Tongsai Bay, is the elegant resort retreat. Set on 25 acres overlooking Tongsai Bay, the hotel has whitewashed, red-tiled hillside cottages, with balconies looking out to sea (though some views are blocked by overgrown foliage), and 24 rooms in the three-story main building. Rooms are stylishly furnished, and some of the split-level rooms incorporate the natural rock. The dining room offers beautiful views over the bay; reserve a table on the terrace. Ko Samui is known for huge succulent oysters and king prawns, and Tongsai gets the best. The duck in Tamarind sauce is also excellent. Service at Tongsai is not as good as it should be for the price. *Tongsai Bay, Ko Samui, tel. 077/421–451, fax 077/421–462; Bangkok reservations, tel. 02/254–0023, fax 02/253–3190. 80 rooms. Facilities: restaurant, bar, pool, tennis, water sports, shuttle to Na Thon and Chaweng. AE, DC, MC, V. $$$$*

★ **Santiburi.** This resort set on 23 acres on the northern coast offers an exclusive hideaway. The standard suites are private bungalows with highly polished wooden floors, even in the huge bathrooms, which have two washbasins, oval bathtubs, and separate shower stalls. The contemporary Thai furnishings give a warm, open feel that's enhanced by an etched glass panel between the living room and bedroom. Sliding doors to the patio add more space. Each bungalow has its own TV, VCR, and CD player, with complimentary CDs and VCR tapes. Ask for a bungalow close to the palm-shaded beach. The main building, like a modern Thai pavilion overlooking the oval swimming pool, has European and Thai restaurants, an open lounge area, shops, and a massage and fitness center. For informal refreshments and meals, guests amble up to the bamboo bar near the beach. Although the Santiburi is a secluded oasis of luxury, you can walk down its driveway to the main road and take a songthaew to any place on the island. There's also a Thai restaurant. *12/12 Moo 1, Tambol Maenam, Ko Samui 84330, tel. 077/425–031, fax 077/425–040; Bangkok reservations, tel. 02/238–4790; U.S. reservations, tel. 800/223–5652. 75 suites. Facilities: 2 restaurants, pool with snack bar, 2 tennis courts, squash courts, fitness center, water sports, CD and video library. AE, DC, MC, V. $$$$*

Boat House Hotel. The Imperial Group's third property on Ko Samui, across the bay from Tongsai, is 36 rice barges, converted into suites. The tightly packed rows of whale-like barges 100 yards in from the shore look like a Jonah's nightmare, but on board, they're superb. On the enclosed upper deck is a lounge with a wet bar; below is a large bathroom with a grand oval tub, a dressing room/lounge area, and the bedroom. The hulls are original; the uncluttered interiors and upper decks are new, with highly polished teak and mahogany beams and paneling. The double beds are just a foot off the floor, while high above are suspended fishing nets. Very nice! Another 176 rooms were built in two wings between the barges and the road. They're less expensive (B3,200 versus B5,400 for a barge suite) but have no sea view. Coral reefs are exposed at low tide, but the swimming is safe and in sheltered waters. *Chengmon Beach, Ko Samui, Surat Thani 84140, tel. 077/421–451, fax 077/421–462; Bangkok reservations, tel. 02/254–0023. 34 boat suites, 176 rooms. Facilities: 2 restaurants, pool, water sports, travel desk, tennis courts, airport bus. AE, DC, MC, V. $$$–$$$$*

The Imperial Samui. Ko Samui's best international resort hotel, this property is attractively laid out at the top of a landscaped garden terrace with steps leading down to the beach. Guest rooms, which fan out from the main building, are standard, with modern furnishings and little appeal except for the view of the beach. Attention is focused on the swimming pool adjacent to the sea; a small island sits in the pool, complete with three coconut trees. The hotel is located at the south end of Chaweng Noi, where the beach isn't crowded and the sea is clean. The restaurant tends to serve too many boring, albeit satisfying, buffets. *Chaweng Noi Beach, Ko Samui, tel. 077/421–390; Bangkok reservations: tel. 02/254–0023, fax 02/253–3190. 77 rooms. Facilities: restaurant, bar, pool, water sports. AE, DC, MC, V. $$$*

Palm Reef Hotel. This new hotel with an enthusiastic staff is on the part of Chaweng Beach that's too shallow for swimming; you need to walk 500 yards along the beach for that. The hotel has a swimming pool with a swim-up bar. The dining room (mostly Western fare) is one floor up, with a view; the Thai restaurant is in a wood-paneled room to the rear. Half the rooms, in two wings that look onto the pool and garden, are simply functional, with small bathrooms and showers only. The more attractive accommodations are on the other side of the dirt road that parallels the beach. They're Thai-style, in small compounds of teak bungalows, like a traditional Thai village. Mattresses are on low platforms above the polished mahogany floor. Large cottages have upstairs mezzanines, air-conditioning, and small terraces. *14/3 Moo 2, Tambon Boput, Chaweng Beach, Ko Samui, Surat Thani 84140, tel. 077/422–015, fax 077/422–394; Bangkok reservations, tel. 02/267–9711. 74 rooms. Facilities: 2 restaurants, 2 pools, tennis courts, airport bus. MC, V. $$*

Samui Pansea Hotel. The Pansea may not be quite as smart as its neighbor, the Imperial Samui, but it costs less. Set back from the beach, rooms come with fans or, for a few more dollars, air-conditioning. Equipment for water sports is available, and the restaurant offers views over the gulf. *Chaweng Noi Beach, Ko Samui, tel. 077/421–384; fax 077/421–385. 50 rooms. Facilities: restaurant, coffee shop, bar, water sports, drugstore. AE, MC, V. $$*

Fair House. Situated on the beach on Chaweng Noi, this hotel offers small, simple bungalows with air-conditioning or overhead fans, and rudimentary private bathrooms. Each bungalow has its own veranda, but only a few have a clear view of the beach. The open-fronted dining room has broad sea views, and the Thai cuisine—with a few Western dishes—is remarkably good. *Chaweng Noi Beach, Ko Samui, tel. and fax 077/421–373. 26 rooms. Facilities: restaurant, bar. MC, V. $*

O.P. Bungalow. Of the inexpensive bungalow cottage hotels that line Chaweng Beach, this is the most efficiently run, and it has clean, simple rooms with hot-water geysers in the bathrooms. The narrow property has four rows of cottages stretching back from the beach to the road (rates are higher close to the beach). The rooms have tile floors and most have twin beds (with a few doubles). Room 502 is a good one to ask for. An open-sided coffee shop down at the beach has reasonably priced Thai and Chinese food. *Chaweng Beach, Ko Samui, Surat Thani 84320, tel. 077/422–424, fax 077/422–425. 38 rooms. Facilities: restaurant. No credit cards. ¢–$*

Excursion from Ko Samui

Though Ko Samui has yet to be completely developed and taken over by resort hotels, like Phuket, the island is no longer off the beaten track. Travelers looking for the simple beach life with few signs of commercialism now head for **Ko Pha Ngan,** 12 km (7.5 mi) north, which is at the turning point of its development. A decade ago, the few international wanderers stayed in fishermen's houses or slung hammocks on the beach. Now guest bungalows, cheap and simple, have sprung up on most of the best beaches, and investors are buying up beach properties. Land worth a million baht three years ago can bring as much as 45 million baht today. For now, though, the lack of transportation to and on the island limits Ko Pha Ngan's development, and one of the world's most idyllic places has yet to be spoiled.

Getting There From Surat Thani, the morning Songserm Express boats depart at 7 AM and 9 AM for Thong Sala, the major town on Ko Pha Ngan, stopping at Na Thon on Koh Samui. One afternoon ferry (sometimes more) departs about 2 PM. From Thong Sala, long-tailed boat ferries travel to all the bays on the island. From Ko Samui, you can also take a small ferry boat at about 10 AM from Bophut to Haad Rin, and in good weather, a long-tailed boat ferry that leaves Maenam on Ko Samui at about 9

AM for Haad Tong Nai Pan (this boat does not and should not run if the seas are high). From Chumphon on the mainland, a ferry travels twice a week to Ko Tao and on to Ko Pha Ngan.

Exploring Since the island's unpaved roads twist and turn, it's easier to beach-hop by boat. In fact, if you want to find the beach that most appeals to you, take a boat trip around the island on the ferries—it takes about nine hours. The southeast tip of the island is divided by a long promontory into **Haad Rin West** and **Haad Rin East,** the island's most popular and crowded areas. Boats from Thong Sala take 40 minutes to reach Haad Rin East; their departure is timed to meet arriving passengers from Songserm's interisland boat. If Haad Rin is too crowded, catch the onward boat up the east coast to **Haad Tong Nai Pan,** a perfect horseshoe bay divided by a small promontory. On the beach of the southern and larger half are several guest houses and a couple of local restaurants. The northern bay, Tong Nai Pan Noi, is the smaller and quieter of the two. Perhaps it has two more years before being developed, but for now it's a beachcomber's paradise. Telephone cables have yet to link it with the world, and though there is a road, no self-respecting kidney will take the incessant bouncing of the four-wheel-drive vehicle negotiating its curves and ruts. Glistening white sand curves around the turquoise waters of this half-moon bay, and coconut trees behind the beach hide the small houses of the villagers. At the ends of the bay are two small resorts.

North of Ko Pha Ngan lies the smaller **Ko Tao,** a Robinson Crusoe island with unpaved roads and no electricity that's also being discovered. Already more than two dozen small guest houses offer basic accommodation, but since the boat stops there only infrequently, the island is still only for those who have time to spare.

Dining **Pannoi's.** The owner of this local restaurant goes fishing in the evening for tomorrow's menu. The guests, barefoot and shirtless, sit at rough-hewn wood tables set in the sand. A meal may consist of tender and succulent *ma pla* (horsefish, much like snapper) and a plateful of barbecued prawns with garlic and pepper. *Haad Tong Nai Pan Noi, no phone. No credit cards.* $

Lodging **Panviman Resort.** This resort has 15 thatched cottages and 10 new stone-and-stucco bungalows, some cooled by fan and others by air-conditioning. In 1993 a new hotel was built. Its rooms, half of which have an ocean view, have twin beds, are fan-cooled, and cost B900. Each bungalow has a balcony, a large bedroom, and a spacious bathroom with a cold-water shower. During the day, electricity is turned off and the rooms become stifling, but who wants to be inside? Outside, a breeze blows in from sea. The circular wood restaurant, cooled by the breezes blowing over the promontory, serves Western food, but the Thai dishes are better and more extensive. Ask for a light hand in the chili department. Guests gather here to watch the nightly video. *Haad Tong Nai Pan. Ko Pha Ngan, Surat Thani, tel. 077/286–900 (the booking office is in Thong Sala); Bangkok reservations, tel. 02/587–8491, fax 02/587–8493. 10 bungalows, 15 hotel rooms, 15 cottages. Facilities: restaurant. MC, V.* $–$$

Tong Tapan Resort. These small thatched cottages on stilts perched on the side of the hill are home to international backpackers. *North end of Haad Tong Nai Pan Noi, no phone. No credit cards.* ¢

Pattaya

Four decades ago, Pattaya was a fishing village on an unspoiled natural harbor 147 km (88 mi) southeast of Bangkok. Discovered by affluent Bangkok residents, it became a weekend playground, replacing Hua Hin and Cha' Am on the southwest coast as vacation destinations. Then came the Vietnam War, when thousands of American soldiers sought release and recreation. With a large U.S. air base at nearby Utapano and a naval base at Cam Ranh, U.S. servicemen hit the beaches at Pattaya in droves and the resort became a boomtown, with a complete range of resort activities to cater to lonely soldiers looking for a good time.

After a few years in the doldrums, Pattaya is getting busier, with many tourists from eastern Europe. The highway traffic between Bangkok and Pattaya on weekends is congested, often stretching the two-hour trip to four. Pattaya has something tacky for everyone, the most obvious being its many bars and nightclubs catering to foreign males. Conveniently located on the side streets are dozens of clinics to treat venereal diseases. Raw sewage flows into the bay, threatening a dose of hepatitis for anyone foolish enough to swim in the once-crystal-clear waters. Even the waters around Ko Larn, the small island 64 km (40 mi) offshore, have been tainted by the effluent, so it's risky to swim there. Pattaya's infrastructure has become so disastrously inadequate that the government has promised US$200 million to start a cleanup process that should include water- and sewage-treatment plants.

If Pattaya were anywhere else but Thailand, it would be positively distasteful. But it is in Thailand, and somehow what is gross is made agreeable by the smiling Thais. Pattaya is Thailand's total beach resort, offering everything from deep-sea fishing to golf, from windsurfing to elephant kraals.

Tourist Information
The **Tourist Authority of Thailand** (382/1 Beach Rd., South Pattaya, tel. 038/428–750) has free brochures and listings of festivities and events. The office is open daily 9–5.

Emergencies
If you need the **police, fire department,** or an **ambulance,** dial 195, or contact the **Tourist Police** (North Pattaya Beach Rd., Pattaya, tel. 038/429–371).

Travel Agencies
Song Asawin Travel Service (Beach Rd., Pattaya, tel. 038/423–704) in the South Pattaya Bus Terminal offers discounts on hotels and transportation. **Malibu Travel Co.** (183/82-84 Post Office La., Pattaya, tel. 038/423–180) arranges tours and travel around Pattaya, and to Ko Samet.

Arriving and Departing
By Plane
By 1995 **Bangkok Airways** (tel. 02/253–4014) should be operating twice-daily flights from Bangkok's Don Muang Airport for B900. These flights land at U-Tapao Airport, 50 km (30 mi) east of Pattaya. Also expected are **Silk Air** flights between Singapore and Pattaya every Tuesday, Wednesday, Friday, and Saturday.

By Taxi
Taxis make the journey from either Don Muang Airport or downtown Bangkok for a quoted B1,500, quickly renegotiated to B1,200 or less. Coming back, the fare is only around B750.

By Limousine/Bus
Direct buses make the three-hour drive between Pattaya's hotels and Bangkok's Don Muang Airport, leaving every two or three hours from 6 AM to 9 PM. **Thai Limousine Service** (ticket desk at airport, or in Pattaya, tel. 038/421–421) has the cleanest, most reliable buses, and they're also air-conditioned. The cost is B200.

By Bus
Buses depart every half hour from Bangkok's Eastern Terminal (Ekkamai) on Sukhumvit Road at Soi 63, about a B70 taxi ride from downtown. They arrive at Pattaya's bus station, in North Pattaya, just off Beach Road. The fare is B53 per person.

By Minibus   Most hotels in Bangkok and Pattaya have a travel-agent desk that works directly with a minibus company. Minibuses leave approximately five times a day and cost B150 per person. An Avis minibus that departs from Bangkok's Dusit Thani hotel for its property in Pattaya is open to nonguests as well.

By Ferry   A new hydrofoil ferry, the *Thepsirinta*, runs daily from the Meanam Hotel pier in Bangkok to Pattaya. The journey takes three hours and costs B350 in second class, B450 in first class. The schedule varies, so check a few days in advance. For information, call: Thai Intertransport, tel. 02/291–9613.

Getting Around
By Minibus   Songthaews cruise the two main streets of Pattaya, which run parallel to the beach. The fare is B5 in Pattaya town, and B10 between Naklua and Pattaya; for the Royal Cliff Resort, the fare is about B50 and to Jontien Beach at least B100.

By Car/ Motorbike   Sedans and Jeeps can be rented for B700–B900 a day, with unlimited mileage. **Avis** (Dusit Resort Hotel, Pattaya, tel. 038/429–901) offers insurance, though not all rental companies do. Motorbikes may be rented for about B250 a day.

Exploring   Pattaya can be divided into three sections, from north to south. To the north, Naklua Beach attracts locals and has few tourist facilities. On a small promontory south of the Dusit Resort Hotel is the picturesque curving bay of Pattaya, which runs alongside Beach Road, lined with palm trees on the beach side and modern resort hotels on the other. At the southern end of the bay is the fun part of town—bars, nightclubs, restaurants, and open-front cafés dominate both Sunset Avenue (the extension of Beach Ave.) and the side streets.

Parallel to Beach Road is Pattaya 2 Road, the main commercial street, which becomes more congested with traffic and local shops the farther south you go. Continuing through town, Pattaya 2 Road climbs a hill leading past Buddha Park on the left and then descends to quieter Jontien Beach, which is now attracting condominium developers and hotels.

Many of Pattaya's diversions are more for the Thai family on vacation than for the foreign visitor, but two of them are worthwhile. The first is elephants. Since teak logging was restricted, this noble beast suffers from high unemployment, and only an estimated 4,000 of them live in Thailand now. At the **Elephant Kraal,** 14 pachyderms display their skill at moving logs in a two-hour show, twice daily. The show also includes demonstrations by war elephants, an enactment of ceremonial rites, and the capture of a wild elephant. Everything is staged, but it's always rewarding to see elephants at work and at play. *On the main highway 5 km (3 mi) out of Pattaya, tel. 038/428–640. Admission charge. Daily shows 2:30 and 4:30.*

The second, a general overview of Thai culture, **Nong Nuch Village** offers a folk show, an exhibition of monkeys picking coconuts, elephants bathing, and a small zoo and aviary. Two restaurants, one Thai and one Western, offer refreshments on rolling grounds covered with coconut plantations. Despite its touristy nature, the village provides a pleasant break from sunbathing on the beach, particularly if you're traveling with children. Hotels will arrange transportation for morning and afternoon visits. *Located 15 km (9 mi) south of Pattaya, 163 km marker on Hwy. 1, Bang Saray, tel. 038/429–321. Admission charge. Open 9–5:30. Daily shows 10 AM and 3 PM.*

Participant Sports

Bungee Jumping If you are one to take a fall, try Kiwi Thai Bungee Jump, off the main road to Jontien Beach. You are hoisted in a metal cage to a height of 46 m (150 ft) and then you jump. Just remember to attach your rubber harness first! *Tel. 038/250–319. Open 1–9.*

Golf **The Royal Thai Navy Course** (Phiu Ta Luang Golf Course, Sattahip, Chonburi, tel. 02/466–1180, ext. Sattahip 2217), located 30 km (18 mi) from Pattaya, is Thailand's longest course at 6,800 yards and is considered one of the country's most difficult with rolling hills and dense vegetation. The **Siam Country Club** (Pattaya, Chonburi, tel. 038/418–002), close to Pattaya, offers a challenging course with awkward water traps and wooded hills.

Water Sports All kinds of water sports are available, including windsurfing (B200 per hour), waterskiing (B1,000 per hour), and sailing on a 16-foot Hobie Catamaran (B500 per hour). Private entrepreneurs offer these activities all along the beach, but the best area is around the **Sailing Club** on Beach Road. Water scooters and parasailing are dangerous and shouldn't be tried for the first time here. Be on the lookout for unscrupulous operators who rent a defective machine and hold the customer responsible for its repair or loss. Parasailing boat operators tend to be inexperienced, making sharp turns or sudden stops that bring the parachutist down too fast. The water near shore is too polluted for diving and snorkeling.

Dining Every type of cuisine seems to be available in Pattaya. Visitors may find it harder to find good Thai restaurants here than other types of eateries, though several rather earthy Thai restaurants are located in the center of town, back from the tourist strip. With the Gulf of Siam at Pattaya's doorstep, seafood is the local specialty.

Buccaneer Terrace. The view of the bay from this rooftop restaurant in the Nipa Lodge Hotel is its prime attraction, although it also offers a good choice of fresh seafood and grilled steaks. *Beach Rd., Pattaya, tel. 038/428–195. Reservations accepted. Dress: casual but neat. AE, DC, MC, V. $$$*

Dolf Riks. The menu here reflects Dolf's many years in Indonesia before settling in Pattaya. A very reasonable *rijsttafel* (a Dutch Indonesian meal consisting of many dishes, including chicken with jackfruit, beef and grated coconut, spicy vegetables and rice) improved by Thai spices is the specialty, but the European dishes are superior, as is the seafood casserole. Only good-quality ingredients are used. The bar is popular with expatriates and the few tourists who find this oasis. *463/28 Sri Nakorn Centre, N. Pattaya, tel. 038/428–269. Reservations accepted. Dress: casual but neat. AE, DC, MC, V. $$$*

Peppermill Restaurant. Tucked away next to P.K. Villa, this distinctly French restaurant takes a classical approach to dining, with an emphasis on flambéed dishes. More creative dishes such as fresh crab in a white-wine sauce and poached fillet of sole with a lobster tail are also offered. Dinner is a special occasion, here, particularly if complemented by a good bottle of wine from the respectable cellar. *16 Beach Rd., tel. 038/428–248. Reservations accepted. Dress: casual but neat. AE, DC, MC, V. Dinner only. $$$*

San Domenico. The Roman owner of this restaurant halfway between Pattaya and Jontien prides himself on his pasta dishes and ice cream, and you might want to try his filling pizzas, excited by Thai spices, or the buffet (B300). Be sure to end your meal with the Italian ice cream that made this Roman an instant success. *Jontien Rd., South Pattaya, tel. 038/426–871. Reservations accepted. Dress: casual. MC, V. $$$*

Angelo's. For Italian food, this is the other good choice. Angelo's is owned by a Milanese who presides over the dining room, and his Thai wife is the chef. Her fortes are lasagna and fish casserole, especially the latter. *N. Pattaya Rd., tel. 038/429–093. Reservations accepted. Dress: casual. MC, V. $$*

Nang Nual. Next to the transvestite Simon Cabaret nightspot, this restaurant is one of Pattaya's better places for seafood, cooked Thai-style or simply grilled. The huge steaks are an expensive treat. The menu has photographs of the finished products to overcome any language barrier. Similar dishes are found at Nang Nual's Jontien Beach branch, located near the Sigma Resort. *214–10 S. Pattaya Beach Rd., Pattaya, tel. 038/428–478. No reservations. Dress: casual. AE, MC, V. $$*

Tak Nak Nam. In a Thai pavilion at the edge of a small lake, this floating restaurant has an extensive menu of Chinese and Thai dishes. Live classical Thai and folk music is played while you dine on such specialties as steamed crab in coconut milk or blackened chicken with Chinese herbs. *252 Pattaya Central Rd., next to the Pattaya Resort Hotel, tel. 038/429–059. Reservations accepted. Dress: casual. MC, V. $$*

Lodging
The Pattaya area has more than 500 hotels. With the exception of the Royal Cliff Hotel, most deluxe hotels line South Pattaya Beach Road, with their choice guest rooms overlooking the bay. Less expensive hotels are generally a block or two from the shore. Hotel tariffs fluctuate widely, depending on the season, the day of the week, and on holiday periods, when they can be more than twice as high as in low season. Lately, the hotels have been discounting their rooms heavily, usually to package tours groups from Eastern Europe. The congestion on Pattaya's beachfront has spawned a rapid development of hotels and condominiums along Jontien Beach, a B150 taxi ride to the south.

Royal Cliff Beach Hotel. Pattaya's most lavish hotel is 1½ km (1 mi) south of Pattaya on a bluff jutting into the Gulf of Siam. The self-contained resort has three wings. Rooms in the Royal Wing are double the price of a standard deluxe room in the main building; for all of these 84 one-bedroom suites there is butler service, breakfast served in the room, and reserved deck chairs. The Royal Cliff Terrace wing has two-bedroom and honeymoon suites with four-poster beds. The swimming pool sits on top of a cliff and overlooks the sea. *Jontien Beach, Pattaya, Chonburi, tel. 038/421–421, fax 038/428–511; Bangkok reservations, tel. 02/282–0999. 700 rooms and 100 suites. Facilities: 4 restaurants, 3 pools, 2 private beaches, 2 flood-lighted tennis courts, 2 squash courts, minigolf course, jogging track, sauna, water sports, pastry shop, boutique shops. AE, DC, MC, V. $$$$*

★ **Dusit Resort Hotel.** On a promontory at the northern end of Pattaya Beach, this large hotel opened in 1989 and offers superb sea views. The spacious rooms feature large bathrooms, balconies, oversize beds, sitting areas, and pastel furnishings. The Landmark Rooms are even more spacious and make extensive use of wood trim. At the Peak restaurant, contemporary French cuisine is served against the backdrop of Pattaya Bay and the gulf. While dinner for two here may set you back $100, it will be the best European dinner in town. While the Dusit is a retreat from the Pattaya tourists, it is also only a B5 songthaew ride along Pattaya Beach Road to where all the action is. *240/2 Pattaya Beach Rd., Pattaya, Chonburi 20260, tel. 038/425–611, fax 038/428–239; Bangkok reservations, tel. 02/236–0450. 500 rooms and 28 suites. Facilities: 4 restaurants, 2 pools, 3 flood-lighted tennis courts, 2 squash courts, fitness center, sauna, water* *sports, billiards and snooker room, table tennis, boutique shops. AE, DC, MC, V. $$$*

Montien. Though not plush, this hotel has a central location and design that take advantage of the cool sea breezes. With the hotel's generous off-season discounts, a room with a sea view can be one of the best values in town. The air-conditioned section of the Garden Restaurant has a dance floor and stage for entertainment. *Pattaya Beach Rd., Pattaya, Chonburi 20260, tel. 038/418–155, fax 038/423–155; Bangkok reservations, tel. 02/233–7060. 320 rooms. Facilities: 2 restaurants, 24-hr coffee shop, pool with snack bar, 2 floodlighted tennis courts, cocktail lounge with live music, meeting rooms. AE, DC, MC, V. $$$*

The Royal Cruise Hotel. Easily recognized by its shiplike exterior, this new hotel employs a nautical motif throughout, with anchor designs on the carpets and guest rooms called cabins. A decor of pastels and teak gives the hotel a comfortable feeling. For a romantic evening, sample the ninth-floor restaurant with its sweeping views of the bay and French-style cuisine. *499 N. Pattaya Beach Rd., Pattaya, Chonburi 20260, tel. and fax 038/424–242; Bangkok reservations, tel. 02/233–5970. 190 rooms and 10 suites. Facilities: restaurant, coffee shop, pool with poolside bar, health center, sauna, business center, travel desk. AE, DC, MC, V. $$$*

Palm Lodge. This no-frills hotel has the benefit of being centrally located, quiet, and inexpensive. Guest rooms are sparsely furnished and don't have carpeting, bathrooms are basic, and the outdoor pool is small. The staff is reliable, however. *Beach Rd., Pattaya, Chonburi 20260, tel. 038/428–780, fax 038/421–779. 80 rooms. Facilities: coffee shop, pool, laundry services. MC, V. $$*

Diamond Beach Hotel. In the heart of Pattaya's nightlife section amid discos and cafés, this hotel is a bastion of sanity. Rooms are clean, and security guards make female guests feel safe. The staff, however, is not particularly friendly or helpful—perhaps that's why you can often find a room here when other hotels are full. *373/8 Pattaya Beach Rd., Pattaya, Chonburi 20260, tel. 038/418–071, fax 038/424–888. 126 rooms. Facilities: restaurant, travel desk, massage room. No credit cards. $*

The Nag's Head. Owned by an Englishman, this small hotel offers clean, inexpensive, air-conditioned rooms with private baths. Its location on a busy road is not the best, but the friendly atmosphere makes this the top choice in the budget category. On the ground floor is an open-front bar and a restaurant inside that serves British fare. *179 Pattaya 2 Rd., Pattaya, Chonburi 20260, tel. 038/418–264. 15 rooms. Facilities: restaurant, bar. No credit cards. ¢*

Nightlife   Entertainment in Pattaya revolves around the hundreds of bars, bar/cafés, discos, and nightclubs. One popular nightspot is the **Pattaya Palladium** (tel. 038/424–922), which bills itself as the largest disco in Southeast Asia. The **Marina Disco** in the Regent Marina Hotel (S. Pattaya Rd., tel. 038/429–568) has a laser light show, live entertainment, and three DJs who keep the activity going until the wee hours of the morning. Bars and clubs stay open past midnight, and some are open much later. Discos usually have a cover charge of B100, and drinks cost about B50. Drinks for any hostess who joins you are B100. Of late, Pattaya has had a rash of AIDS cases and drug-related killings. Caution is advised for night revelers!

Excursion to Ko Samet and Chantaburi

Pattaya is often used as a base for trips farther south to the beach resort of Ko Samet or even to the mining district of Chantaburi. You can visit either of these destinations in a day, but not both.

Getting There   Travel companies will arrange transportation to Ko Samet. Try the **Malibu Travel Centre** (Post Office La., Pattaya, tel. 038/423–180), which has daily 8 AM departures for B120. You can also travel by local bus or by car to Ban Phe and transfer onto the ferry. Buses go to Rayong, where you pick up the minibus (departs from behind the Clock Tower) to Ban Phe. The total journey takes about two hours.

Exploring   If you travel by car, take the main highway (H3) south. A right turn off H3 at the 165-km marker will lead you to the village of **Bang Saray**, 20 km (12 mi) from Pattaya. The village consists of jetties, a fishing fleet, a small temple, and two narrow streets running parallel to the bay. Fully equipped game-fishing craft are tied up to the jetty, and photos to prove fishermen's stories are posted in the area's two hotel bars, Fisherman's Lodge and Fisherman's Inn. It costs about B2,500 to charter one of the faster fishing boats for the day. If you just want to soak up the scene, stop next to the main jetty at the Ruam Talay Restaurant, where most people congregate when they're not at the beach. Windsurfers are available for rent at the beach, just north of the bay at the Sea Sand Club.

Back on H3, drive through Sattahip, a Thai naval base, or you can avoid this busy town by taking bypass H332. The road passes through countryside full of coconut groves and tapioca plantations. **Rayong**, 15 km (9 mi) from Sattahip, is a booming market town, famous for its seafood and *nam plaa*, the fermented fish sauce Thais use as a salt substitute. **Ban Phe** is 20 km (12 mi) farther.

Two ferries from Ban Phe make the 30-minute crossing to **Ko Samet** (fare: B20): One goes to Na Duan on the north shore, the other to An Wong Duan on the east shore. All of the island's beaches are an easy walk from these villages. Ko Samet is known for its beaches; its other name is Ko Kaeo Phitsadan (meaning "sand like crushed crystal"), and its fine sand is in great demand by glassmakers.

Ko Samet has numerous bungalows and cottages, some with and some without electricity. Make sure that your bungalow has mosquito netting: Ko Samet's mosquitoes are malarial. After dusk, cover yourself up or use repellent. Malaria is not very easy to catch, but if you do start showing symptoms, make your way to the Rayong Hospital, which has a malaria clinic.

East of Rayong near the Kampuchea border is Chantaburi, 180 km (108 mi) from Pattaya. Buses from both Rayong and Ban Phe make the 90-minute journey. Much of the jewelry that you find sold in Pattaya contains gemstones from the open-pit mines around this ancient town. Star sapphires and rubies are the two most popular stones. You can take a tour of the mining area and see the 9-m- (30-ft-) deep holes where the prospectors dig.

Beyond Chantaburi is Trat province and the quiet island of **Ko Chang**, only recently discovered by foreign tourists. To reach Ko Chang, you can take the bus from Chantaburi for Trat (2 hours plus) or the bus from Bangkok's Southern Bus Terminal (6 hours). From Trat, take the local bus for a 15-minute ride to the small port of Laen Knob and a boat from there. The only regular boat departs for Ko Chang Resort at 2 PM (90 minutes, fare B300). Once on the island, you can stay at the **Ko Chang Resort** (tel. 039/512–818; in Bangkok, 02/

254–1574), a self-contained complex of clean, rustic bungalows around a reception lounge and dining room (or you can rent a private bungalow, of which there are many available). The island has only beaches to explore and small fishing communities to visit. If this is what you're seeking, go now. It will not last for long; a Holiday Inn is due to open on the island by 1995.

Hua Hin and Cha' Am

Hua Hin's glory days were in the 1920s, when the royal family built a palace there. The entourage would travel the 198 km (123 mi) from Bangkok on special trains, and high society followed. After World War II, the resort lost favor to Pattaya, and Hua Hin became a quiet town once again. Pattaya's seedy reputation has caused Thais and foreign visitors to reconsider Hua Hin and its neighbor Cha' Am as beach resorts close to the capital. In the last several years, the area has enjoyed a boom in the construction of resort hotels and condominiums.

Cha' Am and Hua Hin are low-key destinations. Nightlife is restricted mostly to the hotels. During the day, Hua Hin is a busy market town, but most tourists are at the beach, only coming into town in the early evening to wander through the bazaars before dinner. There is no beachfront road to attract boisterous crowds; so stretches of beach remain deserted. Beaches have gently sloping drop-offs, and the waters are usually calm. The only drawback is the occasional invasion of jellyfish—check for them before you plunge in.

Tourist Information
The **Hua Hin Tourist Information Center** is near the railway station. *114 Phetkasem Rd., tel. 032/512–120. Open daily 8:30–4:30.*

Emergencies
In an emergency, contact the **local police** in Hua Hin (tel. 032/511–027) or in Cha' Am (tel. 032/471–321). The local hospital is in **Hua Hin** (Phetkasem Rd., tel. 032/511–743).

Arriving and Departing
By Plane
Bangkok Airways (tel. 02/253–4014) serves Hua Hin from Bangkok with a daily 25-minute evening flight. Take a taxi from the airport, or ask your hotel to meet you.

By Car
A few hotels, such as the Regent and Dusit Thani, run minibuses between their Bangkok and Cha' Am/Hua Hin properties for a flat fee of B200. Nonguests may use these. Otherwise, you can hire a car and driver for approximately B1,750 or B2,500 to or from the Bangkok airport.

By Train
The train from the Bangkok Noi station in Thonburi takes four long hours to reach Hua Hin's delightful wooden train station (Damnernkasem Rd., tel. 032/511–073).

By Bus
Buses, air-conditioned and non-air-conditioned, depart from the Southern Bus Terminal in Bangkok every half hour during the day. Express air-conditioned buses take three hours to reach Hua Hin's terminal (Srasong Rd., tel. 032/511–654).

Getting Around
Taxis are available, but bicycle *samlors* (small tricycle cabs) are more convenient for short distances. You can walk to most of the sights in town, but if you are staying at a resort hotel in Cha' Am, use the hotel shuttle bus or take a taxi. Tours to nearby attractions are arranged through your hotel. Local buses make it easy to travel between Cha' Am and Hua Hin, as well as points south of Hua Hin.

Exploring
On the east side of the highway at the northern boundary of Hua Hin is the royal summer palace. Every April, the king and queen spend a

month here, during which they celebrate the anniversary of their royal wedding. The palace was completed in 1928 by King Rama VII, who named it Klai Kangwol ("far from worries"). Four years later, while he was staying at Klai Kangwol, the army seized control in Bangkok, demanding that he relinquish absolute power in favor of a constitutional monarchy. He agreed, and the generals later apologized for their lack of courtesy.

The highway to the southern provinces passes through the center of Hua Hin. In fact, it's the town's main street, with shops and cafés lining the sidewalk; a congested street of market stalls and buses runs parallel to the main street. Toward the southern end of town is the quaint wooden railway station. Across the tracks is the respected **Royal Railway Golf Course;** nonmembers can play the par-72 course. You can rent clubs, and a coffee lounge offers refreshments. Lining both sides of Damnernkasem Road, leading to the public beach, are shops for tourists and moderately priced hotels.

On your way to the beach, keep your eyes open for **Nab Chai Hat Lane,** just before the Sofitel, where Damnernkasem Road becomes closed to traffic. Several small restaurants here are excellent places to keep in mind for dinner. Most have their offerings displayed on slabs of ice. You choose the fish, negotiate a fair price, and then take a table and order any other dishes and drinks you want. Farther down Nab Chai Hat, past numerous inexpensive guest houses, is **Fisherman's Wharf.** It's alive with activity in the morning when the catch comes in but is less interesting in the afternoon.

Near the end of the street on the right-hand side, you will see the **Sofitel Central Hua Hin Resort,** formerly the Royal Hua Hin Railway Hotel, which put up royalty and Thailand's elite during the town's heyday. The magnificent Victorian-style colonial building was portrayed as the French Embassy in Phnom Penh in the film *The Killing Fields*. Be sure to wander through the property's well-tended gardens and then along the verandas of the hotel.

If you look south along the coast, you'll see a small hill, **Khao Takiab,** and a small island, **Koh Singto.** You can reach the headland by taking a songthaew, but the fun way to get there is to hire a pony and trot along the beach. The 7-km (4-mi) stretch leads past the Sofitel, the Royal Garden Hotel, the Sai Lom Hotel, and past villas until the beach becomes virtually deserted. You will eventually reach the beach of Khoa Takiab (the village is a little way inland), where, unfortunately, three tall condominiums have been built. At the end of the beach where restaurant stalls abound, dismount for the steep climb past a large statue of the Lord Buddha up to the small Buddhist monastery at the summit—the views are worth the climb. Then if you can, rent a fishing boat at the base of Khao Takiab to cross over to Koh Singto, where you are guaranteed a catch within an hour.

About 40 km (25 mi) south of Hua Hin is the **Sam Roi Yod National Park,** with rice fields, sugar palms, pineapple plantations, and crab farms. The charming fishing village of **Wang Daeng** is typical of coastal Thailand 20 years ago. Farther south, the countryside is even more magnificent, with jungle-clad hills and a curving shoreline. Be sure to travel as far as the fishing village of **Ao Noi** and the city of **Prachuab,** about 90 km (56 mi) south of Hua Hin. For staggering panoramic views, climb the hills at the back of the bay.

Dining and Lodging
The restaurants along Nab Chai Hat in Hua Hin offer a warm ambience and good value, especially for fresh seafood. For Western food, it's best to eat at one of the major hotels. Hotels are completely

booked during Thai holiday weekends, so reservations should be made in advance. At other times, you shouldn't have any problems making reservations. During peak season—October through mid-March—the prices are nearly double those in the off-season.

Dining **Market Seafood Restaurant.** The nautical decor sets the tone for the Royal Garden Resort's excellently prepared gulf seafood—clams, lobsters, mussels, sea-tiger prawns, and crabs. Depending on your taste, these can be cooked with Thai spices (such as lobster with garlic and peppers) or simply grilled. *107/1 Phetkasem Rd., tel. 032/ 511–881. Reservations accepted. Dress: casual but neat. AE, DC, MC, V. $$$*

Sang Thai. For interesting seafood dishes—from grilled prawns with bean noodles to fried grouper with chili and tamarind juice— this open-air restaurant down by Fisherman's Wharf has been consistently popular with Thais. Certainly, the extensive menu is appealing, but you need to close your eyes to the ramshackle surroundings and floating debris in the water. Don't miss the *kang* (mantis prawns). *Naresdamri Rd., tel. 032/512–144. No reservations. Dress: casual. DC, MC, V. $$*

Lodging **Royal Garden Resort.** Adjacent to the Sofitel, this hotel offers accommodations and service equal to those of its neighbor. Because it doesn't have the colonial ambience, however, the prices are a few hundred baht less. The hotel tends to draw a younger set, attracted by the nightclub and the proximity to the beach. Guest rooms are decorated with modern, unimaginative furniture. The hotel's Market Seafood Restaurant is less elegant than Sofitel's Salathai, but serves better food. The Jungle is Hua Hin's hottest disco. *107/1 Phetkasem Rd., Hua Hin 77110, tel. 032/511–881, fax 032/512–422; Bangkok reservations, tel. 02/255–8822. 215 rooms. Facilities: 2 restaurants, coffee shop, cocktail lounge, evening entertainment, pool, tennis courts, water sports, children's playground. AE, DC, MC, V. $$$$*

★ **Sofitel Hua Hin Resort.** Even if you don't stay here, the Old World charm of this tastefully renovated hotel is worth a visit. Wide verandas fan out in an arc, following the lines of the wooden building, which opens onto gardens leading down to the beach. The gardens are splendidly maintained, with scores of different plants plus topiary figures that look like shadows in the night. The lounges around the reception area are open to the sea breezes, and the airiness revives memories of Somerset Maugham. The best guest rooms are those on the second floor with sea views. Less attractive are the units in an annex across the street. Forty more units at the back of the main building should be complete by the end of 1995. *1 Damnernkasem Rd., Hua Hin 77110, tel. 032/512–021, fax 032/511– 014; Bangkok reservations, tel. 02/233–0974. 154 rooms. Facilities: 2 restaurants, coffee shop, bar and nightclub, pool, tennis courts, water sports, conference facilities. AE, DC, MC, V. $$$$*

★ **Dusit Resort & Polo Club.** Although this resort opened in early 1991, the polo grounds and riding stables are still to be added. Perhaps not so many guests will be playing polo, but the game establishes the tone—smart, exclusive, and luxurious. The spacious lobby serves as a lounge for afternoon tea and evening cocktails to the soft tunes of the house musicians. Beyond the ornamental lily pond out front is the swimming pool with bubbling fountains, and beyond that is the beach. The main dining room serves Thai, Chinese, and European fare. Off to the left is the San Marco, an alfresco Italian restaurant; to the right is the Benjarong, in a traditional Thai-style pavilion. All the guest rooms have private balconies and a pool or sea view. *1349 Petchkasem Rd., Cha' Am, Petchburi 76120, tel. 032/520–009, fax*

032/520–010; Bangkok reservations, tel. 02/238–4790. 308 rooms and suites. Facilities: 4 restaurants, 2 bars, pool, children's pool, water sports, boat rentals including speedboats for waterskiing and parasailing, fitness center, 2 squash courts, in-room safes, shuttle service to Hua Hin, car service to Bangkok, and banquet rooms. AE, DC, MC, V. $$$–$$$$

Regent Cha' Am. A modern beach resort, this hotel has everything from water sports to gourmet dining to shopping arcades. The Lom Fang restaurant, overlooking the lake at the back of the hotel, serves excellent fish with a spiced-curry-and-lime sauce. The more formal restaurant, the Tapien Thong Grill Room, offers seafood and steak. Some guest rooms are located in bungalows, a number of which face the beach (no. 309 looks onto the sea and is away from the main building), while others are housed in one of two 12-story buildings set back from the beach. Gardens separate the bungalows, the main building, two large outdoor pools, and two smaller outdoor pools. The gold-sand beach is well patrolled for privacy. In the evening, a small group sings Western songs in Thai. The hotel has its own car service from Bangkok. *849/21 Cha' Am Beach, Petchburi, tel. 032/471–480, fax 032/471–492; Bangkok reservations, tel. 02/251–0305, fax 02/253–5143. 400 rooms. Facilities: 3 restaurants, coffee shop, 2 large and 2 small pools, water sports, nightly entertainment. AE, DC, MC, V. $$$–$$$$*

The Pran Buri Beach Resort. This isolated holiday complex south of Hua Hin offers a collection of small bungalow units along the shore. The first row of bungalows facing the beach is obviously the best. Though simply furnished, guest rooms have their own terraces and come with a minibar, telephone, and TV with in-house VCR. The main lodge contains the bar/lounge and dining room, where Thai, Chinese, and Western food is served. The atmosphere is laid-back, casual, and fun. *9 Parknampran Beach, Prachuapkhirikhan 77220, tel. 032/621–701; Bangkok reservations, tel. 02/233–3871, fax 02/235–0049. 60 rooms. Facilities: pool, 2 tennis courts, fitness center, sailboats, conference center. AE, DC, MC, V. $$$*

Hua Hin Raluek. Centrally located on the main tourist street, this hotel has bungalow cottages in its courtyard. Rooms have huge double beds and not much else, but the price is right. The terrace restaurant facing the street stays open late and is a popular spot from which to watch the parade of vacationers walking past. *16 Damnernkasem Rd., Hua Hin 77110, tel. and fax 032/511–755. 61 rooms. Facilities: restaurant/coffee shop. MC, V. $–$$*

Thanan-Chai Hotel. Located on the north side of Hua Hin, this hotel supplies the basic amenities of clean guest rooms, friendly service, and a coffee lounge that serves breakfast and light fare all day. Its quiet location, friendly staff, and modest price are its assets, but you do have to walk to the beach. *11 Damrongraj Rd., Hua Hin 77110, tel. 032/511–940. 41 rooms. Facilities: coffee shop. MC, V. $–$$*

9 Other Destinations

By Nigel Fisher

As Indochina opens up to international trade and tourism, Bangkok is promoting itself as the hub from which to visit Cambodia, Vietnam, Laos, and Myanmar (formerly called Burma)—though travel in Myanmar is limited. At least eight American tour companies offer trips covering each of these countries singly or in combination, usually departing from and returning to Bangkok. With some exceptions, such as TBI Tours, the cost is substantial—up to 75% higher than you would pay for independent travel.

Cambodia

The instability of the Cambodian truce notwithstanding, it's relatively easy to visit Phnom Penh and Angkor Wat. There are three daily flights between Bangkok and Phnom Penh on Bangkok Airways. Since flights are heavily booked, reservations should be made in advance (tel. 02/253–4014 in Bangkok). Hotels in Phnom Penh are scarce and rudimentary. The best is the **Royal,** one of the few architecturally noteworthy buildings left in the war-torn capital; built in 1923, it became the venue for royal functions and top-level government parties and quickly gained a reputation as the "Raffles of Cambodia." A $30 million renovation should return its facilities and its 200 rooms to their former glory.

Because of the antagonistic political factions (not to mention land mines), travel into the countryside is restricted. The route to Siem Reap/Angkor Wat is open, but since there are no Western hotels in Siem Reap, most travelers find it more comfortable to fly into Siem Reap in the morning, spend the day visiting Angkor Wat, and fly back to Phnom Penh in the evening. You can make tour arrangements (round-trip flight from Bangkok, Phnom Penh hotel, day trip to Angkor Wat, and visas) through a travel agency in Bangkok for approximately US$530. Road travel from Phnom Penh to Ho Chi Minh City, Vietnam, by either hired car or bus poses no problem, except that you must change cars or buses at the frontier. The only traffic across the border is pedestrian, but there is public transportation on either side to Phnom Penh or Ho Chi Minh City.

Laos

Travel conditions in Laos resemble those in Cambodia, minus the volatile politics. Obtaining a Laotian visa in Bangkok takes a week to 10 days and costs US$90; as with Cambodia, travel agents secure the visa for you. Transit visas, which permit visits only to Luang Prabang and Vientiane, may be obtained in approximately three days for US$20. Many travelers heading for Thailand from Hanoi prefer the cheaper transit visa (which is, in any case, the only type issued from Hanoi) because with it they can fly from Hanoi to Luang Prabang (fare: US$80), then travel by land to Vientiane and take the new Friendship Bridge across the Mae Khong, 32 km (20 mi) downriver from Ventiane, to Nong Khai, Thailand—as opposed to paying US$180 for a flight from Hanoi to Bangkok.

Travelers arriving from Bangkok fly into Vientiane (Thai Airways International has three flights a week), those from Hanoi into Luang Prabang. Entry by land is permitted only at Vientiane via the new Friendship Bridge. At present you cannot obtain a Laotian visa in Nong Khai. The situation could change, but probably the best you'll be able to obtain is a day pass to Vientiane.

Officially you are required to sign up for a tour package to travel in the country outside of Vientiane and Luang Prabang. However, if you have a tourist rather than a transit visa, this restriction is seldom enforced.

Myanmar (Burma)

The junta that has ruled the Union of Myanmar since 1988 has recently been relaxing restrictions on tourists in the hope of bringing in foreign currency. Some 20,000 visitors currently enter the country each year. The government hopes to increase that figure to half a million. Visas have become easier to obtain; travelers no longer have to exchange a daily minimum amount of money on arrival; and foreigners are no longer required to stay at government-run hotels. Better yet, independent travel is now possible, though most travelers arrange transport and accommodation through a tour operator.

Journeys International (4011 Jackson Rd., Ann Arbor, MI 48103, tel. 800/255–8735) has eight- and 15-day tours as well as group packages for five to 28 people. **EastQuest** and **Absolute Asia** (*see* Fully Escorted Tours in Chapter 1) offer a variety of packages, from three-day to two-week trips. EastQuest has also teamed up with Bangkok Airways on direct charter flights from Chiang Mai, Thailand, to Pagan, Myanmar, thus avoiding Myanmar Airways, whose reputation for safety ranks as low as Air Vietnam's. Trips can also be arranged in Bangkok: The travel agency (there are dozens of them) will obtain your visa (it takes about 10 days) and book you onto a tour. Typically you fly from Bangkok to Yangon (Rangoon) on either Thai International or Myanmar Airways; then, after one or two nights in the capital, you proceed to Mandalay and Pagan on Myanmar Airways. Other popular tourist destinations are Mt. Pop, Inle Lake, Maymyo, and Thazi. Hotels are still rudimentary; only a dozen meet (and then just barely) international standards. The grandest is the recently renovated **Strand** in Yangon. Rates are high, at around $260 per night—the average citizen's annual income.

Vietnam

Despite masses of red tape, Vietnam places fewer limitations on travel than either Burma, Cambodia, or Laos. The country, shut off from the outside world for 25 years, has the unspoilt beauty of Thailand before the developers set in. Vietnam opened its borders to independent travel only late in the 1980s, and though there is now a steady flow of backpackers working their way up Highway 1 from Ho Chi Minh City (Saigon) to Hanoi, this is still virgin country as far as tourism is concerned. Especially in the south, the Vietnamese extend a natural welcome and will go out of their way to help. This isn't as true in the north, where the people tend to be reticent with foreigners. Not long ago, talking to foreigners could bring down the ire of the secret police—and for many that fear persists.

Visas   A visa is required of all travelers. Until recently, the easiest way to obtain one was through a Bangkok travel agency, but now you can apply in the **United States.** There was no consulate here at press time, but the Mission of the Republic of Vietnam to the United Nations (21 Waterside Plaza, New York, NY 10010, tel. 212/685–8001, fax 212/686–8534) will assist in obtaining your visa through the Vietnamese Embassay in **Canada** (25B Davidson Dr., Gloucester, Ontario K1J 6L7, tel. 613/745–9735, fax 613/744–5072). Your travel agent can also make the arrangements. (By the time you read this, there may be a diplomatic mission in Washington, DC, with the authority to issue visas.) Residents of **Britain** should contact the Vietnamese Embassy (12–14 Victoria Rd., London W8 5RD, tel. 0171/ 937–1912). The usual tourist visa is good for two weeks, but there are four-week visas as well.

Within 24 hours of arriving in Vietnam you must register with the Ministry of the Interior. Your hotel, or a domestic travel service, can do this for you; each hotel you stay in will register you with the police. If you plan to travel overnight outside Ho Chi Minh City or Hanoi, you must get a travel permit from the Ministry of the Interior in either city. These cost about US$30 and are usually easy to obtain. You will have to declare your itinerary, and some destinations may not be permitted. Americans, for example, are often denied Le Dalat. (It's rumored that an American there tried to create an insurrection among the hill tribes.) If travel is arranged by a tour agency, such as Saigon Tourist, the agency will obtain your permit, saving you the hassle of standing in long lines at the Ministry of the Interior.

Tour Agencies Most of the U.S. tour operators who organize trips to Southeast Asia now offer seven- to 14-day packages to Vietnam. They can make hotel reservations for customized trips as well, though you may prefer to deal with a tour operator specializing in Vietnam, such as **South Sea Tour and Travel** (210 Post St., Suite 910, San Francisco, CA 94108, tel. 415/397–4644 or 800/546–7890). **Saigon Tourist** (49 Le Thanh Ton St., Ho Chi Minh City, tel. 08/295834, fax 08/224987) is the largest government-run travel/tour agency in Ho Chi Minh City. A more helpful private agency is **Oscan Enterprises** (Tourist Division, 20 Pham Ngoc Thach St., District 1, Ho Chi Minh City, tel. 08/ 231022, fax 08/231024), run by Ms. Tran Phi Nga in conjunction with a Canadian travel operator.

Currency The unit of currency is the dong, with approximately 11,500 dong to US$1. (The Vietnamese are dollar-hungry, and it's advisable to bring dollars rather than other currencies.) Since the largest bill is 5,000 dong, US$100 in dong practically requires a satchel. Do not use the black-market exchange: The rate you'll get isn't worth the risk of the "Saigon Switch," whereby the roll of 5,000s you thought you were getting turns out to be 1,000s. Dollars are used to pay for major purchases, such as hotels and car rentals, so US$10 per day in dong should more than cover your needs. Carry lots of $1 and $5 bills, but watch out for pickpockets. It is difficult to convert dong back into dollars.

Mail and Telephone The lines at the post office are horrendous, but major hotels have postal services. Mail clerks have a habit of steaming off stamps to make a dong or two, so be sure your stamps are glued on well. Telephone calls are best made from your hotel. Vietnam does not have intercity direct dialing; you must go through the operator. To call the country from outside, dial the country code (84) and drop the first zero of the city code; e.g., to call Ho Chi Minh City from the U.S., dial 011–84–8 and the number.

Language Vietnamese is the national language. In Ho Chi Minh City some form of English is widely spoken, less widely in the countryside. French is more common in the north, but most Hanoi hotels have someone who can speak English.

Precautions Vietnamese food is a delight, but unless you have had shots against hepatitis and typhoid, each meal is a potential disaster. It isn't unusual to see a rat scamper across a dining-room floor. Check with the Centers for Disease Control in Atlanta (tel. 404/332–4559) for recommended inoculations. Except in Ho Chi Minh City and Hanoi, most hotels are pre-1975 and offer few amenities beyond (at best) clean sheets. Even the main road between Hanoi and Ho Chi Minh City frequently disintegrates into a gravel surface pockmarked with axle-breaking craters. Pickpockets in Ho Chi Minh City work fast and often. Dark nighttime streets invite trouble. Stay away from confrontations. At press time the United States was just setting up a diplomatic liaison office; in Ho Chi Minh City it will be at the former U.S. embassy building.

Getting to Vietnam
Flights are expensive. Bangkok has the most frequent flights to Ho Chi Minh City. (Use Thai International rather than Air Vietnam.) Singapore Airlines offers three flights in from Singapore. Cathay Pacific has (expensive) flights from Hong Kong. All these airlines offer less-frequent flights into Hanoi.

Entry by road, by either bus or car, is possible only to Ho Chi Minh City from Phnom Penh, Cambodia.

Getting Around
Flights between Hanoi, Hue, and Ho Chi Minh City are unavoidably on Air Vietnam and fairly expensive (the one-way Ho Chi Minh City–Hanoi fare is US$150). The airline is not known for its safety record. During the rainy season, the turbulent air sends the Soviet-built planes dancing in the sky. Traveling by intercity bus is cheap (under US$2 for an eight-hour journey) but uncomfortable even for those with short legs, padded posteriors, and cast-iron stomachs. Trains are slow and cost about US$20 for an eight-hour trip—10 times more for foreigners than for the Vietnamese. The trip between Ho Chi Minh City and Hanoi takes three days by either road or rail. (The roads are horrendous.) The best way to explore the countryside outside Hanoi and Ho Chi Minh City is to hire a car driver. The cost runs around $100 per 24 hours, including meals and accommodation for the driver.

In the cities there are very few taxis. If you want to tour, hire a car and driver through a tour agency; it costs about US$50 a day, more for intercity trips. The most common mode of city transport is the *cyclo*, a bicycle on which the passenger sits in front, on an uncomfortable cart-seat, while the panting driver pedals from behind. Depending on your negotiating skill and body weight (settle the fee before you get on), count on 4,000 dong (40¢) for a 2-km (1¼-mi) ride.

Ho Chi Minh City

Ho Chi Minh City was once an elegant city. Home to more than 4 million inhabitants, it's a bit shabby now, but it still has its Asian–colonial French hybrid charm. Mostly, though, it's the city's dynamism, reawakened after years of isolation, that captivates the visitor.

Exploring
For amusement tinged with irony, there are three museums celebrating Vietnam's fight for independence, where guides enumerate the virtues of Communism in monotones that do not ring with sincerity. The **Historical Museum** (within the Zoo and Botanical Gardens on Nguyen Binh Khiem St., tel. 08/298146; closed Mon.) gives a good brief overview of Vietnam's 4,000-year history. The **Revolutionary Museum** (65 Ly Tu Trong St., tel. 08/99741) pays tribute to the heroes who fought against the French and the Americans. The **Exhibit of War Crimes** (28 Vo Van Tan St., tel. 08/90325), in the building that once housed the U.S. Information Service, is devoted to capitalist (Chinese and American) atrocities against the Vietnamese. The much-televised former U.S. Embassy is closed to the pub-

lic; it's now the headquarters of the state-owned petroleum company.

Of the several pagodas, the **Giac Lam Pagoda** (118 Lac Long Quan), in the Tan Binh District north of Cholon, is the city's oldest and the best to visit. It dates from 1744 and is built in the Vietnamese style. Fewer than a dozen monks live among the statuary of Buddhas, two goddesses of mercy, Taoist gods, the judges of the 10 regions of hell, and many more characters. **Phuoc Hai Tu,** the Emperor of Jade Pagoda (73 Mai Thi Luu St.), in the Da Kao District, is Ho Chi Minh City's most colorful pagoda; built by the Cantonese in 1909, it's filled with pungent air from burning joss sticks. The **Mariamman Hindu Temple** (45 Truong Dinh St.), in the center of Ho Chi Minh City three blocks from the Ben Thanh Market, is something of an anomoly. There are only about 50 Hindus, all of them Tamils, in the city, but the temple has a loyal following among non-Hindus, including Vietnamese and Chinese, who credit the temple with miraculous powers. Be sure also to visit Ho Chi Minh City's markets. **Ben Thanh Market** (750 yards southwest of the Rex Hotel), the largest, is well worth a stroll—but be wary of pickpockets. The street stalls on **"Liquor Street"** (off Ham Nghi Blvd.) are hilarious: You can purchase a bottle of Johnny Walker Black here for a song—but there's no telling what's on the inside.

Excursions from Ho Chi Minh City   The 200-km (125-mi) network of **Cu Chi Tunnels,** where the Viet Cong hid under the feet of Allied troops, lies 35 km (22 mi) from Ho Chi Ming City as the crow flies, but 75 km (47 mi) by road. A five-hour round-trip tour from the city costs about $20. If you aren't into crawling, a more colorful place to visit is the **Caodai Holy See** at Tay Ninh, a short day trip out toward the Cambodian border.

Caodaiism, a doctrine founded in 1926, fuses Buddhism, Taoism, Hinduism, Confucianism, Vietnamese spiritualism, and Christianity into one religion that worships Cao Dai as the Supreme Being. Today it boasts approximately 2 million adherents throughout Vietnam, with the strongest following in Tay Ninh province. The main temple complex is 4 km (2½ mi) east of the town of Tay Ninh in the small village of Long Hua. Arrive before noon to attend a prayer session, with cloaked and hooded priests marching in procession.

Shopping   Embroidery is a tremendous buy. Try the small **Mai-a-Anh** boutique (81 Mac Thi, off Dong Khoi), as well as **C. Minh Huong** (85 Mac Thi).

Dining   Avoid Madame Dai's **La Biblioteque** (84-A Nguyen Du St., no phone)—it's vastly overrated and reportedly orders food from other kitchens. Try **Thanh Nien** (11 Nguyen Van Chim, tel. 08/225909) for Vietnamese fare popular with the new breed of local yuppies. For pleasant decor, dine at the **City Bar & Grill** (63 Dong Khoi St., no phone), an expat hangout. **Maxim's** (13–17 Dong Khoi St., tel. 08/296676) is still famous for its lavish dinners and dancing. For the homesick, the wood paneling and English club ties pinned to the wall of **Tiger Tavern** (227 Dong Kho St., tel. 08/222738) will remind you of a London pub. British fare at lunch runs under $5.

Lodging   Unless you're on a tight budget, you'll want to stay in District 1, the downtown area of Ho Chi Minh City that's known as Saigon. The other area of Ho Chi Minh, about 6 km (4 mi) from downtown Saigon, is Cholon—crowded and vibrant, with a large Chinese population and many cheap hotels. The best is the renovated **Arc de Ciel** (52–56 Tan Da St., Cholon, tel. 08/452550) for US$35 a night. For a real bargain, you may want to try the small **Comfort** (74 Le Thi Rieng, P. Ben Thanh, Ho Chi Minh City, tel. 08/322454), where $15 will get you an air-conditioned room with a private bath. You can find several dumpy hotels in downtown Saigon, such as the **Majestic** (1 Dong Khoi St., tel. 08/295515), which provides clean sheets and a private bathroom for about US$40; but if your budget allows, you'll be more comfortable at one of the international-style hotels charging around US$90.

Saigon Floating Hotel. The pontoon-supported structure, moored in the Saigon River in the heart of District 1, was earlier a floating hotel in Queensland, Australia—where it went bankrupt. It's ridiculously pricey, but business travelers like its efficient service and its pool (which nonguests may use for US$5). *1-A Me Linh Sq., tel. 08/290783, fax 08/290784. 200 rooms. Facilities: Western-style restaurant, pool, 2 tennis courts, sauna, gym, meeting rooms, business center. V. US$190.*

Continental. This turn-of-the-century grand hotel was the setting for much of Graham Greene's *The Quiet American.* Located across from the Municipal Theatre in the heart of downtown Saigon, it's the preferred place to stay even if some of the rooms (especially the bathrooms) smell a little musty. Service is professional and helpful. Recent renovations did more for the lobby than the guest rooms. During the Vietnam War, the poolside bar—journalists called it the Continental Shelf—was a well-known hangout. *132–134 Dong Khoi St., tel. 08/299201, fax 08/290936. 71 rooms. Facilities: restaurant (Vietnamese and Western fare), small pool. V. US$85–US$120.*

Rex (Ben Thanh) Hotel. Formerly the hotel for U.S. military officers, the Rex boasts a location nearly as good as the Continental's, and the staff is efficient and friendly. Guest rooms are standard, unadorned, and clean. Even if you don't stay here, go up to the rooftop to see the peculiar collection of ceramic animals surrounded by flashing lights. *141 Nguyen Hue Blvd., tel. 08/292185, fax 08/296526. 92 rooms. Facilities: Vietnamese and Western restaurants, pool, 2 tennis courts, post office, photostat service. V. US$40–US$80.*

Hanoi

Hanoi has the old and the new. The old quarter, with its narrow, shophouse-lined streets seething with color and charm, is like a huge bazaar, with some streets specializing in a particular trade, others selling a variety of goods, meats, and vegetables. The newer city is cold, with wide streets and Russian-style government structures. Some buildings attract the curious, like the **Hanoi Hilton** on Hai Ba Trung Street, where American P.O.W.'s were confined, and the **Ho Chi Minh Mausoleum** in Ba Dinh Square, watched over by an unsmiling Praetorian guard. Three days here is probably sufficient for the casual tourist. Ho Chi Minh ran a very effective police state in the north for more than four decades, and the people's spontaneity has yet to return.

Lodging **Pullman Metropole.** This rather austere building was gutted, rebuilt, and reopened in the spring of 1992, so everything is clean and freshly plastered. It even has marble in the foyer! *15 Ngo Ouyen St., tel. 04/266919, fax 04/266920. 109 rooms. Facilities: restaurant (French and Vietnamese fare), outdoor bar, postal and fax services. V. US$152–US$198.*

Khach San Hu'u Nghi (also known as the **Friendship Hotel**). This small and reasonably priced hotel in the heart of the old quarter is usually filled with journalists and Western advisers to the Hanoi bureaucracy. The rooms are basic but clean, and the staff is exceptionally friendly. The bar is an amiable expat hangout. *23 Ouan Thanh St., tel. 04/253182. 38 rooms. Facilities: restaurant (Vietnamese, Chinese, and Western fare), bar. V. US$50.*

Vocabulary

To properly experience the culture of a foreign country, one must feast on its cuisine, learn the history of its monuments, and speak its native tongue. Southeast Asian languages, like its history, are as diverse as its people and customs.

To simplify communications, Fodor's has compiled a vocabulary chart of six languages you may encounter throughout your travels in the region. This easy-reference listing includes important words and significant phrases in English, Cantonese, Malay (which is usually similar to Indonesian), Mandarin, Tagalog, and Thai. Use the phonetical chart to assist you in getting around, asking directions, and dining out.

	English	Cantonese	Malay
Basics	Yes/No	hai/mm'hai	ya/**tee**´-dak
	Please	m'goy	**see**-la/**min**–ta
	Thank you (very much).	doy-jeh/fehseng doh jeh	**tree**-ma **ka**-say (**ban**-yak)
	You're welcome.	foon ying	**sa**-ma **sa**-ma
	Excuse me.	dai'm jee	ma-fkan sa-ya
	Hello	wa´	apa khabar or "hello"
	Goodbye	joy geen	se-**la**-mat **jalan**/ se-**la**-mat **ting**-gal
Numbers	One	yaht	sa-too
	Two	eee	doo-a
	Three	som	tee-ga
	Four	say	em-pat
	Five	m'	lee-ma
	Six	look	e-nam
	Seven	chut	tu-juh
	Eight	baht	la-pan
	Nine	gou	sem-bee-lan
	Ten	sup	se-pu-luh
Days and Time	Today	gäm-yät	**ha**-ree ee-nee
	Tomorrow	ting-yat	**ay**-sok (also **bay**-sok)
	Yesterday	chum-yät	kel-**mar**-in
	Morning	joo-joh	**pa**-gee
	Afternoon	ahn-joh	**pe**-tang
	Night	man-hak	**ma**-lam
	Monday	lye bye **yaht**	**ha**-ree iss-nin
	Tuesday	lye bye **ee**	**ha**-ree se-**la**-sa
	Wednesday	lye bye **som**	**ha**-ree **ra**-boo
	Thursday	lye bye **say**	**ha**-ree **ka**-mees
	Friday	lye bye m	**ha**-ree **ju**-ma-at
	Saturday	lye bye **look**	**ha**-ree sab-too
	Sunday	lye bye **yaht**´	**ha**-ree a-had (also **ha**-ree **ming**-gu)

Mandarin	Tagalog	Thai	English
shee/pu shee	oh-oh/hin-deé	khrap/mai khrap (M)/kha/mai kha (F)	Yes/No
ching	pah-keé	dai prōd	Please
sy-eh sy-eh nee	(mah-rah-ming) sah-lah-maht	khob khun khrap	Thank you (very much).
boo sy-eh	wah-lahng ah-noo-mahn	mai pen rai	You're welcome.
too-eh pu-shee	pah-oó-manh-hiń po	kaw-tōd	Excuse me.
way	kuh-moos-tah/heh-ló	sa-wat dee khrap (M)/sa-wat dee kha (F)	Hello
tsay jen	pah-ah-lam nah pó	sa-wat dee khrap (M)/sa-wat dee kha (F)	Goodbye
ee	ee-sah	nung	One
err	dah-lah-wah	song	Two
san	taht-loh	sam	Three
soo	ah-paht	see	Four
woo	lee-mah	hah	Five
lee-oo	ah-neem	hōk	Six
chee	pee-toh	jet	Seven
bah	wah-ló	paat	Eight
joo	see-yahm´	kaw	Nine
shur	sahm-poó	sip	Ten
chin tien	nga-yohn	wun nee	Today
ming tien	boó-kahss	proong nee	Tomorrow
tso tien	kah-há-pon	moo-ah-wan-nee	Yesterday
shang wu	oo-mah-gah	toan-chao	Morning
sha wu	hah-pon	toan-klang-wun	Afternoon
wan shang	gah-beh	toan-klang-koon	Night
lee-pa-ee	loó-ness	wun-chan	Monday
lee-pa-ayr	mahr-tesś	wun-ung-khan	Tuesday
lee-pa-san	moo-yehŕ-koh-less	wun-poot	Wednesday
lee-pa-soo	hoo-whé-bess	wun-pru-roo-hud	Thursday
lee-pa-wu	bee-yehŕ-ness	wun-sook	Friday
lee-pa-ee-oo	sah-bah-doh	wun-sao	Saturday
lee-pa-tien	leeng-goh	wun-ar-teet	Sunday

	English	Cantonese	Malay
Useful Phrases	Do you speak English?	nay gäng m' gäng ying män	**ta**-hoo-kah ber-ba-**ha**-sa **Ing**-gris?
	I don't speak . . .	ah m' woiy gäng gäng doong wah.	sa-ya **tee**-dak ber-**cha**-kap ba-**ha**-sa
	I don't understand.	äh m' sic	sa-ya **tee**-dak **fa**-ham
	I don't know.	äh m' jee	sa-ya **tee**-dak **ta**-hoo
	I am American/British.	ä hay may gäc yan/ying gäk yan	sa-ya o-rang Amerika/**Ing**-gris
	I am sick.	ä beng **jah**	sa-ya sa-kit
	Please call a doctor.	m goy nay gew yee sung	**see**-la ta-**lee**-pon **dok**-ter
	Have you any rooms?	nay yaw mohfäng	**bi**-lik **a**-da
	How much does it cost?	gay' däh chien	**har**-ga-nya ber-a-pa
	Too expensive	gai' gway	ter-**la**-loo ma-hal
	It's beautiful.	hoh leng	**chan**-tik
	Help!	bong jô	**to**-long
	Stop!	ting jee	ber-**hen**-ti
Getting Around	How do I get to . . .	deem yerng huy . . .	ba-gai-ma-ner boh-lee per-gee-ku . . .
	. . . the train station?	fäw ché jäm	**stay**-shen **kray**-ta a-pee dee **ma**-na
	. . . the post office?	yaw jing gook	pe-**ja**-bat pos dee **ma**-na
	. . . the tourist office?	le hang se'	ja-bat-ban pe-**lan**-chong des **ma**-na
	. . . the hospital?	yee' yuen	**roo**-mah sa-kit dee **ma**-na
	Does this bus go to . . . ?	ga ba se' huy m huy . . .	a-da-kah bas ee-nee per-gee ke . . .

Mandarin	Tagalog	Thai	English
nee fweh sho yung yoo má	mah-roo-nohng hoh kay-yohng mahg-Ing-glehs?	khun pood pas-sa ung-grid dai-mai	Do you speak English?
wo pu fweh sho (thai kway yoo)	hin-deé a-koh mah-roo-nohng mahg-tah-gah-lohg	phom mai pood (Thai)	I don't speak . . .
wo pu lee-oo chee-ay	hin-deé koh nah-ee-een-tin-deé-hahn	phom mai kao chai	I don't understand.
wo pu tung	hin-deé koh ah-lahm	phom mai rue	I don't know.
wo sher may kwo jen/ing kwo jen	ah-ko ay Ah-meh-ree-kah-noh/Ing-glehs	phom pen (American/ ung-grid	I am American/British.
wo sheng ping ler	ah-ko ay may sah-kit	phom mai sa-bai	I am sick.
ching chow ee sung lin	pah-kee-tah-wahg ang dook-tohr	dai-prod re-ak moa mai	Please call a doctor.
nee hay yoo fwang chien ma	may-roh-ohn kah-yong mang-ah kuh-wahr-toh	khun-mee hong-mai	Have you any rooms?
to shaw chien	mahg-kah-noh?	ra-ka tao rye	How much does it cost?
tao kwa la	mah-hal mah-shah-doh	pa-eng goo-pai	Too expensive
chen pee-ow lee-ang	mah-gahn-dah	soo-ay ma	It's beautiful.
choo-ming	sahk-loh-loh	choo-ay doo-ay	Help!
ting	hin-toh	yoot	Stop!
wo tsen yang tao . . .	pah-pah-no pah-poon-tah sah . . .	phom ja pai . . . dai yang-rye	How do I get to . . .
. . . fwa chu chan	ee-stah-syon nahng tren	sa-tai-nee rod-fai	. . . the train station?
. . . yu choo	post oh-pis/tahn-gah-pahn nahng koh-reo	pai-sa-nee	. . . the post office?
. . . kuan kuang choo	oh-pee-see-nah nahng too-ris-moh	sam-nak-ngan tóng-tee-oh	the tourist office?
. . . ee-yuen	oh-spee-tal	rung-pa-ya-bal	. . . the hospital?
chu pu pa shur tao . . . ma	poo-moo-poon-tah bah ee-tohngboos sah . . .	rod-mai-nee pai-nai . . . chai mai	Does this bus go to . . . ?

English	Cantonese	Malay
Where is the W.C.?	say soh gahn herng been doh	**tan**-das **a**-da dee **ma**-na
Left	jäh	**kee**-ree
Right	yäw	**ka**-nan
Straight ahead	chiem mein	troos

Dining Out

English	Cantonese	Malay
Hot/not hot (spicy)	moh´ lät´	pe-das/**tee**-dak pe-das
Please bring me . . .	me goy ne ling lay	to long ba-wa un-tuk sa-ya . . .
Menu	chan pie	**me**-noo
Bill/check	dän	bill
Fork	chä´	**gar**-poo, or "fork"
Knife	bä´ doh	**pee**-sow
Spoon	chee gung	**soo**-doo
Napkin	jee gan	serviette (if paper) or too-ala (if cloth) or "napkin"
Bread	mean bou	**ro**-tee
Butter	ow yôw	men-tay ga or "butter"
Milk	nïh	**soo**-soo
Pepper	woo jew fähn	**la**-da
Salt	yeem	**ga**-ram
Sugar	tông	**goo**-la
Water/bottled water	suy/jun suy	a-yer/a-yer **bo**-tol

Mandarin	Tagalog	Thai	English
chaw soo tsai na lee	sah-ahn ahng bahn-noih	hong-nam yoo tee-nai	Where is the W.C.?
tso	kah-lee-waȟ	sai	Left
yoo	kah-nahn	kuah	Right
ching sung chien tson	dee-reh-tsoh	trong-pai	Straight ahead
la/pu la	mah-hang-hang/ hoo-wahg mah-hang-hang	ped/mai ped	Hot/not hot (spicy)
chin dee keh wo . . .	pah-kee-dah-la moh ah-ko nahng . . .	prod pah chun	Please bring me . . .
tsai tan	meh-noó	rai-kran ar-han	Menu
chang tan	koo-when-tah/ tseh-keh	bill/check (bai-sed)	Bill/check
cha	tee-nee-dohr	som	Fork
tao	kuh-tsee-lee-yo	mead	Knife
tang-sher	kuh-tsa-rah	chen	Spoon
tsan-chin-chu	sir-bee-lee-yeah-tah	kra-dard ched park	Napkin
mien-paw	tee-nah-pie	kha-nom-pang	Bread
nyoo-yoo	mahn-teh-kíll-yah	no-ee	Butter
nyoo-nyai	gaȟ-tahss	nom	Milk
hoo-chao	pee-myeń-toh	pik-tai	Pepper
yen	ah-siń	kloo-ah	Salt
tang	ah-soó-kahl	nam-pan	Sugar
shoo-ay/ping shoe-ay	too-big/too-big sah boȟ-teh	nam/nam koo-at	Water/bottled water

Index

Personal Itinerary

Departure *Date*

Time

Transportation

Arrival *Date* *Time*

Departure *Date* *Time*

Transportation

Accommodations

Arrival *Date* *Time*

Departure *Date* *Time*

Transportation

Accommodations

Arrival *Date* *Time*

Departure *Date* *Time*

Transportation

Accommodations

Personal Itinerary

Arrival   *Date*   *Time*

Departure   *Date*   *Time*

Transportation

Accommodations

Arrival   *Date*   *Time*

Departure   *Date*   *Time*

Transportation

Accommodations

Arrival   *Date*   *Time*

Departure   *Date*   *Time*

Transportation

Accommodations

Arrival   *Date*   *Time*

Departure   *Date*   *Time*

Transportation

Accommodations

Personal Itinerary

Arrival   *Date*   *Time*

Departure   *Date*   *Time*

Transportation

Accommodations

Arrival   *Date*   *Time*

Departure   *Date*   *Time*

Transportation

Accommodations

Arrival   *Date*   *Time*

Departure   *Date*   *Time*

Transportation

Accommodations

Arrival   *Date*   *Time*

Departure   *Date*   *Time*

Transportation

Accommodations

Addresses

Name	*Name*
Address	*Address*
Telephone	*Telephone*
Name	*Name*
Address	*Address*
Telephone	*Telephone*
Name	*Name*
Address	*Address*
Telephone	*Telephone*
Name	*Name*
Address	*Address*
Telephone	*Telephone*
Name	*Name*
Address	*Address*
Telephone	*Telephone*
Name	*Name*
Address	*Address*
Telephone	*Telephone*
Name	*Name*
Address	*Address*
Telephone	*Telephone*
Name	*Name*
Address	*Address*
Telephone	*Telephone*

Fodor's Travel Guides

Available at bookstores everywhere, or call 1–800–533–6478, 24 hours a day.

U.S. Guides

Alaska

Arizona

Boston

California

Cape Cod, Martha's Vineyard, Nantucket

The Carolinas & the Georgia Coast

Chicago

Colorado

Florida

Hawaii

Las Vegas, Reno, Tahoe

Los Angeles

Maine, Vermont, New Hampshire

Maui

Miami & the Keys

New England

New Orleans

New York City

Pacific North Coast

Philadelphia & the Pennsylvania Dutch Country

The Rockies

San Diego

San Francisco

Santa Fe, Taos, Albuquerque

Seattle & Vancouver

The South

The U.S. & British Virgin Islands

USA

The Upper Great Lakes Region

Virginia & Maryland

Waikiki

Walt Disney World and the Orlando Area

Washington, D.C.

Foreign Guides

Acapulco, Ixtapa, Zihuatanejo

Australia & New Zealand

Austria

The Bahamas

Baja & Mexico's Pacific Coast Resorts

Barbados

Berlin

Bermuda

Brittany & Normandy

Budapest

Canada

Cancún, Cozumel, Yucatán Peninsula

Caribbean

China

Costa Rica, Belize, Guatemala

The Czech Republic & Slovakia

Eastern Europe

Egypt

Euro Disney

Europe

Florence, Tuscany & Umbria

France

Germany

Great Britain

Greece

Hong Kong

India

Ireland

Israel

Italy

Japan

Kenya & Tanzania

Korea

London

Madrid & Barcelona

Mexico

Montréal & Québec City

Morocco

Moscow & St. Petersburg

The Netherlands, Belgium & Luxembourg

New Zealand

Norway

Nova Scotia, Prince Edward Island & New Brunswick

Paris

Portugal

Provence & the Riviera

Rome

Russia & the Baltic Countries

Scandinavia

Scotland

Singapore

South America

Southeast Asia

Spain

Sweden

Switzerland

Thailand

Tokyo

Toronto

Turkey

Vienna & the Danube Valley

Special Series

Fodor's Affordables

Caribbean

Europe

Florida

France

Germany

Great Britain

Italy

London

Paris

Fodor's Bed & Breakfast and Country Inns Guides

America's Best B&Bs

California

Canada's Great Country Inns

Cottages, B&Bs and Country Inns of England and Wales

Mid-Atlantic Region

New England

The Pacific Northwest

The South

The Southwest

The Upper Great Lakes Region

The Berkeley Guides

California

Central America

Eastern Europe

Europe

France

Germany & Austria

Great Britain & Ireland

Italy

London

Mexico

Pacific Northwest & Alaska

Paris

San Francisco

Fodor's Exploring Guides

Australia

Boston & New England

Britain

California

The Caribbean

Florence & Tuscany

Florida

France

Germany

Ireland

Italy

London

Mexico

New York City

Paris

Prague

Rome

Scotland

Singapore & Malaysia

Spain

Thailand

Turkey

Fodor's Flashmaps

Boston

New York

Washington, D.C.

Fodor's Pocket Guides

Acapulco

Bahamas

Barbados

Jamaica

London

New York City

Paris

Puerto Rico

San Francisco

Washington, D.C.

Fodor's Sports

Cycling

Golf Digest's Best Places to Play

Hiking

The Insider's Guide to the Best Canadian Skiing

Running

Sailing

Skiing in the USA & Canada

USA Today's Complete Four Sports Stadium Guide

Fodor's Three-In-Ones (guidebook, language cassette, and phrase book)

France

Germany

Italy

Mexico

Spain

Fodor's Special-Interest Guides

Complete Guide to America's National Parks

Condé Nast Traveler Caribbean Resort and Cruise Ship Finder

Cruises and Ports of Call

Euro Disney

France by Train

Halliday's New England Food Explorer

Healthy Escapes

Italy by Train

London Companion

Shadow Traffic's New York Shortcuts and Traffic Tips

Sunday in New York

Sunday in San Francisco

Touring Europe

Touring USA: Eastern Edition

Walt Disney World and the Orlando Area

Walt Disney World for Adults

Fodor's Vacation Planners

Great American Learning Vacations

Great American Sports & Adventure Vacations

Great American Vacations

Great American Vacations for Travelers with Disabilities

National Parks and Seashores of the East

National Parks of the West

The Wall Street Journal Guides to Business Travel

At last — a guide for Americans with disabilities that makes traveling a delight

0-679-02591-X $18.00 ($24.00 Can)

This is the first and only complete guide to great American vacations for the 35 million North Americans with disabilities, as well as for those who care for them or for aging parents and relatives. Provides:

- Essential trip-planning information for travelers with mobility, vision, and hearing impairments
- Specific details on a huge array of facilities, along with solid descriptions of attractions, hotels, restaurants, and other destinations
- Up-to-date information on ISA-designated parking, level entranceways, and accessibility to pools, lounges, and bathrooms

 At bookstores everywhere, or call **1-800-533-6478**